GW01606558

A DICTIONARY OF
Modern German Prose Usage

A DICTIONARY OF
Modern German Prose Usage

BY

H. F. EGGELING
READER-EMERITUS IN GERMAN
IN THE UNIVERSITY OF EDINBURGH

OXFORD
AT THE CLARENDON PRESS

Oxford University Press, Ely House, London W. 1

GLASGOW NEW YORK TORONTO MELBOURNE WELLINGTON
CAPE TOWN IBADAN NAIROBI DAR ES SALAAM LUSAKA ADDIS ABABA
DELHI BOMBAY CALCUTTA MADRAS KARACHI LAHORE DACCA
KUALA LUMPUR SINGAPORE HONG KONG TOKYO

ISBN 0 19 864110 9

© *Oxford University Press 1961*

First published 1961
Reprinted (with corrections) 1967, 1974

Printed in Great Britain
at the University Press, Oxford
by Vivian Ridler
Printer to the University

PREFACE

THE purpose of this volume, which is the outcome of over forty years' teaching in the University of Edinburgh, is to provide teachers and students of German, and others whose calling demands a sound knowledge of standard German prose, with a reliable guide in the many cases of difficulty which that language presents. The author has for many years been urged to compile a reference book of this kind, and he himself always regretted that no such up-to-date work was available in this country—a work dealing with difficulties which are either not discussed at all even in the best grammars, or to which reference can be found only after much laborious search. He can only hope that the present volume will to some extent fill the gap.

The author hesitates to call it a guide to the writing and speaking of 'correct' German, if only because the language written and spoken in one part of the German-speaking countries is not necessarily regarded as correct in other parts. In his address to the Modern Languages Association on 2 January 1958, Dr. Schwarzenberg, the Austrian ambassador, said that he spoke as 'a Viennese, in whose home town all languages are spoken, but none correctly'. This obviously implies that there is such a thing as correct German, and there is a similar implication in the 87th of Platen's *Lebensregeln*—**Rede deine Sprache rein von Provinzialismen und Fehlern gegen die Sprachlehre : es ist der niedrigste Grad von Bildung.** On the other hand, Hugo von Hofmannsthal held that German should be written in an individual manner, otherwise it was bad German. Still, even he presumably differentiated between bad German and incorrect German, and a student who has perpetrated what are vulgarly called 'howlers' can hardly expect his teacher or examiner to accept the excuse that he had been writing in an individual manner!

Assuming, then, that there is such a thing as correct German, the question naturally arises: where is this written and spoken? —a question to which the only possible answer is—nowhere! Every German-speaking country has its own linguistic peculiarities, and standard German prose is that which remains when the whole language has, as it were, been cast into the melting-pot and had its impurities extracted. These impurities are most marked in the more outlying parts of the German-speaking countries, notably in the south—Suabia, Switzerland, and Austria—and for this reason it is open to question whether a student, certainly one in his first years, is well advised to read much of an author like Gottfried Keller. Admittedly, he is one of the best and most entertaining German story-tellers, but many of his Swiss idioms and constructions are never used in central and north Germany, and it is quite possible that some examiners might mark these as incorrect: indeed, the author of this dictionary has himself seen an examination script in which **Er saß ans Feuer** was marked as an incorrect rendering of 'He sat down by the fire', although that is quite a usual way of expressing the standard **Er setzte sich ans Feuer** in Switzerland. So also Keller says **Jukundus anerbot sich, die Mission zu übernehmen,** in which the southern use of the reflexive verb as one with inseparable first prefix is rather frowned upon farther north. And the same applies to the regular southern use of the auxiliary verb **sein,** as contrasted with the northern use of **haben,** with verbs implying a posture or attitude, as in **Hier bin ich oft gestanden** and **Wir sind heute lange im Garten gelegen.**

These are a few simple examples of the numerous difficulties and discrepancies which continually crop up in German, and the present volume is an attempt to guide students along what may be called the right lines, the conclusions arrived at being based on characteristic examples taken from nearly two hundred and fifty German authors, a list of whom will be found in the Appendix at the end of the volume. In this list it has been thought advisable to indicate, as far as possible, when the authors lived—many, of course, are still alive—so that readers might have some idea in which period of the history of the language a particular construction was in use. The great majority of these authors, of course, are modern, but the author has not hesitated to include examples from the classical writers, even the poets, where the examples were appropriate, and more especially where they differ from established modern usage. In particular, these have frequently been quoted in order to show how modern usage has gradually developed: the author has found in practice that students are much less apt to make mistakes when they have had the origin of many expressions and constructions explained to them—such expressions as **allerhand Leute, schlechterdings, wenig Aufhebens machen, Hier ist meines Bleibens nicht,** and constructions like **Er wird**

sicher kommen, er müßte denn krank sein, and **Er kann kaum seine Muttersprache, geschweige denn eine fremde Sprache reden.** Explaining such points has, of course, necessitated reference to earlier periods of the language, especially to Middle High German. Thus, to express a proposition like 'I shall not forget that', one now says **Das werde ich nicht vergessen**, but the Middle High German verb *vergezzen* always took a *genitive* object (now confined in prose to the flower **Vergißmeinnicht**), and the accusative only crept in as a result of confusion between the genitive *es* and the accusative *ez*. And this verb **vergessen** has developed other constructions in the south which are avoided in established prose, as in **Die Angst hatte sie daran vergessen lassen** (Stefan Zweig) and **Er schien auf die Unterredung vergessen zu haben** (Adelbert Stifter). So also Hofmannsthal's **Prinz Eugen war ein Fürstensohn und hatte über diesem** (= **überdies**, 'moreover') **eine fürstliche Seele**, and **Das war jemand anderes Lachen** may be expressed in that author's individual manner, but are certainly not—at least not yet—in accordance with accepted usage.

But the present writer would not like it to be thought that he is against all changes in the language: a language is a living organism and must develop. One way in which it develops is by the introduction of new words, not only indigenous words to express new inventions or discoveries, but also words taken over from other languages. The latter are very appropriate where no German words would exactly express the sense to be conveyed, or where otherwise an awkward circumlocution would be required. Thus, the English adjective 'fair', as used in a proposition like 'That is not fair', has become part and parcel of the German vocabulary, as in **ein fairer Sportsmann** or **ein faires Spiel,** where alternative expressions like **ehrlich** or **anständig** would not quite convey the precise force of the English adjective; and a proposition like **Das ist eben das Unfaire, daß ich ein Versprechen habe geben müssen, aber keines dagegen empfangen habe** (Thomas Mann) no longer comes as a shock, as it would have done not so long ago. And the same applies to propositions such as **Dieses Buch zählt jetzt zu den Bestsellern,** and **Eine tadellos aufgemachte Dame trat herein,** the noun **Aufmachung** having apparently become the recognized expression for a lady's 'make-up'. On the other hand, the present author confesses to having received a real shock when he read, in a translation of a novel of Graham Green's, examples like

Am Abend versammelten sie sich zu ihren Drinks, and **Er mixte die Cocktails**—which reminded him of a German lady who having settled in this country, used to say, **Ich muß das Feuer poken,** and even **Ich habe einen Kalt ge-catched!**—It is, of course, not easy to draw a line here, and it is more than doubtful whether certain expressions used in Thomas Mann's later works should be accepted. He was unquestionably one of the best modern German writers, and his earlier works like *Buddenbrooks* and *Königliche Hoheit* are models of standard prose; but, as a result of spending his last years in America, he came to use expressions which are really not German, but Anglicisms in German clothing, as, for example, when he refers to **die Schule, in der ich aufgebracht worden war,** and even goes so far as to say **Möglicherweise hatte er es in einem kulturgeschichtlichen Buche aufgepickt.** So also a literal rendering of our colloquial 'if you ask me' has anything but a German ring in the proposition **Daß das mit Hexerei zu tun habe, war die Überzeugung früherer Epochen : eine respektable Überzeugung, wenn man mich fragt.**

These are only a few of the many points which are discussed in the present volume. It will be seen from what has been said that this dictionary differs fundamentally from the usual kind: it is mainly concerned with the difficulties which the language presents in grammar and syntax, and with matters which leave the student in doubt as to what is correct and what is not. The only feature which it has in common with other dictionaries is the alphabetical arrangement: this, with the help of numerous cross-references, the author has thought much more convenient than the alternative arrangement in sections based on the various parts of speech—nouns, adjectives, pronouns, etc.—which would have meant much loss of time in finding what was wanted and necessitated a long alphabetical index at the end of the volume. But it is also, to a rather limited extent, a dictionary of more or less synonymous terms; thus, the article on 'room', which explains the difference between some half-dozen possible German expressions, should help students to avoid the mistake of representing a hostess as conducting her guests into the **Speisekammer** ('store-room, larder') instead of into the **Speise-** or **Eßzimmer** ('dining-room')!

But synonyms are more in the nature of side-lines here. What the author had mainly in mind when compiling this volume was to deal with puzzling questions which every teacher and student of German must ask himself—questions like these: should one say **Ich habe viele deutsche** or **deutschen Romane gelesen—Ich erwarte den Besuch einiger guter** or **guten Freunde—Das Buch hat mich** or **mir 20 Mark gekostet—Wir müssen in diese** or **dieser Richtung gehen—Er klopfte an die** or **der Tür—Sie versank in einen** or **einem tiefen Schlaf—Weder er noch sein Bruder war** or **waren da—Ich hängte** or **hing das Bild an die Wand—Sie schrak** or **schreckte aus einem Traum auf—Sie sind nach Amerika übersie′delt** or **ü′bergesiedelt—Er anerkannte mein Recht** or **erkannte mein Recht an—Sie hat** or **ist eine Ehe eingegangen—Er war ein Sohn Wilhelm** or **Wilhelms des Zweiten**—? It is questions such as these that the author has attempted to answer in this dictionary, and he can only express the hope that it will achieve its purpose.

ABBREVIATIONS

abs., absolute(ly).
accus., accusative.
ad fin., at (or near) the end.
adj., adjective, adjectival(ly).
adjs., adjectives.
adj.-subst(s)., adjective-substantive(s).
adv(s)., adverb(s).
antith., antithesis.
ant(s)., antonym(s).
appos., apposition(al), appositive.
art., article.
A-S, Anglo-Saxon.
attrib., attributive.
aux., auxiliary.

cf., compare.
coll., colloquial(ism).
collect., collective(ly).
compar., comparative.
compd(s)., compound(s).
concess., concessive.
cond., conditional.
conj(s)., conjunction(s).
co-ord., co-ordinate.

dat., dative.
def., definite.
dem., demonstrative.
dim., diminutive.
dir., direct.
distrib., distributive.

e.g., for example.
esp., especially.

fem., feminine.
fig., figurative(ly).
fin., at the end.
Fr., French.
fut., future.

G., Goethe.
gen(s)., genitive(s).
Goth., Gothic.

HG, High German.

id., the same (author).
i.e., that is.
imperat., imperative.
impers., impersonal(ly).

indecl., indeclinable.
indef., indefinite.
indic., indicative.
indir., indirect.
insep., inseparable.
interrog., interrogative.
irreg., irregular.
It., Italian.

lang., language.
Lat., Latin.
LG, Low German.
lit., literal(ly).

masc., masculine.
MHG, Middle High German.
MLG, Middle Low German.

neg(s)., negative(s).
neut., neuter.
NHG, New High German.
nom., nominative.
num(s)., numeral(s).

obj., object.
obs., obsolete.
OHG, Old High German.
opt., optative.
ord., ordinal.
orig., original(ly).

part(s)., participle(s).
perf., perfect.
pers., personal(ly).
pluperf., pluperfect.
plur., plural.
poet., poetical.
pos., positive.
possess., possessive.
pred., predicate.
prep(s)., preposition(s).
princ., principal.
pron., pronoun, pronominal.
prov., proverb(ial).

qq.v., to which (plural) refer.
q.v., to which (singular) refer.

recip., reciprocal.
reflex., reflexive.
reg., regular(ly).
rel., relative.
resp., respective(ly).

Sch., Schiller.
scil., namely.
Scot., Scots, scotticism.
sep., separate.
sic, correctly quoted.
sim., similar(ly).
sing., singular.
subj., subject; subjunctive.
subjs., subjects.
subord., subordinate.
subst(s)., substantive(s).
superl., superlative.

synon., synonymous.

temp., temporal.

v.(d.), von (der), in proper names.
viz., namely.
voc., vocative.

The sign $<$ = derived from;
$>$ = leading to, developing into.

Accents are inserted immediately *after* the vowel or diphthong to be accented.

A

Aar: This *masc.* noun is the orig. Germanic word for 'eagle' (Lat. *aquila*), but whereas it was orig. weak, it is now strong, so that MHG *zwên arn* has become **zwei Aare.** Like our 'erne', it is now largely confined to poetry and elevated prose, being replaced in ordinary lang. by **Adler,** a corrupt form of MHG *adel-ar,* i.e. **edler Aar.** Incidentally, the *fem.* **Aar** or **Aare** is the name of the Swiss tributary of the Rhine which flows through Bern, while **die Ahr** is a German river which joins the Rhine below Sinzig.

ab: 1. As an independent adv., **ab** is little used in good prose, except in a few phrases like **ab und zu** ('now and then') and **auf und ab** or **auf und nieder** ('up and down'), used both of walking to and fro and of a vessel at sea, as in **Auf und ab stieg und senkte sich das brave Schiff** (M. Eyth). But it is common in some coll. expressions like **Hut ab!** ('Hats off!') or **Kopf ab!** ('Cut off his head!'), and in the military command **Gewehr ab!** ('Order arms!' as opposed to **Gewehr über!** 'Slope arms!'). In such phrases **ab** is really a sep. prefix, a simple verb being understood (see **ab-**), and this applies also to its coll. use in **Der Knopf ist ab** (i.e. **abgerissen**) and **Wir sind vom rechten Wege ab** (i.e. **abgekommen**). **2.** It is also much used with prep. force in commercial lang.: e.g. **Unsere Preise verstehen sich frei ab Hamburg** ('Our prices are f.o.b. Hamburg')—**Unsere Adresse ist ab 1. Mai** (= **vom 1. Mai ab**) **Hochstraße 20**; and such expressions have found their way into the modern coll. style: cf. **Wir werden ab München** ('after we leave Munich') **in getrennten Kupees reisen** (E. Kästner) —**Ich muß ab morgen** ('beginning tomorrow') **skifahren** (id.).

ab-: 1. The fundamental force of this sep. prefix is not 'down' (which is always suggested by **herab-** and **hinab-**: see 2 and 3), but *'off'*, as in **abbrechen, -kratzen, -schneiden, -wischen,** etc., and esp. in verbs meaning 'to dispossess' a person (dat.) of a thing (accus.) by some means suggested by the simple verb, as **jemandem etwas abgewinnen, -handeln, -kaufen, -locken, -nötigen, -schmeicheln, -schwindeln,** etc. **2.** With verbs implying motion, **ab-** may incidentally suggest downward motion, but its real force is *separation.* Where it approaches **herab-** and **hinab-,** the difference lies either (**a**) in the relation in which the separated objects stand to each other, **ab-** pointing to a close or necessary connexion (cf. **Der Apfel fiel vom Baume ab** and **Der Knabe fiel vom Baume hinab**—**Als er eintrat, nahm er den Hut ab** and **Als er fortging, nahm er den Hut vom Nagel herab**); or (**b**) in the fact that **ab-** points to the object *from* which the falling object has become detached, while the double prefixes point to the object *on* which it falls (cf. **Das Laub fällt vom Baume ab** and **Das Laub fällt auf die Erde herab. 3.** As explained under **her-, hin-** 3, the commonest verbs of motion (**fallen, gehen, kommen, laufen, treten,** etc.), when compounded with a *simple* sep. prefix (**ab-, an-, aus-,** etc.), almost always have more or less *fig.* force and are used with various shades of meaning, while to express *lit.* ideas like falling down (a cliff), going up (a hill), coming up (a street), running into (the garden), etc. requires a double prefix (**herauf-, hinunter-, hinein-,** etc.), it being as exceptional if a simple prefix gives the verb lit. force as it is if a double prefix gives it fig. force. For characteristic examples of the fig. force which a simple prefix gives to these common verbs of motion, see esp. **abfallen, -gehen, -kommen, -laufen**; and the same verbs compounded with **aus-, ein-, unter-,** etc.

abändern: see **change** 1 (*a*).

abblühen: see **aushallen** 3.

abbrechen: see **ab-**; **stop** 1 (*e*).

Abend: 1. This noun is written with a capital letter (cf. **Morgen, Nacht**) in **dieser Abend, des** or **eines Abends, am** or **gegen Abend, zu Abend essen, guten Abend** sagen, but with a small letter in **gestern (heute, morgen) abend, Montag abend,** etc. **2.** The *gen.* is used to express 'in the course of the evening' (e.g. **Ich gehe lieber abends als morgens spazieren**; but a def. time may be added, as in **um 8 Uhr abends**), or it may suggest the idea of a recurrent action: hence distinguish between **Wir gehen Sonntag abends aus** (i.e. every Sunday evening) and **Wir gehen Sonntag abend aus** (i.e. this coming Sunday), the accus. being used here because the idea of def. time enters, as it does in **morgen abend, diesen Abend, jeden Abend,** etc.; cf. **Unsere Truppe spielte regelmäßig alle Abende** (G.), where one now usually says **alle Abend.** Where **abends** is modified by **früh** or **spät,** this may precede or follow: **Wir werden erst spät abends** or **abends spät zurückkommen.**

Abendmahl: see **Mahl** 2.

aber (adverb): The orig. force of this is 'again, anew', as in MHG *nû muoz ich aber singen als ê* (Walther v. d. Vogelweide: 'Now I feel the urge to sing again as I once did'), an idea which is now expressed by **abermals** (see **-mals** 2), substituted in the modern version of the Bible for Luther's **aber,** as in **Sie ward aber schwanger** (Gen. 38. 4). But **aber und aber** is sometimes used to suggest a great profusion, as in **Das Tal verbrannte, wo im Frühjahr die Narzissen aber und aber blühten** (C. Rothe); and one **aber** often serves to modify a word repeated for emphasis: e.g. **Ich fühlte mich von Schranken und aber Schranken beengt** (Chamisso: 'I felt confined by barriers and more barriers')—**Ich habe mich für nichts und aber nichts abgearbeitet** ('I have slaved, and all for nothing whatever, to no purpose'); now esp. before numerals: **Hundert und aber hundert Menschen waren mit Schaufeln beschäftigt, das Kehricht auf die Seite zu häufen** (G.)—**Es hatten sich tausend und aber tausend Leute zusammengefunden.**

aber (conjunction): **1.** The fundamental force of the conj. **sondern** is *separation* (the verb **sondern** means 'to segregate'), hence *dissimilarity,* and finally *antithesis.* It is used to introduce a proposition which *contradicts* a preceding *neg.* statement or idea, for which it substitutes a true affirmative, so that it has much the same force as **im Gegenteil** after a neg. proposition: e.g. **Sie sind nicht reich, sondern arm** (= **im Gegenteil, sie sind arm**). It always follows **nicht nur** ('not only . . . but also'), where it contradicts the adv. **nur:** e.g. **Sie sind nicht nur reich, sondern geradezu steinreich** ('They are not merely rich but actually rolling in money'). The neg. word should be explicitly expressed in the preceding clause: it is only in loose style that **sondern** follows a clause which merely *implies* a negation, as in **Er vermied die Hauptstraße, sondern lief an dem Garten entlang** (Spielhagen: cf. the correct **Er hielt die Hauptstraße nicht inne, sondern bog in einen Seitenweg ein**). **2.** On the other hand, **aber** does *not* contradict; indeed, it concedes the previous point (hence the frequent insertion, in the introductory clause, of a concess. adv. like **allerdings** or **zwar,** qq.v.), but it introduces a *contrast,* so that it may follow either a pos. or a neg. proposition: e.g. **Wir sind zwar ziemlich reich, aber da's können wir uns do'ch nicht leisten** ('True, we are quite comfortably off, but all the same we cannot afford that')—**Müde bin ich nicht, aber hungrig**—**Der Hausrat des Zimmers war nicht überladen und prächtig, aber solid und stattlich** (Hauff). That **aber** contrasts is seen from the fact that it may be a person's *first* word on his entering a room: **Aber was ist denn das für ein Lärm?** (where a previous contrasting idea is implied: 'Everything is quiet outside, but what is all this noise about in here?'). **3.** Not unlike **aber,** but more limited in use, is **allein,** which is little used in ordinary lang. It resembles **aber** in that it does *not* contradict; but while **aber** introduces a contrast, **allein** always has *limiting* force: e.g. **Dichterisches Talent kann man ihm nicht absprechen, allein er besitzt wenig Einbildungskraft.** It is esp. noteworthy that **allein** must always *introduce* its clause, and does *not* affect the word-order: hence distinguish between **Ich reise gern, aber allein reise ich nie** ('. . . I never travel alone') and **Ich habe zwar Zeit und Geld, allein ich reise nie** ('. . . but I never travel'). **4.** See **doch** (conjunction).

abfallen: As explained under **ab-** 2 and 3, and **her-, hin-** 3, this verb is not used with the lit. force of 'to fall down' (a staircase, into a hole, out of a window, to earth from a tree, etc.). This idea of falling to a lower level is expressed by **herab-** or **hinab-,** while that of falling, say, on a smooth floor is suggested by **hin-** or **nieder-** (see **down**): hence cf. **Er fiel die Treppe hinab** and **Er fiel auf der Straße hin** (cf. **stürzen** 1). On the other hand, **abfallen** has only fig. force, with various shades of meaning: e.g. **Hier fällt das Gelände steil ab** ('Here the ground slopes down steeply')—**Er ist vom rechten**

Glauben abgefallen ('He has fallen away from the true faith')—**Bei diesem Handel ist für mich wenig abgefallen** ('This deal has brought me little profit')—**Der zweite Akt fällt gegen den ersten ab** ('The second act shows a falling off from the first, compares unfavourably with the first'); cf. the coll. expression **Sie hat ihn abfallen lassen** ('She has cast him off, given him the cold shoulder').

abgehen: Like **abfallen** (q.v.), this verb has a number of fig. uses, the lit. idea of 'to go down' requiring the use of **hinabgehen.** The following examples illustrate some of the chief senses in which **abgehen** is used: **Der Zug ging Punkt zehn Uhr ab** ('The train left on the stroke of ten')—**Ein Knopf ist mir abgegangen** ('One of my buttons has come off')—**Unser Weg geht hier links ab** ('Our road goes off to the left here')—**Es gehen fünf Prozent ab** ('There is a discount of 5%')—**Das Verständnis für die moderne Kunst geht mir ab** ('To appreciate modern art is beyond me'): see **lack** (verb) 3—**Die Sitzung ging glatt ab** ('The meeting passed off smoothly').

abgelegen: see **abliegen.**

abgewöhnen: see **accustom(ed)** 3 (*a*).

abhalten: This verb can be used lit. in the sense of 'to keep *or* ward off', as in **Die Schutzwand hält den Regen ab,** but is esp. common fig. with objs. like **Sitzung, Versammlung, Prüfung, Gottesdienst, Fest,** etc. ('to hold' a meeting or examination, 'to conduct' a service, 'to celebrate' a festivity, etc.), and with a pers. obj. in the sense of 'to prevent' (see **stop** 2 *b*) as in **Nichts hält mich ab, der Einladung Folge zu leisten** ('There is nothing to prevent me from accepting the invitation'). Here, as with **(ver)hindern** (q.v.), a neg. is sometimes inserted in the dep. clause, but this is better omitted: e.g. **Was hält mich ab, daß ich nicht fluchen darf?** (G.), better **Was hält mich davon ab, zu fluchen?** or **Was hält mich vom Fluchen ab?**—see **negative** (pleonastic) 2 (*a*).

abhanden: see **Hand** 1.

abhängen: 1. As explained under **hängen** 2, *pres.* tense forms now always have the mutated stem-vowel **ä**; *weak* past tense forms (**hängte ab, abgehängt**) are always *trans.*; where an *intrans.* is required, a *strong* form is imperative (**hing ab, abgehangen**), but **hing ab** is now often used with *trans.* force. **2.** *Meanings*: **(a)** *trans.*, **'to take down'** (from a nail, etc.), 'to unhook': e.g. **Sie hängte** (or **hing**) **ihr Kleid vom Haken ab**—**In Köln wird der Speisewagen abgehängt** ('The dining-car is taken off at Cologne'); here belongs its elliptical coll. use in **Er entschuldigte sich und hängte ab** (Frank Thieß: 'He excused himself and rang off'), really = **Er hängte den Hörer an und brach das Gespräch ab** ('He cut off the conversation by hanging up the receiver'); **(b)** *intrans.*, 'to be conditioned by, depend on' (**von**): e.g. **Unser Spaziergang hängt vom Wetter ab**—**Er sagte, seine Bewerbung um die Stelle hinge ganz von dem damit verbundenen Gehalt ab** ('He said his application for the post all depended on the salary attached to it')—**Wenn es von mir abgehangen hätte, wäre die Sache längst erledigt** ('If it had depended on me, the matter would have been settled long ago'); see also **depend** 1 and 2.

abhold: This adj., which is now little used in ordinary prose, means 'ill-disposed', as in **Er ist mir abhold** ('He bears me ill-will'), and is often used in references to an 'adverse' fate or fortune: e.g. **Das Glück hat sich ihm nicht abhold gezeigt** (G.)—**„Wir haben tapfer gefochten", sagte er, „aber das Glück war uns abhold"** (Platen). As these examples show, it is mainly used in the *pred.*, but it is incorrect to say, as some grammars do, that it cannot be used *attrib.*: cf. **Aller Reumütigkeit abholde Naturen halten denjenigen, der einen Fehler frei bekennt, für schwächlich** (Auerbach: 'People who are by nature averse to feelings of remorse regard one who freely confesses a fault as a weakling')—**Der allen politischen Fortschritten abholde Adel stellte sich diesem Vorschlag entgegen** (Mügge).

abholen: see **begegnen** 1 (*a*).

abhören: see **überhören** 2; **accusative** (double) 1 (*c*).

abkommen: To **kommen,** as to other common verbs of motion (cf. **abfallen, -gehen, -laufen**), the prefix **ab-** gives fig. force: cf., on the one hand, **Ich wartete unten an der Treppe, bis die Dame herabgekommen war,** and on the other hand, **Ich glaube, wir sind vom Wege abgekommen** ('I think we have got off our road, taken a wrong turning')— **Können Sie morgen abkommen?** ('Can you get off work, make yourself free tomorrow?')—**Er scheint von seinem Vorhaben abgekommen zu sein** ('He seems to have given up his intention')—**Dieses Muster ist ganz**

abgekommen ('This pattern has gone quite out of fashion').

ablaufen: For the difference between **ab-** and **herab-** or **hinab-**, see **ab-** 2 and 3. Cf. **Der Junge ist den Hügel hinabgelaufen** and **Deine Uhr ist abgelaufen** ('Your watch has run down' or poet. 'Your last hour has come')—**Man hat den Teich ablaufen lassen** ('The pond has been drained')—**Die Frist läuft morgen ab** ('The allotted time expires to-morrow')—coll. **Ich ließ ihn ablaufen** ('I sent him about his business, snubbed him'); trans. **Er hat mir den Rang abgelaufen** ('He has beaten me')—**Er hat sich die Hörner abgelaufen** ('He has sown his wild oats').

ablauschen: see **überhören** 1.

Ablaut: i.e. *vowel-gradation*, change of stem-vowels. Various causes led to such changes (e.g. the shifting of accent), and it would go beyond the purpose of this volume to discuss these causes, which operated at different stages in the development of the language. Characteristic examples are seen in verbs like **binden, band, gebunden,** and in word-groups such as **ziehen, zeugen, Zögling, Zug,** although the latter are not true examples of **Ablaut. 1.** In order to conjugate a MHG strong verb, one must know *four* 'chief parts', not three as in NHG: the additional part one must know is the *plur.* of the past indic., because in most classes of MHG strong verbs the sing. and plur. of the past tense have different stem-vowels: e.g. *ich reit* ('I rode'), plur. *wir riten*—*ich krouch* ('I crept'), *wir kruchen*—*ich lêch* ('I lent'), *wir lihen*—*ich schôz* ('I shot'), *wir schuzzen.* Of this vowel-change in the past indic. there is now only one remnant, viz. **ich ward, wir wurden,** but even here uniformity has been brought about by the formation of the historically wrong sing. **ich wurde,** which has entirely displaced the strong form in ordinary lang. **2.** We still, however, have some other traces of earlier forms. **(a)** The *past subj.* of the MHG strong verb was formed by mutating, where possible, the vowel of the *plur.* of the past indic. (e.g. *wir schuzzen,* 'we shot'—*schüzze ich,* 'If I were to shoot'), and we still have verbs with the vowel **a** in the past indic., but **ü** in the past subj., viz. **helfen, sterben, verderben, werben, werden** and **werfen** (qqv.): cf. **Was würden diese armen Kinder anfangen, wenn ihre Eltern stürben, man sie aus dem Hause würfe und wir ihnen nicht hülfen?** The reason is obvious: there has been a definite striving not only after greater uniformity, but also after word-forms which avoid confusion with others, and it is evident that in the *spoken* lang. (often the determining factor) **ich hälfe** cannot be clearly distinguished from **ich helfe.** In the case of **verbergen,** both **verbärge** and **verbürge** are allowed, although both might lead to confusion: **verbärge** with **verberge,** and **verbürge** with the indic. of **verbürgen** ('to guarantee'). For **stünde,** the alternative form for **stände,** see **past subjunctive** 1 (*c*). **(b)** The following verbs form their past subj. with **ö**, those preceded by † having also *weak* forms: **befehlen, bewegen** (only in the sense of 'to induce'), **empfehlen, erwägen** (see **wiegen** 3), **fechten, flechten, †glimmen, heben, †klimmen, †melken, quellen** (intrans.), **schwellen** (intrans.), **†weben** and **wiegen** (qq.v.). **(c)** The following verbs form their past subj. with **ä** or **ö**, with, on the whole, a preference for **ö**, esp. those preceded by *****: **beginnen, *bersten, *dreschen, *gelten, *gewinnen, *rinnen, *schelten, *schwimmen, sinnen, *spinnen** and ***stehlen** (qq.v.). **3.** Although there are, apart from **werden,** no longer any verbs with different stem-vowels in the sing. and the plur. of the *past* indic., there are a number which have this peculiarity in the *pres.* indic., viz. **dürfen, können, mögen, müssen, wissen** and **wollen:** here the vowel-change from **ich darf** to **wir dürfen,** from **ich mag** to **wir mögen,** from **ich weiß** to **wir wissen,** etc. is explained by the fact that these forms were orig. past tenses which lost their past force and took on pres. force (see **past-present verbs**). **4.** Some verbs which orig. (and still in MHG) formed their past tenses by means of **Ablaut** are now *weak*, notably **bannen, bellen, falten, gellen, hinken, kreischen, kriegen, niesen, rächen** and **waten** (qq.v., and cf. **weben**), while others, which now change their stem-vowel, orig. formed their past tenses by means of 'reduplication' (see **reduplicating verbs**). **5.** For a change of stem-vowel in certain *weak* verbs, see **brennen.**

ableugnen: see **deny** 2 (*b*).

abliegen: This verb is ordinarily used of a remote spot, situated off the beaten track (cf. **distance** 5): e.g. **Der Bauernhof liegt weit von der Eisenbahn ab**—**Er lebt jetzt in einem abgelegenen Dorf.** With *trans.* force, it can be used of lying a specified time, as in **Der Kranke hat mehrere Monate abliegen müssen** (cf. **absitzen** 2). It is only in Switzerland that it is used in the sense of 'to lie down': cf. the example from Th. Mann given under **absitzen** 1.

abmachen: see **agree** 4 (*b*).

abnehmen: As explained under **ab-**, the prefix means 'off', not 'down': cf. on the one hand, **Ich habe das Bild von der Wand herabgenommen,** and on the other hand, **Er hat sich den Schnurrbart abnehmen lassen** ('He has had his moustache shaved off')—**Er hat mir mein ganzes Geld abgenommen** ('He has gone off with all my money')— **Der Priester nahm ihm die Beichte ab** ('The priest heard his confession')—**Du mußt einige Maschen abnehmen** ('You must take in some stitches'); intrans., **Das Fieber hat ab-, nicht zugenommen** ('The fever has abated, not increased': cf. **fail** 3).

abnötigen: see **nötigen** 2.

abreast: An expression like 'three abreast' is rendered by **drei nebeneinander.** For 'abreast of', see **Höhe,** which is also used fig., as in **auf der Höhe der Zeit** ('abreast of the times'); a strictly nautical term here is **dwars** (= '*athwart*'), as in **dwars ab von Helgoland** ('abeam of Heligoland').

abschaffen: see **schaffen** 2 (*b*).

Abscheu: see **Scheu.**

abschmeicheln: see **schmeicheln** 2.

abschöpfen: see **schöpfen.**

abseits: 1. Although properly an adv., this has come also, like **dies-** and **jenseits,** to be used as a prep. (**a**) With *adv.* force, it may imply either rest or motion, so that one can say **Das Dorf liegt abseits** ('off the beaten track': cf. Storm's **Am grauen Strand, am grauen Meer und seitab liegt die Stadt**) as well as **Ich ging etwas abseits** (G.), the latter suggesting not so much the idea of stepping 'aside' to let a person pass (see **bei** 2) as rather that of moving some distance away. In the adv. relation it is also used for our 'offside' in football, as in **Einer der Stürmer** ('forwards') **war** or **geriet abseits.** (**b**) As a *prep.*, it takes a gen. case: e.g. **Er hielt veratmend an** ('paused for breath') **und setzte sich abseits der Straße an den Rain** (H. Hesse)—**Das Pfarrhaus stand hinter der Kirche abseits der anderen Häuser** (Werfel); fig. **Er gratulierte mir, daß ich abseits der Politik in einem Kunstverlag arbeiten kann** (K. Edschmid); cf., as unusual, **Er hat abseits den anderen Gebäuden einen seltsamen Tempel aufgeführt** (Stifter), where **abseits** should be used either as a prep. + gen. or as an adv. followed by **von,** as in **Das Haus lag abseits vom Wege** (Auerbach). **2.** More common than **abseits,** implying less remoteness, is the adv. **beiseite** ('aside'), used esp. with verbs implying motion towards: for examples, see **bei** 2. **3.** On the other hand, **seitlich** is really an adj. meaning 'lateral', but is also used as a prep. + gen.: e.g. **Er fand einen Platz seitlich der Orgel** (Speckmann: 'at one side of, along from the organ').

absence: 1. The idea of absence from a place, when it implies *presence elsewhere* (not *non-existence*: see 2), is suggested by **abwesend** and **Abwesenheit** (cf. **wesen**). Like the antithetical adjectives **anwesend, gegenwärtig** and **zugegen** (see **presence**), the adj. **abwesend** is not really common in every-day language, although the noun is in fairly common use: one would much more readily say **Das Abkommen wurde in meiner Abwesenheit getroffen** ('The agreement was come to in my absence') than **Ich war abwesend, als das Abkommen getroffen wurde**; here the introductory princ. clause would usually take the form **Ich war nicht dabei.** At one time both the noun and the adj. were sometimes used to convey the idea of 'absent-mindedness' (cf. Scott's 'Waverley sat down in silence and with an air of *absence* and abstraction'): cf. the following example, where the reference is to people leaving their home before an advancing enemy and collecting their belongings at the last moment, **Luise geriet ganz aus der Fassung und brachte in Zerstreuung, ja in einer Art von Abwesenheit die unnützesten Sachen zum Aufpacken** (G.); and sim. **Ich schien abwesend, aber nur deshalb, weil ich mehr als gegenwärtig war** (G.)—**Ihre Augen blickten abwesend, wie mit ganz anderen Dingen beschäftigt** (Viebig); but modern usage here prefers the more specific **geistesabwesend. 2.** But **abwesend** and **Abwesenheit** should not be used where 'absence' implies *non-existence,* as in 'despite the absence of a breath of wind' or 'in the absence of any proof'. (**a**) As the adj. **vorhanden** means 'existing, extant' (see **Hand,** 1 *b*), so the noun **Vorhandensein** may merely imply that a thing *is* (see **existence** 2), and **Nichtvorhandensein** that a thing *is not,* available for use for a certain purpose): if the wire in an electric bulb is not burned through when the current is switched on, it is because *there is no air* in the bulb, an idea which a German might express by **Wenn der Draht in einer Glühbirne nicht sofort nach Einschaltung des Stromes durchbrennt, so ist es infolge des Nichtvorhandenseins von Luft in der Birne**; cf. **Mangel** (q.v.) **ist das Fehlen** (see *b*) **oder Nichtvorhandensein von etwas, dessen man bedarf** (Sanders). (**b**) Actually, the verb **fehlen** is not quite identical with **nicht vorhanden sein**: the latter implies non-existence, the former properly suggests that a thing which should be there is somewhere else (see **lack** 1). (**c**) From the last example given under (*a*), it is clear that **Mangel** (q.v.) suggests the non-presence of something of which one *feels the want*. So, in a proposition like **Essen kann ich nicht wegen der Schwierigkeit des Schluckens und der Abwesenheit des Geschmacks** (Heine), it would be better to say **wegen des mangelnden Geschmacks**; on the other hand, in **Nicht darin liegt seine** (*scil.* Guy Mannering's) **Vornehmheit, sondern in der Abwesenheit alles leeren Scheins** (Jul. Schmidt), the meaning is that there *is no* mere show, and that its absence is regarded as a praiseworthy quality, so that it would have been better to say, **sondern darin, daß bei ihm kein leerer Schein vorhanden ist** (or **daß er jeden leeren Schein meidet**). Moreover, the choice of a word may depend on the person's standpoint: while a person who feels the absence of sunshine as a definite drawback would say **Trotz des Mangels an Sonnenschein habe ich angenehme Ferien verbracht,** an angler, who does not want sunshine when he is out with his rod, would say **Trotz fehlenden Sonnenscheins habe ich keine einzige Forelle gefangen.** (**d**) This idea of absence may often be idiomatically expressed by the use of an *antithetical positive*: e.g. **Ein ruhiger Abend, eine vollkommene Windstille** ('the absence of even a breath of wind') **versprachen, das nächtliche Fest zu begünstigen** (G.). But this idea is most often expressed by the use of the suffix **-losigkeit** (cf. los 2 *a*): **Diese Tiere zeichnen sich durch Zahnlosigkeit des vorderen Oberkiefers aus** ('These animals are distinguished by the absence of teeth in the front upper jaw'); sim. **Man bemerkte meine Schattenlosigkeit** (Chamisso). This device is particularly appropriate where both positive and negative ideas are expressed: e.g. **Bewußtsein und Bewußtlosigkeit werden sich beim Komponisten verhalten wie Zettel und Einschlag** (G.)—**Er sieht keinen Zweck seines Wirkens und doch kann er Zwecklosigkeit nicht ertragen** (Sch.); so also in phrases like **sein Verhältnis oder vielmehr seine Verhältnislosigkeit zu diesem Hause** (Kürnberger)—**sein Charakter oder richtiger: seine Charakterlosigkeit.** (**e**) In this connexion, cf. also the expression **in Ermangelung** (see **fail** 1; **Mangel** 2).

absetzen: This verb is rather exceptional in that the prefix here normally has the force of 'down' (see **ab-**): e.g. **Der Fahrgast wurde an der Ecke abgesetzt** ('The passenger was set down at the corner')—**Das Pferd setzte den Reiter ab** ('The horse threw its rider')—**Der König wurde abgesetzt** ('The king was deposed'); fig., **Der Kaufmann setzte seine Waren bald ab** ('The merchant soon disposed of his wares'). Exceptional here also is the *fig.* force of the lengthened prefix **herab-:** e.g. **Der Kaufmann hat sich geweigert, seine Preise herabzusetzen** ('The merchant has refused to reduce his prices')—**Sein Gehalt wurde auf die Hälfte herabgesetzt** ('His salary was cut by half')—**Man sollte die Ehrlichkeit nicht herabsetzen** ('Honesty should not be depreciated, underrated').

absitzen: 1. *Intrans.* (aux. **sein**): Although **sitzen** (q.v. 1) implies *rest*, **absitzen** implies *motion*, but it should not be used in the sense of 'to sit down' (see **niedersitzen** and **her-, hin-** 3), in which sense it is used in Switzerland, as in **Sie saßen vor der Hütte auf die Steinklötze ab** (Federer); cf. **Der Schweizer braucht „absitzen" und „abliegen" für unser „sich setzen" und „sich legen"** (Th. Mann). The only standard intrans. use of **absitzen** is to convey the sense of 'to dismount' (cf. **aufsitzen**): the cavalry officer gives the command **Abgesessen!**—and sim. **Wir saßen ab und nahmen ein Frühstück** (C. F. Meyer)—**Die Pappenheimischen** (Pappenheim's mounted troops) **sind abgesessen und rücken an zu Fuß** (Sch.)—**Wir waren nicht abgesessen, weil wir uns im Sattel sicherer fühlten** (Wassermann). **2.** *Trans.* (aux. **haben**): Here it has the force of 'to sit through' to the end of a specified time: e.g. **Er hatte sein**

Eintrittsgeld gegeben und wollte seine drei Stunden absitzen (Immermann: 'He had paid his entry-money and was going to sit the three hours' till the show began)—**Endlich hatte er seine sechs Schulstunden abgesessen** (Spielhagen)—**Der Verbrecher hatte seine Strafzeit abgesessen** ('had served his sentence, done his time') **und wurde aus dem Gefängnis entlassen.**

absprechen: see **deny** 3.

Abstand: see **distance** 4.

absteigen: 1. Like other verbs implying a change of place, **steigen** requires the longer prefixes **herab-** and **hinab-** to express the lit. idea of descending a hill, a ladder, etc. (see **ab-** and **her-, hin-**); but the shorter prefix **ab-** is used in **von einem Pferde absteigen** ('to dismount' = **absitzen,** q.v.) and in **eine absteigende Tonleiter** (in music: 'a descending scale'). **2.** Noteworthy is the use of **absteigen** in the sense of 'to put up' at an inn, hotel, etc., and here, as with **einkehren** (q.v.), a *dat.* in the prep. phrase is the established rule: e.g. **Der Torwart nannte die „Goldene Sonne" und den „Distelzwang" als die Gasthäuser, in denen vornehme Reisende abzusteigen pflegten** (Jak. Frey)—**In Nürnberg stieg er im „Fürstenhof" ab** (W. v. Scholz)—**Das Gasthaus, in dem wir abstiegen, lag außerhalb** (R. v. Gottschall)—**Es war mir angenehm, aus dem Hotel hinauszutreten, in dem ich abgestiegen war** (Rilke)—**Eine fremde Frau ist in der Schenke abgestiegen** (Waggerl)—**In Meersburg stiegen sie im besten Wirtshaus ab** (H. W. Geißler); cf. the last example given under **schliefen.** For the dat. here, cf. **ankommen, ein-** and **vorsprechen, einsperren,** etc.

abstoßen: Whereas **hinabstoßen** always means 'to push down' to a lower level, as in **Ich stieß ihn die Treppe hinab** or in **den Fluß hinab** (see **ab-** 1), **abstoßen** is used in various specific senses: e.g. 'to push (a boat) off' from the shore or another vessel (see **stoßen** 2 *b*), then 'to leave port, put out', as in **Zwischen salutierenden Matrosen betrat man die Planken** ('stepped on board'), **die Sirene hustete rauh** ('emitted a strident hoot'), **man stieß ab** (Bruno Frank); also as a technical term, e.g. in carpentry ('to plane off'), in music ('to play distinctly, staccato', the notes not being tied), and esp. fig. 'to repel', as in **Sein Benehmen stößt ab** or **Er hat etwas Abstoßendes** (or **Abstößiges**) **an sich** ('There is something repellent about him').

abstürzen: see **stürzen** 1.

Abteil: see **Teil** 2 (*b*).

abtreten: Just as **abfallen** (q.v.) does not mean 'to fall down', so **abtreten** is not used in the sense of 'to step down': one must say **Er trat zu mir herab.** Actually, **abtreten** is mainly confined to a few set expressions like the military command **Abgetreten!** ('Dismiss!') and the stage direction **tritt ab** ('exit'); so also **vom Schauplatz abtreten** is 'to retire' (poet. 'to die') and **von einem Amt abtreten** is 'to resign *or* demit an office'. Otherwise the verb has trans. force: e.g. **Ich habe mir die Hacken abgetreten** ('I have worn away my heels')—**Dieser Teppich ist abgetreten** ('This carpet is worn through')—**Mein Nachbar will mir dieses Ackerstück abtreten** ('My neighbour is going to make over this field to me').

abwechseln: see **change** 2 (*a*).

abwerfen: As distinct from **hinwerfen,** which is used in contexts like **Ich warf mein Buch hin und erhob mich, um den Besuch zu begrüßen,** and **hinabwerfen,** which stresses motion down to a lower level, as in **In Schillers Ballade wirft der König einen goldenen Becher in die Flut hinab** (cf. **aufwerfen**), the fundamental force of **abwerfen** is 'to throw *or* cast *off*' (see **ab-**), any downward motion being accidental. In a proposition like **Das Pferd warf den Reiter ab,** the basic idea is the unseating of the rider, not his falling to the ground: when kicked off, he might conceivably land on a hedge, or even on the branch of an overhanging tree! Other characteristic examples are: **Zu gewissen Zeiten werfen Hirsche das Geweih ab** ('cast their antlers')—**Im Herbst werfen die meisten Bäume die Blätter ab** (of 'deciduous' trees)—**Ich warf zwei Fehlblätter ab** ('I discarded two playing-cards of no value, rags'); and more fig., **Das Unternehmen warf wenig Gewinn ab** ('The enterprise yielded little profit')—**Stundengeben wirft bei uns Musikern nicht viel ab** (R. Wagner: 'Giving lessons does not bring in much money to us musicians').

abwesend, Abwesenheit: see **absence** 1 and 2; **wesen.**

accompany: see **lead** 4 and 5.

accusative absolute: 1. Although not as common as the analogous Lat. *ablative absolute,* and lacking the latter's wide range of application, the German accus. absolute, which expresses some 'attendant circumstance' of an action, is in one respect less limited than the Lat. idiom. Whereas the latter requires a part. in the ablative phrase (in an apparently exceptional expression like *te auctore*, 'at your suggestion', there is a non-existent pres. part. of *esse* understood: lit. 'you being the adviser'), the German idiom is used with either a part., a sep. prefix (the part. of a verb being understood), an uninflected adj. or a prep. phrase: e.g. **Den Blick zu Boden gesenkt, den einen Arm schlaff herabhängend, den anderen gegen die Brust gedrückt, wandte sie sich von mir ab—Den Kopf stolz empor** (*scil.* **-gerichtet**), **die Arme übereinander** (*scil.* **-geschlagen**), **so stand er da—Den Blick starr, kam er auf mich zu—Sie saßen am Tisch, jeder einen Jahrgang einer illustrierten Wochenschrift vor sich** (Ompteda)—**In der einen Hand einen Blumenstrauß, in der anderen ein versiegeltes Papier, trat er in die Kammer** (Bruno Frank). Actually, the accus. here is not 'absolute' at all, it is the direct obj. of an unexpressed pres. part.: **Den Blick zu Boden gesenkt** (*scil.* **habend**), **wandte sie sich von mir ab—Einen Strauß in der Hand** (*scil.* **haltend**), **trat er in die Kammer**; and this explains the use, and the normal position in its clause, of **ausgenommen** (see **except** 1): **Ich habe niemand besucht, meinen Onkel ausgenommen** (*scil.* **habend**: lit. 'having excepted my uncle'). **2.** The unexpressed part. should, of course, refer to the *subj.* of the finite clause, as in the above examples, or in **Dies vorausgeschickt** (*scil.* **habend**), **gehe ich zu meinem Thema über** ('Having—i.e. Now that *I* have—made these preliminary remarks, *I* shall proceed to discuss my subject'); and the grammarians are right in condemning examples like **Ein paar Tage vergangen, wußte ich nicht, ob es schon Zeit sei, die Noten abzuholen** (Grillparzer) or **Die Tür zu, ging das Feuer auf dem Herd aus** (Hopfen), where the subj. of the contracted phrase is obviously not that of the main clause. An exception here is the common expression **gesetzt den Fall,** (**daß**) . . ., '(let us) suppose that . . .', which has become a true accus. abs.: e.g. **Wir können es nicht, aber gesetzt den Fall, wir könnten es** (or **daß wir es könnten**), **was dann?** ('We cannot do it, but suppose we could, what then?'); here, indeed, the accus. is often omitted, as in **Ich hab' es nicht getan, jedoch gesetzt, ich tat's** . . . (Sch.: '. . . but assuming I did . . .'). **3.** Occasionally we find a *nominative absolute*. This use should be confined to cases of 'partitive apposition', i.e. where the nom. in the contracted clause forms a constituent part of the nom. in the finite clause. Thus, it is strictly incorrect to say **Im braunen Reitkleid, ein runder** (for **einen runden**) **Hut auf dem Haupt, lenkte sie aller Blicke auf sich** (Heine), but correct to say **Eine Prozession durchzog die Stadt, voran ein Fahnenträger,** because the standard-bearer formed part of the procession; and sim. **Ich voran, gingen wir in die Halle hinaus** (A. Schaeffer)—**Am Straßenrand stand ein hoher Stein, wie ein Bär, der sich aufrichtet, der gewölbte Bauch groß** (Britting). Cf., with both cases, **Eines Vormittags gingen ihre Eltern, der Graf seinen Schimmel hinter sich, hier vorbei** (Storm). For the fluctuation, cf. in translations of *Macbeth,* **Ist das ein Dolch, was ich vor mir erblicke, der Griff mir zugekehrt?** (Schlegel–Tieck) and **Ist dies ein Dolch, was ich da vor mir sehe, den Griff mir zugewendet?** (Schiller); also **Von der Last der Jahre gebückt, den Schnee des Alters auf dem Scheitel, zahnlos der Mund, aber noch glänzend das Auge, so wohnten sie unter den ihrigen** (A. Schieber).

accusative and infinitive: This construction permits of the substitution, in certain cases, of a noun or pron. in the accus. case, followed by an infin. *without* **zu**, for a finite subord. clause. While fairly common in the earliest periods, it was much less common in MHG, so that we probably owe its extensive use in NHG to the influence of the Lat. idiom; but it seems probable, nevertheless, that the orig. German construction was the *accus. and part.* (q.v.). **1.** (**a**) The accus. and infin. is esp. common after nine verbs (see 1 *d*), viz. **finden** ('to find' the obj. in a certain state), **fühlen, haben** (where the infin. is really pleonastic), **heißen** (q.v. 3 *b*: 'to bid'), **hören, lassen** (q.v.), **lehren** (q.v.), **machen** and **sehen**: e.g. **Ich fand ihn am Feuer sitzen—Ich fühlte meine Pulse heftig schlagen—Er hatte ein Schwert an der Seite hängen—Man hieß mich schweigen—Ich hörte ihn husten—Er ließ mich lange warten—Die Not lehrt uns beten—Der Anblick machte mich beben—Ich sah ihn hinfallen.** (**b**) The Fr. rel. construction after some verbs (e.g. *Nous trouvâmes mon fils qui patinait*) is *not* used in

German. Of course, one can say **Eben sah ich den Herrn, der gestern hinfiel,** where the rel. clause merely identifies the person in question; but where the obj. is not the person or thing, but the *action* suggested by the verb, the rel. construction is never used in German: to render 'I saw him fall' (i.e. in the act of falling) by **Ich sah ihn, der hinfiel** is quite wrong. (**c**) The only alternative German construction is a subord. clause introduced by **wie** (q.v.): **Ich sah, wie er hinfiel** = **Ich sah ihn hinfallen**; and this is often preferred, esp. to avoid one infin. clause depending on another, or a succession of infin. clauses: e.g. **Ich sah, wie er das Kind weinen machte** (for **Ich sah ihn das Kind weinen machen**)—**Noch sehe ich sein Auge sinnend auf den Blättern seines Stammbuches weilen; und deutlich sehe ich, wie dieses Auge nach und nach sich füllt, wie eine Träne in den grauen Wimpern zittert, wie der Mund sich zusammenpreßt, wie der Alte die Feder ergreift und einem geschiedenen Bruder das schwarze Kreuz unter den Namen malt** (Hauff). (**d**) Strangely enough, **fühlen, hören,** and **sehen** are the only verbs of 'sense-perception' which are reg. followed by the accus. and infin.; of the other verbs of this kind, some (like **empfinden** and **vernehmen**) seem never to be so used, while others (**bemerken, erblicken, gewahren, schauen, spüren,** to which might be added **ahnen, glauben, wissen, zeigen**) are only occasionally used in this way (see these verbs). **2.** (**a**) The accus. and infin. having the force of a subord. clause whose subj. is the accus. and whose pred. is the infin., it follows that if the infin. is a trans. verb with a dir. obj., there will be *two* nouns, both in the accus.: e.g. **Ich hörte ihn** (subj.) **ein Lied** (obj.) **singen.** Now, where the subj. is unknown or purposely left vague, it is idiomatically *omitted*: e.g. (without an obj.) **Ich hörte im Nebenzimmer singen,** and (with an obj.) **Ich hörte ein Lied singen,** a word like **jemand** being understood in either case. In the second example, the act. infin. is usually said to have '*pass. force*' ('I heard a song being sung'), and although this was orig. not the case, the true explanation of the idiom (viz. that the infin. has *act.* force, its subj. being unexpressed) was gradually lost sight of, and the infin. did actually come to have *pass.* force. This is evident, for instance, from propositions which contain a *reflex.* pron.: in a sentence like **Das ließ er sich** (dat.) **nicht zweimal sagen** ('He did not wait to be told that twice'), the lit. meaning is 'He did not let (anyone) tell him that twice', so that if the subj. is inserted, the pron. must be a *pers.*, not a reflex. one: **Er ließ niemand ihm das zweimal sagen** (cf. 3). So we say that the infin. has 'pass. force' in propositions like **Ich ließ mir ein Haus bauen** and **Ich sah den Dieb verhaften,** the lit. meanings of which are 'I let (some one) build me a house' and 'I saw (the police) arrest the thief'; so also **Ich hieß den Fremden einführen** is 'I bade the stranger be introduced', but really corresponds to 'A slave announced to him a visit from one of the priests. . . . He *bade introduce the visitor*' (Gissing). It is important to note that in such propositions the true pass. form is *not* used in German: no one says **Ich ließ mir ein Haus gebaut werden** or **Ich hörte ihn gerufen werden.** (**b**) It follows at once that such propositions may be *ambiguous*: **Ich hörte ihn rufen** may mean either 'I heard him calling' or 'I heard him being called'. To avoid this ambiguity, where the infin. has pass. force, the logical subj. is usually expressed by means of **von** or **durch,** as with any pass. verb: e.g. **Ich hörte ihn von seiner Mutter** (or **von irgend jemand**) **rufen**—**Er ließ mich durch seinen Freund grüßen. 3.** Special difficulty arises where the infin. clause contains *pronouns in the 3rd person.* (**a**) If the infin. has *pass.* force, or if its subj. is *omitted,* a *reflex.* pron. refers to the subj. of the *princ.* clause, a *pers.* pron. to some one else: e.g. **Er macht viel von sich reden** ('He is the talk of the town, is making a stir in the world', lit. 'He makes people talk much about him')—**Das läßt sich nicht ändern** ('That cannot be altered', lit. 'That does not let [anybody] alter it'); so also **Er** (A) **ließ sich** (A) **ihm** (B) **anmelden** ('He had himself announced to him, sent in his card to him'). (**b**) If the infin. has *act.* force and its subj. is expressed, a *pers.* pron. refers to the subj. of the *princ.* clause (but see *c*), a *reflex.* pron. to the subj. of the *infin.* clause: e.g. **Er** (A) **hieß ihn** (B) **sich** (B) **hinsetzen**—**Er** (A) **sah ihn** (B) **sich** (B) **ihm** (A) **nähern.** (**c**) To the rule given under (*b*) there is one important exception: a *reflex.* pron. in the infin. clause refers to the subj. of the *princ.*

clause when this reflex. pron. is governed by a *prep.* or a *verbal prefix*: e.g. **Er** (A) **erwartete den Vater auf sich** (A) **losstürzen zu sehen** (Sudermann)—**Sie** (A) **stellte sich** (A) **nicht überrascht, sondern ließ ihn** (B) **ruhig auf sich** (A) **zukommen** (Wassermann)—**Als er** (A) **aufblickte, sah er** (A) **zwei Arbeiter sich** (A) **entgegenkommen** (Storm: 'Looking up, he saw two workmen coming towards *him*', not 'towards each other', which would be expressed by using **einander** instead of sich)—**Der Herzog** (A) **sah einen Staatsmann** (B) **sich** (A) **gegenübersitzen** (C. F. Meyer); cf., as a more complicated example, O. Ludwig's **Er** (A) **eilte hin, hob das Kind in seine** (A) **Arme und stellte es zwischen sich** (A) **und sie** (B); **die Frau** (B) **sah ihn** (A) **den Knaben zwischen sich** (B) **und ihn** (A) **stellen und verstand ihn** (A). **4.** Of the nine verbs given under 1 (*a*), there are five (viz. **heißen, hören, lassen, machen** and **sehen**) which, when used in a *compd.* tense with a dependent infin., have as a rule (cf. 5) the same peculiarity as the *modal aux. verbs* (q.v.) and as **helfen, brauchen** and sometimes **lernen** (qq.v.), viz. that the *past part.* is replaced by the *infin.* form: e.g. **Er hat mich gehen heißen**—**Ernst hatte in seiner Kindheit viel von Feen erzählen hören** (Jul. Wolff)—**Warum hast du das Kind weinen machen?** and here, if the word-order is 'transposed', the aux. *precedes* both infinitives (and any word or phrase closely connected with the first infin.): e.g. **Es wäre besser gewesen, wenn du den Arzt hättest kommen lassen**—**Er sagte, daß er das Kind habe weinen sehen**—**Ich sagte, daß ich sie habe gut Deutsch sprechen hören**—**Er behauptete, daß er den Dieb habe ins Haus schleichen sehen.** **5.** (**a**) Although the infin. form here is still the rule and sounds more idiomatic (indeed, many grammars—and teachers—insist on its use), the fact remains that there is an apparently growing tendency among modern authors to use the *past part.* form, and in this case the aux. in 'transposed' word-order occupies its normal position at the *end* of the clause: e.g. **Auch mir war es, als hätte ich den hageren Reiter vorbeisausen gesehen** (Storm)—**Wer hat dich lachen gemacht?** (Ebner-Eschenbach: no doubt to avoid the harsh combination **lachen machen**)—**Ich habe meinen Vater auf der Höhe seines Lebens schalten gesehen** (W. Schäfer)—**Das, was sie in ihrer Jugend so oft erzählen gehört hatte, glaubte sie nun erfahren zu haben** (Stehr)—**Die anderen hatten sie die Treppe hinuntergehen gehört** (Wassermann)—**Ich habe ihn nie wieder leiden gesehen** (H. Mann)—**Ich hatte die Kinder heranwachsen gesehen** (Werfel)—**Da ließ sich plötzlich die Stimme Quandts vernehmen, der leise hereingetreten war, als er die beiden sprechen gehört hatte** (Wassermann)—**Ich machte mich auf den Weg zu meiner alten Wohnung, in der ich soviele ein- und ausziehen gesehen habe** (Raabe)— **Ihr Blick fiel auf den Spiegel, den man in dem Zimmer stehen gelassen hatte** (A. Reiner)—**Er ging zu der Europakarte, die er auf dem Flügel** ('grand piano') **liegen gelassen hatte** (K. Edschmid). (**b**) The *past part.* form is the rule in the case of **lehren** and **wissen,** and is more usual in that of **fühlen:** where Hebbel says **Sie hätten nichts wissen damit anzufangen** ('They would not have known what to do with it'), one would now say **Sie hätten nichts damit anzufangen gewußt**; and sim. **Wer hat dich singen gelehrt?**—cf. **Ihr habt den Puls der Menschheit niemals durch euer Herz zittern fühlen** (Heyse: more usually **zittern gefühlt**). (**c**) The *part.* form is now always used when the aux. is dropped: e.g. **Wer ihn je malen gesehen** (or **Wer ihn je hat malen sehen**), **wird seine Kunst bewundert haben**—**Schon oben, als er den Wagen vor dem Haus stillhalten gehört, war eine Erstarrung von seinen Gliedern gefallen** (Wassermann). In the pre-classical and classical periods this omission of the aux. with two infin. forms was very common, but this is now avoided. Lessing almost regularly omits the aux. in such cases, esp. where the second infin. is a modal aux.: e.g. **Ich weiß, was hier verlorengegangen und warum es** (insert **hat**) **verlorengehen müssen; darauf bin ich stolzer, als ich auf alles bin, was ich nicht** (insert **habe**) **verlorengehen lassen.** (**d**) The *past part.* form is also the only correct one: (i) when the clause is a contracted one, formed with **zu** and a *perf. infin.*: e.g. **Ich bin mir nicht bewußt, seinen Namen nennen gehört zu haben**—**Ich erinnere mich, den Arzt kommen gelassen zu haben**—**Sie meinten, die Wölfe heulen gehört zu haben** (W. Schäfer)—cf., as incorrect, **Ich meinte, ihn haben rufen hören** (Ponten), which confuses **Ich**

meinte, ihn rufen gehört zu haben and **Ich meinte, ich hätte ihn rufen hören;** (ii) when the whole sentence is in the *pass.*, a use almost confined to **lassen,** and even then only where the dependent infin. has *act.* force, as in **Der Arzt wurde kommen gelassen**—no one says **Das Haus wurde bauen gelassen,** which would be expressed by **Man ließ das Haus bauen;** there is, however, a substitute for the true pass. in the case of **heißen** (q.v. 3 *a* and *b*) and **lehren** (q.v.). **6.** As stated above, the infin. in the accus. and infin. construction has *no* **zu**—it corresponds to the simple infin. in 'I saw him *fall*' or 'I bade him *go*'—and it is important to note that the accus. and infin. *cannot* be used in rendering 'I know him *to* be honest', 'I believe (consider, declare, find, regard, take) him *to* be reliable', 'I acknowledge him *to* be king', 'I expect you *to* be truthful', 'I wish you *to* come', etc. (see **wissen, glauben,** etc.).

accusative and participle: The German accus. and infin. construction (q.v.) probably developed, under Lat. influence, out of the accus. and pres. part.; certainly it seems likely that, in a proposition like **Er hatte einen Freund bei sich stehen,** the infin. **stehen** is a corrupt form of **stehend** ('He had a friend *standing* beside him'). But a *pres. part.* here now has a very limited application, being really only used, though hardly in the spoken lang., after **finden** (q.v.: of finding a person engaged in some occupation), and very commonly in a few phrases after **machen,** where the part. has become a pred. adj.: e.g. **Ich fand die Schwestern vor der Türe sitzend** (G.: usually **sitzen**)—**So oft es auch nötig wurde, sie in ihrem Zimmer aufzusuchen, fand man sie entweder betend oder in frommen Büchern lesend** (E. T. A. Hoffmann: cf. **fand man sie damit beschäftigt, entweder zu beten oder . . . zu lesen**)—**Er flüsterte mir zu, daß er niemals den Anblick vergessen werde, wie er mich schlafend gefunden habe** (Kafka) —**Sie nahm das Kind aus dem Bettchen: ach, sie wußte ja nicht, ob sie es lebend wiederfand** (G. Kinkel: cf. **ob sie es noch am Leben finden würde**); in the case of **machen,** one can only say **Er machte das Kind lachen,** but very common is **Sein Benehmen machte mich rasend** or **wütend** ('furious'), and esp. **Er machte seinen Einfluß geltend** ('He brought his influence to bear'), which is practically fixed (see **gelten** 2). A pres. part. after other verbs, e.g. **denken, glauben, sehen, treffen** (q.v. 2), etc., is only occasionally used in a rather choice literary style, and is better avoided in ordinary prose: e.g. **Er hatte sich ihn sitzend gedacht** (O. Ludwig: cf. **Er hatte gedacht, er würde ihn sitzen finden**)—**Er hat zu Protokoll gegeben** ('stated on evidence'), **daß er das Mädchen von ihres Vaters Dach kletternd und im Walde laufend gesehen habe** (Raabe: better **daß er gesehen habe, wie das Mädchen . . . kletterte und . . . lief**)—**Sie glaubte ihn wachend** (Sudermann: usually **Sie glaubte, er wäre wach**)—**Das Bild zeigt Rubens an einem Tulpenbeet vorbeispazierend** (Heyse: for **wie er . . . vorbeispaziert**)—**Er ging um das Haus herum, in dem er sie tanzend wußte** (O. Ludwig: an awkward way to express **in dem, wie er wußte, sie jetzt tanzte**). On the other hand, a *past part.* is in everyday use: e.g. **Zu meinem Erstaunen fand ich alles verändert** (G.)—**Ich fand deinen Vater in seinem Lehnstuhl eingeschlafen** (Storm)—**Sie fühlte den Apfel aus ihren Fingern genommen** (A. Schaeffer)—**Dann fühlte sie sich am Arm gefaßt und mit jähem Ruck fortgezogen** (Sudermann)—**Er glaubt sich gehaßt** (O. Ludwig)—**Da erlosch die Kerze und er hörte sich im Dunkel flüsternd gerufen** (Ponten)—**Er sah sich belauert, verleumdet, verraten** (Wassermann)—**Er sah seine Mutter in Sorgen verstrickt** (R. v. Gottschall)—**Wir hatten die Straße den Hirschgraben nennen hören, da wir aber weder Graben noch Hirsche sahen, so wollten wir diesen Ausdruck erklärt wissen** (G.)—**Die Frau wußte er mit einem Anstreicher verheiratet** (W. Schäfer); see also **träumen.** The past part. in these examples indicates that the action is completed, so that a state is implied; in several of them (e.g. those from Sudermann and Ponten) an act. infin. 'with pass. force' (see **accus. and infin.** 2 *a*) would idiomatically represent the action as still proceeding: **Sie fühlte sich am Arm fassen** ('She felt herself *being* seized by the arm')— **Er hörte sich im Dunkel rufen** ('In the darkness he heard himself *being* called').

accusative (double): 1. The chief verbs which take an accus. both of the person and of the thing are: **(a) fragen** (q.v.), esp. when the thing is an indef. neut. pron. or an adj.-subst.: e.g. **Hat er dich etwas gefragt?—Das einzige, was er mich**

fragte (= **Die einzige Frage, die er an mich stellte** or **richtete), war, wie ich hieße—Ihre Augen hatten eine Antwort auf alles, was er sie mit deutschen Worten fragte, die sie nicht verstand** (H. Hauser) —**Ich habe Sie Verschiedenes zu fragen** (Wildenbruch: 'I have several questions to ask you'). In this last example, the neut. adj.-subst. may really be an old *gen.*, a common construction in MHG: cf. *ich sage dir gerne*, des *du mich gevrâget hâst* (Hartmann). Apart from cases like the above, **fragen** now usually takes the prep. **nach** when information about a person or thing is asked for: e.g. **Er hat nach dir gefragt** ('He was asking for you') —**Er fragte mich nach der Ursache des Streites**; (**b**) **führen** and **leiten,** less commonly **lenken,** the accus. of the thing being the way along which the person is led or guided (cf. **lead** 1–3): e.g. **Wir werden unerforschliche Wege geführt** (Raabe)—**Komm und leite mich den Pfad** (Grillparzer); (**c**) certain compds. of **hören,** used esp. of a teacher 'hearing' a pupil's lessons, notably **überhören** (q.v.) and **verhören:** e.g. **Er überhörte die Kinder ein auswendig gelerntes Gedicht** (G.)—**Der Lehrer verhörte die Schüler ihre Aufgaben**—in the pass. **Den ersten Vers bin ich, den zweiten ist mein Freund überhört worden**; the same force is suggested by **abhören,** but this prefers a *dat.* of the person, as in **Er hat mir das Gedicht abgehört**; (**d**) **kosten** (q.v.) and **lehren** (q.v. 1). **2.** Some verbs take a double accus. of the person, one a direct, the other a pred. obj.: e.g. **Er hat mich einen Narren genannt (geschimpft, gescholten)**; see also **heißen** 2 and 3 (*a*).

accusative or dative in prepositional phrases: 1. After those preps. which can govern either of these two cases, the *dat.* is used if the place *in* or *at* is suggested, the *accus.* if motion *towards* or *into* is implied. To say that the dat. in such cases expresses 'rest' may obviously be incorrect: motion may quite well proceed *within* a given space, and a *dat.* is the correct case to use in rendering a proposition like 'The young people are dancing in the drawingroom', where the motion proceeds in the room, never extending beyond its limits. But a German's subtle linguistic sense demands that, when a verb of motion is associated with a dat. in the prep. phrase (a combination which obviously implies a clash between two fundamentally different conceptions), the idea of continued motion should be stressed, and this is effected by the use of an additional *prefix of motion*: just as we say 'The children ran *about* in the garden' and 'The horse trotted *round* in a circle', so a German says **Die Kinder liefen im Garten umher** and **Das Pferd trabte im Kreise herum** (see **umher**); and sim. **Er lief hinter mir her**—**Sie ging an mir vorbei**—**Er setzte sich neben mir hin,** etc. (see esp. **ankommen,** and cf. **Richtung**). **2.** (**a**) The accus. in such cases, then, suggests motion *towards* or *into*. Here again a German's more subtle sense of the *direction of activity* should be noted: where we 'stand an umbrella *in* a corner', 'hang a picture *on* the wall' or 'put something *on* a table', a German instinctively uses an *accus.*, as the action is clearly directed towards some object in each case. The accus. is essential with all *simple* verbs which imply such a direction of activity (but see *b*, and cf. **klopfen**): e.g. **Man hängt ein Bild an die Wand, bindet ein Pferd an den Baum, legt ein Buch auf den Tisch, breitet einen Teppich auf den Fußboden, stellt einen Schirm in die Ecke, hängt ein Gewehr über die Schulter,** etc., where the accus. indicates the goal towards which the activity is directed. The same applies, of course, to intrans. simple verbs: e.g. **Ich trat an das Fenster, fiel auf die Erde, ging hinter die Mauer, lief in die Stube,** etc. Where the goal is not specifically referred to, a German almost invariably uses a *compd.* verb: e.g. **Man bindet ein Pferd an** or **fest, hängt ein Bild auf, stellt einen Schirm hin, breitet einen Teppich aus, hängt ein Gewehr über,** etc., where the prefix points not to the activity itself but to the *end* of the activity. (**b**) Even where a compd. verb is used, the goal may, of course, still be added, in which case, as the end of the activity is suggested by the prefix, a *dat.* is really the correct case (but see *c*): e.g. **Man hängt ein Bild an der Wand auf, breitet einen Teppich auf dem Fußboden aus bindet ein Pferd an dem Baum fest,** etc.; and sim. **Er breitete eine Menge Blätter auf dem Tische vor mir aus** (Raabe)—**Er streckte sich in einem Sessel aus** (Keyserling)—**Am folgenden Tage zog der Graf in dem Schloß ein** (Binding)—**Er streckte sich auf dem Rasen hin** (Sudermann)—**Die Alte kauerte neben**

der Gräfin nieder (E. T. A. Hoffmann)—**Koffer und Kisten fielen krachend auf dem Deck nieder** (M. Eyth)—**Eine Droschke fuhr an der Tür vor** (Wildenbruch)—**Sie warf sich in ihrem Lehnstuhl zurück** (Carl Hauptmann)—**Die Bewohner des Hauses eilten vor der Tür zusammen** (C. F. Meyer). In particular, a *dat.* is always used where the prep. phrase indicates a place which stands in a certain relation to some object, and *from* which the motion proceeds, as in propositions like 'He stepped out *from behind* the tree', 'He crept out *from under* the bushes', 'The sound came *from beyond* the wood', etc.: e.g. **Ein kalter Wind kam überm Wald her** (Frenssen)—**Er streifte ihn mit einem Blitze unter seinen buschigen Brauen hervor** (C. F. Meyer)—**„Narrenpossen!" stieß er zwischen den Zähnen hervor** (id.)—**Einige Male hatte ich seine Nase hinter den Fensterscheiben hervorlugen sehen** (Raabe). (**c**) It should be observed, however, that the *accus.* is often employed even with a compd. verb; indeed, this may be essential, notably in connexion with the lengthened prefixes **hinaus, hinein,** etc., which always stress the idea of *continued motion*, not that of a goal which has been reached: so one *cannot* say **Ich stieg auf der Leiter hinauf, lief in dem Garten hinaus, ging in der Stube hinein,** etc., where the *accus.* is the only correct case (see esp. various verbs of motion compounded with **ein-, nieder-** and **ver-**).

accuse: As the fundamental force of **jemanden einer Sache beschuldigen** is 'to lay the blame *or* guilt for something on a person' (and one can do this without actually accusing him), and as **zeihen** and **bezichtigen,** which both imply the actual bringing of an accusation, are now little used (see **zeihen** 1 and 2), the only common expressions for 'to accuse' are **anklagen** and **verklagen.** These differ only in degree, **verklagen** properly referring to less serious charges ('to sue' for a debt, for alimony, breach of promise, etc.), **anklagen** esp. to grave crimes ('to arraign' for murder, 'to impeach' for high treason, etc.): as *Sanders* says, **In der Rechtssprache bezieht sich anklagen auf das peinliche** ('criminal'), **verklagen auf das bürgerliche** ('civil') **Rechtsverfahren: der Staatsanwalt klagt einen des Mordes, des Hochverrats an, der Gläubiger dagegen verklagt den Schuldner, um zu seinem Gelde zu gelangen.** In ordinary lang. the difference is not strictly observed: cf. **Du bist des Hochverrats verklagt** (Sch.)—**Man hat mich manches Lasters angeklagt** (Chamisso).

accustom(ed): 1. The MHG verb (*ge*)-*wōnen*, now obs., meant 'to stay habitually, abide', then 'to be(come) used to' something. The modern adj. **gewohnt** is not, as one might think, the past part. of this old verb, but a corrupt form of the MHG adj. *gewōn*, now with a long stem-vowel and an inorganic **-t,** which latter, however, is absent in the noun **Gewohnheit.** The MHG *gen.* construction in *ich bin des gewōn* ('I am accustomed to that') is still used in poetry and rather elevated prose: e.g. **Nicht des Schwerts gewohnt ist diese Hand** (Sch.)—**Alle schienen seiner unnützen Reden gewohnt** (Novalis)—**Wie bin ich solchen Friedens seit lange nicht gewohnt!** (Storm)—**Für die raschen Siegs gewohnten Römer dauerte der Makedonische Krieg schon zu lange** (W. v. Scholz)—**Es ist, als sei er des Gebrauches seiner Beine nicht gewohnt** (Th. Mann); neg. **Er war dieses Schweigens noch ungewohnt** (E. Engel)—**In dieser Stimme klang etwas, dessen er ungewohnt war** (Sudermann). But through failure to recognize the gen. in **Ich bin es gewohnt** (see **es** 1), the *accus.* came to displace the gen. more and more, and is now, along with **zu**+infin. (cf. **pflegen** 3), the construction in ordinary use: e.g. **Ich bin das gewohnt**—**Du bist die Sprache der Galanterie zu wenig gewohnt** (Lessing)—**Wenn er einmal deine Mitwirkung gewohnt ist, wird er ohne dich sein Geschäft nicht mehr verwalten können** (G.)—**Sie war das Bett, in dem sie lag, nicht gewohnt** (K. Edschmid). The unmutated form **gewohnt,** then, always suggests a *state* (cf. 2); and this form is also used freely as an attributive adj.: **Ich setzte mich an meinen gewohnten** (cf. 4) **Platz. 2.** The verb **gewöhnen** is the causative of the now obs. **gewohnen,** meaning 'to accustom' a person (accus.) to something. That to which the person is made accustomed was at one time expressed by **zu,** as in **Zur Sklaverei gewöhnt der Mensch sich gut** (G.)—**Gewöhnen Sie sich zur Geduld** (Sch.)—**Tausende konnten nicht so bald wieder zur Arbeit gewöhnt werden** (E. Wichert); but the recognized modern construction is **an**+*accus.*: e.g. **Man hat mich an das frühe Aufstehen gewöhnt**—

Ich habe mich daran gewöhnt, früh aufzustehen. While **gewohnt**, then, suggests a state, **gewöhnt** suggests an *action*: where it is apparently used to indicate a state, **worden** is really understood. But the unmutated form has undoubtedly influenced the mutated form in modern times, so that we find examples like **Der Doktor schien diese Art Fahrten gewöhnt zu sein** (Blunck)—**Ich heiße sie Karja, wie sie das gewöhnt ist** (P. Keller)—**Schlechte Behandlung war er gewöhnt** (Kästner); cf., with both forms correctly used, **Er hatte sich an alles gewöhnt, was des Gewohntwerdens bedurfte** (R. Waldmüller). **3.** Noteworthy compounds are: (**a**) **angewöhnen** ('to habituate') and its opposite **abgewöhnen** ('to break of a habit'), both with a *dat.* of the person and *accus.* of the thing: e.g. **Ich habe mir das Frühe Aufstehen angewöhnt** or **das späte Aufstehen abgewöhnt—Man hat sich angewöhnt, von gewissen Romantikern gewisse Dinge zu sagen, und wiederholt sie zu gerne** (Hofmannsthal); (**b**) **entwöhnen,** with the same force as **abgewöhnen,** but with an *accus.* of the person and a *gen.* of the thing: e.g. **Er stieß einen seiner Soldatenflüche, deren er sich** (accus.) **in der Zeit entwöhnt hatte, hervor** (Raabe). **4.** Like **gemein** (q.v.) and our 'common', the adj. **gewöhnlich** has gradually come to have a pejorative meaning, suggesting something 'ordinary', i.e. mediocre, plain, uncouth, inartistic: it should therefore be avoided where it might have such a depreciatory sense: cf. **Dieses Mädchen hat gewöhnliche Züge** ('unrefined features')—**Die jungen Leute waren nicht eigentlich gemeine, aber doch gewöhnliche Menschen** (G.: '. . . not exactly vulgar, but common, ungenteel people'). Where the idea of a *habitual* action is stressed, **gewohnheitsmäßig** may be used, which can, of course, never have such a depreciatory sense.

Achsel: see **shoulder.**

Acht: This fem. noun has three meanings, viz. (i) The figure '8' or an 'eight' in a pack of cards, and here it is written with a capital letter: e.g. VIII **ist eine römische Acht—Die Zahl 688 hat zwei Achten—Ich habe alle vier Achten in der Hand.** The numeral 8, on the other hand, is written with a small letter, and here it may take the coll. form **achte** if nothing follows: e.g. **Wieviel macht acht und zwei?—Es waren unser acht(e)** or **Wir waren zu achten** ('There were eight of us'); cf. **das Achtel,** either the 'eighth part' of something or (in music) a 'quaver'. (ii) Its other common meaning is 'attention, care' (no plur.), now written with a small letter, not only as a prefix, but also in prep. phrases: e.g. **Gib acht auf alles, was der Lehrer sagt!** (see **achten** 1)—**Nimm dich in acht!** ('Take care! Look out!'—see **hüten,** and cf. **Achtung!** 'Attention!')—**Das will ich außer acht lassen** ('I shall disregard that'). (iii) Its third meaning, no longer as common as in medieval times, is 'outlawry, proscription' (as distinct from **der Bann,** 'excommunication'), chiefly used in **jemand in die Acht tun** or **mit der Acht belegen** ('to outlaw a person') and **der** (or **in die**) **Acht verfallen** ('to become an outlaw').

achten: **1.** With the force of 'to heed, pay attention to, take notice of', **achten,** like **achtgeben** (see **observe**), now ordinarily takes the prep. **auf**+accus., while **beachten,** like **beobachten** (see **Obacht**), requires an accus. obj.: e.g. **Kinder, achtet auf das, was eure Eltern sagen!** or **auf die Lehre eurer Eltern!—Er hat die Vorschriften nicht beachtet.** In early NHG the simple verb took a *gen.*, as in **Das Haus Israel achtete mein nicht** (Jer. 3. 20), and this is still used, though not in ordinary lang., esp. where the obj. is a pers. pron.: e.g. **Niemand achtete der** (usually **auf die**) **Musik** (Fontane)—**Er achtete des Weges nicht** (C. F. Meyer)—**Die Wachen umringten ihn, aber er achtete ihrer nicht** (Wassermann)—**Schreie tönten von unten herauf, aber sie achtete ihrer nicht** (Ponten)—**Seine Verschämtheit war überflüssig, denn niemand achtete seiner** (Th. Mann). Here belongs **dessenungeachtet** ('regardless of that, notwithstanding'): see **ungeachtet** 1 (*a*). **2.** The simple verb may also be used in rendering a proposition like 'I regard that as foolish' (**Ich achte das für töricht**), but here modern usage rather prefers the compd. **erachten,** '**as**' being expressed by **für** or (esp. before a noun) **als**: e.g. **Meine wachsende Abneigung gegen die Schule zu begründen, erachte ich für überflüssig** (Th. Mann)—**Ich erachte solche Behandlung als eine Beleidigung**; cf. the common expression **meines Erachtens** ('in my opinion'). With the simple verb, **für** is sometimes omitted, which explains such expressions as **hochachten** ('to esteem highly') and **geringachten** ('to despise'), the pred. adj. having become a sep. prefix. Actually, in **Ich achte das gering,** the orig. construction was probably the accus. and infin., the infin. having dropped out: where Luther wrote **Ich achte es billig sein, euch zu erinnern** (2 Pet. 1. 13), the modern Bible omits **sein.** Out of **hoch achten** there developed, through the omission of **hoch,** the use of **achten** in the sense of 'to esteem', esp. common in the past part.: e.g. **Er ist als Kritiker allgemein geachtet —Er ist ein im ganzen Dorf geachteter Arzt.**

achter(n): see **hinten** 3.

achtgeben: see Acht; **achten** 1; **observe.**

Acker: This noun is used in three senses, viz. (i) 'soil' (now more usually **Boden**), as we speak of clay soil (**Lehmboden**), light soil (**leichter** or **lockerer Boden**), etc.; (ii) its commonest meaning, 'farmland, field', esp. under cultivation, as distinct from land for grazing (**Weideland**); (iii) as a measure, 'acre' (orig. as much as a yoke of oxen could plough in a day), still used in parts of southern central Germany, elsewhere now replaced by **Morgen.** In the first sense it has no plur., in the second the plur. **Äcker,** in the third strictly **Acker,** which is uninflected, as in **zehn Acker Weinberges** (Isa. 5. 10: 'ten acres of vineyard'), and in the dat. **der Ankauf von zwanzig Acker Landes.**

acknowledge: see **anerkennen.**

active with passive force: see **accusative and infinitive** 2 and 3; **accusative and participle ad fin.**; **infinitive** 3 (*a*) and (*b*), with which cf. **zu** 1; **lassen** 3 (*a*) and (*b*); **passive voice** 3 (*b*).

address (forms of): 1. Whereas the pers. pron. **du** (q.v.) and its plur. **ihr** (with poss. **dein** and **euer**) are used in addressing relatives, intimate friends and children, as well as in lyric poetry and prayers to the Deity, the plur. **Sie** (with poss. **Ihr**) is now the established polite form of address (see 2 *c*). Prons. used in direct address are written with capital letters, but **du** and **ihr** (with their poss. forms) only in small letters. **2.** (**a**) At the state opening of Parliament on 4 November 1952 the Queen began her speech from the throne with 'I, Elizabeth', not 'We, Elizabeth', as she would have done at one time: the German Emperor William II always used **„Wir, Wilhelm".** It was as a result of rulers referring to themselves in their decrees as **Wir** that their inferiors addressed them as **Ihr** (plur.: poss. **Euer**), which then became the recognized form of respectful address in polite society till the 14th century: at that time a peasant would say: **„Herr Doktor, das ist schön von Euch, daß Ihr uns besucht."** Sim. a plur. verb was used in addressing or referring to superior officers, dignitaries, etc., and esp. titled people, the poss. **Euer** before the title being generally written in the contracted form **Ew.**: e.g. **„Herr Hauptmann, der Herr Pfarrer bitten, eingelassen zu werden"** (Liliencron: 'Captain, the Padre requests an interview')—**„Erlauben mir Herr Oberst** ('Have I your permission, Colonel'), **auf einige Stunden hinüberzureiten?"** (id.) **—Seit wann interessieren sich der Herr Direktor für Kunst?** (K. Edschmid)— —**„Keine Seele hat sich um ihn gekümmert: Ew. Gnaden sind** ('Your Grace is') **die erste Person, die nach ihm fragt"** (I. Kurz)—**„Ew. Exzellenz dürfen sich nicht darüber täuschen, daß diese Ernennung des Grafen eine Willensäußerung Seiner Königlichen Hoheit in sich schloß"** (Th. Mann: 'Your Excellency must be under no misapprehension here: this appointment of the Count implied an express wish on the part of His Royal Highness'). (**b**) The next step was the use of **Er** and **Sie** (fem.) with a *sing.* verb, which came in at the end of the 16th century. It was regarded as a mark of good breeding to address a gentleman as **der Herr** (= 'sir'), often still with a plur. verb (cf. **Dero**), **Er** being used in a subsequent reference: e.g. **„Der Herr wollen mir gütigst verzeihen, Er hat mich mißverstanden"** (= 'Pardon me, sir, you have misunderstood me'). (**c**) Lastly, at the end of the 17th century, the modern polite use of **Sie** with a *plur.* verb gradually came in, which was the more convenient as it applied to either sex; and the more firmly this mode of address became established, the more did **Er** and **Sie** (sing.), which had till then been the ordinary polite forms, sink to the lowest level, being eventually only used by the educated classes in addressing people of lower social rank, on whom they rather looked down. Thus, a high-born lady, on asking a travelling showman why he was whipping a young bear, and being told **„Lernen muß er!"** asks **„Was hat Er denn gelernt?"** (F. Salten: 'What have *you* learnt?'), sarcastically implying that he had learnt very little; and so also the governor of a castle addresses a servant with **„Wo will Er hin mit den Pferden?"** ('Where do you think you're going with the horses?'). In the classical period, **Sie** (with plur. verb) was replaced by **Ihr**, but this is now regarded as too formal, modern plays being more and more complexioned by the idiom of everyday conversation.

adjectives (attributive): 1. Apart from certain cases where an adj. is not inflected, for which see **adjectives (indeclinable)** and **adjectives (uninflected)**, every attrib. adj. requires an inflectional ending to indicate its case and number. Such endings are either 'strong' or 'weak', according to the context. **2.** A *strong* ending is essential if the adj. has no other qualifying word before it, or has a qualifying word before it which has no inflectional ending, a *weak* ending if the adj. is preceded by a qualifying word which has a strong ending (e.g. the def. art., which is always strong: even **die** has the strong ending **-e,** MHG *die* being disyllabic): e.g. **Guter Rat kommt über Nacht** (prov.: 'Sleep on your problem, you'll find a solution in the morning'), but **Dieser gute Rat kam zu spät—Er tat es mit gutem** Recht, but **Er bestand auf seinem guten** Recht—**Dies sind zwei berühmte Dichter,** but **Die zwei berühmtesten deutschen Dichter sind Goethe und Schiller** (see **kein**)—**Die Anzahl großer Dichter ist verhältnismäßig klein,** but **Hier sind die Werke unserer größten Dichter. 3.** Important points in this connexion are: (**a**) Misleading are the poss. adjs. **ihr, euer,** and **unser,** which only *look* as if they had strong endings; actually, they have none, so that a following attrib. adj. must be *strong*: e.g. **ihr alter Vater—euer neues Haus—unser lieber Freund.** (**b**) In the gen. sing. masc. and neut. the strong forms in **-es** are now little used, being obligatory only in a pron. adj. qualifying a neut. adj.-subst., as in **Das Haus erschien ihm als der Inbegriff alles Schönen** (Sudermann: 'The house seemed to him to be the quintessence of beauty', lit. 'of everything beautiful'), where, as **Schönes** can only be used as a nom. or accus., the attrib. must be strong to show that it is a gen. Elsewhere the strong ending is still allowed in a few expressions like **Sei gutes Muts!** ('Be of good cheer!'), but **Sei guten Muts!** is now more usual; so also **Frischen Mutes konnte ich mich wieder an meine Arbeit setzen** (Raabe)—**Hängenden Hauptes, schwankenden Ganges kam er daher** (Wildenbruch)—**Allen Ernstes** ('In all seriousness'), **du tust ihm Unrecht** (Fontane)—**Seine Bereitschaft zu helfen hatte nichts von der Zudringlichkeit ungebetenen Mitleids** (Zuckmayer); cf. **allen-, jeden-, keinenfalls,** and see **manch** 3, **solch** 2. (**c**) An attrib. adj. following a *Saxon gen.* has a *strong* ending in consequence of the dropping of the art.: cf. **Dies ist das neue Haus meines Onkels,** but **Dies ist meines Onkels neues Haus. 4.** (**a**) Two or more *co-ord.* (i.e. equally important) adjs. should have the same ending, and should strictly be separated by commas, as in **schönes, warmes Wetter,** gen. **infolge schönen, warmen Wetters,** dat. **bei schönem, warmem Wetter.** Fluctuation here is common in the dat. sing. masc. and neut., in reference to which *Sanders* says: **„Ganz entschieden zu mißbilligen ist es, wenn bei nebengeordneten** (co-ord.) **Dativen dem ersten die Endung -em, dem zweiten die Endung -en gegeben wird."** While this strong condemnation is undoubtedly justified in theory, the fact remains that examples of what *Sanders* deprecates occur in practically all modern authors. But even so, it is certainly advisable to give co-ord. adjs. the same ending and to insert a comma, in spite of examples like the following: **Die Leichname wurden nach frommem christlichen Brauch begraben** (Hebbel)—**Er stand vor ihr mit entschlossenem freudigen Antlitz** (C. F. Meyer)—**Seine Schwester war ein schönes Kind mit langem braunen Haar** (G. Keller)—**Sie sah eine weibliche Gestalt mit reichem blonden Haar** (L. Schücking)—**Vor dem Fenster auf schwarzem hölzernen Sockel stand eine Heilandstatue** (Carossa)—**Er war aus Mitteldeutschland gebürtig, mit starkem blonden Schnurrbart** (Th. Mann)—**Hinter der Sänfte ritt auf kleinem weißen Pferde ein junger Adliger** (Dauthendey)—**Sie hatte ein schwarzes Kleid mit weißem hohen Kragen** (K. Edschmid); and even with a comma inserted, which makes it more objectionable, **Er saß auf einem Thron aus blauem, goldgestickten Samt** (Bruno Frank)—**Am Herde stand eine Frau mit rundem, krummen Rücken** (E. Kästner)—**In der Mauer war ein mächtiges, braunes Holztor aus festem, harten Eichenholz** (G. Britting). (**b**) It is different where the second adj. is *subord.*:

as *Sanders* says, **„Anders liegt das Verhältnis, wenn in den attributiven Bestimmungswörtern nicht Neben-, sondern Unterordnung obwaltet, so daß also kein ‚und' zwischengeschoben werden kann und richtig auch kein Komma gesetzt wird."** Thus it is quite correct to say **Er versuchte, die Hose von steifem englischen Leder, die hochgerutscht war, bis auf die groben Schuhe hinunterzuziehen** (Frenssen), because **englisches Leder** means 'moleskin', so that the reference is not to 'stiff English leather' but to 'stiff moleskin', an idea which might have been expressed by **die Hose von steifem Englisch-Leder**; cf. **Er fing an, sich mit den Fetzen seiner englischledernen Jacke die Augen zu wischen** (Sudermann). For the same reason it is quite correct to say **Die dramatischen Probleme Lessings waren nicht die höchsten: Kämpfe von reicherem tragischen Gehalt sind seitdem über unsere Bretter gegangen** (Treitschke), because 'tragic' here is obviously *subord.* **5.** There is much fluctuation also where a noun qualified by an attrib. adj. stands in appos. to a pers. pron., particularly when the latter is not followed by a comma. Contrary to the rule, the *weak* form is fixed in the dat. sing. *fem.* (see below), as in **Lieber Gott, vergilt ihr alles, was sie mir alten** (not **alter**) **Frau getan hat!** (Fontane), and is much more usual in the nom. plur. and the familiar 2nd plur.: e.g. **Wir jungen Leute waren nicht genötigt, uns aufzuopfern** (G.)—**So schwierige Sachen bringen wir vernünftigen Großen am besten selbst in Ordnung** (Speckmann), and sim. **wir alten Soldaten** (id.), **wir kurzsichtigen Menschen** (Heyse), **wir beiden Narren** (Ponten)—cf., as unusual, **Die Mutter blieb zu Hause, wir andere pilgerten zur Stadt hinaus** (H. Hesse); in the 2nd plur., **Ihr stillen Täler, lebet wohl!** (Sch.)—**Ihr nehmt uns alles, ihr reichen Leute!** (Waggerl). On the other hand, a *strong* ending is fixed in the nom. sing., as in **Was soll ich armer Mann (ich armes Weib) anfangen?** and practically fixed in the dat. sing. masc., thus differing from the corresponding fem.: it seems significant that the 1st edition of *Faust* has **Dir Vielgewandten muß ich's sagen,** and later-editions **Dir Vielgewandtem . . .**; and so also **Was erlauben Sie sich, Sie junger Mensch? Mir altem Mann wollen Sie sagen, was ich zu tun habe?** (M. Halbe)—**Haben Sie Erbarmen mit mir unglücklichem Vater!** (Sudermann)—**Der Graf im Rollstuhl empfing sie: „Welche Ehre! Ich weiß, Ihr Besuch gilt nicht mir armem Krüppel"** (Keyserling)—**Mir umgetriebenem Manne steht das an** (Th. Mann)—**Dir jungem Wesen ist es nicht vergönnt, zu trauern** (Raabe); cf. **Mir armen** (usually **armem**) **Schelm geht's nicht gut** (Heine), and sim. **Er setzte mir armen Sünder die Krone auf den Kopf** (Ric. Huch). In the accus. plur. a *strong* form seems preferable, if only to distinguish it from the dat.: cf. **Für uns (junge) Deutsche ist eine Kahnfahrt ohne Gesang Sünde** (Keyserling) and **Uns jungen Deutschen mißfällt eine Kahnfahrt ohne Gesang.** **6.** For the inflection of an attrib. adj. after an indef. num., see **einig, manch, viel, wenig,** etc., and cf. **folgend** 3.

adjectives (indeclinable): The only strictly indecl. adjs. are: **1.** Foreign loanwords denoting *colour* (q.v.): e.g. **Sie band große Bündel mit rosa** (which might have been **lila**) **Bändern** (Fontane)—**Es war ein Strauß gelber und rosa Chrysanthemen** (C. Hauptmann)—**Er trägt ein scharlach Kamisölchen** (Heine), where, however, one would now rather use **ein scharlachrotes Kamisölchen**; and sim. **karmesi'nrot** ('crimson'), **rubi'nrot** ('ruby'), **zinnoberrot** ('vermilion'). Incorrect is the inflected form in **Das Faß war mit oranger Masse gefüllt** (Freytag). Of course, such foreign adjs. can be made German by adding the suffix **-farben** or **-farbig,** as in **ein orange(n)-farbener Teppich, ein cremefarbenes Kostüm, lilafarbige Kleider, eine rosafarbige Tapete,** etc. **2.** Adjs. formed by adding **-er** to place-names: e.g. **Dies ist das Werk eines berühmten Leipziger Professors—Die Londoner klimatischen Verhältnisse sind mit den Wiener** (*scil.* **Verhältnissen**) **kaum zu vergleichen**; a word like **Wiener** or **Berliner** is only inflected when it refers to an inhabitant or a person born there, as in **Die Pariser kann man mit den Londonern kaum vergleichen.** **3.** Adjs. with the suffixes **-hand** and **-lei,** as in **Die Morgenblätter brachten heute allerhand Neues** and **Wir hatten Zeit zur Besichtigung von mancherlei Sehenswürdigkeiten,** where the adjs. were orig. gen. plur. expressions, as explained under **Hand** 2 (*a*) and (*b*). **4.** The cardinal numerals from **vier** upwards; for occasional inflexion here when the noun is not expressed, see

numerals; for the inflexion of **zwei** and **drei**, see **zwei** 2. **5.** Adjs. which are not used attrib., but only in the pred. with **sein, werden**, etc., the commonest being **allein** (q.v.; in coll. speech often **alleine**) —**angst** (see **bang**)—**ansichtig** (q.v.)—**barfuß,** less commonly **barhaupt** (with the attrib. forms **barfüßig, -häuptig**)—**eingedenk** (+gen., as in **Ich bin dessen eingedenk,** 'I am mindful of that')—**feind** (as in **Er ist mir feind:** attrib. **feindlich**)—**gar** (used of food that is 'done, properly cooked'; it is used attrib. in other technical contexts: see **gar** 1)—**gewahr** (q.v.)—**gewärtig** (+gen., as in **Er war dessen nicht gewärtig,** 'He did not expect that': see **gewärtigen**)—**gram** (as in **Er ist mir gram,** 'He bears me a grudge')—**habhaft** (q.v.)—**leid** (as in **Es ist mir leid um sie,** 'I am sorry for her': see **Leid**)—**nutz,** more commonly **nütze** (as in **Diese Maßregeln sind zu nichts nütze,** 'These measures are of no use': the attrib. form is **nützlich**)—**schade** (esp. in **Es ist schade, daß...** 'It is a pity that...') —**schuld** (as in **Er ist an allem schuld,** 'He is to blame for everything': the attrib. form is **schuldig**)—**unpaß** ('unwell, indisposed': see **krank**)—**verlustig** (+gen., 'deprived of', as in **Verbrecher gehen aller Rechte verlustig,** 'Criminals forfeit all rights').

adjectives (uninflected): To be distinguished from adjs. which are invariable —for which see **adjectives (indeclinable)**—are those which, while normally inflected, are in certain cases used in their uninflected form. Such are: **1,** Pos. and compar. adjs. in the pred., as in **Meine Eltern sind krank—Meine Hände sind voll** (for **voller,** see **voll** 3); superl. adjs. are always inflected: cf. **In Südafrika ist es um die Weihnachtszeit am heißesten.** **2.** Attrib. adjs. placed *after* the noun, common in poetry, as in **Es ist ein' Ros' entsprungen aus einer Wurzel zart,** but in prose only where they are really used pred. in a contracted rel. clause: e.g. **Mit ihm kam sein Sohn, ungewöhnlich groß für sein Alter—Er trug einen Zylinderhut, schwarz, lang und rund wie ein Ofenrohr.** **3.** Attrib. adjs. placed *before* the noun (esp. a neut. noun in the nom. or accus.), but left uninflected, also common in poetry, and in prov. expressions: e.g. **Pfui! ein politisch Lied! ein leidig Lied!** (G.)—**Unrecht Gut gedeiht nicht** ('Ill-gotten gain never prospers')— **Bös Ei, bös Küchlein** (cf. 'Like father, like son')—**Gut Ding will Weile haben** ('Good deeds aren't done in a hurry'). At one time this use was quite common in ordinary prose also—endless examples could be cited from the classics—but is now almost confined to a few expressions, esp. with the adj. **gut**, as in **Er war schon ein gut Stück über Sechzig hinaus** (Fontane) and **auf gut Glück** ('at random'), being otherwise generally avoided, so that examples like the following have a distinctly old-fashioned ring: **Es war ein stolz Volk, die Grafen Seeburg** (Raabe)—**Oft vergingen Tage, ohne daß er ein einzig Wort gesprochen hätte** (Sudermann); cf., as a strange example: **Es ist ein verzagtes Herz und kein trotzig Herz** (Fontane), where **Es ist ein verzagtes, kein trotziges Herz** would surely be much more natural. **4.** The first of two attrib. adjs. connected by **und** which form a single idea: e.g. **Zwei blau und weiße Tassen standen neben der Kaffeekanne** (Storm: i.e. two cups with a blue and white pattern)—**Wir redeten von einem grau und roten Papagei** (H. Hesse)—**Sie hatten rosenrot und weißen Speck gegessen** (Ernst)—**An den Wänden hin liefen hohe Regale mit Bänden in braun und weißem Leder** (Fontane: i.e. brown leather volumes with white markings). This use, of course, tends towards the formation of compd. adjs., **eine schwarz, weiß und rote Fahne** becoming **eine schwarzweißrote Fahne.** On the whole, apart from such words denoting colour, this use is now almost confined to expressions in which the two adjs. are more or less synon.: it is possible to say **Mir begegnete ein lang und dünner, ein hager und magerer Kerl—Ich streckte meine müd und matten Glieder aus.** Here belong esp. the set expressions **null und nichtig** ('null and void'), as in **Die Verfertiger dieser null und nichtigen Urkunde sind anklagbar** (Heine), and **gang und gäbe,** orig. used of money which is *given* by one person to another and so *goes from* hand to hand, as in a phrase like **in gang und gäber Münze** ('in current coin of the realm'), and then applied more generally to what is accepted or customary: e.g. **Hierzulande ist das ein gang und gäber Ausdruck** ('That is an ordinary, everyday expression in these parts')—**Er brachte es nicht über sich, was doch gang und gäbe ist, sich selbst vorzuschlagen** (G. Keller: 'He could not find it in his heart to do what is surely quite a usual thing, namely to propose himself' *scil.* as a candidate in the coming election).

adjective-substantives: Although in some cases there is a certain amount of fluctuation (see esp. 2 below), the inflexion of an adj. used as a noun is really quite straightforward. The important thing to bear in mind is that, although as a rule written with a capital letter (cf. 3 below, and see **deutsch** 3), an adj.-subst. is an *adj.* so far as inflexion is concerned, i.e. it takes the inflexional endings of an attrib. adj. **1.** *Adj.-substs. not qualified by an attrib. adj.*: (**a**) An adj.-subst. which is unqualified or is only qualified by an attrib. which has no inflexional ending, must be *strongly* inflected: e.g. **Ich komme als Gesandter des Gerichts** (Sch.)—**Er ist ein Verwandter von mir—Oldendorf ist Abgeordneter durch ein Mehr von zwei Stimmen** (Freytag: 'Oldendorf has been elected a Member by a majority of two votes')—**Die Mädchen verdankten ihren Morgenspaziergängen mancherlei Gutes** (Böhlau)—**Wir sind zu etwas Besserem geboren** (Sch.)—**In diesem Benehmen gab sich deutlich kund, daß ich eine Art von Besessenem war** (H. Hesse: 'My behaviour showed clearly that I was like one possessed': cf. **Art** 1)—**Wir wollen jetzt von etwas Wichtigerem** or **von etwas anderem reden** (but see **jemand** 2)—**In der Gesellschaft befanden sich zwei Deutsche —Darüber gehen die Ansichten Gelehrter auseinander** ('On this point the views of scholars are divided'); cf. **Beamte(r).** (**b**) When qualified by a word (other than an adj.) which has a strong ending (e.g. the def. art., **eines, meine, dieser,** etc.), the adj.-subst. has a *weak* ending: e.g. **Der Gesandte des Gerichts ist hier—Dieser Bediente ist zuverlässig—Wir erwarten den Besuch eines Verwandten—Ich sagte es im Beisein zweier Deutschen—Das Innere des Gebäudes entspricht dem Äußeren nicht—Wir sind mit allem Nötigen versehen—Ich wünsche Ihnen alles Gute** (but **viel Gutes**: see **viel** 1 *d*, and cf. **nichts** 2)—**Ich hatte alles Sehenswerte in der Stadt betrachtet** (W. v. Scholz). In all the above examples, both under (*a*) and (*b*), usage is now established, and very exceptional examples like the following are to be avoided: **Da drang ein Dutzend Anverwandten herein** (G., quoted by *Sanders* with the note **„statt des Nominativs Anverwandte oder des Genitivs Anverwandter"**)—**Er öffnete den Schlag des Wagens, aus dessen Inneren** (for **Innerem**) **er ein Päckchen heraushob** (Wildenbruch). **2.** *Adj.-substs. qualified by an attrib. adj.*: It is here that there is a good deal of fluctuation, and one can only recommend what seems to be the more usual practice. As two co-ord. attrib. adjs. normally have the same case-ending, as explained under **adjectives (attributive)** 4 (*a*), and as an adj.-subst. is really an adj., it follows that an adj.-subst. should have the same ending as a preceding attrib. adj., as in **Er ist ein entfernter Verwandter von mir —Während der Tafel ließ ein durchreisender Fremder sich melden** (Eckermann)—**Ein Dichter ist ein göttlicher Gesandter** (Novalis)—**Ihn haben wahre Gelehrte jederzeit verachtet** (Lessing); and exceptions in the nom. are sufficiently rare to prove the rule: cf. **Ein flinker und wohlunterrichteter Lohnbediente jagte mich durch die Straßen** (G.—*Sanders* says **„gewöhnlich: Bedienter"**). There is no difficulty, of course, where the attrib. adj. has a weak ending: one can only say **Ich erwarte den Besuch eines entfernten Verwandten—Das habe ich von einem durchreisenden Fremden erfahren—Die Zahl der ausländischen Studierenden hat bedeutend zugenommen.** But a *strong* ending in the attrib. adj. is rather more commonly followed by a *weak* ending in the adj.-subst. in certain cases, notably in the *nom. and accus. neut.*, in the *dat. sing.*, and in the *gen. plur.*, and, on the whole, examples like the following can be recommended: **Es ist ein Schloß, dessen Äußeres ein leidliches Innere erwarten läßt** (G.)—**Er erwarb sich durch ein ansprechendes Äußere die scharmantesten Lobsprüche** (Mörike)—**Der Roman** (*scil.* Mörike's 'Maler Nolten') **ist ein organisches Ganze** (H. Maync)—**Unter vielem Verhaßten ist mir das Schreiben das Verhaßteste** (G.)—**Sie war eine beleibte Dame von spießbürgerlichem Äußeren** (Th. Mann)—**Es war ein junger Mann von unauffälligem Äußeren** (Bruno Frank)—**Unterhaltungen deutscher Ausgewanderten** (G.: title)—**Ermüdet von der Arbeit, ging Mozart noch spät ein paar neugieriger Reisenden wegen zu einer musikalischen Soiree** (Mörike). But it must be emphasized that modern examples of strong endings in both adj. and adj.-subst. here (esp. in the nom. and accus. neut.), although apparently not nearly as common as in the classical period, are anything but rare, so that propositions like the following can hardly be condemned: **Der dritte Bruder behielt bis in sein höchstes Alter immer ein wunderliches Äußeres** (G.)—**Der Sarg zeigte sein weißes Inneres** (A. Schaeffer)—**Wer kann ein poetisches Ganzes bearbeiten, ohne seine eigentümliche Schönheit zu zerstören?** (Hofmannsthal)—**Man überschätzt das Sinnliche, wenn man das Geistige nur als einen Notersatz für fehlendes Sinnliches ansieht** (H. Hesse)—**Sie sahen eine Gruppe häßlich gekleideter Reisender** (Bruno Frank). **3.** As stated above, and as the examples show, an adj.-subst. is normally written with a capital letter; but in many everyday set expressions a lower-case letter is used, as in **den kürzeren ziehen** ('to come off second-best, get the worst of it'); and this applies esp. to prep. phrases in which the adj.-subst. loses much of its noun-force, and which to all intents and purposes have become adv. expressions: e.g. **Sie läßt dich aufs herzlichste grüßen** ('She sends you her kindest regards')—**Sie nannte einen Preis für das Zimmer, den er ohne weiteres** ('promptly') **zugestand** (Hofmannsthal)—**Von weitem sehen die Tennisplätze wie ungeheure Spinnennetze aus** (id.)—**Man wollte mich zum besten haben** ('They wanted to make fun of me'); so also **am besten—nicht bei weitem** ('not by a long way')—**fürs erste—im allgemeinen** ('in general')—**im großen und ganzen** ('on the whole')—**vor kurzem** ('a little while ago'), etc.; cf. **Der Arzt plauderte ein langes, verschrieb ein weniges und ging wieder** (Frenssen: 'The doctor chatted a lot, prescribed a little, and went on his way').

admit: 1. In the sense of 'to let in, grant admittance', this is ordinarily expressed by **jemanden ein-** or **zulassen** (qq.v.), more formally by **jemandem Zutritt gewähren.** Thus, **Bei Vorzeigung der Eintrittskarte wurde ich ein-** or **zugelassen**; but only **einlassen** is used of a shoe or a roof which 'lets in' water, and only **zulassen** expresses 'to admit of', as in **Dieser Satz läßt zwei Deutungen zu** ('This sentence admits of two interpretations'), while **vorlassen** is used esp. of admitting to the presence of a person of high standing: **Man ließ ihn bei der Königin vor. 2.** With the force of 'to concede, confess, allow' it can be rendered by several verbs, for which see **confess** 2, and cf. **Wort** 1 (*b*). But our 'I admit', inserted parenthetically in a proposition, is often more idiomatically expressed in German by one of the various 'concessive' advs.: see esp. **allerdings** 1 (*b*), **freilich** 3, and **zwar** 1, and cf. **schon** 2 (*c*) and **wohl** 3 (*a*).

advance: 1. With *trans.* force, the verb **rücken** means 'to move *or* shift' something, as in **den Stuhl ans Fenster rücken** and **den Hut rücken** ('to touch one's hat'); as an *intrans.* verb it is used in some coll. expressions (**jemandem auf die Bude rücken** is student slang for 'to invade a person's digs'), otherwise mainly in military parlance, as in **ins Feld rücken** ('to take the field'). The compd. **anrücken** suggests the *beginning* of a forward movement, while **vorrücken** is the standard expression for an army's 'advancing' in the sense of 'gaining ground': cf., on the one hand, in a reference to 'moves' in a game of chess, **Er läßt erst die Bauern** ('pawns'), **dann die Offiziere anrücken** (A. Eloesser), and on the other hand, **Das Heer ist mehrere Meilen vorgerückt** (cf. 2). The lengthened compd. **heranrücken** is used esp. of time, as in **Die Zeit meiner Audienz rückte heran** (W. v. Kügelgen). **2.** Where 'to advance' has the force of 'to make progress', the usual expression is **vorschreiten,** as in **Die Arbeit schreitet vor,** and **vorgeschritten** is used, as is **vorgerückt,** of a person's 'advanced' age: e.g. **Er steht schon in vorgeschrittenem** or **vorgerücktem Alter. 3.** 'To advance towards a person' is usually expressed by **auf jemanden zutreten** or (implying a closer approach) **an jemanden herantreten,** while **näher treten** is mainly used abs., as in **Bitte, treten Sie näher!** which is the polite way of asking a visitor to 'Come in!'. **4.** If a number of people have assembled or are drawn up, and one 'advances' or 'steps forward' for a specific purpose, the proper expression to use is **vortreten**: e.g. **Der Dorfgeistliche trat vor und sprach den Segen** (Fontane)—**Gefreiter Schmidt trete zwei Schritt vor!** ('Lance-corporal Smith, advance two paces!'); cf., with the verb understood, **Offiziere vor!** ('Officers to the front!').

adverbs formed from adjectives: 1. No one would readily recognize the word **schon** as the adv. corresponding to the adj. **schön,** yet that is actually what it is. Many OHG adjs. ended in *-i*, and to form advs. from such adjs. *-o* was substituted for *-i*; so the adv. corresponding to the adj. *scôni* ('beautiful') was *scôno*. By the MHG period both endings had become *-e*, but the adj. showed mutation of the stem-vowel (see **Umlaut**), while the adv. did not: hence the adj. was *schœne* (> **schön**), the adv. *schône* (> **schon**). Traces of the earlier adv. ending *-e* are still preserved in poetry, as in **Warte nur, balde ruhest du auch!** (G.: *balde* was the MHG adv. from the adj. *balt*, meaning 'brave': see **bald**) and **Schweig' stille, mein Herze!** (Mörike), and esp. in a number of coll. expressions: e.g. **Er drückte sachte an dem Tor und schlüpfte hinein** (G. Keller)—**„Wohin geht die Reise von hier?" „Direkte nach Hause!"** (Immermann)—**Gehe recht geschwinde!** (Spindler)—**In diesen Jahren erweiterte sich seine Kenntnis der musikalischen Weltliteratur rapide** (Th. Mann)—**Hau' ihn feste!** ('Hit him hard!'); cf. **gerne,** often used for **gern,** and, as esp. common, **jemand alleine gehen lassen.** But there is at least one word in the case of which the orig. distinction between adj. and adv. is still usually observed, certainly in the north: one says **Der Weg ist lang,** but **Ich habe lange** gewartet, although even here the form **lang** is often used as an adv., esp. in the south (see **lange**). **2.** Apart from these few remnants, the adj. and adv. forms now coincide, the only difference being, of course, that the adv. has no inflexion: cf. **eine rechte Freude** ('a real pleasure') and **eine recht große Freude** ('a really great pleasure')—**eine auffallende Erscheinung** ('a striking appearance') and **eine auffallend schöne Erscheinung** ('a strikingly beautiful appearance'); and sim. **ein historisch wichtiges Werk—ein vornehm eingerichtetes Zimmer** ('an elegantly furnished room')—**ein kurz zusammengefaßter Bericht** ('a briefly summarized report': see **recent**). **3.** Some words ending in **-lich** are now practically confined to the *adv.* use, esp. **bekanntlich** (e.g. **Er ist bekanntlich steinreich,** 'As everybody knows, he is rolling in money')—**bitterlich** (cf. **bittere Tränen** and **bitterlich weinen**)—**ewiglich** ('eternally')— **freilich** (q.v.)—**kürzlich** ('not long ago': see **recent**)—**schwerlich** (see **hardly**)—**sicherlich** ('undoubtedly'); and the same applies to **gewißlich** ('assuredly') and **wahrlich** ('verily'), now only used in imitation of the Bible, as in **Das ist gewißlich wahr** (1 Tim. 1. 15) and **Wahrlich, ich sage euch, solchen Glauben hab ich in Israel nicht gefunden** (Matt. 8. 10).

advise: see **raten** 2 (*a*) and (*b*).

afterreden: Apart from certain technical and dialectal compds., the prefix **after-** (orig. having the force of **hinter-**, as in **Afterstück,** 'posterior part': cf. **hinten** 3), is almost confined in ordinary lang. to the verb **afterreden,** and even this, meaning 'to speak ill of, slander' (+dat., or now more usually **von**), has a distinctly archaic flavour. It was a favourite expression of Luther's, as in **Afterredet nicht untereinander: wer seinem Bruder afterredet, der afterredet dem Gesetz** (Jas. 4. 11), but ordinarily one expresses this idea by **jemandem Übles nachreden** or **jemanden verleumden** (cf. **Mund** 1 *b*). The prefix is insep. (as in the above example), except in the little used infin. with **zu** and the past part. (**afterzureden, aftergeredet**).

age: see **alt** and **altern.**

ago: see **vor** 2 (*a*).

agree: 1. Used with the force of 'to fall in *or* comply with, accede *or* consent to' a proposal, condition, request, etc., 'to agree' may be rendered by **(a) zustimmen, beistimmen** or, more formally, **beipflichten,** all with a *dat.* obj., which need not, however, be expressed; the first two (which hardly differ: the former seems to be more usual when the reference is to *one* person) properly imply the giving of one's *vote* (**Stimme**) in favour of the proposal, while the last really stresses the idea that one feels it one's *duty* (**Pflicht**) to support it: e.g. **Mein Vater hörte höflich zu und neigte zustimmend sein Haupt** (Rilke: '... signified his assent by a nod')—**Ich stimmte der Ansicht zu, daß er bestraft werden sollte** ('I agreed that he should be punished')—**Die Versammlung stimmte dem Vorschlag des Vorsitzenden bei** ('The meeting agreed with the chairman's proposal')—**Die Besiegten pflichteten den Bedingungen eines Waffenstillstandes bei** ('The vanquished agreed to the conditions of a truce')—cf. also **verstehen** (*b*); **(b) eingehen auf** or **einwilligen in** (both preps. with the *accus.*), the former suggesting that one *enters into* and agrees with the other person's view, the latter that one is *willing* to accede to his wishes (see **willig** and **Wille** 2): e.g. **Er ging sofort auf meinen Plan ein—Die Eltern willigten in die**

Verlobung ihrer Tochter ein or **gaben ihre Einwilligung zur Verlobung ihrer Tochter**; (c) **einverstanden sein** or **sich einverstanden erklären** (both with **mit**), implying that one has come to an *understanding* with the other person and agrees with his standpoint (cf. 4): e.g. **Der Leiter der Schule war** (or **erklärte sich**) **mit den Vorschlägen des Lehrpersonals einverstanden** ('The headmaster agreed to the staff's proposals')—**Einverstanden!** (at a meeting: 'Agreed!'). **2.** Used in the sense of 'to get on with, live *or* exist harmoniously together', it is rendered by **auskommen** or **sich vertragen** (cf. **verstehen** *c*): e.g. **Verwandte kommen oft nicht miteinander aus** ('Relations often disagree')—**Kinder, vertragt euch!** (i.e. 'Don't quarrel!')—**Bier und Obst vertragen sich nicht** or **Bier verträgt sich nicht mit Obst.** **3.** When it means 'to *be in* agreement' (cf. 4 *a*), 'to coincide, correspond with, not differ', it is best rendered by **übereinstimmen** or **einig sein,** the former esp. of things (including *grammatical* agreement), the latter of persons only: e.g. **Meine Ansicht stimmt mit der Ihrigen überein**—**Die zwei Schüler haben das Exempel gerechnet und ihre Resultate stimmen überein** ('The two pupils have done the sum and their results agree')—**Das Zeitwort muß in Zahl und Person mit dem Subjekt übereinstimmen** ('The verb must agree with the subject in number and person')—**Wir sind in diesem Punkt einig** ('We are agreed on this point'). **4.** (**a**) When it means 'to *come to* an agreement', there are quite a number of possible verbs: **sich einigen** or **einig werden, sich verständigen** (rather more formal, used esp. of political parties, parties in dispute, etc. = **zu einer Verständigung kommen**), **sich vereinbaren** ('to come to an amicable settlement': cf. *b* below) and **übereinkommen**: e.g. **Wir konnten uns über den Preis nicht einigen**—**Man einigte sich auf soundsoviel als jährlichen Beitrag** ('An annual subscription of so-and-so much was agreed upon')—**Nach langer Unterredung verständigten sich die beiden Parteien**—**Man vereinbarte sich dahin, den Streit gütlich beizulegen** ('They agreed to settle their differences amicably')—**Wir kamen überein, eine Anzeige in die Zeitung rücken zu lassen** ('We agreed to advertise in the paper')—**Warum sollten die Nationen unter sich einig sein** (see 3), **wenn die Mitbürger nicht miteinander übereinzukommen verstehen?** (G.). (**b**) This idea of coming to an agreement about something may also be expressed by *trans.* verbs, esp. **abmachen, verabreden,** and **vereinbaren**: e.g. **Das wäre also abgemacht** ('So that's agreed upon, settled')—**Als der Antrag auf sofortige Abstimmung gestellt wurde, riefen die Mitglieder alle: „Abgemacht!"** ('On the motion to put the matter at once to the vote, all the members cried "Agreed!".': cf. 1 *c*)—**zur verabredeten Stunde** ('at the hour agreed upon')—**unter den vereinbarten Bedingungen** ('on the conditions agreed upon'). **5.** When used with the force of 'to suit a person's taste, nature, character', as when we talk of food, climate, work, etc., 'agreeing with' one, it is usually rendered by **bekommen** or (in more choice style) **zuträglich sein** (both with the *dat.*): e.g. **Bier bekommt mir nicht** or **ist mir nicht zuträglich** ('Beer disagrees with me')—**Sein Vorwitz wird ihm schlecht bekommen** ('His meddling *or* pertness will have disagreeable results for him, will cost him dear').

ahnden: At one time this was used like **ahnen** (q.v.), indeed, the Romantic writers seem to have preferred the forms **ahnden** and **Ahndung** in references to a presentiment or foreboding, as in **Es war, als ahndete die Prinzessin den Inhalt des Zettels** (Novalis) and **Dunkle Ahndungen beschäftigten meine jugendliche Fantasie** (id.), and Tieck complains that his compositors always altered his MS.: **Wie sie mir meine Ahndung immer in Ahnung umdrucken, obgleich ich diesen Unterschied nicht anerkenne.** Nevertheless, according to modern usage, **ahnden** should only be used in the sense of 'to punish', esp. 'to avenge' (= **rächen**): as *Weigand* rightly says, **In neuester Zeit zieht man ahnen vor** (*scil.* in the sense of 'to have a presentiment'), **um von dem mit „strafen" sinnverwandten ahnden zu unterscheiden.**

ähneln: see **gleich** 1.

ahnen: **1.** This verb, meaning 'to have a presentiment *or* foreboding' (cf. **ahnden**), is used with either a pers. or an impers. subj., in the latter case with a *dat.* of the person: e.g. **Ich ahne etwas Schlimmes**—**Trotz seiner Sicherheit ahnte ihm nichts Gutes** (Heyse). The accus. and infin. after **ahnen** is rare and hardly to be recommended, a **daß**-clause being preferable: cf. **Das Ticken der Uhr wurde immer**

schneller, wie das Klopfen eines Menschenherzens, das Schlimmes kommen ahnt (O. Ludwig), where **kommen** is superfluous in any case; otherwise one might say **. . . eines Menschenherzens, welches ahnt, daß ihm Schlimmes bevorstehe.** In coll. lang. **ahnen** is used with a neg. in the sense of 'to be unable to imagine *or* conceive', as in **Du ahnst nicht, wie ich mich auf deinen Besuch freue. 2.** Whereas **ahnen** is based on a person's *feelings*, which may be so strong that he is convinced of the truth of what he only imagines, **vermuten** (q.v., 'to suppose, conjecture') is based on his *reasoning*: cf. **Was man vermutet, von dem weiß man, daß es nicht völlig gewiß, sondern nur wahrscheinlich sei; was man ahnt, das hält man oft für gewiß, weil das Gefühl für uns den höchsten Grad der sinnlichen Gewißheit hat** (Eberhard). Moreover, while **ahnen** refers to pres. or future time, **vermuten** may refer also to past time: e.g. **Da er gestern nicht kam, vermute** (not **ahne**) **ich, daß er krank war.**

ähnlich: see **gleich** 1; **like** 2 (*b*).

Akt, Akte: Distinguish between **der Akt** (plur. **Akte**), meaning either 'act, action' or (= **Aufzug**) an 'act' as part of a drama or 'pose, posture' (of artists' models), and **die Akte** (plur. **Akten**), meaning 'deed, document'.

all (English): see **all** (German); for '(not) at all', see **gar** 2 and 3, and **überhaupt** 2.

all (German): **1.** Before an otherwise unqualified noun, an attrib. **all** must be *strongly* inflected: e.g. **Aller Anfang ist schwer—Alles Fleisch ist wie das Gras—Alle Menschen müssen sterben.** So also in the gen. sing. masc. and neut.: **Das ist alles Lobes wert—Die Wolken sind das ewige Sinnbild alles Wanderns, alles Verlangens und Heimbegehrens** (H. Hesse); but a weak ending here is permissible if the noun has the strong gen. ending: **trotz allen Fleißes** (Frenssen)—**Sein Vater verlangte allen Ernstes** ('in all seriousness'), **daß er sich entscheiden sollte** (E. Wichert), where **alles Ernstes** would sound very harsh (cf. **every**); and the weak ending is quite established in **allenfalls** (q.v., and cf. **jeder** 1 *b*). In particular, **all** must have strong inflexion before a neut. adj.-subst., the latter having a *weak* ending: hence **alles Gute**, gen. **alles Guten**, dat. **allem Guten**; sim. **Man darf wohl behaupten, daß Shakespeare alles damals in seiner Sprache Vorhandene gelesen hatte** (A. W. Schlegel); cf. **Die Nacht breitete ihren Schleier über alles, Gutes und Böses** (Raabe), where the last phrase stands in appos. **2.** An attrib. adj. or an adj.-subst. after strongly inflected **all** now always has a *weak* ending: **aller wahre Mut—trotz alles gelernten Maßhaltens** (Frenssen)—**mit aller möglichen Geschwindigkeit—alle klugen Leute**, gen. **aller klugen Leute.** Formerly the adj. here sometimes had a strong ending, but this is contrary to modern usage: cf. **Sie hatte alle weibliche** (now **weiblichen**) **Dienstboten entfernt** (E. T. A. Hoffmann); sim. **Kellers „Grüner Heinrich" erzählt, daß er an der Universität alle mögliche Kollegien hörte** (M. Necker), and **Alle schottische Verbannte** (now **schottischen Verbannten**) **lernte ich kennen** (Sch.). But this does not apply to a dem. or poss., or to **beide**, which are always strong (cf. 3): **Ich muß alle diese meine deutschen Bücher verkaufen—Während aller dieser glänzend geführten Unterhaltungen war nur von Savonarola die Rede** (A. Eloesser)—**Alle beide erwähnten Familien sind ausgewandert—Die Übersiedelung aller beider erwähnten Familien findet bald statt. 3.** When **all** is followed by the def. art. or a dem. or poss., it usually remains uninflected, but may take the form **alle**: e.g. **Was nützt all das Reden?—Was will er mit all dem Gelde anfangen?—Die Herzen alle dieses Volks erregt' ich** (Sch.)—**Das währte zehn Jahre, und in alle der Zeit hatte er wenig Muße** (Alverdes)—**Auf der Reise hatte ich Angst vor alle den Großartigkeiten, die ich sehen würde** (H. Hesse)—**Das hatte er unter alle dem, was ihn beschäftigte, allmählich vergessen** (Ompteda); one no longer says **Alles** (for **All**) **unser Bemühen ging verloren** (G.) or **Ich hatte mehr Witz als aller der Pöbel** (Immermann). Where we say 'all Germany', a German says **ganz Deutschland**, and sim. **die ganze Familie** or **alle Familienmitglieder** (not **all die Familie**). **4.** A neut. sing. dem. used subst. may either follow or precede **all.** In either case the dem. has a strong ending, as in **Dieses alles gehört mir**; but where **all** precedes the dem., it may remain uninflected: **All(es) dies gehört mir.** In the dat. sing., **all** now very commonly has a weak ending when it follows the dem.: cf. **Ich habe mir aus allem diesem den ersten fröhlichen Sommer zusammengebaut** (G.) and **Aus**

diesem allen tritt soviel hervor ('From all this so much is clear'), **daß wir uns nicht übereilen sollten** (G.); when **all** precedes the dem. in the dat., it often takes the form **alle,** as in **Von alle dem ahnte ich nichts** (G.), indeed, **alle dem** is now written as one word, a phrase like **trotz alledem** being quite established. **5.** As with us, **all** follows a pers. pron. and is then strongly inflected: **Wir haben alle** (never **Alle von uns haben**) **gut geschlafen —Es geschah vor unser aller Augen— Er hat uns alle beschenkt. 6.** (**a**) The form **alles** should not be used alone as a *gen.*: it might pass in a proposition like **Ich bin alles müde, absonderlich dummer Streiche** (Immermann: 'I am sick of everything, particularly of silly pranks'), but as **müde** (q.v. 1) can take an accus. **dumme Streiche** would be equally correct. Where we say 'I heard all he said', a German says **Ich hörte alles, was er sagte,** and the corresponding gen. is **Ich erinnere mich alles dessen, was er sagte;** sim. **Erspare mir die Wiederholung alles dessen, was ich erdulden mußte** (Chamisso) **—Sie fühlte sich alles dessen beraubt, was ihrem Dasein Inhalt gegeben hatte** (Ric. Huch). (**b**) The invariable form **alles** is added coll. to an interrog. pron. or adv. (from which it is generally separated) to indicate that the reference is to more than one—cf. **was** (**interrogative**) 1 (*b*): e.g. **Was hat er alles gesagt?—Wem sind Sie alles begegnet?—Wovon habt ihr alles gesprochen?—Wo bist du in den Ferien alles gewesen?** (**c**) The form **alles** is also used (rather coll.) of persons in a collect. sense, as in **Als die Polizei erschien, lief alles fort** ('everybody ran off'), and esp. in contexts where it has the force of **lauter** (q.v.): e.g. **Ihr seid hier alles brave Soldaten** (Sudermann)—**Unsere Neffen sind alles Juristen** (A. Zweig)—**Ein Zimmergesell, ein Lagerarbeiter, ein Eisendreher, das sind doch alles an schwere Arbeit gewöhnte Leute** (Speckmann)—**Die Verwandten des Bräutigams sind alles Beamte, die der Braut alles Geschäftsleute** (P. Ernst); cf. **beid. 7.** The invariable form **alle** is used coll. with the force of Scots *done*, as in 'Can you help me out with some potatoes? ours are done', i.e. we have none left: **Können Sie mir mit einigen Kartoffeln aushelfen? Unsere sind alle.** Actually, a past part. like **verzehrt** or **aufgegessen** is understood here, but this is no longer felt, so that one says **Das Brot ist alle** (= **ist alles aufgegessen**); cf. the coll. saying **Die Dummen werden nicht alle** ('There will always be stupid people in this world'). **8.** For the use of **all** with distrib. force, see **every.**

allein (**adjective**): **1.** As now used, this invariable adj.—see **adjectives** (**indeclinable**) 5—has lost much of its orig. force. The MHG expression for 'alone' is *ein*, sometimes inflected, but usually in the stereotyped form *eine* (e.g. *ich muoz iuch eine lân* = **Ich muß euch allein lassen**), and 'quite alone' is generally expressed by *al eine*, so that **allein** should properly suggest the idea implicit in **ganz allein** or **mutterseelenallein.** It is interesting that the form **alleine,** so common in the coll. lang. of the north, is really the orig. MHG form, the final **-e** thus having as historical a basis as it has in **balde, gerne,** etc. (for which see **adverbs formed from adjectives** 1). **2.** A similar loss of force is seen in **vielleicht:** the MHG expression for 'perhaps' is *lîhte*, and *vil lîhte* means 'probably' (cf. *daz ist vil lîhte mügelich* = **Das ist sehr leicht möglich**).

allein (**conjunction**): see **aber** (**conjunction**) 3.

allenfalls: This expression, now always written as one word, with a weak ending in **all** because the noun **Fall** has the strong gen. ending (cf. **all** 1 and see **Fall** 1 *c*), has quite established itself. One now makes a distinction between **allenfalls** and **jedenfalls** (cf. **jeder** 1 *b*); while the latter has retained the orig. force of 'in any case, at any rate', the former has developed the specific sense of 'at most, if need be': cf., on the one hand, **Ich weiß noch nicht, wann er kommen wird, jedenfalls** ('in any event') **nicht vor Ende der Woche,** and on the other hand, **Einem Kranken tut niemand not als einer, der ihm die Arznei reicht und allenfalls ein verschobenes Kissen zurücklegt** (Immermann: 'An invalid only needs some one to hand him his medicine and possibly, *or* at most, rearrange his pillow')—**Sie kramten alles heraus, was sich allenfalls noch brauchen ließ** (Sudermann: 'They rummaged round and fetched out everything that might conceivably still be of use')—**Wenn jemand mit einem gebrochenen Arm zu Ihnen kommt, lassen Sie der Natur doch nicht ohne weiteres ihren Lauf; heilen würde der Bruch allenfalls** ('possibly') **auch ohne Ihr Eingreifen,**

aber schief, unvollkommen (M. Hausmann).

allenthalben: see **halb** 3 (*b*).

allerdings: 1. The MHG gen. plur. *aller dinge* was used with the adv. force of 'in all respects', and Luther still used it in that sense. This is now obs., which seems strange seeing that analogous expressions are in common use, notably **guter Dinge sein** ('to be of good cheer') and **unverrichteter Dinge zurückkehren** ('to return without achieving one's purpose': Lat. *re infecta reverti*); cf. **Er stand unverrichteter Dinge da und starrte in die milde Juniluft** (H. Leip). But out of *aller dinge* there later developed **allerdings,** which was still used in the orig. sense in the 18th century: **Er traute ihm nicht allerdings** (Musäus). Now **allerdi'ngs** is used in two ways: (**a**) coll., as a strong affirmative, to corroborate a previous statement or idea: **„Kann er Geige spielen?" „Allerdings!"** ('That he can! Can't he just!')—**„Es ist ein bißchen frisch heute früh auf offenem Wagen." „Allerdings!"** (Speckmann: 'That 's a fact! You're telling me!'). In some parts of Germany it is also used to correct a previous *neg.* statement, but this idea is better expressed by **doch** (q.v. 1 *a*): e.g. **„Der Briefträger scheint noch nicht gekommen zu sein." „Allerdings ist er** (better **Doch, er ist**) **gekommen"** ('Oh yes, he *has* come'); (**b**) like **zwar, freilich** (qq.v.), with *concess.* force, a limiting 'but'-clause being expressed or implied: e.g. **Man zählt Kleist allerdings** ('it is true, no doubt') **zu den Romantikern, aber eigentlich weist er Züge auf, die ihn von diesen unterscheiden—„Sie haben lange Ferien." „Allerdings** ('I admit that'), **aber ich muß sie mir schwer verdienen!"—Er soll Deutsch sprechen, allerdings nicht fließend. 2.** Formed like **allerdings** are two other expressions which have come into fashion of late, viz. (**a**) **neu'erdings,** used sometimes in the sense of 'anew, again', but esp. in that of 'in recent times'—see **recent** 2 (*a*); and (**b**) **schle'chterdings,** meaning 'quite, absolutely, utterly', in which **schlecht** really has its orig. force of 'simple' (see **bad** 1): e.g. **Das ist schlechterdings** (or **einfach**) **ausgeschlossen** ('That is simply *or* absolutely out of the question')—**Sie gab mir das Versprechen, schlechterdings nichts** ('nothing whatsoever') **gegen meine genaue Instruktion zu tun** (Mörike)—**Vor den Damen vollführte er ein paar** *compliments,* **wie die neue Generation sie schlechterdings nicht mehr zustande brachte** (Th. Mann: '... compliments such as were simply beyond the capacity of the younger generation')—**Man wollte schlechterdings nicht wissen, warum Beethovens Opus 111 nur zwei Sätze habe** (id.: 'They confessed to being quite at a loss to understand why Beethoven's op. 111 had only two movements')—**Was mich störte, war die Farbe ihres Gesichts: sie erinnerte mich schlechterdings** ('positively') **an Gorgonzola** (H. Hesse); cf. also **schlechthin.**

allerhand: The orig. force of this invariable word is 'all kinds of', as explained under **Hand** 2 (*a*): e.g. **In dieser alten Stadt sind allerhand Sehenswürdigkeiten** ('This old town has all manner of objects of interest')—**Er scheint allerhand Interessantes erlebt zu haben** ('He seems to have had all kinds of interesting experiences'). In modern coll. speech it has developed specific meanings: e.g. **„Was war er eigentlich für ein Mensch?" „Ganz ordentlich, gefällig, fleißig, aber das war so ziemlich alles"** ('... that is about all one can say of him'). **„Mich dünkt, das ist schon allerhand"** (Speckmann: 'It seems to me that that is enough to be going on with')—**„Na, das ist aber allerhand!"** (the meaning of which depends on the context and the inflexion of the voice: it may mean 'You don't say! Fancy that!' or, spoken indignantly, 'That 's a bit thick!'); cf. **„Er hat die Stirn** ('effrontery'), **mir seinen Besuch anzukündigen." „Das ist aber allerhand!"** (G. v. d. Vring).

allerlei: see **Hand** 2 (*b*).

allow: see **permit.**

along: see **entlang.**

Alp: Whereas **der Alp** means 'goblin' or 'nightmare' (plur. **Alpe**), **die Alp**(**e**) means 'mountain', but is now practically confined to the plur. **die Alpen** ('the Alps').

als = 'as': 1. (**a**) In a proposition like 'I advise you as a friend' German grammarians distinguish between **„das vergleichende Wie"** and **„das identifizierende Als"**: in other words, while **wie** merely suggests a comparison, **als** has identifying force: cf. **Ich rate Ihnen wie ein Freund** ('I advise you as a friend would') and **Ich rate dir als Freund** ('I advise you in my capacity as your friend'); sim. **Er focht wie ein Löwe und starb als Held**—cf. the example from Ebner-Eschenbach given under **als = 'than'** 5. Where Crabb Robinson, describing his experiences in 1805 in north Germany, then occupied by the French, says that he travelled with a passport which he had procured 'as a Saxon', **als Sachse** would be correct, because his passport identified him as such; and sim. **Er war als Mönch verkleidet,** because his disguise proclaimed him a monk. (**b**) From the above examples it will be seen that the noun idiomatically drops the art. after **als,** but never after **wie.** Care must be taken, of course, to observe the rule of apposition (but see *c*), and even after **als** the art. may have to be inserted to avoid ambiguity. When Antonio, referring to Tasso, says **Als Menschen habe ich ihn vielleicht gekränkt, als Edelmann hab' ich ihn nicht beleidigt** (G.), we assume that the two propositions are parallel, and that **Edelmann** is an accus. obj. like **Menschen**; but if the second proposition stood independently, **Edelmann** would grammatically be taken to refer to the subj. **ich,** a misconception which would be obviated by the insertion of the art.: **Als einen Edelmann hab' ich ihn nicht beleidigt.** Where an attrib. adj. qualifies the noun, its inflexional ending will, of course, make the reference clear: cf. **Er wurde mir als berühmter Künstler vorgestellt** and **Ich wurde ihm als stellvertretendem Direktor vorgestellt,** the **als**-phrase referring to the subj. in the former proposition, to the indir. dat. in the latter. (**c**) Strangely enough, the rule of appos. is *not* usually observed in the *gen.* case, unless an art. precedes the noun after **als:** one says **Ich erkenne die Bedeutung Goethes als Dichter an;** and sim. **Diese Rede bezog sich auf des Staatsministers Eigenschaft als Standesbeamter des großherzoglichen Hauses** (Th. Mann)—**Sein** (*scil.* Th. Mann's) **letztes Werk vor dem Kriege hatte eine Warnung vor der fragwürdigen Rolle des Dichters als Erzieher sein sollen** (A. Eloesser)—**Seine** (which represents the gen. of a pers. pron.) **Bedeutung als Dichter ist nicht zu verkennen**—**Der Schwerpunkt liegt in seiner kompromittierten Ehre als Offizier** (Spielhagen)—**Ein Grund war der Ausbreitung seines** (*scil.* Mörike's) **Ansehens als Dichter hinderlich, seine Eigenschaft nämlich als Schwabe** (E. v. Sallwürk)—**Er sann, soweit** (cf. 2 *b*) **es sich mit seiner Gewissenhaftigkeit als Mensch und Kutscher vertrug, über die Zeit nach, da er mit Andrees gespielt hatte** (Frenssen); and the same applies even where the noun is qualified by an attrib. adj.: e.g. **Er befürchtete, der Ruf des „Paradieses" als fröhlicher Aufenthaltsort möchte leiden** (Ompteda)—**Du weißt, was du deiner Ehre als große Bauersfrau schuldig bist** (Speckmann)—**Hast du einen Freier, der dich trotz deiner Eigenschaft als reiche Erbin zu seiner Frau machen möchte?** (Heyse)—and even **Sie war über den Entschluß des als eingefleischter Hagestolz Verschrieenen aufs höchste verwundert** (Jul. Wolff: 'She was amazed at this decision of a man who was decried as a confirmed bachelor'). In such propositions, a *gen.* after **als,** although, of course, not incorrect, is actually much rarer, esp. where the art. is not inserted: cf. **Da er sich meines Vaters als Geschäftsbeistandes bediente, war er in unserem Hause ein oft gesehener Gast** (Storm)—**Ich fordere von Ihnen das Versprechen, meinen Namen als einer Mithandelnden nicht zu nennen** (H. Hoffmann); but, with the art., **Ich erinnere mich seiner als eines Mannes von hoher Gestalt** (Mörike). (**d**) When associated with a *true reflex.* verb. (i.e. a verb which is used only reflex., e.g. **sich schämen** or **sehnen**), the noun after **als** should agree with the *subj.*, as in **Er sehnte sich noch als alter** (not **alten**) **Mann nach der Heimat, die er als Jüngling verlassen hatte.** In the case of ordinary trans. verbs used reflex., usage fluctuates. Some grammarians would distinguish between **Er erwies sich als guter Klavierspieler** (implying that he proved to be the good pianist he was reputed to be) and **Er erwies sich als guten Klavierspieler** (suggesting that he hitherto had not been known to be a good pianist); but although this distinction may hold good in theory, it is apparently not generally insisted upon; cf. the following examples: on the one hand (**als**+*nom.*), **Er wies sich als gewesener Schmiedegeselle aus** (Polenz—**Er erwies sich als ein besonnener junger Mann** (Fallada)—**Er entpuppte sich als unterhaltender Nachbar** (I. Kurz)—**Er sah einen kleinen Punkt sich nähern, der sich als sein bester Freund entpuppte** (B. E. Werner)—**Er kündigte sich als der Karikaturenzeichner Strobel an** (Raabe); and on the other hand (**als**+*accus.*), **Er bekannte sich als Mitschuldigen** (G.)—**Ein ansehnlicher Mann kündigte sich als Herrn des Hauses an** (G.)—**Der Westwind stürzte sich über den Winter und fing an,**

sich als den Stärkeren zu fühlen (Frenssen); for sim. examples, see **prove. 2.** (a) In propositions like 'I am as tall as he' or 'Do it as quickly as you can', the first 'as' is expressed by **so** (q.v. 1), which is also the most idiomatic expression in *concess.* clauses like 'As clever as he is, he cannot do this sum' (**So klug er auch ist, diese Rechenaufgabe kann er nicht lösen:** see **as . . . as** 2 and so 3). With regard to the second 'as' in such propositions, the grammarians insist that the only correct word is **wie,** and that **als** should only be used after a *compar.* (see **als** = **'than'** 1). But modern authors seem to observe this distinction as little as they do that drawn by *Duden* when he says **„ebenso (in derselben Weise) wie; ebenso (in demselben Grade) als"**, implying that **als** properly expresses *degree,* and **wie** *manner.* Actually, both expressions are used more or less indiscriminately, but **wie** is characteristic of the lang. of every day, while **als** is not much used after a pos. degree except in a contracted clause following **sowohl** (q.v.): cf. **Er ist sowohl dumm als faul** ('stupid as well as lazy') and **Er ist nicht sowohl dumm als** (**vielmehr**) **faul** ('not so much stupid as lazy'). On the other hand, **wie** is reg. used where an 'identifying' **als,** as explained under 1 (*a*) above, occurs in the same proposition, just as **denn** or **wie** is used in such cases after a compar. degree (see **als** = **'than'** 5): e.g. **Er zeigte sich sowohl in seiner Eigenschaft als Berliner wie als Mensch** (Raabe); cf. also **Die Frau trug ihr Haar noch glatt gescheitelt wie als junges Mädchen** (Th. Mann: 'as she did when she was a young girl'). (**b**) Analogous to **sowohl** are the expressions used to render 'as soon (far, often) as'; but here **als** or **wie** is more commonly omitted altogether in finite clauses (see **so** 1 *b* and **wie** 2 b): e.g. **Soviel ich weiß, ist er unverheiratet—Sie schlichen so leise sie konnten durch den Wald** (Ompteda). **3.** For an idiomatic way to render propositions like 'From here you get as fine a view as you will see anywhere' or 'Tonight she sang as well as I have ever heard her sing', see **wie** 2 (*c*). **4.** The only case where **als** has *causal* force is after **um so** followed by a compar. degree, as in **Dein Besuch freut mich um so mehr, als ich dich nicht erwartet hatte** ('Your visit gives me great pleasure, the more so as I had not expected you'). Here **um** is really a prep. meaning 'by' (see **um** 1 d) and its obj. **viel** has dropped out, **um so viel mehr** meaning 'by so much more'; and sim. **Es war ihm um so leichter geworden, als der Graf seiner Situation als Volontär** (see 1 *c*) **mit keinem Worte Erwähnung tat** (Spielhagen: 'He had found it all the easier as the count had made not the slightest reference to his situation as a voluntary worker'); cf. also the first example from Goethe given under **als** = **'than'** 5.

als = **'as if'**: **1.** The conj. **als** has the force of 'as if' when followed by the word-order of a question, whereas **als ob, als wenn** and (rather less commonly) **wie wenn** all require transposed word-order: cf. **Das ist, wie wenn du aus einem kleinen Bürgerhaus stammtest** (Fontane). As such a proposition is not a statement of fact but represents the case as only imaginary or seemingly true, the verb normally stands in the *past subj.* (cf. 'She behaves as if she *were* a child', which she is not); but the pres. subj. is often used to make the imaginary case more vivid, its use in the best prose being limited, however, to cases where the pres. subj. form differs from that of the pres. indic.: e.g. **Er tat, als wäre** (or **sei**) **er krank—Mir war es, als sähe** (better than **sehe**) **ich jemand.** Sometimes we find the *indic.* here, the case being represented as an actual fact, and this use would seem to be on the increase in modern authors, although it is generally avoided in everyday speech: e.g. **Seine Augen gehen immer nach ihr zurück, als will er was sagen und traut sich nicht** (Sudermann)—**Er tut so, als wenn er noch den alten Glauben hat** (Frenssen)—**Es ist, als ob das unendliche Licht herniedersinkt** (Schlaf)—**Mir war, als trat eine Träne in sein Auge** (W. v. Scholz)—**Da ist einer, der auf einer Kiste sitzt: der tut, als wenn er schläft** (H. Hauser)—**Als er dem Dichter begegnet** (see **when** 2 *a*), **tut dieser, als ob er ihn nicht sieht** (P. Ernst) —**Es war ihm, als ob alles Licht erlosch** (E. Wichert)—**Jetzt ist mir, als ob eine ganz neue Zeit kommen muß!** (Th. Mann); cf., as a strange example of fluctuation, **Es war ihr, als könne sie fliegen, flöge über die Erde weg und sah Sonne, Mond und Sterne um sich herumtanzen** (Voigt-Diederichs). **2.** If two or more co-ordinate clauses connected by **und** or **oder** follow this use of **als** = **'as if'**

the question-order is as a rule confined to the *first*, subsequent clauses having normal word-order, unless **als** is repeated: e.g. **Er heftete den Blick auf den Boden, als wären ihm seine Worte entglitten und er müßte** (but **und als müßte er**) **sie nun einzeln auflesen** (Zifferer)—**Er verweilte einen Augenblick, als wollte er etwas sagen und es fehlten ihm die richtigen Worte** (id.)—**Sie sprach immer hastiger, als sprängen ihr die Worte davon und sie müßte ihnen nachlaufen** (A. Reiner). **3.** Where such a clause is contracted, the finite verb not being expressed, **als** is regularly replaced by **wie** (q.v. 2 *d*), as in **Sie fühlte sich wie in einer fremden Welt** (Fontane); cf. the example from W. v. Scholz given under **anwandeln.**

alsbald: see **bald.**

als da: see **als = 'than'** 4.

als daß: This combination is used in two ways. **1.** When **als** has the force of 'than' and is therefore preceded by a compar. degree, it may be followed by an obj. noun-clause introduced by **daß.** Thus, a proposition like 'It is more important that you should go *than that* I should' becomes **Es ist wichtiger, daß du gehst, als daß ich gehe**; and 'What could be more natural than that we should call to ask how he is keeping?' becomes **Was wäre natürlicher, als daß wir bei ihm vorsprächen, um uns nach seinem Befinden zu erkundigen?**—sim. after **ander,** as in **Es blieb nichts andres übrig, als daß wir dort übernachteten** ('There was nothing else for it *but that* we should spend the night there'); cf. also **Sie stolperte mehr, als daß sie ging** (Th. Mann: 'She stumbled rather than walked, did not so much walk as stumble'). **2.** The other use of **als daß** is after a clause in which 'too' precedes an adj. or adv., as in 'This sum is *too* difficult for young children to do.' Actually, this proposition is fundamentally the same as those given under 1 above, because it implies a compar.: cf. 'This sum is more difficult than young children can be expected to do.' So this use of **als daß** is always preceded by **zu** in the previous clause (see below): **Diese Rechenaufgabe ist zu schwer, als daß junge Kinder sie lösen könnten.** Where the subjs. of the two clauses refer to the same person or thing, the *infin.* construction is more usual in ordinary lang., but otherwise **als daß** is essential; cf. the following pairs of examples: **Er ist zu jung, um ins Konzert mitzugehen** and **Er ist zu jung, als daß wir ihn ins Konzert mitnehmen könnten**—**Das Zimmer war zu klein, um uns alle aufzunehmen** ('The room was too small to hold us all') and **Das Zimmer war zu klein, als daß wir alle hätten hineinkommen können** ('The room was too small for us all to get in'); and sim. **Die Entfernung war zu groß, als daß ich sie in einem Tage hätte zurücklegen können** ('The distance was too great for me to cover in a day'). Occasionally we find **als daß** after **so** instead of **zu,** but this has never become established: cf. **Er mußte bei dem Diner im Ratskeller zugegen sein, gedachte aber nicht so lange dort zu bleiben, als daß er nicht hoffte, die Familie abends noch in seinem Hause zu finden** (Th. Mann), where **als** should be omitted.

als ob: see **als = 'as if'** 1.

als = 'than': 1. In a clause expressing comparison, usage fluctuates between **als** and **wie.** The grammarians' distinction between **als** to express degree or intensity, and **wie** to express manner or quality, is not always observed in practice, just as their insistence that **wie** should only be used after a pos. and **als** after a compar. is often disregarded. It is true that **als** is generally used after a compar., after **ander,** and after a word or phrase with neg. force: e.g. **Er hatte nichts Eiligeres zu tun, als mir die Nachricht zu überbringen**—**Was konnte ich anders tun als auf seinen Vorschlag eingehen?**—**Niemand (anders) als er ist imstande, den Plan auszuführen.** But **wie** is freely used here by all standard authors, and not only in coll. passages: cf. **Vielleicht sind die Franzosen glücklicher organisiert wie wir Deutschen** (Heine)—**Es kam anders wie sie gedacht** (Fontane)—**Sie ist um vieles jünger wie du** (Hofmannsthal)—**Sie war so ganz anders wie die anderen** (P. Keller); and in a proposition in which both a pos. and a compar. occur, as in 'He is as clever as, perhaps more clever than, his brother', **wie** is peculiarly appropriate: **Er ist so klug, vielleicht klüger wie sein Bruder**—**Es geht im Leben manchmal so toll oder noch toller zu wie in einem Roman** (Schreckenbach); and so also where another clause introduced by **als** follows, as in **Die Audienz verlief insofern anders, wie sie erwartet hatte, als sie feststellte, daß eine Mäßigung ihrer Abneigung gegen den Fürsten eingetreten**

war (I. Seidel: 'The audience went differently from what she had expected inasmuch as she established the fact that her aversion to the prince had moderated'). **2.** Just as after an 'identifying' **als** (see **als = 'as'** 1 *b*), so here also care must be taken to use the correct case after **als** in a contracted clause: **Er besucht mich öfter als du** ('than you do') is obviously different from **Er besucht mich öfter als dich** ('than he does you'). In the proposition **Hat der König treuere Diener als uns?** (G.), one might think that the nom. **wir** would be more natural (**Hat der König Diener, die treuer sind als wir?**), but the accus. is nevertheless correct, because **Hat der König treuere Diener als wir?** would at once suggest 'Has the king more faithful servants *than we have*?' **3.** In one case the *accus.* in the contracted clause is practically fixed, viz. after **es gibt** followed by a compar.: e.g. **Keinen beschäftigteren Mann gibt es auf einer Hochzeit als den Küster** (Immermann)—**Es gibt nichts Verschiedeneres als uns beide** (A. Schieber)—**Es gab keinen größeren Meister in der Kunst des Halbdunkels als den Doktor Stein** (Raabe)—**Es gab keinen gesunderen Mann als ihn** (Liliencron); and sim. **Du wirst dich für unseren Kandidaten begeistern, es gibt keinen Mann wie ihn** (Blunck). A *nom.* here is rare enough to prove the rule: cf. **Es gibt nichts Lächerlicheres als ein verliebter Mann** (Börne)—**Gab es etwas Reizenderes als der Anblick, den er hier vor sich hatte?** (Hackländer)—**Er war arm, aber es gab ja noch ärmere wie er** (Ompteda). **4.** A proposition like 'He is never in better humour *than when* he is in the company of ladies', with a *pres.* tense in the temp. clause, presents little difficulty: **Er ist nie besser aufgelegt, als wenn er sich in Damengesellschaft befindet**; sim. **Ich habe nie ein schöneres Gefühl für einen Freund, als wenn ich ihm einen Dienst leisten kann** (Immermann). With a *past* tense in the temp. clause, 'than when' may be rendered by **als da** or **als wie**: cf. **Am folgenden Vormittag war die Welt eine andere** (= **eine bessere**) **als wie tags zuvor** (Storm: = **als wie sie tags zuvor gewesen war**); but such propositions are sometimes better rendered in another way: instead of **Sie sehen besser aus, als da ich Sie zuletzt sah**, one prefers to say **Sie sehen besser aus als das letzte Mal, wo ich Sie sah** (or **wie das letzte Mal, als ich Sie sah**). **5.** In MHG 'than' was *denne* or *dan(ne)*: cf. *wîz alsô der snê* ('as white as snow') and *wîzer dan der snê* ('whiter than snow'). With the force of 'than', **denn** (not **dann**) is still used in imitation of earlier usage, esp. in choicer style—cf. **denn** (**conjunction**) 4—as in **Besser ist ein schöner Tod denn solch ein schläfrig Leben** (Hölderlin); but in good prose this use of **denn** is mostly confined to the phrase **denn je** ('than ever') and esp. to contexts in which an 'identifying', a temp. or a causal **als** occurs (see **als = 'as'** 1 and 4): e.g. **Er war um so erstaunter, als** ('as, because') **er nichts weniger denn diese Vorwürfe zu verdienen glaubte** (G.)—**Ich besuche ihn jetzt mehr als Freund denn als Arzt** (Immermann)—**Ich empfand eine Art Scheu, vor die ergraute Frau zu treten, die mir eher als eine gestorbene Vorfahrin denn als eine lebendige Großmutter erschien** (G. Keller)—**Ciano hatte gezeigt, daß er bereit sei, lieber einen Tag als Löwe zu leben, denn hundert als Lamm** (K. Edschmid); cf. **Gustav und Carla verkehrten mehr wie zwei gute Gesellen denn als ein junges Ehepaar** (Ebner-Eschenbach), where **wie** means 'like', and **als** identifies them as a young married couple. In rather more ordinary lang., **denn** is here often replaced by **wie**: e.g. **Als sie wahrnahm, daß ihr Besuch mehr als Störung wie als Freude empfunden wurde, ging sie wieder** (Fontane)—**Diese Frau gefiel ihm tausendmal besser wie als Mädchen** (Viebig)—**Ich mag ihn lieber als ganzen Teufel wie als halben** (Waldau). Needless to say, the following example should not be imitated: **Die ganze Haut ist als nichts andres zu betrachten als als eine Lage von Nervenwürzchen** (Oken). **6.** For propositions like **Ich kam früher an, als ich nicht erwartet hatte**, showing a mingling of 'I arrived sooner than I had expected' and 'I had not expected to arrive so soon', see **negative** (**pleonastic**) 2 (*c*).

als wenn: see **als = 'as if'** 1; **als = 'than'** 4.

als = 'when': see **when** 2 (*a*) and 3.

als wie: see **als = 'than'** 4.

alt: In MHG a gen. was used in expressions like 'three years old', but this is now obs. (see **genitive of measure**). The usual way to express a person's age is now **Er ist sechzig Jahre alt** or **Er zählt sechzig Jahre**; cf. **Ich ging mit sechs Jahren** ('at the age of six') **zur Schule** and **Er starb**

im Alter von neunzig Jahren. At one time imitation of the Fr. idiom (*avoir six ans*) was fairly common, as in **Er hatte fünf Jahre mehr als ich** (G.), and this is still occasionally used even by standard authors: e.g. **Aus diesen Zeichen schloß August, daß er, obwohl er kaum mehr als fünfzig Jahre hatte, kein junger Mensch mehr sei** (H. Hesse); but this is now generally avoided in the best prose, although often used coll. in **Er hat siebzig Jahre auf dem Rücken.** For 'to grow old, to age', see **altern**; for 'to be *or* come of age' (**mündig sein, werden**), see **Vormund.**

alter: see **change.**

altern: 1. The orig. expression for 'to grow old' was **alten** (cf. Walther **v. d.** Vogelweide's *swer sich sô behaltet, daz im nieman niht gesprechen mac, wünneclîche er altet*, 'Who bears himself so that none can speak ill of him, grows old happily'), but this form is now only extant in **veralten** ('to become antiquated'), the past part. **veraltet** being the regular expression for 'obsolete'. **2.** (**a**) The modern form of the verb is **altern.** Most dictionaries represent this as an intrans. verb only, but examples like the following show that standard authors do sometimes use it as a factitive (= **alt machen,** 'to cause to grow *or* look old'): **Der Husten altert mich mehr und mehr** (Chamisso)—**Kummer und Gram haben mich vor der Zeit gealtert** (Spielhagen)—**Der eine Winter schien ihn um zehn Jahre gealtert zu haben** (Heyse). (**b**) Still, the *intrans.* use is much more common, and as its force here obviously implies a change of state or condition, it should, according to rule, require the aux. **sein,** so it is strange that so many authors of repute should have used **haben:** e.g. **Auch diese frischen rotbäckigen Kinder hatten gealtert** (G.)—**Sie mag wohl vor der Zeit gealtert haben** (Sch.)—**Sie hat gar nicht gealtert und ist noch so stattlich wie vor fünfzig Jahren** (Hauff)—**Er hatte allmählich recht gealtert** (Liliencron)—**Auch sie fand, daß die andere gealtert hatte** (Viebig)—**Onkel Harre hatte in den letzten Jahren merklich gealtert** (R. Huch)—**Er hatte ersichtlich gealtert** (Th. Mann). But the strictly correct **sein is** quite as common, indeed, the most recent authors almost seem to prefer it: e.g. **Sie war furchtbar gealtert** (Gutzkow)—**Wie war sie in den drei Jahren meines Fortseins gealtert!** (Stehr)—**Er schien nicht im mindesten gealtert zu sein** (W. v. Scholz)—**Die Räte seines Reiches, die Freunde seines Herzens, alle waren schon gealtert** E. Weiß)—**Hier, im Frieden seines Hauses, ist er niemals gealtert** (K. Lamprecht)—**Seitdem ich ihn kenne, ist er merkwürdig gealtert** (M. Eyth)—**Als ich zu gehen versuchte, war ich zum Greise gealtert** (A. Schaeffer)—**Die Großmutter war gealtert und noch leichter zu hintergehen als früher** (Bergengruen). Here again, as in 2 (*a*), dictionaries apparently disagree, but so many examples of both aux. verbs seem to bear out *Sanders*'s finding: **„Jemand hat oder ist gealtert".**

an: 1. This prep. takes either a dat. or an accus., according as rest at or motion towards is implied. With locative force it expresses close proximity, often direct contact, whereas **neben** suggests proximity to the *side* of a person or thing, without actual contact, unless perhaps in a context like **Er saß ganz dicht neben mir.** If you are cold and wish to warm yourself, you seat yourself **ans Feuer,** not **neben das Feuer** (where you would get less heat), but you hang a picture **an die Wand neben dem Bücherschrank;** and sim. you seat yourself **an den Tisch** (to write a letter) or **zu Tisch** (to have a meal). On the other hand, 'to sit down *beside* a person' is **sich neben** (not **an**) **jemanden** or **zu jemandem setzen,** the latter either implying an intimate relationship or suggesting a desire to have a confidential talk, while the former could apply to a perfect stranger: cf. **Ein Unbekannter setzte sich neben mich** and **Komm, setze dich zu uns!** ('Come and join us!'). Another prep. suggesting nearness is **bei** (q.v. 1 and 2), but here the nearness is more indefinite: one can say **Er saß eine Weile bei uns,** but **bei** more commonly means 'in the vicinity of', as when one addresses a letter to some one in **Godesberg bei Bonn,** or speaks of **die Schlacht bei Fehrbellin. 2.** Out of the fundamental idea of promixity various senses of **an** have developed, the chief of which may be seen from the following examples: (**a**) + *accus.*: **Er richtete die Frage an** ('to') **mich, adressierte den Brief an seine Mutter, begleitete mich bis an die Tür, war damals an die** ('nearly') **vierzig Jahre alt, hat an** ('of') **mich gedacht**; (**b**) + *dat.*: **Er arbeitet an** ('at') **einem neuen Roman, lehrt an** (but **studiert auf**) **der Universität, nimmt an** ('in') **allen Vergnügungen**

teil, hat sich an ('on') **mir gerächt, ist am** ('of') **Fieber gestorben** (see **sterben** 2 *c*)—**Der Blinde erkannte mich an** ('by') **der Stimme und nahm mich am Arm**—**Versündige dich nicht am** ('against the') **Heiligen Geist!**—**Es liegt an** ('rests with') **mir, ihn zu überreden**—**Es liegt mir viel an Ihrer guten Meinung** or **Es ist mir viel an Ihrer guten Meinung gelegen** ('I attach great importance to your good opinion'). Esp. noteworthy is its use (+*dat.*) in the sense of 'in the way of': e.g. **Er ist jung an Jahren, aber reich an Erfahrung**—**Sie erlitten lieber Schläge und was es sonst an Strafen gab** (Villinger: 'They preferred to get a thrashing and suffer whatever else in the way of punishment was meted out to them')—**Sie versuchte zu erkennen, was an Leben hinter ihr lag** (Frenssen)—**Kämpfe, die man mit einem solchen Aufwande an** ('expenditure of') **Geist und Ausdauer führt, werden nach und nach zum Selbstzweck, während die Veranlassung derselben immer mehr an** ('in') **Bedeutung verliert** (Ebner-Eschenbach); and with a neut. adj.-subst., **Sie hatte allein sein wollen, um das in sich zu verarbeiten, was der heutige Tag an Aufregendem und Unbegreiflichem gebracht hatte** (Jul. Wolff).

anbelangen: This double compd. of **langen** means 'to concern', being an alternative expression for **anbetreffen.** Both are now confined to a few set phrases in which the question of separation or non-separation of the first prefix does not arise, such as **was mich anbelangt** ('so far as I am concerned') and **was das anbetrifft** ('as for that'); the pres. parts. are favourite expressions in commercial and official lang.: e.g. **Ihr geschätztes Angebot anbetreffend, so scheint uns der Preis zu hoch angeschlagen** ('With regard *or* reference to your esteemed offer, the price seems to us to be too high'). Both verbs commonly drop one of their prefixes, but strangely enough, not the same prefix, the alternative forms being **anlangen** (q.v.), which is as limited in use as its longer form, and **betreffen** (q.v.), which has a much wider application.

anberaumen: The MHG noun *râm* meant 'goal, end in view', and the verb *râmen* 'to strive' to attain one's end. In course of time these words fell into disuse, being only preserved in the Bavarian dialect, which quite wrongly associated them with **Raum.** The only remnant still in use is the verb **anberaumen** (with **an** sep.), which is mainly used (esp. in the past part. as an adj.) in legal and official lang., with objs. like **Zeit, Tag, Stunde,** etc., in the sense of 'to arrange, settle, fix, agree upon': e.g. **Francesco hatte ihn zu anberaumter Zeit zu unterstützen versprochen** (Platen)—**Der Hochzeitstag war anberaumt und die halbe Stadt dazu eingeladen** (Musäus).

Anbetracht: see **Tracht** 2.

anbetreffen: see **anbelangen.**

anbieten: see **offer** 1 (*a*), and cf. (*e*).

Anblick: see **Sicht** 2 (*c*).

anblicken: see **look** 2 (*a*).

ander: 1. The ord. num. **zweit** (q.v.) does not occur before the NHG period: in MHG, 'second' was *ander*, as when Siegfried says to Gunther *der gesellen bin ich einer, der ander soltu wesen, der dritte sî Hagene* ('I shall be one of the raiding party, you are to be the second, and I want Hagen to be the third'). The only remnant of this earlier sense still in reg. use is the invariable expression **anderthalb,** lit. 'half of the second', i.e. 'one and a half' (see **halb** 1), as in **Das Brett ist anderthalb Fuß breit** and **Ich mußte anderthalb Stunden warten.** Some auctioneers may still, in accordance with the earlier usage, say **Zum ersten, zum andern, zum dritten und letzten!** ('Going, going, gone!'). **2.** As regards inflexion, **ander** takes the reg. adj. terminations: **ein** or **kein anderer, der** or **das andere, etwas anderes** (with *no* gen.), **alles** or **vieles andere** (or **viel anderes:** gen. **alles** or **vieles anderen**), **alle anderen, unter anderem, unter manchem anderen,** etc.; cf. **Herr Baum war Hausbesitzer, Bezirksobmann und noch verschiedenes andere** (Rilke: 'and various other things as well'). Noteworthy points here are that **jemand** or **niemand anders** is practically fixed in the north (see **jemand** 2), and that the gen. sing. masc. and neut., if no art. precedes, has a *weak* ending if the following noun has the *strong* ending, as in **andern Sinnes sein,** where **anderes Sinnes** (Stehr) is contrary to modern usage; sim. always **andernfalls** ('otherwise, or else': see **sonst** 1), less commonly **andernorts** ('elsewhere'), and, with the force of 'next', **andern Tags, Morgens, Abends. 3.** There is some fluctuation in the inflexion of an **attrib.** adj. following **ander** without an art., notably in the plur. The only example given by

Duden is **andere ähnliche Fälle**, and on the whole it seems advisable to treat the two attrib. words as *co*-ordinate and give them both the same ending. *Sanders* is no doubt right in differentiating between **andere schwarzen Anzüge** and **andere, schwarze Anzüge** (with a comma), the former implying more, additional, black suits ('black' being *sub*ordinate), the latter black suits as distinct from suits of other colours (the two attrib. words being *co*-ordinate: cf. **andere, und zwar schwarze Anzüge**). But in practice this almost hair-splitting difference does not seem to be rigidly observed: certainly, in the expression **Angehörige anderer christlicher Sekten** (Stehr), the author is comparing one Christian sect with other Christian sects, not with non-Christian sects. So, as there is a marked preference for **Wir haben noch andere wichtige Vorschläge zu besprechen,** it seems only logical to say **Man hat mich auch anderer unehrlicher Handlungen beschuldigt** ('I have also been accused of other dishonest dealings'). Where the second attrib. is intended to be *sub*ordinate, this can be adequately suggested in the *spoken* lang. by stressing the first. **4.** It would go beyond the scope of this guide to refer to the various idiomatic expressions in which **ander** occurs, but at least one might find space here, because it differs so markedly from the English idiom. The proposition 'Bravery is one thing, foolhardiness another thing' might conceivably be rendered by **Die Kühnheit ist eins, die Tollkühnheit etwas anderes**; but as **etwas** cannot be omitted here, this rendering is rather ineffective, and it is more idiomatic to use **ander** in *both* cases, placing the pred. first: **Ein anderes ist die Kühnheit, ein anderes die Tollkühnheit**; sim. **Ein anderes ist das abgenutzte Wort, ein anderes die lebendige Tat** (Th. Mann: 'Telling of a deed in trite words is one thing, actually doing the deed is another thing altogether').

ändern: see **change** 1 (*a*).

anders: This adv. gen. of **ander** (q.v. 2) is used to express our 'else' after **jemand, niemand,** etc., being treated as invariable in the north, as in **Wir wollen von jemand anders reden** (see **jemand** 2); and sim. with **wo, wie,** etc.: e.g. **Das Buch ist nicht hier, es muß woanders** (or **anderswo**) **liegen**—**Wir müssen diese Frage irgendwie anders anpacken** ('We must tackle this question in some other way'). It is also used as an independent adv.: e.g. **Hier stehe ich, ich kann nicht anders!** (ascribed to Luther)—**Die Sache verhält sich etwas anders** ('The facts are somewhat different')—**Er ist jetzt ganz anders**—**Wie anders die Stadt aussieht!**—**Wir müssen ein Flugzeug benutzen, anders** (or **sonst,** 'otherwise') **kommen wir zu spät an.** Its only other use, which goes far back, is in *conditional* clauses, where it has limiting force, but is practically pleonastic: e.g. **Erwürge mich lieber, habe ich anders Gnade vor deinen Augen gefunden** (Num. 11. 15)—**Unversehens war für sie die Zeit des Aufbruchs gekommen, wenn anders sie den Zug noch erreichen wollte** (Bergengruen).

anderwärts: see **auswärts.**

anerbieten: This verb, used reflex. with the force of 'to offer' to do something, is one of several in connexion with which usage fluctuates as to separation or non-separation of the first prefix (see esp. **anerkennen** and **anvertrauen**). In the south non-separation is the almost generally accepted usage: e.g. **Der Kaplan anerbot sich mich zum Dorfschreiner zu bringen** (G. Keller)—**Er anerbot sich die Mission zu übernehmen** (id.)—**Sie anerbot sich ihn nach Haus zu bringen** (Wassermann). But *Sanders* condemns this practice, and *Duden* allows no insep. forms. Actually, although the verbal noun is quite common (see **offer** 2 *c*), the verb is not much used in the north; when it is, **an** is certainly *sep.*, but the tendency is to treat it like **auferstehen** (q.v.) and drop one of the prefixes (esp. the first) in those parts where separation would take place: e.g. **Er erbot sich** (or **bot sich an**), **mich zu vertreten** ('He offered to take my place') —**Zwei Männer erboten sich, tote Hunde zu liefern** (Bergengruen).

Anerbieten: see **offer** 2 (*c*).

anerkennen: For the difference between this verb and **erkennen** see **recognize** 2.—As the prefix **an** is always accented, it should normally be *sep.*, as in **Es ist jetzt nicht die Jahreszeit, um Geschäfte zu machen, das erkennen wir an** (Kafka); and *Sprach-Brockhaus* expressly characterizes **ich anerkenne** in a princ. clause as **falsch für „ich erkenne an“.** Nevertheless, in the south, non-separation (except in the infin. with **zu**) is almost universal: e.g. **Ihr anerkennt das Recht des Stärkern** (C. F. Meyer)—**Sein Verstand anerkennt**

keine Grenzen (Wassermann)—**Der Papst anerkennt uns nicht** (Bruno Frank)—**Sie stellten sich als anerkennten sie das Recht nicht** (G. Keller). Of all the verbs formed in this way (see esp. **anerbieten** and **anvertrauen**), this is the one in the case of which non-separation has most strikingly spread to the north, so much so, indeed, that *Duden* now allows both forms. But that does not alter the fact that most people in the north still prefer to say **ich erkenne das an,** and in view of this, and esp. of the fact that every one even in the south uses **anzuerkennen,** not **zu anerkennen,** it seems advisable to treat **an** as *sep.* throughout, in spite of examples like the following, which give some indication, however, to what extent the southern idiom has gained ground: **Unser Held, der noch nicht alle Fähigkeit verloren hatte, eine Superiorität außer sich anzuerkennen , anerkannte die dieses Geistes** (Fichte)—**Die Kirche anerkannte ausdrücklich ihre Macht** (C. Hauptmann)—**Ich zeigte ihm meinen Schillerfalter** ('Purple Emperor butterfly'): **er anerkannte seine Seltenheit** (H. Hesse)—**Jeder anerkannte seine Tüchtigkeit** (Th. Mann)—**Er anerkannte das Besitzrecht seines Bruders** (H. Krieger)—**Goethe hatte dem Menschen Schiller mit einer Professur in Jena ausgeholfen, den Dichter Schiller aber kannte und anerkannte er nicht** (Lamprecht)—**Annette anerkannte die zweite Bedingung** (H. Franck)—**Seine militärischen Zeugnisse anerkannten ihn als Kameraden und Untergebenen** (A. Schaeffer)—**Prag anerkennt Henleins Programm als Verhandlungsvorlage** (headline in the *Völkischer Beobachter* of 4/5/1938)—**Mit Dankbarkeit anerkennen wir ihre** (*scil.* the allied troops') **Bemühungen und Opfer** (from the *Kölnischer Kurier* of 9/4/1945, in a translation of General Bradley's speech at Ehrenbreitstein).

anerschaffen: see schaffen 1 (*b*).

Anfall, anfallen: see **attack** 2.

anfühlen: see fühlen 2.

anführen: see **lead** 1.

angaffen: see look 2 (*a*).

Angebot: see offer 2 (*b*); cf. **Gebot.**

angehen: 1. Used abs. with *intrans.* force, this has various shades of meaning: e.g. **Ich wollte die Schuhe anprobieren, sie gingen aber nicht an** ('they would not go on')—**Das Feuer ging nicht an** ('did not catch')—**Morgen gehen die Vorlesungen wieder an** ('The lectures resume tomorrow')—**Nein, das geht nicht an** (or **das ist nicht angängig,** 'that is impossible, that won't do'), **hier muß ich meinen Willen haben** (Lessing)—**Er ist ein angehender Arzt** ('a young inexperienced doctor'), **ein angehender Dreißiger** ('just turned thirty'). **2.** With *trans.* force, it means either 'to solicit, approach' a person (with a request, petition) or 'to concern' (cf. **anlangen**): e.g. on the one hand, **Die Königin, von den Abgeordneten angegangen, ja bedroht, mußte sich dem Vertrage anschließen** (Platen)—**Die Freunde wurden um ihre Meinung angegangen** (H. Maync); on the other hand, **Was geht mich das an?** ('What concern is that of mine?'). In both of these senses the normal aux. is **haben** (*Sanders* says „**haben verdient den Vorzug**"): e.g. **Sie hatten mit einem Schreiben die Herren in Würzburg angegangen und nichts erfahren** (W. Schäfer)—**Das Mädchen schien ihm nicht mehr anzugehören, ihn niemals angegangen zu haben** (Mörike: 'The girl seemed . . . never to have had anything to do with him')—**Vor Zeiten hat man Soldaten gehabt, die den Staat gar nichts angegangen haben** (Auerbach: '. . . who had nothing to do with the state'). But the aux. **sein,** although little used in the north, is fairly common: e.g., meaning 'to approach', **Die Frau stand im Ruf einer Bettlerin, obwohl sie keinen je um ein Almosen angegangen war** (Zahn); cf., as rather unusual in the north, **Das hätte er nur verantworten können, wenn er vorher die Pastorin um ihre Meinung angegangen wäre** (Raabe). So also in the sense of 'to concern', **Was ist er euch angegangen?** (Gotthelf: 'What had he to do with you? What was he to you?')—**Das Portrait** (of the author as a boy) **hängt in meinem Arbeitszimmer, und der Junge mit dem weißen Hemdkragen schaut den Alten mit dem schwarzen Rock so fremd an, als wären sie einander im Leben nie etwas angegangen** (Hansjakob)—**Sie hatten schon allerhand im Halbschlaf gehört, aber es war sie nichts angegangen** (Böhlau)—**Ich habe lange gelitten und dich ist es nichts angegangen** (C. Bulcke). At one time a *dat.* of the person was sometimes used, but this is now very rare: cf. **Nichts auf der Welt ging ihm mehr was** (= **etwas**) **an, wie er keinem mehr was anging** (Polenz).

angehören: see **gehören** 1.

angelegen: see **anliegen** 3.

angeloben: see **promise** 2.
Angesicht: see Sicht 2 (*b*).
angewöhnen: see **accustom(ed)** 3 (*a*).
angle: see **Ecke.**
anglotzen: see look 2 (*a*).
angreifen, Angriff: see **attack** 1.
angucken: see look 2 (*a*).
Angst: The MHG *angest* is a cognate of Lat. *angustiae* (a 'defile', then fig. 'perplexity, straits'), so that it properly suggested the feeling of uneasiness that besets a person who finds himself 'in a tight corner'. But **Angst** now implies a stronger feeling, viz. 'anxiety, fear, alarm', as in **Sie hat Angst vor Gewittern,** while the orig. sense of 'malaise' is really retained in the noun **Bange,** now only used in coll. speech, as in **Haben Sie keine Bange!** (in more select lang. **Haben Sie keine Sorge!** 'Don't worry!'). Actually, **Bange** is formed from MHG *be-ange* (the *e* elided as in **gegessen:** see **essen** 1), where *be-* has intensifying force and *ange* is the adv. corresponding to the adj. *enge* (> **eng**), meaning 'narrow, tight' (see **adverbs formed from adjectives** 1), and **bange** is now used in good style as an attrib. adj. in expressions like **in dieser bangen Stunde** (Sch.: 'in this dread hour') and **aus bangem Traum erwacht** (Uhland: 'awakened from an oppressive dream'), but only in coll. lang. in the pred., as in **Ich bin** (or **Mir ist**) **bange** ('I am frightened') —**Sie war bange um mich** ('She was anxious *or* worried about me'). But the noun and the adj. have become confused, so that one says not only **Du machst mich bange,** but also **Was ist Euch? Ihr macht mir bange** (L. Goldammer: 'What ails you? You frighten me')—**Das ist das einzige, was mir bange macht** (R. Herzog). Incidentally, the same confusion has arisen in the case of **Angst,** and **Mir ist angst und bange** is in common every-day use. As already stated, such expressions in which **bange** stands in the pred. are only coll.; this applies also to the verb **bangen,** as in **Ich bange** or **bange mich** ('I am afraid'), although its impers. use is rather less coll.: **Es bangt mir um** (or **für**) **mein Leben** ('I fear for my life').
anhalten: see **stop** 1 (*c*) and 2 (*b*); for **um jemand anhalten,** see **marry** 1 (*d*).
anhängen: 1. For the mutated root-vowel, and for the various uses of the weak and strong forms, see **hang** and **abhängen** 1. *Meanings*: **(a)** *trans.*: 'to hang (something) on (an object), attach, add': e.g. **Sie hängte** (or **hing**) **sich** (dat.) **die Ohrringe an, hat sich die Ohrringe angehängt— Er hängte, ohne zu antworten, den Hörer an** (Kafka: 'hung up the receiver')—**Plötzlich frug Brigitte: „Sind wir eigentlich arm oder reich, Gabriel?" Daß sie ihrer Frage „Gabriel" anhängte** ('added'), **tat diesem wohl** (Ponten); fig. **Warum hängt sie sich ihm immer an?** ('Why does she always attach herself to, run after him?')—**Die Leute hängen mir immer etwas an** ('People are for ever casting aspersions on me')—**Der Kaufmann hat mir schlechte Waren angehängt** (or **aufgehängt:** 'The merchant has foisted inferior goods on me'); **(b)** *intrans.*: in the lit. sense only in phrases like **Sie hatte einen Schlüsselbund anhängen** ('She had a bunch of keys hanging at her waist') or **Beachten Sie das anhängende Muster** ('Note the accompanying, attached pattern'); otherwise fig. 'to be an adherent of': e.g. **Boll stammte von einer Familie ab, die von alters her** ('for many a long day') **der Kirche angehangen hatte** (Ric. Huch): cf. **Er schien ihr sehr anzuhangen** (Heyse: 'He seemed greatly attached to her'), where we should now use **anzuhängen,** or preferably the simple verb (**Er schien sehr an ihr zu hängen**).
anheben: This verb is not much used in the lit. trans. sense of 'to heave up' (as in raising a sideboard in order to lift a carpet); its usual sense is now 'to begin' (either trans. or, much more commonly, intrans.), esp. 'to begin to speak'. While the past part. is always **angehōben,** the past indic. has two forms, viz. **hōb an** or **hūb an** (cf. **heben** 1 *a*), the latter esp. with the force of 'to begin': e.g. **Die alte Angst hub in ihm wieder an** (Viebig)—**„Ich beschreibe Ihnen also Ihr eigen Werk", hub der alte Herr an** (Mörike)—**Ich hub mein bestes Lied an, daß es weit umher ertönte** (Geßner); but **hob an** is also used here, although perhaps not so commonly: cf. **Die Musik hob wieder an** (St. Zweig)—**Der Auszug** ('evacuation') **von sechshunderttausend Menschen hob um den 20. Januar an** (J. Thorwald). Otherwise the past tense form with the stem-vowel **u** is confined to a choice literary style: e.g. **Er hatte einen Spaten in der Hand und hub neben dem Zelte einen Raum von wenigen Fuß im Geviert aus** (Binding: 'He had a spade in his hand and was digging a hole a few feet square beside his tent').

anheim: This expression was orig. used like **nach** or **zu Hause** (cf. Heim 2 *a*): S. Schaidenreißer (16th century) uses **Er kam spat anheim** and **Der Herr ist nicht anheim**; but in this sense it is now quite obs. According to modern usage it is a sep. prefix, confined to three verbs: **1.** The lit. meaning of **anheimfallen** (+**dat.**) is 'to fall to a person's lot *or* share, become a person's property', fig. 'to fall a prey to': e.g. **Die Krone ist aus Mangel eines Thronfolgers der Nation anheimgefallen** (Wieland)—**Er begann, aus einem Korbe eine Unmenge Fische in die Luft zu werfen, die den heranflatternden Vögeln anheimfielen** (A. Schaeffer); fig. **Ich schwankte zwischen Schlummer und Wachsein, ohne dies zu erreichen oder jenem anheimzufallen** (id.)—**Die Altstadt ist dem Schmutz anheimgefallen** (Immermann)—**Ich fiel einer trotzigen Laune anheim** (G. Keller); sim. **der Vergessenheit anheimfallen** ('to fall *or* sink into oblivion'). **2.** On the other hand, **jemandem etwas anheimgeben** or **anheimstellen** means lit. 'to give *or* put a thing into a person's hand', esp. 'to leave something to some one to deal with, refer it to his judgement': e.g. **Es wäre das beste, wir gäben den Entschluß dem Los anheim** (G.: i.e. 'to let the lot decide, to toss up')—**Er gab ihnen anheim, sich mit dem Präsidenten in Übereinstimmung zu setzen** (Ric. Huch: 'He left it to them to come to an agreement with the president')—**Der Justizrat gab einigen Zeugen anheim** ('gave some of the witnesses to understand, brought it *home* to them'), **daß sie dumme Tröpfe wären** (id.)—**Die Schulvorsteherin gab der Konsulin anheim, der Tochter eine Ermahnung zuteil werden zu lassen** (Th. Mann)—**Sie stellten die Sache einem Höheren anheim** (G. Keller: 'They submitted the case to a Higher Power')—**Ich stellte es dem Schicksal anheim, was es mit mir vorhatte, zu erfüllen** (Chamisso)—**Sie stellte alles meiner Entscheidung anheim** (Lenau)—**Er erwiderte, das hieße soviel, als das Kind einer ungewissen Zukunft anheimstellen** (G. Keller: 'He replied that that would be tantamount to resigning the child to an uncertain future').

anklopfen: see **klopfen** 1 and 2.

ankommen: 1. Whereas **kommen** (q.v.) is a verb of *motion*, **ankommen** is a verb of *rest*, pointing to the moment when the action ceases: hence **Er kam an das Haus**, but **Er kam an dem Hause an**, and it is quite contrary to established modern usage to say **Es sind jetzt sechs Jahre, daß ich auf die Wartburg ankam** (Heine). In fact, every word implying *arrival* at a place requires a dat. in the prep. phrase: see examples under **arrive**, and cf. **Ich kam erst spät nach Hause** (or **in die Stadt**) and **Ich kam erst spät zu Hause an** (or **in der Stadt an**); see also Heim 2 (*a*), and verbs like **einfinden, eintreffen, langen** 2 (*a*) and **get** 2 (*b*). **2.** For **ankommen** with **auf** + accus. in the sense of 'to depend', see **depend** 1 and 2. **3.** Another common meaning of **ankommen** is 'to come over' a person, used of feelings, moods, impulses, etc. (see esp. **anwandeln**). Here there is some fluctuation between the accus. and the dat. of the person: while *Sanders* says **„etwas kommt einen, heute fast überwiegend einem an"**, *Duden* gives only **„mich kommt ein Ekel an"**, and modern usage actually does favour the *accus.*, the dat. having lost ground of late (but cf. 4): e.g. (**a**) with the *dat.*, **Entsetzen möchte einem ankommen** (Lessing)—**Mir kam ein Verlangen zu weinen an** (G.)—**Er sprach wenig, doch je nachdem ihm die Laune ankam, konnte er alle anderen überbieten** (Mörike)—**Mir kam ein Schauer an** (Gellert)—**Es kam ihr die Lust an, Milch zu trinken** (Novalis)—**Es kam ihm wie ein Schwindel an** (L. Goldammer)—**Wie mir einfiel, daß ich allein in dem öden Hause war, kam mir ein Schauder an** (R. Huch); (**b**) with the *accus.*, **Wie der Tod ihn ankam, hatte er ein Leben hinter sich, das sich in zwei verschiedene Hälften teilte** (Fontane)—**Es ging ihm so nahe, daß ihn das Weinen ankam** (Frenssen: 'He was so deeply moved that tears came into his eyes')—**Mich kam ein gewaltiges Erschrecken an** (R. Huch)—**Es kam sie ein Zittern an** (A. Wilbrandt)—**Auch mich kommt mehr als einmal ein solcher Schauder an** (Hofmannsthal)—**Manchmal kommt eine heimatliche Erinnerung mich an** (Th. Mann)—**Wenn ihn die Müdigkeit ankam, streckte er sich auf ein Ruhelager** (Bergengruen); sim. with **es** as subj., **Er konnte tüchtig schaffen, wenn's (= wenn die Lust) ihn ankam** (O. Wildermuth)—**Es kam dich an** ('You felt an impulse'), **ihnen den Arm entgegenzustrecken mit dem Fingerzeichen gegen den bösen Blick** (Rilke). **4.** On the other hand, where **ankommen** is used with an adv. like

schwer, hart, or **sauer** to express the idea that some course of action 'comes hard on' a person, i.e. that he finds it difficult or is reluctant to adopt it, modern usage shows a definite preference for a *dat.* of the person: e.g. **Dieses Geständnis kommt mir etwas sauer an** (Lessing)—**Das kam mir schwer an** (G.)—**Es kommt ihm hart an** (Heine)—**So schwer es mir ankam, lebte ich den Vorschriften des Arztes gemäß** (E. T. A. Hoffmann)—**Ziehenden Schrittes ging er den Berg hinan und wußte nicht, ob ihm das Steigen an sich schwerer geworden, oder ob's ihm nur heute so schwer ankäme** (Binding)—**Ich tat's auf des Kurfürsten Befehl: es ist mir hart angekommen, aber als Soldat mußte ich gehorchen** (E. Wichert). The accus. is now rather rare here: cf. **Der Gang kommt mich sauer an** (Hebel)—**Je älter er wird, desto mehr Dinge treten ihm vor Augen, die noch älter sind als er: es kommt ihn schwer an, Hand an sie zu legen** (Waggerl).

anlangen: Used in the sense of 'to arrive', this compd. of **langen** (q.v.) stands in the same relation to **gelangen** (q.v.) as **ankommen** does to **kommen,** i.e. it points to the moment of *rest,* when the motion ceases (cf. **arrive**): hence **Wir langten endlich an unserem Ziel an**; sim. **in der Stadt, vor dem Hotel, zu** (not **nach**) **Hause anlangen.** The other meaning of **anlangen** is 'to concern' (cf. **betreffen** and **angehen** 2), in which sense it is mainly used in propositions like **Was mich anlangt, habe ich nichts gegen den Vorschlag einzuwenden** ('So far as I am concerned, I have no objection to raise against the proposal')—**Was den Hut anlangt** ('As for her hat'), **so war es ein Strohhut mit einem grünen Band** (Rilke). Here, in commercial and official lang., the longer form **anbelangt** is usually preferred, and it is probable that the shorter form should really not be used in this sense at all, and that it arose through the dropping of the second prefix **be-** (see **anbelangen**).

anlernen: see **lernen** 2.

anliegen: 1. This intrans. verb has several specific, generally lit. meanings: e.g. **Sie trug ein fest** (or **eng**) **anliegendes** ('close fitting') **Kleid**—**Jeder Winkel hat zwei anliegende** ('adjacent') **Seiten**—**Das Schiff lag nach Norden an** ('The vessel stood to the north'). Otherwise its commonest use is with the fig. force of 'to urge, entreat urgently'; in this sense it at one time took an accus. of the person (like **bestürmen**), as in **Er lag den König an, ihm beizuspringen** (Lessing), but this is now obs., the *dat.* having quite displaced the accus.: e.g. **Kaum war ich nach Hause gekommen, als ich den Eltern anlag, uns diesen Mann zum Klaviermeister zu geben** (G.)—**Der Verwalter lag ihm an, ein Paar Rappen zu kaufen** (H. v. Kleist)—**Der Franzose lag mir an, ihn auf die Gemsjagd mitzunehmen** (C. F. Meyer). Obs. here also is the use of the aux. **sein,** as in **Ich bin ihm angelegen, mich zu entlassen** (Rückert), the standard aux. being now **haben:** e.g. **Der Minister hatte mir lange angelegen, ich sollte mich irgend einem Geschäfte widmen** (G.); see 3. **2.** The infin., used as a verbal noun with the force of 'entreaty, urgent request', was a favourite word of Luther's, as in **Wirf dein Anliegen auf den Herrn** (Ps. 55. 22), and this is still in quite common use, as in **Ich habe ein Anliegen an Sie**—**Ich brachte ihm mein Anliegen vor. 3.** The past part. **angelegen** is used as a pred. adj. in the expression **sich** (dat.) **etwas angelegen sein lassen** (lit. 'to let something be near to one's heart', i.e. 'to make it a matter of one's concern, make it one's business'), as in **Ich werde es mir angelegen sein lassen, Ihnen die erwünschte Auskunft zu erteilen** ('I shall make it my business, spare no effort, to let you have the desired information') and **Die Besitzer der Weingüter** ('vineyard plantations') **lassen sich's angelegen sein, die Wächter mit Wein und Speisen zu versorgen** (Heyse: '. . . make a point of supplying the watchmen with plenty of wine and food'); cf. the use of the adj.-subst. in the phrase **nichts Angelegeneres zu tun haben, als . . .** ('to have nothing nearer to one's heart than . . .'): e.g. **Er hatte nichts Angelegeneres zu tun, als mein Geheimnis auszuplaudern** ('He had nothing better to do than let out my secret', i.e. 'The first thing he did was to divulge what I had told him in confidence').

anmaßen: The modern idiom **sich** (*dat.*) **ein Ding** (*accus.*) **anmaßen** ('to arrogate a thing to oneself, presume *or* venture' to do something) has developed (as explained under **es** 2) out of the original **sich** (*accus.*) **eines Dinges anmaßen,** which has now a distinctly archaic flavour: e.g. **Wenn die Rolle von einem Komödianten gespielt wird, der sich dieses Titels an-**

maßen könnte . . . (Lessing)— **Die Scheu Ottiliens, sich jener heiligen Gestalt anzumaßen,** (i.e. Ottilie's reluctance to presume to represent the Virgin in a play) **ward überwunden** (G.)—**Ich will mich keines Ruhms anmaßen, der mir nicht zukommt** (Sch.); more in accordance with modern usage are examples like **Wir maßen uns über sein Hauptverdienst kein Urteil an** (G.)—**Was maßest du dir an,** ('How dare you') **mir falsch Orakel zu verkündigen?** (Sch.).

anmerken: see **lassen** 4.

anmuten: This verb is used in two ways. **1.** (**a**) With a dat. of the person and an accus. of the thing (which may be an infin. or finite subord. clause), it means 'to expect *or* demand something of a person', esp. something unnatural or extravagant: e.g. **Keiner wagt es, ihr etwas Ungebührliches anzumuten** (Möser)—**Das heißt, meiner Geduld zuviel anmuten** (Tieck: 'That is overtaxing my patience'). Actually, **anmuten** is now little used in this sense, being almost entirely displaced by **zumuten,** which has the same construction: e.g. **Mute mir nichts zu, was mir unmöglich ist!** (Wieland: 'Don't expect *or* demand impossibilities from me!'—**Du wirst mir nicht zumuten, einen Mord vor den Richter der Welt hinzuschleppen** (Sch.: i.e. You are surely not suggesting that I should appear before my Maker as a murderer?)—**So etwas kann ihm nicht zugemutet werden** ('That sort of thing cannot be expected of him')—**Ich habe mir zuviel zugemutet** ('I have demanded more from myself than I can manage'); cf. **Das ist eine starke Zumutung!** ('That is really asking too much!'). (**b**) The phrase **jemandem etwas zumuten,** then, implies that one person suggests or hints to another something he has in his mind, and this is precisely the idea conveyed by **jemandem etwas ansinnen,** as in **Sie warf Kalk unter den Stein, und mehreren wurde ein Gleiches zu tun angesonnen** (G.: 'She threw some lime under the foundation-stone, and it was suggested to several other bystanders that they should do the same'); but the suggestion or hint is usually a distasteful or horrifying one to the person receiving it, one that goes against his nature or character: e.g. **Ich weiß, was dir die Königin angesonnen** (Sch. in 'Maria Stuart': 'I know what the queen [Elizabeth] has hinted to you', viz. that he should murder Mary).

2. The other use of **anmuten** is with an impers. subj. and an accus. of the person in the sense of 'to give a person a pleasurable feeling': e.g. **Schon auf der Grenze mutete es mich heimatlich an** (Auerbach: 'Even at the frontier I began to feel at home')—**Ihre Anmut mutet einen an** ('Her gracious manner warms one's heart'). In this sense **zumuten** cannot be used; but cf. **Es ist mir** (or **Mir ist**) **. . . zumute** ('I have a . . . feeling'), with an appropriate adv. inserted, although here the feeling is mostly a strange, uncanny, disagreeable one: **Mir ist sonderbar (unheimlich, schlecht) zumute.**

annehmen: see **get** 1 (*e*).

anordnen: see **befehlen** 3 (*c*).

anraten: see **raten** 2 (*a*).

anrücken: see **advance** 1.

anschaffen: This *weak* trans. verb (cf. **schaffen** 2 *b*) is used esp. with a reflex. dat. in the sense of 'to provide *or* furnish oneself with' something, as in **Ich habe mir einige neue Möbel** (or **Kleider**) **angeschafft.** At one time it was used with the force of 'to give an order for' something (= **bestellen**), as when a waiter says **Sagen Sie mir, was Sie anschaffen** (Gutzkow). *Sanders* represents this as obs., but it is still used in southern dialects in the sense of 'to order, direct' a person to do something: e.g. **Er hatte nachsichtig gelächelt, als er dem Dechanten anschaffte** (= **als er den Dechanten anwies**), **Fis statt F zu singen** (Zuckmayer: 'With an indulgent smile he had directed the Dean to sing F sharp instead of F natural') and **Er saß gewöhnlich und dusselte** (now usually **duselte,** 'dozed') **vor sich hin, und wenn er einmal den Mund aufmachen wollte, bekam er prompt von seiner Frau angeschafft** (= **wurde er . . . angefahren** or vulgarly **angeschnauzt**), **ihn gleich wieder zu schließen** (id.: '. . . he was promptly stormed at by his wife and told to keep his mouth shut').

anschauen: see **look** 2 (*c*).

Anschein, anscheinend: Whereas **Schein** and **scheinbar** (qq. v. 2) may imply that the appearance conflicts with the reality, and even that the appearance is deliberate pretence, **Anschein** and **anscheinend** merely express an opinion based on what strikes the eye, e.g. a natural phenomenon, a person's outward appearance or conduct, etc.: e.g. **Es hat ganz den Anschein, als ob es regnen wollte** ('It looks very much like rain')—**Dem**

Anschein nach zu urteilen ('To judge by his appearance'), **ist der Mann ein Amerikaner—Anscheinend** ('Apparently, so far as one can see') **ist das junge Paar sehr glücklich.**

ansehen: 1. The ordinary expression for 'to look at a person' is **jemand ansehen** (in the north) or **anschauen** (esp. in the south): see **look** 2 (*a*). **2.** A reflex. dat. of interest referring to the subj. is often added, as in **Ich möchte mir das Bild nochmal ansehen** ('I should like to have another look at the picture'). Quite different is the dat. in **jemandem etwas ansehen**: a proposition like **Man sieht ihm sein Alter nicht an** means lit. 'One does not see his age by looking at him', i.e. 'He does not look his age'; and sim. **Niemand würde ihm den Ausländer ansehen** ('No one would take him for a foreigner'), and with a subord. clause as obj., **Man sieht (es) ihr gleich an, daß sie verliebt ist** ('You need only look at her to see she is in love'). The present writer came across an advertisement of a washing-machine with the caption **Sieht man's ihr an, daß sie heute Wäsche hat? Wohl kaum!** ('To look at her, would you say that this was her washing day? Hardly likely!'), the advertisement being accompanied by a sketch of a mother playing with her children while the machine was doing the work. **3.** The verbal noun **Ansehen** is used not only in its lit. sense, as in **Ich kenne ihn nur von Ansehen** ('I only know him by sight') or **Der Fall hat jetzt ein ganz anderes Ansehen** ('The case looks quite different now, has taken a quite new turn'), but also with the fig. force of 'regard, respect, reputation', as in **Er steht hier in hohem Ansehen**; and the past part. **angesehen** is used as an adj. in the sense of 'esteemed, respectable, of high standing': e.g. **Er ist einer der angesehensten Bürger der Stadt—Diese Firma ist im ganzen Lande sehr angesehen.** For **Ansehung,** see **Tracht** 2.

Ansicht: see **Sicht** 2 (*a*).

ansichtig: This adj. is now only used (as is **gewahr,** q.v.) in the pred. with **werden** with the force of 'to catch sight of' (= **erblicken**). The MHG *ansihtic werden* took an accus. obj., and the expression was peculiar in that *an-* was commonly treated as a sep. prefix, so that 'He caught sight of me' was *er wart mich sihtic an*; and this was still in use in early NHG, as in **Sobald er mich wart sichtig an . . .** (H. Sachs). This separation of the prefix has long been obs., but an *accus.* obj. is still quite common, esp. in ordinary lang., while the *gen.* has become almost the rule in more choice prose: e.g. (accus.) **Mittag kam herbei, eh' ich die Freundin wieder ansichtig werden konnte** (G.)—**Als er ihn ansichtig wurde, rief er: „Was treibst du dich hier umher?"** (Immermann); (gen.) **Während sie sich umschauten, wurden sie eines alten Mannes ansichtig, der Gras mähte** (Fontane)—**Das alte Weib blieb stehen, als sie seiner ansichtig wurde** (G. Hauptmann)—**„Da steht ja mein Brauner!" rief er, als er seines Pferdes ansichtig wurde** (Jul. Wolff)—**Dort wurde er zweier Krankenschwestern ansichtig** (Alverdes)—**Die Frau war verschwunden: wenn jemand ihrer ansichtig geworden wäre, so hätte er es erfahren, aber keiner hatte sie zu Gesicht bekommen** (Bergengruen: '. . . but no one had set eyes on her'—see **Sicht** 2 *b*). As the accus. construction was the orig. one, **ansichtig werden** differs from most of the expressions which take an accus. or a gen. (**gewahr werden, müde sein,** etc.): with the latter the gen. was the orig. construction, while the accus. resulted from the NHG **es** (q.v. 1) coming to represent both *ez* (accus.) and *es* (gen.) in MHG.

ansiedeln: see **übersiedeln** 1 (*b*).

ansinnen: see **anmuten** 1 (*b*).

ansprechen: 1. Used with *transitive* force in various senses, viz. 'to speak to, address', like **anreden** (esp. with a request for something); 'to hail' (a ship), like **anrufen**; with fig. force, 'to appeal to, please'; with **für** or an 'identifying' **als**, 'to pronounce to be, characterize as' (a favourite expression of Goethe's, but not so much used now): e.g. **Unterwegs sprach mich ein Bettler um Almosen an—Auf der Überfahrt nach Amerika sprach der Kapitän ein Schwesterschiff an—Das Lied hat eine ansprechende Melodie** ('a nice, catchy tune')—**Das sprachen die Damen für eine Ausflucht an** (G.: 'The ladies represented that as an excuse')—**Manche Figuren in diesem Roman kann man als wohlgeraten ansprechen** (G.); cf. the example from G. Hauptmann given under **beid. 2.** With *intransitive* force, like the more usual **vorsprechen** (q.v. 2), 'to drop in' on a person (with a *dative* in the prep. phrase, and aux. **haben**): e.g. **Am Tage vor Weihnachten sprach Bar-**

bara flüchtig an und brachte einen Pfefferkuchen mit (E. Wichert)—**Es traf sich, daß Konrad bei Herrn Rohde ansprach, um ein Stündchen zu verweilen** (id.).

anstarren: see **look** 2 (*a*).

anstatt: 1. (**a**) This prep. has developed out of MHG *an stat,* a poss. gen. being usually inserted between the two words, as in *er sante mich an ir stat* (Iwein: 'He sent me in her place, instead of her'). This is still in common use in more or less established expressions (see **Statt** 1 *a*), being elsewhere generally expressed by the prep. **anstatt,** often in the contracted form **statt,** with a following gen., as in **statt dessen** ('instead of that'); so also 'in her place' now usually is **(an)statt ihrer** (see 2). At one time a *dat.* was sometimes used instead of a gen., as in **Tut's statt mir!** (Grillparzer), but this should be avoided, except where there is no distinctive gen. ending: e.g. **Statt jenem, den sie gesucht, sahen sie einen Ritter** (M. Greif: 'Instead of the person they had been seeking, they beheld a knight'), where **jenes** would be incorrect, as it is identical in form with an accus. neut., but where an alternative correct expression would be **desjenigen.** The dat. is esp. appropriate in the case of a neut. adj.-subst., as in **Anstatt Gutem hat er Böses angerichtet.** (**b**) It can also stand before a prep. phrase or a subord. or infin. clause: e.g. **Anstatt nach Berlin ist er nach Leipzig gereist**—**Anstatt spazierenzugehen, solltest du arbeiten**—**Sie hätten ihm raten sollen, anstatt daß Sie ihn bestraften. 2.** It is noteworthy that where an expression like 'in your place' does not mean 'instead of you', but 'situated as you were' or 'if I had been you', one does not say **anstatt deiner** or **an deiner Statt,** but **an deiner Stelle:** see **place (noun)** 3.

anstaunen: see **look** 2 (*a*); **wonder** 4.

anstecken: see **light** (**verb**) 2 (*a*).

anstehen: This verb is now used esp. with fig. force: it is possible to refer to a ladder set against a wall as **eine anstehende** (= **an die Wand gestellte**) **Leiter,** but the prefix is redundant in **Der Tisch stand dicht am Fenster an.** Its fig. uses with an *impers.* subj. can be seen from examples like **Der Termin steht auf nächsten Montag an** ('The hearing in court is fixed for next Monday')—**Im Schuldbuch steht noch eine größere Summe an** ('A considerable debt is still outstanding')—**Es steht mir nicht an** (= **Es ziemt mir nicht**), **mit ihm zu verkehren** ('It ill becomes me to associate with him')—**Diese Frage wollen wir anstehen lassen** ('We'll defer that question')—**Damit kann es noch einige Wochen anstehen** (G.: 'That can stand over for some weeks'). With a *pers.* subj., its nearest approach to the lit. sense is seen in its modern application to standing close to others in a queue, awaiting one's turn, as in **Nach meiner Ausweiskarte** ('For my identity-card') **mußte ich eine Stunde anstehen;** otherwise its only accepted sense is now 'to hesitate, scruple', as in **Ich stehe an, mich für einverstanden zu erklären** ('I hesitate to say that I agree') and **Ich stehe nicht an, zu behaupten, daß er schuldig ist;** one no longer says **Ich zwinge meine Tochter nicht; stehen Sie ihr an** ('if you satisfy *or* please her'), **so mag sie zusehen, wie sie glücklich mit Ihnen wird** (Sch.). In all its senses it now usually takes the aux. **haben,** like the simple verb **stehen** (q.v. 1), but **sein** is sometimes used in the south.

anstellen (reflex.): see **stellen** 2; cf. **tun** 3.

anstrengen: see **überanstrengen.**

Anteil: see **Teil** 2 (*a*).

Antrag: see **offer** 2 (*d*).

antragen: see **offer** 1 (*d*).

antreten: As explained under **her-, hin-** 3, the proposition 'He stepped up to me' is **Er trat an mich heran** (not **an**). The sense of **antreten** which is nearest to this is 'to take up a position' for a specific purpose: e.g. **Nach der Pause traten die Tänzer zur Quadrille an** ('took their places for a set of quadrilles'); sim. in **zum Fechten antreten** ('to take one's stand for a fencing bout') and the military command **Antreten!** ('Fall in!'). Otherwise its main use is with *trans.* force, either with inanimate accus. objs. like **Amt** ('to take up an appointment, enter on the duties of an office'), **Dienst** ('to enter service'), **Unterhandlungen** ('to open negotiations'), **Erbschaft** ('to enter on an inheritance'), **Reise** ('to set out on a journey'), as in **Es war noch nicht hell, als die beiden ihre Wanderung antraten** (Fr. Schnack); or with a pers. obj., either of feelings, moods, etc. which 'come upon' one (see **anwandeln**) or with a pers. subj. in the sense of 'to apply to *or* approach' some one, esp. with a request, petition, etc.: e.g. **Ein heftiger Hunger trat mich**

an—Die Versuchung trat mich an, ihm etwas vorzulügen—Ich war bei ihm, als der Tod ihn antrat ('when death surprised him')—**Er hat mich um eine Anleihe angetreten.**

Antwort: see **Wort** 2.

anvertrauen: In connexion with this double compd. of **trauen,** meaning 'to confide' something to the care of a person, 'to entrust' some one with something, usage in the south differs from that in general use in the north (cf. **anerbieten**). Whereas the forms with separation of the first prefix, as in **Ich vertraute es ihm an,** are the only ones officially recognized in the north, the verb is treated as insep. in the south in pres. and past tenses; and while it is true that this has to some extent spread to the north, although not as much as in the case of **anerkennen** (q.v.), it is advisable not to imitate the following examples in good prose: **Ich anvertraue dir Palma: hüte sie!** (C. F. Meyer)—**Deiner Sorge anvertraue ich die Wirtschaft und den Hausstand** (Scheffel)—**Als ich ein Buch Papier überschmiert hatte, anvertraute ich es meinen Freunden** (G. Keller)—**Zuletzt anvertraute er sich seiner Tochter** (Auerbach). It is significant that separation of **an** in the infin. with **zu,** as in **Ich schicke mich an, meine Geständnisse dem geduldigen Papiere anzuvertrauen** (Th. Mann), is firmly established in the south also.

anwandeln: The simple verb **wandeln** (q.v.) is now a rather choice expression, and as an intrans. verb with the force of 'to saunter up' to a person **anwandeln** is almost confined to **angewandelt kommen** (see **kommen** 4 *b*). Very common, however, is its use with an impers. subj. (a feeling, mood, fit, etc.) in the sense of 'to come over *or* seize' a person (cf. **antreten**). Here, in fact, it is in rather more common use than **ankommen** (q.v. 3), but whereas the latter may take a dat. of the person, **anwandeln** now almost invariably takes an *accus.* (aux. **haben**): e.g. **Manchmal wandelte mich ein Verlangen nach solchen abenteuerlichen Dingen an** (G.)—**Was wandelte den Ritter an?** (Sch.: 'What ailed the knight?')—**Ein Heimweh wandelte mich an** (Hofmannsthal)—**Mit einem Male wandelte ihn eine Müdigkeit an** (Waggerl)—**Für Augenblicke wandelte ihn eine böse Lust an** (Bergengruen)—**Als der Sarg versenkt war, wandelte meinen Vater eine Schwäche an** (H. Hesse)—**Die Magd fragte, was ihm zugestoßen sei, und erhielt die Antwort, daß ihn eine plötzliche Schwäche angewandelt habe** (Immermann)—**Ich kann nicht sagen, daß mich ein Schrecken angewandelt hätte** (Fontane)—**Dergleichen Anfälle von Depression hatten mich in früheren Zeiten öfters angewandelt** (Werfel); so also in the pass., **Er stürzte, wie von innerlicher Schwäche angewandelt, jäh zusammen** (W. v. Scholz). A *dat.* of the person here, with the aux. **sein,** once quite common, seems now to be almost obs.: cf. **Es wandelte ihr eine kleine Schwachheit an** (Lessing)—**Was ist dir** (now **hat dich**) **angewandelt?** (Tieck)—**Es war dem** (now **hatte den**) **Jüngling nie eine Lust angewandelt, den Festen des Hofes beizuwohnen** (Novalis).—Incidentally, although **ankommen** can have this force of 'to come over' a person, the corresponding noun for an 'attack, fit, seizure' is never **Ankunft,** but either **Anfall** or **Anwandlung** (cf. **attack** 2).

anweisen: see **befehlen** 3 (*d*).

anwesend, Anwesenheit: see **presence** 1 and **wesen.**

any: This word presents considerable difficulty, as it represents quite a number of German expressions. Actually, it requires a good knowledge of German to determine instinctively which expression is the correct one in a given context. The chief expressions are: **1. irgend** (q.v. 2): e.g. **Hat irgend jemand** (or **irgendwer**) **Kleingeld bei sich?** ('Has any one got change on him?')—**Hat er irgend etwas davon gesagt?** ('Has he said anything about it?')—**Hast du Goethes Gedichte hier irgendwo herumliegen sehen?** ('Have you seen Goethe's poems lying anywhere about here?'); **2. jeder** (q.v. 2 *a* and *b*): e.g. **Ich kann Sie jeder Zeit** (or **zu jeder beliebigen Zeit**) **treffen** ('I can meet you at any time you like')—**Nach dem Bahnhof hätte dich jeder weisen können** ('Any one could have directed you to the railway-station')—cf. **jedenfalls** ('at any rate, in any case'); **3. etwas** (q.v. 1): e.g. **Ist noch etwas Obst übriggeblieben?** ('Is there any fruit left?')—**Wünschen Sie sonst noch etwas?** ('Is there anything else you want?'); **4. welch**—see **welch** (*indefinite*) 1 and 2: e.g. **Hat jemand irgendwelche Klagen vorzubringen?** ('Has anybody any complaints to lodge?')—**„Sie wollen einige Bücher? Was für welche?" „Irgendwelche!"** ('What sort?' 'Any sort!'); **5.** see also **deren** 1 (*b*) and **kein** (*ad fin*).

Anzahl: see **figure** 2.—As explained under **congruence** 1 (*a*) and (*b*), a collective sing. noun like **Anzahl** or **Menge**, when followed by an appos. plur. noun, now usually takes a plur. verb, as in **Eine Anzahl Kinder spielten auf der Straße**, whereas a sing. verb is preferable when the noun following **Anzahl** is a recognizable gen. or is governed by **von**, as in **Seinen Fahnen folgte eine große Anzahl Freiwilliger** (Sch.: cf. . . . **folgten eine große Anzahl Freiwillige**).

Anzug: see **clothes** 3.

anzünden: see **light** (verb) 2 (*b*).

appearance: **1.** (**a**) When this word suggests coming in sight, as in 'At his appearance there was loud applause', it is rendered by an appropriate verbal noun: **Bei seinem Erscheinen** (or **Auftreten,** esp. on a platform, the stage, etc.) **wurde laut geklatscht.** (**b**) At one time **Erscheinung** was used in the above sense, but this idea is now confined to a few expressions, notably **die neuesten Erscheinungen auf dem Büchermarkt** ('the latest publications') and **in die Erscheinung treten,** the latter used of what comes into perceptible existence, takes visual shape, materializes, so that it approaches a 'vision' (cf. **Gesicht** 3) or even an 'apparition': cf. **Meine Einbildungskraft erhöhte des Engels Bild fast bis zur Erscheinung** (G.) and **Daher lassen sich die Geistererscheinungen wohl erklären, . . . ingleichen die Visionen** (G.). Applied to a person, it points not merely to his outward appearance, but also to his bearing and conduct: e.g. **Er ist eine imposante, ja Achtung gebietende Erscheinung** ('He is an imposing, indeed commanding figure'): see below. **2.** A person's mere outward appearance is suggested by the adj.-subst. **Äußeres,** as in **Sein Äußeres erweckt wenig Vertrauen** or **Nach seinem Äußeren zu urteilen, ist er nicht gerade vertrauenerweckend** ('His appearance hardly inspires confidence'). This really implies a comparison or clash between appearance and reality, between what seems and what is: for this see **Anschein, Schein** 2, and **scheinbar** 2, and cf. **look** 1 (*a*).

apposition: **1.** (**a**) An appositive normally stands in the same case as the word it explains: e.g. **Mein Vetter, der Arzt, ist verreist—Meinem Vetter, dem Arzt, habe ich lange nicht geschrieben.** (**b**) The appositive of a whole sentence, or of the idea suggested by a word or phrase, stands in the *nom.*: e.g. **Sie hielt es für praktisch, ihm ein Studio in der Nähe zu suchen, ein Plan, der daran scheiterte, daß es kein leeres Zimmer in der Nähe gab** (K. Edschmid)—**Am See kann ich mich noch zum Angler ausbilden, die insipideste aller Liebhabereien** (Heyse). The same applies to a phrase inserted parenthetically or added as an afterthought: e.g. **In anderthalb Stunden waren wir im Hospital: ein Örtchen, das am Weg auf den Gotthard liegt** (G.)—**Um eins kam er aus der Vorlesung über Handelsrecht, eine Vorlesung, von der er wenig Nutzen gehabt hatte** (Strobl)—**Die Gesellschaft saß an der langen Tafel einer großen Stube des oberen Stockwerks, eigentlich mehr ein Saal** (Stehr)—**Mit seinem „Zauberberg" hat er uns das große Erzählungswerk unserer Zeit gegeben, ein Werk, mit dem er seine Jugend beendet** (A. Eloesser)—**Er spürte eine Sehnsucht nach dem Fluß, der da vorüberfloß, der Fluß, den er immer geliebt hatte** (Viebig); in this last example it would perhaps be more natural to observe the rule of apposition, as it certainly would be in a proposition like **Sie blickte in die Kajüte, ein enger, dreieckiger Raum** (E. Brüning)—cf., as an example of the strict application of the rule, **Keineswegs in die Hände der Großmutter, Maria Annas von Haxthausen, geborener Freiin von Wendt-Papenhausen, legte Annette ihre Gedichte, sondern in die der Mama, Maria Theresias von Droste-Hülshoff, geborener von Haxthausen** (H. Franck). At one time, esp. in Austria, such appositives were for no apparent reason often placed in the *dat.*, as in **Der Kellner sagte, es werde mir gewiß mit der Gesellschaft des Herrn Plessing gedient sein, dem Sohne des Superintendenten** (G.); but this is now rightly condemned and only occasionally used by modern authors, as in **Sie stiegen durch die Annaschlucht hinunter, einer noch vor kurzem verwildert gewesenen Felsenschlucht** (L. Frank). (**c**) The rule of apposition is for the most part *not* observed in the *gen.* of nouns following an 'identifying' **als,** esp. if they are not qualified by an art. or attrib. adj.: e.g. **Ein äußerlicher Grund war der Ausbreitung seines** (viz. Mörike's) **Ansehens als Dichter hinderlich, seine Eigenschaft nämlich als Schwabe** (E. v. Sallwürk); for other examples, see **als** = 'as' 1 (*c*). (**d**) Where an appositive is preceded by **wie,** there is some fluctuation. We can say 'I hate men like him' or 'I hate men such as he (is)', and so also in German: e.g., on the one hand, **Mit einem so armen Mann wie mir** (= **wie mit mir**) **haben Herrschaften aus Ihren Kreisen nichts zu schaffen** (Kästner)—**Der Minister erklärte, die Universitäten würden einem Mann wie ihm verschlossen bleiben** (B. E. Werner); and on the other hand, **Der König brauchte solche Männer wie er** (Raabe: = **wie er einer war**). The second of these examples is probably more usual: cf. **Du hast recht: das ist besser für ein altes Weib wie ich** (Storm: = **für ein Weib, das so alt ist, wie ich bin**)—**In einer Stimmung wie die ihrige wird der natürliche Zufall leicht zum Orakel** (Mörike); and a nom. would be more natural in propositions like **Ich habe niemals einen Menschen so schelten hören wie einen Leutnant** (cf. **wie ein Leutnant schilt**), **der zwischen einem Haufen von Maultieren arbeitet** (Frenssen)—**Eines Tages sah man den Grafen barhaupt über den Platz eilen, wankenden Schrittes wie einen Trunkenen** (Zifferer). **2.** For the appositional construction used for a part. gen. in 'a glass of wine', etc., see **genitive of material** 1–3.

April: see **Monatsnamen.**

arg: see **bad** 4.

Arme(r)sünder: see **Langeweile** 2 (*a*).

Armut: for the fem. gender, see **Mut** 3.

arrive: If a train is scheduled to arrive at a station at 8 o'clock, it may be visualized either as steaming into the station or as being already at a standstill at the specified time. The German lang. is in no doubt, it sees the train *at rest*, for the place of arrival invariably stands in the *dat.*: **Der Zug kommt um 8 Uhr im Bahnhof an.** And this applies to *all* words suggesting arrival: cf. **Die Ankunft des Zuges in der Hauptstadt erfolgt um 8 Uhr**—**Bei meiner Ankunft am Hause meines Freundes erfuhr ich, daß er verreist war**; for characteristic examples, see **ankommen, anlangen, einfinden, einstellen, eintreffen.**

Art: 1. In a phrase like **ein Stück Seife,** the dependent noun, orig. a gen., has become an appos., as explained under **genitive of material** 1. The same applies to a dependent noun after **Art:** e.g. **Unter meines Vaters Papieren befand sich eine Art Tagebuch** ('a sort of diary'). Even when the dependent noun is qualified by an attrib. adj., the commonest construction is appos., the adj. then having a strong ending: e.g. **Ich bin eine Art geborener Beichtvater** (Wassermann)—**Die Kunst ruht auf einer Art religiösem Sinn** (G.)—**Ihre Haare waren zu einer Art lebendigem Helm geflochten** (Kellermann). The appos. construction may, of course, be replaced by a recognizable gen., as in **Mein Vetter möchte gern eine Art unschuldigen Hexenmeisters spielen** (Droste-Hülshoff) and **Sie hatte früher eine Art kleinen Lustspiels geschrieben** (L. Schücking); but here the gen. is little used in ordinary lang., esp. in the case of sing. masc. and neut. nouns (just as one says **Er gab mir ein Stück trockenes Brot,** not **trockenen Brotes,** so also one says **Dies ist eine neue Art** or **Sorte deutscher Käse,** not **deutschen Käses**), so that instead of the gen. the prep. **von** is often used, even in the case of a sing. fem. noun, as in **Hier fand er eine Art von vorläufiger Heimat** (Bruno Frank). As stated above, where a gen. is used, it should be recognizable as such, and an example like **Das äußerte sich in einer Art munteren** (for **munterer** or **von munterer**) **Kameradschaftlichkeit** (Polenz) should not be imitated, although it must be admitted that this lax usage seems to be on the increase. Where **von** is followed by an unmodified adj.-subst., there is considerable fluctuation in the latter's inflexional ending, but here again an example like **Er ist ein armer Teufel, gleichsam so eine Art von Gelehrten** (Chamisso) should not be imitated; a strong ending here would be correct, of course, as in **In diesem Benehmen gab sich kund, daß ich eine Art von Besessenem war** (H. Hesse), but more common is the use, ungrammatical as it is, of the *nom.*, as in **Früh setzte sich in den Köpfen der seinen die Vorstellung fest, daß er ein Gelehrter werden müsse: welche Art von Gelehrter, das stand noch dahin** (Th. Mann: '... what sort of a scholar, that was left an open question'). **2.** The Oxford English Dictionary characterizes a proposition like '*These kind of men have* their uses' as 'common colloquially, though considered grammatically incorrect'. Grammatically incorrect or not, it is certainly the usual way to express such an idea (no one would say 'This kind of men has its uses'), and in German also a plur. verb with **Art** is very common where the dependent plur.

noun has no attrib. qualifying it: e.g. **Diese Art Frauen sind nicht aus gewöhnlichem Fleisch gemacht** (Waggerl). Here the plur. verb is sanctioned by common usage, the dependent noun, orig. a gen., having assumed the function of a nom. in appos. to **Art**, so that **diese Art** is almost like an attrib. adj. (cf. **Derartige Frauen sind . . .**); sim. **Er konnte nicht wissen, welche Art Gäste hier einkehrten** (id.), where **welche Art Gäste** is much like **was für Gäste.** But it is very doubtful whether this use of a plur. verb should be extended to cases where **Art** is followed by a clear gen. or **von**: it is obviously more correct grammatically to say **Diese Art junger Frauen** (or **von Frauen**) **ist aus anderem Fleisch gemacht.** For this, as for a plur. verb used with collect. nouns like **Anzahl, Dutzend, Masse, Menge,** etc., see esp. **congruence** 1 (*a*) and (*b*).

article (**definite**): **1.** The def. art. is the unaccented demonstrative pron., from which it differs in inflexion only in the gen. sing. and plur. and the dat. plur.: see **der** (demonstrative). Being unaccented, it tends to be slurred over in speech, but the literary language recognizes the contracted prep. forms **am, ans, auf, beim, fürs, im, zur,** etc., which are regularly used in set phrases, proverbial expressions and the like, in which the art. has entirely lost its demonstrative particularizing force, the reference being to something quite general: e.g. **jemand zum besten haben** ('to make fun of a person')—**im voraus danken** ('to return thanks in advance')—**jemandem etwas ans Herz legen** ('to impress a thing on somebody')—**mit der Tür ins Haus fallen** ('to blurt out the truth')—**sich** (dat.) **etwas hinters Ohr schreiben** ('to take a thing to heart'), etc. But such contracted forms are inadmissible whenever the art. takes on the slightest particularizing force: hence contrast **„Geht der Junge schon zur Schule?" „Jawohl, er geht zu der** (not **zur**) **Schule, zu der ich selbst früher ging."—Er nahm mich beim Arm** and **Er nahm mich bei dem Arm, den ich mir tags zuvor verrenkt hatte. 2.** Contrary to our idiom, the German def. art. is used: (**a**) For purely formal reasons, when it is necessary to indicate the case of the noun more clearly (esp. in the gen. where the noun has no specific gen. ending) or where its omission would render the proposition ambiguous: e.g. **Ich ziehe Mädchen den Knaben vor** ('I prefer girls to boys')—**Wir sollten den Weg der Tugend wandeln—Er ist ein Mann der Tat—Die Weisheit des Sokrates ist sprichwörtlich.** Strictly speaking, a masc. or neut. sing. with the strong gen. ending would not require the art., but it is nevertheless inserted: e.g. **Man ahnte schon das Herannahen des Winters—Man sollte immer der Stimme des Gewissens folgen.** In certain set phrases in which the noun denotes quality, rank, etc., the gen. construction is replaced by **von** (q.v. 2 *b*): e.g. **Er ist ein Mann von Fach** ('an expert')—**Eine Dame von Adel.** (**b**) The German def. art. is used also before a noun in the sing. which points to an individual as representative of his class, very common in proverbs: e.g. **Der Mensch denkt, Gott lenkt** ('Man proposes, God disposes')—**Den Menschen erkennt man am Gange, den Vogel am Gesange**; in the plur., the art. is usually omitted here, because the reference is not to one individual, but to an indef. number of such individuals: e.g. **Menschen sind keine Engel.** (**c**) Before a collective noun, if the reference is to the whole body as distinct from a part of it: hence always **das Parlament—Er wurde ins Parlament gewählt—Im Herbst stirbt die Natur** (the collective objects and phenomena of the material world); sim. **das Altertum** (all the remains of antiquity). (**d**) Often before names of materials or abstract qualities, when the material or quality as such is referred to, as in **Das Gold ist kostbarer als das Silber** or **Die Liebe wird zur Tugend, wenn sie die Treue krönt**; but the art. is generally dropped in proverbs: e.g. **Gold rostet nicht—Glas in Gold gefaßt bleibt Glas** ('Glass is glass, even when set in gold')—**Alter schützt vor Torheit nicht** (cf. 'There are no fools like old fools')—**Reichtum bringt Sorge.** (**e**) Before most names of definite diseases: e.g. **an der Schwindsucht sterben** ('to die of consumption')—**am Scharlach(fieber)** or **an den Masern erkranken** ('to have an attack of scarlet fever *or* measles')—**vom Schlage gerührt werden** ('to be seized with apoplexy'). (**f**) Before names of seasons (unless when used in the pred.), months (see below), days, meals and, as a rule, sciences: e.g. **Der Frühling naht** (but **Es wird Frühling**; see below)—**Der Februar ist der kürzeste**

Monat—Der Sonntag ist der erste Tag der Woche—Ich gehe vor dem Frühstück spazieren—Ich bin zum Abendessen eingeladen worden—Die Physi'k finde ich schwerer als die Mathemati'k (but **Mathematik studieren**). One always says **im Frühling** and **im Herbst**; for **im Sommer** (**Winter**) one can use **sommers** (**winters**) if the reference is not to a particular summer (winter): e.g. **Ich hoffe, im Sommer** (i.e. *this* summer) **zu verreisen,** but **Wenn sie winters nicht zusammen sein konnten, entschädigten sie sich sommers auf Lustreisen** (G.). In phrases like 'at the beginning (about the middle, towards the end) of July', the art. is commonly dropped: **am Anfang Juli(s)—gegen Ende Februars** (H. Hesse)—**zu Ende Oktobers** (Storm); but most frequently the prep. is also dropped, both nouns being left uninflected: e.g. **Anfang Juli gehen wir aufs Land, werden aber Mitte oder spätestens Ende Augu'st wieder zu Hause sein—Inzwischen war schon Ende März eingetroffen** (id.). **(g)** Before names of streets and squares of a town (except in addresses) and all masc. and fem. names of countries, districts, mountain-ranges, etc.: e.g. **Er wohnt in der Wilhelmstraße—Das Rathaus liegt am Georgsplatz**; esp. in many geographical names: **die Schweiz—der Harz—die Eifel** (the high land between the rivers Moselle, Rhine and Roer)—**die Pfalz** (Palatinate)—**der Breisgau** (the southern part of Baden: cf. **Gau**)—**der Wasgau** (or **der Wasgenwald** or **die Vogesen**, the Vosges Mts.)—**der Spessart** (for **Spechtshart**, 'the forest of the woodpecker': between Frankfurt a. M. and Würzburg). The only neut. here is **das** (no longer **der**) **Elsaß** (Alsace), which only drops the art. in the combination **Elsaß-Lothringen** (Alsace-Lorraine); hence **im Elsaß**, but **in Elsaß-Lothringen. (h)** Before names of persons and countries when modified by an adj. or part., a gen. phrase or a rel. clause: e.g. **der lange Thomas** ('Long Tom')—**das kleine Mariechen** ('little Mary')—**das lustige England** ('Merry England')—**das Frankreich des Mittelalters—Das England, von dem ich spreche, ist nicht das heutige.** When the art. is dropped here (and the adj. consequently has strong inflexion), the phrase is a nom. of address: **Langer Thomas, komm mal her! (i)** Esp. in familiar language, before the unmodified name of a person when the reference is to a definite unmistakable individual: e.g. **Die Liesel hat's gesagt** ('Lizzie said so')—**Mit dem Fritz ist nichts anzufangen** ('There 's no doing anything with Fred'). The *plur.* of the def. art. is placed before the name of a well-known person to suggest the idea of 'persons like . . .': e.g. **Gegen die Unnatürlichkeit des Stoizismus streiten die Lessing und Kleist** (O. Brahm: '. . . authors like Lessing and Kleist')—**Goethes Zeitgenossen und Gefährten: die Hackert, die Kniep, die Tischbein zeichneten treu vor dieser großen Natur** (Hofmannsthal). **(j)** Always before inflected **meist**, unless a possessive precedes: e.g. **die meisten Leute—das meiste Geld—in den meisten Fällen**; but **Er vergeudet seine meiste Zeit** ('. . . most of his time'). **(k)** In the distributive relation, where in English we use the indef. art.: **zweimal die Woche—dreimal des Tages—Wieviel kostet es das Pfund? (l)** To replace the English possessive where no ambiguity arises, esp. where the reference is to parts of the body, clothing, etc.: e.g. **Ich habe es im Halse** ('My throat is sore')—**Er steckte die Hand in die Tasche—Er setzte den Hut auf den Kopf—Der Hund wedelte mit dem Schwanz** (see **mit** 2). The dat. of the person is often added, necessarily to obviate ambiguity: e.g. **Hast du dir die Hände gewaschen?—Der Kopf tut mir weh—Ich habe mir den Fuß verstaucht** ('I have sprained my ankle')—**Den Hut in der Hand, betrat er das Zimmer** (see **accusative absolute** 1); cf. **Er nahm den Hut ab** ('He took off his hat') and **Er nahm mir den Hut ab** ('He took my hat from me'). For a striking example, cf. **Noch steht er lebendig vor mir: die Haare hingen ihm auf die gebräunten Wangen hernieder, listig guckten die blauen Augen darunter hervor; die zerrissenen Beinkleider hatte er bis über die Knie aufgeschlagen, und in der Hand hielt er eine Weidengerte** (Storm).

as: 1. For the difference between **als** and **wie** in a proposition like 'I advise you as a friend', see **als = 'as'** 1. For the difference between **da** and **weil** where 'as' has causal force, see **weil** 2 (*b*), and cf. **als = 'as'** 4. For 'as' used with temp. force, see **when** 2 (*a*) and (*b*). For **'as'** used in expressions like 'as you see', 'as follows', 'as usual', see **wie** 2 (*c*). For the correlative use of 'as' in expressions like 'as good as new' or 'as soon as possible', see **as . . . as** 1, **als** = 'as' 2, and cf. **so** 1 (*b*); for 'as . . . as' used to express a superl. idea, as in 'This is as good a novel as I have ever read', see **wie** 2 (*a*). **2.** To give renderings of all the idiomatic uses of 'as' would go beyond the scope of the present volume, but the following are a few of the commonest ones: 'as a rule' = **in der Regel**; 'as for me' or 'as to that' = **was mich** (or **das**) **an(be)langt** or **(an)betrifft** or **angeht** (see **anbelangen**, and cf. **meinetwegen**); 'as you please' = **wie es Ihnen gefällt** or **beliebt**; 'as much again' = **noch einmal** (or **nochmal**) **soviel**; 'according as' = **je nachdem** (see **je** 2 *b*); 'as it were' = **gleichsam** or **gewissermaßen**; 'As you were!' (military command) = **Befehl zurück!** or (in rifle practice) **Griff zurück!**

as . . . as: 1. (**a**) In a proposition such as 'The water was as clear as crystal', the first 'as' is really *dem.*, the second *rel.* ('The water had that degree of clearness which crystal has'). In German, the first 'as' is expressed by **so**, the second usually by **wie**: e.g. **Das Wasser war so klar wie Kristall—Die Sache ist so gut wie erledigt** ('The matter is as good as settled'); for another idiomatic way to express this idea, see **trotz** 1. Formerly **als** was often used instead of **wie** here, and to *Sanders* (1872) **als** still sounded **„nicht ungewöhnlich"**; but since then **wie** has undoubtedly gained much ground, so that an example like **Er begrüßte den Menschen so freundlich, als seine Stimme es ihm gestatten wollte** (Immermann) does sound a little unusual: in this connexion see esp. **als** = **'as'** 2 (*a*). (**b**) Where **so** modifies common advs. like **bald, oft, viel**, etc., the two words are now written as one when used as *subord. conjs.*, **wie** being generally dropped, as in **Sobald** or **Sowie** ('As soon as') **ich das hörte, benachrichtigte ich meinen Freund**; and this applies equally to cases where the two words are not written as one, as in **Sie half, so gut sie konnte** (W. v. Scholz: 'She helped to the best of her ability'): for other examples, see **so** 1 (*b*). **2.** When 'as . . . as' has *concess.* force, we usually drop the first 'as' and say 'Late as it was, I called on my friend', and sim. one can say in German **Spät, wie es war, sprach ich bei meinem Freunde vor**; but it is much neater and more idiomatic to retain **so** and drop **wie**, as in **So spät es (auch) war, sprach ich** (or **ich sprach**) **bei meinem Freunde vor**: see **so** 3, and word-order 1 (*d*).

ascend: see **climb**.

aside: see **abseits** 2.

astonish(ment): see **wonder** and **Wunder**.

Atlas: This word has two meanings: the gen. sing., whether in the sense of 'atlas' or of 'satin', is either **Atlas** or **Atlasses** (the proper name **Atlas** has only **des Atlas**); but in the plur. one differentiates between **Atlasse** ('different kinds of satin') and **Atlanten** ('atlases').

attack: The correct rendering of this word depends on the context. **1. Angriff** and **angreifen** are used esp. in the lit. sense: **Wir griffen den Feind an** or **machten einen Angriff auf den Feind—Wir rückten zum Angriff vor** ('We advanced to the attack'); cf. **eine Arbeit in Angriff nehmen** ('to attack a piece of work'). **2. Anfall** and **anfallen** are used esp. in a fig. sense: **Er tat es in einem Anfall von Eifersucht** ('in a fit of jealousy': see **anwandeln**)—**Du weißt nicht, daß deine Hoffnungen mein Herz wie Furien anfallen** (Sch.)—**Ihn fiel eine dumpfe Traurigkeit an** (Hofmannsthal)—**Es hat keinen Sinn, von Oscar Wilde so zu sprechen, als ob das Schicksal ihn angefallen hätte wie ein bissiger Köter ein ahnungsloses Bauernkind** (id.). **3.** The insep. **befallen** is used esp. of diseases, fainting fits, etc.: **Eine Ohnmacht befiel mich**; a dat. obj. here, as in **Es befiel ihm eine plötzliche Angst** (G. Keller), should not be used. **4.** A sudden or surprise attack is **ein Überfall**, with an accented prefix, but the corresponding verb has an insep. unaccented prefix: **Er wurde unterwegs nach Hause von zwei Räubern überfa'llen.** This idea can also be expressed by **über jemanden he'rfallen**—cf. **Der Knecht fiel über den Jungen her und trommelte ihm mit einer Blechschale auf den Kopf** (Fr. Schnack) and Goethe's stage direction **Sie fallen übereinander her** ('They come to blows')—and this is also used in contexts like 'He attacked the food that was set before him' (**Er fiel über die ihm vorgesetzten Speisen her**).

auch: 1. The fundamental idea underlying this adv. is *increase* (< Lat. *augere*: cf. our *aug*ment and *eke*), so that its proper meaning is 'also, too, in addition'. But we often use other expressions than 'also' to convey this idea: e.g. **„Ich habe meine Schularbeiten gemacht." „Ich au'ch"**

('So have I')—„**Ich weiß nicht, wie das auf Deutsch heißt.**" „**Ich au'ch nicht**" ('Neither do I')—**Ich ka'nn und wi'll es auch tun** ('I can, and what 's more I shall do it')—**Auch da's noch!** or **Da's fehlte auch noch!** ('That crowns all! That 's the last straw! What next?'). **2.** It is often used to confirm a previous statement: e.g. „**Sie sehen müde aus.**" „**Das bi'n ich auch**" ('So I am')—„**Dieser Satz ist aber gar nicht so schwer zu übersetzen.**" „**Das habe ich auch nicht behauptet: ich sagte nur, er wäre nicht so leicht, wie man auf den ersten Blick glauben möchte**" ('Well, I never said it was . . .'); and hence its use with much the same force as **sogar** ('even'): **Das versteht auch der dümmste Schüler—Ich gehe jeden Tag spazieren, auch bei schlechtem Wetter—Auch da's gefiel ihm nicht** (= **Nicht einmal da's gefiel ihm** 'Not even that pleased him'); and esp. in cond. clauses, as in **Ich würde ihn nicht besuchen, auch wenn ich** (or **wenn ich auch**) **seine Adresse wüßte**—„**Zu einem Spaziergang ist das Wetter nicht gerade einladend.**" „**We'nn auch: gehen wir!**" ('Even so *or* No matter: let 's go!')—**Wie er der Jungfrau Maria seine Bitte vortragen wollte, kam ihm kein schicklicher Spruch in den Sinn, ob** (= **wenn**) **er auch fest daran glaubte, es müsse ein Wunder geschehen** (Zifferer: '. . . even although he firmly believed that a miracle must happen'). **3.** With explanatory force, it gives the reason for a preceding statement or idea: e.g. „**Sie scheinen Aachen gut zu kennen.**" „**Na, ich habe auch lange dort gelebt**" ('Well, after all I lived there a long time')—„**Brahms-lieder singt die Dame mit wirklichem Gefühl.**" „**Dessen Lieder hat sie auch besonders studiert**" ('No wonder *or* So she should, she has made a special study of his songs'). **4.** It has generalizing force in propositions like **Ich nehme es mit jedem auf, wer er auch sei** ('I'll compete with any one, whoever he may be *or* no matter who'), and this idea is emphasized by the insertion of **immer** (q.v. 3) after **auch**, as in **Welche Tür auch immer es sein mochte, er rührte sie nur an, so tat sie sich auf** (A. Schaeffer: 'No matter which door it might be, he only needed to put his hand on it for it to be opened'). **5.** It may imply a certain deference to the wishes of the person addressed: if you call on a friend to see whether he will go out with you, and he seems rather reluctant, you might say either **Ich kann auch den Abend hier bei dir bleiben** ('I can spend the evening with you here, if you like') or **Ich kann auch allein gehen** ('I can easily go alone, if you prefer that'). In such propositions a certain doubt is expressed, and this is also seen in **Kinder, wollt ihr auch a'rtig sein, bis ich zurückkomme?** ('Now, children, you'll be good till I come back, won't you?')—**Du hast versprochen, früh zu Bett zu gehen: kann ich mich auch darauf verla'ssen?** ('I can really depend on that, can I?').

aufbewahren: see **behalten** 2 (*a*).

aufbringen: If a person is upstairs, or standing up on a ladder, and calls to somebody to 'bring up' something, this idea cannot be expressed by **aufbringen,** but only by **heraufbringen** (cf. **ab-** 3, and **her-, hin-** 3). In fact, **aufbringen** is only used with fig. force, e.g. with objs. like **Geld** ('to raise money'), **Mode** ('to introduce a fashion'), **Beweise** ('to furnish proofs'), **Mut** ('to muster up courage'), **Truppen** ('to levy troops'), etc., and with a pers. obj., **jemand aufbringen** ('to exasperate, enrage, infuriate a person'): cf. **Der Konsul war heftig aufgebracht** ('infuriated') **über diesen Streich** (Th. Mann). Although sometimes used in the sense of 'to rear' (young, a brood), it should not be used as an alternative expression for **erziehen** in the sense of 'to bring up' or 'to educate' children: it is not idiomatic German to say **Er fand Anstellung an der Schule, in der ich aufgebracht worden war** (Th. Mann in *Doktor Faustus*) or **Wir erwiesen uns als rechte Kinder des Winkels deutscher Altertümlichkeit, worin wir aufgebracht worden waren** (id.), which is the result of that author's long residence in America (cf. his use of **wenn man mich fragt** given under **fragen** 1).

auferlegen: This verb has the force of 'to impose something on a person' (dat.), and is used esp. with objs. like punishment, penance, duty, tax, etc. As with other sim. verbs (cf. **anerbieten, auferziehen,** etc.), so here also the first prefix, being accented, should normally be *sep.*, the second *insep. Heyne*'s contention that the past tense is „**gewöhnlich: er auferlegte ihm eine Strafe**" is certainly not true of the north, and although *Duden* gives „**ich erlege ihm etwas auf (seltener auch: ich auferlege ihm etwas)**", the fact remains that the vast majority of people still treat **auf-** as sep., and would rather say **Der Beichtiger erlegte ihm eine leichte Schuld auf** than **Der Beichtiger auferlegte ihm eine leichte Schuld** (Auerbach); in particular, separation is quite fixed in the infin. with **zu**, as in **Ich habe leider versäumt, ihm Schweigen aufzuerlegen** (Jul. Wolff). But it is even more common in the north to drop the second prefix altogether in those parts of the verb in which separation would take place, as in **Diese schweren Bemühungen legte ich mir auf** (G.) and **Mein Amt legt mir die Pflicht auf, einem jeden Gehör zu schenken** (Stifter); so also it is more usual to say **Man legt** (rather than **erlegt**) **uns Steuern, Strafen, Zwang auf** (cf. **auferstehen** and **auferwecken**).

auferstehen: This verb is now almost confined to the sense of 'to rise from the dead': cf. **die Auferstehung Christi** ('the Resurrection'). Its first prefix should, of course, be *sep.*, but actually only those parts are in general use in which no separation takes place: **Er wird auferstehen—ist auferstanden—wenn er auferstände.** *Heyne*'s assertion that the past tense is **„er erstand auf, und in neuerer Sprache: er auferstand"** is certainly not in accordance with modern usage, and examples like the following should not be imitated: **Es auferstehen die Toten** (Heine)—**Vielleicht war sie gestorben und auferstand in Liebe** (E. Zahn)—**Das nächtliche Chaos der jagenden Wolken auferstand in höllischem Schein** (C. Hauptmann). It is significant that in contexts where separation would normally take place even Luther drops the second prefix and uses **aufstehen:** e.g., on the one hand, **Am dritten Tage wird er wieder auferstehen** (Matt. 20. 19)—**Nachdem ich auferstehe, will ich hingehen nach Galiläa** (Mark 14. 28)—**Dazu ist Christus gestorben und auferstanden** (Rom. 14. 9); and on the other hand, **Die Verstorbenen stehen nicht auf** (Isa. 26. 14)—**Stehe auf von den Toten!** (Eph. 5. 14). Much less common here, and not to be recommended in prose, is the use of **erstehen;** this is common in Easter hymns, as in **Christ lag in Todesbanden . . . Der ist wieder erstanden** (Luther) and **Halt' im Gedächtnis Jesum Christ, der von dem Tod erstanden ist** (Gellert), but to address people with **Ihr Brüder des** (= **dessen**), **der starb und erstand** (Klopstock) sounds strange to a modern ear, although less so if a prep. phrase is inserted: **. . . der starb und aus dem Grabe** or **zu neuem Leben erstand.** In this connexion see **auferwecken.**

auferwecken: This double comp. of **wecken** has the specific force of 'to raise from the grave', being the factitive of **auferstehen** (q.v.). As with the latter, so so with **auferwecken** Luther drops the second prefix and uses **aufwecken** in those parts of the verb in which **auf-** would be separated: cf., on the one hand, **Euch zuvorderst hat Gott auferweckt seinen Knecht Jesum** (Acts 3. 26), and on the other hand, **Weckt die Toten auf!** (Matt. 10. 8). Another possibility would be to drop **auf-** and use **erwecken,** and while **erstehen,** as explained under **auferstehen,** is now hardly used at all in the sense of 'to rise from the dead', **erwecken** can still be used in that of 'to raise from the dead', if the context makes this specific meaning clear: e.g. **Zuerst hatte ich geglaubt, er wolle das Mädchen von den Toten erwecken** (Bergengruen)—**Es soll davon gesprochen worden sein, daß man dir die Kraft zutraue, Tote zu erwecken . . . Hat Christus den Seinen nicht geboten: Heilt die Kranken, weckt die Toten auf?** (id.).

auferziehen ('to rear, bring up'): Here, as in the case of **auferstehen** (q.v.), those parts are generally avoided where separation of the first prefix would take place; and even where no separation takes place, this double compound is mainly poet., as in **Er sandte mich nach Reims, wo die Gesellschaft Jesu** ('the Society of Jesus') **für Englands Kirche Priester auferzieht** (Sch.) and **Die Kirche, die mich auferzog** (id.). Modern prose usage prefers to drop one of the prefixes, and generally distinguishes between **aufziehen** ('to rear, breed', referring to physical growth and development) and **erziehen** (like **ausbilden:** 'to bring up, educate'): so one always says **Hunde aufziehen,** but **Schüler erziehen**—cf. **Der Säugling wird von der Amme aufgezogen, von den Eltern und Lehrern erzogen** (Sanders).

aufgehen: Like other verbs implying motion from one place to another, when compounded with a simple prefix such as **auf-** (see **aus-, eingehen,** etc.), so **aufgehen** has a large number of specific fig. uses, as distinct from **hinaufgehen,** which has only one meaning, **viz.** 'to go up' a stair, a hill, a ladder, etc. (see **ab-** 3 and **her-, hin-** 3). Thus, **aufgehen** is used with subjs. like **Sonne** ('rise'), **Saat** ('come *or* shoot up'), **Teig** ('rise *or* swell' in an oven), **Naht** ('give way, come apart'), **Knospe** ('open, burst'), **Rechenaufgabe** ('come out exactly' without leaving a remainder), etc. Noteworthy is its use with **in** (+ accus.) in the sense of 'to be converted into' something, and with **in** (+ dat.) in that of 'to lose its identity and be absorbed *or* merged in' something: cf. on the one hand, **Der Plan ging in Rauch auf** ('ended in smoke, came to nothing')—**Es schien, daß sein ganzer Wohlstand in Rauch aufgehen solle** (G. Keller: 'It seemed that his whole fortune was to be eaten up'); and on the other hand, **Die Askese blühte in den Mauern der Klöster und ging nicht bloß in äußeren Formen auf** (K. Lamprecht: 'Asceticism flourished within the walls of the monasteries and did not lose itself in mere outward formalities')—**Schillers Mutter ging in den Mühen und Sorgen des Haushaltes auf** (O. Harnack: 'Schiller's mother was entirely taken up with the worries and cares of house-keeping').

aufhängen: For the mutated stem-vowel, see **hängen** 2 (*a*). As this compd. is always *trans.*, *weak* forms are now the rule, but the strong past tense **hing auf** is permissible as an alternative for the usual **hängte auf** (see **hängen** 2 *b*), and the strong past part. **aufgehangen,** while not nearly as common in the north as **aufgehängt,** seems to be rather more often used than the strong past parts. of other sep. compds. are, although not as often as those of the insep. compds. **be-** and **verhängen** (qq.v.). The following are characteristic examples: **Er hängte** (or **hing**) **seinen Hut auf—Er schimpfte, wenn das so weiterginge, hinge er sich auf** (Voigt-Diederichs: cf. hängen 2 *d*)—**Das Mädchen hat die Wäsche zum Trocknen aufgehängt—Ihr zunächst erhob sich eine Wildhändlerbude** ('game-dealer's stall'), **deren sechs aufgehängte Hasen traurig zu ihr hinüberschauten** (Fontaine); for the strong past part. cf. **Von einem Engländer wird erzählt, er habe sich aufgehangen** (usually **aufgehängt**), **um nicht mehr täglich sich aus- und anzuziehen** (G.)—**Nachdem eine Kerze angezündet war, wurde das Kunstwerk aufgehangen** (Storm)—**Er entledigte sich seines Pelzes, der von den Mädchen aufgehangen wurde** (Polenz). On the whole **aufgehängt** is to be recommended.

aufheben: 1. As pointed out elsewhere (see esp. **ab-** 3 and **her-, hin-** 3), verbs implying motion towards, when compounded with a simple prefix like **auf,** differ from the same verbs compounded with **herauf-, hinauf-** in that the latter are nearly always used in the most lit. sense, while the former almost invariably have fig. force. Thus, in the case of **heben,** one must use one of the longer prefixes to convey the idea of lifting to a higher level, as when one hands up something to a person standing on a ladder, or a saw to some one who has climbed up into a tree to cut off branches: e.g. **Als er oben auf der Leiter stand, hob ich den Eimer Wasser zu ihm hinauf.** On the other hand, when one says **Ich hob den Eimer auf** ('I lifted up the pail'), although no doubt motion to a higher level is implied, the proposition really means 'I did not leave the pail standing on the floor'; sim. **Er hob den Handschuh auf,** which may also suggest 'He took up the gauntlet', i.e. accepted the challenge; and the same applies to picking some one up who has fallen down, where the real sense is to help him on to his feet again (cf. the two examples given at the very end of **her-, hin-** 3). So **hinaufheben** has only *one* meaning, whereas **aufheben** is used in a large number of specific fig. senses, as with objs. like **die Hand zum Schwur** ('to raise one's hand to take the oath'), **ein wichtiges Schriftstück** ('to keep *or* preserve an important document': see **behalten** 2), **eine Sitzung** ('to dissolve a meeting'), **die Tafel** ('to bring a meal to a conclusion': **Die Tafel wurde aufgehoben** = 'The company rose from dinner'), **eine Verschwörung** ('to quash a conspiracy'), **ein Gesetz** ('to repeal a law'), **eine Verlobung** ('to break off an engagement'), **einen Bruch** ('to reduce a fraction to its lowest terms'). Still another use is to suggest that in mathematics one number 'cancels' another, or that in accounting one item 'balances' another, and here **sich aufheben** has *reciprocal* force: **Diese zwei Zahlen** (or **Posten**) **heben sich auf.** This, in fact, is the *only* way to use **sich aufheben**; formerly it could have *reflexive* force, as in MHG *der valke huop sich ûf und flouc in anderiu lant,* and in one of Goethe's stage directions we still find **Abt hebt sich auf** ('The abbot rises from his seat'), but this is now definitely avoided, being replaced by **sich erheben,** and a recent example like **Es fing zu regnen an, Andreas hob sich auf** (Hofmannsthal) should *not* be imitated. **2.** The verbal noun **Aufheben** is now mainly used as the obj. of **machen,** the phrase having the force of 'to make a fuss, ado, stir, commotion', as in **Sie klagte, man hätte ihr die und jene Unbill angetan, aber Aufheben machte sie nicht davon** (E. Zahn: 'She complained that this and that wrong had been done her, but she didn't make a song about it'). But modern usage here prefers the gen. form **Aufhebens,** orig. a part. gen. after an indef. num. like **viel, wenig,** etc. (see **viel** 1 *a* and *b*), but now treated, like the gen. of **Federlesen** (q.v.) and **Wesen** (q.v. 1), as an independent neut. noun, the gen. ending being retained even when no indef. num. precedes it (cf. **übel** 2, **Werk** and **aufsehen** *ad fin.*). The expression **Aufhebens machen** is taken from fencing: cf. **In den alten Fechtstuben wurden vor Beginn des Fechtens die Waffen auf den Boden gelegt und aufgehoben, was mit gewissen rühmenden Worten geschah** (Heyne)—**Viel Aufhebens machte früher ein Kämpfer, der zu Beginn des Kampfes beim Aufheben seiner Waffen unnötigen Lärm verursachte** (Sütterlin). But the orig. sense of the expression is no longer felt, and examples like the following show that it has a quite general application: **In die Kirche geht er nicht: ich glaube, es ist ihm zuviel Aufhebens** (G. Bäumer) —**Ich begreife nicht, was darum soviel Aufhebens im Dorfe ist** (Storm)—**Hier hatte man wenig Aufhebens von der Geschichte gemacht** (Wassermann). Where the indef. pron. on which the gen. depends is omitted, the gen. ending should obviously be dropped, as it is in the example from E. Zahn given above, and in **Das Bewußtsein, in der alten Heimatstadt unbekannt zu sein, genoß er mit schlauer Freude und mit dem Hintergedanken, daß er ohne alles Aufheben wieder verschwinden könnte** (H. Hesse); but actually the gen. form is much more usual here: e.g. **Von solchen Kleinigkeiten macht man nicht groß Aufhebens** (Jul. Wolff)—**Diese Blume** (*scil.* **Löwenzahn,** 'dandelion') **kennt jedes Kind, jeder weiß ihren Namen, aber keiner macht Aufhebens von ihr** (H. Löns)—**Die Menschen haben ihren Gott für ihre Seele so nötig wie Wasser und Brot, von deren täglichem Gebrauch niemand Aufhebens macht** (H. Franck)—**„Ich ging im Walde so für mich hin" . . . Dies waren wohl die ersten Verse Goethes, die mein Gedächtnis aufnahm; warum von solchen Reimen Aufhebens gemacht wurde, verstand ich nicht recht** (Carossa)—**Er sagte sich, daß es jetzt an ihm sei, den verfahrenen Karren ohne Aufhebens aus dem Sumpfe zu heben** (Ric. Huch: 'He told himself that it was now up to him not to make a scene, but to lift the cart out of the bog into which it had skidded'). And this gen. form can even be qualified by an art. or pron. adj.: e.g. **Was machst du denn für ein Aufhebens?** (Böhlau)—**Dort stand die Jupiterstatue des Phidias, von der damals einiges Aufhebens gemacht wurde** (Ebner-Eschenbach).

aufhören: see **stop** 1 (*a*).

auflegen: cf. **auferlegen** *ad fin.*

aufmachen: see **open** 2.

aufnehmen: 1. This verb cannot be used in rendering propositions like 'She took him up his breakfast', an idea which requires the lengthened prefix **hinauf-** (see **her-, hin-** 2); but it is used of 'taking up' such things as a lady's train (**Schleppe**), a fallen stitch (**eine gefallene Masche**), the thread of a conversation (**den Faden eines Gesprächs**), work (**die Arbeit:** after a vacation or a strike), a gauntlet (cf. **den Fehdehandschuh aufnehmen,** but **eine Herausforderung annehmen**), etc. **2.** When used in the sense of 'to admit, receive', it takes the *accusative* in a prep. phrase when the *act* of admission is implied: e.g. **Heute nahm man ein neues Mitglied in die Gesellschaft auf**—**Der Rhein nimmt viele Nebenflüsse in sich** (accus.) **auf**—**Der Redakteur hat den Artikel in die Zeitschrift aufgenommen** ('The editor has accepted the article for insertion in his periodical'); but where 'to receive' a person implies not merely the act of admission but that of making him one of the family circle, one says **jemand bei sich** (or **in seinem Hause**), **aufnehmen;** sim. **Er nahm mich in seinem Palaste auf** (Bürger)—**War es nicht eine Gnade, daß sie mich in ihrem Hause aufnahm?** (Frank Thieß)—**Ich bin in einer Loge aufgenommen** (Lessing: 'in a masonic lodge).

aufnötigen: see **nötigen** 2.

aufrichten: see **aufsitzen.**

aufsagen: see **repeat.**

aufschrecken: see **schrecken** 1 and 2.

aufsehen: 1. If a person is told to look at a plane passing overhead, he will *look up*; and if he is sitting, say, on the top of a step-ladder in the house reading a book, and somebody opens the door and addresses him, he will again *look up* (from his book) but will actually be *looking down*. This illustrates the difference between **aufsehen** and **hinaufsehen:** on the one hand, **Als das Flugzeug vorbeiflog, sah er hinauf,** and on the other hand, **Als er angeredet wurde, sah er von seinem Buche auf.** In the great majority of cases a verb implying motion toward some place (and **sehen** implies that the eye, as it were, travels out into space), when compounded with a simple prefix like **auf-**, has a considerable number of specific, esp. fig. uses (cf. **ab-** 3 and **her-, hin-** 3). In this respect **aufsehen** is exceptional, because its only other use than that explained above is to convey the idea of 'looking up' to a person one admires or respects: **Zu diesem Manne sieht jedermann mit Bewunderung** or **Achtung auf. 2.** In view of the comparatively limited use of the verb, it is all the more strange that the verbal noun **Aufsehen** is such a common expression: e.g. **Diese Nachricht erregte großes Aufsehen** ('This news caused a great stir *or* sensation')—**Dies ist ein Aufsehen erregender Roman** ('This is a sensational novel'); cf. **Eine besondere Atmosphäre der kleinen Stadt schien mich einzuhüllen, ohne daß sie Aufsehens machte** (Binding), with a gen. form which is explained under **aufheben** 2.

aufsitzen: The verb **sitzen** (q.v. 1) normally implies a *state of rest*, and **aufsitzen** may do the same, as in **Ich habe** (SG **bin**) **diese Nacht spät aufgesessen** ('I sat up late last night'). But more commonly it implies *motion*, esp. in the sense of 'to mount a horse' (cf. **absitzen**) or 'to get up on to a vehicle' (cf. **einsitzen**): e.g. **Der Bräutigam hatte schöne Pferde, und sogleich mußte man aufsitzen** (G.)—sim. in the military command **Aufgesessen!** ('Mount! To horse!')—**Der Groom saß hinten auf und fort ging's** (Polenz: 'The groom climbed up behind, and away went the coach'). This compd. is also used coll. of passing from the lying to the *sitting* position as when we say 'Sit up! Here's your breakfast'), but here **sich aufsetzen** or **sich aufrichten** is better: e.g. **Ich war sogleich wach, setzte mich auf und wartete auf die Wiederholung des Rufs** (Stehr)—**Die Schläferin richtete sich im Grase auf** (Heyse); but **sich aufrichten** may also imply passing to the *standing* position, and indeed, this should be its proper function (**aufrecht** = 'upright, erect'): e.g. **Ihr Mann saß am Rand ihres Bettes... Langsam richtete er sich auf** (St. Zweig).

aufstehen: This is one of the compds. of **stehen** (q.v. 3) which always imply motion (here out of a sitting or lying position), and hence always take the aux. **sein,** as in **Ich bin heute sehr früh aufgestanden.** For its use in the sense of 'to rise from the dead', see **auferstehen.** It is also used with the force of 'to arise *or* appear' in propositions like **Es stund** (see **stehen** 1) **hinfort kein Prophet in Israel auf wie Mose** (Deut. 39. 10), but not with subjs. like wind, storm, etc., where **sich erheben** is the usual expression.

auftun: see **open** 2 and 3 (*a*).

aufwecken: cf. **auferwecken.**

aufwerfen: Just as **abwerfen** (q.v.) is not used of throwing something down, say, from the edge of a cliff into the sea, from the roof of a house into the garden, etc., so **aufwerfen** is not used of throwing a a ball high up into the air, a stone up at an attic window, etc.: in such contexts the prefix must be **herauf-** or **hinauf-**, according as the action is viewed from above or below. The chief uses of **aufwerfen** may be seen from the following examples: **Ein heftiger Windstoß warf die Gartentür auf** ('threw . . . open')—**Wirf das Schiebefenster auf, um frische Luft hereinzulassen!—Im Garten hat ein Maulwurf** ('mole') **Erdhügel aufgeworfen—Den Soldaten wurde befohlen, Erdwälle aufzuwerfen—Das Auto warf dicke Staubwolken auf—Sieh mal, wie große Wellen das Schiff aufwirft!—Sie warf Nase und Lippen auf** ('She stuck up her nose and pouted her lips')—**Wer hat diese Frage** or **dieses Thema aufgeworfen?** ('Who raised this question *or* broached this subject?').

aufziehen: see **auferziehen.**

augenfällig: see **scheinbar** 1.

augenscheinlich: see **obvious(ly).**

August: see **Monatsnamen.** Distinguish between **Augu'st,** the name of the 8th month, and **Au'gust,** the proper name Augustus.

ausbedingen: see **dingen** 2.

ausbleiben: see **fail** 5.

Ausblick: see **Sicht** 2 (*c*).

Ausbund: see **Bund.**

ausfallen: As pointed out under **her-**, **hin-** 2 and 3, the simple prefix **aus-** differs from the double prefixes **heraus-** and **hinaus-** in that the former almost always gives a verb of motion fig. force, which the latter hardly ever do: cf. **Das Kind fiel zum Fenster hinaus** (not **aus**) and **Seine Haare fallen aus** (not **hinaus**: 'His hair is getting thin'). Other fig. uses of this verb are seen in examples like **Die Schule fällt morgen aus** ('There will be no school to-morrow')—**Die Ernte fiel letztes Jahr schlecht aus** ('Last year's harvest was a poor one')—**Der Handel ist vorteilhaft ausgefallen** ('The deal has proved profitable'); trans. **Ich habe mir einen Zahn ausgefallen** ('I have fallen and knocked out a tooth').

ausfressen: see **fressen** 1.

ausgehen: Here, as in the case of other verbs implying motion, such as **ausfallen, -kommen, -laufen**, etc. (qq.v.), the prefix **aus-** gives the verb **gehen** fig. force. A proposition like **Er ging zur Tür hinaus** confines attention to the mere act of crossing the threshold; but **Die gnädige Frau ist ausgegangen** implies that the lady has gone out shopping, visiting, for a walk, or the like, so that the proposition really means 'The lady is not at home'. Other fig. uses of this verb are seen in examples like **Ein Erlaß ist ausgegangen** ('A decree has been issued')—**Das Geld ist mir ausgegangen** ('I have run out of money': cf. **fail** 2)—**Ich ging leer aus** ('I got nothing, came away empty-handed': cf. **nachsehen** 1)—**Das Wort geht auf einen Vokal aus** ('The word ends in a vowel')—**Man geht auf mein Verderben aus** ('They are out to ruin me').

ausgenommen: see **except** 1 (*a*) and 2 (*b*).

ausgeschlossen: see **except** 1 (*b*).

ausgleichen: see **gleich** 5.

aushallen: **1.** Verbs denoting a sound, when compounded with **aus-** and **ver-**, refer to the moment when the sound ceases, yet they differ somewhat. In the first place, those with **aus-** properly take the aux. **haben** in a compd. tense, while those with **ver-** nearly always take **sein.** In the second place, those with **aus-** really refer to the final sound, which may be—and generally is—a loud one, whereas those with **ver-** suggest the gradual dying away of the sound: as *Sanders* puts it, **Das Aushallende breitet sich aus, entfaltet sich schwellend, bis es so zu Ende gelangt, das Verhallende nimmt an Stärke ab, bis es allmählich verschwindet und unhörbar wird**; **etwas hat mächtig, brausend ausgehallt, ist leise verhallt.** So also **Der Donner hallt mächtig aus** (Schwab)—**Gottes Gnade hallt in vollem Jubel aus** (Voss). It is true that the difference is not always strictly observed, but an example like **In leisen, dumpfen Schlägen ist das Wetter ausgehallt** (Geibel) is unusual. **2.** The same really applies to other verbs of sound so compounded, notably **klingen** (cf. **sound** 2 *c* and **verschallen** 2): e.g. on the one hand, **Sein Lied hat ausgeklungen** (Freiligrath)—**Als die Glocken ausgeklungen hatten, griff er nach dem Krug** (Heyse)—**Die widerwärtigen Töne** (*scil.* **eines Leierkastens** 'of a hurdy-gurdy') **klangen pfeifend und heulend aus** (Immermann); and on the other hand, **Töne verklingen in den Wellen der Luft, bis endlich alles ruhig ist** (Fr. Schlegel)—**Als die Glocken allmählich verklungen waren, fing der Gottesdienst an** (R. Herzog). **3.** A somewhat analogous difference is seen in the compds. **abblühen** and **verblühen.** The former really suggests that the last flowers are falling (aux. **haben**), while the latter properly points to the state after the flowers have all fallen (aux. **sein**): e.g. **Die Heide hatte abgeblüht** (Storm)—**Der Baum hat abgeblüht** (Waggerl); fig. **Der kurze Sommer des neuen Günstlings war verblüht** (Sch.). Here again there are exceptions: cf. **Schon hat der Lenz verblüht** (Lenau).

ausklingen: see **aushallen** (esp. 2).

auskommen: The same applies to this verb as to **ausfallen** (q.v.). The lit. force of coming from the inside to the outside requires a double prefix, as in **Er kam zu mir heraus** or **Da man mich eingeschlossen hatte, konnte ich nicht hinauskommen** ('. . . I could not get out': cf. **kommen** 3); the simple prefix gives the verb **kommen** fig. force, as in **Ich komme mit meinem Gehalt nicht aus** ('I cannot manage *or* make ends meet with my salary')—**Sie kommen gut miteinander aus** ('They get on well together': cf. **agree** 2). Exceptional, in that the double prefix shows fig. force, are examples like **Bei dem Handel kam wenig heraus** ('The deal brought in little profit') and **Wann kommt Ihr neuer Roman heraus?** ('When is your new novel to be published?').

auslassen: see **miss** 3.

auslaufen: To express the lit. idea of 'to run out' (e.g. into the garden) a German uses a double prefix: **Er lief in den Garten hinaus—Er kam zu mir herausgelaufen**; on the other hand, the simple prefix **aus-** gives the verb fig. force (cf. **ausgehen**, etc.): e.g. **Das Schiff lief aus** ('The vessel put to sea')—**Der Topf ist ausgelaufen** ('The pot has leaked')—**Der Kirchturm läuft spitz** (or **in eine Spitze**) **aus** ('The church-steeple tapers to a point')—**Das Gespräch lief in (einen) Streit aus** ('The conversation ended in a dispute')—**Das Abenteuer lief unglücklich aus** ('The adventure ended disastrously'). Exceptional here is an example like **Es läuft auf eins** (or **auf dasselbe**) **hinaus**, because the double prefix gives the verb fig. force ('It comes *or* amounts to the same thing').

auslernen: see **lernen** 3.

auslöhnen: see **lohnen** 2.

auslöschen: see **löschen** 2.

ausmachen: This verb was at one time used in a number of senses which are now obs. or confined to dialects. Thus, in the proposition **Er begab sich weg, um zu sehen, ob er nicht ein bequemes Quartier für das Ehepaar ausmachen könne** (G.), it probably means 'to discover, hunt around for', in which case one would now prefer to use **ausfindig machen**; but it may possibly mean 'to arrange, settle', in which sense it is still used: cf. **Wir haben die Sache in Güte ausgemacht** ('We have settled the matter amicably')—**Schert Euch 'naus, wenn Ihr was auszumachen habt!** (G.: 'Get out if you have a difference to settle!'). Other common uses are seen in **Das macht eine bedeutende Summe aus** ('That amounts to *or* works out at a considerable sum'), fig. **Das macht mir nichts aus** ('That is immaterial to me, does not matter as far as I am concerned'); more coll., **Nüsse, Erbsen ausmachen** (= **aushülsen**, 'to shell')—**ein Licht ausmachen** (= **auslöschen**, 'to extinguish')—in the past part. used as an attrib. adj., lit. **Das ist eine ausgemachte Sache**, or fig. **Er ist ein ausgemachter Betrüger** or **Schurke** ('He is a downright swindler, an arrant scoundrel'). What seems a rather strange use of the verb is seen in the following two examples from one and the same modern author, Fr. Griese, incidentally the only two which the present writer has come across: **Eine Gestalt kam heran und hinter ihr lief eine andere, aber man konnte nicht ausmachen, was da werden sollte—Sein Gesicht war von einem breitrandigen Hut bedeckt, und es war nicht auszumachen, wohin seine Augen blickten.** Here the verb is evidently used to express our 'one could not *make out*', but this is not an accepted use: one certainly does not use it in rendering propositions like 'At this distance I cannot make out the ship's name' (**Bei dieser Entfernung kann ich den Namen des Schiffes nicht entziffern**), much less 'I cannot make him out' (**Ich kann aus ihm nicht klug werden**).

ausrichten: see **richten** 2 (*b*).

ausschauen: see **look** 1 (*a*).

ausschlafen: While **ausgeschlafen haben** properly covers the whole time spent in sleep and so implies an *action* ('to have had a good night's sleep'), **ausgeschlafen sein** suggests the resultant *state* ('to have had one's fill of sleep and be wide-awake'), but in practice this distinction is not insisted upon: cf. **Geh bald zu Bett, damit du morgen ausgeschlafen bist** (Fr. Schnack). The aux. **haben** is imperative, of course, when the verb is used *trans.* or *reflex.*: e.g. **Er hat seinen Rausch ausgeschlafen** ('He has slept off his intoxication, has slept himself sober')—**Andern Morgens war ich gefaßter** ('more composed'), **ich hatte meinen Ärger ausgeschlafen—Lege dich hin und schlafe dich aus!**

ausschöpfen: see **schöpfen**.

aussehen: see **look** 1 (*a*).

außen: see **inside**.

außer: This prep. (for its use as a conj., see **except** 2) can actually take three cases: **1.** *genitive*: This is quite fixed in **außer Landes** ('abroad'), used with verbs of motion as well as of rest: e.g. **Am Morgen traf die Nachricht ein, der Herzog sei, statt außer Landes verreist zu sein, in dieser Nacht gestorben** (Hauff)—**Unser Bier ist weithin berühmt und wird selbst außer Landes verfahren** (E. Wichert: '... is even exported'). Isolated instances of other nouns in the gen. occur, but these are not so firmly established: **Er wurde für zwei Jahre außer Amts gesetzt** (G. Keller: cf. **seines Amts enthoben**)—**Schon lange außer Amtes** ('retired'), **ging er noch aufrecht einher** (H. Hesse)—**Durch einen Zufall war der Wirt außer Hauses** (E. Toller: = **außer dem Hause** or **nicht zu Hause**—see 2 *a*); cf. **Über alles, was gegen den Herzog zusammentreffen mußte, war Herr von Eichholtz fast außer Leibes** (Fr. Griese: usually

außer sich, 'beside himself': see 2 *a*). **2.** *dative*: This is by far the most common case and is used in three ways: (**a**) It may suggest a position *outside* or *beyond* definite limits. But this use should not be unduly extended: instead of **außer Rom** (G.) and **außer dem Dorfe** (G.), one now says **außerhalb Roms** and **draußen vor dem Dorfe**; cf. also **Sie gehen in dem Raume außer** (for **vor**) **dem Zelte über die Bühne** (Grillparzer: in a stage direction)—**Heinrich war schon außer** (better **draußen vor**) **den Toren der Stadt** (E. Wichert)—**Er spann sich immer tiefer in die Wolken, die ihn von der Welt außer ihm** (better **von der Außenwelt**) **trennten** (O. Ludwig); cf. **Lene war außer ihren Schulstunden** (= **in ihren Freistunden**) **meist unter der Aufsicht der Mutter beschäftigt** (Storm). On the other hand, **außer** + dat. is applicable in less localized contexts, esp. where the noun has fig. force: e.g. **Er sagte, Fratzen lägen außer dem Bereiche der Kunst** (Tieck: '. . . beyond the scope *or* province of art')—**Zwei Knechte schleppten ihn aus dem brennenden Hause in den Garten und legten ihn außer dem Bereich des Qualmes nieder** (I. Kurz: '. . . out of reach of the dense smoke')—**Das lag außer seinem Gedankenkreise** (Droste-Hülshoff: '. . . beyond his mental range'). Coll. usage sanctions **außer dem Hause essen** (or **auswärts essen**, 'to eat out') and **noch außer dem Bette sein** ('not to be in bed yet'), as in **Die Russen, die nachts eintrafen, fanden ihn noch außer dem Bette** (Fr. Griese) and **Es fehlte nicht an Unterhaltung in und außer dem Hause** (G.); and in such expressions the art. is now even omitted: e.g. **Es kam nicht vor, daß Ruth einen Abend außer Haus zubrachte** (Bruno Frank)—**Er wird viel außer Haus sein** (Waggerl)—**Er sagte, seine Tochter wohne seit einiger Zeit außer Hause** (Hofmannsthal)—**Auch wenn er außer Bett war, verbrachte er halbe Tage im verdunkelten Zimmer** (Th. Mann)— **Es war die zweite Nacht, die er außer Bett verbrachte** (A. Reiner). In these last examples the art. has been dropped under the influence of a number of established phrases like **außer Atem, Gefahr, Frage** ('out of the question'), **Hörweite** ('out of earshot'), **Schußweite** ('out of gunfire range'), **Zweifel** ('beyond doubt'), and esp. **außer Dienst**, often abbreviated **a. D.** ('retired', esp. of an officer 'on half-pay'). Here belongs also **außerstande** ('not in a position, unable': cf. 3). (**b**) It may imply *excess* ('besides, in addition to'): e.g. **Er bekam außer dem versprochenen Lohn auch etwas zu essen**—**Außer mir waren noch zwei Freunde eingeladen**; cf. the adv. **außerdem** ('besides, moreover'). (**c**) It may imply *exclusion*: see **except** 2. **3.** *accusative*: This is deprecated by the grammarians, but perhaps too categorically. True, one cannot say **Ich ging außer den Garten** (for **zum Garten hinaus**), nor is it good German to say **Ich geriet außer mich vor Wut** ('I got into a furious rage') or **Ich wollte außer mich kommen** (Waiblinger: 'I nearly went out of my senses'); cf., as examples of the correct usage, **Das brachte mich außer mir** (Spielhagen)—**Ich kam ganz außer mir** (A. Schaeffer). But the accus. has established itself in a number of expressions, esp. in combination with the verb **setzen**: a proposition like **Du bist nun außer unsere Gesellschaft gesetzt** (G. Keller) is looked askance at in the north, but one regularly says **Dieser Brief setzte die Geschichte außer allen Zweifel** (G.: '. . . put the whole matter beyond all doubt') and **Das setzt mich außerstand** (i.e. **außer den Stand**), **dir zu helfen** ('That renders me powerless to help you', lit. That puts me *into* the position of being unable to help you). Here belong some expressions in which, owing to the omission of the art., the case is unrecognizable, but may almost be assumed to be the accus.: **eine Maschine außer Betrieb setzen** ('to stop a machine, put it out of action')—**eine Münze außer Kurs setzen** ('to withdraw a coin from circulation'); cf. **ein Schiff außer Dienst stellen** ('to put a vessel out of commission').

äußer: This, like its ant. **inner** (which latter, incidentally, should not be used as a prep.: see **innerhalb** 2 *c*), is an *adj*. **1.** Where we have the adjs. 'outer, outside, exterior, external' and their ants., the Germans have only **äußer** and **äußerlich**—**inner** and **innerlich**. The longer forms are properly used of something on or below the surface (cf. 'superficial' and 'subcutaneous'), as in expressions like **eine äußerliche Verletzung** ('a superficial wound'), **eine Salbe zum äußerlichen Gebrauch** ('an ointment for external use'); then also **äußerliche Ruhe** ('outward calm', which may be a cloak to conceal **innerliche Unruhe**) and **äußerlich**

unbeschädigt (used of merchandise with the wrapping undamaged). Otherwise the shorter forms are used, as in the following examples in which the longer forms could not be used: **Das Schloß hat zwei Höfe: der äußere ist geräumig, der innere klein —Im inneren Teil der alten Stadt sind lauter enge Gassen**; fig., **So etwas sagt man nur im inneren Familienkreis** ('in the intimate family circle')—**Was ist der innere Wert** ('the intrinsic value') **dieses silbernen Bechers?—Wir müssen wenigstens den äußeren Schein wahren** ('keep up outward appearances')—**Er hat eine Stellung im Ministerium der inneren Angelegenheiten** ('in the Home Office'; in the U.S.A. 'the Department of the Interior')—**Ich sehe es mit dem inneren Auge** ('with the mind's eye'): cf., as very unusual, **Sie beugte sich in horchender Stellung nieder, als müßte nun ihr äußerliches Ohr vernehmen, was sie dem innerlichen nicht zu beantworten getraute** (Jak. Frey). **2.** Esp. common is the use of these words as *neut. adj.-substs.*: e.g. **Das Innere des Hauses mutet freundlicher an als das Äußere—Der Feind drang in das Innere des Landes—Der Trambahnwagen hielt und ich begab mich von der vorderen Plattform, wo ich einstieg, ins Innere** (Th. Mann)—**Frauen geben mehr auf ihr Äußeres als Männer** (see **appearance** 2)—**Man sollte nicht nach dem Äußeren eines Menschen urteilen—Sie hat ein gefälliges Äußere** (see **adjective-substantives** 2). **3.** Also very common are the superl. forms **äußerst** and—to a lesser extent—**innerst**, the former as adj., adj.-subst. and adv., the latter esp. as adj.-subst., but *not* as adv.: e.g. **Der 1. Mai ist der äußerste Zahlungstermin** ('the latest day for payment')—**Im äußersten Fall** or **Wenn es zum Äußersten kommt, verlieren wir wenig** ('At worst we shall not lose much')—**Das ist von äußerster Wichtigkeit** *or* **Das ist äußerst wichtig** ('That is of the utmost importance')—**Ich bin aufs Äußerste gefaßt** ('I am prepared for the worst': cf. the second last example given under **gewärtig** 2 *a*); **Das ist meine innerste Überzeugung** ('That is my profound *or* my most deep-rooted conviction')—**Er hat mir sein Innerstes offenbart** ('He has revealed his inmost heart to me')—**Diese unvermutete Nachricht hat mich bis ins Innerste empört** 'This unexpected news has shocked me to the core').

außerhalb: 1. Like its antithesis **innerhalb,** this prep. is used either of space or of time, its normal case being the *gen.*: e.g. **Viele Deutsche leben außerhalb (der Grenzen) Deutschlands—Außerhalb der Ferien habe ich wenig Zeit, Sport zu treiben**; sim. **außerhalb der Schulstunden, eines Zeitraums,** etc., and fig. **des Gesetzes** (Scots 'outwith the law'). Whereas a *dat.* is fairly common after **innerhalb** (q.v. 2 *a*), and indeed sometimes necessary, it is rare after **außerhalb**: cf. **Der Brunnen lag außerhalb dem Hofe** (Freytag). Where **außerhalb** is used apparently with adv. force, a gen. is really understood or implied: e.g. **Die Familie ist von außerhalb** (*scil.* **des Landes,** 'from abroad') **eingewandert—Die Frauen kamen von außerhalb in die Stadt, um ihre Ehemänner aufzusuchen** (B. E. Werner); sim. in commercial lang., **Wir liefern nach außerhalb** ('We deliver goods to customers living beyond the city boundaries'). **2.** Either the *gen.* or the *dat.* is used with **oberhalb** and **unterhalb,** both used with local force, indicating a point situated at a higher (lower) altitude or farther up (down) a river, valley, etc.: e.g. **Auf einem Hügel oberhalb des Dorfes ragt der Kirchturm empor—Jenes Gestein fanden wir ober- und unterhalb des Neubrunnens** (G.)—**Wir pflegten nach dem „Berg" zu wandeln, einer kleinen Anhöhe in der Ecke des Gartens oberhalb dem ausgetrockneten Bette eines Fischteiches** (Storm)—**Der Garten war eine ziemliche Strecke unterhalb dem Dorf** (Jung-Stilling). A place-name in such contexts is often left uninflected in ordinary lang., esp. in guide-books, etc.: **Oberhalb Forbach wird die Straße einsamer—Unterhalb Boppard mündet das Mühltal in den Rhein**; but **oberhalb des Königsteins, unterhalb des Loreleifelsens,** etc.

äußerlich: see äußer 1.

äußern: Although this is a cognate of our verb *utter*, the two expressions are not used in the same way. Where we speak of a person 'never uttering a word', 'being unable to utter a sound' 'or 'uttering a cry', the Germans use other expressions: **Er sprach kein Wort—Sie konnte keinen Laut hervorbringen** (or **von sich geben**) —**Sie stieß einen Schrei aus.** The verb **äußern** is used esp. with the force of 'to show, manifest' (a feeling, emotion, etc.) or 'to give expression to' (a thought, opinion, wish, etc.): e.g. **Ihr gegenüber äußerte er seine Freude unverhohlen** (Fr. Huch)—**Die Damen äußerten ihre Besorgnis wegen eines Gewitters, das sich zusammenzuziehen schien** (G.)—**Sie äußerte Furcht, ob sie ihn gestern etwa gekränkt habe** (Waiblinger)—**Sie äußerte nicht den mindesten Verdruß über die Untreue ihres Liebhabers** (E. T. A. Hoffmann)—**Er ließ sich, ohne das mindeste Widerstreben zu äußern, nach der nächsten Bank geleiten** (Spindler)—**Ich äußerte den Wunsch, diesen Rechtsgelehrten kennenzulernen** (G.)—**Das ist ein Lieblingswunsch meiner Mutter, den sie schon oft geäußert hat** (Jul. Wolff). So also with a *reflexive* pron. ('to manifest itself'): **Es ist merkwürdig, in wievielen Weisen der menschliche Geist sich äußern kann** (G. Keller)—**Die Krankheit äußerte sich durch Schüttelfrost** ('The disease showed itself in shivers'); but one of the commonest uses of **sich äußern** is with a personal subj., meaning 'to express' (one's views, intentions, etc.), often with the addition of **da'hin** to the princ. clause preceding **daß** ('to the effect that . . .'): e.g. **Ich äußerte mich dahin, daß das Urteil ungerecht wäre**—**Der Hauptmann hatte sich dem Diener gegenüber dahin geäußert, daß er die Kinder abholen würde** (Wildenbruch: 'The captain had expressed his intention to the servant, to the effect that he would call for the children'). It should be noted that the use of the simple verb **äußern** as an alternative of the ordinary **sagen** in a clause introduced parenthetically into spoken words—as in **„Ich verstehe Sie nicht", äußerte er** (Spindler)—is strange to a northern ear.

äußerst: see **äußer** 3.

außerstande: see **außer** 2 (*a*) and 3.

Aussicht: see **Sicht** 2 (*a*).

austauschen: see **change** 2 (*b*).

auswärts: Like **rückwärts** (see **-wärts** 1 and 2), this may convey rest as well as motion outwards: one says not only **Beim Gehen setzt er die Füße auswärts**, but also **Wir wollen heute abend auswärts essen** ('dine out')—**Er wohnt jetzt auswärts** ('out of town')—**Die Familie ist nach auswärts gezogen** (either 'out of town' or 'abroad')—**Diese Firma bezieht allerlei von auswärts** ('from abroad'). Like **rückwärts** also, it has formed an adj., viz. **auswärtig**, esp. common in **das Auswärtige Amt** ('the Foreign Office') and **der Minister des Auswärtigen** ('the Foreign Secretary'); so also **auswärtige Beziehungen haben** ('to have business connexions in other countries'), **auswärtiger Handel** ('foreign trade'), etc. Analogous is **anderwärts**, with the same force as **anderswo** ('somewhere else'); cf. **Die Erinnerung des Verlustes meiner Hoffnungen würde mich wahnsinnig machen, wenn ich sie nicht durch anderwärtige Tätigkeit zu ersticken suchte** (Sch.).

auswechseln: see **change** 2 (*a*).

auxiliary verbs: see **verbs (auxiliary)** and **modal auxiliary verbs.**

B

backen: 1. There are really two verbs **backen**, the one weak (**backte, gebackt**), the other strong (**bük, gebacken**). The *weak* verb is properly *intrans.*, meaning 'to adhere *or* stick together' (like intrans. **zusammenkleben**), while the strong one is its factitive, meaning 'to cause to stick together'. Thus, the basic idea in **Brot backen** is to make the ingredients of the loaf hold together by subjecting it to heat. The intrans. sense of the verb is seen esp. in a proposition like **Leider backt** (not **bäckt**) **der Schnee heute nicht** ('. . . the snow won't *cake* today'); and sim. **Der Schnee lag auf den Zweigen, im Astwerk hängen geblieben, an schwarze Stämme gebackt** (W. Borchert: '. . . plastered against black tree-trunks'). Much more common, of course, is the strong trans. verb, used of 'baking' (bread, fish), 'drying' (fruit: cf. **Backpflaumen,** 'prunes'), 'firing' (tiles), etc.: e.g. **Meine Mutter bäckt eben eine Torte**—**Hat sie diesen Kuchen gebacken?**—fig. **Die Frauen waren braun gebacken von der Sonne** (Kellermann). In the past tense, **bük** (subj. **büke**) is still the standard form, but **backte** is often used coll. here, esp. of drying fruit: in Austria it is even officially recognized. **2.** The past part. commonly drops **ge-** in a few compds. when used as adjs. Firmly established is **hausbacken,** used either lit. or fig.: e.g. **hausbackene Semmeln** ('home-baked rolls')—**hausbackene Verständigkeit** (Heine: 'dry, unimaginative common sense')—**hausbackene Menschen** (Chamisso: 'dull, prosaic people'—cf. L. Stephen's 'Crabbe was one of those simple *homespun* characters'). So also **alt-** and **neubacken,** although here the forms with **ge-** are not uncommon, esp. when used fig.: e.g. **Sie warf den Schwänen die altbackenen Brocken zu** (Th. Mann: 'little bits of stale bread')—**neubackene Brezel** (Auerbach) —**altbackene Lektüre** (Gutzkow: 'fusty, old-fashioned reading matter')—**ein neugebackener Arzt** (Forster: 'a fledgeling medico')—**dies neugebackene Gedicht** (Platen); sim. **frischgebackene Leute der Neuzeit** (Heine).

bad: 1. The adj. **schlecht** is a striking example of a word which has seen better days (cf. **gemein**). Its orig. force is seen in Walther's *mîn sleht hâr ist mir worden rû* ('My once *smooth* hair has become straggly') and Luther's **Was höckericht ist, soll schlecht** (*'plain'*) **werden** (Isa. 40. 4). Out of this last sense, implying an absence of difficulty or trouble, there soon developed the idea of 'simple', in which sense it was regularly used in early NHG: e.g. **Ich hatte Ursache, mich zu verwundern, daß ein so wackerer Herr einen schlechten** ('simple, plain') **Dorfpfarrer um Herberge anredete** (Grimmelshausen)—**Wenn ich anhebe, zu erzählen, so geschieht es schlecht, ohne jede Kunst** (F. Dahn, in a story of the 11th century: 'When I start my story, I shall tell it in a simple, artless style'). In view of the deterioration in meaning which later set in, and to obviate possible misconception, this old use of the adj. is now obs.; but its orig. force is still seen in **schlechterdings** (see **allerdings**), **schlechthin** (q.v.) or **schlechtweg,** meaning either 'plainly, simply, without ceremony' or (= **überhaupt**) 'in general', as in **Rilkes Lyrik ist eine Gipfelleistung der modernen deutschen Dichtung und vielleicht künstlerischer Kultur schlechthin** (R. H. Heygrodt), and esp. in the common expression **schlecht und recht,** as in **Sie ist so schlecht und recht, so unverkünstelt** (Lessing: '. . . so simple and natural') and **Man lebt schlecht und recht, wie ein Schauspieler eine Rolle spielt** (Ponten). But the idea of 'simple, unadorned' soon led to that of 'ordinary, commonplace', and then to that of 'mediocre, below par, bad', as in **schlechte Arbeit** ('poor, inferior work'); cf., with a neat play on the two meanings, **Er hatte seine Sache nicht schlecht und recht sondern rundweg schlecht gemacht** (H. Franck: 'He had done the job, not in a right and proper way, but downright badly'). The final step in this downward trend is seen in a phrase like **ein schlechter Kerl** ('a morally bad, depraved fellow'); cf. 3. **2.** The form **schlicht** is really the LG equivalent of **schlecht,** and it is interesting to observe that the more the HG **schlecht** deteriorated, the more did **schlicht** come to be accepted in the literary lang. with the force which **schlecht** had lost. Now it is only used, like **einfach,** in the sense of 'simple, plain, not ornate, homely', as in **ein schlichtes Kleid**—**der schlichte Mann aus dem Volk** ('the plain, ordinary man') —**schlichte Rede. 3.** Much like **schlecht** as used in its later stages is the adj. **schlimm,** but its orig. meaning was quite different: MHG *slimp* is 'crooked, off the straight' (cf. the Dutch *slimbeenig,* 'bandy-legged'), so suggesting the idea of instability, possible collapse, with attendant disaster, danger to life and limb, privation, etc. Where there is doubt whether the word 'bad' should be rendered by **schlecht** or by **schlimm,** the deciding factor should be whether it has merely *relative* force, indicating inferiority, or implies imminent danger, destruction. Thus, **Wir leben jetzt in schlechten Zeiten** means that, in comparison with 'the good old days', the times are bad, hard (owing to heavy taxation, high prices, etc.), whereas **Wir leben in schlimmen Zeiten** regards only the present conditions and implies a threat of impending disaster, a possible danger of war, revolution, tyranny, oppression, uncertainty of life and liberty and the like. So also one says, on the one hand, **Er spricht ein schlechtes** (not **schlimmes**) **Französisch** (cf. **radebrechen**)—**Ich habe ein schlechtes Gedächtnis**—**Das ist ein schlechter Trost** ('That 's a poor consolation'); and on the other hand, **Die Autofahrt nahm einen schlimmen Ausgang** ('The run ended disastrously')—**Angesichts der neusten Nachrichten aus**

dem Osten können wir auf das Schlimmste gefaßt sein ('. . . we can be prepared for the worst'); cf. the phrase **wenn das Schlimmste zum Schlimmen kommt** (Lessing), lit. 'if the worst is added to the bad', which seems more logical than our 'if the worst comes to the worst' (cf. **Fall** 1 *c*). **4.** Lastly, the adj. **arg** was orig. 'morally bad, wicked, vicious', then, applied to things, 'gross, heinous': thus, **ein arger Schuft** is 'an arrant scoundrel', **ein arger Verstoß** 'a heinous offence', **ein arger** (or **grober**) **Fehler** 'a gross mistake, howler'. This word is used more esp. in the south, where it has degenerated in much the same way as our 'awful(ly)': cf., on the one hand, **Er ist arg bekümmert und gekränkt** (Waggerl: 'He is deeply grieved and offended'), and on the other hand, a coll. expression like **Das ist arg schön** ('That 's awfully pretty').

bald: The MHG adj. *balt* (meaning 'brave', then 'quick to act, daring': cf. **quick** 1 *a*) is now obs., but the adv. **bald** (see **adverbs formed from adjectives** 1) is in every-day use with the force of 'soon', as are the adv. **alsbald** (= **sofort** or **sogleich**, 'at once') and the subord. conj. **sobald** ('as soon as': see **so** 1 *b*): cf. **möglichst bald** (= **sobald wie möglich**, 'as soon as possible': better than **baldmöglichst**). The adv. **bald** led to the formation of the NHG adj. **baldig**, used esp. in expressions like **Auf baldiges Wiedersehen!** ('I hope to see you again soon') and **Um baldige Antwort wird gebeten** ('An early reply will oblige'). The compar. adv. **bälder** ('sooner') is now rare and should be replaced by **eher** (see **ehe** 2): cf. **Bälder, als er gehofft hatte, rollte die Chaise über die Donitzer Brücke** (Kolbenheyer).

bald(e): see **adverbs formed from adjectives** 1 .

Balg: This masc. noun (plur. **Bälge**) is properly used of the 'skin, hide' of animals; also of 'bellows', esp. in the old phrase **die Bälge** (or **den Blasebalg**) **treten** ('to work the bellows' of an organ). It is also used coll. of a 'naughty child, brat', in which sense it is either masc. or neut. (plur. **Bälge** or **Bälger**). Quite different is the fem. **Balge** (plur. **Balgen**), a specifically northern coll. expression for 'bathtub, vat'.

Balken: MHG *balke* was a weak noun (gen., dat. *balken*). In time the final *-n* of the oblique cases crept into the nom., the noun then coming to have strong inflexion, but without mutation of the root-vowel in the plur.: **der Balken, des Balkens, die Balken.** In a number of analogous cases the noun has either **-e** or **-en** in the nom. sing., but the form in **-e** is now more usual in the case of **Friede, Glaube,** and **Wille,** and is practically fixed in **Name** and **Same** ('seed'). On the other hand, the nom. **-en** ending is more usual in the case of **Funken** ('spark'), **Schaden** ('damage': plur. **Schäden**) and esp. **Gefallen** (pleasure, favour': see **Ge-** 4). In this connexion see also **Faden, Fels, Fleck, Hauf, Lump, Tropf.**

Ball: Whether used in the sense of a toy or of a dance, **der Ball** has the plur. **Bälle.** The toy was formerly weak, as in **Ich warf den Ballen weg** (G.), and one still usually distinguishes between **Schneebälle** ('snowballs') and **Schneeballen** ('guelder-roses'). The sing. **der Ballen** ('bale' of cotton, etc.) is unchanged in the plur.

Band, Bande: Distinguish between **der Band** (plur. **Bände**), a 'volume' of poems, etc. (see **Verband**); **das Band** (plur. **Bänder**), a 'ribbon' or 'cord'; **das Band** (plur. **Bande**), a 'fetter, bond, tie'; and **die Bande** (plur. **Banden**), a 'band' (of robbers, musicians, etc.) or a 'cushion' of a billiard-table. The following are characteristic examples: **Der erste Band dieses Werkes fehlt, die anderen Bände habe ich—Das Kind hat sich mit bunten Bändern geputzt—Das Blaue Band kennzeichnet ihn als Ritter des Hosenbandordens** ('The Blue Ribbon distinguishes him as a Knight of the Garter') **—Meine Stimmbänder sind entzündet** ('My vocal cords are inflamed')**—Die Bande der Ehe sind heilig** ('The ties *or* bonds of matrimony are sacred')**—Zwischen den beiden besteht ein festes Band der Freundschaft—Der Mörder wurde gefangen und in Bande geschlagen—In dieser Gegend sollen mehrere Räuberbanden sein—Der Billardball prallte von der Bande ab.**

bange, bangen: see **Angst.**

Bank: Distinguish between **die Bank** ('bench', plur. **Bänke**) and **die Bank** ('money-bank', plur. **Banken**).

barfuß, barhaupt: see **adjectives (indeclinable)** 5.

Bauer: Distinguish between **der Bauer** (gen. **Bauern** or **Bauers**, plur. **Bauern**), meaning a 'peasant, farmer' (see **Nachbar**), also a 'pawn' in chess, and (like **Bube**) a 'knave' in cards; **der Bauer** (gen. **Bauers,** plur. **Bauer**), a 'builder, erector, constructor') now only in compds. like **Orgelbauer,** 'organ-builder' (a man in business as a 'builder' is **Baumeister**); and **das** (now rarely **der**) **Bauer** (gen. **Bauers,** plur. **Bauer**), a 'bird-cage'.—**Bauer** is, of course, a common German surname, no doubt because the bearer orig. came of peasant stock, but here the gen. is **Bauers,** not **Bauern:** cf., in a reference to the modern author J. M. Bauer, **Die bedächtige, überlegende Art des Bauern** ('of the peasant') **ist im Schaffen Josef Martin Bauers am Werke** (H. Arens).

be-: This insep. verbal prefix, really a corrupt form of **bei,** has various functions. The two commonest are: (i) to give an intrans. verb trans. force, and (ii) to alter the force of a trans. verb in such a way that its dir. obj. becomes indir. Thus, under (i), **jemandem drohen** and **jemanden bedrohen—mit jemandem liebäugeln** and **jemanden beliebäugeln—lügen** and **jemanden belügen—viel reisen** and **viele Länder bereisen,** etc.; under (ii), **Häuser bauen** and **ein Grundstück mit Häusern bebauen—Zettel an die Wand kleben** and **die Wand mit Zetteln bekleben—Nägel in etwas schlagen** and **etwas mit Nägeln beschlagen—Butter auf Brot schmieren** and **Brot mit Butter beschmieren,** etc.

beabsichtigen: cf. **beanspruchen** I (*b*).

beachselzucken: see **shoulder.**

beachten: see **achten** I.

Beamte(r): This is contracted from **Beamtete(r),** the past part. of the otherwise now obs. verb **beamten** ('to invest with an office'). It is, therefore, an *adj.-subst.,* and takes the inflexional endings of an attrib. adj. (see **adjective-substantives**): hence **der Beamte,** but **ein Beamter—zwei Beamte,** but **zweier Beamten**; and sim. with an attrib. adj., **Er hatte sich als brauchbarer Beamter bewährt** (Bergengruen).

beanlagen: see **beanspruchen** I (*b*).

beanspruchen: 1. (**a**) An important rule in German is that *verbs formed from nouns are weak.* There is no verb **spruchen,** but **beanspruchen** ('to lay claim to') is formed by giving the noun **Anspruch** the verbal ending **-en** and prefixing **be-** to this artificially constructed verb to give it trans. force. It is therefore a *weak* insep. trans. verb: e.g. **Ich beanspruchte** (= **erhob Anspruch auf**) **meinen rechtlichen Anteil** ('I claimed my lawful share')—**Für den Verlust habe ich Ersatz beansprucht** ('I have claimed compensation for the loss'). (**b**) The same applies to a considerable number of other verbs formed in this way. Besides those referred to under 2 and 3 below, the commonest of these are **beabsichtigen** ('to intend' something), **beaufsichtigen** ('to superintend'), **beargwöhnen** ('to suspect'), **beeindrucken** (q.v.), **beeinflussen** ('to influence'), **beobachten** (see **Obacht**), **bevormunden** (q.v.), **bevorzugen** (q.v.), **verabreden** ('to arrange, agree upon'), **verabscheuen** ('to detest'), **verabschieden** ('to dismiss', reflex. 'to take leave') and **veranstalten** ('to organize'); rather less common are **beanlagen** and **veranlagen** (chiefly used in the past part. with the force of 'gifted, talented', as in Bruno Frank's **Der hochbeanlagte Knabe war nicht viel weniger als ein Wunder gewesen** and Th. Mann's **Er wird studieren: er ist brillant veranlagt**), **beanstanden** ('to object to, call in question') and **verausgaben** ('to pay out'). **2.** Special care is required with those verbs belonging here which end in a simple strong verb. Thus, **beantragen** ('to move' something at a meeting) is not really a double compd. of **tragen,** but is formed from the noun **Antrag** ('to make a motion' is **einen Antrag stellen**), so that it is a *weak* verb: e.g. **Wenn er das beantragt** (not **beanträgt**), **werde ich dagegen stimmen—Er beantragte** (not **beantrug**) **das Übergehen zur Tagesordnung** ('He moved the previous question')—**Ich habe die Annahme des Berichts beantragt** (not **beangetragen**). The same applies to the following verbs, which are treated under their separate heads: **beauftragen, beherbergen, bemitleiden, bewillkomm(n)en, veranlassen** and **veranschlagen**; in this connexion see also **radebrechen** and **ratschlagen,** and cf. **handhaben, wallfahr(t)en** and **willfahren. 3.** There are, of course, many verbs which are actually simple verbs compounded with two prefixes, verbs which are not formed from nouns, and in such cases, where the simple verb is strong, the compd. will be strong also: e.g. **Er behielt den Hut auf** ('He kept his hat on')—**Sie hat ihren Irrtum eingestanden** ('She has acknowledged her mistake')—**Er bereitete sich auf das Examen vor** ('He prepared for the examination'). Here belong quite a number of verbs which show fluctuation between separation and non-separation of the first prefix, and these are treated under their separate heads: see **anbelangen, anbetreffen, anerbieten, anerkennen, anvertrauen, auferlegen, auferstehen, auferwecken, auferziehen, vorbehalten,** and **vorenthalten.**

beantragen: see beanspruchen 2.

beargwöhnen: cf. beanspruchen 1 (*b*).

beaufsichtigen: see beanspruchen 1 (*b*).

beauftragen: There are two ordinary ways of expressing the idea of 'to commission a person to do something', viz. either **jemandem etwas auftragen** (= **einen Auftrag geben**) or **jemanden mit etwas beauftragen;** in other words, the obj. of **auftragen** is what one is commissioned to do, while that of **beauftragen** is the person who is commissioned to do it. Whereas **auftragen** is a true compd. of **tragen** and is therefore *strong,* **beauftragen** is actually formed from **Auftrag** and hence is *weak,* as explained under **beanspruchen** 2: cf. **Er hat mir einen Gruß an Sie aufgetragen** ('He has charged me with greetings to you') and **Er hat mich beauftragt, Sie zu grüßen.**

bedanken: see **danken** 1 (*b*).

bedauern: see dauern 2.

bedeuten: see **deuten** 2.

bedienen: This is the trans. verb corresponding to the intrans. **dienen** (q.v.), but it has a much more limited use than the latter. It is the reg. expression for 'to serve' customers, used of waiters, shop-assistants, etc.: e.g. **Womit kann ich Ihnen dienen?** ('What can I get, offer *or* show you? Can I help you?'), but **In diesem Geschäft wird man gut bedient** ('The service is good in this establishment'). Also very common is the *reflex.* verb: e.g. **Bitte bedienen Sie sich!** the polite phrase for the coll. **Langen** or **Greifen Sie zu!** ('Please help yourself!'); with a *gen.,* **Als ich in Berlin war, bediente ich mich der Gelegenheit** ('I took *or* availed myself of the opportunity'), **meine Freunde aufzusuchen.** The simple verb is used with an accus. of the thing in a few expressions: one no longer uses **ein Amt bedienen** (for **bekleiden:** 'to fill a post'), but a military phrase is **ein Geschütz bedienen** ('to serve a cannon'), and in card-games **Farbe bedienen** (or simply **bedienen**) is the reg. expression for 'to follow suit'; an alternative phrase here is **Farbe bekennen** (not **bekennen** alone), which is also used fig. in the sense of 'to be frank *or* outspoken'.

bedingen, bedingt: see **dingen** 2.

bedürfen: This is one of many verbs which orig. only took a *gen.* case, but which, through failure to recognize a word like **es** (q.v.) as a gen., came later to be associated with an *accus.* obj. Nevertheless, an example like **Er bedurfte jetzt mehr als jemals den guten Willen des Staates** (Sch.) is not so very common, the accus. having really only established itself in the case of unqualified nouns, as in **Trost** or **Hilfe bedürfen,** and esp. in that of indef. neut. expressions like **es, nichts** (q.v.), **das, was,** etc. Actually, *Duden* gives only the gen., and this is still the standard case in good prose: e.g. **Das Christentum bedarf allerdings des Staates nicht, wohl aber der Staat des Christentums** (W. v. Kügelgen)—**Frankreich bedurfte des Friedens, bedurfte der Sicherheit** (Ranke)—**Unter dem Kopftuche glitzerte eine Schnalle hervor, obwohl das rotblonde Haar keines Schmuckes bedurfte** (Sudermann)—**Ihre Taschenuhr schlug die Stunden, ohne wie Repetieruhren eines äußeren Impulses zu bedürfen** (L. Schücking)—**Es scheint mir der schönste Teil meiner Liebe, daß du meiner bedarfst** (Kolbenheyer); so also in the impers. use, as in **Sie sank ohnmächtig zusammen, und er eilte nach stärkenden Mitteln, doch es bedurfte ihrer nicht** (E. T. A. Hoffmann) and **Es hat einiger Mühe bedurft, sie zu einer Unterredung zu bestimmen** (W. v. Scholz); and even indef. expressions often stand in the gen., as in **Nach und nach war der Schlummer, dessen ich so bedurfte, über mich gekommen** (Stifter) and **Begib dich ins Haus und beschaffe dir, wessen du bedarfst** (Bergengruen). The gen. is quite fixed with the adj. **bedürftig,** used pred. with **sein, werden,** etc., as in **Er ist des Trostes bedürftig** (or **benötigt:** see nötigen 2); unusual is a proposition like **Wir sind einander bedürftig** (Zschokke: 'We stand in need of each other'), for **Wir brauchen einander** or **Wir sind einer des anderen bedürftig.**

beeindrucken (not **-drücken**): This is a verb of quite recent introduction, meaning 'to impress' somebody, having been formed (under the influence of **beeinflussen**) from the noun **Eindruck,** so that it is a weak verb (see **beanspruchen** 1). It is now chiefly used pred. in the past part.: e.g. **Frau Rosalie war von den Vorhaltungen**

der Tochter tiefer beeindruckt, als sie sich hatte merken lassen (Th. Mann)—**Irene nickte flüchtig; mag sein, daß sie mich erkannt hatte, doch schien sie nicht sonderlich beeindruckt von dieser Begegnung** (Fr. Thieß)—**„Wie willst du denn helfen?" fragte Karl, wider Willen beeindruckt** (A. Reiner)—**Der Postdirektor war so beeindruckt, daß er persönlich mit der Depesche an den Strand lief** (B. E. Werner).

beeinflussen: see **beanspruchen** 1 (*b*), and cf. **beeindrucken.**

beerben: see **erben.**

befallen: see **attack** 3.

befehlen: 1. This strong verb has two constructions. (**a**) Used in the sense of 'to give an order', it takes an accus. of the thing, a dat. of the person: e.g. **Was du befiehlst, soll geschehen**—**Ich lasse mir nichts befehlen** ('I take orders from no one')—**Mir wurde befohlen, zu Hause zu bleiben.** (**b**) With the force of 'to order (somebody) to appear *or* to go somewhere', or 'to order (something) to be brought', it takes an accus.: e.g. **Er befahl** ('summoned') **seine Wirtin ins Zimmer und gebot ihr** (see 3 *a*): **„Wenn Besuch kommt, bin ich nicht zu Hause!"** (P. Keller)—**Der König befahl ihn mit einer Handbewegung zu sich heran** (Bruno Frank)—**Der Arzt war eilig nach Berlin befohlen worden** (Fr. Griese)—**Er befahl seine Pferde** (G.)—**Der Wirt fragte, welchen Wein der Herr beföhle** (Fontane: see **past subjunctive** 2 *c*. ii)—**„Befiehlst du deine Pfeife, Papa?"** (Sudermann: 'Do you want me to bring your pipe, dad?'). In poetry and choice prose it is used trans. in the sense of 'to entrust, commit', as often in the Bible: **In deine Hände befehle ich meinen Geist** (Ps. 31. 6). **2.** The weak trans. **befehligen** was formerly used, and still is occasionally, like **befehlen** as under 1 (*b*): e.g. **Die Barke wurde befehligt, man stieg ein** (Wieland)—**Ich habe ihn befehligt, das Schloß zu stürmen** (A. Stahr). As a military term it is still so used: e.g. **„Ich bin hierher befehligt", sagte der Offizier** (Hackländer)—**Er war nach Dresden ins Kriegsministerium befehligt worden** (Ompteda); but rather more common here is **beordern** (which is also sometimes used like **befehlen** 1 *b*, as in Fontane's **Er zog die Klingel und beorderte sein Pferd**), while **befehligen** now usually has the force of 'to be in command of' (a regiment, company, squad, etc.), as in **Im letzten Gefecht hatte er einen Sergeanten samt der Kompanie, die dieser befehligte, gefangengenommen** (M. Eyth): cf., as unusual, **Gegen Abend wurde ich befohlen** (for **wurde mir befohlen** or **wurde ich beordert**) **zur Seitendeckung im Busch zu reiten** (Frenssen: 'Towards evening I was ordered to scour the bush and cover the army's flank'). **3.** (**a**) A stronger expression for **befehlen** + dat. is **gebieten,** which, although sometimes used loosely (as in the example from P. Keller given under 1 *b*), really implies absolute power in the person giving the order and precludes disobedience—as *Sanders* puts it **„Der Herr befiehlt seinen Dienstboten etwas, weil er nicht unbedingte Macht über sie hat, wie etwa über Sklaven oder Leibeigene** ('slaves or serfs'); **der Offizier befiehlt den Soldaten etwas, weil er nicht als Oberherr erscheint; der Kaiser kann über eine ungeheure Zahl von Truppen gebieten."** So also it is significant that our Lord's 'commandments' are not **Befehle** but **Gebote,** and that **über ein Volk gebieten** is 'to rule, govern, lord it over a people'. But **gebieten** is also used fig., as in **Der Vorsitzende gebot Ruhe** ('The chairman ordered the assembly to keep quiet, called the meeting to order')—**Man muß seinen Leidenschaften gebieten** ('One must curb one's passions')—**Teures Weib, gebiete deinen Tränen!** (Sch.: '. . . control, restrain your tears!'). The past part. **geboten** is also used as an adj. with much the same force as **erforderlich** ('requisite, necessary'), implying that something is dictated by the circumstances: e.g. **Das Gepäck war größer, als es für den Ausflug geboten schien** (Fontane)—**Er wandte sich an ihn mit der Bitte, nochmals zu prüfen, ob dieser Entschluß geboten sei** (E. Wichert). (**b**) A more formal alternative expression for **befehlen** + accus. of the person (as in 1 *b*) is **entbieten:** e.g. **Der König entbot seinen Leibarzt zu sich** ('The king summoned his physician in ordinary into his presence')—**Er hatte seinen Schwiegersohn aus Kalabrien entbieten lassen** (Platen: 'He had had his son-in-law summoned . . .')—**Er wurde zu seinem Regiment entboten** ('He was ordered to join his regiment'). With a dat. of the person and an accus. of the thing it is a formal expression for 'to send' a message (**Bot-**

schaft), greeting, etc.: **Er entbot mir seinen Gruß.** (c) Although **anordnen** means 'to arrange', it often implies an injunction to do something: e.g. **Alles geschah pünktlich: sie wußte anzuordnen, ohne daß sie zu befehlen schien** (G.)—**Der Tischlermeister sagte: „Mach' das!" und ordnete es so an, daß man seinen Auftrag gern ausführte** (Fr. Schnack); cf. **Der Arzt verordnete** (or **verschrieb**, 'prescribed') **ihm einen Schlaftrunk und ordnete an, daß jemand nachts bei ihm wache.** (d) To this group also belongs **anweisen,** properly 'to allot, assign' something to a person, but esp. 'to direct, instruct' a person to act in some way: e.g. **Man wies mir einen guten Platz an** ('I was directed *or* shown to a good seat') —**Bei seiner Rückkehr nach Rußland wurde ihm die Hauptstadt zum Aufenthalt angewiesen** (M. Eyth: i.e. he was directed not to leave the capital)—**Flüsternd wies sie ihn an, was er zu tun habe** (Bergengruen); cf. **Er befahl mir, zu tun, was Sie befehlen: das sind meine Anweisungen** (M. Eyth: '. . . those are my instructions').

befehligen: see befehlen 2.

befleiß(ig)en: The only MHG form of this verb is *sich vlîzen* (strong: past tense *ich vleiz, wir vlizzen*). The corresponding NHG **sich fleißen** is now obs., the only remnant still extant being **geflissentlich** —see **t** (**inorganic**)—used esp. as an adv. with the force of **mit Fleiß**, 'deliberately'. The strong compound **sich befleißen** ('to apply oneself to, aim sedulously at, cultivate') is still sometimes used, esp. in the past tense: e.g. **Mein Vater befliß sich einer gewissen Reinheit der Sprache** (G.) —**Während sie sich vor den Leuten der friedlichsten Beredsamkeit beflissen, sprachen sie in ihrer Schlafkammer kaum ein Wort miteinander** (G. Keller)—**Bei den Besuchen ihres Sohnes befliß sie sich eines bescheidenen Benehmens** (Ric. Huch); and the part. **beflissen** is quite common in the adj., adj.-subst. or adv. relation: e.g. **Er war beflissen, ein vorzügliches Dejeuner herzurichten** (Fontane: 'He took great pains to serve up an excellent lunch')—**Ich bin beflissen gewesen, die Schuldlosigkeit meines Vaters zu erweisen** (Bergengruen)—**Er ist ein Beflissener der Rechte** ('He is a law student')—**Er fand die Hausfrau höflich und dienstbeflissen** (Kolbenheyer: 'anxious to serve, obsequious')—**Sie kehrten einander den Rücken zu und setzten eilig und beflissen ihre Wege in entgegengesetzter Richtung fort** (Ric. Huch). But otherwise the strong forms have for the most part been displaced in ordinary language by those of the *weak* verb **sich befleißigen:** e.g. **Seit einiger Zeit befleißigt er sich eines besseren Betragens—Du mußt dich wirklich befleißigen, dich besser zu betragen—Es dünkte mich angenehm, in ihr dieselben Ansichten zu entdecken, deren ich mich selber befleißigte** (G. Keller).

befolgen: see **folgen** 1 (*a*) and 2.

before: 1. *Preposition*: see **vor.** In expressions of time, when preceded by a neg., as in 'I shall not see him before Friday', **vor** may be used, but such propositions are more idiomatically rendered by **erst** (q.v. 2 *c*). **2.** *Adverb*: here 'before' is now confined to sequence of time: its earlier use in 'to go before' is expressed by **vorangehen.** When used of time, the appropriate German word depends on whether it is past or present time. A point of time in the *past* is expressed by **vorher** (see **recent** 2 *b*) or **zuvor:** e.g. **Ich war letzte Woche in der Schweiz, wo ich vorher** (or **zuvor**, 'before that time') **nie gewesen war.** When the time is before the *present* moment, it may also be expressed by **zuvor** (never by **vorher**), but much more commonly by **früher** or **eher:** e.g. **Das sagen Sie mir erst jetzt? Sie hätten es mir früher sagen sollen** ('You should have said so before'). In neg. clauses it is generally expressed by **noch:** e.g. **„Sind Sie schon früher hier gewesen?" „Nein, ich war noch nie hier".** **3.** *Conjunction*: see **ehe** 1 (*b*), and cf. **erst** 2 (*c*).

befremden: see **wonder** 3.

befriedigen, Befriedigung: see **satisfaction** (*b*).

befürchten, Befürchtung: see **fürchten** 2.

begeben, Begebenheit: see **occur** 3 (*b*).

begegnen: 1. (a) The two propositions 'Guess whom I met today' and 'Did you meet your friend?' differ in that the former implies an *accidental* meeting, the latter an *arranged* meeting. In the same way **begegnen** properly suggests a chance meeting, the idea being that two people happen to come towards (**gegen**) each other, while a prearranged meeting is really implied by **treffen** (q.v.), the idea being taken from hitting what you aim at: hence, on the one hand, **Rate mal,**

wem ich heute begegnete! and on the other hand, **Hast du deinen Freund getroffen?** Incidentally, 'to meet' a person on his arrival by train, although it implies a meeting by arrangement, is not **treffen,** but **abholen,** as in **Mein Bruder holte mich vom Bahnhof** (or **von der Bahn**) **ab**; cf. **Taxi(s) warten alle** (or die **Ankunft aller**) **Züge ab** ('Taxis meet all trains'). (**b**) Analogous to **begegnen** are **entgegengehen** ('to go to meet') and **entgegenkommen** ('to come towards'). These verbs agree in that the two people approach each other, but do not necessarily meet: cf. **Ich ging meinem Freund entgegen, traf ihn aber nicht** and **Als ich ihn mir entgegenkommen sah, vermied ich ein Zusammentreffen dadurch, daß ich in eine Seitenstraße einbog**; cf. **jemandem auf halbem Wege entgegenkommen** ('to meet a person half-way', lit. or fig.: see **halb** 2 and **entgegen**). **2.** While **treffen** takes an accus. obj. and the aux. **haben,** a *dat.* obj. and the aux. **sein** are now quite established with **begegnen,** as in **Ich entsinne mich nicht, ihm je begegnet zu sein.** At one time it was not infrequently used with **haben,** and even with an accus. obj.: e.g. **Ein Gärtner hatte dem Prinzen dort begegnet** (Sch.)—**Seit der Zeit habe ich ihm zwei- oder dreimal begegnet** (Heine)—**Sie begegneten ihn mit vieler Grausamkeit** (Lessing: see 3 *d*)—**Ich begegnete ihn einmal im Park** (Waldau); cf. **Ein solches Ziel kann man als einen Stern ansehen, nach dem man schifft, wenn man auch nicht weiß, was** [accus.] **man** (now **was** [nom.] **einem**) **unterwegs begegnen werde** (G.). But the use of **haben,** and esp. the accus. obj., are now definitely avoided in good prose, and it comes rather as a shock to read **Halb im Einschlafen träumte er: ihm war es, als begegnete er die Lehrer** (for **den Lehrern**) **vom Gymnasium** (Ompteda). **3.** Besides the ordinary sense of 'to meet', **begegnen** has other shades of meaning. (**a**) It may be, much like **entgegentreten,** used fig., having the force of 'to cope *or* grapple with, take preventive measures against', as we speak of 'meeting' dangers, evils, etc.: e.g. **Wir müssen dieser Gefahr** (or **diesem Übel**) **begegnen**—**Der bürgerliche Krieg entbrennt, wenn wir ihm nicht begegnen** (Sch.). (**b**) It may mean 'to happen to, befall' (cf. **occur** 3 *g*): e.g. **Ihm begegnete das Unglück, daß seine Tochter entführt wurde** (G.)—**In jener Nacht ist mir etwas Seltsames begegnet** (Heine)—**Der Hofschulze kam, was ihm selten begegnete** (= **was bei ihm selten vorkam**), **ganz verstört aus seiner Kammer hervor** (Immermann). (**c**) In the abs. use, it is often used in the sense of 'to be met with *or* found' (cf. **occur** 1), as in **Er war ein Mann besten deutschen Schlages, ein Typ, wie er** ('such as') **in unseren Städten kaum noch begegnet** (Th. Mann). (**d**) In rather choice style, it may mean 'to greet *or* treat' (cf. 4), as in **Man begegnete dem Fürsten mit Ehrfurcht**—**Wilhelm hatte ihr mit entschiedener Verachtung begegnet** (G.). **4.** In the *pass.*, **begegnen** can only be used *impers.*, as in **Diesen Dingen mußte begegnet werden** (Sch., in the sense of 3 *a*)—**Unwürdig seh' ich mir an diesem Hof begegnet** (Sch., with the force of 3 *d*); and sim. **Es ward mir hart begegnet** (Sch.). In these last two examples the trans. **behandeln** would be used in ordinary lang.: **Unwürdig seh' ich mich . . . behandelt**—**Ich wurde hart behandelt.**

beginnen: This verb has undergone various changes since the MHG period. Apart from the fact that it then took a gen. obj. (now obs.) or a simple infin. (now an infin. with **zu**), its past tense and past part. forms were different from those now in use. Where we say **ich begann, wir begannen,** one formerly said *ich began* (or *begunde* or *begonde*), *wir begunnen* (or *begunden*); and our **ich habe begonnen** was orig. *ich hân begunnen.* So also *ob ich begünne* (or *begunde*) is now **wenn ich begänne** or **begönne.** Taken by and large, the subj. form **begönne** is now preferred in the north, **begänne** in the south: e.g., on the one hand, **Mir ist, als ob mir etwas zu entschlüpfen begönne** (Th. Mann), and on the other hand, **Hier wären sie lächerlich, wenn sie von hoher Politik zu reden begännen** (P. Keller)—**Er wäre ängstlich gewesen, daß du zu spielen begännest** (Rilke); for the fluctuation, cf. **Es schien ihr, als ob der starre Zug nachzulassen begönne** (Ompteda) and **Er hatte die Überzeugung, daß in seiner Nachbarin ein leises Interesse für ihn zu erwachen begänne** (id.). Much the same applies to other verbs of this class: see esp. **Ablaut** (2 *c*), and cf. **gelten** 1 (*b*).

begleichen: see **gleich** 5.

begleiten: see **lead** 4, and cf. **leiden** 1 *a*).

begnügen: see **satisfaction** (*e*).

behaglich: see **comfortable** 2.

behalten: 1. The fundamental sense of this verb is 'to keep in one's possession, retain as one's property', as in **Das Kleingeld darfst du behalten** ('You may keep the change'); cf. fig. **Er hat Recht behalten** ('He has been proved right after all, has won his point'). But ordinarily **etwas behalten** does not mean 'to keep safe, preserve' (see 2), but rather 'not to throw away *or* get rid of': when a lady says **Ich werde dieses Dienstmädchen behalten,** there is obviously no suggestion of retaining her as her property, she means that she will 'keep the maid on', not give her notice; and sim. **einen Brief behalten** (i.e. not to destroy it), **etwas im Gedächtnis behalten** (not to forget it), **etwas im Auge behalten** (not to lose sight of it, also fig. to bear it in mind). Almost the only expression in which the idea of security is implied is the past part. **wohlbehalten,** meaning 'safe and sound', as in **Diese Ratgeberin sagte der jungen Dame, daß sie in das Schloß zurückkehren sollte; das tat sie und gelangte wohlbehalten in ihr Schlafgemach** (Musäus); see also **vorbehalten. 2.** (a) The simple verb **wahren** is no longer used as much as it once was, being now largely confined to a few expressions like **den Anstand wahren** ('to observe decorum') and **den Schein wahren** ('to keep up appearances'); cf., as unusual, **Wenn die Zeit kam, daß sich das Gespenst blicken ließ, wahrte sich das Hausgesinde, aus der Kammer zu gehen** (Musäus: '. . . the servants took care not to leave their bedroom', where one would now use **sich hüten,** q.v.). Otherwise **wahren** is now displaced by **bewahren,** which has the specific meaning 'to preserve, keep secure': e.g. **Diese Schätze sollten in einem Museum bewahrt werden —Er hat seine Ehre bewahrt—Diese Lehren hättest du in deinem Herzen bewahren sollen.** So also in the double compd. **aufbewahren,** in which **auf-** (as in **aufheben,** q.v.) suggests a future use: e.g. **Das will ich zu späterer Verwendung aufbewahren** ('I am going to keep that for use at a later date': cf. **einen Notpfennig aufsparen,** 'to lay money by for a rainy day')—**Ich habe die Reste der Mahlzeit zu morgen aufbewahrt** ('I have kept the leavings of the meal for tomorrow')—**Die betreffenden Schriftstücke sind sorgfältig aufbewahrt** ('The documents in question are carefully preserved' for the benefit of posterity). **(b)** The very idea of preserving something implies guarding it against danger or harm, so **bewahren** is most frequently used with the prep. **vor** (q.v.) in the sense of 'to protect *or* shield from' something, much like **behüten** (see **hüten**), as in **Durch Einsalzen kann Fleisch vor Fäulnis bewahrt werden** ('By salting it meat can be preserved from going bad'), and this is esp. common in propositions like **Der König sagte: „Bewahre mich Gott, daß ich etwas Ungerechtes tun sollte!"** (G.: 'God preserve me from committing, *or* God forbid that I should commit, an injustice!'); and hence with **Gott** really understood, the coll. exclamation **Bewahre!** which has entirely lost its orig. sense of 'to preserve' and is used like **Behüte!** (see **hüten** 2 *c*) as an emphatic contradiction: e.g. **„Gehen Sie mit ins Konzert?" „Bewahre! Ich kann diese moderne Musik nicht ausstehen!"** ('No fear! *or* Not on your life! I can't stand this modern music!')— **„Haben Sie das wirklich gesagt?" „Bewahre! Ich habe gerade das Gegenteil gesagt"** ('No, no! I said the very reverse'); cf. **wo** 1. **3.** Even stronger than **bewahren** is **verwahren,** which properly implies keeping so secure that access is very difficult or impossible: e.g. **Der Richter hieß den Verbrecher im Gefängnis verwahren—Es liegt ein ungeheurer Schatz an Gold und Edelsteinen tief unter der Erde im Brocken verwahrt** (Musäus)—**Eine steinerne Treppe führt in die Tiefe in eine geräumige Halle mit drei Türen: zwei davon stehen offen, die dritte ist fest verwahrt mit eisernem Schloß und Riegel** (id.).

behängen: 1. This insep. compd. is always *trans.* The most important point is to differentiate between **hängen** (trans.) and **behängen.** The difference lies in the fact that the dir. obj. of **hängen** corresponds with the indir. obj. of **behängen,** and vice versa. In other words, the dir. obj. of **hängen** is the article which is hung up, while that of **behängen** is the thing on which the article is hung: thus, **Bilder an die Wand hängen,** but **die Wand mit Bildern behängen.** This distinction was orig. observed in English also (cf. Herrick's 'With rich clusters . . . her temple I *behung*'), but most of the English verbs with the prefix *be-* are now obs.: you can 'sprinkle water on the ground' or 'sprinkle the ground with water', but formerly you could either 'sprinkle water **on the**

ground' or '*be*sprinkle the ground with water', just as the wheels of your carriage could 'spatter mud on a pedestrian' or '*be*spatter a pedestrian with mud'. This distinction is still extensively observed in German: characteristic examples are given under **be-** (q.v.). **2.** The past tense is generally **behängte,** as in **Ganz gegen den Brauch behängte sie sich mit allerlei Putz und Tand** (Heyse), but the strong form **behing** is also used, and a little later in the passage just quoted we find **Wie früher ihre eigene Person, so behing sie den kleinen Andree mit allem, was ihr dienlich schien**; sim. **Der Apfelbaum behing sich mit Frühlingsglöckchen** (H. Krieger). In the past part., both weak and strong forms are in common use, **behängt** properly implying an *action*, **behangen** a *state*: e.g. **Den Saal hatte man mit Hautelissen behängt** (G.: 'The hall had been hung with high-warp tapestries')—**Ich hoffe, Ihr Fuhrwerk wiederzusehen bei der Rückkehr von Prag, mit Kränzen behangen** (Mörike)—**Er trug Rohrstiefel, vorn mit einer Troddel behangen** (Auerbach)—**Die Wände waren mit Teppichen behangen** (G. Keller)—**Das Christbäumchen war mit blitzenden Silberstücken behangen** (Stehr); thus, **behängt** would be more usual in the north in the proposition **Sein Diener hatte die Laube mit vergoldeten Kürbissen behangen** (Kopisch): cf. **hängen** 2 (*c*).

behelfen: see **helfen** 1 (*a*).

beherbergen: The vowel sound in the noun **das Heer** ('army') is now a long close one, but was orig. short and open (MHG *hĕr*); the historically correct short sound is retained in **Hermann, Herzog,** and **Herberge** (f. 'shelter, quarters'). It is from this last noun that the verb **herbergen** is formed, which was orig. used of an army encamping, but has now the more general force of 'to lodge, stay', as in **Plato verhält sich zu der Welt wie ein seliger Geist, dem es beliebt, einige Zeit auf ihr zu herbergen** (G.). Esp. common now is the compound **beherbergen** (trans. 'to lodge, take in, give shelter *or* quarters to': cf. our 'to *harbour* evil designs'): e.g. **Der Anblick Friederikens machte mir Vorwürfe, daß ich soviele Nachtvögel** (meaning his 'remorseful thoughts') **bei mir beherbergen mögen** (G.). As these verbs are not really compds. of the strong verb **bergen** (q.v.), but are formed from the noun **Herberge,** they are, according to rule (see **beanspruchen** 1 and 2), *weak*: e.g. **Hier beherbergt** (not **beherbirgt**) **man verspätete Wanderer**—**Ich habe schon manche armen Leute beherbergt.**

behüten: see **hüten** 2 (*b*) and (*c*), and **behalten** 2 (*b*).

bei: 1. The MHG prep. *bî* could be used with an *accus.* with verbs implying motion towards; but although sporadic examples of this occur even down to the classical period, it is now avoided in good prose: cf. **Petrus satzte sich bei die Knechte** (Matth. 26. 58, where the modern Bible has **setzte sich zu den Knechten**)—**Ich bitte mich bei Sie zu Gast** (G., in a letter to Frau v. Stein)—**Er kam auf hundert Schritt bei's Schloß** (Jung-Stilling). This use is now confined to the coll., esp. illiterate lang. of the north, as when a servant says **Euch sollte man ein paar Jahre bei's Regiment** (= **unter die Soldaten** 'into the army') **stecken** (Schreckenbach). **2.** So modern prose usage requires a *dat.* after **bei,** and hence disallows it with *simple* verbs of motion, so that it is incorrect to say **Er setzte sich bei mir**; but it is quite correct to say **Er setzte sich bei mir hin** or **nieder,** because the *compd.* verbs point to the moment when the action ceases (see **accusative or dative . . .**). There are, however, two exceptions to the rule that **bei** cannot be used with a simple verb of motion, viz. **bei Fuß** and **bei Seite,** the former confined to military parlance, the latter in common general use. The military command 'Order arms!' is **Gewehr bei Fuß!** and in narrative this can be used to suggest either the attitude or the action of bringing the rifle *into* the recognized position: e.g. **Der Haustür gegenüber stand Gewehr bei Fuß** ('with ordered arms') **eine Kompagnie Soldaten** (Th. Mann)—**Die Infanteristen setzten das Gewehr bei Fuß und präsentierten es** (id.). The expression **bei Seite** is now written as one word, and **beiseite** is used esp. with verbs of motion ('*to* one side'), as in **Der Diakonus nahm ihn beiseite, um eine Angelegenheit von Wichtigkeit mit ihm zu ordnen** (Immermann); and sim. one says **Er trat beiseite, legte das Buch beiseite, räumte das Geschirr beiseite, schaffte das Gerümpel beiseite,** etc.; cf. also the contracted clause **Spaß** or **Scherz beiseite** ('joking apart') and **beiseite** as a stage direction ('aside').

beibringen: see **lehren** 1.

beichten: see **confess** 1.

beid: Whereas **zwei** stresses the idea of two separate entities, **beid** brings the two into a closer relationship: cf., on the one hand, **Der normale Mensch hat zwei Hände,** and on the other hand, **Mit ei'ner Hand kannst du die Kiste nicht heben, du mußt bei'de (Hände) gebrauchen**; sim. **Er hat zwei Söhne, beide (Söhne) sind verheiratet—Ich hatte zwei Taler in der Tasche, scheine aber beide verloren zu haben,** where the first reference is to two coins, the second rather to their money value, an idea often strengthened by **alle beide.** It is inflected like an ordinary adj., as in **die beiden Söhne** (gen. **der beiden Söhne**), **meine** or **diese beiden Söhne,** etc. After the prons. **wir** and **ihr** it sometimes has a weak ending, as in **Jedermann war ungeduldig, wir beiden aber konnten sehr zufrieden sein** (G.), but **wir beide** is certainly to be preferred, esp. as the strong ending is firmly established after other prons., as in **Hier sind zwei Jungen, sie beide** (not **beiden**) **wollen es gesehen haben** ('. . . they both maintain that they have seen it'). The neut. sing. **beides** is reg. used as a pron., and not only with reference to things: e.g. **Er besitzt beîdes, Geld und Gut—Sie wissen, daß Jena nicht weit von Weimar gelegen ist, beides Orte** ('both of which are towns'), **die man als die wesentlichen Schauplätze von Goethes irdischem Wirken ansprechen kann** (G. Hauptmann). Here the verb reg. stands in the *plur.*: e.g. **Ich gesellte mich zu den zwei Pilgern, beides waren schon über fünfzig** (G.)—**Währenddessen haschte ein Jüngling einen anderen, beides waren Jugendgestalten voller Kraft** (C. F. Meyer).

beiderlei: see **Hand** 3.

Bein: see **bone.**

beipflichten: see **agree** 1 (*a*).

beirren: see **irre** 2 (*b*) (i).

Beisein: see **presence** 4.

beiseite: see **bei** 2, and cf. **abseits** 2.

beißen: For the construction in propositions like 'The dog bit me in the finger', see **schlagen** 2 (*a*).—An interesting coll. imprecation is **Daß dich das Mäusle beiße!** where **Mäusle** (= **Mäuschen**) is a popular corruption of MHG *miselsuht* ('leprosy'). This disease was formerly regarded as a divine punishment, so persons afflicted with it, like Hartman von Ouwe's **Der arme Heinrich,** were banished from society, an idea which led to the modern expression for it, viz. **Aussatz** (from **aus-setzen**). The German imprecation, then, corresponds with our 'A plague take you!', but just as ours later lost much of its force (cf. Shakespeare's 'What a plague mean ye to colt me thus?' i.e. What the deuce do you mean by befooling me in this way?), so also did the German expression: thus, an old man sitting in a tower pouring over an abstruse Latin text says to himself **O, ein grausam gelehrtes Buch! Daß dich das Mäusle** (*scil.* **beiße**), **laßt's mich nur gefaßt haben, dann soll's bald zu End' sein mit dem Hocken hier auf dem Turm** (Raabe: 'Oh, devil take it, just wait till I've mastered it, then I'll soon have done with squatting up here in this tower'); cf. **An der Ecke bemerkte ich einen Knäuel von Menschen: „Kreuzwirt," sagte ich „beißt Euch das Mäuslein, daß Ihr hier Maulaffen feil habt?"** (Fr. Halm: 'What ails you, that you are standing gaping here?': see **Maulaffen**).

beistimmen: see **agree** 1 (*a*).

beiwohnen: see **presence** 4.

bekanntlich: see **adverbs formed from adjectives** 3.

bekennen: see **confess** 2; **bedienen** *ad fin.*

bekommen: see **get** 1 (*a*).

bekreuzen (reflex.): see **kreuzen** 3.

beladen: see **load** (verb) 1 (*c*).

belasten, belästigen: see **load** (verb) 2 (*b*) and (*c*).

belauschen: see **überhören** 1.

beleuchten: see **light** (verb) 1 (*b*).

belieben: 1. (**a**) This verb does not occur before the NHG period. It now has an old-world flavour and is mainly used in formal polite lang., esp. with **zu** + **infin.**, in much the same way as our 'to be pleased *or* to vouchsafe' to do something, as in 'You are pleased to be facetious'. With an *impers.* subj., it takes a *dat.* of the person: **Es beliebt Ihnen, witzig zu sein**; sim. **Es hat ihm nicht beliebt, meine Einladung zu beantworten** (almost 'He has not had the grace to reply to my invitation'). In the same sense it is used with a *pers.* subj., esp. in more or less set phrases used in polite conversation: e.g. **Belieben Sie näher zu treten!** ('Please step in!')—**Wenn Sie zu speisen belieben, so sind Sie wohl so gütig, zu warten** (G.: 'If it is your pleasure to have a meal, perhaps you won't mind waiting')—**Mein Herr beliebte es, mich zu erschrecken**

(A. Schaeffer); with an accus. obj., an infin. is really understood, as in **Man begriff den groben Ton, den sie** (*scil.* **anzuschlagen) beliebte** (A. Döblin: 'Her hearers understood the uncivil tone which she chose to adopt'); the most polite phrase to use when you have not caught a person's words is **Wie beliebt?** ('I beg your pardon?'). The expression **jemandem etwas belieben,** in the causative sense of 'to give a person a liking for something, lay something to a person's heart' seems to be peculiarly Swiss and should be avoided: cf. **Er wollte der Regierung die Erhaltung schöner Bäume als allgemeinen Grundsatz belieben** (G. Keller: i.e. 'He wished to inspire the government with a loving care for the preservation of beautiful trees as a general principle'). **(b)** The part of the verb in ordinary use now is the past part. **beliebt,** used as an *adj.* with the force of 'well-liked, popular, favourite': e.g. **Er ist ein allgemein beliebter Gesellschafter** ('He is a general favourite in company')—**Er macht sich bei allen beliebt** ('He ingratiates himself with everybody'). **2.** The verbal noun **Belieben** is still used formally in a few expressions, esp. **in jemandes Belieben stehen,** as in **„Ich schreibe das nimmermehr!" „Wie Sie wollen: das steht ganz in Ihrem Belieben"** (Sch.: '. . . that is just as you please', cf. our coll. 'that is entirely up to you').

belohnen: see **lohnen** I.

belong: see **gehören.**

bemerken: It is strange that while the accus. and infin. construction is so very common after **sehen,** it is comparatively little used after other verbs of sight-perception. A striking case in point is **bemerken** ('to notice'): for some reason difficult to explain, a proposition like **Nach einer Weile bemerkte ich einen Mann an der Seite des Deiches herabsteigen** (Storm) is surprisingly rare. And rarer still is the use of a pres. part., so common in English: in **Ottilie bemerkte einen Mann neben Charlotten sitzend** (G.), the infin. would certainly sound less objectionable, the alternatives being either the rel. clause **der neben Charlotte saß,** or a **daß**-clause immediately following **bemerkte.** In this connexion see also **erblicken** and **gewahren.**

bemitleiden: This trans. verb, meaning 'to sympathize with, pity' (= **Mitleid fühlen mit**), is not a true double compd. of the strong verb **leiden** (q.v. I *b*), but is formed from the noun **Mitleid,** and hence it is a *weak* verb, as explained under **beanspruchen** I and 2: e.g. **Wir bemitleideten das elternlose Kind.**

benötigen: see nötigen 2.

beobachten: see Obacht and **beanspruchen** I (*b*).

beordern: see befehlen 2.

bequem: see **comfortable** I.

beraten: see **raten** 2 (*b*).

beratschlagen: see **ratschlagen.**

bereit: see **ready** I.

bereitwillig: see **willig.**

bergen: 1. With the force of 'to hide, conceal', this strong verb (cf. **Past subjunctive** 2 *c*) is mainly confined to poetical language: in ordinary language it is now rare in this sense, being generally replaced—e.g. in a proposition like **Ich darf die Wahrheit nicht bergen** (Freytag)—by one of the other verbs given below. But **bergen** is still in common use in the sense of 'to convey to a secure place, save from danger *or* destruction' (= **in Sicherheit bringen**), used in the first instance of salvaging a wrecked ship's cargo, stranded goods, dead bodies, etc., then also in a more general way, esp. in the past part.: e.g. **Es gelang ihnen, das Strandgut zu bergen—Ein Gewitter ist im Anzuge, aber zum Glück ist unser Getreide geborgen** ('. . . our corn is all in')—**Unter diesem Baum sind wir vor dem Regen geborgen** ('sheltered')—**Hier fühle ich mich geborgen** ('Here I feel safe'); cf. **beherbergen** (q.v.). **2.** Where the context implies the conscious and deliberate concealment of some object so that others may not find it, it is ordinarily rendered by the rather prosaic verb **verstecken:** e.g. **Sie versteckte den Brief unter ihrem Kopfkissen;** so also **Verstecken spielen** ('to play hide-and-seek': cf. **viel** I *b*). **3.** A rather more choice expression with the same force is **verbergen** (q.v.), and this verb is used in one sense which neither **verstecken** nor **bergen** conveys, viz. that of 'to prevent from being seen', as in a context like 'A bend in the road *hid* the house from my view', where there is obviously no question of deliberate concealment: **Eine Krümmung des Weges verbarg** (not **versteckte**) **das Haus meinem Blick**—cf. **Ich will mich hier verstecken, der Strauch wird mich ihm verbergen;** so also God's ways are not **versteckt,** but **verborgen,** because He does not deliberately conceal them from us, it is merely that we cannot discern them—cf. **Gott sieht ins Verborgene.** **4.** Where the idea is that of withholding knowledge from others, esp. the knowledge of the truth, of guilt, sins, etc., the verb **hehlen** was formerly used (cf. **Hehl**), but this is now rare, being replaced by the compd. **verhehlen,** which is now always *weak*, as in **Sie verhehlte nicht, daß sie sich ein wenig langweilte** (Th. Mann). The only remnant of the original strong conj. is **unverhohlen,** used as an adj. or an adv. with the force of 'undisguised, unfeigned; openly, frankly'; but even **verhehlen** is hardly an every-day word, ordinary language preferring to use **verschweigen** ('to keep silent about' something), esp. when the silence is prompted by a feeling of shyness or diffidence: e.g. **Er verschwieg dem Mädchen seine Liebe—Er sagte, er habe die Dame ins Wasser fallen sehen, verschwieg aber, daß er sie gerettet habe—Den Namen der Dame bin ich leider genötigt zu verschweigen** (Zuckmayer). **5.** The deliberate concealment of knowledge which one ought to disclose is suggested by **verheimlichen:** e.g. **Er verheimlichte das Verbrechen, das sein Freund begangen hatte—Sie verheimlichten, daß auch sie an dem Irrtum schuld waren.**

berichten: 1. This verb has two constructions. (**a**) With a dat. of the person (which need not be expressed) and an accus. of the thing (which may be a subord. clause or be replaced by **über** + accus. or **von**), it means 'to report something to somebody': e.g. **Das hat man mir so berichtet—Alle Zeitungen haben den** (or **über den** or **von dem**) **Unfall berichtet**; cf. **Berichterstatter** ('newspaper reporter'). (**b**) With an accus. of the person, it means 'to inform'(= **in Kenntnis setzen**), esp. in the past part. with **sein** and an appropriate adv.: e.g. **Die polnischen Großen haben Ende des Jahres, wie ich glaubhaft berichtet bin** ('as I am credibly informed'), **eine Konföderation geschlossen** (E. Wichert)—**In Rußland scheint man mit der Armut fertig zu werden** ('to deal successfully with the question of the people's poverty'), **wenn ich richtig berichtet bin** (B. E. Werner)—**Es ist klar, man hat mich falsch berichtet** (Wassermann). Formerly a gen. of the thing was used here, but this is now practically obs., although in some parts one still says **Ich habe ihn eines Besseren berichtet** ('I have pointed out his mistake to him *or* undeceived him'), where the standard expression is **jemand eines Besseren belehren. 2.** An early use of **berichten** was with the force of 'to set to rights, put in order', but this idea is now expressed by **berichtigen:** e.g. **Einige Druckfehler habe ich berichtigt** ('I have corrected some misprints')—**Wir hoffen, diese Angelegenheit zu berichtigen** ('We hope to settle *or* arrange this matter')—**Der Vogt berichtigt wöchentlich alle Rechnungen** (G.: 'The steward settles all accounts weekly').

bersten: The orig. strong conjugation of this verb (< MHG *bresten*) is still firmly established in the past part., and practically fixed in the past tense: one always says **Das Eis ist geborsten,** and almost always **Das Eis barst**; a less common form is seen in **Auf Seen und Strömen das Grundeis borst** (Bürger: rhyming with **Forst**). With regard to the 2nd and 3rd sing. of the pres. indic., *Sanders* says **„Die schwache Abwandlung kann im Präsens als die heute fast gewöhnlichste gelten“,** and certainly the strong form **birst** would now sound unnatural in an exclamation like **Schrei, bis du berstest!** (Sch.); cf., in an elevated description of the dawn, **Im Osten birst die Nacht und der Morgen dampft durch den Spalt** (Kellermann). On the other hand, the weak past tense **berstete** seems to be avoided. For the subj. form **börste,** see **past subjunctive** 2 (*c*) (ii).

beschaffen: see **schaffen** 1 (*b*) and 2 (*b*).

bescheiden: 1. *Verb*: This compd. of **scheiden** (q.v.), the past part. of which is now always **beschieden** (but see 2), is used in several ways: (**a**) with a dat. of the person and an accus. of the thing, it means 'to allot', now used esp. of what is a person's 'lot' in life: e.g. **Genieße, was dir Gott beschieden!** (Gellert)—**Mir ist viel Glück beschieden** ('Much happiness has been my lot *or* portion'); (**b**) with an accus. of the person, it has the force either of 'to inform' (= **jemandem Bescheid geben:** cf. **berichten** 1 *b*) or of 'to summon' to a specified place: e.g. in the former sense, **Man beschied ihn, daß er sich gedulden solle** (E. Wichert) and **Er bat um Geld, wurde aber ungnädig beschieden** (Fr. Griese: i.e. received a rude reply, was rebuffed), and in the latter sense, **Der General besuchte ihn oft und beschied ihn noch öfter zu sich aufs Schloß** (E. Wichert); (**c**) reflex. **sich**

bescheiden means 'to be moderate' in one's requests, 'to content oneself', as in **Ich habe gelernt, mich mit wenig(em) zu bescheiden** ('I have learned to be content with little'). **2.** *Adjective*: The verb **scheiden** (q.v. 1) is one of the **reduplicating verbs** (q.v.), so its past part. should really be **gescheiden.** This historically correct form is preserved in **bescheiden,** which is never used as the past part. of the verb, however, but only as an adj. Its force derives from the reflex. use of the verb (see 1 *c* above): e.g. **Er hat ein bescheidenes Einkommen** ('He has a moderate *or* modest income, a fair competence')—**Das Mädchen ist sehr bescheiden** ('modest').

beschuldigen: see **accuse** and **zeihen** 1.

Beschwerde, beschwerlich: see **beschweren** 2.

beschweren: 1. This weak verb must not be confused with the strong verb **beschwören** (see **schwören** 2). The two verbs **erschweren** and **beschweren** correspond to the two meanings of the adj. **schwer,** viz. 'difficult' and 'heavy': e.g. on the one hand, **Erschweren Sie nicht meine Pflicht!** (Heyse: 'Don't make my duty more difficult!'), and on the other hand, **Was dein Gewissen beschwert, kann ich von dir nehmen** (id.: 'I can take away from you what weighs heavily on your conscience'): cf. **sich** (dat.) **den Magen beschweren** ('to clog one's stomach') and **das Gedächtnis beschweren** ('to burden one's memory'). The reflex. **sich beschweren** is used in two senses: cf. **Er beschwerte sich nicht mit Besitz, der nur eine Kette sein würde** (H. W. Geißler: 'He did not encumber himself with property which would only be a fetter') and **Ich habe mich bei der Behörde gegen meine Nachbarn beschwert** (= **beklagt:** 'I have lodged a complaint against my neighbours with the authorities'); cf. the two meanings of **Beschwerde** (see 2). **2.** The noun Beschwer (fem. or neut.), meaning 'trouble, inconvenience' is almost obs.: cf. **Ich errege meinen Erben Beschwer** (Immermann). It has now been practically displaced by **Beschwerde** (fem.), used in the sense of either physical 'trouble, ailment' or of 'complaint': e.g. **Er litt keine körperlichen Beschwerden** (Viebig)—**Ich habe eine Beschwerde gegen meine Nachbarn geführt.** In this connexion cf. the adj. **beschwerlich,** used of what is 'troublesome' in the sense of involving laborious effort: e.g. **Er kam nach einer beschwerlichen Reise glücklich nach Hause** (G.)—**Das Wandern fiel ihm beschwerlich, er mußte sich auf den Stecken stützen** (Immermann)—**Sie hat ihr Gemach hier unten, denn die Treppen sind ihr zu beschwerlich** (Storm).

besehen: see **look** 2 (*b*) and (*d*).

besichtigen: see **look** 2 (*c*).

besiedeln: see **übersiedeln** 1 (*b*).

besinnen: see **remember** 1 and 2; for **Besinnen(s),** see **viel** 1 (*b*).

besonders: see **namentlich** 2 (*b*) *ad fin*; cf. **zumal.**

Bestandteil: see **Teil** 2 (*a*).

bestatten: cf. **Statt** 1 (*b*).

bestehen: 1. With *trans.* force, this verb means 'to stand up to, withstand, overcome' (difficulties, dangers, etc.: more commonly **überste'hen**), esp. 'to pass' (a test, an examination: cf. 2 *a*): e.g. **Wir haben die Gefahr glücklich bestanden—Das Schiff hat den Sturm bestanden** ('. . . has weathered the storm')—**Wenn ich meine Prüfung bestehe, erhalte ich eine feste Anstellung.** The only other trans. use now is in the past part., as applied to land on which something is growing, as in **Die ganze Gegend ist mit viel Holz bestanden** (i.e. 'is well wooded'); sim. **ein von kräftigen Kiefern bestandener Hügelrücken** (Heyse: 'a ridge covered with strong pine-trees')—**ein mit Weizen bestandenes Feld** ('a field of growing wheat'). **2.** With *intrans.* force, it is used in a number of ways, and here there is some fluctuation with regard to the *aux.* in a compd. tense (see 3). **(a)** Instead of **eine Prüfung bestehen** (see 1), one can say **in einer Prüfung bestehen** (ant. **durchfallen**); and sim. with **im Kampf** ('to stand one's ground in a fight') and **in einer Probe** ('to pass a test'). **(b)** Another common meaning is 'to be *or* exist': e.g. **Dieses Geschäft besteht schon lange** ('. . . is old-established')—**Solange die Welt besteht, wird es Arme und Reiche geben—Die Gefahr, vor der sie sich fürchtete, bestand nur in ihrer Einbildung**; esp. in the expressions **zu Recht bestehen** and **bestehen bleiben,** as in **Dieses Gesetz bleibt zu Recht bestehen** ('This law is still in force')—**Meine Forderung besteht zu Recht** ('My demand is a legitimate one')—**Der alte Gebrauch bleibt noch bestehen** (G.: 'The ancient custom is still in vogue'). **(c)** With the prep. **auf,** it means 'to insist on *or* persist in', like **beharren** (see **harren** 2). Here **auf** sometimes takes an accus., as in **Die Frauen, die das Mädchen anputzten, bestanden auf ein Paar goldner Schwingen** (G.); but now it far more commonly takes a *dat.*, an accus. being, according to *Duden*, „selten": e.g. **Er bestand hartnäckig auf seinem Sinne** (G.) —**Der Alte bestand auf einer Antwort** (G. Keller)—**Der Hund bestand auf meiner Gesellschaft** ('insisted on keeping me company'), **wenn ich arbeitete** (Th. Mann). (**d**) With the prep. **aus**, it has the sense of 'to consist *of*, be made up *of*' (ingredients): e.g. **Dieses Gericht besteht aus verschiedenen Gemüsen—Dieser Schlaftrunk besteht aus bewährten Hilfsmitteln.** (**e**) With the prep. **in** (+ dat.), it means 'to consist *in*', as in **Meine Arbeit besteht in der Unterrichtung zurückgebliebener Schüler** or **besteht darin, daß ich zurückgebliebene Schüler unterrichte** ('My work consists in teaching backward schoolchildren'). **3.** With regard to the *aux.* used with intrans. **bestehen,** at one time **sein** was quite common: e.g. **Das Mädchen ist sehr wohl bestanden** ('has done her work well, given satisfaction') **und hat ein herrliches Zeugnis davongetragen** (G.); and sim. (with **auf**) **Wie oft bin ich nicht darauf bestanden?** (Lessing)—**Der Arzt war darauf bestanden, daß ich ihm gewisse Gefäße abträte** (G.: '. . . had insisted that I should make over certain vessels to him'). But present-day usage shows a marked preference for **haben,** and an earlier example like the following sounds much more 'modern' than the others given above: **Es wäre ein eigenes Museum entstanden, wenn die Regierung darauf bestanden hätte, daß jedesmal ein Abguß geliefert werden müsse** (G.). **4.** For the past subj. form **bestünde,** see **past subjunctive** 2 (*c*).

besteigen: see **climb** 2.

Betracht: see **Tracht** 2.

betrachten: see **look** 2 (*d*).

betreffen: 1. This verb is used in two senses, viz. (**a**) 'to come upon *or* surprise' a person doing something: e.g. **Es gelang dem Schutzmann, den Dieb auf frischer Tat zu betreffen** ('The policeman succeeded in catching the thief in the very act'—Lat. *furem in flagrante delicto comprendere*)—**Das Kind wurde auf einer Lüge betroffen** (or **ertappt**) : 'The child was caught telling a lie'; (**b**) 'to concern' (cf. **angehen** 2 and **anlangen**): e.g. **Diese Angelegenheit betrifft uns nicht** ('This matter is no concern of ours')—**Die betreffende Dame ist zur Zeit verreist** ('The lady in question is away from home just now')—**Man wende sich an die betreffende** (or **zuständige**) **Behörde** ('Apply to the competent *or* proper authority'). **2.** The noun **Betreff** is now obs., but **in betreff** or **betreffs** (+ gen.) is used in the sense of 'concerning, with regard to, in the matter of': e.g. **Er sparte in allen Dingen, nur nicht in betreff seiner Garderobe, die er bei dem elegantesten Schneider anfertigen ließ** (Th. Mann); cf., as very unusual, **Nach einer Viertelstunde verabschiedete er sich, mit Ermahnungen betreffs Frühnachhausegehen** (for **-gehens**) **reichlich ausgestattet** (Wassermann).

betrinken: see **trinken** 1 (*b*).

betrügen: For the difference between this verb and **täuschen,** see **deceive** 1 and 2. In ordinary prose the compd. has practically displaced the simple **trügen,** which is now almost confined to a few expressions like **Der Schein trügt** ('Appearances are deceptive')—**wenn mich nicht alles trügt** ('if I am not entirely deceived'). Past tense forms are *strong*, and occasional examples of weak forms should not be imitated: cf. **Wenn meine Voraussetzung mich trügte** (for **trog**), **wäre es undelikat, einen Spruch aus Ihrem Munde zu verlangen** (Mörike)—**Betrügt** (for **Betrogen**) **und erregt, glaubte er drohen zu sollen** (Wassermann); cf. **lügen.**

bevor: see **ehe** 1 (*b*).

bevormunden: This verb, meaning 'to be a guardian of' or 'to place under a guardian', is one of many verbs which are formed from nouns, here from **Vormund** ('guardian': see **Mund** 2), and therefore (see **beanspruchen** 1 *a* and *b*) it is an *insep. weak* verb. The same applies to **bevorzugen,** a trans. verb formed from **Vorzug** ('preference'), used not in the ordinary sense of 'to prefer' (which is **vorziehen**), but in that of 'to favour, grant privileges to' a person: e.g. **Es würde mir nie im Traume einfallen, irgend jemanden zu bevorzugen** ('I should never dream of favouring any one')—**Nur wenig Bevorzugte erhielten Zutritt** (Freytag: 'Only a few privileged people were admitted'). Quite different, on the other hand, is **bevorstehen** ('to be imminent', with a dat. 'to be in store for'), which is the verb **stehen** compounded with the *sep.* prefix **bevor-:** hence **Ich fürchte, etwas Schreckliches steht ihm bevor—Dieses Schicksal droht, ihm**

bevorzustehen or **scheint ihm schon immer bevorgestanden zu haben**; for the past subj. of this compd., see **past subjunctive** 2 (*c*).

bevorstehen, bevorzugen: see **bevormunden.**

bewahren: see **behalten** 2 (*a*) and (*b*).

bewegen: see **move** 1 (*a*) and (*b*), and cf. **wiegen**; **Ablaut** 2 (*b*).

bewillkomm(n)en: As the bracketed **n** suggests, this is not a double compd. of **kommen**: it is formed by prefixing **be-** to the noun **Willkommen,** and adding the verbal **-en** (**be-willkommen-en**), and being formed from a noun, it is a *weak* verb (see **beanspruchen** 1 and 2). The form **bewillkommnen,** then, is the historically correct one, but both forms are in common use, so that what *Heyne* says in his dictionary (1889–), viz. **„bewillkommnen ist allein üblich geworden"**, no longer holds good. If anything, the contracted form sounds rather less formal, and a person extending a welcome to guests would generally say **Ich bewillkommne Sie** or **Es freut mich, Sie zu bewillkommnen.** But the contracted form does sound better in those parts of the verb in which a *t*-sound occurs, as in **Die Ehefrau bewillkommt ihn** (Sch. in a stage direction) and **Der alte Mann bewillkommte seinen Gast** (Novalis), where **bewillkommnet(e)** has a less pleasing sound. Yet mere sound can hardly be the deciding factor, as **vervollkommnen** (q.v.) has *no* contracted forms.

bewußt: **1.** It seems strange that although the OHG compd. verb *bi-wizzan* ('to have a thorough knowledge of') was obs. even in MHG, the past part. **bewußt** came to new life in NHG. It is still sometimes used of what one knows well, as when Mephistopheles says **Allwissend bin ich nicht, doch viel ist mir bewußt** (G.: = **Ich weiß viel, aber nicht alles**); but in a proposition like **Das Gespräch bezog sich auf lauter bewußte Personen** (G.), one would now use **bekannte Personen** (= **Personen die man kannte**). In the attrib. use, **bewußt** is used of what one knows about, esp. of what has previously been referred to, as when Sch. speaks of **der bewußte Ring** ('the ring in question'); and so also one distinguishes between **der Bekannte** ('acquaintance') and **der Bewußte** ('the person in question', who need not be referred to by name). **2.** Much more common now is the pred. use of **bewußt** with a pers. subj. ('to be conscious *or* aware' of something), the standard construction being **sich** (*dat.*) **eines Dinges bewußt sein** or **werden,** where the gen. may be replaced by a subord. clause, esp. an infin. clause with **zu** where the two clauses refer to one and the same person: e.g. **Abkürzungen** ('abbreviations') **gebraucht man mechanisch, ohne sich ihres Sinnes bewußt zu werden** (Rilke)—**Erst jetzt wurde sich der Graf alles dessen, was er gehört hatte, voll bewußt** (Fontane)—**Ich bin mir nicht bewußt, ihn beleidigt zu haben**—**Bist du dir bewußt, warum man dich eingeladen hat?** So also **Er begann, allerlei Figuren zu zeichnen, ohne zu wissen, was er tat; als er sich's bewußt wurde, sah er, daß es Halbkreise waren** (id.), where **'s,** orig. a gen., came to be treated as an accus. (see **es**), so that the accus. was eventually used in ordinary lang. in the case of indef. neut. expressions, as in **Ich muß ihn, ohne mir das geringste bewußt zu sein, mit irgend etwas beleidigt haben** (Mörike); but where Lessing says **Ich bin mir noch Kräfte zu bessern Dingen bewußt,** modern accepted usage would require **einiger** or **gewisser Kräfte.** Very occasionally the gen. of the thing is associated with an accus. of the reflex., as in **Dessen bin ich mich völlig bewußt** (Möser), but this should be avoided in good prose.

bezichtigen: see **zeihen** 2.

Beziehung, Bezug: see **relation** 1.

bieten: see **offer** 1 (*a*) and (*b*); for **geboten** (adj.), see **befehlen** 3 (*a*).

billig: **1.** Our word 'bill' has been adopted in German as a fem. noun (plur. **Bills**), but only in the sense of a draft of an Act of Parliament (the real German expression being **Gesetzentwurf**). The ostensible purpose of such Bills is to benefit all classes of the people in a just and equitable way, and this idea serves as a pointer to the meaning of the neg. noun **Unbill** (with fluctuating gender, mostly fem.; plur. usually **Unbilden,** from an obs. sing. **Unbild**), viz. an 'injustice *or* wrong' inflicted on a person, as in **jemandem eine Unbill antun**; cf. the common expression **die Unbilden der Witterung** ('the inclemency of the weather', seen by suffering mortals as a wrong done them by the Clerk of the Weather). **2.** Here belong also the verb **billigen** ('to approve' what one considers right and proper) and the adj. **billig,** the orig. meaning of which is not 'cheap, moderate in price', but 'fair, equitable', as seen in the prov. **Was dem einen recht ist, ist dem anderen billig** ('What 's sauce for the goose is sauce for the gander').

binnen: see **innerhalb** 2.

bis: **1.** (**a**) It is misleading, and indeed incorrect to say, as many grammars do, that **bis** is 'a preposition which governs the accusative'. It is a comparatively recent word: it does not occur before the MHG period, and even then *biz* is rather rare, the standard expression being *unze*. Now, while *biz* was used, not necessarily with *daz*, as a conj. (see 2), it never 'governed' an accus. or any other case; and the same applies to the NHG **bis**. True, it seems to do so in a proposition like **Ich werde bis nächste Woche hier bleiben**, but this accus. phrase does not depend on **bis**: it is an independent adv. expression which can stand on its own legs (as in **Ich werde nächste Woche verreisen**), and which is here merely modified by **bis**. The same applies to examples like **So habe ich mich redlich bis diesen Tag fortgebracht** (Grillparzer) and **Vater ist bald nach Mitternacht abgeholt worden und bis diesen Augenblick noch nicht zurückgekehrt** (Jak. Frey), although here the construction explained under 1 (*c*) is much more common in the north; from the pen of a northern author, **An Liebe war ihr Leben arm bis diesen Tag** (Fontane) is unusual. (**b**) In independent use, **bis** should only stand before certain specific kinds of words, viz. *letters of the alphabet, cardinal numerals* (including hours of the day, dates expressed in figures, etc.), *names of months or of days of the week, church festivals,* unqualified *place-names,* and many *adv. expressions*: e.g. **Ich habe es von A bis Z durchgelesen**—**Das Kind kann schon von eins bis zehn zählen**—**Wir wollen bis elf Uhr warten**—**Der Krieg dauerte bis 1945**—**Ich werde bis Montag hier bleiben**—**Bis Ostern kann ich nicht warten**—**Ich fuhr ihm bis Aachen entgegen**—**Die Beratungen zogen sich bis spät nachts hin**—**Bis wann gedenkst du hier zu bleiben?**—**Wir treffen uns also morgen früh**: **bis da'hin** ('till then') **leben Sie wohl!**—**Er begleitet mich immer bis hierher** ('as far as this'). In fact, apart from a few adv. expressions, independent **bis** should only be placed before words which show *no distinctive case-ending,* never before nouns qualified by an art. or other attrib. word; an example like the following is definitely contrary to northern usage: **Den Kiesgrund hackt man bis eine Tiefe von anderthalb Fuß auf** (Alverdes: 'The gravelly scil is broken up to a depth of 18 inches': cf. the similar but unobjectionable phrase used by the same author in the last example under 1 *d*). (**c**) Otherwise, **bis** requires *to be supplemented by a preposition*. In expressions of *place,* the context must determine the appropriate prep. to use; and here, if the prep. is one which can take either an accus. or a dat., the *accus.* is the correct case: e.g. **Er begleitete mich bis an die Tür, bis auf den Marktplatz, bis hinter die Kirche, bis in das Dorf, bis vor die Stadt**; so also **Er ist bis über beide Ohren verliebt** ('. . . head over ears in love')—**Er steckt bis über die Ohren in Schulden.** In expressions of *time,* one can say **bis um** (or **gegen**) **ein Uhr**; but by far the commonest combination here is **bis zu** (Bergengruen's **Bis an diesen Augenblick habe ich das geglaubt** is unusual). The following pairs of examples are significant: **bis morgen** ('till tomorrow') and and **bis zum Morgen** ('till morning')—**bis heute** and **bis zum heutigen Tage**—**bis Neujahr** and **bis zum neuen Jahre**—**bis Weihnachten** and **bis zum Weihnachtsfest**—**bis Mai** and **bis zum 8. Mai**—**bis 1945** and **bis zum Jahre 1945.** With other prepositions than **zu**, an accus. is correct here also, except in temporal clauses with **vor** ('ago'), where the dat. is firmly established: thus, while no one now says **Du hast bis am** (for **bis an den,** or far more commonly **bis zum**) **Morgen getrunken** (Lessing), one always says **Bis übers Jahr bin ich wieder da** ('I'll be back again by this time next year'), but **Bis vor einigen Wochen wohnte ich in Köln**—**Bis vor kurzem** ('Until recently') **haben wir wenig Regen gehabt.** (**d**) Specially noteworthy in this connexion is the combination **bis auf** (+ *accus.*), because its meaning may be ambiguous. There can, of course, be no ambiguity in propositions like **Er kletterte bis auf den Gipfel des Berges**—**Er stieg bis auf die oberste Leitersprosse** ('. . . on to the top step of the ladder')—**Sagen Sie ihm, er solle bis auf weiteres** ('until further notice') **in der Schweiz bleiben**; on the other hand, **Er hat alle bis auf mich besucht** is quite ambiguous: it probably means 'He has visited everybody *but me*', but it might mean 'He has visited everybody *including even me*'.

Sometimes the wording may make the meaning clear: cf. **Sie kamen bis auf einen um** ('All but one lost their lives') and **Sie kamen bis auf den letzten Mann um** ('They lost their lives to a man') —**Er hat seine Schuld bis auf einige Mark bezahlt** ('. . . all but a few shillings') and **Er hat seine Schuld bis auf den letzten Heller bezahlt** ('. . . to the last penny')—**Das Theater war besetzt bis auf den letzten Platz** (P. Ernst: i.e. there was not a vacant seat), where **bis auf einen Platz** would mean that every seat but one was occupied. The phrase **bis auf** is also used in propositions like **Als ich bis auf eine Meile vom Bahnhof** ('*to within* a mile of the station') **gekommen war, wurde ich aufgehalten—Als er mir bis auf fünfzig Schritt nahe gekommen war, lehnte er sich ans Gemäuer, um mich zu erwarten** (H. Grimm)—**An heißen Tagen durchglühte die Sonne den lockeren Sand bis auf eines Spatenblattes Tiefe** (Alverdes: 'to a spade's depth'). **2.** As a *conj.*, **bis** is used not only in expressions like **zwei bis drei Meilen** or **die Literatur des 14. bis 15. Jahrhunderts,** but also to introduce a final clause, where its orig. form **bis daß** now sounds very formal and is avoided in ordinary lang.: cf. **Man soll die Tore Jerusalems nicht auftun, bis daß die Sonne heiß wird** (Neh. 7. 3)—**Ich ließ dem Kinde eine Tasse Milch vorsetzen: bis daß sie gebracht wurde, zeigte ich ihm die Bilder in meiner Stube** (Wildenbruch, who is rather partial to this older form). For the combination **nicht eher . . . als bis,** see **erst** 2 (*c*); for a pleonastic neg. inserted in a clause introduced by **bis,** see **negative** (pleonastic) 2 (*b*).

bißchen: 1. The noun **der Biß** suggests the action or result of biting: e.g. **Er tat einen Biß in den Apfel—Der Biß eines tollen Hundes ist lebensgefährlich**; cf. fig. **Gewissensbisse** ('pangs *or* qualms of conscience'). The compd. **der Imbiß** means 'a light meal, a little refreshment': **einen Imbiß nehmen** is like our 'to take a snack'. The gender seems to have fluctuated orig., but the neut. is now obs. except in **das Gebiß,** meaning either a 'set of teeth' or a 'bit' (i.e. the mouthpiece of a horse's bridle). **2.** On the other hand, **der Bissen** is a 'mouthful' of food (cf. our 'I haven't had a *bite* of food all day'): e.g. **Vom Brot nahm sie nicht den kleinsten Bissen ein** (G.)—**Als er das beim Frühstück sagte, erschrak ich so, daß mir der Bissen im Munde steckenblieb. 3.** The dim. of **Biß** is now written **bißchen** (with a small letter), which remains uninflected and is only used in *coll.* lang. after an art. or possessive to suggest a small quantity. The *indef.* art. here is *indeclinable,* as it is in the more select **ein wenig**: e.g. **Mutter, gib mir noch ein bißchen Brot—Er war dabei, einen Rucksack mit ein** (not **einem**) **bißchen Wegzehrung zu packen** (H. Leip: 'He was busy packing a rucksack with a little food for the journey')—**Bei ein bißchen gutem Willen wirst du es schon fertigbringen** (Speckmann: 'With a little goodwill you'll manage it all right'); so also in the adv. relation, as in **Sie ist ein bißchen eitel—Sie ziert sich ein bißchen.** The *def.* art. and possessive, on the other hand (which, incidentally, are *not* used before uninflected **wenig**), are always inflected: e.g. **Mit dem bißchen Taschengeld, das ich bekomme,** (or **Mit meinem bißchen Taschengeld**) **kann ich mir so etwas nicht leisten** ('With my little pocket-money I can't afford that sort of thing').

Bissen: see **bißchen** 2.

bitterlich: see **adverbs formed from adjectives** 3.

blau: For this adj., and esp. its use as a subst., see **colour.** Characteristic uses of the adj. are seen in coll. expressions like **mit blauem Auge davonkommen** ('to get off easily' with little damage or loss)—**blau machen** ('to stay off work') and **einen blauen Montag machen** ('to take a Monday off')—**sein blaues Wunder erleben** ('to get the surprise of one's life')—**einen blauen Brief bekommen** ('to receive an official letter, *esp.* a notice of dismissal').

Bleibe: see **bleiben** 3 (*b*).

bleiben: 1. This verb always takes the aux. **sein.** It is not used, as learners are apt to use it, of 'staying' at a friend's house: one does not say **Ich bin ein paar Wochen bei Freunden geblieben,** but **Ich war...bei Freunden zu Besuch** or **Ich habe mich...bei Freunden aufgehalten.** Where **bleiben** is followed by a pred. noun, this stands in the *nom.* case; the accus. here is only used in dialects, and esp. in LG, in which **Er ist und bleibt ein dummer Kerl** takes the form **Hei is un bliwt en dummen Kirl.** The accus. is possible, however, in the accus. and infin. construction: **Laß mich deinen Freund bleiben! 2. (a)** Where we use a pres. part. after 'to remain', **bleiben** takes a *simple* *infin.*, but this is almost confined to cases where the infin. suggests an attitude (see *b*), in which case it has become a real sep. prefix, as in **Ich entschloß mich, noch ein Stündchen liegenzubleiben** (cf. *c*). Where no attitude is implied, an infin. is only sparingly used as a dependent of **bleiben**: one can say **Wir müssen vorläufig hier noch wohnen bleiben** ('. . . go on living here'), and quite established is **Dieses Gesetz bleibt zu Recht bestehen** ('This law is still in force'); on the other hand, one cannot say **Er blieb lesen** (for **Er las weiter** or **Er fuhr zu lesen fort**), and examples like the following are rather unusual: **Bleib hier warten!** (Blunck)—**Die Offiziere blieben halten** (usually **blieben stehen**—see *b*), **um ihre Zigarren anzuzünden** (Hackländer)—**Katten, sagte sie, wäre ein feiner Name, sie müsse so heißen bleiben** (Voigt-Diederichs: cf. **man müsse sie immer so heißen** or **nennen**); and it is only in poetry that one says **O daß sie ewig grünen bliebe, die schöne Zeit der jungen Liebe!** (Sch.), where in prose one would use the adj. **grün** for the verb **grünen**. (**b**) The following are good examples of the compds. suggesting an attitude, most of which have taken on fig. force: **Sehen Sie sich vor, daß Sie nicht mit dem Ärmel an einem Nagel hängenbleiben!** ('Take care your sleeve doesn't get caught on a nail!')—**Dieser Spitzname wird immer an ihm hängenbleiben** ('This nickname will stick to him all his life')—**Das Unternehmen ist hängengeblieben** ('There is a hitch in the enterprise'); **Dieser Schüler wird wahrscheinlich sitzenbleiben** ('This pupil will probably not get his remove to a higher class')—**Als getanzt wurde, blieb sie sitzen** ('When the dancing began, she did not get a partner, was a wallflower')—**Seine älteste Tochter ist sitzengeblieben** ('His eldest daughter has not found a husband'); **Hoffentlich wird der Schlüssel nicht steckenbleiben** ('It is to be hoped the key won't stick in the lock')—**Er blieb in seiner Rede stecken** ('He broke down in his speech'); **Ruhig stehenbleiben!** ('Stand still!')—**Er blieb plötzlich stehen** ('He suddenly stopped, came to a standstill'). (**c**) In one case, **bleiben** is used with the force of **liegenbleiben**, namely, when it means 'to fall in battle': just as one said in MHG *ahzec sîner degene beliben dâ* ('Eighty of his men fell there'), so one now says **Ewald von Kleist blieb bei Kunersdorf** (which does *not* mean that he 'stayed at Kunersdorf'!). (**d**) For a proposition like 'That remains to be seen', see **infinitive** 3 (*a*). **3.** (*a*) The verbal noun **Bleiben** has a rather limited use. The proposition 'Young people do not like staying at home' might be expressed by **Das Zuhause-Bleiben gefällt jungen Leuten nicht,** and one can say **Das Bleiben hier wird mir unerträglich,** but in either case it would be more natural to use the verb. In the proposition **In Paris hab' ich kein Bleiben** ((Chamisso), where the meaning is 'no home *or* fixed abode', **kein Zuhause** or **keine bleibende Stätte** would be more usual; and a more idiomatic way of expressing **In dem öden Hause war heute kein Bleiben** (Sudermann) would be by the use of the gen. form **Bleibens,** for which see **nichts** 3 and 4, and cf. **Wir müssen scheiden, meine Freunde, Eures Bleibens ist hier nicht länger!** (F. Kugler: 'We must part, my friends, you can't stay here any longer!'). (**b**) The fem. noun **Bleibe** is used chiefly in dialects, and has never become an established expression in the literary lang. *Sprachbrockhaus* defines it as **„Herberge, besonders Nachtlager für Wandernde, Obdach"**: cf. **Er ließ ihnen sagen, sie sollten sehen, wie sie in der Alphütte den Winter überstünden, eine andere Bleibe gäbe es nicht für sie** (Zuckmayer: '. . . there was no other accommodation for them').

bleichen: **1.** The only strong form of this verb still in common use is the past part. with the prefix **ver-** (see 2), *weak* forms being otherwise the rule in modern prose, whether used trans. or intrans.: e.g. **Diese Laken müssen gebleicht werden** ('must be bleached')—**Diese bunten Erlebnisse hatten seine Haare gebleicht** (M. Eyth: 'had turned his hair gray')—**Sie hatte früh gebleichtes Haar** (R. Herzog)—**Muschelschalen bleichten rings auf dem Gerölle** (Carossa: 'Cockleshells were whitening among the rubble all around'). In the intrans. sense of 'to grow pale', the usual expression is **erbleichen** (aux. **sein**): e.g. **Meine Nachbarin erbleichte bis zum Tode** (E. T. A. Hoffmann)—**Er taumelte zurück und erbleichte** (Schaffner) —**Die Heide erbleichte wie im Mondlicht** (Kellermann). **2.** The compd. **verbleichen** is sometimes used like **erbleichen** (see 1), as in **Dieses Haarband ist mit seiner Besitzerin verbleicht** (Novalis) and **Napoleons Glückstern**

verbleichte (Treitschke), but its chief use now is in the strong past part. **verblichen,** meaning 'faded': e.g. **Er trug einen verblichenen Regenmantel** (K. Edschmid)—**An den Wänden begannen die verblichenen Tapeten zu blättern** (C. Rothe: 'The faded wallpaper was beginning to peel off')—**Vielleicht liegen in einem Fach seines Schreibtisches ihre verblichenen Briefe** (Rilke)—fig. **Verblichen und verweht sind längst die Träume** (Heine); cf. **Auf dem Fußboden lag ein ausgebleichter** (better **verblichener**) **Teppich** (Stifter). In formal lang. it is applied to persons in the sense of 'deceased': e.g. **Unter den Hauptleuten des verblichenen Königs** ('of the late king') **war Sforza der angesehenste** (Platen)—**Das Begräbnis fand in der Sophienkirche statt, zu der die Verblichenen gehört hatten** (Ompteda)—**In Einträchtigkeit tranken sie auf das Andenken des Verblichenen** (Bergengruen).

Blick: see **Sicht** 2 (*c*).

blicken: see **look** 1 (*b*).

blinken, blinzeln: see **mit** 2 (*b*).

blush: see **röten** 2.

Blüte: see **Fährte.**

Boden: This masc. noun (plur. sometimes **Boden,** now usually **Böden**), is used in several senses, and although the context will generally make the meaning clear, there are certain cases where it might mean two or even three things (see 4). **1.** Its basic sense is 'ground', the earth's surface: e.g. **Ich schlug ihn zu Boden**—**Sie sank ohnmächtig zu Boden**—**Man hat das alte Gebäude dem Boden gleich gemacht** ('razed to the ground, demolished')—coll. **Dies ist der beste Platz auf Gottes Erdboden** ('on God's earth')—fig. **Er hat hier Boden gefaßt** ('taken root here')—**Wir haben etwas Boden gewonnen** ('gained some ground'). In this sense it is also used of the nature of the soil, as in **lockerer** or **fruchtbarer Boden,** and more generally in expressions like **Hier sind wir auf deutschem Boden,** often **auf deutschem Grund und Boden** ('on German soil'), where **Grund** (q.v.) properly points to the sub-soil, esp. in its capacity to bear the weight of what it supports. **2.** The second meaning is 'bottom', which is the same word, as the orig. MHG form was *bodem*: cf. *buosem* (> **Busen,** 'bosom'), *besem* (> **Besen,** 'besom') and *vadem* (> **Faden,** 'thread', as a measure 'fathom'). The sense of 'bottom' is seen in **Der Boden dieses Fasses** (or **dieser Kiste**) **ist beschädigt**—**Dieser Rohrstuhl bedarf eines neuen Bodens**—**Der Boden des Schiffes ist eingestoßen** ('is stove in'); hence **Fußboden** ('floor', really what is at or below the foot), **Bodensatz** ('sediment') and **bodenlos** ('bottomless'), this last used as an adj.-subst. in an expression like **ins Bodenlose versinken** ('to sink into unfathomable depths *or* the abyss') and as a coll. adj. in **Welch bodenlose Unwissenheit!** ('What crass ignorance!') or **Das ist eine bodenlose Frechheit!** ('That is a piece of consummate cheek!'). **3.** The third meaning is 'loft, attic, garret', the idea being taken from adding an upper storey with a new **Fußboden.** This space under the roof of farmhouses is used esp. for drying clothes in wet weather, for storing grain, etc., hence compds. such as **Kornboden** ('corn-loft, granary'), **Heu-, Trocken-, Vorratsboden,** etc., where the north, however, generally uses the simple **Boden. 4.** It is obvious that, taken out of their context, such expressions may be ambiguous: thus, used of a barrel, **auf den Boden stellen** will generally mean 'to set on end', but it might mean 'to put on the floor' or 'to put in the attic'; and sim. **auf dem Boden schlafen** may mean 'to sleep on the floor' or 'to sleep in the loft'. In such cases it is advisable to use a specific word like **Erdboden** ('ground'), **Fußboden** ('floor'), and to add the adv. **oben** in the case of the 'attic' ('*up* in the attic').

bone: Although this word is now ordinarily rendered by **Knochen,** while **Bein** is specifically used of the *leg* (cf. **Dreibein,** 'three-legged stool'), the latter expression originally had the more comprehensive meaning 'bone': cf. Hartmann's *der lewe az daz rêch unz an diu bein,* i.e. **Der Löwe fraß das Reh bis auf die Knochen.** This earlier meaning is still in common use in one or two set phrases (e.g. **Fleisch und Bein**—**Der Schrei ging mir durch Mark und Bein,** '. . . to the very marrow of my bones'), and in certain specific compounds (**Brustbein,** 'breast-bone'—**Hüftbein,** 'hip-bone'—**Schienbein,** 'shin-bone'—**Schlüsselbein,** 'collar-bone'—**Elfenbein,** a corruption of **Elefantenbein,** 'ivory'); cf. the choice collective **Gebein(e),** as in **Angst durchlief die zitternden Gebeine** (Sch.) and **Auf gräßlichen Altären dorret menschliches Gebein** (id.: 'skeletons'). The fundamental idea of *hardness* has suggested the combination **Stein und Bein,** used in a few idiomatic expressions: e.g. **Es friert Stein und Bein** ('It is freezing hard')—**Er schwur Stein und Bein, daß er nichts davon wisse** ('He swore by all that he held sacred that he knew nothing about it').

borgen: 1. Although both **borgen** and **leihen** can be used of giving as well as of receiving on loan, it is, on the whole, advisable to use **borgen** with the force of receiving, and **leihen** with that of giving: cf. **Ich habe mir das Buch aus der Leihbibliothek geborgt.** The verb **leihen** is a rather more select word and hence is always used fig. in expressions like **jemandem sein Ohr** or **seine Aufmerksamkeit leihen** ('to lend one's ear, pay attention to somebody'); cf. **Lord Burleigh leiht dem Gerichte, dem er den Geist geliehn, nun auch den Mund** (Sch.). **2.** (**a**) The compd. **verleihen** is sometimes used in the sense of 'to lend out', as in **Ich habe das Buch an einen Freund verliehen,** but its more usual meaning now is 'to bestow, confer' (titles, decorations, degrees, etc.): e.g. **Man hat ihm den Titel Geheimrat** (or **eines Geheimen Rats**) **verliehen—Seine alte Universität hat ihm den Ehrengrad eines Magisters der freien Künste** ('the honorary degree of M.A.') **verliehen—Der Orden des Eisernen Kreuzes ist ihm verliehen worden**; also fig., as in **Die Anwesenheit der Königin verlieh den Edinburger Festspielen einen besonderen Glanz.** (**b**) The verb **entlehnen** is used esp. of 'borrowing' from an author, as in **Dieser Ausdruck ist (aus) Goethes „Faust" entlehnt.**

box: 1. The expression with the most general application is **Kasten,** a receptacle, not necessarily made of wood, usually serving a specific purpose and hence common in compds: e.g. **Briefkasten, Baukasten** (a child's box of bricks), **Leierkasten** (= **Drehorgel,** 'barrel-organ'), **Malkasten** ('paint-box'), **Schieb-** or **Schubkasten** (a 'drawer' in a table or chest of drawers: cf. 3). In familiar language **Kasten** is used contemptuously of an old building: originally, no doubt, a building erected out of boards—a wooden booth, log-cabin—it is now used quite generally of a large, rambling, old house. **2. Kiste** is really a special kind of **Kasten,** made of wooden boards, usually with a lid for nailing down, a 'packing-case', large or small: the commonest compds. are **Waren-, Bücher-, Zigarrenkiste.** A favourite combination is **Kisten und Kasten,** for all manner of boxes: e.g. **Die Familie war eben erst in das Haus gezogen, Kisten und Kasten standen umher. 3. Lade** was originally also a receptacle made of boards (MHG *lāde* was a 'board, plank') but is now used esp. of a solid wooden box with a hinged lid and lock, a wooden trunk or chest. It was regularly used of the chests in which the old guilds kept their precious documents, etc., and still suggests security. A common compd. is **Schieb-** or **Schublade,** an alternative expression for **Schiebkasten** (see 1): cf. **Er steht am Ladentisch** ('at the counter') **und mustert die Laden und Fächer, die Schachteln und Dosen** (Waggerl). **Truhe** is really the South German expression for **Lade,** and generally suggests a solid wooden chest, often elaborately carved. **5. Schachtel** is a small **Kasten** of a more fragile kind, most frequently a 'cardboard box' (**Pappschachtel**); cf. the familiar expression **alte Schachtel** ('old woman, old maid, hag'). **6. Büchse,** properly a cylindrical receptacle (originally made of *box*wood), is now used in a more general way, but particularly with the force of a 'tin can': cf. **Sparbüchse** (a child's 'money-box') and **Büchsenfleisch** ('tinned meat'). The original cylindrical shape is still seen in the other common modern sense of 'rifle' (from the shape of the barrel): e.g. **Mit der Büchse trifft er** (*scil.* Egmont) **erst, wie keiner in der Welt** (G.). **7. Dose** is usually smaller still, being specifically used for **Schnupftabaksdose** ('snuff-box').

boy: 1. The word **Knabe** is now comparatively little used in every-day lang.: in N and CG, a father says **„Ich habe einen Jungen und zwei Mädchen."** **Knabe** is not only a more select expression but is used in statistics distinguishing between the sexes, in a few compds. like **Knabenschule, -anzug, Chorknabe, Musterknabe,** etc., and in a playful way in the phrase **ein alter Knabe**; but **Junge** is the more general expression in ordinary independent use, as well as in compds. like **Bauernjunge** or **Gassenjunge** ('street arab'), where **-knabe** would sound ridiculous to a German ear. With regard to **Junge,** it should be noted that, although originally an adj.-subst., it is now a real weak noun; the adj.-subst. is only used of the young of animals, as in

In dem Nest ist nur ein Junges—Die Schwalbe hat vier Junge (not **Jungen**) **ausgebrütet.** The ordinary plur. ('boys') is **Jungen,** but the LG plur. form **Jungens** (see **Fräulein**) is now quite common, not only in the north, esp. in addressing sons of the family, while the contracted plur. **Jungs** corresponds to our 'boys' in the navy. **2. Bube** is the SG equivalent of **Junge:** in the south a father would say **„Ich habe einen Buben und zwei Mädel".** In this sense the nom. form **Bub** is to be preferred, as **Bube** ever since the Middle Ages has come to be used as an abusive epithet, much like **Schurke** ('scoundrel'), as one speaks of **ein böser** or **loser Bube;** cf. **Wenn ich Bube genug gewesen, sie zu ermorden . . .** (Sch.: 'If I had been blackguard enough to murder her. . .'); and sim. **bübisch** ('villainous')—**Bubenstück** or **Bubenstreich** ('knavish trick'). **Bube** is also regularly used of the 'knave' in a pack of cards. **3. Bursch** is a 'young fellow'. As in the case of **Bube,** the addition of a final **-e** here often gives the expression a different shade of meaning, generally implying a lower rank or inferior station: a **Bursche** is an officer's 'batman', a **Laufbursche** is a 'messenger-boy' or 'printer's devil'. In student slang, a **Bursch** is a student of later years, as distinct from a **krasser Fuchs** ('fresher').

braten: This verb is normally *strong,* being one of the **reduplicating verbs** (q.v.), but weak forms crept in during the 18th cent., esp. in the past tense, while the past part. resisted any such 'weakening'. But although **er bratet** and **bratete** were sometimes used in the classical period, and occasionally even later, as in **Sie fingen Fische in den Bächen und brateten sich dieselben an einem Feuer, das sie angelegt hatten** (Stifter), these weak forms should *not* be used, but only **er brät, briet, hat gebraten.**

Brauch: see **custom(ary)** 3.

brauchen: 1. Although **mißbrauchen** (see **miß-** 3 *a*) implies 'misuse', the simple verb should not be used in good prose for **gebrauchen** ('to use'): it is mainly in poetry and spoken dialects that it has this force: cf. **Bist du nicht willig, so brauch' ich Gewalt** (G.)—**Der Lehrer brauchte den Stock** (Jung-Stilling)—**Er brauchte derbe Ausdrücke** (Gutzkow). **2.** (**a**) In standard prose it now means 'to need, require', taking an *accus.* or (in poetry and choice prose) a ***gen.*** (cf. **bedürfen**): e.g. **Ich brauche deines Beistandes** (Sch.); cf., in the impers. use, **Was braucht es zur heutigen Kunst noch eines Menschen von Fleisch und Blut?** (C. Hauptmann)—**Es brauchte langen Zuredens, ehe sie zu antworten vermochte** (H. Leip). (**b**) With a following infin. ('to require' to do something), the best prose usage is **Er braucht es nicht zu tun,** although the omission of **zu,** on the analogy of **müssen,** is common in everyday speech—esp., but not only, in the south: cf. **Es kam die Zeit, da sie sich nicht mehr verbergen brauchten** (Fr. Griese)—**Hättest du mehr gelernt, du brauchtest dich nicht durch das Leben schwindeln!** (F. v. Zobeltitz). The only case in which **zu** is generally dropped is where the infin. **brauchen** is itself preceded by **zu;** cf. the following two examples: **Wenn wir direkt im Auto fahren, brauchen wir den langen Umweg über Berlin nicht zu machen** ('If we go direct by car, we don't need to make the long detour via Berlin') and **Der neue direkte Weg ermöglicht es uns** (or **setzt uns instand**), **unser Ziel zu erreichen, ohne über Berlin fahren zu brauchen** ('The new direct road enables us to reach our destination without requiring to go via Berlin'). In this last example, **zu fahren zu brauchen** would sound very harsh, as the similar wording does in **Man lachte, um nicht zu weinen zu brauchen** (Gutzkow); and **zu** is rightly omitted for the sake of euphony in **Man brauchte sich nicht viel Mühe geben** (better than **zu geben**), **den Leutnant zu Gesicht zu bekommen, denn er ging viel spazieren** (Speckmann). (**c**) In a compound tense with a dependent infin., **brauchen** has the same peculiarity as the **modal auxiliary verbs** (q.v.), etc., in that the past part. far more commonly assumes the form of the *infin.*: e.g. **Sie hätte es nie zu erfahren brauchen** (Gutzkow)—**Entdeckungsfahrten nach guten Menschen habe ich nie zu machen brauchen: sie sind mir von selbst in den Weg gelaufen** (Speckmann)—**Man kann nur wünschen, daß Cato nicht geboren worden wäre, so hätte er auch nicht zu sterben brauchen** (Klabund, in a scathing criticism of Gottsched's tragedy **„Der sterbende Cato"**)—**Wenn ich das gewußt hätte, hätte ich mich nicht so zu eilen brauchen** (Zuckmayer)—**Niemand hätte ihn damals**

hindern können, das Haus zu mieten: er hätte niemandes Erlaubnis einzuholen brauchen (K. Edschmid)—**Auf diese Weise hatte sie mit den ihren nicht zu hungern brauchen** (W. Kramp). Much less common here is the reg. past part. form: cf. **Die Leute hatten nur ihre herkömmliche Sonntagstracht anzulegen gebraucht, um malerisch auszusehen** (G. Keller)—**Ich hätte mich nicht zu beeilen gebraucht** (M. Eyth).

braun: see **colour.**

brennen: This represents two verbs which were orig. clearly distinguished, viz. MGH *brinnen* (intrans., strong) and its causative *brennen* (trans., weak). The modern forms are firmly established: whether trans. or intrans. they are **brennen, brannte, gebrannt.** For **Es war mir, als ob etwas im Hause brennte,** see **past subjunctive** I (*b*). Actually, the forms **brannte** and **gebrannt** show the orig. stem-vowel, the infin. of the Goth. trans. verb being *brannjan*, past tense *brannida*. Naturally, the *i* here was more apt to be elided than the *j*, and when the *i* was dropped, there was no feeling that it had ever been there, so that the *a* was not 'mutated' to *e* (see **Umlaut**); but the *j* persisted and caused the 'mutation'. The same applies to other verbs of this class, e.g. **kennen, nennen** and **rennen,** and also to **senden** and **wenden** (< Goth. *sandjan, wandjan*), and the *i* in the past tenses of these words (*sandida, wandida*) naturally resented elision, so that the mutated forms **sendete, wendete** still exist side by side with the commoner forms **sandte, wandte.**

Bruch: Distinguish between **der Bruch** ('break, breach, fracture, fraction') with plur. **Brüche,** and **der** or (more commonly) **das Bruch** ('marshland, bog, swamp') with plur. **Brüche** (masc.) or **Brücher** (neut.): cf. **Geht, Kinder, nicht zu weit ins Bruch!** (Droste-Hülshoff)—**Das Oderbruch wurde urbar gemacht** (Bruno Frank), referring to a wide stretch of low-lying ground along the river Oder north of Frankfurt.

Bube: see **boy** 2.

Buch: In the sense of 'book', this neut. noun has the plur. **Bücher,** but in that of a 'quire' of paper it remains uninflected in the plur.: e.g. **Heute ist eine Bestellung auf zehn Buch Papier eingelaufen** ('An order for ten quires of paper has come to hand today')—**Wir werden mit zwei Buch auskommen** ('We shall manage with two quires'). The same applies to **Ries** (q.v.).

Büchse: see **box** 6.

Buckel: This noun, which incidentally is usually pronounced with an initial *p*-sound, esp. in the north, has two genders. As a *masc.*, with plur. unchanged, it has the same force as **Höcker,** meaning 'hump', e.g. a camel's or a hunchback's, and is often used in coll. speech of a person's 'back', as in **Er hat einen breiten Buckel,** like our 'He has broad shoulders' (used esp. of some one whom one can saddle with all manner of jobs), and **Ich lachte mir einen Buckel** ('I split my sides, nearly doubled up with laughter'); also in vulgar expressions like **Du kannst mir den Buckel 'runterrutschen!** ('Go and be hanged!'). Another meaning is 'knob', like the 'boss' in the centre of a shield, and in this sense it is more usually *fem.*, with plur. **Buckeln.** One must beware of using **Buckel** to render our 'buckle', the German for which is **Schnalle.**

Bund: Distinguish between **der Bund** ('alliance, league') of which the plur. **Bünde** is now usually replaced by **Bündnisse,** and **das Bund** ('bundle, truss'), with plur. **Bunde** or (as a measure) **Bund,** as in **drei Bund Heu** (see **nouns of measure** I). Some confusion seems to have arisen in compds.: thus, in the case of **Ausbund,** meaning 'pattern, model' but now used mainly in expressions like **ein Ausbund von Schönheit, von Häßlichkeit, von Gelehrsamkeit** (respectively a 'paragon' of beauty, the 'quintessence' of ugliness, a 'prodigy' of learning), *Duden* gives the plur. as **Ausbünde** in the north and **Ausbunde** in Austria, while *Sanders* says **„Mehrzahl in der Regel ohne Umlaut",** citing **einige Ausbunde von Übermut** (Eckermann) and **Ausbunde von Liederlichkeit** (Prutz), and *Sprach-Brockhaus* gives only **Ausbünde.** On the other hand, *Duden* allows either **der** or **das Schlüsselbund** ('bunch of keys'), with plur. **Schlüsselbunde:** cf. **Sie fühlte mit der Hand in die Tasche: das Schlüsselbund fand sich an Ort und Stelle** (Musäus).

Bündel: Until recent times this noun was either masc. or neut.: in one of Goethe's poems there occur the two lines **Ihn hat jener Schalk betrogen und ihm den Bündel abgepackt,** while the same poem introduced into his *Wilhelm Meisters Wanderjahre* reads **das Bündel.** In spite of examples like **Was er für einen Bündel angesehen hatte, war ein weißes Tuch**

(Stifter), the neut. has now practically dislodged the masc., which *Duden* no longer allows: cf. the common coll. expression **sein** (not **seinen**) **Bündel schnüren** ('to pack up and go') and **Heut' knüpfe ich mein Bündel und scheide** (Freytag).

Bürde: see **load** (noun) 1.

Bursche: see **boy** 3; cf. **Frauenzimmer** *ad fin.*

C

cause: see **lassen** 3 (*a*) and **veranlassen; Grund** 2.

certain: see **gewiß.**

change: The first step towards determining the correct expression for 'to change' in a given context is to decide to which of two groups of verbs it belongs: the one group implying an *alteration*, the other an *exchange*. **1.** The first group comprises esp. two verbs and their compds., viz. **ändern** and **wandeln.** (**a**) The simple verb **ändern** (trans.) suggests a change in a general way, without any indication of its degree or extent: e.g. **Ich habe meine Meinung geändert—Das ändert nichts an der Sache** ('That does not alter the case'). A partial, usually slight change, a 'modification', is implied in **abändern,** the change being properly effected by taking *off* or *away* (**ab-**) what is imperfect: e.g. **Den Anfang des Briefes muß ich noch abändern—In diesem Takt hat man die Klavierbegleitung etwas abgeändert** ('In this bar the piano accompaniment has been slightly altered'). A more thorough, but not necessarily radical change is suggested by **verändern,** esp. common as a reflex. with intrans. force: e.g. **Seit dem Kriege hat sich die Stadt sehr verändert—Er hat sich zu seinem Vorteil verändert** ('He has changed for the better'); and much the same is conveyed by **umändern,** pointing esp. to the resultant state: **Wir haben unsere kleine Wohnstube in ein Fremdenzimmer umgeändert** ('We have converted our small sitting-room into a spare bedroom'). The same shades of meaning are implied in the derivatives **Änderung, Abänderung, veränderlich,** etc. (**b**) With the force of 'to change', the simple verb **wandeln** is now little used in prose, but two of its compds. are in common use, esp. **verwandeln,** implying a radical change, a transformation into something essentially different, less commonly **u'mwandeln** (sep.), suggesting the result of such a radical change (to be distinguished from the insep. **umwa'ndeln,** 'to walk round' a given space: see **wandeln**): e.g. **Die Szene verwandelt sich** ('The scene changes')—**Die Stadt hat sich verwandelt, man kennt sie kaum wieder—Jupiter verwandelte sich in einen Schwan** (or **wandelte sich in einen Schwan um**)—**Er ist wie verwandelt** ('He's a different man') —**Das Progymnasium ist in eine höhere Bürgerschule umgewandelt** (H. Allmers). Sim. the nouns **Ver-, Umwandlung. 2.** To the second group belong esp. **wechseln** and **tauschen.** (**a**) The former, **wechseln,** properly suggests that something does not remain the same (cf. **Witterungswechsel,** 'a change in the weather'), but this naturally leads to the idea of an *exchange*, one thing being replaced by or substituted for another: e.g. **Ich bin durchnäßt, ich muß die Kleider wechseln** (= **ich muß mich umziehen:** see 3)—**Seit ich ihn zuletzt sah, hat er seinen Wohnsitz gewechselt** (i.e. removed to new quarters)—**Wir wechseln regelmäßig Briefe** (= **stehen in regelmäßigem Briefwechsel**)—**Können Sie diesen Bankschein wechseln?** ('Can you change this banknote?')—**Ich muß dieses Markstück gegen** (or **für**) **Kleingeld wechseln** ('get small change for this shilling'); cf. **Meine Stimme hatte, schon bevor ich sie wechselte** (= **ehe sie sich brach,** 'before it broke': cf. 3), **etwas Schmeichelhaftes für das Ohr** (Th. Mann). Here belong the various compds., viz. **umwechseln,** again pointing to the resultant state, **aus-** and **einwechseln,** the former's obj. being what is *given*, the latter's what is *received* in exchange: e.g. **Ich habe eben mein Buch in der Leihbibliothek umgewechselt—Man wechselte die Gefangenen gegen ein hohes Lösegeld aus** ('The prisoners were handed over for a heavy ransom')—**Einige Teile der Maschine müssen jährlich ausgewechselt werden** (the worn parts being replaced by new ones)—**Ich ließ mir Gold für Silber einwechseln** ('I got my banker to give me gold for silver'); in familiar speech **ausgewechselt** is used of persons, like **verwandelt,** as in **Das Mädchen ist wie ausgewechselt** ('She is not the same girl'). Esp. noteworthy are **abwechseln,** usually intrans. implying alternating acts, periodicity, and **verwechseln** (cf. **vertauschen,** see 3), now always in the sense of 'to mistake' one thing for another, 'to confuse' them: e.g. **Ebbe und Flut wechseln regelmäßig ab** ('The tides alternate regularly')—**In diesem Werk wechseln Prosa und Verse ab—Wir wechselten im Vorlesen miteinander ab** ('We read aloud in turn')—**Ich verwechsele immer diese zwei Namen—Sie sind sich** (dat.) **zum Verwechseln ähnlich** ('They are so like each other that you cannot tell which is which')—**Ich glaube, Sie verwechseln mich mit meinem Bruder.** So also **Zur Abwechselung werde ich heute zu Fuß gehen** ('I'm going to walk today for a change')—**In dem Einerlei des täglichen Lebens muß man ab und zu eine kleine Abwechselung haben** ('In the monotony of daily life one must now and then have a little relaxation')—**Verwechselung dieser zwei Namen ist leicht.** (**b**) Analogous is **tauschen,** which stresses the idea of giving and receiving (cf. **Tauschhandel,** 'barter'). If I get wet and 'change' into dry clothes, that is **die Kleider wechseln,** whereas if two people exchange their clothes, each wearing the other's, that is **die Kleider tauschen.** This idea is emphasized by **austauschen,** esp. with objs. like **Ansichten, Grüße, Glückwünsche,** etc. (cf. **Studentenaustausch,** an 'exchange of students' between universities or countries). The compd. **vertauschen,** while it may have much the same force as the simple verb, as in **Die zwei Schauspieler haben ihre Rollen vertauscht** (cf. our slang 'to swop') and **Er hatte den preußischen mit dem türkischen Dienst vertauscht** (R. Herzog: i.e. had left the Prussian army and joined the Turkish), may also be an alternative expression for **verwechseln,** implying an accidental or deliberate mistake, but in this sense it is only used of things: e.g. **Verzeihung, ich glaube, wir haben unsere Hüte vertauscht!—Ich scheine meinen Schirm mit dem eines anderen vertauscht zu haben;** but **Ich verwechsele** (not **vertausche**) **immer diese zwei Zwillinge. 3.** Other verbs suggesting a change are: **u'mschlagen** (sep., intrans.), used esp. of a sudden change, e.g. in the weather (**Das Wetter ist umgeschlagen**), but also of a voice 'breaking' (**Der Junge ist fast erwachsen, seine Stimme schlägt um**; cf. the example from Th. Mann given under 2 *a* above), and often of moods, feelings, etc.: **Das Mädchen ist unbeständig, ihre Laune schlägt oft um—Jetzt geschah es, daß meine Unruhe plötzlich in einen eiskalten Schrecken umschlug** (Bergengruen)—**Es gibt Menschen, denen jede Dummheit, die sie begehen, in einen Glücksfall umschlägt** (R. Herzog: 'Some people's follies turn out to be lucky strokes'); **u'msteigen,** 'to change' into another train, bus, etc. (**Dieser Zug geht nicht nach Aachen durch, Sie müssen in Köln umsteigen**); **sich umsetzen,** mainly used of a chemical change (**Tut man Schwefelsäure hinzu, so setzt sich das Stärkemehl in Zucker um,** 'By the addition of sulphuric acid the starch is converted into sugar'); **sich umkleiden** or **umziehen** (q.v.), 'to change' into other clothes, usually of a complete change: 'to change one's jacket' is **eine andere Jacke anziehen.**

Chor: This noun is used both in the sense of 'choir, chorus' (of singers and actors), more generally 'band, troop', and in that of the 'choir' as distinct from the 'nave' (**Schiff**) of a church. Its gender fluctuates between masc. and neut., and it is significant that one of the stage-directions in the little play which G. wrote for the inauguration of the theatre in Halle in 1814 has **Der Chor tritt vor,** while the next one, a few lines later, has **Das Chor hat sich geteilt**; and elsewhere G. says **Das unsichtbare Chor fiel in die letzten Worte ein** ('. . . joined in on the last words'). But according to modern practice **der Chor** (plur. **Chöre**) is used, esp. in a good sense, of the singers or of what they sing, and **das Chor** in the depreciatory sense of a disorderly 'band, gang, horde' (*Duden* gives **ein gräßliches Chor,** adding **besonders Kinder**), while **der** or (rather more commonly) **das Chor** suggests the part of a church (plur. **Chore** or **Chöre**): cf., on the one hand, **Das Geläute ruft mich in das Chor** (Chamisso)—**Das Chor ist der wichtigste Teil eines Kirchengebäudes** (Brockhaus); and on the other hand, **Der** (usually **Das**) **Kirchenchor brach ein** ('collapsed') **und einige stürzten in das Schiff** (Gutzkow).

climb: 1. *Intrans.*: (a) The word with the widest application is **steigen** ('to ascend'): e.g. **Als ich auf** (or **in**) **den Baum gestiegen war, sah ich einen Vogel in die Luft steigen—Eine Rauchwolke stieg in die Höhe—Das Barometer steigt** (or **ist im Steigen begriffen**)—**Die Preise der Lebensmittel steigen immer höher**; cf. the coll. expression **Meine Haare stiegen zu Berge** ('My hair stood on end'). But **steigen** may also convey the very opposite idea, although here, apart from its association with the prep. **von** (as in **vom Throne steigen**), a prefix like **hinunter-** must be added, esp. in connexion with an adv. accus.: **Wir sind den Berg hinauf-, hinuntergestiegen.** Where we say 'The road began to ascend gradually', a German says **Der Weg begann anzusteigen.** (b) But the ordinary expression used of people climbing is **klettern,** while **klimmen** (orig. strong, now not infrequently weak) is a more choice expression and generally implies a more arduous ascent: e.g. **Ich begann zu frieren, stand auf und klomm von Stufe zu Stufe treppauf** (A. Schaeffer) —**An den Schultern des alten Riesen klimmten sie hinunter** (Novalis)—**Ich klimmte nach dem Orte, den mir der Treiber wies** (Immermann). **2.** *Trans.* (a) 'To climb a mountain' does not necessarily imply that the summit is reached, and here one must distinguish in German between the prefixes **be-** and **er-** (qq.v.): the former merely brings the action of climbing to bear on some object (a hill, ladder, stair, etc.), while the latter implies that the top is reached: cf. **Wir fingen an, den Berg zu besteigen** and **Es gelang uns, den Berg zu ersteigen**; sim. **Wir bestiegen den Rigi . . . Ein Viertel nach zwei hatten wir die Höhe erstiegen** (G.). In this connexion, it is strange that although **klettern** and **besteigen** are every-day expressions, and **erklettern** and even **erklimmen** are by no means rare, **beklettern** is hardly used at all. Thus, whereas a proposition like **Seit so viel Jahren wurde Fels um Fels beklettert** (G.) is now rather unusual, the following examples are quite common: **Es war der Mühe wert, diese Berghöhen zu erklettern** (G.)—**Er ging durch die Stadt, in deren älterem Teil er vier Treppen eines Hauses erkletterte** (A. Schaeffer)—**Den steilsten, zickzack über Felsen springenden Stieg erklommen wir langsam** (G.)—**Die Gesellschaft kletterte den Berg hinan, und einige der Gewandtesten erklommen auch den höchsten Gipfel** (Eberhard)—**Das müde Pferd erklimmte die Anhöhe** (Gutzkow). (b) But 'to climb a wall' may mean to climb either *on to* or *over* the wall. In the latter case it is necessary to use either an appropriate prep. phrase or a verb compounded with the *insep. unaccented* prefix **über-**, and here again **überstei'gen** (q.v.) is not only more common than **überkle'ttern,** but is obligatory in a fig. sense: e.g. **Um das Haus zu erreichen, mußten wir über eine hohe Mauer klettern** (or **steigen**)—**Wir mußten eine hohe Mauer überstei'gen—Wilde, steinige Höhen mußten überstie'gen werden** (G.)—**Er sagte, wir hätten einen beschwerlichen Weg vor uns, weil wir einen vorgeschobenen Gebirgsriegel mühsam überkle'ttern würden** (G.): 'as we would be climbing over a projecting mountain ridge')—**Als die Flüchtlinge die Mauer überkle'tterten, hörten sie einen Schrei** (P. Ernst)—**Ich hatte den Zaun überkle'ttert und fand mich nun auf der Landstraße** (A. Schaeffer); on the other hand, **Was er mir zumutete, überstie'g** (not **überkletterte**) **meine Kräfte** ('What he expected of me was beyond my strength')—**Das überstei'gt alles!** ('That beats all!').

clothes: 1. The fem. noun **Kleidung** has only collective force, indicating everything put on as a covering of the body; a single garment is **Kleidungstück. 2.** The neut. noun **Kleid** properly denotes only part of **Kleidung,** as seen in compds. like **Unterkleid** ('petticoat') and **Beinkleid** ('knickers, drawers'); the plur. **Beinkleider** is a more select expression for **Hose(n)** ('trousers'). But **Kleid** has come to be used specifically for a lady's 'frock': cf. compds. like **Ausgehkleid** ('outdoor costume') and **Gesellschaftskleid** ('evening frock'); and sim. **Ball-, Hochzeits-, Morgen-, Sportkleid.** The plur. **Kleider,** however, has become the every-day expression for 'clothes' in general, used for wearing purposes. **3.** The masc. noun **Anzug,** on the other hand, is used esp. of a man's 'suit': cf. **Gesellschaftsanzug** (= **Frack,** 'evening dress', whereas a 'frock-coat' is **Gehrock**), **Sakkoanzug** ('lounge suit'), **Schlafanzug** ('pyjamas'), **Badeanzug,** etc. **4.** The neut. noun **Gewand** (plur. **Gewänder,** in poet. lang.

often **Gewande**) was orig. cloth for *winding* round the body (cf. **Leinwand** q.v.); it is now a choice expression suggesting esp. a wide flowing gown or a ceremonious robe: e.g. **Sie waren in schleppende Gewande gehüllt** (Mörike); cf. compds. like **Meßgewand** ('stole, vestment'), **Staatsgewänder** ('robes of state, gala-dress'), etc. **5.** The fem. noun **Tracht** (q.v. I), when used with reference to garments, has *rel.* force, suggesting clothes as indicative of the wearer's status, rank, office, nationality, etc.: cf. compds. like **Amtstracht** ('official robes'), **Bauerntracht** ('peasant's costume'), **Matrosen-, Schüler-, Witwentracht**, etc.; so also the 'kilt' is **die schottische Nationaltracht. 6.** When the reference is to articles which are washed or laundered, as when we talk of 'washing the clothes' or 'hanging out the clothes', the collective sing. **Wäsche** is used: e.g. **schmutzige Wäsche** ('soiled linen')—**die Wäsche zum Trocknen aufhängen. 7.** The MHG *wât* (= **Kleidung**: cf. our 'widow's *weeds*' and Scott's 'Her upper garment was of a coarse stuff called *wad*mal, then much used in the Zetland Islands') is quite obs. in prose, and rare even in poetry: in his ballad **Klein Roland**, Uhland represents the boys whom his shabbily-dressed hero had fought and overcome as bringing him, by way of tribute, **vierfältig Tuch zur Wat**, i.e. cloth in four colours with which to make himself a suit.

collect: see **sammeln**.

colour (words denoting): **1.** See **adjectives (indeclinable)** I and **adjectives (uninflected)** 4. While **Bläue, Röte** and **Schwärze** are real fem. nouns, e.g. **Himmelsbläue, Abendröte, Druckerschwärze** ('printer's ink'), etc., nouns denoting colour are usually expressed by the adjs. written with capitals. These are for the most part left uninflected, esp. those ending in a sibilant (**Weiß, Schwarz**). In the *gen.*, words like **Blau, Gelb, Grün** and **Rot** can take **-s**, as in an expression like **die Pracht des feurigen Rots** (Schücking); indeed, this is imperative if there is no word to show the gen. case, as in **Hier ist der Gebrauch Berliner Blaus** ('Prussian blue') **zu empfehlen.** The *plur.* of such words is generally avoided; when used, it is again usually left uninflected, as in **zwei Eiweiß** ('the whites of two eggs') and in the following reference to a corpse lying in state: **Das Weiß des Kamisols und das Karmesin vom Mantel sonderten sich schroff ab zwischen den beiden Schwarz von Baldachin und Lager** (Rilke). Unorthodox is a plur. in **-s**, as in **Rot dunkelte fast zu Schwarz, und alle Grüns nahmen eine bräunliche Färbung an** (id.). Here one would ordinarily say . . . **alles Grüne nahm eine bräunliche Färbung an**, and this use of the adj.-subst. (**das Blaue**, gen. **des Blauen**) is esp. common after a prep., notably **in**: e.g., on the one hand (*uninflected*), **Frauen und Mädchen zeigten eine farbenprächtige Nationaltracht: das brennende Rot ihrer Kleider, das Blau und Weiß ihrer Tücher glänzte zwischen dem Grün der Bäume hervor** (Roquette)—**Die Bäume schmückten sich mit Dolden: über all dem frischen Grün, dem reinen Weiß und satten Gelb wölbte sich der blaue Himmel** (Frenssen)—**Im Zimmer hatten sich die Farben verwandelt: Blau in schimmeliges Grün, Grün in Grau, und Gelb in ein abgestandenes Weiß** (Rilke); on the other hand (*inflected*), **Das Blaue steigerte sich ins Rote** (G.)—**Die Schwärze ihres Haares spielte ins Blaue** (Kinkel: or **hatte einen Stich ins Blaue**, 'took on a touch of blue')—**Er tat einen Schuß ins Blaue** ('He took a random shot')—**Morgen machen wir eine Fahrt ins Grüne** ('a trip into the country'; cf. **eine Fahrt ins Blaue**, 'a mystery tour' to an unspecified destination)—**Ich streckte mich ins Grüne** ('I lay down on the grass')—**Er hat zweimal ins Schwarze getroffen** ('He has scored two bull's-eyes'). **2.** The following are a few special cases: **Soll ich den Schwarzen oder den Braunen reiten?** ('Shall I ride the black or the bay?')—**Er ist ein Roter** ('a radical')—**Er schwatzt das Blaue vom Himmel herunter** (coll. 'He talks nineteen to the dozen')—**„Kellner, eine Berliner Weiße!"** (i.e. a glass of Berlin **„Weißbier"**, jocularly called **eine Blonde**)—**Ich werde bei Mutter Grün schlafen** (coll. 'I'll spend the night in the open')—**Ich hätte Grün oder Rot angespielt** ('I would have led spades or hearts': spades were green leaves in old German cards)—**Weiß zieht immer an** ('White always makes the first move' in chess).

comfortable: **1.** The adj. **bequem** properly means 'convenient, suitable': cf. **Ein Handkoffer ist bequem zu tragen** ('convenient *or* easy to carry')—**Man sah nicht, daß das meiste** (*scil.* **von dem, was der Sender übertrug**) **reine Lüge war: es**

war bequemer, es nicht zu sehen (K. Edschmid: 'People did not see that the most of the broadcast was a pack of lies: it was more convenient, less bother, not to see it'); and sim. **eine bequeme Ausrede** or **Entschuldigung** ('a convenient excuse'). Hence it suggests a source of bodily ease and comfort, e.g. **ein bequemer Lehnstuhl**; and so also a table is **bequem** if it is of a suitable height, convenient for sitting at, a footpath is **bequem** if it is level or gently undulating, a suit of clothes is **bequem** if it 'sits comfortably'; and so also **es sich** (dat.) **bequem machen** is 'to make oneself comfortable'. Applied to a person, it means 'easy-going, free and easy', often implying indolence, and hence it is also used of a person's bearing, manners, etc., and the following two examples bring out the contrast between an easy, relaxed posture and one in which one observes a certain deportment: **Ich bin der Meinung, daß es nicht erlaubt ist, sich gehen zu lassen und es sich bequem zu machen, sondern daß es unter allen Umständen geboten ist, Haltung zu bewahren** (Th. Mann)—**Aufrecht, in beherrschter Haltung und ohne sich bequeme Abspannung zu erlauben, saß er am Tisch** (id.). Incidentally, the Fr. *léger* has been taken over into German and is often used coll. to express this idea of informality, lack of ceremony, as in **Er hat bequeme** or **legere Manieren**, where **legere** is trisyllabic, pronounced as in Fr., but with the German inflexional ending added. **2.** A room may have **bequeme Möbel**, and yet not be 'comfortable': one need only compare a stiff Victorian 'drawing-room' with a cheerful modern 'lounge' to realize that the latter suggestive expression implies a certain warmth of welcome, a cosy atmosphere, which the former lacks. Such a room is more than **bequem**, it is **behaglich**, implying an absence of formality and stiffness, a free and easy atmosphere, and suggests warmth, friendly social intercourse and companionship. This adj., in fact, approaches **traulich**, which implies intimacy: cf. **eine trauliche Ecke** ('a cosy corner'), **ein trauliches Plauderstündchen** ('an hour's intimate chat'), etc. **3.** A step farther is implicit in **gemütlich**, of which there is no exact single equivalent in English. It implies qualities which affect one's whole being—mind, heart and soul—put one at one's ease and in a good mood, and make one feel jolly and entertain warm feelings towards one's fellow men. It follows that one cannot say **ein gemütlicher Lehnstuhl**, but one can speak of **eine gemütliche Gesellschaft, ein gemütlicher Abend**, etc.; cf. the coll. **Er ist ein gemütliches Haus** ('He 's a jolly, sociable fellow').

common: see **gemein.**

conceal: see **bergen.**

concessive clauses: A concessive clause may, of course, be a princ. one, as in 'I admit that you did it with the best intentions, but . . .', and to express this in German presents little difficulty: **Ich gebe** or **gestehe zu** (or simply **Zugegeben** or **Zugestanden**), **daß Sie es in bester Absicht getan haben, aber...** But this idea can be expressed equally well by dropping 'I admit that' and inserting a concessive *adv.* in the 'that'-clause: 'You doubtless did it . . ., but . . .', and there are several German advs. which are used in this way: see **allerdings** 1 (*b*), **freilich** 3, and **zwar** 1; cf. also **auch** 4, **immer** 3, and **schon** 2 (*c*). Otherwise the concessive clause is a subord. one, introduced by a *conj.*, for which see **ob** 2 (*c*), **obgleich** and **trotz** 2. For other idiomatic ways of expressing such clauses, see **so** 3 and **wie** 2 (*a*): e.g. **So gern sie auch plauderte, jetzt sehnte sie sich nach Ruhe** ('Much as she liked to chat, she now longed for quietness')—**Sei dem, wie ihm wolle** (or **Wie dem auch sein mag**), **ich ändere meine Pläne nicht** ('Be that as it may, I shall not alter my plans')—**Soviel es auch kosten mag** (or **Es koste, was es wolle** or **Einerlei, was es kostet**), **ich setze meinen Plan durch** ('Cost what it may, I shall carry out my plan')—**Welche Summe er auch** (**immer**) **fordert, ich bezahle sie** ('No matter what amount he demands, I shall pay it'). For the position of the verb after a concessive clause, see **word-order** 1 (*d*) and 3 (*d*).

confess: 1. The correct expression for 'to confess' (to a priest) is **beichten,** used either abs. (= **Beichte tun** or **ablegen**) or with an accus. obj., as in **Verklagt das Herz dich keiner andern Sünde, die du noch nicht gebeichtet?** (Sch.). **2.** Whereas **bekennen** is strictly 'to make known' (= **bekanntmachen**), esp. 'to confess' voluntarily what one is not obliged to divulge, **gestehen** really implies a certain hesitation or reluctance to disclose something: thus, with an obj. like **Schuld**

('guilt'), either verb can be used, according as the confession is voluntary or not. De Quincey's 'Confessions of an English Opium Eater' are **Bekenntnisse** (not **Geständnisse**), but a hesitant lover may be so carried away that he makes a **Liebesgeständnis** (not **Liebesbekenntnis**). The double compd. **eingestehen** emphasizes the reluctance, often implying that the confession is made under pressure (e.g. in cross-examination), as when a person may be tortured into confessing to what he has not done. The proposition **Ich konnte dir nicht bekennen, was ich mir selbst nicht eingestehen wollte** (Lewald) implies great reluctance to confess what the speaker's conscience has urged him to disclose. The verb **gestehen** is also often used with a force which **bekennen** never has, viz. that of 'to confess, admit, concede', as in **Gestehe, daß ich glücklich bin!** (Sch.) and in the common phrase **offen gestanden** ('to be frank, to tell the truth'); and **zugestehen** has much the same force (cf. **Wort** 1 *b*), being used esp. with an accus. of the thing and a dat. of the person, as in **Klugheit muß man ihm zugestehen** ('It must be admitted that he is clever'); cf. **Ich gestehe (zu), daß der Schein gegen mich spricht, trotzdem bekenne ich mich aber nicht für schuldig** (Sanders). Other verbs used with the same force of 'to admit, concede' are **zugeben** and **einräumen**: e.g. **Er gibt zu, ein Unrecht begangen zu haben—Zugegeben** ('Granted'), **daß ich mich geirrt habe, so rechtfertigt das sein Benehmen gegen mich nicht—Jedermann wird einräumen, daß wir in schlechten Zeiten leben**; cf., in grammar, **ein einräumender Nebensatz** ('a concessive clause').

congruence: 1. *congruence of number*: **(a)** In ordinary lang. we say 'There *are* a lot of people here', and this corresponds exactly to **Es sind eine Menge Leute hier,** because **Leute** here was orig. a part. gen. (see **genitive of material**). Strictly, of course, the verb should be sing., but as **Leute** is unrecognizable as a gen., it is now treated as an appos., and the idea of plurality is so prominent that this appos. has become the subj. and made the verb plur.; sim. **Hinter dem Sarge her gingen eine Menge Leute** (Volkmann-Leander)—**An einer Stelle des Ufers lagen eine Masse Kieselsteine** (Wildenbruch)—**Eine große Gesellschaft Seiltänzer und Gaukler waren eingezogen** (G.)—**Ein Paar** (q.v.) **flammende Augen starrten ihn an** (Sudermann)—**Auf der Bahn gingen ein Dutzend junge Leute** (G.). While a plur. verb is more usual where the collect. noun suggests a number of loosely connected individual components, a sing. verb is, of course, not wrong, and is indeed really more correct in the case of a compact group: e.g. **Ein Schwarm Bienen flog** (not **flogen**) **an mir vorbei—Es kam ein Trupp Bauernburschen die Straße herauf** (Ric. Huch)—**Am gedeckten Tisch saß schon eine Anzahl Offiziere** (Ompteda). Analogous is the use of a plur. verb in 'These sort of books are rare', for which see **Art** 2. **(b)** Different from the examples given above are propositions like **Eine Menge hübscher Frauen waren da** (Bruno Frank) and **Ein Haufe von jungen Offizieren waren dabei, Pferde zuzureiten** (Frenssen), where the collect. sing. noun is followed by a recognizable gen. phrase in the former, and by **von** in the latter. Here a plur. verb should really be incorrect, and an uncompromising grammarian like *Wustmann* is justified in condemning it where a gen. or **von** replaces the appos. construction: **„Es stört in hohem Grade"**, he says, **„wenn man Sätze lesen muß, wie: Außer den Seen müssen noch eine Menge kleiner Kanäle benutzt werden—Dem Reichsdeutschen treten in dem schweizerischen Schriftdeutsch eine Menge von Besonderheiten entgegen."** But the fact remains that propositions like those here condemned are quite common in modern standard authors, although the appos. construction would undoubtedly be preferable: cf. **Aus seinen Westentaschen starrten ein halbes Dutzend gespitzter Bleistifte hervor** (Th. Mann)—**Eine Menge junger Mädchen standen plaudernd zusammen** (Gerstäcker)—**An dem Altar brannten eine Menge geopferter Kerzen** (Perkönig)—**Er ließ das Wasser über seinen Kopf rinnen: es war, als streichelten ihn ein Dutzend feiner Frauenhände** (id.)—**Es standen eine Unzahl von Leuchtern auf Tischen** (A. Schaeffer)—**Nur eine Handvoll revolutionär gerichteter Studenten nahmen an den Vorlesungen teil** (Th. Mann)—**Die junge Dame hatte einen grünen Gürtel, in dem ein Paar halboffener Rosen steckten** (Hofmannsthal: see **stecken** 2 *b*); all the same, the plur. verb does sound strange in **Hier wohnten ein Paar frommer Hausleute**

(Möser, where the reference is to a married couple), but quite correct in **Hier wohnten ein paar** ('a few') **fromme Hausleute.** (**c**) Two *sing.* (not plur.) nouns connected by **und,** esp. without an art., often form one collect. idea, and in this case the verb stands in the *sing.*: e.g. **Tod und Leben stehet in der Zunge Gewalt** (Prov. 18. 21)—**Himmel und Erde lag ihm weit entfernt** (Novalis)—**Ich will nicht, daß mein eigen Fleisch und Blut mich über die Schulter ansehen soll** (Lewald)—**Mir verging Hören und Sehen** (G.)—**Zufrieden jauchzet groß und klein** (G.)—**Es regte sich jung und alt** (Sch.)—**Hoch und niedrig** ('Rich and poor') **strömte herbei—Er hat die Welt in Flammen stehen sehen und kann die dämonische Beleuchtung nicht vergessen, in der damals Gut und Böse, Schön und Häßlich, Hoch und Niedrig an ihm vorüberzog** (Heyse)—**An ihm ist Hopfen und Malz verloren** ('He is past reclaiming, a hopeless case')—**Gleich und gleich gesellt sich gern** ('Birds of a feather flock together': cf. the example from Immermann given under **-gleichen** 1); so also with three nouns, as in **Da sieht man wieder einmal, daß Alter, Erfahrung und Grämlichkeit nicht vor Torheit schützt** (Raabe) and **Sie betraten die Kaserne, aus der Signalblasen, Lärm und Pfeifen ertönte** (Ompteda). (**d**) Two *sing.* nouns connected by **oder,** with or without a preceding **entweder** (for **weder . . . noch,** see **weder** 1) require a *sing.* verb, and examples like the following are not to be recommended: **Wenn Onkel Hans oder Johann kamen, war es für uns Kinder ein Fest** (Hebbel)—**Wolf oder Bär kommen selten davon, wenn ein Lappe ihnen aufs Blatt hält** (Th. Mügge: 'A wolf or a bear seldom gets away alive when a Laplander draws a bead on him') —**Die Konsulin oder Klara verlasen einen Abschnitt aus der Bibel** (Th. Mann)—**Sie telegraphierte, der Herr Doktor oder Marion würden kommen** (B. E. Werner). There is fluctuation where the connected words are pers. prons., but the verb usually agrees with the nearest pron.: e.g. **Du oder ich bin verrückt—Ich oder du bist verrückt—Du oder dein Bruder ist verrückt.** (**e**) A *sing.* verb is really also correct with **sowohl . . . als** or **wie** ('as well as': see **sowohl** 2), as in **Sowohl er als sein Bruder war da**; but as such propositions so obviously convey the idea of plurality, a plur. verb is very common: e.g. **Sowohl du als ich sind eingeladen** (= **Wir sind beide eingeladen**)—**Diese Zurückweisung haben sowohl Fichte als Hegel erfahren** (Varnhagen v. Ense, which *Sanders* quotes, adding the note **„gewöhnlich: hat"**)—**Ringsum war alles still: Ida sowohl wie Mama schliefen noch** (Th. Mann). The same applies to **wie** without a preceding **sowohl,** to **samt** (q.v. 1), and to **nebst** (prep. + dat.: 'along *or* together with', esp. in references or invitations to a married couple): e.g. **Mutter wie Tante verrieten dem Vater nichts—Er wie sein Sohn zögerten keinen Augenblick, sich zu entscheiden** (K. Edschmid)—**Goethe wie Mörike greifen nach dem, was ihnen in der Wirklichkeit lebenswarm gegenübertritt** (H. Ilgenstein)—**Auch Doktor Langhans nebst Frau kamen an** (Th. Mann). (**f**) For a plur. verb used politely or obsequiously in addressing a person of higher rank in society, see **address** (forms of) 2 (*a*) and (*b*). **2.** *congruence of gender*: When a masc. or neut. noun is used with reference to one of the female sex (**Fräulein, Mädchen, Weib, Schatz,** etc.), a subsequent reference in a pron. should strictly be masc. or neut., as the case may be, but modern usage undoubtedly favours the *fem.*: e.g. **Als Kind ging das schöne Annerl mit ihrer Großmutter in die Scharfrichterei** (Brentano) —**Große Ehre für mich, dies Ding** (q.v.) **heimzuführen** ('to marry this female *or* creature'), **während ihr Herz kalt ist wie Eis!** (Th. Mügge)—**Einst lebte ein junges Fräulein allein am Rhein; sie wurde nur von einer alten Haushälterin betreut** (K. Edschmid)—**Diesem jungen Frauenzimmer** (q.v.) **habe ich versprochen, sie eine Strecke zu geleiten** (Immermann)—**Ich gewahrte die Hand eines Frauenzimmers, an deren kleinem Finger ein Brillant funkelte** (E. T. A. Hoffmann)—**Ich gab dem geliebten Geschöpfe die Hand und sagte zu ihr . . .** (G.)—**Sein Liebchen war noch nicht erkaltet, und schon war die Flamme in dem Herzen ihres Ungetreuen verloschen** (Musäus)—**Dieses Mädchen hatte ein herrliches Zeugnis, man konnte nichts als Gutes an ihr finden** (G.)—**Das Mädchen ward ein muntres Geschöpf, deren Gesicht so glatt war wie ihr Gemüt** (Novalis)—**Die Dame hatte ein Kammermädchen, wie man sie nur wünschen mochte** (G.: see **wie** 2 *a*)—**Er sieht sein Schätzel an: die wendet sich** (G.); even a rel. pron. immediately following such a noun may be fem., as in **Ich vermisse mein Weib, die mich erheitert** (Waiblinger), but cf. **Sie ist ein Wesen, das von ihrer Art nicht lassen kann** (Gutzkow). In their fairy-tales the brothers Grimm in such cases almost always use the strictly grammatical prons., but this is now rather unusual: e.g. **Die Großmutter wußte nicht, was sie dem Kinde geben sollte. Einmal schenkte sie ihm ein Käppchen von rotem Sammet, und weil ihm das so wohl stand und es nichts anderes tragen wollte, hieß es nur das Rotkäppchen. Eines Tages sprach seine Mutter zu ihm . . .** etc.; cf., on the other hand, in a more modern tale, **Weil das Mädchen schöner war als sieben andere zusammen, so nannten die Leute sie Siebenschön ; und dabei war sie so sittsam, daß, wenn sie zur Kirche ging, was sie fleißig tat, sie immer einen Schleier trug, damit die Leute sie nicht angaffen sollten . . .** etc. The strict grammatical usage does in fact sound rather unnatural in a quite modern novel: **Das Fräulein beschäftigte sich eifrig mit seinem Teller** (W. Kramp).

copy: see **nachahmen.**

corn: see **Getreide** 1 and 2.

cost: see **kosten** and **Kost(en).**

create: see **schöpfen** 1 and 2.

cross (verb): see **quer** 1; **über-** 1.

custom(ary): 1. The noun **Gewohnheit** (cf. **accustomed** 1) suggests what a person does mechanically and almost unconsciously because he has long been in the 'habit' of acting in that way (**weil er schon seit lange gewohnt ist, so zu handeln, und gewöhnlich so handelt**). **2.** Analogous is **Sitte,** which is used in this sense more esp. of a nation, social class, etc., the course of action having become generally recognized as a norm of decent behaviour: e.g. **Das ist hierzulande nicht Sitte** ('That is not *done* in this country'); cf. the prov. expression **Ländlich, sittlich,** which suggests that people should conform to the customs of the country in which they are living ('When in Rome, do as the Romans do'). And hence **Sitte** came to be used of people's 'manners', whether good or bad, and applied to an individual as well as to a class, as in **Er ist ein Mann von feinen Sitten. 3. (a)** Common combinations are **Sitte und Brauch** and **Sitten und Gebräuche,** the second noun in each phrase pointing to what has been 'in use' for a long time and become an established 'usage': cf. the expression **nach altem Brauch,** and the often quoted **Ein tiefer Sinn wohnt in den alten Bräuchen** (Sch.). **Gebrauch** is now more common than **Brauch,** being esp. used of a custom which is part of the ritual observed by a society, guild, etc., e.g. by Freemasons. **(b)** The adj. **gebräuchlich** has a wider application, being used of anything that is in accordance with common usage, as in **Diese Redensart** or **Diese Ausdrucksweise ist überall gebräuchlich,** i.e. **wird überall gebraucht**; and much the same applies to **üblich,** which suggests that something is in general use because it has been 'practised' (**ausgeübt**) for a long time: so one speaks of **übliche Preise** ('ordinary prices'), **die üblichen Bedingungen** ('the usual conditions'), etc.

D

da: 1. *Adverb.* **(a)** Used of *place,* this means 'there, yonder', as opposed to **hier**: e.g. **Ihr Buch liegt da drüben** ('over there')—**Dieser Junge zählt elf Jahre, der da** ('that one there') **erst acht**—**Wir fahren zuerst nach Berlin, von da nach Wien**; cf. **hier und da** ('here and there') with **da und da,** as in **Ich habe ihm geschrieben, mein Freund wohne da und da** ('my friend's address was so and so'). In coll. lang. **da** is often used for 'here': e.g. **Ach, da bist du ja endlich!** ('Ah, here you are at last!')—**Er versprach, um 1 Uhr hier zu sein, aber es ist schon 2 Uhr und er ist immer noch nicht da** ('but . . . he is not here yet'); cf. the third example given under **stop** 1 (*a*). **(b)** Used of *time,* it means 'then' (q.v. 2 *b*): e.g. **Er war letzte Woche hier, da** (= **zu der Zeit**) **war ich aber verreist**—**Ich wollte eben ausgehen, da kam Besuch** (= **als Besuch kam**); cf. its superfluous use to introduce a princ. clause after an **als**-clause, as in **Als ich am Bahnhof ankam, da stand der Zug**

schon da (see **so** 2). **2.** *Subordinate conjunction.* (**a**) Here **da** most commonly has *causal* force ('because, as'), for which see **weil** 2 (*b*), **denn** (conjunction) 2 and 3, and **so** 2 (*b*). (**b**) Its use as a *rel.*, meaning 'where' or 'when', was very common at an earlier period: e.g. **Dem wäre es besser, daß . . . er ersäuft würde im Meer, da es am tiefsten ist** (Matt. 18. 6)—**Ihr sollt kein neu Brot . . . essen bis auf den Tag, da ihr eurem Gott Opfer bringet** (Lev. 23. 14)—**Es ist schön, wenn wir uns alter Zeiten erinnern, besonders in einem Augenblick, da wir eine Höhe erreicht haben, von welcher wir uns umsehen können** (G.). This is still in use, as in the examples from Frenssen and Th. Mann given respectively under **als = 'as'** 1 (*c*) and **so** 2; but in such propositions **da** now sounds rather choice and is usually replaced by **wo**: see **when** 2 (*b*) and cf. **als = 'than'** 4. **3.** For its use as a prefix to preps. and advs., see **da(r)-** and cf. **dabei**, etc., and esp. **darein.**

dabei: This is often used with a following **zu**+infin. or a finite clause in appos. to the pron. implicit in **da-**: e.g. **Als er kam, war ich eben dabei', ihn anzurufen** ('. . . I was just ringing him up')—**Er bleibt dabei, daß der Plan mißlingen wird** ('He persists in maintaining that the plan will miscarry'). Otherwise it has independent adv. force with different shades of meaning: **Sie ist kränklich, aber dabei heiter** ('She is ailing, but cheerful for all that')—**Das hat keinen Zweck, es kommt nichts dabei heraus** ('There is no point in that, nothing is to be gained by it')—**Wenn's einmal eine komische Frauenrolle darzustellen gibt, ist sie dabei** (F. A. Hohenstein: '. . . she is always ready to join in *or* take it on')—**Wenn Unfug getrieben wird, ist er immer dabei** ('When there is mischief afoot, he always has a hand in it'). See **presence** 4, and cf. **absence** 1.

dadurch: This is in some ways different from the other preps. compounded with **da(r)-**. The phrase 'through it', in a reference to something previously mentioned, as in 'Do you see that gateway there? Well, to get to the castle you must go through it', is expressed by **da durch** (two words), **durch** being prefixed to the verb: **Um zu dem Schloß zu gelangen, müssen Sie da durchgehen** ('go through there'). Written as one word (in which case the (accent falls on the prefix), it always suggests a way of attaining some end, corresponding to 'in that way' or 'by so doing', as in **Wir wollen diesen kürzeren Weg nehmen, da'durch gewinnen wir etwas Zeit.** Another way to express this is **Wir werden da'durch Zeit gewinnen, daß wir diesen kürzeren Weg nehmen**; and here it is important to note that even where the subjs. of the two clauses refer to the same person, as in this example, an infin. with **zu** can never be used—cf. **da(r)-** 1 (*c*): it is quite wrong to say **Man kann dadurch viel lernen, andere Länder zu bereisen** (for **daß man andere Länder bereist**).

dafür: see **da(r)-**. At one time **dafür** and **davor** (q.v.) were used almost indiscriminately: e.g. **Grauen hat mich betäubt: ich habe in der Nacht keine Ruhe dafür** (Isa. 21. 4), where, in accordance with present-day usage, the modern version has **davor**; on the other hand, Goethe's Reynard says **Kann ich davor, wenn Braun** (the bear) **mit blutiger Platte zurückkehrt?** where the modern expression is **Kann ich etwas dafür?** ('Can I help it? Am I to blame for it?'). One now distinguishes clearly between these two words, and **davor** could not be used in the following examples: **Hier ist ein schönes Buch, ich habe nur 10 Mark dafü'r gegeben**—**Er ist gerade da'für berühmt** ('That is just what he is famous for')—**Da'für wird man hierzulande gestraft** ('For that sort of offence people are punished in this country')—**Er ist ein Taugenichts, ich wenigstens halte ihn dafü'r** ('at least I consider him one')—**Als der Antrag gestellt wurde, waren die meisten dafü'r** ('in favour')—**Ich bin dafü'r, daß wir spazierengehen** ('I vote we go for a walk'). The rel. use is now avoided, esp. when the reference is to people, as in **Ich bin nicht der, dafü'r ihr mich haltet** (Acts 13. 25), where one would now use **für den.**

daheim: see **Heim** 2 (*a*).

daher, dahin: **1.** With **da-** accented, these two advs. point to a definite locality from or to which the motion proceeds: e.g. **„Sie sind hier? Ich glaubte, Sie wären in Köln." „Eben da'her bin ich gekommen"** ('That is just where I have come from') or **„Da'hin fahre ich auch in einer Stunde"** ('That is just where I am going in an hour'). But actually, in such propositions, the two parts are usually separated, both being accented: **Da' komme ich eben he'r**—**Da' fahre ich in**

einer Stunde hi'n; cf. Luther's hymn **Vom Himmel hoch da komm' ich her.** Other idiomatic uses: **Also da'her der Lärm auf der Straße!** ('So *that's* the reason for the noise in the street!')—**Ich hoffe, in acht Tagen zurückzukommen, bis da'hin** ('till then') **bleiben Sie gesund und munter!** (see **then** 2 *b*)—**Es ist mit ihm da'hin gekommen** (or **Er hat es da'hin gebracht**), **daß man ihn entlassen mußte** ('Things came to such a pass *or* He went so far that he had to be dismissed')—**Er äußerte sich** (or **seine Meinung**) **da'hin, daß der Plan unausführbar wäre** ('He expressed his view to the effect that the proposal was impracticable')—**Ihre Meinung ging da'hin, Gott habe den Mönch richten wollen** (Bergengruen: 'She gave it as her opinion that God had wished to condemn the monk')—**Sie einigten sich da'hin, die Bitte auszuschlagen** ('They reached a final agreement to refuse the request'); see **dahinstehen.** It is noteworthy that **daher** (not **dahin**) can be used with *rel.* force: e.g. **Es scheint, daß nach der Starrsucht** ('catalepsy, seizure') **mein Gedächtnis lange schwach geblieben, dahe'r** (= **weswegen,** 'as a result of which') **ich auch nicht viel gelernt** (Spindler). **2.** With **-her** and **-hin** accented: **Der Junge kam dahe'rgelaufen** (= **herangelaufen,** 'came running up' from a place unknown or left vague)—**Die Tage, von denen Sie sprechen, sind längst dahi'n** ('are long past'; for **Diese Frage wollen wir dahi'ngestellt sein lassen,** see **dahinstehen**).

dahinstehen, dahinstellen: As **dahin** implies motion, and **stehen** implies rest, the compd. **dahinstehen** can only be used fig., **etwas dahi'nstehen lassen** having the force of 'to let something stand over, remain undecided' (see below): e.g. **Den Preis für Verköstigung und Bedienung ließ sie zunächst noch dahi'nstehen** (Th. Mann: 'As to the charge for board and service, she left that open for the present')—**Für dich hat die Tante Geld und Liebe: was davon wichtiger ist, stehe dahi'n** (Fontane: '. . . which of the two is the more important, let that remain undecided'). In contrast, **dahinstellen** can be used both lit. and fig., according to the accent: cf. on the one hand, **Stellen Sie den Tisch nicht hie'rher, sondern da'hin!** ('Put the table over there, not here!'), and on the other hand, **Diese Frage wollen wir dahi'ngestellt sein lassen** (= **dahi'nstehen lassen,** 'leave in abeyance')—**Sie hatten sich zu der Fahrt verabredet: ob die Anregung von Jeanette ausgegangen war, blieb dahi'ngestellt** (Th. Mann: 'They had arranged the trip, whether at Jeannette's instigation remained an open question').

dahinter: see **da(r)-.** The following idiomatic uses of this word are worth noting: **Dies ist das Rathaus, dahi'nter** ('behind it') **ist der Dom**—fig. **Es steckt etwas dahi'nter** ('There is more in this than meets the eye' or 'There is something mysterious going on here')—**Er steckt mit dahi'nter** ('He has a hand in it too, is one of the accomplices')—**Hier geht irgend etwas vor sich: wenn ich nur dahi'nterkommen könnte!** ('There is something going on here: if only I could get to the bottom of it!'). See **da(r)-** 3.

daneben: see **da(r)-.** There are only one or two idiomatic expressions in which this occurs: e.g. **Das große Gebäude dort ist das Theater, das dane'ben** ('the one next to it') **ist die Hauptpost**—**Der Schütze hat dane'ben geschossen** ('has missed his mark'); coll. **Nein, da hast du dane'ben geschossen** ('No, you are quite wrong there, very wide of the mark')—**An der einen Stelle griff der Klavierspieler dane'ben** ('At one place the pianist struck a wrong note').

Dank: 1. It is strange that whereas the corresponding English word no longer has a sing., **Dank** has *no plur.*: where we say 'Many thanks!' a German says **Vielen** (or, more coll., **Schönen**) **Dank!**—cf. **Dank wissen** (see **wissen** 3 *a*). To suggest 'expressions of gratitude', recourse is had to **Danksagungen,** as in **Der Knecht war unter vielen Danksagungen fortgegangen** (Stifter); cf., as a bold example of an unrecognized plur., **Dies war der erste echte Dank, den er seit Jahren bekam: Schein-Danke** (= **nichtssagende Ausdrücke des Dankes,** 'empty *or* insincere expressions of gratitude') **hörte er jeden Tag mehr als genug** (A. Schaeffer). It is possible that our 'thanks' was orig. a *gen.*, a governing word having dropped out: cf. **Was Danks** ('What in the way of thanks') **habt ihr davon?** (Luke 6. 34, where our version has 'What *thank* have ye?'). But the orig. force of **Dank** had nothing to do with its modern sense of 'gratitude': it was the noun corresponding to the verb **denken,** and so meant 'thought', an idea now expressed by **Gedanke** (MHG *gedanc*). The idea of 'thought' gradually led to that of 'intention, wish' (MHG *dankes* was used adv. in the sense of 'voluntarily', and ***un-dankes*** in that of 'unwillingly'), and this is still preserved in **Niemand kann es ihm zu Danke machen** (G.: = **Niemand kann es ihm recht machen,** 'No one can please *or* satisfy him', lit. 'No one can do it in accordance with his wishes'). This last idiom may suggest how the idea of 'gratitude' developed: if a person's wishes have been carried out to his liking, he will naturally feel grateful. **2.** The prep. **dank** ('thanks to') is simply the noun written with a small letter. Orig. it governed a noun in the gen. case (which is still allowed in Austria), but the *dat.* is now the usual construction, esp. with masc. or neut. sing. nouns (with fem. sing. nouns the case is of course problematical): e.g. **Dank meinem Einfluß** (or **meiner Bemühung) hat er eine gute Stelle bekommen.**

danken: 1. (**a**) This verb always takes a *dat.* of the person; the old gen. of the thing is now expressed in prose by the prep. **für,** but is unconsciously preserved in **Gott** (dat.) **sei es gedankt!** (lit. 'God be thanked because of it!'). But it can be used with an accus. of the thing in the sense of 'to owe *or* be indebted' to a person for something, although **verdanken** is to be preferred here in good prose: e.g. **Was dank' ich dir nicht alles!** (Sch.)—**Ihm, nicht mir, dankt ihr das Unheil** (Hackländer: 'You have to thank him, not me, for the harm done'); cf. the example from W. v. Scholz given under **inne** (*c*). (**b**) The comp. **bedanken** is esp. used reflex., **sich bedanken** having the same force as **danken**; but the dat. of the person with the simple verb is replaced by the prep. **bei** with the reflex. compd.: e.g. **Ich habe mich bei ihm für seine Hilfe bedankt.** Without the reflex. pron., **bedanken** is now only used in the *pass.*: e.g. **Sei bedankt** (not **gedankt**) **für dein Anerbieten!—Für den Brief sollst du vielmals bedankt sein** (Speckmann). An accus. of the thing as the obj. of **bedanken** is very rare, and the following example should not be imitated: **Ich hob die Hand grüßend an den Kalabreser, was** (for **wofür sich**) **der andere mit einem Lüften seines Jägerhütchens bedankte** (Alverdes: 'I touched my broad-brimmed slouch-hat by way of greeting, which the other acknowledged by raising his Tyrolese hunter's hat'); otherwise **was** could be retained and **erwiderte** substituted for **bedankte. 2.** The every-day expression **Danke!** is really the 1st sing. pres. indic. of the verb with the pers. pron. understood. Of special interest in this connexion is the use of **danken** with *neg.* force. If a German is offered something to eat or drink, he says **Danke!** if he does not wish anything; cf. **Er erschien hastig zum Tee, nahm keinen Zucker, schlug eine Zigarette aus und dankte auch für Brot** (K. Edschmid: i.e. he refused a cigarette and would not take any bread either)—**Die Eltern haben mich gebeten, ihren kranken Jungen zu besuchen: ich solle sogleich kommen, dem früheren Hausarzt hätten sie für fernere Besuche gedankt** (Carossa: i.e. they had told their family doctor to discontinue his visits). The author of the present volume once heard a lady, whose little girl had been offered another cake, say **Das Kind dankt!** (lit. 'The child says No, thank you!' i.e. 'She has had enough!').

dann: 1. This adv. may have *temp.* or *cond.* force (see **then** 1 and 2 *a*), or it may replace **so** after a cond. clause (see **so** 2 *ad fin.*). Still another use, esp. with **auch** later in the clause, is to introduce a final point or argument, as in **Dann müssen wir auch bedenken, daß . . .** ('We must also bear in mind that . . .'), where, however, **sodann** is preferable. Distinguish between **dann und wann** ('now and then': see **wann**) and **dann und dann** ('at such and such a time'), as in **Ich habe ihm dann und wann geschrieben und das letzte Mal gesagt, ich würde ihn dann und dann treffen**; cf. **da und da** (see **da** 1 *a*). **2.** The expression **von dannen** is an adv. of *place*, meaning 'away (from there)', like **von da fort.** It is very common in the Bible, as in **Da Jesus von dannen ging, sah er einen Menschen am Zoll sitzen** (Matth. 9. 9), and at that time it was also used with rel. force, as in **Von dannen** ('thence') **schifften sie gen Antiochien, von dannen** ('from whence') **sie verordnet waren zu dem Werk . . .** (Acts 14. 26): cf. **da**(r)**-** 2. This is now confined to choice prose, and indeed it has never lost its biblical flavour: cf. **Mit steifen Beinen ging er durch die Säulenhalle von dannen** (Th. Mann).

dannen: see **dann** 2.

da(r)-: 1. (**a**) When prefixed to a prep., this represents a 3rd pers. pron. referring to something impers. previously mentioned, as in 'Where is the new chair?' 'You are sitting *on it*' (**darauf**, coll. **drauf**)—'He saw two letters on the table and stretched out his hand *for them*' (**griff danach**). Important here is the distinction between **darein** and **darin**, for which see **darein**. Exceptional preps. in this connexion are **halb** and **wegen**, which substitute **des-** for **da-**, and **ohne**, which has no such combination now, **darohne** being obs., so that one says **ohne es** (or **sie**), **ohne dasselbe** (or **dieselben**). (**b**) In such expressions the accent ordinarily falls on the prep. (**dara'n**), but shifts for the sake of emphasis to the prefix (**da'ran**) which then represents a dem. pron.: e.g. **„Sie hätten nach dem Arzt schicken sollen." „Da'ran habe ich nicht gedacht"** ('*That* is something that did not occur to me'). (**c**) The German lang. is esp. rich in idioms based on these adv. expressions, and some of the most noteworthy of these are given under **daran, dabei, darein**, etc. Very common is their use with a following clause in appos. to the pron. implicit in **da(r)-**, usually **zu**+infin. if the subjs. of the two clauses refer to the same person or thing: e.g. **Ich habe darauf bestanden, ihn zu begleiten** ('I have insisted on accompanying him')—**Er ist damit beschäftigt, Briefe zu beantworten** ('He is engaged in answerin letters'); with different subjs., **Ich bin davon überzeugt, daß er zuverlässig ist** ('I am convinced [of the fact] that he is reliable'). Exceptional here is **dadurch**, which is never followed by an infin. clause: cf. **Ich habe ihn da'durch beleidigt, daß ich ihn nicht eingeladen habe** ('I have offended him by not inviting him': not **ihn nicht eingeladen zu haben**). **2.** These expressions are sometimes used to represent *rel.* prons., and although this use seems to be on the increase, it still generally sounds somewhat old-fashioned and reminiscent of Luther's Bible: cf. **Tue mir kund den Weg, darauf ich gehen soll** (Ps. 143. 8: '. . . the way wherein I should walk')—**Der Vater lüftete die Gardine, dahinter** ('behind which') **der Fünfjährige schlief** (A. Schaeffer)—**Die Au ist das Flüßchen, daran ursprünglich unsere Stadt gelegen war** (Th. Mann)—**Von einer Nische sah ein Bild nieder, darauf ein Mönch abgemalt war** (Stifter)—**Er verkaufte sein Schiff, draus er nicht viel herausschlug** ('out of the sale of which he didn't make much'), **und kaufte sich das Haus, drin wir jetzt wohnen** (Fontane)—**Wir werden bei Rilke durch Parke geführt, darin verwitterte Brunnen und Steinbilder stehen** (Manfred Schneider)—**Die Kinder saßen um den Stuhl, darum** ('round which') **sie Rosen gewunden hatten** (W. Schäfer)—**Zu der Zeit, davon** ('about which') **ich rede, lag am Ende des Dorfes ein sauberes Häuschen** (M. v. Bülow). Of this rel. use *Sanders* says **„Im allgemeinen gilt für die gewöhnliche Prosa hier nach dem heutigen Sprachgebrauch wo(r)- als die Regel"**; but actually a rel. pron. governed by a prep. is preferable in references to something concrete, and **wo(r)-** in references to something abstract, as in the following pairs of examples: **Der Fluß, an dem** (or **welchem**) **unser Haus steht, ist tief** and **Das ist etwas, woran ich nicht gedacht habe**—**Der Berg, auf den ich gestiegen bin, heißt der Brocken** and **Das ist ein Thema, worauf ich nicht eingehen werde** ('which I shall not go into')—**Das Gebäude, aus dem er eben tritt, ist das Rathaus** and **Dies ist ein Gedanke, woraus ich nicht klug werde** ('of which I can make nothing')—**Sie hat die Handarbeit, mit der sie beschäftigt war, nicht vollenden können** and **Das ist ein Vorschlag, womit ich nicht einverstanden bin** ('to which I cannot agree'). **3.** It is important to distinguish between **dahinter** and **da hinten**, between **darüber** and **da drüben**, between **darunter** and **da unten**: e.g. **Sehen Sie den Baum dort? Dahinter** ('behind it') **hat sich jemand versteckt**; but **Unser Haus ist hier vorn, mein Freund wohnt da hinten** ('Our house is here in the foreground, my friend lives back yonder')—**Bald kommen wir an den Fluß, eine Brücke wird eben darüber** ('across it') **gebaut**; but **Diese Stadt heißt Köln, da drüben** ('across the river there') **liegt Deutz**—**Hier wächst ein Rosenstrauch, darunter** ('below it') **soll jemand begraben liegen**; but **Da unten** (coll. **Da drunten**, 'down there') **im Tale ist eine alte Ruine.**

daran: see **da(r)-**. This word, which often takes the coll. form **dran** (q.v.), is used in a large number of idiomatic expressions: e.g. **Gespenster? Nein, da'ran glaube ich nicht** ('Ghosts? No, I don't believe in *them*')—**Es mag etwas Wahres dara'n sein** ('There may be some truth in it')—**Bin ich jetzt dran?** ('Is it my turn now?')—**Er hat alles dara'n gesetzt, den Freund zu retten** ('He has done his utmost to save *or* has staked his all on saving his friend')—**Es liegt mir wenig dara'n, ob er kommt oder nicht** ('I don't much care whether he comes or not')—**Was liegt dara'n?** ('What does it matter?')—**Ich fürchte, der Arme wird dara'n glauben müssen** ('I fear the poor man is nearing his end': probably from MHG *sich gelouben* + gen. in the sense of 'to abandon, renounce'—cf. 'to give up the ghost')—**Ich war drauf und dran, den Einbrecher niederzuschießen** ('I was within an ace of shooting the burglar')—**Der Hauptmann war drauf und dran, einen Diener zu nehmen** (Ompteda: 'The captain was just on the point of engaging a servant').

darauf: see **da(r)-.** The number of idiomatic expressions connected with this word is a particularly large one. In the lit. sense, it can express either rest on or motion on to something, so that in a proposition like **Dieser Stuhl ist wacklig, niemand will darau'f sitzen,** it would be equally correct to say **niemand will sich darau'f setzen.** Other uses are seen in the following examples: **Er hat uns letztes Jahr besucht, starb aber kurz darau'f** ('shortly after that')—**Ich habe seine Adresse vergessen, kannst du dich darau'f besinnen?** ('can you recall it to mind?')—**Er ist durchaus ehrlich, da'rauf können Sie sich verlassen** ('on that you can rely')—**Ich habe ihm einen Brief geschrieben, er hat aber noch nicht darau'f geantwortet**—**Ich bin neugierig darau'f, was er sagen wird**—**Wir haben ihn um seinen Rat gebeten: wir halten viel darau'f** ('we set great store by it')—**Er geht darau'f aus, uns ins Verderben zu bringen** ('He aims at *or* is bent on ruining us')—**Er weiß nicht, ob er mitgehen wird, es kommt darau'f an, was für Wetter es ist** ('it depends what sort of weather it is')—**Wir wollen es darau'f ankommen lassen** ('We'll leave it to chance' or 'We'll wait and see')—**Seit er seinen reichen Onkel beerbt hat, läßt er viel drau'fgehen** ('Since he came into his rich uncle's fortune he is very extravagant *or* throws his money about'); cf. **Er ist ein Drau'fgänger** ('He is a dashing, go-ahead, reckless fellow')—**Ich werde bestimmt kommen, meine Hand drauf!** ('my hand on it! Take my word for it!'); cf. the combination **drauf und dran,** for which see **daran** *ad fin.* As with other words of this kind, so here also the rel. use is now avoided: cf. **Tue mir kund den Weg, darauf ich gehen soll** (Ps. 143. 8).

daraus: see **da(r)-.** This means 'out of it *or* them' (or 'out of that *or* those' if the prefix is accented): e.g. **Diese Tassen sind schmutzig, da'raus trinken wir nicht** ('We shan't drink out of those')—**Wir hatten einen Ausflug für gestern geplant, aber es wurde nichts darau's** ('but it came to nothing')—**Was? ihr wollt bei diesem Sturm im Meer schwimmen? Kinder, da'raus wird nichts** ('that is out of the question')—**Schlittschuhlaufen? Nein, ich mache mir nichts darau's** ('I don't care for *or* fancy it')—**Ich habe den Satz dreimal gelesen, aber ich werde nicht klug darau's** ('but I can make nothing of it')—**Eben ist ein Brief gekommen: ich entnehme darau's, daß es dem Patienten besser geht** ('I gather from it that the patient's condition has improved')—**Wenn dem so ist, so folgt darau's, daß wir den Versuch werden aufgeben müssen** ('If that is the case, it follows that we shall have to give up the attempt'). It must be distinguished from **da draußen:** cf. **Auf der kleinen Insel da draußen** ('out yonder') **wohnt niemand**—cf. **da(r)- 3.**

darbieten: see **offer** 1 (*c*).

darein, darin: 1. (**a**) In these expressions the prefix **dar-** represents a pron., as explained under **da(r)-** 1. (*a*) and (*c*). While **darin** ('in it *or* them') is in very common use, **darein** ('into it *or* them') is now rare, and indeed obs. where the idea of motion into a place or locality is suggested (but see *b*): instead of **Wir kamen dem Tale näher und endlich darein** (G.), one would now say . . . **und endlich in dieses** (or **dasselbe**) **hinein**; sim. **Sehen Sie dieses Glas: unsere Namenszüge sind dareingeschnitten** (G.: = **darin eingeschnitten**)—**Der Segen war fort aus meiner Hütte, sobald Sie einen Fuß darein** (= **in dieselbe**) **setzten** (Sch.)—**Er zog seinen Rock vom Leibe und hüllte sie darein** (Storm: = **hüllte sie in diesen ein**)—**Er besorgte eine Tasche: darein** (= **in diese**) **tat er das Nötigste** (C. Rothe)—**Ich entfaltete das Papier und fand einige Worte darein geschrieben** (H. Hesse: ordinarily **darin niedergeschrieben**)—**Sie schenkte mir eine Birne, und ich bat sie, den ersten Biß darein zu tun** (id.: usually **ich bat sie, zuerst hineinzubeißen**). The form **darin** is particularly applicable with verbs which can take either a dat. or an accus. in an accompanying prep. phrase, esp. those compounded with **ver-** (q.v. 2 *a*): cf. **In Schrecken hob sie die Hände, um ihr Gesicht darein zu vergraben** (Stehr) and **Sie fiel ins Meer und fühlte sich darein versinken** (Hauser), where in both cases **darin** would be much more usual. (**b**) In point of fact, **darein** is now little used except as an adv. suffix to **hinter-** and **oben-**, and as a sep. prefix to a limited number of verbs, in the former case always, in the latter usually, in the contracted form **drein**: e.g. **Wenn man den Schaden hat, bekommt man den Spott obendrein** (q.v. and cf. **überdies**: 'as well, in addition, into the bargain')—**Ein alter Leiermann kam die Straße heraufgehumpelt, die ganze Dorfjugend hinterdrein** (= **hinter ihm her**, 'after him, in his wake')—**Junge, du mußt nicht immer dreinreden!** ('put in a word, interrupt the conversation'); esp. in the reflex. verbs **sich dreinmischen** or **dreinmengen** ('to poke one's nose in, meddle in what doesn't concern one'), **sich dreinfinden** ('to reconcile oneself', as in **Der Krieg hat eine ganz neue Lage geschaffen, man wird sich dreinfinden müssen**) and **sich dreinfügen** or **dreinschicken** ('to resign oneself': cf. **Das ist mein Schicksal, ich muß mich dreinschicken**). Otherwise, **darein** is used fig. in good prose with the verbs **legen** and **setzen** and objs. like **Ehre, Ehrgeiz, Stolz,** etc., to anticipate an infin. clause: e.g. **Alle hatten etwas zu berichten, und sie legten Ehre darein** ('made it a point of honour'), **es auf eine lustige Art zu tun** (Waggerl)—**Er schien seinen Ehrgeiz darein gesetzt zu haben** ('to have made it his ambition'), **das Grundstück zu kaufen** (Th. Mann)—**Als er majorenn wurde, setzte er seinen Stolz darein, noch mehr zu verschwenden** (Tieck: 'When he came of age, he took pride in throwing still more money about')—**Der Gast setzte sein größtes Vergnügen darein** ('made it his chief pleasure'), **sich von der Tochter des Hauses bedienen zu lassen** (Spindler). But although the use of **darein** is now very limited, and modern authors mostly avoid it, that is no excuse for using **darin** with verbs which require **in** + accus.: it is really incorrect to say **Die Männer vertrieben sich die Zeit mit Johlen und Lärmen; der Schrei einer weiblichen Stimme mischte sich darin** (Sudermann) or **Ihr müßt euch darin finden** (Speckmann). But such propositions are significant, as showing the authors' reluctance to use the old-fashioned, rather precious form **darein**. **2.** The *rel.* use of **darein** (= 'into which') is even rarer than that of **daran, darauf,** etc. with rel. force (see *Sanders's* comment given under **da(r)-** 2), so that an example like **Ich habe in die Grube gesehen, darein man mein Liebstes versenkte** (Auerbach) is very unusual; cf., as correct, **Sie fühlte den schrecklichen Zustand, worein** (or **in den**) **ihn diese Worte versetzt hatten** (G.) and **Sie hatten ihre eigenen Gegenstände der Unterhaltung, worein sonst niemand eingeweiht werden konnte** (Mörike): see **wo(r)-**.

darüber: see **da(r)-**. The following examples show some of the most characteristic uses of this word: **Bald werden wir an den Fluß kommen: man hat unlängst eine neue Brücke darü'ber gebaut**—**Das ist eine schwierige Frage, wir wollen darü'ber noch sprechen**—**Ich bin froh darü'ber, daß ihr mein Geschenk so gefallen hat**—**Wir haben gestern abend viel musiziert, da'rüber verging die Zeit sehr schnell** ('that made the time pass quickly')—**Also hat er Ihnen das übelgenommen? Da'rüber wundere ich mich nicht** ('So he is offended with you for that? That does not surprise me')—**Ein glückliches Familienleben: da'rüber geht nichts!** ('there is nothing to match *or* beat that')—**Ich war darü'ber hinaus, was die Nachbarsleute von mir denken würden** (Tieck: 'I was past caring what my neighbours would think of me')—**Es ist möglich, daß der Versuch mißlingen wird, aber da'rüber brauche ich mir noch keine grauen Haare wachsen zu lassen** ('but I don't need to worry about that yet')—**Eine Zeitlang war ich mit meinem Freunde in Zwist, aber da'rüber ist nun Gras gewachsen** ('For a time I had a quarrel with my friend, but that is forgotten now, a thing of the past'); cf. the combination **drunter und drüber**, for which see **darunter** *ad fin.*

darum: see **da(r)-**. As with **daran, darin,** etc., so here also **dar-** is accented when the pron. it represents has *dem.* force: e.g. **„Sie wollten mir doch ein Buch leihen?" „Eben da'rum bin ich gekommen"** ('It 's just for that reason I have come'); with a following adversative (esp. **doch**), it assumes the force of 'nevertheless', as in **Das Werk ist nicht gerade hervorragend, aber da'rum doch ganz lesenswert** ('but quite worth reading for all that') and **Es klingt zwar unglaublich, aber da'rum kann es doch wahr sein**—cf. its now unusual use as a rel. in **Er galt für einen**

Juden, darum ('in spite of which') **er aber nicht minder sorgfältig gepflegt wurde** (Chamisso). With the accent on **-um**, it is used in propositions like **Es fehlen mir zehn Mark, jemand muß mich daru'm betrogen haben—Helfen Sie mir, ich bitte Sie daru'm!—Es ist mir einzig daru'm zu tun, ihn zu überzeugen, daß ich recht habe** ('My sole aim is to convince him that I am right')—**Es ist, als wäre es dem Erzähler** (*scil.* Hermann Grimm) **überall darum zu tun, mehr auf Hörer als auf Leser zu wirken** (Heyse: 'It is as though the novelist's object was to make all his tales appeal more to the listener than to the reader'); **Ich habe diese Arbeit mit allem, was drum und dran hängt, übernommen** ('I have taken on this job with all it implies')—cf. the subst. use of this last coll. combination in **Einige helfende Hände hatten** (*scil.* **in der Feuersbrunst**, 'in the conflagration') **auch dieses Tischchen mit allem Drum und Dran gerettet** (Frenssen: i.e. with everything on it) and **Der Maler hatte in München nicht nur das Handwerk, sondern auch das gesellschaftliche Drum und Dran gelernt** (O. Flake: 'In Munich the artist had learned not only his craft but also the social conventions it brought with it').

darunter: see **da(r)-**. The following are some characteristic uses of this expression: **Da ist ein großer Baum, daru'nter finden wir Schutz vor dem Regen—Ich habe die Schrift durchgelesen: da'runter kann ich meinen Namen nicht setzen** ('I can't put my name to *that*')—**In diesem Geschäft verkauft man nur Gegenstände zu 20 Mark und daru'nter** ('and less')—**Da sind alle die Dokumente, es sind wichtige Briefe daru'nter** ('There are important letters among them')—**Dieser Satz ist zweideutig** ('ambiguous'): **was verstehen Sie daru'nter?** ('What do you understand by it *or* what do you take it to mean?')—**Bei uns ist augenblicklich alles drunter und drüber** ('Everything is topsy-turvy *or* upside down in our house just now')—**Sie besorgte das Haus, und wenn sie fort war, ging alles drunter und drüber** (E. v. Sallwürk: 'She ran the house, and when she was away everything got into a state of confusion'). See **da(r)- 3**.

dative: see **accusative or dative . . ; dative -e; passive 1** (*a*) and **2**. As mentioned under **genitive (possessive) 1** *ad fin.*, the poss. pron. **sein** was formerly, esp. in the classical period, often inserted after a Saxon gen. in coll. speech: e.g. **Nimm meinen Ring und gib mir des Majors seinen dafür!** (Lessing: = **gib mir den des Majors dafür**)—**Wenig Tage nach des Herrn Grafen seiner Abreise starb mein Gemahl** (Gellert)—**Als ich hinaustrat, sah ich Marx Sievers seinen Ältesten herunterkommen** (Storm). In such contexts the gen. was commonly replaced by the *dat.*, as in **Da ist dem Kerl sein Platz** (G.), and in modern popular lang. there seems to be a preference for the dat.: e.g. **Es war dem Kleinen sein Eigentum** (Wildenbruch: = **Es war das Eigentum des Kleinen**).

dative -e: In MHG the dat. sing. ending *-e* in masc. and neut. nouns was almost fixed, the exceptions being nouns ending in *-el*, *-en*, and *-er*, and the latter still holds good: one can only say **im Spiegel—im Magen—zum Mädchen—mit dem Dampfer.** In ordinary language the final **-e** is disappearing more and more, the general tendency being to drop it in *un*-modified monosyllabic nouns and usually before words beginning with a vowel, but to insert it between two accented syllables. Thus, one ordinarily says **ein Ring von Gold**, but **ein Ring vom feinsten Golde** (cf., in the old folksong, **ein Ringlein von Go'lde ro't**); so also **einen Mord mit Blut büßen**, it being only for the sake of the metre that **-e** is inserted in **Nur mit Blute büßt sich ab der blut'ge Mord** (Sch.). Luther's **Gebet Gotte, was Gottes ist** (Matt. 22. 21) now sounds very harsh, and the **-e** is rightly dropped in the modern version; but one still says **dem Go'tte I'sraels.** In particular, the **-e** is omitted in phrases like **Arm in Arm gehen—von Haus zu Haus wandern—von Jahr zu Jahr warten—Kopf an Kopf stehen—von Mund zu Mund gehen**—but is retained in a number of set prep. expressions such as **heutzutage—zutage kommen** ('to come to light')—**nach Hause gehen** and **zu Hause bleiben—zugrunde richten—jemandem etwas zuleide tun—beileibe nicht!** ('not on your life!')—**außerstande sein** and **zustande bringen**; and so also usually in **jemand zu Rate ziehen** ('to consult somebody'): cf. **Lysander ging mit sich zu Rate** (Bergengruen: '. . . communed with himself'). In other expressions either form is used, as in **Mir ist traurig zumut(e)—zu Bett(e) gehen—jemand zu Tisch(e) laden**, etc., the deciding factor often probably being euphony.

dauern: There are really two verbs **dauern**, one derived from Lat. *durare*, the other connected with **teuer**. **1.** The former, meaning 'to last, en*dure*, continue' (cf. **ein dauerhafter Stoff**, 'a durable material'), is a LG word (**duren**) which has spread to all parts and largely gained the ascendancy over the HG **währen** (q.v.). It is used esp. of the passage of time: e.g. **Es wird noch lange dauern** (or, more choice, **währen**), **ehe** or **bis . . .** ('Itwill be a long time yet before . . .')—**Die Vorstellung dauerte drei Stunden—Der Lärm war groß und dauerte eine Weile fort** (G.). It has a wider application than **währen**, its pres. part. being often used as an adj. or adv.: e.g. **Er hat eine dauernde** (or **feste**, 'permanent') **Anstellung bekommen—Ich habe mich nun dauernd in Berlin niedergelassen**; cf. **Wir haben seit einer Woche andauernd** (or **andauernden** = 'continuous') **Regen. 2.** The original force of the other verb **dauern** was 'to be precious', an idea which may still be dimly seen in the expression **sich etwas nicht dauern lassen**, lit. 'not to let a thing be too precious', i.e. 'to set little store by a thing', implying readiness to give it up, i.e. 'not to grudge' it, as in **Die Ritter ließen sich das Blut nicht dauern** (Sch.: '. . . risked their lives'). But relinquishing something precious is inevitably accompanied by feelings of regret and pity, which explains the modern use in **Es dauert mich, ihn beleidigt zu haben** or **daß ich ihn beleidigt habe** ('I regret having offended him')—**Der arme Mann dauert mich** (= **tut mir leid**, 'I am sorry for *or* pity the poor man': see **erbarmen**). Whereas the subj. of **dauern** is the person or thing which excites pity, that of the trans. compound **bedauern** is the person in whom pity is excited: e.g. **Ich bedaure den armen Mann—Die Frau ist zu bedauern** ('. . . is to be pitied')—**Wir bedauern lebhaft, Sie gestern verfehlt zu haben** ('We are very sorry to have missed you yesterday').

davon: see **da(r)-**. Used with a verb of motion, this does not suggest departure from a specified place, but is merely an alternative expression for **fort** or coll. **weg** ('off, away'): cf. **Wir brachten einen Tag in London zu und reisten von da** (or **von dort**, not **davon**) **nach Frankreich**; but **Als ich nach ihm griff, lief er davo'n.** The following examples give its other main uses: **Vor Ihrem Hause ist jemand verunglückt: was wissen Sie davo'n?** ('What do you know about it?'), in the reply to which the accent might shift: **Da'von weiß ich nichts** ('That I know nothing about')—**Was haben wir nun davo'n?** ('What do we get out of it?')—**Ich kam mit einem Schrecken davo'n** ('I came out of it with nothing worse than a fright')—**Er kam mit einem blauen Auge davo'n** ('He came off cheaply, had a narrow escape'); so also with an appos. infin. or finite clause: **Ich rate Ihnen davo'n ab, diese Aktien zu kaufen** ('I advise you against buying these shares') —**Das kommt davo'n, wenn man sich nicht vorsieht** ('That comes of not taking care')—**Spazierengehen? Das hängt davo'n ab, ob sich das Wetter aufklärt** ('That depends on whether it clears up').

davor: see **da(r)-**. This is now clearly distinguished from **dafür** (q.v.). There are not so many idioms here as with most of the other preps. compounded with **da(r)-**, but the following are worth noting: **Als wir uns der Haustür näherten, stand ein grimmiger Hund davo'r—Das Bergsteigen ist mit Lebensgefahr verbunden, aber da'vor scheinen leidenschaftliche Bergsteiger keine Angst zu haben—Gegen Mitternacht zog ein schweres Gewitter auf, ich konnte davo'r nicht einschlafen** ('I could not fall asleep for it')—**Kind, hüte dich davo'r, in den Fluß zu fallen!** (see **hüten** 2 *a*)—**Ich schrak davo'r zurück, ihm diese schlechte Nachricht mitzuteilen** ('I shrank from giving him this bad news') —**Mein guter Stern bewahrte mich davo'r** (Sch.: 'My lucky star saved me from that').

dazu: Here, as with **daran**, etc., the accent falls on the *prefix* (**da**) when it stands for a dem. pron., but on the *prep.* (**zu**) when the prefix stands for a pers. pron.: e.g. in the former case, **Er will versuchen, diese Felswand hinaufzuklettern: da'zu gehört Mut** ('that requires courage')—**Sie wollen sich ein größeres Haus bauen lassen? Da'zu würde ich Ihnen jetzt nicht raten** ('That I should not advise you to do just now')—**Also da'zu alle diese Vorbereitungen!** ('So *that* is the purpose of all these preparations!'); in the latter case, **Hier sind zwei Mark, und noch zwei dazu'** ('and two more to add to them')—**„Man hat vorgeschlagen, heute einen Ausflug zu machen: was sagen Sie dazu'?"** ('What do you say to the proposal?'); **„Was? Ich soll meine Arbeit lassen und einen**

Ausflug mitmachen? noch dazu′ bei diesem kalten Wetter?" ('. . . and in this cold weather too?')—**Der Junge ist dreist, und noch dazu′ frech** ('The boy is pert, and impertinent as well *or* into the bargain')—**Diese Vorrichtung dient dazu′, den Ofen schneller zu heizen** ('This contrivance is for the purpose of heating the oven more quickly'). It is used esp. with **kommen**: e.g. **Er scheint viel Geld zu haben: wie er wohl dazu′ gekommen ist?** ('I wonder how he came by it')—**Dazu′ kommt noch, daß es zu kostspielig sein würde** ('What 's more, it would be too expensive')—**Ich komme einfach nicht dazu′, Briefe zu schreiben** ('I simply cannot find time to write letters')—**Ich möchte gern wissen, wie ich dazu′ komme, zu der Feier eingeladen zu werden** ('. . . how I come to be invited . . .')—**Wie kommen Sie dazu′, mir so etwas zuzumuten?** ('How could you bring yourself to expect such a thing of me?' i.e. How dare you come to me with such a suggestion?—see **anmuten**). The earlier rel. use is now obs.: cf. **Ergreife das ewige Leben, dazu′** ('whereunto') **du berufen bist** (1 Tim. 6. 12).

dazwischen: see **da(r)-**. Here the prefix **da-** necessarily represents a pers. pron. in the 3rd *plur.*, the reference being to something that separates at least two objs., as in **Hier werden jetzt zwei Häuser gebaut, aber dazwi′schen ist reichlich Platz für ein drittes.** With a verb of motion like **kommen, treten,** etc., it is somewhat unlike **daran, darauf,** etc. in that it can be used of people, in which case its basic sense is that of prevention: e.g. **Als die Knaben sich schlagen wollten, trat ich dazwi′schen** ('I intervened' to prevent a fight)—**Wir wollen uns morgen treffen: hoffentlich kommt nichts dazwi′schen** ('it is to be hoped that nothing will occur to prevent our meeting').

deceive: **1.** The verb **täuschen** implies no intention of deliberate deception: its force is merely to cause a person to confuse one thing with another, as when one says **Die Zwillinge sind sich täuschend ähnlich,** i.e. are so like each other that one cannot tell which is which. It is esp. common in expressions which suggest confusion between the appearance and the reality: e.g. **Ich habe ihn falsch verstanden, mein Ohr hat mich getäuscht,** i.e. my ear misled me into thinking he said something which he actually did not say; sim. **Ich glaube ihn gesehen zu haben, ich mag mich aber täuschen**—**Wie konnte sie sich so täuschen lassen?** (P. Keller). But such confusion may, of course, easily cause disappointment, as in **Er hat meine Erwartungen getäuscht** or **Ich habe mich in meinen Hoffnungen getäuscht,** where the simple verb closely approaches the compound **enttäuschen**: cf. **Ich hatte mich auf das Konzert gefreut, es hat mich aber sehr enttäuscht.** **2.** Where a deliberate deception is suggested, the most general expression is **betrügen** ('to deceive, cheat, swindle'), the prep. **um** being used to indicate what one has been swindled out of: e.g. **Er hat mich um eine große Summe betrogen.** Unusual now is a proposition like **Die Zauberei täuschte ihn um seine Lust** (Arnim): cf. **Die Zauberei täuschte ihn derart, daß ihm alle Lust verging.** **3.** Analogous is **hinterge′hen** (insep.), properly implying deceitful conduct behind a person's back ('to impose upon'): e.g. **Er wunderte sich über die Ruhe, mit der ihn der junge Mann so lange hinterga′ngen hatte** (H. Hesse)—**Er hat sich erdreistet, mich in meiner Abwesenheit zu hinterge′hen** ('He has had the audacity to impose upon me during my absence').

deinesgleichen: see -gleichen 1.

denen: see **der** (demonstrative) 2, esp. the example from Th. Mann under 2 (*b*).

denken: **1.** This verb has a number of constructions, viz. (**a**) an *accus.* obj., esp. a neut. pron. or adj.-subst., also a noun with a pred. adj.: e.g. **Denke, was du willst: was ich denke, darf ich sagen** (Sch.)—**Manche Leute denken immer das Schlechteste von ihren Nachbarn** (see *e*)—**Das Übrige können Sie sich denken** ('I leave the rest to your imagination')—**Eine Reise ins Ausland denke ich mir sehr lehrreich** ('I fancy a journey abroad to be very instructive'); (**b**) a *gen.* obj. in the sense of 'to think of, bear in mind', now only in poetry and elevated prose (cf. **gedenken**): e.g. **Denkt nicht des Irrtums meiner Jugend!** (Sch.); (**c**) **an**+*accus.*, which has displaced the gen. in ordinary language: e.g. **Der brave Mann denkt an sich selbst zuletzt** (Sch.)—**Ich denke ernstlich daran, auszuwandern** ('I am thinking seriously of emigrating')—**Ich denke nicht dran!** (coll., 'Nothing is further from my mind!'); (**d**) **auf**+*accus.*, in the sense of 'to meditate on' some goal to be reached, 'to consider means, make plans' to achieve some end, 'to direct one's thoughts' towards something: e.g. **Er denkt** (or **sinnt**) **auf Rache** ('He is meditating revenge')—**Die Männer denken mehr auf das Einzelne, die Weiber mehr auf das, was im Leben zusammenhängt** (G.)—**Ein jeder denkt auf seinen Vorteil** (Chamisso: 'Every one has an eye to the main chance')—**Sie wußte nichts mehr mit sich anzufangen: man mußte darauf denken, ein stilles Asyl für sie ausfindig zu machen** (Mörike: 'She was at her wit's end: thoughts must be directed towards finding a quiet sanctuary for her')—**Vor allem soll ein junger Mensch darauf denken, wie er sich nützlich erzeigen kann** (G. Keller)—**Er muß jetzt darauf denken, wie er dem Übel begegnen kann** (F. Griese); (**e**) **von** (or **über** + *accus.*) with the force of 'to think of, have an opinion about' something: e.g. **Denke nicht niedrig von mir!** (G.: 'Don't think meanly of me!')—**Was denken Sie von der jetzigen internationalen Lage?**—**Ich will dir sagen, was ich über sein Betragen denke**; (**f**) **zu** + *infin.*: e.g. **Er dachte mich zu betrügen** ('He thought to deceive me')—**Was denkst** (usually **gedenkst**) **du zu tun?** ('What do you propose to do?'); (**g**) the *accus. and infin.*, now practically obs. and not to be recommended: cf. **Nun denke dir die Vettel vor mir herumtanzen** (Sch.: 'Now picture to yourself the old hag dancing about in front of me'), and, as a particularly objectionable example from a modern author, **Mein Vater rückte den Wandschirm zur Seite und enthüllte die sitzende Gestalt eines schönen Mädchens, das uns gläsern anstarrte. Es war gespenstisch, sie ohne Bewegung hinter dem Wandschirm gesessen haben zu denken** (A. Schaeffer: '. . . It was eerie to think of her as having sat motionless behind the screen'). Equally rare now is the **accus. and part.** (q.v.). **2.** For **gedacht** with the force of 'above-mentioned, referred to previously', see **gedenken** (*a*) (ii).

Denkmal: see **Mal** 1.

denn (**adverb**): **1.** Inserted in a question, **denn** implies a lively interest or impatience on the part of the questioner, or makes the question less abrupt: e.g. **Wo bleibt er denn nur?** ('Where on earth can he be?')—**Man hat Sie ja lange nicht gesehen: sind Sie denn krank gewesen?**—**Wie heißt du denn?** ('Tell me your name, will you?'). Sim. in an indir. question: **Auf die Frage, über welche Beschwerden sie denn zu klagen habe, sah sie den Arzt ratlos an** (Carossa). **2.** In a semi-exclamatory statement, it intensifies a previous remark, being often introduced by **so** or **also**: e.g. **So hat er denn seinen Plan durchgesetzt** ('So he *has* carried his point')—**Das ist denn doch zuviel verlangt** ('But that is really asking too much'). So also **denn auch** with confirmatory force: **„Ich werde mit meiner Frau sprechen", sagte er, und das tat er denn auch** (Fontane: '. . . and so he did'). **3.** To express 'I shall go home tomorrow unless I am ill' in MHG, one said *ich wil morne heim gân, ich ensî dan ungesunt*, where the neg. *en-* and the adv. *dan* could be omitted. This old idiom is still used in choice style, but the neg. is omitted and **denn** (not **dann**) retained, the word-order being that of a *princ.* clause, although the force of the clause is subord.: e.g. **Ich will morgen nach Hause gehen, ich sei denn krank**; sim. **Er entfernte sich niemals weit, er sagte es ihr denn** (G.: '. . . without telling her')—**„Ich lasse dich nicht fort", rief sie, „du sagst mir denn, was du im Sinn hast"** (E. Wichert: '. . . unless you tell me what you have in mind')—**Er wird von seiner Meinung nicht weichen, Ihr überzeugtet ihn denn einer besseren** (id.: 'He will never alter his opinion, unless you should convince him of a better one'). So also in the common phrase **es sei denn**, as in **Was sie getan hat, kann ich dir nicht sagen, es sei denn unter vier Augen** ('. . . unless we are alone together'), often with a following **daß**-clause ('unless it be that . . .'): e.g. **Er schrieb emsig und ohne Aufenthalt, es sei denn, daß er die Feder in das Tintenfaß tauchte** (Th. Mann: 'He wrote rapidly without stopping, except to dip his pen into the inkstand')—**Die Gräben** ('trenches') **lagen leer da, es sei denn an Stellen, an denen noch gebaut wurde** (J. Thorwald); cf. **except** 2 (*b*). The same idea is idiomatically expressed in another way, viz. by using **denn** with *the past subj. of* **müssen**: e.g. **Es wird kein Feind die Schwelle überschreiten, er müßte denn über meine Leiche gehen** (Jak. Frey), which may be explained thus: 'No enemy shall cross my threshold; if he should do so, *he would have to* step over my dead body'; sim. **„Sie werden Palmas Übertritt** ('conversion') **nicht wünschen?" „Nein, Palma müßte sich denn dafür entscheiden"** (Zobeltitz)—**Er gehört zu denen, die ein Vogel in der Luft nicht**

verwundern kann, es müßte denn ein künstlicher Vogel sein (Waggerl)—**Er frug Ernst, auf welche Weise hier das meiste Geld verdient würde, worüber ihm dieser jedoch keine Auskunft geben konnte, sie hätte denn lauten müssen: im Stegreif** (Jul. Wolff: '. . . a question to which, however, the only answer the latter could have given him would have been by seizing the opportunity'). **4.** Another idiomatic use of **denn** is seen in the expression **geschweige denn** ('not to mention'): see **geschweigen.** In a proposition like **Das Gehalt war zu gering, als daß ein einziger, geschweige denn eine Familie davon leben konnte** (Ric. Huch) the pers. pron. **ich** is really omitted, the lit. meaning being 'The income was too small to support a single man, (and having said that,) I keep silent about a family', i.e. '. . . a single man, *far less* a family'; sim. **Sie vertragen nicht einmal guten, geschweige denn schlechten Wein** (G. Keller: 'They can't even stand a good wine, *let alone* a bad one')—**Die alte Dame hatte die Veränderung ihrer Lage noch nicht begriffen, geschweige denn innerlich verarbeitet** (W. Kramp: 'The old lady had not yet grasped her altered circumstances, *much less* fully appreciated what these meant for her'). Sometimes **denn** is dropped here, but it sounds rather more idiomatic to insert it: cf. **Einen Kadetten, sagte sie, könne sie nicht einmal lieben, geschweige heiraten** (Fontane)—**Ein ehrenhafter Soldat vergreift sich nicht an einem Gefangenen, geschweige an einem Verwundeten** (Schreckenbach)—**Es war ein Boot, in dem man kaum über einen See fahren konnte, geschweige übers Meer** (Kellermann)—**Sie saßen eine Viertelstunde lang, ohne einander anzusehen, geschweige, daß sie zusammen geredet hätten** (Immermann).

denn (conjunction): **1.** As a coord. conj. with normal word-order, **denn** (= MHG *wande*) has causal force, being used to introduce an explanatory statement which gives the *logical* reason for the previous assertion, the reason being one which can be readily verified: e.g. **Es muß sehr kalt sein, denn** ('for', as is evident) **der Teich ist zugefroren.** Such a proposition can also be expressed by reversing the clauses, making the second the introductory princ. one, and the first a subord. one introduced by **also** or **folglich,** giving the logical deduction: **Der Teich ist zugefroren, also muß es sehr kalt sein.** **2.** A somewhat stronger expression for **denn** here is the subord. conj. **da,** introducing a clause which generally *precedes* the logical reason: **Da der Teich zugefroren ist, muß es sehr kalt sein.** **3.** Whereas **denn** and **da** give the logical reason, the subord. conj. **weil** (q.v.: = MHG *sît* or *sît daz*) gives the *real* or *moral* reason for a statement (the cause of some fact or phenomenon, the motive of some action, etc.): e.g. **Der Teich friert zu, weil es kalt ist** (the actual cause) or, reversing the clauses, **Es ist kalt, daher** or **deswegen** ('for that reason') **friert der Teich zu.** It is correct, then, to say **Es muß kalt sein, denn der Teich friert zu,** but incorrect to say **Es muß kalt sein, weil der Teich zufriert**; so also cf., on the one hand, **Du kannst nichts lernen, denn du bist unaufmerksam** (i.e. I conclude from your inattentiveness that you will learn nothing), and on the other hand, **Du kannst nichts lernen, weil du unaufmerksam bist** (i.e. Your inattentiveness is the real cause of your not learning anything). It is important to note that the answer to a question asking 'why?' or 'for what reason?' is always introduced by **weil,** never by **da:** e.g. **„Warum** (or **Weswegen** or **Aus welchem Grunde**) **ist er denn nicht gekommen?" „Weil er krank ist."** **4.** At one time **denn** was very commonly used with the force of 'than': e.g. **Man muß Gott mehr gehorchen denn den Menschen** (Acts 5. 29)—**Keins der Gefolge bestand aus weniger denn zwanzig Bedienten** (G.). Although this use still occurs occasionally, as in **Alle Beleidigungen, die ihm während seines mehr denn sechzigjährigen Lebens zuteil geworden waren, traten ihm jetzt frisch vor die Seele** (Raabe), and esp. before **je,** as in **Jetzt sehne ich mich mehr denn je** ('more than ever') **nach den Ferien** and **Ihre Mutter, so kleinlaut sie auch geworden war, erschien ihr herrschsüchtiger denn je** (W. Kramp), its main function is now to replace the normal **als** in propositions in which an identifying or temp. **als** also occurs, as explained under **als** = 'than' 5; cf. **Das betrachten wir eher als eine Tugend denn als einen Fehler** (G. Keller).

deny: 1. The verb **verneinen** (ant. **bejahen**) means 'to give a negative answer to' (a question) or 'to contradict' (an assertion): e.g. **Er verneinte meine Frage —Das läßt sich nicht bloß bezweifeln son-**

dern geradezu verneinen (Heine)—**Wer kann dies mit Gewißheit bejahen oder mit Gewißheit verneinen?** (Wieland). **2.** (a) Much like **verneinen** with reference to assertions is **leugnen,** 'to deny, not to admit' (ant. **zugestehen**): e.g. **Ich leugne nicht, das gesagt zu haben**—**Ich leugne nicht, daß er das gesagt hat**—**Das ist nicht zu leugnen** ('That is undeniable'). (b) With a direct accus. obj. other than an indef. neut., the compound **ableugnen** is more usual, as in **eine Schuld ableugnen**; esp. with an additional dat. of the person: e.g. **Das hieße, den Göttern die Vernunft ableugnen** (Sch.: 'That would be as much as to say that the gods were not reasonable beings'). (c) The commonest compound is **verleugnen:** as *Sanders* says, **„Zum Leugnen und Ableugnen gehört immer ausdrückliches Aussprechen, daß etwas nicht ist; verleugnen kann man auch durch Schweigen, durch eine Handlung usw.: wer etwas verleugnet, der weiß, daß es ist, und spricht oder handelt doch so, als ob es nicht wäre."** This explains expressions like **Karte verleugnen** (in card-playing: 'not to follow suit', although one has a card of the required suit in one's hand)—**Als der Diener meldete, daß jemand mich sprechen wollte, ließ ich mich verleugnen** ('When the servant announced that somebody wished to see me, I told him to say I was not at home'). In this sense, it is a favourite word of Luther's: cf. **Ehe der Hahn krähet, wirst du mich dreimal verleugnen** (Matt. 26. 34: 'Before the cock crow, thou shalt deny me thrice', i.e. thou wilt say that thou dost not know me); and this leads to the sense of 'to deny, renounce, give up': e.g. **Will mir jemand nachfolgen, der verleugne sich selbst** (Matt. 16. 24: i.e. let him practise self-denial)—**Nicht das Vaterland und nicht der Väter Glauben möcht' ich verleugnen** (Platen). **3.** Analogous to **ableugnen** is **absprechen,** 'to deny, refuse' something to a person, i.e. to say that he lacks something (**sagen, daß ihm etwas abgehe**—see **lack** 3): e.g. **Talent kann man ihm nicht absprechen** ('It cannot be denied that he is talented.') **4.** Here belongs also **versagen** (q.v. 1 and 2).

depend: 1. In ordinary language there is often little distinction drawn between **ankommen** (+ **auf** + accus.) and **abhängen** (+ **von**), and indeed, they approach each other closely. Properly, whereas **ankommen** implies a definite, generally vital *condition,* **abhängen** lays stress on the close, often necessary *connexion* between the things referred to. Actually, both these ideas are implicit in our verb 'to depend', of which *The English Oxford Dictionary* gives two shades of meaning: (i) 'to be contingent on *or* conditioned by' (e.g. 'The value of a book does not depend on its size') and (ii) 'to be connected with in the relation of subordination' (e.g. 'Their peasants now depend upon the Czar's officers'). The following examples may make this distinction clearer: on the one hand, **Das Dienstmädchen hat gekündigt und sucht eine neue Stellung; es kommt ihr besonders auf gute Behandlung an** ('The servant-girl has given notice and is looking for a new situation; her main concern is good treatment', i.e. good treatment would be the main condition of her accepting a situation); and, on the other hand, **Die Anzahl der Winkel in einem Dreieck hängt von der Anzahl seiner Seiten ab** (Eberhard: 'The number of angles in a triangle is conditioned by the number of its sides', where there is a clearly defined, necessary connexion between the sides and the angles of the geometrical figure). **2.** But while the use of **abhängen** is strictly limited, **ankommen** has a wider application, being used in a number of idiomatic expressions where **abhängen** cannot be used: e.g. **Auf Geld kommt es hier nicht an** ('This is not a question of money')—**Auf ein paar Mark soll es mir nicht ankommen** ('I shan't let a few shillings stand in the way')—**Es kommt mir weniger darauf an, was er tut, als wie er es tut** ('With me the question is not so much what he does as how he does it')—**Worauf es hier hauptsächlich ankommt, ist, eine Entscheidung zu treffen** ('The main question here is to come to a decision')—**Dem Durstigen kommt es auf die Schale nicht an, sondern auf die Früchte** (H. v. Kleist: 'To a thirsty person the dish is of no consequence, what matters is the fruit in the dish')—**Wir wollen es auf den Versuch ankommen lassen** ('We'll put the matter to the test': cf. risk *ad fin.*)—**Das kommt ganz darauf an!** ('That all depends!': cf. the last example given under **je** 2 *b*).

der (demonstrative): 1. Used like an *attrib. adj.* Here the various forms are the same as those of the def. art., the two expressions being actually the same, the only difference being that the dem. is accented, while the art. is not. It follows that this use of the dem. is much more common in the spoken lang., where it can be accented, than in print, where often, if the sense is to be clear, the stress should be indicated by italics or spaced letters. Thus, the sense of the proposition **Nein, in der Stadt wohnt er nicht** depends on the accent: if this falls on **Stadt**, the meaning is 'No, he lives out of town', but if it falls on **der**, the meaning is 'No, that is not the town in which he lives'. **2.** Used as a *subst.*: (**a**) Here, if no dependent prep. phrase or rel. clause follows (as in 'those of us' or 'those who were present'), its forms are those of the art. in the nom. and accus. sing. and plur., and in the dat. sing. (for other cases, see *b* below): e.g. **Ein Schutzmann ist an der Tür: was de'r wohl will** ('I wonder what *he* wants')—**Der Inhalt der „Idylle vom Bodensee" ist ungefähr de'r:...** (E. v. Sallwürk: 'The story of [Mörike's] "Idyll of the Lake of Constance" is roughly this: . . .')—**Karl** (or **Marie**) **Schmidt? De'n** (or **Die'**) **habe ich lange nicht gesehen—Seine Söhne? Nein, die' kenne ich nicht.** Where a prep. phrase or a rel. clause follows, modern usage rather prefers the appropriate forms of **de'rjenige** (see **dies** 2 *d*): e.g. **De'rjenige, welcher der letzte im Zimmer war, hat vergessen, das Licht abzuschalten** or **abzuknipsen** ('The person who was the last in the room has forgotten to switch off the light'), which is obviously better than to begin with **De'r, der der letzte...**; sim. **Die'jenigen, welche die** (better than **Die', die die**) **Prüfung bestanden haben, sind auf dieser Liste aufgezeichnet.** (**b**) In the gen. sing. masc. and neut. the form **dessen** is practically fixed (des is sometimes used, but should preferably be avoided), and definitely established is the dat. plut. of all genders, viz. **denen**: e.g. **Ich bin ihm vor einem Jahre begegnet: ich erinnere mich dessen ganz deutlich** ('I remember that very clearly') —**Heinrich trat in die Stelle, die Rudolf eingenommen hatte: er wohnte in dessen** (i.e. Rudolph's) **Stube, benutzte dessen Bücher** (Raabe)—**Ich spreche nicht von meinen eigenen Büchern, sondern von denen meines Bruders—Mehrere Gäste erkannten ihn nicht: das machte gewiß der Knebelbart** ('imperial') **aus, und das sagte ich denen auch, denen es nicht hatte beikommen wollen, daß er es sei** (Th. Mann: '. . . and I told that to those to whom it had never occurred that it could be he'). In the gen. sing. fem. and the gen. plur. of all genders there is much fluctuation, the forms **der, deren,** and **derer** having become hopelessly confused; the form **der** is not nearly as common as the other two—in **An der Wand hing eine Tafel, wo die Namen aller de'r standen, die im Kriege gefallen waren** (Raabe), **all de'rjenigen** would be more usual—but **deren** and **derer** are so common and so bewildering that it has been thought advisable to treat them in separate articles.

der (relative): In the north by far the commonest rel. pron. is **der, die, das**; there **welch** sounds rather formal, while **so** (q.v. 4 *a*) is almost obs. **1.** In particular, **der** is now almost always used where the antecedent is a *pers. pron.*: it is rather unusual for a woman to say **Da soll ich eine Heimat finden, ich, welche niemals eine rechte Heimat gehabt habe** (Raabe); cf. **welch (relative)** 4. Until fairly recent times a *1st* or *2nd* pers. pron. was usually repeated after **der** when this was the *subj.* of its clause, the verb agreeing with the pers. pron., and this is still done in select prose (but see 2): e.g. **Im Herbste stellte er eine Treibjagd an, ich aber, der ich nicht jage, blieb daheim** (Storm)—**Ihr Alten, die ihr mit ihm jung gewesen** (*scil.* **seid**), **sehet den Toten noch einmal an!** (id.)—**Wie kann man Vertrauen zu Ihnen haben, der Sie keinen Glauben haben?** (A. Eloesser); cf. **Du Phrasenmacher, welcher** (better **der**) **du ein Dichter sein willst!** (Raabe). A *3rd* pers. pron. is only repeated in *indir.* speech: e.g. **Sie sagten, daß sie, die sie Deutsche wären, nicht in Herden arbeiten könnten** (Frenssen), where the dir. speech would be **Wir, die wir Deutsche sind, können nicht in Herden arbeiten**; cf. **Es war ihr, als sei dies eine Schande, nicht nur für ihn, sondern auch für sie, die sie seine Schwester war** (Bergengruen), an indir. expression of what she was saying to herself: **Dies scheint mir eine Schande . . . für mich, die ich seine Schwester bin. 2.** There seems to be a growing tendency among modern authors, however, to drop the repetition of the pers. pron. and make the verb stand in the *3rd* pers.: e.g. **Dies bringt uns zum Lachen, und das ist für mich, der ebenfalls lacht, der rührendste**

Anblick der Welt (Th. Mann)—**Ich sitze hier in meiner Stube, ich, der achtundzwanzig Jahre alt geworden ist** (Rilke)—**Wie kann es sein, daß du, die doch verzichtete, ihn noch immer liebst?** (H. Franck)—**Wagst du's, an ihrem Herzen zu zweifeln, der, was er ist, nur ihrem Herzen dankt?** (Grillparzer)—**„Ja", sagte sie, „ich denke, wenn du mich siehst, die soviel Kummer erlebt hat und doch noch munter ist, das kann dir gut tun"** (Frenssen)—**Sie, der an der Wahrheit des schottischen Ossians zweifelte, hören Sie jetzt mich!** (Herder)—**Es ist unverzeihlich, daß Ihr, der seine Schwäche kennt, ihn noch aufreizt** (C. F. Meyer); for the fluctuation, cf. **Warum sitzt du, der über all diese Dinge die Überschau hat, da oben und läßt das Dreinreden uns, die wir nichts davon verstehen?** (Blunck). **3.** But one must be on one's guard here. It would be incorrect to repeat the pers. pron. and let the verb agree with it in a proposition like **Warst du es nicht, der meine Liebhaberei anzufeuern wußte?** (G.), because the antecedent here is not **du,** but the pred. **es,** the meaning being 'Were you not *the person who* knew how to encourage me in my hobby?'; and sim. **Da ich es bin, der das Geld verdient, so muß ich auch in der Lage sein, mir über jeden Kreuzer Rechenschaft ablegen zu können** (H. W. Geißler: 'As I am the one who earns the money, I must be in a position to account to myself for every farthing')—**„Ich bin es"; sagte sie, „die dich in Sünde gestürzt hat"** (C. F. Meyer)—**Also Ihr seid es, der das Genie des Obersten aus den Windeln gewickelt hat!** (id.); for other examples, see **es ist** 1 (*c*).

deren: The forms **deren** and **derer** (q.v.) should really be clearly distinguished, but unfortunately they are often confused even by the best authors (see esp. 2 *b*). The form **deren** is correctly used in two ways: **1.** It may be the gen. sing. fem., or the gen. plur. of all genders, of the *dem.* pron. **der:** see **der (demonstrative)** (**a**) Here it is often used as a substitute for the *poss.*, in order to obviate possible ambiguity: e.g. **Sie traf die Schneiderin nicht zu Hause und mußte sich von deren Mutter Maß nehmen lassen** (Stehr), where **deren** makes it clear that the reference is not to her own mother (which **ihrer** would at once suggest), but to the dressmaker's mother; sim. **Darauf verließ Margarete das Gemach, begleitet von ihrer Tochter und deren** (i.e. her daughter's) **Kindern** (Jul. Wolff). (**b**) Its other common use is with *partitive* force: e.g. **„Arme? De'ren haben wir hier genug"** ('Poor people? We have plenty of *them* here'), where the gen. depends on **genug**—**Seit des Pfarrers Tode hatte er nur in Berufspflichten das Witwenhaus betreten; jetzt gab es deren nicht mehr** (R. Waldmüller), the gen. depending on **mehr**—**Hier hast du statt des versprochenen Guldens deren zwei** (Jul. Wolff); and the word on which the gen. depends may even be unexpressed: **„Feinde? Er hat deren** ('some'), **namentlich am bischöflichen Hofe"** (C. F. Meyer), where one more ordinarily would use **welche:** see **welch (indefinite)**; sim. **Es gibt Fälle, ja es gibt deren, wo Verzweiflung Pflicht ist** (G.)—**Freiheitskämpfe haben einen eigenen Zauber, und ich danke Gott daß die Geschichte** ('history') **deren in Fülle zu verzeichnen hat,** (Fontane)—**Sie wird wohl einen Bankier heiraten: hoffentlich einen christlichen, wenn's deren** ('any such') **noch gibt** (id.)—**Sein affektiertes Wesen ist nur eine kleine Schwäche, wie jeder Mensch deren hat** (Ompteda)—**Da sie im Märchen bewandert war, gab sie deren oft zum besten** (Speckmann). (**c**) Where we use 'of that, of those' with reference to, and to avoid the repetition of a previous noun (as in 'In view of my father's objections and *those* of his friends the motion was withdrawn'), German usage fluctuates: der or **deren** may be used of things, der or (more usually) **derer** (q.v. 1) of persons, but **derjenigen,** although rather prosaic, is applicable in both cases: e.g. **Angesichts der Einwände meines Vaters und der(en)** (or **derjenigen**) **seiner Freunde wurde der Antrag zurückgezogen**—**Ich erinnere mich seiner Drohungen und deren der anderen Verschwörer**—**Ungeachtet meiner Einrede und der(en) meines Bruders ging der Antrag durch**; for the fluctuation cf., in a reference to persons, **Er hatte wenig Geschmeidigkeit in der Behandlung der Menschen, weder der, die seinesgleichen waren, noch derer, die über ihm standen** (Jul. Schmidt). **2.** (**a**) It may be the gen. sing. fem., or the gen. plur. of all genders, of the *rel.* pron. **der:** e.g. **Das ist die einzige Schulfreundin** (or **Das sind die einzigen Schulfreundinnen**), **deren ich mich erinnere.** With poss. force, it immediately precedes a noun, which then loses its art. (as does our 'whose'); and hence, if the noun is qualified by an attrib. adj., **this**

must be *strongly* inflected: **Dies ist die Dame, deren ältester Sohn neulich verunglückt ist—Der Oberst hat Feinde, in deren besonderem Interesse es liegt, ihm mein Vertrauen zu rauben** (C. F. Meyer); for other examples, see **derer** 1, **genitive (possessive)** 3, and **von** 1 (*c*), and cf., as incorrect, **Noch jugendlich schien mir diese alte Frau, deren am Tage vielleicht scharfen** (for **scharfe**) **Züge in der Dämmerung weicher wurden** (W. v. Scholz). So also with a dependent num. or **jeder**: e.g. **In den Ecken hockten Spieltische, an deren einem** ('at one of which') **zwei Professoren Schach spielten** (St. Zweig)—**Es zeigte sich ein reinlicher Platz mit Bänken, von deren jeder** ('from each of which') **man eine hübsche Aussicht gewann** (G.)—**Er wies ihnen drei Zellen an, in deren jeder ein Bett stand** (Jul. Wolff). **(b)** It is here that confusion has arisen. Even the least narrow-minded of the grammarians condemn the use of the form **derer** as a *rel.* pron., and insist that, in examples like the following, it is incorrect, **deren** being the only correct form: **Eine stille Wut überfiel ihn, derer er nicht Herr werden konnte** (Ompteda)—**Es entstanden Streitigkeiten, infolge derer** ('in consequence of which') **er Italien verlassen mußte** (Jul. Meyer)—**Sie ging in den Park zu bestimmten Stunden, während derer** (see *c* below) **die Herrschaften dort zu promenieren pflegten** (Böhlau). If standard authors were as agreed on this point as the grammarians, it would certainly cause fewer headaches among our learners of German, but unfortunately this is by no means the case; the following additional examples show to what extent this incorrect use of **derer** has spread: **Begannen sie von der Heimat zu sprechen, offenbarten sie eine Herzlichkeit, derer sie fähig sein mochten** (Jul. Roth)—**Es gibt Einzelheiten aus dieser Zeit, derer ich mich genau entsinne** (Bonsels)—**Er zeichnete die Bilder aller Verwandten, derer er habhaft werden konnte** (E. Wiechert)—**Seitdem sind lange Wochen verflossen, während derer Sie sich von der Welt zurückgezogen haben** (Th. Mann)—**Einige Sekunden, während derer das Haus** ('the audience') **den Atem anhielt, vergingen, bevor sich der Beifall entlud** (H. Mann)—**Dahi'n** ('Gone') **waren die Abende, während derer sich Herren und Gesinde zu einer großen Familie einten** (Fr. Griese)—**Nach zehn Minuten, während derer niemand sich auch nur geräuspert hatte, kam er zurück** (Werfel)—**Das geschah nur um der einen Frau willen, wegen derer die Dörfer in Unruhe waren** (Blunck). Nevertheless, the fact remains that this rel. use of **derer**, which incidentally has no historical basis, is not 'officially' recognized, and students would be well advised to avoid it. **(c)** In the proposition **Die Krone, der mein Fürst mich würdig achtete, soll keiner mir bezweifeln** (G.), the gen. form **der** is used for metrical reasons and would be replaced by **deren** in prose. It will have been observed that, in the 'incorrect' examples given under (*b*), the commonest phrase is **während derer.** In this connexion it should be noted that it is not incorrect to say **Nach einer Weile, während der er aufs Tischtuch niedersah, fing er wieder zu sprechen an** (W. v. Scholz), as **während** (q.v.) may take a dat. as well as the normal gen., so that here both **während deren** (gen.) and **während der** (dat.) are quite correct; and sim. **„Wie machst du das?" fragte er nach einiger Zeit, während der er vor sich hingestarrt hatte** (G. Engel); and the same applies to **wegen** (q.v. 2, and cf. 3 below), as in **Ich brachte eine Flasche hervor, wegen der mich meine Nachbarn beriefen** (G.: '. . . for which my fellow travellers took me to task'). **3.** Instead of **wegen der(en)**, it is more common to use **derentwegen**, less frequently **deretwegen** (not recommended by *Duden*), both with inorganic **t**: e.g. **Da ist das Haus mit der berühmten Treppe, derentwegen Reisende von weither kommen** (C. Rothe)—**Er wandte das Gespräch von der Angelegenheit ab, derentwegen Juliane hier war** (Jul. Wolff)—**Die Universität hat ihr Gepräge von den Sitten der Studenten, derentwegen Jena lange berüchtigt gewesen** (F. A. Hohenstein)—**Er schämt sich, ein Deutscher zu sein, der üblen Dinge halber** (see **halb** 3 *c*), **derentwegen sich die Deutschen in der Welt einen verhaßten Namen gemacht haben** (B. E. Werner); cf., as incorrect, **„Dann kann ich wohl wieder gehen?" „Bevor die Entscheidung, dererwegen ich dich rufen ließ, gefallen ist?"** (H. Franck). In this connexion cf. **Er wollte der Frau, um deretwillen es geschehen war, Schuld geben** (Blunck) and **Da habe ich der** (= **derjenigen**, 'to her') **das Wiederkommen versprochen, um derenwillen ich** diese weite Reise mache (Storm), for which see Wille 3.

dere(n)twegen, -willen: see deren 3 and Wille 3.

derer: 1. (a) In good prose the form **derer** is only used as the *gen. plur.* of the *dem.* pron. **der,** and only where the reference is to *persons,* whereas **deren** (q.v. 1 *c*) is used in sim. references to *things,* as in **Bei dem Studieren der Wissenschaften, besonders deren** ('of those'), **welche die Natur behandeln, ist die Untersuchung so nötig als schwer** (G.). It should *not* be used as a gen. sing. fem.: as *Sanders* says, **Weil „derer" für die Mehrzahl gilt, vermeidet man im allgemeinen den Genitiv der weiblichen Einzahl,** and indeed, the use of **derer** now so inevitably suggests a reference to more than one person that the final rel. clauses in the following examples almost come as a shock: **Er wollte auf das Wohl derer trinken, die fern von ihm war** (Ompteda)—**Man setzte alle Hoffnung auf die Heimkehr derer, welche man in der Burg Amme nannte** (H. Franck), where **derjenigen** would be a better expression. The above examples show, however, that when one sees the word **derer,** one immediately expects a following rel. clause (or its equivalent: see 2), so that its proper force is 'of those people who *or* whose . . .', as in **Wir Knaben waren alle gute Aristokraten, mit Ausnahme derer, die vom Lande kamen** (G. Keller). Hence, as **deren** (q.v. 2) can have rel. force, *both* forms frequently occur in one and the same proposition: e.g. **Bald lud er den Haß derer auf sich, deren Beschützer zu sein er berufen war** (E. T. A. Hoffmann: 'He soon incurred the hatred of those whose protector he was appointed to be')—**Seine Gesichtszüge hatten jenes Lächeln derer, die viel erlebt haben und deren Herz ein gutes Gedächtnis besitzt** (Wildenbruch)—**Betrachte die Worte der Erkenntnis derer, deren Namen die Erinnerungskraft der Menschen bewahrt hat** (Bonsels)—**Einige derer, welche der Frau ein Almosen verweigerten, machten ihrem Unmut über Schnorrereien Luft, deren Berechtigung man nicht nachprüfen könne** (H. Franck: 'Some of those who refused to give the woman alms gave vent to their displeasure at begging, the justification for which could not be tested'). (b) Unlike **deren,** the form **derer** can never immediately precede a noun ('of those people' is simply **derer,** never **derer Leute**). and should *not* be used as a *rel.* pron. To the examples of this incorrect rel. use given under **deren** 2 (*b*) may be added: **Sie war diejenige unter den Geschwistern, derer** (for **deren**) **er in Liebe gedachte** (Fr. Griese)—**Er gebrauchte die altmodische Sprechweise, derer sich einfache Leute zu bedienen pflegen** (Bonsels) —**Die Weihnachtsbäckerei erforderte alle Künste, derer wir fähig waren** (E. Wiechert). **2.** Here belongs the use of **derer** in the gen. of aristocratic family names: thus, **die von Schleh** are 'those who are members of the family **von Schleh**', and the gen. of such phrases is firmly established: **Die blaue Flagge derer von Schleh wehte vom Turme** (C. Hauptmann) —**Was seine Aufmerksamkeit am meisten an sich zog, war das Stammhaus derer von Stallburg** (G.)—**So ist denn, wie so vieles Schöne auf dieser Erde, auch das Geschlecht derer von Gemperlein erloschen** (Ebner-Eschenbach)—**Er träumte davon, daß dieser Sproß berufen sein müsse, das Geschlecht derer von Rheinstein dereinst wieder zu altem Ansehen zu bringen** (R. Herzog).

dergleichen: see -gleichen 2 (*a*); cf. like 2 (*a*).

derjenige: see der (demonstrative) 2 (*a*); dies 2 (*d*).

derlei: see Hand 2 (*b*); -gleichen 2 (*a*). For its use as a rel. pron., cf. **Ein Falter saß auf einem Steine und sonnte die schimmernden Flügel, derlei** ('the like of which') **der Herr niemals gesehen hatte** (Stifter).

Dero: This archaic form (actually the OHG gen. plur. of *der*) was formerly used before titles, in addressing or referring to people of high rank, as in **Dero Gnaden** ('Your *or* his Grace, Worship'): it was associated with a plur. verb, and could also be used without the actual title: e.g. **Ich werde sprechen zu seiner Exzellenz: „Dero Herr Sohn** ('Your Excellency's son') **haben ein Auge auf meine Tochter; meine Tochter ist zu schlecht** (see bad 1) **zu Dero Herrn Sohnes Frau"** (Sch.)—**Ich erbitte mir Dero Erlaubnis** (Chamisso). Rather later the form **Ihro** came to be used in this way: e.g. **Wann befehlen Ihro Gnaden die Pferde?** (G.)—**Empfangen Ihro kaiserliche Hoheit meine Glückwünsche** (Beethoven).

derweil: see weil 1.

desgleichen: see -gleichen 2 (*b*).

dessen: This is the gen. of **der** used either

as a dem. or as a rel. pron. As a *dem.* pron., it is esp. common in association with **alles,** as in **Ich erinnere mich noch deutlich alles dessen, was er mir erzählte:** see **all** 6 (*a*) and **genitive** I, and cf. the plur. **deren** (q.v. I *b*). Its use as a *rel.* pron. is seen esp. in propositions like **Da drüben steht Herr Müller, dessen einziger Sohn mein intimster Freund ist** and **Sie gingen in den Saal hinunter, an dessen einem Ende** ('at the one end of which') **der Eßtisch bereit stand** (W. v. Scholz); cf. **deren** 2 (*a*).

desto: This is derived from OHG *des diu* (> MHG *deste*), combining the gen. and the instrumental cases of the art., the former having causal force (as in **deshalb, deswegen**), the latter suggesting a measure or amount. The modern word is only used, like **um so** (q.v. 2, and cf. **als** = **'as'** 4 and **um** I *d*), before a compar. adj. or adv. in the sense of 'by so much (the more)', following a sim. phrase introduced by **je** (q.v. 3).

deucht(e), gedeucht: see **dünken** I.

deuten: 1. The fundamental idea suggested by this simple verb is 'to make comprehensible, explain', as in **einen Traum deuten** ('to interpret a dream') or **das Gesetz deuten** ('to expound the law'); cf. **Sie haben meine Absichten falsch gedeutet** ('You have misconstrued my intentions'). It was out of this idea that the other use of the verb developed, viz., with the prep. **auf** + *accus.*, to convey the idea of 'to point to, indicate': by pointing to a thing you make it plain to what you are referring: cf. **Alles deutet auf schlechtes Wetter. 2.** This may serve as a pointer to the fundamental sense of the compound **bedeuten,** viz. 'to cause to be understood, give to understand', which is obvious from a proposition like **Was soll das bedeuten?** ('What is the meaning of that? What is that meant to convey? What does that imply?'); so also **Daß ich mich matt fühle, hat nichts zu bedeuten** (Rilke: 'That I am feeling tired means nothing, is of no consequence'). The only real difficulty which arises in connexion with **bedeuten** is a grammatical one. *Sanders* distinguishes between **jemandem bedeuten,** with much the same force as **zu verstehen geben** or **andeuten** ('to give to understand, drop a hint') and **jemanden bedeuten,** in the sense of **anweisen** or **belehren** ('to direct, instruct, inform'); but he adds **„Mitunter berühren sich die Begriffe und gehen ineinander über."** *Sanders*'s admission that the shades of meaning sometimes approach and merge into each other seems to be borne out by the following examples, the sense of the verb, whether with an accus. or a dat. of the person, apparently ranging from mere information or hint to what is a virtual injunction, so that there is really no fundamental distinction between the two groups: (**a**) with an *accus.* of the person: **Sie bedeutete ihn** ('indicated to him') **mit einem Winke der Hand, Platz zu nehmen** (Wildenbruch)—**Der Offizier bedeutete ihn** ('explained to him'), **daß der König unmöglich jeden selbst sprechen könne** (E. Wichert)—**Der Wirt bedeutete den Schutzmann** ('informed the policeman'), **daß alles in Ordnung sei** (A. Eloesser)—**„Bleiben Sie hier!" bedeutete** ('directed') **ihn Louis** (Gutzkow); and in the *pass.*, **Sie wurde von dem Vater bedeutet** ('Her father pointed out to her'), **daß sie dem Geschick zu besonderem Dank verpflichtet sei** (I. Kurz)—**Was meine Vaterstadt betrifft, so sei der Ausländer bedeutet** ('let me explain to a foreign reader'), **daß sie südlich von Halle gelegen ist** (Th. Mann); with a *dat.* of the person: **Ich ahnte, sie bedeutete mir** ('suggested to me'), **ich müßte etwas tun** (Rilke)—**Ulrich bedeutete ihm** ('pointed out to him'), **es sei nicht die mindeste Zeit zu versäumen** (Ompteda)—**Der Schiffsoffizier bedeutete ihm** ('informed him'): **„Herren dürfen kein Rettungsboot besteigen, solange nicht alle Frauen und Kinder eingeschifft sind"** (Max Nordau)—**Der Polizist bedeutete ihr** ('drew her attention to the fact'), **daß Unterhaltung hier verboten sei** (B. E. Werner)—**Er händigte einem Angestellten eine Flasche Wein und bedeutete ihm** ('directed him'), **sie den armen Leuten draußen zu überreichen** (Ric. Huch)—**Sie bedeutete** ('instructed') **dem Chauffeur, langsamer zu fahren** (St. Zweig); in the *pass.*, with impers. subj., **Nach Tisch wurde dem Knaben bedeutet** ('the boy was told'), **daß er schlafen zu gehen habe** (id.)—**Auf meinen Brief wurde mir bedeutet** ('I was informed'), **daß sämtliche Bilder vernichtet seien** (Bruno Frank).

deutsch: 1. This adj. was *diutisc* in OHG, from the noun *diot* (= **Volk**), so that it properly meant **volkstümlich,** used esp. of the lang. spoken by ordinary people, as contrasted with Latin, used by scholars. It is now written with a small letter in propositions like **Hierzulande wird die deutsche Sprache weniger gelehrt als die französische**, but with a capital in **die Deutsche Akademie, der Deutsche Bund** (1815), **das Deutsche Reich**, etc. **2.** In the sense of the 'German language', it is an *indeclin. neut.* (cf. 3): e.g. **Er spricht gut** (or **ein gutes**) **Deutsch—Ich habe ihm einiges Deutsch beigebracht—Mich drängt's, . . . das heilige Original in mein geliebtes Deutsch zu übertragen** (G.)—**Das ist schlechtes Deutsch—Die Schweden schrien dem jungen Mann in gebrochenem Deutsch drohende Worte zu** (A. Wilbrandt)—**Sie entschuldigte sich in einem Deutsch, das nicht ohne fremden Anklang war** (R. v. Gottschall)—**Er fing an, in fließendem Deutsch zu reden** (A. Schaeffer); cf. **Zwischen dem ruhigen Englisch konnte man ängstliches Spanisch und aufgeregtes Französisch hören** (M. Eyth). But it is written with a small letter in what are practically adv. phrases, like **Wie heißt** 'dog' **auf deutsch?**—*Hôtel* **zu deutsch: Gasthof**—cf. **Deutsch reden** ('to speak German') and **deutsch reden** ('to be outspoken, speak bluntly'). **3.** Applied to *persons*, the German word differs markedly from sim. expressions referring to other nationalities: whereas the latter are real *nouns*, either strong (**Engländer, Amerikaner, Norweger, Italiener, Spanier,** etc.) or weak (**Schwabe, Schotte, Franzose, Schwede, Russe,** etc.), the German word is an *adj.-subst.*, with the inflexional endings of an attrib. adj.: e.g. **Er ist ein geborener Deutscher—Es waren drei Deutsche anwesend—So denken alle Deutschen—Er sagte es im Beisein zweier Deutschen.** So also **Wie kannst du Deutscher so etwas sagen?** and **Wir Deutsche beten mit dem Herzen** (Ponten); but there is fluctuation here in the plur.: while *Duden* allows both **wir Deutsche** and **wir Deutschen**, *Sanders* favours the latter, which *Volksbrockhaus*, however, characterizes as **„weniger gut"**. The neut. **das Deutsche** suggests what is specifically German, but it is used of the language in **etwas aus dem Deutschen** or **ins Deutsche übersetzen.**

Dezember: see Monatsnamen.

Dickicht: see Käfig.

diejenige(n): see dies 2 (*d*); welch (relative) 3.

Diemen: see Getreide 2.

dienen: 1. The obj. of this verb always stands in the *dat.*, the corresponding trans. verb being **bedienen** (q.v.). **2.** The simple verb is used with several shades of meaning, just as our verb 'to serve' is: e.g. (**a**) with a *pers.* subj.: **Es soll geschehen, daß er nicht mehr den Fremden dienen muß, sondern dem Herrn** (Jer. 30. 8–9)—**Er dient jetzt als Chauffeur bei Herrn Braun—Mein Sohn dient bei der Luftwaffe** ('is in the air force')—**Er würde seinen Mitmenschen zum Gelächter dienen** (G.: 'He would be a laughing-stock to his fellow-men')—**Damit kann ich Ihnen leider nicht dienen** ('I'm sorry, I can't oblige you with that'); (**b**) with an *impers.* subj.: **„Wozu dient diese Vorrichtung?"** ('What purpose does this apparatus serve?') **„Sie dient dazu, den Strom zu unterbrechen"** ('It serves the purpose of cutting off the current')—**Laß dir das als** (or **zur**) **Warnung dienen!** ('Let that be a warning to you!'); (**c**) in the *pass.* (see impersonal verbs 3): **Damit ist mir nicht gedient** ('That does not serve my purpose')—**Ich kann Ihnen einen Fahrplan geben, wenn Ihnen damit gedient ist** ('I can give you a time-table if that is of any use to you'); cf. **Mein Sohn ist ein von der Pike auf gedienter Offizier**, where the past part. has *act.* force ('My son has risen from the ranks to be an officer').

dies: 1. This dem. adj. is inflected like an attrib. adj., except in the gen. sing. masc. and neut., where the ending **-es** is quite established: **dieser Mann**, gen. **dieses Mannes.** Used as a pron., the form **dieses** (or far more commonly **dies**) is left uninflected when used with the verb **sein** and a pred. noun to indicate identity, the verb then agreeing in number with the *pred.* noun: e.g. **Dies ist die Dame, von der ich eben sprach—Dies sind alle meine Bücher** (i.e. 'These are all the books I have got', as distinct from **Dies sind alles meine Bücher**, 'All these books are mine')—**Sind dies Ihre Töchter?**—The form **dieses** should not be used as the gen. of the *pron.*: 'I don't remember this' is **Ich entsinne mich dessen nicht**; but an exception is made in the expression for 'the bearer' of a letter delivered by hand, where a noun is really understood: cf. **Bitte geben Sie dem Überbringer dieses** (*scil.* **Briefes** or **Schreibens**) **sofort hundert Kronen!** (St. Zweig). Notice that one usually says **alles dies** or **dieses alles. 2.** (**a**) While the various forms of **dies** point to something near at hand, those of **jener** suggest something more remote in time or place:

cf. **Dieser Garten** (hier) **ist schöner als jener** (dort) and **dieses und jenes Leben** ('this life and the life to come'). So these two expressions are used to render 'the former' and 'the latter', as in **Von den zwei Gedichten, die Sie vorgelesen haben, ziehe ich dieses jenem vor** ('. . . I prefer the latter to the former'). (**b**) The only other regular use of **jener** is with a following rel. clause or its equivalent, showing the reference to be to something definite and well known. It is obvious that a statement beginning with 'On that terrible night' requires an explanatory clause or phrase to make the reference clear to a listener or reader: 'On that terrible night on which the Tay Bridge collapsed.' This use of our dem. corresponds exactly to that of **jener**: **In jener schrecklichen Nacht, in welcher die Tay-Brücke einstürzte**; sim. **Mich überschlich jenes bedrückende Gefühl, welches man beim Betreten eines verwunschenen Schlosses empfindet** ('There crept over me that oppressive sensation which one feels on stepping into an enchanted castle'). But the reference must be to something definite and unmistakable: it is only in popular ballads and the like that **jener** is used in a vague way, as in **Da droben auf jenem Berge . . . da drunten in jenem Tale**—cf. Burns's 'O wert thou in the cauld blast on *yonder* lea . . .'. (**c**) It follows that the various forms of **jener** have a much more limited use than our 'that, those'. To express a proposition like 'Who is that man over there?' or 'Have you seen those ruins the speaker mentioned?' a German would use not **jene**(r), but simply the def. art.: **Wer ist denn der Mann da drüben?—Hast du die Ruinen gesehen, die der Redner erwähnte?** Our students are far too apt to use **jener** in such contexts, and Thomas Mann pokes fun at the foreigner's fondness for it in his *Doktor Faustus*: **Adrian war sofort immer mit allen Söhnen Albions** (i.e. **Engländern**) **bekannt, redete ihre Sprache mit ihnen und wußte komisch ihre Versuche im Deutschen nachzuahmen, ihre Ausländer-Schwäche für das Pronomen „jener, jenes", wie sie also sagten: „Besichtigen Sie jenes!" wenn sie nur sagen wollten: „Sehen Sie das da!"** ('Look at that!'). (**d**) In particular, it is quite incorrect to use **jene Schüler** in rendering the proposition 'I shall punish those pupils who come late tomorrow', where obviously the late-comers are unknown when these words are spoken. Here the reference is to 'the pupils, whoever they may be', and the correct rendering is **Ich werde diejenigen Schüler bestrafen, welche morgen spät kommen,** where incidentally the correct accentuation is **die'jenigen,** not **dieje'nigen** as our students are apt to say; sim. **De'rjenige, der das Buch entliehen hat, wird ersucht, dasselbe möglichst bald zurückzubringen** ('The reader who has borrowed the book is requested to return it as soon as possible'). Admittedly, the forms of **derjenige** are rather prosaic—see **welch (relative)** 3—but they are at least correct in such contexts; the alternative is to use the forms of the determinative **der,** which must then be strongly accented: **Die' Schüler, die morgen spät kommen, werden bestraft.**

diesseit(**s**): see **jenseit**(s).

dieweil: see **weil** 1.

Ding: **1.** Of special grammatical interest in connexion with this every-day word is its use in the *gen.*, either in adv. expressions or as an independent noun. Such expressions are **aller-, neuer-, schlechterdings** and **unverrichteterdinge** (for all of which see **allerdings** 1 and 2) and the common phrase **guter Dinge sein** ('to be of good cheer, in good spirits': cf. **genitive (adverbial)** 3 *c*). In MHG, *vil dinges* (lit. 'much of thing') could be used to express **viele Dinge,** and in course of time *vil* could be omitted, leaving a gen. which eventually came to be treated as an independent word, as in the case of **Aufhebens machen, Rats erholen,** etc. (see **viel** 1 *a*). According to modern usage, **das Dings** is used in a half playful, half slightly contemptuous way of any little, trivial object, esp. of a young animal or small child (cf. our 'poor little thing'), as when Storm refers to a little girl as **das kleine Dings** and G. Keller to an older one as **ein Ding von sechzehn Jahren.** **2.** In much the same way the expression **Dingsda** (also **Dingskirchen**) has become fixed in reference to a place, or a person, whose name one cannot at the moment recall or does not care to specify: e.g. **Wir waren kürzlich in . . . Dingsda zusammen** (Immermann)—**Dingsda . . . wie heißt das Land? . . . Amerika** (Mörike); cf. J. Schlaf's village sketches entitled **„In Dingsda"** and **Herr** (or **Frau**) **Dingsda** ('Mr. *or* Mrs. Thingummy'). **3.** In the plur., the reg. form is Dinge, but **Dinger** is the form generally used as the plur. of **Dings** referred to above: e.g., contemptuously, **„Wenn ich nur wüßte, ob ich meine Orden anlege...“ „Lassen Sie die Dinger weg!“** (Speckmann: 'I wonder whether I am expected to wear my decorations . . .' 'Leave the silly things off!')—**Die Zigaretten, diese kleinen Dinger mit gelbem Mundstück, waren Toms Leidenschaft** (Th. Mann)—**Draußen im Dunkel waren die Schneeflocken fast unsichtbar, diese winzigen Dinger, die den Fußgängern um die Nase wirbelten** (I. Frapan); sim. in references to animals: **Er phantasierte von Robbenjagd** ('He raved about seal-hunting'), **und daß man das nächste Mal die Büchse mitnehmen müsse, „denn die Dinger haben ein festes Fell“** (Fontane)—**Ich kann diese Dinger mit den schlenkrigen Gliedern** (viz. 'mosquitoes') **nicht vertragen** (Dauthendey)—**Man fischte eins von diesen seltsamen Dingern** (a 'jellyfish') **heraus** (Voigt-Diederichs); so also more playfully of girls, as in **Ihr armen Dinger!** (G.) and **Wir Mädchens** (see **Fräulein**) **sind sonderbare Dinger** (Lessing).

dingen: 1. This simple verb ('to hire, engage') and its compound **verdingen** ('to let out on hire, put to service') are no longer used as much in the language of the north as they once were, being now generally replaced by other expressions (e.g. **einen Wagen mieten, ein Dienstmädchen in Lohn nehmen,** etc.): a proposition like **Ich muß eine Magd dingen** (G. Keller) now has a rather archaic southern flavour. The historically incorrect strong forms **dang, gedungen** (formed on the analogy of **dringen, singen,** etc.) are officially recognized along with the weak forms, but the latter are now more usual: even in the classical period the past indic. was almost invariably **dingte,** and **gedungen** was mainly used, as it still is, of 'hired' assassins, murderers, etc.: e.g. **Zum Sklaven dingtet ihr den sonst so freien, jetzt bedrängten Mann** (G.)—**Sie sind gedingt** (or **gedungen**), **euch zu töten** (Sch.)—**Er ist ein gedungener Handlanger** (id.: '. . . a hired accomplice')—**Seid ihr Straßenräuber? Wer hat euch gedungen?** (Bruno Frank). **2.** The only compound still in every-day use is **bedingen,** meaning either 'to stipulate, postulate, demand' (as a condition of success) or 'to cause, produce' (as a result of given conditions). Here also the strong forms are practically obs., an exception being the past part. of the double compound **ausbedingen** ('to stipulate'), as in **Das hat er sich** (dat.) **als eine Sache der Ehre ausbedungen** (Federer)—**Die Uhr war sein letztes Weihnachtsgeschenk, das er selber sich ausbedungen hatte** (A. Schaeffer). Otherwise *weak* forms are quite fixed, esp. the past part. **bedingt** ('conditional, qualified'), used with adj. force, and its opposite **unbedingt,** used either as an adj. or as an adv.: e.g. **Im Norden hat die Urbarmachung des meist unfruchtbaren Bodens großen Fleiß und zähe Ausdauer bedingt** (i.e. hard work and perseverance were demanded as the only condition on which the cultivation of the poor soil was possible)—**Bodenbeschaffenheit und Klima haben besondere Pflanzenarten bedingt** (i.e. conditions of soil and climate have produced special flora)—**Dem Angeklagten wurde eine bedingte Begnadigung zuteil** (i.e. the accused was released on ticket of leave, his release being conditional on his good behaviour)—**Der Lehrer verlangt unbedingten Gehorsam** ('. . . implicit obedience')—**Morgen muß ich unbedingt** ('without fail') **verreisen**—**Das ist unbedingt nötig** ('absolutely essential').

Dingsda: see **Ding** 2.

distance, distant: 1. The words **fern** and **Ferne** point to some vaguely located *remote* spot, without any indication as to the extent of the intervening space: e.g. **Ich sah ein Licht in der Ferne—Sie kamen aus fernen Ländern zusammen—Er wohnt fern von Menschen.** As the spot referred to has only a vague relation to that occupied by the speaker, **fern** and **Ferne** cannot really be qualified by any word indicating how far away the spot is, but at most by an equally vague term which emphasizes the remoteness: e.g. **Er lebt in einem sehr fernen Lande—Auf dem Wasser hört man Geräusche aus großer** or **weiter Ferne;** one no longer says **Meine Augen wenden sich nach Norden, wo, kaum eine Meile fern** (cf. 3), **der graue Kirchturm aufsteigt** (Storm, in a story of the 17th century). **2.** Whereas **fern** refers to the remote *end* of a space, **weit** (q.v.) refers to the space itself: hence **Wir haben noch weit** (not **fern**) **zu gehen—Wie weit ist es bis zur Stadt?—Wir sind noch weit vom Ziel.** The noun **Weite** is the regular expression for 'width' (like **Breite, Höhe,**

Länge), as in **Die Weite der Tür beträgt drittehalb Fuß** ('The door is 2½ ft. wide'), but is otherwise little used in prose, except with fig. force: of a person with a 'wide outlook' one might say **Er hat eine ungewöhnliche Weite des Blicks. 3.** In contradistinction to **fern** and **Ferne,** which point to a vaguely remote spot, **entfernt** and **Entfernung** indicate the relative distance between two spots, and when used lit. of extension in space they must be qualified by some word or phrase which suggests, however vaguely, the distance between the two points: e.g. **Das Dorf liegt 10 Kilometer von der Stadt entfernt** (not **fern**)—**In einiger Entfernung** (or **Nicht weit entfernt,** 'At some distance, A little way off') **sah ich einen Mann stehen—Ich bin weit davon entfernt, so etwas zu behaupten** ('I am far from making such an assertion'); these expressions, then, should *not* be used without some modification, as in **Seitwärts erblickte ich in der Entfernung** (for **in der Ferne** or **in einiger Entfernung**) **einen Schimmer** (Roquette). The intervening space, which must, of course, be *large* in the case of **fern** and **Ferne,** may be quite *small* in that of **entfernt** and **Entfernung:** e.g. **Diese zwei Punkte sind nur drei Zoll voneinander entfernt.** The only contexts in which **entfernt** should be used without some qualification are those in which we use 'remote *or* distant' with fig. force as in 'a remote likeness' or 'a distant relative': e.g. **Die Kinder sind sich nur entfernt ähnlich** or **Es besteht nur eine entfernte Ähnlichkeit zwischen den Kindern—Er ist ein entfernter Verwandter von mir—Diese vier Menschen standen miteinander in entfernten verwandtschaftlichen Beziehungen** (Rilke); cf. also **Wir liefen nun in der Irre und fühlten uns nicht entfernt so sicher wie vorher** (Fr. Griese: 'We had lost our way and did not feel anything like as safe as before')—**Er hat nicht den entferntesten Grund zur Klage** ('He has not the remotest *or* slightest cause for complaint')—**Ihre Mantilla ließ sich mit den kostbaren Spitzenüberwürfen der anderen Damen nicht im entferntesten vergleichen** (Werfel: '. . . could not even remotely be compared with the exquisite lacework scarves of the other ladies'). A proposition like **Er zog sich auf seine entferntesten Güter zurück** (W. Alexis) is not incorrect, because the adj. implies the relative distance between his several estates. **4.** Much the same as **Entfernung** is **Abstand;** but whereas the former indicates the distance between two points, the latter considers the points themselves and is used esp. of things that stand upright (**stehen**): e.g. **Telegrafenstangen werden in regelmäßigen Abständen errichtet** (cf. 5 and 6)—**Der Abstand zwischen diesem und jenem Baum beträgt vier Meter;** and as one says **Die Sterne stehen am Himmel,** so one speaks of a planet's distance from the sun as **der Abstand eines Planeten von der Sonne;** sim., in a riding-school, riders in single file must **Abstände halten,** i.e. must keep at a safe distance from each other, and so also **Ich folgte nahe hinter ihm, der Abstand zwischen uns blieb derselbe** (Rilke). **5.** As **Abstand** is used of things that stand, so **Entlegenheit** should properly be used of things that lie (**liegen**); but while the former may imply a short distance, the latter always indicates things far apart: one cannot use it, say, of two adjacent trees that have been blown down, but one can say **Die Entlegenheit zwischen den zwei Städten beträgt 20 Kilometer.** And so **entlegen** has come to be used esp. of a 'remote, out-of-the-way' spot: **Er wohnt in einem entlegenen Dorf, in einem weltentlegenen Tal,** etc. (cf. **abliegen**). **6. Zwischenraum** indicates the *space* between two points, and may also have the temp. force of 'interval' (**Intervall** is mainly used in music): one can say **Zwischen dem Hause und dem Tor ist ein Abstand** (or **Zwischenraum**) **von 20 Meter,** but **Der Zwischenraum** (not **Abstand**) **zwischen dem Haus und dem Tor ist mit Fliesen belegt** ('The space between the house and the gate is paved with flagstones').

doch (adverb): This word, which always has *adversative* force, so that the idea of 'but' is always implied, may be either accented or unaccented, and some of its unaccented uses are not easy to explain, because the sense may vary with the intonations. **1.** *accented*: (a) used to correct a preceding erroneous neg. statement or impression: e.g. **„Sie brauchen ja noch nicht fortzugehen." „Do'ch, ich muß"** ('Yes, I must': really 'That 's what you say, but I must')—**„Er ist doch** (unaccented: see 2) **noch nie in Berlin gewesen?" „Do'ch, er war letzten Sommer da"** ('Oh yes, he was there last summer')

—**Niemand war zu sehen: do'ch, an einem Fenster, eine Frau in weißem Kleid** (G. Britting); so also **do'ch nicht** (cf. 2 *b*) corrects a preceding erroneous pos. idea: **„Sie bleiben wohl noch einige Zeit hier?" „Do'ch nicht, ich muß morgen abreisen"**; (**b**) used much like **dennoch** or **trotzdem** with the force of 'all the same, in spite of everything': e.g. **Obwohl man mir abgeraten hat, werde ich do'ch hingehen**—**„Hast du gehört, daß er seinen Vater überredet hat?" „Also do'ch?"** ('So he *did* talk him over after all?' in spite of my conviction to the contrary)—**„Ich glaube nicht, daß er kommen wird." „Aber wenn er do'ch käme, was dann?"** ('But what if he *did* come?' contrary to your expectation). **2.** *unaccented*: (**a**) If A says to B **„Unser Freund wollte mich gestern aufsuchen, ist aber nicht gekommen"**, B might reply **„Aber er ist doch kra'nk."** Here **doch** approaches **ja** (q.v.); but whereas **ja** would be used to remind A of something he knew but had apparently forgotten at the moment ('But he is ill, you know'), **doch** here expresses surprise that A had evidently not heard of his friend's illness ('You seem not to know, but surely you must have heard that he is ill'); sim. **„Das hätte man mir doch sa'gen sollen!"** (i.e. I haven't heard about that, 'but surely I ought to have been told!'), and in a neg. question, to express a confident expectation of a neg. reply: **„Du siehst blaß aus, du bist doch nicht krank?"** ('You're looking pale, but you're not ill, are you?'). (**b**) In an *imperative* proposition, **doch**, although unaccented, has persuasive, pressing, often reassuring force, generally implying disinclination on the part of the person addressed to do what he is told: e.g. **„Aber se'tzen Sie sich doch!"** (i.e. Why remain standing? 'Do sit down!')—**„Schlage doch das Wort im Wörterbuch nach!"** (either with mere persuasive force: 'I'm sorry to trouble you, but you might look this word up in the dictionary', or spoken in irritation: 'If you don't know what the word means, for goodness' sake look it up!')—**„Na** (coll. for **Nun**), **komm doch!"** would be said to reassure a child to whom one had previously said **„Komm mal her!"** but who showed reluctance to approach ('Oh come on! I'm not going to hit you'); so also **ni'cht doch** (cf. **do'ch nicht**: see 1 *a* and **doch nicht**: see 2 *a*) corrects and denies a preceding affirmative statement or impression, or indicates disapproval of a suggestion made: e.g. **„Wir können wohl noch eine Stunde hier bleiben?" „Ni'cht doch, der letzte Zug fährt in zehn Minuten"**—**„Vater, darf ich dein Taschenmesser haben?" „Ni'cht doch, du könntest dich in den Finger schneiden."** (**c**) In an *optative* proposition, **doch** expresses an eager desire for the fulfilment of the wish: e.g. **„Ach, wäre ich doch zu Hause geblieben!"** ('Oh I *do* wish I had remained at home!')—**„Wenn er doch nu'r käme!"** ('If only he would come!'). (**d**) Immediately after **oder**, it has the force of 'at least, at all events': e.g. **Er ist krank, oder doch kränklich** ('He is ill, or at least ailing')—**Der Patient hat eine Stunde geschlafen, oder doch hingedämmert** ('The patient has slept, or at least dozed, for an hour')—**Es galt, Spuren zu finden, die zum Ermordeten hinzulaufen schienen oder doch hinlaufen konnten** (Bergengruen: 'The important thing was to find clues which seemed likely to lead, or if not that, which might possibly lead, to the murdered man'). Analogous is the use of **so doch** with limiting force after a neg. cond. clause, esp. common where both clauses are contracted: e.g. **Das hat gewisse Veränderungen zur Folge gehabt, wenn nicht in meinem Charakter, so doch in meiner Weltanschauung** (Rilke: 'That has effected certain changes, if not in my character, certainly in my outlook on life'). **3.** The insertion of **doch** in the word-order of a question gives the proposition the force of a subord. clause of *reason*, as in **Viele Kaufleute gestatteten ihrem Frauenzimmer eine Spazierfahrt, war auf solche Weise doch die Gelegenheit geboten** ('because in this way an opportunity offered'), **die prächtigen Pelze zu zeigen** (E. Wichert); for other examples, see **word-order** 3 (*h*).

doch (conjunction): There is no fundamental difference between **doch** and **aber** (q.v.); the former, besides having a wider application, partly in view of its various adv. uses, is the stronger expression, having, much like **jedoch** (q.v.), the force of 'however, yet': e.g. **Er ist ein liebevoller, doch strenger Vater.** It should be noted that in a finite clause **doch** is used either with or (rather less commonly) without influence on the word-order: e.g. **Ich möchte wohl spazierengehen, doch habe ich** (less usually **doch ich habe**)

zuviel zu tun. Here **doch** may be replaced by **jedoch,** and one can also say **ich habe jedoch zuviel zu tun;** but in such a proposition one generally avoids **ich habe doch zuviel zu tun,** because in this word-order **doch** almost always has *adv.* force, as explained under **doch (adverb)** 2 (*a*): 'You think I have plenty of time, but believe me, I have too much to do'.

Dorn: There is some fluctuation in the plur. forms of this masc. noun. The form in general use is **Dornen,** used either in the collect. sense of 'thorns', as in **Rosensträucher haben Dornen,** or in that of 'thornbushes', as in **Hier wachsen viele Dornen;** but **Dorne** is specifically used of different 'varieties of thornbushes': e.g. **Hagedorne** ('hawthorns'), **Schwarzdorne** ('blackthorns'), etc. The third form **Dörner** appears to be chiefly used as a technical expression, e.g. 'punches' for making or enlarging holes, 'tongues' of a buckle, etc.; but see **Leiche.**

Dose: see **box** 7.

double negative: see **negative (pleonastic).**

down: 1. This word expresses different ideas in propositions like 'He tripped over a stone and fell down' and 'Halfway up the cliff he slipped and fell down', the latter obviously implying a fall to a lower level. In German a clear distinction is made: cf., on the one hand, **Er stolperte über einen Stein und fiel hin** (see 2 and 3 below) or **nieder** (q.v., and see 3 below), and, on the other hand, **In halber Höhe der Klippe** (see **halb** 2 *b*) **glitt er aus und fiel hinunter** or **hinab. 2.** As pointed out under **her-, hin-** 2 (*b*), **hin-** is the usual prefix in the north for 'down' in connexion with verbs suggesting a position or attitude, as in 'to fall, lie, sit', etc. (but see **niedersitzen** and **niederlassen**): e.g. **Sie legte ihr Buch hin und stand auf—Ich legte** (or **streckte**) **mich der Länge nach hin—Ich setzte mich hin und fing zu schreiben an—Erschöpft sank sie hin—Sie stellte die Lampe hin—Ermüdet warf er sich hin** (but **Er warf sich in den Fluß hinunter**). **3.** (**a**) But the fact remains that verbs compounded with **hin-** are often somewhat prosaic, so that **nieder-** (which is rather more select, certainly in the north) is often preferred in good prose (cf. *b*). And it should be noted that such verbs compounded with **nieder-,** as with **hin-,** properly point to the *end* of the action, so that a *dat.* is almost the rule in an accompanying prep. phrase (cf. **accusative** or **dative** . . . 2 *b* and *c*): e.g. **Er kauerte neben ihr nieder** (Kellermann)—**Sie kniete neben den Kindern nieder** (Frenssen: see **knien**)—**Da kniete er vor ihr nieder** (Ebner-Eschenbach)—**Er sinkt im hohen Grase nieder** (Novalis)—**Er erkletterte den Zaun und sank jenseit desselben im Graben nieder** (Sudermann)—**Der Alte warf sich vor mir nieder** (G.). (**b**) But there are cases where **nieder-** is established even in the north, **hin-** sometimes conveying a different meaning. Thus, **hin-** cannot be used in contexts like the following: **Sie schämte sich und blickte** (or **schlug die Augen**) **nieder** ('cast down her eyes')—**Er bückte sich nieder** ('He bent down')—**Ich fühle mich niedergedrückt** (= **niedergeschlagen,** 'depressed')—**Sie ist mit einem Kinde niedergekommen** ('She has been delivered of a child')—**Er ließ sich im Lehnstuhl nieder** (see **niederlassen**)—**Das alte Haus ist niedergerissen** ('has been demolished'; but **Ich ließ mich vom Zorn hinreißen,** 'I let myself be carried away by my anger')—**Er drohte, mich niederzuschießen—Ich saß nieder** (= **Ich setzte mich hin:** see **niedersitzen**).

Drache: Distinguish between **der Drache,** gen. and plur. **Drachen** ('dragon'; also 'box-kite' with self-recording meteorological instruments) and **der Drachen,** gen. **Drachens,** plur. **Drachen** ('kite' which children fly; not the bird 'kite', for which see **Weih**).

dran, drauf, etc.: For these contracted forms, which are in every-day use in familiar lang., esp. in more or less set expressions, see **daran, darauf, darein** 1 (*b*), **darum, darunter,** etc. Quite established are a few combinations of two such expressions, notably **drauf und dran, drum und dran,** and **drunter und drüber,** for which see respectively **daran, darum,** and **darunter** *ad fin.*

drängen: 1. The fundamental difference between **dringen** and **drängen** is that the former is a strong intrans., the latter a weak trans. verb: cf., on the one hand, **Er drang in das Haus,** and, on the other hand, **Er drängte mich in die Ecke;** so also **Der Feind drang bis Köln vor** ('. . . pressed on as far as Cologne') and **Er drängte sich immer vor** ('He was always pushing himself forward'). Where **dringen** means 'to force one's way', the aux. is always **sein,** as in **Er ist in das Haus**

gedrungen; but **haben** is used in the case of **auf etwas** (accus.) dringen ('to press for *or* urge something'), and usually also in that of **in jemanden dringen** ('to urge a person'): e.g. **Der König hat darauf gedrungen, Eleonore zu entlassen** (Fr. Griese)—**Er hat sich, ohne daß ich in ihn gedrungen hätte, über seine Situation ausgesprochen** (Spielhagen); less commonly, **Sie sagte, sie sei in ihn gedrungen, davon Abstand zu nehmen** (Fontane). **2.** In spite of the fundamental difference between the two verbs, each has to some extent encroached upon the functions of the other. (**a**) In some cases **dringen** has assumed trans. force, esp. in the past part. Thus, while the weak form is fixed in **Es drängt** (not **dringt**) **mich, an Sie zu schreiben,** one usually says **Ich fühle mich gedrungen, an Sie zu schreiben,** probably because **sich gedrängt fühlen** more naturally suggests the lit. force of 'to feel oneself being pushed': cf. **Die Schweizerin sah sich gedrungen** ('found herself impelled') **den Deutschen Mangel an nationalem Selbstbewußtsein vorzuwerfen** (O. Walzel). 'To force (the acceptance of) something on a person' is **jemandem etwas aufdrängen,** but strong forms have crept in here also, esp. again in the past part.: e.g. **Man drängte ihm Nachrichten auf, vor denen er gern die Ohren verstopft hätte** (W. Alexis)—**Papa hat mir das Geld aufgedrängt** (G. Keller)—**Er nahm sich vor, dem Wirt sein aufgedrungenes Mittagsmahl zu bezahlen** (id.)—**Ich will dir gestehen, daß ich dir diesen Pirschgang aufgedrungen habe, um etwas mit dir zu besprechen** (G. Bäumer: 'I'll confess I have pressed you to come stalking with me in order to discuss something with you'); so also **Bei dem Gespräch beteiligte sie sich nur mit wenigen** (*scil.* **ihr**) **abgedrungenen Worten** (E. Wichert: 'The only part she took in the conversation was to say a few words which were forced from her'). The strong form is fixed in **notgedrungen** ('impelled by necessity'), as in **Notgedrungen vertröstete ich mich auf die folgende Woche** (Bruno Frank: '. . . I consoled myself with hopes for the following week'). (**b**) The factitive **drängen,** then, properly demands an accus. obj., as in **Meine Gläubiger drängen mich** ('My creditors are dunning me'; but **Meine Gläubiger dringen auf Zahlung,** 'My creditors are pressing for payment') and **Wenn sie ihre Bilder betrachten, drängt eine frohe Erinnerung die andere** (Speckmann: 'When they look at their snaps happy memories follow closely on each other'); and it is noteworthy that the prefixes **be-** and **ver-** are only combined with **drängen,** never with **dringen:** e.g. **Es ist vorauszusehen, daß Karl Polen schwer bedrängen wird** (E. Wichert)—**Aus der Regierung hat man ihn verdrängt** (Fr. Griese). But the personal obj. of **drängen** is often unexpressed, so that it practically assumes intrans. force, as in the common phrase **Die Zeit drängt** ('Time presses'); and sim. **Die jetzige Lage drängt zur Entscheidung** ('The present situation urges us to come to a decision') —**Er drängte zur Heimkehr** (Jul. Wolff: 'He pressed the party to return home'). Esp. common here are examples where the reflex. **sich** is really understood, **drängen** thus closely approaching **dringen.** Yet there is a definite distinction: **dringen** always implies the use of force to overcome resistance, while **drängen** suggests a crowd (**Gedränge**) pressing forward without hostile intent: cf., on the one hand, **Die feindlichen Truppen drangen** (not **drängten**) **durch das Tor in die Stadt,** and, on the other hand, **Zuerst drängte** (not **drang**) **alles nach der Kirche** (Frenssen); and sim. **Volk aus allen Ständen drängte um den Katafalk** (W. Alexis)—**Michael folgte der Menge, die gegen den Teich drängte** (Zifferer)—**Sie drängten gleichzeitig aus der Tür** (Blunck) —**Nun drängten alle heran, die Unterschrift des Königs zu sehen** (E. Wichert); cf. fig. **An den Schloßberg drängten Wiesen heran** (G. Britting). Even where the reference is to a single person, the implication is that he has to elbow his way through a crowd, as in **Er spürte, daß jemand auf ihn zudrängte** (Stehr). Not really in accordance with accepted usage, therefore, are examples like **Die Blüten drängten aus der Knospenhülle** (Storm)—**Die Luft drängte durch die Fenster** (G. Bäumer)—**Die Schwester** ('nurse') **drängte darauf, daß man die Kranke ins Krankenhaus brachte** (id.)—**Nach einer beinahe schlaflosen Nacht des Papstes drängte der Arzt auf Absage der vorgesehenen Empfänge** (Werfel: '. . . the doctor urged that the projected receptions be countermanded'). **3.** Three *participles* are used with adj. force: (**a**) **dringend** ('pressing, urgent'), as in **Ich habe eine dringende Bitte an Sie**; (**b**) **gedrängt:**

e.g. **Das Zimmer war gedrängt voll** ('The room was packed')—**Wir saßen gedrängt** (cf. Waggerl's **Zusammengedrängt kauern die Hütten im Tale**)—**eine gedrängte Schreibart** ('a terse, concise style')—**eine gedrängte Übersicht** ('a condensed summary, synopsis')—cf. (*c*); (**c**) **gedrungen:** e.g. **Der Wärter war ein kleiner, gedrungener Mensch** (Bruno Frank: 'The warder was a small thickset man'), where the weak form is much less common: cf. **Es war ein junger Bursche von kräftiger, aber gedrängter Figur** (W. Alexis).

draußen: see **außen.**

drei: Like the MHG second num. (see **zwei** 1), the third had three forms in the nom. and accus., only that here the form *drî(e)* was used for both masc. and fem., while *driu* was neut. For the inflexion of **drei,** see **zwei** 2 and 3. An interesting coll. phrase is **alles dreies,** with a strong sing. neut. ending, having collective force, formed on the analogy of **alles beides:** e.g. **Er ißt und redet zugleich, und ich glaube, er gäbe wer weiß was darum, wenn er noch dazu trinken könnte, und das alles dreies auf einmal** (Lessing: i.e. he would give anything to be able to eat, talk, and drink all at the same time)—**Ich bin eigentlich alles dreies** (Fontane: viz. **Kind, Narr und Poet**).

dreierlei: see **Hand** 3.

drein: For this contracted form of **darein,** used as a suffix in **oben-** and **hinterdrein,** and as a prefix to **finden, reden, schicken,** etc., see **darein** 1 (*b*).

dress: see **clothes.**

dringen: see **drängen.**

drinnen: see **außen.**

drohen: This form of the verb ('to menace, threaten') only became established towards the end of the 17th century: Luther always wrote **dräuen** (< MHG *dröuwen* or *dreuwen*), as in **Esau dräuet dir, daß er dich erwürgen will** (Gen. 27. 42), but this earlier form is now only used in poetry: cf. **Vernahmst du nicht mein dräuendes Verbot?** (Wildenbruch, in a ballad). The person threatened now always stands in the *dat.*, as in **Der Gattin Feinde drohen auch dem Gatten** (G.), while that with which he is threatened is expressed by **mit,** as in **jemandem mit einer Strafe, mit Rache, mit dem Tod drohen.** It is also freely used with an impers. subj., as in **Nahes Unheil droht dir** (Sch.), and it is significant that the accus. obj. **sie** in the proposition **Vater, bring' Er die Tochter weg, sie droht eine Ohnmacht** (Sch.) was altered to **ihr** in later editions. An accus. of the thing is sometimes used in expressions like **Jeder Schritt drohte den Brüdern einen jähen Fall** (Platen: 'At every step the brothers were threatened with a sudden fall'), but this is now little used: instead of **Das Haus droht den Einsturz,** one prefers to say **Das Haus droht einzustürzen.** A dir. accus. obj., however, is always used with **bedrohen:** cf. **Lasset uns ernstlich sie bedräuen** (Acts 4. 17)—**Der Richter bedrohte ihn mit Gefängnis;** and so also in the pass., **Das Land wurde mit Krieg bedroht,** whereas the simple verb can be used only *impers.*: e.g. **Zu dieser Zeit ward der alten strengen Tragödie mit einer Revolution gedroht** (G.).

drüber, drum, drunter: see **dran.**

du: For this pron., see **address (forms of)** 1, and **der (relative)** 1 and 2. The degree of intimacy in which two people stand towards each other is suggested by the use of the reflex. verbs **sich duzen, ihrzen** and **siezen,** according as they use **du, Ihr** and **Sie** in addressing each other: e.g. **Bisher haben die beiden sich gesiezt, seit gestern aber duzen sie sich**—**Sie duzt sich jetzt mit ihm.** To express this intimate relationship, Mörike says **Ich und der Komödiant stehen du und du,** but the established expression is now **auf du und du stehen,** as in **Er steht mit den allerhöchsten Herrschaften auf du und du** (Fontane). The verb **duzen** has led to the formation of nouns compounded with **Duz-:** e.g. **Er stand mit allen Künstlern auf dem Fuße des Duzkameraden** (R. v. Gottschall)—**Hier entfaltete sich Hoffmanns innige Freundschaft mit Devrient, einem von den wenigen Menschen, mit denen er Duzbrüderschaft geschlossen hat** (Bergengruen). When two people decide to become **Duzbrüder,** they go through a little ceremony in which they face each other, drink each other's health with their right arms interlocked, and then shake hands: this is familiarly known as **Brüderschaft trinken.**

dulden: 1. The fundamental sense of this verb is 'to suffer', used either abs. or with an obj., 'to endure, submit patiently (geduldig) to something', while the compd. **erdulden** requires an obj. and intensifies the idea of enduring to the end: e.g. **Große Seelen dulden still** (Sch.)—**Die Liebe . . . duldet alles** (1 Cor. 13. 7)—**Was**

bis dahin muß erduldet werden, erduldet's! (Sch.). Out of this developed the use of **dulden,** like that of our 'suffer', in the sense of 'to tolerate, let something happen *or* continue' without taking steps to prevent or stop it (cf. **leiden** 2): e.g. **Er duldet, daß seine Tochter oft ins Kino geht—Die Frau wollte nicht dulden, daß er schwöre** (Auerbach: 'His wife would not suffer him to take the oath'); sim. with an impers. subj., **Diese Angelegenheit ist dringend, sie duldet** (or **leidet**) **keinen Aufschub** ('. . . admits of no delay')—**Es ist spät: hast du etwas auf der Seele, was keinen Aufschub bis morgen früh duldet?** (Freytag); and this led to the modern impers. use with an accus. of the person in propositions like **Der Prinz saß im Regen auf einem Faß: es hatte ihn im Hause nicht mehr geduldet** (G. Britting: '. . . he could not bear to remain longer indoors'). The compd. **gedulden** is only used *reflex.* with the force of 'to wait patiently', as in **Er sagte, Andreas möge sich bis morgen gedulden** (Hofmannsthal). **2.** A more general expression for 'to suffer', which is often synonymous with **dulden,** is **leiden** (q.v. 2 for examples). While **dulden** in its orig. sense requires a pers. subj., **leiden** can be used of things, as in **Bei dem Luftangriff hat Dresden schwer gelitten** (not **geduldet**). But the two verbs may convey different meanings: e.g. **Ich muß bitten, Ihre Sprache zu ändern, ich kann solche Ausdrücke nicht dulden** (Jul. Grosse), i.e. I cannot go on listening to such language, whereas **leiden** here would suggest dislike; cf. **Sie konnte alles dulden, ohne zu leiden** (G.: 'She could put up with anything without suffering').

dünken: 1. This irreg. weak verb was orig. only used with an impers. subj., meaning 'to seem' (cf. 3). Its MHG forms were *dunken* (or *dünken*), *dûhte, gedûht,* and the mutated past subj. *diuhte* (> **deuchte**) gradually crept into the indic., even the pres. indic., which explains the modern forms **deucht, deuchte, gedeucht.** In course of time, however, the reg. weak forms **dünkt, dünkte, gedünkt** established themselves also, and modern usage recognizes both forms; but the fact remains that **deucht, deuchte** now have a rather archaic flavour, and modern authors show a very decided preference for **dünkt, dünkte.** The older forms even led to the formation of an infin. **deuchten** (past tense **deuchtete**), but these forms are now obs.: cf. **Es fängt mir an zu deuchten, wir stehen hier am Pranger** (Sch.). **2.** The Goth. word (*þugkjan*) reg. took a dat. of the person (*mis þugkeith* = **mir dünkt**); but in MHG the accus. was rather more usual (*daz dunket mich guot* = 'That seems good to me'), and in NHG either case is allowed: e.g., with accus., **Wir beklagen uns oft, daß der guten Tage so wenig sind, und, wie mich dünkt, mit Unrecht** (G.)—**Bald schadenfroh, bald traurig dünkte ihn ihr Blick** (Federer); with dat., **Dieser Tag dünkte ihm der glorreichste seines Lebens** (G.)—**Besonders bewunderungswürdig dünkte dem Jungen der Damm** (Federer)—**Diese Jahre dünkten ihm ein unverlierbarer Besitz** (C. Rothe)—**Die ganze Welt dünkte ihr jetzt so ganz anders als ehedem** (Zifferer). **3.** In all the examples just given the subj. is impers., but it need no longer be: cf. **Jetzt meinte sie ihn zu erkennen: ein Schauspieler dünkte er sie, den sie als Mädchen von fern geliebt hatte** (St. Zweig). The *reflex.* verb in particular almost demands a pers. subj. and a pred. adj. or noun: **Er dünkt sich klug** exactly corresponds to our 'He thinks himself clever'; cf. **Ich dünke mich** (much like our 'I flatter myself'), **verständlichere Dinge gesagt zu haben als irgend ein Schriftsteller** (Lessing). In such propositions the reflex. pron. is now always accus., and an infin. with **zu** may be added: **Das Kind dünkt sich klug zu sein—Er dünkt sich ein vornehmer Herr** (or **einen vornehmen Herrn**)—**Vor seinen Richtern hatte er sich bisher einen Helden gedünkt** (Riehl). The infin. without **zu** is no longer used: it is significant that modern versions of the Bible have added **zu** in Luther's **Dünke dich nicht weise sein** (Prov. 3. 7); cf. also the coll. use of the reflex. with pred. **etwas** or **etwas Rechtes,** as in **Jeder dünkte sich etwas** (G.: 'Every one had a high opinion of himself').

durch-: 1. As this verbal prefix is used both sep. and insep., and as usage fluctuates to some extent, the chief verbs compounded with it are discussed under their respective heads. The broad rule is that if the compd. is *intrans.,* its prefix is *sep.* (aux. **sein**), and if it is *trans.,* the prefix is *insep.* (aux. **haben**). The following are a few characteristic examples which are not discussed elsewhere in the present volume: **durchreisen:** e.g. **Wir sind zuerst nach Berlin du'rchgereist** (i.e. without making a stay *en route*), **haben aber dann fast ganz Deutschland durchrei'st** (i.e. covered nearly the whole country in our travels)—**durchreiten:** e.g. **Es war ein großes Gedränge auf der Straße, aber es gelang uns, du'rchzureiten,** but **Wir durchri'tten die Stadt, obwohl die Straßen gedrängt voll von Menschen waren**—**durchschlängeln:** e.g. **Unten im Tal schlängelte sich ein Bach du'rch,** but **Ein Bach durchschlä'ngelt das Tal**; sim. **Das Tal ist von dem Fluß Oreto durchschlä'ngelt** (G.)—**durchschwimmen:** e.g. **Dort verengte sich der Fluß so sehr, daß es fast unmöglich war, du'rchzuschwimmen,** but **Nach abgeschlossener Studienzeit sah ich mich wie den Fisch, der erst noch sein helles Reich durchschwa'mm, mit einem Mal ans Trockene geworfen** (Mörike: i.e. he felt like a fish out of water); **Hättest du den Ozean durchschwo'mmen, so sähst du Well' auf Welle kommen** (G.). A striking example of such verbs used trans. is **Ist nicht Deutschland von einem Ende zum andern durchrei'st, durchkreu'zt** (see 2 *b*), **durchzo'gen** (see **durchziehen**), **durchkro'chen und durchflo'gen?** (G.). **2.** (**a**) Some compds. are only used with *sep.* prefix, notably **durchfallen,** esp. fig., as in **Er ist im Examen du'rchgefallen** ('failed') and **Das Theaterstück fiel du'rch** ('was a failure')—**durchführen,** esp. fig., as in **Er hat seinen Plan du'rchgeführt** ('carried out his plan') —**durchkommen:** e.g. **Das Gedränge war derart, daß es fast unmöglich war, du'rchzukommen** and **Gott sei Dank! ich bin in der Prüfung du'rchgekommen**; and to these one might add some that are only very rarely used with insep. prefix: e.g. **du'rchhauen** ('to thrash'), **du'rchmachen** (e.g. **Er hat viel du'rchgemacht,** 'He has come through a lot'), **du'rchnehmen** (e.g. **Der Lehrer hat vergessen, die unregelmäßigen Zeitwörter du'rchzunehmen,** 'to go through the irregular verbs'); see **durchsitzen.** (**b**) On the other hand, in the following the prefix is always or practically always treated as *insep.*: **durchkreuzen,** as in **Hier durchkreu'zen sich die zwei Straßen** (sim. **durchque'ren:** see **quer**)—**„Es ist furchtbar, in die Hände der Fremden zu fallen": diesen Satz und seine bittere Wahrheit durchda'chte und durchli'tt ich oft in jenen Tagen des Zusammenbruchs und der Übergabe** (Th. Mann: referring to Germany's collapse and capitulation)—**Das Papier ist durchlö'chert** ('perforated')—**Mich ergriff frohe Lust, den Park zu durchschwei'fen** (R. v. Gottschall: 'to stroll through the park') —**Seit drei Wochen durchstrei'fe ich die Normandie die Kreuz und die Quer** (Heine: see **quer**). (**c**) And there are some verbs which are used with the prefix either *sep.* or *insep.* indiscriminately: thus, one can say **Ich habe das ganze Haus durchsu'cht** or **du'rchgesucht**—**Wir haben die halbe Nacht durchwa'cht** or **du'rchgewacht**; and sim. **Ich habe alles durch(ge)stöbert** or **durch(ge)forscht** ('rummaged, searched through everything')— **Die Zimmer sind durch(ge)wärmt,** although in these last cases the *insep.* forms are more usual: see **durchsuchen,** and cf. **Er durchstö'berte manche Bücher** (Wieland)—**Kein Platz blieb undurchfo'rscht, nichts wurde undurchstö'bert gelassen** (Immermann).

durchblättern: 1. Used with an *insep.* prefix, this properly implies a cursory glance through the pages of a book, periodical, etc., the verb then approaching **durchflie'gen** and **durchlau'fen** (qq.v.): e.g. **Man braucht das alberne Buch nur zu durchblä'ttern, um zu sehen, daß es nichts taugt** (Wieland)—**Er fing an, Bücher zu durchblä'ttern** (H. Grimm). **2.** With a *sep.* prefix (and this seems to be more usual now), it should really suggest a somewhat closer perusal, but actually, as the following examples show, the distinction is not strictly, if at all, observed: **Ich habe die Abhandlung mehr du'rchgeblättert als gelesen** (Lessing)— **Er blätterte eine Mappe abgegriffener Zeitschriften du'rch** (Speckmann)—**Ich blätterte Reisealbums und Tagebücher du'rch** (H. Hesse)—**Ich saß im „Goldenen Löwen" und blätterte die Ortszeitung du'rch** (W. v. Scholz)—**Er nahm das Buch und blätterte es schnell von hinten nach vorne du'rch** (Th. Mann).

Durchblick: see **Sicht** 2 (*c*).

durchblicken: This verb is used very much like **durchschauen** (q.v.). (**a**) With *sep.* prefix, it is always *intrans.*, whether used lit. with the force of 'to cast a glance, have a peep' (e.g. through an opera-glass) or fig. in the phrase **etwas du'rchblicken lassen** ('to let something appear *or* be understood, to hint at *or* suggest something'): e.g. **Die Berge waren**

klar, der Himmel blickte an verschiedenen Stellen blau du'rch (G.)—**In seinem Brief ließ er du'rchblicken, daß er fast mittellos war** (i.e. reading between the lines one gathered that he was almost destitute)—**Als er sich neulich mit uns unterhielt, hat er du'rchblicken lassen, daß er vielleicht ins Ausland reisen würde** (i.e. he did not say it in so many words, but hinted at the possibility of his going abroad). (**b**) With *insep.* prefix, it is always *trans.* being used esp. in the sense of 'to see through, penetrate', not so much with a person or some bad quality as obj. (cf. **durchschau'en**), but rather with words like 'secrets, intentions', etc.: e.g. **Ich habe ihr Geheimnis durchbli'ckt** ('I have fathomed her secret')—**Es ist leicht, seine Absichten zu durchbli'cken** ('It is easy to see through his intentions').

durchbrechen: 1. With *sep.* prefix, this verb can be either *trans.* (aux. **haben**) or *intrans,* (aux. **sein**): e.g. **Er nahm den Stock in die Hand und brach ihn mitten du'rch**—**Die Armee hat sich du'rchgebrochen** ('The army has fought its way through')—**Das Eis ist unter ihm du'rchgebrochen** (or **eingebrochen**); cf. *fig.*, **In seiner Jugend wünschte Goethe Professor zu werden; . . . als man ihm ganz andere Ämter übertragen hatte, brach doch immer wieder der Lehrer in ihm du'rch** (W. Bode: '. . . the didactic urge every now and again reasserted itself'). **2.** With *insep.* prefix, the verb is always *trans.* (aux. **haben**): e.g. **Schäumend durchbra'ch der Bach seinen Damm**—**Es war ihm geglückt, die feindlichen Reihen mit seiner Reiterei zu durchbre'chen** (E. T. A. Hoffmann: 'He had succeeded in breaking through *or* penetrating the enemy's ranks with his cavalry')—**Bei der Untersuchung stellte es sich heraus, daß an dem Bahnübergang das Auto die Schranken durchbro'chen hatte** ('At the inquiry it was established that the car had crashed through the barriers at the level crossing') —so also *fig.* **Er hat die Schranke der guten Sitte durchbro'chen** ('He has overstepped the bounds of propriety'); cf. also **durchbro'chene Stickerei** ('open-work embroidery') and **Sie schritten die breite Treppe mit dem durchbro'chenen Holzgeländer hinunter** (Th. Mann: 'They stepped down the staircase with its carved open-work banisters').

durchbringen: The prefix of this verb is always *sep.*, the aux. **haben**: e.g. **An der Grenze gelang es ihm, eine Kiste Zigarren** (*scil.* **unverzollt**) **du'rchzubringen** ('At the frontier he succeeded in smuggling a box of cigars through')—**Der Arzt hat den Kranken eben noch du'rchgebracht** ('The doctor just managed to pull the patient through')—**Sie bringt ein kümmerliches Leben du'rch** (G.: = **Sie schlägt sich kümmerlich du'rch,** 'She lives in straitened circumstances')—**Er brachte das ihm hinterlassene Vermögen in kurzer Zeit du'rch** ('In a short time he squandered the fortune that had been left him').

durchdenken: see **durch-** 2 (*b*).

durchdringen: 1. With *sep.* prefix, this is used in the *intrans.* sense of 'to force one's way through' (aux. **sein**): e.g. **Eine Menschenmenge war zusammengelaufen, aber ich drang** (or **drängte mich**) **du'rch**—**Es gelang der Reiterei, du'rchzudringen**—**Der Regen ist bei uns du'rchgedrungen** ('The rain has come through in our house') —*fig.* **Bei der Besprechung drang er mit seiner Meinung du'rch** ('At the discussion he carried his point'). **2.** With *insep.* prefix, it always has the *trans.* force of 'to penetrate' (aux. **haben**): e.g. **Ein Schrei durchdra'ng die Nacht**—**Das Stöhnen der Kamele durchdra'ng das Ohr** (G.) —**Der Verfasser hat sich von den Überzeugungen seines Vorgängers durchdru'ngen** (G.: i.e. identifies himself with his predecessor's convictions'). The past part. esp. indicates a state of being strongly affected with some feeling: **Der Herzog schläft, und alle Diener sind von Schmerz durchdru'ngen** (G.). The pres. part. usually takes the accent of the *insep.* verb: **durchdri'ngende Kälte** ('intense cold')—**ein durchdri'ngender Verstand** ('a penetrating mind, a keen understanding').

durchfahren: In the *lit.* sense of the verb the prefix is *sep.*: e.g. **Der Torweg war so niedrig, daß es unmöglich war, du'rchzufahren** (cf. durchreiten and **durchkommen**: see **durch-** 1 and 2 *a* respectively); but when the verb is *trans.* with *fig.* force, durch- is *insep.*, as in **Ein Schauder durchfu'hr mich** ('A shudder ran through me').

durchfallen: see **durch-** 2 (*a*); fail 6.

durchfliegen: With *sep.* prefix, this is used *intrans.* in the lit. sense, as in **Vor kurzem flog eine Kette Rebhühner hier du'rch** ('A little while ago a covey of partridges flew past here'); in student slang, **Er ist im Examen du'rchgeflogen** (= **du'rchgefallen,** 'failed'). With *insep.* prefix, it is *trans.*, used either *lit.* or *fig.*:

e.g. **Käfer durchflo'gen die sonnenhellen Räume** (J. Kerner)—**Flugzeuge durchflie'gen die Lüfte schneller denn je**—**Sie durchflo'g alle die Zimmer** (Gutzkow: 'She flew *or* dashed through all the rooms'); esp. in the sense of 'to read hurriedly, skim over, glance through' (cf. **durchblättern**): **Sie öffnete das Schreiben und durchflo'g begierig seinen Inhalt** (Fr. Halm)—**Ich habe den Brief nur flüchtig durchflo'gen.**

durchführen: see **durch-** 2 (*a*).

durchgehen: **1.** The use of this compd. as a *trans.* verb with *insep.* prefix is little used, which seems strange, seeing that analogous verbs are commonly so used, notably **durchlau'fen, -rei'sen, -schrei'ten,** etc.; but in fact one now rather avoids propositions like **Er durchge'ht die Stadt** (Voß), or the first example given under **durchwandeln,** preferring to say simply **Er geht durch die Stadt.** Certainly *not* to be recommended is the *trans.* use of **durchge'hen** with the aux. **sein,** as in **Unsere Erdkugel ist große Umwälzungen durchga'ngen** (W. v. Humboldt: = **hat ... durchgemacht**)—**Er ist viel Leid durchga'ngen** (H. Blunck: better **Er hat viel Leid erfahren** or **Ihm ist viel Leid widerfa'hren**). **2.** Very common, on the other hand, is the verb with *sep.* prefix used *intrans.* (aux. **sein**) or *trans.* (aux. **haben**): e.g. *intrans.*, lit. in **Der Bach ist nicht tief, ich bin eben du'rchgegangen**—**Traumartig ging er durch die Knechte du'rch** (better **zwischen den Knechten durch**), **die ihm schweigend Platz machten** (Hofmannsthal); and esp. *fig.* in **Geht dieser Zug nach München du'rch?** ('Is this a through train to Munich?')—**Der Antrag ging du'rch** ('The motion was carried')—**Das Pferd ist mit ihm du'rchgegangen** ('has bolted with him')—**Die Phantasie ging mit ihm du'rch** (Treitschke: 'His imagination ran away with him')—**Der Lehrer hat einen Fehler hier du'rchgehen lassen** ('has not marked a mistake here'); *trans.*, **Man gätet** (now **jätet**) **hier fleißig, die Männer gehen das ganze Feld du'rch** (G.: 'They are very busy weeding here, the men go over *or* work through the whole field'); so also 'to go through' a list, documents, etc. (cf. **durchlaufen** 2): **Sie hat im Telephonbuch die Liste der Rechtsanwälte du'rchgegangen** (K. H. Strobl)—**Hat der Schüler alle seine Aufgaben du'rchgegangen?** On the whole, however, the *trans.* use here with *lit.* force is avoided in a compd. tense, except in **Er hat seine Schuhe** (or **Sohlen**) **du'rchgegangen** (see **durchlaufen** 1, and **durchsitzen**); one no longer says **Ich habe eine Menge Konditorladen du'rchgegangen** (Heine).

durchirren: This verb is practically always used with *trans.* force, the prefix being *insep.* (aux. **haben**): e.g. **Schlaflos durchi'rrte sie zur Nachtzeit den Park** (E. T. A. Hoffmann).

durchkommen: see **durch-** 2 (*a*).

durchkreuzen: see **durch-** 2 (*b*).

durchkriechen: With *sep.* prefix, this has the *lit. intrans.* sense of 'to crawl *or* creep through': e.g. **Hier ist eine Lücke in der Hecke, da sind die Kinder wahrscheinlich du'rchgekrochen.** With *insep.* prefix, it has *trans.* force, the obj. being the thing through which something crawls: **Die Kinder haben die Hecke durchkro'chen**; cf. the last example given under **durch-** 1, and the example from G. under **durchwandeln.**

durchlaufen: **1.** With *sep.* prefix, this is properly *intrans.* when used in the *lit.* sense (aux. **sein**), as in **Der Bote lief zwischen den zwei Menschenreihen du'rch,** but is *trans.* (aux. **haben**) in the sense of 'to wear through', as in **Knaben laufen ihre Schuhe schnell du'rch**—**Die Sohlen werden bald du'rchgelaufen sein** (G.): see below. **2.** With *insep.* prefix, it is always *trans.*: e.g. **Ich durchlie'f die ganze Stadt nach einem Arzt**—**Vor einigen Tagen bin ich hier angekommen und habe schon die Stadt durchlau'fen** (G.)—**Franz hatte die Staatsschule mit Auszeichnung durchlau'fen** (J. Schaffner: '. . . had passed through . . . with distinction'). Esp. common is its use in the *fig.* sense of 'to run through, glance over' a document, etc., as in **Ich hatte die Bibel mehrmals durchlau'fen und mich mit derselben sprungweise bekannt gemacht** (G.); but here the prefix can also be *sep.* (cf. **durchgehen** 2 and **durchlesen**): e.g. **Haben Sie die Vorrede du'rchgelaufen?** (Lessing)—**Er lief die Bekanntschaften du'rch, die ihm jene Schrift verschafft hatte** (G.: 'He ran through the list of acquaintances . . .'); cf. as unusual, with **sein** as aux., **Lasset uns einen Blick auf die Völker werfen, deren Geschichte wir du'rchgelaufen sind** (Herder).

durchleiden: see **durch-** 2 (*b*).

durchlesen: The prefix of this verb is sometimes treated as *insep.*, as in **Er**

legte die Blätter auf den Tisch, nachdem er sie durchle'sen hatte (Mörike), but this use may easily imply no more than dipping into or skimming through a document, like **durchflie'gen** (q.v.). Where a more thorough perusal is intended, it is advisable to treat the prefix as *sep.*: e.g. **Er las das Stück mit Aufmerksamkeit du'rch** (G.)—**Möge es dir gefallen, alles, was ich dir zu erzählen im Begriff stehe, bis ans Ende du'rchzulesen** (E. T. A. Hoffmann).

durchlöchern: see **durch-** 2 (*b*).

durchmessen: This verb is always *trans.*, the prefix being either *sep.* or *insep.* in the *lit.* sense, but *insep.* in a *fig.* sense: e.g. **Geschwind ans Werk! Noch einmal durch-'gemessen, ob auch alles paßt!** (G.: 'Come on now, set to work! Check over the measurements, to make sure they are all correct!': cf. **Du'rchmesser**, 'diameter')—**Der Architekt durchma'ß die Baustelle mit geübtem Auge** ('measured the building-site with an expert eye'); now esp. in the sense of 'to walk *or* stalk across (*or* through), cross, traverse': e.g. **Er sprang auf und durchma'ß das Zimmer mit großen Schritten** (R. Herzog)—**Die Wanderer hatten wohl schon zehnmal Park und Garten auf und ab durchme'ssen** (Gutzkow)—**Arndt war langlebig, hat er doch beinahe ein Jahrhundert durchme'ssen** (H. v. Sybel: = **durchle'bt**)—**Die ganze Skala wird durchme'ssen** (Fr. v. d. Leyen: 'The whole gamut is gone through')

durchqueren: see **durch-** 2 (*b*); **quer**.

durchreisen, durchreiten: see **durch-** 1.

durchschauen: Like the simple verb **schauen** (q.v.), this is esp. characteristic of the south: in the north one generally uses **durchsehen** (q.v., but see 2). **1.** With *sep.* prefix, it has *intrans.* force, meaning 'to (take a) look through', as in **Hier ist ein Loch in der Mauer, da kann man du'rchschauen**—**Dies ist mein neuer Feldstecher** ('binoculars'), **schauen Sie mal du'rch! 2.** With *insep.* prefix, it is always *trans.*, the accus. obj. being not what one looks through, but what one sees, what one penetrates with one's eye, then also fig. what one grasps, fully understands: e.g. **Durchschau'e diese Brust!** (G.: 'Look into my heart!')—**Beim Musizieren schien sein Blick die Dinge träumerisch zu durchschau'en** (Th. Mann)—**Alles Mögliche beruht auf Theorien, die noch kein Mensch durchschau't hat** (M. Eyth). But its commonest use now—and this applies equally to the north (where **durchsehen** is not used in this way)—is in the sense of 'to see through' a person (i.e. to see him in his true colours) or a person's game, tricks: e.g. **Jetzt durchschau'e ich dich!**—**Man hat seine niederträchtigen Schliche durchschau't** (Gutzkow: 'People have seen through his dirty tricks').

durchschlängeln: see **durch-** 1.

durchschweifen: see **durch-** 2 (*b*).

durchschwimmen: see **durch-** 1.

durchsehen: This verb is practically only used with *sep.* prefix, either (like **du'rchschauen**, q.v. 1) with *intrans.* force (where the prefix often takes the lengthened form **hindu'rch-**), as in **Ein Nebel überzo'g die Berge, nur ein wenig blauer Himmel sah du'rch** (G.), but esp. with *trans.* force in the sense of 'to look through, examine, scrutinize' (documents, etc.): e.g. **Der Lehrer ist damit beschäftigt, einige Arbeiten** ('exercises, compositions') **seiner Schüler du'rchzusehen**—**Wir haben Ihre Rechnung du'rchgesehen: sie stimmt** ('We have gone through your account: it is in order'). It is esp. noteworthy that **durchse'hen** is *not* used, as **durchschau'en** reg. is, of 'seeing through' somebody, some one's tricks, etc.

durchsetzen: With *sep.* prefix, this means 'to carry through, accomplish', esp. in the face of obstacles: e.g. **Ich hoffe, meinen Plan du'rchzusetzen** ('I hope to carry out my plan')—**Er hat seinen Willen du'rchgesetzt** ('He has asserted his will, carried his point, had his way')—**Der Antrag wurde du'rchgesetzt** ('The motion was carried')—**Er war fast abgewiesen worden, verstand aber, seinen Empfang du'rchzusetzen** (Th. Mann: 'He was almost turned away, but managed to gain admittance'). With *insep.* prefix it is mostly used in the past part. in the sense of 'interspersed, pervaded' with something: e.g. in geology, **Links fand sich Quarzgestein, mit Schwefelkies durchse'tzt** (G.: 'quartz interspersed with iron sulphide')—**Die Luft war mit einem Geruch von Eau de Cologne durchse'tzt** (Th. Mann: 'The air was pervaded *or* laden with the scent of eau-de-Cologne').

Durchsicht: see **Sicht** 2 (*c*).

durchsitzen: The prefix of this verb is almost always *sep.*, whether it means 'to wear holes in something' by sitting on it (e.g. trousers, sofas, etc.) or 'to sit up' (e.g. all through the night), the accus. being a dir. obj. in the former case, an adv. accus. of time in the latter: e.g. **Da war ein schmutziges Bett, ein dreibeiniger Tisch und ein Stuhl mit du'rchgesessenem Polster** (P. Ernst)—**Ich habe manche Nacht du'rchgesessen, um mir über die Kostenberechnung klar zu werden** (M. Eyth: 'I have sat up many a night in order to be clear about the calculation of the costs'). Incidentally, this verb is *not* used of 'sitting through' (i.e. to the end of) a concert, meeting, etc. (cf. **Ich habe dem Konzert bis zum Ende beigewohnt**); nor is **du'rchstehen** used of 'standing through' a football match, etc.: it is *not* good German to say **Das Gespräch dauerte zwei Stunden, und viel Selbstverleugnung war nötig, es du'rchzustehen** (Th. Mann), which is probably the result of the author's long stay in America.

durchstehen: see **durchsitzen** *ad fin.*

durchstreichen: This verb is always *trans.* With *insep.* prefix it has the sense of 'to roam *or* wander through': e.g. **Er durchstri'ch einige Straßen der Stadt** (Mörike)—**Als das Kind gegen Abend nicht zu finden war, fing man an, die umliegenden Wälder zu durchstrei'chen** ('to scour the surrounding woods'). The aux. is **haben,** as in **Ich hatte schon als Kind die dunkeln Gänge des Klosters mit schaurigem Behagen durchstri'chen** (G.); cf., as not to be recommended, **Er schrieb von den Sitten mancher Länder, die er durchstri'chen war** (Heinse). With *sep.* prefix, it usually has the force of 'to draw a line through, strike out': **Ganze Sätze mußten du'rchgestrichen werden** (Rilke); but in this sense the prefix is sometimes used as *insep.*

durchstreifen: see **durch-** 2 (*b*).

durchsuchen: see **durch-** 2 (*c*), and cf. (with *sep.* prefix) **Er sah sich um, suchte alles du'rch und fand keine Spur von dem Schalk** (G.: 'He looked about him, searched all over the place, and found no trace of the little minx')—**Wir haben alles du'rchgesucht: von dem Gelde ist nichts zu finden** (Storm); (with *insep.* prefix) **Er durchsu'chte des Vaters Schlafgemach** (Gellert).

durchtreiben: With *sep.* prefix, this has the *lit.* sense of 'to drive through' (trans.), as in **Als wir am Torweg ankamen, wurden gerade Kühe du'rchgetrieben.** With *insep.* prefix, it orig. meant 'to examine *or* study closely' in order to master the contents, but this is now obs.; it is now only used in the past part. as adj. meaning 'crafty, cunning, sly', as in **Er ist ein durchtrie'bener Vogel** (Heyse: 'He is a cunning dog, a sly customer').

durchwandeln: This rather select word (see **wandeln**) is now nearly always used as a *trans.* verb with *insep.* prefix: e.g. **Die Schloßzimmer, die ich zu durchge'hen** (q.v.) **hatte, um zu meinem Vater zu gelangen, durchwa'ndelte ich in abgemessenen Schritten** (Platen)—**Ich besaß die Arbeitsfreudigkeit des jungen Technikers, bereit, die Rosenpfade des Daseins zu durchwa'ndeln** (M. Eyth). The normal aux. is **haben,** as in **Manchen Wald habe ich durchwa'ndelt, manche Ruine durchkro'chen** (G.); cf., as *not* to be recommended, **Schon oft war ich die Allee durchwa'ndelt** (E. T. A. Hoffmann)—**Ich glaubte, ich sei den Appenin durchwa'ndelt** (Seume). Very unusual (perhaps Austrian?) is the *trans.* use of the verb with *sep.* prefix, esp. with *fig.* force, as in **Alle Formen deiner Mißgunst hatte ich du'rchgewandelt** (St. Zweig: 'I had passed through all the stages of your ill-will').

durchwandern: This is chiefly used with *insep.* prefix, being treated like **durchlau'fen** (q.v.): e.g. **Ich rate dir, die Zimmer des zweiten Stocks zu durchwa'ndern** (E. T. A. Hoffmann)—**Er tat den Vorschlag, die kleinen Kantone zu besuchen, die er schon durchwa'ndert habe** (G.)—**Aus Rom berichtete Goethe, er habe die wunderbare Stadt durchwa'ndert** (W. Bode); *fig.* **Er hatte das ganze Gebiet ägyptischer Weisheit durchwa'ndert** (Sch.). The aux. is normally **haben,** as in the last examples, but **sein** is sometimes used, esp. in the south: cf. **Wie klein ist der Raum, den ich durchwa'ndert bin!** (Novalis)—**Das ganze Dorf war ich schon durchwa'ndert** (P. Keller)—**Daher kam es, daß ihm alles Land, das er durchwa'ndert war, zum Friedhof wurde** (Stehr). Definitely not to be recommended is the use of the verb with *sep.* prefix as a *trans.*, as in **Er hätte gern die ganze Insel du'rchgewandert** (Stifter: for **Er hätte gern die ganze Insel durchwa'ndert** or **Er wäre gern durch die ganze Insel gewandert**).

durchweben: see **weben** *ad fin.*

durchweg: see **weg** 2.

durchziehen: With *sep.* prefix, this is used both *intrans.* and *trans.*, the former with the force of 'to pass through *or* along', as in **Eben ist eine Prozession hier du'rchgezogen,** the latter with several shades of meaning: e.g. **Ziehe den Faden**

du'rch! (Pull the thread through!')—**Quer durch das Feld hat der Bauer einen Graben du'rchgezogen** ('. . . has cut a ditch through it': cf. below); also *fig.*, like **du'rchhecheln**, in the sense of 'to criticize adversely, pull to pieces, run down': **Wir zogen die Gesellschaft gehörig durch** (G.) —**Dein Epigramm hat mich trefflich du'rchgezogen** (Lessing). With *insep.* prefix, it is always trans.: e.g. **Amerika hatten wir von Osten bis zum äußersten Westen durchzo'gen** (A. Schaeffer)—**Das Feld ist mit einem Graben durchzo'gen** ('The field is crossed by a ditch'); cf. the first example from Goethe given under **durch-**. The *insep.* verb should *not* be used with the aux. **sein**: cf. **Ich bin das Land durchzo'gen und habe allerlei Gewerbe versucht** (Musäus), where **bin** should be replaced by **habe** and the later **habe** omitted.

dürfen: This modal aux. is one of the past-present verbs (q.v.), implying permission to act in a certain way: e.g. **Im Konzertsaal darf man nicht rauchen** (or **darf nicht geraucht werden**)—**So etwas dürfen unsere Kinder nicht** (*scil.* **tun**). In a compd. tense the past part. takes the infin. form, unless the dependent infin. is unexpressed: cf. **Bei aller Tragik seines Lebens darf Beethoven doch glücklich gepriesen werden, denn er hat sich vollenden dürfen** (K. Lamprecht) and **So etwas haben unsere Kinder nie gedurft** (but **nie tun dürfen**). The MHG *durfen* was much used with an infin. in the sense of 'to need *or* require to', as in *des dorft er sich niht schamen* ('Of that he had no reason to be ashamed'), and this was still in use in the pre-classical period, as in **Vor mir dürfen Sie sich Ihres Unglücks nicht schämen** (Lessing), but in such contexts one now uses **brauchen** (q.v.): **Dessen** (or **Ihres Unglücks**) **brauchen Sie sich nicht zu schämen.** Formerly **dürfen** could be used with a *gen.* in the sense of 'to stand in need of', as in **Die Starken dürffen des Arztes nicht** (Matth. 9. 12), but this is now avoided in good prose. *Sanders* rightly represents it as **„im allgemeinen veraltet und durch bedürfen** (q.v.) **ersetzt"**, and in the above quotation **bedürfen** is used in the modern version of the Bible. But although the use of the simple verb should now be avoided in this sense, it is not actually obs., indeed, it is still used in good prose in the south, esp. in Austria: e.g. **Es war ihnen so leicht, mich zu beschädigen, daß sie keiner Hilfe dazu durften** (Rilke). Noteworthy is the modern idiomatic use of the *past subj.* in modest or cautious expressions of opinion: e.g. **Es dürfte geraten sein, den Versuch aufzugeben** ('It might be advisable to give up the attempt').

Dutzend: 1. Like other nouns of measure (q.v.), **Dutzend** takes the normal plur. ending when used distrib., but no ending in the plur. in a collect. sense after numerals: e.g. **Es standen Dutzende von Leuten auf dem Bahnsteig**—**Die Menschen kamen zu Dutzenden herangelaufen;** but **Ich habe drei Dutzend Eier gekauft** (cf. Mandel). In expressing a proposition like 'Half a dozen men stood about', the adj. **halb** may be inflected in the normal way or left uninflected, and in the former case the verb is usually sing., in the latter plur.: cf. **Im Hof stand ein halbes Dutzend Soldaten** (Britting) and **Wie können sich ein halb Dutzend kluge Leute so lange bei einem Schreibfehler aufhalten!** (G.); cf. congruence 1 (*a*). **2.** Treated like **Dutzend**, of course, are **Hundert** and **Tausend:** e.g. **Zweihundert Vögel** (but **Hunderte von Vögeln**) **flogen übers Meer**—**Man versammelte sich zu Hunderten, ja zu Tausenden.** But **Million,** being fem., inflects in the plur.: e.g. not only **Wir haben Millionen Arbeitslose** (B. E. Werner: 'millions of unemployed'), but also **Im Kriege sind drei Millionen Soldaten gefallen**—**Er soll ein Vermögen von zwei Millionen haben.**

E

-e: 1. For a final **-e** in certain advs. (e.g. **lange, gerne**), see **adverbs formed from adjectives** 1. **2.** For a final **-e** in the dat. sing. of masc. and neut. nouns (e.g. **mit sich zu Rate gehen, zu Hause bleiben**), see **dative -e**.

eben: 1. The *adj.* **eben** properly implies the absence of humps or depressions: hence **ebener Boden** ('level ground'), **ebenes Land** ('flat land')—cf. **Was ungleich ist, soll eben werden** (Isa. 40. 4: see bad 1) and in geometry, **eine schiefe Ebene** ('an inclined plane'); so also **zu ebener Erde wohnen** ('to live on the ground floor', on the street level) and fig. **seinen ebenen Schritt gehen** ('to keep the even tenor of one's way'). **2.** The *adv.* **eben** has various shades of meaning, depending on whether it is accented or not, but in either case *it never means 'even'*. (a) When *accented,* it mostly corresponds to our 'just' (cf. **recent** 2 *b*): e.g. **Der Brief ist e'ben** (or more emphatic **soe'ben) angekommen** (cf. **gerade** 2)—**Ich war e'ben im Begriff, auszugehen—„Wo ist Karl?" „Er war e'ben hier"** ('He was here a moment ago')—**Mit meinem Gehalt komme ich e'ben aus** ('With my income I can just make ends meet')—**Ein Schinken für sechs Mann reicht e'ben zu** (Immermann: '. . . will just go round')—**Die Nachtigallen schlugen so leise, daß man sie e'ben noch hören konnte** (Fontane: '. . . that one could just hear them and no more'); so also to strengthen **so,** as in **Sie hätten e'benso gehandelt** ('You would have acted in just *or* exactly the same way')—**Ich war e'benso klug wie vorher** ('I was just as wise as before, none the wiser'). A common coll. expression is **Na e'ben!** used in reply to some startling news to indicate that one has already heard it: **„Karl soll verunglückt sein." „Na e'ben!"** ('I know! Yes, just fancy! Isn't it awful!'). (b) When *unaccented,* it can also sometimes be rendered by 'just', but other expressions may bring out the sense more clearly: e.g. **„Wie hat er nur soviel Geld erwerben können?" „Er ist eben gewe'ckt"** (with explanatory force: 'It 's just that he is shrewd'—to be distinguished from **Er ist e'ben geweckt,** 'He has just been wakened')—**„Das Essen ist bereit: was machen wir, wenn unsere Gäste nicht bald kommen?" „Na, wir fangen eben o'hne sie an"** ('Well, we'll just begin without them'); sim. after **nicht,** as in **Er ist nicht eben gewe'ckt** ('He is not exactly what you would call bright')—**Eine von den Häusern beschattete, nicht eben rei'nliche Gasse führte hinein** (Th. Mann). Where the identity of a person or thing is emphasized, we generally use 'very': e.g. **Eben di'ch suche ich** ('You're the very man I'm looking for')—**Eben da'rum** (or **de'swegen) bin ich hier** ('That 's the very reason I'm here')—**Eben da'vor mußt du dich hüten** ('That 's the very thing you must guard against')—**Eben da'rauf kommt es beim Einkauf eines Teppichs an** ('That is the very thing you must look for when buying a carpet'); sim. **Dieser junge Mann war erfüllt von dem Gedanken der Würde aller staatlichen Dinge, und eben die'ser junge Mann mußte um eben die'ser Dinge willen eben die'se Würde verleugnen** (Bergengruen).

echo: see **sound** 1 and **widerhallen.**

Ecke: The commonest expression for 'corner' is **die Ecke.** The form **das Eck,** although recognized in Austria and used occasionally elsewhere, as in **Er lehnte sich gemächlich im Eck des alten Ledersofas zurück** (W. v. Scholz), is little used as an independent noun, but reg. in geometrical compds. like **Dreieck** ('triangle'), **Vier-, Acht-, Vieleck** ('polygon'); in various place-names such as **Rolandseck, Waldeck,** and **das Deutsche Eck** (at the confluence of the Rhine and the Moselle); and as a prefix in nouns like **Eckschrank** ('corner cupboard'), **-brett** ('corner bracket'), **-fenster, -pfeiler, -stein,** etc. The two expressions **die Ecke** and **der Winkel** regard the junction of two lines or planes from different standpoints, the former from the *outside,* the latter from the *inside.* Whereas we think of a triangle as containing three interior *angles,* the Germans look on it as a figure with three exterior projecting *corners,* as seen from the word **Dreieck**; but its angles are obviously interior, and hence **Ein Dreieck hat drei Winkel, von denen mindestens zwei spitz** ('acute') **sein müssen und höchstens einer recht** ('right') **oder stumpf** ('obtuse') **sein kann.** It follows that **Winkel** cannot be used in examples like **Er bog links um die Ecke—Mein Freund wohnt gleich um die Ecke—Das Kind hat sich an der Tischecke gestoßen.** But in ordinary lang. **Ecke** has largely displaced **Winkel,** as when one says **Das unartige Kind mußte zur Strafe zehn Minuten in der Ecke stehen** or **Die Alte saß in der Kaminecke** ('in the ingle-nook'); indeed, apart from its use in geometry, **Winkel** now implies remoteness, seclusion or secrecy: e.g. **Das junge Paar saß in einem lauschigen Winkel** ('in a cosy corner')—**Das Dorf liegt im entlegensten Winkel des Landes—Dieses Volk lebt in einem vergessenen Winkel Europas** (Sch.); cf. the combination of both words in **Er durchspähte alle Ecken und Winkel** (Immermann: 'every nook and corner'), and the fig. use of **Winkel** in **Er ließ mich in die verborgensten Winkel seiner Seele blicken** (G.: 'into the most hidden recesses of his soul')—**Er durchforschte alle Winkel des Gedächtnisses** (Immermann)—**Er durchsuchte alle Winkel in seinem Kopf, ein Mittel zu finden** (Wieland: 'He ransacked his brain to find an expedient').

ehe: 1. (**a**) The MHG adv. *ê* had the force of 'once, formerly' (= **früher**), and occasional examples of this occur in the classical period and even later: cf. **Mit drei Schritten mess' ich dein Grab, du, der du ehe so groß warst!** (G.)—**„Du bist doch noch meine Mutter?" „Deine Mutter! Eh' nanntest du mich so"** (Sch.). This adv. use is now obs. in prose, but cf. **ehemals,** reg. used in the sense of 'formerly, at one time'. (**b**) According to modern usage, **ehe** is only a subord. *conj.*, and like its alternative **bevor** and its ant. **nachdem** (q.v.), it requires a finite verb, an infin. with **zu** being impossible: e.g. **Ehe ich ihn besuchte** (never **Ehe ihn zu besuchen**), **ging ich auf die Post.** Sometimes a neg. is inserted in an **ehe**-clause, but as explained under **negative** (**pleonastic**) 2 (*c*), this should be avoided in good prose, so that examples like the following should not be imitated: **Einen so zarten Punkt durfte ich nicht gegen ihn berühren, ehe er mir nicht das Recht dazu gab** (Roquette), which would much more idiomatically take the form **Einen so zarten Punkt durfte ich gegen ihn nicht eher berühren, als bis er mir ein Recht dazu gab** (see **erst** 2 *c*)—**Sie hat gesagt, sie könnte keinen Bissen zu sich nehmen** ('that she couldn't eat a bite'), **ehe sie nicht dem Hausherrn gedankt hätte** (Wildenbruch)—**Ich finde nicht Ruhe, ehe ich nicht mein Gewissen erleichtert habe** (Jul. Wolff). **2.** Although **ehe** is no longer used as an adv., the compar. **eher** is only so used, its force being, like that of our 'sooner', either temporal or preferential ('rather'): e.g. **Je eher, desto** (or **je** q.v.) **besser** ('The sooner, the better') —**Hätten Sie nicht eher** (or **früher**) **kommen können?**—**Er ist eher klein als groß** ('He is short rather than tall')—**Ich würde eher** (or **lieber**) **verhungern als um Almosen bitten** ('I would rather starve than ask for charity'); cf. **erst** 2 (*c*). The superl. is mainly used in **ehestens** and **am ehesten**: e.g. **Er wird ehestens** (or **frühstens**, 'at the earliest') **in drei Tagen ankommen**—**So ließe sich der Plan am ehesten ausführen** ('In that way the plan would be most readily carried out').

Ehe: see **marry** 2 (*e*).

ehebrechen: This verb, meaning 'to commit adultery', is now only used in the infin. without **zu**, being elsewhere replaced by **die Ehe brechen** (or **Ehebruch begehen**): e.g. **Du sollst nicht ehebrechen** —**Sie drohte, die Ehe zu brechen**—**Sie hat die Ehe gebrochen.**

ehelichen: see **marry** 1, and cf. **Er wollte die Tochter ehelichen, doch stieß des Pärchens Wunsch auf väterlichen Widerstand** (Th. Mann).

Ehrfurcht: see **Furcht** 2.

eifrig: see **idle** 2.

eigentlich: see **really** 2.

eignen: 1. It is strange that this verb has now such a limited use, esp. as the adj. **eigen** ('own'), the noun **Eigenschaft** (the 'peculiar quality' of a person or thing) and the compd. **sich** (dat.) **etwas aneignen** ('to appropriate something') are so common. At one time **jemandem etwas eignen** was used in the sense of 'to give a person something as his possession', but this is now practically obs., being replaced by **jemandem etwas zu eigen geben**; cf. **Ich hoffe, mancher zu gefallen, der ich mich wohl eigen möchte** (G.: '. . . to whom I might devote myself'). Almost obs. also is its *intrans*. use meaning 'to belong to': cf., as a modern example, **Mit Schauder setzte er den Fuß in das Haus, das einst der Familie Kindler geeignet** (= **gehört**) **hatte** (Raabe). Nowadays **eignen** is almost confined to the *reflex*. use with the force of 'to be suitable': e.g. **Er eignet sich nicht zum Lehrer** ('He is not cut out for teaching')—**Er eignet sich nicht dazu, diese schwere Aufgabe zu bewältigen** ('He has not the qualifications to accomplish this arduous task')—**Dieses Buch eignet sich nicht für Kinder** ('is unsuitable for children'); cf. the common part. **geeignet** (= **passend**), as in **Ich werde ihn bei geeigneter Gelegenheit zu Rate ziehen** ('I shall consult him when a suitable opportunity offers'). **2.** The reflex. verb **sich ereignen** has no connexion with **eignen,** but is derived from **Auge,** as explained under **occur** 3 (*c*), and hence is properly used of an occurrence (**Ereignis**) which strikes the *eye*; and the same applies to the now obs. impers. use of **es eignet** with reference to a supernatural manifestation, like **es spukt** (see **umgehen**), as in **Es eignete sich sogar am**

Tage in dem gräflichen Hause (Musäus: 'The apparition haunted the count's house even in the daytime'), implying that the apparition was actually seen.

eilen: At one time this was used as a *trans.* verb in the sense of 'to urge' a person to do something (like **drängen,** q.v.), but this is now obs. It is still used occasionally as a *reflex.* verb with the force of 'to hasten' to do something, as in **Ich eilte mich, über die Schwelle zu kommen** (Börne) and **Er eilte sich in der Arbeit, was er nur konnte** (Gutzkow: 'He hurried on with his work as fast as he could'), but here **sich beeilen** is now much more usual. It can also be used *impers.,* as in **Mir eilt es nicht** (Heyse: 'I am in no hurry'), but this is more common without a dat. of the person: **Eilt es** (or **die Sache) denn so?** ('Is the matter so urgent?'), which might be expressed **Ist es denn so eilig?** or **Hat es denn solche Eile?** Most common of all the constructions is the *intrans.* use, and where quick *motion* is implied, the aux. is **sein,** otherwise **haben:** cf., on the one hand, **Er hat nicht geeilt** (or **sich nicht beeilt), meinen Brief zu beantworten,** and on the other hand, **Ich bin ihm zu Hilfe in seine Wohnung geeilt** (*not* **Ich habe mich ... in seine Wohnung beeilt).**

eilig: see **quick** 2.

ein: 1. *Indefinite article*: **(a)** This is inflected in the normal way, but like the poss. adjs. it has no ending in the nom. masc. and the nom. and accus. neut., so that a following attrib. adj. must have a strong ending there: **ein armer Mann—ein Wahnsinniger; ein kleines Kind, ein Ganzes.** There is fluctuation where a neut. adj.-subst. is qualified by an attrib. adj., but where the art. has no ending the adj.-subst. is now preferably weak, as in **ein reizendes Äußere** ('an attractive exterior'): see **adjective-substantives** 2. **(b)** The art. remains uninflected in expressions like **ein paar** ('a few'), **ein wenig, ein bißchen,** etc., and in coll. lang. also before numerals to indicate an approximate number: e.g. **Ich sah alles mit ein wenig nach rechts geneigtem Kopfe an** (Rilke)—sim. **mit ein paar Freunden—bei ein bißchen gutem Willen** (Speckmann); **Sie pflegten so ein vier Wochen** ('about four weeks') **am Ort zu bleiben** (Storm)—**Der Jagdmeister des Königs wird mir schon ein fünf bis sechs Schweinchen ablassen** (A. Kopisch: '. . . will let me have half a dozen piglets or so')—sim. **ein anderthalb Jahr** (Gutzkow: 'some eighteen months'). Now obs. is **Laß doch die Dirne einen Tag oder zehn bei uns bleiben** (Gen. 24. 55), i.e. **etwa** (or coll. **ein) zehn Tage;** but this idea is also expressed coll. in another way, viz. by adding **-er** or **-ner** to the noun, and inserting this noun between the art. and the numeral: e.g. **„Deshalb hast du dich mit allen geschlagen?" „Nein, nicht mit allen: nur mit ein Stücker viere"** (Storm: 'And for that you fought with them all?' 'No, only with about four of them')—**Es mag jetzt ein Stückener acht Wochen her sein** (G. Engel: 'It may be a matter of eight weeks ago'); sim. **ein Tager sechs** (Varnhagen v. Ense)—**vor ein Jahrer fünfzehn** (R. Prutz). **2.** *Numeral*: see also **einer** and **eins.** As a numeral, **ein** is inflected in the normal way: e.g. **Der Name des einen Schülers ist Max, des anderen Karl—Sein eines Auge war mit einer Schwäche behaftet** (Th. Mann); and here there is even a plur., as in **Die einen gingen zu Fuß, die anderen fuhren im Auto.** But it is often left uninflected in **ein(er) und derselbe** ('one and the same'), **ein(es) oder das andere** ('one or the other); so also **An ein und demselben Punkte** ('At one and the same place') **wurden zwei Gespräche angeknüpft** (Raabe).

ein-: 1. The fundamental force of this sep. prefix is that of *motion into*; but this motion may imply destruction **(Fenster einschlagen, -werfen),** diminution **(einschrumpfen),** acquisition **(einkaufen, -wechseln)** or inducement to sleep **(einschläfern, -wiegen). 2.** Most common verbs implying motion, when compounded with a *simple* prefix like **ein-** (e.g. **eingehen, -kommen, -ziehen,** etc.), have various more or less distinct shades of meaning, often with fig. force: thus, **eingehen** and **einkommen** (qq.v.) are used in a number of different ways, but *not* now generally to express mere translocation from the outside to the inside, an idea which requires the use of **hineingehen** and **hereinkommen** (see **her-, hin-** 2, and **accusative or dative . . .** 2 *c*). **3. (a)** Where a verb compounded with **ein-** is associated with a prep. which may govern either an accus. or a dat., the *accus.* is the only correct case where the context implies that the motion is *still proceeding* (cf. *b*): e.g. **Er trat in die Stube ein—Laßt uns in dieses Abteil einsteigen**

—**Wir bogen in einen Seitenweg ein**—**Der Feind fiel in unser Land ein**, etc. (**b**) But there are cases where either the accus. or the dat. may be associated with **ein-**, the determining factor being whether the motion is regarded as completed or not; if it *is* completed, then obviously a *state* is suggested, so that the *dat.* is the correct case to use, whereas if the motion is still proceeding, an *action* is implied, in which case the *accus.* is required. The case, in fact, depends on the mental picture that presents itself to the writer: in a proposition like **Warum haben England und Frankreich uns nicht den Krieg erklärt, als wir im Rheinland einmarschierten?** (B. E. Werner), what the author has in his mind is not the moment when the troops were crossing into the Rhineland (an idea which would properly be expressed by **als wir in das Rheinland hineinmarschierten**), but the time when they were already in occupation there. For sim. examples see esp. **ankommen** 1; also **einführen, -kehren, -nisten, -schiffen, -schließen, -sprechen, -stellen,** and cf. **absteigen.** (**c**) The *dat.* is very commonly associated with the *past part.* of such verbs, as this part of a verb by its very name implies completed action, esp. when it is combined with **sein** (as distinct from **werden,** which properly implies an action), or with verbs of rest like **ruhen, sitzen, stehen,** etc.: e.g. **Der Sonne Pracht ist tief im Nebel eingehüllt** (G.)—**Eine Perle ruht in stillen Schalen eingeschlossen** (G.); and cf. the following pairs of examples: **Er kleidet seine Gedanken in schöne Worte ein** and **Dieser Gedanke ist in schönen Worten eingekleidet**—**Er schlug** (or **wickelte**) **das Buch in braunes Papier ein** and **Das Buch war in braunem Papier eingeschlagen** (but **Das Buch wurde in braunes Papier eingeschlagen**)—**Sie sperrte sich in ihre Kammer ein** (B. E. Werner: 'She *went into* her room and locked the door') and **Der Dieb ist im Gefängnis eingesperrt**—**Ich trug seinen Namen in mein Notizbuch ein** and **Sein Name steht in meinem Notizbuch eingetragen,** etc.

einbegreifen: This verb is chiefly used in commercial lang. in the past part. **einbegriffen,** meaning 'included' (cf. **einschließen**): **Das wird, alle Spesen mit einbegriffen** ('all charges included'), **200 Mark kosten.**

einbrechen: This verb is now almost always used *intrans.*: one might conceivably use **ein altes Gebäude einbrechen** in the sense of 'to demolish an old building', but **abbrechen** or **niederreißen** would be much more usual there. In any case the simple prefix **ein-** may give **brechen** *fig.* force (see **her-, hin-** 2 and 3): e.g. **Der Knabe ertrank, als das Eis einbrach**—**Der Knabe ist auf dem Eise eingebrochen**—**Unter der Last des Schnees brach das Dach ein** ('. . . the roof fell in')—**Der Feind ist in das Elsaß eingebrochen** ('. . . has invaded Alsace'). So also **Die Nacht bricht ein** ('Night is falling'), although here **bricht herein** is much more common; but **bei einbrechender Nacht** is quite usual, and **bei Einbruch der Nacht** is definitely fixed (cf. **Der Tag bricht an** and **bei Tagesanbruch**). Another very common use of **einbrechen** is in the sense of 'to break in' (of a burglar), and here the aux. is either **haben** or, more commonly, **sein:** cf. **Im Finstern bricht man in die Häuser ein** (Job 24. 16)—**Wie ein Dieb war das Fieber in das Haus eingebrochen** (Wildenbruch)—**O Gott, hat jemand hier eingebrochen?** (Waggerl); a dat. in the prep. phrase is possible when the verb is used impers., as in **In unserem Hause wurde diese Nacht eingebrochen** ('There was a burglary in our house last night').

einer: 1. Written with a capital letter, in which case it less frequently takes the form **Einser,** this is a masc. noun meaning 'unit', i.e. a number less than 10, as distinct from 'tens, hundreds', etc. (**Zehner, Hunderter,** etc.): cf. **Die Amerikaner fangen alles, was sie beginnen, mit sechs Nullen hinter den Einern an** (K. Edschmid: i.e. they only deal in millions). **2.** Written with a small letter, **einer** has much the same force as the indef. **man** (q.v.), which it provides with oblique cases. But these latter are in common use only in the dat. and accus., as in **Gewöhnlich bedankt man sich, wenn einem ein Geschenk gegeben wird.** The gen. **eines** here is for the most part avoided now: cf. **Sollen das Worte eines** (better **eines Menschen**) **gewesen sein, der nicht weiß, was er spricht?** (Immermann); sim. **Ist es uns nicht erlaubt, nach der Herkunft eines zu forschen, der sich unter uns drängt?** (W. Alexis)—**Für ein paar Stunden durfte sie froh sein, mit der Freude eines, der aus Kerkermauern wieder zur Sonne emporsteigt** (St. Zweig). But the gen. **eines** is reg. used in propositions like **Der Name eines der Mitglieder** ('of one of the members') **ist Meier**; sim. **Ich hatte Empfehlungen an den Präsidenten eines der obersten Gerichtshöfe** (Hofmannsthal)—**Sie erwartete das Kommen eines der übrigen Ärzte** (Bergengruen)—**Sie war auf Kosten eines ihrer Verwandten in Deutschland erzogen worden** (K. Edschmid)—**Er reiste am Abend ab, neben dem Chauffeur eines der Lastautos** (id.). For **unsereiner,** see **eins** 3.

einerlei: see **Hand** 2 (*b*).

einfahren: As in the case of **abfallen, einführen,** etc. (qq.v.), so here also the simple prefix implies *fig.* force: whereas 'to drive into the town' is **in die Stadt hineinfahren** (or **hereinfahren,** viewed from the speaker's standpoint), **einfahren** is used in specific cases: e.g. **Die Bergleute sind** (*scil.* **in die Grube**) **eingefahren** ('The miners have gone under ground')—**Der Zug fuhr** (or **lief**) **pünktlich ein** ('The train came in on time'). In an accompanying prep. phrase the case is normally, of course, the accus.; a dat. here, on the analogy of **ankommen, einkehren** or **sich einfinden** (qq.v.), is unusual and not to be recommended: cf. **Der Bauer fuhr in der Kreisstadt ein** (Polenz)—**Es war am 1. Juli, als Marinke im Dorfe einfuhr** (Sudermann). With *trans.* force, **einfahren** is used in the sense of 'to break in' (a horse to the driving-reins), and of 'to run (a car) in': **Das junge Pferd** (or **Unser neues Auto**) **ist noch nicht eingefahren.** Here also belongs its use by farmers with the obj. unexpressed: **Morgen fahren wir ein** or **Morgen wird eingefahren** ('We'll begin to carry [*Scots* lead in] tomorrow'), where **das Heu** or **das Getreide** is understood.

einfallen: The same applies to this verb as to **ab-, ausfallen,** etc. (qq.v., and see **her-, hin-** 3): one says **Das Kind beugte sich zu weit über den Fluß und fiel hinein** (not **ein**), but **Das Gebäude fiel plötzlich ein** (not **hinein**) = **stürzte ein,** 'collapsed'. Other specific uses are seen in propositions like **Der Feind fiel in die Stadt ein** ('invaded the town')—**Regenwetter ist eingefallen** ('has set in')—**Die Kapelle fiel ein** ('The band struck up')—**Hier fällt der Chor ein** ('Here the chorus joins *or* comes in')—**Er fiel mir in die Rede ein** ('He interrupted me as I was speaking')—**Sie hat eingefallene Wangen** ('hollow cheeks'). But its commonest fig. use is in the sense of 'to come to mind' (see **occur** 2): e.g. **Wie heißt er doch? Sein Name fällt mir im Augenblick nicht ein—Was? Ich soll mit ins Konzert gehen? (Das) fällt mir nicht im Traume ein!** ('I should never dream of it!')—**Als er sie küßte, sagte sie: „Was fällt Ihnen ein?"** (indignantly: 'The idea! How dare you?'). Incidentally, **einfallen** is not used to express our military order 'Fall in!' the German equivalent of which is **Antreten!**

einfinden: This verb is only used *reflex.* and should strictly mean 'to find one's way into (a place)', but actually it seems never to be so used, which is all the more surprising as **finden** (q.v.) and many of its compounds are often used, with or now commonly without the reflex. pron., in the sense of 'to find one's way'; and even in an example like **Sie mußten sich wieder in die gewohnte Ordnung einfinden** (Auerbach), where the verb has fig. force ('They had to adapt themselves again to the old order of things'), one would generally use **sich finden** or **sich hineinfinden.** The only regular force of **sich einfinden** is now 'to arrive, turn up' (esp., but not necessarily, of a number of people), which explains the *dat.* case in an accompanying prep. phrase (see **arrival**): e.g. **Auf dem Platze hatten sich viele Zuschauer eingefunden** (G.)—**Unterdessen hatte sich das Hochzeitgefolge im Hofe eingefunden** (Immermann)—**Die übrigen Gäste fanden sich nach und nach in der Halle ein** (Heyse)—**An Theaterabenden versäumt er selten, sich vor dem Schauspielhause einzufinden** (Hebbel)—**Sie pflückte einige Haselnüsse, bevor sie sich in der Küche einfand** (Voigt-Diederichs)—**Barbara fand sich zur bestimmten Stunde im Gefängnis ein** (E. Wichert).

einführen: As explained under **her-, hin-** 2 and 3, a double prefix is necessary with **führen** if it is to have the lit. force of 'to lead *or* conduct (a person) in': e.g. **Ich führte die Gesellschaft in das Schloß hinein.** On the other hand, the simple prefix **ein-** implies *fig.* force—not that of 'to carry' crops from the fields to the stackyard (see **einfahren**), but that of 'to introduce' (esp. something new; not one person to another, which is **vorstellen**). In an accompanying prep. phrase the case may be either accus. or dat., the former stressing the *act* of introducing, the latter pointing to the *state* after the introduction and hence used esp. with a past part.; cf. on the one hand, **Ich ward wohl empfangen und in manche**

Familie eingeführt (G.)—**Wir sollten versuchen, diese Sitte in unser Land einzuführen**; and, on the other hand, **Das ist eine Sitte, die schon längst in unserem Lande eingeführt ist** ('That has long been an established custom in our country')—**Ich wollte ihn bei uns** (i.e. **in unserem Hause**) **einführen, aber er verbat sich das** (H. Grimm: really 'I wished to take him in and make him feel at home with us . . .'); cf. **Als ich zurückkam, fand ich ihn in unserem Kreise eingebürgert** (Immermann: '. . . I found him established as a member of our circle').

Eingang: see **entrance**.

eingedenk: see **adjectives (indeclinable)** 5.

eingehen: **(a)** *Intrans.*, to express the *lit.* idea of 'to go in, enter', one must now use the double prefix **hinein-** (cf. **her-**, **hin-** 2 and 3; **abfallen**, **eintreten**, etc.): **Er ging zur Tür** (or **in das Haus**) **hinein.** At an earlier period the simple prefix **ein-** was used in this sense, as in Luther's **Gehet ein durch die enge Pforte** (Matt. 7.'13), and this is still preserved in a few Biblical expressions like **zum ewigen Leben** or **in die ewige Ruhe eingehen**; cf. **Eine provenzalische Sage behauptet, jeder fallende Stern sei eine irrende Frauenseele, die ins Paradies eingehe** (Sudermann)—**Herr, schenke ihr ein reines Herz, auf daß** (= **damit**) **sie eingehe in die Wohnungen des ewigen Friedens** (Th. Mann). Otherwise **eingehen** is now always used with various more or less *fig.* meanings: e.g. **Eine große Ladung ist heute eingegangen** ('A large cargo has come in, been imported, today')—**In diesem Hause gehen viele Künstler aus und ein** ('Many artists frequent this house')—**Alles geht ihm leicht ein** ('He is quick of apprehension, picks things up easily')—**Das Tuch ist beim Waschen eingegangen** ('The cloth has shrunk in the wash')—**Letzten Winter sind alle meine Rosen eingegangen** ('All my roses died last winter')—**Beim Ausbruch des Krieges ging das Geschäft ein** ('On the outbreak of war the shop put up its shutters')—**Die Zeitung ist eingegangen** ('The paper has stopped publication')—**Man ging auf alle meine Bedingungen ein** ('They agreed to all my conditions')—**Er ging in alle Einzelheiten ein** ('He entered into all the details': cf. **eingehend**, 'in detail'). **(b)** *Trans.*, **Ich gehe jede Wette ein** ('I'll bet you anything')—**Die zwei Länder gingen ein Bündnis ein** ('The two countries entered into an alliance')—**Die Mutter war wenig geneigt, die von mir eingegangenen Kontrakte zu realisieren** (Hebbel). Used with this trans. force, **eingehen** should normally take the aux. **haben**, as it does in **Die ersten Worte bestätigten ihm, daß er eine neue Pflicht eingegangen habe** (G. Keller); but modern usage seems to favour **sein**: e.g. **Er ist eine Wette eingegangen** (C. F. Meyer)—**Ich wäre jede Bedingung eingegangen** (Hofmannsthal: 'I would have accepted any conditions')—**Das Heer ist eine Konföderation eingegangen** (E. Wichert)—**Wie kam er wohl am schnellsten aus den Verpflichtungen heraus, die er eingegangen war?** (G. Engel)—**Jetzt erst kam er zur rechten Überlegung, wie große Verantwortung er eingegangen war** (C. Rothe)—**Die Ehe war sie auf den Wunsch ihrer Eltern eingegangen** (Jul. Wolff)—**Es hieß, daß sie entwichen und mit einem Franzosen die Ehe eingegangen sei** (Th. Mann).

eingestehen: see **confess** 2.

einhalten: For the *intrans.* use of this verb, see **stop** (*verb*) 1 (*b*). As a *trans.* verb, it is not used to express an idea like 'to hold one's breath in' (=**den Atem anhalten**), but in ordinary, non-technical language it generally has the force of 'to observe punctually', esp. of conditions, formalities, set or appointed times, etc.: e.g. **Ich verlasse mich darauf, daß Sie die vereinbarten Bedingungen einhalten** ('I rely on your observing *or* fulfilling the conditions agreed upon')—**Die üblichen Formalitäten wurden eingehalten** ('The usual formalities were observed')—**Sie werden ersucht, den Zahlungstermin** (or **Zahltag**) **einzuhalten** ('You are requested to pay on the due date')—**Eine bestimmte Tagesstunde ist ihm verdrießlich: selten, daß er sie einhält** (G., of a person who rarely 'keeps' an appointment)—**Auf dieser Strecke halten die Züge den Fahrplan meistens nicht ein** ('On this section the trains generally don't keep to the time-table').

einig: **1.** As an adj., this orig. meant 'single, sole, only', in which sense it was in use down to the classical period: e.g. **Du vermagst nicht ein einiges Haar weiß oder schwarz zu machen** (Matt. 5. 36)—**Dann wäre mir das einige Verdienst** ('my one and only merit') **entwischt** (Sch.). But apart from a phrase like **der dreieinige Gott** ('the Triune God'), this is now obs., **einzig** being used instead: cf. **Sie sind der einzige Mensch, dem ich auf solche**

Reden antworte (Sch.), where the 1st edition reads **der einige Mensch.** The orig. sense is still dimly seen, however, in propositions like **Wir sind über den Preis einig** or **haben uns darüber geeinigt** ('We are of one mind *or* agreed as to the price': cf. **agree** 4 *a*). **2.** But the commonest modern use of **einig** is as an indef. pron. adj. or pron., meaning 'some, a few, several', and in this sense it is used not only in the plur., but also (unlike the more choice expression **etlich,** q.v.) in the sing. **(a)** The inflexion of **einig** presents no difficulty: it should always have a *strong* ending. Indeed, the only case in which a weak ending is at all possible is the gen. sing. masc. and neut., and then only when the following noun itself has the strong **-(e)s** ending; but there a weak ending is rightly characterized by *Sanders* as **„nicht gut"**: cf. **Die meisten Leute erwehren sich dieses Fehlers** ('avoid this mistake') **vermittelst einigen** (better **einiges**) **empfangenen Unterrichts** (Varnhagen v. Ense). **(b)** The chief difficulty in this connexion is where **einig** is followed by an attrib. adj. On the whole, a *weak* ending in the adj. (as in the last example under *a* above) is to be recommended in all cases *except the nom. and accus. plur.*, where a *strong* ending, as after **viel** (q.v. 2 *c*) and **etlich** (q.v.), is now almost established (but see **manch** 5). Characteristic examples are: **Dazu gehört einiger frohe Mut** or **Dazu bedarf es einiges frohen Mutes—Wir gingen zusammen, ich mit einigem inneren Widerstreben** (H. Hesse)—**Außer einigem bescheidenen Hausrat hinterließ er nur drei Falken von hohem Wert** (Bergengruen)—**Man hat hier die Namen einiger vaterländischen Autoren weggelassen** (G.: cf. *c* below)—**Das scheidende Licht küßte die Spitzen einiger hochstämmigen Lorbeerbäume** (Hackländer); and sim., in an adj.-subst., **Die Anmerkungen bringen einiges Biographische** (Otto Braun, in his preface to selections from Herder)—**Die Einleitung gibt neben einigem Biographischen eine Übersicht über des Dichters Stellung in der Literaturgeschichte.** But in the nom. and accus. plur. a strong ending is almost fixed, as in **Vor der Tür spielten einige kleine Kinder**; and sim. **Im Vordergrunde ist eine Felsenplatte, auf die sich einige hilflose Menschen retten** (G.). Exceptions do occur, of course, esp. in the neut. sing.: cf. **Der Erbauer des Hauses hatte einiges überflüssiges** (usually **überflüssige**) **Geld besessen** (Böhlau); and sim. **Einiges slawisches Blut floß in ihren Adern** (Th. Mann). **(c)** By far the greatest fluctuation occurs in the *gen. plur.*, where a strong ending in the adj., characterized by *Sanders* as **„minder gut"**, is by no means uncommon: e.g. **Es ist verfehlt, Beethoven als Kompositum einiger vorhergegangener menschlicher Größen erweisen zu wollen** (K. Lamprecht)—**Die Sonne warf ihre Strahlen durch die Scheiben einiger aus der Schweiz heimgebrachter Glasgemälde** (L. Schücking)—**Die Maske ließ sich vermittels einiger schwarzer Schnüre befestigen** (A. Schaeffer)—**Eine neue Verfassung wurde trotz des Widerspruchs Krögers und einiger anderer störrischer alter Herren zum Staatsgesetz erhoben** (Th. Mann)—**Der junge Fürst war auf den Rat einiger vertrauter Männer angewiesen** (A. Neumann).

einkehren: This is the verb most commonly used in the sense of 'to put up' at a hotel or an inn. As the fundamental idea is not *entering*, but *staying at* the inn, a *dat.* is the recognized case in the prep. phrase, as it is with **absteigen** (q.v. 2): e.g. **Ein Getümmel zog eine Anzahl Menschen nach dem Tore des Gasthofs, in welchem Wilhelm eingekehrt war** (G.)—**Erkrankt durch Übermüdung, mußte er im** Hôtel de Dieu **einkehren** (Heine)—**Wo** (not **Wohin**) **wollt Ihr denn einkehren?** (E. Wichert)—**Gegen sonstige Gewohnheit kehrte er im Kruge ein** (id.)—**Eines Abends geschah es, daß er in der Polizeihütte zur Rast einkehrte** (H. Grimm); sim., with personified abstract subjs., **Fleiß und Rührigkeit kehrten unter seinem Dache ein** (Spindler)—**So war denn wieder das Glück in dem Häuschen eingekehrt** (Villinger). Occasional examples of an accus. should not be imitated: cf. **Er kehrte in ein Wirtshaus ein** (H. v. Kleist)—**Es ist mir bedenklich, daß er ins „Schwarze Kreuz" einkehrt** (Zschokke)—**In Ilmenau war es, wo er in das Haus zum Löwen einkehrte** (Jul. Rodenberg); and definitely to be condemned is **Er fragte nach einem Hotel, worein bessere Fremde kehrten** (C. Hauptmann: for **wo . . . Fremde einkehrten**). The basic idea being *rest at*, not *motion into* the place, one would rather expect the aux. to be **haben,** but as two of the above examples show, this is not so: the recognized aux. is **sein,** and an example like **Es ist mir, als habe ein Engel bei mir eingekehrt** (M. Kaufmann) is very unusual.

einkommen: This is not used in the sense of 'to enter' (see **ein-** 2), but esp. of money 'coming in', hence **Er hat ein jährliches Einkommen** von zehntausend Mark ('His income is ten thousand marks a year'). The only other common use of **einkommen** is with the prep. **um** in the sense of 'to apply *or* petition for' something: e.g. **Jedermann scheint jetzt um eine Gehaltserhöhung einzukommen** ('Everybody seems to be applying for an increase of salary just now')—**Er war um einen plötzlichen Urlaub eingekommen** (R. Herzog: 'He had applied for immediate leave of absence').

einladen, Einladung: see **load** (verb) 1 (*a*); **load** (noun) 2.

einlassen: This is rather exceptional in that **jemand einlassen** can be used to convey the lit. idea 'to allow a person to enter, admit him' (= **hereinkommen lassen**); cf. **Mein einer Schuh läßt Wasser ein** ('My one shoe is letting in water', i.e. is not water-tight). It is also used with the force of 'to insert' something, an accus. in the accompanying prep. phrase suggesting an action, while a dat. implies a fixed state: cf. **Spiegel werden in die Wand eingelassen** (G.) and **In der Kirchenmauer war ein Grabstein eingelassen** (Hofmannsthal); so also **Sie ließ sich in ein Gespräch mit mir ein** ('She joined *or* let herself be drawn into a conversation with me')—**Auf solche Händel lasse ich mich nicht ein** ('I shall not become involved in, shall have nothing to do with, such dealings').

einlaufen: Like other verbs of motion compounded with **ein-** (q.v. 2), **einlaufen** is only used *fig.*, the lit. sense of 'to run in' requiring the prefix **herein-** or **hinein-**, as in **Die Kinder kamen hereingelaufen, als es zu regnen anfing.** On the other hand, **einlaufen** is mainly used as in the following examples: **Der Zug lief pünktlich** (*scil.* **in den Bahnhof**), **das Schiff** (*scil.* **in den Hafen**) **ein**—**Das Kleid ist beim Waschen eingelaufen** (i.e. 'has shrunk': see **eingehen**)—**Das Auto muß sich noch einlaufen** ('is not yet run in')—**Mit der Morgenpost sind wichtige Briefe eingelaufen** ('have come in, to hand'); sim. **Vom Regimentskommando war abends ein Schriftstück eingelaufen** (J. F. Perkonig: like **eingegangen**). In prep. phrases with **in, an,** etc., the *accus.* is the normal case, as in the phrases inserted in the first example above, but very occasionally a dat. is found, as with **eintreffen** (q.v.): cf. **Zwei Minuten bevor der Expreßzug auf der Station einlaufen sollte, stieß er auf einen wartenden Lastzug** (J. Roth).

einlegen: As in the case of other common verbs of motion (see **abfallen, eingehen,** etc.), so here also the simple prefix **ein-** gives **legen** *fig.* force, the lit. idea of 'to lay (a thing) in' (a receptacle) requiring a double prefix: cf. **Ich holte einen Korb und legte die Eier hinein** and **Ich habe sechs Dutzend Eier eingelegt** ('I have preserved six dozen eggs'). Other fig. uses of **einlegen** are seen in examples like **Der Ritter legte die Lanze ein** ('The knight couched his lance')—**Die Tischplatte ist mit Elfenbein eingelegt** ('The table-top is inlaid with ivory')—**Er hat versprochen, ein gutes Wort für mich einzulegen** ('He has promised to put in a good word for me')—**Damit hat er wenig Ehre eingelegt** ('He has gained little honour by that')—**Ich habe dagegen Verwahrung eingelegt** ('I have entered a protest against it'). Exceptional here is the coll. expression **Man hat mich gründlich hineingelegt** ('I have been fairly taken in, imposed upon'), where the double prefix has fig. force.

einlernen: see **lernen** 2.

einleuchten: see **obvious(ly)** *ad fin.*; **light** (verb) 1 (*c*).

einmal: The meaning of this word depends on the *accent*. **1.** With the accent on **ein-**, it is primarily an iterative adv. meaning 'once', as distinguished from **zwei-, drei-mal,** etc.: e.g. **Ei'nmal eins ist eins** (hence **das Einmaleins,** 'the multiplication table': see **eins**)—**Ich bin nur ei'nmal in Frankreich gewesen**—**Ich habe ihm das nicht ei'nmal, sondern drei'mal gesagt**—**Wenn du so etwas noch ei'nmal sagst, werde ich dich bestrafen** (for the last two examples with a different accent, see 2). Other idioms: **Ich habe ihm das ei'nmal über** (or **um**) **das andere gesagt** ('over and over again, time and again')—**Es fing auf ei'nmal** (or **mit ei'nmal** or **mit ei'nem Male**) **zu regnen an** ('all at once')—**Ich kann nicht ausgehen, ei'nmal** (or **erstens:** see **erst** 2 *e*) **weil ich beschäftigt bin, sodann weil ich einen Schnupfen habe** ('in the first place . . ., in the second place . . .')—**Im Juli hatten wir viel Regen, aber im August noch ei'nmal soviel** ('as much again, twice as much'). **2.** With the accent on **-mal,** it is used esp. to suggest a vague, unspecified time, as in our stereotyped 'once upon a time' in fairy-tales: **Es war einma'l ein König . . .**; or the time may be future, as in **Es wird einma'l eine bessere Zeit kommen.** Then, it is used, esp. in the shorter form **mal,** in imperat. propositions to moderate the bluntness of a command: e.g. **Komm mal her!** ('Come here, will you?')—**Sehen Sie mal!** ('Oh, look!') **Da kommt ein Reiter angaloppiert!** The expression **nicht einmal,** with only a slight accent on **-mal** and the main accent on a following word, means 'not even': e.g. **Nicht einmal der Leh'rer konnte diese Aufgabe lösen—Ich würde das nicht tun, nicht einmal wenn er mich darum bä'te.** So also **noch einmal** simply means 'again' in a proposition like **Ich mußte das Gedicht noch einmal** (usually **nochmal**) **aufsagen.**

einnisten: 1. The simple verb **nisten** (lit. 'to build a nest', fig. 'to take root, be established') takes the *dat.* in an accompanying prep. phrase: e.g. **Die Tauben nisten in den hohlen Löchern** (Jer. 48. 28) —**Die Sorge nistet im tiefen Herzen** (G.). **2.** In the fig. sense, however, the reflex. compd. **sich einnisten** ('to become established, settle') is much more usual. Sometimes an accus. in the prep. phrase is found here, as in **Dieser Mensch hatte sich in sein Vertrauen eingenistet** (Spielhagen, implying an *act*: 'This person had wormed himself *into* his confidence'); but much more common is the *dat.*, suggesting the *state* of being already established (cf. **einführen**): e.g. **Die Fremden nisteten sich im südlichen Venn** (a district south of Aachen) **schon ein** (C. Rothe)—**Im Wuppertal hatten sich die Menschen mit ihrer Industrie eingenistet** (W. Schäfer)—**In diesem Hause hatte der Maler sich eingenistet** (Dauthendey)—**Er hatte mich auf die Bahn des Abenteuerlichen gebracht, das sich so leicht im kindlichen Gemüt einnistet** (E. T. A. Hoffmann)—**Im brachen Feld hat Schierling** ('hemlock') **sich eingenistet** (Schlegel)—**Efeu hatte sich in den Ritzen des Mauerwerks eingenistet** (Immermann); cf. **Sie zweifelten nicht, daß der Satan sich in Davids Gliedern festgenistet hatte** (Waggerl).

einräumen: see confess 2.

eins: 1. Written with a capital letter, this is a fem. noun denoting the figure 1, and the other numbers are treated in the same way: e.g. **Die Zahl 12 fängt mit einer Eins an—Die Zahl 11888 hat zwei Einsen und drei Achten—Eine Million hat sechs Nullen nach der Eins**; cf. **das Einmaleins** ('the multiplication table') and the example given under **einer** 1. So also in class-marks, etc., as in **Dieser Schüler hat eine Eins, der da eine Zwei bekommen.** To be distinguished from **die Eins** is **der Einer** (sometimes **Einser**), for which see **einer** 1. **2.** Otherwise **eins** is now written with a small letter, as in many idioms: e.g. **Punkt eins** ('On the stroke of one o'clock') **müssen wir am Bahnhof sein—Ich habe es eilig, aber eins** ('one thing') **muß ich dir noch sagen—Da sind zwei Bücher: eins davon ist ein Roman—Sie hätten ihm eins versetzen sollen** ('You ought to have dealt him a blow')—**Trinken wir noch eins!** (see **trinken** 1 *a*)—**Es läuft auf eins hinaus** ('It comes *or* amounts to the same thing')—**Es ist mir alles eins** ('It 's all one *or* the same to me')—**Hierin sind wir eins** (= **einig,** 'in agreement')—**Blitz und Donner waren eins** ('simultaneous')—**Er lief mit eins** (= **mit einem Male, plötzlich,** 'all of a sudden') **zur Tür hinaus—Ich kam aus dem Wald heraus und fand mit eins das schöne liebliche Wasser** (Stifter). **3.** The expressions **unser einer** (fem. **eine,** neut. **eines**) mean **lit.** 'one of us', but these are now written as one word and used esp. in the sense of 'people like us, people of our social class' (cf. our coll. 'the likes of us': see **-gleichen** 1), being often a mere circumlocution for 'I' or 'we': e.g. **Es ist zu gut hier für unsereinen** (C. Rothe). Esp. common is the neut. **unsereins,** convenient as referring to people of either sex: e.g. **Wenn unsereins** (here: hardworking girls like us) **am Spinnen war, stand sie bei ihrem Buhlen** (G.)—**Herr, unsereins ist übel dran** (Sch.: 'a fellow like me is badly off')—**Mir war nicht eingefallen, daß Beethoven vorhanden war, daß er Brot essen und Luft atmen könne wie unsereins** (Rich. Wagner: 'It had never occurred to me that Beethoven could be a living being, could eat bread and draw breath like the rest of us')—**„Kommst du nach dem Theater gleich heim?" „Unsinn! Unsereins will doch auch sein bißchen Erholung"** (R. Herzog: 'Nonsense! A fellow like me wants his occasional bit of fun'); sim. in the gen., **Er mußte immer was** (= **etwas**) **Besonderes haben und war niemals unsereins Freund** (Ponten: '. . . and was never on friendly terms with the likes of us'). The neut. has even become an invariable form, so that one can say **Er ist zu vornehm, um mit unsereins** (or **unsereinem**) **zu verkehren** ('He is too genteel to associate with us').

einschiffen: It is not wrong to say **Gestern ist die Familie nach Brasilien eingeschifft** ('The family embarked for Brazil yesterday'), but the verb is much more commonly used with *trans.* force: e.g. **Ich schiffte mich nach Brasilien ein—Diese Waren sollen nach Amerika eingeschifft werden** ('These goods are to be shipped to America')—**Wir müssen noch viele Truppen nach Korea einschiffen** ('We must embark many more troops for Korea'); and this use has even been extended to the 'entraining' of soldiers: **Als die Truppen auf dem Festlande landeten, wurden sie sofort in Eisenbahnzüge(n) eingeschifft** ('On landing on the continent, the troops were immediately entrained'), where, rather strangely, the *dative* seems to be the more usual case: cf. **Ich hatte am Abend vorher, als ich mich auf der „Florida" einschiffte** ('when I went aboard the *Florida*'), **keine Lust gehabt, Menschen zu sehen** (Dauthendey).

einschlagen: 1. *Trans.*: not only 'to drive (a nail) in' or 'to smash (a door, window) in', but also 'to wrap' (something in paper, etc.: see **ein-** 3 *c*), and 'to take, turn into' (a road), as in **Wir haben den falschen Weg eingeschlagen. 2.** *Intrans.*: (**a**) with the aux. **haben:** either 'to shake hands' on the conclusion of a bargain, as in **Schlag ein!** ('Give me your hand on it!') and **Wir haben den Handel abgeschlossen und darauf eingeschlagen** ('We have struck the bargain and shaken hands on it'), or esp., used of bombs, lightning, etc., 'to strike': e.g. **Der Blitz schlug in die** (or **der**) **Kirche ein**; but always **Irgendwo** (not **-wohin**) **hatte der Blitz eingeschlagen** (Waggerl)—**Im Dunkeln sah er, wo die Bomben eingeschlagen hatten** (B. E. Werner)—fig. **Diese Nachricht hat in ihn wie ein Blitz eingeschlagen** (C. Bulcke)—**Nun** ('Now that': see **nun** 2) **das Glück wie der Blitz eingeschlagen hat, möchte man am liebsten heulen** (E. Kästner)—cf. **Blitzartig war** (usually **hatte**) **in mir die Überzeugung eingeschlagen** ('the conviction had flashed across my mind'), **daß die Folgen meines Planes unausdenkbar sein mußten** (F. Thieß); (**b**) with the aux. **sein:** 'to thrive, progress' (much like **geraten**, ant. **fehlschlagen**): e.g. **Das Getreide schlägt gut ein** ('The corn promises well')—**Das Unternehmen ist nach Wunsch eingeschlagen** ('The undertaking has made the hoped-for progress'); sim. **Mehrere Versuche waren fehlgeschlagen** (A. Schaeffer).

einschließen: The commonest meaning of this verb is 'to shut *or* lock in', and here (see **ein-** 3) the place of confinement may stand either in the accus. or in the dat., the former properly suggesting the action, the latter the resultant state (but see **schließen** 1). e.g. **Der Kurfürst schloß sich ins Lager ein** (Sch.) and **Zuletzt schloß er sich in seinem Zimmer ein** (Wassermann); cf. **Die Tante schloß sich einen ganzen Tag in ihre Kammer ein** (Heyse), where **in ihrer Kammer** would seem more natural, as the duration of the confinement is emphasized. Other uses of the verb are seen in the following examples: **Das Dorf ist von hohen Bergen eingeschlossen** ('shut in')—**Das feindliche Heer schloß die Festung ein** ('surrounded, invested')—**Die in Klammern eingeschlossenen Wörter können ausgelassen werden** ('The words enclosed in brackets can be omitted')—**Ich will Euch in mein Gebet einschließen** (Sch.: 'I'll include you in my prayer'); so also **In der Rechnung ist das Porto eingeschlossen** ('Postage is included in the account'), but this idea is more usually expressed by **einbegriffen** (see **einbegreifen**) or by **einschließlich,** which has become a prep., esp. in accounts, price-lists, etc.: e.g. **einschließlich Porto und Verpackung** (or **des Portos und der Verpackung:** 'packing and postage included *or* paid'); cf. the unusual dat. (not given by *Duden*) in **Alle Rechte, einschließlich dem der Übersetzung und Verfilmung, vorbehalten** (on the title-page of J. Thorwald's **„Es begann an der Weichsel":** 'All rights reserved, including translation and film rights').

einschreiten: Verbs of motion compounded with **ein-** (q.v. 2) nearly always have only *fig.* force, and this applies particularly to **einschreiten,** which is never used in the sense of 'to stride in', but only in that of 'to step in', i.e. 'intervene' (in a dispute, etc.) or, with **gegen,** 'to proceed against' a person: cf., on the one hand, **Ohne anzuklopfen schritt er in das Haus hinein,** and, on the other hand, **Als ein Aufruhr auszubrechen drohte, schritt die Polizei ein—Sie hatten nicht zu befürchten, daß die Obrigkeit gegen sie**

einschreiten würde (Sudermann: '. . . that the authorities would take legal action against them').

einsehen: This verb is now little used with *intrans.* force, although a schoolboy who has left his book at home may say to his neighbour **Laß mich mit einsehen!** ('Let me look on with you!'). In particular, it cannot be used to render expressions like 'to look in' through a window or 'look into' a room, where the prefix **hinein-** is required, or 'to look in' to see a friend, which is **jemand aufsuchen** or **bei jemandem einsprechen** (q.v.) or **vorsprechen.** But **einsehen** is quite common as a *trans.* verb, and here its most frequent use is to express our 'to see' in the sense of 'to understand' (= **begreifen**): e.g. **Jetzt sehe ich meinen Irrtum ein** ('Now I see my mistake')—**Sehen Sie die Notwendigkeit einer solchen Handlungsweise ein?** ('Do you see the necessity for such a course of action?')—**Sie konnte den Zweck dieser Maßregeln nicht einsehen** or **Sie konnte nicht einsehen, was diese Maßregeln bezweckten** ('She could not see the purpose of these measures'). The only other standard modern use of **einsehen** is with the force of **prüfen,** 'to scrutinize, inspect, examine' (documents, etc.): e.g. **Er war auf dem Amt gewesen, wo er den Vertrag eingesehen hatte** (Auerbach)—**Ich bat den Rechtsanwalt, das Testament einzueshen** (Fr. Thieß)—**Sie können mir Ihre Herren nach Hause mitgeben, um meinen Paß einzusehen** (Bruno Frank: 'You can let your men accompany me home to examine my passport'). Such expressions are mainly characteristic of official lang., and even more official is **Einsicht nehmen** or **gewinnen in** (+ accus.). While **Einsicht** is now used esp. with fig. force, as in 'a man of deep insight', the verbal noun **Einsehen** is only used as an obj. of **haben,** really 'to have a sympathetic understanding': thus, **Haben Sie ein Einsehen!** is much like our coll. 'Have a heart!' (i.e. 'Be sympathetic!'); and so also **Wir hatten eine Landpartie veranstaltet, und das Wetter hatte ein Einsehen** ('We had arranged a picnic, and the weather was kind'). Incidentally, our 'clerk of the weather' is popularly identified in Germany with St. Peter: hence the expression **Petrus meint es heute gut** ('The clerk of the weather is favourably disposed today, has given us a fine day').

einsitzen: 1. This verb implies the same clash between two conflicting ideas as does **einstehen** (q.v.), but whereas the simple verb **sitzen** (q.v. 1) should not be used like **sich setzen** ('to seat oneself'), **einsitzen** is one of several compounds of **sitzen** (q.v. 5) which do imply motion, its force being 'to (step in and) take one's seat in a conveyance': e.g. **„Sitzet nur ein! . . ." Beim Einsitzen durfte der Pudel nicht zurückbleiben** (G.: 'Step in' . . . When we took our seats, the poodle could not be left behind')—**Gegen Abend saßen sie ein und fuhren ab** (Stifter) cf. **Sie bat, auf dem Kahne fahren zu dürfen, und ich setzte mich mit ihr ein** (G.: usually **setzte mich ... hinein**). **2.** Occasionally **einsitzen** is used *trans.* with the force of 'to press (a thing) down by sitting (on it)', esp. of a chair which has developed a hollow through long usage: e.g. **Das Ruhebett war eingesessen** (Gotthelf)—**Der mit Leder gepolsterte Stuhl war tief eingesessen** (A. Wilbrandt)—**Die Stühle kamen ihm so dürftig vor mit ihren eingesessenen Sprungfedern** (Ompteda); and the past part. is often used of one who has settled somewhere as a resident: e.g. **Er stammt aus der Schweiz, siedelte sich aber vor vielen Jahren hier im Norden an und ist nun ganz eingesessen—Der Küster begrüßte einige Ortseingesessene** ('some of the locals') **und trat dann zu mir** (W. v. Scholz).

einsprechen: With the force of 'to look in' (to see a person), this verb is no longer as common as it once was, being replaced by **vorsprechen,** less commonly **an-** or **zusprechen** (qq.v.). Like these, it is used with a *dat.* in the prep. phrase, and with the aux. **haben:** e.g. **Weyland sprach von Zeit zu Zeit bei Freunden ein** (G.)—**Täglich sprachen Menschen im Hofe ein** (Immermann)—**Heute abend sprech' ich auf ein Gericht Karauschen bei euch ein** (H. v. Kleist: 'I'm going to drop in on you this evening for a dish of carp'); cf. **Auf dem Rückwege bin** (now **habe**) **ich bei meinem Bruder eingesprochen** (Lessing).

einsperren ('to shut in, lock up'): As in the case of **einschließen** (q.v.), so here also an accompanying prep. phrase can have either an *accus.* or a *dat.*, according as the *act* of incarcerating or the *state* of being incarcerated is implied (cf. **ein-**, 3 *c*): cf., on the one hand, **Am Vorabend des Wahltags werden alle Fremden aus**

der Stadt gewiesen und die Juden in ihre Gasse eingesperrt (G.), and, on the other hand, **Gretchen als Missetäterin im Kerker eingesperrt!** (G.) and **Kam Besuch, so schlich er gleich aus dem Zimmer und sperrte sich im Ziegenstall ein** (Kästner: where the fundamental idea is that he turned the key and was then safe in the goat-shed).

einspringen: In accordance with what is almost a rule, viz. that the prefix **ein-** gives a verb *fig.* force, **einspringen** is not used in the lit. sense of 'to jump in' (see **ein-** 2; and esp. **her-** 2), but only in that of 'to take the place of, act as substitute for' somebody, generally at a moment's notice. The following is a characteristic example, the reference being to the national German card-game *Skat*, normally played by three players: **„Spielen Sie Skat?" „Danach fragen Sie einen alten Feldsoldaten?" „Schön: der dritte muß gleich nach Hause, Sie können für ihn einspringen"** (Speckmann); sim. **„Mit deinem verletzten Bein wirst du doch nicht ins Theater gehen wollen?" „Wer spielt meine Rolle?" „Da kann doch ein anderer einspringen!"** (P. Ernst).

einstecken: **1.** The lit. force of 'to stick *or* put' (a thing into a hole, receptacle, pigeon-hole, etc.) normally requires the lengthened prefix **hinein-** (which is often pleonastic): e.g. **Man grub ein Loch und steckte den Pfahl hinein—Ich steckte dem Kinde etwas Watte in den hohlen Zahn—In welches Fach hast du das Dokument hineingesteckt?**—and the lengthened prefix is also used of 'poking one's nose' into something: **Es ärgert mich, daß er immer die Nase in meine Angelegenheiten hineinsteckt** (cf. the last two examples under 2). **2.** On the other hand, **einstecken** is used specifically with the force of 'to put (something) into one's pocket' and 'to pocket' (an insult, etc.), as well as 'to put' (a person in gaol): e.g. **Melina steckte die Grobheiten ein** (G.)—**Summe ich einen französischen Psalm, so bin ich gleich ein Ketzer und werde eingesteckt** (G.): cf. **Geld einstecken** ('to pocket money') and **Geld in ein Unternehmen hineinstecken** ('to invest, sink money, in an undertaking').

einstehen: This verb seems to imply a clash between two essentially different conceptions, **ein-** being a prefix of *motion*, and **stehen** a verb of *rest*; but we do find very occasional examples of the simple verb **stehen** implying motion, and several of its compds. are only so used (see **stehen** 3, and cf. **auf-** and **einsitzen**). This applies also, but to a more limited extent, to **einstehen**: it is never used like **in ein Zimmer eintreten** (q.v.), but frequently with the fig. force of **für jemand eintreten**, viz. 'to act as a substitute *or* be a guarantee for a person' (cf. 'to step into the breach'). Rather nearer to the lit. sense is its use in the following example, where an artist, on hearing that a young lad is anxious to learn to paint, says **Wo ist der Bube? Er kann morgen bei mir einstehen** (Zifferer: = **Er kann kommen, um bei mir in der Lehre zu stehen,** 'He can come and be my apprentice'). In this latter sense one would usually say **Er ist gestern bei mir eingestanden**; but where the verb has *fig.* force, the aux. would rather be **haben** in the north.

einstellen: The proposition 'He put the ladder upright in the shed' is **Er stellte die Leiter in den Schuppen.** In this lit. sense the prefix **hinein-** may be added, but not the short prefix **ein-** (see **her-**, **hin-** 3), **einstellen** being only used in specific cases, generally with *fig.* force: e.g. **Arbeiter** or **Diener einstellen** ('to take on workmen, engage servants'), **einen Feldstecher** or **photographischen Apparat einstellen** ('to focus a field-glass, camera'); sim. **das Radio einstellen** (= **einschalten**), often with the station or country as obj., as in **Sie stellte die Schweiz ein** (B. E. Werner: 'She tuned in to Switzerland'). Then, from the idea of putting in an obstacle, it takes on the sense of 'to bar, stop' (cf. **stop** 2 *b*), as with objs. like **Arbeit** ('to strike, down tools'), **Zahlung** ('to suspend payment'), **Verkehr** ('to bar, close a road to traffic'), **das Feuer** ('to cease fire'), etc. That it is not used *lit.* as in **etwas in die Stube hineinstellen,** is seen from examples in which it is combined with a dat. in prep. phrases: e.g. **Er stellte sein Pferd in dem ältesten Kruge des Fleckens ein** (E. Wichert: 'He stabled his horse at the oldest inn in the market-town')—**Darf ich mein Auto für die Nacht hier** (not **hierher**) **einstellen?** ('May I garage my car here for the night?'). So also *reflex.*, like **sich einfinden** (q.v.), with the force of 'to arrive, put in an appearance', not only of persons, as in **Er stellte sich pünktlich am verabredeten Ort ein,** but also of symptoms, pains, attacks, etc., as in **Mein körperliches Übel stellte sich wieder ein** (G.: 'My old complaint set in again'). Here belongs the artificially formed neut. noun **Stelldichein,** really the imperat. **Stelle dich ein!** ('Be sure to turn up!'), now used in the sense of an 'appointment, arranged meeting, rendezvous', esp. an 'assignation' with one of the opposite sex: **Er hat ein Stelldichein mit dem Mädchen** ('He has a date with the girl').

eintreffen: Apart from the abs. sense of 'to be realized *or* fulfilled' (of hopes, fears, suspicions, etc.), as in **Meine Ahnung ist eingetroffen** (Wieland), this verb is only used with the force of 'to arrive', and hence (see **arrive**) the *dative* is necessary in an accompanying prep. phrase: e.g. **Die Gäste trafen alle am verabredeten Orte ein—Nach halbstündiger Verspätung traf** (or **lief**) **der Zug endlich im Bahnhof ein—Als sie in der Halle eintraf, standen die anderen schon vor der Hoteltür** (Kästner).

eintreten: As pointed out under **her-, hin-** 2 and 3, a verb of motion used in its *lit.* sense normally requires a double prefix (**herab-, hinein-**, etc.), whereas the same verb compounded with a simple prefix (**ab-, ein-**, etc.) as a rule has only *fig.* force (see **abfallen, -gehen**, etc.). Viewed from this angle, **eintreten** is exceptional in that it is often used with *lit.* force: one can say **Er trat in das Zimmer ein** or **hinein,** and indeed the simple prefix is perhaps more usual where there is no prep. phrase: e.g. **Als ich „Herein!" rief, trat ein Fremder ein.** But **eintreten** is also used *fig.*, in which case the double prefix is inadmissible: this applies esp. to its use with phrases like **in eine Gesellschaft** ('to become a member of a society'), **ins Heer** ('to join up'), **in ein Amt** ('to enter on the duties of a post'), **für jemand** ('to intercede *or* act as substitute for a person': cf. **einspringen, -stehen**); so also, used abs., **Heute ist Regenwetter eingetreten** ('Rain has set in today'). Unlike **eintreffen** (q.v.), which suggests the moment when the motion has ceased, **eintreten** points to the motion as still proceeding, so that the prep. **in** requires an *accus.*: it is contrary to accepted usage to say **Als sie in dem** (for **das**) **Zimmer eintraten, unterbrach sich der Pastor** (B. E. Werner).

Eintritt: see **entrance.**

einverleiben ('to incorporate'): *Duden* gives **„er verleibt ein und er einverleibt"**, but the latter is esp. South German, as in **Die Waschfrauen einverleibten die Witwe in ihrem Verbande** (G. Keller: 'The washer-women admitted the widow to their union'), and separation of the first prefix is certainly the rule in the north, as in the case of **anerkennen, anvertrauen, auferlegen,** etc. (qq.v.): e.g. **Sie verleiben einem fremden Leichnam moralisches Leben ein** (Jean Paul)—**Er sehnte sich, dieses verlassene Wesen an Kindes Statt seinem Herzen einzuverleiben** (G.).

einverstehen: At an earlier period this verb was used reflex. with **über** + accus. in the sense of 'to agree' with an opinion, etc.: e.g. **Darüber hast du mit meinem Vater oft dich einverstanden** (Lessing); now it is practically only used with **mit** in the expressions **einverstanden sein** and **sich einverstanden erklären:** e.g. **Einverstanden!** (at meetings: 'Agreed!')—**Ich erkläre mich mit ihm** (or **mit seinem Vorschlag**) **einverstanden;** cf. Burleigh's words to Queen Mary: **Ihr wart mit Babington einverstanden** (Sch.: 'You had an understanding with Babington').

einwechseln: see **change** 2 (*a*).

einwerfen: Like other verbs compounded with the simple prefix **ein-** (q.v.), this is not used in a general way of throwing something, say, into a hole or river, an idea which is expressed by the simple verb or by the use of the longer prefix **hinein-.** It is, in fact, only in certain specific cases that **einwerfen** is used: e.g. **Die Kinder haben ein Fenster eingeworfen** ('The children have [thrown something and] smashed a window')—**Wenn du an der Post vorbeigehst, sei so gut und wirf diesen Brief ein!** (i.e. in the letter-box)—**Da der Fußball über die Seitenlinie gestoßen wurde, mußte ihn einer der Läufer wieder einwerfen** ('As the ball was kicked over the touch-line, one of the halves had to throw it in again')—**Er schwieg, als wolle er den anderen Gelegenheit geben, ein Wort einzuwerfen** (W. v. Scholz: '. . . as if he wanted to give the others a chance to put in a word')—**Gegen meinen Vorschlag warf** (or **wandte**) **sie ein, daß er schwer auszuführen sei** ('She objected to my proposal as being difficult to carry into execution').

einwilligen: see **agree** 1 (*b*).

einwohnen: see **inne-** 4.

einzeln, einzig: see **single.**

eitel: The orig. force of this adj. is 'empty',

in which sense it is still used *fig.* as we speak of 'empty, frivolous chatter' (eitles Geschwätz) or '*idle* conjectures' (eitle Vermutungen): cf. **Der Herr weiß die Gedanken der Menschen, daß sie eitel sind** (Ps. 94. 11)—**Das ist das einzige Reelle, alles andere ist eitel** (G.)—**Mit eitler Rede wird hier nichts geschafft** (Sch.). The idea of emptiness led to that of vanity, and 'vain, conceited' (= **eingebildet**) is its commonest modern meaning, as in **Er ist ein eitler Geck** (Heine: 'He is a conceited fop') or **Sie ist eitel auf ihre schlanke Figur.** But its fundamental force is still seen in its use in the sense of 'nothing but' (like **lauter**, q.v. 2), orig. no doubt 'void of other ingredients', and in this sense it is now usually left uninflected: e.g. **Wollt Ihr mir die Rose geben? Seht, diesen Beutel eitel Gold** ('this bag of pure gold') **sollt Ihr dafür bekommen** (Platen)—**Er war beschämt, denn er fühlte, daß sein Freund seine Worte für eitel Ausflucht hielt** (Ric. Huch: '. . . that his friend thought his words a mere excuse')—**Bei seinem ersten Auftreten** (*scil.* on the stage) **war er schwarz gekleidet, und dennoch ging eitel Glanz von ihm aus** (Th. Mann).

else: see **ander** 1; **jemand** 2; **nichts** 2; **sonst** 1 and 2.

empfangen: see **get** 1 (*c*).

entbehren: see **miss** 2 (*c*).

entbieten: see **befehlen** 3 (*b*).

entfallen: see **escape** 2.

entfalten: see **falten** 1.

entfernt, Entfernung: see **distance** 3.

entgegen: see **gegen.**

entgegengehen, -kommen: see **begegnen** 1 (*b*).

entgehen: see **escape** 1; **miss** 4 (*b*).

entkommen: see **escape** 1.

entlang: 1. This word, the commonest expression for 'along', was orig. an *adv.*, and it is still so used, esp. in conjunction with a prep. phrase, as in **Ich ging am Flusse entlang.** This is probably the reason why, when it came to be used as a *prep.*, it had no fixed construction, so that usage fluctuated considerably; and its orig. force no doubt also explains why it could *follow* the noun—which it still far more commonly does. Where the noun is a fem. sing., it is, of course, doubtful whether the case is gen. or dat.: cf. **Der Dorfweg führte ein Stück entlang der Grenze** (Polenz); but the presumption is in favour of the *dat.*, as the gen. of masc. and neut. nouns is now rare here (cf. 2): examples like **Dann kam das fremde Volk wie eine Schar schnatternder Gänse des Wegs entlang** (Frenssen) or **Entlang der Ufer** (*scil.* des Nils) **prangte schon das glänzende Grün eines kleinen Zuckerrohrfeldes** (M. Eyth) sound rather strange nowadays. Here the *dat.* is quite common, more esp., it is true, in the south (Duden represents it as „schweizerisch"), but the north definitely prefers the *accus.*, which, after all, seems the most natural case, being a good example of the *accus. of extent.* The following few examples of the *accus.* might be multiplied indefinitely: **Ein Zaubergesang strömte den Berg entlang** (G.)—**Der Wind streift die Heide entlang** (Chamisso)—**Vorsichtig tastete sich Michael die Wand entlang** (Zifferer)—**Sie schlichen die Wände entlang** (H. Hauser); for the *dat.* (which Moritz Heyne's dictionary condemns as „tadelhaft"!), cf. **Der Anblick wird immer schöner, je mehr man dem Pincio** (one of the hills of Rome) **entlang wandelt** (Waiblinger)—**Sie spazierten dem Gitter des Stadtparkes entlang** (Schnitzler)—**Sie schritten dem Kanal entlang** (H. Kesten)—**Mein Langohr trottete einem Kanal entlang** (M. Eyth)—**Herr und Hund ergehen sich gern dem Hang entlang** (Th. Mann). **2.** The other common expression, but not so much favoured in the north, is **längs,** which is only used as a *prep.* and always *precedes* the noun. The latter stands either in the *gen.* or in the *dat.*, preferably the dat., certainly to avoid harsh-sounding propositions like **Die Leute saßen längs des Flusses;** sim. **Längs eines öden Tals** (in the north more usually **Ein ödes Tal entlang**) **streckt sich ein See** (Wieland)—**Dörfer ragten längs des Tals auf** (H. Kesten); cf., as more usual, **Büsten der römischen Könige standen längs den Wänden** (C. F. Meyer).

entlegen, Entlegenheit: see **distance** 5.

entlehnen: see **borgen** 3.

entpuppen: This verb comes from the noun **Puppe** in its sense of 'pupa, chrysalis, cocoon', and **sich entpuppen** is used lit. of a butterfly 'bursting its chrysalis'; but **sich als etwas entpuppen** is in common use with the *fig.* force of 'to turn out *or* prove to be something', generally implying surprise: e.g. **Er entpuppte sich als Betrüger** ('He turned out to be a swindler'). The case of the noun following **als** may be either nom. or accus., according as it is regarded as referring to the subj. **er** or to the reflex. **sich**: see examples given under **als** = **'as'** 1 (*d*) and **prove.**

entrance, entry: Eingang is properly the door by which one enters a building, while **Eintritt** is the act of entering it: cf., on the one hand, **Er begegnete mir am Eingang** (not **Eintritt**) **zur Kirche,** and on the other hand, **Ein Schließer** ('door-keeper') **lud zum Eintritt** (G.). A notice often to be seen on a door runs **Eintritt verboten!** ('No entry! No admittance!'), and it is significant that the alternative form this notice may take is not **Eingang verboten!** but **Verbotener Eingang!** implying that the door in question is not to be used by people wishing to enter the building; so too, one can only say **Eintrittsgeld** and **Eintrittskarte.** But while **Eintritt** is practically confined to the force of 'entering', **Eingang** has a wider application, sometimes approaching **Eintritt** rather closely: e.g. **Er gestattete mir den Eingang** (= **Er gewährte mir Zutritt,** 'He granted me admission')—**Ich werde versuchen, mir Eingang zu verschaffen** ('I shall try to gain admission') —**In diese Vereinigung war der Eingang nicht leicht zu erlangen** (Bergengruen); fig. **Diese Ideen werden hier nie Eingang finden** ('These ideas will never find favour *or* acceptance here')—and esp. in commercial language: **Nach Eingang des Betrages** ('on receipt of payment') **werden wir die bestellten Waren abschicken—Wir bestätigen hiermit den Eingang** ('arrival') **Ihrer geschätzten Bestellung.** The gen. is used as an adv. or a prep. (+ gen.) in the sense of 'at the beginning (of)', as in **Ich bin gewillt, den eingangs dieser Aufzeichnungen zugesicherten Freimut mit Mäßigung zu verbinden** (Th. Mann: 'I propose to combine the candour which I promised at the beginning of these records with moderation'); so also **ausgangs** is used for 'at the end (of)', as in the first example quoted under **genitive (adverbial)** 2.

entraten: see **miss** 2 (*a*).

entschieden: see **scheiden.**

entschlüpfen: see **slip** 1.

entsinnen: This compd. of **sinnen** (q.v.) is only used *reflex.* ('to remember, recall to mind'), its standard constructions being a *gen.* obj. (see below), a perf. infin. with **zu** when the subjs. of the two clauses refer to the same person, or a subord. clause: e.g. **Kannst du dich seines Namens entsinnen?—Ich entsinne mich nicht, den Brief empfangen zu haben—Endlich entsann er sich, wo er das Buch hingetan hatte—Mir ist, als entsänne ich mich, daß die Büchsen auf dem Kamin stehen** (Rilke; cf. **Ablaut** 2 *c*). For the precise force of the verb, see **remember** 2, where other examples are given. The use of the preps. **an** and **auf** instead of the normal gen. case, on the analogy of **jemand an sein Versprechen erinnern** and **sich auf einen Namen besinnen** (see **remember** 1–3), is very rare and not to be recommended: the standard dictionaries give only the gen., and although *Curme* gives **auf** (not **an**) as an alternative construction, he cites no examples. The present writer, so far as his recollection goes, has met the prep. use in the work of only one modern author, viz. B. E. Werner: **Er entsann sich genau an diesen Sonntag—Er entsann sich auf den letzten Brief Helenes, der wie ein Abschiedsbrief geklungen hatte.** An interesting example, but hardly to be recommended, is **Ich kann mich nichts mehr davon entsinnen** (Novalis), where **nichts** is used as what it orig. was, viz. the gen. of MHG *niht* ('of nothing': see **nichts** 1); here one would now say **Ich kann mich an nichts mehr davon erinnern,** or better still—as **sich erinnern** prefers a gen. (see **remember** 3 *c*)—**Ich kann mir nichts mehr davon ins Gedächtnis zurückrufen.**

entstehen: This compd. of **stehen** is now only used in the sense of 'to come into existence, arise' (out of), 'result' (from), its aux. being always **sein**: e.g. **Daraus entstand Hader und Streit** (G.)—**Plötzlich war eine Schlägerei entstanden** ('Suddenly a free fight had broken out')—**Aus diesem Unternehmen ist mir wenig Gewinn entstanden** ('Little gain has accrued to me from this enterprise', i.e. it has brought me little profit). For the past subj. forms, see **past subjunctive** 2 (*c*).

entweder: **1.** In a proposition in which two *sing.* nouns connected by **oder,** with or without a preceding **entweder,** form the subj., the verb requires to be in the *sing.*, as in **Entweder Karl oder sein Bruder wird kommen**; as **oder** here obviously excludes the idea of plurality, the use of a plur. verb is incorrect (see **congruence** 1 *d*, and cf. **weder** 1). **2.** In English, we commonly use 'either . . . or' after a neg. expression, as in 'The things which a boy is set to learn at school . . .

are things which do *not* require the exercise *either* of the highest *or* the most useful faculties of the mind' (Hazlitt). It should be specially noted that this is not in accordance with the German idiom, which requires **weder . . . noch** in such propositions (see **weder** 2).

entwischen: see **escape** 1 (*a*).

entwöhnen: see **accustom(ed)** 3 (*b*).

entzünden: see **light (verb)** 2 (*c*).

equal: see **gleich** 1.

er-: 1. The orig. force of this insep. verbal prefix, viz. 'from within', is still seen more or less dimly in a few verbs like **erpressen** (esp. fig. 'to extort'), **erschließen** ('to disclose'), **erschöpfen** (see **schöpfen** 1), etc. **2.** The orig. idea led to that of 'transition' or 'resultant state' (aux. **sein**): e.g. **erblühen** ('to burst into bloom': see 3 *b*), **erkalten** ('to grow cold'), **erröten** ('to blush'), etc. **3.** Out of this there developed its most fruitful meaning, viz. 'to obtain *or* attain to'. **(a)** This is seen in compds. like **erbitten** ('to obtain by request'), as in **Ich habe mir die Erlaubnis erbeten, ins Konzert zu gehen** (i.e. obtained by *request*), with which cf. **Was ihm zu wissen unentbehrlich schien, erfragte er** (H. Hesse: i.e. found out by *inquiry*); sim. **erflehen** ('to get by entreaty'), **erlangen** (see **langen** 2 *b*), **erlernen** (see *b* below), **erraten** (see **raten**), **erreichen** (cf. **langen** 1 *a*), **erringen** ('to obtain by an effort, win'), **ersteigen** (see **climb**), **erstürmen** ('to take by storm'); cf. **In der politischen Arena ersiegte** (usually **erkämpfte**) **Börne den Kranz von Eichenlaub** (Heine). So also characteristic modern examples like **Unter ihrem Nachlaß befand sich eine Menge Kleinigkeiten, die sie erbettelt, erstoppelt** (lit. 'gleaned', i.e. 'picked up') **hatte** (Immermann)—**Er erheiratete eine bedeutende Mitgift** (Th. Mann)—**Das unermeßliche Du der Natur läßt sich so wenig erjagen, wie es sich erträumen läßt** (H. Franck)—**Die Ratten drängten sich an den Schemel und suchten diesen zu erklettern** (Fontane)—**Drei Katzen stellten sich ein, um schnurrend den gewohnten Morgentrunk zu erschmeicheln** (Speckmann)—**Er hatte erschnoben** (lit. 'sniffed out', i.e. 'snooped round and discovered'), **daß ich ein Tagebuch führte** (P. Keller)—**Das blinde Mädchen ertastete den Zugdraht der Klingel** (E. Toller: i.e. 'groped about until she found the bell-pull')—**Seine Gestirne hatten es stets so gut gemeint, daß ihm nichts umsonst zukam: er hatte alles erarbeiten, erstreben und erzwingen müssen** (K. Edschmid). **(b)** In a number of cases **ver-** (q.v. 3) expresses the opposite of **er-**, either negating the force of the simple verb or giving it a bad sense: e.g. **erblühen** ('to bloom') and **verblühen** ('to fade, wither')—**erkaufen** ('to acquire by purchase') and **verkaufen** ('to lose possession of by sale')—**erkennen** ('to recognize') and **verkennen** ('to fail to recognize, mistake, one thing for another')—**erlernen** ('to gain a knowledge of by study') and **verlernen** ('to unlearn, forget what one has learnt')—**erziehen** ('to bring up') and **verziehen** ('to bring up badly, spoil'); cf. the past parts. **erwachsen** ('grown up') and **verwachsen** ('grown out of shape, deformed').

erachten: see **achten** 2.

erbarmen: In MHG this verb was used with an accus., less commonly a dat., of the person in the sense of 'to excite to pity, move to tears'. The dat. is now obs., but was in use in comparatively recent times, esp. in the south, as in **Die Singvögel mag ich nicht schießen, sie erbarmen mir** (Stifter). And even the accus. is now almost confined to the south: cf. **Der Jammer des deutschen Volks erbarmet mich** (Sch.)—**Du erbarmtest mich, als ich dich trostlos sah** (Gotthelf). In the north it is not wrong to say **Das erbarmt mich,** but one generally prefers to use another verb, e.g. **dauern** (q.v. 2) or **jammern.** The main use of **erbarmen** now is as a *reflex.*, with a gen. or **über** + accus., as already in early NHG: **Der Gerechte erbarmet sich seines Viehs** (Prov. 12. 10)—**Erbarme dich über meinen Sohn!** (Matt. 17. 15).

Erbe: Distinguish between **der Erbe** ('heir'), gen. and plur. **Erben,** and **das Erbe** ('inheritance'), gen. **Erbes,** no plur., **Erbschaften** being used instead.

erben: It is important to distinguish between **erben** ('to inherit') and its chief compds. The accus. obj. of the simple verb is that to which one falls heir, not the person from whom one inherits it, but the obj. need not necessarily be expressed: e.g. **Er lebt seit einiger Zeit auf großem Fuße, er muß (viel Geld) geerbt haben** ('He has been living in grand style for some time, he must have come into a lot of money')—**Seine musikalische Veranlagung hat der Junge von der Mutter geerbt** 'The boy has inherited his musical gifts from his mother'); and the same idea is conveyed by the not very common compd. **ererben** ('to gain possession of through inheritance'), as in **Ein Herzogtum ererbt zu haben, war ihm nichts, aber er hätte sich eines erringen können, das wäre ihm etwas gewesen** (G.: 'To have fallen heir to a duchy meant nothing to him, but he might have won a duchy by his own efforts, and that *would* have meant something to him'). Formerly **beerben** was used in this way, as in **Beerbe du, was ich beerben soll, denn ich mag's nicht beerben** (Ruth 4. 6), but this use is now obs.; according to modern usage the obj. of **beerben** is the person from whom one inherits something, as in **Alle kamen und wollten ihn beerben** (C. F. Meyer). On the other hand, **vererben** means 'to bequeath' and takes a dat. of the person (or **auf** + accus., esp. in the reflex. use) and an accus. of the thing: e.g. **Er hat ein großes Vermögen hinterlassen und mir alles vererbt—Seine Kunstschätze hat er der Nation vererbt** (or **vermacht**)—**Die Vaterlandsliebe des Vaters vererbte sich auf die Söhne** (Treitschke)—*fig.* **Diese Krankheit vererbt sich oft von Geschlecht zu Geschlecht** ('is often transmitted from one generation to another').

erbieten (sich): see **anerbieten.**

erbleichen: see **bleichen** 1.

erblicken: Strangely enough, although 'to catch sight of' (see **ansichtig** and **Sicht** 2 *b*, and cf. **look** 1 *b*) so closely approaches 'to see' in sense, and **sehen** is so regularly associated with the accus. and infin., **erblicken** hardly ever is: *Sanders* characterizes as „**selten**" the proposition **Da erblickte ich den Vater aus einer Ritze sich schleichen** (G.). Modern usage prefers to make the subj. of the infin. clause the obj. of **erblicken**, following it up with either a *rel.* clause or one introduced by **wie,** the former where the important obj. is the person or thing referred to (as in 'She caught sight of a strange figure standing near her'), the latter where the real obj. is the idea suggested by the infin. (as in 'He caught sight of some one falling into the river'). Thus, in the former case, **Sie erblickte dicht neben sich einen Mann stehen** (A. v. Sternberg) would more usually take the form **Sie erblickte einen Mann, der dicht neben ihr stand**; and the same applies to **Er erblickte eine malerische Hütte aus dem Wasserspiegel sich erheben** (W. Tesche). On the other hand, instead of **Da erblickte sie sich** ('She suddenly had a mental picture of herself') **im Kreise von vielen Kindern an einfach gedecktem Tisch sitzen** (O. Ludwig) it would be more usual to say **Da erblickte sie sich, wie sie . . . an einfach gedecktem Tisch saß**; and sim. the first example given above would preferably take the form **Da erblickte ich den Vater, wie er sich aus einer Ritze schlich.** As the examples show, **erblicken** *must* have an accus. obj.: one cannot say **Ich erblickte, daß** (or **wie**) **ein Mann auf mich zukam.** Other more or less synon. verbs which rarely take an accus. and infin. are **bemerken, gewahren** and esp. **schauen** (qq.v.).

Erbteil: see **Teil** 2 (*c*).

Erde: for **auf Erden,** see **Frau** 2.

erdulden: see **dulden** 1.

ereignen, Ereignis: see **occur** 3 (*c*).

ererben: see **erben.**

erfragen: For the difference between this verb and **erbitten,** see **er-** 3 (*a*), and cf. **Als er an die Grenze kam, erfragte er den Weg nach der Hauptstadt** (Platen).

erfreuen: see **freuen** 2.

erhaben: see **heben** 1 (*b*).

erhalten: see **get** 1 (*d*).

erhängen: see **hängen** 2 (*d*).

erheben: see **heben** 3 (*c*) and 4.

erhellen: see **light** (**verb**) 1 (*c*).

erinnern: see **remember** 3.

erkennen, Erkenntnis: see **recognize.**

erklettern, erklimmen: see **climb** 2.

erkranken: see **krank** 2.

erlangen: In this compd. of **langen** (q.v.) the prefix **er-** suggests 'success in reaching' that to which one extends one's hand (see **er-** 3); it is now used esp. of 'attaining to' such objects as **Ehre, Ruhm, Gunst, Glück,** etc.: cf. **Wir möchten das früh so sehnlich gewünschte, endlich spät erlangte Glück genießen** (G.).

erlauben, Erlaubnis: see **permit; leave** (**noun**).

erlauschen: see **überhören** 1.

erläutern: see **lauter** 1.

erleuchten: see **light** (**verb**) 1 (*b*).

erlöschen: see **löschen** 2.

ermangeln, Ermangelung: see **fail** 1 and 5; **lack** 2; **Mangel** 2; **miss** 1 (*b*).

eröffnen: see **open** 2.

erraten: see **raten** 1.

erröten: see **röten** 2.

ersäufen: see **fressen** 2.

erschaffen: see **schaffen** 1 (*a*).

erschallen: see **schallen** 2, and cf. **Im Dunkel kam ein Boot näher: Stimmen erschallten** (W. v. Scholz).
Erscheinung: see **appearance** I.
erschmeicheln: see **schmeicheln** 2.
erschöpfen: see **schöpfen**.
erschrecken: see **schrecken** 1–3.
erschweren: see **beschweren** I.
ersehnen: see **sehnen**.
ersparen: see **spare** I (*a*).
erst: **1.** *Ordinal numeral*: (**a**) This is an attrib. adj. or adj.-subst., inflected in the normal way: e.g. **der erste (am ersten) Mai—bei erster Gelegenheit** ('at the first opportunity')—**Ich fahre selten erster Klasse—Sie hat den ersten besten Mann geheiratet** ('She married the first man that came along')—**Er ist in den ersten dreißiger Jahren** (Auerbach: 'in his early thirties': see **-zig**)—**Unser Jüngster ist der Erste der Klasse—Er ist einer der Ersten der Stadt** ('one of our most prominent citizens'); sim. in prep. phrases: **Ich bekomme mein Gehalt immer am Ersten** (coll. = **am ersten Tag des Monats**)—**Ich habe fürs erste** (= **vorläufig**, 'for the present') **genug zu tun—Zum ersten, zum zweiten, zum dritten!** (at auctions: 'Going, going, gone!'); so also **Mein Name ist der hundertunderste auf der Liste**, the Swiss forms of which should be avoided—cf. **Ich bitt' zum hundertundeinten Male** (Federer) and **Wenn man schon hundertmal getäuscht worden ist, überlegt man es sich zum hunderteintelmal gehörig** (J. A. Lux) and, as unusual in the north, **seine tausendundeinste Seele** (Fontane). (**b**) In a proposition like 'He was the first to arrive', we use a Gallicism which has of late also found its way into German, esp. in the south: e.g. **Die ersten, jene Veränderung zu bemerken, waren ihre Kinder** (St. Zweig)—**Der Lehrer war der allererste, laut zu erklären, der Junge müsse auf die Universität** (Th. Mann); but this idea is better expressed in other ways: cf. **Er war der erste, der ankam** or **Er kam als erster an** or **Er kam zuerst an** (cf. 2 *e*). (**c**) The inflected compar. **erster** is used, often without the def. art., in the sense of 'the former', with **letzter** ('the latter') expressed or implied: e.g. **Das Ehepaar hatte zwei Söhne, von denen der erstere** (or **deren ersterer**) **früh starb, der letztere noch lebt—Der Versammlung wohnten sowohl Herren als Damen bei; erstere waren in der Mehrzahl.** **2.** *Adverb*: (**a**) Used of the first in a sequence (cf. *e* below), often in prov. expressions: e.g. **Erst wäge, dann wage!** (lit. 'First weigh [the pros and cons], then venture!' i.e. 'Look before you leap!')—**Erst die Pfarre, dann die Quarre!** (lit. 'First the manse, then the squalling baby!' 'First the nest, then the nestlings!' i.e. 'Don't get married until you can keep a wife and family!'); sim. **Ja, ich gehe gern mit, aber erst** ('first, before I do': see **recent** 2) **muß ich mich umziehen.** (**b**) In *temp.* and (esp. after **doch**) *opt.* clauses: e.g. **Wenn wir erst oben sind** ('Once we have reached the summit'), **haben wir eine schöne Aussicht—Ist der Junge erst aus der Schule, wird nichts mit ihm anzufangen sein** ('Once the boy has left school, there will be no putting up with him' or 'he'll be a handful')—**Ach, wären wir doch erst zu Hause!** ('Oh, if *only* we were at home!'). (**c**) Used with the force of 'not until, not earlier than, not more than': e.g. **Sie kommt erst morgen an** ('She is not arriving till tomorrow')—**Ich kann Sie erst um acht Uhr treffen** ('I can't meet you before 8 o'clock')—**Das Kind kann noch nicht zählen, es ist ja erst** ('only', see **nur** I) **zwei Jahre alt—Ich habe ihn erst gestern noch gesehen** ('I saw him no longer ago than yesterday', where the omission of **noch** might suggest 'I did not see him till yesterday'). Of course, a proposition like 'He won't arrive till tomorrow' may take the form **Er wird vor morgen nicht ankommen**, but **Er wird erst morgen ankommen** is more idiomatic; and this applies esp. where the proposition consists of two finite clauses: **Er kam erst, als er gerufen wurde** is more idiomatic than **Er kam nicht, bis er gerufen wurde.** Indeed, this last example only becomes idiomatic when **nicht, bis** is replaced by **nicht eher, als bis**: e.g. **Er erwachte nicht eher, als bis die Sonne durch die Fenster schien** (Jul. Grosse)—**Ein Verlangen überkam sie, ihn nicht eher zu verlassen, als bis er ihr vergeben hatte** (St. Zweig)—**Sein Zeigefinger verfolgte die gedruckten Zeilen, wenn er las, und rückte nicht eher von der Stelle, als bis das Wort gelesen war** (Th. Mann)—**Sie werden Euch nicht eher vor die Augen kommen, als bis Ihr sie rufen laßt** (Jul. Wolff); rather less common here is **nicht früher**, as in **Das Städtchen erblickt man nicht früher, als bis man davor steht** (Heine) and **Der Doktor entfernte sich**

nicht früher, als bis der Pfiff der Lokomotive ertönte (Zifferer). Sometimes the word **als** is omitted in such propositions, but it is better to insert it: cf. **Es dünkte mir unmöglich, die Welt eher zu verlassen, bis ich das alles hervorgebracht, wozu ich mich aufgelegt fühlte** (Beethoven)—**Sonnabends ging sie zum Einkauf und kam nicht eher zurück, bis sie den Geldbeutel geleert hatte** (Stehr)—**Sie ließ die Knaben nicht eher vorüber, bis sie jeden geküßt hatte** (Wildenbruch); see also **negative (pleonastic)** 2 (*b*). (**d**) Here belongs the expression **erst re'cht.** Take the proposition **Ich hielt mich noch eine Woche bei meinen Freunden auf, dann wurde mir aber der Abschied erst re'cht schwer** ('I stayed another week with my friends, but by that time the parting had become all the more difficult'), where **erst re'cht schwer** approaches **um so schwerer** (see **um so** 2, and **als** = **'as'** 4). Here the last clause was orig. **erst da'nn wurde mir der Abschied recht schwer** ('Not till then did the parting become really difficult': see **recht** 3); but eventually both **erst** and the accent shifted their positions, **erst re'cht** becoming an independent phrase which could be used without the adj. or adv. which **recht** orig. modified: e.g. **Als der Junge laut schrie, drohte ihm der Vater mit dem Stock, da schrie er erst re'cht** (like **um so lauter**, 'all the louder') —**Er hat mir geraten, nicht auszugehen; nun gehe ich erst re'cht!** ('now I'm all the more determined to go!': almost 'now I'll go just to spite him!'); sim. **Er sagte, ich sollte zu Hause bleiben; nun erst re'cht nicht!** (see **gerade** 2 *ad fin.*)—**Mein Mann trägt Ihnen nichts nach, und ich natürlich erst re'cht nicht** (Bergengruen: 'My husband bears you no malice, and I, of course, all the less'). (**e**) Noteworthy in this connexion are: **erstens** ('in the first place': see **zunächst** 2), as in **Ich kann jetzt nicht mitgehen: erstens habe ich viel zu tun, zweitens erwarte ich Besuch** (see also **einmal** 1), and **zuerst,** the latter being either like **als erster** (see 1 *b*) or 'at first, to begin with', as in **Da ich fremd war, fühlte ich mich zuerst sehr einsam.**

erstaunen, erstaunlich: see **wonder** 4.

erstehen: This is now almost obs. as an intrans. verb, practically its only use being in the trans. sense of 'to acquire by purchase', properly used of a person who stands and bids at an auction, then coll. quite generally: **Ich habe dieses Bild billig erstanden.**

ersteigen: see **climb** 2.

erst recht: see **erst** 2 (*d*).

ertappen: see **surprise** 3.

ertränken: see **fressen** 2.

ertrinken: see **trinken** 1 (*b*).

erübrigen: As a trans. verb with a pers. subj., this means 'to save *or* lay by' (money, etc.) or 'to spare *or* set aside' (time for a specific purpose: see **spare** 1 *b*): e.g. **Ich habe mir soviel erübrigt, daß ich mir ein Bauerngut kaufen kann** (Auerbach)—**Für seine Kinder erübrigt er sonnabends immer ein paar Stunden—Da'zu werde ich schwerlich die Zeit erübrigen** ('I doubt very much whether I shall find the time for that'). With an impers. subj. it is much like **übrigbleiben,** used of what is left over or remains to be done: **Das ist das einzige, was mir noch zu tun erübrigt** ('That is the only thing I still have to do'). The *reflex.* verb is only used with an impers. subj. in the sense of 'to be unnecessary *or* superfluous', as in **Es erübrigt sich, hier auf das Nähere einzugehen** ('It is unnecessary here to go into further particulars')—**An diese Namen erinnere ich mich und ungefähr auch an die Physiognomien ihrer Träger, die hier zu beschreiben sich erübrigt** (Th. Mann: '. . . whom I need not describe').

erwägen: see **wiegen** 2; **Ablaut** 2 (*b*).

erwähnen: Of all the common verbs which orig. took a gen. and later an accus. of the thing (see **genitive** 2), this is probably the one which has discarded the gen. in ordinary lang. more than any other: some authorities now characterize the gen. as obs. Only a few examples of the orig. construction need be given: **Eines Glücksfalls muß ich erwähnen** (G.) —**Hamlet erwähnt seiner Erziehung auf einer Universität, wiewohl es zur Zeit des historischen Hamlet noch keine Universitäten gab** (A. W. Schlegel)—**Sie erwähnte der herrlichen Oper, deren Darstellung sie in Paris gesehen** (E. T. A. Hoffmann) —**Ich beschloß, mir von der Sache nichts merken zu lassen und ihrer nicht zu erwähnen** (Stifter); in more recent authors the gen. is much rarer: cf. **Sie erwähnte gewisser Opfer, die sie bringen mußte** (Baumbach)—**Sie erwähnte des Abenteuers** (Binding). The accus. in such propositions is much more in accordance with present-day usage, and is, indeed fixed where the obj. is an indef. expression or a pers. pron.: everybody now says **Ich habe das** (not **dessen**) **nicht erwähnt,** and in the example from Stifter given above one would replace **ihrer** by **sie**; cf. also, in the pass., **Das** (not **Dessen**) **wurde nicht erwähnt—Vorerwähnten Meistern folgten Nachahmer** (G.)—**Obenerwähntes Werk ist vergriffen** ('The work referred to above is out of print': cf. **folgend**). If the original construction is not entirely obs., it may be because it is firmly established with the circumlocution **Erwähnung tun,** as in **Dessen** (not **Das**) **tat ich keine Erwähnung.**

erziehen: see **auferziehen.**

es (see also **es gibt, es ist** and **impersonal verbs**): **1.** The very form and sound of **es** suggest a *gen. sing.*, and historically that is just what it is: in MHG the nom. and accus. of the neut. pers. pron. was *ez*, the gen. *es*. But in course of time **es** came to represent all three cases, with the result that many expressions in which a gen. was originally the only correct case were misunderstood, the gen. having been mistaken for one of the other two cases. Thus, *mich nimet es wunder* is lit. 'Surprise *because of it* seizes me', but gradually the gen. here came to be regarded in NHG as a nom., and the noun *wunder* to become a sort of sep. prefix, which explains why it is written with a small letter; and **Es** (nom.) **nimmt mich wunder** quite naturally led to **Das nimmt mich wunder** (cf. **Wunder** I). In the same way, *ich wart es gewar* ('I became aware *of it*') led to **Ich ward das** (or **ihn**) **gewahr.** Sim. a proposition like **Deine Hilfe ist mir not** ('Your help is necessary to me') has developed out of *dîner helfe* (gen.) *ist mir nôt* ('I stand in need *of your help*'), and **Ich weiß dir deine Freigebigkeit großen Dank** (A. König) out of *ich weiz dir dîner milte* (gen.) *grôzen danc* ('I give thanks to you *on account of your generosity*'). This misconception explains why so many verbs and adjectives take either a gen. or an accus., the historically correct gen. being now for the most part characteristic of a rather choice literary style, and being displaced by the accus. in ordinary language: cf. verbs like **bedürfen, brauchen, erwähnen, genießen, pflegen, vergessen,** and adjectives like **ansichtig, fähig, gewahr, gewohnt, habhaft, los, müde, satt, überdrüssig, wert, würdig,** etc. (cf. also **nichts** I). **2.** This confusion between the cases is particularly noteworthy in a number of verbs used *reflex.*, where the orig. gen. **es** has come to be regarded as an accus., and hence the orig. accus. **sich** to be treated as a *dat.* The commonest of these verbs are **sich erinnern** (see **remember** 3 *c*) and **sich versehen** (q.v. 2 *c*); see also **anmaßen, getrauen** and **vermuten. 3.** In contradistinction to the other pronouns, **es** is a very weak word which cannot as a rule be accented. It is for this reason that one cannot express **Ich weiß es nicht** in 'inverted' word-order: instead of **Es weiß ich nicht** one must say **Das weiß ich nicht.** It follows that as a prep. is 'proclitic', i.e. 'leans forward' on the word it governs (which presupposes that this word can, as it were, support the weight of the prep.), **es** should not be used as the accus. obj. of a prep. Some authors, it is true, esp. Swiss authors, continually use **durch es, für es,** etc., and certainly such a phrase is less objectionable when the reference is to a *person*, as in **Bring mir dein Kind, ich will für es sorgen** (Grimm) and **Er trat zum Bett des Kindes hin und beugte sich über es** (Zuckmayer); but otherwise this use is now generally avoided in good prose, and examples like the following are not to be recommended: **Dies Dach war in zu guter Ordnung, als daß wir uns auch nur den geringsten Riß durch es** (better **durch dasselbe**) **hätten vorstellen können** (Raabe: 'This roof was in too good a condition to let us imagine even the smallest crack in it')—**Von neuem wälzte es sich** ('Again the mob came surging up') **gegen das herzogliche Reithaus heran und in es hinein** (id.)—**Wie das Haus querab zum Dampfer lag** ('As the steamer came abreast of the house'), **sah ich daß man durch es hindurchsehen konnte** (H. Hauser)—**Das Abenteuer hatte ihn erregt, die durch es entzauberten Empfindungen verwirrt** (Binding). Admittedly, **dasselbe** is a rather prosaic expression, but it is nevertheless preferable to **es** after a prep.

escape: **1.** (**a**) With the force of 'to free oneself' from confinement, threatening danger, etc., this is usually rendered by an appropriate verb compounded with the insep. prefix **ent-.** Thus, **entgehen** (see *b*) properly implies escape by walking, **entlaufen** by running, etc. Obviously, a person making his escape from prison or from an armed guard does not normally walk away at a leisurely pace, so that a word like **entlaufen** or **entspringen** is appropriate in such cases; **entweichen** and **entrinnen** are choice expressions, less specific in sense; **entschlüpfen** implies cleverness in 'slipping' out of a guard's clutches, while **entwischen** suggests adroitness in seizing the favourable opportunity. (**b**) Specially important is the difference between **entgehen** and **entkommen.** As **kommen** (q.v. 3) does not necessarily imply movement towards the speaker, but is regularly used like our 'to get' in propositions such as 'I could not get into the house' or 'He was going to wire me when he got to London', so **entkommen** does not mean 'to come away' (**fort-** or **wegkommen**), but implies escape (not necessarily towards the speaker) from a situation into which one has 'got', while **entgehen** esp. indicates that one has avoided 'getting' into such a situation. In other words, **entkommen** implies the recovery of freedom, **entgehen** the evasion of capture (cf. **miss** 4 *b*): so **Er entkam der Haft** is only used of one who has actually been in custody, **Er entging der Haft** of one who has avoided being taken into custody; and sim. **Sie wunderte sich, wie dies ihrer Aufmerksamkeit hatte entgehen können** (Bergengruen). **2.** To express propositions like 'His name *escapes* (i.e. eludes) me at the moment', the best rendering is obtained by the use of **entfallen:** e.g. **Sein Name ist mir** (or **meinem Gedächtnis**) **im Augenblick entfallen.**

es gibt: see **es ist, es sind** 2.

es ist, es sind: 1. (**a**) If some one says **Es ist ein Mann an der Tür,** and on being asked who it is, replies **Es ist ein Bettler,** he has made two statements which, similar as they look, are yet essentially different. In the first, the real subj. is **Mann** (it is merely a more idiomatic way of saying **Ein Mann ist an der Tür**), while **es** is a grammatical subj. which 'anticipates' the real subj. that has been placed after the verb, and without which the proposition would normally be a question, not a statement: it is only in lively coll. speech and in poetry, esp. folk-songs, that the word-order of a question is used in narrative style, as in Goethe's **Sah ein Knab' ein Röslein stehn ... Lief er schnell, es nah zu sehn.** In the second proposition, on the other hand, the real subj. is **es** (used for the sake of brevity for **der Mann an der Tür**) and **Bettler** is the pred. It follows at once that if the reference is to more than one, the verb must stand in the *plur.* in either case: in the first proposition because the real subj. *is* plur. (**Es sind zwei Männer an der Tür** = **Zwei Männer sind an der Tür**), in the second because the real subj. *represents* a plur. (**Es sind zwei Bettler** = **Die Männer an der Tür sind zwei Bettler**). The distinction is important in 'inverted' and 'transposed' word-order. (i) In the first proposition (where we say '*there* is or are'), it is obvious that there would be no point in inserting an 'anticipatory' **es** at all, unless the verb separates the two subjects; in other words, **es** automatically drops out, unless the verb separates it from the real subj.: e.g. **Eben war ein Mann** (not **war es ein Mann**) **an der Tür—Er sagte, daß ein Mann** (not **daß es ein Mann**) **an der Tür sei.** And the same applies, of course, to an 'anticipatory' **es** with any other verb: e.g. **Es erhob sich ein Sturm—Gestern erhob sich** (not **erhob es sich**) **ein Sturm—Er sagte, daß sich** (not **daß es sich**) **ein Sturm erhoben habe.** One must, therefore, be on one's guard in rendering any sentence in which 'there', as used here, does not introduce a princ. clause, or is preceded by an adv. expression or subord. clause: thus, 'Among my pupils there are two very lazy ones' = **Unter meinen Schülern sind** (not **sind es**) **zwei sehr faule**—'As I stood at the door, there suddenly appeared a large crowd in the street' = **Als ich an der Tür stand, erschien** (not **erschien es**) **plötzlich eine große Menschenmenge auf der Straße.** (ii) In the second proposition, on the other hand (where we say '*it* is, *they* are'), **es**, being the real subj., does not ordinarily drop out, no matter where the verb stands (but see *b* below): e.g. **Sieh mal nach, wer an der Tür ist: wahrscheinlich ist es ein Bettler—Als ich fragte, wer an der Tür sei, sagte man mir, daß es ein Bettler sei** or **daß es zwei Bettler seien.** (**b**) There is, however, one special case where we use 'it' to express an 'anticipatory' **es**, viz. where the real subj. is an *infin.* or *noun* clause. In this case **es** only drops out when the real subj. stands *first*: e.g. **Es ist mir eine Freude, Sie kennenzulernen,** in 'inverted' order: **Eine Freude ist es mir, Sie kennenzulernen**; but **Sie kennenzulernen ist mir** (not **ist es mir**) **eine Freude**; and sim. **Es ist sonderbar** (or **Sonderbar ist es**), **daß er nicht gekommen ist,** but **Daß er nicht**

gekommen ist, ist sonderbar. **(c)** When 'it is' is followed by a *pers. pron.*, **es** never introduces the clause, and the verb agrees with the pers. pron.: e.g. **Bist du es? Ja, ich bin es—Ach, Sie sind es?** ('Oh, it 's you, is it?'). In this case, if a *rel.* clause follows, the antecedent of the rel. pron. is really **es**, so that the verb is in the *3rd* person—see **der (relative)** 3: e.g. **Ich bin es, der es getan hat** (lit. 'The one who did it is I'); sim. **Du, Johannes, wirst es nicht sein, der mich noch elender machen will** (Storm)—**Heute wird diese Empfindung um so stärker sein, weil gerade Sie es sind, der ihn so gesehen hat** (Spielhagen). Analogous are propositions like 'It is his carelessness that surprises me': here also the real antecedent is **es** ('The thing that surprises me is his carelessness'), so that the correct rel. pron. is **was**: e.g. **Es ist seine Nachlässigkeit, was mich verwundert—Nicht Furcht war es, was seine Hartnäckigkeit endlich besiegte** (Sch.)—**Es war eine große Neigung, was sie zusammenführte** (Fontane); for other examples, see **was (relative)** 2 (*c*). **2.** Fundamentally different from **es ist** or **sind** is the expression **es gibt** ('there is, there are'): here **es** is the real subj. (so that it never drops out), and the verb is always *sing.* and requires an *accus. obj.* (for a contracted 'than'-clause after **es gibt**, see **als (than)** 3). One naturally wonders how **es gibt** ever came to have the force of 'there is'. The young hero of Schiller's ballad **Der Taucher,** who, after diving into the whirlpool to recover the golden goblet, tells of what he saw down below, uses a suggestive expression when, referring to some horrible marine monster which had come at him, he says **Da kroch's heran:** unable to put a specific name to this monster, he refers to it as **es.** This vague, non-committal way of suggesting something which one either cannot or will not name specifically is also seen in the idiom **In diesem Hause geht es um** ('Something walks in this house', i.e. 'This house is haunted'), and the same really applies to **es gibt.** Although the orig. force of the phrase is no longer vividly felt, **es** is here, in fact, a non-committal term for the hidden power which regulates the laws of nature and determines man's life and experience, the obj. of **es gibt** being the result of such laws and experience, something brought about by evolution, by natural conditions or operations, by what we call 'force of circumstances', etc. Thus, **In Afrika gibt es viele wilde Tiere** suggests that the conditions existing in Africa have been favourable for the propagation of many different species of wild animals by natural evolution; sim. **Diesen Sommer hat es hier viel Regen gegeben,** i.e. climatic conditions here have produced much rain this summer—**Hoffentlich gibt es keinen Krieg,** i.e. it is to be hoped that the present state of international relations will not lead to war. But it should be noted that, with **es gibt,** the reference is always a more *general* one than with **es ist,** as the following pairs of examples show: **Es gibt hier viele Vögel** and **Es sind zwei Vögel in diesem Baum—Es gibt rote und schwarze Johannisbeeren** and **Es sind sechs Johannisbeersträucher in meinem Garten—Es gibt viele Löwen in Afrika** and **Im Zoologischen Garten sind mehrere Löwen.** The obj. of **es gibt** may be a sing. noun denoting an individual or object, as in **Es gibt einen Gott,** but is much more usually a plur., a collective, an abstract or a material noun. **3.** As pointed out under 1 (*a*) above, **es** 'anticipates' the subj. in **Es ist jemand an der Tür.** It has, of course, the same force in propositions like **Es wundert mich, daß er nicht gekommen ist** and **Es lohnt sich nicht, den Versuch zu machen,** where the subord. and infin. clauses are the real subj. (**Daß er nicht gekommen ist, wundert mich—Den Versuch zu machen lohnt sich nicht**). The same applies also to propositions in which **es** is not the subj. but the obj., as in **Ich halte es für möglich, daß er kommen wird;** but here **es** is obviously pleonastic, so that it is often omitted, esp. before an infin. clause: e.g. **Ich habe (es) mir vorgenommen, morgens früher aufzustehen—Er wünscht sehr, Sie kennenzulernen—Ich weiß genau, daß er verreist ist** (cf. **Ich weiß es genau: er ist verreist**).

essen: 1. Many German words show the elision of an unaccented **e**: e.g. **Angst** (< *angest*), **bleiben** (< *belîben*), **gleich** (< *gelîch*), **glauben** (< *gelouben*), **Gnade** (< *genade*), etc., and in ordinary lang. one generally says **grade** for **gerade.** An elision of **e** is also seen in the past part. **gegessen,** which is formed not by inserting a second **g** for the sake of euphony, but by prefixing **ge-** to the MHG past part. *gezzen*, which is contracted from *ge-ezzen*; but **ge-** has been prefixed to **fressen** (q.v.), which is a contracted form of **ver-essen.** **2.** In a few cases the neg. particle **un-** has been prefixed to past parts. in the coll. lang. to give these *act.* force. Thus, **ungegessen** is used not only of food which has not been consumed, but also of a person who has not had a meal: e.g. **Sie beschloß, mit den Kindern ungegessen schlafenzugehen** (G. Keller)—**Der Vater stieß den Teller von sich und ging ungegessen zu Bett** (Ponten)—**Seine Verzweiflung, den Gast ungegessen zu Bett schicken zu müssen, ist mit Worten nicht zu schildern** (H. Kurz)—**Es war gegen vier Uhr, und er war noch von früh an ungegessen und ungetrunken** (C. Hauptmann); so also **„Ich will nicht ungefressen bleiben", sagte der Wolf und fraß das unschuldig Lämmlein** (Luther)—**Ungefrühstückt ging ich hin** (Sch.).

etlich: This indef. pron. (or pron. adj.), meaning 'some, several', was very common in early NHG, when it could be used in the sing. as well as in the plur.: cf. **Indem er säete, fiel etliches** ('some seeds fell') **an den Weg** (Matt. 13. 4). Now it is practically confined to the plur. use, but is little used in ordinary lang., being for the most part displaced by **einig** (q.v.). In the nom. and accus. plur., a following attrib. adj. has *strong* inflexion, as after **viele, einige**: e.g. **Etliche ihnen zu Ehren geladene Gäste waren bereits erschienen** (Fontane)—**Im Winkel hatte er etliche schlanke Peitschen bemerkt** (Kolbenheyer). It is still sometimes used before a *num.*, as in **etliche zwanzig Kühe,** where the real meaning is not 'about twenty cows' (= **etwa zwanzig Kühe**), but 'twenty odd cows', having developed out of **etliche und zwanzig Kühe.**

etwa: 1. This adv. no longer has the force of 'somewhere' (= **irgendwo**), as MHG *etewâ* had, but is now used in two ways. (a) Before numerals it means 'about' (= **ungefähr**): e.g. **Es waren etwa hundert Leute da**—**Ich mußte etwa zehn Minuten warten**—**Das Dorf liegt etwa elf Kilometer von Berlin entfernt**; and analogous are propositions like **So etwa sagte er** ('That was pretty much what he said') and **Das ist etwa** ('roughly') **der Inhalt des Romans.** (b) In other contexts it has two meanings. It may convey no more than that something may conceivably happen: e.g. **Sollten wir etwa** ('by any chance') **in Köln den Anschluß verpassen, werden wir dort übernachten müssen**; sim. **Komme ich etwa ungelegen?** ('Do I happen to come at an inconvenient time?'). In *neg.* propositions its force is not so easy to define. The question **Er ist doch nicht krank?** means 'Surely he isn't ill?' and if **etwa** is inserted after **nicht,** it implies that the speaker has drawn a conclusion from what has just been said: 'But surely I am not to understand from what you say that he is ill?'); and so also **Er hat dich doch nicht etwa betrogen?** ('Surely you don't mean to say that he has swindled you?')—**Denken Sie nicht etwa, daß ich mich in seine Gunst stahl** (Sch.: 'Don't think, as you might do, that I curried favour with him')—**Du mußt nicht etwa denken, daß ich dich ärgern will** ('Now don't jump to the conclusion that I want to annoy you'). **2.** From the adv. the adj. **etwaig** (trisyllabic) has been formed in recent times, used only attrib. with the force of 'possible': e.g. **Nimm für etwaige Fälle** ('for possible contingencies') **hundert Mark mit!**—**Die Mutter fürchtete ein etwaiges neues Zerwürfnis zwischen den zwei Söhnen** (Ompteda: 'The mother feared there might be a renewed break *or* quarrel between her two sons').

etwas: 1. Used as an indecl. indef. pron. in the sense of 'something' or 'anything' (cf. **any**), **etwas** can be used in every case except the gen.: thus, one says **Es ist etwas geschehen**—**Ich entsinne mich, so etwas gehört zu haben** ('I recall having heard something like that')—**Sie dünkt sich etwas** ('She rather fancies herself, thinks she is a somebody')—**Er wird es noch zu etwas bringen** ('He will get on in the world'), but not **Eben erinnere ich mich etwas, was ich Ihnen sagen sollte,** where **an etwas** is imperative; so also 'to take possession of something' is not **sich etwas bemächtigen,** but **von etwas Besitz ergreifen.** It is rather strange that **etwas** has become an every-day expression, for the MHG *etewaz* was comparatively rare: where we now say **Ich habe etwas Geld,** people then said *ich hân iht geldes,* where *iht* is the now obs. pos. of *niht* ('nothing'), so that the lit. meaning of this phrase is 'I have something (in the way) of money' (cf. **nichts** 2). The old part. gen. is still extant in propositions like **Ich habe etwas Neues** gehört, only that **Neues** here is no longer treated as a gen., but as an accus.

in appos. to **etwas** (see **adjective-substantives** 1 and 2); and so also in the dat., **Ich komme mit etwas Neuem—Gehen wir zu etwas anderem über!** ('Let us pass on to another matter!'). As these examples show, the adj.-subst. must have a strong ending: it is now regarded as incorrect to say **Du hattest eine Vorahnung von etwas Entsetzlichen, was dich betreffen müsse** (Tieck). **2.** The other use of **etwas** is as an *adv.*: e.g. **Das Wetter ist etwas kühl** ('rather cool')—**Der Hauptmann war etwas bezecht** (C. F. Meyer: 'somewhat intoxicated')—**Es geht ihr heute etwas besser** ('She is feeling a little better today')—**Sie sollten sich etwas ausruhen** ('You should take a little rest').

euer: see **unser** 1 and 2.

euresgleichen: see **gleich** 2.

every: see **all** and **jeder.** The gen. **jedes** meaning 'of everybody' should be accompanied by a word which makes the case clear: **Ich erinnere mich noch jedes einzelnen** (or **eines jeden**) **der Anwesenden.** Note the common use of the collect. **all** with distrib. force in expressions like 'The trains run every few minutes' or 'We stopped and rested every five miles': **Die Untergrundbahn fährt alle** (more formally **aller**) **zehn Minuten—Die Brandung dröhnte, als ob alle zwei Sekunden eine Häuserreihe einstürzte** (Kellermann: 'The breakers thundered as if a row of houses collapsed every two seconds')—**Alle Kilometer lag ein totes oder sterbendes Tier** (Frenssen); sim. **alle zwei Tage** or **jeden zweiten Tag** or **einen Tag um den anderen** ('every second day').

evident(ly): see **obvious(ly).**

Ew.: see **address** (forms of) 2 (*a*).

ewiglich: see **adverbs formed from adjectives** 3.

Examen: Most books of reference still give **Examina** as the only plur. form of this neut. noun, but in ordinary lang., esp. among pupils and students, the sing. form is used in the plur. also: e.g. **Meine verschiedenen Examen habe ich, das letzte sogar mit Auszeichnung, bewältigt** (W. Schäfer: 'I managed to pass my various examinations, the final even with distinction')—**Ist es nötig, uns hier im Urwald nach Examen zu fragen?** (H. Blunck); cf. **Prüfung heißt im landüblichen Deutsch Examen: Plural indeklinabel** (H. Kurz).

except: 1. (**a**) The normal construction of **ausgenommen** is a *preceding* dependent *accus.* The reason for this case and word-order should be obvious: **ausgenommen** is the past part. of the trans. verb **ausnehmen** ('to except'), and in **Er hat alle seine Freunde besucht, mich ausgenommen,** the word **habend** is really understood (lit. 'having excepted me'): see **accus. abs.** 1, and cf. 'I question if there 's anybody can tell the tale but mysell, aye *out-taken* the laird' (Scott, *The Antiquary,* ch. 24). But through misconception **ausgenommen** came to be regarded as a real prep. taking an accus., and was placed before its dependent like most preps.: **Alle hat er besucht, ausgenommen mich.** And a further step led to its use as a co-ordinate *conj.* connecting parallel phrases (cf. 2), the case of the dependent coinciding with that of the corresponding word in the preceding phrase: e.g. **Keiner hat es bemerkt, ausgenommen ich—Keinem hat er es gesagt, ausgenommen mir**; and where the earlier phrase has a prep., this is generally repeated in the second: e.g. **Mit keinem verkehrt er hier, ausgenommen mit mir.** Where the case concerned is the *gen.*, the orig. construction is certainly to be preferred: **Ich kann mich seiner mancherlei Vorschläge nicht mehr erinnern, den wichtigsten ausgenommen** is better than . . . **ausgenommen des wichtigsten.** When it is associated with a neg. particle, **ausgenommen** always stands last: e.g. **Alle haben mich besucht, meine Feinde nicht ausgenommen.** (**b**) A sim. development is seen in the case of **ausgeschlossen** ('excluding'): **In der Versammlung waren alle Stände vertreten, den Adel ausgeschlossen** (*scil.* **habend**) led naturally to . . . **ausgeschlossen der Adel. 2.** (**a**) With the force of 'except', **außer** normally takes a *dat.* case. Its occasional use as a co-ordinate conj., like **ausgenommen,** should, on the whole, perhaps not be imitated. Where the case concerned is the accus., it might pass, as in **Wir konnten die Berge, die das Tal einschließen, sehen, außer den Montblanc, der mit Wolken bedeckt war** (G.) or **Wilhelm konnte nichts merken außer das Wasser** (H. Grimm), although in the latter example it would be much more usual to say **Er konnte nichts andres merken als das Wasser**; but in the nom. case, although occasionally used, the phrase rather grates on the ear: e.g. **Niemand kommt mir entgegen, außer ein Unverschämter, der mir lieber den**

Eintritt verweigert hätte (Lessing), where modern usage would certainly prefer either **außer einem Unverschämten** or, better still, **Niemand anders kommt mir entgegen als ein Unverschämter . . .**; and sim. **Niemand kann mir helfen, außer ich selbst** (Fulda)—**Ich soll ihm nicht nachsterben dürfen? Wer soll das dürfen außer ich?** (Binding), where again **Wer anders . . . als ich?** would be much more usual. But **außer** is very commonly used to connect parallel prep. phrases, the prep. being usually repeated, as in **Sie war es nicht gewohnt, was sie dachte und fühlte, gegen irgend einen Menschen, außer gegen Justus, frei zu äußern** (Spielhagen). (**b**) To connect independent propositions with a finite verb in each, **außer** and **ausgenommen** are quite commonly used when followed by a subord. conj.: e.g. **Ich gehe vormittags immer spazieren, ausgenommen wenn** ('unless *or* except when') **es regnet**—**Die Kinder dürfen überall herumlaufen, außer wo schon gesät worden ist**—**Er hat mir nie geholfen, außer damals, als meine Eltern starben.** Very occasionally we find **außer** used alone as an independent conj. (cf., in Gen. 32. 26, 'I will not let thee go, *except* thou bless me'), but the best authors seem to avoid this—strangely enough, seeing that several other expressions have developed along sim. lines, notably those with the prefix **so-** (**sobald, soviel,** etc.: see **so** 1), **ungeachtet** and **zumal** (qq.v., and cf. **kaum**): e.g. **Das Berghaus hat sicher ein Gastzimmer, und darin will ich mich, außer** ('unless') **Sie jagen mich hinaus** (better **außer wenn Sie mich hinausjagen**), **drei Tage festsetzen** (Suttner)—**Bestimmt werde ich kommen, außer ich wäre tot** (F. Schwarzenburg), which would be more idiomatically expressed in a neg. cond. clause introduced by **es sei denn, daß**: see **denn (adverb)** 3.

exchange: see **change (verb)** 2 and 3.

existence: **1.** To express a phrase like 'to lead a miserable existence', the Germans say **ein elendes Dasein führen,** where the verbal noun merely implies the idea of *being here* (**da** being commonly used for **hier,** as in **Da bist du endlich!** 'Here you are at last!'); and sim. **Heutzutage ist der Kampf ums Dasein schwer**—**Ein Nichtgläubiger leugnet das Dasein Gottes.** Analogous is **Beisein,** the noun which corresponds to **dabei sein** (see **presence** 4). **2.** The adj. **vorhanden** (see **Hand,** 1 *a*) properly suggests that a thing is 'at hand', and so 'extant, available, to be had', as in **Es war in dem Zimmer nur soviel Platz vorhanden, daß man zwei Schränke hatte aufstellen können** (Kafka); but **vorhanden sein** may imply no more than that a thing 'exists', an idea which we often express by the verb 'to be': e.g. **Nimm dich in acht: es ist Gefahr vorhanden** ('Take care: there is danger'). The noun corresponding to this use of the adj. is **das Vorhandensein**: e.g. **Der Mann schien über irgend etwas zu stolpern, es war aber nichts da; und doch schien er an das Vorhandensein eines Hindernisses zu glauben, denn er sah sich nach der Stelle um** (Rilke). For the corresponding negative noun, **das Nichtvorhandensein,** see **absence** 2 (*a*).

F

Faden: Distinguish between **der Faden,** plur. **Fäden,** meaning 'thread', and **der Faden,** plur. **Faden,** a nautical expression meaning 'fathom', in ordinary lang. usually **die Klafter,** plur. **Klaftern,** but **Klafter** as a measure of depth.

fähig: It is only in late MHG that this adj. first occurs, and then in the now obs. compd. form *gevaehic*. It is obviously derived from the verb *vâhen* (> **fangen**), and its early NHG meaning seems to have been 'able to hold *or* contain': cf. **Der Becher ist eines Nösels fähig** (K. Stieler: 1691), where **Nösel** is an old liquid measure. But this idea of holding or containing no longer applies, the adj. now having the general sense of 'able, capable'. Its normal construction is a *gen.*: e.g. **Sie könnten eines so häßlichen Streiches fähig sein?** (Lessing)—**Wer von euch ist denn der Freundschaft fähig?** (Nietzsche)—**Sie war starker Empfindungen fähig** (Fontane); and sim. **Er ist jedes göttlichen Gefühls unfähig** (Hölderlin). The gen. is esp. common in a number of compds. as in **Er hat eine heiratsfähige Tochter** ('a marriageable daughter')—**Soviel ich weiß, ist er zahlungsfähig** ('solvent')—**Der arme Mensch ist nicht ganz zurechnungsfähig** ('not quite responsible'). In the proposition **Dieser Mann ist alles fähig** (Heine), **alles** is presumably a gen., but it naturally came to be treated as an accus. (see **es** 1, and cf. **all** 6 *a*); still, the accus. is not as common with **fähig** as with words like **müde, gewohnt, satt,** etc. (qq.v.), and should at least be confined to indef. neut. expressions like **das, so etwas,** etc.; and even there good prose usage prefers either the gen. construction or the prep. **zu:** e.g. **Er schwelgte in Vorstellungen eines schöneren Lebens, soweit seine Phantasie dessen fähig war** (H. Hesse)—**Wer ihn jetzt gesehen hätte, würde haben ahnen können, wessen er fähig war** (Polenz)—**Mussolini war gewisser Gefühle mächtig, die** (better **deren**) **andere Diktatoren nicht fähig sind** (K. Edschmid)—**Er ist zu allem fähig—Ich wüßte nicht, wozu mein Herz fähig wäre** (G.)—**Er ist ein gerissener Bursche, zu allerhand fähig** (G. v. d. Vring: 'He is an artful dodger, up to all manner of tricks')—**Er erzählte mir, daß Beethoven, zu größeren Arbeiten unfähig, sich damit beschäftigte, schottische Lieder aufzuschreiben** (Th. Mann).

fahren: 1. This verb orig. meant 'to *fare*, go, wander', and its factitive is **führen,** really 'to cause to go', hence 'to guide' (see **lead**). The old meaning is seen in the old folksong **Ich fahr' dahin** ('I am going away' out into the world), in **Fahr wohl!** ('Farewell!' now generally **Leb wohl!**) and in **fahrende Sänger, Schüler** ('wandering minstrels, travelling scholars'). Out of this developed the sense of 'to get on', as in 'You might go far and *fare* worse': cf. **Du bist heute schlecht gefahren** (G.: 'You have fared ill today'—cf. 2). Used as above, **fahren** is now practically obs., but the orig. sense is still seen in its common use to suggest a sudden quick movement: e.g. **Aus den Wolken fuhr ein greller Blitz hernieder, und unwillkürlich fuhr ich zurück** ('. . . I started back')—**Der Schreck fuhr mir in alle Glieder** (Platen: 'The sudden fright darted *or* shot through my every limb')—**Er wollte vor Wut aus der Haut fahren** ('He felt like jumping out of his skin with rage')—**Als mitten in der Nacht jemand an die Haustür klopfte, fuhr ich in die Kleider** ('. . . I flung on my clothes')—**Der Kutscher fuhr mit der Rechten dankend an seinen Hut** (Fontane: '. . . raised his right hand smartly to his hat by way of thanks'); cf. **Es kann mir nicht nachgesagt werden, daß ich im Zorn auf irgend jemand losgefahren sei** (G.: 'No one can say behind my back that in a passion I had stormed *or* railed at anybody'). **2.** The commonest meaning of **fahren** now is 'to drive', either *intrans.* in the sense of to be conveyed, as contrasted with walking, or *trans.* in that of to guide a vehicle or to give a lift to somebody. As a trans. verb, it of course takes the aux. **haben;** with intrans. force it takes **sein** if conveyance from one place to another is implied, but **haben** if the way of driving is referred to (cf. **laufen, reiten,** etc.): e.g. **„Sind Sie zu Fuß gekommen?" „Nein, ich bin mit der Elektrischen gefahren"—Wir sind gestern spazierengefahren** ('We went for a drive yesterday')—**„Ich habe kein Rad und liebe es nicht, Auto zu fahren . . . Seit wann fährst du Motorrad?"** (G. v. d. Vring; '. . . How long have you been motor-cycling?')—**Fahren Sie einen „Volkswagen"?—Er hat ein Kind tot gefahren—Auf der Autobahn fährt es sich leicht** ('It is easy to drive on an Autobahn')—**Er näherte sich dem Ufer** (in a boat), **fühlte sich aber in einiger Entfernung davon angehalten: er hatte sich fest gefahren** (G.: '. . . he had run aground')—**Der Kutscher hat heute schlecht gefahren. 3.** Esp. noteworthy in this connexion is the distinction between the two uses of **fortfahren.** In the *lit.* sense it means 'to drive away' (intrans.) and takes the aux. **sein,** while with *fig.* force it corresponds to our intrans. use of 'to continue' and takes **haben:** cf., on the one hand, **Er ist eben auf seinem Rad nach der Stadt gefahren,** and, on the other hand, **Er hat eben fortgefahren, sein Rad zu reparieren** or **Er hat eben mit der Reparatur seines Rades fortgefahren** (cf. the example from G. given under **willfahren**). The other expression for 'to continue' is **fortsetzen,** which is *trans.* and requires an accus. obj.: hence, either **Er hat zu studieren fortgefahren** or **Er hat seine Studien fortgesetzt.**

fahrenlassen: This is written as two words when it means 'to let (some one) drive', as in **Ich bat meinen Vater, mich fahren zu lassen;** but **fahren** has become a sep. prefix when the verb has the *lit.*

sense of 'to let (something) go, relax one's hold', or the *fig.* force of 'to give up, relinquish': e.g. **Er ließ ihren Arm fahren** (Wildenbruch: in more ordinary lang. **Er ließ . . . los**)—**Wollen Sie gefälligst meinen Arm fahrenlassen?**—**Er hat seinen Anspruch fahrenlassen** ('He has renounced his claim': more ordinarily **Er hat . . . aufgegeben**).

fahrlässig: see **idle** 2.

Fährte: This is one of a number of nouns which are really plur. forms that have come to be treated as sing. In most cases the old sing. is now obs., the plur. form retaining the orig. sing. meaning: such are **Ente** ('duck', the plur. of MHG *ant*), **Esche** ('ash-tree' < *asch*), **Hüfte** ('hip', with inorganic **t** < *huf*, plur. *hüffe*), **Locke** ('lock of hair' < *loc*), **Säule** ('pillar' < *sûl*, plur. *siule*), **Träne** ('tear' < *trahen*), **Tücke** ('malice' < *tuc*), **Woge** ('wave' < *wâc*) and **Zähre** (south German = **Träne** < *zaher*). In other cases both forms are still in use, the plur. having developed an independent meaning of its own: e.g. **Blüte** ('blossom', really the plur. of **Blut**), **Fährte** ('spoor, track', plur. of **Fahrt**), **Gräte** ('fish-bone', plur. of **Grat**: cf. **Rückgrat**, 'spine'), **Schläfe** ('temple', plur. of **Schlaf** q.v.), **Stätte** ('place', plur. of **Statt** q.v. 1 *b*) and **Trümmer** ('fragment', plur. of **Trumm**, q.v.).

fail: Of this verb there are numerous possible renderings, according to its various uses. **1.** Its fundamental force, 'to be absent, lacking' (see **fehlen**) is now almost confined to the conditional pres. part., as in a proposition like 'Failing conclusive proof, the accused cannot be found guilty', which might be idiomatically rendered by **In Ermangelung** (see **Mangel** 2) **schlagender Beweise kann der Angeklagte nicht schuldig gesprochen (befunden, für schuldig erklärt) werden**; cf. **Wir hoffen mit dem Flugzeug zu reisen, sonst** (or **wenn das nicht angeht**, 'failing that') **mit der Eisenbahn** (in this connexion see **zuwider** *ad fin.*). **2.** Another common meaning is 'to be running short': e.g. **Unsere Vorräte an Nahrungsmitteln werden knapp** or **gehen aus** ('Our supplies of food are failing'). **3.** Used of health, eyesight, etc., it conveys the sense of 'to lose strength, flag': e.g. **Des Kranken Kräfte haben abgenommen** or **nachgelassen** ('The invalid's strength has failed')—**Seine Hörkraft nimmt seit einiger Zeit ab** ('His hearing has been failing for some time'). **4.** The idea of 'to be wanting' may lead to that of 'to give no help', even 'to disappoint': e.g. **Die Stimme versagte mir** ('My voice failed me')—**Mir sank der Mut** ('My courage failed me')—**In der höchsten Not ließ er mich im Stich** ('He failed me in the hour of my greatest need')—**Ich finde keine Worte** (or **Worte reichen nicht aus**), **meine Entrüstung auszudrücken** ('Words fail me to express my indignation'). **5.** It may also convey the sense of 'to omit' to do something: e.g. **Er versäumte (es), den Brief zu beantworten** ('He failed to reply to the letter'—cf. **miss** 1 *c*)—**Versäume** (or **Vernachlässige**) **niemals deine Pflicht** *or* **Versäume** (or **Unterlaß**) **es niemals, deine Pflicht zu tun** ('Never fail in your duty'); and in a neg. proposition: **Er sagte, er werde nicht verfehlen** (or **ermangeln**), **der Sitzung beizuwohnen** ('He said he would not fail to attend the meeting'). Another idiomatic way to express this idea of 'to fail, omit' to do something in a neg. proposition is to use the impers. **nicht ausbleiben**: e.g. **Er war durch den kinderlosen Haushalt verwöhnt, und so konnte es nicht ausbleiben, daß Klein-Anna ihn nicht selten störte** (D. Speckmann: '. . . so it was inevitable that little Annie should disturb him fairly often *or* so Annie could not fail to disturb him occasionally'). **6.** Yet another sense is that of 'to be unsuccessful': e.g. **Er ist in der Prüfung durchgefallen** ('He has failed in his examination')—**Mein Plan hat fehlgeschlagen** ('My plan has failed')—**Der Versuch, den Berg zu ersteigen, ist ihm mißlungen** ('He has failed in his attempt to climb the mountain'). **7.** Lastly, there is the sense of 'to go bankrupt': e.g. **Er ist bank(e)rott** (or **zahlungsunfähig**) **geworden** *or* **Er hat Bank(e)rott** (slang **Pleite**) **gemacht.**

Fall: **1.** (**a**) The lit. sense of this noun is seen in **Er tat einen schweren Fall** ('He had a bad fall')—**jemand zu Fall bringen** ('to cause a person to fall, trip him up', also 'to ruin *or* seduce')—**Hochmut kommt vor dem Fall** (Prov. 16. 18). (**b**) **Fall** is also used in grammar of the 'cases' in declension, **der erste, zweite, dritte** and **vierte Fall** being 'the nom., gen., dat. and accus. case' respectively; but these are now more usually called **der Wer-, Wes-, Wem-** and **Wenfall.** The story goes that a man out rowing fell in three times: the first time he fell **in das Wasser**, the second time **in des Wassers, denn es war der zweite Fall,** and the third time **in dem Wasser, denn es war da tief** (a play on **Dativ**). (c) **Fall** also represents our 'case' in the sense of an occurrence, circumstance, state of affairs, etc.: e.g. **Das ist durchaus nicht der Fall** ('That is by no means the case')—**Der Arzt behandelt augenblicklich einen sonderbaren Fall** ('a strange case')—**Das gilt in neun von** (or **unter**) **zehn Fällen** ('That holds good in nine cases out of ten'). This use is esp. common in set prep. phrases, as in **Wenn es regnet? Nun, in dem** (or **diesem**) **Fall bleiben wir zu Hause** ('In that case we'll stay at home'); but such ideas are often neatly expressed by the use of the gen. of the noun as a suffix: e.g. **Ich komme auf jeden Fall** or **auf alle Fälle** or **jedenfalls** ('I shall be there in any case *or* at any rate': *not* **allenfalls**, q.v.); sim. **im Notfall** or **nötigenfalls** ('in case of need')—**im schlimmsten Fall** or **schlimmstenfalls** ('at worst, if the worst comes to the worst': see **bad** 3)—**in dem gegebenen Fall** or **gegebenenfalls** ('in the case in question', also 'if the occasion should arise')—**andernfalls** (see **ander** 2). **2.** But **falls** is not only used as a suffix: it has acquired independent force as a *subord. conj.*, meaning 'in case, if': e.g. **Falls es regnen sollte, bleiben wir zu Hause,** where **im Fall daß es regnen sollte** is not nearly so common. It is esp. useful where a **wenn**-clause occurs, as in **Wenn du, falls es regnen sollte, einen Schirm mitnimmst, wirst du nicht naß werden.**

fallen: The only interesting grammatical point in connexion with this verb is that, while it normally is *intrans.* (aux. **sein**), it can be used *trans.* (aux. **haben**) with an obj. indicating the result of a fall. Where we can only say 'He has fallen and wounded his forehead', a German says **Er hat sich** (dat.) **eine Wunde in die Stirn gefallen**; sim. **Die Bombe fiel ein tiefes Loch in unseren Garten—Ein Geschrei weckt mich, ich springe herunter und finde, daß mein Neffe sich eine Brausche** ('lump *or* swelling') **gefallen hat** (G.). Of the numerous idiom. uses of **fallen** with preps., the following are worth noting: **Das Kind fiel der Länge nach** ('full length') **auf die Erde** or **zu Boden—Ich fiel aus den Wolken** or **dem Himmel** ('I was thunderstruck')—**Er fiel aus der Rolle** (*lit.* of an actor who forgets his part, *fig.* of a person who acts out of character)—**Sie fiel mit der Tür ins Haus** ('She blurted out *or* dropped a bomb-shell')——**Sie ist nicht auf den Mund gefallen** ('She has the gift of the gab'): of a lady who trips over a man's foot, gets up and rages at him, one might say **Gefallen ist sie, aber nicht auf den Mund!**

falten: 1. Like **halten,** this was orig. one of the **reduplicating verbs** (q.v.), with strong forms (MHG *vielt, gevalten*), but, unlike **halten,** it is now a *weak* verb, the only surviving remnant of the strong conj. being the past part. **gefalten,** which is still occasionally used for the normal **gefaltet** in the adj. relation: one now always says **Er faltete die Hände** and **Hast du die Hände gefaltet?** (implying an action), and usually says **Er stand mit gefalteten Händen** (G.), but it is not incorrect to say **„Was hilft es mir, stolz zu sein?" winselte er mit gefaltenen Händen** (Ponten) or **Man übergab ihm den zusammengefaltenen Brief** (Jul. Wolff). But there is one compd. which is invariably *weak*, even in the past part., viz. **entfalten** ('to unfold'): cf. **Ihr habt gesehen, wie sie mit entfalteten** (not **entfaltenen**) **Händen mich segnete** (G.)—**Die Blumen haben sich entfaltet** ('have opened, unfolded, their petals'). **2.** Much the same applies to **spalten** ('to split, cleave'), except that here the *strong* past part. is much more common than the weak one when an action is implied. While it is permissible to say **Er hat Holz gespaltet,** the form **gespalten** is much more usual, and is quite fixed in the adj. relation, as in expressions like **ein gespaltener Gaumen** ('a cleft palate'), **eine gespaltene Lippe** ('a cracked lip'), **gespaltene Hufe** ('cloven hooves'), etc.; so also **Das Gesicht war von einer großen Wunde gespalten** (Rilke)—**Er hat am Kopf eine Wunde, die Hirnschale ist ihm gespalten** (A. Meissner)—**Es war, als hätte sich der Berg gespalten** (Heyse)—**Er hat das Bild mit gespaltenen Birkenzweigen eingerahmt** (Waggerl)—**Inmitten des gespaltenen Gewölkes sah der blaue Himmel nieder** (J. Ludwig); *fig.* **Ich fühle mein Wesen in zwei Teile gespalten** (G. Keller)—**In unserem Glauben sind wir gespalten** (Frenssen). **3.** To the same class belongs **salzen** ('to salt'), the past part. of which is now invariably *strong*: e.g. **Ich habe gesalzene Häringe gekauft—Die Suppe ist zu stark gesalzen**; *fig.* **Er macht gern gesalzene Witze** ('spicy jokes')—**„Ich werde ihm einen Brief**

schreiben", rief ich, „einen gepfefferten!" und eine Stunde später war der Brief, leidlich gesalzen ('a pretty sharp one'), **im Briefkasten** (M. Eyth); sim. the compd. **versalzen** ('to oversalt'), as in **Die Suppe ist versalzen**; *fig.* **Ich sah, wie gründlich ich mir das Verhältnis zu den Leuten versalzen hatte** (H. Hesse: 'I saw how completely I had spoiled my relations with the inhabitants of the place').

Faß: For expressions like **zwei Faß Wein,** see **nouns of measure** I (*a*).

fast: see **adverbs formed from adjectives** I.

Fasten: see **Weihnachten.**

faul: see **idle** I.

Februar: see **Monatsnamen.**

Federlesen: This verbal noun is used in the same way as **Aufheben** and **Wesen** (qq.v.) with the force of 'fuss, to-do'. Its use may have been suggested by the behaviour of a fussy servant who 'picked fluff' from the dress of his master or of some one with whom he wished to curry favour; but whether this be the true explanation or not, the expression **Federlesen machen** is now used in a general way in the sense of 'to be fussy *or* ceremonious', being usually associated with a neg.: e.g. **Man hatte nicht das geringste Federlesen mit ihnen gemacht** (Schreckenbach: 'Not the slightest fuss was made over them, They were treated without the least ceremony'). Actually, it is much more common to use the *gen.* form here, which was orig. a part. gen. depending on an indef. pron. like **viel** (q.v. I *a* and *b*), as in **Hierzuland macht man nicht viel Federlesens** (Federer: much like . . . **macht man keine Umstände,** 'one doesn't stand much on ceremony'); but the gen. form has now become quite established as an independent noun (cf. **nichts** 4): e.g. **Der Herzog war ohne Federlesens in Rede und Haltung** (Kolbenheyer: 'The Duke was unceremonious in speech and bearing').

fehl: The masc. noun **Fehl** was common in early NHG—Luther is fond of expressions like **jemandem seine Fehle vergeben** ('to forgive a person his trespasses')—but this use is now confined to Biblical or poet. lang., being elsewhere replaced by **Fehler.** But **fehl** is still used in the pred. in **fehl am Ort sein,** either *lit.*, as in **Er sah, daß er fehl am Ort war** (B. E. Werner: 'He saw that he had come to the wrong place *or* had lost his bearings') or *fig.*, as in **Strenge ist hier fehl am Ort** ('To act with severity *or* apply the full rigour of the law is out of place here'); cf. **Hier ist jede Scheu ganz fehl am Platze** (Th. Mann: 'This is no place for reserve'). It is esp. common as a sep. prefix of certain verbs, notably **fehlgehen** ('to go wrong *or* astray'), **fehlrechnen** ('to miscalculate'), **fehlschießen** ('to miss the mark'), **fehlschlagen** ('to miscarry'): e.g. **Gehen Sie geradeaus, Sie können nicht fehlgehen** (see **fehlen** 2 *b* and **irre** I)—**Du hast fehlgerechnet** (Heyse)—**Er schoß fast nie fehl** (Hackländer)—**Mehrere Versuche waren fehlgeschlagen** (A. Schaeffer)—**Alles ist fehlgeschlagen und hat sich zum Unglück gewandt** (Th. Mann: 'Everything has gone wrong and turned out disastrously'); cf. compd. nouns like **Fehlgeburt** ('miscarriage'), **-schluß** ('false inference'), **-tritt** ('false step, *faux-pas*'), **-zug** ('wrong move' in chess).

fehlen: 1. For the *trans.* use of this verb in the sense of 'not to hit' (a target, etc.), see **miss** I. **2.** *Intrans.*: (**a**) For its use with the force of 'to be absent', as in **Gestern fehlten zwei Schüler,** see **lack** I. (**b**) With the meaning 'to err, go astray', it was formerly used with a gen. of what is sinned against, but this is now obs.: it is significant that the rel. clause in Luther's **Verflucht sind, die deiner Gebote fehlen** (Ps. 119. 21) has been altered in the modern version to **die von deinen Geboten abirren** (cf. **irre** 2 *b*). In the abs. use, to suggest a moral lapse, **fehlen** is still in use, as in Queen Mary's confession **Ich habe menschlich, jugendlich gefehlt** (Sch.) and **Wo haben wir gefehlt, daß uns so Ungeheuerliches geschehen ist?** (Frenssen: 'Wherein have we sinned, that such a disastrous fate should have befallen us?'), but such a moral transgression is usually suggested by **einen Fehltritt tun.** Even where it is used of 'taking a wrong road', as in **Ich will Sie bis zum Kreuzweg begleiten, dann können Sie nicht fehlen** (Roquette), one generally uses **fehlgehen** (cf. **fehl**) or **irregehen** (cf. **irre** I) or **den rechten Weg verfehlen** (see **miss** I *b*).

fehlgehen: see **fehlen** 2 (*b*) and **irre** I.

feind: see **adjectives (indeclinable)** 5.

Fels, Felsen: Both these forms are recognized, but the second (with gen. **Felsens**) is much more common; in spite of examples like **Auf einem Vorsprung dieses Felsen erblickt man die Überreste der**

alten Burg (Mörike), the shorter form (with gen. **Felsen**) is now mainly characteristic of poetry and elevated prose.

fern, Ferne: see distance 1; cf. adverbs formed from adjectives 1.

fertig: see ready 1 and 2.

Fetzen: see rag 3.

Fichte: see Kiefer 2 (*c*).

Figur: see figure 1 (*c*).

figure: 1. The following three expressions should be distinguished: (a) **Form:** Although in a few cases used of something concrete, as in **etwas in eine Form** ('mould') **gießen** or **einen Hut über die Form schlagen** ('to block a hat'), this word really suggests an abstract conception, viz. the *form* or *shape* of a body, as distinct from its *matter* (**Stoff**) or *content* (**Gehalt**, q.v.): e.g. **Die Erde hat die Form einer Kugel—Mein Hut verliert seine** (or **kommt aus der**) **Form—Die Form dieses Gedichts ist auffallend.** In a fig. sense it is used, often in the plur., of the prescribed *etiquette* observed in polite society: **die Formen des gesellschaftlichen Lebens—Dieser junge Mann hat gute Umgangsformen**; and it is also used in grammar, of the *voice* of a verb (**die tätige Form**, 'active voice'—**die leidende Form**, 'passive voice'), and in modern times, borrowing the English idiom, of a person's *bodily fitness* (**Er ist außer Form**, 'not in form'—**in Form bleiben**, 'to keep fit'). (b) **Gestalt:** properly used of the form in which a body, esp. a living body, presents itself to the eye of the beholder, not as an abstract conception but as a three-dimensional quality inseparable from a concrete body, and hence often applied to such a body itself. When we say 'A tall gaunt figure approached me', we do not think of an abstract shape or outline, but of a concrete living being with certain distinguishing attributes: hence **Eine lange hagere Gestalt nahte mir—Gott erschien auf Erden in menschlicher Gestalt**; *fig.* **Jetzt zeigt er sich in seiner wahren Gestalt** ('in his true colours')—**Der Vorschlag nimmt festere Gestalt an** ('is taking shape'). (c) **Figur:** used of the *outline of* a body, the lines bounding a figure in the plane of vision: e.g. **Ein Dreieck ist eine geometrische Figur—Diese Dame hat eine schöne Figur** (referring to the *lines* of her body, as they present themselves to another's eye); *fig.* **Er spielt eine klägliche Figur** ('He cuts a poor figure'). With concrete force, it is used mainly of a carved or sculptured 'figure', esp. one of small size: e.g. **eine kleine Holzfigur** or **Figur aus Holz—Schachfiguren** ('chessmen'). **2.** Entirely different from the nouns given above is **Ziffer**, i.e. an *arithmetical figure*, a sign representing a particular number (hence **Zifferblatt**, the 'dial' of a clock). To express a number *as such*, the Germans use **Zahl** (q.v.); to express a number *of objects*, they use **Anzahl** (q.v.). Thus, 'five' is a **Zahl**, whose corresponding **Ziffer** is '5'; and if a child has written a large number of fives, he will have written **eine große Anzahl (von) Ziffern** (in this case **Fünfen**).

finden: 1. When used of finding some one engaged in an action or occupation, **finden** may take an **accusative and infinitive** (q.v. 1 *a*, and cf. **treffen** 2), and it is possible that the infin. here is a corrupt pres. part. Examples of the pres. part. itself are rare; on the other hand, a *past* part. is very common, implying a state, attitude, etc., and here the infin. **sein** may really be understood: instead of **Ich fand ihn Briefe schreiben** one usually prefers to say **Ich fand ihn damit beschäftigt, Briefe zu schreiben.** For various examples of these constructions, see **accusative and participle.** It is noteworthy that a subord. finite clause is required when **finden** is used of discovering or learning a fact, and esp. in the modern sense of 'to be of opinion': e.g. **Sie werden finden, daß ich mich nicht geirrt habe—Ich finde, daß er sich sehr schlecht betragen hat**; cf. the coll. idiom **„Nein, wie ich das finde!"** ('Oh, I think that 's dreadful!'), presumably contracted from **Nein, frage mich nicht, wie ich das finde!** ('Don't ask me what I think of that—words fail me!'). **2.** The reflex. **sich finden** (cf. 3) is used: (a) with an *impers.* subj., meaning 'to be found', as in **Dieses Wort findet sich nicht im Wörterbuch** (see occur 1); cf. the coll. **Das wird sich finden**, as in **„Was fangen wir an, wenn der Zug Verspätung hat?" „Das wird sich schon finden"** ('Don't worry, we'll decide that *or* find a solution when the time comes'); (b) with a *pers.* subj., in the sense of 'to find oneself in *or* adapt oneself to' a state or situation: e.g. **Ich finde mich in der Lage, dir zu helfen—Ich kann mich in die neue Lage nicht (hinein)finden.** **3.** While the reflex. may also be used with the force of 'to find one's way', as in **Der Busch ist so dicht, daß du dich nicht hindurchfinden würdest** (Ponten) and **Man kann sich in diesen engen Straßen schwer zurechtfinden,** this idea is now usually expressed by the *intrans.* use of **finden** and its compds., a use that is quite modern: e.g. **Am Ufer drängte sich das Volk, so daß er manchen Rippenstoß aushalten mußte, ehe er zum Rhein fand** (W. Schäfer)—**Die alte Baronin hatte endlich von Stuttgart nach Daylesford gefunden** (Feuchtwanger)—**Könnt ihr immer noch nicht nach Hause finden?** (Blunck: implying 'Isn't it high time you were going home?'); and sim. in compds., **Als Kind war ich oft durch die unbekannten Straßen gestreift und hatte doch immer wieder heimgefunden** (Fr. Thieß)—**Wie hat sie denn hergefunden?** (H. Hauser)—**Sie hielten den Atem an, daß er nicht den Trompetenklang übertönte, der jetzt zu ihnen herfand** (G. Britting)—**Geht zu einem erfahrenen Menschen und laßt euch von ihm sagen, wie ihr aus der Not herausfindet** (Frenssen)—**Aus den Wirrnissen fand er gar nicht heraus** (Zuckmayer)—**Ihn beklemmte der Wald: standen die Stämme nicht da, wie um ihn gestellt, daß er nicht mehr herausfände?** (H. E. Busse)—**Er konnte von dieser Insel nicht wegfinden** (H. Leip: i.e. 'He could not tear himself away from this island')—**Kennen Sie die Irrgärten** ('mazes'), **in die man lief und aus denen man nicht wieder zurückfand?** (Blunck)—**Endlich fanden die beiden lange Getrennten wieder zusammen** (Stehr); cf. *fig.* **Es dauerte einige Minuten, bis er zu sich fand** (W. v. Scholz: 'It was some minutes before he came to himself again').

fir: see Kiefer.

Fleck(en): Originally this word had the force of a 'place' or 'spot', and one still says **sich nicht vom Fleck rühren** ('not to move from the spot') and **das Herz auf dem rechten Fleck haben.** In a wider sense, it means a 'piece of ground', esp. in the dim. form: **ein hübsches Fleckchen Erde.** Later it came to mean a 'spot, mark, stain', the plur. being either **Flecke** or (rather less commonly) **Flecken:** cf. **Sie fand dunkle Flecken auf dem Teppich: waren es Weinflecken?** (Waggerl); in some districts **Flecken** is still used coll. with the force of 'measles' (**die Masern** or **Röteln**). Sometimes **Fleck** is also used of a 'patch' for mending a hole, but here one now prefers to use **Flicken.** The sing. form **Flecken** is now quite fixed when the reference is to a 'small town' or 'large village' which enjoys certain privileges, esp. the right to hold regular markets: hence always **ein Marktflecken.**

fliehen: Where we say 'He fled *from* a threatening danger', a German usually says **Er floh vor einer drohenden Gefahr,** the idea being that the danger was in front of or facing him. With *trans.* force, the verb is used in the sense of 'to shun', being a stronger expression than **meiden:** e.g. **Er scheint uns zu meiden, ja zu fliehen** (G.)—**Haltet mich nicht für einen Menschenfeind: ich habe die Welt nicht geflohen, sondern in dieser Höhle nur eine Ruhestätte gesucht** (Novalis: '. . . I have not renounced the world: I have only sought a resting-place in this cave')—**Er war so erregt, daß ihn der Schlaf floh** (Ompteda: 'He was so excited that sleep forsook him'). Instead of **Ich habe die Welt nicht geflohen,** Novalis might have said **Ich bin nicht vor der Welt geflohen**; the two constructions are confused in **Ich bin ihr Wirken geflohen** (Gutzkow), which should not be imitated. The historically correct pres. forms with the vowel-sound **eu** (< MHG *iu*) are obs. except in poetry and archaic prose: cf. **Fleuch zu meinem Bruder Laban** (Gen. 27. 43, where the modern version has **Flieh . . .**)—**Fleuch auf der Stelle!** (Sch.).

Flur: In the north a distinction is almost reg. made between the HG **die Flur** ('meadow, pasture-land': plur. **Fluren**) and the LG **der Flur** ('entrance-hall, lobby': plur. **Flure**): cf., on the one hand, **Der Sommerabend senkt sich auf die stille Flur** (Grillparzer), and on the other hand, **Er lief über den Flur und die Treppe hinauf** (Immermann). As the masc. gender was only used in the north, it is not surprising that when the sense of 'lobby' spread to the south, the word was used as a fem. noun in that sense also: but to avoid possible confusion, southern authors prefer to express 'lobby' by **Hausflur.** Although this fem. use is officially allowed, it is perhaps advisable to observe the northern distinction, i.e. not to imitate such examples as **Es ließen sich Stimmen in der Hausflur vernehmen** (Spindler)—**Damit trat sie in die Hausflur** (Schnitzler)—**Ich sah mich in der halblichten Hausflur um** (H. Hesse)—**Die Werkstatt war dunkel, ich stolperte durch eine finstere Hausflur** (id.); cf. **„Gute**

Nacht!" rief er und stürzte auf die Hausflur hinaus (Hebbel), where the use of the fem. is no doubt a result of the northern author's long residence in Munich.

Föhre: see **Kiefer** 2 (*a*).

Folge: see **Grund** 2.

folgen: 1. (**a**) This verb takes a *dat.* obj., both in the lit. sense of 'to follow, walk behind' (a person) and in the fig. sense of 'to obey' (a person), 'to act in accordance with' (a rule, precept, advice) or 'to follow' (an argument, a course of events); but with *lit.* force it takes the aux. **sein,** with *fig.* force **haben:** e.g. **Ich gehe voran, bitte folgen Sie mir!—Sie folgt den Abgehenden** (dat. plur.) **mit den Augen** (Sch.: in a stage direction)—**Er ist mir auf den Fersen gefolgt;** but **Wenn du mir damals gefolgt hättest, es wäre alles gut geblieben** (G.)—**Sie meinten, daß ich nur deshalb in der Schule nichts lernte, weil ich der Lehrersfrau nicht folgte, doch habe ich dem Schulmeister auch nicht gefolgt** (W. Schäfer)—**Hattet Ihr's schon jemals zu bereuen, mir gefolgt zu haben?** (Jul. Wolff: 'Had you ever occasion to regret having taken my advice?')—**Sie hatte dem Vorgange mit Aufmerksamkeit gefolgt** (C. F. Meyer). With an impers. obj. **folgen** + dat. is often replaced by **befolgen** + accus. (cf. 2). (**b**) The only other constructions are the preps. **aus** ('to follow from', as a logical deduction) and **auf** + accus. ('to follow' in the temporal sense of 'to come after, succeed'): e.g. **Aus dem Gesagten folgt, daß der Versuch mißlingen wird** ('It follows from what has been said that the attempt will fail')—**Was folgt daraus?—Auf Regen folgt Sonnenschein—Ein Unglück folgt auf das andere** ('Misfortunes never come singly'); in references to succeeding to a throne either **auf** or a dat. is used, as in **Friedrich der Große folgte Friedrich Wilhelm dem Zweiten** or **auf Friedrich Wilhelm den Zweiten. 2.** As with most other verbs which take a dat., so also with **folgen** the pass. is generally avoided (cf. **passive voice** I. iii): instead of **Mir wurde gefolgt** one prefers to use **Man folgte mir,** and to treat the verb as a trans., as in **Man muß voraufgehen, wenn man gefolgt sein will** (Möser), is definitely bad German; cf., correctly with an impers. obj., **Es wäre besser gewesen, wenn sein Rat befolgt worden wäre.** There are, however, two exceptions: (a) the past part. can be used in a *contracted* clause to suggest a concomitant circumstance: thus, while a proposition like **Der Fürst wurde von seinen Offizieren gefolgt** is to be condemned, **Von seinen Offizieren gefolgt, betrat der Fürst den Saal** is sanctioned by usage, and sim. **Vom Jammer gefolgt, schreitet das Unglück** (Sch.); of special interest here is the following example, describing a Catholic festival, **Das Hochwürdigste wurde vom Bischof getragen, von Geistlichwürdigen umgeben, von östreichischen Kriegern begleitet, gefolgt von zeitigen Autoritäten** (G.: 'The host was carried by the bishop, surrounded by ecclesiastical dignitaries, accompanied by Austrian soldiers, followed by temporal office-holders'), where the word-order at the end is significant: if **gefolgt** had been placed at the very end, the clause would have been a finite one like the three preceding ones (**Das Hochwürdigste . . . wurde von zeitigen Autoritäten gefolgt**), which, as pointed out above, would not be good German. (**b**) The past part. with pass. force is also allowed in the accus. and part. construction, esp. with *reflex.* verbs (cf. **schmeicheln**): e.g. **Ich glaubte mich gefolgt** ('I believed I was being followed')—**Sie war gewohnt, sich von Verehrern gefolgt, geschmeichelt und bewundert zu sehen** (Wieland). **3.** In propositions like 'The following examples will suffice', the def. art. is very commonly omitted in German, in which case, of course, the attrib. part. must be strongly inflected: **Folgende Beispiele werden genügen.** The same applies, esp. in epistolary and commercial lang., to expressions like 'the above-mentioned *or* aforesaid particulars', 'the gentleman in question', etc., for which there are several common German words, esp. **obig, vorerwähnt, vorbenannt, vorstehend, genannt** and **gedacht** (this last a favourite word of Goethe's, but not so common now): e.g. **Gedachter Edelmann zeigte mir einen kleinen Ring** (G.)—**Ich werde aus obigem Grunde** ('for the reason stated above') **der Versammlung nicht beiwohnen—Infolge vorerwähnter Umstände** ('in consequence of the aforesaid circumstances') **muß ich Ihre Bitte leider abschlagen—Das Pferd, auf welchem Goethe in vorbenannten Angelegenheiten** ('in connexion with the matters referred to') **umherritt, hatte den Stallnamen „Poesie" erhalten** (K. v. Lyncker). The only difficulty that arises here is where an attrib. adj. follows such expressions, as in 'The following short report was submitted', and here there is so much fluctuation in the inflexion of the adj. that no hard and fast rule can be laid down: **Folgender kurze(r) Bericht wurde vorgelegt** (cf. **vorliegen** *ad fin.*)—**Vorstehender wunderliche Brief war schon lange geschrieben** (G.)—**Gedachter junger Mann empfiehlt sich durch eigenes Talent** (G.)—**Obenerwähnter junger Mann hatte die Verhältnisse des Berliner Schauspiels schlecht begriffen** (Heine); on the whole, a weak ending seems to sound better in the nom. and accus. sing. neut., in the dat. sing. masc. and neut., and in the gen. plur.: **Glücklicherweise wird genanntes herrliche Werk fortgesetzt** (G.)—**Er gab folgendes witzige Gedicht zum besten—Aus obigem zwingenden Grunde muß ich Ihre freundliche Einladung leider ablehnen—Infolge vorerwähnter schwierigen Umstände werden wir nicht reisen können.** Of course, the art. may be inserted in all such propositions, in which case no difficulty arises: **Das folgende schöne Gedicht solltest du auswendig lernen—Der Dichter des erwähnten schönen Gedichts ist unbekannt.**

Form: see figure 1 (*a*).

former: see erst 1 (*c*).

fortfahren, fortsetzen: see fahren 3.

fragen: 1. Whereas **bitten,** like the rather more formal **ersuchen,** means 'to ask' in the sense of 'to request', **fragen** is 'to ask' a question: cf. **Man bat mich, den Kranken zu besuchen,** and **Man fragte mich, ob ich den Kranken besuchen wollte**; see **accusative (double)** 1 (*a*). The impers. reflex. **es fragt sich** means 'it is questionable': see the example from Novalis given under 2 below. Incidentally, our coll. expression 'if you ask me', used with the force of 'to my thinking' in props. like 'He requested my friend to lend him some money: a strange request, if you ask me', should be rendered by **meines Erachtens** or **meiner Meinung nach** or **nach meinem Dafürhalten**; the use of **wenn man mich fragt** in such a context is not a German idiom, and an example like **Daß das mit Hexerei zu tun habe, war die Überzeugung früherer Epochen: eine respektable Überzeugung, wenn man mich fragt** (Th. Mann in *Doktor Faustus*) is a result of the author's long residence in America. For a similar 'un-German' use, see **aufbringen** *ad fin.* **2.** The verb **fragen** orig. had only *weak* forms, like **klagen, sagen, wagen,** etc. Incorrect strong forms crept in from the north in the 18th century under the influence of **schlagen, tragen,** etc. (cf. **jagen**): e.g. **Was frägst du?** (W. Alexis)—**Es frägt sich, ob wir die Natur wahrhaft begreifen lernen können** (Novalis)—**Niemals frug ein Kaiser nach mir** (G.)—**Ich müßte mich schämen, wenn deine Brüder mich frügen, was ich gesehen habe** (Ponten). It seems significant that strong forms which Schiller often used at first, esp. in the past indic., were altered to weak ones in later editions. But these strong forms eventually became so common that they are now allowed by *Duden,* although they are condemned by *Sanders* (and *Wustmann,* of course) and are represented as dialect forms by *Sprach-Brockhaus.* On the whole, weak forms are to be recommended in good prose, and it is noteworthy that the past part. is invariably weak: cf. its use in commercial lang. with the force of 'in demand', as in **Deutschland hat noch ansehnliche Bestände dieses zur Zeit sehr gefragten** (or **gesuchten** or **begehrten**) **Holzes** (Speckmann: referring to oak).

Frau: 1. The MHG *vrouwe* was almost invariably *weak,* and the form **Frauen** in the gen. and dat. sing. was common in the early NHG period and even down to the 18th century, esp. in poetry: e.g. **In einer Frauen Hand ist ein anmutiger Zweig gewaltiger als Schwert und Waffe** (G.)—**Nun fand er sich unmittelbar an seiner Frauen Türe** (G.: '. . . at his lady-love's door'). This is now obs., except in references to the Virgin Mary, e.g. in names of churches, nunneries, hospitals, etc., such as **Unsrer lieben Frauen Kirche. 2.** Apart from **Frau,** one or two other fem. nouns are very occasionally used in poetry with weak endings in the oblique cases of the sing., but such forms are now obs. in standard prose: e.g. **Röslein auf der Heiden** (G.)—**Sind diese Ulmen nicht Kinder unsrer Sonnen?** (Sch.)—sim. in the proverb **Es ist nichts so fein gesponnen, es kommt doch endlich an die** (or **ans Licht der**) **Sonnen** (i.e. There is no secret that will not eventually come to light; cf. 'Murder will out'); but an example like **Wie ich in meiner Zellen gesessen bin, da hätte ich singen und jauchzen mögen** (Heyse) is very exceptional in prose. There is, however, one phrase in which the weak dat. sing. of a fem. noun has firmly established itself: cf., on the one hand, **Er lag auf der Erde** ('He lay on the ground') and **Wir wohnen zu ebner Erde** ('We live on the ground-floor'), and, on the other hand, **Alle Schuld rächt sich auf Erden** ('. . . here on earth'). It should be added, however, that a weak gen. sing. fem. ending is seen in many compound nouns in which the first component part was a weak noun in MHG, e.g. **Hosenträger, Katzenfell, Kirchenstuhl, Sonnenschein, Stubentür, Wochenende**, etc.

Frauenzimmer: see **congruence** 2. This word is no longer used, as it once was, to suggest the private room of the mistress of a house, nor yet a 'ladies' room' (**Damenzimmer**). It gradually came to be used of the women who retired to such a room, and in the 17th century of a single woman. Nowadays it is a playful or rather disrespectful term for one of the female sex. A similar development from a place where people meet to one of those meeting there is seen in **Bursche** (from **Börse**, Fr. *bourse*) and **Kamerad** (cf. Ital. *camerata*, 'sleeping apartment').

Fräulein: see **Mädchen** 1 and 2.

freien: see **marry** 1 (*d*).

freilich: This adv. (see **adverbs formed from adjectives** 3) is no longer used, as MHG *vrîlîche* was, in the sense of 'freely, without restraint'; it is wrong to use it in rendering expressions like 'to speak freely' (= **frei heraus sprechen**), 'to confess freely' (= **offen gestehen**), 'to spend money freely' (= **eine offene Hand haben** or **mit dem Gelde um sich werfen**). According to modern usage, it conveys three ideas: **1.** It may serve as a strong *affirmation*, either in answer to a question or emphasizing the correctness of a preceding *pos.* statement or idea: e.g. **„Darf ich eintreten?" „Ja, freilich!"** ('Certainly!' American 'Sure!')—**Auf die Frage, ob er den ihm erteilten Auftrag ausgerichtet habe, antwortete er „Freilich!"—„Ihr seid ernstlich krank." „Ja freilich!"** (Sch.: 'I am that!' slang 'You're telling me!'). It is sometimes used to correct a preceding *neg.* statement, as in **Der Junge kann ja noch nicht zählen." „Freilich kann er das!"** ('Of course he can!'), but this is better expressed by **„Natü'rlich kann er das!"** or **„Do'ch, das kann er!"**: see **doch (adverb)** 1. **2.** It may have *explanatory* force, to give the reason for the preceding statement, in which case it usually immediately follows **aber**: e.g. **Er sieht recht müde aus, aber freilich, es ist ein weiter Weg hierher**; in such a proposition there is really a clause understood after **freilich**, which explains why a *comma* (to indicate a short pause) is inserted after **freilich**, and *normal* word-order is used in the next clause (= **aber freilich muß man eins bedenken: es ist ein weiter Weg hierher**, 'but, of course, one thing must be remembered, it's a long way he's come'). **3.** Like **allerdings** (q.v.), it often has *concessive* force, a limiting 'but'-clause being either expressed or implied: e.g. **Dieser Satz ist freilich** ('no doubt, it is true') **leicht zu verstehen, aber schwer ins Deutsche zu übersetzen—Ich stimmte seinem Vorschlag zu, freilich mit einigem Widerstreben** ('I agreed to his proposal, but with some reluctance, I confess')—**Lavaters Anregungen brachten mein künstlerisch beschauliches Wesen in Umtrieb, freilich** ('I must admit') **nicht zu meinem augenblicklichen Vorteil, indem meine Zerstreuung sich nur vermehrte** (G.).

fressen: 1. In the lit. sense of 'to eat', this corrupt form of **ver-essen** is now only applicable to animals, as in **Das Tier muß krank sein, es will nicht(s) fressen**; cf. the example from Luther given under **essen** 2. But **fressen** is also used of what 'eats' into or spreads through something, as in **Das Feuer wird die Hütten fressen** (Job 15. 34); and so also of lichens (**Flechten**), dry-rot (**Trockenfäule**), cancer (**Krebs**), ulcers (**Geschwüre**), etc., and *fig.* of what 'eats up' money, or esp. of 'consuming' passions and emotions: e.g. **Dieses Unternehmen wird viel Geld fressen—Zu tief hat schon der Haß gefressen** (Sch.)—**Hör' auf, mit diesem Gram zu spielen, der wie ein Geier dir am Leben frißt** (G.). Applied to human beings, it is a vulgar expression, used of a 'dirty' eater, or one who gobbles his food; but a few coll. expressions belonging here are in common use: e.g. **Er hat einen Narren an ihr gefressen** ('He dotes on, is infatuated with, her')—**Das Geschenk war mir ein gefundenes Fressen** ('The present came as a godsend', was the very thing I wanted), so also **allerlei Streiche ausfressen** ('to be up to all sorts of tricks'); cf. **Während seiner Universitätszeit hatte er die tollsten Sachen ausgefressen** (R. Herzog: 'When at the university he had played the maddest pranks'). **2.** The correct expression for 'to drink', as applied to animals, is **saufen,** so that 'to water the horses' might be rendered by **den Pferden zu saufen geben,** but here one generally uses **die Pferde tränken,** which is the causative of **trinken.** Like **fressen, saufen** is a vulgar expression when used of persons, as in **Er säuft wie ein Bürstenbinder** or **wie ein Loch** ('He drinks like a fish') and **Er hat seinen Freund unter den Tisch gesoffen**; cf. **Er ist ein Saufaus** (unchanged in gen. and plur.) or **Saufbold** ('He is a drunkard')—**Säuferwahnsinn** ('delirium tremens'). Distinguish between **ersäufen** ('to drown' an animal), **ertränken** ('to drown' a person: reflex. 'to drown oneself') and **ertrinken** ('to be drowned': cf. **trinken** 1 *b*).

freuen: 1. With a *pers.* subj., **freuen** is now almost confined to the *reflex.* use: a proposition like **Ihr freut den König nicht mit Eurer Nähe** (Wildenbruch) is rare even in poetry (see 2). According to modern practice **freuen** is used: (**a**) with an *impers.* subj.: **Das freut mich—Es freut uns, daß Sie uns besuchen wollen—Es hat mich gefreut, Ihre Bekanntschaft zu machen**; (**b**) as a *reflex.*: still sometimes in rather choice prose with the earlier *gen.*: **Mein Geist freuet sich Gottes, meines Heilandes** (Luke 1. 47)—**Eine Stunde vor meiner Abreise trat Wilhelm bei mir ein, ich freute mich seiner** (R. Wagner)—**Sie freute sich des Sturmes** (Frenssen). Here, in ordinary prose, a *prep.* is used: as *Duden* says, **Man freut sich über Geschehenes, am Gegenwärtigen, auf Künftiges**; i.e. **Ich habe mich über Ihr Geschenk gefreut—Ich freue mich an Ihrem Erfolg** ('I am glad of your success')—**Ich freue mich auf Ihren versprochenen Besuch** ('I am looking forward to your promised visit'); cf. **Die Mißwollenden halten sich darüber auf** ('The evil-minded view with disfavour'), **daß Goethe in Italien malt, während seine Amtsgenossen für ihn schwitzen müssen; die Wohlmeinenden freuen sich seiner** (or **an seiner**) **Freude, und man freut sich schon auf die Erzählungen des Heimgekehrten** (F. A. Hohenstein). **2.** The compd. **erfreuen** is rather stronger than **freuen,** and is esp. common with a *pers.* subj.: **Sie haben mich mit Ihrem neulichen Besuch erfreut—Ich bin über diese Nachricht erfreut** (cf. **froh**)—**Wir erfreuen uns an Ihrem Glück**; the *gen.* is firmly established in **Ich erfreue mich einer guten Gesundheit** ('I am enjoying good health').

Friede: see **Balken.**

frieren: The impers. use of this verb is more idiomatic than the pers. use: the best rendering of 'I am freezing' is **Es friert mich** (or **Mich friert**), and 'My feet are freezing' is **Mich friert an den Füßen**; cf. **Er saß da mit einem Gesichtsausdruck, als fröre ihn** (Th. Mann) and **Sie fror** (Gutzkow: where **Sie** may be either nom. or accus.). A dat. of the person here, as in **Dem Kandidaten fror sehr** (Raabe), should not be used; but it is good German to say **Mir froren die Finger,** which is a more idiomatic way of saying **Meine Finger froren.** Noteworthy compds. are seen in **Meine Pflanzen sind alle erfroren** ('killed by the frost')—**Der Kahn am Ufer ist eingefroren—Der Bach ist zugefroren**; also **Es gefriert,** which is the scientists' expression for temperature at or below freezing-point (**Gefrierpunkt**; cf. **Siedepunkt,** 'boiling-point').

fristen: The fem. noun **Frist** properly suggests a space of time allowed for carrying something into effect, as when a person is granted a certain time in which to pay a fine: **Dem Schuldner wurde eine Frist von zwei Wochen bewilligt**; cf. **Daniel bat den König, daß er ihm Frist gebe** (Dan. 2. 16)—**Der Tod vergönnte ihm eine traurige Frist** (Sch.). So the verb **fristen** really means 'to put off, delay', esp. 'to reprieve, spare the life of' a person (cf. **spare** 2 *a*); but its main use now is with the obj. **Leben** (or **Dasein**) in the sense of 'to support life, gain a living', generally with an adj. or adv. suggesting a modest or meagre subsistence: e.g. **Aller Güter beraubt, fristete die evangelische Kirche ein ärmliches Leben** (Treitschke)—**So berichtet Musäus, der Verfasser der „Volksmärchen", der damals in Weimar als Gymnasialprofessor ein bescheidenes Dasein fristete** (F. A. Hohenstein); rather less common is the use of the reflex. in this sense, as in **Er fristete sich mühsam** (or **kümmerlich**) **durch die Kriegsjahre.**

froh: The MHG adj. *vrô*, when it meant 'glad of, rejoicing at, pleased about', was always associated with the *gen.*, as in *des wâren si vil vrô* ('Of that they were very glad'), and this case is still used in a choice literary style: e.g. **Thomas Mann ist allmählich jünger geworden, aber auch tatkräftiger und froh der Verantwor-**

tung, die der Ruhm ihm auferlegt hat (A. Eloesser)—**Er lächelte leise, froh der gelungenen Flucht** (Kolbenheyer)—**Sie wurden ihrer Liebe nicht mehr froh** (Tovote: i.e. 'Their married life was never happy again'). Sim., one can still say **Ich werde meines Lebens nie mehr froh**; but in ordinary lang. the usual construction of **froh**, as of **erfreut** (see **freuen** 2), is **über** + accus.: e.g. **Ich bin froh über das Gelingen seines Planes** (or **froh, daß ihm sein Plan gelungen ist**).

frohlocken: This compound of **locken**, meaning 'to shout with joy', shows some fluctuation in pronunciation, although to a lesser extent than is shown by **liebkosen** (q.v.). Duden says **„Die Betonung auf der zweiten Silbe kann heute als die übliche gelten"**, and **frohlo'cken** is certainly much more common than **fro'hlocken**; indeed, the only part of the verb in which the prefix is often accented is the past part., where **gefro'hlockt** is an alternative form of **frohlo'ckt.** But whether the prefix is accented or not, it should not be treated as sep.: one always says **Ich frohlocke** (not **Ich locke froh**) and **Dies ist nicht die Zeit zu frohlocken** (not **frohzulocken**). An example like **Ich habe frohgelockt** (Chamisso) is not in accordance with modern usage, and in quoting it *Sanders* rightly says **„statt gefrohlockt"**.

fuchteln: see **mit** 2 (*a*).

fühlen: **1.** It is rather strange that this verb is so common, as MHG *vüeren* is actually rare: indeed, it was really through Luther's constant use of it that it spread to the south, where previously **empfinden** (< *entvinden* or *emphinden*) had been the established expression; and even now **empfinden** is very much less used in the ordinary lang. of the north, where it sounds a little pedantic. If any distinction can now be drawn between the two verbs, it is that the feeling suggested by **fühlen** is basically more physical (its orig. force was 'to ascertain by touching with the fingers'), and that suggested by **empfinden** more spiritual: thus, **empfinden** cannot be used of feeling sick or insulted, of feeling some one's pulse, of feeling one's way in the dark, etc., but one can say **Als mein Freund starb, empfand ich seinen Verlust sehr tief.** On the other hand, **fühlen** has a wide application, as the following examples show: **Ich fühlte einen plötzlichen Schmerz im Rücken**—**Er ließ mir seine schlechte Laune fühlen**—**Der Arzt fühlte mir den** (or **an den**) **Puls**—**Er fühlte nach seinen Papieren in der Tasche** (Immermann: 'He groped in his pocket for his papers')—**Ich werde ihm auf den Zahn fühlen** (*fig.* 'I shall sound him'): in the pass., **Es ward ihm scharf auf den Zahn gefühlt** (Scheffel); *reflex.* **Danke, ich fühle mich besser** (never **Ich fühle besser!**)—**Ich fühlte mich elend** (Tieck)—**Können Sie sich in meine Lage fühlen?**—**Er fühlte sich in der Dunkelheit nach Hause**; with an accus. and infin. or part., **Ich glaubte, ich fühlte mein Ende herannahen**—**Ich fühlte mich von Schauder ergriffen** (Grillparzer)—**Ich fühle mich geschmeichelt** (see **schmeicheln** 1, and cf. **passive voice** 1. iii)—**Als er aus dem Wagen trat, fühlte er sich umringt, bewillkommt** (W. Alexis)—**Wer zu häufig badet, fühlt seine Nervenkraft erschlaffen, sein Blut überreizt** (Heyse). **2.** There is one important point here: to express our 'It is cold' in the sense of 'It is cold to the touch, feels cold', **sich anfühlen** should be used: e.g. **Seine Hand fühlte sich eisig an** (Gutzkow)—**Sein Hemd fühlte sich feucht an** (Bruno Frank); cf., as a far-fetched example, **Es ist eine Haut, der man Glätte und Kühle mit den Augen anfühlt** (H. Hauser: i.e. You need only look at the skin to see that it is smooth and cool to the touch).

führen, Führung: see **lead** 1 and 2; **accusative (double)** 1 (*b*).

Funken: see **Balken**; cf. **Wir ruderten durch den engen Kanal, in den kaum ein Sonnenfunken herabdrang** (H. Leip).

für: see **vor**.

Furcht: **1.** The two expressions **die Furcht des Todes** and **die Furcht des Kindes** differ fundamentally in that the gen. is *objective* in the former (death is what is feared) and *subjective* in the latter (the child is beset with fear). The objective gen. is permissible where ambiguity is out of the question, as in **die Furcht Gottes**, but is otherwise usually replaced by the prep. **vor** (cf. **fürchten** 1), as in **die Furcht vor Dieben, vor Gespenstern,** etc.; sim. **Ich versuchte, die Furcht des Kindes vor Gewittern zu beruhigen.** Whereas we can talk of a person's 'fears', all the authorities agree that **Furcht** has *no plur.*, and although occasional examples do occur, like **all meine Hoffnungen und Furchten** (Heine) and **Sie vergaß ihre Fürchte und**

Ängste (W. v. Scholz), these are so rare that they are negligible. For a makeshift plur., see **fürchten** 2. **2.** What has been said above applies equally to the compd. **Ehrfurcht** ('awe'): cf. as a rare example of the plur. **Wir halten es für Pflicht, die Sittlichkeit zu üben, wie es die Ehrfurcht vor uns selbst verlangt, welche aus den drei Ehrfurchten entsprießt, zu denen wir uns bekennen** (G., referring to three kinds of self-reverent awe, which he calls the ethnical, the philosophical and the Christian).

fürchten: 1. This verb can be used abs., as in **Wenn ich einmal zu fürchten angefangen, hab' ich zu fürchten aufgehört** (Sch.), but generally requires an obj. (which may be a subord. clause) or the prep. **für** ('to fear *for*' a person): e.g. **Wir Deutschen fürchten Gott, sonst nichts auf der Welt** (Bismarck)—**Seine Wirtin war mürrisch, er fürchtete sie** (H. Kesten)—**Ich fürchte Oranien, und ich fürchte für Egmont** (G.)—**Ich fürchte, wir werden den Zug verpassen**; but much more common than **fürchten** with an accus. obj. is **sich fürchten** with the prep. **vor** (cf. **Furcht** 1): **Sie fürchtet sich zu Tode vor Gewittern** ('She is mortally afraid of thunderstorms'); cf. **Sie war gesund und fürchtete krank zu werden; sie lebte unangefochten und fürchtete sich vor Nachstellungen** (Bergengruen). **2.** The compd. **befürchten** requires an accus. obj. or subord. clause, and generally implies fear of some untoward event or threatening evil: e.g. **Der Arzt befürchtet den baldigen Tod des Patienten** or **daß der Patient bald sterben wird**—„**Glauben Sie, daß er sterben wird?**" „**Das befürchte ich**"—**Es steht zu befürchten, daß das Unternehmen mißlingen wird** ('It is to be feared that the enterprise will fail': see **infinitive** 3 *a*). So also **Was ich befürchtete, ist eingetroffen** ('What I feared has come true'), which might take the form **Meine Befürchtung hat sich verwirklicht**, and it is the plur. of this noun that is used as the plur. of **Furcht** (q.v. 1), which is now only used in the sing.: e.g. **Alle meine Befürchtungen sind eingetroffen.**

fürliebnehmen: see **vor** 1.

Fuß: 1. In ordinary references to a person's 'feet', **Fuß** is inflected in the normal way, as in **Das Kind kann schon auf den Füßen stehen**—fig. **Er steht auf eigenen Füßen** ('He is independent')—**Ich habe mir die Füße wund gelaufen**—**Er warf sich ihr zu Füßen**; but the sing. is used in many idiomatic expressions: e.g. **Sie leben auf großem Fuße** ('They live in style')—**Wir stehen auf vertrautem Fuß mit ihm** ('We are on intimate terms with him')—**Wir kamen trockenen Fußes** ('dryshod') **nach Hause.** The strange expression **stehenden Fußes** (= **sofort**, 'immediately') —see the example from Sch. given under **genitive (adverbial)** 3 (*b*)—is explained by J. Grimm in his *Deutsche Rechtsaltertümer* as being an old legal term applied to an accused person in court, who, if he was dissatisfied with the court's verdict, must object 'then and there', „**zur Stelle, unverwandtes Fußes im Fußstapfen** (*stante pede*)": he quotes a law-book of the 15th century, which states that the objection must be lodged „**unverzogelich** (= **unverzüglich**) **und standes Fußes, e** (= **ehe**) **er hinder sich trede**" (i.e. without delay, before he moves a foot to withdraw), failing which the verdict will stand. The (late?) Latin *stante pede* almost seems to have been adopted as a recognized German phrase meaning 'promptly, at once', in which sense it is not uncommonly used by standard modern authors, as in **Sie sagte, sie habe stante pede dem Gendarmen gesagt, das müsse ein Irrtum sein** (St. Zweig); and certainly, in the corrupt form **stantepeh, it** is a favourite coll. expression in LG. **2.** Used as a measure of twelve inches, it retains its sing. form in the plur. after numerals, but takes the *unmutated* plur. form when used with distrib. force (see **nouns of measure** 1 *a*, and cf. **Zoll**): thus, one says **Die Bretter sind vier Fuß lang,** but **Ich habe die Bretter nach Fußen** (not **Füßen**) **gemessen.** On the other hand, the *mutated* form is used in references to metrical feet: **Der Pentameter hat fünf, der Hexameter sechs Füße.**

G

gang und gäbe: see adjectives (uninflected) 4.

gar: 1. The *adj.* gar, now mainly used in the pred., is the ant. of **roh** in its orig. sense of 'in a raw state' (see **rough** 2), and hence implies that the thing referred to has been subjected to some kind of treatment and is ready for use, as in **Das Metall wird bald gar sein** (G.: i.e. 'ready for casting'). Its commonest application in ordinary lang. is to food, as in **Das Fleisch ist noch nicht gar** ('not done yet', i.e. not properly cooked); sim. **halbgar** ('underdone'). **2.** (a) The *adv.* **gar** was at one time used with the force of 'quite, entirely': where Luther says **Sollen wir denn gar untergehen?** (Num. 17. 13), one would now use **ganz,** strengthened **ganz und gar,** because, although **gar** can modify an adj. or adv., it is no longer used to modify a verb. Thus, one can say **Sie sind ein gar** ('very') **willkommener Gast** and **Ich freue mich gar sehr** ('very much indeed'), but not **Ich freue mich gar.** (b) A proposition like **Ich bin so gar ein armer Mann** (Uhland: where one would now say **Ich bin ein so gar armer Mann**) has led to the compd. **sogar** ('even'), and sometimes **gar** alone is used in this sense: e.g. **Ich heiße Magister, heiße Doktor gar** (G.)—**Sie ist ein Kind von zehn oder gar noch weniger Jahren**; sim. **„Ich finde sie kindlich." „Kindlich? Warum nicht gar kindisch?"** ('Why not go farther and say childish?'). It is an expression like the last one that led to the elliptical exclamation **Warum nicht gar!** implying a strong contradiction: e.g. **„Laß das Kind schlafen, es wird sein letzter Schlaf sein." „Warum nicht gar!"** (Spindler: 'Nothing of the kind! What an idea!' probably contracted from 'Why not even say he is already dead?')—**„Hier handelt es sich um eine Beschmutzung meiner Ehre." „Warum nicht gar!"** (O. Ernst: 'My honour is at stake here.' 'Nonsense! Don't you believe it!'); other neg. expressions of this kind are **I wo!** (see **wo** 1), **Bewahre!** (see **behalten**) and **Behüte!** (see **hüten** 2 *c*). **3.** Esp. common now is the use of **gar** in *neg.* propositions: e.g. **Es ist gar kein Wunder** or **gar nicht zu verwundern, daß er sich gekränkt fühlt**—**Ich kann mir gar nicht denken, was er will** ('For the life of of me I can't think what he wants'); hence distinguish between **nicht gar klug** ('not very clever') and **gar nicht klug** ('not at all clever'). Incidentally, our 'not at all' has a wider application than **gar nicht**: cf. 'Thank you!' 'Not at all!' (**Bitte sehr!**)—'Don't think you're not wanted, not at all!' (**Durchaus nicht!** or **Keineswegs!**): see **überhaupt** 2.

Garbe: see **Getreide** 2.

gären: This is the NHG form of MHG *jesen* ('to ferment': cf. 'yeast'), past tense *jas, jâren,* part. *gejesen.* The modern strong forms are **gōr, gegōren,** reg. used in the lit. sense: **Der Wein hat** (sich) or **ist zu Essig gegoren**; cf., as rare and not to be recommended, its trans. use in **Die Frühlingsnacht gor den Saft im Boden** (Fr. Griese: '. . . caused the sap in the soil to ferment'). Strong forms are also sometimes used with fig. force, as in **Was in ihm gor, verbarg er** (Blunck: 'He did not betray his inward agitation'), but here, in the impers. use, *weak* forms are now almost the rule: e.g. **Es gärt unter dem Volk** ('The people are in a ferment')—**Ein Gemisch von Lebensliebe und Lebensverachtung gärte in ihm** (Auerbach: 'Love and contempt of life vied with each other in his breast')—**Wie es in mir gärte!** (Gutzkow: 'What a turmoil raged within me!')—**Es gärte in ihm von dunklen Schmerzen** (Heyse: 'Vague pains smouldered in his breast')—**Die Seefahrt war bewegt gewesen, und noch gärte in meinem Blut ein schlaftrunkenes Gefühl** (St. Zweig).

gather: see **sammeln.**

Gaul: see **Roß** *ad fin.*

Ge-: The gender of nouns with this prefix can only be learned by experience, as all three genders are abundantly represented. Some which one would expect to have the same gender actually differ: thus, **Gefühl, Gehör** and **Gesicht** are neut., while **Geruch** and **Geschmack** are masc. A few have different meanings according as they are masc. or neut.: see esp. **Gefallen, Gehalt, Gemahl, Gespiele,** and cf. **Gefährt. 1.** The majority of such nouns are *neut.*, many having collect. or verbal force: e.g. in the former class, **Gebein** (see **bone**), **Gebirge, Gefieder,**

Gepäck, Geschrei, Gesträuch (see **Strauch**); in the latter class, **Geflüster, Geheul, Gemurmel, Geplätscher, Geschwätz, Gezwitscher**; see **Gerumpel.** The commonest other neut. nouns are **Gebet, Gebiet, Gebot** (q.v.), **Gedicht, Geleit, Gemälde, Gemüse, Gemüt, Gerät, Geschäft, Geschenk, Geschlecht, Geschöpf, Gesetz, Gespenst, Gewand, Gewicht, Gewitter. 2.** Those ending in **-er** which suggest an agent are *masc.*, such as **Gebieter, Geleiter, Gesellschafter,** and also **Gebrauch, Gedanke, Gehilfe, Gehorsam, Genuß, Gesang, Gewinn. 3.** Those ending in **-in, -heit** and **-keit** are *fem.*, as are also **Gebärde, Gebühr, Geburt, Geduld, Gefahr, Geschichte, Gestalt, Gewalt.**

ge-: 1. The orig. force of this verbal prefix, preserved in English only in archaic words like 'y-clept' (AS *geclypod*), was perfective, indicating the point at which an action or state was completed, or a new state or condition entered into. In MHG, *ge-* could be placed before any part of a simple verb, e.g. before a pres. to give it future force (cf. *des ge-lerne ich vil,* 'By that I shall learn much'), and before a past to give it pluperf. force (cf. *dô ich sanc,* 'While I was singing', and *dô ich ge-sanc,* 'When I had sung'); but even at that period its orig. force was no longer vividly felt, except perhaps in its use with verbs implying an attitude (cf. *sitzen,* 'to be sitting', and *ge-sitzen,* 'to sit down') or when associated with the so-called **past-present verbs** (q.v.). The idea of completion inherent in *ge-* led to its assuming what is now its main function, viz. to mark the *past part.*, that part of a verb which most clearly points to a completed action or state. Several MHG verbs, which in themselves implied the passing from one state, condition, or position to another (notably *komen, vinden,* and *werden*) obviously required no *ge-* in the past part., and such unprefixed forms occur frequently in later periods, esp. in intentionally archaic contexts, in poetry, dialects, etc.: e.g. in the old Christmas hymn **Es ist ein Ros' entsprungen . . . und hat ein Blümlein bracht**; sim. **Ich weiß, der Herr hat Gnade funden vor Saladin** (Lessing, imitating a common expression of Luther's)—**Ich wollt', Ihr wär't eher kommen** (G.)—**Dem Weislingen haben sie das Geleit geben** (G.)—**Wär mein Lieb nur blieben treu, sollte mir nicht bangen** (Mörike). Noteworthy in this connexion is esp. the distinction now observed between **worden** and **geworden** (cf. 2 *a* below, and see **werden** 3). Incidentally, the orig. force of the prefix may still be dimly perceived in some of the simple verbs compounded with **ge-**: e.g. **jemandem gehorchen** ('to hear a person out' and act in accordance with his wishes, i.e. 'to obey') or **gedenken** (either 'to think out completely' and then take action, i.e. 'to make up one's mind, intend', or 'to think completely of' and impress on one's mind, i.e. 'to remember'). **2.** Verbs which do not now take **ge-** in the past part. are: (**a**) **werden,** when used to form the pass. voice; (**b**) those whose first syllable is unaccented (e.g. those compounded with a single insep. prefix) and a number of verbs, mostly Germanized foreign words, some used only in coll. lang., such as **krakeelen** (coll. 'to brawl, kick up a row'), **kredenzen** ('to taste wine' before offering it to some one), **posaunen** ('to play the trombone, noise abroad'), **rumoren** ('to rummage'), **scharmützeln** ('to skirmish'), **spektakeln** ('to make a noise'), **stibitzen** (coll. 'to steal, pinch'), **trompeten** ('to blow the trumpet'); (**c**) those with double prefixes, the second of which is unaccented, e.g. **anerkennen, ausverkaufen**; (**d**) those ending in **-ieren** and **-eien,** even if compounded with a sep. prefix, e.g. **(ein)studieren, (aus)marschieren, prophezeien**; (**e**) the verbs **heißen, lassen,** and **sehen** (qq.v.), when an infin. depends on them in a compd. tense, e.g. **Ich habe ihn kommen sehen. 3.** Some verbs show fluctuation; esp. **frohlocken, offenbaren, überanstrengen, übersiedeln, widerhallen, willfahren,** and those compounded with **miß-** (qq.v.).

gebären: 1. This strong trans. verb, meaning 'to bring forth, give birth to', must not be confused with the weak verbs **gebaren,** more commonly **gebärden,** both used reflex. with the force of 'to behave, conduct oneself', esp. in expressions like **Er gebärdet sich wie toll** (Börne: 'He carries on like a madman'); cf. **trotz seines unwirschen Gebarens** (Auerbach: 'despite his brusque behaviour'). **2.** For 'to be born', see **passive voice** 2 (*b*); cf. **Frau Schmidt ist eine geborene** (abbreviated **geb.**) **Müller** ('*née* Müller')—**Er ist zum Herrscher geboren** ('a born ruler').

Gebein: see **bone.**

geben: **1.** Of the numerous uses of this verb with an accus. obj. only those seem to call for notice here in which we do not use 'to give' in English: some of the commonest of these are **Gas geben** ('to accelerate' a car)—**Karten geben** ('to deal cards')—**jemandem recht geben** ('to admit that a person is right')—**ein Paket auf die Post geben** ('to post a parcel')—**viel auf etwas geben** ('to set great store by something')—**etwas zum besten geben** ('to contribute something [a round of drinks, a story, etc.] by way of entertainment')—**sich zufrieden geben** ('to rest content')—**Der Schmerz wird sich bald geben** ('The pain will soon pass off'). **2.** For **es gibt,** see **es ist** 2; **als** = **'than'** 3; infinitive 3 (*a*).

gebieten: see **befehlen** 3 (*a*).

Gebiß: see **bißchen** 1.

geboren (**sein**): see **gebären** 2; **passive voice** 2 (*b*).

Gebot: The noun **Bot** is no longer used in standard prose, having been superseded by **das Angebot** (see **offer** 2 *a* and *b*). Although the shorter compd. *das* **Gebot** is still used to a limited extent with much the same force, e.g. for a 'bid' at an auction, as in **Ich machte ein Gebot auf 100 Mark, wurde aber überbo'ten,** it is now almost confined in the best prose to the sense of an 'order, injunction' (see **befehlen** 3 *a*). But **Gebot** is stronger than **Befehl** in that it implies an order issued by a person with absolute authority, so precluding the possibility of disobedience: as *Sanders* says, **Gebot ist der Befehl eines Gebietenden, dessen Wille zwingende Gewalt übt,** and this explains why 'the Ten Commandments' are **die zehn Gebote** (not **Befehle**). It has lost some of its force, however, in the common expression **jemandem zu Gebot(e) stehen** (like **zur Verfügung stehen,** 'to be at a person's disposal'): e.g. **Eine solche Geldsumme steht mir augenblicklich nicht zu Gebote** ('I cannot *command* such a large sum of money at the moment')—**Wenn Sie meine Hilfe benötigen, stehe ich** (or **ich stehe**) **Ihnen zu Gebote** ('If you need my help, I am at your service').

geboten: This is the past part. of both **bieten** and **gebieten**: for the former, see **offer** 1 (*a*) and (*b*); for the latter, see **befehlen** 3 (*a*).

Gebrauch, gebräuchlich: see **custom(ary)** 3.

gebrauchen: see **brauchen** 1.

gebrechen: see **lack** (**verb**) 1 (*b*).

gedacht: see **denken** and **gedenken**; also **folgen** 3.

gedenken: **1.** With a *gen.* obj., this verb is used (**a**) in the sense of 'to think of, bear in mind', being rather more formal than the simple verb with **an** (see **denken** 1 *b* and *c*): e.g. **Es ist liebenswürdig von dir, daß du des Freundes Zustand bedenkst, allein erlaube mir dich aufzufordern, auch deiner, auch unser zu gedenken** (G.)—**Gedenke der Stunde, gedenke des Orts!** (Wildenbruch: spoken to a woman in prison about to be burned as a witch)—**Gedenke doch dessen, was du ihr schuldest** (G. Keller)—**Wenn er seines Vaters gedachte, konnte er sich nur auf die Ohrfeige besinnen** (see **remember** 1), **die er einmal von ihm erhielt** (R. v. Gottschall); for the *pass.* of such propositions, see **impersonal verbs** 3. So also the verbal noun **Gedenken,** as in **Behalten Sie mich in freundlichem Gedenken** (or more usually **Angedenken**: 'Keep me in kindly remembrance'), but esp. in **seit Menschengedenken** ('in living memory, since time immemorial'); (**b**) like **erwähnen,** with the force of 'to mention': e.g. **Er gedachte meiner mit keiner Silbe** ('He never once alluded to me')—**Mit keiner Silbe wurde daran erinnert** (see **remember** 3 *a*), **daß er als Gefangener hier saß, auch seines vergangenen Schicksals gedachte niemand** (Bruno Frank); so also in the expression **nicht zu gedenken,** as in **Er wurde des Diebstahls verklagt, anderer Vergehen nicht zu gedenken** ('He was accused of theft, not to mention other misdemeanours'). Here belongs also the past part. **gedacht,** used as an attrib. adj. in the sense of 'afore-said, above-mentioned', for which see **folgen** 3. **2.** With a *dat.* of the person and an *accus.* of the thing, it has the force of 'to bear some one a grudge for something': e.g. **Diese beleidigende Behandlung werde ich ihm gedenken** ('I'll not forget the insulting way he has treated me')—**Das gedenk' ich dir!** ('I'll pay you back for that!'). **3.** With **zu** + infin., it is used like **vorhaben** or **beabsichtigen** ('to intend'): **Wann gedenken Sie abzureisen?**—**Den nächsten Morgen gedachte er Melina zu besuchen** (G.).

gedrängt, gedrungen: see **drängen** 3.

gedulden: see **dulden** 1.

Gefahr: The prep. 'at' in a phrase like 'at one's own risk' is expressed by **auf** (+accus.), and 'at the risk of doing something' is **auf die Gefahr hin, etwas zu tun**: e.g. **Er tat es auf eigne Gefahr—Ich sagte ihm meine Meinung auf die Gefahr hin, ihn zu beleidigen**; but where the subjs. are different, **Ich tat es auf die Gefahr hin, daß er sich beleidigt fühlen würde.** 'To run a risk' is **Gefahr laufen** (aux. **haben**): e.g. **Ich hätte Gefahr gelaufen, mich zu verschnappen** (Lessing: 'I should have run the risk of letting the cat out of the bag'); see **risk.**

Gefährt: Distinguish between **das Gefährt** (strong, plur. **Gefährte**), meaning 'vehicle', and **der Gefährte** (weak, gen. and plur. **Gefährten**), meaning 'companion'.

Gefallen: Distinguish between **der Gefallen,** as in **Wollen Sie mir einen Gefallen tun?** ('Will you do me a favour?'), and **das Gefallen,** as in **An solchen Dingen finde ich kein Gefallen** ('I take no pleasure in such things').

gefallen: This verb means 'to please' (+ *dat.*), as in **Die Aufnahme, die ich fand, hat mir sehr gefallen** ('I was very pleased with the reception I got')—**Tun Sie, wie es Ihnen gefällt** ('Do as you please'). With a pers. subj., it usually suggests, not pleasure, but fondness (see below): a proposition like 'You would please me if you accepted my invitation' is best rendered by **Sie würden mir einen Gefallen** (q.v.) **tun** or **mir eine Freude bereiten, wenn Sie meine Einladung annähmen.** A question which a student might naturally ask himself is: How did a compd. of **fallen** come to have the force of 'to please'? It seems probable that it was orig. taken from throwing dice, an expression like **Es gefiel mir gut** having the force of 'The dice fell favourably for me', which naturally pleased me; cf. the MHG *wünschet daz mir heil gevalle* (Walther: 'Wish me that salvation may be my lot'). The commonest English way to express the verb is by using 'to like' (q.v. 1 *b*), as in **Das Mädchen gefällt mir** ('I like the girl')—**Wie gefällt Ihnen diese Musik?** to which the reply might be **Sie gefällt mir nicht übel** ('I rather like it *or* I can't say I dislike it': see **mißfallen** under **miß-** 5); so also the expression **sich** (dat.) **etwas gefallen lassen,** as in **Ew. Majestät wolle sich gnädigst gefallen lassen, mir einen Adelsbrief zu geben** (Thümmel: 'May it please your Majesty to raise me to the nobility by letters patent'), which led to the ordinary modern use in the sense of 'to put up with something': e.g. **Er ist gutmütig und läßt sich alles gefallen** ('He is easy-going and will put up with anything')—**Eine solche Behandlung lasse ich mir nicht gefallen** ('I'll not stand such treatment').

geflissentlich: see **befleiß(ig)en.**

gegen: The MHG prep. *gegen* (contracted into *gein,* then weakened to *gen,* the latter very common in early NHG, esp. before place-names, as in **gen Jericho**) was mainly used in the sense of 'towards', and nearly always with a *dat.,* while 'against' was usually expressed by *wider,* which took an *accus.* A dat. after **gegen** is now obs., but survived even to the classical period: cf. **Ihr werdet gegen der Menge wenig sein** (G.). In MHG, then, *er kom gegen mir* meant 'He came towards me *or* to meet me', where one now says **Er kam auf mich zu** ('towards me') and **Er kam mir entgegen** ('to meet me'). Here **entgegen** is a sep. prefix, but it is also used as an independent prep. (placed either after or—more usually—before the dat., thus differing from **gegenüber,** q.v.) in the sense of 'against, contrary to', so it is important to distinguish between **Er ist entgegen meinen Wünschen gekommen** ('He has come contrary to my wishes') and **Er ist meinen Wünschen auf halbem Wege entgegengekommen** ('He has met my wishes half-way').

Gegenteil: see **Teil** 2 (*b*).

gegenüber: This word, meaning 'opposite', can be used as an *adv.,* as in **Er wohnt in dem Hause gegenüber** ('across the street'), but even then it is really a *prep.,* the word it governs being understood. The latter, when expressed, now always stands in the *dat.,* and may follow, but far more commonly precedes, the prep., necessarily so if it is a pron. The dat. is fixed even with verbs implying motion: one says not only **Er saß mir gegenüber,** but also **Er setzte sich mir gegenüber**; sim. **Man stelle die Zeugen mir gegenüber!** (Sch.: 'Let the witnesses be brought before me face to face!'). Formerly the dat. was often inserted between **gegen** and **über,** indeed, some authors in the classical period, esp. Goethe, did this almost regularly: e.g. **Der Vetter saß gegen uns über—Der Platz des neuen Hauses, gegen dem Schloß über, wurde gebilligt—Sie wagten nicht, einander anzusehen, ob sie gleich gegen einander über standen,** now ordinarily **obgleich sie sich gegenüberstanden** (for the past subj. of **gegenüberstehen,** see **past subjunctive** 2 *c*). This separation of the two parts is now avoided in the lang. of the north, but that it is not obs. can be seen from a recent southern example like **Man setzte das Mädchen gegen dem Grafen über** (Rilke). Sometimes **gegenüber von** is used, esp. before place-names: instead of **Mannheim gegenüber** ('across the river from Mannheim') one can say **zu Oggersheim, gegenüber von Mannheim** (Hebel). With more fig. force, it is used in the sense of 'to(wards)', as in **Ihr gegenüber ist er immer höflich** and **Er äußerte sich mir gegenüber da'hin, daß ihm die moderne Musik verhaßt sei** ('He gave me it as his opinion that modern music was odious'). Noteworthy is its use as a neut. subst., now rarely of things, as in **Die Sonne erleuchtete das Gegenüber** (G.: 'The sun lit up the land-scape across the valley'), but commonly of a person standing or sitting opposite one, one's *vis-à-vis*: e.g. **Er forschte nach dem Eindruck, den er auf sein Gegenüber hervorbringen würde** (Gutzkow).

Gegenwart, gegenwärtig: see **presence** 3; cf. **-wärts** 2 and **gewärtig(en)** *ad fin.*

Gehalt: 1. As a *masc.* noun (cf. 2), this is much like **der Inhalt,** but while the latter is mostly used of the 'contents' of a parcel, a volume, etc., as in **ein kurzer Inhalt eines Romans** ('a short summary of a novel'), **Gehalt** properly suggests the 'content' or 'proportion' of an ingredient, as we speak of the sugar 'content' of milk: cf. **Diese Münzen haben einen geringen Gehalt an Silber.** Then **Gehalt** is often used *fig.* of that part of a thing which gives it its intrinsic value, the 'substance' or 'inner qualities' as distinct from the 'form' or 'outward appearance': e.g. **Die meisten Leute achten mehr auf das Äußere als auf den Gehalt—Der Gehalt des Lebens bestimmt seinen Wert** (Sch.). **2.** The other meaning of **Gehalt** is 'pay, salary', and in this sense it was formerly also masc., as in **Er hat 600 Reichstaler jährlichen Gehalt** (Lessing)—indeed, the south still prefers the masc.: cf. **Der kleine Witwengehalt reichte gerade zu dem Kleiderbedarf hin** (G. Keller) and **Ich hoffte, Sie würden einen erhöhten Gehalt verlangen** (M. Eyth); but in the north it is now almost always *neut.*: **Man hat mir ein höheres Gehalt bewilligt.**

gehen: The MHG infin. of this verb was *gân* or *gên*, the former earlier form being contracted from *gangen* (Scots 'gang'), so that it is really one of the **reduplicating verbs** (q.v. 2); the historically correct past tense **gieng** has now been replaced by the LG **ging. 1.** As with other common verbs of motion (see **laufen, reiten**), so also with **gehen** the normal aux. is **sein,** as in **Diesen Weg** (adv. accus.) **bin ich oft gegangen**; but **haben** is correct in the trans. use in propositions like **Ich habe mich lahm gegangen** ('I am lame from walking'); cf. **Er klagte, daß er sich** (dat.) **Blasen unter die Füße gegangen** (Heine: '. . . that he had raised blisters on the soles of his feet with walking', **habe** being understood). Sometimes **haben** is also used in the north where the verb loses its local force, e.g. with the impers. **es geht,** as in **Es hat gut gegangen** (Viebig: 'Things have gone *or* passed off well'). **2.** Where we say 'The old man came hobbling up the street', a German says **Der Alte kam die Straße heraufgehumpelt** (see **kommen** 4). Strangely enough, this use of a past part. does not apply to **gehen**: cf. **Er ging humpelnd die Straße hinauf**; but a past part. is correct where it implies a condition or state, not a mode of progression, as in **Er ging gebückt** ('bent with age') **die Treppe hinauf** or **Er ging zerlumpt** ('clothed in rags') **die Dorfstraße entlang.** In a few set expressions an infin. without **zu** is used where the emphasis lies not so much on **gehen** as on the idea expressed in the infin.: e.g. **Bei schönem Wetter gehe ich morgens spazieren—Seine Brüder sind Schlittschuh laufen gegangen, er aber liegt in seinem Bette, denn er muß frühe schlafen gehen** (Sudermann)—**Ach, könnt' ich betteln gehen über die braune Heid'!** (Storm)—**Sie ging einige Besorgungen machen** (Zuckmayer)—**Sie ging zu einer Nachbarin schwatzen** (C. Busse)—**Der Doktor war einen Kranken besuchen gegangen** (W. Kramp). **3.** Noteworthy is the *impers. pass.* use of **gehen** when the subj. is not a specific one or is left vague: just as one says **Es wird getanzt** ('Dancing is going on' or, on an invitation card, 'There will be dancing') and **Andern Morgens wurde spät aufgestanden** ('Next morning everybody rose late'), so also **Mit den Hühnern wurde zu Bett gegangen** (Polenz: 'The family retired to bed in the early hours', cf. 'at cock-crow')—**Es wurde zu Tisch gegangen** (id.: 'The company went in to dinner'). **4.** See **open** 3 (*b*).

gehorchen: see **obey**; cf. **gehören**.

gehören: **1.** The basic force of this verb is 'to belong to, be the rightful possession of' somebody. How a compound of **hören** came to have this meaning may be seen by considering the analogous **gehorchen**: a bondman (**ein Höriger**) really belonged to, was one of, the chattels of his superior and had to 'listen to' and 'obey' his orders. With this force, **gehören** takes a *dat.* case: e.g. **„Wem gehört dies Buch?" „Meinem Bruder."** At one time the dat. of a pers. pron. might be replaced by the corresponding poss. pron., as in **Alle die Konturen, die er zeichnet, gehören mein** (G.), but this use is now confined to a few dialects and is avoided in good prose.—A closer and more intimate connexion is implied in the double compound **angehören,** used esp. of persons: e.g. **Verkünde der Geliebten, daß ich ihr ewig angehöre!** (G.)—**Ich bin dein Kaiser: mir angehören ist deine Ehre** (Sch.). **2.** (**a**) The bondman referred to above was only *one* of his overlord's possessions; and **gehören** soon developed the subsidiary meaning of 'to be part of' a larger whole, in which sense it requires the prep. **zu**: e.g. **Er gehört nicht zu uns** ('He is not one of our party')—**Brahms gehört zu den größten deutschen Komponisten—Dieses Geschlecht gehörte zu den besten des Landes** (Ranke)—**Der Judenhaß gehörte zum guten Tone** (Treitschke: 'Hatred of the Jews was one of the marks of good breeding'); cf. the reflex. **Das gehört sich nicht** ('That is unseemly'), and the adj. **gehörig,** as in **Der Fensterladen klapperte im Winde, weil er nicht gehörig befestigt war** (Hebbel: 'The shutter rattled in the wind because it had not been fastened properly'). (**b**) Analogous is the use of **gehören** with other preps. to suggest that somebody or something properly belongs to a certain class and therefore ought to be incorporated in it: e.g. **Dieser Dieb gehört ins Gefängnis** ('This thief should be imprisoned')—**Der Trauring gehört an den dritten Finger—Dieser Schuh gehört an den rechten Fuß—„Wohin gehört dieses Buch?" „In das oberste Fach"** ('Where does this book go?' 'On the top shelf'). The prep. phrase here may be replaced idiomatically by a past part.: e.g. **Er gehört geschlagen** (B. Kellermann: 'He ought *or* deserves to be thrashed')—**Ich wüßte noch mehr Fenster in hiesiger Stadt, die eingeworfen gehören** (A. Schieber: 'I could tell you of other windows in this town which ought to be smashed in').

gehorsamen: see **obey.**

gelahrt: This alternative form of the past part. of **lehren** has historic foundation: beside the normal MHG forms *lêrte, gelêr*(*e*)*t,* there arose in the north the forms *lârte, gelârt.* While the past tense with the stem-vowel **a** is quite obs., the past part. **gelahrt** is still in use, although not in the verbal sense of 'taught' (cf. **lehren** 1 *ad fin.*). In the MHG period a person was *gelêrt* if he could read and write; in NHG **ein Gelehrter** is 'a learned person, a scholar'. So also **gelahrt** is used, often with the prefix **hoch-**, in the sense of 'learned, scholarly', but this use is now practically confined to rather supercilious or contemptuous references to the 'intellectuals': e.g. **Träume sind Schäume** (prov. 'Dreams are mere froth *or* empty shadows'), **mögen auch die hochgelahrten Herren davon halten, was sie wollen** (Novalis); cf. **Die Gelahrtheit läßt sich ohne Pedanterie nicht denken** (G.).

gelangen: There are three important points to be noted in connexion with this compd. of **langen** (q.v.): (*a*) it is a *weak* verb, so its past tense **gelangte** must not be confused with **gelang** (from **gelingen**); (*b*) it is *intrans.*, and hence requires a prep. phrase to complete its sense (usually **an, in** or **nach** in the lit. sense, **zu** in the fig. sense); and (*c*) contrasted with **anlangen** (q.v.), it implies the *action* of reaching a spot, not the state after the spot is reached. The following examples illustrate these points: **Wir gelangten an unser Ziel—Es gelang uns, in das vom Feinde umringte Dorf zu gelangen—Der verlorene Ring ist wieder in meinen Besitz gelangt—Endlich gelangte ich nach Hause** (not **zu Hause**, but cf. **Ich langte zu Hause an**)—**Abends gelangte ich nach Paris** (not **an** or **in** with place-names which have no art.)—**Ich bin zu der Überzeugung gelangt** ('I have become convinced'), **daß der Plan unausführbar ist—Der Plan gelangte leider nicht zur Ausführung** ('Unfortunately, the plan failed of execution')—**Er ist zu hohen Ehren gelangt** ('He has attained to high honours': cf. **erlangen**).

Gelaß: see **room 6.**

gelb: For the subst. use of this adj., see colour, and cf. **das Gelbe im Ei** or **das Eigelb** (= **der** or **das Dotter**, 'the yolk of an egg': see **weiß**). The adj. is used coll. in propositions like **Sie war gelb vor Neid** (we say 'She was green with envy') and **Es wurde mir grün und gelb vor den Augen** ('I felt giddy, My head was going round').

Geld: In ordinary lang. this noun, like our 'money', is only used in the sing., the plur. being used much like our 'funds', esp. with attrib. adjs., as in **ausstehende und eingehende Gelder** ('monies owed and owing') and **Staats-** or **öffentliche Gelder** ('public funds'); but our coll. 'to be in funds' is **bei Gelde sein**. For the gen. sing. in **eine Summe** or **ein Haufen Geldes**, see genitive of material 2 (*b*).

gelegen, gelegentlich: see **liegen** 4.

Geleit, geleiten: see lead 4.

gelernt: see **lernen** 2.

gelingen ('to succeed, be successful', with *strong* forms: **gelang, gelungen**): This verb is only used with an *impersonal* subj., a *dative* of the person, and the aux. **sein:** one says not only **Es ist ihm gelungen, den Berg zu ersteigen**, but also **Der Versuch, den Berg zu ersteigen, ist ihm gelungen**; and sim. **Sein gelungener Versuch, den Berg zu ersteigen, hat mich erfreut.** So also its opposite **mißlingen,** for which see **mißfallen,** 2 (*a*).

geloben: see promise 2.

gelten: 1. (a) The fundamental force of this verb is 'to be worth, have a certain value', as in **Dieser Bankschein gilt 20 Mark.** The following examples illustrate other shades of meaning: **Dieser Fahrschein gilt nicht mehr** or **ist nicht mehr gültig** ('is no longer valid')—**Was gilt die Wette?** ('How much do you bet?')—**Es gilt!** ('Agreed! Done!')—**Eine solche Entschuldigung lasse ich nicht gelten** ('I can't accept that sort of excuse')—**Galt diese Bemerkung mir?** ('Was that remark meant for me?')—**Er hat immer als mustergültiger** (or **für einen mustergültigen**) **Schriftsteller gegolten** ('He has always been reckoned to be a standard author')—**Es galt, ihn zu überzeugen** ('It was a case of trying to convince him'). **(b)** According to *Duden*, the past subj. of **gelten** is **„gölte (jetzt auch: gälte)"**: see **Ablaut** 2 (*c*). Actually, there is no objection to the form **gälte** in propositions like **Sie blieb unbeweglich sitzen, als gälte alles, was er sagte, nicht ihr** (Heyse) and **Mit schwerem Herzen hatte sie von ihm Abschied genommen, als gälte es einer langen Trennung** (Ompteda), because even if these words were spoken or read out, it would not matter if the listener took **gälte** to be the pres. subj. **gelte.** But the forms with **ä** should not be used where there might be confusion with the pres. *indic.*, as in **Man behandelte sie, als ob sie für Verbrecher gölten** (not **gälten,** which would sound the same as the indic. **gelten**). **2.** Of special interest is the expression **geltend machen,** almost the only example in common use of a *pres.* part. in the accus. and part. construction (q.v.), which is used either with certain impers. nouns or with a reflex. pron. as obj. Thus, **Er machte seinen Einfluß geltend** means 'He exerted his influence, brought his authority to bear'; and sim. with objs. like **Anspruch** ('to assert a claim'), **Gesetz** ('to enforce a law'), **Ansicht** ('to urge an opinion'); cf. **Er macht sein Recht an die Krone geltend** (Wieland: 'He vindicates his right to the crown')—**Wer ist so gebildet, daß er nicht seine Vorzüge gegen andere geltend machte?** (G.). The infin. form here, as in **Der Meister hatte sein Vermögen auf alle mögliche Weise gelten gemacht** (G.), is now hardly used at all. So also **sich geltend machen,** with a pers. subj., is 'to assert oneself', with an impers. subj. 'to make itself felt': e.g. **Ich fühlte das Alter sich bei mir geltend machen** ('I felt old age beginning to tell on me').

gelüsten: This verb, meaning 'to covet, have a craving for' something, has practically displaced the simple verb **lüsten,** and a proposition like **Ich verharrte im Hause und lüstete nicht ins Freie** (G. Keller: '. . . felt not the least desire to go out') has a decidedly archaic flavour; and indeed even **gelüsten** is a choice expression, hardly used in every-day prose. It is now almost confined to the *impers.* use, the obj. being expressed by the prep. **nach** or by an infin. with **zu:** e.g. **Es gelüstete ihn nach Ruhm—Es gelüstete ihn (danach), Ruhm zu ernten.** Formerly a gen. obj. was quite common, as in **Laß dich nicht gelüsten deines Nächsten Hauses** (Exod. 20. 17), but this is contrary to modern usage, not only because of the gen. obj. **Hauses,** but esp. because a gen. can now never be preceded by a *Saxon genitive* (q.v., and cf. **von** 1 *a*); one would now, therefore, have to say **nach**

deines Nächsten Hause. Sometimes a dat. of the person is used, as in **Es gelüstete ihm, ihr ein Zeichen zu geben** (W. Schäfer), but the accus. is the recognized case. In this connexion see **verlangen.**

Gemach: see **room** 5.

Gemahl: In the sense of 'husband', this is naturally a *masc.* noun; its use as a *neut.* in the sense of 'wife' (= **Gemahlin**) is confined to the lang. of poetry: cf. **Auf dem Throne sitzen der König und sein Gemahl** (Uhland).

gemein(sam): 1. The adj. **gemein** (Lat. *communis*) is properly used of what is 'common' to one or more individuals, classes, etc., as in **nichts miteinander gemein haben** ('to have nothing in common') or **gemeine Sache mit jemandem machen** ('to make common cause with some one'); so also **das gemeine Wohl** ('the common weal'), where, however, as the idea is common to all, **allgemein** would be more appropriate. **2.** But **gemein** underwent the same deterioration as 'common' (or as **schlecht:** see **bad** 1): what is common to all becomes 'ordinary', so that **gemein** came to be much like **gewöhnlich** (cf. **accustomed** 4): e.g. **der gemeine Mann** ('the man in the street')—**im gemeinen Leben** ('in every-day life')—**ein gemeiner Soldat** or **ein Gemeiner** ('a private')—**das Haus der Gemeinen** or **das Unterhaus** ('the House of Commons'); cf. the neg. **ungemein** ('uncommon'), used esp. adv. in the sense of 'exceedingly', as in **Er ist ungemein reich** or **Es freut mich ungemein, das zu hören.** From the idea of 'ordinary' it was a short step to that of 'vulgar, low': **ein gemeiner Kerl** ('a blackguard')—**ein gemeiner Verbrecher** ('a low criminal'). It is mainly in order to obviate the possibility of any misunderstanding that, to express the idea of 'in common' as explained under 1, the form **gemeinsam** is often preferred: cf. the example from C. F. Meyer given under **zwei** 2 (*b*).

Gemisch: see **mix(ture)** 2 (*b*).

Gemüt: This word has no equivalent in English, and the same applies, of course, to the adj. **gemütlich** (see **comfortable** 3). Our nearest approach to it is the expression 'heart and soul', suggesting a person's feelings, disposition, character, etc., reflecting his whole personality and determining his actions. When Egmont says of the Duke of Alba **Er hat kein Gemüt gegen uns Niederländer,** he means that the sentiments which the Duke entertains towards the Dutch are antagonistic because he cannot feel with them, because his whole outlook differs from theirs, because his heart is steeled against them. Sim. **Wir sind ein Herz und ein Gemüt** (Sch.: i.e. We have the same sentiments, feelings and outlook towards our fellow men).

genannt: see **folgen** 3.

genießen: The orig. *gen.* construction was common down to recent times and is still used in a rather elevated style: e.g. **Laß mich der neuen Freiheit genießen!** (Sch.)—**Schlaft wohl, genießt einer erquickenden Ruhe!** (Stifter)—**Er genoß mehr eines geschäftlichen als eines persönlichen Ansehens** (Fontane)—**Geld ausgeben zu dürfen, war ihm ein lang ersehntes Vergnügen, dessen er jetzt schwelgerisch genoß** (H. Hesse)—**Wir setzten unsere Fahrt nach Ettal fort, das wegen seiner Abtei eines guten architektonischen Rufs genießt** (Th. Mann). But even in the classical period the *accus.* was not rare, and this has now practically displaced the gen. in ordinary lang. (cf. **genitive** 2): e.g. **Abends nahm ich mir vor, den Sonnenaufgang zu genießen** (G.)—**Ich beschloß, da ich diese Ansicht genossen hatte, noch höher zu steigen** (Stifter); in particular, the accus. is always used when the obj. is food or drink. While the MHG *geniezen* always took a gen., the simple verb *niezen* (now obs.) took an accus. of the person, meaning 'to be of use to': an expression like *ez sol mich niezen* would now take the form **Es wird mir Nutzen bringen** or **von Nutzen sein.**

genitive: The inflexional gen. is still in common use not only after many prepositions (cf. 6 below), but also in expressions like **der Sohn des Arztes** ('gen. of origin'), **das Haus meines Onkels** ('possessive gen.')—see **genitive (possessive)**—**der Gesang der Vögel** ('subjective gen.') and **die Errichtung des Denkmals** ('objective gen.'); but even so, there is ample evidence that the inflexional gen. has long been in a state of gradual decline—the man in the street generally favours the use of the prep. **von** (q.v. 1), which is often necessary in the best prose style also, as in **der Verkauf von vier Gemälden** (see 1). The following points are noteworthy as evidence of the decline referred to: **1.** Axiomatic in good modern German is the avoidance of a gen. form which might be another case. Thus, MHG *allez* (nom. and accus.) and *alles* (gen.) having both become **alles,** modern usage frowns upon the use of this form as a gen. unless it is modified in some way to make the case clear. It is for this reason that in a proposition like **Dank für Ihre lebendige Beschreibung alles, was Sie umgibt** (G., in a letter of September 1775 to Auguste v. Stolberg), modern usage demands **alles dessen, was Sie umgibt;** and sim. the forms **einiges, manches, vieles,** etc. cannot be used as gen. when standing alone—cf. **Sollen das Worte eines sein, der nicht weiß, was er spricht?** (Immermann), where one would now say **eines Mannes** or **Menschen.** For the same reason it is strictly incorrect to say **jenseit mancherlei Gewässer** (H. Franck), which would be correct if the suffix **-lei** (q.v.) were omitted, and **während Monate tiefster innerer Glaubenszerrüttung** (id.), where **während einiger Monate** would be an obvious improvement. **2.** In MHG the gen. was quite established as the obj. of many verbs and adjectives. Typical examples are *wünschen* and *gewon* (now **gewohnt:** see **accustomed**), and when we now say **Ich wünsche es** or **Ich bin es gewohnt,** we are actually using the MHG idiom, only that we no longer regard **es** here as the gen. which it orig. was, but treat it as an accus. (see **es** 1 and 2); and hence we say **Ich wünsche das, bin das gewohnt,** where the MHG gen. *des* was quite fixed. While **wünschen** now only takes an accus., most verbs in this class still take a gen. in poetry and choice prose but an accus. in ordinary language; and much the same applies to the adjectives, only that in their case the old gen. is often replaced by a prep. phrase (**frei von Schuld, reich an Gütern, unschuldig am Morde**). The commonest words of this kind which retain the old gen. in elevated style, but take an accus. in ordinary prose, are: (*verbs*) **bedürfen, begehren, brauchen, entbehren, erwähnen, genießen, gewahren, pflegen, spielen, vergessen, wahrnehmen;** (*adjs.*) **ansichtig, fähig, gewahr, gewohnt, los, müde, satt, überdrüssig, wert.** Most of these words are discussed under their respective heads. **3.** MHG nouns which depended on other nouns denoting quantity, measure or kind stood in the gen. Where we now ordinarily say **ein Stück Brot, ein Haufen Holz, eine ArtTagebuch, etc.,** the uninflected dependent noun has replaced the old gen. (see **genitive of material**). **4.** A gen. after adjs. like **lang, hoch, tief, alt,** etc. is now practically obs. (see **genitive of measure**). **5.** When we say **etwas Gutes, nichts Wichtiges, viel Schönes,** etc., we are also using the old gen. construction, but we now treat such expressions as *appositional* and say **mit etwas Schönem,** etc. (see **nichts** 2). **6.** The old gen. has resisted change most stubbornly after the majority of preps., but even here other cases have crept in, esp. after **dank, entlang** and **längs, gemäß, ob,** and **zunächst** (qq.v.). **7.** For other important points in connexion with the gen., see **als = 'as'** 1 (*c*); **passive voice** 1 (ii); **Proper names** 2; **viel** 1 (*a*)–(*d*); **von** 1 (*c*) and 3; **zwei** 2 (*a*).

genitive (adverbial): 1. *Adv. expressions of place:* e.g. **Unser Haus ist das zweite linker Hand—Halben Weges zwischen B. und O. trat er auf den eine Schräglinie bildenden Fahrweg** (Fontane: see **halb** 2 *a* and **unterdessen**)—**Es finden sich aller Orten und Enden** ('here, there and everywhere') **herrliche Sachen** (here 'pictures'), **von denen nicht viel Redens ist** (G.: for the gen. **Redens,** see **viel** 1 *a*); sim. in official lang., **Das ist höheren** or **geeigneten Orts gemeldet worden** ('That has been reported to a higher *or* to the proper authority'). **2.** *Adv. expressions of time* (indef. or recurrent time, or the period of time between def. limits): e.g. **Eine Frau von ausgangs vierzig stand vor ihr** (Fontane: 'A woman of close on fifty stood before her'—cf. **entrance,** *ad fin.*)—**Ich schicke dir dieser Tage** ('one of these days') **meine Tragödien** (Heine)—**Ich habe mich verlobt, nächster Tage** ('in a few days') **ist die Hochzeit** (Wildenbruch)—**Für tagsüber hat er den Sportanzug** (E. Kästner: 'For day-wear he has his sports suit'), in which sense **untertags** is used in the south: see **unterdessen** *ad fin.*—**Bei schönem Wetter gehe ich abends spazieren;** sim. **morgens, vormittags, nachts** (see **Nacht**)—**Man hatte unsere Zusammenkünfte seit Jahren sonntags fortgesetzt** (G.)—**Ich habe einen Freund, einen lahmen Mann, der seinen Stuhl winters wie sommers hart am Fenster hat** (Rilke), but usually **im Herbst,** the adv. form **herbstens** being mainly used in poetry. Of course, def. and indef. time may approach each other more or less closely, 'this day' or 'the same day' being obviously more def. than 'some day': hence **eines Tages**, but **diesen Tag, denselben Abend**; cf., as unusual, **Am folgenden Tage** (which might have taken the form tags **darauf** or **andern Tages**) **überschritten sie die Paßhöhe und gelangten desselben Abends ins Tal** (E. Zahn)—**Jedes Tages** (for **Jeden Tag**) **begab sie sich zu den Karmelitern, um die Frühmesse zu hören** (E. T. A. Hoffmann). **3.** *Adv. expressions of manner*: **(a)** e.g. **Sie befragten sich des genauesten** (or **aufs genaueste**, 'in the most searching manner') **nach unseren Umständen** (G. Keller)—**Meine Reiseerlebnisse werde ich Dir später des näheren** ('more in detail') **berichten** (C. F. Meyer)—**Ich habe es euch schon eines** (usually **des**) **öftern** ('repeatedly') **bewiesen** (id.)—**Sein Vater verlangte allen Ernstes** ('in all seriousness'), **daß er sich entscheiden sollte** (E. Wichert). Here belong also the numerous advs. ending in **-weise** and **-maßen,** which were orig. written as two words: e.g. **begreiflicher-, glücklicher-, natürlicher-, unnötigerweise—bekannter-, einiger-, folgendermaßen** (cf. **Maß** *c*). **(b)** Idiomatic here is the adv. use of the gen. of a sing. noun modified by an attrib. adj.: e.g. **Ich kam unverrichteter Sache zurück** ('I returned without effecting my purpose') —**Der Kerl fährt erster Klasse, als ob er was Besseres wäre wie wir** (Ompteda). This use is esp. common in the case of masc. and neut. nouns denoting parts of the body, corresponding to our 'with bowed head', 'with blazing eyes', 'with tottering steps', etc.: e.g. **Nach Uri fahr' ich stehenden Fußes** (Sch.: 'at once, forthwith')—**Der Alte zog den Kahn gegen das Land, damit Victor trockenen Fußes** ('dryshod') **aussteigen konnte** (Stifter)—**Klopfenden Herzens rannte sie die Stufen hinauf** (Binding)—**Sie wandelte gesenkten Hauptes durch den Garten** (id.)—**Sie sprach zurückgelegten Hauptes mit Zorn** (Th. Mann: 'She spoke in anger, her head thrown back')—**Barfuß und bloßen Hauptes zog er im Dorfe ein** (Waggerl)—**Schwankenden Ganges kam er daher** (Wildenbruch)—**Johannes wandte sich ihm bittenden Auges zu** (W. Schäfer)—**Offenen Mundes wies er auf ein zweistöckiges Gebäude** (Bruno Frank)—**Gereckten Halses** ('With craned necks') **stellten sich die Bürger auf die Zehen** (id.) —**Der Marschall führte ihn raschen Schrittes in das zweite Stock** (Werfel). Here belongs also the expression **seines Zeichens,** to indicate a person's trade, profession, etc. (cf. **Kennzeichen**): e.g. **Er ist seines Zeichens ein Fuhrmann** (Hackländer: 'He is a carter *or* carrier by trade') —**Es ist mein Freund Monsieur Tourbillon, seines Zeichens** ('by profession') **ein französischer Sprachlehrer** (Raabe)—**Mein Unteroffizier ist seines Zeichens Studienrat** (B. E. Werner). **(c)** The adv. use of the gen. is very common in the pred., esp. after **sein**: e.g. **Mein Freund und ich sind gleichen Alters** ('of the same age')—**Ich bin entgegengesetzter Meinung** ('of the opposite opinion')—**Er war damals vorzüglicher Dinge** ('in capital spirits': see **Ding** I) . . . **Er war, sage ich, damals aufgeräumt** (Th. Mann)—**Er war schlechter Laune** ('in a bad mood')—**Beim Unterricht war er langsamen und abgewandten Geistes** (Th. Mann: 'During lessons he was slow and inattentive')—**Du bist des Todes** ('You are doomed, a dead man')—**Er gilt ärztlich nicht für ersten Ranges** (Fontane: 'As a medico he is not thought to be at the top of his profession').

genitive of material, time, etc.: 1. A MHG noun depending on another noun denoting quantity, measure or kind stood in the *gen.*: e.g. *ein stücke tuoches* ('a piece of cloth'), *ein trunc wazzers* ('a draught of water'), *ein leip brôtes* ('a loaf of bread'); sim. with weak fem. and all plur. nouns: *ein phunt wollen* ('a pound of wool'), *ein stranc sîden* ('a skein of silk'), *ein houfe buoche* ('a pile of books'). NHG unmodified fem. or plur. nouns have no distinctive gen. ending, so when, retaining the old idiom, we say **ein Stück Seife, ein Pfund Wolle, ein Strang Seide, ein Haufen Bücher,** we treat the construction as **appositional**, and extend this use to masc. and neut. sing. nouns also: **Geben Sie mir ein Stück Brot und ein Glas Wasser!—Auf einmal hörte sie das Getrappel von einer Herde Schafe** (Brentano)—**Ein warmer Tag schmolz die letzten Reste Schnee und Eis hinweg** (Mörike)—**Er setzte sich mit dem Paket Briefe aufs Sofa** (Storm)—**Er lief mit einem Paar Schuhe unter dem Arm durch die Gassen** (Jul. Wolff)—**Er wurde zu fünf Jahren Zuchthaus verurteilt** ('Sudermann: 'He was condemned to five years penal servitude'). **2. (a)** But the inflected gen. of unmodified masc. and neut. sing. nouns is surprisingly common in modern authors and would seem to be on the increase. Still, it is significant that such gens. are never used in the spoken lang. —no one would ask for **ein Glas Wassers** —and examples like the following, most of which are from ordinary narrative, have a distinctly archaic ring: **Vom wilden Thymian** ('wild thyme') **stieg eine Wolke Wohlgeruchs empor** (Immermann) —**Der Kätner hatte eben einen Eimer Wassers aus seinem Brunnen aufgezogen** (Storm)—**Keiner hatte seit dem frühen Morgen einen Tropfen Wassers gekostet** (Bruno Frank)—**Weiße Säulen Rauches stiegen gen Himmel** (M. Eyth)—**Die Nüstern der Pferde stießen heiße Ströme Dampfes aus** (H. Hoffmann)—**In die Zelle sah durch ein hoch angebrachtes Fenster ein Stück Himmels herein** (W. v. Scholz)—**Er brachte zwei Flaschen Schnapses** (H. Grimm)—**Wieviel Fetzen Papiers bedeckte ich mit Versuchen, die väterlichen Schriftstücke nachzubilden!** (Th. Mann); and sim. after nouns denoting time, the dependent gen. being often a verbal noun: **In jener halben Stunde Schlafs träumte ihr folgendes** (A. Schaeffer)—**Ich fuhr aus mancher süßen Stunde Schlafs erschreckt zu Höcht** (H. Leip, where **zu Höcht** is LG. for **in die Höhe**)—**Nach einer halben Stunde Schlummers erwachte sie** (Carossa)—**Einige Zeit Zuhörens ließ mich den Faden durch dieses Labyrinth erkennen** (Grillparzer)—**Nach einer Stunde Wanderns kamen sie auf einen Abhang, der von Wald entblößt war** (Stifter)—**Die vierzehn Tage Wartens hatten mich ungeduldig gemacht** (M. Eyth)—**Nach einer Weile Reitens wandte sich der Bote um** (Rilke)—**Nach einer kurzen Zeit Gehens rief er den Diener zu sich** (Bergengruen). **(b)** The only common unmodified gens. here are those of **Geld, Gold** and esp. **Weg** (cf. **viel** I *a*): e.g. **Er hatte eine große Summe Geldes verloren** (Th. Mann)—**Man kam zu dem Schluß, den Eltern eine Summe Geldes zu schicken** (Polenz)—**Welch ungeheures Faß! und jeder Römer** ('hock-glass, rummer') **ein Stück Goldes wert!** (Hauff)—**Ich gebe dir eine Tonne Goldes** (Rilke)—**Man pries ihn glücklich, daß er in den Besitz einer so großen Menge Goldes gekommen sei** (Allmers); **Er begleitete den Gast eine Strecke Wegs** (O. Ludwig)—**Sie ließ es sich nicht nehmen, mich ein Stück Weges zu begleiten** (G. Keller)—**Unterdessen waren sie eine Weile Wegs zusammengegangen** (Blunck)—**Es war gegen Mitternacht, und noch hatten sie eine gute Stunde Wegs** (Viebig)—**Ich hatte noch anderthalb Stunden Weges vor mir** (H. Hesse)—**Der Hund legte die zwanzig Kilometer Weges zurück** (Th. Mann). **3. (a)** In the proposition **Mit dem Vorsetzen einer Tasse Tees hatte sie die Pflichten erfüllt, die ihr Vater ihr auferlegte** (Ebner-Eschenbach), **Tees** is presumably an appos. gen., attracted into the case of the preceding noun, but actually this construction is unusual in the gen. of unmodified nouns, esp. if both nouns are masc. or neut.: one says **ein Faß Wein,** but never **der Preis eines Fasses Weines.** It is significant that Storm in such cases treats a phrase like **ein Stück Vieh** ('a head of cattle') as if the two nouns formed a comp., only the dependent noun taking the gen. ending: **Ich entschloß mich zu dem Verkauf eines Stück Viehs**; and sim. **Es kam zu einem Prozeß wegen eines Stück Ackerlandes.** In the dat. of unmodified nouns, on the other hand, the appos. construction is not uncommon, as in **Erfahrung in dieser Art Dingen zu sammeln, hatte er kaum Gelegenheit gehabt** (Polenz), although in **dieser Art Dinge** would be more usual (see **Art**). **(b)** But both the gen. and the appos. construction are quite common where the dependent noun is modified by an adj.: e.g., in the *gen.*, **Ich genoß viel Vergnügen an den Haufen alten Eisens, die in dem Magazin lagen; das schönste Gedicht von Schiller hätte ich um solch einen Berg alten Gerümpels gegeben** (Hansjakob)—**Auf einer langen Tafel standen zwei mächtige Keulen kalten Fleisches** (M. Eyth)—**Die Krankenschwester legte einen Packen frischer Wäsche auf das Bett** (Alverdes)—**Vor ihm stand eine große Tasse heißen Kaffees** (Frenssen)—**Das fremde Volk kam wie eine Schar schnatternder Gänse des Weges entlang** (id.)—**Auf der Tafel hatte sie eine Menge** (q.v.) **gespitzter Bleistifte verteilt** (Th. Mann); and in *appos.*, **Er hatte sich auf die Loggia zurückgezogen, um einen Zug frische Luft zu tun** (Fontane: 'to get a breath of fresh air')—**Er kam sich überflüssig vor, wie ein Fetzen weggeworfenes Papier** (Viebig)—**Nun erschien ein Fleckchen blauer Himmel zwischen den Nebelbänken** (Kellermann)—**Der Gedanke, Klosterbruder zu werden, behagte ihm so wenig wie einem Vaganten dreißig Tage**

grauer Regen (J. F. Perkonig)—**Sie erhielt beim Krämer ein Dütchen** ('a small paper bag') **gerösteten Kaffee, ein Stück guten Schinken und ein halbes Pfund frische Butter** (G. Keller)—**Man hatte ihm eine harte Semmel und ein Stück alten Käse gereicht** (C. Hauptmann)—**Wir brauchen so eine Art** (q.v.) **starken Mann mit militärischem Spektakel** (B. E. Werner)—**Ich warf eine Handvoll trockenen Tang auf das Feuer** (Frenssen)—**Ihr fürchtet euch vor dem Paar schwarzen Augen** (Kopisch). **(c)** In many cases the man in the street favours the use of **von** here, and indeed, **von** is quite common even in more select prose, esp. in contexts like **Er holte eine Flasche von dem besten Wein, den er im Keller hatte**— **Ich habe mir einige Ellen von diesem roten Tuch gekauft**—**Ich ging mit zwei von meinen Freunden spazieren**—**Es standen Hunderte von Kindern herum**; in ordinary lang. one says **Es waren nur zwei von uns da,** in more elevated style **Es waren unser nur zwei da**—cf. **Die Möwen umkreisten mich wie eine Wolke, und mich erfaßte eine mythische Furcht, denn es waren ihrer so viele** (Kellermann), more ordinarily **es waren so viele von ihnen.**

genitive of measure: This use of the gen. was quite established in MHG after certain adjs.: Siegfried's sword was *zweier spannen breit,* the central knob on Kriemhilde's shield was *drîer spannen dicke,* and sim. one said *zweier jâre alt, drîer tage lanc,* etc. But the gen. here has now been almost entirely displaced by the *accus.*: no one says **Das Brett ist eines Fußes breit** or **Der Graben ist eines Meters tief** or **Das Kind ist dreier Jahre alt.** But the gen. of measure was still in common use in early NHG, as in **Da er unter das Volk trat, war er eines Hauptes länger denn alles Volk** (1 Sam. 10. 23)—**Die Wunde ist eines Nagels tief** (Schottel: 17th century); and sim., in deliberately archaic lang., **Neben der Teekanne erblickte ich ein seltsam Zierat, fast eines Fußes hoch** (Storm)—**Ich meinte einen Schatten schreiten zu sehen, aber nur eines Atemzuges lang** (id.), and modern examples like the following sound very old-fashioned: **Er ist eines Hauptes länger als alle vorigen Heiderieter** (Frenssen)—**Hinten in der Stube brannte ein kleines Nachtlicht, nur eines Funkens groß** (A. Schieber: cf. **nicht größer als ein Funke**)—**Das Faserwerk der Wurzeln der vom Sturm aus der Erde herausgezerrten Fichten war armsdick** (Jul. Rodenberg). The only remnants of the earlier construction still in use are the adjs. **hoch, tief,** and occasionally **schwer,** with the gen. prefix **manns-**: e.g. **Der Weg ist überall, wo Bäume stehen, mannshoch** ('to the height of a man') **mit Schnee bedeckt** (H. Hauser)—**Die über mannshohen Laubengänge waren mit dem Segen dieses Jahres beladen** (Heyse)—**Einige Fuß hoch am Berg war eine Höhle geöffnet, wenig über mannshoch und kaum so breit** (A. Schaeffer)—**Er besaß ein Barometer, ein halbmannshohes Stück von der altmodischen Art** (Bergengruen)—**Die Angelrute besteht aus vier halbmannshohen Bambusstecken** (Alverdes)—**Den beiden Töchtern sind vier kleine, kaum anderthalb mannshohe Zimmer zugewiesen** (H. Franck)—**Das niedrige Dach der Sennhütten ist hinten in die Halde gebaut, strebt aber vorne dreimannshoch empor** (Federer); cf. **Das Gelände senkte sich etwa um drei Mannshöhen bis auf den Spiegel des Flusses** (Speckmann)—**Unter ihm, kaum mannstief, lag die stille Flut des Sees** (Federer)—**Das Mädchen half die mannsschweren Körbe tragen** (C. Rothe); cf. also **halben Wegs** and **halbwegs** (see **halb** 2 *a*).

genitive (possessive): 1. As in English, an attrib. poss. can either follow or precede a noun in German: just as we say 'the house of my father' or 'my father's house', so a German says **das Haus meines Vaters** or **meines Vaters Haus,** the latter being known as the *Saxon genitive.* As a noun qualified by a Saxon gen. loses its art., it follows that if the noun is modified by an attrib. adj., this must have *strong* inflexion: cf. **das große Haus meines Vaters** and **meines Vaters großes Haus**; sim. **in meines Onkels großem Garten**—**Goethes lyrische Gedichte.** At an earlier stage a poss. pron. (esp. **sein**) was often inserted after a Saxon gen. in coll. speech, as in **Er reichte ihm die Hand, drückte des Emirs seine mit Kraft** (Wieland: = **Er . . . drückte die des Emirs mit Kraft**); for other examples, see **dative.** **2.** Another important point here is that *a Saxon gen. cannot precede a noun which is itself in the gen.*: in other words, it is wrong to say **Von hier aus sieht man die Front meines Freundes Hauses.** There is no grammatical objection to **Man sieht die Front des Hauses meines Freundes,** but such a sequence of sibilants undoubtedly grates on the ear, and this is probably the main reason why, in such cases, recourse is generally had to the use of the prep. **von** before the modifying gen.: **Während jener Sitzung hatte er an der Seite von des Senators Vater dem Pöbel getrotzt** (Th. Mann)—**Ich stand neben dem Kopfende von meines Herrn Bett** (A. Schaeffer); cf. **Er überschritt die Schwelle zu seines Vaters Zimmer** (R. Herzog: 'He crossed the threshold *of* his father's room'), which avoids the harsh sound of **die Schwelle des Zimmers seines Vaters.** Such a sequence of sibilants arises only, of course, when the nouns are masc. or neut., but the rule applies—or should apply—equally to fem. or plur. nouns, and it is really incorrect to say **Er bewunderte die Sorgfalt ihrer Hände Arbeit** (C. Rothe: better **die sorgfältige Arbeit ihrer Hände**) or **Die kleinen Städte sind immer geneigt gewesen, mit den großen Städten gemeinsame Sache zu machen, um sich des Adels Übermacht zu erwehren** (E. Wichert: for **um sich der Übermacht des Adels zu erwehren**). That the *sound* of such gen. sing. masc. and neut. phrases may have led to the rule seems borne out by the fact that the rule is sometimes not observed in the case of unmodified fem. or plur. nouns, or of neut. nouns modified by an adj. with a *weak* ending: e.g. **Ich lache der Fürsten Herrschsucht und Ränke** (G., using **lachen** + gen. in the old sense of 'to laugh at, snap one's fingers at')—**Trotz der Frau Amalie abwehrenden Kopfschüttelns . . .** (Raabe). Still, these are clearly contrary to the rule, and on the whole they should not be imitated. **3.** In this connexion it should be noted that **dessen** and **deren** are real Saxon gen. forms (see **deren** 2 *a* and **von** 1 *c*). In other words, these cannot stand before nouns which are in the gen. case: one cannot say **Heute wurde ich einer Dame vorgestellt, deren Namens ich mich nicht erinnern kann** (a proposition in which **an deren Namen** would be correct, or which could take the form **. . . auf deren Namen ich mich nicht besinnen kann**; see **remember**); so it gives one a shock to read **Die Gräfin war in Begleitung ihrer Tochter und deren Gemahls** (Keyserling). An example like **Er wurde Erzieher dessen kränklichen Sohnes** (L. Herrig) is rightly condemned by *Sanders*, who substitutes **von dessen kränklichem Sohne**; cf., as correct, **Er begehrte, den Herrn allein zu sprechen, zur großen Verwunderung von dessen Gattin** (Jul. Wolff). So also it is really careless to say **Sie machte ihn eines Abends mit Hilfe der Schwester und deren Liebsten betrunken** (Frenssen: for **mit Hilfe der Schwester und des Liebsten derselben**) and **Der Kupferstecher hatte, um das Werk zu vollenden, die Hilfe seiner Nachbarn und deren Verwandte** (for **der Verwandten derselben**) **in Anspruch nehmen müssen** (Böhlau).

genitive (predicative): see **genitive (adverbial)** 3 (*c*).

genitive (Saxon): see **genitive (possessive)** 1–3.

genug: **1.** Where this word modifies an *adj.*, it generally follows the latter, as in English: e.g. **Ein Auto halte ich mir nicht, weil ich nicht reich genug bin** or **Ich bin nicht reich genug, mir ein Auto zu halten.** In the latter example, the infin. clause is often introduced by **um**, but this is better omitted, esp., of course, in a proposition like **Die junge Dame ist alt genug, allein** (not **um allein**) **nach Deutschland zu reisen, um die deutsche Sprache zu erlernen.** **2.** In MHG the adj. *genuoc* was either inflected regularly or used as an invariable indef. numeral (cf. **nichts, viel,** etc.), and in the latter case the verb stood in the *sing*. Thus, a proposition like 'Plenty of ladies sat there' might be expressed *genuoge vrouwen sâzen dâ*, but more usually took the form *genuoc vrouwen saz dâ* (lit. 'Enough *of* ladies was seated there'). Although one now usually says **Er hat Geld genug** or **genug Geld,** the earlier gen. use is still occasionally found, as in **Meister Bölzlein hatte Grundes genug, jeder Meinungsverschiedenheit mit dem Wirt auszuweichen** (Jak. Frey); cf. **Er hatte ein Belobigungsschreiben** ('a commendatory testimonial') **erhalten und konnte davon nicht genug Rühmens machen** (E. Wichert), where, however, **Rühmens** (q.v.) is no longer felt as a gen. Ungrammatical as it really is to use a *plur.* verb where **genug** is associated with a *gen.* plur., it is nevertheless fixed in a proposition like **Der Worte sind genug gewechselt!** (Speckmann: 'We've had enough arguments pro and con!'). The most firmly established gen. here is the expression **Manns genug,** as in **Er ist Manns genug, sich zu verteidigen** ('He is man enough, i.e. quite well able to defend himself')—**Da der Mann nicht Manns genug war, hatte die Frau sich ermannen müssen, die Zügel des Burglebens zu ergreifen** (H. Franck); and it can even be used of the fair sex, as in **Die Mädchen waren Manns genug, vergnügt zu sein** (Böhlau). The gen. here is so fixed that it can actually be used *without* **genug**, as in **Er schien wieder Manns geworden** (Blunck: 'He seemed to have regained his courage'); cf. **viel** 1 (*c*).

genügen: This verb is used in two ways: **1.** With an *impers.* subj. it means 'to suffice': e.g. **Halt! das genügt** ('Stop! that will do')—**Sein Gehalt genügt ihm nicht** ('His salary does not satisfy him')—**Diese Portion genügt für zwei** ('This helping is sufficient for two')—**Das wird zu meinem Zweck genügen** ('That will serve my purpose'); sim. in the part., **Dafür habe ich genügende Beweise** ('Of that I have ample proof')—**Die Arbeit dieses Schülers ist genügend** ('satisfactory, fair': cf. **satisfaction** *b* and *e*). **2.** With a *pers.* subj. and a dat. obj., it means 'to comply with' (wishes, orders), 'to satisfy' (conditions), 'to execute' (duties): e.g. **Ich werde Ihren Wünschen genügen**—**Er empfahl sich mit dem Versprechen, allen Anordnungen zu genügen** (W. Müller)—**Diese Maßregeln genügen allen Anforderungen** ('satisfy all requirements'); in the pass., **Dieser schwierigen Aufgabe wurde genügt** (Bruno Frank: 'This arduous task was executed'). Obs. now is **sich** (accus.) **an etwas genügen** ('to rest content with something'), for which one says **sich mit etwas begnügen** (contracted from **be-genügen, as begleiten** is contracted from **be-geleiten**: see **lead** 4, and cf. **satisfaction** *e*).

Genugtuung: see **satisfaction** (*a*).

gerade: This word has been formed by prefixing **ge-** to the OHG adj. (*h*)*rad* or (*h*)*rat*, meaning 'quick, nimble, smart' (cf. our '*ready* wit'), and in southern dialects **gerade** is said to be still used in that sense. **1.** *Adjective*: In modern prose **gerade** (coll. **grade**) means either 'straight', both lit. and fig., or, applied to numbers, 'even' (ant. **ungerade**, 'odd'): e.g., in the former sense, **Der gerade Weg ist der kürzeste**—**Halte dich gerade!** ('Hold yourself straight *or* erect!')—**Er ist ein gerader Mensch** ('an honest, upright person': cf. 'He is straight')—**Ich beschloß, ganz offen und gerade gegen ihn zu sein** (G.: '. . . to be quite frank and straightforward with him')—**Entrüstet fand ich diese geraden Seelen** (Sch.: 'I found these good honest souls indignant'); before numbers, **Zwei und vier sind gerade, drei und fünf ungerade Zahlen**—**Er hatte eine Neigung, fünf gerade sein zu lassen** (Fontane), the idiom **fünf gerade sein lassen** having the force of 'not to be over-particular, to let mistakes pass, shut one's eyes to *or* wink at shortcomings' (cf. **ein Auge zudrücken**). **2.** *Adverb*: with various shades of meaning: **(a) Er wohnt mir gerade gegenüber** ('straight across the road from me': ant. **schräg gegenüber**, see **quer** 2) —**Es ist gerade** ('on the stroke of') **Mitternacht**—**Ich kam gerade recht** ('just at the right time')—**Er war gerade** (or **eben**: see **recent** 2) **im Begriff, auszugehen** ('just on the point of going out')—**„Du wolltest doch zur Post gehen?" „Da komme ich gerade** (or **eben**) **her"** ('That 's just where I have come from')—**Die Division ging gerade auf** ('The division sum came out exactly' without a remainder)—**Er sagte, ich sollte nicht ausgehen: nun gra'de!** ('now I'm all the more determined to go, now I'll go just to spite him!'), where **grade** = **erst recht** (see **erst** 2 *d*). **(b)** Here belong the expressions **geradeaus** ('straight on'), as in **Um nach Bonn zu kommen, müssen Sie geradeaus fahren; geradewegs** or **geradenwegs** (now rarely **geradeswegs**), meaning 'straight, in a beeline', as in **Diese Schlüssel trage ich itzt** (obs. = **jetzt**) **geradeswegs zum Polizeileutnant** (Sch.)—**Sie entschlüpfte aus der Hintertür und begab sich geradewegs zur Weidestelle ihres Schafes** (H. Hoffmann)—**Geradewegs aus dem Schloßtor heraus lief ein breiter Weg** (Britting)—**Er sagte, er wollte geradenwegs in die Kirche kommen** (Ompteda)—**Er nahm den Fußweg, der geradenwegs zur Höhe führt** (H. Leip)—**Wir können dem Göttlichen nicht geradenwegs ins Antlitz schauen** (W. Bode); **geradezu,** used to modify either an adj. or adv., as in **Das ist geradezu beleidigend** ('That is positively, *or* nothing less than, insulting'), or as a pred. adj., as in **Er ist etwas geradezu** ('He is rather blunt, outspoken'); **nachgerade,** meaning 'now gradually', esp. 'by this time, by now': e.g. **Unser vertrauter Umgang fängt nachgerade an, mir zuwider zu werden** (Sch.)—**Diese Maskerade wird uns nachgrade langweilig** (Heyse)—**Du hättest das Gedicht nachgerade auswendig lernen**

können ('You might have committed the poem to memory by this time', after all the time you have been learning it by heart); **schnurgerade** ('straight as an arrow'), as in **Hier läuft der Weg mehrere Kilometer schnurgerade** (or **in schnurgerader Richtung**)—**Die Katze lief mit schnurgerade gestrecktem Schwanz weg** (I. Frapan).

geraten: This strong verb, the past part. of which, **geraten,** is also that of **raten** (q.v.), corresponds to our coll. 'to get' (into a rage, debt, etc.): e.g. **Er geriet in Wut, in große Verlegenheit**—**Der Brief geriet an die falsche Adresse** or **in falsche Hände**; here we often use other idioms: **Das Haus geriet in Brand** ('The house caught fire')—**Er geriet außer Fassung** ('He lost his self-control')—**Wie bist du auf diesen Gedanken geraten?** ('How did you hit on this idea?'). Analogous is its other meaning, 'to turn out' (well or badly), suggesting the condition into which something 'gets': **Die Ernte ist gut** or **schlecht geraten,** the latter often expressed by **mißraten** (see **mißfallen** 2 b); and here belongs the phrase **aufs Geratewohl** (= **auf gut Glück,** 'at a venture'), implying a hope that things will turn out well, as in **etwas aufs Geratewohl versuchen**; cf., as quite incorrect, **Die Augen wurden dem Knaben verbunden, der nun mit dem Stock aufs geradewohl zuschlagen mußte** (Ompteda), the reference being to a game in which a blindfolded person is spun round and then tries to strike an object lying on the floor.

geräumig: see **room** 1 *ad fin.*

Geräusch: see **sound** 3 (*a*).

gering: 1. For **niemand Geringeres als . . .** ('no less a person than . . .'), see **jemand** 3.—The word is written with a small letter not only in an expression like **nicht im geringsten,** but also in the phrase **vornehm und gering** when used in the generalizing sense of 'all classes of humanity, everybody', as in **Alles, vornehm und gering, war auf den Straßen, um die Königin zu begrüßen**; on the other hand, where the reference is to individuals, a capital letter is used: e.g. **Es waren sowohl Vornehme als Geringe in der Versammlung. 2.** It has become a real sep. prefix in a verb like **geringschätzen,** used with the fig. force of 'to esteem lightly, look down upon, despise', but not in the lit. sense of 'to rate at a low figure': hence **Er hat mich geringgeschätzt,** but **Es kostet, gering geschätzt, drei Mark** (Duden). The insep. use of the prefix, as in **Der Doktor fühlte sich geringschätzt** (W. Schäfer), is contrary to accepted modern usage, the more so as **gering** is always accented in such verbs.

geringachten: see **achten** 2.

geringschätzen: see **gering** 2.

gern: 1. The NHG expression **ein Ding begehren** ('to desire *or* covet a thing') was in MHG *eines dinges gern,* and closely related to this verb was an adj. *gern* ('desirous of, eager for'). But even at that period the adj. was rare and eventually died out, so it is strange that the adv. not only survived but became such a common expression in NHG. Actually, the coll. form **gerne** is historically more correct, being derived from OHG *gerno* (see **adverbs formed from adjectives** 1). It is possible that the old adj. is still extant as a pred. in a proposition like **Ich habe sie gern** ('I am fond of her', lit. 'I hold her as something for which I crave': cf. **like** 1 *a* and *b*), but if so, this is no longer felt. The adv. is now used in the sense of 'gladly, willingly': thus, if a person is thanked for some service he has rendered, a polite way to say 'Not at all' or 'Don't mention it' is **Es ist gern geschehen** (lit. 'It was done with pleasure'); we often use other expressions, as in **Ich möchte gern tanzen** ('I should like to dance')—**Das glaube ich gern** ('I can readily believe that'). A strange idiom is the combination **gut und gern,** used to suggest an approximate amount or degree, 'about', esp. 'not less than': e.g. **Das Paket wog gut und gern 100 Pfund** ('at least 100 pounds')—**Der Stock maß gut und gern anderthalb Fuß** (Th. Mann: 'The stick was quite 18 inches long')—**Mit meinem kleinen Wagen bin ich gut und gern meine 14000 Kilometer ohne Panne gefahren** (Fr. Thiess: 'In my small car I have done a good 14,000 kilometres without a puncture')—**Sie ist gut und gern ihre 40 Jahre alt** ('She is forty if she 's a day'). **2.** The compar. and superl. forms **gerner, am gernsten** are now confined to dialects and avoided in good prose: in propositions like **Ich bliebe gerner zu Hause** and **Ich habe euch am gernsten gehabt** (Sch.) one now uses **lieber, am liebsten**: cf. **bald.**

Geruch: In the lit. sense, this *masc.* noun (see **Ge-**) means either a 'sense of smell' (= **Geruchssinn**) or 'scent, odour': e.g.

Sie hat einen feinen Geruch—Ein Geruch von allerlei Drogen ('drugs') **war um sie her** (Zifferer)—**Dieses Fleisch gibt einen üblen Geruch von sich—Jagdhunde gehen dem Geruch nach** ('follow the scent'); sim. **Diese Blumen haben einen angenehmen Geruch**, but this is better expressed by **Duft** ('fragrance'). With fig. force, it means 'reputation', esp. 'evil repute': e.g. **Er steht im Geruch der Heiligkeit** ('He has an odour of sanctity')—**Dadurch könntest du in üblen Geruch kommen** (Hauff)—**Hatte ihr Neffe gefehlt, so kam** (a vivid indic.) **sie selbst in den Geruch, seine Mitverschworene zu sein** (Werfel: 'If her nephew had broken the law, she herself would be suspected of being his accomplice').

Gerumpel: Distinguish between **Gerumpel** and **Gerümpel:** the former has *verbal* force, a 'rumbling' noise or the 'jolting' of a cart; the latter *collect.* force, 'lumber, rubbish' (cf. **Rumpelkammer,** 'lumber-room').

gerundive infinitive: see **infinitive** 1–3; cf. **zu** 1 and the last five examples given under **genitive of material** 2 (*a*).

gesamt: see **samt** 2 (*a*).

geschehen: The uses of this verb are explained under **occur** 3 (*a*). Additional examples of its act. sense of 'to happen, come to pass': **Es geschah, daß ich zu der Zeit verreist war** ('It so happened that I was away from home at that time')—**Was auch geschehen mag, mein Entschluß steht fest** ('No matter what happens, my mind is made up')—**Es ist um ihn geschehen** ('It is all up with him'). With regard to its use in the pass. sense of 'to be done', this has a rather limited application, occurring mainly in more or less set phrases: thus, one can say **Das kann so nicht weitergehen, es muß etwas geschehen** ('Things can't go on like this, something will have to be done'), but not **Die Arbeit muß besser geschehen** (for **getan werden**); other examples: **Wenn er das getan hat, so geschah es wohl unabsichtlich** ('. . . it was no doubt done unintentionally')—**Gern geschehen!** (lit. 'It was done gladly', used like our 'Not at all! *or* Don't mention it!' after one has been thanked for something); cf., as a dialectal use which is not good German, **Was hat zu geschehen?** ('What requires to be done?')—see the last two examples given under **haben.**

Geschmack: see **taste** 1.

Geschöpf: see **schöpfen** 1; **congruence** 2.

Geschrei: see **Schrei.**

geschweigen: This compd. of **schweigen** (q.v.), meaning 'not to refer to *or* mention, to pass over in silence', has a very limited use, being now confined to the 1st sing. pres. indic., and the infin. with **zu** (with a gen. obj.). But in the pres. indic. use, the pron. **ich** is now omitted altogether, and **geschweige,** usually followed by **denn,** has become a sort of conj. without influence on the word-order. Thus, one no longer says **Ich geschweige der Drohung des Bruders** (Bürger: now **Ich schweige zu der Drohung des Bruders**), but propositions like the following are very common: **Wurde er aus seinem Berufe herausgedrängt** ('If he were sacked'), **so würde er Geschichten schreiben, die niemand lesen, geschweige denn** ('much less') **kaufen würde** (Ompteda); for other characteristic examples, see **denn** (adverb) 4, and cf. Luther's **Das ist nicht menschlich, schweige** (now **geschweige**) **denn christlich.** The infin. use conveys the same idea, as in **Corinna steckt sieben Felgentreus in die Tasche, nächststehender Anverwandten ganz zu geschweigen** (Fontane: 'Corinna is a match for seven girls like the Felgentreus, let alone our nearest relatives').

geschwind: see **quick** 1 (*b*).

Geschwister: In standard prose this is now only used as a collect. *plur.* in the sense of 'brothers and sisters', as in **Keins von ihren Geschwistern war um sie** (G.). Its earlier use in the sing., as in **des Kindes älteres Geschwister** (Lessing), occurs very occasionally in more recent times, but is now practically displaced by **Geschwisterkind:** cf. **Dein Vater freite sie als eine Sechzehnjährige: dein Geschwister** ('sister') **ist nicht älter** (C. F. Meyer)—**Ohne ein Wesen, das ihr wie ein Geschwister zu Hilfe kam, hätte sie die Unerbittlichkeit des Krieges nicht ertragen** (Binding).

Gesicht: This, the only *neut.* compd. of Sicht, is used in three senses, viz. (1) still in a few expressions (with no plur.), the 'sense of sight' (= **Sehvermögen, Gesichtssinn**: see **Sicht** 2 *b*); (2) its commonest meaning (with plur. **Gesichter, but cf. singular** 3), 'face', also 'grimace', as in **Gesichter schneiden**; (3) 'vision' (with plur. **Gesichte**): e.g. **Ihr Geist war ganz von Gesichten erfüllt** (G.)—**Was Beethoven vor allem charakterisiert, ist die Fülle der Gesichte** (K. Lamprecht)—**Bald wuchs**

Scholz in die volle Gestaltung seiner Gesichte hinein (H. M. Elster)—**Hoffmanns „Nachtstücke" treten als unmittelbare Gesichte seines Inneren hervor** (K. Martens).

gesinnt, gesonnen: see **sinnen** 1 and 3.

Gespiele: As a *masc.* noun this means 'playmate'; as a *neut.* it has verbal force (= **das Spielen**), generally used in a derogatory sense: **All dies Gespiele führt zu nichts** ('All this playing leads nowhere *or* is to no purpose').

Gestalt: see **figure** 1 (*b*).

gestatten (see **Statt** 2): This is a slightly more formal expression than the ordinary **erlauben:** e.g. **Man gestatte mir die Bemerkung** (or **Es sei mir gestattet, zu bemerken**), **daß . . .** ('Permit me to observe that . . .'); it is esp. common in official or business correspondence: e.g. **Wir gestatten uns, Ihnen hierdurch die Mitteilung zu machen, daß . . .** ('We hereby beg to inform you that . . .').

gestehen: see **confess** 2.

Gesträuch: see **Strauch.**

get: In a reference to the pensions of retired officers, a staff reporter of the *Observer* writes 'The older they get, the less they get', thus neatly illustrating the two main uses of the English verb (trans. 'to receive', intrans. 'to become'). **1.** With *trans.* force: (**a**) The commonest expression for 'to get, obtain' is **bekommen.** Being a compd. of **kommen,** this is properly used of getting what *comes* to one in the natural course of events: e.g. **Hoffentlich bekommen wir bald besseres Wetter**—**Sie bekommt oft Hustenanfälle**—**Die jungen Vögel haben Federn bekommen**—**Im Frühling bekommen die Bäume neue Blätter**; and sim. **Ich bekam heute einen Brief aus China** (the letter came to hand through the normal channel). Esp. noteworthy is the use of **bekommen** with a pred. *past part.*: e.g. **Er stand am Hackstock** ('chopping-block') **und versuchte die neue Axt, die er geschenkt bekommen hatte** ('. . . which had been given to him as a present')—**Der Gast bekam Käse und Brot vorgesetzt** ('The customer had bread and cheese set before him')—**Wasser müssen Sie unten in der Küche holen, falls es Ihnen nicht gelingt, Wasser gelegt zu bekommen** (K. Edschmid: '. . . in case you don't succeed in getting water laid on')—**Im Laboratorium saßen Leute, die Blut entnommen bekamen** (id.: '. . . who were having blood taken from them' for transfusion, where, of course, the people are not *getting* anything). Quite different is the intrans. impers. use of **bekommen** with a dat. of the person, meaning 'to agree with', as in 'Something I ate yesterday hasn't agreed with me', for which see **agree** 5. (**b**) Much the same as **bekommen** is **kriegen** (orig. to get by striving, fighting), which, however, is mainly coll. and rather avoided in good prose. Characteristic examples are **Warte, du kriegst's!** ('Just you wait, you'll catch it!')—**In diesem Roman kriegen sie sich** (i.e. the hero and heroine get married)—**Das kriegt er noch von mir zu hören** ('He'll get to hear about that from me yet', i.e. I'll give him a piece of my mind). (**c**) The best word for 'to get, receive' is **empfangen,** which really suggests the idea of *catching* (**fangen**) or grasping something, but without implying that this is the rightful property of the recipient (see *d*): thus, **ein Empfangsschein** is 'a receipt', given to the person, not necessarily the owner, who takes delivery of something (**etwas in Empfang nehmen**); so also it is used of 'receiving' a visitor at the door, which may be done by a maidservant (cf. *e*). Obviously, **empfangen** and **bekommen** may approach each other closely, and they are in fact often used indiscriminately; but the former is a more select expression, cf. the polite ending to a letter **Empfangen** (never **Bekommen**) **Sie die Versicherung meiner Hochachtung!** (a formal way of expressing our 'Yours respectfully'). (**d**) The idea that the recipient of an article is the actual owner is properly suggested by **erhalten,** which implies that the person *holds* it as his property (cf. 'obtain', from Lat. *tenere*, 'to hold'): e.g. **Ich habe das Geld richtig erhalten** (the money was owing to me)—**Er hat die Stelle erhalten, um die er sich bewarb**; and so, of course, one can also say **Ich habe Ihren Brief erhalten.** (**e**) Quite different is **annehmen** ('to accept' something, i.e. not to refuse it). The only expression in which this can be used with the force of 'to receive' is **Besuch annehmen,** not in the sense of opening the door to visitors, but in that of not refusing to see them, i.e. of being 'at home' to callers. **2.** With *intrans.* force: (**a**) Expressions in which 'to get' is used with a pred. *adj.* present little difficulty: cf. **alt, dick, müde werden** ('to get old, fat, tired'); but it is noteworthy that such ideas are often expressed by independent verbs: e.g. **Er beginnt zu altern** (q.v.)—**Ermüde dich nicht!**—**Die Luft verdünnt** (ant. **verdichtet**) **sich**—**Er hat sich betrunken** ('He has got drunk')—**Sie hat sich erholt** ('She has got better')—**Die Lage hat sich gebessert** ('The situation has got better, improved')—**Ich habe mir alle meine Sorgen vom Halse geschafft** ('I have got rid of all my worries'). (**b**) On the other hand, where there is a pred. *adv.* or *prep.*, specific verbs have mostly to be used, the commonest being **kommen,** generally with a prefix: e.g. **Ich kam spät nach Hause**—**Die Tür war verriegelt, ich konnte nicht hinaus- or hineinkommen**—**Es gelang mir, den steilen Abgrund hinunterzukommen**—**Der Verkehr war so stark, daß wir nicht durch- or weiterkommen konnten**—**Er kam mit dem Schrecken davon** ('He got off with a fright'; cf. also **escape**). Other verbs are seen in **Scher dich hinaus!** ('Get out!')—**Er ist in Schulden geraten** (q.v.)—**Er macht auf der Schule gute Fortschritte** ('He is getting on well at school').

Getränk: see **trinken** 2 (*a*).

getrauen: see **trauen** 2 (*b*).

Getreide: 1. This collect. noun orig. meant whatever the earth brings forth (MHG *getregede* = **was der Erdboden trägt**), but is now specifically used of indigenous *grain*-crops, viz. **die Gerste** ('barley'), **der Hafer** ('oats'), **der Roggen** ('rye') and **der Weizen** ('wheat'). Where the reference is to exotic crops like 'maize' (**der Mais**), the Germans use **das Korn,** properly grain-*seed* ('maize' is also called **türkisches Korn**); but just as in Scotland 'corn' is generally understood to refer to *oats,* so in Germany **Korn** is often specifically used for *rye.* **2.** At harvest-time (**Erntezeit**), when the grain is 'led in'—**wenn (das Getreide) eingefahren wird**—special expressions are used in different parts of the country for words like 'shock', 'stack', 'barn', etc., but **die Garbe** ('sheaf') is in almost universal use. *Southerners* mostly use **der Garbenhaufen** (or **die Puppe**) for a 'shock' of sheaves set up in a field to dry (a 'stook' in Scotland, a 'stitch' in Wessex according to Hardy: cf. **Steg** 4 *c*), **der Schober** for a 'stack', and **die Scheuer** for a 'barn'. On the other hand, in the *north,* a 'shock' is usually called **die Hocke** or, now less commonly, **die Mandel** (q.v., which Voss defines as **„eine Hocke von 15 Garben"**), a 'stack' **der Diemen** or in some districts **die Miete,** and a 'barn' **die Scheune.** In Spielhagen's *Plattland,* a farmer says **„Was nicht ins Fach kommt, setzen wir in Mieten, und was wir nicht in Mieten setzen, bleibt in den Hocken stehen"**, where **Fach** is that part of the **Scheune** adjoining the **Tenne** ('threshing-floor') in which the grain is stored, and which is sometimes called **Banse**; cf. **Er hielt nichts vom Einmieten der Kartoffeln** (B. E. Werner: 'He did not think much of clamping potatoes').

getreulich: see **adverbs formed from adjectives** 3.

gewahr: This adj. is now practically confined to the pred. use with **werden** in the sense of 'to become aware of, perceive'. Its orig. construction was a *gen.*, as in **Unter den Kindern ward ich eines närrischen Jünglings gewahr** (Prov. 7. 7), and this is still used, esp., but not only, in a choice literary style: cf. **Ein Maschinengewehrschütze** ('machine-gunner') **wurde seiner gewahr und traf ihn in das linke Bein** (Alverdes); sim. 'before I became aware of it' is **ehe ich dessen** or **es gewahr wurde.** But through failure to recognize the gen. in phrases like **es** or **nichts** (qq.v.) **gewahr werden,** the gen. was gradually displaced in ordinary lang. by the *accus.*, which *Sanders* characterizes as **„heute überwiegend"**, and which is not confined to indef. expressions: e.g. **In diesem Kinde werde ich den Charakter ihrer Mutter gewahr** (G.)—**Zaudre nicht lange! und daß** ('see to it that') **kein Auge dich gewahr wird!** (Sch.)—**Nun ward er mich gewahr** (Stehr). Both cases are also used after **ansichtig werden** ('to catch sight of'), but there the accus. was the orig. construction (see **ansichtig**).

gewahren: The orig. *gen.* construction of this verb ('to become aware of': cf. **gewahr** and **wahrnehmen**) is replaced in ordinary lang. by the *accus.*: expressions like **eines Felsenriffs gewahren** (Sch.) or **sein gewahrend, erschrak Diomedes** (Bürger) are only used in a choice literary style. Like **bemerken** and **erblicken** (qq.v.), **gewahren** is only very occasionally followed by the accus. and infin.: cf. **Ein Licht gewahrt er aus der Hütte schimmern** (Platen) and **Er gewahrte den Jungen wie eine große Raupe um den Baumstamm hängen** (Storm), where a **daß**-clause would be much more usual.

gewährleisten: The fem. noun **Gewähr** means 'guarantee, security, surety, bail', and **Gewähr leisten** (+**für**) is 'to guarantee, stand bail for' something, as in **Für die Wahrheit seiner Aussage hat er Gewähr geleistet** ('He has vouched for the truth of his evidence'). But in modern times the noun in this expression has become a prefix, and **gewährleisten** is treated as an *insep.* trans. verb: e.g. **Die Stadt Neapel gewährleistete den Vertrag** (Platen)—**Der Verkäufer ist bereit, die Haltbarkeit seiner Nahrungsmittel zu gewährleisten** ('The seller is prepared to guarantee that his provisions will keep').

Gewand: see **clothes** 4.

gewärtig(en): 1. The verb **gewarten** ('to wait for, look forward to'), although in use until comparatively recent times (esp. in the infin.), is now *obs.*: cf. **Deine Nachkommen haben viel Gutes zu gewarten** (Jer. 31. 17)—**Wir haben einen guten Tag zu gewarten** (G.)—**Was hätte sie von einem solchen Manne zu gewarten?** (Mörike). **2.** (**a**) The adj. **gewärtig** means either 'willing to serve' or (now as a rule) 'expectant, on the look out for' (+ *gen.*): e.g. in the former sense, **Möget ihr künftig dem Könige treu und gewärtig bleiben** (G.)—**Ich biete Ihnen meine stets gewärtige Freundschaft** (R. Herzog); in the latter sense, **Alle Fragen bestürzen, deren wir nicht gewärtig sind** (Lessing: 'Any question for which we are unprepared is disconcerting')—**Er ist jedes Winks gewärtig** (Sch.)—**Vor dem Hause hatte sich das Gesinde, der Abfahrt ihres Herrn gewärtig, versammelt** (Fr. Halm)—**Ich wußte, daß der Tod unser kluger Bruder ist, der die rechte Stunde weiß und dessen wir mit Zuversicht gewärtig sein dürfen** (H. Hesse)—**Des Äußersten gewärtig** ('Prepared for the worst'), **begab ich mich in meines Vaters Zimmer** (Th. Mann). In the proposition **Die Einzelheiten sind mir heute nicht mehr gewärtig** (A. Schaeffer) the adj. is presumably a mistake or misprint for **gegenwärtig** ('present to my mind, clear in my memory': see **presence** 3). (**b**) The verb **gewärtigen,** a rather choice expression, means 'to expect', but unlike its ordinary alternative **erwarten** (trans.) it orig. took a *gen.*, as the *reflex.* verb still does: e.g. **Wer konnte so freudigen Besuchs sich gewärtigen?** (H. v. Kleist) and **Sie versuchen, auszukundschaften, wessen sie sich gewärtigen müssen** (H. Grimm). With the simple verb, on the other hand, the *accus.* has now practically established itself (as explained under **es** 1): e.g. **Wenn man nichts Übles gewärtigte, so kam das Unglück** (Th. Mann)—**Sein Benehmen der Braut gegenüber war erfüllt mit dem Zartgefühl, das man von ihm zu gewärtigen berechtigt war** (id.)—**Das Kommando suchte gegen die Brücke vorzudringen, wo Fühlung mit dem Feind** ('contact with the enemy') **zu gewärtigen war** (Hofmannsthal).

gewiegt: see **wiegen** 1 (*b*) and 4 (*b*).

gewillt: see **Wille** 2 (*b*).

gewinnen: The same applies to this verb as to **beginnen** (q.v.), the past subj. here also having two forms, viz. **gewänne** or (rather more usually in the north) **gewönne** (see **Ablaut** 2 *c*): cf., on the one hand, **Es ist keine Stelle dieser Tafeln** ('panels, pictures'), **die nicht durchs Vergrößerungsglas gewönne** (G.); and, on the other hand, **Er hatte nicht geglaubt, daß ein guter Geist Macht über ihn gewänne** (Auerbach)—**Glauben Sie, daß es recht wäre, wenn wir sie für uns gewännen?** (P. Keller: '. . . if we won her over?'). The past part. is now always **gewonnen** (< MHG *gewnnnen*): cf. the prov. **Frisch gewagt ist halb gewonnen** ('Well begun is half done') and **Wer nicht wagt, gewinnt nicht** ('Nothing venture, nothing win *or* have').

gewiß: 1. (**a**) The adjs. **gewiß** and **sicher** both mean 'certain, sure', but they approach this idea from different angles. While **gewiß** is connected with **wissen,** and so implies that one *knows* a fact and relies on its being true, **sicher** is from Lat. *securus*, meaning 'free from care *or* mental worry', so that one has no doubts. Hence one can say **Von diesem Ereignis habe ich gewisse** or **sichere Nachricht.** On the whole, however, **sicher** is to be preferred here, because **gewiß** has come to lose some of its orig. force: just as we say 'on a *certain* day in January' or 'certain people', the reference being to something not clearly specified, so also in German one says **An einem gewissen Tage im Januar ereignete sich Folgendes** and **Es gibt gewisse Menschen, die nie seekrank werden**; cf. **eine Dame in gewissen Jahren** ('a lady of a certain age'). But **sicher** has not undergone this change, so that a tradesman may say **Herr Müller ist ein sicherer Kunde** ('a safe, trustworthy customer'), **aber ich habe gewisse Kunden** ('some customers' whom I shan't mention), **die nicht regelmäßig zahlen.** (b) And this deterioration is also seen in the *adv.* use of **gewiß.** It may be a strong affirmative, as in **„Gehen Sie morgen mit?“ „Gewiß!“** ('Certainly!' where **„Sicher!“** is rather more coll., like our 'Sure!'); but here again it may lose much of its force: e.g. **Er wollte mich gestern besuchen, kam aber nicht: er ist gewiß verreist** ('he is probably *or* no doubt out of town'); cf. **gewissermaßen** ('to some extent'). **2.** To express 'safe' from danger, etc., one can only use **sicher,** as in **Hier sind wir sicher vor Gefahr** *or* **vor Feinden,** but either expression can be used with a *gen.* in the sense of 'sure, certain of' something: e.g., on the one hand, **Dessen bin ich gewiß** ('Of that I am certain')—**Er ist seiner Sache gewiß** ('He is certain of his facts, sure of his ground')—**Er war seiner Niederlage gewiß** (A. Döblin: 'He was sure he was going to be defeated')—in the neg., **Wenn unsere alten Meister ihre Münster aufführten, der Vollendung des Werkes ungewiß** ('erected their cathedrals and were uncertain whether the work would be completed'), **so bauten sie den einen Turm** (Uhland); on the other hand, **Des** (usually **Dessen**) **bin ich sicher** (Wassermann)—**Hier ist man seines Lebens nicht sicher** ('You are in danger of your life here')—**Es mußte Zeit vergehen, bis er seiner selbst sicher war** (A. Eloesser: 'Some time had to elapse before he was sure of himself'). It was failure to recognize the gen. in **Ich bin es gewiß** (see **es** 1) that led to **Es ist mein Bruder, das bin ich gewiß** (G.), but this accus. has never become established (as it has with **gewohnt, müde, satt, wert,** etc.), and should be avoided; cf. **Er meinte nun des Kurfürsten Zustimmung sicher sein zu dürfen** (E. Wiechert), where the gen. **Zustimmung** is strictly against the rule that a noun in the gen. should not be preceded by a Saxon gen.—cf. the examples from the same author and C. Rothe given under **genitive (possessive)** 2.

gewißlich: see **adverbs formed from adjectives** 3.

gewogen: see **wiegen** 1 (*a*), 2, 3, 4 (*a*).

gewöhnen: see **accustom(ed)** 2.

Gewohnheit, gewohnt: see **accustom(ed)** 1; **custom(ary)** 1.

gewöhnlich: see **custom(ary)** 1; **gemein** 2.

Gicht: This fem. noun forms the plur. **Gichten** when used as a technical term (one of its meanings is the 'mouth' of a blast-furnace), but has no plur. when used with its ordinary force of 'gout', in which sense it requires the def. art., as do the names of other diseases—see **article (definite)** 2 (*e*): **Er leidet an der Gicht.** The plur. form **Gichter** is used, esp. in the south, for 'convulsive fits' (usually **Krämpfe** or **krampfhafte Zuckungen**), particularly with reference to children: e.g. **Die Kinderkrankheit, die im nördlichen Deutschland „das Schäuerchen“ genannt wird, heißt im südlichen Deutschland „die Gichter“** (Benecke)—**Die Mutter versank in die Betrachtung des von Gichtern geschüttelten Knaben . . . Johann hatte wieder seine Gichter bekommen, der Anfall der Krämpfe wurde immer heftiger** (Spindler); more fig. **Ich weiß eine Zeit, wo du beim Anblick einer Krone Gichter bekommen hättest** (Sch.: '. . . when the sight of a crown would have sent you into fits')—**Ich bekomme Gichter beim bloßen Gedanken** (Mörike).

giddy: see **schwindeln** 1.

Gift: This noun was orig. *fem.* and meant 'gift, present' (= **Gabe, Geschenk**), but apart from **Mitgift** ('dowry'), which is still always fem., this is now obs. The *neut.* **Gift** ('poison') is really the same word, taken presumably from the idea of 'giving' or administering something injurious to life, just as our 'poison' is really the same word as 'potion'. In this bad sense it was at one time sometimes used as *masc.*, as in **Ich habe den Gift an Tausende gegeben** (G.) and **Noch spür' ich den Gift nicht** (Sch.: 'I don't feel the poison working on me yet'), but *Duden* allows the masc. gender only in the coll. fig. sense of 'anger', as an example of which he gives **einen Gift (= Zorn) auf jemanden haben** ('to be angry with a person').

Glas: Used as a measure or amount, this noun remains unchanged in the plur. (see **nouns of measure** and **genitive of material**): cf. **Er stellte drei Gläser auf den Tisch,** but **Er trank drei Glas Wein;** it is really not in accordance with the spirit of the German lang. to say **Ich trank drei oder vier Gläser schweren Weins** (Hofmannsthal) or **Ich hatte mich mit ein paar Gläsern Bier betäubt** (St. Zweig). In nautical parlance, **Glas** is used of the half-hourly divisions of a four hours' watch, and here the plur. is generally **Glasen;** in other words, where we speak of 'eight bells', meaning 12, 4, or 8 o'clock, a German sailor uses **acht Glasen**: cf. **Ich hörte vier Glasen schlagen** (Gerstäcker: here 6 o'clock). But the invariable form **Glas** is now used here also, as in **Es hatte sieben Glas geschlagen, halb zwölf Uhr nachts** (H. Hauser), so perhaps **Glasen** is now mainly used by older seamen; for the fluctuation, cf. **Von vier Glas an bis zu den nächsten vier Glasen stand er als Taillemann** (id.: 'From 2 to 6 o'clock he was on duty as winchman').

Glaube: see **Balken.**

glauben: **1.** With a *dat.* obj., **glauben** has the force of 'to put one's trust in, rely on the trustworthiness of': e.g. **Ich glaubte seiner Versicherung** (or **Ich glaubte ihm auf seine Versicherung hin**), **daß er mir das Geld zukommen lassen würde—Ich kann Ihren Worten nicht glauben, die Tatsachen sprechen dagegen—Ich glaubte** (= **traute**) **meinen Ohren nicht. 2.** With an *accus.* obj. (cf. 3), it means 'to think something true *or* in accordance with the facts', being esp. common with indef. neut. expressions, and often associated with a dat. of the person as the source of the statement: e.g. **Das kann ich dir unmöglich glauben**; cf. **Er glaubt wunder** (or **wunders**: MHG *gelouben* could take a gen. obj.), **wie klug er ist** ('He thinks himself mighty clever')—**Wir glaubten wunder, was Ihnen widerfa'hren** (Gutzkow: 'We believed all manner of things had befallen you', i.e. 'We wondered what on earth had happened to you'). And the accus. obj. may, of course, take the form of a subord. clause: **Ich glaube ihm nicht, daß er da gewesen sei—Er glaubt selbst nicht, was er sagt. 3.** With the force of 'to believe *in* (the existence of)', **glauben** was at one time used with an *accus.*: e.g. **Glauben Sie kein Schicksal, keine Macht, die über uns waltet?** (G.)—**Die Unsterblichkeit, insofern sie geglaubt wurde, stand in dunkler Ferne** (Schlegel). In this sense, however, the simple accus. is now avoided, being replaced by **an** + *accus.*: e.g. **Wer glaubt heutzutage an Gespenster?—Wen die falsche Welt verläßt, der glaubt an Gott und Sterne** (Eichendorff); cf. the idiom **daran glauben müssen** ('to resign oneself to *or* suffer one's fate'). A rather far-fetched distinction is made in **Wenn man den Teufel glaubt, muß man sich hüten, nicht an ihn zu glauben** (Tieck: 'If one believes that there is a devil, one must beware of relying on him'): cf. **negative (pleonastic)** 2 (*a*). **4.** (a) In rendering 'I believe him to be honest', one says **Ich glaube, daß er ehrlich ist** or **Ich erachte ihn als** (or **halte ihn für**) **ehrlich**: no one says **Ich glaube ihn ehrlich sein.** It is true that the **accusative and infinitive** (q.v. 6) is occasionally found after **glauben,** but this use has never become established, and examples like the following should, on the whole, not be imitated: **Er saß noch manche Stunde, bis er alles schlafen glaubte** (Storm)—**Von Zeit zu Zeit glaubten die Vorfahren das Ende der Welt bevorstehen** (R. v. Schaukal)—**O Gott, sie ist tot, da wir sie leben glaubten** (A. Schaeffer). Nor yet does one say **Ich glaube ihn ehrlich zu sein,** although this was also possible at an earlier period, as in **Er glaubte es nach dem Geschmack seiner Landsleute zu sein** (Lessing) and **In jedem Stiche** ('engraving') **glaubte man eine Grazie versteckt zu sein** (Möser). According to modern usage, the infin. with **zu** is confined to cases where the subj. of **glauben** and that of the infin. refer to one and the same person: e.g. **Ich glaube, gehört zu haben, daß er krank ist.** But it is probable that, in the examples of the accus. and infin. given above, the infin. is a corrupt *pres. part.* with **zu sein** understood—cf. **Er sagte ihr, er hätte sich ausgezeichnet unterhalten, worüber sie sehr erstaunt war, da sie ihn den ganzen Abend schlafend** (*scil.* **zu sein?**) **geglaubt hatte** (W. v. Kügelgen) and **Er stellte fest, daß man, wenn man sie schlafend glaubte, Stimmen in ihrem Zimmer vernommen habe** (W. v. Scholz); and this seems the more likely as the *past part.* is very common in such propositions: e.g. **Er glaubte sich betrogen** ('He believed himself to have been defrauded')—**Neulich glaubte er sein Zimmer erbrochen** (G.: 'He believed his room had been broken into recently')—**Die Eltern glaubten ihr Kind erhöht** (Chamisso)—**Er glaubte sein Lager gesichert** (C. F. Meyer)—**Der alte Soldat glaubte sich zu früh verabschiedet** (Bruno Franck: 'The veteran thought he had been discharged before his time'); cf. **Wir glaubten dich weit in der Ferne** (G.) and **Er glaubte sich der Letzte seines Stammes** (Gutzkow), which are difficult to explain otherwise than by assuming that **zu sein** is understood. In this connexion, see also **accusative and participle.** **(b)** The obvious rendering of a proposition like

'He is a man whom I believe to be honest' is **Er ist ein Mann, den ich für ehrlich halte.** In order to use **glauben** here, a circumlocution is necessary which is actually not as clumsy in German as it would sound in English, viz. 'He is a man, of (**von**) whom I believe that *he* is honest': **Er ist ein Mann, von dem ich glaube, daß er ehrlich ist** (in this connexion see esp. **von** 5 and **wissen** 3 *a*); sim. **Aus den Saiten der Geigen wurden Töne gelockt, die ich noch niemals vernommen hatte, und von denen ich glaubte, daß nur vom Himmel Herabgestiegene sie spielen könnten** (E. Wiechert).

gleich: 1. *Adjective*: Strictly speaking, **gleich** implies complete agreement between the things compared, i.e. *equality, identity*, while **ähnlich** suggests a merely approximate agreement, i.e. *resemblance*. This distinction is generally observed: **Sie verfolgen gleiche Zwecke** is not exactly the same as **Sie verfolgen ähnliche Zwecke**, the former implying that both parties have exactly the same ends in view, the latter that the ends differ to some extent but are closely related; and it is significant that **gleich** now has no degrees of comparison. In the following examples **gleich** could not be replaced by **ähnlich: Teilen Sie diese Linie in drei gleiche Teile!—Die zwei Knaben stehen im gleichen Alter—Deutsch und Englisch spricht er mit gleicher Fertigkeit** ('with equal fluency')—**Ich zahlte es ihm mit gleicher Münze heim** ('I paid him back in his own coin')—**Es ist mir ganz gleich** (= **einerlei**, 'all the same to me'), **ob er kommt oder nicht** (cf. **like** 2 *a*). On the other hand, **gleich** cannot be substituted for **ähnlich** in contexts like **Sie ist ihrer Mutter sehr ähnlich—Das sieht dir ähnlich** ('That's just like you, what I should have expected of you'). **2.** *Adverb*: In the adv. use, **gleich** may have two meanings: cf. **Die Knaben sind gleich alt** ('of the same age') and **Wenn man ihm Vorwürfe macht, wird er gleich** (= **sogleich**, 'at once') **zornig.** As a rule the exact meaning will probably be clear from the context: **Gleich darauf klopfte es an die Tür** can only mean 'Immediately afterwards . . .', and **Er spricht die zwei Sprachen gleich fließend** only '. . . with equal fluency'. But occasionally ambiguity may arise, as in **Sie sind gleich bereit zu lachen** (G.), and in such cases **sogleich** should be used for 'at once', and an expression like **in gleichem Maße** for 'equally'. **3.** Here belong two expressions in which **gleich** has become **glich**, viz. **männiglich** (q.v. for the explanation how this developed and how it is used) and **jeglich.** The latter, a favourite word of Luther's, now confined to a choice style and replaced in ordinary lang. by **jed-**, has developed out of OHG *êo-gilîh*, MHG *ie-gelîch*, meaning 'any, every': e.g. **Ein jegliches hat seine Zeit** (Eccles. 3. 1: in every-day lang. **Jedes Ding hat seine Zeit**)—**Ängstlich klopft Erwartung in jeglicher Brust** (Sch.: = **in jeder** or **jedermanns Brust**).

gleichen: The difference between **ähnlich** and **gleich** (see gleich 1; **like** 2 *a* and *b*) applies also to the two verbs **ähneln** and **gleichen** (both+*dat.*). Although they occasionally approach each other closely (cf. **Sie gleichen** or **ähneln sich wie ein Ei dem anderen**, 'They are as like as two peas'), **ähneln** merely suggests *resemblance*, while **gleichen** properly implies *equality, identity*. Modern usage recognizes only the strong forms **glich, geglichen,** and this applies also to compds. At one time, when, esp. in poetry, the verb could have factitive force ('to make equal, level'), weak forms were used: e.g. **Er gleichte sich diesem oder jenem Helden** (i.e. he assumed the outward shape of some hero), **und in dieser Gleichung war der Gott nicht zu erkennen** (Heine)—**Wie hast du meiner Stirne Falten gegleicht!** (Thümmel: 'How you have smoothed out the lines on my forehead!' where one would now use **geglättet**). This factitive use with weak forms is now obs., so the idea of 'making equal' must be expressed in some other way: cf. **Du mußt alle Figuren gleich groß machen—Die allgemeine Not macht alle Leute gleich—Sein Ziel ist, alle Stände bürgerlich gleichzustellen** ('His aim is to level all social classes').

-gleichen: 1. The adj. **gleich** (q.v.) may, of course, be used as an adj.-subst.: e.g. **Es hätte Mühe gekostet, in der Toten die Gleiche** ('the same person') **zu erkennen, die noch jüngst bei der Arbeit zu sehen gewesen war** (Bergengruen); and sim. **ein mir Gleicher** ('one exactly like me, an equal'). But this latter idea is more idiomatically expressed by means of the fossilized suffix **-gleichen,** which is attached to the gen. forms **der** and **des** (see 2 *a* and *b*), to **meines, deines, etc.,**

and to the preps. **ohne** and **sonder.** These forms are invariable, used irrespective of gender or number, and now only rarely preceded by an art.: **ein dergleichen Fest** (G.) now usually takes the form **ein derartiges Fest.** The precise origin of these forms is obscure. Earlier examples suggest that they may orig. have been weakly inflected adj.-substs., as in Luther's **Es ist sein Gleiche nicht im Lande**; but another possible explanation is that a noun was really understood after **-gleichen,** so that **dergleichen Leute** was **Leute der gleichen Art,** and **unseresgleichen** was **Leute unseres gleichen Standes**—an explanation which seems to gain support from the common use of these forms after preps. At all events, usage is now quite established: e.g. **So etwas tut meinesgleichen nicht** ('People like me don't do that sort of thing')—**Sie hatte eine Jugend verlebt, wie wenige ihresgleichen** (R. Herzog)—**Er sprach zu ihr wie zu seinesgleichen** (Böhlau: 'He spoke to her as to people of his own class')—**Im Notfall trank er unter seinesgleichen** ('among his fellows') **ein Glas Bier** (H. Hesse)—**Ein Mensch kann fast alles ausstehen, aber von seinesgleichen verstoßen sein, das kann er nicht ausstehen, denn der Vogel fliegt mit seinesgleichen** (Immermann)—**Er begriff, daß das Fenster zu seiner und seinesgleichen Abschreckung angebracht sei** (H. Mann: 'He realized that the window had been set in there to scare him and people like him away'); and so also **Er war ein Held ohnegleichen** ('He was a hero beyond compare')—**Es war ein windstilles Wetter von fünf Grad Frost, ein Februartag sondergleichen** (Th. Mann) —**Das ist eine Frechheit sondergleichen** ('That's an unparalleled piece of impertinence'). **2.** Esp. noteworthy in this connexion are **(a) dergleichen,** used as an adj. or a noun, as sing. or plur., for any case of any gender, and (like **desgleichen,** for which see *b*) as a dem. or a rel. (cf. **derlei**): e.g. **Mir würde dergleichen** ('that sort of thing') **nicht passieren** (Schreckenbach)—**Wie können Sie auf dergleichen** (or **auf einen derartigen**) **Verdacht kommen?** (Lessing: 'How can such a suspicion cross your mind?')—**Der Herr soll ein Botanikus sein: dergleichen Schlages liebt** (= **Leute solchen Schlages lieben,** 'People of that kidney love') **alles, was wild zusammenwächst** (Storm)—**Etwas dergleichen** (= **So etwas**) **erinnere ich mich von ihm gehört zu haben** (Sch.: 'I remember having heard him say something of that sort'); cf. the common phrase **und dergleichen mehr,** often contracted **u.dgl.m.** ('and so on, etc.') and its use as a rel. pron. (cf. **derlei**), as in **In jenen fernen Ländern konnten ungläubige Heiden Martern an ihm ausüben, dergleichen** ('the like of which') **man im gottesfürchtigen Schwabenland weder kannte noch ahnte** (R. Huch)—**Er fand sie an einem Handschuh stickend, dergleichen damals zu den wichtigsten Modedingen gehörte** (Muellenbach); **(b) desgleichen,** a much less common form, used only in the masc. and neut. sing., but representing any case, and now largely displaced by **dergleichen,** which has a much wider application; indeed, it is now used esp. (like the legal and official term **ingleichen**) as a particle with the force of 'likewise, ditto': e.g. **So gehe hin und tu desgleichen** (Luke 10. 37)—**Nun zog er sein Schreibzeug und einen Briefbogen hervor, desgleichen ein blaues Kuvert** (H. Hesse)—**Er gab seine Zustimmung, ich desgleichen. (c)** The forms referred to above are fossilized gens., but, as pointed out, **-gleichen** was orig. in all probability a subst., and this seems borne out by the fact that the two parts of these compd. expressions were written as separate words, as in **Ich bin deines Gleichen** (G.). So also **deren** and **dessen Gleichen** were at one time commonly used with rel. force, as in **Sie hat Augen, deren Gleichen ich in meinem Leben noch nie gesehen habe** (Wieland) and **Hier ist ein Platz, dessen Gleichen in der Welt vielleicht nicht wieder zu sehen ist** (G.). Such expressions have now been almost entirely displaced by the shorter compd. forms, being now only very occasionally found: cf. **Ihr Gebaren war von einer Anmut übergossen, deren Gleichen er noch nicht gesehen hatte** (H. Hoffmann) —**Unsere Gegend wurde von einem Zyklon heimgesucht, dessengleichen in unserem Lande weder vorher noch später gesehen worden ist** (H. Hesse).

gleiten: This verb, meaning 'to glide', and its compounds (e.g. **ausgleiten,** for which see **slip** 1) had orig., and as a rule still have, *strong* forms (**glitt, geglitten**). Weak forms, which *Duden* characterizes as **„selten"**, were used occasionally in the classical period, and even later, but should now be avoided, the more so as they have no historical basis, being probably the result of confusion with **begleiten,** with which gleiten has no connexion (see **lead** 5): cf. **Als ich sie die Felsentreppe hinunter begleitete, glitt sie auf den ausgetretenen Stufen aus.** The following are examples of the incorrect weak forms: **Wir gleiteten auf dem Strom dahin** (Wieland)—**Nun gleitete der Kahn den Fluß hinab** (G.)—**Geßler ist vom Pferde herabgegleitet** (Sch., in a stage direction)—**Unsere Gespräche gleiteten wie ein Gewässer weg** (Hölderlin)—**Von Wien bis hier** (*scil.* Paris) **Regen und Schnee, auf den schwäbischen Alpen sogar Eis, daß die Pferde gleiteten** (Grillparzer)—**Er begann im Dunkeln die Treppe hinabzusteigen, gleitete auch bald auf den verwitterten Steinstufen aus** (G. Keller).

Glück: All the dictionaries agree in representing this as a noun which has *no plur.* Actually, the plur. does occur, but it is so very rare, esp. in modern literature, that it can be regarded as nonexistent: cf. **Was es doch für sonderbare Glücke** (= **Glücksfälle**) **gibt!** (Fontane: 'What strange fortunes one comes across!'). The expression 'to wish a person luck *or* happiness' is **jemandem Glück wünschen;** although a compd. verb **glückwünschen** occasionally occurs, as in **Sie waren glückwünschen gekommen** (Ompteda: 'They had come to wish him a happy birthday') and **Die Mädchen glückwünschten ihr** (Auerbach), it has never really established itself, which seems the more strange as the trans. **jemanden zu etwas beglückwünschen** ('to congratulate a person on something', e.g. on an honour conferred on him) is by no means uncommon.

gönnen: see **permit** 4; **past-present verbs** 3.

Gunst: see **permit** 4.

Grad: 1. Distinguish between **der Grad,** meaning 'degree' (see 2)—**der Grat** (plur. **Grate,** less commonly **Gräte**), 'ridge'—**die Gräte,** really the plur. of **Grat,** now sing. (plur. **Gräten**), 'fish-bone' (cf. **Rückgrat,** 'spine'). **2.** The plur. of **Grad** depends on the context. In a distrib. sense it is **Grade,** as in **Es gibt drei Grade der Steigerung** ('There are three degrees of comparison')—**Er hat sich zwei akademische Grade erworben** ('He has taken two University degrees'); but when used collect. as a measure, it retains the sing. form in the plur. (see **nouns of measure** 1 *a*), as in **Das Thermometer steht auf 68 Grad Fahrenheit, das heißt, auf 20 Grad Celsius und 16 Grad Reaumur.** In non-scientific lang. the sing. is much used in expressions like **Das interessiert mich in hohem Grade** ('That interests me greatly')—**Seine Klage ist bis zu einem gewissen Grade berechtigt** ('His complaint is to some extent justified')—**Die Lage ist im höchsten Grade peinlich** ('The situation is exceedingly awkward')—**Er ist mir im höchsten Grade unsympathisch** ('He is intensely antipathetic to me, I dislike him ever so much').

grain: see **Getreide** 1 and 2.

gram: see **adjectives (indeclinable)** 2.

Grat, Gräte: see **Grad** 1; **Fährte.**

grau: For the subst. use of this adj., see **colour,** and cf. the coll. expressions **sich** (dat.) **über etwas** (accus.) **keine grauen Haare wachsen lassen** ('not to worry about something *or* take a thing too much to heart')—**alles grau in grau malen** ('to paint everything in gloomy colours, take a dismal view of things')—**das graue Elend haben** (= **einen Katzenjammer haben,** 'to have a hangover' after too much liquor).

grauen: 1. There are two verbs **grauen,** one meaning 'to become gray' (as used of the sky at dawn), the other 'to feel a horror of, shudder at' (**vor**). With a *pers.* subj., the latter is now little used, except as a reflex., as in **Man müßte sich grauen, zu Bett zu gehen** (Alexis). Much more common is the *impers.* use, generally with a *dat.* of the person: *Duden* gives only **Mir graut vor dir,** and sim. **Es graute ihm vor der Versuchung** (Heyse). Much the same applies to the now rather more usual form **grausen** (see **gruselig**), which is almost always used *impers.*, but which may also take an *accus.* of the person: e.g. **Dem Vater grauset's** (G.)—**Wenn sie jetzt in die Wirtschaft der Mutter kam, grauste es sie** (Viebig)—**Es grauste sie, wenn von Menschenfressern die Rede war** (K. Edschmid); cf., with the case uncertain, **Die Lockungen und Drohungen der Stadt waren seltsam vermischt: uns grauste vor Einsamkeit, und doch trieb ein Verlangen uns vorwärts** (Hofmannsthal). **2.** Analogous is **schaudern** ('to shudder'), used with either a pers. or (rather more commonly) an impers. subj.: e.g. **Der Anblick machte mich vor Ent-**

setzen schaudern—Bei dem Anblick schauderte es mir or mich.

grauselig: see gruselig.

grausen: see grauen, and cf. gruselig 2.

greifen: cf. langen 1 (*b*).

grob: see rough 3.

grün: For the subst. use of this adj., see **colour.** The adj. is used in a number of coll. idioms: e.g. **auf keinen grünen Zweig kommen** ('not to get on in the world')—**jemandem grün sein** ('to be well-disposed towards some one', neg. 'to bear some one a grudge')—**sich an jemandes grüne Seite setzen** ('to sit down at some one's left side', the side of the heart).

Grund: 1. As explained under **Boden** (q.v. 1 *ad fin.*), **Grund** really implies ability to support what rests on it. In some cases the two nouns may approach each other closely: thus, the 'bottom' of the sea may refer to the water at the bottom (**Meeresboden**) or to the earth immediately below the water (**Meeresgrund**). A person taking soundings with a lead (**Senkblei**) will naturally measure the depth to the **Grund**, not to the **Boden**; and so also **keinen Grund finden** ('to be out of one's depth')—**zu Grunde gehen** (of a ship, 'to sink'; fig. of a person, 'to be ruined')—**einer Sache auf den Grund gehen** ('to go *or* get to the bottom of something')—**jemanden zu Grunde richten** ('to ruin *or* destroy some one'), etc. That **Grund** implies ability to support something is obvious from its common use in the fig. sense of 'basis, foundation' or of 'reason' (see 2): e.g. **Seine Behauptung ist ohne jeden Grund** ('His assertion is quite unfounded')—**Er hat keinen Grund zur Klage** ('He has no cause for complaint')—**Alles hat seinen Grund** ('There is a reason for everything'). **2.** It is important to distinguish between **Grund** and **Ursache.** The former means 'reason, ground' (ant. **Folge,** 'result, outcome'), the latter 'cause' (ant. **Wirkung,** 'effect'): cf. **Augustin hatte wohl Gründe, aber keine Ursache, die Äbtissin zu besuchen** (H. W. Geissler)—**Der Mensch sieht nur die Wirkungen; die Ursachen sind ihm unbekannt** (G.)—**Dieses sind natürliche Folgen natürlicher Ursachen** (Immermann); in the proposition **Die Bosheit sucht keine Gründe, nur Ursachen** (G.), **Ursachen** has the rather unusual sense of 'motives' or 'excuses' (**Beweggründe** or **Vorwände**).

gru'selig: 1. This is now the more usual form of **grau'selig,** meaning 'gruesome, hair-raising, creepy', as in **eine grauselige Geschichte** (Auerbach), which might have been simply **eine grausige Geschichte.** Incidentally, **grauselig** has no connexion with the adj. **selig,** the **e** of the former being short, but is derived from MHG *grûwesal* with the addition of the adj. ending *-ic*, which caused the *a* to mutate to *æ*, as explained under **-selig** 2. Although the noun **Grausal** (a 'ghastly figure *or* shape', a 'monster') is now hardly used at all, it was not uncommon a century ago, as in **Nun ist der Reiter dem Grausal nahe** (Tieck); on the other hand, **Scheusal** (< MHG *schiuwesal* = **Vogelscheuche,** 'scarecrow') is still in quite common use in the same sense as **Grausal. 2.** The adj. **grauselig** is formed from the noun **Graus,** meaning 'horror', but more usual in this sense is now the verbal noun **Grausen** (see **grauen** 1), as in **In diesem Buch** (*scil.* **„Tausendundeine Nacht"**) **ist kein Platz für Grausen** (Hofmannsthal).

guess: see **raten** 1.

guide: see **lead.**

gut und gern: see **gern** 1.

H

haben: 1. See **verbs (auxiliary). 2.** Of the many uses of **haben** as an independent verb, the only one which seems to call for notice here is its infin. construction. (**a**) The infin. *without* **zu** is confined to propositions like **Sie hatte einen Ring am Finger stecken,** for which see **accusative and infinitive** 1 (*a*) and cf. **accusative and participle.** (**b**) The infin. *with* **zu** is used in propositions like **Ich habe einen Brief zu beantworten,** where the infin. is gerundive and really has pass. force (**einen Brief, der zu beantworten ist**). The omission of the accus. obj. here leads to propositions in which **haben zu** approaches **müssen**: e.g. **Sie haben dafür zu sorgen, daß alles glatt geht** ('You have to see to it that everything runs smoothly'), where an obj. like **Pflicht** ('duty') is understood; sim. **Wir haben uns nach den Regeln zu richten** ('We have [no choice but] to conform to the regulations') and **Ich habe mit der Königin zu reden** (Sch.: 'I have [a need] to speak with the queen'). Apart from such examples, in which there is a pers. subj. and an obj. is implied, the infin. with **zu** is only used in dialects, esp. with an impers. subj., the commonest infin. here being **geschehen** (q.v.) in its pass. sense of 'to be done': e.g. **Noch ehe ich heute einschlief, mußte ich wissen, was am nächsten Morgen zu geschehen hatte** (M. Eyth: = **was . . . getan werden mußte**, 'what had to be done next morning')—**Der Flieger ging umher, um zu sehen, was für die Herrichtung des Flugfeldes zu geschehen habe** (Binding: 'The airman went round to see what required to be done in the way of laying out the landing-ground'). Such expressions should be avoided in good prose. **3.** For the coll. expression **Hat sich was!** see **impersonal verbs** 4 (*b*); for **habend,** see **participle (present)** 2.

habhaft: Like **ansichtig** (q.v.), this indecl. adj. is only used in combination with **werden** in the sense of 'to get hold *or* become possessed of'. Its orig. construction was a *gen.* obj., and this is still the rule in choice prose, and also in more ordinary lang. in the south: e.g. **Wenn ich nur wüßte, wie ich des verabredeten Preises habhaft werden soll!** (G. Keller)—**Von Schmetterlingen und Käfern fing ich zusammen, wessen ich habhaft werden konnte** (id.); fig. **Er dachte über den Traum nach, und es war ihm unlieb, daß er seiner nicht habhaft werden konnte** (Jul. Grosse: '. . . he was annoyed that he had no vivid recollection of it', lit. that he could not get a grip of it). But through the influence of **es** (q.v. 1) the *accus.* has become common in the lang. of every day: e.g. **Unter allen Umständen gibt's gute Kinder, die sich mit Planen beschäftigen, dich habhaft zu werden** (G.: see **Plan**)—**Er ritt auf allen Pferden, die er habhaft werden konnte** (Stifter).

Habicht: see **Käfig.**

Hader: see **rag** 4.

Haft: Distinguish between **die Haft** ('custody, arrest'), with no plur., and **der Haft** ('clasp, hook'), with plur. **Hafte** or **Haften**: cf. **etwas mit Haften** (or **Haken**) **befestigen** ('to fasten with hooks and eyes').

halb: 1. Used as an attrib. adj., this is inflected in the reg. way, as in **Er erhob sich mit halbem Leibe** (Immermann: 'He half rose'); but if qualified by an art. or poss., the latter always *precedes* **halb:** e.g. **Der Prozeß zog sich ein halbes Jahr hin** ('dragged on for half a year')—**Darüber ging das halbe Jahr hin—Er hat sein halbes Vermögen verloren.** It remains uninflected before place-names which have no art., and may remain so in fractions (cf. **Dutzend** 1): e.g. **Er hat halb Europa** (but **die halbe Schweiz**) **durchreist—Das Geschäft hat drei(und)-einhalb** (or **drei und ein halbes**) **Prozent abgeworfen—Seit zweieinhalb Jahren leitete er die Klinik** (K. Edschmid); it is never inflected when suffixed to an ordinal numeral, as in **anderthalb** (q.v.) and **fünftehalb Mark** (lit. half of the 5th mark, i.e. $4\frac{1}{2}$ marks). **2.** There are several ways of rendering 'half-way': (**a**) The best way to suggest a point lying 'mid-way' between two places is seen in examples like **Sie eilte zur Tür, blieb aber auf halbem Wege** stehen (Jul. Wolff)—**Auf halbem Heimweg** ('Halfway home') **kam ihm das Vesperläuten entgegen** (W. v. Scholz); so also **sich auf halbem Wege treffen** ('to meet halfway', either lit. or fig.), and with a verb of motion, **Der Wagen ist hier, ich gebe Ihnen Pferde auf halben Weg** (G.). Sometimes the art. is inserted here, or an adv. gen. is used: e.g. **Sie begegnen sich meist auf dem halben Weg** (Viebig)—**Halben Wegs zwischen den zwei Dörfern lief ein Graben, über den eine Brücke** führte (Fontane)—**Plock liegt etwa halben Weges zwischen Warschau und Thorn** (Bergengruen). Another way to express the same idea is seen in **Das Haus lag auf der Hälfte des Weges** (Immermann)—**Auf der Hälfte der Treppe kam ihm Rauch entgegen** (E. Wichert); cf. **Eine Tür war bloß angelehnt, er öffnete sie zur Hälfte** (G. Keller)—**Das Dorf bestand nur zur einen Hälfte aus Häusern: daran schloß** sich **ein Schwarm von Zelten** (Britting); see also **halbwegs.** (**b**) Analogous expressions are used to express 'halfway up *or* down': e.g. **Zwei Leute bewegten sich hügelabwärts; auf halber Höhe blieben sie stehen** (Bergengruen)—**In halber Höhe des Berges saß**

ein Bursch unter den Reben (Heyse)—**Bücherbehälter waren rings bis zur halben Höhe des Raumes angebracht** (I. Seidel: 'Bookshelves were fitted up halfway up the walls round the room')—**Seine Lider hoben sich bis zur halben Höhe des Auges** (K. Edschmid: i.e. he half opened his eyes). For analogous prep. phrases, used to express 'abreast of', see **Höhe. 3.** (**a**) Besides its use in fractions (see 1), **-halb** is used as a suffix to **außer, inner, ober** and **unter** to form preps., for which see **außerhalb.** (**b**) The suffix **-halben** (orig. the dat. plur. of the obs. fem. noun **Halbe,** meaning 'side, direction') is now added to possessives to form advs., with an inorganic **t** inserted: thus, **meinethalben** has developed out of the dat. plur. **meinen Halben,** and sim. **deinet-, dessent-, derenthalben,** etc. Actually, these expressions are no longer as common as they once were: 'for my sake' is more usually expressed by **um meinetwillen,** and the later sense of **meinethalben,** viz. 'as far as I am concerned, for all I care', is mostly expressed by **meinetwegen** (q.v.); but one still says **Zwischen den Bäumen standen allenthalben** ('on all sides') **steinerne Zwerge** (Stifter). (**c**) The form **halber** (really the masc. of the adj. **halb**: see **voll** 3) has established itself as a prep. meaning 'for the sake of, because of' (cf. our 'on my be*half*'), thus approaching **wegen** (q.v.) in sense, and is always placed *after* the noun, which stands in the *gen.*: e.g. **Des Friedens halber traten die zwei Parteien in Verhandlungen ein—Seit vier Tagen stecke ich Hustens halber** ('because of a cough') **im Turme** (Droste-Hülshoff). Where the noun is not qualified by an art. or attrib. adj., **halber** has now generally become attached to it as a suffix, the result being an adv. expression written with a small letter, as in **Er ist gesundheitshalber** (or **krankheits-, sicherheits-, vorsichtshalber**) **zu Hause geblieben;** and this applies esp. to nouns with an unrecognizable gen., such as **ehrenhalber;** cf. **Er hat das Gut Schulden halber übernommen** (Jul. Grosse), where accepted usage requires either **schuldenhalber** or **der Schulden halber.**

-halben, -halber: see **halb** 3 (*b*) and (*c*) respectively.

halbmannshoch: see **genitive of measure.**

halbwegs: As explained under **halb** 2 (*a*), the most idiomatic rendering of a phrase like 'halfway to the town' is **auf halbem Wege zur Stadt,** an idea which is also expressed by the adv. **mittewegs,** used esp. with the prep. **zwischen:** e.g. **Er erlangte einen vorteilhaften Sitz mittewegs zwischen der Akademie und des Oberamtmanns Wohnung** (G.). The adv. **halbwegs** is also sometimes used in this lit. sense, as in **In einiger Entfernung, halbwegs nach Neumark hinunter, stand ein alter Mann und hackte Holz** (Zuckmayer) and **Man muß das Trinkwasser halbwegs des Berges holen** (Auerbach: usually **auf halber Höhe des Berges**—see **halb** 2 *b*); but **halbwegs** is now generally used coll. with the fig. force of 'tolerably, passably' (cf. 'middling'); e.g. **Wenn er nur halbwegs vernünftig ist, wird er seinen Plan aufgeben—Du bist froh, wenn nur deine Kleider halbwegs anständig sind** (Ompteda)—**Sie beschloß, niemals ein schönes, ja nicht einmal halbwegs anziehendes Dienstmädchen zu nehmen** (L. Winder)—**Er mußte überlaut schreien, um seine Zwischenreden halbwegs verständlich zu machen** (Th. Mann).

Halfter: This noun, meaning 'halter', is used either as a *masc.* or *neut.* (plur. Halfter) or, more commonly, as a *fem.* (plur. Halftern). In Austria all three genders are officially recognized.

halfway: see **halb** 2 (*a*) and (*b*); **halbwegs.**

Hall: see **sound** 1 (*b*).

halten (*intrans.*): see **stop** 1 (*c*).

Hand: Although **Hand** now has the plur. **Hände** (unless where it is used as a measure of distance or amount, when it is generally treated as invariable: e.g. **zwei Hand breit—drei Handvoll Mehl:** see **nouns of measure** 2), it did not orig. mutate the root-vowel, and remnants of the unmutated forms are still in use: **1.** Thus, the OHG dat. plur. *hantum* (> **Handen**) is still extant in **Der Brief ist mir leider abhanden gekommen** ('has been mislaid, got lost'; cf. Heine's use of this form with a playful afterthought: **Als ich das nasse Fußzeug mit Pantoffeln vertauscht hatte, kam mir einer derselben abhanden, oder vielmehr abfüßen**)—**Es sind Vorräte genug vorhanden** ('at hand, available': see **existence** 2)—**Es ist keine Gefahr vorhanden** ('There is no danger') —**Dies ist das einzige vorhandene Exemplar** ('the only copy available, extant')—also, in commercial language, **Adressieren Sie den Brief zuhanden** (or **zu Händen,** abbreviated **z. H.**) **des Herrn Soundso** ('c/o Mr. So-and-so'); cf. **Er schrieb**

zunächst die Adresse, an Fräulein Weber in der Hirschgasse, zu eignen Handen (H. Hesse: as we mark a letter 'Personal'). Analogous expressions with other prepositions are now obs.: cf. **Sie zeigte sich überall tätig und ging der Mutter in allem an Handen** (G.: 'She . . . lent her mother a helping hand in all the housework') and **Gern hätten uns die Mönche einen Abdruck der Medaille gegeben, es war aber nichts bei Handen, was zu einer Form tauglich gewesen wäre** (G.), where in both cases **zur Hand** would now be used. **2.** (**a**) The MHG noun *hant* meant not only 'hand', but also 'kind', so that *liute aller hande* meant 'people of all kinds'; and sim., with the gen. placed first, *maniger hande spîse* ('food of various kinds'), *drîer hande kleit* ('three kinds *or* changes of clothes'). This gen. plur. has survived in the invariable suffix **-hand,** as in **allerhand** (q.v.); so also **mancherhand, vielerhand,** etc., which are, however, not nearly as common as **allerhand.** (**b**) Analogous is the other invariable suffix **-lei,** with the same force as **-hand.** In MHG there were three words *lei*(*e*): one meant 'layman' (> **Laie**); another meant 'rock *or* cliff' (cf. **Lorelei** or **Lurlei,** 'the rock on which gnomes lurk', and place-names in the Moselle valley like **Bullay, Schwarzlay,** etc.); and the third meant 'kind, sort', as in *aller leie dinc* ('things of all kinds'), which eventually took the form **allerlei Dinge** (cf. **viel** 1 *b*). This **-lei** has a much wider application than **-hand,** as the following examples show: **Das ist mir einerlei** (That 's all one to me')—**Künstler beiderlei Geschlechts** (Th. Mann: 'Artists of both sexes')—**Haben Sie öfter derlei Ohnmachten?** (St. Zweig: 'Do you have these sorts of fainting-fits often?')—**Seine Frau war eine stille Frau, vor der er sich keinerlei Zwang aufzuerlegen brauchte** (L. Winder)—**Er hatte mancherlei Merkwürdiges zu berichten** (E. Wichert)—**Ein rechter Reisender soll solcherlei Seltsamkeiten nicht vorbeigehen** (Storm: see **pass** 2 *b*)—**Sie hatten sich in hunderterlei Hinsicht verändert** (K. Edschmid)—**Tausenderlei wollte sie wissen** (Fr. Schnack: 'She asked a thousand questions')—**Sie hatte zehnerlei Dinge zugleich zu tun** (Waggerl); and such expressions can be used freely after the def. art. or a poss.: e.g. **Er übernimmt es, sie mit den vielerlei Geschäften in Haus und Hof bekannt zu machen** (id.)—**Die allerlei neuen Gestalten machen mir ein buntes Schauspiel** (G.)—**Man konnte die verschiedenerlei** ('various') **Empfindungen der Kirchgänger wahrnehmen** (C. Rothe)—**Es ist gut, etwas Abwechslung in das ewige Einerlei des Alltagslebens zu bringen** ('. . . into the endless monotony of every-day life')—**Euer einerlei Geschwätz!** (Mörike: 'Your monotonous idle chatter!'); cf. also **Leipziger Allerlei** (a dish of mixed vegetables) and **Meister Allerlei** ('Jack of all trades').

Handhabe: This fem. noun, meaning 'handle', may be used in the lit. sense, as in **Er besah sich einen Stock, dessen Handhabe mit Leder beschlagen war** (Mörike) and **Die silberne Schale hatte zwei Widderköpfe als Handhaben** (C. Bulcke), but on the whole **der Handgriff** is now more usual in this sense, as in **Es war ein Stock aus dunklem Holze mit einem rund gebogenen Handgriff** (Rilke); it is still in common use, however, with fig. force: cf. **Die Erfindungen boten nirgends eine Handhabe dar, bei welcher er sie anpacken konnte** (G. Keller:' Nowhere did the inventions offer a handle by which he could lay hold of them'). Cf. **handhaben.**

handhaben: In MHG a distinction was usually made between the contracted and the uncontracted forms of *haben*, the former (*ich hân, hâte*, or *hete*, etc.) being used as the aux., the latter (*ich häbe, häbete*, etc.) with the force of **halten;** so **handhaben** really means 'to hold one's hand on' a thing, hence now 'to handle, ply, wield' (a weapon, instrument, etc.), and fig. 'to deal with, manipulate, manage, administer'. Being formed from the noun **Handhabe** (q.v.), it is a reg. *weak* verb (see **beanspruchen** 1), with uncontracted forms, viz. **handhabte, gehandhabt:** e.g. **Wie geschickt du diese Waffe handhabst!**—**Er rief einem Manne zu, der emsig die Nadel handhabte** (Jak. Frey)—**Ich verfolgte die Bewegungen, mit denen die Musiker ihre Instrumente handhabten** (Th. Mann)—**Sie saß da und handhabte schweigsam ihr goldenes Besteck** (Bruno Frank)—**Die Fliegenklappe wußte der Wirt so geschickt zu handhaben, daß er auf dem Rande eines Glases eine Fliege treffen konnte, ohne das Glas umzustürzen** (Auerbach); also fig., **Die absolute Monarchie ist die schlechteste oder die beste Regierungsform, je nachdem sie gehandhabt wird** (Bruno Frank)—**Ich**

werde das Testament so handhaben ('execute'), **daß der Erlös den Gläubigern zugewandt wird** (Bergengruen)—**Die Art und Weise, wie der Lehrer den Unterricht handhabte** ('conducted'), **hatte etwas ungemein Gewinnendes** (Ompteda)—**Er war lange in Paris gewesen und handhabte die Formen der höfischen Manieren mit viel Geschick** (E. Wichert).

hängen: 1. The OHG lang. distinguished between *hâhan* (strong trans.: past tense *hiang*, part. *gihangan*), *hangên* (weak intrans.) and *henchan* (weak trans. > **henken**—see 2 *d* below). That confusion resulted later is hardly surprising, and the grammarians of the 17th and 18th centuries, whose chief aim was to differentiate clearly between trans. and intrans. forms, were at least actuated by sound motives when they fixed the *strong* verb **hangen** (**hing, gehangen**) as *intrans.*, and the *weak* verb **hängen** (**hängte, gehängt**) as *trans.* **2.** This grammatical rule holds good, in the main, to this day, but it has been modified in one or two respects. (**a**) In all *pres.* tenses (pres. indic. and subj., infin., pres. part., and imperat.) the unmutated forms are no longer used at all in ordinary prose, having been displaced by the mutated forms (which are, of course, common to both verbs in the 2nd and 3rd sing.): it is only in poetry or very choice prose that a proposition like **Die Bilder hangen an der Wand** is now used. In other words, **ich hänge, sie hängen,** etc. are now always used in ordinary prose, whether with trans. or intrans. force: **Die Bilder hängen an der Wand** and **Wir hängen die Bilder an die Wand.** (**b**) In the *past* tense the rule holds good that the form **hängte** is invariably *trans.*, and that where an *intrans.* form is required, it must be **hing** (subj. **hinge**). But it is esp. noteworthy that, despite the grammarians' protests, modern authors continually use the strong form **hing** with *trans.* force (cf. **schrecken** 2), and the following examples might be multiplied indefinitely: **Er hing die Schnur wieder an ihre Stelle** (G.)—**Ich hinge lieber alles Bücherschreiben an den Nagel** (Heine: 'I would rather give up all literary work')—**Ein wenig Geld hatte ich übrig, also hing ich meine literarischen Verpflichtungen an den Nagel** (H. Hesse)—**Sie hing sich an seinen Arm** (Fontane)—**Froh, ein vertrautes Gesicht zu sehen, hing ich mich an seinen Arm** (Sudermann)—**Mit dem gesunden Arm fuhr er nach dem Öllicht zu seinen Häupten: er hing sich daran, daß die Ketten rissen** (E. Zahn)—**Dann hingen wir unsere Lumpen über die Büsche zum Trocknen** (Frenssen)—**Ich nahm den Helm ab und hing ihn über den Arm** (H. Hauser). In view of such examples it seems idle to protest, the more so as these authors are actually restoring to the strong past tense its historic right to be used with trans. force. In other words, then, we *must* say **Das Bild hing an der Wand,** and we *may* say **Ich hing das Bild an die Wand;** and it is perhaps significant that in one expression, viz. **den Kopf hängen** ('to hang one's head'), the strong past tense is almost invariably used: e.g. **Sie hing den Kopf** (Freytag)—**Es war ein schwüler Morgen, manche Feldblume hing das feine Köpfchen** (J. Ludwig); with other parts of the body, **hängenlassen** is more usual, as in **Der Hund ließ den Schwanz** or **die Ohren hängen.** (**c**) In the *past part.*, on the other hand, the grammarians' rule still practically holds good: we cannot say **Das Bild hat an der Wand gehängt,** but only **Das Bild hat an der Wand gehangen.** Strangely enough, however, authors who freely say **Ich hing das Bild auf** seem reluctant to say **Ich habe das Bild aufgehangen**; cf. the following four examples from Fontane: **Sie hing den Korb an ihren Arm**—**Er hing ihr das Umschlagetuch um**—**Sie hatte sich in seinen Arm gehängt**—**Sie hat mir das Kettchen umgehängt**; and the following two from C. F. Meyer: **Die Alte hing ihm das Pulverhorn um**—**Ein Mädchen hatte sich ihm an den Hals gehängt.** Examples like the following are certainly not in accordance with ordinary prose usage in the north: **Vor die Gasflamme hatte man einen Bogen Löschpapier gehangen, um die Blendung zu mildern** (Ompteda)—**Er hatte den schwarzen Rock an den Zaun gehangen** (C. Hauptmann)—**Die Säbel hatte er wieder an ihren Ort gehangen** (Binding). (**d**) The weak trans. **henken** is now only used of hanging a criminal, as in **Eben waren etliche Spione gefangen und sollten stracks gehenkt werden** (Hans Hoffmann), but in ordinary lang. it has largely been displaced by **hängen** or **aufhängen** or esp. **erhängen,** although **Henker** is still the regular word for 'hangman', besides being often used in oaths like our 'devil, deuce': **Zum Henker!**

('Devil take it!')—cf. **Henkersmahlzeit,** really a condemned criminal's last meal, coll. a 'farewell dinner'. **3.** (**a**) What has been said of **hängen** applies also to its **sep.** compds. (see **ab-, an-, aufhängen,** etc.): the weak forms are always trans., the strong past tense intrans. or (despite the grammarians) trans., the strong past part. usually intrans. (but see **aufhängen** 2 *b*). (**b**) The *insep.* compds. are always *trans.*, their dir. obj. being the indir. obj. of the simple verb (see esp. **be-** and **verhängen**), and here both weak and strong forms are very common; in the past part. one should distinguish between the **weak** form denoting an *action*, and the *strong* form denoting a **state**: cf. **Man hat die Fenster mit Gardinen verhängt** and **Die Fenster sind mit Gardinen verhangen.**

hängenbleiben: see bleiben 2 (*b*).

happen: see **occur** 3; **geschehen.** Propositions like 'I happened to meet him *or* It so happened that I met him last night' can be neatly expressed by using the adv. **zufällig** ('by chance'): **Ich traf ihn zufällig gestern abend**; cf. **Der Zufall wollte es, daß ich ihm gestern begegnete** ('As good luck would have it, I ran across him yesterday').

hardly: For this adv. there are two common expressions which approach each other, yet differ. **1.** Used in statements of *fact*, as in 'I can hardly (= almost not) hear a word' or 'I had hardly (= only just) got home when it began to rain', it is expressed by **kaum** (q.v. for the ways to use it, and cf. below). **2.** In statements of *opinion*, expressing *doubt*, it is rendered by **schwerlich**—which, incidentally, is no longer used in the sense of 'heavily, greatly', as in **Ich habe schwerlich gesündigt** (2 Sam. 24. 10), where the modern version has substituted **schwer.** If you measure a stick and find it is not quite long enough for your purpose, you can say **Er ist kaum lang genug**; but if you look at it and think it will be just too short, you say **Er wird schwerlich lang genug sein.** So also **Der Raum ist kaum groß genug** implies that you have established the fact that the space is too small, whereas **schwerlich** here would suggest that you are afraid it will prove too small; sim. **Wir werden schwerlich den Zug erreichen** ('I doubt whether we shall catch the train'). So it is wrong to say **Ich war schwerlich am Bahnhof angekommen, als der Zug abfuhr,** but correct to say **Ich werde schwerlich am Bahnhof ankommen, ehe der Zug abfährt.**

harren: 1. This verb, meaning 'to wait' for something (esp. eagerly), is rare in MHG, and it was Luther who first used it freely. In modern times it has lost some ground, being mainly used in imitation of the Bible or in poetry, and replaced in ordinary lang. by (**sehnsüchtig**) **warten** (q.v. 1): cf. **Harre in Geduld, bis Gott deiner Eltern Sinn wendet!** (Immermann). Luther used it with either a gen. or **auf** + accus.: e.g. **Ich harre des Herrn . . . Meine Seele wartet auf den Herrn** (Ps. 130. 5–6)—**Siehe, das ist unser Gott, auf den wir harren** (Isa. 25. 9). The prep. construction is the usual one now, but the gen. still occurs: e.g. **Bald schritt ich über den Markt, allwo die Bäcker, vieler Käufer harrend, ihre Schragen** ('stalls') **geöffnet hatten** (Storm)—**Er war früh aufgestanden, um sich an eine Arbeit zu machen, die seit geraumer Zeit der Erledigung harrte** (Fontane)—**Sie saßen des Dampfers harrend** (= **auf den Dampfer wartend**) **am Hafen** (H. E. Busse). **2.** Rather more common is the compd. **beharren,** used like **bestehen** (q.v. 2 *c* and 3) with the force of 'to insist on, persist in, adhere to' (an opinion, standpoint, etc.), with **auf** + *dat.*: e.g. **Ich muß auf meiner Abschlagung ihrer Bitte beharren —Trotz aller Versuche, ihn zu überreden, beharrte er auf seinem Standpunkt—Der Händler beharrte auf seinem Kopf** (Bergengruen: 'The tradesman stuck to his point, was obstinate'). The usual aux. is now, as with **bestehen, haben,** but **sein** is sometimes used in the south, as in **Der Priester war** (better **hatte**) **auf der Entfernung der Bilder beharrt** (Marriot: 'The priest had insisted on the removal of the pictures').

Harz: Distinguish between **das Harz** ('resin', plur. **Harze**; hence **harzig,** 'resinous') and **der Harz** ('the Harz Mountains'). Although the growing timber on these mountains is largely coniferous, their name seems to have no direct connexion with resin: it is a corrupt form of MHG *hart* ('forest'), as are also **die Hardt** (in the Palatinate) and **der Spessart** (in Lower Franconia), the latter < MHG *spehtes hart,* i.e. **Spechtswald** ('forest of the woodpecker'). In references to these mountains it is necessary to insert the def. art.: **Der Brocken ist der höchste Berg im Harz—Der Weg von Aschaffen-**

burg nach Würzburg geht mitten durch den Spessart.

hastig: see quick 2.

hauen: **1.** The MHG verb *houwen* (> **hauen**) was one of the **reduplicating verbs** (q.v.), with past tense *hie* or *hiu* (for *hiew, hiuw*), past part. *gehouwen*; hence the modern forms in **Er hieb den Jungen mit dem Stock, hat ihn gehauen**—sim. **Sie war frech, ich habe sie riesig verhauen** (Ompteda: 'thrashed her soundly'). The proper sense of the verb is 'to *hew*, cut', then 'to strike, thrash'; cf. **weder gehauen noch gestochen**, an expression taken from fencing (**hauen und stechen** = 'to cut and thrust'), now only used fig. of what is 'neither one thing nor another', something one cannot 'make head or tail of': cf. **Eure Reden sind Geschwätz, gehauen nicht und nicht gestochen** (H. v. Kleist: 'Your speeches are a hotch-potch of idle chatter, without rhyme or reason'). For propositions like 'I struck him in the face', where the pers. obj. may be either the accus. or the dat., see **schlagen**. **2.** The *weak* forms **haute, gehaut** were fairly common at one time, as in **Er haute die Axt in den Baum** (Klopstock), and indeed, they have a historic foundation: there were two OHG verbs, *houwan* (strong) and *houwôn* (weak). But although these weak forms are not used in the best prose—*Duden* says **„du hiebst (häufig, aber nicht gut: hautest), gehauen (nicht gehaut)"**—the fact is that they are often used in familiar lang. by standard authors, the strong forms now sounding rather 'refined': e.g. **Da haute ihm Stoltenkamp eins** ('dealt him a blow') **über die Schulter** (R. Herzog)—**Er gab ihm die Geige in die Hand, und dabei packte ihn ein solcher Zorn, daß er sie ihm beinahe um den Kopf gehaut hätte** (R. Hohlbaum)—**Er hat das Mädel furchtbar gehaut** (A. Reiner)—**Es war weniger schlimm, durchgehaut zu werden, als sich noch einmal gegen den Stärkeren zur Wehr zu setzen** (id.); cf. the rather unusual adj. use of the past part. in **Sie zerquälte sich den Kopf, wie das nur möglich sei, daß so ein Lump sich durch seine gehauten Praktiken unter die Diener der Kirche eingeschlichen habe** (Werfel: 'She racked her brains to think how such a scoundrel could possibly have wormed his way among the servants of the church by his sharp practices'), probably based on the common coll. expression **jemand übers Ohr hauen** ('to cheat *or* swindle a person'). In this connexion cf. the coll. expression **Haue** (for **Hiebe**) **kriegen** ('to get a thrashing').

Hauf(en): The short form **Hauf**, common in Luther's Bible, is now almost obs., the only remnant of earlier usage, apart from the dims. **Häufchen** and **Häuflein**, being the expression **zuhauf** (< MHG *ze hûf*), used in poetry and choice prose with the force of 'in crowds, altogether', as in a well-known hymn by J. Neander: **Kommet zuhauf! Psalter und Harfe, wacht auf!** In more recent times the form **Haufe** (gen. **Haufens**) was used esp. of a 'crowd', and this is still permissible: cf. **Es zieht ein Haufe das Tal herab** (Uhland); but modern usage prefers the longer form **Haufen** both in the sense of 'heap, pile' and in that of 'crowd': thus, **ein Heuhaufen** is a 'haycock' (Scots 'coll'), and sim. **ein Ameisenhaufen** ('ant-hill'), **Schnee-, Steinhaufen**, etc., and **Ihr seid ein Haufen Elender** (G. Keller: 'You are a pack of miserable creatures'); so also **einen Plan über den Haufen werfen** ('to throw a plan overboard') and **jemand über den Haufen rennen** ('to rush along and knock a person down'). For expressions like 'a heap of stones' or 'a pile of books', see also **genitive of material** 1 and 5, and cf. **Masse** and **Menge**.

Haupt: This was the orig. German word for 'head', but it is now a rather choice expression, used esp. as we speak of 'the head of a party' or 'crowned heads', being elsewhere displaced in ordinary lang. by **Kopf** (q.v.). In OHG it was *houbit*, which became *houbet* in MHG, the labial consonant *b* preventing the mutation of the stem-vowel; but the form *höubet* arose in Central Germany and gradually spread to other parts, which explains the modern established plur. **Häupter.** The historically more correct plur. form **Häupte** is still in use but confined to the *dat.* with the prep. **zu**: cf. **Unter einem Mandelbaume lag er wie entseelt** ('lifeless'); **Angiolina warf sich ihm zu Häupten** (A. Kopisch)—**Zu ihren Häupten** ('overhead') **funkelte ein früher Stern . . . Plötzlich begann es zu sausen über ihren Häuptern** (B. Kellermann). Noteworthy are the use of the distrib. sing. in propositions like **Alle Anwesenden entblößten das Haupt** ('All those present uncovered their heads') and the unchanged plur. in expressions such as **zwanzig Haupt Vieh** ('twenty head of cattle'); in this last connexion, see **überhaupt** (< MHG *über houbet*), orig. used of a rough calculation of numbers, e.g. in an assembly of people, a large herd of cattle, etc.

head: see **Haupt** and **Kopf.**

heben: 1. This verb is always *strong*: it is only an illiterate person who could say **Hättest du die eine Zigarre aufgehebt, hättest du morgen auch was zu rauchen** (H. Hesse). The established past tense forms are now **hōb, gehōben,** but remnants of earlier usage are still preserved. **(a)** Thus, **hūb** (< MHG *huop*) is still sometimes used, not so much in the simple verb, as in **Ich nahm einen Hebel und hub** (now usually **hob**) **den Stein** (Kopisch), but esp. in the compound **anheben** (q.v.) used in the sense of 'to begin'. The past subj. is usually **höbe**: cf., as unusual, **Ich überhübe mich, wollte ich ihnen gleich sein** (Rilke: 'I should be conceited if I presumed to be their equal'). **(b)** In MHG the past part. form was always *gehăben*, and this is preserved (but with lengthened stem-vowel) in **erhāben.** Whereas **erhōben** is always used with *verbal* force, implying an *action*, **erhāben** is only used as an *adj.*, implying a *state*, and always with *fig.* force: cf., on the one hand, **Kein einziger Schüler hat die Hand erhoben—Er ist in den Adelstand erhoben worden** ('He has been knighted *or* raised to the peerage'); and, on the other hand, **erhabene Arbeit** ('relief, chased work')—**halberhaben** ('bas-relief')—**ein erhabener Anblick, Stil, Gedanke** ('imposing, lofty, noble')—**Vom Erhabenen zum Lächerlichen ist nur ein Schritt** ('From the sublime to the ridiculous . . .')—**Er ist über jeden Verdacht erhaben** ('He is above all suspicion'). **2.** When not associated with a prep. phrase indicating the place *on to* which a thing is raised (as in **ein Kind auf den Stuhl heben**—see 3 *a*), the simple verb **heben** is not nearly as common as some of its compounds (see 3). Apart from its specific use with objects like **ein untergegangenes Schiff** ('to raise a sunken vessel'), **einen Schatz** ('to dig up a treasure') or **jemandes Mut** ('to raise a person's courage'), it is mainly used, often fig., with a prep. phrase pointing to the place *from* which the thing is raised: e.g. **eine Tür aus den Angeln heben** ('to take a door off its hinges')—**den Gegner aus dem Sattel heben** ('to unhorse an adversary, supplant a rival')—**ein Kind aus der Taufe heben** ('to stand godfather to a child'); and the past part. is used with *fig.* force in expressions like **ein gehobener** ('elevated') **Stil—gehobene Stimmung** ('high spirits'). For **sich heben,** see 4. **3.** Of the compounds, the ones which should be distinguished are: **(a) herauf-** and **hinaufheben,** with only *one* meaning (see **her-, hin-**), viz. 'to lift to a higher level' *and leave there*, the prefix being really pleonastic when an appropriate prep. phrase is added: e.g. **einen Korb vom Fußboden auf den Tisch, jemandem ein Bündel auf die Schulter, ein Kind auf die Mauer (hinauf)heben. (b) aufheben** (cf. 4 *c*), with various specific meanings, e.g. 'to annul, cancel, repeal', etc.; its fundamental force is 'to pick up', i.e. 'not to leave lying', then 'to keep, not to throw away', as in **Hier ist meine ganze Bibliothek: es sind eher Bücher, die ich nicht wegwerfe, als die ich aufhebe** (G.); where it approaches *(a)*, the object is raised *temporarily* for a particular purpose, the idea of leaving it at the higher level being absent: e.g. **die Hand zum Schwur, die Faust zum Schlage aufheben—Bei seinem Herannahen hob ich die Augen von meinem Buche auf—Indem sie in das Auto stieg, hob sie ihr Ballkleid auf**; cf. **Nach aufgehobener Tafel** ('after rising from table' at the end of a meal) **wurde die Gesellschaft zu einem Spaziergang eingeladen** (G.). **(c) erheben** (cf. 4 *a*), 'to raise', with objects where **aufheben** is not used, e.g. with **Stimme, Geschrei, Gelächter, Einwände** or **Einwendungen** ('objections'), **Steuern** ('taxes'); also 'to raise' to a higher social rank (e.g. **in den Adelstand erheben,** 'to raise to the peerage'), or 'to extol' (e.g. **in den Himmel erheben,** 'to laud to the skies'); and in mathematics, 'to raise' to a higher power (**in** or **auf eine höhere Potenz erheben**) as contrasted with **einen Bruch aufheben** ('to reduce a fraction'). It is never used with the force of 'not to leave lying' (hence always **den Handschuh aufheben,** either *lit.*, or *fig.* 'not to refuse a challenge'); on the other hand, **Der Berg erhebt sein Haupt bis in die Wolken.** In some cases there may be a clear distinction, e.g. between **einen Gefallenen aufheben** (lit., not to leave him where he has fallen) and **einen Gefallenen erheben** (fig., to raise one who has sunk low). **4. (a)** In the *reflex.* use, by far the commonest expression is **sich erheben** ('to rise, arise'): e.g. **sich vom Stuhl, vom Schlum-**

mer, *fig.* **über alle Schicksalsschläge erheben—ein Wind, ein Gewitter, ein lautes Gelächter, eine Schwierigkeit erhob sich,** etc. (**b**) On the other hand, **sich heben** is hardly used at all, unless in conjunction with **lassen** (as in **Der schwere Stein ließ sich nicht heben**) or with another verb expressing its opposite (e.g. **Ihre Brust hob und senkte sich**). (**c**) In **sich aufheben,** the pron. has only *reciprocal*, not *reflex.* force: e.g. **Diese zwei Zahlen heben sich auf** ('. . . cancel each other')—**Es gibt Lagen, in denen Furcht und Hoffnung sich wechselseitig aufheben und in eine dunkle Fühllosigkeit verlieren** (G.); on the other hand, a stage direction like **Der Abt hebt sich auf** (G., for **erhebt sich**) sounds very unnatural today, as does also **Lianen schlangen sich an den Ahornriesen empor, die sich aus Geröll aufhoben** (Blunck).

Hehl: This noun, meaning 'secrecy' (cf. **bergen** 4 and 5), is now used esp. as an obj. of **haben** or **machen** in *neg.* propositions (cf. **ohne Hehl,** 'without dissimulation, frankly'). The thing kept secret orig. stood in the *gen.*, as in MHG *si hete des hæle* (= **Sie verheimlichte das,** 'She made a secret of that, kept it secret'), and the gen. is still used in good style: e.g. **Seiner Empfindungen machte er kein Hehl** (Gutzkow)—**Der Dichter hatte der Sache kein Hehl** (id.)—**Er hatte dessen kein Hehl, daß er ein Sterbender sei** (Treitschke); so also **Er hat es keinen** (now always **kein**) **Hehl, daß wir um seinetwillen hieher berufen sind** (Sch.)—**Er hatte es kein Hehl, daß ihn jeder Mensch interessierte** (Heyse). In the last two examples, **es** (q.v.) is really a gen., but it came to be treated as an accus., thus leading to **Er macht das kein Hehl,** which now, however, usually takes the form **Er macht kein Hehl davon** or **daraus:** cf. **Er machte daraus kein Hehl** (K. Edschmid)—**Je größer ein Dichter selbst ist, um so weniger macht er aus seinen Anleihen ein Hehl** (H. Maync: 'The greater poet a man is, the less does he make a secret of having borrowed from others').

Heide: Distinguish between **die Heide** ('heath, moorland'; also = **Heidekraut,** 'heather'), with plur. **Heiden,** and **der Heide** ('heathen, pagan'), with gen. and plur. **Heiden.**

Heim, heim-: 1. While **das Heim** is a 'home' in the intimate family sense, as we speak of 'a comfortable home' or 'a home of one's own', **die Heimat** conveys the wider sense of 'homeland, native country *or* district': cf. **Das junge Paar hat noch kein eigenes Heim** and **Nach längerem Aufenthalt in der Fremde kehrte das Paar in die Heimat zurück**; and there is the same distinction between the two adjs.: **Der Fremde fühlte sich bald ganz heimisch bei uns—Börne konnte den heimatlichen Dialekt nie ganz verleugnen** (Heine). **2.** (**a**) The form **heim** is the accus. of the noun used as an adv. prefix of motion in **heimgehen, -kehren, -kommen,** etc., while the corresponding adv. of rest is **daheim:** hence **Als er schließlich daheim ankam** (but **heimkam**), **war er noch nicht müde** (Fr. Schnack). Actually, **Heim** and **heim-** are esp. characteristic of the south; in the north one prefers **nach Hause gehen** and **zu Hause bleiben,** and the latter phrase has led to the modern noun for 'home', viz. **Zuhause** (neut.): e.g. **Wir erzählten uns von unserem Zuhause** (W. v. Scholz)—**Schiller beginnt, sich in Jena ein zweites Zuhause zu schaffen** (F. A. Hohenstein)—**Warum in die Ferne fahren, da man ein solches Zuhause sein eigen nennt?** (H. Franck)—**München war nicht sein Zuhause** (A. Eloesser). But in a number of verbs **heim-** is in regular general use, often with *fig.* force: the chief of these are **heimfallen** (in law: 'to revert to the former possessor'), as in **Es war ihm nicht möglich, das Haus wie ein heimgefallenes Lehen an sich zu bringen** (Zifferer)—**heimführen** ('to take a bride to her new home')—**heimleuchten** (*lit.* 'to light a person [dat. or accus.] home' with a lantern, *fig.* 'to give a person [dat.] a piece of one's mind' or 'to send somebody packing'): e.g., on the one hand, **Es kam vor, daß die Damen sich bei Besuchen verspäteten und heimgeleuchtet werden mußten** (E. Wichert) and, on the other hand, **Du bist gerade der Rechte, ihnen heimzuleuchten** (Gerstäcker: 'You are the very one to send them about their business')—**heimsuchen** (*fig.*, often in the Bible, 'to afflict, punish, visit'): **Kein Übel wird sie heimsuchen** (Prov. 19. 23)—**Ich bin ein eifriger Gott, der da heimsucht der Väter Missetat an den Kindern** (Exod. 20. 5)—**heimzahlen** (*fig.*, with a dat. of the person, 'to requite, pay someone back in his own coin'): **Noch nie ist mir mein Vertrauen mit**

Verrat heimgezahlt worden (C. F. Meyer) —less commonly **heimgeben** (*fig.*, like **heimleuchten** or **heimzahlen**): e.g. in the former sense, **Er lachte, wenn er an Georg dachte: dem hatte er es heimgegeben** (Raabe) and in the latter sense, **Er kann mit nächstem** ('soon, presently') **die Freude haben, seinem Nebenbuhler den Spott auf die schönste Art heimzugeben** (Sch.). (**b**) The lengthened prefix **anheim-** is now practically confined to the verbs **fallen, geben** and **stellen**: for examples, see **anheim-**. In the case of **stellen,** the shorter prefix **heim-** was once used, but this is now obs.: cf. **Es ist besser, ich stell's dem Himmel heim** (Sch.).

Heirat, heiraten: see marry 2 (*c*) and 1 (*a*) respectively.

heischen: This trans. verb, meaning 'to ask for, solicit' (=**bitten um**) or 'to demand' (= **fordern**), although hardly obs., is now very little used, esp. in the north. The standard MHG form is *eischen* (> our *ask*), the modern initial cons. having crept in in the 13th century, probably under the influence of **heißen.** It was orig. a *weak* verb, but in late MHG (again under the influence of **heißen**) the strong past tense *iesch* appeared, so that it joined the class of *reduplicating verbs* (q.v. 3); but apart from an occasional use of the past part. **geheischen,** strong forms eventually died out, so that the verb is now *weak* again: e.g. **Die jungen Kinder heischen Brot** (Lam. 4. 4)—**Meine Mutter ging bei den Geistlichen um, Hilfe heischend** (Rosegger)—**Er ging, das Gasthuhn zu heischen** (Scheffel)—**Seid Ihr geheischen worden?** (Immermann: 'Have you been summoned *or* cited?').

heißen: This is one of the 'reduplicating verbs' (q.v.) and is used in the following ways: **1.** With the force of 'to be named': e.g. **Der erste normannische König von England heißt Wilhelm der Eroberer.** **2.** With the force of 'to call' a person something, with a *double accus.* (becoming a double *nom.* in the pass.): e.g. **Sie hieß ihn einen dummen Jungen—Er wurde ein dummer Junge geheißen.** **3.** With the force of 'to bid, order', with several constructions: (**a**) It may take an accus. both of the person and of the thing, the latter being always a neut. pron., esp. **was:** e.g. **Tu, was dein Herz dich heißt** (G.), which is probably the accus. and infin. construction (see *b*), the infin. **tun** being unexpressed; sim. **Du weißt, daß du mir Gehorsam schuldig bist in allem, was ich dich heiße** (Sch.)—**Er tat, was ihn sein Instinkt hieß** (Binding). In the classical period a dat. of the person is sometimes found here, as in **„Denken Sie an Lotten!" „Brauchen Sie mir das zu heißen?"** (G.) and **Der Herr hat's ihm geheißen** (Sch.), but this use is now almost confined to the *pass.*, where it is the rule (cf. *b*): e.g. **Von wem wurde dir** (not **wurde dich**) **das geheißen?**—cf. **Er tat verwundert, wie ihm geheißen war** (Sudermann). (**b**) The commonest construction is the *accusative and infinitive* (q.v. 1 *a* and 2 *a*): e.g. **Er hieß die Kinder schweigen—Man hieß ihn sich hinsetzen—Sie hieß mich ihr folgen.** At one time a dat. of the person was sometimes used here, as in **Wann hieß ich dir die Schrift an Burleigh geben?** (Sch.), but this is now avoided. On the other hand, there seems to be a growing tendency to use an infin. *with* **zu** here, esp. where the verbs are some distance apart: e.g. **Sie nahm die Kinder zu sich an den Tisch und hieß sie mit glücklichem Lächeln, sich zu ihren Seiten zu stellen** (Th. Mann)—**Sie hieß den Diener die jungen Herrschaften zu holen** (R. Herzog)—**Eine unaussprechliche Ergriffenheit hieß ihn, sie an sich zu ziehen** (Binding). Here, no doubt under the influence of **befehlen,** the accus. is now occasionally replaced by the dat., as in **Dann hieß sie ihr, den Nonnen den Befehl zu überbringen** (H. Franck), but this is not to be recommended (but see below). When the accus. and infin. (q.v. 4) is used in a *compd.* tense, the past part. normally assumes the infin. form, as in **Er hat sie schlafen gehen heißen** (C. Bulcke), but modern usage rather prefers **Er hat sie geheißen, schlafen zu gehen**; sim. **Ich habe keinen Augenblick gehabt, an dem mein Herz mich geheißen hätte, Ihnen zu schreiben** (G.). Here also a dat. of the person has crept in, as in **Er hatte sich niedergeworfen und den Hirten geheißen, ein Gleiches zu tun** (C. Hauptmann); but this should really be confined to the *pass.*, where it is the established construction in the north: one says **Dem** (not **Der**) **Kutscher wurde geheißen, die Pferde anzuspannen**—cf., as a southern example unusual in the north, **Die Fremden wurden** (for **Den Fremden wurde**) **geheißen, gleich zum Mittagstisch zu kommen** (Hofmannsthal).

The past part. with **ge-** is also fixed in a contracted *perf.* infin. clause, as in **Ich erinnere mich, dich das tun geheißen zu haben** (or **dich geheißen zu haben, das zu tun.**) **4.** Other idiomatic uses are seen in **Ich gehe abends spazieren, das heißt** ('that is'), **wenn es nicht regnet—Was soll das heißen?** ('What is the meaning of that?')—**Was heißt** au revoir **auf deutsch?—Wie heißt doch jene Stelle im „Faust"?** ('Now, how does that passage in *Faust* run?')—**Es hieß, er sollte heute kommen** ('The story went that he was to come today')—**Hier heißt es vorsichtig sein!** ('Caution is indicated here, Here it is a case of being on one's guard').

helfen: 1. (**a**) With a *pers.* obj., the MHG verb *helfen* could take either a dat. or an accus., the former with the force of 'to assist', the latter esp. with an impersonal subj. in the sense of 'to be of use, avail': thus, in two successive verses of the Nibelungenlied we find *waz hilfet iuch* (accus.: the dat. would be *iu*) *des kapelânes tôt?* ('In what way does the chaplain's death benefit you?') and *er wolde sîn genesen ob im iemen hülfe* ('He thought he would not lose his life if some one helped him'). This personal accus. was in use down to the classical period: Luther wrote **Was hülfs den Menschen, so er die ganze Welt gewünne . . . ?** (Matth. 16. 26), where the modern version reads **Was hülfe es dem Menschen, wenn er . . . gewönne . . . ?** (for these verbal forms, see *past subjunctive* 2); sim. **Was helfen mich tausend bessere Empfindungen?** (Sch.). In post-classical times the distinction is sometimes made between **jemandem helfen** ('to assist a person') and **jemanden wohin helfen** ('to help in getting a person to some place'), the latter expression pointing not so much to the action of giving help as to the *result* of such action, as when one helps a fugitive to a place of safety or helps a person on to his feet after he has fallen down: e.g. **Ich habe dieses Geschlecht aus den Toren geholfen** (Chamisso: 'I have helped to manœuvre this family out of the town')—**„Iven", rief er, „hat das Pferd dir Leids getan?" und suchte seinen Knecht vom Boden aufzuhelfen** (Storm: '. . . tried to set his groom on his feet again'); cf. **Meine Kunst hat mich wider Erwarten fortgeholfen** (Tieck: 'Contrary to my expectation my art has helped me on, enabled me to make a living'). But even in such propositions the *dat.* is now the recognized case, as in **jemandem auf die Beine** or **in den Wagen helfen.** The same applies to the compounds of **helfen,** the only exception being **behelfen,** which is now only used with an accus. of the reflex. pron.: e.g. **Du mußt dich mit wenig behelfen lernen** ('You must learn to content yourself *or* get along with little'); cf. **Der neue Knecht ist sehr unbeholfen** ('. . . clumsy, loutish'). (**b**) An *impers.* accus. obj., really a Low German idiom with which we are familiar in English, too, is common in the coll. speech of the north and has spread to other parts but is avoided in good prose; it is used esp. with words like **was, viel, nichts,** etc., as in **Er weiß, wie verhaßt mir diese Ermahnungen sind: sie helfen nichts** (G.: '. . . they are of no avail')—**Was konnten sie es helfen, daß dieser Tag ein Sonntag war?** (Voigt-Diederichs: exactly like our 'How could they *help it* that today **was a** Sunday?'), where, in standard prose, the first clause would be **Was konnten sie dafür**; for 'I could not help doing that', see **umhin. 2.** A dependent infin. after **helfen** prefers to drop **zu** in short propositions like **Ich half ihr den Korb tragen**; but **zu** is often inserted in longer sentences: cf. **Ich half ihr, den Korb, der zu schwer für sie war, nach Hause zu tragen.** In a *compd.* tense the past part. may assume the *infin.* form, esp. where the two verbs stand together (cf. **accusative and infinitive** 4); rather more select than **Ich habe ihr geholfen, den schweren Korb zu tragen** is **Ich habe ihr den schweren Korb tragen helfen**; and sim. **Er hatte die Adresse an den König unterzeichnen helfen** (Sudermann)—**Ein gütiges Schicksal hatte ihn gesund bleiben lassen und alle Anwandlungen von Schwäche überwinden helfen** (H. Leip). In 'transposed' word-order, the aux. immediately *precedes* both infin. forms: e.g. **Es waren zwei Unteroffiziere, die manche Schlacht hatten verlieren helfen** (Hebbel); and in the proposition **Er war überzeugt, Stefan habe den Streich anstiften helfen** (H. Hesse: '. . . Stephen had helped to instigate the trick'), the subord. clause might have taken the form **daß Stefan den Streich habe anstiften helfen.** But the past part., not the infin. form, is used where the aux. is unexpressed, as in **Mein Freund barg einige Ertrinkende auf**

einem Floß, das er bauen geholfen (M. Nordau: 'My friend brought some drowning people to safety on a raft which he had helped to build'), where the rel. clause might have been expressed **das er hatte bauen helfen.**

hemmen: see **stop** 2 (*b*).

henken, Henker: see **hängen** 2 (*d*).

herab-, herauf-, etc.: see **her-, hin-** 3; **Reinfall.**

heranrücken, herantreten: see **advance** 1 and 3.

herausstellen: This is used lit. in propositions like **Hausfrauen werden gebeten, die leeren Milchflaschen früh herauszustellen** ('. . . to put the empty milk-bottles out early'); but it is esp. used *reflex.* in the fig. sense of 'to turn out (to be)': e.g. **Er stellte sich als** (**ein** or **einen**) **Betrüger heraus** ('He proved to be *or* It turned out that he was an impostor': cf. **als**='as' 1 *d*)—**Ich hatte mich als guter Verwalter herausgestellt** (G. Keller: 'I had proved myself to be a good manager')—**Seine Unschuld hat sich** (*scil.* **als außer Zweifel**) **herausgestellt** ('His innocence has proved to be beyond doubt', i.e. 'has been established'); see **prove.**

Herberge, herbergen: see **beherbergen.**

herein-: see **her-, hin-** 3; **Reinfall.** The following are a few examples which show the difference between the simple prefix **ein-** and the lengthened prefix **herein-: Die Nacht brach herein** ('Night fell') and **Diese Nacht brach jemand bei uns ein** ('Somebody broke into our house last night')—**Ich holte das weinende Kind herein** ('I fetched the weeping child in') and **Ich holte das Kind bald ein** ('I soon overtook the child')—**Er trat zu mir herein** ('He stepped into my room') and **Er trat für mich ein** ('He stood up *or* interceded for me').

herfallen: see **attack** 4. Distinguish between **Sie fielen übereinander her** ('They came to blows')—**Der Schieferdecker fiel vom Dach herab** or **herunter** ('The slater fell down from the roof')—**Es fiel anders aus, als man erwartet hatte** ('Things turned out differently from what had been expected')—**Er fiel aus der Rolle heraus** ('He acted out of character, was not his usual self')—**Sein Name fällt mir im Augenblick nicht ein** ('His name escapes me for the moment')—**Er stolperte auf der Schwelle und fiel zur Tür herein** ('He stumbled on the threshold and fell in through the door': see **nach** 3 *d*, and cf. **Reinfall**).

her-, hin-: 1. The fundamental difference between these sep. prefixes is that **her-** implies motion *towards*, **hin-** motion *away from* the speaker: cf. **Komm hierher!** and **Geh dorthin!—Wo kommst du her?** and **Wo gehst du hin?** In the everyday language of the north this distinction is not always observed as strictly as it should be, **her-** being often used instead of **hin-,** esp. when followed by a second prefix (cf. 3), in which case, if the latter begins with a vowel, the double prefix is commonly contracted in coll. speech to **'raus, 'rein,** etc., irrespective of the direction in which the motion is proceeding (see **Reinfall**): a German from the north instinctively says **Lauf mal 'rüber** (=**hinüber**) **zur Post!** ('Run across to the post-office!'). But *Sanders* goes too far when he condemns an example like **Ich klopfte an seine Tür: „Ich wollte dir guten Abend sagen, darf ich hereinkommen?"** (Spielhagen), where the speaker, as it were, is anticipating his friend's **„Herein!"** and where **hineinkommen** would sound quite unnatural since it almost invariably conveys the sense of 'to get in', as in **Das Haus war verschlossen, also konnte ich nicht hineinkommen** (cf. **kommen** 3). Still, *Sanders* is right in insisting that the essential difference between **her-** and **hin-** should be strictly observed in good prose. **2.** But **her-** and **hin-** have each developed specific independent uses. (**a**) Thus, **her-** may suggest the idea of motion, not directed towards the speaker but proceeding in a a constant local relation to some person or thing, as when we say 'The child trotted along in front of its mother' or 'As I drove down the street, a man ran along beside my car', where **her-** is associated with a *dat.* in the prep. phrase because the relative position of the two moving bodies remains constant: hence, **Das Kind trippelte vor seiner Mutter her—Als ich die Straße hinunterfuhr, lief ein Mann neben meinem Auto her;** and sim. **Ich hörte jemand hinter mir herschleichen—Als er vorbeigegangen war, blickte ich hinter ihm her.** Moreover, **her-** need not necessarily suggest motion at all, but may imply *rest* in relation to some centre of interest, as in **Es standen viele Leute um mich her.** (**b**) On the other hand, one of the commonest meanings of **hin-**, esp. in the north, is *down* (q.v. 2) in phrases like 'to put, lay, set, throw down', where **nieder** is rather more select and not always applicable (see **down** 3): one says regularly **Ich setzte mich in der Ecke hin—Ich will mich eine halbe Stunde hinlegen—Ich stellte die Lampe hin—Ich warf mein Buch hin** (but **Ich warf mein Buch in den Garten hinunter**: see 3); cf. **Er fiel auf der Treppe hin** and **Er fiel die Treppe hinab**, the former implying that he fell as he went up or down the staircase, the latter that he fell headlong down the stairs. **3.** But the commonest use of **her-** and **hin-** is as an additional prefix to verbs implying motion which already have a sep. prefix, as in **herab-, heran-, hinein-, hinüber-,** etc. It should be realized that verbs like **ab-** or **einfallen, aus-** or **ü'ber-** or **u'nter-gehen, ein-** or **vorspringen**, etc. are not generally used with the mere *lit.* force of motion from one place to another. Thus, **ablaufen** does not mean 'to run down' (a street), nor **einspringen** 'to jump in' (a river), nor **u'ntergehen** 'to go down' (a hill). The fact is that verbs of motion compounded with a *simple* prefix like **ab-, an-, ein-, vor-,** etc. almost invariably have quite a number of different shades of meaning, being mostly used with *fig.* force, while the *lit.* sense of motion downwards from above, from the outside to the inside (or vice versa), from one side to the other, etc. requires the use of a lengthened prefix like **hinab-, herein-, hinunter-,** etc. When somebody knocks at your door, you call **„Herein!"** (not **„Ein!"**), and sim. 'He went down into the valley' is **Er ging ins Tal hinab** or **hinunter** (not **ab** or **unter**). This difference is almost axiomatic: it is as exceptional for a simple prefix to have *lit.* force (cf. **eintreten**) as it is for a lengthened prefix to be used with *fig.* force (cf. **hinauslaufen**). It would occupy too much space here to enumerate all compound verbs of motion (the most characteristic ones are treated under their special heads, e.g. **ab-, aus-** and **eingehen, ab-, aus-** and **einfallen**, etc.); but the following pairs of examples are typical: **Das Schiff ging mit Mann und Maus unter** ('The vessel sank with all hands') and **Ich ging die Straße hinunter—Das Geschäft ging ein** ('The shop put up its shutters') and **Er ging in den Saal hinein—Die Zeit ist abgelaufen** ('The time has expired') and **Er kam den Berg herabgelaufen—Das Wasser ist übergelaufen** ('The water has overflowed') and **Er ist zum Bäcker hinübergelaufen—Er sprang für mich ein** ('He took my place at short notice, stepped into the breach for me') and **Er sprang in den Fluß hinein—Als das kleine Mädchen hinfiel** (cf. 2 *b*), **hob ich es wieder auf** ('. . . I set her on her feet again') and **Ich hob das kleine Mädchen auf die Leiter hinauf** (cf. **accusative or dative . . .** 2 *c*).

hersagen: see **repeat.**

herum-: see **umher-**. For the contraction **'rum-**, see **her-, hin-** 1 and **Reinfall.**

herunter-: see **her-, hin-** 3; **Reinfall.** Distinguish between **Als das Haus zu brennen anfing, brachte er seine Kinder glücklich herunter** ('. . . he brought his children down to safety') and **Er hat seine Kinder gut u'ntergebracht** ('He has provided well for his children')—**Komm schnell herunter!** ('Come down quickly!') and **Kann ich hier für die Nacht u'nterkommen?** ('Can I put up for the night here?').

hide: see **bergen.**

hin-: see **her-, hin-** 1, 2 (*b*) and 3; **down; nieder-.**

hinab-, hinauf-, etc.: see **her-, hin-** 3.

hinaus-: As explained under **her-, hin-,** the great majority of verbs compounded with such a prefix have *lit.* force, as in **Ich trat** (or **rannte**) **in den Garten hinaus—Ich stieß den Eindringling zum Hause hinaus** ('I pushed the intruder out of the house': see **nach** 3 *d*). But **hinaus-** is somewhat exceptional in that it forms quite a number of compds. which have *fig.* force: e.g. **Diese Fenster gehen nach dem Garten hinaus** ('look into the garden') —**Es kommt auf eins hinaus** ('It comes to the same thing')—**Sein Brief lief darauf hinaus, daß es ihm an Geld mangelte** ('His letter amounted to this, that he was short of money')—**Es soll mich wundern, wo das hinauswill** ('I wonder what the upshot of this will be')—**Die Sitzung zog sich stundenlang hinaus** ('The meeting dragged on for hours').

hinausgehen: see **her-, hin-; hinaus-; open** 3 (*b*).

hindern: As explained under **negative (pleonastic)** 2 (*a*), a subord. clause depending on a verb of prevention, prohibition, restraint, etc. often has a pleonastic neg. expression inserted in it. This is now esp. characteristic of the coll. lang., and should, on the whole, be avoided in good prose, unless where ambiguity might arise, as sometimes after **warnen** (q.v.). But such a superfluous neg. was very common in the classical period (see **sich hüten** and **verbieten**), esp. after **hindern** and its comp. **verhindern**: e.g. **Was hindert mich, daß ich nicht eine der Schnuren** (now much more commonly **Schnüre**) **ergreife und sie eurem Rücken anmesse?** (G.: 'What is there to prevent me from seizing one of the cords and applying it to your back?')—**Er hinderte, daß das Gespräch nicht zu Ruhe kam** (Tieck: 'He prevented the conversation from flagging')—**Ich verhinderte, daß die Truppen sich dem Kastelle nicht zu nahe wagten** (G.)—**Dadurch verhinderte ich, daß ihnen dieser Fensterladen nicht sogleich ins Gesicht fiel** (Sch.).

hinein-: see her-, hin- 1–3; **Reinfall.**

hinrichten: see richten 2 (*a*).

Hinsicht: see Tracht 2.

hinten, hinter: **1.** The form **hinten** is an *adv.*, meaning 'at the back, behind', and preceding preps. are used to express motion to or from a position at the back: e.g. **Er stand vorn** ('in front'), **ich ganz hinten** ('at the very back')—**Wir wohnen hinten hinaus** ('in the back premises')—**Das Pferd schlug hinten nach mir aus** ('The horse lashed out at me')—**Ich wurde nach hinten gedrängt** ('I was pushed to the back')—**Ich wurde von hinten angefallen** ('I was attacked from behind'); see 3 below. **2.** The form **hinter** is used as an *adj.*, as in **Die hinteren Zimmer sind kleiner als die vorderen** ('The back rooms are smaller than the front ones') or **Dieser Schüler sitzt auf der hintersten Bank** ('on the back bench'); but its commonest use is as a *prep.*, its case depending on whether rest at or motion towards a specified spot is intended: cf., on the one hand, **Er stand hinter mir** and **Er trat hinter mich** (i.e. 'He stepped into the vacant place behind me'); but, where both are in motion, **Ich lief die Straße entlang, er lief hinter mir her.** The accus. is used in a number of fig. expressions: e.g. **Ich bin ihm hinter die Schliche gekommen** ('I have seen through his tricks, have found him out')—**Er hat mich hinters Licht geführt** ('He has deceived me': cf. **hintergehen**)—**Schreibe dir das hinter die Ohren!** ('Make a special note of that! Take that to heart'). **3.** In nautical lang. **hinter** and **hinten** are mostly replaced by **achter** and **achtern** respectively: e.g. **Ich stand achter dem Großmast** (H. Leip: 'I was standing abaft the main-mast'); so also in many compds., such as **Achterdeck** ('poop'), **Achtersteven** ('stern-post'), etc. Actually, **achter** is a LG corruption of **after,** a prefix now obs. in ordinary lang. except in a few words like **(von) jemandem afterreden** (q.v.: 'to speak ill of, slander a person'): **Er scheint (von) mir afterzureden** or **aftergeredet zu haben**; **Er brachte mich nach aftern** (id.: 'He took me aft').

hinter- (verbal prefix): It is only in coll. lang. that this is treated as *sep.*, as when a person unable to swallow something might say **Ich kriege es nicht hi'nter** or **'ru'nter** (like our 'I can't get it down'; for **'runter**, see **her-, hin-** 1 and **Reinfall**). In good prose the prefix is always *insep.*, giving the compd. *fig.* force, and there are actually only half a dozen such verbs in common use, viz. **hinterblei'ben,** used esp. in the past part. as an adj.-subst., **die Hinterblie'benen** meaning 'the survivors', esp. those a dead person leaves behind, 'the relicts'—**hinterbri'ngen,** used of 'news, information' delivered in secret: cf. **Man hinterbra'chte ihm die Bewegungen seiner Gegner** (L. v. Ranke)—**hinterge'hen**: see **deceive** 3, and cf. **Meine Mutter im Grab? Du hinterge'hst mich!** (Sch.)—**hinterla'ssen**: see **leave** (verb) 3 (*b*)—**hinterle'gen** ('to deposit' money, etc.)—**hintertrei'ben** ('to frustrate, thwart'), as in **Er hintertrie'b die Heirat** (Sch.).

hinterdrein: see **darein** 1 (*b*).

hinunter-: see **her-, hin-** 3; **Reinfall.**

hinzu-: This sep. prefix is chiefly used with **kommen** and **setzen**, either *lit.*, as in **Wir beide saßen zuerst allein, aber später kamen** (or **setzten sich**) **zwei Freunde hinzu** ('two friends joined us'), or esp. *fig.*, as in **Die Sorgen vermehrten sich; hinzukam, daß er an der Treue seiner Geliebten zweifelte** (R. v. Gottschall: 'His troubles increased; a further *or* an additional worry was that he doubted his lady-love's loyalty') and **Er sagte, daß er bald nach Frankreich reisen wolle, und setzte** (or **fügte**) **hinzu** ('and added'), **daß er wohl mehrere Wochen dort zubringen werde.**

hire: see **dingen** 1.

hochachten: see **achten** 2.

hochfahrend: see **Hoffart.**

Hochzeit: see **marry** 2 (*b*).

Hocke: see **Getreide** 2.

hocken: see **knien.**

Hoffart: Although its first vowel is now *short*, this noun has no connexion with **hoffen** but is a corrupt form of MHG *hôchvart*, used orig. in the good sense of 'noblemindedness' (=**Edelmut**), then in the bad sense of 'arrogance' (cf. **Hoch-, Übermut**), which is the only meaning of the modern word: and so also the adj. **hoffärtig** (< *hôchvertic*) only means 'haughty, arrogant'. At one time the idea of haughtiness was also implicit in the verb **hochfahren,** as is seen from examples like **Fahre nicht hoch, halte dich an deinesgleichen!** (Luther: 'Don't be uppish *or* affect superiority, associate with people like yourself!') and **Habt ihr euch an Gott gewendet und Erhörung erlebt durch göttliche Huld, so beseitiget jetzt allen Übermut und anmaßliches Hochfahren!** (G.: '. . . lay aside all pride and presumptuous arrogance!'). One can, of course, say **Die Rakete fuhr hoch in die Luft** ('The rocket shot up high into the air'), but **hoch** here is an adv., not a prefix. Actually, the verb **hochfahren** is no longer used fig. implying haughtiness, which is the more surprising as the part. **hochfahrend** is reg. used as an adj. with much the same force as **hoffärtig.**

hoffen: for 'it is to be hoped that . . .', see **infinitive** 3 (*a*).

Höhe: This noun is in common use in prep. phrases to indicate a point lying 'midway' between two places: see **halb** 2 (*b*). It is also used in nautical parlance —as our 'height' once was: cf. 'Spain lyeth in the same height with the Azore Islands' (1622)—to point to a spot defined by a parallel of latitude: thus, in a reference to a vessel lying 'off' some place, one says **Das Schiff lag auf der Höhe von Dover** or **auf der Höhe des Kaps der Guten Hoffnung;** and sim., with a verb implying motion, **Kurz nachher kamen wir auf die Höhe von Madeira** (G. Forster: 'Presently we came *abreast* of Madeira'). This idiom has also been extended to places on land, and not necessarily on sloping ground: e.g. **Seine Sachen wurden von Matrosen nach seiner Wohnung befördert; in der Höhe des Hauses** ('abreast of the house') **kamen ihnen einige junge Leute entgegen** (E. Wichert)—**An der Ecke vom Marktplatz sah er den Stadtsekretär herankommen, und als die beiden Herren auf gleicher Höhe waren** ('were abreast of each other'), **griffen sie an die Hüte und grüßten sich** (Fallada). A coll. idiom is **Das ist die Höhe!** ('That 's the limit! That beats all!').

Hohe(r)priester: see **Langeweile** 2 (*a*).

hohnlächeln, -lachen, -sprechen: Here the noun **Hohn** ('scorn') has become a real verbal prefix. The prefix is *sep.* throughout in **hohnsprechen** (+ dat.); in **hohnlächeln** and **-lachen** (+ dat. or gen.) it is sep. in the infin. with **zu** and in the past part., but modern usage prefers to treat it as *insep.* in pres. and past tenses: e.g. **Sein Benehmen spricht jedem Schicklichkeitsgefühl hohn** ('His behaviour shows contempt for all sense of decency')—**Das Rechtsverfahren sprach der Gerechtigkeit hohn** ('The legal procedure made a mock of justice')—**Die Ergrimmte hohnlachte** (Spindler: 'The furious woman gave a scornful laugh')—**„Allerdings", hohnlachte der Buchhalter** (Hackländer)—**„Ja, darauf freue ich mich", hohnlachte er** (Jul. Wolff)—**„Jetzt hohnlach' ich deiner"** (Wildenbruch).

hören: 1. In propositions like **Kaum waren zwei bis drei Stunden verflossen, so hörte Karl draußen Stühle rücken und Fenster öffnen und zuschlagen** (W. Müller), the three infins. are usually said to have *pass. force*, and, indeed, we do use the pass. in such cases in English: 'Charles heard chairs being moved outside and windows being opened and slammed.' But in point of fact, as explained under **accusative and infinitive** 2 (*a*), they are *act.* infins. with a subj. like **jemand** or **Leute** understood, and the same applies to **Ich hörte im Nebenzimmer seufzen** (Immermann) and **Sie war noch nicht lang auf dieser Burg angelangt, als sie eines Abends an ihrer Türe klopfen hörte** (Platen); cf. 'We *heared tell* as he'd sold his own land' (Geo. Eliot). But where the infin. is a trans. reflex., it actually does take on pass. force, as in **Der Angeklagte hörte sich verurteilen** ('The accused heard himself being sentenced'), where, if the subj. of the infin. were expressed, the reflex. pron. would have to be a *pers.* one: **Er hörte den Richter ihn verurteilen.** It follows that such propositions may be ambiguous: in **Ich hörte den Arzt rufen** the doctor might be either calling or being called, according as he is the subj. or the obj. of **rufen.** And the same ambiguity is possible, though less likely, in **Als er aus einem bösen Traum auf-**

schrak, hörte er sich rufen. In such cases it is better to use a subord. **wie**-clause to make the meaning clear. **2.** In a compd. tense, where **hören** has a dependent infin. (cf. 'I have heard tell . . .'), the past part. **gehört** may assume the infin. form, as in **Mir ist, als hätte ich schon davon reden hören** (Novalis), but **gehört** is now quite common: see examples under **accusative and infinitive** 4 and 5, and cf. **Einmal hat doch jeder auf seinem Weg still gestanden und hat Gottes Flügel rauschen gehört** (Frenssen)—**Hast du mich nicht pfeifen gehört ?** (J. Schaffner)—**Ich habe keinen Wagen kommen gehört** (St. Zweig). Incidentally, **Ich habe das sagen hören** has led to the verbal noun **Hörensagen** ('hearsay'): **Ich weiß das nur vom Hörensagen.**

Horn: This neut. noun has two plur. forms, viz. **Horne** ('varieties of horn') and **Hörner** ('horns' of an animal; also 'horns' in an orchestra).

Huf, Hufe: Distinguish between **der Huf** meaning 'hoof' (plur. **Hufe**) and **die Hufe,** properly a 'hide' of land (plur. **Hufen**), then simply 'land, estate': cf., on the one hand, **Laß die armen Waisen von deines Pferdes Huf zertreten werden !** (Sch.), and, on the other hand, **Das Glück lächelte ihm nicht auf der eignen Hufe** (Spindler: 'Fortune did not smile on him when he had a holding of his own').

Hüfte: see **Fährte.**

huldigen: This has entirely displaced MHG *hulden.* As the fundamental idea is that of 'homage, allegiance', the verb presupposes a person or thing *to* whom or which homage is rendered, so the obj. naturally stands in the *dat.* case: e.g. **Die Menge huldigte dem König**—**Huldige dem Genius!** (Hölderlin); and sim., by extension, **einer Ansicht huldigen** ('to subscribe to, profess an opinion')—**der Mode huldigen** ('to follow the fashion'). So also in the impers. *pass.* **Dem Könige wurde von allen gehuldigt;** cf. the occasional use of the past part. in the pers. pass. relation (like **schmeicheln,** q.v.): **Ihr wollt gehuldigt sein** (Kosegarten: better **Ihr wollt, daß man Euch huldige**).

Hundert: see **Dutzend.**

hurtig: see **quick** 4.

Hut: Distinguish between **der Hut** ('hat') and **die Hut** ('protection'). The latter is common in expressions like **in Gottes Hut stehen** and **jemand in seine Hut nehmen,** and esp. in **auf der** (or **seiner**) **Hut sein** (= **sich in acht nehmen,** 'to be on one's guard'), a following 'against' being most idiomatically rendered by **vor** (q.v. 2 *b*): e.g. **Sei auf der Hut vor Aufwallungen des Zorns!** (Platen: 'Beware of giving vent to outbursts of anger!'): see **hüten** 2 (*a*).

hüten: 1. This verb is formed from **die Hut** (q.v.), its basic force being 'to protect from harm, take care of, guard', as in **Der Hirt hütet das Vieh** (cf. **warten** 2); then, from the idea of not leaving what you are guarding, came the sense of 'to remain in', as we use 'to keep' one's bed, room, etc.: **Ich habe mich erkältet und muß das Bett** or **Zimmer hüten. 2.** (**a**) The reflex. **sich hüten** is like **auf der Hut sein** or **sich in acht nehmen** ('to be on one's guard'), as in **Man hüte sich vor Taschendieben !** ('Beware of pickpockets !')—**Hüte dich vor allzuvielem und schnellem Lesen!** (Platen: see **vor** 2 *b*). A following dep. clause implies *negation*: **Hüte dich, zu fallen!** = **Nimm dich in acht** (or **Sieh dich vor**), **daß du nicht** fällst! and sim. **Mein Vater hatte sich gehütet, dieses Werk anzuschaffen** (G.: coll. 'My father had taken jolly good care not to buy this work')—**Er hütete sich, den Volkskrieg zu ermuntern** (Freytag)—**Ich werde mich hüten, bei diesem Wetter auszugehen!** ('Catch me going out in this weather!'). In such propositions a neg. was sometimes inserted in the dep. clause, as explained under **negative (pleonastic)** 2 (*a*), and this is still common in coll. speech. Thus, **Wir müssen uns hüten, daß wir nicht Übles stiften** (G.) is a mingling of 'We must beware of causing mischief' and 'We must take care not to cause mischief'; sim. **Wir hüteten uns, nicht zu lügen** (G.)—**Hüte dich, daß du nicht zu nah an das Schloß kommst!** (Jung-Stilling). (**b**) The same applies to the compds. **behüten** ('to protect, save') and **verhüten** ('to avert, prevent'): e.g. **Gott möge mich behüten, daß ich nicht je wieder in den Fall komme** (G.)—**Verhüt' es Gott, daß ich nicht Hilfe brauche!** (Sch.: 'God forbid that I should ever stand in need of help!')—**Der Himmel verhüte, daß der Schwätzer nicht in dem Tale verweilt** (Tieck)—**Er sagte, man müsse verhüten, daß ich nicht wieder einen Trödler aufsuche** (G. Keller). Such pleonastic negs. are better avoided in good prose. (**c**) Noteworthy is the exclamatory **Behüte!**

This is really a contraction of **Gott behüte mich** (or **uns**) **davor!** but came, like **Bewahre!** (see **behalten**), to be used as a strong contradiction: e.g., in a reference to a liqueur, **„Selbstgemacht, Herr Wirt?" „Behüte! Veritabler Danziger!"** (Lessing: 'By no means! *or* Anything but! Real Danzig Goldwasser!')—**Das kleine Mädchen stammelte: „Hansel wird doch nicht sterben, Papa?" „Behüte!" versicherte der Vater** (Spindler: really 'God forfend!' i.e. 'Good gracious, no!').

I

ich: The 1st pers. pron. **ich** (gen. **meiner,** in poetry often **mein**) can by its very nature have no plur., but the noun **das Ich** has a plur. as well as a gen. sing. This noun is used with reference either to a person's 'individuality', the *ego* which distinguishes him from the *non-ego* (**das Nicht-Ich**), or to one part of his individuality, as is suggested by expressions like one's 'other *or* better self'. But usage fluctuates: it is either treated as invariable, remaining **Ich** in all cases and both numbers, or it can take the ending **-s** in the gen. sing. and the plur., so that one can say **Gedenke deines besseren Ich(s)!** ('Think of your immortal soul!') and **Jeder Mensch hat zwei Ich(s).** Very unusual, and not to be recommended, is the ugly plur. **Iche,** as used in the following mod. example: **Wenn Annette die wenigen Blätter prüfend überflog, die sie daheim ihrem Inneren abrang, so müssen immer zwei Iche vor ihr gestanden haben: ein lebendiges und ein totes Ich. Welches von beiden Ichen war sie in Tat und Wahrheit?** (H. Franck).

idle: 1. A man who is *idle* is not necessarily *lazy*: he may be industrious but either temporarily out of work or having a short break in his labours. On the other hand, an *idle* pupil suggests a *lazy* boy who shirks work, or at least is *indolent,* a sluggish worker. Similarly, a German distinguishes between **arbeitslos** ('out of work') and **müßig** (see below), and between **träge** ('indolent') and **faul** ('lazy'). But there is no hard and fast line: **Muße** means 'leisure, free time', and the fundamental idea of **müßig** is seen in a proposition like **Mein Amt läßt mir wenig Zeit, müßig zu sein;** yet **Müßiggänger** ('idler') generally implies disinclination to work: cf. the proverb **Müßiggang ist aller Laster Anfang** (much like 'Satan finds some mischief still for idle hands to do'). **2.** Analogous expressions are **lässig** and two of its compounds. The simple word implies reluctance to take trouble (cf. Lat. *lassus,* 'weary'), suggesting the the attitude of a person who 'can't be bothered'. The true antithesis of **lässig** is therefore **eifrig**; but it is apt to descend in the scale, as when Luther says **Einem Lässigen** ('the *slothful* man') **gerät sein Handel nicht, aber ein fleißiger Mensch** ('the *diligent* man') **wird reich** (Pr. 12. 27). The compound **fahrlässig** is properly used of one who lets things drift along (cf. *laisser aller*), hence 'easy-going, inattentive, negligent', while **nachlässig** goes still farther, suggesting 'careless', whether in outward appearance or in actions.

-ig: There is an important difference between this adj. termination and **-lich** in connexion with nouns denoting time, esp. **Tag, Jahr, Monat,** and **Woche.** The forms **tägig, jährig, monatig,** and **wöchig,** which are now hardly ever used without a numerical prefix (**jährig** is sometimes used for **einjährig,** esp. of young animals: **ein jähriges Kalb**), imply duration throughout the period suggested, while **täglich, jährlich, monatlich,** and **wöchentlich** (not **wöchlich**) imply recurrence after the suggested interval: e.g., on the one hand, **Wir hatten diesen Sommer einen dreimonatigen Aufenthalt in der Schweiz** ('a stay of three months in Switzerland'), and, on the other hand, **Er macht uns regelmäßig einen dreimonatlichen Besuch** ('a regular visit every three months');

sim. **Ich habe jedes Jahr einen zweiwöchigen Urlaub** and **Diese Zeitung erscheint wöchentlich zweimal**; cf. also **ein Einjähriger** (who serves for a year in the army) and **ein jährlicher Beitrag** ('an annual subscription'). But the distinction is not always observed as strictly as it should be. Thus, in the proposition **Als sie die Urkunde unterzeichnete, fand sie noch die Rechnung über ihre Verköstigung während der elfmonatlichen Haft** (Riehl) the adj. should obviously be **elfmonatigen** ('during her eleven months' imprisonment'); and so also **Es kam ein Donnerwetter, das in einen vierwöchentlichen** (for **vierwöchigen**) **Landregen überzugehen drohte** (M. Eyth: '. . . a thunderstorm which threatened to turn into a general four-weeks' rain'). The result of this incorrect usage is that one is sometimes left in doubt as to the meaning: the proposition **Wenn ich mißgünstig wäre, würde ich dich beneiden, im Besitz eines zweimonatlichen Urlaubs** (Hackländer) presumably refers to a long leave of two months, but should properly suggest a short leave every two months.

ihrer: see **unser** 1.

ihresgleichen: see gleich 2.

Ihro: see **Dero.**

ill: see **krank.**

Imbiß: see **bißchen.**

imitate: see **nachahmen.**

immer: **1.** Our usual expression for this adv. of time is 'always'. We sometimes use 'ever' in this sense in choice lang., as in 'It was ever thus', ordinarily in 'Good-bye for ever!' or 'He is for ever boasting'; but apart from such expressions (**Es war schon immer so—Lebwohl auf immer!—Er prahlt immer**), and from the special cases referred to under 3 below, **immer** should not be used to render 'ever': see esp. **je** 1, and cf. **Seitdem ich ankam, hat es immerzu** or **andauernd geregnet** ('It has rained ever since I arrived'). **2.** (**a**) Before a compar. adj. or adv., **immer** suggests a progressive action or state, an idea which we usually convey by repeating the compar.: e.g. **Der Zug fuhr immer langsamer** ('slower and slower')—**Die internationale Lage wird immer schlimmer** ('worse and worse'). (**b**) The combination **immer noch** or **noch immer** indicates that the action or state is unduly prolonged, which we often suggest by a stressed 'still' or 'yet': e.g. **Es regnet immer noch** ('It is *still* raining', as if we hadn't had enough)—**Ist er immer noch nicht gekommen?** ('Has he not come *yet*?', he should have been here long ago). **3.** Idiomatic is the use of **immer** in *concess.* clauses to express the idea suggested by our 'ever' used as a generalizing suffix to prons. and advs., as in 'whoever, whatever, wherever, however', etc. Such concess. clauses do not absolutely require the insertion of **immer**—cf. **Was du tust, bedenke das Ende** or **die Folgen**! ('Whatever you do, think first what the effect will be!')—but the insertion of **immer** at once suggests a concess. clause, which **was du tust** need not do, of course (cf. **Was du tust, geht mich nichts an,** 'What you do is no concern of mine'). In such concess. clauses **immer** may be replaced or amplified by an unstressed **auch** (q.v. 4): e.g. **Wer immer auch** (in prose usually **Wer auch immer**) **die Reiterei geführt, . . . der ist des Todes schuldig** (H. v. Kleist: 'Whoever it was that led the cavalry, . . . he has forfeited his life')—**Was für Entschuldigungen er auch immer vorbringen mag, er hatte kein Recht, so zu handeln** ('Whatever kind of excuses he may offer, he had no right to act as he did')—**Wie** (or **So**: q.v. 3) **sehr er sich auch immer anstrengt, er scheint wenig Fortschritte zu machen** ('No matter how much he exerts himself, he seems to make little progress')—**Niemand verläßt die Festung, aus welcher Ursache immer!** (E. Wichert: 'No one will leave the fortress, no matter for what reason!')—**Es war ausgemacht, der Vorfall sollte geheimgehalten werden, aber aus** (unusual for **durch**) **wessen Schuld immer, diese Übereinkunft war durchbrochen worden** (Bergengruen: 'It was agreed that the incident should be kept secret, but whoever might have been responsible, this agreement had been broken')—**Er hielt sich** (dat.) **das Kind fern, aus welchem Grunde immer** (Th. Mann: 'He kept the child away from himself, whatever the reason may have been')—**Wo der Attentäter sich auch immer verborgen haben mag, die Polizei wird ihn schon fassen** ('No matter where the cut-throat may have hidden, the police will get him, you may be sure')—**Ermitteln muß man den Täter, wo auch immer** (G. v. d. Vring: 'The culprit must be discovered, wherever he may be')—**Unter wessen Tür der Fremde auch immer trat, er fand die Hausfrau höflich** (Kolbenheyer: 'No matter into whose house he stepped, he found the housewife polite').

imperative mood: 1. The only true imperat. forms are those of the familiar 2nd sing. and plur., as in **Lauf schnell und wirf diese Postkarte in den Briefkasten!**—**Karl, benimm dich!**—**Kinder, seid artig und schlagt euch nicht!** Otherwise *subj.* forms are used: e.g. **Spreche ich ganz offen!** ('Let me speak quite candidly!')—**Sehen wir in die Zukunft!** ('Let us look to the future!')—**Behalten wir das im Auge!** ('Let us keep that in view!')—**Gott sei Dank!** (see **passive voice** 2 *b* ii)—**Ihre Majestät, sie lebe hoch!** ('Long live Her Majesty!')—**Man glaube nicht** (or **Glaube niemand**), **daß ich spaße!** ('Let no one think I am joking!')—**Sehe jeder zu, daß er pünktlich kommt!** ('See that every one comes punctually!'). **2.** The following are substitutes for the imperat.: the modal aux. **wollen,** as in **Wollen wir das annehmen!** (Storm: 'Let us assume that!' which might have been **Nehmen wir das an!**) and **Wollet das nicht von mir heischen!** (id.: 'Don't demand that of me!'); a princ. clause, to express a peremptory order, as in **Du schweigst!** ('Hold your tongue!'); a subord. **daß**-clause, as in **Daß du ja' reinen Mund hältst!** ('Be sure you keep this dark!'), where a preceding imperat. clause like **Sieh zu** is understood ('See *or* Be sure you don't blab!'). **3.** For a past part. and an infin. used with imperat. force, see **participle (past)** 3.

impersonal verbs: 1. These are quite normal so far as conjugation is concerned, except that (i) as their subj. is **es** (which in certain cases is understood), they are confined to the 3rd pers. sing., and (ii) that their pass. use is very limited (see 3). **2.** The impers. use of verbs has a very wide application. **(a)** Like our 'it', **es** commonly refers to natural phenomena, weather conditions, times of day, etc.: e.g. **Es ist kalt**—**Es friert Stein und Bein** ('It is freezing hard')—**Es wetterleuchtet** (q.v.)—**Es ist noch früh am Tage**—**Es wird gleich eins schlagen,** etc. **(b)** Common also is the use of **es** to suggest an agent which is deliberately left vague because it is unknown or not clearly understood: e.g. **Es klopft**—**Es hat geklingelt** or **geschellt**—**Es raschelte in den Zweigen** ('There was a rustling sound in the branches')—coll. **Bei ihm rappelt es im Kopfe** or **im Oberstübchen** (*lit.* 'There is something rattling in his upper story', i.e. 'He has a screw loose'); and here belong not only **es gibt** (fully explained under **es ist, es sind** 2), but also common expressions like **Es lief mir kalt über den Rücken** or **Es überlief mich eiskalt** (Heyse: 'Cold shivers ran down my spine')—**Es geht mir gut**—**„Wie steht's?“ „Es steht schlecht“** ('How are things going?' 'They're going badly'). This use of **es** is esp. effective in references to what is mysterious or supernatural: **Es geht nicht mit rechten Dingen zu** ('There is something uncanny here')—**Hier spukt es** ('Something queer *or* weird is going on here', esp. 'This place is haunted')—**Nachts geht es in dem alten Schlosse um** ('A ghost walks at night in the old castle'). **(c)** In many cases the impers. use replaces the pers. use: e.g. **Es freut** (or **Ich freue**) **mich**—**Es wundert** (or **Ich wundere**) **mich**—**Es eilt mir** (or **Ich habe es eilig:** see **eilen**)—**Es ist mir angst und bange** (see **Angst**). **3.** An idiom which deserves special mention, because there is nothing like it in English (although it occurs in Lat.), is the impers. use of some verbs which take a gen. or a dat. With these verbs, when used in the *passive,* the gen. or dat. does *not* become a nom. (as the accus. obj. of a trans. verb does), but remains a gen. or dat., and the subj. **es** drops out in inverted word-order. Thus, **gedenken** (q.v.), meaning 'to think of, remember', takes a gen., as in **Wir gedenken Eurer** (Storm), and the *pass.* of such a proposition is seen in the opening lines of a well-known hymn of Gellert's, viz. **Dies ist der Tag, den Gott gemacht, Sein** (gen.) **werd' in aller Welt gedacht** ('Let Him be remembered all over the world'); cf. Lat. *servorum miserebat* ('The slaves were pitied'). So also **verzeihen** ('to forgive') takes a dat. of the pers., hence in the *pass.*, **Um deinen lieben Sohn** (= **Um deines lieben Sohnes willen**) **soll dir verziehen sein** (Uhland: 'You shall be forgiven for your dear son's sake': Lat. *tibi ignoscetur filii tui cari causa*). So also with **dienen** (q.v. 2 *c*: 'to serve'): **Damit ist mir nicht gedient** lit. 'With that it is not served to me', i.e. 'That does not serve my purpose *or* is of no use to me'—with **raten** (q.v.: 'to advise'): **Es ist mir** (or **Mir ist**) **geraten worden, von meiner Forderung abzustehen** ('I have been advised to waive my claim')—with **schmeicheln** (q.v. 2:

'to flatter'): **Dem Künstler wurde von allen Anwesenden geschmeichelt** ('The artist was flattered by all those present') —with **trauen** (q.v.1: 'to trust'): **Ihm wird allgemein getraut** ('He is trusted by one and all')—with **widersprechen** (q.v., 'to contradict'): **Dem Redner wurde von einem der Zuhörer lebhaft widersprochen** ('The speaker was sharply contradicted by one member of the audience')—with **widerstehen** (q.v. 1: 'to resist'): **Dem Feinde konnte nicht widerstanden werden** ('The enemy could not be resisted': Lat. *hostibus resisti non potuit*). **4.** (a) Another idiomatic use of certain impers. verbs which has no counterpart in English is their *reflexive* use to represent an activity, condition or state not so much as an individual experience but in its general application, and here **es** is retained in inverted word-order: e.g. **Hier sitzt es sich sehr bequem** ('It is very comfortable sitting here')—**Auf diesem Pfade geht** or **spaziert es sich gut** ('It is easy walking on this path')—**„Wieder produktiv werden": das sagt sich leicht** (Hofmannsthal: 'To start writing again, that is easily said')—**„Das hört sich ganz gut an", sagte Wendelin, als Georg mit seiner Verteidigungsrede fertig geworden war** (A. Meissner: 'That doesn't sound at all bad, said W. when G. had concluded his speech for the defence'). (b) Here presumably belongs the expression **Hat sich was,** a coll. development out of **Es hat sich** as formerly used in the sense of **Es verhält sich**: cf. **Es hat sich nicht so** (in the orig. version of 2 Sam. 20. 20: 'The matter is not so'). If, as seems likely, this is how the modern coll. idiom arose, it was orig. a strong affirmative, but it now always has ironic force and suggests that the preceding expression or statement is misapplied, esp. that the very reverse is true, an idea which we often express coll. by 'Rubbish!' or 'Nonsense!' or by common slang expressions like 'My foot' or 'I don't think' (cf. Dickens' 'You're a amiably-disposed young man, sir, I don't think'): e.g. **„Nirgends Rat in meinem Unglück!" „Rat, Majestät? Hat sich was zu raten"** (Sch.: 'No one to give me advice in my plight!' 'Advice, your Majesty? Nonsense, you don't require advice')—**Gut? Ja, es hat sich was mit dem „gut", böse sollte es heißen** (J. G. Kohl: 'Good my foot! it should have been bad').

indessen: This word, although rather more common than the shorter form **indes** is not nearly as common as it once was, esp. with *temp*. force. In an example like **So flossen einige Stunden vorüber; indessen** (adv., 'meanwhile') **hatte die Fürstin vernommen, daß wir Deutsche seien** (G.), one would now prefer **unterdessen** (q.v.) or **inzwischen**; and in **Damit beschäftigten sich diese Männer, indessen** (conj., 'while') **wir uns an Wein und Brot erquickten** (G.), the more usual expression would now be **während** or **dieweil** (see **weil** 1). Still fairly common, however, is the use of **indessen** with *adversative* force, as in **Das habe ich irgendwo gehört, ich weiß indessen nicht, von wem** (Rilke), but even here **jedoch** or **aber** would be more usual in ordinary lang.

induce: see **bewegen** under **move** 1 (*b*).

infinitive: 1. Although the infin. and the gerund were orig. distinct (as in Lat.: *amare* and *amandum*), the gerund is now only recognizable in the gen. (see 2); otherwise the two are identical in form, except that the gerund is written with a capital. This so-called *gerundive infinitive* (see 3) is a neut. verbal subst. in the exact sense, possessing properties both of a verb and of a subst. In its verbal capacity it can govern a case (the *gen.*, which replaces the accus. obj. of the verb) and be modified by an adv. (generally in the form of a prefix); in its subst. capacity it can be qualified by an art. or adj., can be inflected (in the gen.), can be governed by a prep., and can be the subj. or the obj. of a verb. The following examples illustrate these points: **Das viele Rauchen hat mich heiser gemacht—Infolge (des) vielen Rauchens bin ich heiser—Nicht Streitens wegen kam ich her** (Sch.)—**Das Betreten des Rasens ist verboten—Ich bin des Tanzens müde—Das Langsamgehen mag ich nicht—Leb wohl! Auf baldiges Wiedersehen!** In ordinary lang., verbal nouns standing alone prefer to be qualified by the art.; it is mainly in poetry, proverbs, notices, etc. that they remain unqualified: e.g. **Reden ist Silber, Schweigen ist Gold—Raten ist leichter als Helfen —Irren ist menschlich—Rauchen verboten!—Parken verboten!** Some gerundive infins. have become real nouns, e.g. **Leben, Wesen, Einkommen, Verderben, Vertrauen,** etc. **2.** As stated above, the gerund could be inflected: its gen. ending was orig. in MHG *-ennes*, its dat. *-enne*; but gradually these were shortened to

-ens and *-en*, which are both still in regular use: cf. **Es ist Schlafenszeit** (< *ez ist slâfennes zît*) and **Es ist Zeit, zu schlafen** (< *ez ist zît ze slâfenne*). What we now call the *infinitive with* **zu,** then, is really the dat. of the gerund governed by the prep. **zu:** thus, **Ich hoffe, dich zu sehen** really means 'My hope is (directed) to the seeing (of) you', and **Ich habe keine Zeit, Briefe zu schreiben** is 'I have no time (to devote) to the writing (of) letters'. The origin of such expressions is no longer felt, of course, but that the infin. here is really a noun is clear from propositions like **Das zu beweisen** (subj.) **ist nicht leicht—Es freut mich, Sie kennenzulernen** (in appos. to **Es**)—**Sie begann zu weinen** (obj.). **3.** (**a**) The gerundive infin. represents something to be done as fit, possible or necessary, and it should be noted that, whereas in English we here use either the *act.* ('I am to blame', 'This house is to let') or more commonly the *pass.* ('This house is to be sold', 'It is to be hoped *or* feared', 'That remains to be seen'), the Germans invariably use *the act. with pass. force.* This is esp. common after **sein** and **finden,** and after **es gibt, es bleibt** and, in a few expressions, **es steht:** e.g. **Es ist hier manches Interessante zu sehen—Sie ist noch zu haben** (coll.: lit. 'She is still to be had', i.e. 'She is not married yet')—**Als ich zurückkehrte, fand ich allerlei zu erledigen—Es gab wichtige Sachen zu besprechen—Es bleibt abzuwarten** ('It remains to be seen'), **ob er kommen wird —Es steht zu hoffen** ('It is to be hoped'), **daß sein Zustand sich bessern wird—Sie fand, wie zu erwarten stand, den Kaufpreis zum Lachen gering** (Th. Mann)—**Er überschlug** ('estimated') **den Profit, der für ihn zu erwarten stand** (Zifferer)—**Die Ärzte erklärten, daß er das Predigen aufgeben müsse, widrigenfalls das Schlimmste zu befürchten stand** (R. Huch: '. . . failing which *or* otherwise the worst was to be feared'). (**b**) Of special importance in this connexion is the use of such a gerundive infin. with pass. force placed *attrib.* before a noun, a use which resulted from confusion between the gerund (the dat. of which ended in *-enne*) and the pres. part. (which ended in *-ende*). The latter form gradually encroached upon the special province of the former, so that *ze slâfende* eventually became an alternative form of *ze slâfenne*, and it was an easy and natural step from there to the attrib. use of what looked like a pres. part. This explains how **Das Haus ist zu verkaufen** ('The house is to be sold, is for sale') led to **Dies ist das zu verkaufende Haus** ('This is the house to be sold'), where the attrib. phrase has the force of a rel. clause. The following are a few characteristic examples of this use: **Ich hatte meine sämtlichen Schriften mitgenommen, um die von Göschen zu besorgende Ausgabe zusammenzustellen** (G.: '. . . the edition which was to be undertaken by Göschen') —**In den Vorzimmern erwarteten die Herren den zu feiernden General** (Liliencron: '. . . awaited the arrival of the general who was to be fêted'); and sim., with **zu** inserted after a sep. prefix, **Als man die einzuladenden Gäste** ('the guests who were [*or* would have] to be invited') **zusammenrechnete, da waren es sechzehn** (Storm)—**Der Kirchenchor intonierte die von der Gemeinde mitzusingenden Lieder** (Zuckmayer: lit. '. . . the hymns which were also to be sung by the congregation', i.e. in which they were to join). The important points to notice, then, are (i) that the gerundive infin. used attrib. takes the pres. part. form; (ii) that it always has pass. force; and (iii) that this use is confined to *trans.* verbs which take an *accus.* obj. This last point is esp. important: 'the order which is to be executed' is **der zu befolgende Befehl,** not **der zu gehorchende Befehl** (because **gehorchen** takes a dat.); sim. 'the friend to be assisted' is **der zu unterstützende** (not **zu helfende**) **Freund,** and 'the express due this morning' might be **der heute früh zu erwartende Schnellzug,** but not **der . . . einzutreffende Zug** (because **eintreffen** is intrans.). The following example, in which the intrans. **geschehen** is so used, is therefore strictly incorrect, but as **geschehen** sometimes has the pass. force of 'to be done', and as the sentence is undoubtedly neat, its use may perhaps be excused: **Er wußte, daß man das Geschehene sich eher gefallen läßt, als daß man in ein noch zu Geschehendes einwilligt** (G.: 'He knew that people are more ready to acquiesce in what has already been done than to agree to what is still to be done'). **4.** With purely verbal force, the *infinitive without* **zu** is chiefly used in the *accus. and infin.* construction (q.v.); after the **modal auxiliary verbs** (q.v.); after **lassen** and, in certain cases, **bleiben, lehren** and **lernen** (qq.v.), also

helfen (q.v. 2); and after verbs of motion like **gehen, fahren, reiten,** etc. (see **gehen** 2); see also **was (interrog.)** 5.

ingleichen: see **-gleichen** 2 (*b*).

inmitten: see **mitten.**

inne-: At one time **inne** was used as an independent adv. meaning 'inside, in the middle', as in **Allda kreuzigten sie ihn, und mit ihm zween andre zu beiden Seiten, Jesum aber mitten inne** (John 19. 18: '. . . Jesus in the midst'). According to modern usage, however, it is a sep. prefix, used mainly in four verbs: **1. innehaben,** meaning either 'to occupy' (a house, a seat, etc.), 'to fill' (a post) or fig., like **beherrschen,** 'to be a master of, have expert knowledge of' (a branch of learning): e.g. **Er hat den Flügel des Schlosses inne** (Sch.)—**Er soll ein Zimmer in einem Hotel innehaben** (Th. Mann)—**Sie hatte den Sofaplatz inne** (id.)—**Es ist ihm gelungen, eine Stelle als Buchhalter innezuhaben—Dies ist ein Wissensgebiet, das er vollständig innehat**; cf. **Er war Chefarzt einer großen Klinik und Inhaber einer Professur der medizinischen Fakultät** (Zuckmayer). **2. innehalten,** meaning either (*trans.*) 'to obey, comply with' (laws, instructions), 'to keep' (a date, an appointed time), 'to follow, observe, adhere to' (a habit, mode of action), or (*intrans.*), like **einhalten** (q.v.), 'to stop, pause': e.g. **Jeder ist verpflichtet, die Gesetze innezuhalten—Er hat den Zahlungstag nicht innegehalten—Der Pastor sprach in dem Plauderton, den er auch auf der Kanzel innezuhalten liebte** (Th. Mann)—**Durch meine Ankunft gestört, hatten sie mit Spielen innegehalten** (G.: = **hatten sie ihr Spiel unterbrochen**)—**Er hielt im Schritt inne** (Blunck: = **Er hielt den Schritt an**). **3. innewerden,** meaning 'to become aware *or* conscious of, perceive, realize', orig. (and for the most part still) + *gen.*, as the verb is little used in ordinary lang.: e.g. **Besser denn alle beide** (*scil.* **Lebendige und Tote**) **ist, der . . . des Bösen nicht innewird** (Eccles. 4. 3) —**Ich habe lange gebraucht, bis ich dessen innewurde, was ich meiner Vaterstadt Berlin danke** (W. v. Scholz); occasionally, + accus., the result of confusing MHG *ez* and *es* (see **es** 1); as in **Er war das Verhältnis zwischen Gott und Mensch innegeworden** (Ranke). **4. innewohnen,** no longer used with a pers. subj. in the *lit.* sense of 'to dwell in' a place, but only *fig.* of what is 'inherent *or* innate in' somebody or something (dat.): cf. 'The body which man's spirit inhabits and *indwells*' (H. S. Holland, 1882). Formerly this idea was more commonly expressed by **inwohnen,** but this is now obs. according to *Duden,* who gives the example **Auch alten Methoden kann Gutes innewohnen** ('Even antiquated methods can have their good points'); for the earlier use, cf. **Es ist ein Gespenst, dem kein Geist inwohnt** (Tieck)—**Tatsache ist, daß jeder geheimen Verbindung Verderbnis inwohnt** (Börne). In this sense **einwohnen** was also formerly used, as in expressions like **die einem Menschen einwohnende Natur** (G.) and **die uns einwohnende Kraft** (Heine); but this verb is now practically confined to the *reflex.* use with a pers. subj. in the sense of 'to adapt oneself' to something, esp. 'to become acclimatized': e.g. **Sie wußte sich in dem unbequemen Hause nicht einzuwohnen** (Görres)—**Er schrieb, er sei jetzt drüben in Amerika ganz eingewohnt** (W. v. Scholz); less commonly now with **in** + accus., as the predominant idea is that of being *settled* in a place: cf. **Ich hatte mich in diese Gesellschaft eingewohnt** (G.).

innen: see **inside.**

inner: see **äußer** 1–3.

innerhalb: 1. *preposition*: (**a**) Like **außerhalb** (q.v.), this is used both of space and (rather less commonly) of time (see 3). The normal case after it is the *gen.*, but the *dat.* should be used where the gen. would be unrecognizable as such: *Sanders* says **„Es heißt: innerhalb dieses Zeitraums, dagegen: innerhalb acht Tagen, weil acht Tage sich nicht als Genitiv durch die Form bemerkbar macht".** So also **Innerhalb vierzehn Tagen verließen ihn die Angstvorstellungen** (Stehr)—**Ich muß innerhalb drei Tagen in Wien sein** (V. Baum). But authors in the north seem rather to dislike the simple dat. here, preferring to use **innerhalb von** where the gen. is inapplicable: cf. **innerhalb vier Wänden** (G. Keller) and **innerhalb von vier Wänden** (Raabe). (**b**) Special care is required here in *rel.* clauses. Modern practice condemns a proposition like **Er überlebte Firdusi kaum ein Jahr, innerhalb welches er das Werk zu Ende schrieb** (G.) and substitutes **dessen** for **welches,** because the latter is not specifically gen. in form; and so also one says **Er hatte nur eine Woche** (or **zwei Jahre**)

innerhalb deren er das Werk zu Ende schreiben mußte. But the insertion of **von** is advisable, or even necessary, where **dessen** or **deren** is a *Saxon* gen.: e.g. **Wir wohnen in einem Bezirk, innerhalb von dessen Grenzen** (in einer Gegend, innerhalb von deren Grenzen) **keine Fabriken errichtet werden dürfen** ('. . . within the boundaries of which no factories may be erected'). On the other hand, **welch** is the correct expression where 'which' has *adj.* force: **Die Stadt erstreckt sich bis zu den zwei Flüssen, die sie fast umringen, innerhalb welcher Grenzen** (or **innerhalb von welchen Grenzen**) **keine Fabrik errichtet werden darf.** (**c**) The prep. form **innert,** used esp. of time, should be avoided, being peculiarly Swiss and practically unknown in the north. With regard to its case, *Duden* says explicitly **„innert eines Jahres, nicht: einem Jahre"**, but presumably the same applies here as in the case of **innerhalb,** the dat. being used where there is no distinctive gen. ending; at all events, the official Swiss Milk Supply regulations require inspectors to report **„innert zehn Tagen".** To be avoided also is the use of **inner** as a prep. of space, which seems to be esp. Austrian: cf. **Neben der Hoftür war eine Holzbank inner der Mauer** (Hofmannsthal). **2.** Rather more common than **innerhalb** used of *time* is **binnen,** which as a prep. of *space* is now almost confined to a few compds. like **Binnenhafen, Binnenmeer** ('inland sea'), **Binnenhandel** ('home trade'), etc.; the large lake in Hamburg called **die Alster** narrows at one point, where a bridge separates the **Binnenalster** from the **Außenalster.** The case after **binnen** is either the *gen.*, as in **Kleine Geschäfte waren imstande, sich binnen weniger Jahre zu Großhandlungen zu entwickeln** (Th. Mann), and sim. **binnen weniger Nächte** (Speckmann), or, now more usually, the *dat.*: e.g. **Der Hund hatte binnen wenigen Minuten die letzten Spuren ihrer Morgenarbeit vernichtet** (H. Hoffmann); and the dat. is obligatory in expressions like **binnen kurzem** ('in a short time') and in the idiom **binnen heute** (or **hier** or **jetzt**) **und . . .** ('between now and . . .'): e.g. **Binnen kurzem hatte sie die Vorstadt erreicht** (Fontane)—**Binnen heute und drei Monaten haben wir Krieg** (id.)—**Fichte hat einen Aufsatz binnen heut' und acht Tagen** ('by this day next week') **zu liefern versprochen** (Sch.)—**Ich werde zornig werden, wenn Sie binnen hier und dem neuen Jahre an Ihre Abreise gedenken** (Lessing: '. . . if you think of leaving before the New Year')—**Der Geist stellte es mir frei, binnen jetzt und der folgenden Mitternacht** ('by next midnight') **drei Wünsche zu äußern** (K. Scheffler).

innerlich: see **äußer** 1.

innerst: see **äußer** 3.

inner(**t**) (prep.): see **innerhalb** 1 (*c*).

insgesamt: see **samt** 2 (*b*).

inside: 1. *Adverb*:—The German expressions for 'inside' and 'outside' depend on whether the context implies rest or motion. Thus, 'Come inside!' is **Kommt herein!** and 'Children, run outside!' is **Kinder, lauft hinaus!** whereas 'It is warmer inside than outside' is **Es ist drinnen wärmer als draußen.** Here the shorter forms **innen** and **außen** were formerly often used, as in **Er ging aus dem Hospital und setzte sich außen vor die Türe hin** (G.), but these forms are now little found in independent use. Actually, the longer forms are contractions of **da** and **innen** or **außen,** but all feeling for this has been lost, so that one says **Warum stehen Sie da draußen? Hier drinnen ist es wärmer** ('Why stand out there? It is warmer in here'). But the shorter forms are still in use in compds. (see 3) and in propositions like **Der Becher ist sowohl innen wie außen vergoldet** ('gilded both inside and out'); but esp. after the preps. **nach** and **von:** e.g. **Die Fenster gehen nach innen, die Tür nach außen auf** ('open inwards . . . outwards')—**Er trat auf die Straße und schloß die Tür von außen zu** (A. Wilbrandt)—**Wallenstein hatte in dem ansehnlichsten Hause der Stadt Wohnung genommen; eine von außen angelegte Wendeltreppe** ('a spiral stair built on from outside') **führte zu seinen Zimmern** (L. v. Ranke)—**Von außen gesehen** ('Seen from outside'), **macht das Gebäude einen imposanten Eindruck, aber die Innenräume** (cf. 3) **sind klein**—**Ich habe die Innenseite des Kissenüberzugs nach außen gekehrt** ('I have turned the pillow-case inside out')—fig. **Ich kenne diesen Ort** (**von**) **innen und außen** or **in- und auswendig** ('I know this place inside out, every stone in it'). **2.** *preposition*:—see **außerhalb** and **innerhalb. 3.** *Noun*:—Expressions like 'the inside, outside of a building' are best rendered by **das Innere, Äußere eines**

Gebäudes (see **äußer** 2), but in other contexts a compd. noun is often more appropriate: e.g. **Die Gebrauchsanweisung ist auf der Innenseite des Deckels angegeben** ('The directions for use are given on the inside of the lid')—**Die Außenwand ist wetterdicht—Die alten Pferdebahnwagen hatten Sitze für Innen- und Außenpassagiere**; cf. modern expressions in sport like **Das erste Rennen wurde von einem Außenseiter gewonnen** ('was won by an outsider') — **Dieser Fußballspieler ist der linke Innenstürmer** ('the inside left').

invite: see **laden** 1, 2, and 4.

inwohnen: see **inne-** 4.

inzwischen: see **indessen.**

irgend: 1. In independent use this adv. suggests a bare possibility, being esp. common in expressions like **Komm, wenn du irgend kannst!** ('Come if you possibly can!')—**Ich werde Sie, wenn irgend möglich** ('if at all possible'), **nächste Woche besuchen—Die Gelegenheit war so günstig wie nur irgend möglich** (Ompteda)—**Wenn es morgen irgend** (= **etwa,** 'by any chance') **regnen sollte, schieben wir die Landpartie auf. 2.** But its commonest use is as a modifier of inflected **ein,** indef. prons. and advs. to increase the indefiniteness still more, being written as a sep. word before **jemand** and **etwas,** but elsewhere as a prefix: e.g. **Ich werde schon irgendeinen Ausweg finden** ('Never fear, I'll find some way or other out of my difficulty')—**Wenn irgend jemand** (or **irgendeiner,** coll. **irgendwer,** 'any one, no matter who') **anklingeln sollte, sagen Sie, ich wäre beschäftigt—Der Junge muß irgend etwas** (coll. **irgendwas**) **angerichtet haben** ('The boy must have been up to some mischief or other')—**Hat jemand irgendwelche Vorschläge zu machen?—Das Buch ist nicht hier, es muß irgendwo anders sein—Das Geld muß irgendwie** ('somehow or other') **geschafft werden—„Wohin sollen wir gehen?" „Irgendwohin"** ('Anywhere you like'). It is strange that **irgend** has become such a common expression, as the MHG *iergen(t)* was much rarer than *iender(t)*, which is now obs.; and it is equally strange that the adv. form **irgends** (= **irgendwo,** 'anywhere') is so much less common than the neg. **nirgends** ('nowhere'), which is an everyday expression.

irre: Apart from the expression **irre Reden führen** ('to rave, talk wildly'), **irre** is not much used as an attrib. adj., but rather in the pred. after verbs: e.g. **Er war ganz irre im Kopf** ('He was quite bewildered *or* in a state of mental aberration')—**Was sprichst du da Fürchterliches? Bist du irre?** (Binding: 'What dreadful things are you saying? Are you out of your mind?')—**Ich fange an, irre an ihm zu werden** ('I am beginning to have my doubts about him *or* to lose confidence in him'); in most cases, indeed, **irre** is now treated as a sep. prefix, esp. in **irrereden** ('to talk incoherently'); **irreführen** ('to lead astray, mislead'); **irregehen** (lit. like **fehlgehen,** 'to lose one's way' [cf. **fehlen** 2 *b*], *fig.* 'to err, deviate from the right path'); and **irremachen** ('to perplex'), esp. common in **sich nicht irremachen lassen** ('not to let oneself be disconcerted *or* put out': cf. **irren** 2). Nor is the adj. much used as a subst.: 'an insane person' is **ein Irrsinniger**—cf. compds. like **Irrenanstalt** ('lunatic asylum'), **Irrgarten** ('maze'), **Irrwisch** ('will-o'-the-wisp') and esp. **Irrtum** ('error'), as in **im Irrtum sein** or **sich im Irrtum befinden** ('to be mistaken').

irren: 1. With *trans.* force, this verb is now only used *reflex.*: e.g. **Wenn ich mich nicht irre, ist er augenblicklich verreist** ('If I am not mistaken, he is away from home just now')—**Ich habe mich geirrt, die Sache verhält sich etwas anders** ('I was wrong, the facts are somewhat different'); one no longer says **Wenn ich den König irrte?** (Sch.: 'What if I were to mislead *or* deceive the king?'), where one would now use **irreführen** (see **irre**) or **täuschen** (see **deceive** 1). With *intrans.* force, **irren** is used either *lit.* or *fig.*: e.g. **Ich irrte durch die Stadt** ('I wandered through the town': cf. Musäus' **Er wanderte den ganzen Tag in der Irre herum**)—**Irren ist menschlich** ('To err is human')—**Es irrt der Mensch, solang er strebt** (G.). **2.** Apart from **abirren** (see **fehlen** 1 *b*), the commonest compds. are **beirren** and **verirren:** the former ('to confuse, perplex') is esp. used in **sich nicht beirren lassen** ('not to let oneself be put out': cf. **irremachen** under **irre**), while the latter is now only used reflex. with lit. force ('to lose one's way, go astray'), cf. **verirrte Schafe** ('lost sheep').

J

ja: This coll. expression is used to convey quite a number of different ideas, which are difficult to reproduce in precise words, mainly because its exact meaning in a given context depends largely on accent and intonation, esp. when it is combined, as it frequently is, with other adv. particles. **1.** *Accented* (with a long vowel): (**a**) With the force of 'yes' it is used in propositions like **Er beantwortete die Frage mit „Ja"—„Ist er verreist?" „Ich glaube, ja"** ('I think he is'); cf. **Sie hat ihr Jawort gegeben** ('She has accepted him'). The affirmation is often emphasized by the addition of another adv.: e.g. **ja gewiß** ('yes indeed'), **ja wahrhaftig** ('yes, really'), **ja natürlich** ('yes, of course'); and here belongs **ja′ doch** as an expression of impatience or irritation, as in **„Kommst du denn nicht?" „Ja′ doch!"** ('Yes, yes, I'm coming!'). It has the force of 'indeed, nay', when it corrects or amplifies a previous expression: e.g. **Er soll krank sein, ja schwer krank—Das Wetter war schlecht, ja abscheulich.** The introductory expression **nun ja′** (in every-day speech usually **na ja′**) implies agreement with what has just been said, but is mostly followed by a reservation or qualification: e.g. **„Vater, darf ich auf der Straße spielen?" „Na ja′, aber sieh dich vor den Autos vor!"** ('Oh all right, but watch the traffic!')—**„Sie hätten ihn um etwas Geld angehen können". „Na ja′, aber das hätte er vielleicht übelgenommen"** ('Why yes, but he might have been offended'). (**b**) Idiomatic is the use of a strongly accented **ja** to suggest the idea 'without fail', as in **Kommen Sie ja′ rechtzeitig!** ('Be sure you come in good time!') and **Grüßen Sie ihn ja′ von mir** ('Now remember to give him my kind regards!'); and esp. in *neg.* propositions to express 'on no account': e.g. **Vergiß ja′ nicht, die Rechnung zu bezahlen!** ('Whatever you do, don't forget to pay the bill!')—**Der Arzt hatte dem Kranken eingeschärft, ihn ja′ zu rufen, sobald er seiner bedürfe** (Ompteda: 'The doctor had urged his patient not to hesitate a moment to call him as soon as he required his services')—**Auf der Reise bis Koblenz blickten sie aus dem Fenster, damit ihnen ja′ nichts entginge** (id.: '. . . so that they might be sure not to miss anything'). **2.** *Unaccented* (with a short vowel): (**a**) It is most frequently inserted in a statement which is explanatory, or which assumes that the person addressed knows the facts, although he may have forgotten them at the moment —cf. **doch** (adverb) 2 (*a*): e.g. **Wir gehen am besten zu Fuß, es ist ja nicht weit** ('. . . it 's not far, you know')—**Sollen wir noch ein Stündchen plaudern? Es ist ja erst neun Uhr—Es hat wenig Zweck, ins Konzert zu gehen: es ist ja so wie so′ zu spät** ('. . . it 's too late anyway, as you can see')—**„Warum ist denn dein Bruder nicht gekommen?". „Du wei′ßt ja, daß er verreist ist"** ('But I told you he was out of town'). (**b**) The expression **ja so′** introduces a statement indicating that the speaker has either been under a misapprehension, and has had some fact explained to him, or has been reminded of something he had forgotten: e.g., on the one hand, **„Ich dachte, deine Schwester wollte mitkommen?" „Das wollte sie auch** ('And so she did'), **aber sie hat nicht abkommen können". „Ja so′, dann müssen wir ohne sie gehen"** ('Oh well, in that case we'll have to go without her')—**„Der Hund hat nicht mich, sondern meinen Bruder gebissen" „Ja so′, das ist etwas anderes"** ('Ah, that 's another matter'); and, on the other hand, **„Wissen deine Eltern schon, daß du morgen nach Berlin mußt?" „Ja so′, ich wollte ihnen ja schreiben!"** ('Oh yes, that reminds me, I meant to write them, didn't I?').

jagen: This verb is now *weak*. At one time, through the influence of verbs like **fahren, graben, laden** (q.v.), etc., the strong past form **jug** was sometimes used (cf. **frug**: see **fragen**), but this is quite obs.: cf. **Der Postillion jug** (now **jagte**) **durch die Gassen zum Tore hinaus** (E. T. A. Hoffmann).

Jahr: see **nouns of measure** 1 (*b*). For the difference between **-jährig** and **jährlich**, see **-ig.**

Januar: see **Monatsnamen.**

je: 1. The commonest meaning of **je** is 'ever', in which case it is slightly accented. In MHG, 'always' was *ie* (> **je**) or *iemer*

(= *ie*+*mêre* > **immer**), the former used of past time, the latter of future time. This distinction no longer holds good, but one clearly distinguishes between **Haben Sie je** or **jemals** ('ever') **in Berlin gewohnt?** and **Haben Sie immer** ('always') **in Berlin gewohnt?** So also **Wenn du je nach Deutschland kommen solltest, hoffe ich, daß du mich aufsuchst—Es ist kälter als je** ('It is colder than ever'): cf. **denn (conjunction)** 4—**Wer hätte es sich je träumen lassen, daß so etwas geschehen würde!** ('Who would ever have dreamed that the like of that would happen!'). **2.** In certain cases **je** has *distrib.* force, being then also slightly accented: (**a**) before numerals as in **Er gab den Kindern je einen Apfel** ('He gave each of the children an apple') and **Je das dritte Kind in der Klasse mußte ein Gedicht aufsagen** ('Every third child in the class had to repeat a poem'); (**b**) in the expressions **je nach** (prep.) and **je nachdem** (conj.), meaning 'according to' and 'according as' respectively: e.g. **Wir wurden je nach Verdienst belohnt** ('Each of us was rewarded according to his merit')—**Die Kinder wurden gelobt oder bestraft, je nachdem sie fleißig oder faul gewesen waren—Hoffmann begleitete auf dem Klavier und malte alles mit Tönen aus, je nachdem es grausig, zärtlich oder rührend war** (Bergengruen); cf., elliptically, **„Gehst du ins Konzert?" „Je nachdem!"** ('That depends!' i.e. I shall go or not go, according to circumstances: cf. the last example given under **depend** 2). **3.** Another common use of **je** is before a compar. adj. or adv. in expressions like 'the more the merrier', in which case it is unaccented. In such propositions the first 'the' is always **je,** the second either **je** (esp. in short pithy phrases) or **desto** or **um so** (qq.v.): e.g. **Es glückte dem Freunde, ihn zu überzeugen, daß er sich je eher je lieber** ('the sooner the better') **eine neue Tätigkeit suchen müßte** (E. Wichert)—**Das Gefühl seiner Abhängigkeit von Gott setzte sich je länger je mehr in Furcht um** (K. Lamprecht)—**Ihn drückte je länger je mehr die Regelmäßigkeit dieses Lebens** (H. Hesse)—**Der Bär bewegte seine je näher je riesiger werdenden Glieder auf den Schützen zu** (L. Goldammer)—cf. **das Jelängerjelieber** (the popular name of the 'honeysuckle'); but **Je höher man hinaufsteigt, eine desto** (or **um so**) **schönere Aussicht hat man.** Normally, the rel. clause precedes, as in the last example, but the order may be reversed: e.g. **Die Berge wurden dunkler, je tiefer die Sonne stand, und gewannen ein desto schöneres Blau, je glänzender der Strahl des Abends das Laub der Bäume färbte** (Stifter)—**Der Bankier benahm sich desto lustiger, in je gefährlicherer Laune er sich befand** (Th. Mann).

jedenfalls: see **all** 1; **jeder** 1 (*b*); **wenig** 4 (*b*).

jeder: 1. (**a**) This indef. num., like its archaic alternative **jeglicher** (see **gleich** 3 *b*), is now only used in the sing., the plur. being obs.: cf. **Wo wir uns der Sonne freuen, sind wir jede** (now always **alle**) **Sorgen los** (G.). It is used both as an adj. and as a subst., and may be preceded by the indef. art., as in **Das weiß (ein) jedes Kind**; but in the subst. use the art. must be inserted in the *gen.*: **Das ist eines jeden Pflicht** (not **Das ist jedes Pflicht**). *Duden* apparently allows **Er erinnert sich noch jedes von euch** ('every one of you'), but **eines jeden** or **jedes einzelnen** is certainly preferable in good prose (see **every**). (**b**) An attrib. adj. after **jeder** has *weak* inflexion, as in **ein jeder rechtschaffene Bürger,** gen. **eines jeden rechtschaffenen Bürgers.** In the adj. relation without the art., the normal gen. is **jedes,** and this is imperative before a weak subst., as in **Das ist jedes Beamten Pflicht**; but **jeden** is permissible if the noun has the strong ending: e.g. **Ich pochte an die Tür jeden Turmes** (C. F. Meyer)—**Das Gäßchen war mit Menschen jeden Geschlechts und Alters vollgepfropt** (Fr. Halm)—**Du bist jeden Schamgefühls bar!** (Th. Mann)—**Das Wunder ist das liebste Kind jeden Glaubens** (A. Schaeffer). *Sanders* represents this as **„nicht nachahmenswert",** and *Duden* gives **„jedes Schlages (besser als: jeden Schlages)",** but as the weak ending is firmly established in **jeden-, allen-, besten-, widrigenfalls,** etc., and very common in **allen Ernstes** (see **all** 1), **guten Mutes,** etc., it would seem natural to allow both forms and let the sound decide: **jeden Schlages** is certainly more euphonious, while **jedes Spaßes** is particularly harsh. (**2**) (**a**) Idiomatic is the use of **jeder** where we use '*any*': e.g. **Er will sein Haus um jeden Preis** ('at any price') **verkaufen—Er muß jeden Augenblick kommen** ('He will be here any moment now')—**Jede Entschuldigung gilt** ('Any excuse will do')—**Mit einem Stück Draht öffnet er dir jedes Schloß** (Kellermann)—**Sie war ohne jede Spur von Anmaßung**

(K. Edschmid); esp. common with **ander** after a compar. and als ('than'): e.g. **Ich ahnte bereits, daß die Musik mehr zu sagen vermag als jede andere Kunst** (E. Wiechert)—**Er wußte, sie liebte diesen Wein mehr als** jeden anderen (Fr. Huch) —**In diesem Lande ist das leichter als in** jedem andern (A. Schaeffer)—**Die Angst, den Besitz zu verlieren, war stärker als** jedes andere Gefühl (B. E. Werner)—**Ihre Meinung gilt mir mehr als die jedes anderen.** (**b**) Often the collect. **all** is used for the distrib. jeder here (cf. **every**): e.g. **Es ist alles andere als** ('anything but') **Sommerwetter—Ich gehe unter allen Umständen** ('in any case') **früh nach Hause—Wie kommt es, daß ohne allen Anlaß eine Person uns so lebendig in den Sinn kommt, daß wir darüber staunen?** (E. T. A. Hoffmann); cf. **Mit Esperanto kann man sich überall** ('anywhere') **verständlich machen—Er bemerkte, er schlafe überall, und legte sich auf den Fußboden** (A. Schaeffer). **3.** Out of the distrib. masc. **jeder Mann** there has developed the collect. num. **jedermann** ('everybody'), which only inflects in the *gen.*, **jeder**- remaining invariable: e.g. **Das Kätzchen war zutraulich gegen jedermann** (G. Keller)—**Er hatte die Gabe, jedermann davon zu überzeugen, daß er unter ei'ner Decke mit ihm stecke** (M. Eyth: 'He had the gift of being able to convince one and all that they were fellow conspirators of his') —**Er kam lächelnd und schüttelte jedermann** (dat.) **die Hand** (H. Hesse)—**Er verkehrt mit jedermann** ('He'll associate with anybody')—**Das ist nicht jedermanns Sache** ('That is not in everybody's line' or 'It is not every one who is cut out for that').

jedermann: see **jeder** 3.

jeglich: see **gleich** 3.

jemand, niemand: 1. These indef. prons. have an inorganic final *t*-sound, the MHG forms being *ieman* and *nieman*. The modern forms can inflect in the normal way: **Hast du unterwegs (irgend) jemanden getroffen?—Ich bin niemandem begegnet.** Inflexion is necessary in the gen., as in **Das ist niemand(e)s Angelegenheit** ('That is nobody's business'), but in the accus. and dat. the *uninflected* forms are strongly favoured in the north, where **Ich habe niemand getroffen** and **Ich bin niemand begegnet** are almost universal; and even G. Keller says **Wem gehören die Goldgülden? Niemand gehören sie.**[1] What is now regarded as definitely wrong in good prose is the earlier use of a *weak* ending in the *dat.*, as in **Ich werde keine Heimat haben, ich gehöre niemanden an** (Stifter) and **Wir werden von niemanden gestört** (W. Alexis), where **niemandem** would not be wrong, but **niemand** much more usual in the north. **2.** To render the expression 'some one else', the north always uses **jemand anders,** in MHG *ieman anders*, where *anders* is a gen. sing., a noun being really understood ('somebody of another name *or* stamp'). In MHG it could also take the form *ander ieman*, where *ander* is the contracted gen. plur. *anderer*, again with a noun understood ('some one of other people'), and in the south, esp. in Austria, **jemand anderer** is still almost the rule: e.g. **Jemand anderer erzählte von zwei jungen Mädchen** (Wassermann)—**Es war niemand anderer als Doktor Franck** (Zifferer). But southern authors do not regard **anderer** here as the gen. plur. which it orig. was, but treat it as a nom. sing. masc., and therefore inflect it in the oblique cases: e.g. **Die Blumen ließ sie niemand anderen begießen** (W. v. Scholz), which the author might have expressed by **Die Blumen erlaubte sie niemand anderem zu begießen —Er hatte niemand anderen, mit dem er den Fall besprechen konnte** (Zuckmayer). In all these examples the stereotyped form **anders** is to be recommended, and indeed *Duden* gives only **„von jemand anders reden"**; but in the dat. the form **jemand anderem** is often used, as in **Sie beschäftigte sich mit niemand anderem als diesem Sohn Albions** (Fontane), and esp. where there is no prep. to indicate the case: e.g. **Sie sprach einen Fluch über den Schatz aus, daß er niemals jemand anderm angehören sollte** (G. Keller)—**Es wird ratsam sein, wenn Sie Ihre Protektion jemand anderem zuwenden** (A. Reimer)—**Wißt ihr nun, daß ihr euer Gold niemand anderem zu geben habt?** (Dauthendey). A *weak* ending here is now rightly condemned, and examples like the following should not be imitated: **Nehmt meine Tat mit ins Grab! Nie hat mich die Eitelkeit versucht, sie jemand anderen** (for **anderem** or, better, **anders**) **zu erzählen** (Lessing)—**Schon war er im**

[1] In the present volume the forms **jemanden** (accus.) and **jemandem** (dat.) are often used to make the case clear.

Begriff, sich zu jemand anderen zu wenden (G.)—**Liebe in Gedanken an jemanden andern als an dich war mir unausdenklich** (St. Zweig); cf., as unusual even in the south, **Ich sah, daß der Tisch, an dem ich zu sitzen pflegte, von jemandem anderen** (for **von jemand anders**) **eingenommen war** (Rilke). The *gen.* of such expressions is generally avoided; if unavoidable, it would take the form **jemandes anderen**; cf., as an example of Austrian usage not to be recommended, **Das war jemand anderes Lachen** (Hofmannsthal: for **jemandes anderen Lachen**, 'some one else's laugh'). **3.** The MHG expression for 'some stranger' was *ieman vremder*, where again *vremder* is a gen. plur. ('some one of strangers'), and **jemand Fremder** is still the usual southern idiom, **Fremder** being here also treated as a nom. sing. masc. and inflected, as in **Sie spannte ihre Augenbrauen hoch, als wenn man jemand Lästigen** ('some bore') **wegweisen will** (St. Zweig) and **In ihm brütete ein Gefühl, das er endlich als Eifersucht eingestand, gegen niemand Faßbaren, gegen jeden Möglichen** (A. Zweig: i.e. jealousy of no one 'tangible', no one in particular). But, in the north, usage is quite established: just as one says **jemand anders**, so also one says **jemand Fremdes**, but while **anders** generally remains in that form, **Fremdes** is treated as a *neut. sing.* and inflected as such: e.g. **Er wollte abwarten, bis jemand Fremdes das Lesezimmer betreten** (Ompteda)—**„Wer ist da?" „Jemand Bekanntes"** (G.: 'Some one you know')—**Ich dachte nicht, daß Ihr oder sonst jemand Wichtiges käme** (Jak. Frey: 'I didn't expect either you or any other important visitor')—**In der Hochzeitsgesellschaft befand sich niemand Geringeres als Fräulein B.** (Polenz: '. . . no less a person than Miss B.')—cf. **Sie sagt mir, das Spuken käme immer mal wieder, namentlich wenn wer Neues** (coll. for **jemand Neues**) **im Hause erschiene** (Fontane: 'She tells me the ghost walks every now and then, particularly when a new visitor appears in the house': see **wer** 2 *c*); so also in the accus., **Habt Ihr jemand Liebes hier zur Ruhe gebracht?** (I. Kurz: 'Have you buried some one dear to you here?'), and in the dat., which is established in the south also, **Er streifte durch Haus und Gehöft, wobei er oft erregt mit jemand Unsichtbarem sprach** (Stehr)—cf. **Der Brief muß von jemand Hohes sein** (G.), which *Sanders* rightly characterizes as **„ungewöhnlich"**, and which should not be used. The gen. is generally avoided, as in the case of **jemand anders**: here again it would have to take the form **jemandes Fremden** (not **jemand Fremdes**, which can only be nom. or accus.).

jene(r): see **dies** 2.

jenseit(s): This adv., meaning 'on the other *or* far side', is now mainly used as a *prep.* (+ gen. or **von**, formerly also + dat.) with the force of 'beyond, across', as opposed to **diesseit(s)**, 'on this side of'. Where Luther wrote **disseid** and **jenseid**, the modern version has **Wir wollen nicht mit ihnen erben jenseit des Jordans, sondern . . . diesseit des Jordans** (Num. 32. 19), and a well-known story of Storm's is entitled **Von jenseit des Meeres.** All the same, modern prose usage seems to show a definite preference for the forms with a final **s**: e.g. **In der Ferne glänzte das Kloster Johannisberg, einzelne Lichtpunkte lagen dies- und jenseits des Flusses** (G.)—**Von jenseits des Wassers** ('From across the river') **war das Lachen zweier Spaziergänger vernehmbar** (Bruno Frank); **das Jenseits** ('the next world'). In rather more loose style, a point lying on the far side of a street, frontier, etc., is also suggested by the prep. **über** (q.v. 1 *a* and *b*); cf. also **quer** 1 (*a*).

jetzt: see **nun** 1 and 2.

Joch: This neut. noun is used in the various senses of our 'yoke': e.g. the wooden contrivance used for carrying two pails or for coupling two oxen at the plough; the two animals so coupled (whence its fig. sense of 'restraint, oppression'); also an old measure of land, 50–60 acres (cf. 'The originals mention certain persons by name, with the number of yokes and acres belonging to them': 1772). For the sing. form used in the plur., as in **zwei Joch Ochsen**, see **nouns of measure** 1 (*a*).

Juli: see **Monatsnamen.**

Junge: This was orig. an adj.-subst., and it is still so used, as in **Junge und Alte** ('Young and old people'); in particular, the *neut.* is quite fixed in the sense of the 'young' of animals: e.g. **Unsere Katze hat ein Junges (zwei Junge) geworfen—Die Jungen, die unsere Katze geworfen hat, sind alle tot.** On the other hand, in the sense of 'boy', the masc. has become a regular *weak noun*: **ein** (or **der**) **Junge,**

des Jungen, die (or zwei) Jungen. For the LG plur. **Jungens**, see **Mädchen** 2.

jüngst: see recent 1 (*a*) and (*b*).

Juni: see **Monatsnamen**.

K

Käfig: This noun, meaning 'cage, bird-cage', has developed out of MHG *kevje*, which was orig. fem. (< Lat. *cavea*). According to present-day usage it is *masc.* (the only gender given by *Duden* and *Sprach-Brockhaus*), but it was commonly treated as neut. in comparatively recent times: cf. **Ich tat die jungen Vögel gleich ins Käfig** (Mörike). The earlier form **Käficht**—see *t* **(inorganic)**—is now obs.: cf. **Was für ein Tor i ch war, daß ich ins Käficht zurückwollte!** (Sch.: i.e. 'into captivity'). In point of fact, the gender of nouns with the suffix **-icht** (which mostly has collect. force) fluctuates somewhat: thus, **Dickicht** ('thicket'), **Röhricht** ('reed-bed'), **Spülicht** ('dish-water, slops') and **Tannicht** ('fir-plantation': cf. **Kiefer** 2) are always *neut.*, while **Kehricht** ('sweepings') is either masc. or neut. Always *masc.* is **Habicht** ('hawk'), but this does not really belong to the above group, as the suffix does not suggest a collect. idea: it has developed out of MHG *habech*.

Kamin: This noun, meaning 'fireplace', with the accent on the *last* syllable, is now almost always treated as *masc.*; but it was formerly not infrequently used as a neut. (e.g. by G. and Sch.), and the neut. is occasionally found in more recent authors, as in **Manchmal kam ein Windstoß durch das Kamin herunter** (M. Eyth).

Kammer: see room 4.

Kante: This fem. noun means 'edge, border, margin', e.g. of a table, a cliff, even the sea (**Tisch-, Felsen-, See-** or **Meereskante**): the expression **auf die Kante legen** is lit. 'to lay edgewise' (of boards, bricks, etc.)—cf. **Geld** or **einen Notpfennig auf die hohe Kante legen**, 'to save, lay by money (for a rainy day)'. The plur. **Kanten** is used esp. in the trade as a 'lace edging' to a handkerchief, garment, etc., but it has become a *sing. masc.* in the north in the sense of a 'crust, heel, outside slice' of a loaf, as in **Er war damit beschäftigt, Fett auf einen Brotkanten zu streichen** (B. E. Werner).

Kate: This is a characteristically northern expression, meaning a peasant's small 'cottage', the peasant being **der Kätner**. The form **die Kate** is the only one given by *Duden*, and Storm always uses **it**; but the alternative form **der Katen** seems to be used in eastern Mecklenburg—cf. **Er ging mit ihr zusammen den Weg zur Kate** (Fr. Griese) and **Er kaufte den alten baufälligen Katen dicht am Waldrande** (id.).

Kauderwelsch: The verb **kaudern** means 'to gobble', expressing the cry of a turkey-cock (**Puterhahn**). The adj. **welsch** was used in connexion with the language, customs, etc., of those who spoke a non-Germanic, Romance language (cf. Goethe's **Nun hatte ich zum erstenmal einen stockwelschen Postillio'n**, i.e. a driver who was Italian to the backbone), and as Italian pedlars used to go about in south-west Germany in the Middle Ages, speaking a language which the German peasants could not understand, **Kauderwelsch** came to be used in the sense of unintelligible 'gibberish, jargon'. It can also be used as an *adj.* (Mörike's pet starling spoke to the poet **in seiner kauderwelschen Sprache**), and from it the insep. verb **kauderwelschen** was formed, as in **Ich habe den Mann nicht verstanden, er hat allerlei gekauderwelscht.** In this connexion see also **radebrechen.**

kauern: see **knien.**

kaum: **1.** There are two ways of expressing a proposition like 'The morning had scarcely dawned when he set out' (see hardly). The straightforward rendering is **Der Morgen war kaum angebrochen, als er sich auf den Weg machte.** The other way, which is rather more idiomatic, is to start with a subord. clause introduced by **kaum daß** (see 2) and follow it up with a princ. clause (often introduced by **so** or **da**): **Kaum daß der Morgen anbrach, so begab er sich auf den Weg** (Novalis); sim. **Kaum daß er erschienen war, ertönten die ersten Takte der Polonaise** (Wildenbruch). This even led to the omission of **daß**, so that **kaum** became a real *conj.*, as did **nun** (q.v. 2), **ungeachtet** (q.v. *b*) and **zumal** (q.v.); but this is a peculiarly southern, esp. Austrian usage, and examples like the following are not to be recommended: **In jedem Hause, kaum sie eintrat, wußte sie sich nützlich zu machen** (Rosegger)—**Kaum diese Worte gesprochen waren, wandte sie sich um und verschwand hinter der Tür** (id.)—**Ich vermochte mich seiner im ersten Augenblick nicht zu entsinnen; kaum er aber seinen Namen nannte, erinnerte ich mich sofort** (St. Zweig)—**Kaum er den Mund öffnete, wurde er niedergeschrieen** (A. Döblin). **2.** The combination **kaum daß** is also used in another way, viz. to introduce, not a temp. clause as under 1 above, but a clause of result. Thus, in the proposition **Stille war es: die Bäume hörten zu flüstern auf, die Bienen ließen ihr Summen, kaum daß die Blumen zu atmen wagten** (Zifferer), the last clause emphasizes the silence and is much like **ja, es war so still, daß die Blumen kaum zu atmen wagten**; sim. **Das Wetter ist prachtvoll, kaum daß ein Lüftchen geht** (Fontane)—**Sie hielt eine leidenschaftlich bewegte Rede, kaum daß sie sich Zeit ließ, Atem zu schöpfen** (Th. Mann)—**Er scheint das Musizieren fast aufgegeben zu haben, kaum daß er sich jemals ans Klavier setzt** ('He seems almost to have given up his music, indeed, he hardly ever sits down at the piano').

keep: see **behalten.**

Kehricht: see **Käfig.**

kein: As this neg. (< Goth. *nih-ain*, 'not one') has no inflexional ending in the nom. sing. masc. and neut. when qualifying a noun, a following attrib. adj. must be *strong*: just as one says **ein (mein, dein) guter Vater**, but in the plur. **meine (deine) lieben Eltern**, so also **kein großer Dichter**, plur. **keine großen Dichter.** At an earlier period this rule was not strictly observed in the plur., indeed, *Campe*'s dictionary (1807–11) demands **keine frohe Tage**, and *Weigand*'s (1873) still gives **keine große Aussichten**, but adds **„doch ist schwache Form des Adjektivs heute üblicher".** Modern usage here is quite fixed, and the strong adj. endings in an example like **Gewiß sind in ganz Deutschland keine unbescholtenere Mädchen und keine treuere Frauen als in Schwaben** (Novalis) would be marked as bad mistakes. In this connexion it is noteworthy that although one always says **allenfalls** (q.v.), and sim. **jeden-, besten-, schlimmsten-, gegebenenfalls**, etc., **keinesfalls** is much more common than **keinenfalls**, and **keineswegs** ('on no account, by no means') is firmly established. For **kein** qualifying a partitive gen., see **nichts** 4, and cf. **Leid.** When used subst., **kein** must, of course, be inflected strongly: e.g. **Keiner von den Knaben konnte die Frage beantworten—Geld? Ich habe keins.** For the double neg. in propositions like **Er durchstrich die Gänge des Parks: umsonst! Nirgends keine Seele war zu sehen** (G.), see **negative (pleonastic)** 1 and 2 (*a*).

keineswegs: see **kein** *ad fin.*

kennen: see **wissen** 2, and cf. **Ich kenne ihn nicht, aber ich weiß um ihn** ('I don't know him, but I know about him'). For **Es war mir, als kennte ich die Dame,** see **past subjunctive** 1 (*b*).

kennenlernen: It seems illogical to give, as *Duden* does, **kennen lernen** as two words, and **kennengelernt** as one word, seeing that the dependent infin. has now to all intents become a real sep. prefix: **„Wo lernten Sie ihn kennen?" „Ich habe ihn noch nicht kennengelernt, hoffe aber, ihn bald kennenzulernen."** In a compd. tense the past part. of **lernen** may assume the infin. form, as in the case of the **modal auxiliary verbs** (q.v.): e.g. **Schon vor der Abreise von Amerika hatte er sie kennenlernen** (R. v. Gottschall). But this alternative part. form of **lernen** is actually little used now with dependent infins. other than **kennen**: cf., as a striking example, **Er hatte den Architekten näher kennenlernen und sein Talent schätzen gelernt** (G.). The reg. past part. form is, indeed, just as common even with **kennen**: see the examples given under **lernen** 1 (*b*), and cf. **Diese Druckerei war kleiner als die anderen, die ich kennengelernt hatte** (M. Eyth). One important point is that the infin. form *cannot* be used in the *perf. part.* and should be avoided when the aux. is omitted in a subord. clause—see **verbs (auxiliary)** 2 and 3: e.g. **Er behauptet, mich schon kennengelernt zu haben** (never **kennenlernen zu haben**)—**Maria hatte Mörike, der sie in Ludwigsburg kennengelernt** (better than **kennenlernen**), **völlig in ihre Fesseln geschlagen** (E. v. Sallwürk)—**Sie hörte mir zu, wenn ich von der Kanzlei erzählte, wo wir uns kennengelernt** (Grillparzer).

Kerl: For the LG plur. **Kerls** (HG **Kerle**), see **Mädchen** 2.

Kiefer: **1.** There is no connexion between **Kiefer** (*masc.*, plur. **Kiefer**), 'jawbone', and **Kiefer** (*fem.*, plur. **Kiefern**), 'pine-tree': the former is connected with **kauen** ('to chew'), while the latter is a corrupt form of **Kien-föhre** (see 2 *a*), **Kien** being a specific term for 'resinous wood' (**harzreiches Holz**). **2.** The various common conifers (**Zapfenträger** or **Nadelhölzer**) are apt to be confused: even botanists do not seem to agree, so there is some excuse for a proposition like **Diese hohen Personen standen in einem Tannicht** ('fir-plantation'), **und der Landgraf, vor Alter schwach, hielt sich an eine Fichte.** But the following may be taken as the most generally accepted distinguishing features: (**a**) **Föhre** is the SG term for **Kiefer,** i.e. 'pine, Scotch fir' (Lat. *pinus silvestris*); (**b**) **Tanne** (cf. *c*) is the 'silver fir', bearing *erect* cones (Lat. *abies pectinata*); (**c**) **Fichte** (or **Rottanne**) is the 'spruce fir' or 'Norway spruce', with *pendent* cones (Lat. *abies* [or *picea*] *excelsa*): this is the traditional Christmas tree, popularly called **Tannenbaum**; (**d**) **Lärche** is the 'larch', the only deciduous conifer (Lat. *larix*).

kind: For 'a kind of . . .', see **Art.**

Kiste: see box 2.

kite: see **Drache** and **Weih.**

Klang: see **sound** 2 (*c*).

klappen, klappern: see **mit** 2 (*b*).

Kleid(ung): see **clothes** 1 and 2 (*a*).

Kleingeld: This is the ordinary expression for 'small change, coppers' (see **change** 2 *a*): e.g. **Kannst du mir ein paar Groschen leihen? Ich habe leider kein Kleingeld.** To 'give' change is **herausgeben,** to 'receive' change **herausbekommen,** and in familiar speech these verbs are often used without the obj.: e.g. **Sie haben mir nicht richtig herausgegeben** ('You've given me the wrong change')—**„Worauf warten Sie denn?" „Ich bekomme noch heraus"** ('I've still to get some change').

klemmen: **1.** The noun **Klemme,** really an instrument for clamping or pinching, is now mainly used coll. with the fig. force of 'a tight corner, fix, predicament', as in **Ich bin** (or **stecke**) **in einer Klemme** or **Ich half ihm aus der Klemme. 2.** (**a**) The *weak* verb **klemmen** properly means 'to pinch, squeeze': e.g. **Ich habe mir den Finger in der Tür geklemmt—Die Fessel klemmt der Jungfrau zarte Hände** (Sch.); cf. the slang phrase **etwas klemmen** ('to steal or *pinch* something'). So also, in the sense of 'to squeeze, press, stick' a thing firmly into a space, as in **ein Buch zwischen andere Bücher, den Hut unter den Arm, die Brille auf die Nase klemmen** (cf. **Klemmer,** 'pince-nez'). Occasionally, it is now even used with intrans. force: **Unter seinem Arm klemmte** (= **stak**: see **stecken** 2 *b*) **die Aktentasche** (E. Brüning). (**b**) Esp. noteworthy in this connexion is the compd. **beklemmen,** now used only with the *fig.* force of 'to oppress', and here the strong past part. **beklommen** (showing confusion with **klimmen**: see **climb** 1 *b* and 2 *a*) has firmly established itself to suggest a state of feeling oppressed: cf., on the one hand, implying an *action,* **Wie beklemmt mich dieser Anblick!** (Tieck)—**Etwas, das in der Luft zu liegen schien, beklemmte mich** (G.)—**Ein Angstgefühl hatte mir das Herz beklemmt**; and on the other hand, implying a *state,* **Mir ist so beklommen zumute—Die Trauer des Unbekannten schloß Wilhelms beklommenes Herz auf** (G.)—**Bleich stand er und beklommen** (Freiligrath); so also the strong part. form would be more strictly correct in **Plötzlich wird mir die Bettdecke vom Leibe gerissen: „Donnerwetter!" rufe ich beklemmt und setze mich aufrecht** (G. Keller).

Klepper: see **Roß** *ad fin.*

klettern: see **climb.**

Klima: According to *Duden,* the plur. of this neut. noun is **Kli'mas** or **Klima'te**; but the latter, the only form given by *Sprach-Brockhaus,* is little used in the north and mainly confined to the south: it is, indeed, the only form officially recognized in Austria.

klimmen: see **climb.**

klingen: see **sound** 2 (*c*) and **aushallen** (esp. 2).

klopfen: **1.** This is the best expression for 'to knock' (at a door, etc.). In this sense the verb **pochen** (see 2) is often used, but this properly implies a louder knocking and has a more limited application: thus, it cannot be substituted for **klopfen** in expressions like **Er klopfte** ('clapped *or* tapped') **mir** (or **mich**) **auf die Schulter** (see **schlagen** 1 and 2 *c*) or **Ich klopfte bei ihm auf den Busch** ('I sounded him, tried to worm the secret out of him'). In the *abs.* use, it is more common to use the compd. **anklopfen,** as in **Ich trat an das Haus und klopfte an,** where the prefix points to the *end* of the action. **2.** As the simple verb implies an action directed towards some object, a prep. phrase accompanying it should normally require an *accus.* case: **Ich klopfte an die Tür** (like **Ich band mein Pferd an den Pfahl, hängte das Bild an die Wand,** etc.: cf. *accusative or dative* . . . 2). But in point of fact the *dat.* is quite commonly used by all standard modern authors: e.g. **Eine Stunde darauf klopfte er an der Tür einer Dachkammer** (Heyse)—**Sie klopfte an der Pforte** (G. Keller)—**Der Oberst klopfte an der Wohnstubentür** (Viebig)—**Ein fremder Finger klopfte an seiner Tür** (H. W. Geissler); so also **Es ist ein Wunder, daß sie gerade an seiner Tür pochte** (C. Hauptmann)—**Alexander pochte an der Tür seines Bruders** (A. Schaeffer). The dat. seems to be esp. common with an impers. subj., the person inside not knowing who is outside: e.g. **Eines Abends klopfte es an meiner Tür** (H. Hesse)—**Vor einigen Tagen klopfte es an meiner Tür** (Kästner)—**Sie wunderte sich, daß sie** (*scil.* **jemand**) **an der verschlossenen Haustür klopfen hörte** (A. Wilbrandt: cf. **accusative and infinitive** 2 *a*) —**Gegen acht Uhr pochte es an der Tür** (Wassermann); and sim. with the verbal noun: **Hier unterbrach ihn ein Klopfen an der Tür** (Heyse)—**Ein Pochen an der Tür brachte sie zu sich** (Mörike)—**Ich vernahm leise Tritte und gleich darauf ein Pochen an meiner Tür** (Roquette)—**Die Sonne stand schon hoch, als er durch ein Pochen an seiner Tür geweckt wurde** (Jak. Frey). With the compd. **anklopfen,** which indicates the *end* of the action, the dat. is almost fixed: **Er klopfte am Fenster an.**

Knabe: see **boy** 1.

kneifen: 1. There are two forms of the verb meaning 'to nip, pinch', viz. **kneifen** (HG) and **kneipen** (LG), the former being *strong* (**kniff, gekniffen:** the only forms given by *Duden*), the latter *weak* (*Duden* adds **„scherzhaft: geknippen"**). But the LG word has spread to other parts (even to Austria), and has influenced the HG word, so that one occasionally finds weak forms of the latter, as in **Er kneifte** (for **kniff**) **ihr die zarten Wangen** (Auerbach) and **Der Hund wurde in den Schwanz gekneift** (G. Keller, for **gekniffen**). In a proposition like 'He pinched me in the arm', the pers. pron. may be either dat. or accus., as explained under **schlagen** (q.v.), but the accus. is much more common when associated with a prep. phrase: one says either **Er kniff mir den Arm** (= **meinen Arm**) or **Er kniff mich in den Arm**; so also **Er kneift den Hund in den Schwanz** (Freiligrath)—**Er kniff ihn kräftig unter den Arm** (C. F. Meyer)—**Einer kniff die Magd in die Backen** (Freytag); and in the LG form, **Miller kneipt sie in die Ohren** (Sch., in a stage direction)—**Er kneipt mich in die Backen** (Grillparzer)—**Seine Frau kneipt mir ins Ohr** (Börne: usually **mich ins Ohr** or **mir das Ohr**). Incidentally, **kneifen** is always strong when it has the coll. force of 'to shirk, back out of' (an engagement,etc.), in which sense **kneipen** is not used: cf. **Er ist ausgekniffen** ('He has cleared out, made off', slang 'done a bunk'). **2.** A different word is **kneipen** (weak), used in students' slang in the sense of 'to drink, tipple', which is formed from **die Kneipe** ('beer-house, pub'): e.g. **Wir haben den ganzen Abend gekneipt:** cf. **Machen wir einen Kneipbummel!** ('Let 's do a pub-crawl!'). **3.** The strong past forms of **kneifen** should not be confused with the verb **kniffen,** a *weak* verb meaning 'to make a crease in' (cloth, paper, etc.), esp. 'to fold (together)': cf., as an example containing both verbs, **Er war bemüht, ein zusammengeknifftes Zeitungsblatt unter die Lampenkuppel zu klemmen, und dann fiel ein heller Strahl in seine Augen, die er zusammenkniff** (A. Schaeffer: 'He was busily engaged in squeezing a folded newspaper under the lampshade, and then a bright light shone in his eyes, which he screwed up'); so also **die Seite eines Buches einkniffen** ('to dogs-ear the page of a book').

kneipen: see **kneifen** 1 and 2.

knien: The three verbs **hocken** ('to squat'), **kauern** ('to cower, crouch') and **knien** ('to kneel') are the only verbs implying an *attitude* which can be used *without* a prefix to convey the idea of *motion* as well as of *rest*. Where *rest* is implied, northern usage definitely favours the aux. **haben,** as with other verbs suggesting an attitude (cf. **sitzen** 2); where *motion* is implied, the aux. **sein** is fixed, and if there is *no* prefix (see below), the *accusative* in an accompanying prep. phrase is imperative: cf. **Sie hockten auf fauler Streu** (Heine: 'They were squatting on a litter of rotted straw') and **Mit einem**

leichten Sprung hockt ihm der Teufel auf den Rücken (G.: 'With a light step the devil jumps up and squats *down* on his back')—**Sie kauerte da vor ihm** (Voigt-Diederichs: 'She was crouching there in front of him') and **Sie kauerte in die Ecke** ('She crouched *down* in the corner')—**Sie hat** (SG **ist**) **oft neben ihm gekniet** ('She has often *been* on her knees beside him') and **Sie war neben ihn gekniet** (O. Ludwig: 'She had *gone down* on her knees beside him'). But, in point of fact, it is much more usual to emphasize the idea of motion by the addition of the prefix **hin-** or **nieder-** (see **down**, and cf. **niedersitzen**), and as these prefixes point to the *end* of the action, a *dative* in the prep. phrase is the appropriate case: e.g. **Götter werden vor dir niederknien** (Sch.)—**Mühsam kniete er neben dem Jungen nieder** (Ebner-Eschenbach)—**Sie kniete vor der mit Kränzen behangenen Nische nieder** (id.)—**Ich kniete mit ihr vor dem Kreuze hin** (Heyse); cf. the two examples **Die Prinzessin fiel zu den Füßen des Königs, der Sänger kniete an ihre Seite** (Novalis) and **Ich kniete vor dem Bilde der himmlischen Mutter nieder** (id.).

kniffen: see **kneifen** 3.

knirschen: see **mit** 2 (*b*).

Knochen: see **bone.**

knock: see **klopfen.**

kommen: 1. The 2nd and 3rd sing. pres. indic. forms with mutated vowel (**kömmst, kömmt**), although historically more correct (the OHG endings were *-ist, -it*), and still used coll. in certain districts, are now obs. in good prose. **2.** When associated with a prep. which can take either an accus. or a dat., the *simple* verb requires the *accus.*, but with **ankommen** the *dat.* is essential (see **arrive**): hence **Er kam an die Tür,** but **Er kam an der Tür an. 3.** The motion implied is normally *towards* the speaker: e.g. **Kommen Sie her!—Woher kommst du?** (in ordinary lang. usually **Wo kommst du her?**) But **kommen** also expresses our intrans. '**to** *get*', in which case, of course, the motion may be *away from* the speaker: e.g. **Schreibe mir, wenn du nach Berlin kommst—Gestern ging ich zu meinem Freunde, aber als ich hinkam** ('when I got there'), **erfuhr ich, daß er verreist war** (cf. also **entkommen,** for which see **escape,** 1 *b*). **4** (**a**) In expressing 'He came *running*', **the** Germans use the *past* part., not the pres.: **Er kam gelaufen.** This use of the past part. is no longer confined, as it used to be, to verbs of *motion*, but has been extended in more recent times to verbs conveying a *sound*: one says not only **Das Mädchen kam auf mich zugestürzt—Das Kind kam die Treppe heruntergesprungen—Der Alte kam in die Stube gestolpert**; but also **Vom nächsten Feldwege her kam das Geräusch knarrender Heuwagen herübergeklungen** (H. Hesse)—**Die Alte kam an ihrem Stock hereingehustet** (Storm)—**Ein Mädchen kam in Holzschuhen vorbeigeklappert** (Kellermann)—cf. the example from Prutz given under **schleifen** 3—**Also Ihr seid der seltene Vogel, der von der Burg heruntergezwitschert kommt!** (Jul. Wolff: 'So you are the rare bird that comes whistling down from the castle!')—**So eine javanische Feldstraße morgens ist die reine Wettrennbahn: was einem da alles entgegengelaufen, -geflogen, -gemeckert und -geflötet kommt, das ist ganz wunderlich** (Dauthendey). In this last example, both motion and sound occur in the same proposition, the words of sound referring to different subjects; where these refer to the same subject, the motion is usually expressed in a past part., the sound in a pres. part.: e.g. **Heulend kam der Sturm geflogen** (Sch.)—**Ihre Beiden** ('Her two children') **kamen heulend in die Stube hereingestürzt** (Viebig)—**Das Vieh** ('cattle') **kam brüllend die Dorfstraße entlanggezogen.** Very occasionally other verbs than those of motion and sound are so used, but this is not yet in accordance with accepted usage: cf. **Eine Ziege kam in die Stube geguckt** (P. Keller: for . . . **kam an die Tür und guckte in die Stube**). (**b**) This idiomatic use of the past part. is esp. common in the case of verbs compounded with **an-**: e.g. **Des Landvogts Reiter kommen angesprengt** (Sch.)—**Angefahren kamen nun Kammerjungfern** (G.); cf., as a bolder example, **Mit der Dunkelheit kam der alte Bürgermeister mit einer Kerze angezittert** (W. Schäfer: = **kam zitternd angehumpelt**). In point of fact, as the past part. obviously implies completed action, it seems probable that **an-** here has come to be misplaced, and that, instead of being prefixed to the part., it should actually be prefixed to **kommen**; in other words, that in a proposition like **Ich winkte ihm zu, als er angeritten kam,** the subord. clause should properly be **als er geritten ankam** ('when he arrived, having ridden'). Otherwise it is not easy to explain why the past part. should so frequently be used with **kommen,** and so rarely, if ever, with **gehen** (q.v. 2). **5. Kommen** and its compounds are much used to express our intrans. 'to get', as in 'I got home', 'I could not get in', etc., for which see **get** 2 (*b*) and cf. **geraten.**

können: 1. This is one of the **past-present verbs** (q.v.), which explains the stem-vowel change in the pres. tense (**ich kann, wir können**) and the weak past tenses. **2.** In a compd. tense with a dependent infin., the past part. assumes the form of the infin., as in **Er hat es tun können** ('He has been able to do it'); but the normal part. form is used when the dependent infin. is not expressed: e.g. **Er hätte es getan, wenn er es gekonnt hätte**—**Ich hätte es nicht zugeben dürfen** (q.v.), **aber ich habe nicht anders gekonnt** (Auerbach: '. . . but I could not do otherwise' = **ich habe nichts anderes tun können**). The same applies when the aux. is understood, but here it is advisable to insert the aux. and use the two infin. forms: cf. **Infolge des Unfalls war sein Mundwinkel verzerrt, der so lieblich lächeln gekonnt** (A. Schaeffer: better **der so lieblich hatte lächeln können**). In MHG, a proposition like 'He could have done it' was *er künde ez getân haben*; in NHG this is expressed by **Er hätte es tun können,** because **Er könnte es getan haben** rather suggests 'He *might* have done it', i.e. 'It is quite possible that he did it'. **3.** A quite recent use, found esp. in works of literary criticism, is that of the past part. **gekonnt** as an *adj.* in the sense of 'able, accomplished, masterly': e.g. **Heute ist der Stil Thomas Manns meisterlich gekonnt** (Strich)—**Die Bilder von Heinrich sind ausführlicher, die von Thomas gekonnter** (A. Eloesser). But this use is anything but firmly established, and indeed sounds very stilted, esp. in the attrib. relation, as in **eine nicht gekonnte** (i.e. 'inexpert, clumsy') **Behandlung entgegengesetzter Inhalte** (B. v. Münchhausen).

Kopf: The MHG *kopf* or *koph* orig. meant 'container', esp. 'drinking-vessel, beaker' (cf. our *cup*); later, in accordance with the barbarous practice of drinking out of the skulls of slain enemies, it was used with the force of 'skull, brain-pan', and eventually with that of 'head', in which sense it has largely displaced the orig. expression **Haupt** (q.v.). In the proposition **Er war zwei Köpfe größer als seine Frau** (K. Edschmid), it would be more in accordance with the spirit of the language to say **zwei Kopf größer,** as explained under **nouns of measure.** On the other hand, **Köpfe** is the only correct form in the sense of 'individuals', as in **Der Haufe mochte hundertundfünfzig Köpfe zählen** (Sudermann: 'The crowd might be 150 strong'). When tossing a coin to decide a chance, we ask a person to cry 'head(s) or tail(s)': here the German expression used to be **Kopf oder Wappen,** but since the value has been substituted for a ruler's head on the obverse of a German coin, **Kopf** has been replaced by **Zahl:** e.g. **„Wir werden einen Groschen hochwerfen: ich nehme Wappen." Er warf die Münze hoch. „Hurra!" rief ich, „Zahl!"** (E. Kästner); cf. **Ich kann aus diesem Mischmasch nicht klug werden** ('I can't make head or tail of this hotch-potch').

Korn: see **Getreide** 1.

Kost, Kosten: 1. The fem. noun **Kost** (which has *no* plur.) is really a later development out of the now obs. sing. of **Kosten** (see 2). Its orig. meaning was the 'cost of food', but it is now only used with the force of 'food, fare, board': e.g. **schmale** or **magere Kost** ('slender fare, short commons')—**bürgerliche Kost** ('good plain cooking')—**Kost und Wohnung** or **Logis** ('board and lodging')—**kostfrei** ('without having to pay for one's board': contrast **kostenfrei** given under 2)—**Kostgeld** ('board wages')—**kein Kostverächter sein** ('not to be fastidious about food')—**jemand in Kost nehmen** or **verköstigen** ('to take a person as boarder'; a 'boarder' is usually **Pensionär**); cf. **Dort fand sie gegen ein geringes Entgelt Aufnahme und Verköstigung** (Werfel: 'There she was received as a boarder at a low charge')—**Der Preis des Zimmers, Verköstigung und Bedienung eingeschlossen, erwies sich als sehr mäßig** (Th. Mann). **2. Kosten** is now only used in the *plur.* and means 'cost, expense(s)'. Luther often used the sing. **Kost** in this sense, but this is now obs., and the plur. has been substituted in the modern version of the Bible, as in **Die Kosten sollen vom Hause des Königs gegeben werden** (Esra 6. 4); so also one now always says **die Kosten bestreiten** ('to defray the expenses')—**auf seine Kosten kommen** ('to recover one's outlay')—**kostenfrei** or **kos-**

tenlos ('free of all charges'). A proposition like 'I know that to my cost' is better expressed by **Das weiß ich aus bitterer** (or **aus teuer erkaufter**) **Erfahrung**; for 'at all costs', see **jeder** 2 (*a*). The compd. **Unkosten** properly implies a needless, often relatively excessive expense, but is often used much like **Kosten**: e.g. **Er hat sich in Unkosten gestürzt** ('He has run into needless expense'); cf. **Reise-, Kriegskosten,** etc.

kosten: There are two quite different verbs **kosten**: one means 'to cost' (Lat. *constare*, Fr. *coûter*), the other 'to taste' (Lat. *gustare*, Fr. *goûter*); for the latter, see **taste** 2 (*b*). The amount which a thing costs, i.e. the price paid, stands in the *accus.*: e.g. **Die Äpfel kosten das Stück einen Groschen** ('a penny each')—**Sag' ihm die Wahrheit, es wird nicht den Kopf kosten** ('. . . he won't take your head off'). With regard to the case of the person paying the price, usage fluctuates: *Duden* gives **„Es kostet mich oder mir . . .“**, but *Sanders* says **„Der persönliche Dativ dürfte im allgemeinen in der heutigen Sprache überwiegen: der Akkusativ klingt unserm Ohr in den meisten Fällen geziert.“** In point of fact, the accus. seems to be quite common where the price is a specific sum of money or an indef. expression: e.g. **Es hat mich zwei Mark** (or **nichts**) **gekostet—Die gute Kost** (q.v. 1) **und das Quartier, das hat ihn keinen Groschen gekostet** (Waggerl)—**Zahlen Sie mir, was mich die Kleider kosten** (G.). But in other contexts the accus. now does sound a little strange, and the majority of modern authors seem to prefer the *dat.*: cf., on the one hand (with the *accus.*), **Sprechen will ich, und sollte es mich mein Leben kosten** (Hauff) —**Es kostete mich keine Anstrengung, zwei Stunden bei Tische zu sitzen** (Rilke) —**Es kostete sie keine Überwindung, ihr Anliegen vorzubringen** (Zifferer)—**Dieses Begebnis kostete ihn viel Ruhe und Nervenkraft** (W. v. Scholz)—**Er hatte sich einer Operation unterziehen müssen, die ihn eine seiner Nieren gekostet hatte** (Th. Mann)—**Es mußte ihn Mühe gekostet haben** (W. Kramp); and on the other hand (with the *dat.*), **Sie hielt das Papier in Händen, das ihrem Mann das Leben kosten sollte** (W. Schäfer)—**Es kostete ihm keine Anstrengung** (W. Bode)—**Es hat mir Qualen genug gekostet** (Sch.)—**Ein Prozeß hatte der Witwe ihr Vermögen gekostet** (Chamisso)—**Ich entsann mich jenes Vorfalls, der einer Offizierswitwe ihren einzigen Sohn gekostet hatte** (Storm)—**Der Graf nickte dem Türhüter zu, obgleich es ihm Mühe kostete** (Ponten)—**Viele schrieben ihm Briefe, die ihm den Hals hätten kosten können** (K. Edschmid)—**Wenn Ihnen diese Begegnung unangenehm ist, so kostet es Ihnen nur ein Wort, mich nie wiederzusehen** (Jul. Grosse). For the idiom **teuer zu stehen kommen**, see **teuer.**

kraft: see **vermöge.**

krank, kranken, kränken: 1. The adj. **krank** only dates from the MHG period, and was even then not very common. Its orig. force was that of 'thin, slender, weak': of a warrior in the Nibelungenlied we are told that the din of battle had made *sîne witze kranc* (i.e. made his senses weak, so that he lost consciousness), and Walther even says that a man with few friends was *an friunden kranc* (**arm an Freunden**). It is strange that a word of such comparatively recent introduction should have become the ordinary expression for 'ill', and have almost displaced the old German word, viz. Goth *siuks* (> '*sick*') which in its NHG form **siech** is hardly used in ordinary lang., being in any case confined to cases where the complaint is a long wasting disease. Whereas **krank** implies a specific illness, **kränklich** is 'ailing', indicating an abnormal state of health, a susceptibility to a feeling of 'indisposition'; while **krankhaft** suggests either some visible symptom of a possible illness (e.g. **eine krankhafte Gesichtsfarbe**) or esp. a pathological state of mind: a person with a **krankhafte Phantasie** has a 'morbid' imagination and is subject to hallucinations—Tieck pities **den armen krankhaften Tasso.** A passing indisposition, as when one is 'out of sorts', is suggested by **unpaß** or **unpäßlich**—see **adjectives** (indeclinable) 2—which are used coll. for the more select **unwohl. 2.** The verb **kranken** properly means 'to *be* ill', and **erkranken** 'to *fall* ill', but the former is now only used fig.: one says **Er ist plötzlich erkrankt,** but **Ist er krank?** (not **Krankt er?**); on the other hand, the *fig.* use of the simple verb is quite common, as in **An diesem Fehler krankt unser Adel** (G.: 'Our aristocracy is afflicted with this failing'). The verb corresponding to **kränklich** is **kränkeln,** while

kränken is now only used, like **beleidigen,** in the sense of 'to offend': cf. on the one hand, **Er kränkelt fast jedes Jahr, ohne eben krank zu sein** (Voss: 'He is in indifferent health nearly every year without being really ill'), and on the other hand, **Als Menschen hab' ich ihn vielleicht gekränkt, als Edelmann hab' ich ihn nicht beleidigt** (G.)—**Man kann nicht leben, ohne andere zu kränken und daran zu kranken** (O. E. Hesse: 'without offending others and so suffering oneself').

krankhaft, kränklich: see **krank** I.

kreuzen: 1. With *trans.* force, this is used in propositions like **Er kreuzte die Arme auf der Brust—Er warf sich in den Lehnstuhl und kreuzte die Beine—Die zwei Fechter kreuzten die Klingen** ('crossed swords')—**Um neue Blumen zu schaffen, kreuzt man zwei verschiedene Arten—Unsere Briefe haben sich gekreuzt —Hier kreuzen sich mehrere Eisenbahnlinien. 2.** With *intrans.* force, it is chiefly used in the sense of 'to cruise', as in **Da es gerade Ebbe war, so daß unser Schiff nicht einlaufen konnte, kreuzten wir vor dem Hafen (hin und her)**; fig. **Allerlei verworrene Pläne kreuzten in meinem Gehirn** (E. T. A. Hoffmann). **3.** Distinguish between the two verbs **kreuzigen** and **bekreuzen.** The former means 'to crucify' (= **ans Kreuz schlagen**): Our Lord is often referred to as **der Gekreuzigte,** and the verb is used fig. in **das Fleisch kreuzigen** ('to mortify the flesh'). The reflex. **sich (be)kreuzigen** is sometimes used in the sense of 'to make the sign of the cross', as in **Was hab' ich nicht schon erlebt im Walde: manches sonderbare Geschöpf, bei dem der Mensch sich kreuzigt** (L. Schücking); but here **sich bekreuzen** is much more usual: cf. the exclamation **„Gott sei uns gnädig!"** followed by the stage direction **Sie bekreuzen sich und entfliehen** (Sch.).

kreuz und quer: see **quer** I (*a*).

kriegen: see **get** I (*b*).

Kunde: Distinguish between **die Kunde** 'information': plur. **Kunden**) and **der Kunde** ('customer': gen. and plur. **Kunden**).

kurz, kürzlich: see **recent** I (*a*) and 2 (*a*); **adverbs formed from adjectives** 3.

Kurzweil: see **Langeweile** 2 (*b*).

L

lack (noun): see **Mangel.**

lack (verb): 1. (a) To express the idea that something *is not there,* esp. if it ought to be there, a German uses **fehlen.** Thus, if a teacher calls the roll, and one boy is absent, another will say **„Fehlt!"**; if a set of an author's works is incomplete, the bookseller will say **„Es fehlen leider zwei Bände"**; and if you send a person to make a purchase, and the change he brings back is two marks short, you naturally say **„Hier fehlen 2 Mark!"** The idea of incompleteness or absence is also seen in examples like **Es fehlen** ('It wants') **nur 5 Minuten an drei Uhr—Es fehlte wenig, so wäre er ertrunken** ('He was within an ace of being drowned': see **miss** I *e*); cf. the coll. **Was fehlt dir?** ('What 's wrong with you?'). Instead of **Das nötige Geld fehlt mir,** one can say **Es fehlt mir am nötigen Gelde**; and sim. **Wir wurden ein starkes Volk, aber es fehlte uns an guten Formen** (Frenssen: '. . . but we lacked society manners')—**Es fehlte ihm an festen Schuhen, dicken Strümpfen und einem starken Winterrock** (O. Ernst)—**Er ordnete eine pompöse Leichenfeier an und ließ es an nichts fehlen, alle alten Gebräuche zu beobachten** (G. Keller: lit. 'let nothing be wanting', i.e. 'spared no pains to observe all the old customs'). **(b)** A stronger, more select, esp. poet. expression for **fehlen** is **gebrechen,** which properly implies a complete or almost complete lack: so Antonio says to Tasso **Wenn es dir an Fassung ganz gebricht, so soll mir's an Geduld gewiß nicht fehlen** (G.); sim. **Suche eine schöne, aber unbemittelte Frauensperson, welcher es an Freiern gebricht** (G. Keller); cf. the example from *Sanders* given under 2 below. It should be noted that while one says **Es gebricht** or **gebrach ihm an Geld,** the past part. **gebrochen** is quite obs. in this sense. **2.** It is but a short step from the idea of being absent to that of *being missed,* and **fehlen** may suggest that also, as when a son, writing to his father on his engagement day, says **Du fehlst mir gerade heute** (P. Keller: 'I miss you today of all days'). But this idea that the absence of a thing is felt as a real *want* is particularly suggested by **mangeln:** cf. **Ein neugeborenes Kind hat keine Zähne und braucht auch keine, also ist bei ihm das Fehlen der Zähne kein Mangel** (see **absence** 2 *c*); so also **Woran es mir mangelt, davon habe ich nicht genug; woran es mir gebricht, davon habe ich sehr wenig oder gar nichts** (*Sanders*)—**Was man** (*scil.* during the Carnival revelries in Rome) **unangenehm empfindet, ist, daß die innere Fröhlichkeit den Menschen fehlt und es ihnen an Geld mangelt** (G.). Whereas **mangeln** is used with an *impers.* subj. and a *dat.* of the person (its use with a pers. subj. and an accus. obj., as in Gotthelf's **Sie mangelt bar Geld,** is characteristic of SG, esp. Switzerland, and should be avoided), the compd. **ermangeln** (see **fail**) now prefers a *pers.* subj. and a *gen.* obj.: e.g. **Ein Herz, das sucht, fühlt wohl, daß ihm etwas mangle** (G.), but **Sie ermangelten aller Waffen und aller Fähigkeit, sich zu schützen** (G.). The impers. use of the compd. is now avoided: in the proposition **Der Hausfrau soll es nicht an Kohl noch an Rüben im Topf ermangeln** (G.) one would now use the simple verb, and the same applies to **Wir müssen neue Mittel ausforschen, weil es an den herkömmlichen ermangelt** (G., for **weil wir der herkömmlichen ermangeln**). **3.** Another expression with much the same force as **mangeln,** but with a more limited application, is **abgehen,** always with an *impers.* subj. and a *dat.* of the person, and properly implying that the person feels a lack of something desirable or necessary: e.g. **Wir wollen diese vorsorglichen Anstalten loben; nun geht uns aber das Notwendigste ab, ein tüchtiger Mann, der das alles zu handhaben weiß** (G.). It is esp. used where the lack refers to some part of a person's mental or spiritual make-up, social qualities, etc.: e.g. **Was ihm an Begabung abgeht, ersetzt er durch Fleiß**—**Ihr Benehmen zeigt deutlich, daß ihr jedes Taktgefühl abgeht**—**Vielen Leuten scheint jedes Verständnis für klassische Musik abzugehen**; in a letter to a friend, Storm maintains **daß ihm der Sinn für Politik und Geschichte abgehe.**

Lade: see **box** 3.

laden: see **load (verb).**

Laden: As a *masc.* noun, this has two meanings, viz. 'shop' and 'window-shutter'. Actually, the two are closely connected: the MHG weak fem. *läde* meant 'board, plank' (cf. our *lath*), and the first shops were loose planks on trestles or simple wooden booths. In the plur. the forms **Laden** and **Läden** are both officially recognized in either sense, but in the north the mutated form is almost fixed in the sense of 'shops', while the unmutated form is rather more commonly used for 'shutters': for the fluctuation, cf. **Die Laden des unteren Geschosses waren dicht verschlossen** (H. Grimm) and **Die Läden waren geschlossen, doch hatten sich ihre Augen an die Dunkelheit gewöhnt** (G. v. d. Vring). The precise sense can, of course, be suggested by the use of the compds. **Kaufladen** and **Fensterladen.**—Different is the *neut.* **Laden,** a verbal noun without a plur. (see **load** 2): e.g. **Bis der Befehl gegeben wird, ist das Laden der Gewehre verboten** (= **ist es verboten, die Gewehre zu laden**)—**Das Laden** (or **die Ladung**) **des Schiffes hat länger gedauert, als man erwartete.**

Ladung: see **load (noun)** 2 and **load (verb)** 1 (*a*) *ad fin.*, and cf. the last two examples given above.

Land: In the sense of 'country, state', this has the plur. **Länder,** as in **Frankreich ist eins der Länder Europas.** On the other hand, **Lande** is used to suggest the territories of a state, the various component parts of a political whole, so that **deutsche Lande** embraces Prussia, Bavaria, Saxony, etc.; and sim. **die Rheinlande** includes those parts through which the Rhine flows, viz. Baden, Alsace, the Palatinate, etc.; cf. **die Niederlande** ('the Netherlands').

landen: As a *trans.* verb (aux. **haben**), this means 'to put ashore, disembark' (passengers, cargo) or 'to bring to earth, ground' (planes); and it is now also used in boxing slang of 'landing' a blow, as in **Er hat seinem Gegner einen Knockout gelandet.** With *intrans.* force (aux. **sein**), it means 'to come *or* go ashore' or 'to come to earth, be grounded': e.g. **Ihr bewohnt eine berühmte Insel: schon Äneas ist hier gelandet** (Porten)—**Auf dem Platz schwirrten die Propeller zahlloser Flugzeuge, die während der Nacht gelandet waren** (Binding); in coll. lang. it is also used as we speak of a person 'landing' in gaol or in a madhouse (**im Gefängnis** or **Irrenhaus landen**).

lange: The distinction between the adj. **lang** and the adv. **lange** (see **adverbs formed from adjectives** 1) is almost always observed in prose in the north: e.g., on the one hand, **Der Weg ist lang—Zwei Meilen? Nein, so lang ist der Weg nicht;** on the other hand, **Wir sind noch lange nicht am Ziel** ('We are nowhere near our destination yet')—**Solange ich lebe** ('As long as I live'). It is only in southern dialects that **lange** is used as an adj. in the pred.: cf. **Das Leben ist unermeßlich lange** (for **lang**), **solange man noch jung ist** (Stifter). But **lang** is used as an adv. in **über kurz oder lang** ('sooner or later') and in **Tage (Monate, Jahre) lang,** as well as in poetry for metrical reasons, as in **So komme, was da kommen mag, / So lang du lebest, ist es Tag** (Storm); cf. **längst.**

langen: 1. This *simple* verb (cf. 2) is rather frowned upon in modern times: it is now characteristic of the coll. language, esp. in the north. (**a**) Out of its original meaning, viz. 'to become long', there developed, first, the now obsolete intrans. sense of 'to extend, stretch' (Luther says **Deine Gewalt langet bis an der Welt Ende:** Dan. 4. 19), then that of 'to be (long) enough, to suffice', and finally, with trans. force, 'to extend' (the hand), 'to pass *or* hand' (something to a person). In these last senses **langen** is displaced in the literary language by **reichen:** e.g. **Dieses Stück Zeug reicht eben noch zu einem Kinderkleidchen aus** (coll. **langt . . . zu einem Kleidchen**: 'This piece of cloth is just long enough for a child's frock')—**Ich wäre gern nach Paris weitergereist, aber dazu reichte** (coll. **langte**) **mein Geld nicht** ('. . . my purse wouldn't stretch to that')—**Die untersten Zweige waren zu hoch, als daß ich hätte hinaufreichen können** ('The lowest branches were too high for me to reach up to them')—**Sie reichte** (not **langte**) **ihm die Hand zur Ehe;** cf. **Lange mir mal das Tauende da!** (as a sailor instinctively expresses 'Hand me over that bit of rope!'). (**b**) But **langen** is also used where **reichen** would not be appropriate, viz. with the force of 'to dive, thrust one's hand' (e.g. into one's pocket), 'to reach out' (for something) or trans. 'to take *or* fetch' (a thing out of a bag, etc.): e.g. **Das kleine Mädchen langte** (in good style **griff**) **in die Tüte** ('. . . dived into the paper bag')—**Der Lehrer langte** (= **griff**) **nach seinem Rohrstock—Er langte** (= **holte**) **einen Groschen aus der Tasche. 2.** It is both strange and regrettable that the simple verb **langen** should have lost face, the more so as at least four of its compounds are used in the best literary style, viz. **an-, er-, ge-,** and **verlangen** (qq.v., and cf. **anbelangen**).

Langeweile: 1. As a rule, an adj. which is prefixed to a noun to form a compd. remains invariable, losing its power to inflect: thus, inflexional changes in words like **Blaustrumpf, Lautsprecher, Hochschule,** etc., appear only in the noun, not in the adj.-prefix (**Blaustrümpfe,** etc.). **2.** (**a**) But there are a few words of this kind in which the two component parts, although joined to form a single word, *both* inflect: cf. **der Hohepriester** ('the High Priest'), but **ein Hoherpriester—des Hohenpriesters—die Hohenpriester,** but **zwei Hohepriester;** sim. **der Armesünder** ('the condemned criminal'), but **ein Armersünder—die Armensünder—zwei Armesünder.** (**b**) Esp. interesting in this connexion is the compd. **Langeweile.** Although the form **La'ngweile** is allowed, and the corresponding adj. and verb are always **la'ngweilig** and **la'ngweilen** (cf. Freytag's **Sieh nicht so gela'ngweilt aus!**), **Langewei'le** is the form much more commonly used. Whereas its ant. **Ku'rzweil** ('pastime, amusement') is quite fixed, the adj.-prefix remaining invariable (but cf. **Ich blieb nur eine kurze Weile**), **Langeweile** may be treated either as a true compd. or as a loosely constructed one, the adj.-prefix being sometimes left uninflected, but now far more commonly inflected as if it were a separate attrib. adj.: cf. on the one hand, **die Göttin der Langeweile** (Heine)—**vor Langeweile** (Eichendorff)—**Zu den Nazis war er aus Langeweile gegangen** (Fallada); and on the other hand, more in accordance with modern usage, **Aus Langerweile betrachtete er das Firmament** (Ompteda)—**An diesen Naturbildern fuhren unsere Väter in geschlossenem Reisewagen, von Langerweile geplagt, vorüber** (Rilke)—**Mein Klavierspiel hatte ich aus Trotz und Langerweile aufgegeben** (E. Wiechert)—**Aus Langerweile fressen sie** (*scil.* the crew of a passenger liner) **einander beinahe auf** (H. Hauser); with an attrib. adj., **Sollen wir nichts tun, um uns aus der erbärmlichen Langenweile zu retten?**

(G.)—**Er war bewegt, wie ein Mann, der von tödlicher Langerweile erlöst ist** (Th. Mann); for the fluctuation, cf. **„Sie liebte doch den Baron?“ „Aus Langerweile! Man kann aus Langeweile zum Verbrecher werden, warum nicht lieben?“** (R. v. Gottschall).

Langohr: According to modern usage, this word is now little used with the force of 'long ear': in **Was für ein Esel streckt sein Langohr aus diesem Geschwätze?** (Sch.) one would now say **sein langes Ohr.** It is now generally treated as a *masculine* noun meaning 'an animal with long ears', occasionally 'a hare', as in **Man weiß, daß der Langohr hier sein Lager hat** (Coler), but much more commonly 'a donkey': e.g. in the proverbial saying **Ein Esel heißt (nennt, schilt, schimpft) den anderen Langohr** ('The pot calls the kettle black')—**der gute Langohr** (Nicolai)—**Gleich mußte nun Titania erwachen und aus dem Langohr ihren Liebling machen** (Schlegel).

längs: see **entlang** 2.

längst: Beware of using this adv. in reference to a *point* of time in the remote past: one says **Das geschah vor langer Zeit** and **Ich bin ihm einmal in Berlin begegnet, aber das ist nun lange her** (see **lange**). On the other hand, **längst** means 'for a long time', not as used in 'I lived in Berlin for a long time', which is **Ich wohnte lange** or **lange Zeit in Berlin,** but in a proposition like 'I have known that for a long time now' (**Das weiß ich schon längst**); sim. **Er muß schon längst in Paris angekommen sein, aber da er nur einen Tag dort bleiben wollte, wird er längstens** (= **spätestens**, 'at latest') **in zwei Tagen wieder hier sein.** Strangely enough, **unlängst** ('not long ago') can be used of a point of time in the recent past: **Ich begegnete ihm unlängst in Berlin** (see **recent** 1).

Lappen: see **rag** 1.

Lärche: see **Kiefer** 2 (*d*).

Lärm: see **sound** 3 (*a*).

lassen: 1. As explained under **leave (verb)**, the fundamental force of **lassen** is not 'to leave', but 'to let' (implying permission). It is true that a German usually expresses 'Leave me alone!' by **Laß mich allein!** but a dependent infin. is really understood here: **Laß mich allein sein!** i.e. 'Let me be alone!' (cf. our old-fashioned 'Let me be!'). And the same is true of propositions like **Ich kann das Rauchen nicht lassen** (i.e. **nicht bleiben lassen**: 'I can't leave off *or* give up smoking'—cf. our obs. 'I can't let smoking be')—and even of **Er ließ sein Leben für seinen Freund** ('He gave his life for his friend': really 'He let his life pass away for his friend'). **2.** So the normal construction of **lassen** is the **accus. and infin.** (q.v.), i.e. an infin. *without* **zu.** A proposition like **Die Bedienung in diesem Hotel läßt viel zu wünschen übrig** ('The service in this hotel leaves much to be desired') seems to contradict the rule, but here the infin. **bleiben** is also understood, **zu wünschen** being a contracted rel. clause, the meaning being 'The service . . . lets much that is desirable remain unperformed.' **3.** (**a**) The pers. accus. is often idiomatically dropped when the reference is clear from the context: e.g. **Mein Vater läßt Sie grüßen** ('My father sends you his kind regards', lit. '. . . lets [me] greet you')—**Ich muß mir das Haar schneiden lassen** ('I must get my hair cut': really 'I must let [the barber] cut my hair'); cf. **schließen** 2. Where the accus. is dropped, the act. infin. is usually said to have *passive force* (see **passive voice** 3 *b*): cf. **Ich ließ mein Pferd beschlagen** ('I caused my horse to be shod', but really 'I let [the blacksmith] shoe my horse'). And in time, as the true explanation of such constructions was lost sight of, the infin. did actually take on passive force, as is shown by propositions like **Ich ließ mein Pferd vom Hufschmied beschlagen** (*lit.* 'I let my horse be shod by the blacksmith') and **In „Maria Stuart“ läßt Schiller die Königin vom Henker hinrichten** ('. . . Schiller has the queen executed by the hangman'). (**b**) This omission of the pers. accus. is esp. common in many idiomatic expressions in which the dependent infin. is *reflex.* Here the pron. ought to be a *pers.*, not a *reflex.* one, but the reflex. is nevertheless quite fixed. Thus, the proposition **Das Paket läßt sich tragen** ('The parcel is not too heavy to carry') is *lit.* 'The parcel lets [a person] carry it', i.e. **Das Paket läßt einen Menschen es tragen;** sim. **Das läßt sich nicht beweisen** ('That cannot be proved', *lit.* 'That lets [no one] prove it')—**Er läßt sich** (*dat.*) **nichts vormachen** ('He won't let himself be imposed upon': cf. **Er läßt niemand ihm etwas vormachen**). **4.** At an earlier period the pers. accus. was often replaced by a *dat.* in certain set expressions, esp. with **wissen**

lassen and **sehen lassen.** This *dat.* is probably due to French influence (cf. *faire savoir, faire voir quelque chose à quelqu'un*), and although it is still used in coll. lang., and occasionally even in standard works, it is contrary to good modern prose usage: cf. **Wollen Sie dem** (for **den**) **Prinzen nicht wissen lassen, mit wem Sie eine Verbindung vollziehen werden?** (Lessing)—**Er ließ ihr** (for **sie**) **seinen Plan sehen** (G.)—**Du kannst ihm** (for **ihn**) **von deinen Absichten wissen lassen** (Ompteda). The same applies to **merken lassen,** except that the *dat.* is still almost the rule in the case of a *reflex.* pron.: e.g., on the one hand, **Er meinte, man müsse den Kindern** (for **die Kinder**) **nicht merken lassen, wie lieb man sie habe** (G.); on the other hand, in the proposition **Ich fürchtete mich, ließ mich es aber nicht merken** (G.), **mir** would be more in accordance with modern usage—sim. **Ich fürchte, ich habe mir merken lassen** (see 5), **wie widerwärtig mir das alles war** (Spielhagen). The *dat.* here probably shows the influence of **anmerken,** which requires a pers. *dat.*: e.g. **Man merkt es ihm sofort an, daß er Junggeselle ist** ('You have only to look at him to see that he is a bachelor')—**Niemand schien mir meine Gefühle anzumerken** ('No one seemed to read my feelings in my face')—**Hoffentlich wird mir keiner meine Enttäuschung anmerken** ('I hope I shan't betray my disappointment to anybody'). **5.** When **lassen** is used in a *compd.* tense with a dependent infin., the past part. almost always takes the form of the *infin.*, as in the example from Spielhagen given above: see **accusative and infinitive** 4 and 5, and **verbs (auxiliary)** 3.

lässig: see **idle** 2.

Last: see **load (noun)** 1.

lasten: see **load (verb)** 2 (*a*).

lauern: see **umlauern.**

laufen: The ordinary meaning of **laufen,** one of the **reduplicating verbs** (q.v.), is 'to run', but it implies a less high speed than **rennen** (q.v.): cf. **Er wendete sich nach der Stadt, durch deren Straßen er mehr rannte als lief** (Tieck); so also the race between the hare and the tortoise is a **Wettlauf,** while a horse-race is a **Wettrennen.** Indeed, in some cases **laufen** does not imply running at all: one commonly says **Das Kind läuft noch nicht** ('cannot walk yet'), and a person who has missed the last bus may say **Ich habe zu Fuß laufen müssen.** Like other verbs of motion **laufen** ordinarily takes the aux. **sein,** but **haben** is quite correct where the idea of getting quickly from one place to another does not arise: an athlete in training for a race can say **Ich habe eine Stunde gelaufen, um in guter Form zu bleiben**; and sim., more fig., **Das Faß muß die ganze Nacht gelaufen** (or **geleckt**) **haben** ('The barrel must have been leaking all night')—**Die Kerze hat gelaufen** ('The candle has guttered'); cf. **Die „Anna Hollmann" hatte fast vierzig Jahre gelaufen** (Frenssen: 'The good ship A.H. had been sailing the seas for almost forty years'). Of course, **haben** is the only correct aux. where the verb has real trans. force (cf. **gehen** 1, **fahren** 2 and **reiten**), as in **Ich habe mich wundgelaufen** ('I am footsore from walking *or* running so much') and **Den linken Fuß hatte ich mir beim Aufstieg des Berges wundgelaufen** (P. Alverdes); cf. **Sie fragten ihn, ob er durchgelaufene Füße habe** (Ompteda). With other accus. objs. usage is not so fixed: cf., on the one hand, **Ich hätte Gefahr gelaufen, mich zu verschnappen** (Lessing: 'I'd have run the risk of letting the cat out of the bag'), and, on the other hand, **Es ist kaum anzunehmen, daß diese Leute das Risiko eines Kampfes gelaufen sein werden** (Spielhagen); and so also either aux. can be used with expressions like **Schlittschuh laufen** ('to skate'), **Spießruten laufen** ('to run the gauntlet'), **Sturm laufen** ('to make an assault'), etc.; cf., with a cognate accus., **Wenn ich bedenke, was für einen Gang mein Leben später gelaufen ist, kann ich die Sorge der Mutter verstehen** (W. Schäfer).

lauschen: This verb means 'to listen intently' or esp. 'to eavesdrop': e.g. **Wir lauschten auf seine Worte—In verborgnen Winkeln lauscht die Schar verschworener Verräter** (G.); cf. **Horchen heißt, auf etwas mit gespannter Aufmerksamkeit hören, lauschen hat den Nebenbegriff des Heimlichen, Versteckten** (Eberhard); so also **jemanden belauschen** and **jemandem etwas ablauschen** (see **überhören**).

Laut: see **sound** 2 (*a*).

lauter: **1.** Used as an adj. and inflected in the normal way, this implies freedom from impurities and hence is used of 'pure' metals, 'clear' spring-water, etc. It is a rather select expression, generally standing in the attrib. relation, and is mostly replaced in ordinary lang. by other words: e.g. **lauteres** (= **reines**) **Gold—lauteres** (= **klares**) **Wasser.** It is also used fig., as in **Die Nachricht stammt aus lauterer Quelle** ('from a reliable source') and **Seine Absichten sind nicht lauter** ('open to suspicion'). Strangely enough, although the adj. is rather choice, the verb **erläutern** is a common expression with the fig. force of 'to explain, interpret': volumes of poems are often published **mit Erläuterungen** ('with explanatory notes'). **2.** A phrase like 'pure gold' implies that the object contains *only* gold, and hence **lauter** is in everyday use with the force of 'nothing but' (cf. **all** 6 *c*, and **eitel** 2). In this sense it is *indecl.*, more adv. than adj., qualifying plur. or collect. sing. nouns: e.g. **Die Gesellschaft bestand aus lauter Männern —Das sind lauter Lügen** ('a pack of lies') **—Was er sagte, war lauter Unsinn** ('all nonsense').

lazy: see **idle.**

lead: **1.** The most general expression for 'to lead' is **führen,** which is really the factitive of **fahren** (q.v.), so that its fundamental force is 'to cause to *fare*' in a certain direction: e.g. **Ich führte sie am Arm—Dieser Weg führt in den Wald, nach der Stadt, zum Rathaus**; cf. **Haben Sie einen Schwarzwaldführer?** ('Have you a guide to the Black Forest?'). Incidentally, the compd. **anführen** can take a *sing.* pers. obj. when used *fig.* with the force of 'to hoax, impose upon', but only a *plur.* in the *lit.* sense, as in **ein Heer** or **Truppen anführen**; cf. **Welcher von euch Jungen ist der Anführer?** ('Which of you boys is the ring-leader?'). **2.** The verb **lenken** implies an endeavour not to let the obj. deviate from the desired course, and generally presupposes incapacity on the part of the obj. to keep to the right path, hence used esp. of a higher power or of a person with better knowledge and more insight: e.g. **Der Mensch denkt, Gott lenkt** ('Man proposes, God disposes') **—Dieses Pferd läßt sich schwer lenken— Es gelang ihm, das Auto durch die Schneewehe** ('snowdrift') **zu lenken—Der Lehrer lenkte die Aufmerksamkeit der Schüler auf eine besonders wichtige Regel.** **3.** The verb **leiten** (cf. **leiden** 1 *a*) emphasizes the idea of guiding the obj. safely to its destination, implying a definite purpose or intention: e.g. **Ich leitete den Blinden über die Straße—Er leitete das Gespräch auf die bevorstehenden Wahlen** —cf. words like **Wasserleitung** ('water-supply') and **Blitzableiter** ('lightning-conductor'), etc.; hence also used of an authority entrusted with the direction or management of some concern, business, institution, etc., with objs. like **Geschäft, Schule, Unternehmen**; cf. **Ein Offizier führt seine Abteilung, ein Feldherr leitet die Schlacht** (Eberhard), and distinguish between **die Führung übernehmen** ('to take the lead') and **die Leitung übernehmen** ('to undertake the management'). **4.** The compd. **geleiten** is a more formal expression for the word generally used in the sense of 'to accompany', viz. **begleiten,** which is *not*, as one might think, a compd. of **gleiten** (q.v.), but a double compd. of **leiten** (= **be-geleiten**) and therefore always *weak*: e.g. **Er begleitete mich bis Berlin—Sie hat mich** (or **das Lied**) **auf dem Klavier begleitet.** To the idea of accompaniment **geleiten** adds that of protection: e.g. **Du geleitest mich durchs Leben, sinnende Melancholie** (Lenau)—**Er geleitete** (in ordinary lang. **brachte,** 'saw') **die junge Dame nach Hause**; cf. **jemandem das Geleit geben** ('to escort a person') and **ein sicheres Geleit** ('a safe-conduct').

leave (noun): When used with the general force of 'permission' (as in 'I beg leave to inform you . . .'), this is expressed by **Erlaubnis,** whereas a soldier's 'leave', i.e. permission to absent himself, is expressed by **Urlaub**: cf. **Er bat um Erlaubnis, mitzugehen** and **Er bat um vierzehn Tage Urlaub.** Actually, the unaccented short prefix in **Erlaubnis** and the accented long prefix in **Urlaub** (but always short in **Urteil**) are different forms of the same prefix, both having developed out of Goth. *us-*, which changed to *ur-* before a following *r* (**erlauben** < *uslaubjan*). The form **er-,** which dates from the OHG period, has now for the most part supplanted **ur-**, which is only retained in a few nouns and adjectives, the corresponding verbs generally having **er-**: thus **Urkunde** corresponds to **erkennen, Ursprung** to **erspringen** (now supplanted by **entspringen**); and sim. **Urlaub** corresponds to **erlauben,** while **Urteil** gives both **erteilen** and **urteilen.** The trans. forms **beurlauben** ('to grant leave of absence to') and **beurteilen** ('to judge of, criticize') are formed like **beanspruchen** (q.v.).

leave (verb): 1. When some one says 'Leave me alone!' or 'I have left my umbrella somewhere', the first idea that occurs to us is probably that of 'departure from'; but actually, 'leave' does not originally imply this idea at all, being a cognate of **bleiben** (< MHG. *belîben*, 'to remain, be left'). In the corresponding German idiom, the verb **lassen** (q.v. 1) is used, which is a cognate of 'let' (< Goth. *letan*), so that the idea of 'departure' or 'desertion' does not enter. **Laß mich allein!** and **Ich habe meinen Regenschirm irgendwo gelassen** are really examples of the accus. and infin. construction, the infin. being understood; lit. 'Let me [be] alone!' and 'I have let my umbrella [stand] somewhere'. The same applies to expressions like 'to leave a person in the lurch' (**jemand im Stich lassen,** which originally meant 'to let a person stand exposed to his adversary's sword-thrust'), 'to leave no stone unturned' (**kein Mittel unversucht lassen**), etc. **2.** Where the idea of 'departure from' does enter, the usual expression is **verlassen,** which incidentally requires an accus. obj., so that one cannot render 'When does the train leave?' by **Wann verläßt der Zug?** but by **Wann geht der Zug ab?** From the idea of 'departure' to that of 'desertion' is a short step: hence **Man verließ mich in der Not—Er fühlte sich von allen verlassen—eine öde, gottverlassene Gegend. 3.** The English 'to leave behind' has two shades of meaning: (a) **zurücklassen** is used of a person in motion leaving an object in the rear (e.g. **Er überholte mich und ließ mich bald weit zurück**) or of leaving something behind of which one has not given up possession (e.g. **Ich habe meine Bücher irgendwo zurückgelassen**); (b) **hinterla'ssen** (*insep.*) indicates either leaving a mark or impression behind (e.g. **Der Wagen hinterließ tiefe Spuren auf dem sandigen Boden**) or esp. of leaving something behind with which one has definitely parted, particularly of a deceased person 'leaving' money, etc. (e.g. **Als er abreiste, hinterließ er einen Gruß für Sie—Der Verstorbene hat über eine Million Mark hinterlassen**); where there is a reference to the person to whom money is left, **vermachen** is more usual (e.g. **Er hat mir tausend Mark vermacht**). **4.** Where 'to leave' has the force of 'to resign, surrender' (as in 'He left me to my fate'), the correct expression is **überla'ssen** (*insep.*): e.g. **Er überließ mich meinem Schicksal—Das überlasse ich dir** ('I leave that to you')—**Die Wahl hat er mir überlassen** ('He has left the choice to me').

Lebtag: This word, which is now only used with an attrib. poss. adj., is really the contracted form of the plur. **Leb(e)tage,** as still used in the modern version of the Bible: **Versammle mir das Volk, daß sie meine Worte hören und lernen mich fürchten alle ihre Lebetage auf Erden** (Deut. 4. 10: '. . . all the days that they shall live upon the earth')—**Ich werde in Demut wandeln all meine Lebtage** (Isa. 38. 15: 'I shall go softly all my years'). But the established form is now **mein (dein, unser) Lebtag,** an adv. accus. of duration: e.g. **Mein Lebtag denk' ich dran** (Sch.: 'I'll remember it all my life') —**Das werd' ich mein Lebtag nicht verwinden** (id.: 'I shan't get over that till my dying day')—**Er sagte, es sei ihm lieb, daß er von der ganzen Sippschaft sein Lebtag kein Wort mehr hören werde** (Heyse: '. . . that he would never again hear from any of his relatives so long as he lived'). As **mein Lebtag** obviously looks like a sing., *Duden* rightly warns against using **meinen Lebtag.** The adv. gen. plur. **meiner Lebtage** (Wieland), although possible, is not nearly as common.

legen: see put 1.

lehren: 1. Whereas **beibringen** takes an *accus.* of the thing and a *dat.* of the person (**einem Schüler fremde Sprachen beibringen**), and **unterrichten** an *accus.* of the person and a *prep. phrase* (**einen Schüler in fremden Sprachen unterrichten** see below and 3), the normal construction of **lehren** is a *double accus.* (**einen Schüler fremde Sprachen lehren**). A pers. *dat.* here, as in **Er bekam ein jährliches Gehalt, zwei Schülern die Malkunst zu lehren** (G.), is frowned on by grammarians, and perhaps not to be recommended; but in point of fact it is surprisingly common, and indeed apparently on the increase, in modern standard authors, and in the face of examples like the following, which might easily be multiplied, it is now more than doubtful whether one is justified in condemning it outright as „falsch", which *Sprach-Brockhaus* does: **Das ist das Beste, was ein Mensch sich selbst und anderen lehren kann** (Storm)—**Der Junge machte eine**

tiefe Verbeugung, wie sie ihm die Mutter gelehrt hatte (Ompteda)—**Wo ist der Gott, der der Liebesleidenschaft jemals Weisheit lehrt?** (Dauthendey)—**Niemand hatte dem Mädchen diese Künste gelehrt** (Polenz)—**Der Pfarrer fragte, ob der Herr das Geschick habe, den Kindern die Reinheit des Herzens zu lehren** (Blunck)—**Der Jüngling lehrte den Leuten in Weimar das Baden** (W. Bode). But the *dat.* is the rule in the *pass.*: e.g. **Uns anderen ist das nicht gelehrt worden** (G.)—**Ihm wurde, sobald er denken konnte, gelehrt, mich zu hassen** (Hackländer)—**Es war ihm gelehrt worden, nur Verheirateten die Hand zu küssen** (Ompteda); cf. **Ich tat, was ich** (unusual for **mir**) **gelehrt wurde** (Immermann). In the *abs.* use of 'to be taught', it is advisable to use **unterrichten**, as in **Es war in Wien, wo er unterrichtet wurde,** where **gelehrt wurde** would rather suggest 'became a scholar' (**Gelehrter wurde**: see **gelahrt**). **2.** (**a**) The normal rendering of 'to teach a person (how) to do something' is **lehren** with the accus. and infin., as in **Die Mutter lehrte das Mädchen stricken** (**hat es stricken gelehrt**: see *b*); but where **lehren** and the dependent infin. are some way apart (separated by an obj. of the infin., an adv. phrase, etc.), the infin. is rather more commonly preceded by **zu**: e.g. **Ich brauche dich nicht zu lehren, ein jedes Gut nach seinem Wert zu schätzen** (G.)—**Mein Vater hatte mich gelehrt, meinen Namen zu schreiben** (Hauff)—**Wer hat dich gelehrt, das Köpfchen so nach der linken Seite hinüberhängen zu lassen?** (Raabe). (**b**) In a compd. tense one usually says **Er behauptete, er habe das Kind rechnen gelehrt** (see **accusative and infinitive** 5 *b*); the alternative infin. form, as in **Er hat mich rechnen lehren** (cf. **heißen** 3 *c* and **lernen** 1 *b*), is no longer as common as it once was: cf. **Er hat mich bedauern lehren** (now usually **gelehrt**), **daß die Gewalt eines Fürsten an den Grenzen seines Landes endet** (Bruno Frank). **3.** Another verb meaning 'to instruct' is **unterweisen** (insep.). Whereas **unterrichten** properly implies a systematic course of instruction in a subject, but is then also used more loosely in the sense of 'to inform', as in **Da'von hat man mich schon unterrichtet** ('I have already heard *or* been informed of that'), **unterweisen** really means 'to direct' along certain lines, esp. 'to point out' a certain course of action, as in **Ich will dich unterweisen und dir den Weg zeigen, den du wandeln sollst** (Ps. 32. 8); so also formerly, like **lehren,** with a double accus. (now obs.), **Er wird ihn unterweisen den besten Weg** (Ps. 25. 12). But the distinction between the two verbs is no longer vividly felt: one says not only **Man hat mich unterwiesen, wie ich an mein Ziel gelangen kann,** but also **Herr Braun hat mich im Französischen unterwiesen,** in which latter proposition **unterrichtet** would be a more ordinary expression, and indeed more strictly correct, as a progressive course of instruction is suggested; and the same applies to **In den Tanzstunden unterwies er uns in den Schritten** (G.).

-lei (as in **aller-, einerlei,** etc.): see **Hand** 2 (*b*).

Leichdorn: see **Leiche.**

Leiche: This fem. noun is now confined to the sense of 'corpse', but MHG *lîch* meant 'body' (= **Körper**), whether alive or dead. Its applicability to a living body is still seen in **Leichdorn** (plur. **-dorne** or more commonly **-dörner**: see **Dorn**), used in some parts for the standard **Hühnerauge** ('corn' on the foot or hand) and properly meaning 'thorn in the body', the expression being probably suggested by the sharp stinging pain caused by a corn.

Leid: This noun (with no plur.) was orig. the neut. of the MHG adj. *leit* ('sad, painful'), and some of the old idioms are still in use: e.g. **Er tut mir leid** ('I am sorry for him'); see **adjectives (indeclinable)** 5 —**Ich tue dir nichts zuleide** (< *ich entuo dir niht ze leide*, 'I'll do nothing to harm you'). In propositions like **Erlkönig hat mir ein Leids getan** (G.) or **Mir war ganz unheimlich: ich dachte, er könne sich** (dat.) **ein Leids angetan haben** (Storm: '. . . I thought he might have taken his life'), the expression **ein Leids (an)tun** might at first sight be thought to be analogous to **ein Aufhebens machen** ('to make a fuss'), but actually the two phrases are different: **Aufhebens** is a partitive gen. now treated as a nom. or accus. (see **Aufheben** and **viel** 1 *b*), while **Leids** is really the neut. sing. of the MHG adj. *leit,* so that **ein Leids tun** was orig. *ein leidez tuon* ('to do a distressing thing'). Nowadays **ein Leids** is archaic, one usually says **sich ein Leid antun** and **jemandem ein schweres Leid zufügen;** but **viel Leids** is still fairly common, and even **kein Leids** is still in use (cf. the example from Heyse given under **viel** 1 *a ad fin.*).

leiden: 1. It seems a far cry from **Er mag an einer unheilbaren Krankheit leiden** ('He may be suffering from an incurable disease') to **Er mag das Mädchen gern leiden** ('He is very fond of the girl'), and in order to understand how the latter idiom developed, it is necessary to trace the history of the verb, at least from the MHG period, when there were two quite different verbs: (**a**) The one is *lîden* (strong: past tense *leit*, part. *geliten*), used either *intrans.* meaning 'to go, proceed', or *trans.*, meaning 'to suffer something to proceed', i.e. to do nothing to prevent it. In the sense of 'to proceed', the verb is now obs., but its weak factitive **leiten** (really' to cause to go', hence 'to lead, guide') is still an every-day expression (see **lead** 3), as are its compds. **verleiten** ('to lead astray, tempt') and **begleiten** ('to accompany': see **lead** 4). (**b**) The second MHG verb is *leiden* (weak), used with a dat. of the person in the sense of 'to be(come) repugnant to' or 'to cause to be(come) hateful to'. In both these senses the simple verb is now also obs., but its compd. **jemandem etwas verleiden** (*weak*) is still in common use, meaning 'to give a person a dislike for something', often 'to spoil' (a person's pleasure or enjoyment): e.g. **Diese Unannehmlichkeiten verleideten mir meine Arbeit** or **die Freude an meiner Arbeit** ('These vexations made my work distasteful to me')—**Hier ist mir kein Tag erschienen, den mir nicht jemand verdorben oder verleidet hätte** (G.)—**Mir ist das Leben verleidet** (Auerbach: 'I have no more pleasure in, *or* am sick of, life'). Weak also, incidentally, although its basic sense is 'to suffer', is **bemitleiden** ('to sympathize with'), for which see **beanspruchen** 1 and 2. **2.** As explained above, one of the meanings of *lîden* was 'to suffer something to happen', and when it happens to oneself, it implies that one is acted upon by some external force, and hence the NHG form **leiden** (**litt, gelitten**) stands in contrast to **wirken** or **tätig sein**: cf. **Der Romanheld muß leidend, wenigstens nicht in hohem Grad wirkend sein** (G.); and so also **Jedes transitive Zeitwort hat zwei Formen, und zwar eine Tätigkeitsform** or **tätige Form** ('active') **und eine Leideform** or **leidende Form** ('passive'). From this idea of being acted upon came the general sense of 'to suffer (from)', with objs. like **Hunger, Mangel, Not, Unrecht,** etc., or with a prep. phrase, as in **an der Schwindsucht, durch den Krieg, unter einem Druck leiden.** Such expressions imply submission to external forces, and this is seen esp. in neg. propositions, where it is synonymous with **dulden** (q.v.): e.g. **Er litt nicht, daß man ihn so schlecht behandelte** ('He would not tolerate such bad treatment'); with an impers. subj., **Das Unternehmen leidet keinen Aufschub** ('The enterprise admits of *or* brooks no delay')—**Es leidet mich keinen Augenblick mehr im Hause** ('Not for another moment can I stand being cooped up indoors')—**Plötzlich kam das Heimweh über mich, und es litt mich nicht mehr im fremden Lande** (Spindler)—**Sie luden mich ein, den Sommer dort zuzubringen, aber es litt mich nicht eine Stunde bei ihnen** (Jul. Grosse: '. . . but I could not bear to be with them for a single hour'). Then, applied to pos. propositions, it came to imply raising no objections, and finally to putting up willingly or even gladly with something (cf. 'to suffer fools gladly'), as in **Er hat sich so von seiner Krankheit erholt, daß er jetzt Freunde um sich leidet**; and hence its modern coll. sense of 'to be fond of, like', as in **Er mag sie gern leiden—Er kann die allzuhöflichen Damen ebenso wenig leiden als die allzugroben Wirte** (Lessing): cf. **like** 1 (*b*).

leihen: see **borgen.**

Leinwand: see **clothes** 3.

leisten: This verb is derived from the MHG noun *leist* ('footprint, spoor'), so its orig. force was 'to follow a track'. According to modern usage, however, it is much like **aus-** or **verrichten** (see **richten** 2 (*c*)), meaning 'to perform, execute, accomplish', and used esp. with an indef. obj. or a neut. adj.-subst.: e.g. **Wir haben heute viel geleistet** ('We have got through a lot of work today')—**Dieser Schüler hat Tüchtiges geleistet** ('This pupil's performance has been excellent')—**Es ist unmöglich, Unmögliches zu leisten** ('It is impossible to accomplish impossibilities'). Otherwise it is mainly confined to a number of set expressions, its chief objs. being **Bürgschaft** ('to go bail'), **Dienste** ('to render services'), **Eid** ('to take an oath'), **Folge** ('to render obedience', also 'to accept' an invitation), **Gehorsam** ('to obey'), **Gesellschaft** ('to accompany'),

Hilfe ('to give help'), **Verzicht** (with **auf** + accus., 'to waive a claim to'), **Widerstand** ('to offer resistance'). In familiar lang. it is also used in the sense of 'to indulge in, afford': e.g. **Das kann ich mir leisten** ('I can rise to *or* afford that')—**Kostspielige Vergnügungen können wir uns nicht leisten** ('We cannot indulge in expensive amusements').

leiten: see **lead** 3; **accusative (double)** 1 (*b*); cf. **leiden** 1 (*a*).

Leiter: Distinguish between **der Leiter** ('leader, guide', plur. **Leiter**) and **die Leiter** ('ladder', plur. **Leitern**).

lenken: see **lead** 2; **accusative (double)** 1 (*b*).

lernen: **1.** (**a**) A dependent infin. without **zu** is used with **lernen** to express 'to learn (how) to do' something, but **zu** is usually inserted when the two verbs are some way apart: e.g. **Ich muß mich wohl ohne die Eltern behelfen lernen** (Heyse)—**Man muß lernen, sich in die neuen Umstände zu fügen**—**Die Stunde reifte heran, wo Mörike gelernt hatte, den leisen Stimmen der eigenen Seele Worte zu leihen** (E. v. Sallwürk). (**b**) In a compd. tense the past part. of **lernen** may assume the infin. form (cf. **helfen** 2; **lehren** 1), but most modern authors seem to prefer the part. form, except in the case of **kennenlernen** (q.v.): cf., on the one hand, **Ich habe mich in England an viel gewöhnen lernen** (Sch.)—**Ich habe die Notwendigkeit verehren lernen** (Chamisso)—**Nachdem er das Altertum hat verstehen lernen, kommt er nach dem Morgenlande** (Tieck); and, on the other hand, **Sie hatte einsehen gelernt, wie hoch jede wahre Neigung zu schätzen sei** (G.)—**Ich habe über die alte Zeit nachdenken gelernt** (Novalis)—**Sie hat die Welt verehren gelernt** (P. Keller)—**Erst durch die Belehrung Wagners habe ich Mozart verstehen gelernt** (H. v. Wolzogen)—**Die Kraft der Griechen habe ich bewundern gelernt** (H. Bahr)—**Prinz Eugen hat die deutsche Sprache nie beherrschen gelernt** (Hofmannsthal). **2.** In dialects **lernen** is used, like Scots 'to learn', in the sense of 'to teach': cf. **„Gib acht, daß der Junge den Unterschied zwischen lehren und lernen kapiert"** (coll. = **begreift**), **warnte sie ihren Mann: dieser sagte für beide Fälle lernen** (K. Edschmid). This is avoided in good prose, of course, but it is noteworthy that **gelernt** is used as an adj. to indicate that a person has served his apprenticeship in a trade, completed a full course of study for a profession, etc., and that **jemanden zu etwas** (or **jemandem etwas**) **an-** or **einlernen** has the force of 'to teach *or* train a person for some occupation': e.g. **Ich bin ein gelernter Jurist** (Gutzkow: 'I am a professional lawyer': cf. **ein gelehrter Jurist**, 'a learned lawyer')—**Die Schüler machten gute Fortschritte, gerade weil er kein gelernter Lehrer war** (Th. Mann)—**Die beiden Knechte faßten ihren verunglückten Herrn mit der Zartheit gelernter Krankenschwestern** (Zuckmayer); **Die durch natürliche, nicht angelernte Bildung bevorzugte Frau schlug Fesseln um den Dichter** (L. A. Frankl)—**Des Vogels Gesang, zum Teil von dem früheren Besitzer angelernt, ist unbeschreiblich schön** (Mörike)—**Ich lernte ganze Stellen** ('passages') **und rezitierte sie wie ein eingelernter Sprachvogel** (G.: 'like a bird trained to speak', cf. 'like a parrot')—**In der gezierten Gesellschaft machte er die eingelernten Redeformen und Verbeugungen mit** (W. Schäfer: i.e. he did as the rest of the 'refined' company, speaking and bowing as he had been brought up to do)—**Mein musikalischer Geschmack ist ein im Opernhause mühsam eingelernter** (Droste-Hülshoff).

letzter: see **erst** 1 (*c*).

leuchten: see **light (verb)** 1 (*a*).

leugnen: see **deny** 2.

Leumund: see **Mund** 1 (*b*).

-leute: see **Mann** 2 (*b*).

-lich: see **adverbs formed from adjectives** 3. For the difference between this termination and **-ig** in adjs. of time (e.g. **jährlich** and **jährig**), see **-ig**.

Licht: Two plur. forms of this noun occur, and at one time there was a tendency to distinguish between **Lichter** in the sense of 'lights' and **Lichte** in that of 'candles'. But this distinction has never been insisted upon, and **Lichter** is now the form most generally used in either sense, while **Lichte** (which, if used, always means 'candles') seems to be becoming more and more rare, so that examples like the following can now be regarded as rather precious: **Einige Lakaien hatten für das Abbrennen der tropfenden Lichte zu sorgen** (A. Schaeffer)—**Die Lichte des Weihnachtsbaumes waren herabgebrannt** (Th. Mann).

lieb, lieber: see **gern** 2.

liebkosen: This compd. of **kosen**, meaning 'to caress, fondle', shows some fluctuation in its forms, due mainly to the fact that the accent may fall either on the prefix (**lie'bkosen**) or on the verb (**liebko'sen**). The former is now much more usual, but even so, **lieb-** is never separated in pres. and past tenses: no one says **Ich koste das Mädchen lieb.** The chief fluctuation occurs in the infin. with **zu** and in the past part. *Sanders* gives **liebzukosen** and **geliebkost** as the most generally accepted forms, but while this is certainly true of the *part.* (**liebko'st** is much less common, and **liebgekost** seems only to occur in poetry), modern usage definitely prefers the *infin.* **zu liebkosen,** which is the only form given by *Duden.* With regard to the construction, a *dat.* obj. was formerly quite common, e.g. **Der Vater trat zu Ginnistan und liebkoste ihr** (Novalis), and is still occasionally found, as in **Sie sah ein Gerippe, dem sie mit Zärtlichkeit liebkoste** (Hans Franck); but the *accus.* is now much more usual in prose. The following are some characteristic examples: **Er liebkoste sie** (E. Wichert)—**Zu seinen Füßen saß ein Jüngling, welcher eine Ricke** ('a doe') **liebkoste** (Hans Franck)—**Du bist geliebkost worden** (Fontane)—**Das Mädchen zuckte bei der Berührung einer Katze, die sie sonst immer geliebkost hatte, jähe zusammen** (W. v. Scholz)—**Von dieser Bank aus geht der Blick auf die Figur der ruhenden Flora, die vom Amor liebko'st wird** (Bruno Frank: usually **geliebkost wird**)—**Nun fing das Gespenst ihn zu liebkosen an** (Eichendorff); cf. the following two examples from poetical works, where the now unusual infin. form **liebzukosen** is required for the sake of the metre: **Und hat ein Wort zum Ohre sich gesellt, / Ein andres kommt, dem ersten liebzukosen** (G.)—**Ich bin zu alt, der Amme liebzukosen** (Schlegel).

liegen: 1. Like other verbs indicating an attitude of rest (see esp. **stehen** and **sitzen**), **liegen** is used with the aux. **haben** (even in the south **sein** is very rare, but see 4), preps. like **auf, in, unter,** etc. taking a *dat.*, as in **Auf ärztlichen Rat hin** ('On medical advice') **habe ich zwei Wochen im Bett gelegen, und zwar auf dem Rücken;** and so also in fig. expressions like **Die Brüder haben sich wieder mal in den Haaren gelegen** ('. . . have been fighting *or* at loggerheads again')—**Diese beiden haben immer unter ei'ner Decke gelegen** (or **gesteckt:** '. . . have always intrigued *or* conspired together')—**Das liegt auf der Hand** ('That is evident, obvious')—**Es liegt an dir, ihn zu überzeugen** ('It 's up to you to convince him')—**An deiner guten Meinung liegt mir viel** ('I attach great importance to your good opinion'). **2.** Whereas **sitzen** and **stehen** (qq.v.) are occasionally used in the south as verbs of motion (= **sich setzen** and **sich stellen**), **liegen** in the sense of **sich legen** is very rare even in the south: cf. **Die Pferde lagen** (for **legten sich**) **ins Geschirr** (Gotthelf: = **zogen kräftig an,** 'strained at their traces' to draw the heavy load). **3.** As a *trans.* verb, **liegen** is only used in propositions like **Ich habe mich** (or **mir den Rücken**) **wund gelegen** (also **Ich habe mich durchgelegen:** 'I have bedsores on my back from lying so long'). **4.** Apart from its use in a compd. tense, the past part. **gelegen** is used in other ways. Thus, it commonly has the sense of 'situated', as in **Das Dorf ist** (not **hat**) **am Rhein gelegen** (= **liegt am Rhein**). With fig. force, it means 'important, of consequence': e.g. **Es ist mir viel an dem Ergebnis der Unterhandlungen gelegen** ('I attach great importance to the outcome of the negotiations': cf. 1)—**Daran ist mir wenig gelegen** ('That is of little consequence to me'). On the other hand, it may have the temp. force of 'suitable, convenient', as in **Ich werde Sie zu einer gelegeneren Zeit** ('at a more convenient time') **aufsuchen—Mortimer starb Euch sehr gelegen** (Sch.: 'Mortimer's death came at a very opportune time for you'). Hence **Gelegenheit** ('opportunity') and **gelegentlich,** the latter used either in the sense of 'when an opportunity arises', as in **Ich werde Sie gelegentlich besuchen,** or as a prep.+*gen.*, as in **Wir hatten gelegentlich unseres Besuches** ('on the occasion of our visit') **das Vergnügen, sie kennenzulernen** (Speckmann)—**Er hatte eine schwere Krankheit bestanden, gelegentlich welcher sein Herz „gewandert" war** (Th. Mann).

liegenbleiben: see **bleiben** 2 (*a*) and (*c*).

lift: see **aufheben.**

light (verb): This English word is used in a variety of ways: cf. 'to light a fire, a pipe'—'to light up a room'—'to light a person to his room'—'to light up' (of a face), etc. In German two groups of verbs must be clearly differentiated:—**1.** (**a**) The simple verb **leuchten** is always *intrans.*, used either in the sense of 'to give out light, shine', or (with a *dat.*) in that of 'to give light' to a person in order that he may see where he is going or what he is doing: e.g. **Der Himmel ist klar, die Sterne leuchten hell—Ich leuchtete ihr die dunkle Treppe hinunter—fig. Ihre Augen leuchteten vor Freude**; cf. also **Die Flamme leuchtete auf** ('. . . flared up')—**Die Lampe leuchtete in die Nacht hinaus.** (**b**) The two insep. compds. **beleuchten** and **erleuchten** are always *trans.*, both meaning 'to shed light on, light up' some object, the distinction being one of degree, **be-** here indicating light as opposed to darkness, and **er-** implying a bright light as opposed to a dim light: cf. **Das Zimmer war nur schwach beleuchtet** and **Zum Empfang der Königin war die Stadt festlich erleuchtet**; and fig. **Er will den Fall näher beleuchten** ('He is going to throw further light on the case') and **Er ist ein erleuchteter Kopf** ('He is an enlightened, well-informed man'). In particular, the prefix **be-** must be used when the reference is to the system of lighting, not to the amount of light supplied: e.g. **Hat das Haus elektrische oder Gasbeleuchtung?—Was für Straßenbeleuchtung hat die Stadt?** (**c**) An alternative, slightly more select expression for **erleuchten** is **erhellen**: e.g. **Der Kronleuchter erhellte den ganzen Saal**; but this verb has a wider application, being used both reflex., with the intrans. force of 'to become bright', and impers. (with **aus**) in the sense of 'to be manifest': e.g. **Ihre Züge erhellten sich** or **hellten sich auf** ('Her features lit up')—**Aus der Aussage der zwei Zeugen erhellte, daß der Angeklagte schuldig war** ('It was obvious from the evidence of the two witnesses that the accused was guilty'). Analogous to this impers. use of **erhellen** is that of **einleuchten** (+ dat. of the person): e.g. **Das leuchtet jedem ein** ('That is clear to every one')—**Seine Beweggründe leuchteten uns allen ein** ('His arguments carried weight with us, convinced us all'): see **obvious(ly)**. **2.** A fundamentally different group is that of trans. verbs which mean 'to set alight':—(**a**) In this sense **anstecken** was a favourite expression of Luther's, but has lost caste in modern times; it is now a rather prosaic word but is very common in the coll. speech of the north: **Steck' dir die Pfeife an!** ('Light your pipe!')—**Sieh dich vor, sonst steckst du das Haus an** ('Take care, or you'll set the house on fire'). (**b**) In good prose style this idea is suggested by **anzünden**: e.g. **Der Küster zündete die Kerzen auf dem Altar an.** (**c**) The insep. compound **entzünden** has a wider use: it is not so much used, like **anzünden**, in the sense of 'to put a light to', but has much more commonly the *lit.* or *fig.* force of 'to inflame', as in **Mein Hals ist entzündet** (cf. **Er ist an Lungenentzündung erkrankt**)—**Die schlechte Behandlung hat seinen Haß** (or **hat ihn zu Haß**) **entzündet—Aufwiegler entzündeten das Volk zum Bürgerkrieg** ('Agitators stirred the people up to civil war'); and **entzünden** is the only verb in this group which can be used reflex., in which case it means 'to catch fire' or esp. fig. 'to be inflamed': e.g. **Eine Flamme wilder Wut hat sich unter dem Pöbel entzündet.**

like: 1. *Verb*: (**a**) In many contexts, 'to like' is ordinarily expressed by the use of the adv. **gern** (q.v.), esp. in 'to like to . . .': e.g. **Möchten Sie gern spazierengehen?** or **Haben Sie Lust, spazierenzugehen?** ('Would you like to go for a walk?')—**Möchten Sie gern, daß ich Ihren Brief aufgebe?** ('Would you like me to post your letter?')—**Sie singt gern** ('She likes to sing'). (**b**) With an *accus.* obj., the simple verb **mögen** is common in everyday lang., as in **Ich mag sie nicht** ('I don't like her') and **Nein, Sauerkraut mag ich nicht**, where an infin. is really understood: **Ich mag sie nicht leiden** (q.v.)—**Sauerkraut mag ich nicht essen.** So also **jemand** or **etwas gern haben**: e.g. **Ich habe kleine Kinder** (or **alle Blumen**) **gern—Er hat es nicht gern, wenn man zu leise spricht** ('He does not like people to speak in too low a voice'). A question like 'How do you like Berlin?' is best rendered by **Wie gefällt Ihnen Berlin?** (cf. **Wie es Euch gefällt**, 'As You Like It': see **gefallen**), but 'How do you like living in Berlin?' by **Wohnen Sie gern in Berlin? 2.** *Adjective*: This can be rendered in various ways. (**a**) Where *similarity* i.e. *sameness* is implied, as in the phrase 'in like manner', one says **in gleicher Weise** (see **gleich**); cf. **gleichfalls** ('likewise') and **Wer sollte denn dergleichen stehlen?** (Storm: 'Who would steal the like of that?'): see **-gleichen.** (**b**) Where the context suggests *resemblance*, the usual expression is **ähnlich,** as in **Diese Brüder sehen sich gar nicht ähnlich** ('. . . don't look like each other') and **Das sieht ihm ähnlich!** ('That 's just like him!'

i.e. just what one might expect of him). (**c**) (**i**) Very often we use 'like' where a German uses **wie**: e.g. **Er betrug sich wie ein Wahnsinniger** ('He behaved like a madman')—**Sie sieht wie eine Ausländerin aus**—**Das Schloß sah eher wie ein Museum als wie ein Landhaus aus** (K. Edschmid: see als = than 5)—**Manches, was wie Teilnahme aussieht, ist bloß Neugier** (Fontane)—**Er lief wie besessen die Treppe hinunter** ('He ran downstairs like mad')—**Wie der Herr, so der Knecht** or **Diener** ('Like master, like man'). But many English idioms are expressed in other ways in German: e.g. **Sie gleichen sich wie ei'n Ei dem anderen** ('They are as like as two peas')—**Gleich und gleich gesellt sich gern** ('Like draws to like, Birds of a feather flock together')—**Es geht nichts über die Behaglichkeit** ('There 's nothing like comfort')—**Dazu wäre er frech genug** ('That would be just like his cheek')—**Aus Tanzen macht er sich nichts** ('He doesn't like dancing' = **Er tanzt nicht gern**)—**Sein zweiter Roman ist bei weitem nicht** (or **ist nicht entfernt**) **so gut wie sein erster** ('His second novel is nothing like as good as his first'). (**ii**) A special difficulty arises in connexion with expressions such as 'a house like this': in the *dat.* should one say **in einem Hause wie dieses** or **wie diesem?** Actually, **wie** here introduces an elliptic subord. clause—'a house (such) as this *is*' —and of course there is no difficulty where the verb 'to be' is expressed, as in **Das will bei einem Mädchen, wie ich bin, mehr sagen als bei anderen** (Immermann) or, with an inflected num. **ein-** inserted, **Dies ist doch eigentlich ein fader Ort, besonders für einen jungen Mann, wie du einer bist** (St. Zweig). But the verb 'to be' is ordinarily omitted, in which case the fact that a verb is understood is often lost sight of, the noun or pron. following **wie** being then ungrammatically attracted into the case of the previous noun to which it refers. The strictly correct *nom.* was more usual in the 19th century, but modern usage rather prefers the oblique case. Thus, on the one hand, in the *nom.*, **Von Männern wie Ihr** (*scil.* **seid**) **werde ich nicht gern verlassen** (C. F. Meyer)—**Der König brauchte solche Männer wie er** (Raabe)—**Auf Halunken wie Ihr muß man ein fleißiges Aufsehen haben** (Jul. Wolff: 'On rascals like you one must keep a sharp eye')—and sim. **in einem kleinen Kreis wie der gegenwärtige** (Mörike), **für ein altes Weib wie ich** (Storm), **hinter einem Tisch wie dieser** (G. Keller), **in Augenblicken wie dieser** (Th. Mann), **in einem Staat wie der unsrige** (Fontane). On the other hand, in the *dat.*, **Das ist das Beste, was einer jungen Frau wie dir passieren kann** (id.)—**Es hieß, Universitäten würden einem Mann wie ihm verschlossen bleiben** (K. Edschmid)—**Selbst an einem Tage wie diesem konnte sie die Erinnerung an den Krieg nicht wegweisen** (id.); in the *accus.*, **So geschmackvolle Dinge wie diesen kleinen Strohhut und diesen Sonnenschirm meinte er in seinem ganzen Leben nicht gesehen zu haben** (Ebner-Eschenbach)—**Ich habe niemals einen Menschen so schelten hören wie einen Leutnant, der mit zwanzig Mann zwischen einem Haufen von Maultieren arbeitete** (Frenssen)—**Eines Tages sah man den Grafen wankenden Schrittes wie einen Betrunkenen über den Platz eilen** (Zifferer); in the *gen.*, **Diese Zeiten sind der Förderung einer Aufgabe wie der meinigen nicht eben günstig** (Th. Mann). It is perhaps significant that Duden's *Stilwörterbuch* gives only **in einer Zeit wie der unsrigen.** In this connexion see also **apposition** 1 (*d*) and **als** = **'than'** 3 and 5.

likewise: A favourite expression of Luther's is seen in contexts like **Er nahm das Brot . . . desselbigen gleichen auch den Kelch** (Luke 22. 19–20), but while this is no longer used, the shorter form **desgleichen** is very common (see **-gleichen** 2 *b*). In more ordinary lang. other expressions are now used to convey 'in the same way': e.g. **Unter diesen Umständen hätte ich in gleicher Weise** or **ebenso gehandelt** (cf. eben 2 *a* and like 2 *a*)—**„Auf Ihr Wohl!" „Gleichfalls!"** or **„Ebenfalls!"** ('Good health!' 'The same to you!').

lila: see **adjectives (indeclinable)** 1.

links: see **recht** 4.

load (noun): 1. The two words **Last** and **Bürde** have much the same force, both indicating something—usually, but not necessarily, something heavy—which presses on that which supports its weight; hence the two expressions are often used indiscriminately, as in **Jede Last nahm er auf sich, wie ein Sklave, der für den geliebten Herrn nicht genug Bürden tragen kann** (Fr. Huch). But **Bürde** is not only a much more choice expression than Last (it is common in poetry) but has a more limited range in that its support must be a living being, whereas that of **Last** may be animate or inanimate: one can say **Er lud dem Esel eine zu schwere Last** (or **Bürde**) **auf**, but only **Die Säulen waren nicht stark genug, die Last des Gebäudes zu tragen.** With *fig.* force, either expression may be used of what is oppressive or irksome: Goethe's minstrel, refusing the golden chain with which the king wishes to reward him, says, **Gib sie dem Kanzler . . . und laß ihn noch die goldne Last zu andern Lasten tragen,** where the sing. refers to the heavy chain, the plur. to the Chancellor's arduous duties; so also one speaks of **die Bürde des Amtes** (of the burdens connected with a responsible post), **die Last der Jahre,** etc., but such things as oppressive taxes, monetary encumbrances and the like are called **Lasten:** cf. **Ich zahlte meine Steuern und trug meine Lasten** (Immermann). As indicated above, **Last** is much more common in ordinary lang., occurring esp. in many idiomatic expressions: e.g. **Ihr Brief hat mir eine große Last vom Herzen gewälzt** (G.)—**Sein Gemüt arbeitete unter der Last schwerer Erinnerungen** (Immermann)—**Ich möchte Ihnen nicht zur Last** (or **nicht lästig**) **fallen** ('I should not like to be a burden to you') —**Man hat ihm zweierlei zur Last gelegt** ('Two things have been laid to his charge'). **2. Ladung,** apart from its use as a verbal noun, as in **Die Ladung** (or **Das Laden**) **lebensgefährlicher Waren auf das Schiff ist verboten,** points to the material, or the amount of material, which comprises a load, e.g. the 'charge' with which a gun is loaded (**eine Ladung Schrot,** 'a charge of shot'), esp. a 'cart-, waggon-, shipload' (**eine Wagenladung Kohlen**—**Die Schiffsladung ist gelöscht,** 'The cargo is landed *or* discharged'). It is no longer used in the sense of 'invitation', which is expressed by **Einladung:** but cf. **load (verb)** 1 (*a*) *ad fin.*

load (verb): 1. (**a**) The MHG distinction between the strong verb *läden* meaning 'to load' and the weak verb *läden* meaning 'to invite' is no longer observed: in both senses **lāden** is now *strong* (**lud, geladen**), the only remnants of the weak conjugation being the 2nd and 3rd sing. pres. indic. forms **du ladest, er ladet** (which are recognized alternative forms of the rather more choice **du lädst, er lädt,** and can be used in either sense) and the imperative **lade! ladet!** for which there are no alternatives. With the force of 'to invite', the simple verb is now only used in a few rather formal phrases like **jemand zu Tisch** (or **zu Gast**) **laden,** being elsewhere entirely displaced by **einladen,** which can also be used of 'stowing' luggage in a conveyance, as in **Der Kutscher saß auf dem Bock, während der Gepäckträger die Handkoffer einlud** (Th. Mann); but **laden** is still regularly used of 'summoning' or 'citing' a person to appear in a court of law: e.g. **Ich bin zu morgen vor Gericht** (or **als Zeuge**) **geladen worden**—cf. **Ich habe zu morgen eine gerichtliche Ladung** ('citation') **erhalten.** (**b**) When the simple verb **laden** means 'to load', it is all-important to note that its *direct* obj. is not the conveyance on to which the thing is loaded (see *c*), but *the thing to be conveyed*: e.g. **Die Männer luden Heu auf den Wagen** (or **Kohlen in das Schiff**)—*fig.* **Ich habe eine große Schuld** (or **Sünde**) **auf mich geladen.** The only exception here is that the simple verb is always used of loading fire-arms: **eine Flinte mit Schrot** ('shot') **laden,** and hence **Er hatte eine mit Schrot geladene Flinte.** (**c**) The simple verb, then, corresponds to English usage when we speak of 'loading hay on a cart'. But we can also speak of 'loading a cart with hay', and to express such a proposition, in which the *dir.* obj. is the *conveyance,* the Germans must use the compound **beladen** (see **be-**): e.g. **Die Männer haben den Wagen mit Heu, das Schiff mit Kohlen beladen**—**Da ist ein mit Kohlen beladenes Schiff**—cf. *fig.* **Kommt her zu mir alle, die ihr mühselig und beladen seid** (Matt. 11. 28). **2** (**a**) The simple verb **lasten** is now practically confined to the *intrans.* use, meaning 'to weigh, press heavily' on something, and is used esp. with *fig.* force: e.g. **Das Femgericht lastete noch auf einem großen Teile des Vaterlandes** (G.)—**Die Sorge um die Zukunft seiner Kinder lastete auf ihm**—**Die ganze Verantwortung lastet auf meinen Schultern.** (**b**) On the other hand, the compd. **belasten** is only used *trans.,* and has much the same force as **beladen,** except that, like **lasten,** it generally has *fig.* force: e.g. **Es ist zu bedauern, daß Schulkinder ihr Gedächtnis mit unnützem Kram belasten müssen** ('It is regrettable that school-children must charge their memory with useless lumber')—**Das Gut ist mit schweren Schulden belastet** ('The estate is encumbered with heavy debts': cf. **Auf dem Gut lasten schwere Schulden)**—**Trotzdem der Krieg längst vorüber ist, sind wir immer noch mit Steuern übermäßig belastet** ('. . . overburdened with taxes')—**Das arme Kind ist mit einer erblichen Krankheit belastet** ('. . . afflicted with a hereditary disease'). It is also much used in commercial language: e.g. **Wir haben Ihr Konto mit diesem Betrag belastet** ('We have debited your account with this amount'). (**c**) Different from **belasten** is **belästigen,** which means 'to trouble, incommode, inconvenience': e.g. **Es tut mir leid, Sie mit dieser Angelegenheit belästigen zu müssen** ('I am sorry to have to trouble *or* bother you with this matter').

lobpreisen: This verb is *trans.*, meaning 'to sing a person's praises, extol'. It is treated as *insep.* in the pres. tenses (the past tenses are now little used), but *sep.* in the past part. and the infin. with **zu:** e.g. **Alle Engel lobpreisen dich** (Zifferer)—**Lobpreiset den Herrn!—Wir haben Gott lobgepriesen, und haben allen Grund, ihn lobzupreisen**; for the now rare past tense, cf. **Der Pastor lobpries die Eigenschaften der Dahingeschiedenen** (Th. Mann: 'The parson extolled the virtues of the departed lady').

lobsingen: This has the same force as **lobpreisen** (q.v.) and is treated in the same way, except that it requires a *dat.* case: e.g. **Lobsinget dem Herrn!—Dem Gott Israels wurde lobgesungen.** The past tenses are quite obs.

locker: see **loose** I.

lohnen, löhnen: 1. The MHG verb *lônen* took a dat. of the person and a gen. of the thing, and in *ich wil es dir lônen* ('I shall reward you for it') the gen. *es* came later to be treated as an accus. (see **es** I), so that the modern idiom is **Ich will dir das lohnen.** But the gen. is still used in a rather choice style and is firmly established *reflex.* in ordinary prose in **Das lohnt** (or **verlohnt**) **sich nicht der Mühe** ('That is not worth the trouble'). A dat. of the person alone has a more *fig.* force—**Ich habe Ihnen übel gelohnt** is 'I have served you ill'—and a dat. of the thing, as in **Solchen Taten kann nur Gott lohnen** (G.), is now almost obs. In such propositions modern usage prefers **Ich muß ihn für seine Güte belohnen** and **Solche Taten sollten belohnt werden. 2.** The mutated form **löhnen** is only used with an accus. of the person (esp. a soldier, servant, labourer, etc.) in the sense of 'to pay, give wages to': **einen Arbeiter löhnen = einem Arbeiter seinen Lohn geben;** cf. **Soldaten auslöhnen** ('to pay soldiers off').

look (verb): 1. (**a**) While **sehen** properly suggests a more or less accidental, instinctive action, **schauen** really implies a more conscious, deliberate action: cf., in Schmeller's *Bavarian Dictionary*, **Ich schaue alleweil und sehe doch nichts.** Actually, however, **schauen** is esp. characteristic of the south; in the north it is a rather select expression, little used in ordinary lang.: where a northerner says **Auf Wiedersehen!** a southerner says **Auf Wiederschauen!** (see also **zusehen** I). But there is at least one case where the southern expression is to be preferred: 'to look out for somebody' whom you are expecting or hoping to see is **nach jemand ausschauen,** as in **Er öffnete das Fenster und schaute nach seinem Freunde aus.** Here **ausschauen** is preferable, because **aussehen nach** usually has the force of 'to have the appearance of': cf. **„Reiste er allein ab?" „Allein? Nicht doch! Er hatte einen Herrn bei sich, der nach etwas Vornehmem aussah"** (Sch.: '. . . who looked distinguished, aristocratic')—impers., **Es sieht nach Regen aus** ('It looks like rain'). So also in the north one always says **Sie sehen** (not **schauen**) **blaß aus,** and **aussehen** would be used in propositions like **Keiner von beiden wußte, wie komisch sie ausschauten** (Zuckmayer: 'how funny they looked') and **Auf dem Bilde stehen rechts zwei im Dunkeln, die schauen ganz wie ein Liebespaar aus** (G. v. d. Vring). (**b**) The intrans. **blicken** (cf. **Sicht** 2 *c*) implies a fleeting look, a 'glance' (see also **lugen**), and the corresponding trans. **erblicken** (q.v.) is 'to catch sight of': cf. **Ich blickte hin und her, konnte aber meinen Freund nicht erblicken.** The proposition **Diese amerikanischen Damen blicken nicht, sie schauen nur** (Lenau) does not seem a very convincing way to suggest the idea that these ladies look at you without seeing you, that their eyes are blank. **2.** There are various ways of rendering 'to look at', the choice depending partly on the degree of concentration involved, partly on the facial expression of the observer. (**a**) There are, first, several *trans.* verbs with the prefix **an-,** indicating that the eyes are directed towards some object. The commonest of these are **ansehen** (in the south **anschauen**) and **anblicken** (coll. **angucken,** pronounced **ankucken** in the north), the latter implying a more cursory glance; with more specific force, **anstarren** or, more forcibly, **anglotzen** ('to stare wide-eyed at'), coll. **angaffen** ('to gaze with astonishment at'). (**b**) As distinct from **ansehen,** the verb **besehen** implies a somewhat closer look at a thing: **Im Museum sieht man sich** (*dat.*) **möglichst viel an und besieht die interessantesten Gegenstände.** (**c**) A step further is suggested by **besichtigen,** which means 'to inspect', as when an expert 'examines' damage done and reports. (**d**) Finally, **betrachten** implies a deeper insight, the observer's intellectual, emotional and artistic sense being brought into play: cf. **Ein Gemäldehändler besieht ein Gemälde von allen Seiten, um zu untersuchen, ob es aucht nicht schädlich sei; der Künstler aber betrachtet es, um die Kunst an demselben zu bewundern und darüber nachzudenken** (Eberhard); and that the intellectual faculty plays an important part here is clear from the common use of **Betrachtungen** (über + accus.) to express an author's 'thoughts' or 'reflections' on a special subject.

loose: 1. Where this adj. suggests that a thing is no longer firmly attached to something else, has become 'slack', it is rendered either by **locker** or by **lose:** thus, either expression may be used of a 'loose' tooth, knot, screw, etc. (cf. **los** 1). But where the reference is to the loose connexion between the component parts or ingredients of something, without any suggestion of one thing having become detached from another, the correct expression is **locker,** not **lose:** e.g. **lockerer Boden** ('light soil' or soil which has been 'loosened by digging')—**lockeres Gebäck** ('light pastry'). On the other hand, **lose** specifically suggests that two things are not closely or firmly attached: e.g. **Nun soll ich diese losen Blätter** ('loose sheets of paper') **alle sammeln** (G.)—**Ihre losen Haare flatterten im Winde—Die Mauersteine lagen lose aufeinander** (i.e. were not cemented); *fig.* **Sie hat eine lose Zunge** or **einen losen Mund** ('She is a chatterbox' or esp. 'She has a malicious tongue')—**Er ist ein loser Vogel** ('He is a gay dog')—**Er führt ein loses Leben** ('He is leading a dissolute life')—**Er hat uns einen losen Streich gespielt** ('He has played us a roguish prank'). **2.** The word **schlaff** is used of something (e.g. a rope) which hangs 'loose, slack', as opposed to **straff** ('taut'): hence **ein schlaffes Seil straff ziehen—eine schlaffe Saite spannen** ('to tighten a violin string')—**Bei völliger Windstille hängen die Segel schlaff.** The LG form of **schlaff** is **schlapp** (cf. **ragged** 3), which has established itself coll. in the literary language in a few compounds like **Schlapphut** ('slouch-hat, wide-awake') and **Schlappschwanz** ('weakling, slacker'); cf. **eine schlappe Haltung** ('a slouching carriage', esp. 'an unsoldierly bearing') and **schlapp machen** ('to be a slacker').

Lorelei: see **Hand** 2 (*b*).

los: 1. It may be assumed that **los** and **lose** were orig. two forms of one and the same word, but modern usage differentiates them. Whereas **lose** is an adj., used esp. in the *attrib.* relation and inflected in the ordinary way (see **loose** 1), **los** is invariable and mostly used in the *pred.* That the sense of 'loose' was orig. common to both forms is clear from examples like **Das Kind hat einen losen Zahn** and the coll. expression **Bei ihm ist eine Schraube los** ('He has a screw loose'); but while **lose** always suggests that the thing referred to is still attached to something else, **los** now mostly implies complete detachment. **2.** The idea of complete detachment inherent in **los** is seen esp. (**a**) in numerous adjs. formed from nouns by attaching **-los** as a suffix with the force of 'bereft of, without' (= our *-less*): e.g. **atem-, heimat-, hoffnungs-, wolkenlos,** etc. (cf. **absence** 2 *d*); and (**b**) in a number of verbs compounded with the sep. prefix **los-** (cf. 3), as in **Laß mich los!** ('Unhand me!'). The orig. gen. case after **los sein** and **loswerden** is still used in poetry and elevated prose, as in **So ward ich meiner Bande los** (Sch.: 'Thus was I freed from my fetters') and **Er ward seines Feindes los** (Chamisso: 'He escaped from his enemy's clutches'); but here the gen. is now replaced in ordinary lang. by the prep. **von:** e.g. **Der Hund ist von der Kette los—Bindet die Pferde von den Bäumen los!** (Freiligrath)—**Goethe schritt weiter aus, als müsse er von den trüben Gedanken loskommen** (Kolbenheyer)—**Ich sagte mich von allen Pflichten gegen sie los** (G.: 'I renounced all obligations towards her'). But where **los sein** and **loswerden** have taken on the common force of 'to be *or* get rid of', the *gen.* has been entirely displaced by the *accus.*: e.g. **Ich will Gott danken, wenn ich dich Narren wieder los bin** (Lessing)—**Man nannte die drei Brüder nur die drei Hasen, welchen Spitznamen sie lange nicht loswurden** (G.)—**Ins Fremdenbuch setzte er nicht seinen Familiennamen, sondern Müller, und war somit seinen wirklichen Namen los** (W. Schäfer)—**Tags darauf starb er, und die Stadt war einen Kostgänger los** (H. Hesse)—**Die Italiener wurden den Verdacht nicht los, es solle ihnen gezeigt werden, wie man in Deutschland alles besser machen könne** (K. Edschmid)—**Die Kühe brüllten: sie hatten Hunger und wollten die Milch los sein** (Fr. Schnack: '. . . they wanted to be milked'). **3.** Out of this idea of freedom or riddance another sense of **los** developed, implying the sudden commencement of an action, after all ties, as it were, have been got rid of. This use is common in many coll. expressions, such as **Nun los! es wird spät** ('Come on, let's start, it's getting late')—**Was ist denn los?** ('What's the matter? What's up?' really 'What has started?')—**Hier scheint nicht viel los zu sein** ('There doesn't seem to be much doing here'); and esp. in many compd. verbs: e.g. **Ein Gewitter brach los**—**Eine Schlägerei ging los** ('A brawl started')—**Ich drückte los** ('I pulled the trigger')—**Schieß los!** ('Fire ahead!')—**Die Jungen schlugen aufeinander los** ('The boys came to blows').

löschen: 1. The *weak* verb **löschen** is reg. used with *trans.* force with objs. like **Licht** ('to extinguish'), **Durst** ('to quench'), **Staub** ('to lay'), **Tintenklecks** ('to blot' with **Löschpapier**, 'blotting-paper'), etc.: see also **load (noun)** 2. **2.** The *strong* verb **löschen** always has *intrans.* force ('to be extinguished, go out'), but here the simple verb is now little used (cf. St. Zweig's **Hinter mir löschten die Lichter**), being usually replaced by one of the compds., viz. **auslöschen** (which, however, more often has the trans. force of 'to put out' a light), and esp. **erlöschen** and **verlöschen.** *Duden* only allows the old forms here (**Das Licht erlischt, erlosch, ist erloschen**), but the modern tendency is very definitely towards *weak* forms here also (cf. esp. **schrecken**), as the following examples show: **Die Lichter löschten aus** (G. Keller)—**Irgend jemand trug eine Laterne, aber sie löschte bald aus** (Viebig)—**Der Abend kommt, der Wald löscht aus** (Waggerl)—**Es geht mir wie einem Hause, dem zur Nachtzeit das einzige Licht erlöscht** (Stehr)—**Sofort erlöschten alle Lichter** (M. Eyth)—**Im Osten blitzte eine Sternschnuppe** ('shooting star') **auf und erlöschte nach kurzem Fluge** (Jul. Wolff)—**Hier und da schloß sich ein Fenster und die letzten Lichter verlöschten** (id.)—**Wenn bloß** ('If only') **dieses grellweiße Licht dort oben verlöschte!** (Bruno Frank)—**Die Kerzen in den Kandelabern verlöschten** (A. Neumann)—**Die halb angerauchten Zigaretten verlöschten zischend im Wasser** (K. Edschmid)—**Das Licht ward immer kleiner und verlöschte endlich** (H. Grimm).

lose: see **loose** I; **los** I.

lot: For 'a lot of money, people', etc., see **genitive of material** (esp. 3 *b*); **Masse; Menge; viel** I.

Lüge: for the expression **Lügen strafen,** see **strafen.**

lugen: This is a characteristically southern, esp. Swiss and Austrian verb, meaning 'to look intently' (cf. **look** I *a*), as when a Swiss shepherd-boy is told **Lug', ob das Vieh sich nicht verlaufen** (*scil.* **hat**)! (Sch.). It is only occasionally used farther north: e.g. **Der Halbmond lugte** ('peeped') **scheu aus dem dunklen Gewölk** (Heine)—**Alles drängte zum Treppengeländer und lugte** ('peered') **hinunter** (Th. Mann).

lügen: In MHG a clear distinction was made between *ligen* (with a short stem-vowel: 'to be reclining') and *liegen,* later *liugen* ('to tell a lie'), and when the former came to be written as **liegen,** the latter took on the modern form **lügen.** Both verbs were—and still are—*strong*: **liegen, lag, gelegen—lügen, log, gelogen.** On no account should historically quite wrong weak forms be used: it is carrying 'poetic licence' too far, even for the sake of the rhyme, to say, as Sch. once does, **Wer mit Schritten eines Niebesiegten / Wandert dort vom Felsenhang? / Ha! wenn meine Augen mir nicht lügten, / Das ist eines Römers Gang.**

Lump, Lumpen: Modern usage distinguishes between **Lumpen** (gen. **Lumpens**), meaning 'rag' (for synonyms, see **rag, ragged**) and **Lump** (gen. **Lumps,** plur. **Lumpe** or more commonly **Lumpen**), meaning 'some one clothed in rags, tramp', esp. 'scamp, scoundrel'; hence the distinction between **Lumpensammler** ('rag and bone man') and **Lumpengesindel**

or **-pack** ('riff-raff'). For this distinction between a short form denoting a person and a longer form denoting a thing, cf. **Tropf(en)**.

lüsten: see **gelüsten**.

lustwandeln: This artificially constructed compd. of **wandeln** (q.v.), dating from the 17th century, means 'to stroll, saunter'. Its prefix is now always *insep.*, its aux. either **sein** or (perhaps more usually) **haben**: e.g. **Meine gnädige Frau Herzogin lustwandelt im Park** (Heyse)—**Im Schatten der Linden lustwandelte man auf und nieder** (Kolbenheyer)—**Eine lange Allee gab Gelegenheit, im Freien zu lustwandeln** (G.)—**So kostumiert war** (or **hatte**) **sie dort gelustwandelt** (Immermann).

M

machen: **1.** Apart from the practically fixed expression **geltend machen** (see **accusative and participle**), the normal construction of **machen** is the **accusative and infinitive** (q.v. 1 *a*, 4 and 5). At an earlier period the infin. *with* **zu** was used in the case of one or two verbs, notably **lachen**, as in **Was mich so herzlich zu lachen macht, das hat auch seine ernsthafte Seite** (Lessing) and **Das macht mich zu lachen** (G.), but this is not in accordance with accepted modern usage. Quite different, however, is the expression **zu schaffen machen**, which requires a *dat.* of the person: hence distinguish between **Der Aufseher machte die Arbeiter tüchtig schaffen** ('The foreman made the labourers work hard') and **Womit machst du dir zu schaffen?** ('What are you busy with?'), and esp. **Seine Söhne machen ihm viel zu schaffen** ('His sons are a great worry to him'). **2.** Noteworthy is the familiar use of **machen** in the sense of 'to hasten', as in **Mach' schnell!** ('Hurry up!'). It is much used with a **daß**-clause: e.g. **Mach', daß du fortkommst!** ('Get out of here! Clear out!')—**Sie erschrak und machte, daß sie zum Zimmer hinauskam** (Bergengruen: 'She gave a start and bolted from the room').

Mädchen: **1.** As this noun is neut., a qualifying art., poss. or attrib. adj. must be *neut.*, as in **ein kleines Mädchen**. Sim. **das junge Fräulein**—**Mein gnädiges Fräulein!**—**Teures Weib!** etc.; one no longer says **Ich wollte mich eben empfehlen, als meine Fräulein B. hereintrat** (G.). So also one should strictly say **Das kleine Mädchen erzählte seiner Mutter, was es erlebt hatte**; but modern usage prefers **Das kleine Mädchen zeigte ihrer Mutter den Brief, den sie geschrieben hatte**—see **congruence** 2. **2.** In the familiar speech of the north, **Mädchen** and **Fräulein** commonly take the LG ending **-s** in the plur.: thus, Heyse speaks of **Fräuleins, die schon eingesegnet sind**, and Minna v. Barnhelm's cultured lady's-maid and friend says **Er weiß, daß der Weg zu den Fräuleins durch die Kammermädchens geht** (Lessing), while even a duke can say **Macht nicht solches dummes Zeug, ihr Mädchens** (Böhlau). This applies also to **Kerl** and esp. **Junge** (q.v.): e.g. **Jetzt muß ich die Pfaffen scheren: ich kann die Kerls nicht ausstehen** (G.)—**Stelle mich vor ein Heer Kerls wie ich!** (Sch.)—**Jungens müssen sich prügeln** (Wildenbruch). But this use should be confined to coll. speech and to the nouns given above: it is only an uncultured labourer who would say **Siehst du, da gibt es Männers, die von allen Weibers geliebt werden und die dabei gegen Damens sehr stolz sind** (G. Engel). **3.** Different is the common familiar use of a surname, title or profession in the plur., as in **Müllers sind augenblicklich verreist** ('The Millers are away from home just now') and **Wir waren gestern abend bei Müllers** ('We were at the Millers last night'): see **Proper names** 3 (*a*).

Mahl ('a meal'): **1.** This is actually the same word as **Mal** (q.v. 2), the idea of a 'point of time' having been specifically applied to the hour at which a meal is taken, and then to the meal itself. It is now a formal expression for a 'banquet', used esp. in compds. like **Fest-, Gast-, Hochzeitsmahl,** whereas the word for an ordinary meal is **Mahlzeit,** commonly used as a coll. greeting when men meet at lunch-time, and in the polite formula

Gesegnete Mahlzeit! on the conclusion of a meal. **2.** The *plural* is either **Mahle** or **Mähler,** of which the former, being rather more choice, is the usual form in the case of the compds. given above, and is practically fixed in that of **Abendmahl** ('the Lord's supper'), as distinct from the everyday expressions **Abendbrot, -essen** or **-mahlzeit** ('supper'). In this ordinary sense, some (esp. SG) dialects use **Nachtmahl:** e.g. **Wir nahmen nun das Nachtmahl ein** (G. Keller)—**Die Magd rüstete den Tisch zum Nachtmahl** (Heyse); and this has even led to the formation of a verb **nachtmahlen,** so that one says in the south **Wir haben schon genachtmahlt** for the standard **Wir haben schon zu Abend gegessen.**

Mai: see **März** and **Monatsnamen.**

Mal: 1. The original force of this neut. noun, in which sense it is now little used except in compds., was a 'sign, mark', esp. a disfiguring mark, a 'scar', as in **Muttermal** ('birthmark, *mole*'), **Wunden-** and **Nägelmal** (used esp. of our crucified Lord's scars), and in the case of these nouns the *plur.* form is **-male:** Thomas would not believe that Christ had appeared to the other disciples until he had seen **die Nägelmale in seinen Händen** (John 20. 25). This force of **Mal** led to that of a distinguishing or commemorative landmark, a 'memorial', as in **Grabmal** ('tombstone') and esp. **Denkmal** ('monument'), and in such expressions there is considerable fluctuation in the plur.: if any distinction might be made between **Denkmale** and **Denkmäler,** it is that the latter is more usual in ordinary language, esp. when used in the *lit.* sense, while the former is a somewhat more dignified form, often used with *fig.* force: cf. **Herabgestürzt seh' ich die Denkmäler alter königlicher Pracht** (Sch.) and **Sie zerstörten alle Denkmale der Literatur** (G.); but this distinction is by no means strictly observed: cf. **Im Hofe** (*scil.* **des Akademischen Instituts zu Ferrara**) **erquickten mich einige alte Denkmale** (G.)—**Ich wuchs in einer altstädtischen Umgebung auf, deren Baudenkmale weit zurückreichten** (Th. Mann)—**Man legte Promenaden an und zierte sie durch freundliche Ruhesitze und Denkmale** (Kolbenheyer)—**Briefe gehören unter die wichtigsten Denkmäler, welche der einzelne Mensch hinterlassen kann** (G.). Here also belongs **Merkmal** (a distinguishing 'feature, characteristic, symptom'), with the plur. **Merkmale.** With regard to the simple word, the following example is interesting: **Als wir klein waren und „Kriegen" spielten, da gab es immer ein „Mal", ein abgegrenztes Fleckchen, wohin man laufen konnte und wo man nicht abgeschlagen werden durfte** (Th. Mann), referring to the game of 'tig' (**der Zeck**) and the 'home *or* base' (Scot. 'den') to which one ran for safety. **2.** It might be thought that **Mal** meaning 'mark' and **Mal** meaning 'time' are quite different words, but they are one and the same, the force of 'time, occasion' being derived from the shadow-line on a sun-dial, marking the time of day (cf. **Mahl** 1). This use of the word requires the plur. **Male:** cf. **mehrere Male** and **zu wiederholten Malen** ('repeatedly'): see **-mal**(s).

-mal(s): 1. The form **-mal** is suffixed to cardinal numerals and **halb** to form *iterative* adverbs: e.g. **einmal** (q.v.)—**Einmal eins ist eins** (cf. **das Einmaleins,** 'the multiplication table')—**Dreimal drei ist** (*not* **sind**) **neun**—**Diese Kiste ist anderthalbmal so groß wie jene** ('This box is half as large again as that one'). From these iterative adverbs, adjectives have been formed by adding **-ig:** e.g. **Nach dreimaliger Aufführung der Oper erkrankte die erste Sängerin. 2.** There is some fluctuation between the forms **-mal** and **-mals** in other derivative adverbs. On the analogy of the numerals, one says **ein dutzendmal** (plur. **dutzendemal**), **ein paarmal** ('two or three times'), **ein andermal, diesmal, einigemal, manchmal, jedesmal** or **allemal** (cf. **Wenn er mich besucht, bin ich allemal verreist** and **Solche Behandlung verbitte ich mir ein für allemal,** 'Once for all, I won't put up with any more of such treatment'). On the other hand, **-mals** has established itself in expressions exemplified in the following propositions: **Bei herannahender guter Witterung gedachte ich, die schönen Tage des vorigen Jahres abermals zu genießen** (G.), i.e. 'once again': see **aber** (adverb)—**Er bestand aber und abermals darauf** (G.: 'He insisted on it over and over again')—**Ich war damals noch auf der Schule** (see then, *2 b*)—**Die Verhältnisse waren ehemals** (or **vormals**) **besser** ('Conditions were better formerly, in the old days')—**„Warst du jemals in der Schweiz?" „Jawohl, mehrmals, aber niemals in Italien"—„Also, auf Wieder-**

sehen; nochmals ('once again') **besten Dank!"** (but usually **Sage das Gedicht nochmal her!**)—**Als Junge habe ich die Ferien oftmal(s) hier verbracht—Ich bitte vielmals um Entschuldigung** (but **Wievielmal geht 4 in 12?**)—**Diese Gedichte sind herrlich, zumal** ('especially') **die Naturgedichte.**

man: This is only used in the nom., its oblique cases being borrowed from **einer** (q.v. 2). In point of fact, **einer** is slightly more definite than **man,** and really approaches **jemand** in sense, but this difference only arises in propositions consisting of two clauses, in both of which the indef. person is referred to in the nom. case: in such a context, if **man** is used in the first clause, it must be repeated in the second, whereas the subsequent reference to **einer** is not **einer,** but **er.** Thus, the couplet **Wenn jemand eine Reise tut, so kann er was verzählen** (M. Claudius: where **verzählen** is an obs. HG form of LG **vertellen**) is generally misquoted **Wenn einer eine Reise tut, so kann er was erzählen;** and this might also take the form **Wenn man eine Reise tut, so kann man** (not **er**) **was erzählen.** It is significant that Goethe, in his autobiography, says **Was einer in der Jugend wünscht, hat er im Alter genug,** but continues a few pages later **Ich werde mit Zufriedenheit jenes Wort wiederholen können: Was man in der Jugend wünscht, hat man im Alter genug.**

manch: 1. This indef. pron. or pron. adj. has either *distrib.* or *collect.* force, and may therefore represent or qualify both sing. and plur. nouns, the former corresponding to 'many a' (see 2), the latter to 'many', but suggesting more than **einig** (q.v.) and fewer than **viel** (q.v.). **2.** Just as we say 'many a man', so also in German the indef. art. may follow **manch,** in which case the latter is always *uninflected,* as in **manch ein gutes Kind,** gen. **manch eines guten Kindes.** The reverse order, so common in the case of **solch** (q.v. 1), is now obs.: one no longer says **ein mancher Bauer** (Schelling). **3.** As a *pron. adj.* **manch** normally has *strong* inflexion when no other qualifying word follows it, as in **mancher Mensch,** plur. **manche** (gen. **mancher**) **Menschen.** The uninflected form here was common at one time and is still used in poetry, esp. in the neut. sing., as in **Manch Herze schwoll** (Uhland), but this is little used in modern prose. In the gen. sing. masc. and neut. one can only say **Das ist manches Menschen Meinung;** but a *weak* ending is permissible where the noun has the strong gen. ending, so that **manchen Mannes** is not incorrect: cf. **Sie sehen, daß ich mit der Arbeit fertig geworden bin, wenn es gleich wegen manchen Zögerns und Säumens den Anschein nicht hatte** (G.); in this connexion see **solch** 2. **4.** When it is used as a *pron.,* the gen. is not used: one does not say **Das ist manches Meinung** or, in the plur., **Das ist mancher Geschmack** (for **mancher Leute Geschmack**). **5.** When followed by an attrib. adj., **manch** may remain uninflected, the adj. then being *strong,* but is more commonly strongly inflected, the adj. then being preferably *weak,* as in **Wie auf manches andere im deutschen Lande, so bin ich auch auf unsere guten Wirtshäuser stolz** (Fr. Ratzel) and **Es war der Spielplatz mancher vergessenen** (or **manch vergessener**) **Kindergeneration** (R. Waldmüller); but before a neut. adj.-subst. **manch** must be inflected, as in **Wie verwundert war er, als sie ihm in Gefolg so manches Unerfreulichen** (which might be **nach so manchem Unerfreulichen**) **sagte, sie hoffe, daß alles sich wieder geben werde** (G.). Sanders, quoting expressions like **mancher freier Mann** (Möser) and **in so manchem verdrießlichem Buche** (Tieck), says **„Diese Beispiele widerstreben dem heutigen Sprachgefühl so entschieden, daß sie nur zur Bestätigung der Regel dienen können";** and so also gen. expressions like **mancher ähnlicher Erlebnisse** (Speckmann) and **trotz mancher komischer Züge** (B. E. Werner) are contrary to accepted modern usage, which prefers the weak ending **-en** in such cases. But the strong ending would, of course, be essential if **mancherlei** were used instead of **mancher** (see **Hand** 2 *b*). Rather less uncommon here are two strong endings in the nom. and accus. plur., on the analogy of **viele** or **einige berühmte Dichter** (see **viel** 2 *c* and **einig** 2 *b*), but here also one prefers to say **Manche dummen Kerle haben Spottlieder auf ihn gemacht** (Fontane), and the following examples are hardly in accordance with accepted present-day usage: **Nie verfällt Hans Sachs der schmutzigen Witzelei wie manche unsaubere** (better **unsauberen**) **Talente des 16. Jahrhunderts** (Erich Schmidt)—**Im Anfang machte ich**

manche unglückliche Experimente (H. Hesse)—Ich ging bis Schottland hinauf und machte manche nutzbringende Bekanntschaften (Th. Mann)—In dieser Zeit kamen manche junge Männer an den Hof (Bergengruen).

mancherhand, mancherlei: see **Hand** 2.

Mandel: The two commonest meanings of this fem. noun (plur. **Mandeln**) are 'almond' and 'tonsil' (**Mandelentzündung** = 'tonsilitis'); but it was formerly also used to suggest 'fifteen' units (cf. **Getreide** 2), so that **zwei Mandel** = **dreißig,** (**Stück**) or **ein halbes Schock** (q.v.): thus, eggs used to be sold in fifteens, **vier Mandel Eier** being the equivalent of the modern **fünf Dutzend Eier.** For the collect. use of the sing. form in the plur. after numerals, as in the above examples, see **nouns of measure.**

Mangel: 1. (**a**) The verb **fehlen** implies that something *is not there* (see **lack** 1), and the *masc.* noun **Mangel** (cf. 3) may suggest little more than that: e.g. **Bei dem Mangel aller Beweise einer Schuld wurde der Angeklagte freigesprochen—In den Kaufläden war eine Unmenge Waren, aber ein Mangel an Käufern;** cf. the adj. **mangelhaft,** as used, for example, of a manuscript of which parts are *missing,* as distinct from **fehlerhaft,** which implies not incompleteness but inaccuracy. But **Mangel** is used esp. of a lack which is felt as a real *want* (see **absence** 2 *c*), particularly a lack of necessities, as in **Mangel leiden** ('to suffer privation'). As the above examples show, the construction is either a *genitive* (where that case is recognizable) or **an** + *dative;* the use of **von** here, as in **Ich machte ihn aufmerksam auf den Verfall der Mauern und den Mangel von Toren** (G.), is now avoided (cf. the correct **auf das Fehlen von Mauern**). But the gen. should not be used where ambiguity might arise: **der Mangel eines Freundes** may mean either the *lack,* or the *privation,* of a friend, the former an objective, the latter a subjective gen.; and to obviate misconception, a proposition like 'I feel the lack of a faithful friend' is best rendered by **Ich vermisse einen treuen Freund** (see **miss** 2 *b*). (**b**) It should be noted that the plur. **Mängel** (cf. 3) is now only used of 'defects, imperfections, shortcomings': e.g. **In den Volksliedern findet man unreine Reime und ein holpriges Versmaß; dafür sucht die Melodie alle Mängel der Metrik zu verhüllen** (K. Breuer); *fig.* **die erblichen Mängel der Menschen** (G.: cf. 'man's original sin'). **2.** On the other hand, **Ermangelung** requires an objective *gen.* (see below): e.g. **Bei Ermangelung nötiger Vorsicht entstand bald Mangel** (Joh. v. Müller: 'In consequence of the lack of requisite foresight privation soon reared its head'). In modern usage it is largely confined to the combination with the prep. **in,** as in the common expression **in Ermangelung eines Besseren** (*faute de mieux*). Where a gen. is not recognizable as such, the prep. **von** must be used: e.g. **in Ermangelung von Beweisen** ('for want of proof'), but with an attrib. adj. better **in Ermangelung triftiger Beweise. 3.** To be distinguished from **der Mangel** is **die Mangel** (plur. **Mangeln**), meaning 'mangle', which developed out of MHG *mange,* a 'catapult' used for hurling stones in war, and later for the peaceful operation of pressing garments, etc.

mangeln: see **lack (verb)** 2.

Mann: 1. The gen. sing. of **Mann** is **Mann(e)s,** but the **e** is always dropped in adjs. like **mannshoch** (see below), and as a rule in the phrase **Manns genug** ('man enough'), used not only in a proposition like **Er ist Manns genug, sich zu verteidigen,** but even in **Die Mädchen waren Manns genug, vergnügt zu sein** (Böhlau) and, with **genug** omitted, **Er schien wieder Manns geworden** (Blunck: 'He seemed to have regained his courage'); cf. as rather exceptional, **Da der Mann nicht Mannes genug war, hatte die Frau sich ermannen müssen, die Zügel des Burglebens zu ergreifen** (H. Franck). The adj. **mannshoch** is a convenient way to express 'as tall as a man': e.g. **Einige Fuß hoch am Berg war eine Höhle geöffnet, wenig über mannshoch und kaum so breit** (A. Schaeffer)—**Der Weg ist überall mannshoch mit Schnee zugeweht** (H. Hauser); and so also **Die Angelrute besteht aus vier halbmannshohen Bambusstecken** (P. Alverdes)—**Das niedrige Dach der Sennhütte ist hinten in die Halde gebaut, strebt aber vorne dreimannshoch empor** (Federer)—**Die übermannshohen Laubengänge waren mit dem Segen dieses Jahres beladen** (Heyse); cf. **Das Gelände senkte sich etwa um drei Mannshöhen bis auf den Spiegel der Werle** (Speckmann)—**Unter ihm, kaum mannstief, lag die abendstille Flut des Sees** (Federer)—**Das Mädchen half die mannsschweren Körbe**

tragen (C. Rothe). **2.** (**a**) There are three plur. forms of **Mann:** persons of the male sex are **Männer** (see *b*), but **Mann** in a collect. sense (see **nouns of measure** I *a*), while **Mannen** means 'vassals': e.g. **Sowohl Männer als Frauen waren eingeladen—Er wurde als Gefangener in das nächstliegende Gebäude geführt, und zwölf Mann wurden damit betraut, ihn zu bewachen** (Wassermann)—**Zwei Mann hoch fand sich die Polizei ein** (H. Hesse)—**Alle Mann hoch** or **an Deck!** ('All hands on deck!'). (**b**) In compds., the plur. **-männer** is fixed where the reference is to an object in human shape, such as **Hampelmann** ('jumping Jack') and **Schneemann,** and in a few nouns like **Bieder-** and **Ehrenmann** ('man of sterling quality, honourable gentleman'), **Gewährsmann** ('guarantor'), **Leiermann** ('organ-grinder'), **Staatsmann** ('statesman'). In certain cases—esp., but not necessarily, where both sexes are implied—the reg. plur. form is replaced by **-leute,** as in **Edelleute** ('people of noble birth'), **Geschäfts-** and **Kaufleute, Hofleute** ('courtiers'), **Land-** and **Landsleute** (the former 'peasants', the latter 'compatriots'); also usually **Hauptleute** ('captains'), **Spielleute** ('minstrels, strolling musicians'), etc. Elsewhere either form is used, as in **Fuhr-, Schutz-, See-, Steuer-, Zimmermänner,** or **-leute.** In this connexion, distinguish between **Ehemänner** ('husbands') and **Eheleute** ('married couple'), and between **Dienstmänner** ('porters, commissionaires'), **Dienstleute** ('servants' of either sex') and **Dienstmannen** ('vassals').

männiglich: In OHG, 'every' was *iogilîh* (> **immer gleich**), but this idea could also be expressed by *gilîh* preceded by the gen. plur. of a noun, as in *manno gilîh* (lit. 'the likes of men', i.e. **jeder Mensch**). It is this OHG combination which developed into the NHG **männiglich,** a word no longer much used in ordinary prose, but once common, esp. in official documents. Although Goethe, in a letter to Schiller, uses the phrase **zu männiglicher Verwunderung** ('to everybody's astonishment'), it is now usually treated as indeclin., having the force of 'one and all' or 'everybody, individually and collectively'. It may represent any case except a gen., as may be seen from the following examples: in the *nom.*, **Man hatte vereinbart, daß man sich männiglich verpflichten wolle, Punkt vier Uhr in Halensee zu sein** (Fontane: 'It had been agreed that all the members of the party should pledge their word to be in Halensee on the stroke of four o'clock'); in the *accus.*, **Er trieb allerhand Späße, welche männiglich ergötzten** (G. Keller: 'He played all sorts of pranks, which delighted everybody') and **Sie haben ihm Beistand geschworen wider männiglich** (Grillparzer: 'They have sworn to support him against all comers'); in the *dat.*, **Es war männiglich bekannt** ('known to one and all'), **daß Meister Hänni der geschickteste Haarkünstler der Stadt sei** (Jak. Frey) and **Männiglich bekannt sind die giftigen Jämmerlichkeiten, welche man in München gegen mich ausübte** (Heine: 'Everybody knows to what spiteful indignities I was subjected in Munich'). It is chiefly in this combination with **bekannt** that the expression is now used, esp. in a contracted **wie**-clause, as in **Madame Kummerfelden war, wie männiglich bekannt, früher Schauspielerin gewesen** (Böhlau), and here all feeling for the orig. dat. case is now lost, so that it is virtually an adv., much like **allgemein** ('universally').

mannshoch: see **genitive of measure; Mann** I.

Mark, Marke: 1. As a *fem.* noun, **Mark** has two meanings: (*a*) 'mark, shilling', in which sense it remains unchanged in the plur., as in **zwei Mark fünfzig** ('half a crown'), single shilling pieces being expressed by **Markstücke** (cf. **nouns of measure** 2); and (*b*) 'frontierland', with plur. **Marken** ('marches'). **2.** As a *neut.* noun, **Mark** means 'marrow', with no plur. **3.** On the other hand, **Marke** (*fem.*) has a number of meanings, e.g. 'sign, mark, postage-stamp', etc.; cf. **Lebensmittelmarken** ('food coupons')—**Woher die Marken, um den Gästen wenigstens kleine Schnitzel bieten zu können?** (K. Edschmid: 'Where are we to get coupons, so that we can offer our guests at least small chops?').

marry, marriage: 1. (**a**) The verb in most general use is **heiraten,** really (like the now little used **ehelichen** q.v.) a *trans.* verb, although the obj. is frequently understood, as in **Sie behauptet, sie werde nie heiraten.** The most important point in connexion with **heiraten** is that the subj. and obj. must be of *opposite* sexes, so that **sich heiraten** can only have *reciprocal*, not reflexive, force: e.g. **Die jungen Leute wollen sich** (= **einander**) **heiraten,** but *not* **Er will sich heiraten**; cf. **Heiratsantrag** ('proposal of marriage': see **offer** 1 *d* and 2 *d*). (**b**) The compound **verheiraten** and the more formal **vermählen** both mean 'to *give* in marriage': e.g. **Er hat seine Tochter an den ersten besten Mann verheiratet** ('He has given his daughter to the first man that came along'); hence **sich verheiraten** or **sich vermählen** (lit. 'to give oneself in marriage') is the usual expression for 'to get married', the past part. being regularly used to suggest the married state: e.g. **Er ist mit meiner Schwester verheiratet—Ist sie verheiratet, oder noch ledig?—Meine Schwester und ich haben uns an demselben Tage verheiratet** ('My sister and I got married on the same day')—**Sie sind doch verheiratet, oder, wie es poetischer heißt, vermählt?** (Jul. Grosse)—**Trinken wir auf das Wohl des neuvermählten Paares!** ('Let us drink the young couple's health!'). (**c**) When used of the person who joins two people in wedlock, 'to marry' is rendered by **trauen** (+ *accus*): e.g. **Welcher Geistliche hat das junge Paar getraut?** cf. **Ich lasse mich kriegstrauen** (Viebig: used of a 'war-wedding')—**Eines Tages gestand er mir, daß er verheiratet sei, kriegsgetraut, wie er sagte** (Alverdes). (**d**) The verb **freien,** at one time very common, is now little used; it takes either an accus., like **heiraten,** or the prep. **um,** in which case it has the force of 'to woo, court', but this idea is now more usually expressed by **werben** or, even more commonly, by **anhalten,** as in **Er hat um meine Tochter** (or **um die Hand meiner Tochter**) **angehalten.** The only expression connected with **freien** still in current use is the jocular phrase **auf Freiersfüßen gehen** ('to go a-wooing'). **2.** *Nouns*: (**a**) The actual wedding ceremony is **Trauung,** as in **Die Trauung fand nicht in der Kirche sondern auf dem Standesamt statt** ('The wedding was not held in the church, but in the registrar's office'); a parson might say **Ich habe diese Woche drei Trauungen gehabt.** (**b**) **Hochzeit** (pronounced with a *short open* o) is MHG *hôchgezît*, a 'festival' of any kind, but now embraces all the celebrations connected with a wedding, including the reception, lunch, dance, etc.: e.g. **Die Einladungen zur Hochzeit sind abgeschickt—Die Hochzeitsfestlichkeiten zogen sich bis spät nachts hin.** (**c**) **Heirat** is 'matrimony' or 'match', often with verbal force: e.g. **Wir sind durch Heirat verwandt** ('We are related by marriage') —**Er hat eine gute** (**reiche**) **Heirat geschlossen** ('He has made a good match, married money')—**Die Heirat ist rückgängig gemacht** ('The engagement has been broken off, the wedding will not take place')—**Schnelle Heirat, lange Reue** ('Marry in haste, repent at leisure'). (**d**) **Verheiratung** and **Vermählung** always have verbal force ('disposal in marriage'): e.g. **Durch die Verheiratung seiner Tochter an diesen vermögenden Mann hat er ihr eine glückliche Zukunft gesichert.** (**e**) **Ehe** is 'the married state, conjugal life' (**Ehestand**): e.g. **Sie leben in glücklicher Ehe** ('Theirs is a happy married life')—**Die Ehe ist getrennt worden** ('The marriage has been dissolved') —**Er hat seine Tochter einem wohlhabenden Mann zur Ehe gegeben**; cf. also **ehebrechen.**

März: The MHG nouns *merz* or *merze* ('March') and *meie* or *meige* ('May') were weak, and weak forms are still used, but only in poetry, folksongs and dialects: e.g. **Im Märzen der Bauer die Rößlein einspannt** (Volkslied)—**Der Winter ist vergangen, ich seh des Maien Schein** (id.) —**Kommt die Schneeschmelze zu Anfang des Märzen, dann macht euch bereit** (C. F. Meyer). According to modern prose usage, **der Mai** is the name of the month, while **die Maien** are young green branches used for decoration: e.g. **Alle Hüte schmücken sich mit grünen Maien** (Sch.). For the inflexion of names of the months, see **Monatsnamen.**

Maß: 1. The noun **das Māß** means either 'measurement' (plur. **Māße**) or 'measure' of corn, wine, etc. (plur. **Māße,** collect. **Māß**: see **nouns of measure** 2): cf., on the one hand, **Ich habe mir das Maß zu einem neuen Anzug nehmen lassen** ('I have been measured for a new suit') and **In der Möbelliste waren die Maße genau angegeben** (Fr. Schnack), and, on the other hand, **Wir fragten, ob es denn wahr sei, daß es Herren geglückt, acht rheinische Maß in 24 Stunden zu sich zu nehmen** (G.: '. . . that gentlemen had managed to consume eight Rhenish measures in 24 hours'). In this latter sense of 'tankardful, quart-pot', the noun is now more commonly *fem.*: e.g. **Er trank eine halbe Maß Ungerwein** (Hebel)—**Bei jeder Hoch-**

zeit erhielt er eine Maß Wein (Raabe). The following example combines the two senses neatly: **Der Tischler hatte nicht nur beim Barbier das Maß genommen, sondern auch in der Brauerei** (Fr. Schnack: 'The joiner had not only taken the measurements at the barber's, but had also had a mug of beer in the brewery'). **2.** A different word is **die Mäße** (to be distinguished from **die Măsse,** q.v.), meaning 'moderation'. This was common in MHG (*diu mâze* was then one of the distinctive features of society manners and good breeding: 'modest behaviour, self-control'), but it is now chiefly used in the expression **über alle Maßen** ('immoderately, exceedingly'), and esp. in the *gen.* in adv. compds. like **anerkanntermaßen** ('as is generally acknowledged'), **einigermaßen** ('to some extent, somewhat'), **folgendermaßen** ('as follows') and **gewissermaßen** ('after a fashion, as it were').

Masse: The orig. meaning of this fem. noun is 'mass, lump' (of rock, metal, etc.), as in **Gebirgsmasse** ('massif'); cf. **in Masse verkaufen** ('to sell in the lump *or* in bulk'). This led to its use to suggest a large quantity, either of a lump or of individual components: cf. the example from Wildenbruch given under **congruence** 1 (*a*). In this sense it is now a less refined expression than **Menge** (q.v.): e.g. **Er hat eine Masse Geld** ('a lot of money')—**Tüchtige Ärzte haben wir eine ganze Masse** (K. Edschmid: 'Of competent doctors we have quite a lot')—**Die Wirtin wußte einer solchen Masse von Gästen genugzutun** (G.: 'The innkeeper's wife managed to satisfy such a crowd of guests'); cf. **Die große rohe Masse** ('populace, masses'), **welche die einen das Volk, die anderen den Pöbel nennen** (Heine). So also **in Masse** (= **in Menge**), as in **Deutsche Tragödien habe ich in Masse gelesen** (Platen: 'I have read any amount of German tragedies')—**Man stattete Besuche in Masse ab** (G. Keller: 'We paid endless visits').

Mäßlieb: This name for a 'daisy' is now usually replaced by **Gänseblümchen.** Its forms are anything but fixed. In Brockhaus's *Encyclopaedia* we find **Die bekannteste Art dieser Pflanzengattung ist das Gänseblümchen oder die Maßliebe**; cf. **Die Maßlieben dringen aus dem Boden** (G.). But more usual is **das Maßlieb,** the plur. of which is given as **Maßliebe** by Duden, as **Maßliebs** by Sprach-Brockhaus. The origin of the word is doubtful: one suggestion is that it is connected with **Matte** ('meadow')—cf. Dutch *Madelief*—which seems more likely than a connexion with 'moss': cf. **die Bescheidenheit eines Schneeglöckchens, eines Moosliebchens, eines Veilchens** (A. Schwegler: 1847).

Mast: Distinguish between **der Mast** (= **Mastbaum,** 'mast' of a ship), with plur. **Maste(n),** and **die Mast** ('fattening' of cattle, etc., or 'mast, fodder' for feeding swine), with plur. **Masten.**

Maulaffen: It would be a waste of time to consult a treatise on monkeys in order to find the English equivalent of this word, for the simple reason that there are no such animals. **Maulaffen** is a corruption of a LG expression: where we say 'to stand gaping', a person speaking *Plattdeutsch* says **dat Mul apen hollen,** in HG **das Maul offen halten** ('to hold one's mouth open'). This explains the modern coll. phrase **Maulaffen feil halten** or **haben** ('to gape'), as used in the example from Fr. Halm given under **beißen** *ad fin.*

Mäusle: For this SG contraction of **Mäuslein** ('little mouse'), see **beißen.**

measure: see **nouns of measure**; **Maß.**

meet: see **begegnen** 1 (*a*) and 2; **treffen.**

meiden: cf. **fliehen.**

meinesgleichen: see **-gleichen** 1.

meinetwegen: As explained elsewhere (see **wegen**), the second part of **meinet-, deinetwegen,** etc., was orig. a dat. plur., having developed out of **von meinen wegen:** when **von** dropped out, as it gradually did, **meinen wegen** was unintelligible, and **meinetwegen** was artificially coined to convey the sense of the orig. expression, viz. 'on my account'. But **meinetwegen** has also developed another shade of meaning: a father, on being asked by his boy whether he might go to see a film, might reply **„Meinetwegen!"** ('So far as I am concerned, you may', i.e. 'I have no objections'); cf. **„Meinetwegen kannst du dich zum Henker scheren!"** ('You can go to blazes for all I care!')—cf. **halb** 3 (*b*).

melken: Weak forms of this verb are displacing the orig. strong ones more and more, but while the pres. forms **er milkt** and **milk!** are practically obs., the strong past forms are still in fairly common use, esp. the part. **gemolken,** which is, indeed, quite established when applied to milk:

one can say **Ich habe die Kühe gemelkt** or **gemolken,** but only **Diese Milch ist frisch gemolken.** The past tense **molk** (< MHG *malc,* plur. *mulken*) is represented by Duden as **„mundartlich"**, and it is mainly in southern, esp. Austrian, dialects that the strong forms are now used: cf. **Einige Male fand er ihn, als er eigenhändig die Ziegen molk** (G. Hauptmann)—**Das Vieh ist gemolken** (Waggerl)—**Das meiste Vieh stand hinter den Hütten und wurde gerade abgemolken** (Federer)—**Ich trank die schäumende Milch, die ein Frauenzimmer in einen Holzeimer niedermolk** (Hofmannsthal). The verb **melken** is really the factitive of **milchen** ('to give *or* yield milk') and should therefore not be used intrans., but **eine melkende Kuh** is sometimes used for **eine Milchkuh** ('a milchcow').

Menge: In the phrase **eine Menge Frauen,** as explained under **congruence** 1 (*a*), **Frauen** was orig. a *gen.*, but being unrecognizable as such, became an *appos.* (cf. **Masse**) and forced the verb into the plur.: **Es befanden sich in dem Zimmer eine Menge Hirschgeweihe** (Stifter). Where the gen. is recognizable, or replaced by **von,** the verb should obviously be *sing.*, as in **Eine Menge durcheinandergeworfener Steine lag herum** (id.); but even here a plur. verb, though strictly incorrect and perhaps unrecommendable in the best prose, is not uncommon: see examples under **congruence** 1 (*b*) and cf. **Von dem Flur waren links und rechts eine Menge roher Holzkabinen abgeteilt** (H. Böll). The phrase 'in large quantity *or* numbers' is expressed by **in Menge** or *coll.* **die Menge,** the latter already occurring in early NHG: **allerlei Wein die Menge** (Neh. 5. 18: 'store of all sorts of wine')—**Dieser Winter war eine schwere Zeit für die Tiere, die kleineren erfroren in Menge** (H. Hesse)—**„Wir haben doch Pulver genug?" „Pulver die schwere Menge"** (Sch.: 'Any amount of powder'). For **eine Menge Geldes,** see **genitive of material** 2 (*b*), and cf. **Jetzt fiel ihm eine Menge anderes ein** (Hofmannsthal: 'Now he recalled a lot of other things'), where **anderes,** really a gen., is now treated as an appositive.

mengen: see **mix(ture)** 1.

merken: for **merken lassen,** see **lassen** 4.

Merkmal: see **Mal** 1.

Messer: Distinguish between **der Messer** ('measurer'; also 'meter', instrument for measuring) and **das Messer** ('knife'), both with gen. **Messers** and plur. **Messer.**

Miete ('stook'): see **Getreide** 2.

Million: see **Dutzend.**

mindestens: see **wenig** 4 (*b*).

mischen, Mischung: see **mix(ture)** 1 and 2 (*a*).

miss: 1. (**a**) With the force of 'not to hit' (a target, etc.), **fehlen** is now mainly used abs., as are always **fehl-** or **vorbeischießen** and **daneben schießen:** e.g. **Es ist noch hell, Ihr könnt nicht fehlen** (Jul. Wolff)—**In der blinden Hitze hat er daneben geschossen** (Mörike); in **Wenn ich den einen Wolf auch nicht fehle, kommt mir der andere auf den Hals** (Goldammer) and **Das Reh konnte nicht gefehlt werden** (Immermann) the compd. **verfehlen** would be more usual (see 1 *b*), and this is even more true of the orig. gen. construction, as in **Eurer wahrlich hätt' ich nicht gefehlt** (Sch.: 'I certainly would not have missed you'). Here belongs the *fig.* expression **weit gefehlt,** as in **Sie war nicht mehr jung: wer auf dreißig riet, hatte nicht weit gefehlt** (Auerbach: '. . . was not wide of the mark') and **Ich dachte, sie würde sich mit dem Menschen vereinigen; aber weit gefehlt** ('far from it'), **sie ergriff die Feuerzange und warf sie ihm an den Kopf** (Hebbel). (**b**) Where the obj. is expressed, the best rendering in the sense of **nicht treffen** is **verfehlen** (+ accus. or, in elevated style, gen.), used in a general way to suggest failure of attainment: e.g. **die Scheibe** or **den Weg verfehlen**—**Das Unternehmen wird seinen Zweck verfehlen** ('. . . will not achieve its purpose')—**Er hat seinen Beruf verfehlt** ('He has missed his vocation'); and sim., with a pers. obj., **In dem Gedränge verfehlte ich meinen Freund.** It is also used with **zu** + infin., like **ermangeln** (see **fail** 5), as in **Ich werde nicht verfehlen, mich rechtzeitig einzufinden** ('I shall not fail to turn up in good time'). The past part. is used freely as an adj.: **Das Experiment war verfehlt** ('unsuccessful, a failure')—**ein verfehltes Verfahren** ('a mistaken, wrong mode of procedure'). (**c**) Analogous are **verpassen** and **versäumen,** both used of 'missing' trains, opportunities, engagements, etc.: e.g. **Ich habe meinen Zug verpaßt**—**Er hat den deutschen Unterricht versäumt**—**Ich muß das Versäumte nachholen** ('I must make good the omission, make up leeway')—**Dadurch, daß Sie nicht ins Konzert**

gegangen sind, haben Sie wenig versäumt ('You did not miss much by not going to the concert'); and **versäumen** is also used with an infin. clause: cf. **Ich habe die Sitzung versäumt** and **Ich habe (es) versäumt, der Sitzung beizuwohnen.** (**d**) By extension, 'to miss' may mean 'to fail to obtain' something desirable, as in 'You should see the abbey by moonlight, or you will *miss* much of its charm'; here a good phrase is **verlustig gehen** (+ *gen.*): **Sie sollten die Abtei bei Mondschein sehen, sonst gehen Sie des Reizes zum großen Teil verlustig** (or **sonst geht Ihnen ein gut Teil des Reizes verloren**). (**e**) Here belongs also a proposition like 'I narrowly *missed* being taken prisoner', an idea which is expressed in several ways: e.g. **Es fehlte nur wenig, so wäre ich gefangengenommen**—**Ich wäre um ein Haar gefangengenommen** ('I was within a hair's breadth of being taken prisoner')—**Ich entging mit knapper** (or **genauer**) **Not der Gefangennahme.** **2.** (**a**) The simple verb **missen** means 'to be without' what one once possessed: e.g. **Verliere das Buch nicht, ich möchte es nicht missen** (cf. the last example given under (*c*) below). Here **missen** approaches the more choice expression **entraten,** 'to get on without, dispense with' (generally + *gen.*, and mainly used in the infin.), as when Queen Mary, referring to the servants from whom she has been separated, says **Ihrer Dienste kann ich entraten, doch beruhigt will ich sein, daß die Getreuen nicht leiden und entbehren** (Sch.: see *c*). (**b**) The compd. **vermissen** means 'to feel the absence *or* loss of' what should be there, or what one expected to find. In Schiller's *Der Graf von Habsburg*, the emperor, at his coronation banquet, says **Wohl glänzet das Fest . . . doch den Sänger vermiss' ich . . .** (he sees the glitter and pomp, but no minstrel whom he expected to see); see other examples under (*c*), and cf. the past part. **vermißt,** where we use the *pres.* part.: **Er wurde als vermißt gemeldet** ('He was reported missing')—**Er galt als vermißt und wurde für tot erklärt** (Fr. Griese). (**c**) A stronger expression is **entbehren,** the real force of which is 'to do without' something whose absence or loss one feels very keenly (+ *gen.* or, in ordinary lang., *accus.*), as in **Gott hat mich nicht ei'nen Tag des Notwendigen entbehren lassen** (Auerbach), and hence often used abs. 'to practise renunciation': e.g. **Ein Herz, das sucht, fühlt wohl, daß ihm etwas mangle** (see lack), **ein Herz, das verloren hat, fühlt, daß es entbehre** (G.)—**Ich soll entbehren, soll mich mäßig zeigen** (G.)—**Ich hab' gelernt verlieren und entbehren** (Grillparzer); but it may also merely suggest absence or lack, as in **Seine Behauptung entbehrt jeder Grundlage** ('His statement is entirely unfounded'). The precise force of these various expressions is well brought out in the following quotation: **Wehe dem, dessen man entraten und den man missen kann, den man, wenn man ihn nicht hat, auch nicht vermißt, und den man, wenn man ihn vermißt, entbehren kann** (Eberhard); cf. **Unmöglich schien es ihm, sich von ihr zu trennen: sie war nicht mehr ein Besitz, den man vermißt, aber nicht entbehrt** (H. Grimm). **3.** There are several other shades of meaning of 'to miss', which must be rendered in different ways: e.g. **In seiner Übersetzung ins Deutsche hat der Schüler einen ganzen Satz ausgelassen** ('. . . has missed out a whole sentence')—**Bei der Verteilung der Geschenke wurden zwei Kinder überga'ngen** ('missed, passed over': see **übergehen** 2) —**Wir wollen das nächste Kapitel überspri'ngen** ('miss out, skip')—**Was er eben sagte, habe ich leider überhö'rt** ('Unfortunately I missed, did not catch, what he said just now': see **überhören**).

miß-: **1.** The MHG prefix *misse-* (a form now extant only in the nouns **Missetat,** 'misdeed', and **Missetäter,** 'evil-doer') was much more extensively used with verbs than the modern **miß-,** many of the earlier verbs having become obs., like *missegân* ('to miscarry') and *missetuon* ('to do wrong'). Some that have survived (e.g. **mißgreifen**) are hardly used at all, while others are limited in scope: one says **Sie lachte mißtönend** (Bruno Frank), but avoids **Ihr Lachen mißtönte**—yet **Mißgriff** and **Mißton** are quite common. **2.** The conjugation of verbs compounded with **miß-** shows much fluctuation, mainly because the prefix may be accented or not. Thus, in the case of **mißtrauen** (+ *dat.*, 'to mistrust, distrust'), one ordinarily says **„Ich mißtrau'e diesem Mann"**; but if one person says **„Ich traue diesem Mann"**, another may say **„Und ich mi'ßtraue ihm"**. But even when there is no such juxtaposition of positive and negative ideas, the accent may shift in one and the same verb, and this applies esp. to the *past part.*, where several verbs have alternative forms, with or (more usually) without an introductory **ge-**, the prefix **miß-** being accented in the former case but unaccented in the latter. Still, the general tendency nowadays, certainly in the case of *simple* verbs compounded with miß- (for others, see 6), is undoubtedly to treat the prefix as *insep.* and *un*accented: e.g. **Mißtrau't er dir?—Er scheint dir zu mißtrau'en—Er hat dir mißtrau't,** where **gemi'ßtraut,** although allowed, is much less common. **3.** (a) A typical example of such a verb with alternative part. forms is **mißbrauchen** ('to misuse, abuse'). Here, as in the case of **mißtrauen** (see 2), the form without **ge-** is the more usual one, but that with **ge-** is by no means rare: cf., on the one hand, **Ich habe das Leben mißbrau'cht** (C. F. Meyer)—**Sie hatten einem Buben Vertrauen geschenkt, nun hatte dieser ihr Vertrauen mißbrau'cht** (H. Hesse)—**Es tut mir leid, die Gastfreundschaft mißbrau'cht zu haben** (Ponten)—**Der Bürgermeister war trotz seiner mißbrau'chten Uniform bei guter Laune** (W. Schäfer); and, on the other hand, **Ihr sehet, wie mein Name gemi'ßbraucht wird** (Sch.)—**Sie erzählte uns Hexengeschichten, und der Schornstein, der von den Mächten der Hölle gemi'ßbraucht wurde, flößte uns Entsetzen ein** (Hebbel)—**Man konnte nicht sagen, daß sie ihre Macht gemi'ßbraucht hätte** (Jul. Wolff)—**Der Ursprung des Bösen im Menschen besteht oft in der von anderen gemi'ßbrauchten Freiheit seines Willens** (Fr. Griese). (b) The same applies to **mißhandeln** ('to maltreat'), and **mißbilligen** ('to disapprove of'), but here the part. without **ge-** is much more usual: e.g. **Er mißha'ndelt seine Diener, scheint sie zu mißha'ndeln—Damit kann ich die mißha'ndelte Ordnung wieder heilen** (Sch.)—cf., as unusual, **Emilie wurde von einem Knaben gemi'ßhandelt** (Hebbel) and **Der gemi'ßhandelte Dichter, unfähig, seine Wut zurückzuhalten, eilte aus dem Zimmer hinaus** (W. Müller); **Frau Lotte mißbi'lligte seine Absicht** (Zifferer)—**Alle meine Schritte werden mißbi'lligt** (Sch.)—**In der Stube fand er alles in Ordnung, nur der Wandspruch wurde von ihm mißbi'lligt** (H. Hesse)—cf., as less common, **Er hatte dieses Spiel gemi'ßbilligt** (Jul. Wolff). **4.** (a) The part. with **ge-** is also allowed in **mißachten** ('to disregard, slight'), **mißarten** ('to degenerate'), **mißdeuten** ('to misinterpret') and **mißleiten** ('to mislead, lead astray'), but here again **ge-** is more usually omitted: e.g. **Ich habe mich über die Klage gewundert, daß die Poesie jetzt mißa'chtet sei** (G. Keller)—**Man hat mich mißa'chtet** (Speckmann)—**Hatte sie ihn bei seiner Ankunft mißa'chtet, so schob sie ihm jetzt das Frühstück wie einem Landstreicher hin** (W. Schäfer)—**Sein Schweigen wird mißdeu'tet** (Bismarck)—**Andere haben seine Jugend mißlei'tet** (Heyse). In some of these verbs **miß-** was formerly used as a *sep.* prefix, but examples like the following are now obs.: **Keine dergleichen Schrift dürfte mi'ßzuachten sein** (G.: now **zu mißa'chten**)—**Du wagst es, meine Bemühung, der Freundin beizustehen, mi'ßzudeuten?** (G.: for **zu mißdeu'ten**). (b) On the other hand, **ge-** inserted *after* **miß-** is practically fixed in the case of a number of verbs which are now little used except in the part. with adj. force, notably **mißbilden, mißschaffen,** and **mißstimmen:** e.g. **Ein mi'ßgebildeter** ('deformed') **Körper und eine schöne Seele sind wie Öl und Essig** (Lessing)—**Ist jemand hier, der mi'ßgeschaffene** ('misshapen') **Füße hat?** (H. v. Kleist)—**Das Klavier ist mi'ßgestimmt** ('out of tune'); fig. **Ich war sehr mi'ßgestimmt** ('very depressed, in a very bad mood'). **5.** The following verbs never have **ge-** in the part.: **mißfallen** (+ dat., 'to displease'), **mißgönnen** (+ dat. and accus., 'to begrudge'), **mißkennen** ('to misunderstand': now usually **verkennen**), **mißraten** ('to turn out badly, miscarry', with aux. **sein:** cf. 6), and the impers. verbs **mißglücken** and **mißlingen** ('to be unsuccessful, fail', with aux. **sein:** for the latter cf. 6): e.g. **Er mißfä'llt mir, hat mir immer mißfa'llen** ('I dislike, have always disliked, him')—**Sogar ihr Bild wird ihm mißgö'nnt** (Wieland); in the infin. **Sind uns die bunten Lumpen zu mißgö'nnen?** (G.: in a reference to the fancy-dress worn at Shrove-tide jollifications)—**Er glaubte, er sei als Dichter seiner Zeit voraus und müsse daher mißka'nnt werden** (Bergengruen)—**Karl ist der einzige mißra'tene Sohn in der Familie** ('Charles is the only black sheep in the family')—**Mein Plan ist mir mißglü'ckt** or **mißlu'ngen.** The same applies to **mißhören** ('not to hear rightly' what is said), but this idea is now more commonly expressed by **überhö'ren** (q.v.

2 *b*): cf. **Er kann mich kaum mißhö'rt haben** (Bismarck)—**Ich konnte die Worte mißhö'rt haben** (C. F. Meyer). **6.** The verb **mißraten** (see 5) is really a contracted form of **miß-geraten,** i.e. of the simple verb **raten** compounded with *two* prefixes (see **geraten**), just as **mißlingen** stands for **miß-gelingen,** only that the simple verb **lingen** is now quite obs. Two common verbs of this kind retain both prefixes, viz. **mißbehagen** (+ dat., 'to displease, cause discomfort'), a double compound of the obs. **hagen** ('to surround with a hedge', thus giving a feeling of security, and hence of comfort) and esp. **mißverstehen** ('to misunderstand'). Here usage is quite fixed: although always *accented,* **miß-** is *insep.*, the only exception being the *infin.* of **mißverstehen**: e.g. **Seine Nähe mi'ßbehagt ihr, hat ihr immer mi'ßbehagt, scheint ihr zu mi'ßbehagen**; so also **Der Alte mi'ßverstand den Ausdruck seines Schwiegersohnes** (Stehr)—**Wie mi'ßverstand Luther die Bibel zuerst!** (K. Lamprecht)—**Er hat das mi'ßverstanden**; but **„Es beliebt dir", versetzte er, „mich mi'ßzuverstehen"** (Hebbel)—**„Was heißt das?" fragte ich, um nicht etwa etwas Wichtiges mißzuverstehen** (K. Edschmid)—**Der Pastor empfing einen nicht mi'ßzuverstehenden Wink, seine Pfarre mit einer anderen zu vertauschen** (R. Herzog). An example like **„Wie verstehen Sie mich gründlich miß!"** (Immermann: 'How completely you misunderstand me!') is now rightly condemned in good prose; it is only in a playful way that one says **„Verstehe mich nicht miß!"** for the correct **„Mi'ßverstehe mich nicht!"**—The only other verb of this kind still in use is **mißgestalten** ('to deform'), a double compd. of the obs. **stalten,** now only used in the past part. with adj. force like **mißgebildet** and **mißgeschaffen** (see 5): e.g. **Ich wollte lieber einen mi'ßgestalteten Menschen lebendig geschaffen haben als die schönste tote Bildsäule des Praxiteles** (Lessing)—**Vor Ankunft der Königin hatte man die Anordnung gemacht, daß sich keine mi'ßgestalteten Personen, keine Krüppel auf ihrem Wege zeigen sollten** (G.).

missen: see miss 2 (*a*).

mit: **1.** This prep. requires a *dat.* case. In a proposition containing two preps. which take the same case, one can say **Ich werde ihn vor oder nach dem Konzert sprechen**; but it is rather careless to say **Sie dachte, die Dinge würden mit oder ohne den Mann ihren Lauf nehmen** (G. Keller: for **mit dem Mann oder ohne ihn**); cf. **um** 1 (*a*). Notable expressions in which we use other preps. than 'with' are: **mit der Eisenbahn** ('by train')—**mit drei Jahren** ('in one's third year')—**mit einem Male** or **mit ein(em)mal** or coll. **mit eins** ('all at once')—**mit einem Wort** ('in a word')—**mit anderen Worten** ('in other words'). **2.** (**a**) Noteworthy is the use of **mit** with many verbs where we mostly use a dir. obj. Thus, 'to throw stones at a person' is either **Steine** or **mit Steinen nach jemandem werfen**: cf. **Man kann sagen, daß Thomas Mann in einem Glashaus sitzt und eben deshalb bittet, nicht mit Steinen zu werfen** (A. Eloesser)—**Die anderen warfen nach ihm mit Schneebällen** (Kästner)—**Der Junge blieb liegen, wir warfen mit Tannenzapfen nach ihm** (Werfel); so also in the common coll. expressions **mit dem Gelde um sich werfen** ('to fling one's money about') and **mit der Wurst nach der Speckseite werfen** (lit. 'to throw the sausage to get the flitch of bacon', i.e. 'to throw a sprat to catch a whale'). Sim. **Er fuchtelte mit der Peitsche hin und her** (Gutzkow: 'He waved *or* swished his whip to and fro'); **Sie fuchtelte mit der Gabel** (Kästner: 'She waggled her fork about')—**Er schlug ein Bein über das andere und pendelte mit seinem Lorgnon** (H. W. Geissler: 'He crossed his legs and swung his monocle to and fro'). (**b**) This use of **mit** is esp. common in connexion with parts of the body, as in the following examples, in which the verbs are arranged alphabetically: **Er blinkte mit den Augen** (Gutzkow)—**Unaufhörlich blinzelte der Blinde mit den leeren Augen** (Alverdes)—**Er klapperte mit den Zähnen** (I. Seidel)—**Ein schöner Hahn klappte mit den Flügeln** (R. Waldmüller)—**Ich knirschte mit den Zähnen** (G.: 'I gnashed my teeth')—**Mein Alter nickte mit dem Kopfe** (Raabe); fig. **Die Büsche nickten mit ihren Zweigen** (Fallada)—**Er schnalzte mit der Zunge** (Brentano: 'He clicked his tongue')—**Ich schnappte mit den Fingern** (Heine), more usually **Sie schnippte vergnügt mit den Händen** (Spielhagen)—**Sie schüttelte den Kopf** or **Sie schüttelte finster mit dem Haupte** (Storm)—**mit den Füßen stampfend** (Sch., in a stage direction)—**Er schritt, mit den Händen tappend, voran** (Hackländer: 'He felt his way forwards')—**Sie tippte mit der Fußspitze auf den Boden** (Fallada: 'She tapped her toe on the floor'); **Er tippte sich mit den Fingern an die Stirn** (Alverdes: to convey the opinion that somebody is crazy); **Er tippte ihm mit dem Zeigefinger auf die Brust** (I. Seidel)—**Zuweilen trappelten** (or **trampelten**) **sie heftig mit den Füßen** (id.)—**Er trommelte mit der Hand auf die Türe** (id.)—**Die Alte wackelte mit dem Kopfe** (G.: 'The old dame wagged her head'); **Der Esel wackelte mit den Ohren—Mein Hund leckte mir die Hand und wedelte mit dem Schwanz** (Kellermann)—**Der Hund blickte ihm entgegen und wedelte mit der buschigen Rute** (W. Kramp)—**Er wedelte wild mit seinen langen Armen durch die Luft** (K. Edschmid)—**Er winkte erst mit der Hand, dann mit einem Taschentuch** (Fallada)—**Die Bachstelze** ('wagtail') **wippt mit dem Schwanz** (in the north the wagtail is often called **Wippsterz** or LG **Wippstart**: cf. our 'red*start*'); **Die Elster** ('magpie') **wippte wohlgefällig mit dem Schwanze** (Immermann)—**Der Hund zuckte mit den Ohren** (Kellermann); cf. **mit keiner Wimper zucken** ('not to bat an eyelid') and **die** (or **mit den**) **Achseln zucken** ('to shrug one's shoulders')—**Sie nickten ihm zu und zwinkerten dabei mit den Augen** (Alverdes). **3.** An idiomatic use of **mit** is to suggest that a person or thing is *one of several*, as in **Dieser Gasthof ist mit der beste in der Stadt** ('This hotel is one of the best in the town'). Here **mit** seems to have become an adv., but actually a dat. is understood: 'With (some others) this is the best in the town'; sim. **Ich konnte es nicht mehr mit ansehen** ('I couldn't bear to be an onlooker any longer')—**Er erklärte den Mädchen, sie lebten in einer Zeit, von der man in Jahrtausenden noch reden würde: das trug zu ihrem Selbstbewußtsein mit bei** (Böhlau: '. . . that helped to contribute to their sense of their own importance').

Mitgift: see **Gift**.

mitnichten: see **nichts** I.

mitten: This is an *adv.*, mostly combined with an appropriate prep. Thus, 'in the centre of the town' is **mitten in der Stadt**; and sim. **Sie stellte die Vase mitten auf den Tisch—Ein Fußweg läuft mitten durch den Garten—Ich stand mitten unter der Menschenmenge.** On the other hand, **inmitten** is a *prep.*, taking a gen. or (much less commonly) a dat.: **Inmitten des Gedränges überkam mich eine Ohnmacht—Die Tage und Nächte des Vaters sind nichts als Werk: er bleibt inmitten der Seinen** ('in the midst of his family') **ein Einsiedler und Junggeselle** (O. E. Hesse); but where the gen. would not be recognizable as such, **inmitten von** should be used, as in **inmitten von Gewittern** (Freytag). It is only in southern dialects that **mitten** is used as a prep., and an example like **Sie stellte das Geschirr mitten des Tisches** (W. v. Scholz) should not be imitated in good prose.

mittewegs: see **halbwegs**.

mix(ture): **1.** There are two verbs which should properly be distinguished: while **mengen** (cf. 'mingle'—and 'among' < MLG *mang*, still in common use in NLG **mank**) is properly used of mixing things which are still separate in the mixture, as when flour and currants are mixed, **mischen** really implies that the ingredients, when mixed, are indistinguishable, as in the case of whisky and water. But **mischen** has a much wider application than **mengen**, being quite fixed in expressions like **Farben mischen** ('to mix paints'), **Karten mischen** ('to shuffle cards'), **gemischte Metalle** ('alloys'), **gemischte Ehen** ('mixed marriages'), **eine gemischte Gesellschaft, gemischte Gefühle**, etc. Either verb may be used reflex. (with **in** or **unter** + *accus.*) to convey the sense of 'mixing' in a crowd, etc., or 'meddling' with, 'interfering' in something: e.g. **Ich menge** or **mische mich ungern in die Angelegenheiten anderer Leute.** **2.** (**a**) **Mischung** suggests either the verbal force of mixing things, or the resultant mixture in a general way: **Aus der Mischung von Grün und Gelb entsteht Blau—Das Geheimnis der Mischung** (Ganghofer: referring to the secret of a certain alloy). (**b**) **Gemisch** is only used of a completed mixture, as in **Meine Schwester war das sonderbarste Gemisch von Strenge und Weichheit, von Eigensinn und Nachgiebigkeit** (G.); but it is apt to take on a depreciatory meaning, as when Wieland refers to a certain fricassee as **ein ekelhaftes Gemisch**, or Goethe to a medley of sounds as **ein barbarisches Tongemisch** (cf. **der Mischmasch**, 'hotchpotch'). (**c**) **Mixtu'r** (fem.) is the recognized expression for a *medicinal* mixture.

Möbel: This is the Fr. word *meuble*, introduced into German about the middle of the 18th century, and at first written **Meubel.** It soon became completely Germanized as **Möbel** (neut.), which exists side by side with the native expression **Hausrat** (masc.) or (esp. collect.) **Hausgerät** (neut.). There was at first considerable fluctuation, as often with foreign loan-words: Lessing uses it as *fem.*, which explains the plur. form **Möbeln,** as in **Ein Hagelwetter schlug die Spiegelscheiben der Hinterseite des Hauses zusammen, beschädigte die neuen Möbeln und verderbte** (see **verderben** 2) **einige schätzbare Bücher** (G.)—**Die Magd räumt auf und verändert nach Gutdünken die Stellung der Möbeln** (Heine: '. . . shifts the furniture as she thinks fit'); but we also find **Ein großes Portrait der Großmutter kann zu den Möbels ihrer Enkelin unmöglich mehr passen** (G.). Both of these plur. forms are now obs.: the established form is **Möbel.** The sing., then, means a 'piece of furniture' (*Sanders* defines it as **ein Stück des Hausgeräts in den Zimmern**), and indeed the neut. **Möbelstück** is now almost more commonly used than the sing. **Möbel.**

modal auxiliary verbs: This is the name given by grammarians to the verbs **dürfen, können, mögen, müssen, sollen,** and **wollen** (qq.v.). Being **past-present verbs** (q.v.), they now, with the exception of **sollen,** have different stem-vowels in the sing. and the plur. of the pres. tense: **ich darf, wir dürfen—ich kann, wir können—ich mag, wir mögen—ich muß, wir müssen—ich soll, wir sollen—ich will, wir wollen.** But the chief difficulty which these verbs present is that they have two past part. forms, viz. weak forms (**gedurft, gekonnt, gemocht, gemußt, gesollt, gewollt**) and forms which are identical with the infin. The former are used as independent past parts., the latter in compd. tenses with a dependent infin.: cf. **Das habe ich nicht gedurft** with **Das habe ich nicht tun dürfen.** But what makes these verbs specially troublesome is that analogous expressions often have different shades of meaning: thus, 'He would have been able to do it' (**Er hätte es tun können**) is obviously different from 'He might have done it' (**Er könnte es getan haben**); and 'He has had to do it' (**Er hat es tun müssen**) is quite different from 'He must have done it' (**Er muß es getan haben**). These difficulties, and other uses of these modal auxiliaries, are explained under the verbs themselves. For the position of the aux. **haben** in compd. tenses used in subord. clauses, and for the result of omitting the aux. in such clauses, see **verbs (auxiliary)** 2 and 3, and **accusative and infinitive** 4; see also **passive voice** 2 (*b*) (iii).

modified vowels: see **Umlaut.**

Moment: Distinguish between **der Moment** (= **Augenblick,** 'moment' of time) and **das Moment** ('momentum, motive, impulse'), with the accent in either case on the *last* syllable: cf., on the one hand, **Der günstige Moment war vorüber** (Sch.)—**Warten Sie einen Moment!** and, on the other hand, **In diesen Worten liegt das erregende Moment des Dramas** ('These words set the play in motion, are the starting-point of the plot'). It is not used to express a phrase like 'something of little moment', which is **etwas von geringer Wichtigkeit.**

mögen: 1. The MHG verb *mugen* or *mügen* implied physical ability, the bodily strength enabling one to do something (cf. **Macht** and Fr. *pouvoir*), while *kunnen* or *künnen* implied mental ability, esp. the knowledge how to do something (cf. **kennen** and Fr. *savoir*): e.g., on the one hand, *er mohte ez niht getragen* ('He could not carry it', and, on the other hand, *er konde videlen* ('He could play the fiddle'). This distinction is no longer observed: **können** is used in both senses, but the orig. force of **mögen**—see **modal auxiliary verbs** and **past-present verbs** 1—is still sometimes dimly seen in the compd. **vermögen** (q.v.), while that of **können** may be idiomatically expressed by **sich auf etwas verstehen** (q.v. *b*). **2.** In course of time **mögen** developed various uses, viz. (**a**) It may suggest a possibility or probability: e.g. **Ich habe ihn lange nicht gesehen: er mag verreist sein** (= **er ist vielleicht verreist**)—**Als ich nach Hause kam, mochte es Mitternacht sein;** in the subj., **Ziehen Sie den Überzieher an, Sie möchten sich sonst erkälten** ('otherwise you might catch cold'): see (*b*) *ad fin.* (**b**) It may suggest an inclination, liking, fondness for something, now its commonest use (see **like** 1 *b*, and cf. **leiden** 2 *ad fin.*): e.g. **Kaffee mag ich nicht** (*scil.* **trinken**), **ich ziehe Tee vor** ('I don't like coffee, I prefer tea')—**Ich mag den Kerl nicht leiden** ('I dislike the fellow')—**Bei schlechtem Wetter mag ich nicht ausgehen;** the past subj. has pres. force, as in **Möchten Sie**

gern spazierengehen? ('Would you care to go for a walk?')—**Ich möchte nicht, daß er schlecht von mir denke** ('I should not like him to think ill of me'); in a compd. tense, **An deiner Stelle hätte ich nicht gehen mögen** ('If I had been you I should not have cared to go'), but with the dependent infin. omitted, **„Warum sind Sie nicht mitgegangen?" „Ich habe nicht gemocht".** Confusion between the idea of possibility and that of fondness may arise, as in **Man sagte mir, daß er es getan haben möchte,** which may mean either 'I was told that he might have done it' or 'I was told that he would have liked to do it'; where such ambiguity is possible, it is advisable to express the former proposition by **Man sagte mir, daß er es vielleicht getan hätte.** (**c**) It may have concessive force: e.g. **Ich mag tun, was ich will,** or **Was ich auch tun mag, es ist niemandem recht** ('Do what I may *or* No matter what I do, no one is satisfied') —**Ich mag mich irren** ('I grant you I may be wrong'). (**d**) It may express a wish or a hope, esp. in the subj.: e.g. **Möge Ihnen der Versuch gelingen!** ('May you succeed in the attempt!')—**Möchte mir gestattet sein, meine Meinung zu äußern** ('I hope I may be permitted to state my view'); so also **Möchte er doch Vernunft annehmen!** ('I wish he were sensible! If he would only listen to reason!')—**Sie schimpfen auf mich? Mögen sie schimpfen!** ('They are running me down? Let them!' i.e. I wish them to be allowed to go on, I couldn't care less!).

Monat: We now distinguish between **Mo'nat** ('month': cf. **nouns of measure** 1 *b*) and **Mond** ('moon'), but they are really two forms of the same word (< MHG *mande* or *mânt*). In the sense of 'month', **Mond** was quite common at one time (as was our 'moon', cf. Shakespeare's 'twice six moons' and Scots *towmond*, 'twelvemonth'), esp. in old names of some months, such as **Brachmond** (June), **Heumond** (July), **Nebelmond** (November) and **Julmond** (December); and the plur. is still used in elevated style: **Einige Monde waren vergangen, seitdem er den Thron bestiegen hatte** (Sudermann)—**Nach mehreren Monden trat der erste große Schmerz in mein Leben** (L. Schücking)—**Goethe wartete geduldig Monde lang, bis die Musen sich zu ihm herabließen** (W. Bode)—**Sie war keine Hausfrau, aber welcher Ehemann merkt das in den Honigmonden?** (R. Herzog: = **in den Flitterwochen,** 'on his *honeymoon*'). Both **Monat** and **Mond** are now strong, but some MHG forms were weak (in Num. 3. 15 Luther wrote **eins Monden alt**: cf. **genitive** 4), and this explains poet. compds. like **Mond(en)nacht, Mond(en)schein,** etc. For the difference between **-monatig** and **monatlich,** see **-ig.**

Monatsnamen: 1. One can say **Vor Mai** or **März** (q.v.) **wird er nicht kommen** or **Ich werde erst nach Juli zurückkehren**; but the prep. **in** requires the insertion of the art.: **Das Kind wird im** (not **in**) **Oktober drei Jahre alt sein. 2.** In the gen. sing., the names of the months (see **Monat**) may be inflected, but are now more usually left uninflected: cf. **Es war um die Zeit des Oktobers** (Frenssen) and **Schon jetzt, um die Mitte des Oktober, war das Laub vergilbt** (Th. Mann). Where the art. is not expressed, the *gen.* form is now generally avoided in prose: in ordinary lang. it is left uninflected, esp. in expressions like **am** 3. (i.e. **dritten** [*scil.* **Tag des**]) **April—Anfang Juli** ('at the beginning of July')—**Ende Mai. 3.** Where such names are used in the plur. (cf. 'my first two Januaries in Germany'), the reg. ending **-e** is used in the first five months of the year, and **-s** in the next two, while the others remain uninflected: hence, **Meine ersten zwei Februare in Deutschland waren sehr kalt—Die zwei letzten Julis waren naß—Die vergangenen drei Oktober habe ich in der Schweiz verlebt.**

Mond: see **Monat** 1.

move: There are three verbs which approach each other closely. **1.** The one in commonest use and with the widest application is **bewegen** (cf. **wiegen**): (**a**) Used *lit.* in the sense of 'to shift' something, or *fig.* in that of 'to touch, move' (to tears), **bewegen** now always has *weak* forms: e.g. **„Was fehlt Ihnen?" „Ich kann den rechten Arm nicht bewegen"—So schwer die Kiste war, er bewegte sie leicht von der Stelle—Die See ist heute sehr bewegt** ('rough')—**Dieses Klavierstück sollte bewegter gespielt werden** ('more quickly, *più moto*')—**Ihr Gesang hat mich tief** (or **zu Tränen**) **bewegt.** To express our *intrans.* use of 'to move', the *reflex.* is required in German: **Der Festzug bewegte sich langsam durch die Stadt.** (**b**) With the strong forms **bewog, bewogen,** it now only means 'to induce, prevail upon' (cf. **vermögen** 2): e.g. **Was**

bewog ihn wohl zur Abreise? ('I wonder what induced him to set off on a journey')—**Er hat mich (dazu) bewogen, ihn zu begleiten.** Formerly, weak forms were sometimes used in this sense, but this is contrary to modern usage: cf. **Weil er schlecht mit Kleidern versehen war, bewegte** (now **bewog**) **er meine Schwestern, daß sie ihm ein neues Kleid gaben** (G.). **2.** Much like **bewegen** with *lit.* force is **regen,** which properly points to the *beginning* of a movement: e.g. **Der Vogel begann die Flügel zu regen—Der Verwundete konnte kein Glied regen;** and here also our *intrans.* use requires a *reflex.* pron.: **Die Hähne krähn, schon regt sich's im Palast** (Sch.: 'the palace is already astir')—**Die Liebe regte sich in ihr** ('Love stirred in her breast'). **3.** MHG *rüeren* is simply 'to set in motion' (*ein wint ruorte ir schif,* 'A wind caused their vessel to get under way'), but **rühren** now implies *freedom* of movement, as in the military word of command **Rührt euch!** ('Stand easy!'); sim. **Rühre dich nicht von der Stelle!** ('Don't move away! Stay where you are!' while **Rege dich nicht!** is 'Don't budge!')—**Der Gefangene war an Händen und Füßen gebunden und konnte sich infolgedessen nicht rühren—Ich bat ihn um Hilfe, aber er rührte keinen Finger.**

müde: 1. Just as we distinguish between the *lit.* and the *fig.* uses of the word 'tired' (cf. 'I am tired after my long walk' and 'I am tired of his complaints'), so the Germans make the same distinction in the use of **müde:** cf. **Wer von der Arbeit müde ist, den hat sie müde gemacht; wer ihrer müde ist, der mag sie nicht fortsetzen** (Sanders); so also, on the one hand, **Ich bin von dem vielen Reden müde** (Gellert), and, on the other hand, **Ach, wie bin ich der Dichter müde!** (Nietzsche). The gen. in the fig. use is still very common in good prose: e.g. **Ich bin des Treibens müde** (G.)—**Es war eine lange Fahrt: wenn die Chausseen meiner so müde sind als ich ihrer, so werden sie sich freuen, daß wir auseinanderkommen** (Droste-Hülshoff)—**Sie erklärten, Frankreich sei des Joches von Napoleon müde** (Ranke)—**Er war des Alleinseins müde** (H. Hesse). But in an expression like **Ich bin es müde,** the old gen. **es** (q.v. 1) came to be regarded as an accus., and this is the case now used in ordinary lang., as in **„Seid Ihr mich schon müde?" „Euch nicht sowohl als Euern Umgang"** (G.: 'Are you tired of me already?' 'Not so much of you as of your company'). **2.** An analogous expression used with the gen. or the accus. is **überdrüssig** ('tired *or* weary of, bored with'—see also **verdrießen** and esp. **satt**): e.g. **Diese Unglückliche ist des Lasters überdrüssig** (Sch.)—**Ich bin meiner Weisheit überdrüssig** (Nietzsche)—**Er war der Lehrer, der Mitschüler, ja des Schulhauses gründlich überdrüssig** (W. v. Scholz)—**Sie hatte so viel nachgedacht, daß sie des logischen Denkens überdrüssig war** (L. Winder). As, according to modern usage, a word like **alles** can no longer be used alone as a *gen.* (see **all** 7), it came to be treated as an *accus.* in a proposition like **Ich bin alles überdrüssig** (Lessing), and this explains the ordinary expression **Ich bin das** (for the more choice **dessen**) **überdrüssig;** but Lessing may have used **alles** above as an accus., for he also says **Die letzte Hälfte des Werkes bin ich bald überdrüssig geworden.**

Muff: Apart from some technical uses (e.g. 'socket-joint', usually **die Muffe**), this noun is used in the north much like **Schimmel** in the sense of 'mould, mildew', and the adj. **muffig** has spread to other parts: cf. **Hier riecht es muffig** or **ist eine muffige Luft** ('There is a musty smell here') and **Sie stiegen treppab und traten in die muffig schwüle** ('muggy') **Straße hinaus** (Fontane). But the commonest meaning is 'muff' (for warming hands), in which sense there is much fluctuation: Duden gives both **der Muff** (plur. **Muffe**) and **die Muff** or **Muffe** (plur. **Muffen**), whereas Sprach-Brockhaus gives only what is certainly the commonest form, viz. **der Muff** (plur. **Müffe**), and characterizes the fem. as **„veraltet".** All the same, Th. Mann's use of the masc. in **Der Muff hing an einer goldenen Kette** is rather unusual: he much more commonly uses the fem., as in **Sie drückte die braune Muff gegen ihre Wangen—Dort saßen, die Hände in halb enthaarten Pelzmüffen, beleibte Weiber;** cf. also the example from the same author given near the end of the article on **stecken.**

Mund: 1. (a) With the force of 'mouth', **der Mund** is applied to human beings (in references to animals one uses **das Maul**), as well as to a limited number of objects such as a cannon or a mine; on the other hand, the 'mouth' of a river is **die**

Mündung (cf. **münden**). The plur. is comparatively little used, most idioms preferring the sing.: e.g. **Wenn Erwachsene sprechen, müssen kleine Kinder den Mund halten—Die Leute standen mit offenem Munde da—Wir versprachen alle, reinen Mund zu halten** ('We all promised to keep the secret'). It is the more surprising that as many as three plur. forms are recognized: to **Munde** and (rather more commonly) **Münde** modern usage has added **Münder,** as in **Er behauptete, die Sänger hätten kaum die Münder geöffnet** (Th. Mann). (**b**) One might be tempted to think that the masc. noun **Leumund** (no plur., 'reputation') was derived from the idiom **in aller Leute Mund sein** ('to be the talk of the town'), but this would be incorrect. The word is not **Leu-mund,** but **Leum-und,** in which the suffix is another form of that seen in **Jugend** (for **Jung-end**) and **Tugend** (from **taugen**), while the first part of the word is connected with **verleum-den** ('to calumniate, slander'). **2.** In old German there was also a fem. noun *munt,* meaning 'hand' (cf. Lat. *manus*), then 'protection' or 'power, authority': according to Grimm's 'Deutsche Rechtsaltertümer', *munt* was the legal term for the *potestas* exercised by the male over the female—cf. 'All Germanic immigrants seem to have recognized a corporate union of the family under the *mund,* or authority of a patriarchal chief' (Maine, *Ancient Law*: 1861). These ideas are still seen in the word **Vormund** (q.v.). In the old sense of 'hand', **Mund** is now quite obs., unless it is preserved in the proverb **Morgenstunde hat Gold im Munde** (cf. 'Early to bed and early to rise makes a man healthy, wealthy and wise' and 'The early bird catches the worm'), which W. Borchardt, however, prefers to regard as a poetical personification of the golden rays of the sun, a contention which he supports by citing similar ideas occurring in other countries, e.g. in Norway, where gold coins fall from the sun's mouth when he speaks.

münden: This verb and its compounds are properly used of a tributary flowing into a river, a river flowing into the sea (the 'mouth' of a river is **Mündung**), a path striking a highroad, etc., and hence their normal construction is **in** + *accus.*: e.g. **Die Saale mündet in die Elbe, die Elbe in die Nordsee—Sie suchte die Stelle, wo der Steig in die Landstraße eingemündet hatte** (E. Wichert); sim., in a comparison between Lenau's early nature poetry and his later works, **Emilie hing mehr an dem ursprünglichen, gebirgshellen Quell seiner Poesien als an dem Strom, in den soviele fremde Bäche eingemündet hatten** (R. v. Gottschall)—**Lachen drang durch mehrere Türen, die auf den Korridor mündeten** (Th. Mann)—**Der Weg mündete rechts und links in Seitenpfade aus** (Immermann: 'The road divided into footpaths to right and left'); cf., in a wider application, **An der Wand war ein Kessel angebracht, in den eine Dampfleitung mündete** (H. Hauser: '. . . a boiler into which a steampipe led'). Although the *accus.* is the normal case in the prep. phrase, a *dat.* is not infrequently found, the idea in the author's mind being the end or culminating point of the action suggested by the verb: e.g. **Ihr Pfad schien im Himmel zu münden** (E. Kästner: 'Her path seemed to end in heaven')—**Der Garten kam bis an den im Hof mündenden Fahrweg heran** (I. Seidel: 'The garden extended as far as the drive which ended in the courtyard'). The dat. is esp. common where the verb is used with fig. force: e.g. **Der erlösende Übermut mündete in einem beglückenden Spaß** (A. Zweig: 'The tension was relieved by merriment which culminated in cheerful hilarity')—**Er traf Maßnahmen, als müßte die Folge der Ereignisse notwendig in einem peinlichen Glaubensprozeß ausmünden** (Stehr: '. . . as though the events must inevitably culminate in a painful religious controversy'); cf., in a reference to Frederick the Great, **Seine Gedanken mündeten da, wo sie jetzt immer zu münden pflegten, bei dem Werk, dessen Vollendung er nun nicht mehr erlebte, der Justizreform** (Bruno Frank: i.e. his thoughts always reverted to, concentrated on, the great work which he would now not live to see finished, the reform of the judicature).

Muselmann: This corrupt form of *Moslem* has established itself in German side by side with the weak form **Muselman;** the plur. is **Muselmänner** in the north, while the alternative weak **Muselmanen** is allowed in the south.

Muße, müßig: see **idle.**

müssen: 1. Like the other **modal auxiliary verbs** (q.v.), so **müssen** also belongs to the class of **past-present verbs** (q.v.). The verb **sollen** (q.v.) really implies that something may or may not be the case, may or may not happen. The proposition **Man sagt, daß der Verurteilte sterben soll** ('that the condemned man is to die') implies a possibility that he may be reprieved, so that his execution need not necessarily take place. So also **Er soll reich sein** ('He is said to be rich'), but this is only a rumour, and the rumour may be false—**Kinder sollten gehorsam sein** ('Children should be obedient'), but they often are not. The verb **müssen,** on the other hand, properly implies no such possibility one way or the other, but suggests that something cannot but be the case or happen—even if the condemned man were to be reprieved, he *must* die some time; sim. **Die Ärzte haben alle Hoffnung aufgegeben: er muß sehr krank sein** ('he must be very ill'), that is the only possible conclusion one can draw. But the two ideas may approach each other, esp. in the subj.: one can say **Eigentlich sollte** or **müßte ich nach Hause gehen** ('I really should *or* ought to be going home'), where **sollte** implies that the urge comes from without (those at home are expecting me), and **müßte** that the urge comes from within (my conscience or sense of duty tells me to go): (see **sollen** 1). So also **Als er das sagte, mußte ich lachen** ('I could not help laughing'), I could not resist the urge to laugh —**Ach, natürlich, ich mußte gerade verreist sein, als er vorsprach** ('Oh, of course, he *had* to call just when I was out of town'), fate decreed that I should be away. **2.** Distinguish between **Er muß es getan haben** ('He must have done it': no one else can have done it) and **Er hat es tun müssen** ('He has had to, has been obliged *or* forced to, do it'); in the latter case, the reg. past part. **gemußt** replaces the infin. form **müssen** when the dependent infin. **tun** is understood: **„Warum hat er das getan?" „Er hat gemußt."**—For the idiomatic use of the past subj. to express a neg. cond. clause introduced by 'unless', see **denn (adverb)** 3.

Mut: Although **Mut** is *masc.*, some of its compds. are *fem.* The reason for this is that whereas the masc. ones were true compds. of the OHG noun *muot*, the fem. ones were abstract nouns derived from adjs. ending in *-muoti*; in MHG this became *-müete*, then, through confusion, *-muote*, and finally dropped the final *-e*, so that both groups now end in **-mut.** In general, words denoting the milder, less aggressive qualities are *fem.*, viz. **An-, De-, Groß-, Lang-, Sanft-, Schwer-, Wehmut**; the others, denoting more manly qualities—or their opposites—are *masc.*, viz. **Edel-, Hoch-, Klein-, Gleich-, Über-, Un-, Wankelmut.** Incidentally, the fem. **Armut** has no connexion with **Mut:** it is actually not **Ar-mut,** but **Arm-ut,** the ending being another form of that in **Heim-at** (see also **Wermut**).—For **Sei gutes** (or **guten**) **Mutes,** see **adjectives (attributive)** 3 (*b*); for **zumute,** see **anmuten.**

mutation of vowels: see **Umlaut.**

N

na: see **nun** 3.

nach: 1. This prep. is really the same word as the adj. **nah(e):** in MHG the word for 'near' was *nâch*, which dropped the *c* before inflexional endings (*nâher*, etc.). So the word orig. implied a state of rest 'in the proximity of' a person or thing (see **Nachbar**); but when **nach** became a prep., the idea of rest gave way to that of motion 'towards the proximity of' something. The use of **nach** with the force of 'for' with verbs like **fragen, verlangen, sich sehnen,** etc., can then be explained as a mental operation directed towards a specific goal. The temporal force of **nach** ('after') probably developed out of the idea of 'in the proximity *behind*' something, which then led to that of 'following after' it. Its other common use in the sense of 'according to', as in **meiner Meinung nach,** may orig. have implied an approximate rather than a categorical expression of opinion, or have suggested an opinion which one 'follows', by which one is guided (**nach welcher man sich richtet**). **2.** It follows that the preps. **nach** and **zu,** suggesting motion towards something, approach each other closely. In many cases, indeed, either prep. can be used: one can say **Er lief nach dem** or

zum Bahnhof — Ich ging nach der or **zur Kirche — Der Weg nach dem** or **zum Dorfe geht steil bergan,** etc. In the north there was until recent times a definite preference for **nach** here (e.g. in Storm, Frenssen, etc.); but more modern authors seem to lean more to the southern use of **zu. 3.** And it is important to note that **zu** (not **nach**) is used in the following relations: **(a)** to suggest a state of *rest* in expressions like **Er studiert auf der Universität zu Bonn** and **Ich wurde zu** (or **in**) **Berlin geboren** (but **nach Bonn reisen, nach rechts gehen, nach Norden blicken**), and esp. in names of inns or hotels, as in **der Gasthof zum Adler** or **zur Post;** also in every-day expressions like **zu Bett liegen, zu Tisch sitzen** (for a meal), **zu Hause sein** or **bleiben,** as distinct from **nach Hause gehen** (but cf. the first example under *c* below); **(b)** to suggest a state of **motion** towards a **person**: e.g. **Das Kind lief zur Mutter—Wir gehen heute abend zu Onkel Fritz** or **zu Schmidts** (see **Proper names** 2 *c*)—**Er kam zu mir hergelaufen—Er hatte mich aufgefordert, zu ihm nach Halle zu kommen** (Th. Mann); cf. **Die vom Plattdeutschen** (i.e. LG) **herstammende Vorliebe des Norddeutschen für „nach" als Richtungspräposition ging früher so weit, daß man von Ungebildeten hören konnte: „Ich gehe nach Großmutter", und es kam vor, daß Kinder erst in der Schule lernen mußten, daß sie bei Personen „zu" sagen müßten** (M. Tamsen); **(c)** in specific cases to suggest *motion* towards a *goal*, esp. in numerous idioms: e.g. *lit.*, **Der Bettler ging von Haus zu Haus—Das Konzert ging zu Ende—Die Haare standen mir zu Berge** ('My hair stood on end')—**Er kroch zu Kreuze** ('He repented', esp. 'He humbled himself, ate humble pie'); *fig.*, suggesting a purpose, **Sie ist zur Erholung verreist** ('She has gone away to recuperate')—**Er tat es mir zuliebe** ('He did it to please me')—**Kommen Sie zur Sache!** ('Come to the point!')—**Ich zog ihn zur Rechenschaft** ('I called him to account')—**Man hat ihn zum Abgeordneten gewählt** ('He has been elected an M.P.')—**Der Einbrecher schlug ihn zum Krüppel** ('The burglar made a cripple of him, broke every bone in his body'); **(d)** to indicate the place *through* which the motion proceeds: e.g. **Er warf den Ball zum Fenster hinaus** ('He flung the ball out through the window')—**Er kam zum Fenster hereingeklettert** ('He came climbing in by the window'); the use of an accus. here instead of **zu** + dat., on the analogy of **die Straße entlang, den Berg hinauf,** etc., seems to be peculiarly Austrian: cf. **Er taumelte die** (for **zur**) **Türe hinaus** (St. Zweig).

nachäffen: see **nachahmen** 2.

nachahmen: 1. This is one of several verbs compounded with **nach-** which have the force of 'to imitate', but which differ somewhat in sense according as the obj. stands in the accus. or the dat. As Sanders says, **Wer mich nachahmt, dem bin ich nur ein Gegenstand, den er kopiert; wer mir nachahmt, dem bin ich eine Persönlichkeit, nach der als Muster er sich bildet:** in other words, an accus. suggests the idea of copying, while a dat. implies an endeavour to emulate, a difference neatly brought out in the proposition **Sie müssen nicht das Werk, sondern dem Meister nachzuahmen suchen** (Lichtenberg). Other characteristic examples are: with the *accus.*, **Christian ahmte mit Geschick die Lehrer nach** (Th. Mann)—**Diesen jungen Leuten fiel es leicht, die Manieren von Männern nachzuahmen** (H. Hesse)—**Sie ahmte das Quaken der Kröte nach** (Zuckmayer); with the *dat.*, **Ich ahme berühmten Männern nach** (Hagedorn)—**Die Stadt Meißen ahmte größeren Städten nach** (H. Hesse); in **Als Kind wagte ich, den Terenz nachzuahmen** (G.), the accus. is no doubt used deliberately to suggest mere copying, not emulation. A *dat.* of the person is fixed, however, where there is also an impers. dir. *accus.* obj., as in **Er ahmt mir alles nach,** which might take the form **Er ahmt mich in allem nach;** cf. the example from A. Eloesser given under 2 below. Incidentally, the idea of taking something as one's model and striving to emulate it is always conveyed by **nacheifern,** which therefore takes a dat.: e.g. **Eifere deinen Vorfahren nach!** (Ompteda). **2.** Used like **nachahmen** + accus. are the two verbs **nachmachen** and **nachäffen,** the latter always in a depreciatory sense (= **wie ein Affe nachahmen,** 'to ape, mimic'): e.g. **Sie üben sich, alle Vögel mit Pfeifen nachzumachen** (G.)—**Ich ergötzte die Meinigen damit, daß ich mit Hilfe zweier Stöcke das Gebaren des Violinisten nachzumachen suchte** (Th. Mann)—**Die Kinder machten Tierstimmen nach** (Zuckmayer)—**Die Bürger Lübecks haben Thomas Mann zur Rede gestellt: was hatte**

er ihnen (*scil.* die Art und Weise) **nachzumachen, wie sie essen und trinken, wie sie handeln und wandeln** (A. Eloesser: '. . . what right had he to [let the characters in his 'Buddenbrooks'] copy the table manners and behaviour of the inhabitants of Lübeck'); **Sie ärgern sich, weil sie sich nachgeäfft fühlen** (Rilke)—**Die Vesperglocke klang vom Turm, und eine Kuckucksuhr in der Stube äffte sie nach** (H. Leip). **3.** The verb **nachbilden** is only used with an impers. accus. obj. with the force of 'to copy, reproduce' something, as when a potter makes a vase after a certain model or pattern: **Die griechische Vase hat der Töpfer geschickt nachgebildet;** but it can, of course, be used in a bad sense, as of a forger who 'counterfeits' coins, etc., as in **Ein Falschmünzer bildet echte Münzen nach;** cf. the example from Th. Mann given under **genitive of material** 2 (*a*).

Nachbar: As explained under **nach** 1, the first part of this noun is really the adj. **nah** (< MHG *nâch*), while the second part is a corrupt form of MHG *bûr* (= **Bauer**, 'peasant'), so that one's *nâchbûr* or *nâchgebûr* was a peasant whose croft was near to or bordered on one's own. The modern word is therefore inflected like **Bauer** (q.v.): gen. sing. **Nachbars** or **Nachbarn**, plur. **Nachbarn.**

nachbilden: see **nachahmen** 3.

nachdem: 1. Like **ehe, bevor, seitdem,** etc. (qq.v.), the temporal conj. **nachdem** cannot be followed by an infin. with **zu,** but requires a finite verb: a proposition like 'After visiting me he went straight home' can only take the form **Nachdem er mich besucht hatte, ging er geradewegs nach Hause.** In the narrative style its regular construction is the *pluperf.*, as in the example just given; sim. **Nachdem er fortgegangen war** (not **fortging**), **schrieb ich einen Brief.** With a perf. tense it has *future-perf.* force, but here **wenn** is to be preferred: e.g. **Nachdem** (better **Wenn**) **ich den Brief geschrieben habe** (= **haben werde**), **hoffe ich, spazierenzugehen. 2.** As an adv., **nachdem** is sometimes used in the sense of 'thereupon, thereafter', but here **darauf** or **danach** is much more usual: cf. **Nachdem kam eine kräftige Suppe auf den Tisch** (Gutzkow)—**Er schickte einen seiner Diener zum Pfarrer; nachdem verließ er das Haus** (I. Kurz). Quite established, however, is the expression **je nachdem,** which has come to be used as a subord. conj.: e.g. **Ich werde offen oder zurückhaltend gegen ihn sein, je nachdem er sich benimmt** ('I shall be frank or reserved with him, according to the way in which he behaves')—**„Habt Ihr im Sinn, über die Religion zu spotten, oder vor ihr zu zittern?" „Spotten oder zittern, je nachdem** ('according as') **du mir antwortest"** (Sch.); so also, used elliptically, **„Wie wollen Sie es anfangen?" „Je nachdem"** ('How are you going to set about it?' 'That depends').

nacheifern: see **nachahmen** 1.

nachgerade: see **gerade** 2 (*b*).

nachhängen: Of all the compds. of **hängen,** this one presents least difficulty: apart from the mutated stem-vowel in all *pres.* tense forms (see **hängen** 2 *a*), it is now quite reg., always *strong* (**hing nach, nachgehangen**), always *intrans.* (+ dat.), and only used *fig.* with the force of 'to give oneself up to' (meditation), 'give free play to' (thoughts, fancies), 'indulge in' (day-dreams), etc.: e.g. **Er hing seinen glücklichen Träumen nach** (G.)—**Ich pries mich glücklich, meiner Neigung nachgehangen zu haben** (G.)—**Er nahm sich, während er bis dahin allerhand unklaren Gedanken nachgehangen hatte, fester ins Verhör** (Fontane). Actually, the basic idea is 'to pursue, follow': the MHG verb *hengen* (the factitive of *hâhen*, hence meaning 'to cause to *or* let hang' = **hängenlassen**) was esp. used in the idiom *einem rosse* (or *hunde*) *hengen*, where the accus. obj. *daz seil* is understood, so that the meaning is 'to let a horse's rein (a dog's lead) hang loose' so that he may press forward, an idea which is now expressed by **verhängen** (q.v. 2), and which is still seen in **einem Hirsch nachhängen,** used by hunters with the force of 'to press after a stag' by not holding the dog in. As *hengen* was a weak verb, *weak* forms of **nachhängen** would really be historically correct, but they have now been entirely superseded by *strong* forms, so that occasional examples like the following should not be imitated: **Er hängte** (for **hing**) **seinen schwermütigen Schwärmereien nach** (Sch.)—**Ich habe oft stundenlang allerlei Phantasien nachgehängt** (Lichtenberg: for **nachgehangen**).

nachher: see **vorher, vorhin** 1 (*b*).

nachlassen: see **fail** 3.

nachlässig: see **idle** 2.

nachmachen: see **nachahmen** 2.

nachreden: see **afterreden.**

nachsehen: 1. In the sense of 'to follow (a departing person) with one's eyes', this verb takes a *dat.*, as in the well-known song **Nun leb' wohl, du kleine Gasse,/nun ade, du stilles Dach!/Vater, Mutter sahn mir traurig/und die Liebste sah mir nach** (v. Schlippenbach: 1833); and hence the expression **das Nachsehen haben** (= **leer ausgehen,** 'to get nothing, come away empty-handed'), the idea being that one looks after a person who goes off with something. Also with a *dat.* of the person, but with an *accus.* of the thing added, it means 'to overlook, excuse, condone', as in **Wir haben ihm diese kleine Schwäche nachgesehen** ('We have excused this little weakness of his')—**Sieh doch einem Alten etwas nach!** (Lessing: = **Hab' doch Nachsicht mit einem Alten!** 'Be a little lenient with an old man!'). **2.** In the abs. use with a following subord. clause, it means 'to investigate', as in **Ich will nachsehen, ob er kommt** ('I'll go and see whether he is coming')—**Sieh mal nach, wo die Kinder sind!** And this led to its common modern use with an accus. of the thing in the sense of 'to examine, inspect': e.g. **Er hatte die Bremsen nachgesehen** (W. Schäfer: 'He had tested *or* seen to the brakes')—**Ich gehe oft in den Wald die Kaninchenschlingen nachsehen** (H. Hauser: 'I often go into the wood to inspect the rabbit-snares')—**Die Patronen wurden zur Hand gestellt und die Gewehre gründlich nachgesehen** (Fr. v. Bülow: 'The cartridges were placed within reach and the rifles thoroughly examined').

nachsprechen: see **repeat.**

nächst, nächstens: see **nahe** 3 (*a*) and (*b*) respectively.

Nacht: The OHG noun *naht* did not orig. mutate the stem-vowel in the plur., and the dat. plur. *nahtun* is preserved in **Weihnachten** (q.v.). But later the noun became merged in the '*i*-declension', the result being the modern plur. **Nächte.** Incidentally, the gen. sing. *nahti* is still extant in **Nachtigall** (< *nahti-gala*, 'singer of the night', from *galan*, 'to sing'). Our adv. phrase 'at night' is **nachts** or **des Nachts,** formed on the analogy of **tags, abends;** and sim. 'one night' is **eines Nachts,** never **einer Nacht.** Where we say 'I dreamt last night', a German says **Ich** (or **Mir**) **träumte diese** (or **vergangene**) **Nacht;** but 'I saw him last night' is **Ich sah ihn gestern abend.** See also **nouns of measure** 1 (*b*).

Nachteil: see **Teil** 2 (*a*).

Nachtmahl: see **Mahl** 2.

nachtwandeln: see **wandeln.**

nah(e): The MHG adj. for 'near' is *nâch* (inflected *nâher*, etc.), the uninflected form being still extant in **Nachbar** (q.v.). **1.** *Positive*: In contexts implying **rest, nahe** can be used as a prep. (+ dat.) in the sense of 'near to, not far from': e.g. **Der Herzog bot ihm einen Sessel nahe dem Fenster an** (A. Neumann)—**Sie hätte ihm gern eine Wohnung nahe ihren Verwandten eingerichtet** (K. Edschmid); cf., usually with a preceding *dat.*—**Sie war böse und den Tränen nahe** (id.)—**Sie war einer Ohnmacht nahe** ('She nearly fainted')—**Man glaubte, die Welt sei ihrem Untergang nahe** (where **nahe** has almost become a sep. prefix). But much more common in a locative sense is the *adv.* use of **nahe** with a following prep., which latter will, of course, take an *accus.* where motion towards is implied: e.g. **Das Haus steht ganz nahe bei der Kirche—Sie saßen nahe am Fenster—Der Fremde trat nahe an mich heran—Setze dich nicht zu nahe ans Feuer!—Sie ist schon nahe an die fünfzig** ('She is already approaching her fifties')—**Ich war nahe daran, das Leben zu verlieren;** cf. **Er stand nahe bei mir** (*lit.*) and **Er stand mir nahe** (*fig.*: 'He was a close friend of mine'). **2.** *Comparative*: Here, in the lit. sense, the *adv.* use is almost fixed: e.g. **Er wohnt näher** an **der Stadt als ich—Er ist kürzlich umgezogen, und zwar näher an die Stadt.** But the *dat.* (esp. of a pers. pron.) is common where **näher** has become a sep. prefix and the compd. has taken on *fig.* force: thus, **etwas näher bringen** is 'to bring *or* move something nearer', while **jemandem etwas näherbringen** means 'to explain, bring something home, to a person'; so also **Er trat näher an mich heran** ('He came nearer to me') and **Er trat mir näher** ('He became more intimate with me')—**Er stand näher bei mir als du** (lit.) and **Er stand mir näher als du** ('He was a closer friend of mine than you'). Noteworthy are some phrases in which only the compar. is used: **Bitte, treten Sie näher!** (the polite way to say 'Come in!)—**Kennst du ihn näher?** ('Are you intimately acquainted with him?')—**Ich habe nichts Näheres erfahren** ('I have heard no details')—**Näheres in meinem nächsten Brief** ('Particulars in my next letter'). **3.** *Superlative*: **(a)** The prep. use of

nächst is rather rare with lit. force (cf. *b*): e.g. **Sie hatte ihre Äcker verkauft und nur einen schönen Baumgarten nächst** ('next to') **dem Haus behalten** (G. Keller); sim., in a stage direction, **Vor des Stauffachers Hause an der Landstraße nächst der Brücke** (Sch.), where **dem Haus, der Brücke zunächst** (q.v. 1) would now be more usual. But 'the nearest town' is **die nächstgelegene** (or, even more commonly, **die am nächsten** gelegene) **Stadt,** as **die nächste Stadt** might suggest 'the next town' (see *b*); and so also **meine Nächsten** ('those near and dear to me')—**bei nächster Gelegenheit** ('at the first opportunity'). (**b**) The commonest meaning of **nächst** is 'next', as in **Ich hoffe, Sie nächster Tage** ('in the course of the next few days') **zu besuchen,** etc. Noteworthy here is the prep. use of **nächst** corresponding to our 'next after': e.g. **Nächst unserem Vater im Himmel habe ich alles meinem alten Meister zu verdanken** (Novalis)—**Nächst den rastlosen Wolken weiß ich kein schöneres Bild des Wanderns als ein Schiff, das in großer Ferne fährt** (H. Hesse)—**Es war, nächst meiner ersten Jugend, die einzige Zeit meines Lebens, in der ich mich meinen Neigungen hingeben konnte** (W. Schäfer)—**„Nächst Gott", sagte er, „dankt Ihr die Rettung vornehmlich** ('mainly') **Eurem eigenen festen Willen"** (E. Wichert). Cf. also **demnächst** and **nächstens,** both meaning 'soon, shortly': e.g. **Er behauptete, daß die Engländer demnächst die Reichshauptstadt angreifen würden** (B. E. Werner).

Name: for the nom. sing. form **Namen,** as in **Heute sind alle Könige und Fürsten vergessen, Homers Namen aber ist in aller Mund** (P. Ernst), see **Balken.**

namentlich: 1. The verb **namen** (= **nennen**) is now obs., and the same practically applies to the compound **benamen,** although the past part. **benamt** ('named') is still very occasionally used, and to the alternative form **benamsen,** which was quite common in the classical period and even later: e.g. **Lange benamten wir dich den Humpler** (Voss: 'For long we called you the Hobbler, the Man with the Limp')—**Unser Blick irrte auf wunderlich benamste Inseln** (G.: '. . . islands with strange names'). **2.** From the simple verb comes the word **namentlich,** which should properly be **namendlich,** being formed from the pres. part. of **namen,** as **hoffentlich** is from **hoffen.** The word is often misconstrued by learners, who use it like **nämlich,** i.e. in the sense of 'namely', a meaning which it never has. Actually, it is used either (**a**) as an *adj.*, meaning 'nominal, by name': e.g. **Er hat mich namentlich ganz aus diesem Streit gelassen** (Lessing: 'He has not referred to me by name in this dispute')—**Der Vorsitzende verordnete eine namentliche Abstimmung** ('The chairman ordered a vote by name')—**Der Lehrer rief die Schüler namentlich auf** ('The teacher called the roll of his pupils'); or esp. (**b**) as an *adv.*, meaning 'especially', used much like **zumal** (q.v.) where one of a number or class is singled out, one condition or occasion stressed, etc.: e.g. **In diesem Jahre ist das Obst gut geraten, namentlich die Pflaumen—Ich gehe gern spazieren, namentlich wenn die Sonne scheint.** As these examples show, it is mostly used to introduce a sort of particularizing afterthought, following a general statement; it is not so common in propositions like 'What I *particularly* like about him is his frankness', which would rather be expressed **Was mir an ihm besonders** (or **vor allem**) **gefällt, ist seine Offenherzigkeit.**

names of persons: see **Proper names.**

nämlich: cf. **namentlich** 2.

naseweis: see **weis-.**

neben: see **an** 1.

nebst: see **congruence** 1 (*e*).

negative (pleonastic): 1. In German a double neg. orig. implied a strong negation: the MHG neg. particles *en-* and *ne-* were reg. associated with words like *niht, nie, nieman, kein,* etc. (cf. **nichts** 1). But eventually the Lat. rule, according to which two negs. cancel each other and make the proposition a pos. one, became the rule in German also, although occasional examples of a double neg. to express a neg. idea are found in comparatively recent authors, as in **Keine Spur der Entflohenen kam nirgendwo** (for **irgendwo**) **zutage** (Heyse: 'Not a trace of the fugitives came to light *any*where'). There is, however, one case where a double neg. is still the rule, viz. where a neg. *precedes* the neg. combination **weder . . . noch,** for which see **weder** 2. **2.** (**a**) Elsewhere a double neg. to express a neg. idea is now avoided in good prose: one no longer says **Er hatte es sich zum Gesetz gemacht, von keinem Menschen . . . nicht**

eine Feige anzunehmen (G.). This applies also to propositions which *imply* a negation, esp. those containing a prohibition, prevention, interdict, warning, etc.: one no longer says, or should not say, **Es besteht hier ein Verbot, keine Kühe zu schlachten** (G.), which is a mingling of the two propositions 'It is forbidden to kill any cows' and 'An order is in force to kill no cows'; so also **Es ist bei Strafe verboten, nichts** (for **etwas**) **in die Kanäle zu schütten** (G.). Examples of this are found in other langs.: thus, the Greek neg. partcile μή (*mê*) was reg. used after verbs of contradicting, denying, etc., and in English one could once say 'They would *hinder* . . . that *no* great armie should be made out of France against them' (1587) and 'The design was to *prevent* that *no* body might be sent to meet me' (1723). This use has persisted longer in German than in other cognate langs., but examples like the following should now be avoided: **Mignon sah sie an, als wenn sie sie warnen wollte, sich nicht zu verraten** (G.)—**Es herrschte bei einem Teile der Einwohner eine stärkere religiöse Strömung, welche jedoch nicht verhinderte, daß nicht einige vom Wege zum Tempel Gottes abschweiften** (G. Keller)—**Nicht fluchen! Aber wie sollte man's hindern, daß es nicht kam?** (Viebig: 'No curses! But how to prevent them from escaping one's lips?'); in this connexion, see esp. **hüten** 2 (*a*), and cf. **abhalten.** (**b**) A sim. confusion between two ideas explains the pleonastic insertion of a neg. in clauses introduced by **bis, ehe, ohne** and **seit** (qq.v.): e.g. **Bis du nicht einen Entschluß faßt, ist dir jeder Ausgang untersagt** (Jul. Grosse), a confusion between 'Until you come to a decision' and 'So long as you don't come to a decision'—**Liliencron ruhte nicht, bis nicht der Ausdruck das feinste Kleid seiner Gefühle wurde** (K. Lamprecht)—**Sie versicherten, nicht eher das Schloß verlassen zu wollen, bis sie nicht ihre Monarchin mit eignen Augen gesehen hätten** (Platen)—**Ich kann nicht schlafen, ehe meine Mutter mir nicht verziehen hat** (Jul. Wolff: cf. **ehe** 1 *b* and **erst** 2 *c*)—**Er konnte nicht leben, ohne nicht des Tages geknallt zu haben, schoß aber regelmäßig vorbei** (Immermann: 'He could not live without firing his gun every day, but he invariably missed')—**Wie habt Ihr denn gelebt, seit wir uns nicht gesehen haben?** (Stifter), where the last clause should properly be **seit wir uns zuletzt sahen**; sim. **Vierzehn Jahre waren es, seit der Vater kein Wort mit seinem Sohne sprach** (Auerbach). While perhaps permissible in coll. speech, such pleonasms should be avoided in a careful prose style. (**c**) The same applies to a pleonastic neg. in clauses introduced by **als** ('than'), an idiom quite common at one time, but now unusual (Sanders says **„Diese Weise wird heute im allgemeinen vermieden"**): e.g. **Er ist ein Goldschmied, sehr fleißig bei seiner Kunst, die ihm mehr einbringt, als die Musik nicht tun würde** (G.)—**Dieses Wort machte auf ihn einen peinlicheren Eindruck, als er sich nicht gestehen wollte** (C. F. Meyer); cf. Fr. *C'est plus vrai que vous ne le croyez* (Delavigne). **3.** A strange construction is the use of **nicht** in exclamations to convey a strong affirmative, as in **Wie erschrak sie nicht, als sie ihre Hand kohlschwarz aus dem Wasser zog!** (G.: 'What a fright she got when she drew her hand from the water and found it as black as coal!'), probably the result of mingling the two propositions 'What a fright she got' and 'Did she not get a fright?' This is still very common in coll. lang., esp. in exclamations introducing **alles**: e.g. **Was du nicht sagst!** (cf. 'Well, I never! Do you tell me that? You don't say!')—**Was man nicht alles erlebt auf dieser wunderlichen Welt!** (Jul. Grosse: 'Oh, the things one experiences in this queer world!')—**Was wurde in diesen Gesprächen nicht alles erörtert!** (Rilke: 'What an endless variety of things were discussed during these conversations!')—**Welch eine herrliche Gabe ist nicht die Phantasie!** (Th. Mann); cf. **Werk** *ad fin.*

neuerdings: see **allerdings** 2 (*a*); **recent** 2 (*a*).

neuerlich: see **recent** 1 (*b*).

neulich: see **recent** 1 (*a*).

never: 1. Although **immer** (q.v.) is used by all Germans in the sense of 'always', the corresponding neg. **nimmer** is hardly used at all in the north, being there replaced by **nie(mals).** The word **nimmer** is specially characteristic of the south, being elsewhere only used with intensifying force in **nie** (or **nun**) **und nimmer**, and in a few compds.: e.g. **Das werde ich nie und nimmer tun**—**Du verlangst, daß ich ihm verzeihe? Nimmermehr!**—**Sie trennten sich auf Nimmerwiedersehen** ('They parted, never to meet again'). In the proposition **Gemacht hat er's nicht, nun und nimmer, darauf schwör' ich** (Sch.: 'He never did it, I'll swear to that'), the time referred to is past, but in modern southern usage the reference is almost always to the future ('no longer' or 'never again'), where the north uses **nicht mehr**: e.g. **Ich kann es vor Schmerzen nimmer aushalten** (Hebel)—**Er verblieb länger als nötig in der Fremde und dachte schließlich überhaupt nimmer an die Heimkehr** (H. Hesse). **2.** But 'never' has a rather wider application than **nie(mals)**, which only has the force of 'not ever, never at any time'. Thus, in a reference to a person who has been dumb from birth, one can say **Er sprach nie**; but this expression cannot be used in rendering a proposition like 'I asked him several questions, but *he never spoke*', which would be expressed by **Ich stellte mehrere Fragen an ihn, aber er sprach kein Wort** (or **überhaupt nicht**). Sim., in rendering 'As he walked down the street, I called after him, but he *never* looked round', one would say **Als er die Straße hinunterging, rief ich ihm nach, aber er sah sich nicht** (or **kein einziges Mal**—not **nie**) **um**; cf. **Ich hatte ihn gebeten, mich gestern zu besuchen, aber er kam nicht** ('but he never came').

next: Care is required in translating 'next' into German, esp. where we use it in the adv. relation, because, although **nächst** (q.v.) is often applicable, it does not meet every case. The following examples show how a German would express himself:—**1.** *Adjective*: (**a**) with *temporal* force: 'He won't arrive till next week' = **Er kommt erst nächste Woche an**—'He only came next day' = **Er kam erst am nächsten** (or **folgenden**) **Tage** (or **tags darauf**)—'I could meet you on the Sunday after next' = **Ich könnte dich am übernächsten Sonntag** (or **Sonntag über acht Tage**) **treffen**; (**b**) with *locative force*: 'He is in the next room' = **Er ist im anstoßenden Zimmer**—'He lives next door' = **Er wohnt hier nebenan**—'The Smiths live in the next house but one' = **Schmidts wohnen im zweitnächsten Hause.** **2.** *Adverb*: 'He sat next to me' = **Er saß neben mir** (or **mir zunächst**: q.v. 1)—'She was standing next to the door' = **Sie stand am nächsten** (or **dicht**) **an der Tür** (or **der Tür zunächst**)—'He earns next to nothing' = **Er verdient fast** (or **so gut wie**) **gar nichts**—'What shall we do next?' = **Was sollen wir jetzt anfangen?**—'What did he do next?' = **Was tat er darauf?**—'When next I see him I shall ask him' = **Wenn ich ihn das nächste Mal sehe** (or **Das nächste Mal, wenn ich ihn sehe**), **werde ich ihn fragen**—'It is your turn next' = **Du bist der nächste dran** (or **an der Reihe**)—'I come next after you' = **Ich komme gleich** (or **unmittelbar**) **nach dir an die Reihe**—'Next after Goethe's poems I like Heine's best' = **Nächst Goethes Gedichten** (see **nahe** 3 *b*) **gefallen mir Heines am besten.**

nichts: **1.** The MHG expression for 'nothing' is *niht* (< *ni-wiht*, 'not a whit'), a noun, inflected in the reg. way (gen. *nihtes*, dat. *nihte*, accus. *niht*), and NHG **nicht** is really the MHG accus. used as an adv., just as our 'nothing' was once used: cf. 'I nothing doubt the power of your tribe' (Scott's *Fair Maid of Perth*, ch. 14). To express 'nothing whatever', *nihtes niht* was used (i.e. 'nothing of anything')—see **negative** (**pleonastic**)—but *niht* might be omitted here, and it is what then remained, viz. *nihtes*, that has given us the NHG **nichts.** No one, of course, now recognizes this as a gen.: even when the historically correct gen. is used, as in **Ich bedarf nichts**, one regards the obj. as an accus. (see **es** 3, and cf. the example from Novalis given under **entsinnen**); and in **Er fing wegen nichts Streit an** (Kellermann), **nichts** is treated as a dat. (cf. **wegen nichts anderem**). The MHG dat. is still preserved in **zunichte**, used with **werden** ('to come to nothing') and **machen** ('to frustrate, destroy'), as in **Das alles machte meinen Traum zunichte** (Kolbenheyer); and in **mitnichten** ('not at all, by no means'), which may have developed out of *mit nihte n(iht)*, and which was common in early NHG and is still sometimes used in formal speech in imitation of earlier usage: e.g. **Sie hießen ihn Zacharias, aber seine Mutter antwortete: Mit nichten, sondern er soll Johannes heißen** (Luke 1. 60)—**„Ach, der Herr Pineiß belieben zu scherzen!" „Mitnichten!" rief Pineiß** (G. Keller)—**„Ihr verbietet mir Euer Haus?" stammelte Konrad. „Mitnichten", beschwichtigte Rohde** (E. Wichert). **2.** Like other MHG indef. neut. expressions, *niht* was normally associated with a part. gen. (cf. **viel** 1 *a*): e.g. *niht schœners* ('nothing of greater beauty', Lat. *nihil pulchrioris*, Fr. *rien de plus* *beau*); and where the gen. was a plur., the verb was still sing., as in *hie ist niht schœner bluomen* ('Here there is nothing in the way of pretty flowers'). Actually, one still uses the MHG idiom in **nichts Schöneres,** but the relation is now treated as *appositional* (cf. **etwas** 1 and **wenig** 1): hence **Eine Zeitlang sprach man von nichts anderem als seinem Schauspiel** (Ina Seidel), although, when the reference is to a person, one still prefers to say **von niemand anders sprechen** (see **jemand** 2). **3.** That the subst. force of these indef. expressions was still felt in early NHG is evident from an example like **Wenn ich mit Menschen- und mit Engelzungen redete und hätte der Liebe nicht** (lit. 'nothing *of* charity'), **so wäre ich ein tönend Erz oder eine klingende Schelle** (1 Cor. 13. 1), and the orig. gen. is still used in certain more or less set expressions, esp. in the case of verbal nouns: e.g. **Hier ist meines Bleibens nicht** (*lit.* 'Here there is nothing of my staying', i.e. 'This is no place for me', esp. 'It's getting too hot for me here'); and sim. **Ich weiß mir nicht Rats** (lit. 'I know nothing of advice for myself', i.e. 'I am at my wits' end': see **Rat** 2). **4.** As explained under **viel** 1 (*b*), all feeling for the orig. construction is now lost, some of these gen. forms having become independent nouns through dropping the very word which caused them to be in the gen., as in **Ich weiß mir Rats.** Such gen. forms occur most commonly in neg. propositions, which usually take the form of a verbal noun qualified by uninflected **kein:** e.g. **Jetzt hatte er kein Bleibens mehr an diesem Ort** (Mörike)—**Hier in Neapel ist kein Besinnens mehr** (G.: 'Here in Naples one cannot collect oneself now')—**Er mußte sie sehen: es war kein Haltens mehr** (H. Grimm: '. . . there was no keeping him back')—**Es war kein Hehlens mehr** (Storm: 'There was no keeping the secret now')—**Fort mußt du, davon ist kein Redens mehr** (E. Wichert: 'You must get away, we need waste no more words about that').

Nichtvorhandensein: see **absence** 2 (*a*); cf. **Hand,** 1 (*b*).

nicken: see **mit** 2 (*b*).

nie: see **never** 1 and 2.

nieder-: see **down** 1 and 3.

niederkommen: This is a good example of a verb of motion compounded with a *simple* prefix which is never used in a *lit.* sense (see **her-, hin-** 3). The expression 'to come down' (a hill, from the sky, etc.) requires the lengthened prefix **hernieder-** (in more ordinary lang. **herunter-**), as in **Ich kam vom Walde hernieder, da stand noch das alte Haus** (Eichendorff). On the other hand, **niederkommen** is only used in the *fig.* sense of 'to be delivered of' (a child): **Sie ist mit einer Tochter niedergekommen** ('She has given birth to a daughter'). Incidentally, as there is no lengthened prefix **hinnieder-,** 'to go down' is **hinunter-** or **hinabgehen.**

niederlassen: This is used lit., like the more ordinary **herunterlassen,** of 'letting down' inanimate objs. such as **Vorhang, Fahne, Zugbrücke,** etc., but certainly *not* fig., as in our coll. 'to let a person down' (**jemand im Stich lassen**). It is esp. common as a *reflex.* in the sense of 'to sit down', and as it then points to the moment when the action ceases, a *dat.* in prep. phrases is now the rule (see **down** 3): e.g. **Sie ging ins Wohnzimmer zurück, wo sie sich auf dem alten Platze niederließ** (R. Herzog)—**Es gelang ihr, die Erschöpfte zu bewegen, sich in einem Fauteuil niederzulassen** (Ebner-Eschenbach)—**Sie ließ sich langsam in einem ihrer Plüschsessel nieder** (E. Kästner)—**Während ich mich setzte, ließ er sich wieder vor dem Schreibtische nieder** (Wildenbruch); cf., as much less common, **Sie antwortete, sich ermüdet auf die** (usually **der**) **Bank niederlassend: „Prosit!"** (Spindler). The *dat.* is esp. fixed where the reflex. means 'to settle down' in a place: **Er beabsichtigt, sich als Arzt in unserer Stadt niederzulassen—Wo** (not **Wohin**) **hat er sich niedergelassen?**

niederlegen: This verb is regularly used of 'laying down' not only objects like **ein Buch, die Waffen** (= **die Waffen strecken**) or **ein Amt** ('to demit an office'), but also a personal obj., as in **die Kinder nieder- or hinlegen** (= **ins Bett legen**). As in the case of other verbs compounded with **hin-** or **nieder-** (q.v.), the *dat.* in a prep. phrase is the usual case: e.g. **Ich legte den Befehl auf dem Tische des Hauses nieder** (Bismarck)—**Als er sie ruhig atmen hörte, hob er sie auf und legte sie bequem auf dem abhängigen Boden nieder** (Heyse) and sim. with a *reflexive* pron. in the sense of 'to lie down': **Er legte sich am Ufer nieder** (Waiblinger)—**Ich legte** (or **streckte**) **mich auf dem Sofa nieder.**

niedersitzen: Like **ab-, auf-** and **ein-**

sitzen (qq.v.), this verb implies motion. As pointed out under **down** 2, the prefix generally used in the north to express 'to sit, kneel, fall down' is **hin-**, but it is noteworthy that in **ab-**, **niedersitzen** and **sich niederlassen** (q.v.) **hin-** cannot be substituted for **nieder-**: cf. **Er stand und getraute nicht niederzusitzen** (G.), where one could use **sich hinzusetzen**, but not **hinzusitzen**; so also **Er strich sich wie erwachend über die Augen und saß zum einfachen Essen nieder** (R. Waldmüller). As these verbs usually point to the moment when the action ceases, preps. like **an, auf, in**, etc. preferably take a *dat.*: cf. **Er setzte sich auf einer Bank hin** (G.)—**Sie setzte sich in der Sofaecke nieder** (R. Herzog)—**Sie saßen am Teetisch nieder** (Th. Mann); so also **Laß uns dort** (not **dorthin**) **niedersitzen!** (Heyse), where **niedersitzen** is obviously preferable as it avoids the harsh repetition of the reflex. in **Laß uns uns dort hinsetzen!** An *accus.* in such prep. clauses is much less common: cf. **Als sie hoch oben zwischen den Bergen waren, ließ er sie ins Moos** (usually **im Moose**) **niedersitzen** (Heyse); sim. **Man lud mich ein, auf einen Teppich niederzusitzen** (Mörike).

niederstürzen: This compound of **stürzen** (q.v.) is not used of falling down to a lower level (see **down** 1), but, like **hinfallen,** of a person falling down in the street, or esp. of impetuously going down on one's knees. If knees are specially mentioned, they will stand in the *accus.* case, while the place where the action takes place is expressed by the *dat.* case: e.g. **Sie stürzte auf der Straße nieder** (or **hin**)—**Sie stürzten sich vor den Altären nieder** (Sch.)—**Sie stürzte vor dem Sarge auf die Knie nieder** (G.). The same idea is conveyed by **sich niederwerfen**: e.g. **Die Kinder warfen sich vor den Eltern** (*scil.* **auf die Knie**) **nieder** (G.).

niemals: see **never** 1 and 2.

niemand: see **jemand**.

niesen: see **schnauben** 1 (*b*).

nimmer: see **never** 1.

nisten: see **einnisten** 1.

noch: **1.** *Adverb*: **(a)** With *temp.* force ('still, yet'): e.g. **Es regnet immer noch** ('It is *still*, has never stopped, raining')—**Indem wir noch sprachen** (i.e. Before we had finished speaking), **klopfte es an die Tür**—**Ich bin auch jetzt noch derselben Ansicht** ('Even now I am still of the same opinion')—**Das wirst du noch bereuen** ('You'll live to regret that some day')—**Heute vor acht Tagen um diese Zeit: weißt du noch?** ('. . . do you remember?')—**Ich habe ihn erst gestern noch gesehen** ('I saw him no longer ago than, as recently as, yesterday'); sim. in neg. clauses: **Ich bin noch lange nicht fertig** ('I am not nearly ready yet')—**Er wohnt noch nicht sehr lange hier** ('He has not been living here very long yet')—**Ich bin noch nie im Ausland gewesen** ('I have never been abroad yet'); **(b)** suggesting something *additional*: e.g. **Bringen Sie mir noch ein Glas Bier!** ('Bring me another beer!')—**Noch eins, ehe wir auseinandergehen!** ('One other point before we separate!')—**Sag' das Gedicht noch (ein)mal auf!** ('Recite the poem once more!')—**Ist sonst noch etwas zu besprechen?** ('Is there anything else to discuss?')—**Das fehlte gerade noch!** (coll. 'It just needed that! That caps everything!')—**Auch de'n Schrecken noch!** (coll., like our slang 'That puts the lid on it!'); **(c)** before a *compar.*: **Dieses Dorf ist noch schöner gelegen** ('still *or* even more beautifully situated')—**Das wäre noch schöner!** (coll., iron., 'That would crown all!'); **(d)** with *concess.* force, generally in the form **auch no'ch so** modifying an adj. or adv., to express our 'ever so' or 'however', as in 'Don't beat the child, even if he has been ever so naughty!': **Schlage das Kind nicht, wenn es auch no'ch so unartig gewesen ist**; sim. **Ich täte es nicht, wenn er mich auch no'ch so dringend darum bitten sollte** ('I would not do it, were he ever so pressing')—**Sie hatten Dinge erlebt, von denen heutzutage kein no'ch so wilder Junge sich eine Vorstellung machen kann** (Böhlau: 'Their experiences had been such as no boy, however wild, could conceive nowadays,')—**Nie hätte ein auch no'ch so frommer Gutsherr sich eine so große Kirche erbaut** (G. Britting: 'Never would a landed proprietor, however devout, have built himself so large a church'). In such propositions, the insertion of **auch** is not essential, although it is more idiomatic to retain it; but the same idea can be expressed without **noch,** in which case **auch** comes later in the sentence: **Schlage das Kind nicht, so u'nartig es auch gewesen ist!**
2. *Conjunction*: esp. in the combination **weder . . . noch** ('neither . . . nor'), for which see **weder.** In English, 'nor' can introduce a proposition following a *pos.*

statement, as in 'Nor among the friends of Socrates must the jailer be forgotten' (Jowett). As this is merely another way of expressing the pos. idea that the jailer must be added to the number of friends previously referred to, **noch** would be incorrect in a German rendering, which would run thus: **Unter den Freunden des Sokrates darf auch** (unaccented) **der Gefängniswärter nicht vergessen werden.**

noise: see **sound** 3.

nominative absolute: see **accusative absolute** 3.

nor: see noch 2; **weder.**

Nord: **1.** The cardinal points have two forms in German: **der Nord** (gen. **des Nordes**) and **der Norden** (gen. **des Nordens**); and sim. with **Ost(en)**, **Süd(en)**, **West(en)**. The form **Nord** is much less common than **Norden** in ordinary language, being chiefly used with an art. in the sense of **Nordwind**: e.g. **Nicht wehte diesmal ein förderlicher Nordost, sondern leider von der Gegenseite ein lauer Südwest, der allerhinderlichste** (G.)—**Im Sturme schlagen sich die Winde, der wilde Süd, des Nordes rauhe Macht, der mut'ge Ost** (Sch.)—**Ein frischer Südost trieb sie in den Ozean** (Frenssen). The short forms are also used, esp. in nautical parlance, of the points of the compass, as in **Von dem Vorlande, das nach Nord und Süd hinläuft, können wir die Erde** ('soil') **nehmen** (Storm), but the longer forms are much more common in this sense, although never in that of the wind coming from the direction in question: e.g. **Ich gehe, mich in des Nordens Wäldern zu verbergen** (Sch.)—**Ein paar Habichte flogen von Westen nach Osten** (G.)—**Es ging immer weiter, Tag und Nacht, immer nach Süden** (Frenssen); for the fluctuation, cf. **Sie zogen nach Süden und Südwest** (Kellermann). In such prep. phrases the art. is frequently omitted, the only exception being **im** (not **in**) **Norden.** **2.** Expressions like 'to the north of . . .' are usually rendered by **nördlich** (+ gen. or, necessarily where the noun has no specific gen. ending, **von**): e.g. **nördlich der Donau**—**östlich von Paris**; cf. **Der Großvater hatte in seiner Jugend eine Esche osten der Haustür gepflanzt** (Storm, using a north-German provincialism.) Where we say 'the north of Germany, the east of Europe', etc., the Germans prefer **das nördliche Deutschland, das östliche Europa,** etc., or they use a compd. like **Norddeutschland**; but 'in the west (east) of Prussia' is **im westlichen** (**östlichen**) **Preußen** or **im Westen** (**Osten**) **Preußens,** *not* in **Westpreußen** (**Ostpreußen**), which are the names of two Prussian provinces in the extreme northeast of Germany.

nördlich: see **Nord** 2.

nötigen: **1.** This trans. verb implies bringing pressure to bear on a person, and so fluctuates between 'to force' (**zwingen**) and 'to press' (**drängen**): e.g., in the former sense, **Ich wurde veranlaßt, ja genötigt** ('induced, nay obliged'), **an den Übungen Anteil zu nehmen** (G.)—**Ein plötzlicher Regenguß nötigte uns, in ein Kaffeehaus einzutreten** (Sch.)—**Ich sah mich genötigt, ihm einen Verweis zu erteilen** ('I found myself under the necessity of reprimanding him'); in the second sense, **Er nötigte mich, hereinzukommen** ('He pressed me to come in')—esp. of pressing food and drink on a person, as in the familiar expression **Greift zu, genötigt wird nicht!** ('Help yourselves, don't wait to be pressed!'). **2.** The same difference applies to the compds. **abnötigen** and **aufnötigen**: cf. **Er hat mir ein Versprechen abgenötigt** ('He has forced a promise from me') and **Sobald ich eintrat, wurde mir eine Erfrischung aufgenötigt** ('As soon as I entered, I had a little refreshment pressed upon me'). The only other common compd. is **benötigen** ('to stand in need of'): this orig. always took a *gen.*, but eventually the MHG gen. obj. in *ich benôte es* came to be regarded as an *accus.* (see **es** 1), which led to **Ich benötige das**; the part of the verb in most common use is the past part. used in the pred., as in **Da ich Geldes benötigt war** (= **Da ich Geld nötig hatte**—cf. **bedürfen** *ad fin.*), **entschloß ich mich, den Handel zu beendigen** (C. F. Meyer: 'As I stood in need of cash, I decided to close the deal').

nouns of measure, etc. (**plural of**): **1.** (a) After numerals, *masc.* and *neut.* nouns expressing measure, amount, weight, extent, etc. (for *fem.* nouns, see 2) normally retain their collect. sing. form in the plur., but take the plur. form when used in a distrib. sense: e.g. **Wir haben sechs Faß Rheinwein bestellt,** but **Im Keller stehen sechs leere Fässer**—**In der Ebene stand mit dreißigtausend Mann** (regarded as a single unit) **der älteste Heerführer** (Wassermann), but **In dem Abteil saßen sechs Männer.** (i) The following are characteristic examples of the collect. use, some of the nouns in which are treated under separate heads: **Drei weitere Blatt** ('sheets of notepaper') **hatte sie noch mit Bleistift geschrieben** (K. Edschmid)—**Der Bauer fuhr mit zwanzig Bund Stroh in die Stadt—Schiller war mit sechs Fuß zwei Zoll der längste Mann in Weimar** (K. Lamprecht); cf. the example given under **anheben** *ad fin.*—**Eine Bestellung auf zwei Dutzend Hemden und zwölf Paar wollene Strümpfe ist eingelaufen—Sie sagte, daß es einen Falken gegeben habe, für den ein Landgut von 600 Joch Weizenboden geboten worden sei** (Bergengruen)—**Mehr als vier Kopf** (see below) **am Tage vertrage ich von dem Zeug nicht** (Speckmann: 'I can't stand more than four pipefuls of that weed a day')—**Am Ufer lagen Kähne mit Platz für sechs Mann** (C. Rothe)—**Das Zimmer hat eine Länge von zehn Meter—Dieser Artikel kostet nur fünfzig Pfennig—Ich habe drei Sack Kartoffeln gekauft—Zuweilen sehe ich dort einen bloßarmigen Mann sein neun Schuh** (= **Fuß**) **großes Gemüseäckerchen umgraben** (Th. Mann)—**Das Haus ist drei Stock hoch—Ihm gehörte ein Hof von zwanzig Stück Rindvieh** (A. Schaeffer)—**Er hinterließ eine Schuldenlast von einer halben Million Taler** (Fr. Griese). (ii) The use of the normal plur. form in such propositions is really not in the spirit of the German lang., and *Sanders* rightly characterizes examples like the following as **„minder korrekt"** or **„nur vermeintlich korrekter"** (i.e. thought to be more correct): **Es fehlten ihm zu sechs Fuß nur wenige Zolle** (E. Wichert)—**Das Quecksilber liegt wenige Grade unter Null** (F. Thiess: 'The thermometer registers a few degrees below zero')—**Er pflügte mit zwölf Jochen** (1 Kings 19. 19)—**Was über der zehn Kirchtürme hohen Wand lag, lachte noch in der gelben Sonne des Abends** (Federer)—**Sachte** ('Gradually') **gewöhnte man die Dame an unsere Höhe von 2200 Metern** (id.)—**Gegen das Versprechen eines Honorars von 50 Pfennigen lieferte Emil dem Franz die mathematische Arbeit im Abgangsexamen** (H. Hesse)—**Ich fange an, einige Stücke Vieh zu verkaufen** (Frenssen). The same applies to **Er überragte Ludwig um zwei Köpfe** (Bruno Frank), but it is noteworthy that the plur. form **Köpfe** is correct when it means 'individuals', as in **Die Zuschauer mochten tausend Köpfe zählen** (or **stark sein**) and **Das Offiziersdetachement von etwa sechzig Köpfen versammelte sich gegen zehn Uhr abends** (A. Neumann). (**b**) Somewhat exceptional are the nouns **Schritt, Jahr,** and **Monat.** In the case of **Schritt**, both the sing. and the plur. forms are used, the former esp. with the force of 'paces', the latter mostly in the fig. sense of taking 'steps' towards some end: e.g. **Durch einen kurzen Gang von drei Schritt Länge näherte er sich der Portiere** (Stehr)—**Nach den ersten hundert Schritt lahmte das Pferd** (Hofmannsthal)—**Man sah ihm den Kriminalkommissar auf hundert Schritt an** (K. Edschmid: 'You could tell at a hundred yards that he was a C.I.D. commissary')—**Bleib mir drei Schritt vom Leibe!** (coll. 'Don't come near me! Keep your distance!'); but **Ältermann** ('Alderman') **Sturm versprach, die nötigen Schritte zu tun** (Bergengruen). With regard to **Jahr** and **Monat,** while the sing. forms may be used collect. in ordinary lang. in the nom. and accus., there is a definite preference for the plur. forms in good prose, indeed, these are practically fixed in the gen. and dat.: thus, while one commonly says **Das mag schon hundert Jahr her sein** (Heine) and **Vier Monat mochte das Fohlen alt sein** (G.), one now rather avoids propositions like **Es waren Knaben von ungefähr anderthalb Jahr** (Seume) and **Ich bin seit vier Monat hier** (Heine), where **Jahren** and **Monaten** are much more usual; and sim. in the gen., **Er ist heute nach Ablauf zweier Monate** (or **von zwei Monaten**) **aus Deutschland zurückgekehrt.** The plur. form is now also firmly established in the case of **Tag** and **Nacht:** one no longer says **Wir tanzen schon drei Tag und Nacht** (G.). **2.** All *fem.* nouns of measure, etc., normally require inflexion in the plur., esp. those ending in **-e,** and it may be that **Jahr** and **Monat** have been influenced here by **Minute, Sekunde, Stunde, Woche,** etc. In any case, usage is quite fixed: one can only say **zwei Flaschen Wein,** whether the reference be to individual bottles or to the quantity contained in them; and so also **Das Tuch ist drei Ellen lang—Ich war zehn Jahr und drei Wochen alt** (H. Hesse)—**Ein Weg führt nach einem viereinhalb Stunden entfernten Dorf** (id.). Exceptional here are **Mark** and **Maß** (qq.v.), the latter of which is fem. in the south in the sense of a 'measure' of wine, etc.: these retain their sing. form in the plur., as in **Das Buch kostet zehn Mark** and **Er hat drei Maß Bier getrunken.** Here belongs also **Hand,** which usually remains unchanged in the sense of 'handbreadths', but often takes the plur. form in that of 'handfuls': e.g. **Diese Bretter sind zwei Hand breit—Das Pferd ist zwölf Hand hoch—Die Köchin bat mich, zwei Handvoll** (or **Händevoll**) **Mehl zu holen—Sie kam mit zwei Handvoll Zucker zurück**; but in a distributive sense, **Ich konnte die Tür nicht aufmachen, weil ich beide Hände voll hatte.**

November: see **Monatsnamen.**

null und nichtig: see **adjectives (uninflected)** 4.

number: see **figure** 2.

nun: **1.** *Adverb*: Whereas **jetzt** points to the present moment or a moment in the immediate future, **nun** (or coll. **nu,** which is the historically correct form) considers the present moment in its relation to the immediate past: cf., on the one hand, **Ich habe jetzt keine Zeit, den Brief zu beantworten,** and on the other hand, **Ich habe den Brief geschrieben, nun muß ich ihn auf die Post geben**; so also **Karl ist jetzt in Deutschland, soll aber nun bald nach Amerika gehen.** The point of time referred to may, of course, be in the past, as in **Der Vater war kürzlich gestorben, nun starb auch die Mutter**; and the past time may be merely implied, as when a person says **Was fangen wir nun an?** ('What shall we do now?'). It follows that in many contexts either **jetzt** or **nun** can be used: 'from now on, henceforth' is either **von jetzt ab** or **von nun an,** the former suggesting the starting-point, the latter implying a comparison with what has gone before. **2.** *Conjunction*: MHG *nû* was used not only as a temporal adv., but also as a causal conj. ('now that, because'), and **nun** (not **jetzt**) can still be used with this force (cf. **zumal**). One can, of course, say **Nun, da wir alle versammelt sind, können wir zu Tisch gehen,** but here the word **da** (and the comma preceding it) can be omitted altogether, and this use of **nun** as an independent conj. has become very common in modern prose: e.g. **Nun es dämmerte, kam sie ein Grauen an** (Mörike)—**Nun es zu dämmern begann, kamen sie an die Bootslände zurück** (W. v. Scholz)—**Nun die Kinder angekleidet waren, ging es endlich zum Frühstück** (G. Keller)—**Nun du das weißt, gib dich über alles andere zufrieden** (Heyse)—**Nun der Winterfrost gekommen war, konnte sie nicht recht einschlafen** (Sudermann)—**Nun es Sommer geworden ist, habe ich sie in die Schule genommen** (P. Keller)—**Nun das Problem gelöst war, lag in der Sache kein Reiz mehr für mich** (W. Schäfer)—**Als du ein Knabe warst, gelobtest du, meine Ehre zu schützen; nun du ein Mann bist, wirst du nicht anders denken** (Binding); cf., as unusual, with temporal force, **Nun** (for **Als**) **er fragte, wie es ihm ergangen sei, erfuhr er, was ihn sehr betrübte** (E. Wichert). **3.** *Interjection*: With exclamatory force, **nun** is, of course, only used in conversation, as in **Nun, wie geht's?** ('Well, how are you?') or **„Was sagen Sie dazu?" „Nun, ich bin ganz Ihrer Meinung"** ('What do you say to that?' 'Oh well, I am entirely of your opinion'). In familiar speech it usually takes the form **na** (with short vowel), which has developed quite a number of different shades of meaning. It may express impatience (**Na, bist du noch nicht fertig?—Na, wird's bald?** 'Well, how long am I to be kept waiting?', almost like 'Come on, get a move on!'), or surprise (**Na, so was!** 'Well, I never! Why, who would have thought it?'—**Na, das fehlte noch** or **gerade!** 'Well, that beats all!'), or displeasure (**Na, aber wie konntest du dich auch so betragen?**), or curiosity (**Na, ob er wohl kommen wird?**), or a warning (**Na, warte nur, das wird dir schlecht bekommen!** 'Just you wait, you'll pay dearly for that!'); and it may also suggest doubt, or have appeasing force, in which case it is often repeated: e.g. **Na, na, wenn die Sache nur nicht schief geht!** ('Well, well, I hope things won't go wrong!')—**Na, na, ruhig Blut** or **nicht so hitzig!** ('Now then, keep cool, don't get excited!').

nur: **1.** This adv., meaning 'only', has developed out of OHG *ni wâri* > MHG *newære*, i.e. (**wenn es**) **nicht wäre,** 'if it were not'—cf. **es sei denn** ('unless it be'), for which see **denn (adverb)** 3; its orig. force is still seen dimly in **Er hat keine anderen Freunde hier, nur mich** (really 'unless it be me'). It therefore has limiting force, much like the more coll. **bloß** (LG **man**): e.g. **Er ißt kein Fleisch, nur Gemüse—Er tat es nur mir zu Gefallen—Ich kenne ihn nur von Ansehen** ('only by sight')—**Sie tu't nur so** ('She's only pretending')—**Er ist nicht nur dumm sondern auch faul—Wenn ich nur wüßte, wem das Buch gehört—Wenn er nur käme!** So also when used as a *conj.* to introduce a qualifying statement: **Ich will es gern tun, nur weiß ich nicht, wie ich es anfangen soll—Der Roman ist gut, nur müßte er etwas kürzer sein.** The limit is definitely fixed in the case of **nur**, thus differing from **erst** (q.v. 2 *c*), which points beyond the limit: hence distinguish between **Ich war nur zwei Tage in Berlin** (I could not stay longer) and **Ich war erst zwei Tage in Berlin, als der Krieg auszubrechen drohte** (I had meant to stay longer). **2.** In *imperat.* propositions, **nur** has persuasive, reassuring force: e.g. **Komm nur, ich tue dir nichts!** ('Oh come on, I'm not going to hurt you!')—**Treten Sie nur ein!** ('Just step in!')—**„Soll ich nach dem Arzt schicken?" „Nein, laß nur, es geht mir schon etwas besser"** ('No, don't trouble, I'm feeling a little better'); iron., **Warte nur, es wird Schläge setzen!** ('Just you wait, you'll catch it!'). **3.** Elsewhere it has generalizing force: e.g. **Er scheint soviel Geld zu bekommen, wie er nur will** ('. . . as much money as ever he wants'); esp. in questions expressing doubt: **Woher hat er nur soviel Geld?** ('Where on earth has he got so much money?')—**Wie ist so etwas nur möglich?** ('How is that sort of thing at all possible?')—**„Mama, was ha'st du nur? Mir wird angst und bange!"** (Fontane: 'Mother, whatever is wrong with you? I'm really getting anxious!').

nutz, nütze: see **adjectives (indeclinable) 5.**

O

ob: 1. *Preposition*: This use is preserved in a few southern place-names and dialects, but is otherwise confined to poetry and choice prose. With the locative force of 'over, above' it takes a dat., with that of 'on account of' a dat. or a gen.: e.g. **Österreich ob der Enns** (Upper Austria, bounded by the river Enns)—**Rothenburg ob der Tauber** (cf. Boat *of* Garten)—**Ob dem Altar hing eine Mutter Gottes** (Sch.)—**Wie eine Gewitterdecke hing alles ob den Häuptern** (Federer: usually **zu Häupten**)—**Die Erde zitterte ob dem furchtbaren Krachen** (Hackländer)—**Sie empfand einen Schmerz ob den Worten, die sie hörte** (Jak. Frey)—**Die Mutter schüttelte den Kopf ob soviel Unverstand** (Speckmann)—**Ihr seid verwundert ob des seltsamen Gerätes in meiner Hand** (Sch.)—**Die Treppe herauf kam, als die Musik pausierte, in Verwirrung ob der vielen Herrschaften, der jüngste Lehrling des Kontors** (Th. Mann)—**Der Student zitierte noch einmal, selber verwundert ob des melodischen Tonfalls** (Raabe); cf. **Ich war darob** (= **darüber**) **verwundert. 2.** *Subordinate conjunction*: **(a)** In indirect questions with the force of 'whether': e.g. **Ich fragte ihn, ob er wüßte, wieviel Uhr es sei—Ob er wohl kommen wird?** (with a preceding princ. clause understood: **Ich frage mich, ob . . .** or **Ich möchte gar zu gern wissen, ob . . .**)—**Ob uns die See, ob uns die Berge scheiden, so sind wir eines Stammes** (Sch.)—**Morgen gehe ich spazieren, einerlei, ob** ('no matter whether') **es regnet oder nicht—Dann kommen mir Gedanken, ob gesund, ob krank, das mag ich selber nicht bestimmen** (Droste-Hülshoff). Where we say 'I looked down the street to see whether my friend was coming', a German idiomatically omits the words 'to see' altogether: e.g. **Wir überschritten die Grenze: alles sah sich um, ob denn das fremde Land anders aussehe wie Preußen** (Liliencron)—**Sie sah über die Bucht nach Freestedt hinüber, ob von dort ein Zeichen käme** (Frenssen)—**Er horchte, ob er denn nicht das Gebetglöcklein hören könnte** (Stifter); indeed, the idea of 'looking' need not be expressed at all: **Nicht immer war Wasser da** (in S.W. Africa): **oft mußten wir graben, ob wir ein wenig fänden** (id.)—**Sie saßen die ganze Nacht am Lager des Verwundeten, ob sie noch etwas erfahren möchten, was er zu künden hatte** (Schreckenbach). **(b)** In careless speech we often use 'if' in the sense of 'whether', as in 'He asked me if I would accompany him,' and in point of fact this exactly corresponds to

Er fragte mich, ob ich ihn begleiten würde, because MHG *ob(e)* = NHG **wenn,** 'if' (*er wolde genesen sîn ob im iemen hülfe* = **Er glaubte, er würde am Leben bleiben, wenn ihm jemand hülfe**), a use now obs., but common in early NHG: e.g. **Ob jemand sündiget, so haben wir einen Fürsprecher bei dem Vater** (1 John 2. 1). This earlier use of ob explains **als ob,** for which see **als** = **'as if'.** (**c**) Analogous is the expression **ob auch,** the orig. sense of 'even if' (now usually **auch wenn**) leading to that of 'although' (see **obgleich**): e.g. **Ob auch die Nacktheit nicht schön ist, ist sie einem lieber als das falsche Prunkgewand** (Ponten). In such propositions **ob** and **auch** are often separated, esp. by a pers. or reflex. pron., as in **Ob ihm auch das Blut in den Adern erstarrte, der junge Mann schaute nicht auf** (M. Nordau); indeed, separation is fixed where the subj. of the clause is a pers. pron.: e.g. **Ob er auch** (not **Ob auch er**) **vorwärtsstrebte, es gelang ihm nicht, rechtzeitig anzukommen.** (**d**) In coll. lang. it introduces a surprised question following a previous question, as in **„Kennt Ihr denn dieses Gefühl?" „Ob ich es kenne?"** (G.), where words like 'Need you ask' are understood; and this led to the use of **Und ob?** as an emphatic affirmation of assent, as in a reference to the young men who joined up in 1914: **„Es waren gute Jungen." „Und ob?"** (Th. Mann: 'Weren't they just? You bet they were!'—like our modern slang 'You're telling me!').

ob-: 1. Most of the verbs compounded with **ob-** are now almost obs. A few past part. forms like **obbemerkt, -benannt, -erwähnt** ('above-mentioned': cf. **folgen** 3) are still used in commercial letters, but examples like the following have a rather strange ring: **Wir wollen bekennen, einigermaßen besorgt gewesen zu sein, es möge hier einige Gefahr obschweben** (G.: 'We confess to having felt some fear that a certain danger threatened')—**Sie dachte an die Ähnlichkeit, die zwischen dieser Lage und jener damaligen obschwebte** (Bergengruen)—**Er gedachte obzusiegen** (G. Keller: 'He planned to get the upper hand')—**Luther hat in dem wiederholten Kampfe obgesiegt** (Lamprecht). Still fairly common, however, is **obwalten** ('to prevail'—cf. **walten** *ad fin.*): e.g. **Dergleichen Dramen waren dem ehrbaren Bürgersinn gemäß, der immer mehr obzuwalten anfing** (G.); and **unter obwaltenden Umständen** ('in present circumstances, as things are') is in regular use. **2.** But the compd. in most frequent use is **obliegen** (+ dat.), no longer used in its old sense of 'to be victorious', as in **Der Herr wird seinen Feinden obliegen** (Is. 42. 13), but either with a pers. subj. with the force of 'to occupy oneself with, devote oneself to' some activity (e.g. **dem Studium der Chemie obliegen**), or esp. with an impers. subj. and a dat. of the person meaning 'to be incumbent on, devolve upon': e.g. **Wer mehr tut, als ihm obliegt, der wagt vielleicht mehr, als ihm recht ist** (Freytag)—**Als erste Pflicht liegt uns Philologen die Herstellung korrekter Texte ob** (H. Mayne). Orig. the prefix **ob-** was *sep.*, as in the last example and in **Sie lag ihrer häuslichen Arbeit ob** (Spindler) and **Diesem Spiel pflagest** (see **pflegen** 1) **du morgens obzuliegen** (H. Kurz); its insep. use originated in Austria, from where it spread to the north, so much so that *Duden* now allows both **es liegt mir ob** and **es obliegt mir,** while *Sprach-Brockhaus* has only **ich obliege** and **es obliegt mir**; but both of these authorities recognize only **obzuliegen** and **obgelegen,** so that an example like **Anstatt still den Reparaturarbeiten zu obliegen, wagte er es, zu reden** (P. Karlson) must be condemned. But the fact remains that, as **ob-** is always accented, it should really be *sep.*; indeed, *Sanders* characterizes the insep. use as **„falsch",** while *Wustmann* sees in it a sign that all feeling for correct usage has become blunted: **„Wir sollten uns gegen diese Verwirrung wehren, die ein Zeichen trauriger Verlotterung des Sprachgefühls ist".** So, until usage is firmly established, it seems advisable to treat **ob-** as always *sep.*; but the following examples show to what extent the insep. use has spread: **Der staatlichen Justiz obliegt die Pflicht, die allgemeine Sitte zu schützen** (St. Zweig)—**Die Sorge um seine geistliche Entwicklung oblag zum größten Teil Arthurn, der ein Jahr älter war als er** (I. Seidel)—**Es fehlte nur noch, daß sie rotlackierte Fingernägel hatte; aber ihren Händen, das konnte er gleich feststellen, oblag viel rauhe Arbeit** (H. E. Busse)—**Mein Hund obliegt diesen Übungen im Sinne einer gymnastischen Morgentoilette** (Th. Mann)—**Ich wandte mich dem Studium der klassischen Sprachen zu und oblag demselben auf den Universitäten Jena und Halle** (id.);

but cf., from the same author, **„Zunächst liegt es uns ob, die Quelle zu besuchen", sagte Thomas.** With regard to the aux., *Sprach-Brockhaus* distinguishes between **ich bin** (**meinen Pflichten**) **obgelegen** and **es hat mir obgelegen**; but this distinction seems rather far-fetched: in spite of an example like **Er hatte mit meinem Vater die Rechte studiert und war nachmals** ('later') **den Künsten obgelegen** (Storm, in a story set in the 17th century), the north prefers to use **haben** throughout (as with the simple verb **liegen**): cf. **Seine Frau stammte aus dem Reiche und hatte einst dem Gesang obgelegen** (Th. Mann).

Obacht: This compound of **Acht** ('attention') is mainly characteristic of the south. Where a southerner says **Gib während meiner Abwesenheit Obacht auf die Kinder!** ('Look after the children while I am away!'), a northerner prefers to use the simple noun, which has become a sep. prefix and is therefore written with a small letter: **Gib** (or **Habe**) **auf die Kinder acht!** In common use everywhere, on the other hand, is the verb **beobachten** (see **observe**), with a strictly incorrect pronunciation in most parts, viz. **be-ö'-bachten** (instead of **be-ob-achten**).

oben: The fundamental force of this adv. is 'on *or* at the top' of something (ant. **unten**): cf. **oben auf dem Berge** and **unten im Tale**; so also **Mein Schlafanzug liegt oben im Koffer** ('My pyjamas are lying uppermost in the trunk'). Distinguish between **oben wohnen** ('to live upstairs, in the upper flat') and **weiter oben wohnen** ('to live farther up the street'). By extension it is used of a higher position in rank, order, etc.: e.g. **oben in der Klasse sitzen** ('to be at the top of the class')—**oben an der Tafel sitzen** ('to sit at the head of the table')—**Der Befehl kam von oben** ('The order came from a higher authority'). As this last example shows, it may be governed by a prep.; sim. **Bitte bemühen Sie sich nach oben!** ('Kindly walk upstairs!')—**Das Glas war bis oben voll** ('The glass was full to the brim')—**Er musterte mich von oben bis unten** ('He eyed me from head to foot, from top to toe')—**Die Arbeiter haben alles von oben nach unten gekehrt** ('The workmen have turned the place upside down'); fig. **Behalte den Kopf oben!** ('Don't lose your head! Keep cool!') —**Man behandelte mich von oben herab** ('I was treated haughtily').

obendrein: see **darein** 1 (*b*), and cf. **Laß dir obendrein** (or **überdies** q.v.) **raten, von deinem Vorhaben abzustehen** ('What's more, be advised to give up your intention').

oberhalb: see **außerhalb** 2.

obey: With a pers. obj., this is usually expressed by **gehorchen** (+ *dat.*). At one time it could be used in the pass. as if it were trans., as in **Ein großer Herr will gehorcht sein** (G.), but this is no longer permissible: cf. **Ein großer Herr will, daß man ihm gehorche.** By extension, it is also used of obeying a person's words, orders, advice, etc., but with an obj. like **Vorschriften** ('instructions') the correct verb is **befolgen** (+ *accus.*); cf. also **folgen** 1 (*a*) and **leisten.** It is rather strange that whereas **jemandem Gehorsam bezeigen** or **gehorsam sein** are reg. used for 'to obey a person', the verb **gehorsamen,** at one time quite common, is now practically obs.: propositions like **Du betrübest mich, statt deine Pflicht zu tun und mir zu gehorsamen** (Spindler) and **Ich habe dir nicht gehorsamt** (C. F. Meyer) now sound very strange.

obgleich: 1. As explained under **ob** (q.v. 2 (*c*)), the combination **ob auch** can have the concess. force of 'although', in which case the two words must be separated if the subj. is a pers. pron.; and the same applies to the combination **ob gleich,** as in **Man fand ihn in einem sonderbaren Zustand, denn ob er gleich noch lebendig war, schien er doch tot zu sein** (Fr. Griese). But it is much more common now in ordinary prose to write these two words (not **ob auch**) as one and say **Obgleich er lebendig war, schien er tot zu sein**; and this applies equally to the alternative expressions **obschon, obwohl, obzwar** and **wiewohl.** As these are all subord. conjs., the verb must, of course, go to the end, as in **„Wann darf ich nach Thurneck wiederkehren?" „Wann Ihr wollt, obschon ich gern Euch länger bei mir sähe"** (H. v. Kleist): it is an offence against established usage to say **Der Graf war gut gewachsen, obzwar andere hielten sich besser** (Rilke). **2.** As in English, all these words can be used in a *contracted* clause: e.g. **Obgleich in Jahren** ('Although up in years'), **nahm er an allem teil** (G.)—**Auch ich, obgleich ein Landmann, dünkte mich glücklich, ein städtischer Aristokrat zu heißen** (G. Keller)—**Das Hilfszeitwort „sein"** ('the aux. verb *to be*') **wird zuweilen**

obgleich im allgemeinen nicht nachahmenswert, weggelassen (Sanders)—**Obgleich eben erst von einer weiten Fahrt zurückgekehrt, erzählte er eine Schnurre nach der anderen** (Speckmann)—**Ich muß es, obzwar mit Bedauern, verlassen** (Moltke)—**Er war ein unleidlicher Grobian, wiewohl ein großer Mann** (Th. Mann).

obig: see **folgen** 3.

obliegen: see **ob-** 2; cf. **Ich betrachtete es als meine Obliegenheit, den Gatten von dem Vorgefallenen zu verständigen** (Th. Mann: 'I regarded it as my bounden duty to inform the husband of what had happened').

obschon: see **obgleich** 1 and 2.

obschweben: see **ob-** 1.

observe: When a person says 'Did you observe that man who passed us just now?' he uses the word 'observe' in a loose way to suggest a casual act of perception, like 'Did you happen to notice that man?'. This idea is suggested in German by **bemerken** (q.v.). A more conscious and deliberate perception is expressed by **achtgeben** (see **Acht** and **achten** 1), as in **Gib auf diesen Mann acht** ('Keep your eye on this man'). A further step is seen in **beobachten** (q.v.), implying a more concentrated attention, esp. a sharp watch on a person's actions, a close examination of a thing to discover its nature or character (hence used of scientific observation), or an observance of rules, proprieties, etc.: e.g. **Der Erzieher beobachtet ein Kind, um die Natur desselben zu studieren** (Eberhard)—**Ein Astronom beobachtet die Gestirne, ein Botaniker die Entwicklung einer Pflanze**—**Die Mitglieder werden ersucht, die Vorschriften zu beobachten.**

obsiegen- see **ob-** 1.

obtain: see **get** 1.

obvious(ly): Where this expression, or 'evident(ly)', occurs in a factual statement which is based on the evidence of *sight*, it is best rendered by **sichtlich** (sometimes strengthened by the prefix **offen-**) or **augenscheinlich:** e.g. **Sie langweilten sich sichtlich** (K. Edschmid: i.e. you had only to look at them to see that they were bored)—**Er schwieg eine Weile und kämpfte sichtlich, ob er erzählen solle oder nicht** (Jul. Grosse)—**Es ist augenscheinlich, daß ein Kreis rund ist**—**Er ist augenscheinlich schlecht gelaunt.** But such a statement may be the result of a *mental* process, based on a clear understanding of the circumstances, and in this case the correct expression is **offenbar:** e.g. **Es ist meine offenbare Pflicht, es der Polizei zu melden**—**Nach dem, was der Arzt sagt, hat der Kranke ein offenbares Bedürfnis nach Ruhe**—**Diese Beweisführung ist offenbar falsch** ('This argument is obviously wrong'); cf. **Er ist sichtlich** ('as one can see') **verrückt** and **Er ist offenbar** ('evidently') **verrückt, sonst hätte er das nicht getan.** A good expression for 'to be obvious to' (a person) is **einleuchten** (+ dat.), as in **Daß der Angeklagte gelogen hatte, leuchtete jedem** (or **jedermann**) **ein:** see **light (verb)** 1 (*c*).

obwalten: see **ob-** 1.

obwohl, obzwar: see **obgleich** 1 and 2.

occur: This word is used in three senses which must be distinguished in German. **1.** With the force of 'to be met with, be found', as of a plant that occurs in a certain locality, or a passage to be found in a certain chapter, it is usually expressed by **vorkommen** (cf. 3 (*g*) below) or **sich finden,** rather less commonly by **begegnen** (q.v. 2, and cf. 3 (*g*) below): e.g. **In dieser Gegend kommen Steinkohlen vor**—**Dieser Ausdruck kommt erst im Neuhochdeutschen vor**—**Die betreffende Stelle findet sich im dritten Kapitel des Romans. 2.** When it means 'to come to mind', **einfallen** (q.v.) or **in den Sinn kommen** is generally used, with a dat. of the person: e.g. **So etwas zu tun, fällt mir nie ein. 3.** When it means 'to happen, take place', there is a large choice of expressions, which, however, differ to some extent. (a) The verbs with the most general application are **geschehen** (q.v.) and **passieren,** the latter only in coll. speech. Actually, **geschehen** is a rather colourless word, its proper force being that of Lat. *fieri*, 'to be done': e.g. **Dein Wille geschehe** ('Thy will be done')—**Was Sie befehlen, ist schon geschehen**—**Ein Wunder ist geschehen** ('A miracle has been performed', which is really the passive of **ein Wunder tun**)—**Es ist töricht, Geschehenes zu beklagen** ('It's useless to cry over spilt milk'); cf. **Das geschieht ihm recht** ('That serves him right'). That this verb really has passive force is seen from the fact that it is the intrans. verb corresponding to the factitive **schicken** as used in its early sense of 'to cause to happen'; cf. Luther's **Gott schickte es wunderbarlich, daß . . .** (lit. God miraculously caused it to happen that . . .', i.e.

'God ordained that . . .'). It is precisely because **geschehen** lacks pith that one of the more pregnant verbs given below is so often preferred, and it is significant that **geschehen** is more frequently used with indef. expressions like **es, etwas, nichts,** etc., than with specific nouns, of which the only common ones are **Unglück** and **Unfall.** (**b**) Much like **geschehen** is **sich begeben,** which, however, although the noun **Begebenheit** is quite common, has a rather Biblical flavour: **Es begab sich, daß . . .** ('It came to pass that . . .'). (**c**) The reflex. **sich ereignen** has no connexion with **eigen** (see **eignen** 2) but is a corruption of **sich eräugen,** a derivative of **Auge** (MHG *erougen* or *eröugen* = **vor Augen stellen, zeigen**; Lessing still uses **eräugen**), so it is properly used of an occurrence (**Ereignis**) that catches the *eye*, and then more generally of one which attracts special notice; e.g. **Am 1. November 1755 ereignete sich das Erdbeben von Lissabon** (G.)—**Ein Vorfall** (cf. (*d*)) **hatte sich ereignet, der die Gäste etwas wider Lisbeth einnahm** (Immermann). (**d**) The two verbs **vorgehen** and **vorfallen** (both used absolutely, and esp., like **geschehen,** with indef. expressions) differ mainly in that the former suggests an occurrence (**Vorgang**) that is gradual or continuous, the latter an occurrence (**Vorfall**) that is sudden and unexpected: cf. **Was geht denn hier vor?** ('What's *going on* here?') or **In diesem Winter ging im Hause eine merkwürdige Veränderung vor** (O. Ernst) and **Eben ist etwas Entsetzliches vorgefallen.** (**e**) Rather more choice expressions for **vorfallen** are **sich zutragen** and **zustoßen,** which differ mainly in that the former is generally used absolutely, while the latter, which is particularly appropriate in connexion with mishaps, accidents, disasters, etc., requires a dat. of the person: e.g. **Ein sonderbarer Vorfall hat sich neulich zugetragen—Eben ist meinem Vater ein Unfall zugestoßen: er ist die Treppe hinuntergestürzt.** (**f**) The choice expression **widerfahren** (insep., always with a dat.) properly suggests, as does **begegnen,** what comes *up against* a person, what he *meets with,* what *befalls* him; but it is always associated with nouns indicating the treatment he meets with at the hands of his fellow men as a result of his actions, nouns suggesting good or evil, honour or disgrace, justice or injustice, praise or censure, etc.: e.g. **Es soll ihm kein Leids widerfahren** (G.)—**Ihm widerfuhr größere Ehre, als er verdiente—Mir ist großes Unrecht widerfahren—Man ließ ihm Gnade widerfahren** ('He was shown mercy')—**Man ließ ihm Recht widerfahren** ('Justice was meted out to him'). (**g**) **Vorkommen** and **begegnen** (q.v.) may also be used to suggest an occurrence (although the nouns **Vorkommnis** and **Begegnis** are much less common), but even here their fundamental force is that given under 1 above: **So etwas kommt bei uns nicht vor** means 'That sort of thing does not happen, is not done, in our house *or* country', i.e. 'You won't come across it with us'.

oder: see **congruence** 1 (*d*) and **weder** 1; **sonst** 1.

Ofen: The plur. of this masc. noun is now always **Öfen:** the unmutated form, although historically correct and still used very occasionally, e.g. by Mörike, and more recently by Rilke, who says **Die Zimmer waren kalt, die Ofen rauchten,** is not recognized and should not be used.

offen: see **open** 1.

offenbar: see **obvious(ly).**

offenbaren: In the past part. of this verb, the forms with and without **ge-** are both in use, the former esp. of 'revealed' religions, the latter in more ordinary contexts: according to *Sanders,* **Heutigem Sprachgebrauch gemäß gilt offenbart überwiegend in nicht kirchlichem Sinn, geoffenbart dagegen im kirchlichen von Wahrheiten, die auf übernatürliche Weise dem Menschen kundgeworden; vgl.** (= cf.) **ein offenbartes Geheimnis, die geoffenbarte Religion.** Luther almost always uses the form without **ge-**: e.g. **Es soll das Recht offenbart werden wie Wasser** (Amos 5. 24)—**Im dritten Jahr ward dem Daniel etwas offenbart** (Dan. 10. 1); **Deine Propheten haben dir deine Missetat nicht geoffenbart** (Lam. 2. 14) is quite exceptional. On the whole, *Sanders*'s distinction seems still to be observed: cf. **Die Bibel kündete ihm, was sein Herz ersehnte: dauernde Gottesgewißheit, den Glauben an die in ihr geoffenbarte Wahrheit** (K. Lamprecht)—**Derart Dinge sah er nicht, weil sie ihm nicht offenbart wurden** (K. Edschmid).

offer: 1. *verb*: (**a**) In expressing propositions like 'May I offer you a cup of tea?' or 'I offered him a tip', the Germans do not use the simple verb **bieten** (see (*b*)), but the compd. **anbieten,** which implies the option of acceptance or rejection of what is offered: **Darf ich Ihnen eine kleine Erfrischung anbieten?—Ich bot ihm ein Trinkgeld an**; (**b**) the simple verb **bieten,** apart from a few phrases like **Ich bot ihr meinen Arm** or **Für diese Ware hat er einen zu geringen Preis geboten** ('He has made too low an offer for this commodity'), is particularly used in cases where the idea of acceptance or rejection hardly arises, and here we often use other words in English: e.g. **Er bot mir die Hand** ('He held out his hand to me' or 'He lent me a helping hand')—**Er bot mir Trotz** ('He bade me defiance')—**Eine gute Gelegenheit bot sich** ('A good opportunity presented itself')—**Albert trat in die Stube: man bot sich** (dat.) **einen frostigen „Guten Abend"** (G.: '. . . we wished each other an icy Good evening')—**So etwas lasse ich mir von ihm nicht bieten** ('I shan't stand that sort of treatment from him'); (**c**) rather more select than the simple verb is **darbieten,** which is esp. used as a reflex.: e.g. **Eine herrliche Aussicht bot sich unseren Augen dar** ('A glorious view presented itself to our eyes'); (**d**) a more formal expression than **anbieten** is **antragen,** used of offering not trivial things like a tip or a drink, but such things as a post, friendship, services, etc., and esp. one's hand in marriage: **Er trug** (or **bot**) **mir das Amt** or **seine Dienste an**—Faust says to Margaret: **Darf ich wagen, meinen Arm und Geleit Ihr anzutragen?** (G.)—**Er hat ihr die Hand zum Ehebunde angetragen**; (**e**) for 'to offer *to do something*', see **anerbieten. 2.** *noun*: To each of the verbs given above there is a corresponding noun: (**a**) The one corresponding to **bieten** is **das** (in the north generally **der**) **Bot,** now obs. except in some dialects: cf. **Güter gegen den höchsten Bot anschlagen** (Möser: presumably 'to shake hands on a sale of goods at the highest price offered'); (**b**) the noun corresponding to **anbieten** is **das Angebot,** which has supplanted **Bot** and is therefore used in quite a general way, particularly of a commercial offer (= **Offerte**): e.g. **Das Angebot Ihrer Hilfe ist sehr verführerisch** ('The offer of your help is very tempting') —**Unser Angebot versteht sich einschließlich Porto** ('Our offer includes postage')—**Laut Angebot** ('as per offer')—**Die Preise richten sich nach Angebot und Nachfrage** ('Prices are determined by supply and demand')—cf. **Gebot**; (**c**) although the verb **anerbieten** (q.v.) is no longer much used, the verbal noun **das Anerbieten** is in very common use, being employed where an infin. is expressed or implied: e.g. **Er erbot sich, sie zu begleiten, und sie nahm sein Anerbieten dankbar an—Ich bedaure, von Ihrem freundlichen Anerbieten keinen Gebrauch machen zu können** ('I am sorry not to be able to avail myself of your kind offer'); (**d**) a more formal expression, corresponding to **antragen,** is **der Antrag,** used esp. of an offer of marriage: e.g. **Ich fühle mich durch den Antrag dieses Amtes sehr geehrt** ('I feel greatly honoured by the offer of this post')—**Er hat ihr einen Antrag** (= **Heiratsantrag**) **gemacht.**

öffnen: see **open** 2 and 3 (*a*).

oft: Although the compar. and superl. forms **öfter** and **öftest** can be inflected, esp. in certain adv. phrases, as in **Das habe ich ihm schon des öfteren** (= **öfters**) **gesagt** ('I have already told him so on various occasions') and **Ich verbringe die Ferien manchmal am Meer, aber am öftesten** ('most frequently') **im Gebirge,** it is only in some southern dialects that they are used as attrib. adjs., as in **Solche öftere Erzählungen taten ihm wohl** (Auerbach: 'Such often repeated stories did him good'). In particular, the use of the pos. oft as an attrib. adj. is quite contrary to accepted usage, and an example like **Das Vergangene ist müde von zu oftem** (for **häufigem**) **Erinnern** (Rilke) should never be imitated.

Ohm: There are three nouns **Ohm.** The one (masc.) is contracted from **Oheim,** meaning 'uncle'; the other two are technical expressions, one (masc. or **neut.**) really the name of a famous physicist of last century which came to be used in electricity as a unit of resistance ('ohm' or 'ohmad'), the other (neut.) an old liquid measure ('aam'), about two-thirds of a 'hogshead' (**Oxhoft**). In these technical senses its plur. remains unchanged, as in **Ein Fuder hat zehn Ohm** (Hebel); in that of 'uncle' it is usually **Öhme,** the mutated initial vowel being also used in the sing.: cf. **einer meiner Öhme** (Heine) —**der Öhm und Ahnherr dieses Kaiserhauses** (Sch.). It is now almost confined to dialects, being replaced ordinarily by **Onkel.**

ohne: 1. This prep. now always takes an *accus.* In MHG, *âne* was commonly used with a gen. (which usually preceded it), and occasional NHG examples even of the dat. are found, but these are now obs.: one no longer says **Ich bin ohne Gleichem** (Lessing) or **Ich beschloß, den Abend ohne einer weiteren Maßregel bei ihm zuzubringen** (Stifter); cf. the coll. maxim **Bescheidenheit ist eine Zier, doch weiter kommt man ohne ihr!** in which the dat. is playfully used for the rhyme. The only remnants of earlier usage still extant are **ohnedem,** sometimes used for the much more usual **ohnedies** ('apart from that, besides, moreover'), as in **Er hatte ohnedem eine gute Flinte bei sich** (G.), and **zweifelsohne** (< MHG *zwîvels âne*, 'without doubt'), used mostly as an adv., but occasionally also as a pred. adj.: e.g. **Die Augustiner-Eremiten waren zweifelsohne** ('undoubtedly') **einer der strengsten Orden** (K. Lamprecht)—**Wer sollte, wenn es zum letzten kommt, nicht wünschen, ganz zweifelsohne vor seinem Richter zu stehen?** (Fontane: 'Who, when his end comes, would not wish to stand before his Maker free of all unbelief?'). In an example like **„Ja, bezaubernd bin ich", antwortete sie ohne Rühmens, im Tone einer klaren Erkenntnis** (A. Zweig), the prep. seems to take a gen., but this gen. form is now treated as an accus., an indef. numeral being really understood, as explained under **viel** 1 (*a*) and (*b*). In the coll. style **ohne** is often used independently in the pred. as a sort of adv., but actually an accus. obj. is understood: e.g. **Die Vorstellung war gar nicht so ohne** ('The performance wasn't at all bad', really 'wasn't without its good points'). **2.** The English pres. part. after 'without' is sometimes expressed by a neg. **daß**-clause, as in **Er kehrt nie von einer Reise wieder, daß ihm nicht ein Dritteil seiner Sachen fehle** (G.: 'He never returns from a journey without a third of his luggage having got lost'); but this idea is much more usually expressed by **ohne zu** + infin., or (necessarily where the subjs. of the two clauses are different) by **ohne daß**, esp. with a subj. of cautious statement: e.g. **Er kehrte heim, ohne seinen Freund getroffen zu haben** or **ohne daß ihm ein Bekannter begegnet wäre**—**Der nächste Tag verging, ohne daß sich die Schwestern gesehen hätten** (Fontane)—**Eine Weile umstrich er das Haus, ohne daß er den Mut gefunden hätte, einzutreten** (H. Hesse)—**Ein Jahr mochte vergangen sein, ohne daß ich seiner gedacht oder an ihn erinnert worden wäre** (A. Schaeffer); cf. the example from this last author given under **wonder** 4. As **ohne** implies a negation, a pleonastic neg. expression should not be inserted into its clause, the only permissible exception in good prose being where **weder . . . noch** occurs in the clause: see **weder**, and esp. **negative (pleonastic)** 2 (*a*) and (*b*).

ohnegleichen: see -**gleichen** 1.

ohnerachtet, ohngeachtet: These are older spellings of **unerachtet** and **ungeachtet** (q.v., and cf. **ungefähr**): e.g. **Ohnerachtet die Hauptstadt so nahe lag** ('Notwithstanding that the capital was so near'), **hatten sie das Gewühl der Menschen zu vermeiden gesucht** (Novalis)—**Die Gegend war fruchtbar, ohngeachtet die Hügel ein abschreckendes Ansehen hatten** (id.).

ohngefähr: see **ungefähr.**

Oktober: see **Monatsnamen.**

once: see **einmal**; **erst** 2 (*b*).

only: see **nur** 1; **erst** 2 (*b*) and (*c*); **single.**

open: 1. The adj. **offen** is used in the pred. with **halten, lassen** and **stehen,** but 'to throw a window open' is not **ein Fenster offenwerfen:** cf., on the one hand, **Er hielt die Tür offen, bis ich hinausgetreten war**—**Ich habe das Fenster offengelassen** (or **offenstehen lassen**), and, on the other hand, **Sie warf das Fenster auf** (Freiligrath)—**Ein Windstoß warf das Fenster auf** (Immermann); sim. **Er stieß das Fenster auf. 2.** The *trans.* verb 'to open' (a door, box, etc.) is usually rendered by **öffnen** or **aufmachen,** in rather more choice language by **auftun;** but the compound **eröffnen** is used of opening a meeting, a ball, an account, hostilities, etc. Where we, referring to a theatre, concert or the like, say 'The doors open at 7 o'clock', the Germans do not use **Tür** at all, but say **Die Kasseneröffnung** (i.e. the opening of the box-office) **findet um 7 Uhr statt. 3.** In rendering the *intrans.* verb 'to open', special care is necessary. **(a)** In a phrase like 'The door opened', the commonest expression is **aufgehen** (which is particularly appropriate in a proposition like 'This door does not open easily': **Diese Tür geht schwer auf**), while **auftun** and **öffnen** here require the reflex. pron., as in **In diesem Augenblick tat** (not **machte**) **sich die Tür auf**—**Nach einer Weile hörte sie die Haustür sich öffnen** (L. Schücking). In this connexion, one should not be misled by a proposition like **Er hörte die Tür öffnen**: here the infin. is *trans.* and Tür its obj., a subj. being understood, i.e. **Er hörte (jemand) die Tür öffnen** (see **accus. and infin.** 2 (*a*)). Where we say 'School opens today' and 'A new shop has opened', a German says **Die Schule geht heute an** and **Ein neuer Laden hat sich aufgetan**; it is quite contrary to accepted usage to say **Er vernahm, der Gasthof habe gerade erst eröffnet** (H. Leip). (**b**) 'To open *or* give' on to a street, garden, staircase, etc., is **gehen** (not **geben**!) with a suitable prep.: e.g. **Dieses Zimmer geht auf den Marktplatz—Die Wohnstube geht nach Norden—Meine Fenster gehen auf einen schmalen Kanal** (G.)—**Für die kleine Luke, die in den Garten ging, hatte sie einen Vorhang genäht** (Zifferer). Where appropriate, as in all the examples just given, the compd. **hinausgehen** is even more common; but where one room opens into another, **hinaus-** is obviously unsuitable: cf. **Die Studierstube ging in eine Schlafkammer (hinein)**.

orange: see **adjectives (indeclinable)** 1.

order: see **befehlen**.

order of German words: see **word-order**.

ornament: **1.** The verb **putzen** means, in the first instance, 'to remove dirt from', as in **Stiefel, Fenster, Messer putzen**. Then it comes to mean 'to add something bright to', generally small personal ornaments (a brooch, ribbon, etc.), esp. such as are of little intrinsic value, gaudy, not artistically beautiful, as in **Der Schäfer putzte sich zum Tanz mit bunter Jacke, Band und Kranz** (G.); cf. **Viele Menschen lehnen sich gegen Putz auf** ('object to ornaments *or* to dressing up') **und verlangen, die Frauen nur in einfachen Kleidern zu sehen** (G.)—**Die Mutter flocht den Mädchen grüne Bänder in die langen Zöpfe**; so **aufgeputzt** ('dressed up') **stolzierten sie über den Markt** (Böhlau); or it may imply the idea of vanity, as when one speaks of **die Putzsucht der Frauen**. **2.** Rather more choice expressions are **Schmuck** and **schmücken**, which suggest something beautiful and valuable: 'to set with pearls' is **mit Perlen schmücken** (not **putzen**), and **Schmuck** (plur. **Schmucksachen**) implies a fine piece of jewellery, not a cheap trinket: e.g. **Sie hatte außer der Perle auf ihrer Stirn nichts von Schmuck angetan** (Carl Hauptmann)—**Ach, welche Armbänder! welcher Halsschmuck!** (G.); so also one always speaks of **Brautschmuck**, using the more dignified expression for a solemn occasion. **3.** The idea of artistic beauty is even more pronounced in **zieren**, and so **Zierde** (now more common than **Zier**) points to something artistically complete in itself which beautifies its surroundings, and is often used with *fig.* force: e.g. **Dieses Gebäude ziert den ganzen Marktplatz** (or **ist eine Zierde des ganzen Marktplatzes**); so also Schiller refers to the brave knights who had gone out and tried to slay the dragon as **die Zierden der Religion**, as we speak of 'the flower of chivalry'. And here there are two derivative nouns: (**a**) **Zierat** (with fluctuating gender, cf. **die Heimat** and **der Monat**; now mostly *masc.* but usually with the fem. plur. form **Zieraten**) is a small beautifying object, like a drawing-room ornament, etc.: e.g. **Neben der Teekanne und den Tassen erblickte ich ein seltsam Zierat aus rotem Ton gebildet** (Storm)—**Die abgefallenen Stücke dieser Zierat gingen unter der Dorfjugend als gangbare Münze** (G. Keller: referring to bright buttons which 'passed for current coin among the youngsters of the village'); (**b**) **Verzierung** suggests ornamentation on a larger scale, e.g. in architecture: **Es sind Zieraten im eigentlichsten Verstande** ('in the real sense'), **denn sie sind kaum Verzierungen** (G. Forster)—**Die Verzierungen des Schlosses sind geschmackvoll: der Baumeister hat eine besondere Liebhaberei zu Vögeln, die er mit andern Zieraten angenehm zusammenstellt** (G.)—**Im Schloß sind angenehme Verzierungen, die aber doch einen umherschweifenden Geschmack verraten** (G.); cf. **Ein alter, reichverzierter Erker schmückte das Haus** (Böhlau).

Ort: see **place (noun)** 1.

Osten, östlich: see **Nord**.

Ostern: see **Weihnachten**.

outside: see **inside**.

overhear: see **überhören** 1.

P

Paar: 1. Written with a capital letter, this means 'pair, couple', with the distrib. plur. **Paare**, collect. **Paar** (see **nouns of measure** 1 *a*): e.g. **Er benötigte eines Paares weicher Schuhe** (E. Wichert)—**Sechs Paare traten zum Tanz an**—**In der Gesellschaft befanden sich drei neuvermählte Paare**—**Schuhe werden nur nach Paaren** (or **paarweise**) **verkauft**; but **Im Schrank hat er neun Paar solcher Schuhe** (Britting)—**Sie kam mit zwei Paar neuer Schuhe zurück. 2.** Written with a small letter, it is only used with an art. or pron. adj. in the sense of 'a few', being then *indecl.*: e.g. **Diese paar Wochen im Ausland haben meine Gesundheit wiederhergestellt**—**Nach ein paar im Ausland verbrachten Wochen kehrte er nach Hause zurück**—**Mit ein paar harten Worten verurteilte er das Betragen Onkel Christians** (Th. Mann)—**Georg hatte nach ein paar Löffeln die Suppe von sich gestoßen** (B. E. Werner)—**Er löschte die Flamme mit ein paar Handvoll Wasser** (Stehr: cf. **nouns of measure** 2). One can say either **ein paar Kinder** or **ein paar der Kinder**, and both take a *plur.* verb (cf. **congruence** 1): e.g. **Ein paar der Freunde traten an ihn heran** (Sudermann).

participle (past): 1. (a) The past part. of a *trans.* verb (for intrans., see (*b*) below), expressing a condition or state resulting from a completed action, can be used *attrib.* to qualify a noun: e.g. **Dies ist ein gut gebautes Haus.** But this use has a wider application in German than in English in that the attrib. part. can be modified by adv. and esp. prep. phrases: thus, 'He lives in a house overgrown with ivy, separated from the street by a large garden' is best rendered by **Er bewohnt ein mit Efeu überwachsenes, durch einen großen Garten von der Straße getrenntes Haus.** But this should not be overdone, as some standard authors are fond of doing, esp. in descriptive passages. If a proposition begins with the words **Seit einem Jahrzehnt bewohnte die Familie . . .**, the reader is justified in expecting the accus. obj. to follow reasonably soon; yet in the following example the obj. is separated from the verb by such a long string of attrib. phrases that by the time he reaches it, the reader may easily have forgotten how the sentence began: **Seit einem Jahrzehnt bewohnte die Familie in einer ruhigen, mit Linden bepflanzten, nach Peter von Cornelius benannten Straße ein gartenumschlossenes, mit dem etwas verjährten, aber behaglichen Mobiliar im Stil von Rosaliens Vermählungszeit ausgestattetes Häuschen**—and as though that were not enough to be going on with, the author adds a long rel. clause—**das einem kleinen Kreis von Verwandten und Freunden . . . öfters zu anständig aufgeräumten, nach Landesart auch gern ein wenig weinseligen Abendfeiern gastlich offenstand** (Th. Mann). This proposition is so overloaded with what grammarians call *pycnometochia*, i.e. the too frequent use of part. phrases, that the average reader may well give up the struggle long before he reaches the end. And even where the attrib. words are adjs., or parts. which have become adjs., a proposition should not be as overloaded as the following one is: **Ein Dichter ist ein auf allen Gebieten ernsthafter Tätigkeit unbedingt unbrauchbarer, einzig auf Allotria bedachter, dem Staate nicht nur nicht nützlicher, sondern sogar aufsässig gesinnter Kumpan, ein innerlich kindischer, zur Ausschweifung geneigter und in jedem Betracht anrüchiger Scharlatan** (A. Eloesser). It is sentences like these that have caused people in other countries to poke fun at the German lang., and they are quoted here as **„abschreckende Beispiele"**, i.e. as warnings against the undue use of such attrib. phrases. For an example of this construction which is not to be recommended, see **sollen** 3 (*b*); **(b)** *intrans.* verbs which take the aux. **sein** can also be used *attrib.*: one can say **das eingestürzte Haus, der umgefallene Baum**, etc., and even **das früher dort gestandene Gebäude** (Storm: 'the building which used to stand there'), although unusual in the north, is permissible, as **stehen** (see **sitzen** 3) is used in the south with **sein**. But this does not ordinarily apply to intrans. verbs which take **haben**: *Duden* rightly condemns as „falsch" expressions—used in news reports, wedding notices, etc.—like **die stattgefundene** (for **abgehaltene**) **Versammlung** or **die gestern stattgehabte**

(for **vollzogene**) **eheliche Verbindung**; cf. **In der Kapelle waren Tafeln, die hier stattgefundene Vermählungen meldeten** (K. Edschmid). So also it is really incorrect to say **Im Umkreis standen die, die bloß aus Neugier sich eingefunden hatten, darunter der schon stark gefrühstückte Kantorssohn** (Fontane: '. . . among them the organist's son, who had already had a substantial breakfast'); but in point of fact, the past parts. of verbs meaning 'to eat, drink, breakfast', etc., have become sanctioned by coll. usage in an act. sense; and sim. in the *neg.*, as in **Lieber ungegessen ins Himmelreich als mit allen Taschen voll Proviant in die Hölle!** (Anzengruber: 'Better to go to heaven on an empty stomach than to hell with one's pockets stuffed with victuals!'); for other examples, see **essen** 2, and cf. Lat. *impransus, incenatus.* **2.** (a) Very common in English is the use of a past part. after 'having', as in 'Having said that he left the room'. The corresponding use of **habend** is always clumsy and should be avoided, esp. in the attrib. relation (cf. (*b*)): the proposition **Das Häuschen trug die Spuren eines hier heftig getobt habenden Kampfes** (Liliencron) would certainly be better expressed by means of a rel. clause (. . . **die Spuren eines Kampfes, der hier heftig getobt hatte**). But in certain common elliptical clauses the past part. of a trans. verb may be explained by the omission of **habend** (see **accusative absolute**): thus, one can say **Das gesagt** (*scil.* **habend**), **verließ er das Zimmer**; and sim. **Dies vorausgeschickt, fing er seinen Vortrag an** ('Having made these preliminary remarks he began his lecture')—**Dies Geschäft erledigt, ging man zur Tagesordnung über** ('Having disposed of this business the meeting passed on to the order of the day'). And such clauses are even used where they are strictly less correct: it is obvious that if **habend** is understood, it must refer to the *subj.* of the princ. clause, which is not the case in **All das erwogen, drängt sich mir eine Frage auf** (Fontane). (**b**) In the case of *reflex.* verbs, the attrib. use of the past part. should be avoided altogether: the expression **das sich verbreitete Geheimnis** (G.) in the sense of 'the secret which had spread abroad' is not good German, and **alle sich erhoben habenden Schwierigkeiten** (Raabe: 'all the difficulties which had arisen') is clumsy, to say the least. And this applies even more to trans. verbs with act. force when associated with an accus. obj.: it is taking more than a liberty with the lang. to say **das den Grafen befallene Unglück** (G.) for **das Unglück, das den Grafen befallen hatte.** (**c**) There is nothing really incorrect in a proposition like **Diese Worte richteten sich gegen seinen dreimal verheiratet gewesenen Vater** (Fontane), where the attrib. past part. is deliberately used to convey the idea that the married state applied to past time (**gegen seinen dreimal verheirateten Vater** might suggest that he was still married—and to three wives!); but here also a rel. clause would be much more natural (**gegen seinen Vater, der dreimal verheiratet gewesen war**). **3.** The past part. is used coll. with *imperative* force in a limited number of peremptory commands, warnings, etc., esp. in **Rauchen verboten!** and **Eintritt verboten!** ('No smoking!' 'No admittance!'). Elsewhere the simple infin. is used, notably in **Einsteigen!** ('All aboard! Take your seats!'), **Abfahren!** (called by the stationmaster to the guard) and **Schritt fahren!** ('Drive slowly!' esp. of horse traffic); **Als sie in den Wagen stiegen, sagte er: „Langsam fahren!"** (C. Bulcke). With other verbs either form is used: cf. **Das nächste Mal aufgepaßt!** (Böhlau: 'Next time keep your eyes open!')—**Plötzlich ertönte das scharfe Kommando: Stillgestanden! . . . und nach dem Frühstück: Aufstehen! Wegtreten!** (Ompteda: '. . . Stand! Dismiss!'). In an expression like **Nichts verraten!** ('Keep it dark!') the verb may be either the infin. (= **Du sollst nichts verraten!**) or the past part. (= **Nichts soll verraten werden!**); but that the exact explanation of such a phrase is not felt is evident from an expression like **Reinen Mund gehalten!** ('Mum 's the word! Don't blab!'). **4.** Other uses of the past part. are seen in **Er kam gelaufen** (see **kommen** 4) and **ungefrühstückt** (see **essen** 2). See also **accusative and participle, ein-** 3 and **passive voice.**

participle (present): 1. This part of the verb is not used nearly as much in German as it is in English (cf. **accusative and participle; werden** 4). There are, of course, many parts. which have become adjs., e.g., in the case of *trans.* verbs, **eine beleidigende Bemerkung** ('an insulting remark')—**ein erregender Roman** ('an exciting novel')—**ein reizendes Bild** ('a charming picture')—**ein überraschendes Resultat** ('a surprising result')—**ein ohrzerreißendes Gekreisch** ('ear-splitting shrieks')—and of *intrans.* verbs, **ein vorübergehendes Gewitter** ('a passing thunder-storm')—**Nach langer Fahrt durch nicht enden wollende Wälder** ('through forests that seemed never to be going to end') **erreichte er sein Ziel** (M. Eyth); cf. **Es ist jetzt zehn, also nachtschlafende Zeit** (Fontane: 'time we were in bed'). **2.** In particular, the pres. part. of **sein** is practically never used, and that of **haben** only in a few expressions like **der wachthabende Offizier** ('the officer on guard-duty') and esp. **eine wohlhabende Familie** ('a well-to-do family'). So, to express propositions such as '*Being* ill (*Having* had to leave town), he could not accept my invitation', a German uses a causal clause: **Da er krank war** (or **sich erkältet hatte**), **konnte er meine Einladung nicht annehmen**—or he uses two princ. clauses: **Er war krank, und darum konnte er . . .** A subord. **daß**-clause is necessary after **dadurch**, as in **Ich vermied ihn dadurch, daß ich einen Umweg machte** ('I avoided him by going a round-about way'), but after other compds. of **da(r)-** an infin. clause is used: **Er war damit beschäftigt, seinen Koffer zu packen** ('He was engaged in packing his bag')—**Ich war drauf und dran, auszugehen, als er mich anrief** ('I was just on the point of going out when he rang up'). An introductory part. clause is possible in rendering propositions like 'Leaving the road we followed a path through the wood', but even here a German feels reluctant to say **Den Weg verlassend, folgten wir einem Pfad durch den Wald,** preferring to use two princ. clauses ('We left . . . and followed . . .'). These few examples illustrate the German disinclination to use pres. part. constructions, and this is also seen in some idioms which can only be explained by assuming the omission of a part., as in **Einen Brief in der Hand** (*scil.* **haltend**), **trat er bei mir ein** (see **accusative absolute**) and **Ich habe den ganzen Roman gelesen, das erste Kapitel ausgenommen** (*scil.* **habend**: see **except** I). **3.** For propositions like **Hier ist eine zu bezahlende Rechnung** ('Here is an account that has to be paid'), where **bezahlend** is a pres. part. in *form* only, see **infinitive** 3 (*b*) and cf. **zu** I.

pass: 1. In nautical language, **passieren** is regularly used with the force of 'to sail past *or* across' some place: e.g. **Wir haben** (or **sind**) **das Kap der Guten Hoffnung passiert**; cf. **Man sagt von jemand, dem es im Kopf übergesprungen ist** (= coll. **der übergeschnappt ist**): **er hat die Linie passiert** (Kant: 'A person who has gone crazy is said to have crossed the Line'). In modern times this use has been extended to travelling on land, and **die Grenze passieren** (= **überschrei'ten**, 'to cross the frontier') has become a common phrase; so also **Als der Wagen Lodi** (a town in Lombardy) **passiert hatte, senkte sich der Abend auf die Erde** (Hackländer)—**Als er das Palais passierte, sah er zu der zweiten Etage hinauf** (Fontane)—**Als er den Korridor passierte, hörte er hinter einer Tür Seufzer ausstoßen** (Kafka). But, on the whole, this use of the verb is avoided in good prose, and is in any case confined to passing a place, as in the above examples: one does not say **Er passierte mich. 2.** The usual way to express the idea of passing a place or a person is to use the appropriate verb of motion compounded with **vorbei-** or **vorüber-**, for examples of which see **vorbei**, and cf. **im Vorübergehen** (*en passant*) and **Ich halte mich vorübergehend** (not **vorbeigehend**) **hier auf** (i.e. 'temporarily').

passieren: see **occur** 3 (*a*); **pass** I.

passive voice: 1. The pass. of a verb is generally formed by combining the uninflected past part. with the various parts of **werden** (q.v. 3), which then has *no* **ge-** in the past part. In the case of trans. verbs, the accus. obj. of the act. becomes the subj. of the pass., while the subj. of the act. is expressed by **von** or **durch,** the former indicating the *agent*, the latter the *means*: e.g. **Ich bin soeben von meinem Vater durch einen Rippenstoß geweckt worden.** On the other hand, intrans. verbs, trans. verbs which have no obj., and verbs which take a gen. or dat. can only be used *impers.* in the pass., the gen. or dat. being retained, and the subj. **es** being dropped unless it stands first (see **impersonal verbs** 3): e.g. (i) with *no obj.*, **Es ist nach dem Arzt** (or **Nach dem Arzt ist**) **geschickt worden**—**Eifrig wurde gelesen, hastig gefrühstückt und dann kräftig geraucht** (Ebner-Eschenbach)—**Da wurde genäht, gestickt, gestrickt, gestopft und endlos geplaudert** (Böhlau)—**Gehustet und geniest und geschnoben**

wird über die Maßen in unserem Hause (Storm: 'There is an unconscionable amount of coughing, sneezing and nose-blowing going on in our house')—**Madame S. beehrt sich, ihre Gäste zum Tee zu bitten: es wird getanzt** (F. v. Zobeltitz: '. . . there will be dancing')—**Sobald ich eine Anstellung gefunden habe, wird geheiratet** (Kästner: 'As soon as I find a job, we'll get married')—**Du bist erhitzt, jetzt wird ausgeruht!** (Roquette: '. . . you're going to have a good rest now!')—**„Ich muß in die Küche." „Nein, jetzt wird liegengeblieben"** (A. Reiner: '. . . No, you'll stay in bed')—**In den Zwischenpausen wurde Soldaten gespielt** (Ompteda: 'In the intervals they played at being soldiers'); (ii) with the *gen.*, **Seiner wird jährlich an seinem Geburtstage in Ehren gedacht** ('His memory is honoured every year on his birthday')—**Das heilige Wort „Heimat" wurde mit Verachtung genannt und des Vaterlandes wurde gespottet** (Frenssen); (iii) with the *dat.*, **Mir wurde gedroht**—see also **begegnen** 3. Contrary to the rule, a few verbs which take a dat. are in special cases used *pers.* in the pass., esp. **folgen** and **schmeicheln,** occasionally **huldigen** and **widersprechen** (qq.v.) **2.** (**a**) When **sein** is substituted for **werden,** the word **worden** is really understood, the reference being not to an action still proceeding, but to a completed action, i.e. a *state,* so that the past part. is to all intents a pred. adj.: thus, **Das Korn wurde geschnitten** suggests that the corn was being cut, **Das Korn war geschnitten** that it had been cut; sim. **Dann war er in die Droschke gehoben** (Wildenbruch) really means 'Next moment he was in (had been lifted into) the cab'. (**b**) But **sein** is used instead of **werden** to form the pass. in certain cases, viz. (i) in rendering 'to be born', esp. with reference to a person still alive: e.g. **„Ich bin in Berlin geboren . . . Wo sind Sie eigentlich geboren?"** (I. Seidel); of a deceased person one says **Goethe ist** (or **wurde**) **1749 geboren,** but **Goethe war damals noch nicht geboren** ('G. had not yet been born at that time'); (ii) now almost always in the *imperat.*, where propositions like **Dein Name werde geheiliget** (Matt. 6. 9) or **Ewig werde dein gedacht, Bruder!** (Sch.) now have a definitely archaic flavour; cf., as examples of modern usage, **In Gottes Namen sei der Versuch gemacht!** (G.)—**Gesegnet seien unsere Sterne!** (Raabe)—**Erde, du unsere Mutter, sei gegrüßt!** (Forbes-Mosse)—**Das sei Gott** (dat.) **geklagt** (Droste-Hülshoff)—**Es werde** (now usually **sei**) **hier nur eins bemerkt** (Frenssen); (iii) very commonly in the infin. when associated with one of the **modal auxiliary verbs** (q.v.): here **werden** is not incorrect, cf. **Daran mochte der Graf nicht erinnert werden** (Heyse)—**In Hannover mußte umgestiegen werden** (Speckmann)—**Es sollte in dem Ort gefüttert, gerastet und Mittag gehalten werden** (Mörike)—**Frauen wollen noch immer geraubt werden** (Kellermann: see below); but **sein,** although apparently little used with **dürfen,** is much more common with the others: e.g. **Das kann nicht gemeint sein—Nur von dir möchte ich gut genannt sein** (Heer)—**Was gesagt sein muß, muß leise gesagt sein** (O. Ludwig)—**Wenn durchaus gestritten sein muß, dann sei es auf würdigem Kampfplatze** (Ebner-Eschenbach)—**Weil es ein solcher Freudentag ist, soll auch allen Sündern vergeben sein** (Heyse). This use of **sein** is esp. common with **wollen:** e.g. **Ich wollte nicht genannt sein** (Chamisso: 'I did not want my name to be mentioned')—**Die Toten, welche hier begraben liegen, wollen nicht beklagt sein** (Raabe)—**Sie fühlte, daß diese kindliche Natur anders angefaßt sein wollte** (Ompteda: 'She felt that a person with such a childlike nature required to be handled in another way'); for other examples, esp. of such propositions with an impers. subj., where **wollen** often has an idiomatic force which **werden** lacks, see **wollen** 2. (*a*). **3.** (**a**) After certain verbs, e.g. **hören** and **sehen,** an act. infin. is often used with pass. force, as in **Ich hörte ihn zu fünf Jahren Gefängnis verurteilen** ('I heard him being sentenced to five years' imprisonment') or **Ich sah ihn verhaften** ('I saw him being arrested'); but actually the construction here is the accus. and infin., the accus. being understood: 'I heard (the judge) sentence him . . .'—'I saw (a policeman) arrest him'. (**b**) This is esp. common after **lassen,** as in **Man ließ** (*scil.* **jemand**) **den Arzt holen**; that such an act. infin. eventually comes to have real pass. force is seen from an example like **Eine solche Beleidigung lasse ich mir von niemand bieten** (lit. 'I let such an insult be offered to me by no one', i.e. 'I'm not going to put up with an insult like that from any one'), which has developed out of **Eine solche**

Beleidigung lasse ich niemand mir bieten; cf., as a clumsy example not to be imitated, **Er lächelte mit einem sich nicht beschreiben lassenden Ausdruck der Milde** (= **mit einem Ausdruck der Milde, der sich nicht beschreiben läßt,**) **auf mich hernieder** (A. Schaeffer). **4.** (**a**) For certain past part. forms used coll. with act. force, like **Ich ging ungefrühstückt ins Geschäft,** see **essen** 2 and **participle (past)** 1 (*b*). (**b**) For expressions like **die zu bezahlende Summe,** where the pres. part. form has pass. force, see **infinitive** 3 (*b*).

past-present verbs: 1. In most classes of MHG strong verbs the stem-vowel in the *plur.* of the *past. indic.* differs from that of the *sing.* (see **Ablaut** 1). This vowel-change is now preserved only in **ich ward, wir wurden** (although the sing. has been superseded in ordinary lang. by **ich wurde**); but a sim. change is seen in the *pres.* tense of **dürfen, können, mögen, müssen, wissen** and **wollen** (qq.v., and cf. **modal auxiliary verbs**). The change from **ich darf** to **wir dürfen,** etc., is explained by the fact that these were orig. *past* tense forms which later assumed pres. force, so that new past tense forms had to be found (and these, incidentally, are all *weak*). That the pres. forms of these so-called past-present verbs were orig. past is proved not only by this vowel-change, but also by the fact that their 1st and 3rd sing. are identical (**ich darf, er darf**), and that their 3rd plur. ends in **-en** (**sie dürfen**), whereas the 3rd plur. pres. indic. in MHG ends in *-ent*, the past indic. in *-en*. **2.** How such past tense forms came to have pres. force will be best understood by considering the Greek verb *οἶδα* (*oida*), which means 'I know', but is actually the perf. tense of an obs. verb meaning 'to perceive'. In point of fact, this word has lost an initial consonant, the so-called 'digamma' (a sound not unlike German *w*), so that there is an obvious close connexion between the Greek word, the Lat. *vidi*, our 'to *wit*', and the German **ich weiß**: like the Greek perf., the German past orig. meant 'I have perceived'—and so 'I know'. The other past-present verbs have all undergone a sim. development, although the change in meaning there is not so obvious; in the case of **dürfen,** the cognate **darben** ('to be in want') suggests that **ich darf** once had the force of 'I have lacked the permission', which implies that permission was later obtained—hence 'I am allowed'. **3.** In MHG the list of these verbs was a slightly longer one: it included NHG **sollen** (< *ich sol, wir suln*), **gönnen** (< *ich gan, wir gunnen*), **taugen** (< *ich touc, wir tugen*), and one (*ich tar, wir turren*, past *ich torste*) which is obs. in NHG, but preserved in our English 'dare, durst'.

past subjunctive: 1. (**a**) The past subj. of a *weak* verb is normally the same as its past indic.: e.g. **Ich wäre froh, wenn er mich lobte.** (**b**) Exceptional are (i) the verbs **brennen, kennen, nennen** and **rennen,** which have the stem-vowel **a** in the past indic. (see **brennen**), but **e** in the past subj. It is true that occasional examples of **brännte** etc., are found, as in **Mir ist, als kännte ich dich schon lange** (Ponten) and **„Wenn man nur den Mann kännte,"** **meinte der Ratsherr** (Federer), but these forms are not to be recommended: *Duden* says expressly **„du kenntest (nicht: känntest)"**; and so also **Es wäre schrecklich, wenn das Haus niederbrennte**; (ii) the verbs **bringen** and **denken,** which have **brächte** and **dächte**; (iii) the verb **wissen** (q.v. 1). **2.** In the case of *strong* verbs, the past indic. and subj. forms always differ. (**a**) If the stem-vowel of the indic. cannot mutate, the subj. differs from the indic. only by the insertion of **e**: e.g. **Es wäre besser, wenn er mehr spazierenginge (wenn du mehr spazierengingest).** (**b**) If the stem-vowel of the past indic. is capable of mutation, the mutated form marks the subj.: e.g. **Ich würde nicht weinen, wenn er mich schlüge—Wir sähen besser, wenn wir auf den Zehen ständen** (see 3)—**Er wäre böse, wenn er nicht alles in Ordnung fände.** But although **a** normally becomes **ä** in the past subj., a number of verbs of this class show other forms, for which see **Ablaut** 2. (**c**) Noteworthy here are esp. **stehen** (q.v. 1) and its compds., in which the historical subj. forms with **ü** (< MHG *stüende*), although sounding rather choice and not used in coll. speech, are almost as common in prose as those with **ä**, esp. in 'as if' clauses: e.g. **Ich hatte ein Gefühl, als stünde der Tod hinter mir** (Wildenbruch)—**Es war, als stünden geliebte Tote neben mir** (H. Hesse)—**Es war, als stünde man in einer Zauberkugel** (M. Eyth)—**Er meinte, daß alles mir zu Gesichte stünde** (Th. Mann); sim. in compds.: **Sie drohte, Florenz zu verlassen, wenn er darauf bestünde,**

sie zu sehen (I. Kurz)—**Er wußte nicht, was ihm bevorstünde** (Stehr)—**Die Boten benahmen sich, als wenn der Weltuntergang bevorstünde** (A. Döblin)—**Er war bereit, ihm das Geld zu schenken, damit keine Schwierigkeiten entstünden** (Rilke)—**Er konnte es kaum erwarten, bis er ihr gegenüberstünde** (Jul. Wolff)—**Er blickte sie verwundert an, als verstünde er sie nicht** (Zifferer)—**Er fragte nicht, ob wir das verstünden** (Th. Mann). **3.** (**a**) The past subj. is reg. used in *indir.* speech (where the pres. subj. is more formal and should be avoided if it has the same form as the indic.), and also in subord. clauses implying unreality, doubt, etc., as in those introduced by 'as if' (see **als** = **'as if'**): cf. **Es wurde den Brüdern schwer, voneinander zu gehen: nicht daß sie sich um den Hals gefallen wären** (Wildenbruch: '. . . not that they threw *or* it was not as if they had thrown their arms round each other'). But it is also used idiom. in *dir.* discourse to make a statement less blunt, more polite, esp. more cautious, implying that the statement may possibly be incorrect: e.g. **Dürfte** (less blunt than **Darf**) **ich Sie um Feuer bitten?** ('Might I trouble you for a light?')—**Ich dächte, es wäre Zeit, aufzubrechen** ('I rather think it is time to set out—or am I wrong?'). A sim. cautious statement is seen in propositions like **Es gibt wohl keinen zweiten Dichter, der die Schwächen der menschlichen Natur tiefer erkannt hätte als Gottfried Keller** (M. Necker)—**Es gab wohl keinen Ort in Mitteleuropa, wo mehr Vögel gesungen hätten als hier** (Schmidtbonn)—**In dem Friedhof war kein Grab, das nicht Marmortafel und Eisengitter gehabt hätte** (id.) (**b**) Not easy to explain are common statements, used, say, by the leader of a discussion group, **Na, so weit wären wir!** or **Das wäre also erledigt!** Of the meaning there is no doubt: they both express satisfaction that the discussion has reached a stage or a conclusion—the former means 'Well, we have got so far anyway', the latter 'So that is settled!'. But why past subj.? Is it because the upshot has been doubtful during the discussion? This might explain the former example, where the discussion is not yet concluded, but surely hardly the latter. Another explanation, suggested by R. M. Meyer, is that such a statement is **„ein in die direkte Rede eingesprengtes Stück indirekter Rede“**, i.e. that the subj. is that of an *indir.* statement transferred to *dir.* speech: cf. **Wir können nun sagen, daß wir so weit wären.** Whatever the explanation may be, the subj. is certainly in reg. use in such contexts. (**c**) The past subj. of **wünschen** and **wollen** are used to introduce a wish: **Ich wünschte** or **wollte, ich wäre reich!** (cf. **wünschen** 2 (*d*) and **wollen** 1); the pres. indic. here would rather suggest a blunt command, as in **Ich wünsche, daß das geschehe!** (practically 'See that it is done!').

pendeln: see **mit** 2 (*a*).

permit: 1. The usual expression for this verb is **erlauben** (+ dat. of person), which really has the neg. force of 'not to forbid', as in **Ist das Rauchen hier erlaubt?**—see **leave** (noun). **2.** More formal, and more positive, is **gestatten** (q.v.). **3.** Analogous is **zulassen** (cf. **admit**), which is used in the sense of 'to suffer *or* tolerate' what one either cannot or will not prevent, and usually implies passive disapproval, as when one allows something to be done or to continue which one views with disfavour: the question **Warum ließen Sie das zu?** implies an additional clause like **wenn Sie es doch mißbilligten**, or **wenn Sie es doch hätten verhindern können. 4.** The verb **gönnen,** one of the **past-present verbs** (q.v.), was in OHG *gi-unnan,* just as the noun **Gunst** was *gi-unst.* It properly has the neg. force of 'not to grudge', as in **Ich gönne ihm sein Glück**; but the compd. **vergönnen** has more positive force, emphasizing the idea of **Gunst** and meaning 'to allow as a favour', and so is used esp. of permission granted or vouchsafed to man by God: e.g. **Er starb ohne daß es ihm vergönnt gewesen wäre, sein Lebenswerk zu vollenden.**

Pfennig: Although the normal plur. form **Pfennige** is always used in a distrib. sense (as in **die Pfennige zählen**, 'to count one's pennies', or **nach Pfennigen rechnen**), it should really not be used, as it sometimes is in careless writing, in references to a sum of money, where the collect. sing. form is the correct one to use: thus, there should be a clear distinction between **zehn Pfennige** (i.e. ten pfennig pieces) and **zehn Pfennig** (an amount of money, approx. a penny)—see **nouns of measure** 1 (*a*). It is interesting that the 1875 issue of German postage stamps was inscribed

Pfennige, but this was altered to **Pfennig** in the 1880 issue; most recent issues simply bear a numeral, only in a few isolated cases is the abbreviated form Pf. or Pfg. added.

Pferd: see **Roß.**

Pfingsten: see **Weihnachten.**

pflegen: **1.** The MHG verb *phlegen* had only strong forms, and these are still in use, but with a change of stem-vowel, viz. pflōg, gepflōgen (< *phlăc, gephlĕgen*). The orig. past indic. form with the stem-vowel *a* is now obs., but was used in the south as late as the 19th century: e.g. **Er hatte sich enger an mich geschlossen als alle übrigen, so daß wir eine besondere Freundschaft pflagen** (G. Keller); cf. **In Begleitung seines Hofmeisters, mit dem er gern der** (see 2) **Unterhaltung pflag, kam er oftmals auf Besuch** (Storm, using the archaic form intentionally in a tale of the 17th century), and the example from H. Kurz given under **ob-** 2. **2.** The MHG verb always took the *gen.* case, and this construction is still in use in choice lang., esp. in more or less set phrases as with **der Ruhe** ('to take one's ease *or* rest'), **der Liebe** ('to enjoy the pleasures of love'), **seines Amtes** ('to discharge the duties of one's office'), **Rats** ('to take counsel'); cf. **Die alten Teile der Klosterschule, in denen noch die Väter der jetzigen Generation der Wissenschaften gepflogen hatten, waren der Erde gleichgemacht** (Th. Mann). But the *accus.* can now be freely used in such contexts, even with the strong forms of the verb, although these are not used in the everyday lang.: e.g. **Er pflog geistliche und weltliche Gespräche mit ihr** (id.)—**Das war das Gespräch, das er mit einem Bauern pflog** (Auerbach)—**Im stillen pflog er mit sich selber Rat** (I. Kurz)—**Sie sagten, nachdem sie Rat gepflogen hatten, „Wir geben dir drei Rätselfragen auf"** (Rilke)—**Sie ritten heim; in beiden wirkte das gepflogene Gespräch noch lange nach** (Jul. Wolff: '. . . the conversation they had held left an impression on both of their minds for a long time'). **3.** One of the commonest uses of **pflegen** is to suggest that something 'usually' happens, is done 'as a rule', an idea which we often express by 'I am used to . . .', and here the subj. may be either *pers.* or *impers.* In MHG this use was followed by a simple infin., but now the infin. requires **zu**: e.g. **Er pflegt morgens spazierenzugehen**—**Im Sommer pflegt es im Süden sehr heiß zu sein.** Its force, then, approaches that of **gewohnt sein** (see **accustom** 1 and 2), but the latter naturally stresses that a thing is done as the result of an acquired *habit* and is therefore properly used only with a *pers.* subj.: thus, one says **Die Schwalben pflegen** (not **sind gewohnt**) **im Herbst nach Süden zu ziehen,** because it is an instinct, not a habit; cf. **Dieser Schüler pflegt in seinen schriftlichen Arbeiten grobe Fehler zu machen, das bin ich von ihm gewohnt** (i.e. he usually makes bad mistakes, and I have become accustomed to expect them from him)—**Ich bin es nicht gewohnt, daß man mir schmeichelt: man pflegt mir eben nicht zu schmeicheln.**

Pfund: Like other words denoting measure, weight, etc., this retains its sing. form in the plur. after numerals when it has *collect.* force (see **nouns of measure** 1 (*a*)), but takes the plur. ending when used *distrib.*: cf. **Das Paket wog drei Pfund** and **Es ist ein Paket von drei Pfund (Gewicht)**, but **Der Zucker wird nach Pfunden abgewogen** ('Sugar is weighed by the pound').

pick up: see **aufheben** 2 and 3.

pine: see **Kiefer.**

place (noun): There are several expressions which approach each other more or less closely, but really convey different ideas. **1. Ort**: In MHG, *daz* (less commonly *der*) *ort*, besides suggesting a 'place' in a general way, had various specific shades of meaning, e.g. a 'terminal point' (*unz an daz ort* = **bis zu Ende**; in mining, **Ort** is still used of the 'end' of a gallery), a 'sharp-pointed end' of an instrument or weapon (*diu ort ir swerte* = 'the points of their swords'; cf. **das** or **der Ort**, a shoemaker's 'awl'), and a 'point' of the compass, 'direction' (cf. Luther's **Ich will die vier Winde aus den vier Örtern des Himmels über sie kommen lassen,** Jer. 49. 36, and Kingsley's 'the four *airts* of heaven'). In modern times, when the *masc.* gender has gained the ascendancy over the neut., and the plur. **Orte** over **Örter** in good prose, **Ort** suggests a 'place' or 'spot' in a wide sense, and specifically a place where people have converged and settled down together: e.g. **Ich habe meine Wertpapiere an einen sicheren Ort gebracht** ('I have lodged my securities in a safe place')—**Die Verhandlungen wurden an einem dritten Ort abgehalten** ('The negotiations were conducted in the house of a third party *or* on neutral ground')—**am angeführten Ort** (contracted **a.a.O.,** *loco citato,* 'in the passage quoted above')—**Dieser Ort zählt eine Million Einwohner**; it is also often used in combination with **Stelle** (see 3), as in **Alles ist an Ort und Stelle** ('Everything is in its proper place') or **Wir werden bald an Ort und Stelle sein** ('We shall soon be at our destination'). **2. Platz** is either an open space in a town, a 'square' (e.g. **Schloßplatz, Bismarckplatz,** etc.) or, more generally, the space occupied by or reserved for a person or thing: e.g. **Im Theater gibt es Sitz- und Stehplätze—Dieser Platz ist belegt** ('This seat is reserved')—**Er nahm auf dem Sofa Platz — Behalten Sie Platz!** ('Keep your seat! Don't get up!')—**Bitte, Platz machen!** ('Make room, please!'); cf., with specific force, **Er ist auf dem Platze geblieben** ('He fell on the field of battle': cf. Barber's 'Bot the best of thair cumpany left ded in the *plass*'). **3. Stelle** always has *relative* force, indicating a place or spot in its relation to its surroundings: e.g. **Baustelle** ('building-site', as distinct from adjoining sites)—**An einigen Stellen ist der Bergpfad gefährlich — In diesem Roman sind zwei herrliche Stellen** ('passages')—**Er sucht eine Stelle als Schreiber** ('a situation as clerk', where he will be above or below other employees; cf. a maid looking for a 'place')—**An deiner Stelle hätte ich anders gehandelt** (see **anstatt** 2)—**an erster Stelle** ('in the first place, first and foremost'). **4. Statt** and **Stätte:** see **Statt** 1 (*a*) and (*b*).

place (verb): see **put.**

Plan: In all senses of this noun, e.g. 'plain', 'plan' (of a city), 'time-table' (= **Fahrplan**), and esp. 'plan, intention', its plur. is now **Pläne:** *Heyne* says **„Die Mehrzahl Plane mehr in älterer Sprache, Pläne heute allgemein geworden"**, and **Pläne** is the only form given by *Duden* and *Sprach-Brockhaus.* This is all the more surprising as **Plane** was at one time almost the rule: cf. **Ich machte neue Plane und überlegte, was zu tun sei** (G., who almost invariably used the unmutated form)—**Ein solches Gesindel sollte meine Plane zerschlagen?** (Sch.)—**Von den seltsamen Planen, mit denen ich Euch oft unterhalten habe, habe ich die meisten aufgegeben** (Stifter).

Platz: see **place** (noun) 2; **room** 1.

pleasure: see **Vergnügen; Gefallen** (under **Ge-** 4 (*a*)).

pochen: see **klopfen** 1 and 2.

Polster: This is now generally treated as a *neut.* noun—*Duden* gives its gender as **„sächlich und (seltener) männlich"**, and *Sprach-Brockhaus* has **„das (vielerorts auch: der) Polster":** cf., on the one hand, **Senkt sein Haupt aufs kühle Polster** ('cushion') **nieder** (G.), and on the other hand, **Der Anhänger** ('side-car' of a bicycle) **ist aus Aluminium gebaut und besitzt roten Lederpolster** (K. Edschmid: '. . . is padded and covered with red leather').

prahlen: Where we 'boast *of*' our ancestors, a German 'boasts *with*' them: **Er prahlt** (or **brüstet sich**) **mit seinen Ahnen.** In the proposition **Ich möchte nicht gern Prahlens machen** (Zelter), the gen. form is used as an accus. in the same way as **Aufhebens, Federlesens, Rühmens,** etc. (qq.v., and see **viel** 1 *b* and *c* for the explanation of this use); but it is now unusual in the case of **Prahlen.** But a common coll. alternative expression for **Prahler** ('boaster, swaggerer') is **Prahlhans** (gen. **Prahlhansen** or **-hanses,** plur. **-hänse**), and we even find **Prahlhanserei** (Heine) with the force of an 'addiction to boasting' (**Prahlerei**).

prefixes (verbal): 1. (a) These are either 'separable' (**trennbar**) or 'inseparable' (**untrennbar**), i.e. in certain cases the prefix is detached from the verb, in others it is never detached. The insep. prefixes are *unaccented,* apart from very exceptional cases like **In diesem Satz ist der Ausdruck „be'denken" falsch, es sollte „ge'denken" heißen;** the sep. prefixes are *accented,* being orig. separate words, either advs. or preps. (**eintreten, hinfallen**) or nouns (**stattfinden, teilnehmen**) or adjs. (**gutheißen, losmachen, totschlagen**) or prep. phrases (**instand setzen, zustande bringen,** written as two words, but as one in the verbal nouns **das Instandsetzen, Zustandebringen**). Separation of the sep. prefixes takes place in the simple tenses of princ. clauses, in questions commencing with the verb, in cond. clauses in which **wenn** is omitted (which orig. were questions: see **word-order** 3 (*b*)) and in **daß**-clauses in which **daß** is omitted (see **word-order** 1 (*c*)): e.g. **Ich gehe jeden Morgen aus — Geh heute nicht aus! — Gehen Sie heute aus? — Gehst du aus, so bleibe ich zu Hause — Er sagte, er ginge nicht aus.** In the past part., infin. and gerundive, **ge** and **zu** stand between the sep. prefix and the verb: **Ich habe viele Gäste eingeladen — Wieviel Gäste wünschen Sie einzuladen? — Hier ist eine Liste der einzuladenden Gäste**; in the case of an insep. prefix, there is *no* **ge** in the past part., and **zu** precedes the infin. and gerundive as a separate word: **Ich habe seinen Namen vergessen — Ich bitte Sie, meine Adresse nicht zu vergessen.** (**b**) In poetry, a simple sep. prefix is often treated as insep., as in **Aufsteigt der Strahl** (C. F. Meyer) and **Aufgeht noch einmal das Portal** (Freiligrath), and this is sometimes extended to prose by southern authors, esp. Auerbach; but this, as H. Kurz rightly says, **„widerspricht dem Geist der deutschen Sprache"**. But it is noteworthy that many verbs have double prefixes (one of which is always sep., as in **au'fbewahren, ei'ngestehen, bea'nspruchen, vera'nlassen**; no verbs have two insep. prefixes, see **vergewissern**), and here, in the case of a few verbs in which the sep. prefix stands first, this is not infrequently treated as insep. (see esp. **a'nerkennen** and **a'nvertrauen**). (**c**) Some prefixes, notably **durch-, über-, um-** and **unter-**, can be either sep. or insep.: see esp. **durch-**, and headwords like **übergehen, übersiedeln, umgehen, unterlaufen**, etc. **2.** For the difference in meaning between **ab-, auf-**, etc., and **heran-, hinauf-**, etc., see **ab-** 3 and **her-, hin-** 3.

prepositions: 1. For the purposes of the present volume it is unnecessary to give a complete list of the German preps.: for some of the chief difficulties connected with these, see esp. **accusative or dative . . .**, and special articles on words like **außer, entlang, ob, ungeachtet, von, während, wegen, zunächst**, etc. **2.** There is nothing objectionable in the juxtaposition of two preps. in sentences like **Ich habe lange keine Nachricht von zu Hause** or **Er begleitete mich bis nach Hause**; cf. also the combination **von wegen** referred to under **wegen** 1. But when a prep. is separated from the noun it governs by an attrib. part. phrase introduced by another prep., the resulting juxtaposition of the two preps. undoubtedly strikes a jarring note. Thus, a proposition like **Er hat eine gute Sammlung nach der Natur gemalter Bilder** has a much more pleasant sound, and is more lucid, than **Er hat eine gute Sammlung von nach der Natur gemalten Bildern**; and the same harshness and lack of lucidity is seen in **Das Dokument befindet sich unter zu Hause aufbewahrten Papieren** and **Die Geschichte ist reich an im Kriege vollführten Heldentaten.** One would think that any author with a sense of style would agree with *Sanders* when he says **„Solchen Zusammenstoß vermeidet man gern als hart und unübersichtlich"**, and with *Wustmann* when he characterizes such a clash as **„für jeden Menschen von feinerem Gefühl eine der beleidigendsten Spracherscheinungen"**. But apparently modern authors are deficient in such an instinctive sense of good style, and it is to be regretted that examples like the following seem to be on the increase: **Denkt euch, wie solch ein ödes Haus zwischen mit Luxus ausstaffierten Prachtgebäuden sich ausnehmen muß** (E. T. A. Hoffmann: 'Just imagine how such a bare house is bound to look between richly ornamented mansions')—**An über Tonnen gelegten Brettern hatten sie gesessen** (Storm)—**Er strich mit vor Alter zitternder Hand den langen Bart** (E. Wichert)—**Es war ein feingekleideter Herr mit am Kinn ausrasiertem Bart** (L. Frank)—**Sie sah ihn mit in Tränen schwimmenden Augen an** (Th. Mann)—**Die Firma galt jetzt für im** (better **als im**) **Rückgange begriffen** (id.)—**Mit nach oben geworfenen Armen rannte er durch die Zimmer** (Wassermann)—**Sie wich mit von sich gestreckten Armen zurück** (A. Schaeffer). Such jarring examples are the more surprising as the clash can generally be easily avoided, often by the insertion of a single word, otherwise by the use of a short rel. clause: cf. **Er strich mit der vor Alter zitternden Hand den langen Bart—Sie saßen an einigen über Tonnen gelegten Brettern—Sie wich mit weit von sich gestreckten Armen zurück—Sie sah ihn mit Augen, die in Tränen schwammen, an. 3.** Although the preps. **mit** and **ohne** take different cases, it is quite usual to say **Er faßte den Entschluß, niemals zu heiraten, weder mit noch ohne Schwiegermutter** (Jul. Wolff), because the fem. noun has the same form in the dat. and the accus. But where the dat. and accus. forms differ, it is doubtful whether the use of the figure of speech known as *zeugma* is to be recommended. Purists, of course, condemn propositions like **Auf das weibliche Geschlecht übte er, ob mit ob ohne seinen Willen, eine unwiderstehliche Anziehungskraft aus**

(A. Schaeffer)—**Über zweihundert Kerzen brannten um und neben dem Hochaltar** (G.)—**Er hörte nicht das Geschrei der Möwen, die um oder über ihm flogen** (Storm)—**Vom Marktplatz herunter kam der Bürgermeister, den durch den Sturm angerichteten Schaden in und um die Stadt zu beschauen** (Raabe). Although strictly incorrect, such examples might perhaps be allowed, if only because there is unquestionably something harsh and clumsy about alternative phrases like **um den und neben dem Hochaltar** or **um den Hochaltar und neben demselben,** and **in der Stadt und um dieselbe**; but where one of the cases concerned is the gen. sing., the use of *zeugma* seems particularly harsh, as when H. Graef gives to one of his literary essays the title **Goethe vor und während des Tasso,** where surely **vor und während dem Tasso** would have been the obvious phrase to use. On the other hand, Storm could quite well have said **um ihn oder über ihm**; cf. **Von dort waren die lückenhaften Stadtmauern, sowie durch sie und über ihnen die Reste der Tempel zu sehen** (G.).

presence (cf. absence): **1.** The words **anwesend** and **Anwesenheit** suggest no more than occupation of part of a given space (**anwesend** = **an einem Ort seiend:** see **wesen**); so, if one says **Er war während der Revolution in Paris anwesend,** one does not necessarily imply that he took part in, or even witnessed, what went on (see 4). **2.** Rather more is implied by the use of **zugegen,** which suggests participation in some incident *towards* (gegen) which one's interest is directed: e.g. **Er war bei der Krönung zugegen,** i.e. he was an interested spectator at the coronation ceremony (see 4). **3.** A further step is implied by the use of **gegenwärtig** and **Gegenwart,** which not only stress a person's interest directed *towards* something (the second part, as in **aufwärts,** etc., is connected with Lat. *versus*), but above all suggest the exertion of a strong *influence* by that which excites his interest: e.g. **In ihrer Gegenwart verjüngt man sich** ('Her presence has a rejuvenating influence')—**Er ist ein Mann von schöner Gestalt und Gegenwart** (G.: i.e. a 'presence' which makes an impression on people)—**Ewig wird mir ihr Bild gegenwärtig sein** (G.); so also always **Gott ist überall gegenwärtig,** because He influences all things (not **anwesend,** because He does not occupy a part of space). Hence its force of the 'present', as distinct from the 'past' and the 'future', because we are esp. influenced by the conditions of the moment: **Ich will das Gegenwärtige genießen, und das Vergangene soll mir vergangen sein** (G.); cf. **jemandem etwas vergegenwärtigen** ('to represent something vividly to a person', as if he were actually seeing or experiencing it), esp. with a reflex. dat., as in **Er schloß die Augen, wie um sich das Vergangene recht zu vergegenwärtigen** (W.v.Scholz: 'as if to conjure up a clear picture of the past'). **4.** Actually, the adjs. given above are not so much used in ordinary lang. (at a roll-call a German says **Hier!** not **Anwesend!**); usually the idea of being present at something is expressed by **dabei sein,** with the noun **Beisein** (e.g. **Warst du dabei, als die Schlägerei entstand?** — **Er sagte es im Beisein zweier Zeugen**), or, in choicer style, by **beiwohnen** (+ *dat.*): e.g. **Haben Sie der Sitzung beigewohnt?** In particular, the adjs. given above are no longer used of things: one no longer says **Die zoologische Sammlung ist hier in Hanau nicht mehr anwesend** (G.), but rather **Die Sammlung befindet sich nicht mehr hier.**

pretend: see **stellen** 2; **tun** 3; **wollen** 2 (*c*).

promise: 1. The commonest rendering of this verb is now **versprechen,** as in **jemandem etwas versprechen** or **versprechen, etwas zu tun**; so also **goldene Berge versprechen** ('to make extravagant, impossible promises')—**Die jetzige Lage verspricht nichts Gutes** ('The present situation bodes ill')—**ein vielversprechender Schüler** ('a very promising pupil')—**Sie hat sich ihm versprochen** ('She has pledged her troth to him'). **2.** It is surprising that **versprechen** was orig. not so used. MHG *versprechen* meant 'to reject, refuse, deny', while 'to promise' was then expressed by *lŏben* or, more commonly, *gelŏben*: a striking example from the Nibelungenlied is *Kriemhilde wolde Sîfriden niht* versprechen, *ouch* lobte *er si ze wîbe* ('K. would not refuse S., and he promised to take her to wife'). While the simple verb **loben** now only has the force of 'to praise', the more select compound **geloben** is still used with that of 'to give a solemn promise, swear' to do something (cf. **ein Gelübde ablegen,** 'to make a vow'); so always **das Gelobte Land** ('the promised *or* Holy Land'). Cf. also **the**

doubly compounded **angeloben,** really **an** (or **in**) **die Hand** (or **mit Handschlag**) **geloben,** 'to promise *or* swear by shaking hands': e.g. **Er gelobte ihr ewige Treue an.** **3.** Another choice expression is **verheißen,** which stresses the solemnity of the vow and implies a certainty of its fulfilment; it is because of this implication that it is common in references to the Deity, as in **Was Gott verheißet, das kann er auch tun** (Rom. 4. 21).

proper names of persons: 1. There is considerable fluctuation in the declension of these, but the modern tendency seems to be to alter the name as little as possible, even **Jesus Christus** being now used for all cases, although the older oblique case-forms are still generally preferred: gen. **Jesu Christi,** dat. **Jesu Christo,** accus. **Jesum Christum.** Formerly proper names often took a weak ending in the dat. and accus., and this still holds good in familiar lang., as in **Als sie öffnete, stand Rudolf auf dem kleinen Flur und sagte, daß er Vatern holen sollte und Hedwigen auch** (Fontane); but elsewhere examples like the following now sound very old-fashioned: **Ich lasse Moritzen ungern allein. . . . Ich habe ihn aufgemuntert, an Herdern zu schreiben** (G.)—**Die Baronesse hatte schon mit Charlotten über Ottilien gesprochen** (G.)—**Sie dankte Theobalden für sein letztes Schreiben** (Mörike). To be esp. avoided is the earlier inflexion of names like **Agnes,** ending in a sibilant, as in **Ich rede von Agnesen** (id.). **2.** The only case which requires to be clearly shown is the *gen.* (**a**) Names ending in a sibilant may still, in accordance with earlier usage, form their gen. in **-ens,** as in **Das ist Fritzens Buch,** and this has been extended to other names in familiar lang., as in **Mariens Schirm**; cf. **Es ist hier die rechte Stelle, ein Bruchstück aus dem Nachlaß Annettens von Droste einzuschalten** (L. Schücking). But even this gen. ending often sounds old-fashioned, and one prefers other forms, e.g. **Elises Tante, Goethes Werke, Brahms' Symphonien, die Reden des Demosthenes,** etc. (**b**) After an art. or other determinative word, a proper name now usually remains uninflected: where Goethe uses **Die Leiden des jungen Werthers,** one now would use **des jungen Werther,** and sim. **Das Jahrhundert des zwölften Karl und des großen Peter war zu Ende** (Bergengruen)—**Es war des Römischen Kaisers Friedrich berühmte Schrift** (id.)—**Am folgenden Tage hatte er es nicht erwarten können, seinen Platz in dem Atelier des Meisters Teodor zu erobern** (Carl Hauptmann); so also **seit des Kaisers Napoleon Kontinentalsperre** (R. Herzog) and **das Bild Armin des Cheruskers** (Zifferer). (**c**) A difficulty arises in references to a monarch or ruler with a Roman numeral after the name. It is obvious that in propositions like **Über der Tür der Kapelle malten die Brüder Zucchari die Exkommunikation Heinrich IV** (Waiblinger) and **Heute war auch die seit dem Tode Friedrich Wilhelm IV meist leerstehende herrschaftliche Loge besetzt** (Fontane) the numeral represents the gen. **des Vierten,** but as a numeral cannot be given a gen. ending, it is better to give the name the ending in such cases, as in **Das gleiche Licht ist auf der Szene Richards III mit dem Stallknecht** (Hofmannsthal) and **Das Innere der Burg war zu Beginn der Regierung Johann Albrechts III einer umfassenden Verschönerung unterzogen worden** (Th. Mann). That in accordance with the tendency to leave a name unaltered one should *say* **Richard des Dritten,** and yet have to *write* **Richards III,** is, of course, absurd, and hence many authors prefer to inflect both name and numeral, as in **Ich erfuhr, daß er Friedrichs des Vierten Gemahlin meinte** (Rilke). The only important point is that the gen. case should be instantly recognizable as such. Where the prep. **von** indicates a title of nobility, as in **Friedrich von Schiller,** one says **die Werke Friedrich von Schillers**; but where the prep. merely serves to identify a person's birthplace or home, one says **die Gedichte Walthers von der Vogelweide.** **3.** (**a**) Where we say in familiar lang. 'We are going to the Smiths this evening' or 'I was at the Browns last night', a German drops the art.: **Wir gehen heute abend zu Schmidts — Ich war gestern abend bei Brauns.** This is really a gen. sing. with **Haus** or **Familie** understood, but is felt as a plur., so that one says **Schmidts haben jetzt Besuch**; and so also **Sie waren zu Schopenhauers eingeladen** (Böhlau) and, in a reference to a name ending in **-s, Die Köchin war sieben Jahre bei Fuchsens gewesen** (Wassermann). This use is also extended to titles, professions, etc.: **Die Gesellschaft bei Apothekers war eigentümlich beschäftigt** (Böhlau)—**Heute abend geht sie zu Pastors**

(Blunck: 'to the Manse')—**Ein Eckstübchen erinnerte ihn an das Rauchzimmer bei Kommerzienrats** (H. Hoffmann). (**b**) The plur. of the def. art. is used before an uninflected name to suggest 'people like': thus **die Lessing und Kleist** (O. Brahm) means 'dramatists like L. and K.', and sim. **Zu den Offenbarungen des Inneren, mit denen die Richard und Iago** ('characters like R. and I.') **ihre Taten einleiten, finden sich Kleists Helden nicht geführt** (id.)—**Goethes Zeitgenossen und Gefährten: die Hackert, die Kniep, die Tischbein** ('such artists as . . .') **zeichneten treu vor diesen Denkmälern** (Hofmannsthal). It is not in accordance with modern practice to give such names a strong plur. ending, as in **Wir besaßen nunmehr, wo nicht Homere, doch Virgile und Miltone** (G.) and **Hätt' ich nur einige Jean Paule da!** (Stifter).

prospect: see **Sicht** 2 (*a*).

prove: The verb **beweisen** is the ordinary expression for 'to prove' used *trans.*, as in 'to prove the truth of a report *or* that a report is true'. It may also be used *reflex.* to express our *intrans.* use in a proposition like 'The report proved to be true' (where 'to be' is rendered by **als**), but here **sich erweisen** is rather more common: **Das Gerücht erwies sich als wahr.** Where **als** is followed by a *noun* in such propositions, this may stand either in the *nom.* (agreeing with the subj.) or in the *accus.* (agreeing with **sich**): cf. **Er bewies sich als einen klugen Mann** (G.) and **Er erwies sich als teilnehmender Gesellschafter** (G.). The same applies to several other verbs used reflex. in much the same sense, notably **zeigen, erzeigen, entpuppen** (q.v.) and **herausstellen** (q.v.), and to **glauben** ('to believe oneself to be'—with **als** omitted), **betrachten** ('to regard oneself as'), etc.; to the examples given under **als** = **'as'** 1 (*d*), the following may be added: **Er zeigte sich als bedeutender General** (G.), **als einen scharfsinnigen Beobachter** (G.)—**Er glaubte sich der letzte seines Stammes** (Gutzkow)—**Ich betrachte mich immer als einen Reisenden** (G.)—**Ich sah mich als einen Fremdling in diesem Kreise** (Sch.).

Pult: As this noun, meaning a sloping 'writing-desk' or 'music-stand', is derived, like our *pulpit*, from Lat. *pulpitum* ('staging, stage'), it is historically neut. At one time it was not uncommonly treated as masc., but this is now rare, and *Duden* gives only **das Pult:** cf. **Ich rannte an den Pult und schrieb das Gedicht von Anfang bis zu Ende herunter** (G.).

put: 1. This verb can be used with a great variety of objs.: you can put money in your pocket, salt in the soup, a thief in prison, a glass on the table, a child to bed, your daughter to a boarding-school, etc. There is no single German word with such a wide application, and the correct rendering of the English word in a given context is mainly determined by the resultant posture of the obj.: a vertical, upright position requires the use of **stellen** (q.v.: the factitive of **stehen,** i.e. 'to cause to stand'), a horizontal, recumbent position that of **legen** (the factitive of **liegen,** i.e. 'to cause to lie'), a sitting position that of **setzen** (q.v.: the factitive of **sitzen,** i.e. 'to cause to sit'), and a secure position (e.g. on a hook, in a receptacle, etc.) that of **stecken** (the factitive of the *intrans.* **stecken** [q.v.], i.e. 'to cause to stick'). It is imperative that the appropriate expression should be used: it is absurd to say **Die Mutter stellte das Kind ins Bett** or **Sie legte die Tasse Tee auf den Tisch.** The following are some characteristic correct examples: **Man stellt ein Glas Wein auf den Tisch, einen Stuhl an die Wand, einen Blumentopf ins Fenster, ein unartiges Kind in die Ecke, einen Soldaten vor ein Kriegsgericht — Man legt ein Buch auf den Tisch, einen Teppich auf den Fußboden, einen Toten ins Grab, die Hände in den Schoß, den Arm um ein Mädchen — Man setzt den Hut auf den Kopf, jemand auf den Thron, ein Huhn auf Eier, sich ans Feuer** or **in einen Lehnstuhl — Man steckt Geld in die Tasche, sich** (dat.) **Watte in die Ohren, einen Schlüssel ins Schloß, einen Dieb ins Gefängnis, einen Ring an den Finger, einen Braten an den Spieß, eine Feder an den Hut. 2.** But obviously even these four verbs do not cover the whole ground: not one of them, for instance, is applicable to the case of putting one's daughter to a boarding-school, or even of putting salt in the soup, as the salt can hardly be regarded as safe and secure there in the sense in which documents are secure when they have been 'stuck' in a pigeon-hole. The only verb that answers cases like these is one which suggests no specific posture, viz. **tun,** which is not confined, however, to such cases, but is used in ordinary lang. in quite a general way:

e.g. **Er tat sein Kind in die Schule** or **seine Tochter in eine Pension — Du hast vergessen, Salz an die Suppe zu tun — Er sollte sein Geld auf die Bank tun—Der Papst tat den Kaiser in den Bann** ('The Pope excommunicated the Emperor')—**Hast du deine Schulbücher in die Mappe getan? — Tu das an seinen rechten Platz! — Wo hast du die Zeitung hingetan? — Junge, tu das Messer weg! 3.** It will be observed from these examples that the *simple* verbs meaning 'to put' require the *accus.* in an accompanying prep. phrase with **an, auf, in,** etc. With some *compd.* verbs a *dat.* is quite correct, indeed, strictly more correct, as the prefix points not to the action as still proceeding, but to the moment when the action has ceased. Thus, while **sich setzen** demands an accus., **sich hin-** or **niedersetzen** can be used with a dat.: e.g. **Er setzte sich auf einer Bank nieder** (G.); and sim. **Sie legte sich auf das Sofa,** but **auf dem Sofa hin— Er stellte die Lampe auf den Tisch,** but **auf dem Tisch hin.** There is no hard and fast rule—an accus. is sometimes used even with a compd. verb; the only fixed rule is that with *simple* verbs of this kind the *accus.* is imperative (cf. **accusative or dative . . .** 2).

Putz, putzen: see **ornament** 1.

Q

quer: 1. (a) This has developed out of MHG *twerch* which corresponds to our 'a-*thwart*'. Its basic force is 'across' but it is an *adv.* not a prep. It properly suggests a right-angle crossing: cf. **Querbalken** ('cross-beam'), **Querholz** (e.g. the horizontal piece of a cross), **Querschiff** ('transept'), etc. But geometrical precision is often not insisted upon: cf. **eine Straße überque'ren, den Marktplatz durchque'ren** ('to cross a street, the market-place'); and a right-angle crossing is clearly not implied in propositions like **Eine Furche war quer übers Land gezogen** (Zuckmayer) and **Wie ein aufgescheuchtes Wild war er stundenlang querfeldein geflohen** (F. Kugler: 'Like a startled quarry he had fled for hours across country'—cf. **Querfeldeinlauf,** 'cross-country race'); cf. **Er saß aufrecht, ein bißchen quer zum Tisch** (C. Bulcke: 'obliquely to the table')—**Am Ende des Saales stand ein Tisch, der Quere nach aufgestellt** (Kafka). Here belongs the phrase **kreuz und quer** or (in) **die Kreuz und Quer(e),** meaning 'hither and thither, in all directions', as in **Ich ritt die Kreuz und Quer** (Chamisso). **(b)** So **quer** (or **verquer,** esp. in the Berlin dialect) often has fig. force: e.g., with an impers. subj., **Ich kann kaum einen Tag abwesend sein, ohne daß alles quer geht** (Hauff: '. . . without everything going wrong': cf. Scots 'to gang agley')—**Ihm war viel verquer gegangen** Fontane)—**Diese Fragen kamen dem Wirte quer** (Freytag: 'These questions embarrassed the landlord'); with a pers. subj., **Der Kerl ist quer im Kopf** (Prutz: 'The fellow is cross-grained'), whence the common expression **Querkopf** ('a perverse, obstinate person'), as in **Mein älterer Bruder galt für einen Querkopf** (G. Keller); cf. also **jemandem in die Quere kommen** ('to get in a person's way', impeding or thwarting his progress: e.g. **Da kam mir ein Jude in die Quere** (Chamisso). **2.** In contrast to the fundamental sense of **quer,** the adj. **schräg** always implies an oblique direction or position, esp. a deviation from the perpendicular or horizontal (cf. 3): e.g. **Er bog um die Ecke und ging schräg über die Straße** (A. Schaeffer)—**Mein Freund wohnt mir schräg** (ant. **quer** or **gerade**) **gegenüber —Das Haus hat ein schräges** ('sloping') **Dach—Die Mütze wurde schräg auf das Ohr gedrückt** (Gaudy: see 3); cf. **Die windgeschrägten Pappeln waren von Schrapnellkugeln zerfetzt** (Zuckmayer: cf. Scott's 'the wind-swung oak'); so also **Schräg-** or **Kursivschrift** ('italics'). **3.** The same idea of 'off the straight' is conveyed by **schief,** esp. if the thing should normally be straight: e.g. **In Pisa steht der berühmte schiefe Turm — Das Bild hängt schief — Der Leutnant zog seine Mütze keck-schief** (Zuckmayer: i.e. set his cap at a jaunty angle); and so also with the force of 'deformed', as in **Ihr Mann hieß „der schiefe Leopold", denn er hatte eine lahme Hüfte** (id.)—**Das arme Mädchen war schief gewachsen** (P. Keller)—**Der Kerl hatte eine rote, etwas schiefe Nase** (Eichendorff). Like **quer, schief** often has *fig.* force: from the *lit.* **einen schiefen Mund haben** comes the *coll.* **ein schiefes Maul ziehen** ('to pout, look sulky, make a wry face'); sim. **jemand schief ansehen** ('to look askance at a person')—**in ein schiefes Licht kommen** ('to appear in a wrong light'); and esp. **schief gehen** in the sense of 'to go wrong, turn out badly', as in **Hackert sah wohl, daß das Ganze schief ging** (G.); cf. also the coll. expression **Da bist du schief gewickelt** ('You're wrong *or* much mistaken there').

Queue: Distinguish between **die Queue** ('queue, line of people') and **das Queue** ('billiard-cue'); in either case the plur. is **Queues.**

quick: 1. (a) The orig. force of MHG *snel* was 'fit, strong, brave', esp. 'eager to fight', out of which the later meaning 'quick' developed; and it is interesting that the adv. **bald** shows a sim. development, the MHG adj. *balt* meaning 'brave, courageous'. The NHG **schnell** properly suggests nothing more than speed, without any implication of a motive for quick action: **Lauf schnell zur Post!** means no more than that the person addressed is not to loiter on his way; so also **Sprich nicht so schnell!—Die Zeit drängt: du mußt dich schnell entscheiden — Ein Schnellzug legt die Strecke in kürzerer Zeit zurück als ein Personenzug — Diese Ware hat einen schnellen Absatz** ('This commodity finds a brisk, ready sale'). (**b**) Much the same is implied by **geschwind,** properly used of what comes and quickly disappears (**ver-schwinden**); the adj. is not as common as **schnell** in the north, but the noun **Geschwindigkeit** is the reg. expression for 'speed, velocity', as in **Dieses Flugzeug übertraf alle anderen an Geschwindigkeit. 2.** The words **eilig** and **hastig** really imply an impulse, the former esp. an impulse from outside, the latter one from within: e.g. **Eilig ist, wer zu einer Verrichtung nicht viel Zeit hat, hastig, wer aus innerer Unruhe alles geschwind verrichtet** (Eberhard); sim. **Halte mich nicht auf! Ich habe es eilig** (= **Ich bin in Eile, muß eilen** or **mich beeilen**), **sonst verpasse ich den Zug! — Er ging mit langen Schritten wie einer, der schnell, aber ohne Hast nach Hause möchte** (Fr. Griese). A normally phlegmatic person may on occasion be **eilig**, i.e. 'in a hurry', but one who is constitutionally of a 'quick, hasty' nature is **hastig. 3.** Much like schnell is **rasch,** which often suggests that a person is '*over*-hasty' (cf. our rash) or that something is done 'precipitately': cf. **die rasche Jugend** (Sch.)—**ein rascher, übereilter Entschluß. 4.** Analogous is **hurtig,** from MHG *hurte* ('collision, clash'), a characteristically southern expression little used in the north: cf. **Mach hurtig! Zieh die Naue ein!** (Sch.: 'Hurry up, Be quick! Pull in the boat!').

R

radebrechen: This is the usual form which the verb takes in the north, while the south seems to favour **radbrechen.** Its orig. force was 'to break on the wheel', the assumption being that it was formed from an obs. noun **Rad(e)breche** (cf. **Flachsbreche,** an instrument for breaking flax), and this would explain the fact that it is an *insep. weak* verb (see **beanspruchen** I): e.g. **Die Knie sind mir wie geradbrecht** (G.: 'I feel as if my knees were broken'). This lit. sense is now expressed by **rädern,** while **radebrechen** is confined to the *fig.* use, suggesting a fumbling, unskilful way of doing something, as in **Er radebrechte ein paar Kartenkunststücke** (Werfel: 'He made clumsy attempts at a few card-tricks'), but used esp. with the force of 'to murder' a language, as we talk of speaking '*broken* German': e.g. **Sie radebrechten Französisch** (Treitschke)—**„Langweilig** (for the correct **Langweiliger**) **Frosch!" radbrechte Hassan** (C. F. Meyer). Occasional examples of strong forms, as in **Er radebricht** (Heyse), are incorrect.

rag: 1. Lappen orig. denoted a hanging

part of anything, like our *lap* in its old sense of 'a piece that hangs down at the bottom of a garment' (cf. the dim. **Ohrläppchen,** 'the *lobe* of the ear'). In modern use, however, its main force is that of a piece of cloth, generally torn off, for which a practical use can still be found: e.g. **Staublappen** ('duster'), **Wischlappen** ('dish-cloth'), **Waschlappen** ('washing-cloth', also applied contemptuously to a person who is a 'milksop, molly-coddle'); and one can mend a torn garment by putting on a **Lappen** or **Flicken** ('patch'). **2. Lumpen** (see **ragged** 1) was orig. used with much the same force as **Lappen,** but now generally implies a quite worthless rag, fit only to be given to a **Lumpensammler** ('ragman'). The sing. is now rare, but the plur. is the usual expression for 'torn, ragged clothes', as in **ein in Lumpen gehülltes Weib.** The shortened form **Lump** is now only used of persons, with the force of 'ragamuffin, tatterdemalion', esp. one of low mind, a 'scamp, scoundrel' (cf. 4): hence the familiar expression **sich nicht lumpen lassen** ('not to prove oneself stingy', really = **sich nicht für einen Lump ansehen lassen**). **3. Fetzen** is even stronger than **Lumpen,** and may be used of other things than clothes: e.g. **Der Sturm riß die Fahne in Fetzen** ('The gale tore the flag to shreds *or* ribbons')—in 1914, the German chancellor characterized the agreement guaranteeing the neutrality of Belgium as **ein Fetzen Papier** ('a scrap of paper'); applied to clothes, it is the equivalent of our 'tatters', as in **Dem Landstreicher hing der Anzug in Fetzen vom Leibe** ('The tramp's suit hung about him in tatters')—cf. fig. **keinen Fetzen an jemandem lassen** ('to tear a person's character to shreds'). **4. Hader** in the sense of 'cloth, rag' (older than the same word meaning 'dispute, quarrel', and probably unconnected with this) is now little used: cf. **Ein altes Weib mit einem Wischhader in der Hand** (Droste-Hülshoff). The common SG opprobrious epithet **Haderlump** ('scoundrel, knave') shows an interesting combination of two synonymous terms.

ragged: 1. Although **Lumpen** (see **rag** 2) is the ordinary expression for 'rags', **lumpig** is no longer much used for 'ragged', having esp. become a coll. expression, used contemptuously with the force of 'mean, paltry': e.g. **Der lumpigste Ladenschwengel** ('the meanest counterjumper') **hat heute das Recht, sentimental zu werden** (Heine)—**Wozu soll ich dieses lumpige** ('miserable') **Leben noch leben?** (Sudermann); esp. of a 'paltry' sum of money: **lumpige zehn Mark.** This sense is also often implied in nouns compounded with the prefix **Lumpen-,** with either *lit.* or *fig.* force: e.g. **Lumpengeschäft** ('rag and bone shop'), **Lumpenhandel** or **-kram** ('trade in rags and bones'), **Lumpengesindel, -pack, -volk** ('rabble, riff-raff'), **Lumpenkerl, -hund** ('scoundrel, blackguard'); cf. **Ich habe es mir für ein Lumpengeld erstanden** ('I picked it up for an old song, dirt-cheap' = **spottbillig**). **2.** The two words **zerlumpt** and **zerfetzt** differ in several ways: in the first place, **zerfetzt** is the stronger expression, implying a greater degree of raggedness, just as **Fetzen** is stronger than **Lumpen** (see **rag** 2 and 3); in the second place, while **zerfetzt** is a true *past part.* (**zerfetzen** = 'to tear to shreds, hack in pieces'), **zerlumpt** is now only an *adj.*, the verb **zerlumpen** being quite obs.; and in the third place, while **zerlumpt** refers only to clothing, but may be used either of the clothes themselves or of their wearer (**ein zerlumpter Mensch** = **ein Mensch in zerlumpten Kleidern**), **zerfetzt** cannot be used of the wearer of such clothes, but may refer to clothes or anything else: thus **ein zerfetzter Mensch** can only mean 'a hacked *or* mutilated human body', not 'a person in rags'; sim. **eine von Kugeln zerfetzte Fahne** ('a flag tattered *or* riddled with bullets')—**Warum hast du die Blume zerfetzt?** ('Why have you torn off all the petals of the flower?') **3.** Other possible renderings of 'ragged' are seen in examples like **zerrissene Wolken — zackige Felsen — ein zottiges Fell — unordentlich** or **schlapp marschieren** (of soldiers marching in a ragged fashion). The word **schlapp** is really the LG form of **schlaff** (see **loose** 4).

raise: see **aufheben.**

rasch: see **quick** 3.

Rat: 1. When used pers. with the force of 'councillor', this noun has the plur. **Räte,** but when used impers. in the sense of 'counsel, advice', it has *no* plur., **Ratschläge** being used instead if required. **2.** As explained under **viel** 1 (*a*) and (*b*), and **nichts** 3 and 4 (cf. also **pflegen** 2), the gen. **Rats** has come to be used as an accus. obj. In the common expression **Ich weiß mir nicht Rats,** the gen. really depends on **nicht** (= MHG *niht*, 'nothing'), the lit. meaning being 'I know nothing (in the way) of advice to give myself', i.e. 'I don't know where to turn, I am at my wits' end'. But the form **Rats** is used even without the indef. neut. word on which it depends, that is, without the very word which causes it to be a gen., so that it has really become an accus. obj., being esp. common after **holen, einholen,** or much more commonly **erholen,** in the sense of 'to seek advice' from (**bei**) a person: e.g. **Sich bei ihr Rats zu holen, verbot ihm sein Stolz** (Sudermann)—**Wackere Bürger hatten sich oft bei ihm Rats erholt** (Hauff)—**Es waren Briefe von Fremden, die sich in allerlei Herzensnot Rats bei ihm erholten** (Auerbach)—**Er stieg die Treppe hinauf, weil er sich für seine Reise Rats erholen wollte** (Fontane)—**Unsere Wohnung war von Bittstellern umlagert** ('Our house was besieged by supplicants'), **die Rats einholen wollten** (Ric. Huch). Other gen. forms used in the same way are **Aufhebens** and **Rühmens** (qq.v.).

raten: This is one of the **reduplicating verbs** (q.v.) and is used in two distinct senses, viz. 'to guess' and 'to advise'. **1.** With the force of 'to guess', it is used three times in the following example: **„Er muß heiraten? Hab' ich's geraten?" „Du hast es geraten, aber nun rate auch weiter: wen soll er heiraten?"** (Jul. Wolff), in which it has the accus. obj. **es** the first two times, an interrog. obj. clause the third time. A strict grammarian would say that the verb is wrongly used the first two times, and actually he would be justified: **raten** should properly be only used in the sense of 'to have *or* hazard a guess' (at something: **auf** + accus.), whereas 'to guess something correctly' is **etwas erraten** (cf. **er-** 3). Thus, one can only say **„Rate mal** (see 3 below), **wem ich heute begegnet bin!"** which would be followed either by **„Nein, du hast falsch geraten"** or by **„Ja, du hast es erraten"**; it is only in rather loose coll. lang. that the simple verb is used for a correct guess. **2.** (**a**) With the force of 'to advise', **raten,** like the rather stronger **anraten,** takes a *dat.* of the person and an *accus.* of the thing, which latter may be an infin. clause with **zu,** less commonly a **daß**-clause: e.g. **Wer riet dir das (an)? — Er will die Einladung abschlagen: haben Sie ihm das** (or **dazu**) **geraten?**—in the pass., **Mir wurde geraten, meinen Plan aufzugeben** (see **impersonal verbs** 3). The past part. has come to be used as an adj. in the sense of 'advisable', as in **Bei dem drohenden Gewitter wäre es geraten** (superl. **am geratensten**), **Unterkunft zu suchen**; and it is also, of course, the part. of **geraten** (q.v.). (**b**) The compd. **beraten** has several meanings, esp. 'to advise' (with an *accus.* of the person), 'to provide' (a person with something) and 'to discuss, take counsel' (with an accus. of the thing or **über** + accus.): e.g. **Vom Arzt beraten, entschlossen sie sich, den Augenarzt kommen zu lassen** (G.)—**Ich bin mit allem Nötigen gut beraten** (or **versehen**) — **Wir haben (uns) lange darüber beraten. 3.** Like all 'reduplicating' verbs, **raten** is a *strong* verb, so that the 2nd sing. imperat. should really be **rat!** but the weak form **rate!** is almost always used. Other weak forms, as in **Was ratet er?** (A. Neumann: for **Was rät er?**), should never be used, the only exception being the phrase **raten und taten** (formed from an expression like **jemandem mit Rat und Tat beistehen**), of which *Sanders* gives the past tense **ratete und tatete.**

ratschlagen: This verb (*intrans.*, 'to take counsel') and its compd. **beratschlagen** (*trans.*, 'to deliberate on' something, or *reflex.* with intrans. force), being formed from the noun **Ratschlag,** are *insep. weak* verbs (see **beanspruchen**): e.g. **In voller Ratlosigkeit ratschlagte man über dies Unikum** (Raabe)—**„Ja," brummte der Alte und ratschlagte weiter** (Blunck)—**Sie ratschlagten, was zu tun** (Scheffel: 'They deliberated what was to be done'), where **sei** or **wäre** is understood: see **was (interrogative)** 5—**Ich begann zu ratschlagen, ob ich ihr die Sache entdecken wolle oder nicht** (G. Keller)—**Es blieb nichts übrig, als einen Wagen stehen zu lassen** (i.e. to leave one wagon-load of household goods behind): **nun ward geratschlagt, was das Entbehrlichste sei** (G.: 'now there was some discussion what we could most easily do without'); **Sie beratschlagten** (*scil.* **die Frage**), **was für eine Marschroute sie nehmen sollten** (Eichendorff), where the princ. clause might be **Sie beratschlagten sich.** Very occasional strong forms, as in **Er ratschlägt** (G.), should not be imitated.

rauh: see **rough** 1.

Raum: see **room** 1.

Rauschen: see **sound** 3 (*b*).

ready: 1. The two expressions **fertig** and **bereit** are often confused. While **fertig** merely indicates that the person has finished something or that some work is finished, as in **Meine Arbeit ist fertig** or **Ich bin mit meiner Arbeit fertig** (cf. **Ich bin mit ihm fertig,** 'I'll have nothing more to do with him'), and that the person is prepared for what is to come, even if it may go entirely against his inclinations, **bereit** implies his willingness to take the next step (see **Wille** 2 and **willig,** and cf. **bereitwillig**); in fact, while **fertig** looks to the past and the present, **bereit** points particularly to the future. It almost follows that **fertig** is not followed by an infin. with **zu**; but although one does not say **Er ist fertig zu reisen,** it is possible to say **Er ist zur Reise fertig** (or **reisefertig**), i.e. he has made his preparations, so that there is nothing to prevent him from setting out; sim. **Er hatte seine Rechnung berichtigt und war zum Aufbruche fertig** (Stifter). On the other hand, **Er ist zur Reise bereit** (or **bereit zu reisen**) implies that he is not only ready, but quite 'prepared', i.e. willing to set out. As **fertig,** then, implies that a person has accomplished a job or made all preparations for a possible eventuality, it has come to be used to suggest that he is proficient in his profession and has not much more to learn: e.g. **Er spricht fertig** (or **mit Fertigkeit**) **Deutsch** ('He speaks German perfectly, like a native')—**Sie ist eine fertige Klavierspielerin** ('She is a finished *or* accomplished pianist'); and as *Eberhard* neatly says, **Der fertigste Spieler ist nicht immer bereit zu spielen,** because he may not be in the mood or may be out of practice. **2.** But although **fertig** is not used with **zu** + infin., it does practically have the force of **bereit** in some compds.: e.g. **bußfertig** ('contrite, willing to atone') —**dienstfertig** ('ready to serve')—**friedfertig** ('peace-loving, wanting to preserve peace'); and *Eberhard* again says appositely **Auch der Friedfertigste wird nicht unter entehrenden Bedingungen bereit sein, Friede zu machen, noch der Dienstfertigste zu schimpflichem Dienst bereit sein.**

really: Of the various possible renderings of this adv., there are esp. two which students find difficulty in distinguishing. **1. wirklich:** As an adj., this word implies the antithesis of what only *appears to be and is not*, or of what is *purely imaginary*. The Romantic poets turned their backs on **die wirkliche Welt,** in which Schiller says everything is **„Schaum und Schein"** (see **appearance**). So the adv. **wirklich** means 'actually, in point of fact', much like **tatsächlich** or **in der Tat:** e.g. **Man glaubte allgemein, sie stelle sich krank oder bilde sich nur ein, krank zu sein, aber der Arzt sagt, sie sei wirklich krank** (i.e. her illness was neither feigned nor imagined, but genuine)—**Ich weiß wirklich nicht, was ich tun soll** ('I really, positively don't know what to do'—I'm not just saying so). **2. eigentlich** (with an inorganic t): This adj. is commonly used in the sense of 'literal' (as against **uneigentlich** or **übertragen,** 'figurative'), in which sense it approaches **ursprünglich** ('original'). This may serve as an index to the precise force of **eigentlich:** it points to the distinctive, intrinsic qualities of a thing, to what, from its origin and by its nature, it can call peculiarly its own (**das, was ihm ursprünglich eigen** or **eigentümlich ist**). Thus, in a proposition like **Der Liederkomponist Franz hieß eigentlich Knauth,** the meaning is that his 'real', i.e. original surname was Knauth, but that the family assumed that of Franz; **wirklich** here would suggest that some one had questioned the fact: cf. **„Er hieß doch ursprünglich nicht Knauth?" „Doch, wirklich!"** ('Surely Knauth wasn't his original name?' 'Yes, it actually was!'). If a person has said that he would be unable to attend a meeting and turns up after all, he might say, **„Ja, ich bin wirklich gekommen, aber eigentlich hätte ich nicht kommen sollen"**; here we can use 'really' in both propositions, but **wirklich** points to his having in fact come, while **eigentlich** implies that properly, strictly speaking, his original reasons for saying he wouldn't come still held good. Sim., where there is a reference to 'Greece *properly* so called, as distinguished from Macedonia' (Paley), a German would say **Das eigentliche Griechenland im Gegensatz zu Mazedonien,** just as, in rendering a proposition like 'A few poets of the older school continued to write during the first few years of the Augustan epoch, but cannot *properly* be regarded as belonging to it' (Cruttwell), he would say, **Einige Dichter der älteren Schule setzten während der ersten paar Jahre des**

Augusteischen Zeitalters ihre poetische Tätigkeit fort, können aber nicht eigentlich als diesem angehörig betrachtet werden. Other characteristic examples which may be helpful are: **Wir wollten damals eigentlich** ('really', i.e. according to our original intention) **ans Meer reisen, es war aber verboten—„Der Angeklagte verdiente eigentlich eine mehrtägige Haft, kam aber mit einer Geldstrafe davon." „Ach, wirklich?"** i.e. 'The accused really (strictly, in accordance with the evidence) deserved a few days' imprisonment, but was let off with a fine.' 'Oh, really, is that a fact?'—**Ich weiß wirklich nicht, was er eigentlich wollte, als er mich besuchte** ('I positively don't know what he really wanted when he called on me', i.e. he wished me to think he had come for this or that reason, but I don't know what the original purpose of his visit was).

receive: see **get** 1.

recent: 1. (a) There are several words which express our adv. 'recently', esp. **unlängst** (see **längst**), **kürzlich** (see 2 *a*), **jüngst** and **neulich,** of which the first three suggest an indef. time in the not distant past ('a short time ago, not long ago'), while the last exactly expresses our 'the other day, a day or two ago' (= **vor ein paar Tagen**). Strangely enough, not one of these expressions is ordinarily used as an *adj.*: **unlängst** and **kürzlich** are always advs. (for the latter, cf. **adverbs formed from adjectives** 3), and an example like **Er zürnt noch von dem neulichen Ballabend her** (Wildenbruch: 'He is still angry at what happened at the ball held the other evening') is unusual. As for **jüngst**, it is a rather choice expression, hardly used in every-day lang., and almost confined to phrases like **die jüngste Vergangenheit** ('the recent past'), **Thomas Manns jüngstes** ('latest') **Werk,** etc. (b) The want of a corresponding adj. has been keenly felt. Where 'recent' is contrasted with 'ancient', the compar. **neuer** is often used: P. F. L. Hoffmann defines **jüngst** as **„in neuerer Zeit, der alten entgegengesetzt"**, and **die neuere Literatur** is practically 'modern literature'; but one cannot use it to render phrases like 'his recent visit' or 'your recent letter', where **sein mir unlängst abgestatteter Besuch** and **der kürzlich von Ihnen erhaltene Brief** are at best poor makeshifts. Here, in fact, the only adj. is one of comparatively 'recent' introduction, viz. **neuerlich.** This was orig. an *adv.*, and it is still so used: e.g. **Dieses Paar hatte sich erst neuerlich zusammengefunden** (G.)—**Er begann sich neuerlich** ('of late') **vor dem Schlaf zu fürchten** (J. Schaffner)—**Herrn Paulsen hatte er neuerlich einen Tyrannen geheißen** (H. Hoffmann)—**Sie gewöhnte sich neuerlich, in ihm einen mißratenen Sohn zu erblicken** (Bergengruen). But its use as an *adj.* is now rapidly gaining ground in the sense of 'recent', as well as in that of 'renewed, fresh': e.g. **Unsere Villa hat sich durch neuerliche Möbelanschaffungen verschönert** (Th. Mann)—**Sie schrieb, sie halte es für gefährlich, davon zu reden, bevor ein neuerlicher Spruch des Rats ergangen sei** (Fr. Griese)—**Hastig gab sie das Signal zum Halten und stieg zu neuerlicher Verwunderung des Chauffeurs plötzlich aus** (St. Zweig). **2.** (a) To come back to advs., it is noteworthy that **kürzlich** now always has the force of **vor kurzem** ('not long ago') and is no longer used, as it once was, with the force of 'briefly, in a few words': here one now uses **kurz,** which would be substituted in examples like **Die Steinarten erwähne ich nur kürzlich** (G.)—**Nur kürzlich muß ich dir melden, daß deine Hoffnung vereitelt ist** (Sch.)—**Lassen Sie mich kürzlich den Verlauf der Posse erzählen** (Mörike). The only other adv. corresponding to 'recently' is **neuerdings,** formed like **allerdings** (q.v.): e.g. **Bis dahin waren die Menschen insgesamt ein Ganzes für mich gewesen; neuerdings lernte ich, wie lohnend es ist, Einzelne zu studieren** (H. Hesse). (b) To be distinguished from the advs. given above, which imply a lapse of at least some days, are **vorhin** and **eben,** which refer to a point of time in the immediate past: e.g. **Als ich vorhin** ('a little while ago') **die Straße entlang ging, begegnete ich meinem Freunde — Du erwähntest vorhin** ('a minute ago'), **daß dein Freund krank ist**; and **eben** in this last example would correspond exactly to our 'just now'. Incidentally, **vorhin** must not be confused with **vorher,** which latter indicates a point of time before something happened or will happen, not before the present moment: e.g. **Ich bin eben** ('just') **aus der Schweiz zurückgekehrt, wo ich vorher** ('before that') **nie gewesen war**—**Ich reise in einer Stunde nach Berlin, aber vorher** ('first') **muß ich noch zur Bank gehen**: cf. **erst** 2 (*a*).

Recht: 1. This noun is really the neut.

sing. of the adj. **recht** (q.v.) used subst., and in some common expressions it is actually written with a small letter: thus, where we say 'He *is* right', a German says **Er hat recht,** not **Er ist recht,** which is used *coll.* in the sense either of being in one's right senses, as in **Er ist nicht recht bei Troste** ('He's not in his right mind, is not all there') or of being on the right road, as in **Damit ich das Haus nicht verfehlte, rief ich einen Bedienten, der versicherte, ich sei recht** (G.); so also **Ich habe wieder mal recht behalten** ('I was right again after all')—**Da muß ich ihm recht geben** ('I must admit, I think he's right there'). **2.** The noun **Recht** is used in several senses, viz. **(a)** 'right, claim, title': e.g. **Er hatte kein Recht, das zu tun—Er hatte ein gewisses Recht zu diesem Ehrennamen** (G.) — **Ich bestehe auf meinem Recht — Er wollte mir mein gutes Recht streitig machen** ('He wanted to dispute my right *or* claim')—**Er tat es mit Fug und Recht** ('He had every right to do it')—**Jedes Volk hat ein Recht auf Selbstbestimmung** ('Every nation has the right of self-determination')—cf. **Stimmrecht** ('the right to vote'); **(b)** 'justice': e.g. **Recht sprechen** ('to administer justice')—**Gnade für Recht ergehen lassen** ('to show mercy *or* be lenient, instead of inflicting the just punishment')—**Ich habe mir Recht verschafft** ('I have seen justice done to me', often 'I have taken the law into my own hands'); **(c)** 'law' (see 3): e.g. **das römische, bürgerliche Recht** ('Roman, Civil Law')—**Er studiert die** (or **ist ein Student der) Rechte** ('He is a law-student')—**Er ist Doktor beider Rechte** ('He is an LL.D.')—cf. **Handelsrecht** ('mercantile law'), **Völkerrecht** ('international law'), etc., and see **bestehen** 2 (*b*). **3.** The reg. gen. sing. is **Rechts,** as in **von Rechts wegen** ('by rights')—**Er hat es auf dem Wege des Rechts erlangt** ('He obtained it by taking legal proceedings'); but in some legal expressions the form **Rechtens** is quite established, esp. in the pred.: e.g. **Das ist bei uns Rechtens** (Sch.: 'That is in accordance with our law')—**Du kannst froh sein, daß ich dir den Schaden nicht vom Lohne abziehe, wie Rechtens wäre** (Immermann: '. . . as would be my legal right')—**Er breitete eine in aller Form Rechtens ausgestellte Vollmacht auf dem Tische aus** (Storm: '. . . a power of attorney made out in strictly judicial form')—**Man führe ihn vor die Stadt und tue, was Rechtens!** (Hebbel: '. . . deal with him according to the law!')

recht: 1. As an *adj.* this is used in most of the senses of our 'right': e.g. **Dies ist weder ein spitzer noch ein stumpfer, sondern ein rechter Winkel** ('This is a right angle, neither acute nor obtuse')—**Er streckte mir die rechte Hand entgegen** (see 2 and 4)—**Du kommst gerade zur rechten Zeit — Sind wir auf dem rechten** (or **richtigen**) **Weg?—Ganz recht!** ('Quite right!'). In other examples we use an expression like 'real': **Ein rechter Schütze hilft sich selbst** (Sch.: 'A real *or* true marksman. A bowman of the right stamp can take care of himself')—**Ich habe mir rechte Mühe gegeben** ('I have taken real trouble')—**Ich habe keine rechte Lust, hinzugehen** ('I really don't feel inclined to go'); cf. **Hier geht es nicht mit rechten Dingen zu** ('There's something queer *or* uncanny going on here'); for **schlecht und recht,** see **bad** 1. **2.** Very common is its use as an *adj. subst.*: e.g. **ein Rechter** (e.g. in boxing, 'a right-hander')—**an den Rechten kommen** ('to meet one's match') —**die Rechte** ('the right hand' or 'the conservative side' in parliament)—**das Rechte tun** ('to do what is right')—**nach dem Rechten sehen** ('to see that everything is in order'). **3.** As an *adv.* it is much used, esp. in coll. expressions, to modify verbs: e.g. **Geht diese Uhr recht? — Das geschieht ihm recht** ('That serves him right')—**Das verstehe ich nicht recht** ('I don't quite understand that')—**Ich weiß nicht recht, wie ich es anfangen soll** ('I don't quite know how to set about it') —**Er versucht, es jedem recht zu machen** ('He tries to please everybody'). As a modifier of adjs. and advs. it really has no exact equivalent in English: thus, **ein recht guter Schüler** properly implies that the pupil is more than 'good', but less than 'very good', and unfortunately 'quite good' in such a context has taken on a rather depreciatory meaning (cf. 'fair', 'not bad'); but 'very' is the nearest approach in propositions like **Wir waren recht erfreut, Sie zu sehen — Wollen Sie mir einen Gefallen tun?" „Recht gern!"** ('. . . Very gladly!')—**Das ist alles recht schön, aber . . .** ('That is all very well, but . . .'), while 'quite' is perhaps nearer the mark in **Wir hatten zuletzt recht schönes Wetter — Daraus werde ich nicht recht klug** ('I can't quite make head or tail of it'); for **erst recht,** see **erst** 2 (*d*). **4.** It seems strange to us that the adjs. **recht** and **link** ('right' and 'left') hardly occur before the NHG period: the usual MHG expressions were *zese* (= Lat. *dexter*) and *winster* (= Lat. *sinister*). The forms **rechts** and **links** are really the gen. sing. of the adjs. used adv. with the force of 'on *or* to the right, left': e.g. **Der Gasthof liegt links an der Landstraße — Rechts fahren!** ('Keep right!'). With the force of motion towards, they can be preceded by **nach,** and motion from requires the prep. **von:** e.g. **Unser Weg biegt hier (nach) rechts ab — Der Wind kam von links her.** The two advs. can also be used as *preps.* ('to the right *or* left of . . .'), taking either a gen. or **von,** the latter necessarily before prons.: e.g. **Das Bild zeigt uns die freiste Aussicht: links des Zuschauers eine mäßig entfernte Stadt, rechts des Zuschauers ein Tempelgebäude** (G.)—**Rechts von ihm sah man mehrere Geschichtswerke aufgeschlagen** (Frenssen)—**Der Oberst gab Befehl, den Marsch abzubrechen, rechts und links der Straße Rast zu machen** (W. v. Scholz). Of course, in such propositions the adj.-subst. forms **die Rechte** or **Linke** can be used (see 2), so that **links des Zuschauers** might be replaced by **zur Linken des Zuschauers,** and **rechts von ihm** by **zu seiner Rechten.**

Rechtens: see **Recht** 3.

rechtfertigen: The prefix of this compd. of **fertigen,** which means 'to justify', is always accented, but never separated: hence, in the infin., **zu re′chtfertigen,** and in the past part., **gere′chtfertigt.**

rechts: see **recht** 4.

recognize: 1. The verb **erkennen** means: **(a)** 'to know again, recollect' what one has previously perceived, often strengthened by the addition of the sep. prefix **wieder-:** e.g. **Du wirst ihn leicht am Gange (wieder)-erkennen** ('You will easily recognize him by his walk')—**Obwohl ich ihn lange nicht gesehen hatte, erkannte ich ihn sofort wieder; (b)** 'to give a judgement, pronounce a verdict': e.g. **Man erkannte ihn für schuldig** ('He was found guilty')—**Das Gericht erkannte auf den Tod** ('The court pronounced sentence of death')—**Der Richter hat auf drei Jahre Zuchthaus erkannt** ('The judge has passed sentence of three years' penal servitude'). **(c)** In this connexion, a clear distinction is now made between **die Erkenntnis** ('knowledge, insight': cf. **der Baum der Erkenntnis,** 'the tree of knowledge') and **das Erkenntnis** ('verdict', as in Ranke's **Über Religionsstreitigkeiten nahm der Papst das oberste Erkenntnis in Anspruch**). **2.** Distinct from **erkennen** is **anerkennen,** 'to recognize' in the sense of 'to acknowledge', as in 'I recognize him as king'. For the fluctuation between separation and non-separation of the first prefix, see **anerkennen.**

reduplicating verbs: 1. Many Goth. strong verbs formed their past tense by means of reduplication. Just as the perf. tense of Gk. *poiein* ('to make') is *pe-poika,* and that of Lat. *pendere* ('to hang') is *pe-pendi,* so those of Goth. *haitan* (> **heißen**) and *slêpan* (> **schlafen**) are *hai-hait* and *sai-slêp* (where *ai* has the open *e*-sound, as in *set*). This method of forming a past tense had disappeared entirely by the OHG period, reduplication having been displaced by **Ablaut:** thus, Goth. *hai-hait* had become *hiaz* (> **hieß**) and *sai-slêp* had become *sliaf* (> **schlief**). **2.** In NHG nearly all strong verbs which orig. reduplicated can be recognized by two characteristics: (i) the vowel of the past part. is the same as that of the infin.; and (ii) the past tense has the diphthong **ie** throughout: e.g. **heißen, hieß, geheißen—laufen, lief, gelaufen—rufen, rief, gerufen—schlafen, schlief, geschlafen—stoßen, stieß, gestoßen,** etc. The only NHG verb which has one historically incorrect form is **scheiden,** the MHG past part. *gescheiden* having become **geschieden** under the influence of another class of strong verbs which did not reduplicate in Goth. (**bleiben, meiden, schreiben,** etc.); but the historically correct form is preserved in the adj. **bescheiden** (q.v.). To the reduplication class belongs also **gehen, ging, gegangen,** the orig. MHG infin. of which was *gân* (contracted from *gangen*), the past tense *gienc* (until recent times written **gieng**) and the part. (*ge*)*gangen* or *gegân*. **3.** Quite a number of reduplicating verbs have become *weak* in NHG, notably **bannen, falten** (q.v.), **(um)halsen, heischen** (q.v.), **salzen** (see **falten** 3), **schalten, schweifen, spalten** (see **falten** 2), **spannen, wallen, walten;** in this connexion see **braten** and **hauen** 2.

refuse: see **versagen** 1 and 2; **weigern** 1 and 2.

regen: see **move** 2.

reichen: see **langen** I.

Reif: Distinguish between **der Reif** (plur. **Reife**, but not very common), meaning 'hoar-frost'—**der Reif** (plur. Reife) or **der Reifen** (plur. **Reifen**), meaning 'hoop' or (mainly poet.) 'ring'—and **die Reife** (no plur.), meaning 'ripeness, maturity' (cf. **das Zeugnis der Reife**, 'Leaving *or* Higher School Certificate, Attestation of Fitness' admitting to a university).

Reigen, Reihe(n): Distinguish between **die Reihe** (< MHG *rihe*) and **der Reihen** or, more commonly, **Reigen** (< MHG *reie* or *reige*). The former is the ordinary expression for a 'row, rank, tier', in mathematics 'progression, series': e.g. **Unsere Theaterplätze sind in der dritten Reihe—in Reih' und Glied** ('in rank and file'); cf. **Du bist jetzt an der** (or **kommst jetzt an die**) **Reihe** ('It is your turn now')—**Bei Tisch machte** or **bildete man bunte Reihe** (i.e. ladies and gentlemen sat alternatively)—**in alphabetischer Reihenfolge** ('in alphabetical order'). The second word, now mainly confined to poetry, is a kind of 'dance' (like our obs. 'ray'), orig. no doubt one in which the dancers followed each other in a row; the Erlking uses it when he says **Meine Töchter führen den nächtlichen Reih'n**, which students have sometimes actually been known to take to be a reference to the river Rhine (**der Rhein**)!—Another meaning of **der Reihen** is the 'instep', now more usually **der Spann**.

Reinfall: As pointed out under **her-, hin-** I, verbal prefixes like **herauf-** and **herunter-** are reg. contracted in the coll. lang. of the north into **rauf-** and **runter-** (the only exception being **herab-**); indeed, the initial apostrophe is now commonly dropped, although it is advisable to insert it in the case of **rein-** where there is a possibility of confusion with the adj. **rein.** Moreover, these contractions are often even used for **hinauf-** and **hinunter-**. If you are upstairs and call to somebody to come up, you ordinarily say **Komm mal rauf!** and later you might say **Jetzt kannst du wieder runtergehen.** Commonest of all are **raus-** and **rein-**: an exclamation of displeasure like **Scher dich hinaus!** ('Get out!') can take the rude form **Raus!**—and sim. **Es fängt an zu regnen: wir müssen reingehen**; but when some one knocks at your door, you say **Herein!** (not **Rein!**). Esp. interesting here is the verb **hineinfallen.** It is used both in the *lit.* sense of 'to fall in' (into a hole, etc.) and with the *fig.* force of 'to come to grief *or* come off badly', esp. 'to be taken in' or (to use a slang expression) 'to be sold', and the contracted form **reinfallen** is so common in a proposition like **Wir sind hier gründlich reingefallen** ('We have been properly taken in here') that the noun **Reinfall** has become an established expression everywhere, used either of a 'take-in' or of something that has disappointed one's expectations, ideas which we often express by the slang words 'sell' or 'flop'. Thus, 'The insurrection proved a thorough sell' (Palgrave) = **Der Aufstand erwies sich als ein gründlicher Reinfall**; and sim. 'The performance was a complete flop *or* failure' = **Die Vorstellung war ein vollständiger Reinfall**; cf. the humorous saying **Das war ein Reinfall bei Schaffhausen** ('a mighty flop'), with a play on **Rheinfall** (the Falls of the Rhine between Basle and the Lake of Constance, **zwischen Basel und dem Bodensee**).

Reis: Distinguish between **der Reis** ('rice'), with plur. **Reise** (better **Reisarten**, 'kinds of rice'); **das Reis** ('shoot, twig'), with plur. **Reiser**; **die Reise** ('journey'), with plur. **Reisen**; and **das Reisig** ('brushwood'), with no plur.

reiten: Like other verbs of this kind (see esp. **fahren** 2 and **laufen**), **reiten** takes the aux. **sein** when an intention to proceed from one place to another is implied: e.g. **Der Bauer ist in die Stadt geritten, um Geschäfte zu verrichten—Wir sind, glaube ich, in die Irre geritten** (i.e. off the track leading to our destination). On the other hand, **haben** is used when the verb has trans. force, when the reference is to the rider's way of handling his horse, and generally also when the action is an exercise or sport: e.g. **Ich habe mich steif geritten** ('I have been riding till I am stiff': cf. **gehen** I)—**Ich habe heute den Schimmel, nicht den Schecken geritten** ('I have been riding the white horse today, not the piebald one')—**Er hat ein Kind über den Haufen** (or **zu Boden**) **geritten** (or **Er hat ein Kind u'mgeritten**, 'He has ridden a child down': see below)—**Der Stallmeister sagte, ich hätte gut geritten—Du hast seitdem geritten und geschwärmt** (Freiligrath: addressed to a circus-rider). Elsewhere usage is not so fixed: with a cognate accus. one usually says **Ich bin diesen Weg schon oft geritten—Wir sind**

(im) Galopp geritten; and in the proposition **So hab' ich nie geritten, nie so toll gejagt** (G.), **bin ich** would be more natural as the purpose of riding so hard was to get to his destination quickly. In particular, **sein** is always used with sep. compds. like **aus-, fort-, hinauf-, spazierenreiten**, etc.: cf. **Ich bin durch die Stadt (du'rch-)geritten** with **Ich habe die Stadt durchri'tten** — **Er ist u'mgeritten** ('ridden a round-about way') with **Er hat das Dorf umri'tten** ('ridden round the outskirts of the village'). For **Er kam angeritten,** see **kommen** 4 (*b*).

relation: 1. The most general term expressing a connexion or relationship between persons or things is **Beziehung** (cf. 3): e.g. **Seine Bemerkungen hatten keine Beziehung** (= **bezogen sich nicht**) **auf mich** ('His remarks did not relate, had no reference to me')—**Wir haben freundschaftliche Beziehungen zu ihm angeknüpft** ('We have entered into friendly relations with him')—**Frankreich brach die Beziehungen zu Deutschland ab** ('France broke off diplomatic relations with Germany')—**Diese zwei Fragen haben keine** (or **stehen in keiner**) **Beziehung zueinander** ('These two questions have no bearing on each other')—**Er ist in jeder Beziehung für den Posten geeignet** ('He is in every respect fitted for the post'). With the same force, **Bezug** is esp. common in commercial correspondence: e.g. **Wir nehmen Bezug** (= **Wir beziehen uns**) **auf Ihren geschätzten Auftrag** ('We beg to refer to your esteemed order'); cf. **bezügliche Fürworter** ('relative pronouns'). **2.** Connexion through relationship by blood or marriage is expressed by **Verwandtschaft** (cf. **verwandt**), properly conveying the abstract force of 'kinship', but also used collectively of 'kinsfolk': e.g. **Zu der Hochzeit hat man die ganze Verwandtschaft** (= **sämtliche Verwandten**) **eingeladen**; but it is also used of things that are 'akin', i.e. closely allied or related: e.g. **chemische Verwandtschaft** ('chemical affinity'). **3.** A special kind of **Beziehung** is suggested by **Verhältnis.** As *Sanders* says, **Verhältnis bezeichnet die Beziehung, worin etwas zu etwas andrem steht, die Art und Weise, wie es sich in Bezug auf etwas verhält,** i.e. the respect or degree of relationship in which the two stand to each other: e.g. **Im Verhältnis zu der Arbeit ist der Lohn gering** ('In proportion to the work the pay is poor')—**In der Versammlung waren die Männer und die Frauen im Verhältnis von zehn zu eins** ('. . . in the proportion of ten to one')—**in umgekehrtem Verhältnis** ('in inverse ratio')—**Er hat ein Verhältnis mit ihr** ('He is on an intimate footing with her'); cf. the *coll.* **sein Verhältnis** ('his girl friend'). Esp. common is the plur. **Verhältnisse,** used with the force of 'circumstances, means' or simply 'state of affairs': e.g. **Die Familie lebt in guten Verhältnissen** ('. . . in easy circumstances')—**Meine Verhältnisse erlauben mir, viel zu reisen** ('My means permit me to travel a lot')—**Seit dem Kriege haben sich die Verhältnisse hier gebessert** ('. . . conditions have improved').

relative clauses: see the various rel. prons. **der, was, welch, wer,** and also **da(r)-** 2 and **so** 4 (*a*). For contracted rel. clauses used attrib., as in **eine mit Efeu überwachsene Ruine,** see **participle (past)** 1 (*a*) and (*b*); and for the sim. attrib. use of the gerund, as in **die zu lösende Aufgabe** ('the problem to be solved'), see **infinitive** 3 (*b*). For propositions like 'He is a man whom I know to be honest' or 'Here is a letter which I wish you to read', see **von** 5.

remember: 1. The basic force of **sich besinnen** is 'to meditate' (cf. **Ich habe mich eines besseren besonnen,** 'I have thought better of it'), and hence it is reg. used (with **auf** + accus.) to suggest the conscious mental process involved in trying to recall something to mind of which one has only a dim recollection (cf. the quotation from Eberhard given under 2 below). If I am asked a person's address, I might say **Warten Sie mal, da muß ich mich erst besinnen**; and sim. **Eben begegnete ich Herrn . . ., wie heißt er doch? Ich kann mich im Augenblick auf seinen Namen nicht besinnen** — **Besinnen Sie sich doch, wo Sie das Buch hingetan haben! 2.** On the other hand, **sich entsinnen** (q.v.) points, as does **sich erinnern** (see 3), not to the whole mental process, but to the *end* of the process, the successful outcome of the attempt to recall a thing to mind: as Eberhard says, **Was keinen sonderlichen Eindruck gemacht hat, woran wir lange nicht gedacht haben, das scheint aus unserem Gedächtnis verlöscht zu sein, wir müssen uns lange besinnen, ehe wir uns dessen entsinnen; daher besinnt man sich, ob, und entsinnt sich, daß man etwas getan habe**; and sim. **Jetzt, wo Sie**

mir die Einzelheiten des Vorfalls ins Gedächtnis zurückgerufen haben, entsinne ich mich deutlich—**Ich entsinne mich genau, den Brief beantwortet zu haben.** **3.** (**a**) The simple verb **erinnern** properly means 'to remind' a person (accus.) of a thing (**an**+accus.): e.g. **Ich erinnerte ihn an sein Versprechen**; sim., with the pers. obj. understood, **Diese Musik erinnert an** ('is reminiscent of') **Mozart.** The only other standard meaning of **erinnern** is 'to criticize adversely, take exception to, animadvert upon' something, used esp. in the infin. with **zu** with an indef. neut. obj.: e.g. **Er sagte, er habe nur eins zu erinnern: die Hütte scheine ihm zu klein** (G.: 'He said he had only one criticism to make, namely that he thought the hut too small')—**Nach der ersten Aufführung ließ er Stellen, bei denen er etwas zu erinnern hatte, wiederholen** (G.: 'After the first performance he made them repeat certain passages in connexion with which he had some fault to find')—**Es blieb mir nichts zu erinnern, ich mußte meine Diener loben** (Chamisso)—**Er war zu einer Besichtigung** ('inspection') **gekommen und hatte nichts zu erinnern gefunden** (R. Herzog); cf. **Was Ihre Erinnerung in Rücksicht auf die Entwicklung betrifft** ('With regard to your criticism of the working out of the plot'), **war es mir unmöglich, Ihren Wunsch zu erfüllen** (Sch., in a letter to Goethe). (**b**) In the extreme north the simple verb **erinnern** is reg. used with an accus. obj. in the sense of 'to remember' (see **c**): e.g. **Erinnerst du den Garten?** (Storm)—**Deutlich erinnere ich sein Gesicht** (Frenssen)—**Ich erinnere das wie heute** (Th. Mann). Although, as the following additional examples show, this trans. use has spread to other parts, even to Austria, it should, on the whole, be avoided in good prose: **Was in jener Nacht geschah, erinnerst du nicht?** (A. Schaeffer)—**Die Mama küßte die Kinder herzlicher, als es eines von beiden erinnerte** (H. Franck)—**Goethe gewöhnte sich damals, wie Sie erinnern werden, zwischen dem Gebirg und dem flachen Lande hin und her zu wandern** (Carossa)—**Ich erinnere ein anderes Gedicht, das du früher gerne hattest** (Hofmannsthal)—**Es standen eine Menge Geschichten in dem Buch: ich erinnere nur noch zwei** (Rilke); sim. in the pass., **Die Melodie war wie ein erinnerter Traum** (G. Bäumer). (**c**) In the example from H. Franck given above, **es** (q.v.) may conceivably be the old *gen.*, a case which is also sometimes used in the north, as in **Du erinnerst vielleicht der Verhandlungen** (Storm), and which is certainly the standard construction in good prose of the commonest expression for 'to remember', viz. **sich erinnern.** Although properly suggesting a recurrence to mind without conscious effort, this reflex. verb is often used synonymously with **sich entsinnen**, the latter being a rather more select expression (see also **gedenken**). As 'to remind a person of something' is **jemand an etwas erinnern** (see above), it is not surprising that 'to remember something' not infrequently takes the form **sich an etwas erinnern,** but although this use, which came mainly from Austria, has undoubtedly spread to other parts, good prose style distinguishes between **Ich erinnerte ihn an sein Versprechen** and **Ich erinnerte mich meines Versprechens,** and between **Ich erinnerte ihn daran** and **Ich erinnerte mich dessen.** Here it should be noted that it is incorrect to say **Ich erinnere mich alles, was er gesagt hat**; standing alone, **alles** cannot be used as a gen. (see **all** 6 *a*), so the only correct rendering of 'I remember everything he said' is **Ich erinnere mich alles dessen, was er gesagt hat.** (**d**) It is, then, in accordance with standard good prose usage to say **Das ist das einzige, dessen ich mich erinnere.** When Goethe says **Das einzige, was ich mir zwischen Emmendingen und Zürich erinnere, ist der Rheinfall bei Schaffhausen,** he is using an interesting idiom which can easily be explained: it is the result of confusing the dat. and the accus. forms **sich.** In an example like **Wenn du dich's erinnerst, . . .** (Böhlau), the **'s** is a gen. case, and the same should apply to **Er erinnert sich's**; but it is not surprising that **sich** here came mistakenly to be regarded as *dat.*, and hence **'s** to be treated as an *accus.*, so that 'He reminds himself of it' became 'He recalls it to himself'. This idiom, however, has never really established itself; indeed, the only case in which the accus. of the thing and the dat. of the person is imperative is where the less common comp. **zurückerinnern** is used, as in **Wenn ich mir die Jahre zurückerinnere, da Sie und Eduard das schönste Paar bei Hof waren, . . .** (G.), where the introductory clause is like an amalgamation of **Wenn ich mich der Jahre erinnere**

and **Wenn ich mir die Jahre ins Gedächtnis zurückrufe.** In this connexion cf. **anmaßen, getrauen** (see **trauen** 2 *b*), **vermuten, versichern** (q.v. 2) and **versehen** (q.v. 2 *c*).

remind: see **remember** 3 (*a*).

rennen: This verb properly suggests a higher speed than **laufen** (q.v.), corresponding to our 'to race', implying that the person exerts himself to the utmost. In ordinary lang. it is used much like our 'to rush *or* tear' (along the street, down the stair, etc.), but actually a much more common expression in that sense is **stürzen** (q.v.). If the basic idea contained in **rennen** is that of getting speedily from one place to another, the aux. is **sein**; but **haben** is correct, of course, when the verb has trans. force, as in **Er war im Nebel verschwunden, nachdem er einen Handwerksburschen auf der Treppe über den Haufen gerannt hatte** (Raabe: '. . . after knocking a travelling journeyman head over heels in his mad rush down the stairs'). For the form **rennte** in a proposition like **Wenn du renntest, würdest du den Zug eben noch erreichen,** see **past subjunctive** 1.

repeat: Distinguish between **Man hat mich gebeten, zu wiederholen** (q.v.), **was ich vorhin sagte** ('I have been asked to repeat what I said before'),—**Du sollst mir diesen Satz nachsprechen** ('You are to repeat this sentence after me')—and **Ich mußte das auswendig gelernte Gedicht her-** or **aufsagen** ('I had to repeat *or* recite the poem I had learned by heart').

Rest: Used of what is 'left over' (**was übrigbleibt**), including architectural 'remains', arithmetical 'remainders', the 'remains' or 'leavings' of a meal, etc., this masc. noun has the plur. **Reste:** e.g. **Altäre, Stücke von Säulen und dergleichen Reste** (G.)—**Ich kann diese Rechenaufgabe nicht lösen: ich habe dreimal versucht und jedesmal sind die Reste verschieden** ('I can't do this sum: I have tried three times and the remainders are different each time')—**Gestern wurden seine irdischen Reste zu Grabe getragen** ('His mortal remains were interred yesterday')—**Wir haben schon zu Mittag gegessen, du mußt mit den Resten vorliebnehmen** ('. . . you will just have to make the best of what is left')—**Von der Decke** ('ceiling') **schwebte ein Kronleuchter, in dem noch Reste von Wachskerzen staken** (Th. Mann); cf. in students' slang, **Rest weg!** ('Drink up!'). The plur. **Rester** is used esp. in the haberdashery trade of 'remnants' of material, while **Resten** is characteristic of the extreme south and should be avoided.

richten: 1. The basic sense of this verb is 'to cause to go in the right direction' (**Richtung**), as in **Sie richtete den Blick auf mich** or **in die Höhe**—**Das Schiff wurde nach Süden gerichtet**—*fig.* **Ich werde mich nach dir richten** ('I shall be guided by you'); so also 'to direct the course of the law' i.e. 'to judge, condemn'. **2.** The basic force is also seen in many compounds, notably **(a) hinrichten** ('to execute' a criminal, properly to cause him to go away out of this world); **(b) ausrichten,** lit. 'to send out towards the proper destination', is used with words like **Gruß** ('to convey a greeting' to somebody), **Auftrag** ('to deliver a message'), **Botschaft** ('to execute a commission'), and very commonly with indef. expressions like **viel, wenig, nichts,** etc. ('to accomplish'); **(c) verrichten** ('to carry out *or* transact in a due and proper manner'), as with nouns like **Geschäfte, sein Amt, seine Gebete** ('to perform one's devotions'); cf. **unverrichteter Sache zurückkehren** ('to return without achieving one's purpose' =**ohne etwas ausgerichtet zu haben**). In connexion with this idea of 'to perform, accomplish', see also **leisten** and **voll-.**

Richtung: In a proposition like 'The town lies in this direction', where the verb is one of *rest,* a *dat.* in the prep. phrase is the obvious case to use: **Die Stadt liegt in dieser Richtung.** With a verb implying *motion,* the accus. is sometimes used here, as in **Sie war in die Richtung weggestürzt, aus welcher der Schrei gekommen war** (Britting)—**Ich sah, daß er in eine bestimmte Richtung blickte** (Wassermann—the eye, as it were, travelling out into the distance)—**Wenn sie aufsah, blickten ihre Augen in meine Richtung** (A. Döblin); but these examples are far outnumbered by those with a *dat.*: e.g. **Er ging an den Fenstern vorbei in der Richtung nach dem Stall** (E. Wichert)—**Er ging langsam in der Richtung des Gartenhauses** (Bergengruen)—**Ich ging die Boulevards in einer Richtung hinauf und in der entgegengesetzten Richtung zurück** (Rilke)—**Sie mußte in der Richtung, die sie eingeschlagenh atte, weitergehen** (H. Franck)—**Ich lief in der Richtung des Weges, den wir gekommen waren** (Frenssen)—**Axtschläge belehrten ihn, in welcher Richtung**

er vorzudringen hatte (Speckmann)—**Er schritt in der Richtung des Hotels** (Th. Mann)—**Er schritt nun in der Richtung nach Reichenbach** (G. Hauptmann)—**Er eilte in der Richtung nach dem Viale von dannen** (I. Kurz)—**Eine heftige Bewegung des Schiffes warf ihn in der Richtung nach der Kajütentreppe** (M. Eyth)—**Er schloß das Fenster und ging in der Richtung zur Haupttreppe** (Kafka)—**Sie wandte den Blick in der Richtung, die des Abts Zeigefinger wies** (Scheffel)—**Ich sah rechts und links in verschiedenen Richtungen** (Stifter).

Ries, Riese: Distinguish between **das Ries** (a 'ream' of paper), with plur. **Riese** or (as a measure) **Ries**, e.g. **Von den fünf Ries Papier, die wir unlängst erhielten, haben wir nur noch zwei Buch** (q.v.); **der Riese** ('giant'), *weak* (**des Riesen, die Riesen**); and **die Riese** ('coif'; also a 'timber-slide' for sending lumber down a mountainside), with plur. **Riesen.**

rise: see **erheben** 2.

risk: see **Gefahr.** The best expression for 'to risk one's life' is **sein Leben aufs Spiel setzen,** but in more familiar lang. one says **das Leben riskieren.** The neut. noun **Risiko** is properly used of risk in commerce and insurance, but has found its way into ordinary lang.: cf. **Es geht auf dein Risiko** ('It is at your own risk') —**Ich werde es darauf ankommen lassen** ('I'll risk it, take my chance').

roh: see **rough** 2.

Röhricht: see **Käfig.**

room: 1. Whereas **Platz** (see **place** 2) is always a *bounded* space with definite limits, **Raum** properly implies *unbounded* space: **Dreifach ist des Raumes Maß** (Sch., referring to the three dimensions); so also **Himmelsraum** ('the expanse of the heavens') and **der unermeßliche Raum der Zeit** ('the endless space of eternity'). But it also comes to suggest a limited space: **ein leerer Raum** is a 'vacuum', and **Zwischenraum** (see **distance** 5) is an 'intervening space' or 'interval'; and so **Raum** is sometimes used also of an apartment in a house, but only in quite a general way, properly with reference to the amount of space it occupies: **Wieviel Räume** (or **Räumlichkeiten**) **sind in dieser Wohnung?**—cf. **Maschinenraum** (the 'engine-room' in a ship) and the adj. **geräumig** ('spacious, roomy'). **2.** Of the more specific expressions for a 'room', **Stube** is the most homely. It is, in fact, the same word as our *stove*, which was orig. used in the sense of a 'sweating-room', then in that of a room with a heating apparatus: cf. 'As for our *stooves*, we have not hitherto used them greatlie, yet doo they now begin to be made in diuerse houses of the gentrie, who build them not to worke and feed in as in Germanie and elsewhere, but now and then to sweat in' (1587: Harrison, *England*)—'When a certain Frenchman came to visit Melanchthon, he found him in his *stove*, with one hand dandling his child, and in the other hand holding a book' (1642: Fuller, *Holy and Profane State*); cf. also 'stove-plants', i.e. hot-house plants. **Stube,** then, is properly a room that can be heated, and so esp. a small living-room: hence **Wohnstube** ('parlour'), **Kinderstube** ('nursery'), **Bauernstube** (see 3). **3. Zimmer** was orig. 'timber' for building purposes, being related to Lat. *domus*, which was first a 'timber-building'. **Zimmer** is now the best expression for a 'living-room', suggesting something more select and formal, less 'cosy' than **Stube.** It eventually came to be associated more particularly with *town*-life: a genuine **Bauernhaus** had no **Zimmer,** only **Stuben** —indeed, visitors there were taken into **die gute Stube** ('the best room'), a phrase which began to die out, however, after the 1914–18 war. So **Zimmer** is a rather colourless, unpoetic expression, as used e.g. by those who 'let rooms' and who refer to their lodger as **Zimmerherr;** where people in a small way speak of **Eßstube** and **Schlafstube,** the 'better classes' use **Speisezimmer** (cf. 4) and **Schlafzimmer.** Hence always **Gesellschaftszimmer** ('salon, drawing-room'), **Empfangszimmer** ('reception-room'), **Audienzzimmer** ('audience-chamber'), **Gastzimmer** ('spare room'; but **Gaststube,** 'coffee-room, commercial room' in an inn). A lady looking for accommodation is told that there *is* a vacant room, **dies dürfe aber kein Zimmer, sondern nur eine Kammer** (see 4) **genannt werden** (E. T. A. Hoffmann). **4. Kammer** denotes esp. one of the other, generally smaller rooms of a house, really implying security or privacy (cf. **in camera,** i.e. in the judge's private chamber, not in open court). In independent use it esp. suggests a *bedroom*, as in the common advertisement **Stube und Kammer zu vermieten** ('Sitting-room and bedroom to let'); cf. **Mägdekammer** ('maid's room'). Then also of rooms other than living-rooms, e.g. **Speisekammer** (not 'dining-room', but 'pantry'), **Vorratskammer** ('store-room'), **Dachkammer** ('attic'), **Rumpel-** or **Polterkammer** ('lumber-room'). The idea of privacy, aloofness, is further seen in **Handelskammer** ('Chamber of Commerce'), **Schatzkammer** ('Treasury, Exchequer'), **Ständekammer** (Council Chamber'), etc. **5.** Like **Stube, Gemach** shows an interesting development. The orig. force of MHG *gemach* was 'quietness, ease, comfort', a meaning still preserved in the exclamation **Nur gemach!** ('Gently! Not so fast!') and in the adj. **gemächlich** ('easy-going, without hurry, moving at a comfortable pace'). Gradually the noun came to be applied to the *place* where one takes one's ease and has home comforts. Now, however, it is the most select expression of all, being used mainly in poetry or of sumptuous apartments in a mansion or palace: e.g. **die Privatgemächer eines Fürsten—Prunkgemach** ('state-room'); cf. **Er eilte durch die großen Gemächer nach einem kleinen Hinterstübchen** (Tieck). **6.** Still another expression here is **Gelaß.** This has, for the most part, retained much of its orig. force, viz. a place where things are left (**gelassen**) or stored, as when **ein finsteres Gelaß** (Hackländer) is used of a coach-house, or **diese Gelasse** (Gutzkow) of cupboards. It is, therefore, now little used of a living-room in a house, as it once was: cf. **Es war das einzige Gelaß, welches noch Fenstern hatte** (Immermann)—**Das übrige Gelaß war für die Freunde eingerichtet** (Waldau). A significant example is **Das Haus war einstöckig, mit acht Zimmern und kargen Gelassen für den Dienst** (Bruno Frank: i.e. store-rooms, servants' quarters, etc.).

rosa: see **adjectives (indeclinable)** I.

Roß: This is the ordinary expression for a 'horse' in the south, while the north uses **Pferd.** That the latter was not used in the south is proved by a riddle dating from the early 16th century: the person was asked **in welchem Land kein Pferd sei?** and the answer was **Schwaben!** In the north, **Roß** is a select word, being used in ordinary lang. only of thoroughbreds, race-horses, etc., otherwise mainly in poetry: one speaks of **ein edles Roß,** also of **ein Kampf-** or **Streitroß,** but of **ein Acker-** or **Bauernpferd**; cf. **Das Fohlen Wittekinds, ein Schlachtroß weiland** ('once a charger'), **sank zum Ackerpferde** (Freiligrath). It is significant that a 'packhorse, sumpter' is **Packpferd** in the north, **Saumroß** in the mountainous regions of the south. Incidentally, the standard plur. of **Roß** is **Rosse,** the form **Rösser** being only used in southern, esp. Austrian dialects: cf. **Die Knechte striegelten die schweren Bierwagenrösser blank** (Zuckmayer—who, although born near Mainz, lived many years near Salzburg). —The word **Gaul** suggests a heavy cart-horse as opposed to a riding-horse, but is often used in a derogatory sense, like **Klepper,** which implies an ill-conditioned, bony 'jade' or 'hack'.

rot: For the subst. use of this adj., see **colour.** Like **blau, grün, schwarz,** etc., the adj. **rot** is used in several coll. expressions: e.g. **bis über die Ohren rot werden** ('to blush to the roots of one's hair')—**keinen roten Heller haben** ('not to have a brass farthing')—**jemandem den roten Hahn aufs Dach setzen** ('to set fire to a person's house')—**ein rot angestrichener Tag** ('a red-letter day')—**so rot wie ein gesottener Krebs** ('as red as a turkey-cock').

röten: 1. The *intrans.* use of this verb in the sense of 'to be *or* become red', as in **Der Morgen rötet** (Tieck), is avoided now; here modern usage requires a reflex. pron.: e.g. **Der östliche Himmel hat sich gerötet—Im Fieber rötet sich das Gesicht.** In other words, **röten** should only be used with *trans.* force: e.g. **Sie sah ihn an: er hatte ein gerötetes** ('flushed') **Gesicht, und sie erriet, daß ihn ein heißes Getränk so gerötet hatte. 2.** On the other hand, **erröten** is always *intrans.*, being confined to the sense of 'to blush' (aux. **sein**); e.g. **Bei seinen Schmeichelworten errötete sie bis an die Ohren** (= **wurde sie bis über beide Ohren rot**)—**Sie errötete vor Scham** —cf. **Ich errötete über der** (usually **über die**) **Bosheit** (Sch.). The infin. with **zu** after **erröten** is now rare: cf. **Ich errötete bei dem Gedanken, was er gesagt hätte** ('I blushed to think what he would have said')—**Sie errötete, als sie ihn diesen Vorschlag machen hörte** ('She blushed to hear him make this proposition'). The infin. is the only form of the verbal noun: **Ohne Erröten** (not **Errötung,** but cf. **Ohne zu erröten,) darf ich meinen Irrtum eingestehen.**

rough: It is important to distinguish between the following three expressions:

1. rauh (MHG *rûch*: cf. **Rauchwerk** = **Pelzwerk,** 'furs') is used (**a**) in the *lit.* sense to suggest roughness *as perceived by the senses,* i.e. with the force of 'not smooth' (ant. **glatt**), 'uneven' (ant. **eben**) or 'harsh' (ant. **mild**), so that it may be applied not only to nouns like **Haut, Fell, Hals, Stimme,** but also to **Pfad, Gegend, Klima, Witterung,** etc.; (**b**) with *fig.* force, either of persons or—more commonly—of actions, behaviour, language, etc., implying no more than *a lack of exterior polish or refinement*: e.g. **Mein Vater war ein strenger, rauher Mann** (G.)—**Sein Mund spricht rauhe Worte, doch sein Herz ist treu** (Sch.)—**rauhe Sitten** ('rude, primitive customs')—**die rauhe Seite herauskehren** ('to cut up rough'). **2. roh** (MHG *rô*) is our *raw,* with the same root as *crude*: (**a**) used *lit.*, it indicates the natural, unwrought state of a thing, before subjection to any process of dressing or manufacture: e.g. **rohes Fleisch**—**Rohseide** ('raw silk')—**Roheisen** ('pig iron')—**rohe Steine** ('unhewn stones', as they come from the quarry)—**aus dem Rohen gearbeitet** ('roughly finished'); (**b**) as applied to behaviour, morals, etc., it implies *a lack of moral backbone, of all sense of decency*: e.g. **ein roher Kerl** ('a coarse, brutal fellow')—**rohe Gewalt** ('brute force')—**eine rohe Ausdrucksweise** ('coarse, vulgar, indecent language'). **3. grob** (the orig. meaning of which, viz. 'thick, bulky', is now confined to a few expressions like **grobes Geschütz,** 'heavy artillery') is used (**a**) *lit.*, with the force of 'coarse, not fine': e.g. **grober Zucker** ('granulated sugar', as opposed to 'icing sugar')—**grobes Hafermehl** ('coarse, pin-head oatmeal')—**grobes Brot, Tuch, Papier**—**grobkörnig** ('coarse-grained')—cf. **die grobe Arbeit verrichten** ('to do the rough *or* dirty work, the drudgery'); (**b**) *fig.*, either in the sense of 'gross, glaring' (**ein grober Fehler** is 'a howler', **ein grober Verstoß** 'a flagrant offence', **ein grobes Verbrechen** 'a heinous crime', **eine grobe Lüge** 'a downright lie') or, applied to behaviour, etc., with the force of 'rude, offensive': e.g. **ein grober Kerl** (= **ein Grobian,** 'an insolent fellow')—**eine grobe Antwort** ('a brusque answer')—**jemand grob anfahren** ('to come down gruffly on some one')—cf. the proverb **Auf einen groben Klotz gehört ein grober Keil** ('One rude word deserves another').

rücken: see **advance** 1.

rückwärts: see **-wärts** 1 and 2.

rufen: This is one of the **reduplicating verbs** (q.v.). In OHG it had two forms, *hruofan* (strong) and *hruofen* (weak). The now obs. weak past tense **rufte** was still in fairly common use in the classical period: e.g. **Das Parterre rufte, bis Voltaire heraustreten mußte** (Lessing)—**Er rufte einen seiner Leute** (Sch.). A quite incorrect past subj. is seen in **Nichts rührte sich: rüfe** (for **riefe**) **ich, so wüßte der Teufel, ob ich jemals gehört würde** (Dauthendey). With regard to the construction, a *dat.* of the person or animal called was the only case in standard MHG, and this has to some extent persisted into modern times: e.g. **Er rief seinem Hund, der in einem Winkel gelegen hatte** (Storm)—**Sie rief ihrem Mädchen** (Gutzkow)—**Wer ruft mir?** (O. Ernst). A dat. is, indeed, even now more usual where a dependent clause follows, although here the compd. **zurufen** is more usual: **Man rief mir (zu), schnell zu kommen** or **daß ich kommen sollte.** But otherwise the *accus.* is now practically fixed: everybody says **Man hat mich gerufen,** and while **zurufen** can only take a dat., all the other compds. require an accus., as in **jemanden ab-, an-** ('to ring up'), **herein-, zurückrufen,** etc.

Rühmens: For the use of this partitive gen. as a nom. or accus., see **viel** 1 (*b*) and (*c*), **nichts** 3 and 4, and cf. **Ich eilte, den Saal zu sehen, von dem man viel Rühmens machte** (G.)—**Er begehrte, die kunstreiche Nähterin zu sprechen, von der soviel Rühmens gemacht werde** (Musäus)—**Er hatte ein Belobigungsschreiben** ('a good testimonial') **erhalten und konnte davon nicht genug Rühmens machen** (E. Wichert); see also **Aufheben, prahlen, Rat** 2, and the example from A. Zweig given under **ohne** 1.

rühren: see **move** 3.

S

Sack: see **nouns of measure** 1 (*a*).

-sal: see **-selig** 2. Nouns ending in -sal fluctuate somewhat in gender. A few are either neut. or (now far more commonly) fem., such as **Drangsal, Mühsal, Saumsal** and **Trübsal**; others are definitely neut., viz. **Irrsal, Labsal, Rinnsal, Scheusal, Schicksal** and **Wirrsal.** Nouns in which

-*sal* was weakened to **-sel** (which often implies inferiority, insignificance) fluctuate also: masc. are **Häcksel** (sometimes neut., esp. in Austria), **Stöpsel** and **Wechsel**; neut. are **Anhängsel, Geschreibsel, Rätsel** and **Überbleibsel**; the only fem. is **Amsel**, but this may not belong here at all (< OHG *amisala*, 'ouzel').

salzen: see **falten** 3.

Same: see **Balken.**

sammeln: 1. The basic idea in this trans. verb is 'to gather together *or* into a heap', as in **Holz zu einem Feuer** or **gefallenes Laub sammeln**—cf. **Du wirst feurige Kohlen auf sein Haupt sammeln** (Rom. 12. 20); then, more specifically, 'to gather *or* collect', not only with concrete nouns like **Münzen** or **Briefmarken** (cf., with **Geld** understood, **für die Armen sammeln**), but also with words like **Kräfte, Erfahrungen**, etc.; so also an author's 'collected' works are **gesammelte Werke.** Where we use 'to gather' with intrans. force, as of clouds (cf. 2), it is necessary to use the reflex. in German: **Gewitterwolken sammelten sich im Westen** (= **zogen sich . . . zusammen**). **2.** With a *pers.* obj., the simple verb is only used in a few expressions like **ein Heer sammeln** or **Volk um sich sammeln**, and reflex. with fig. force, **Ich muß mich sammeln** ('I must collect my thoughts'). Elsewhere the compd. **versammeln** is the rule: e.g. **Zu Weihnachten hatten die Eltern ihre ganze Familie um sich versammelt—Als Hauptfigur, um welche sich die übrigen am glücklichsten versammeln ließen, war mir Egmont aufgefallen** (G.). Here again the *reflex.* corresponds to our *intrans.*, and it is noteworthy that, where a prep. phrase is used to indicate the meeting-place, the case after **an, in, vor**, etc. is now almost always the *dat.*: e.g. **Die Bürger versammelten sich am Fluß, in der Kirche, vor dem Rathaus—Die Welt versammelt sich an Fenstern und Türen** (Jean Paul); and so also **Wo** (not **Wohin**) **sollen wir uns versammeln?** and in the pass., **Wir wurden in einem Saale versammelt** (G. Keller). Of course, this verb can be used with other preps. with which this point does not arise: e.g. **Die Leute versammelten sich um den Redner—Zu den Seinigen versammelt werden** ('to be gathered to one's people'), **ist so ein herzlicher Ausdruck** (G.), after Luther's **Ich werde versammelt zu meinem Volk** (Gen. 49. 29).

samt: 1. This was orig. an *adv.*, but this is now confined to **samt und sonders** ('collectively and individually, one and all'), as in **Die Räuber wurden samt und sonders verhaftet** ('. . . arrested in a body')—**Die Möbel waren samt und sonders fadenscheinig** (Ompteda). Otherwise **samt**, often compounded with **mit-**, is now a *prep.* (+ *dat.*), meaning 'along with'. It is a rather formal expression (cf. **nebst**), used where there is a close connexion: e.g. **Der König betrat den Saal samt seinem Gefolge—Herein kamen Vater und Mutter mitsamt drei Kindern—Der Alte samt seiner Frau machte Lärm über den Skandal** (Jul. Grosse)—**Das Schiff ging samt Mannschaft und Passagieren unter.** The plur. verb in **Ein Sofa, samt etlichen Sesseln, harrten vornehmer Gäste** (Sudermann) is, of course, strictly incorrect, and although this is in some cases sanctioned by usage (see **congruence** 1 *e*), the author's commas really condemn it: it would be permissible, but not to be recommended, if the commas were omitted. **2.** (**a**) Although **samt** is limited in scope, there are two derivative *adjs.* in common use, viz. **gesamt** and **sämtlich.** The former, really the contracted past part. of MHG *samenen* (> **sammeln**), is used attrib. with collect. *sing.* nouns, the latter with similar *plur.* nouns: thus, 'all the relatives' is either **die gesamte Verwandtschaft** or **sämtliche Verwandte** (see below), 'the whole population of the town' either **die gesamte Stadtbevölkerung** or **sämtliche Stadtbewohner**, and 'all the officers' either **das gesamte Offizierkorps** or **sämtliche Offiziere**; cf. also **Die bäurische Bevölkerung Italiens war an dem gesamten Ideengut** ('ideology') **des Faschismus gar nicht interessiert** (K. Edschmid) and **Goethes sämtliche Werke.** With regard to the inflexion of an attrib. adj. or an adj.-subst. after **sämtlich**, the same applies as in the case of **viel** (q.v. 2 *c*): nom. and accus. **sämtliche ordentliche Mitglieder**, gen. usually **sämtlicher ordentlichen Mitglieder**; cf. **Er wohnte nicht mehr im Wirtshaus, dessen sämtliche alten** (better **alte**) **Räume er vermietete** (Zuckmayer), and sim. **Die Heiligenstatuen erwiesen sich zumeist, wenigstens sämtliche neuern, als Fabrikarbeit gewöhnlicher Art** (H. Hesse). (**b**) As an *adv.*, **sämtlich** is only used in propositions like **Die Verwandten hatten sich sämtlich** ('to a man, one and all') **eingestellt.** The only other adv. is **insgesamt**, which was formerly used in the same way, as in **Saladin liebt sein** (now **seine**) **Geschwister insgesamt** (Lessing) and **Wir setzen eine Formel auf, worin wir uns dem Herzog insgesamt verschreiben** (Sch.); but it is now mostly used in commercial lang. with the force of 'altogether, making a total of', as when a waiter or shopgirl might say **Die Rechnung beträgt insgesamt sechzig Mark.**

sämtlich: see samt 2.

satisfaction, satisfy: The word 'satisfaction' seems to have two fundamental meanings, viz. the 'acceptance of a challenge' and the 'gratification of a desire'; out of the former there has developed the idea of making 'amends', out of the latter that of a 'feeling of contentment', the result of release from uncertainty or uneasiness. The following examples, embracing both nouns and verbs, indicate how these ideas may be expressed in German: (a) **Er fühlte sich beleidigt und forderte Genugtuung** (where satisfaction with weapons is implied, as in a duel, **Satisfaktio'n** is also still used)—**Was konnte boshafter sein, als einen Unschuldigen, dessen Leiden man verursacht, zu verspotten und weder an Genugtuung** ('redress') **noch Entschädigung** ('reparation') **zu denken** (G.)—**Die Frau Professor hatte die Genugtuung** ('satisfaction'), **wegen ihrer Kochkunst in der ganzen Bekanntschaft berühmt zu sein** (Böhlau)—**Ich habe mit Genugtuung erfahren, daß Ihre Gesundheit völlig wiederhergestellt ist**; (b) **Ein Gefühl innerer Befriedigung** (or **Zufriedenheit**) **beschlich sie**—**Er drang auf sofortige Befriedigung seiner Forderungen** (cf. *c* and *e*)—**Warte, bis ich meinen Hunger befriedigt** (or **gestillt**) **habe**—**Soviel der Junge auch ißt, er scheint nie befriedigt** (= **satt**) **zu sein** (cf. **Dieses Gericht ist sehr sättigend,** 'This dish is very satisfying')—**Ich bin leider außerstande, deine Neugier zu befriedigen**—**Die Leistungen dieses Schülers sind befriedigend** ('fair') or **genügend** ('satisfactory'); (c) **Die Zufriedenstellung seiner Kunden** ('To give satisfaction to his customers') **ist erste Pflicht eines Händlers**—**Er konnte die Forderungen nicht ganz befriedigen, hat aber seine Gläubiger** ('creditors') **durch eine Teilzahlung zufriedengestellt** (Sanders); (d) **Ich habe die Überzeugung gewonnen, daß er diesem Posten gewachsen ist** ('I am satisfied that he is equal to this post')—**Er hat mich von seiner Ehrlichkeit überzeugt** ('He has satisfied me as to his honesty'); (e) **Seine Erklärung genügt mir nicht** ('I am not satisfied with his explanation')—**Du hast meinen Bedingungen nicht genügt**—**Laßt euch** (*dat.*) **an diesem Geständnis genügen** or, in more choice style, **Laßt euch** (*dat.*) **dieses Geständnis Genüge tun** (Sch.: 'Let this confession satisfy you'), an idea ordinarily expressed by **Begnügt euch** (*accus.*) **mit diesem Geständnis** or **Gebt euch** (*accus.*) **mit diesem Geständnis zufrieden** ('Rest content with this confession').

satt: This adj. is properly used of a person who is 'satisfied' after a meal—cf. **satisfaction** (*b*)—as in **Ich bin satt**—**Er hat sich an dem, was man ihm vorsetzte, satt gegessen und getrunken** ('He has eaten and drunk his fill of what was set before him'); and this reflex. idiom has been applied *fig.* to a few other verbs, esp. **sehen,** as in **Ich konnte mich an der schönen Aussicht nicht satt sehen** ('I could not get enough of, take my eyes off, the lovely view'); less commonly **Die Tochter spielte den Flügel, und so schön, daß wir uns kaum satt hörten** (Mörike: '. . . so beautifully that we could have gone on listening indefinitely'). It is possible to say **ein satter Magen** ('a full stomach'), but actually the attrib. use of the adj. is rather rare, the only common phrases here being with words denoting colour: 'rich colours' are **satte Farben.** In the *lit.* sense of the adj., the food or drink orig. stood in the gen. case, as in **Am Morgen sollt ihr Brotes satt werden** (Exod. 16. 12), but this is now almost obs. The *gen.* is still used in choice lang., however, where **satt** has come to mean 'sick *or* tired' of something: just as one said in MHG *ich bin es* (gen.) *sat,* so Luther said **Ich bin der Brandopfer satt** (Jes. 1. 11); and sim. **Man wird der Weiber bald satt** (G.)—**Als wir des musikalischen Vergnügens satt waren, gingen wir vor das Haus** (G. Keller)—**Er ist der Schönheit satt, die ein Geschrei der Gassen geworden** (A. Eloesser)—**Ich bin deiner übersatt** (C. F. Meyer)—**Ich bin es satt, des eklen Schauspiels** (Tieck). But the gen. **es** was gradually confused with the accus. (see **es** 1), as with **müde** and **überdrüssig** (see **müde** 1 and 2), and the accus. is now the normal case in ordinary lang.: e.g. **Du mußt eine reiche Frau nehmen, so eine wird man nimmer satt** (G.)—**Die kleinen Städte bin ich satt** (Platen)—**Er hatte keinen Haß**

auf seinen Hauslehrer, er war nur seinen Eifer von Herzen satt (W. Schäfer)—**Wir müssen von hier weg: die Damen sind uns satt** (K. Edschmid)—**Auch die Lerche hatte das Singen satt und war verstummt** (Britting); cf. a common idiom like **Ich habe** or **bekomme es satt, mich von ihm an der Nase herumführen zu lassen** ('I am [getting] sick of being made a fool of by him').

Sau: The ordinary plur. form of this noun ('sow') is **Säue**, but hunters, foresters, etc., use **Sauen** of 'wild sows'.

saugen: This is the NHG form of the MHG strong verb *sûgen* ('to suck'), while that of the corresponding weak factitive *sougen* ('to suckle') is now **säugen.** The latter is still always weak, but like many other orig. strong verbs, **saugen** has developed weak forms. *Duden* recommends the strong forms, but *Sanders* says **„Die schwache Abwandlung ist auch bei unsern besten Schriftstellern üblich"**, and *Heyne* goes further and represents the weak forms as **„jetzt in gewöhnlicher Rede bevorzugt"**. The following are some characteristic examples of the strong forms: **Christian sog an seiner Pfeife** (J. F. Perkonig)—**Scheffel hat an dem Borne mittelalterlicher Dichtung gesogen** (A. Hausrath)—**Der Nachtregen war längst von einer dampfenden Morgenhitze aufgesogen** (W. Schäfer)—**Vom Fenster her kam ein süßer Duft, den die feine Nase des geistlichen Herrn behaglich einsog** (Heyse)—**Er hatte jedes Wort begierig eingesogen** (Fontane). But the following quotations give a good idea of the extent to which the use of weak forms has spread in modern times: **Der Boden saugte die Feuchtigkeit in sich** (G.)—**Er riß die Krebse auseinander und saugte den Saft aus dem Geflechte der Füße** (Stifter)—**Dicke Efeuranken saugten ihre Kraft aus den Baumstämmen** (H. Hauser)—**Der Kaiser wär nicht so arm, wenn nicht soviel Blutegel** ('leeches') **an dem Mark des Landes saugten** (Sch.)—**Söldner und Pfaffen saugten am Marke des Volks** (Platen)—**Der Junge saugte am Daumen** (I. Seidel)—**In einer Schüssel war Honig: eine Biene saß am Rand und saugte eifrig** (G. Britting)—**Ihre Lippen preßten sich auf seinen Mund und saugten sich daran fest** (Viebig)—**Ihre Augen saugten sich an den leuchtenden Fenstern fest** (G. Engel)—**Wunderbar war es, zu fühlen, wie Rilkes Sprache sich mit Farben vollsaugte** (St. Zweig)—**Da war es wieder, dieses Gefühl eines Glückes, das alle vernünftigen Gedanken aufsaugte** (W. Kramp)—**Sein Blick folgte dem Licht des Scheinwerfers, der das Dunkel der Straße in sich hineinsaugte** (id.); for the fluctuation, cf. **Die Bienen saugten fleißig an den Nektartropfen, selbst die Spinne kroch herbei und sog gewaltig** (G.).

save: Distinguish between **Geld sparen** ('to save money': see **spare** 1 *a*)—**seine Kräfte aufsparen** ('to save one's strength' for some labour or effort)—**sich Mühe ersparen** ('to save oneself trouble')—**den Schein wahren** ('to save appearances')—**jemand vor dem Untergang bewahren** ('to save somebody from ruin')—**jemand vom Ertrinken retten** ('to save a person from drowning').

Saxon genitive: see **genitive (possessive)** 1–3.

scarcely: see **hardly.**

Schachtel: see **box** 5.

schade: see **adjectives (indeclinable)** 5.

Schaden: see **Balken.**

schadenfreuen: The noun **Schadenfreude,** suggesting a feeling of malicious gratification at another person's misfortune—Valentine Williams refers to it as 'that untranslatable German portmanteau word for pleasure in another's discomfiture'—is an every-day expression, and the same applies, though to a lesser extent, to the adj. **schadenfroh**; but the verb **sich schadenfreuen** has never become established, and its use is not to be recommended: cf. **Es erschien ein Etwas auf dem Antlitz, das sich über die Demütigung zu schadenfreuen schien** (O. Ludwig), where one would rather say **das Schadenfreude . . . auszudrücken schien.** These expressions do not occur before the NHG period: cf. Luther's **Sie freuen sich über meinen Schaden** (Ps. 35. 15).

schaffen: 1. With *strong* forms: **(a)** This verb and its compd. **erschaffen** are the reg. expressions for 'to create', in which sense **schöpfen** (q.v.) is no longer used: e.g. **Gott schuf den Menschen ihm zum Bilde** (Gen. 1. 27)—**Er ist dazu** (or **dafür**) **wie geschaffen** ('He is the very man for it')—**Sie sind füreinander wie geschaffen** ('They are made for each other, an ideal couple'). **(b)** The only other strong compds. are **u'mschaffen** ('to re-create, metamorphose'), **anerschaffen** ('to implant in the act of creating') and **beschaffen** (only in the *past part.*, suggesting a state: 'constituted, conditioned'—but cf. 2 (*b*)): e.g. **Ich kann nicht anders sagen, als daß ich zu einem neuen Menschen umgeschaffen wurde** (W. Müller: '. . . that I was made a new man of'); **Gott hat dem Kamel einen Höcker anerschaffen** ('When God created the camel, He gave him a hump')—**Das Vieh hat alles besser als die Menschen: es trägt seinen Rock anerschaffen auf seinem Leibe** (Immermann)—**Wenn Gott den Menschen erschaffen hat, so ist ihm der aufrechte Gang anerschaffen** (G.); **Ich bin nun einmal von Natur so beschaffen** ('That's just the way I'm built')—**Dein Betragen ist nicht so beschaffen, daß es einen vorteilhaften Eindruck machen könnte** ('Your behaviour is not of the kind *or* not calculated to make a favourable impression')—**Wie ist's mit deinen Geldmitteln beschaffen?** (coll.: 'How are you off for cash?'); for **zu schaffen machen**, see **machen** 1. **2.** With *weak* forms: (**a**) The simple verb means 'to be active, busy', then esp. trans. 'to effect, accomplish': e.g. **Mit eitler Rede wird hier nichts geschafft** (Sch.)—**Ich habe heute tüchtig geschafft** ('I have got through a lot of work today')—**Ich habe mit ihm nichts zu schaffen** ('I have no dealings with him')—**„Kann ich noch zum Zug kommen?" „Das schaffen Sie kaum"** (K. Edschmid: 'Can I still catch the train?' 'You'll hardly manage that'). It is also much used in the sense of 'to get, procure' with objs. like **Geld, Hilfe, Mittel, Rat,** etc. (= **verschaffen**: see *b* below), and in that of 'to remove': e.g. **etwas beiseite** or **aus dem Wege schaffen**—**sich** (*dat.*) **etwas vom Halse schaffen** ('to get rid of' a burden)—**Übelstände aus der Welt schaffen.** (**b**) So also all compds. not implying creation are *weak*: e.g. **Diese Mißbräuche sind alle abgeschafft** ('have been got rid of, remedied')—**Ich habe mir ein Auto angeschafft** ('I have acquired a car': see **anschaffen**)—**Wer hat das Geld beschafft?** ('Who procured *or* raised the money?')—**Er verschaffte mir eine gute Stellung** ('He got me a good post').

Schall: see **sound** 1 (*a*).

schallen: **1.** The MHG verb *schellen* was strong (past tense *schal,* past part. *geschollen*), meaning 'to resound' and used esp. of the clash of shields and spears in a hand-to-hand fight. Now **schellen** is a *weak* verb, suggesting a ringing sound, esp. the sound of bells. It is still sometimes used in its earlier sense, as in **Alle Glocken im Hause schellten** (Gutzkow), but much more commonly in that of 'to ring *or* pull a bell' (= **klingeln, die Klingel ziehen**): e.g. **Ich habe dreimal geschellt, aber niemand öffnete**—**Soll ich nach dem Kellner schellen?** ('Shall I ring for the waiter?') **2.** On the other hand, the MHG *schallen* was a weak verb, meaning 'to make a noise, create a din'; but the sound now suggested by **schallen** may be of almost any kind and any intensity (see **sound** 1): cf. **ein leiser Schall** ('a gentle sound') with **schallendes Gelächter** ('a roar of laughter'); so also **Ihr Schrei schallt mir noch in den Ohren** ('Her cry is still ringing in my ears'). With regard to the conjugation, it is still predominantly *weak,* but strong past forms (really taken from MHG *schellen*: see 1) are sometimes used in choicer prose: e.g. **Aus einiger Entfernung schollen Musikklänge her** (G. Britting)— **Es war sehr still, nur selten einmal scholl aus den Ställen ein Wiehern oder Hufschlag** (Bruno Frank). These strong forms are particularly common in the two compds. **erschallen** and **verschallen,** the former esp. when used with *fig.* force, as in **Sein Ruhm** or **Ruf erscholl durch das ganze Land** ('His fame resounded throughout the country'). The compd. with **ver-** means 'to fade out, die away' (like **verklingen**), and here also strong forms are sometimes used: e.g. **Der Kranz war aufgesteckt, bunt flatterten die Bänder in der Luft und eine kurze Rede verscholl im Winde** (G.: '. . . was lost in the wind'). Sim. **Die Nachtigallen waren längst verschollen** (Heine); but the past part. in this *lit.* sense is now generally avoided, being mainly used *fig.*, occasionally of something old-fashioned, characteristic of a by-gone age, as in **Acht Läufer, Mützen von verschollener Form auf dem Kopfe, schritten paarweise voran** (Bruno Frank), but esp. of people of whom nothing has been heard for a long time, who have disappeared and are often presumed dead: e.g. **Der Sohn ist vor Jahren über See gefahren und seitdem verschollen**—**Dieser Brief war sein letztes Lebenszeichen, niemand vernahm seitdem das geringste von ihm: er blieb verschollen** (Th. Mann)—**Der Erbe ist für verschollen erklärt worden** ('The heir has been declared dead in the eyes of the law').

scharlach: see **adjectives (indeclinable)** 1, and cf. **colour (adjectives denoting)**.

Schatz: see **congruence** 2.

schaudern: see **grauen** 2.

schauen: see **look** 1 (*a*), and cf. 2 (*a*).

Scheck: Distinguish between **der Scheck** (gen. and plur. **Schecken**) or, much more commonly, **die Schecke** (plur. **Schecken**), meaning a 'dappled animal', esp. a 'piebald horse'—and **der Scheck** (plur. **Schecks**), meaning a 'cheque'.

scheiden: Whether used *trans.*, as in **eine Ehe scheiden** ('to annul a marriage') and **sich scheiden lassen** ('to get a divorce'), or *intrans.*, as in **von einem Freunde scheiden** ('to part from a friend') and **aus einem Amt scheiden** ('to resign from a post'), this verb is now always *strong* (**schied, geschieden**): one no longer says **Tag und Nacht scheidete sich** (Musäus). It is really one of the **reduplicating verbs** (q.v. 2), indeed, it is the only verb in that class which is irreg., its past part. being **geschieden, not gescheiden,** as it should be historically. The same applies, of course, to its compds., as seen esp. in one or two past parts. which have become adjs., as in **Sein Austritt aus der Gesellschaft ist ein entschiedener Verlust** ('His resignation . . . is a decided *or* definite loss') and **Darüber sind die Meinungen verschieden** ('Opinions on this point differ considerably'). The only past part. which has retained its historically correct form as an adj. is **bescheiden** (q.v. 2).

Schein: 1. The fundamental force of this noun is 'what strikes the eye' (**das ins Auge Fallende**), esp. 'light, brightness', as opposed to darkness. This is seen esp. in compds. like **Sonnen-, Mond-, Lampen-, Fackelschein** and **Scheinwerfer** ('spotlight'). A later development is the sense of a 'visible proof of something', now esp. a 'certificate, ticket, label', as in **Geburtsschein** ('certificate of birth'), **Empfangsschein** ('receipt'), **Bankschein** ('banknote'), **Schuldschein** ('IOU'), **Gepäckschein** ('luggage ticket'), etc. **2.** What first strikes the eye when one looks at a thing is its outward 'appearance', and here **Schein** has two shades of meaning which may approach each other closely. The one is the mere way or shape in which a thing presents itself to the eye, esp. the general aspect of circumstances or events, to express which we generally use the plur. 'appearances': e.g. **Der Schein spricht gegen mich** ('Appearances are against me, not in my favour')—**Laß dich nicht durch den Schein trügen** ('Don't be misled by appearances')—**Ich darf hoffen, daß ich nicht nach dem Schein gerichtet werde** (Sch.). Such examples imply a contrast between what merely seems and what actually is, and this is emphasized in an adj. like **scheintot,** applied to a person who looks dead, but is really only in a trance; cf. also the prov. **Der Schein trügt** ('Appearances are deceptive'). And this idea of contrast leads to the second shade of meaning, where a person acts in a certain way merely for the sake of appearance, *pretending* to be what he is not: thus, **scheinheilig** or **scheinfromm** implies that the person is not truly devout, but wishes to be thought so by others, that he is, in fact, 'hypocritical, sanctimonious'; and sim. **Er tut nur so zum Schein** ('He is just pretending for show') —**Er hat mich unter dem Schein der Freundschaft besucht** (i.e. 'under the cloak of friendship'). The difference between appearance and pretence is suggested by **anscheinend** and **scheinbar** (see **Anschein** and **scheinbar** 2).

scheinbar: 1. At one time this word had a somewhat wider application than it has now. In a proposition like **Die Römer bestatten die Leiche und stellen des Verstorbenen Bildnis an dem scheinbarsten Orte des Hauses auf** (Lessing: 'The Romans bury the corpse and set up an image of the deceased in the most conspicuous place in the house'), one would now replace **scheinbar** by **augenfällig** (from **in die Augen fallen,** 'to catch the eye'); and where the same author talks of a body suspended in the air **ohne eine scheinbare Ursache, welche die Wirkung seiner Schwere verhindert** ('without any apparent, *i.e.* perceptible cause preventing the operation of gravity'), modern usage would probably prefer a word like **erkennbar** or **wahrnehmbar.** It is rather strange that this use of **scheinbar** with reference to what 'strikes the eye' should have fallen into disuse, the more so as the corresponding *neg.* expression is still so common: where Goethe refers to theatrical costumes as being **wenig scheinbar,** one would now use **unscheinbar** ('insignificant-looking, unimpressive') or **unansehnlich. 2.** According to modern usage, **scheinbar** has two possible meanings, and it is sometimes not easy to be sure which of these the author wishes to convey. **(a)** It may mean no more than 'so far as one can see, to judge by what the eye sees', and some authorities even limit its use to this sense, as when the *Sprach-Brockhaus* gives as its only meaning **„soviel man erkennen kann"** and *Weigand* explains it as **„äußerlich wahrzunehmend"**. That the expression often has this force is certain: few readers would take it to mean anything else in propositions like **Er saß, scheinbar** ('apparently') **in Gedanken vertieft, am Feuer—Sie gab sich scheinbar Mühe, gegen ihn weniger unliebenswürdig zu sein als früher** (Speckmann)—**Einem scheinbar unwichtigen Impuls folgend schlug er die Richtung zum Tal ein** (L. Frank)—**Ein kleines Mädchen spielte im Schoße der Mutter, die scheinbar unbeschäftigt auf dem Sofa saß** (Storm). On the whole, however, this idea of 'so far as one can judge by appearances' is now more commonly expressed by **anscheinend** or **dem** (or **allem**) **Anschein nach** ('to all appearance'). (**b**) Despite the view expressed by the authorities quoted above, modern usage seems definitely to favour the other meaning, suggesting *what only seems to be but is not*, **scheinbar** thus emphasizing the specific sense of **Schein** (q.v. 2). While *Sanders* gives its sense as **„dem möglicherweise nicht mit der Wahrheit übereinstimmenden Anschein nach beurteilt"**, thus admitting the *possibility* that the appearance may not correspond with the fact, *Heyse* represents the non-conformity between appearance and fact as the very *differentia* of the expression in modern usage: **„den Schein von etwas habend, im Gegensatz zu Wahrheit und Wesen."** In a phrase like **Er hörte mir nur scheinbar zu**, the insertion of **nur** makes it clear that he was not really listening, and **ein scheinbarer Vorwand** obviously implies that the pretext is merely a specious one. The distinction between appearance and reality is well brought out in the following examples: **Bei der Operation war nur die eine langfingerige Hand des Chirurgen mit ihren scheinbar zufälligen, in Wirklichkeit aber methodischen Bewegungen sichtbar** (E. Weiss)—**Er blickte in die Augen der scheinbar so freundlichen, in Wirklichkeit so grausamen Damen** (F. Kafka)—**Einmal war die Rede von allerlei wirklichen und scheinbaren Genies** (W. Bode); cf. **Wenn Mozart, durch Berufsarbeiten abgemüdet, nach frischem Atem schmachtete, war den erschlafften Nerven häufig nur in neuer Aufregung eine scheinbare Stärkung vergönnt** (Mörike: implying that the new excitement only seemed to be but was not really a tonic for his flagging energies). (**c**) And this idea of appearance as distinct from reality may easily go a step farther and suggest deliberate *pretence*. In a proposition like **Er blätterte scheinbar gleichgültig in seinem Buche fort** (Heyse), the author may wish to convey no more than that the man was unconcerned so far as one could judge, but more probably wishes to suggest that he was merely pretending to be unconcerned, an idea which is clearly implied in **Er wurde leichenblaß und bückte sich scheinbar nach der entfallenen Serviette, um seine Verlegenheit zu verbergen** (Spindler: i.e. he wished it to be thought that he stooped down merely to pick up his table-napkin, but actually did so in order to conceal his embarrassment). On the whole, then, in order to obviate the possibility of misconception, it would seem advisable to confine the use of **scheinbar** to cases of contrasted appearance and reality, and to use **anscheinend**, as indicated under 2 (*a*), where no such contrast is implied.

schellen: see **schallen** 1.

schelten: The only recognized forms of this verb are *strong*: past tenses **schalt, schölte** (see **past subjunctive** 2 *c* ii), **gescholten.** The weak imperative sing. **schelte!** (for **schilt!**) is sometimes used coll. . . but the weak pres. indic. favoured by certain Swiss authors should never be used: cf. **Er herrscht mich an und scheltet** (for **schilt**) **wie immer** (Federer); sim. **„Wenn du nur Leute verschrecken kannst!" scheltet er ernst** (id.: where the comparatively rare compd. verb **verschrecken** is also characteristic of the south, being elsewhere replaced by **erschrecken**—see **schrecken**). In these examples the verb is used abs. ('to scold'), but it can take either an accus. or **auf** + accus., as in **Wie unverständig war es, als du ehemals auf eine Nation schaltest** (G.: '. . . when you inveighed against a nation'). Its other common use is in the sense of 'to call' a person by a disparaging name: e.g. **Er hat mich dumm** (or **einen Dummkopf**) **gescholten—„Junge, man könnte dich ein Mädchen schelten"** (G.). The only compd. form in general use is the past part. of **beschelten**, esp. the neg. **unbescholten** ('blameless, of good reputation'): cf. **Daß wir unbescholten sind, gibt uns das Recht, uns auch einmal schelten zu lassen** (G.).

scheren: There were two MHG verbs *schërn*, one strong (*ich schir—ich schar, wir schâren—geschörn*), the other weak. The strong verb meant 'to cut, shave, shear' or *fig.* 'to annoy, molest', the weak verb 'to remove, get rid of'. All these meanings are still preserved, but the modern tendency is towards *weak* forms: of strong forms, the pres. **du schierst, er schiert** and the imperat. **schier!** are now almost obs., but the past forms **schōr, geschōren** are still preferred when the meaning is 'to cut, shear'. The following are characteristic examples: *lit.* **Er hat sich das Haar scheren lassen** (cf. the idiom **sein Schäfchen scheren,** 'to feather one's nest')—**Er erzählte von einem fürchterlichen Unwetter und von acht Schafen, denen der Blitz die Wolle bis auf die Haut abschor** (Waggerl: '. . . whose wool a lightning-flash had shorn off to the skin')—**Sie behauptete, es sei zum Lachen, wenn sie sich Andree in der Kutte mit geschorener Platte vorstellen sollte** (Heyse: '. . . if she were to picture A. to herself in a cowl with shorn pate') —**Sieh, wie der Busch vom Winde geschoren ist** (Ponten: 'See how the wind has stripped off the leaves of the shrub'); *fig.* **Jetzt muß ich die Pfaffen scheren, ich kann die Kerls** (cf. **Fräulein** 1) **nicht ausstehen** (G.: 'Now I must vex the priests, I can't stand these fellows')—**Was schert mich Weib, was schert mich Kind?** (Heine: 'What are wife and child to me?') —**Mag ihm das alte Gebäude auf den Kopf fallen, was schiert's** (now usually **schert's**) **mich?** (Raabe: '. . . what do I care?'). In coll. speech the strong past part. is esp. common in the neg. form **ungeschoren,** usually in the expression **jemand ungeschoren lassen** ('to leave a person alone, unmolested'): e.g. **So lebte die fromme Frau in tiefem Frieden und blieb ungeschoren** (G. Keller)—**Macht, was ihr wollt, nur laßt mich ungeschoren** (G.: '. . . don't bother me')—**Stehst du am Ziel, dann steure ich dir nach; bis dahin laß mich ungeschoren** (Tieck: '. . . till then leave me in peace')—**„Die Treppe ist breit genug für uns beide", sagte Konrad, „laßt mich ungeschoren vorbei!"** (E. Wichert: '. . . let me pass unmolested!'). The MHG weak verb is now confined to the coll. use of the **reflex.** with the force of 'to remove oneself' from **a** person's presence, 'to take oneself off, clear out', and vulgarly to the phrase **sich den Teufel um etwas scheren** ('not to care a hang about something'): e.g. **Scher dich hinaus!** ('Get out!')—**Scher dich zum Kuckuck!** ('Go to blazes!')—**Wer im Herzen jung ist, schert sich den Teufel um Brotsorgen** (L. Winder: 'Whoever is young at heart doesn't trouble his head *or* care a brass farthing about his daily bread'); cf. **Ich schor** (now **scherte**) **mich den Teufel um den Krimskrams hier** (Immermann: 'I didn't care a fig for all this trash'). As a technical expression in weaving, **scheren** has the force of 'to stretch *or* warp' (threads, ropes, etc.); cf. **Wir fingen einmal einen Stör von vier Metern Länge, und Matten schor ihm ein Ende Leine durch Maul und Kiemen, knotete eine Schlinge, band den freien Tamp am Bootsbord fest und warf den Fisch wieder ins Wasser** (H. Leip: 'Once we caught a sturgeon measuring four metres, and M. passed a bit of rope tightly through its mouth and gills, knotted a loop, fastened the loose end of the rope to the gunwale and threw the fish back into the water').

Scheu: Like the adj. **scheu** (see **shy** 1), the noun **Scheu** may imply no more than 'timidity', reluctance to approach what may threaten danger, as in **Sie trat ohne Scheu an den Fremden heran,** but is esp. used to suggest a feeling of 'awe', as when one enters a cathedral: **Beim Eintritt in den Dom empfand ich eine fromme** or **ehrfurchtsvolle Scheu.** As this example shows, its gender is *fem.*; at an earlier period it was sometimes treated as masc. (G. used **der Vogelscheu** where we now use **die Vogelscheuche,** 'scarecrow'), but this is now obs. except in the compd. **Abscheu** ('aversion, loathing') which is always *masc.*: e.g. **Dieser schreckliche Anblick flößte mir den größten Abscheu ein—Eine Scheu, die** er **sich nicht erklären konnte, machte es ihm unmöglich, seine Absicht auszuführen: er haßte Regine nicht mehr, sein Abscheu war gewichen** (Sudermann).

scheuen: In the *intrans.* use (aux. **haben**), this is used of animals which are **scheu** (q.v.), esp. of horses which 'shy' at something, as in **Das Roß scheute an** (now always **vor**) **meinem Neffen** (Sch.). Otherwise it is used *trans.* in the sense of 'to be afraid of', esp. **'to shy at, fight shy of,**

steer clear of, avoid' something (esp. trouble, expense, etc.: see **spare** 1 (*a*)): e.g. **Ein gebranntes Kind scheut das Feuer—Ich tue recht und scheue keinen Feind** (Sch.)—**Er hat keine Baukosten gescheut** ('He has grudged no building-expenses')—*fig*. **Seine Taten scheuen das Tageslicht**; so also very commonly *reflex.*: **Ich scheue mich vor dem bevorstehenden Umzug in unser neues Haus** ('I dread the coming removal to our new quarters')—**Er scheut sich davor, die Extraarbeit zu unternehmen.** The MHG *sich schiuhen* took a *gen.*, and this case is sometimes still used in NHG, both with the simple verb and with the reflex., now esp. in choice style: e.g. **Fast scheu ich mich des Sonderlings** (Lessing)—**Sie scheute der Mühe nicht** (Rilke).

Scheuer, Scheune: see **Getreide** 2.

Scheusal: see **gruselig** 1 and **-sal.**

schicken: cf. **occur** 3 (*a*).

schief: see **quer** 3.

Schild: Distinguish between **der Schild** (plur. **Schilde**) meaning 'shield, escutcheon'—and **das Schild** (plur. **Schilder**) meaning 'sign-board, notice-board, name-plate', also 'badge' (e.g. as worn by porters, etc.).

Schlaf, Schläfe: At one time **Schlaf** was used not only in the sense of 'sleep' but also with reference to that part of the human head which we call the 'temple': e.g. **Da nahm Jael einen Nagel . . . und schlug ihm den Nagel durch seinen Schlaf** (Judges 4. 21)—**Sie verändert das Gesicht nicht, und ich habe auch nicht gesehen, daß sie einmal die Hand nach dem Schlafe zu bewegt hätte** (G.); and in this sense it is very occasionally found even later, as in **Der Hauptmann flog vom Sattel mit durchgespaltnem Schlaf** (Geibel). So also in the plur.: **Seine Schläfe waren eingesunken und das ergraute Haar war struppig um dieselben herum** (Stifter)—**Sie sprengten ihm Wasser ins Gesicht und rieben ihm die Schläfe** (Heyse); but this plur. **Schläfe** eventually established itself as a *fem. sing.* (cf. **Fährte**), with a new plur. **Schläfen**, and these are the accepted forms in modern times: cf. **Er streckte ihn mit einem Schusse durch die Schläfen nieder** (C. F. Meyer).

schlafen: see **reduplicating verbs** 1 and 2.

schlaff, schlapp: see **loose** 2.

schlagen: **1.** This verb can be used either trans. or intrans.: cf. **Ich schlug ihn mit der Faust** and **Ich schlug mit der Faust auf den Tisch.** In both these cases the art. replaces a poss. ('*my* fist'), and this idiom is esp. common where the art. is combined with the dat. of a pers. pron., as in **Er drückte mir Geld in die Hand** (= **Er drückte Geld in meine Hand**). It is this idiom that explains why a *dat.* of the pers. pron. is possible in a proposition like 'I struck him on the head with my fist': one can say either **Ich schlug ihn mit der Faust auf den Kopf** or **Ich schlug ihm . . . auf den Kopf,** the latter being a more idiomatic way of saying **Ich schlug auf seinen Kopf**; and so also **Er schlug** ('patted') **ihm . . . auf die Schulter** (Ompteda), or **Drauf schlug ich ihn ins Gesicht** (G.)—**Sie holte aus** ('She lifted her arm'), **um ihn ins Gesicht zu schlagen** (Bergengruen). Of course, this applies only to contexts in which the pers. pron. is associated with *a prep. phrase*: cf. **Einige Leute schüttelten ihm** (not **ihn**) **die Hände und klopften ihn** (see 2 (*c*)) **auf die Schulter** (id.). In this connexion *Sanders* says **Wo es möglich erscheint, ist der Dativ vorzuziehen, also lieber „Er schlug ihm (statt ihn) auf die Backe"**; but with some verbs of this kind the accus. is rather more usual (see below). **2.** The same choice of a dat. or an accus. is possible with the following verbs: **(a) beißen**: e.g. **Dann wird eine Schlange . . . das Pferd in die Fersen beißen** (Gen. 49. 17)—**Der Caro** (a dog) **hat manchen Bauerlümmel in die Wade gebissen** (Kotzebue)—**Ich biß mich in die Zunge, um mich zu erwecken** (Chamisso)—**Ich biß mir auf die Zähne** (Spielhagen); on the whole, the accus. is rather more common here: one usually says **Der Hund hat mich in den Finger** (or **mir den Finger**) **gebissen**—**(b) hauen** (q.v.); cf. **Er griff seine Schwertscheide und hieb dem Heribald flach über den Rücken** (Scheffel), but usually **Man hat mich übers Ohr gehauen** ('I have been swindled')—**(c) klopfen** (q.v.): e.g. **Wurm klopft ihn auf die Schulter** (Sch., in a stage direction)—**Der Kleine klopfte ihm auf die Schulter** (Freytag)—**(d) kneifen** (q.v.)—**(e) schneiden**: one usually says **Ich habe mich in den Finger** (or **mich beim Rasieren in die Backe**) **geschnitten**, and sim. **Er hat den Herzog mehrmals in das Fleisch geschnitten** (Immermann) and **Diese Undankbarkeit schneidet mich durch die Seele** (Möser); but also **Es schneidet mir durch die Seele** (Auerbach)—**In die Seele schnitt**

mir's (Sch.)—**Da er sie so unglücklich sah, schnitt es ihm ins Herz** (Ompteda).

schlecht: see **bad** 1, 2, and 3.

schlechterdings: see allerdings 2 (*b*).

schlechthin: In this adv., as in **schlechterdings** and **schlechtweg** (see **allerdings** 2 and **weg** 2), we see the orig. meaning of **schlecht**, viz. 'plain, simple' (see **bad** 1): e.g. **Diese Bewunderer Beethovens konnten ihm bei den Werken seiner letzten Periode schlechthin nicht folgen** (Th. Mann: 'These admirers of Beethoven were simply unable to follow his last works': these were quite beyond them). Then, just as 'simply' may mean 'absolutely' (cf. Kingsley's 'Your political economy is simply undeniable'), so **schlechthin** may have the same force: cf. **Ihr verdanke ich schlechthin alles, was ich geworden bin** (W. Kramp).

schlechtweg: see **weg** 2.

schleifen: 1. *Strong* forms of this verb are fixed when it means 'to sharpen, grind' (tools, weapons), 'to polish' (wood, etc.) or 'to cut' (glass, precious stones): e.g. **Herschel erbaute seine Teleskope selber, schliff selber die Spiegel** (A. Schaeffer)—**Das Glas war geschliffen mit einer Blumenranke, und hineingeschliffen war der Name Rosa** (id.)—**Ein Sonnenstrahl blitzte in den fein geschliffenen Kelchen** (C. F. Meyer)—**Ich hatte damals einen Kleiderkasten geschliffen** (W. Schäfer)—cf. **In den Reisfeldern schliff der Abendwind die Blätter gegeneinander** (Hackländer); so also **ein geschliffener Degen, geschliffene und ungeschliffene Edelsteine**, and *fig.* **geschliffene** ('polished') **Verse, Manieren,** etc.—**ein ungeschliffener Tölpel** ('an unmannerly lout'). **2.** *Weak* forms are fixed (**a**) when the verb has *intrans.* force (cf. 3), meaning 'to trail *or* scrape' (along the ground): e.g. **So groß war der Kranz, den die Mädchen trugen, daß er auf dem Boden schleifte** (G. Britting)—**Die unteren Äste der Buche schleiften auf dem Boden** (Fr. Schnack)—**Sie schleifte durch das Zimmer** (Kafka)—**Es klang, wie wenn Schleppenkleider über die Diele hinschleiften** (Fontane)—**Das Gartentor schleifte über den Kies** (Zifferer)—cf. **Der Wind schleifte über die Heide** (Kellermann); (**b**) when it is used *trans.* in the sense of 'to cause to trail', i.e. 'to drag' (along the ground) or 'to raze to the ground': e.g. **Der Junge schleifte einen Streifen bunten Papiers im Schnee nach** (Zifferer)—**Hektors Leiche wird rückwärts am Wagen zu den Schiffen geschleift** (Voss)—**Hitler ging greisenhaft und schleifte den linken Fuß nach** (J. Thorwald)—**Als Wittner durch das Lokal ging, merkte Georg, daß er den verwundeten Fuß leicht nachschleifte** (K. Edschmid)—**Die Befestigungen unserer Stadt waren längst geschleift und in Anlagen umgewandelt** (Speckmann); cf., in music, **geschleift zu spielen** (i.e. *legato*) and *coll.* **jemand an den Haaren in eine Abendgesellschaft schleifen** ('to drag some one by main force to a party'). **3.** There is some fluctuation, but with a definite preference for *weak* forms, when the verb means 'to shuffle' or, like **schlittern,** 'to slide' (on the ice): e.g. **Die Straßenjugend schleifte auf den mit Schnee bedeckten Trottoirs** (Hackländer)—**Alle erdenklichen Arten von Pantoffeln kamen geschlurft, geschleift, geklappert** (Prutz: see **kommen** 4 (*a*))—**Ich lief in den Hof und schliff** (usually **schleifte**) **auf dem Eise hin und her** (Carossa).

schleißen ('to split', esp. 'to slit'): While *weak* forms of this verb are allowed in Austria, *strong* forms are practically fixed elsewhere. Its commonest use is in the past part., esp. compounded with the prefixes **ver-** and **zer-:** e.g. **Breite, mit verschlissener** ('threadbare') **Seide bespannte Armstühle umgaben die Feuerstelle** (Th. Mann)—**Er war in einen viel zu weiten und völlig zerschlissenen** ('tattered') **Waffenrock gekleidet** (Alverdes).

schlicht: see **bad** 2.

schliefen: This strong intrans. verb is now almost confined to southern dialects, being replaced ordinarily by **schlüpfen.** It is used esp. of animals 'slipping' or 'stealing' into a hole for cover: e.g. **Das Füchslein schloff behend durchs Loch** (Rückert)—**Droben im Boden grub der Junge eine Schlafhöhle in den Heuhaufen und schloff wie ein Dachs in die Röhre** (Fr. Schnack: 'Up in the loft the boy dug a sleeping-place in the heap of hay and slipped in like a badger into his sett'); cf. fig. **Wir stiegen zuweilen in kleinen, warm durchsonnten Städten ab** (see **absteigen** 2), **durch die das Leben hinschloff** (Kurt Matthies: '. . . through the streets of which life jogged on').

schließen: 1. When used of locking some one or something in a room, the simple verb **schließen** requires an *accus.* in the prep. phrase: **Die Mutter schloß das unartige Kind in den Keller.** Here the sep. prefix **ein** could be added at the end, but actually **einschließen** (q.v.) rather prefers a *dat.* in the prep. phrase, pointing to the resultant state after the action, i.e. to the time when the child is *in* the cellar and the key turned in the lock (see **accusative or dative** . . . 3 (*b*)). **2.** To be noted is the use of **schließen** in the sense of 'to draw a conclusion, infer'. It can take an accus. obj., but only when this is an indef. neut. expression like **das, etwas,** etc., as in **Das kann man aus seinen Worten nicht schließen**; or its obj. can be a subord. clause, as in **Aus Ihrem Brief darf ich wohl schließen, daß es Ihnen gesundheitlich jetzt besser geht.** Otherwise what is inferred is expressed by **auf** + *accus.*: e.g. **Aus dem Wetterbericht können wir auf heftigen Regen schließen** (lit. 'From the weather forecast we can infer heavy rain', i.e. 'The forecast predicts heavy rain'); esp. idiom. are such propositions with **lassen** (q.v. 3 *a*): e.g. **Seine Kleidung ließ auf einen Lehrling schließen** (Spindler: lit. 'His dress let [one] infer an apprentice', i.e. 'His dress proclaimed him an apprentice *or* To judge by his clothes he was an apprentice')—**Seine Stimme war gedämpft, sie ließ auf Kopfschmerzen schließen** (Th. Mann: 'His voice was muffled and argued a headache').

schlimm: see **bad** 3.

schlüpfen: see **schliefen**; **slip** 1.

Schlüsselbund: see **Bund.**

schmecken: see **taste** 2 (*a*).

schmeicheln: **1.** In the pre-classical period, an *accus.* obj. after **schmeicheln** (cf. 2) was quite common, as in **Schwiegermutter eines Prinzen zu sein, schmeichelt die meisten Mütter** (Lessing), and examples of this earlier use are occasionally to be found in modern authors: e.g. **Den Zaren hatte es geschmeichelt, daß er an den Höfen in Paris und Wien aufgenommen war** (Fr. Griese). But the orig. *dat.* is still the recognized construction: one always says **Ich schmeichle mir, ein gutes Geschäft gemacht zu haben.** So also, in the *pass.*, the *impers.* construction is the normal one (see **impersonal verbs** 3), the *pers.* construction being to some extent sanctioned by usage: cf., as a significant example, **Ich bin das erste Mädchen, das ihm schmeichelt, und hoffe, das erste zu werden, das von ihm geschmeichelt wird** (Lessing). This use is now so far recognized that it is generally employed where a *state*, as distinct from an *action*, is implied: one still prefers **Ihr wurde von allen Männern geschmeichelt,** but examples like **Ich war geschmeichelt und nickte** (H. Hesse), **„Du langweilst dich mit mir?" lachte Ernst, der nicht sonderlich geschmeichelt war** (Jul. Wolff) and **Sie kamen sich geschmeichelt vor** (A. Döblin) are quite common, and **Ich fühlte mich geschmeichelt** is quite established, as is also the past part. used as an adj.: e.g. **Felix strich sich mit geschmeicheltem Lächeln über das Kinn** (Sudermann)—**Sie überreichte dem verdutzten und geschmeichelten Knaben ein Kleinod** (Carossa); cf. **folgen** 2 (*b*) and **widersprechen.** So also, of a 'flattering' portrait, one says **Der Maler hat ihr geschmeichelt,** but **Das** (not **Dem**) **Bild ist entschieden geschmeichelt**; sim. **Das ist sein Bild: es ist etwas geschmeichelt** (Rilke)—**Ich habe sein Bild, zwar keine geschmeichelte Miniatur** (Bruno Frank). **2.** As a *trans.* verb, it has the force of 'to coax' a person into a certain action or state: e.g. **Die Mutter sitzt im Grase mit dem Söhnlein, das die Sonne in lächelnden Schlaf schmeichelt** (Hölderlin); cf. also the *fig. reflex.* use in **Die Stimme schmeichelte sich** ('glided gently, stole') **ins Herz** (Frenssen) and **Diese Lieder Geibels schmeicheln sich ins Ohr** (S. Waetzoldt). Definitely trans. is the compd. **erschmeicheln** ('to obtain by coaxing'), as in **Drei Katzen stellten sich ein, um den gewohnten Morgentrunk zu erschmeicheln** (Speckmann); and sim. **abschmeicheln,** which requires a dat. of the person: **Er hat es mir abgeschmeichelt** ('He has coaxed me into parting with it').

Schmuck, schmücken: see **ornament** 2.

schnalzen, schnappen: see **mit** 2 (*b*).

schnauben: **1.** (a) This verb, meaning 'to snort', is generally *weak*, as MHG *snouwen* was: cf. **Saulus schnaubte . . . wider die Jünger des Herrn** (Acts 9. 1)—**Im gleichen Augenblick schnaubte das schwarze Ungetüm** (a railway engine) **an uns vorüber** (M. Eyth). But the strong past forms **schnob,** less commonly **geschnoben,** are fairly common in poetry, as in **Der Tauwind . . . schnob durch Welschland** (Bürger), and even in prose, esp. used of excited or enraged people (cf. **wutschnaubend**): e.g. **Sie horchte auf den Sturm, der draußen um die Kirche schnob** (Bergengruen)—**Er sprang auf: „Satteln!" schnob er, „ich muß fort!"** (Jul. Wolff)—**Der alte General schnob Feuer und Flammen über den Schwindler** (Jul. Grosse). For the strong part., cf. the example from P. Keller given under **er-** 3. (**b**) In the proposition **Da schnaubete der Knabe siebenmal** (2 Kings 4. 35) Luther uses the verb with the force of 'to sneeze', and Storm does the same playfully in the example quoted under **passive** 1 (i); but 'to sneeze' is properly **niesen,** while **sich** (accus.) **schneuzen** or sich (*dat.*) **die Nase schneuzen** is 'to blow one's nose'. **2.** Another form of schnauben is **schnaufen,** really LG, always *weak*, used esp. with lit. force: e.g. **Die Pferde schnauften und tosten** (G.) —**Ihr schnauft ja wie die Bären** (Tieck). In this connexion cf. the common expression **(sich) verschnaufen,** meaning 'to recover one's breath' (= **wieder zu Atem kommen**): e.g. **Nach dem Tanze machten wir ein paar Touren gehend im Saale, um zu verschnaufen** (G.)—**Ich bin schnell gelaufen: warte, bis ich (mich) ein wenig** verschnauft habe.

schnaufen: see schnauben 2.

schneiden: see schlagen 1 and 2 (*e*).

schnell: see **quick** 1 (*a*).

schneuzen: see schnauben 1 (*b*).

schnippen: see **mit** 2 (*b*).

Schnur: There are two entirely different nouns **Schnur** both fem., and both with the alternative plur. forms **Schnuren** and (now far more commonly) **Schnüre.** The one, meaning 'daughter-in-law' (= **Schwiegertochter**), was common in early NHG, as in **Naemi machte sich auf mit ihren zwo** Schnüren (Ruth 1. 6), but is now almost, if not quite, obs. The other is still an everyday expression, having much the same force as **Bindfaden:** thus, it is used *lit.* of 'string' for securing a parcel, of 'cord' for a window-blind, etc. (cf. **Perlenschnur,** a 'string of pearls'), and *fig.* in expressions like **bei der Schnur bleiben** ('to keep within bounds'), **über die Schnur hauen** ('to go too far, kick over the traces'), and—now rather less commonly—**von der Schnur leben** ('to live on one's capital', perhaps taken from the idea of having to open one's purse-strings). In other fig. expressions the dim. form is used: e.g. **wie am Schnürchen gehen** ('to go like clock-work', probably suggested by a puppet-show), **etwas am Schnürchen haben** ('to have a thing at one's fingers' ends'), and **jemand am Schnürchen haben** ('To have a person on a string, under one's thumb').

schnurgerade: see gerade 2 (*b*).

Schober: see **Getreide** 2.

Schock: With the force of 'three score', this noun retains its sing. form in the plur. after numerals, as in **zwei** Schock **Garben** ('120 sheaves'): see **nouns of measure,** and cf. **Mandel.**

schon: 1. This expression orig. meant 'beautifully', being the adv. corresponding to the adj. **schön** (see **adverbs formed from adjectives** 1). As the two words are used now, there would seem to be no connexion whatever between them, but in the 16th century one still said **Er kundt auf der Harpfen schon spielen** (B. Waldis: 'He could play the harp beautifully'). **2.** (**a**) The ordinary meaning of **schon** is 'already', as in **Geht der Junge schon zur Schule?—Ich hatte schon gefrühstückt, als der Briefträger kam.** But in course of time different shades of meaning have developed, and in some of these we use other expressions than 'already': e.g. **Sind Sie schon in der Schweiz gewesen?** ('Have you been to Switzerland before?')—**Das erfuhr ich schon letzte Woche** ('I heard that as long ago as last week': cf. **erst letzte Woche,** either 'no longer ago than last week' or 'not till last week'—see **erst** 2 (*c*))—**Schon anderen Morgens erhielt ich die Nachricht** ('I got the news the very next morning')—**„Es sieht nach Regen aus". „Es regnet schon jetzt"** ('It's raining at this very minute')—**Was? Du willst schon wieder Geld?** ('What? You want money again?' so soon after the last time I gave you some?)—**Das schon an sich sollte ihn überzeugen** ('That in itself, apart from any other argument *or* to go no farther, should convince him') —**Schon der Gedanke** (or **Der bloße Gedanke**) **ist empörend** ('The very idea is shocking')—**Seine Anwesenheit schon allein störte mich** (Ompteda: 'His mere presence flustered me')—**Nur so weiter! Mir schon recht!** (Lessing: 'Carry on! It's quite all right as far as I'm concerned': cf. our slang 'It's okay by me!') —**„Mache dieser Kinderei ein Ende!" „Das kann ich nicht". „Weil du nicht willst". „Oh ich will schon, aber Wollen und Können sind zweierlei"** (Fontane: 'Oh I want to all right, but it's one thing to want to, and another thing to be able to'). (**b**) Idiomatic is the use of **schon** with *reassuring* force: e.g. **Haben Sie keine Sorge: es wird schon alles gut gehen** ('Don't worry: you can depend upon it *or* never fear, everything will go all right') —**Ich werde dich schon rechtzeitig wecken**

('You can rely on my waking you in good time'). (c) In a *concess.* clause it has the force of 'I admit, I grant you', with a following qualifying remark: e.g. **„Das Wetter hat sich gebessert". „Das ist schon richtig** (or contracted **Das schon**), **aber kalt ist es immer noch"** (cf. our '*Quite*, but it's still cold'); here also belongs the elliptical expression **Wenn schon, denn schon** ('What's worth doing at all is worth doing well'; also 'As well be killed for a sheep as for a lamb' or simply 'If a job is to be done, get on with it!').

schonen: see spare 2 (*a*).

schöpfen: In view of the fact that **Schöpfer, Schöpfung** and **Geschöpf** are the regular expressions for 'creator', 'creation' and 'creature' respectively, it is strange that **schöpfen** is no longer used, as it was to a limited extent at an earlier period, in the sense of 'to create' (for which see **schaffen**). Its *lit.* sense now is 'to *scoop*, ladle, draw' (milk from a pail, soup from a tureen, water from a well, etc.), but it is also used *fig.* with objs. like **Atem** ('to draw breath'), **Mut** ('to take courage'), **Hoffnung** ('to derive hope'), **Verdacht** ('to conceive suspicion'); cf. **aus einem Schriftsteller schöpfen** ('to borrow from an author'). So also in a few compds.: e.g. **Hast du das Fett von der Brühe und den Rahm von der Milch abgeschöpft?** ('Have you skimmed the fat off the broth and the cream off the milk?': cf. **abgerahmte Milch,** 'skim milk')—**Ich habe das Boot ausgeschöpft** (H. Hauser: 'I have bailed out the boat', which might have been expressed by **leer geschöpft**). But by far the commonest compd. is **erschöpfen,** used now not so much in the lit. sense (although it is not incorrect to say **In diesem trocknen Sommer haben wir unseren Brunnen völlig erschöpft**), but esp. with the fig. force of 'to exhaust': e.g. **Ich bin** (or **Meine Kräfte sind**) **erschöpft—Meine Geduld war erschöpft—Der Kritiker hat sein Thema erschöpft.**

schräg: see quer 2.

schrauben: This verb was orig. *weak*, and weak forms are still the rule, whether used lit. or fig.: e.g. **Sie schraubte die Lampe höher** ('She turned *or* screwed up the lamp')—**Der Kronleuchter brannte schon, aber die niedrig geschraubten Flämmchen waren kaum sichtbar** (Fontane)—**Der Kartoffelmangel und die neue Mißernte schraubten** ('forced up') **die Preise zu furchtbarer Höhe** (Waldau); sim. in compds., as in **Er schraubte das Licht aus** (Dauthendey)—**Der Sarg ward zugeschraubt** (Federer: 'The coffin-lid was screwed down')—**Er legte die Bücher in eine Kiste, deren Deckel er fest schraubte** (Stifter)—**„Ach, Sie sind es!" rief die Frau mit einer hochgeschraubten** ('high-pitched') **Stimme** (W. Kramp). The past part. **geschraubt** is used fig. of words, style, etc., in the sense of 'laboured, affected, stilted': e.g. **Er flößte ihnen durch geschraubte, fremdländische Redensarten eine gewisse Scheu ein** (I. Kurz)—**Er stotterte ein paar Worte zur Begrüßung zusammen, viel förmlicher und geschraubter, als sonst seine Art war** (E. Wichert)—**An dem englischen Leben beanstandete der Graf vor allem die geschraubte** ('strained, forced') **Kirchlichkeit** (Fontane). The historically incorrect strong forms **schrob, geschroben** should not be used, the only one in common use being **verschroben,** used *lit.* in the sense of 'distorted', but esp. *fig.* with the force of 'crotchety, eccentric': **ein verschrobener Kerl** is 'a crank'.

schrecken: 1. This simple verb is now comparatively little used (the past part. **geschrocken** hardly at all), being usually replaced by a compd., esp. **erschrecken.** *Weak* forms are imperative when the verb has the *trans.* force of 'to frighten, startle', *strong* forms normally when it has the *intrans.* force of 'to get a fright' (but see 2): e.g., on the one hand, **Er erschreckt mich jedesmal, wenn er die Tür heftig zuschlägt—Warum erschrecktest du das Kind?—Erschrecke mich nicht!** and on the other hand, **Sie erschrickt, wenn er die Tür so heftig zuschlägt—Als es laut klopfte, erschrak ich—Erschrick nicht!** So also in the past parts.: **Du hast mich erschreckt** (an action) and **Ich war über sein Betragen erschrocken** (a state). **2.** Despite the grammarians' protests, however (and *Duden* explicitly differentiates between the weak and the strong forms in the way exemplified above), the fact remains that modern authors continually use *weak* forms with *intrans.* force, esp. in the past tense, and notably in the compds. **auf-, zurück-** and **zusammenschrecken** ('to start up, recoil, give a start'): e.g. **Jemand zupfte ihn am Ärmel, er schreckte auf** (Viebig)—**Sie schreckte aus einem Traum auf** (E. Wichert)—**„Line!" rief Fräulein Dewitz, da schreckte sie auf** (G. Engel)—**Er**

wunderte sich, daß Heinz nicht aufschreckte (Federer)—**Unwillkürlich schreckte der Gewarnte auf** (St. Zweig)—**Da er eben im Einschlafen war, schreckte er von einer leichten Berührung auf** (A. Schaeffer)—**Er sank eine Minute lang in Betäubung, schreckte aber sofort wieder auf** (H. Hesse)—**Da klopfte es: ich schreckte auf** (M. Eyth)—**Die Tante schreckte aus dem Schlaf auf** (Keyserling)—**Als er sich in einer häßlichen Phantasie als Mörder sah, schreckte er vor dieser Vorstellung zurück** (id.)—**Da vernahmen sie so namenloses Geheul aus dem Krankenzimmer herabschrillen, daß alle zusammenschreckten** (G. Engel); for the fluctuation cf. **Sie hat ihre Welt in sich, und sie schreckt auf, sobald etwas von außen daran stößt: das drängt sie in sich zurück, daß sie zusammenschreckt . . . sie saß verträumt da und schrak zusammen, wenn man sie anredete** (W. v. Scholz). Used as they are by so many authors of repute, these weak intrans. forms clearly show the present-day tendency; but as they are not yet recognized officially, it might still be advisable—notably for examination purposes!—to observe the rule given under 1 above. For other weak forms used intrans., see esp. **hängen** and **löschen**. **3.** Of **schrecken** and its compds. the only one that is used *reflex.* is **erschrecken**, which then has the same force as the intrans., viz. 'to get a fright'. Here, strangely enough, although *weak* forms are imperative in pres. and past tenses, the past part. rather prefers the *strong* form: cf. **Ich erschreckte** (not **erschrak**) **mich** with **Das Kind muß sich erschrocken haben** (W. Kramp).

Schrei: This noun (*masc.*) suggests a single 'cry, scream, shriek', as in **Sie tat einen Schrei des Entsetzens** or **Sie stieß einen Schrei des Entsetzens hervor** ('She uttered a cry of horror'); cf. **der letzte Schrei** (= **die neuste Mode,** 'the latest fashion, Fr. *le dernier cri*). In the compd. **Geschrei** (*neut.*) the prefix **Ge-** (q.v.) gives the noun *collect.* force, as in **Als er vor die Menschenmenge trat, erhob sich ein wildes Geschrei**; cf. **Viel Geschrei und wenig Wolle** (= **Viel Lärm um nichts,** 'Much ado about nothing'), which seems to be taken from an early mystery-play in which the devil shears the bristles off a sow—cf. 'Humph, quoth the Dee'l when he clip'd the sow, a great cry and little woo' (Kelly: *Sc. Prov.* 1721).

Schritt: For the plur. forms of this noun, see **nouns of measure** 1 (*b*).

schüchtern: see **shy** 2.

Schuh: This noun is sometimes used as a measure of distance (= **Fuß**), in which case—see **nouns of measure** 1 (*a*)—its *sing.* form is used collect. in the plur. after numerals, like our 'two *foot* six': e.g. **Auf Holzböcken, ein bis zwei Schuh über dem Boden, lag eine ausgehakte Tür** (Sudermann)—**Ihr Leben sei zu Ende, schrieb sie: fünf Schuh Erde über sich, anderes sei für sie nichts zu wünschen** (Bruno Frank).

Schuld: This fem. noun means either 'debt, indebtedness' (with plur. **Schulden,** used esp. of money debts) or 'fault, blame, guilt' (no plur.): e.g. in the former sense, **Mein Gut ist mit einer Schuld von tausend Pfund belastet** ('My estate is encumbered with a debt of £1,000')—**Er steckt tief in Schulden** ('He is deep in debt')—**Er ist in Schulden geraten** or (stronger) **hat sich in Schulden gestürzt** ('He has run *or* rushed into debt'); in the latter sense, **Ich trage die Schuld an allem** or **bin an allem schuld** ('It is all my fault, I am to blame for everything')—**Ich habe mir nichts zu Schulden** (or **zuschulden**) **kommen lassen** ('I have incurred no blame, am not guilty of anything'). The noun **Schuldigkeit** may imply financial indebtedness, but more usually means 'obligation, duty': hence distinguish between **Das ist meine Schuld** ('I am to blame for that') and **Das ist meine** (*coll.* **verdammte**) **Pflicht und Schuldigkeit** ('That is my bounden duty').

schuld: see **adjectives (indeclinable)** 5.

Schulter, schultern: see **shoulder.**

schütteln: For propositions like **Er schüttelte mit dem Kopf und zog ein finsteres Gesicht** (Chamisso), see **mit** 2 (*b*).

schwarz: For the subst. use of this adj., see **colour.** Like most other adjs. of colour, it is used coll. in a number of expressions: e.g. **eine Bekanntmachung an das schwarze Brett anschlagen** ('to put up a notice on the notice-board')—**schwarz fahren** ('to use another person's car without his permission')—**schwarz werden** (in card-games, 'not to take a trick'); hence **jemand schwarz machen** ('not to let a player take a trick') and **auf Schwarz reizen** ('to declare one will take all the tricks')—**der Schwarze Peter** (really 'the knave of spades'), hence **Schwarzen Peter spielen** ('to play Old

Maid', the Germans discarding the knave of spades where we discard the queen of hearts).

schweigen: This verb is now always *strong* and has *intrans.* force, meaning 'to be silent' or 'to stop' (e.g. of music, bird-song' etc.). The MHG *swîgen* took a gen. when it meant 'not to speak about *or* mention', and Luther still wrote **Ich schweige der Freuden** (Ps. 39. 3), but this is now almost obs., being replaced by **über**+accus. or esp. **von**; the gen. is still in use, however, with the compd. **geschweigen** (q.v.). Obs. also is the earlier use of the verb as a trans. in the sense of 'to silence a person', now expressed by **jemand zum Schweigen bringen:** where Luther says **Die Gottlosen müssen geschweigt werden** (Ps. 31. 18) one would now say **müssen zum Schweigen gebracht werden**; and the first phrase in **Schweige deine Zunge und bewahre unser Geheimnis!** (Musäus) would be expressed by **Schweig still!** or **Halt den Mund!** or **Halt reinen Mund!**—indeed, this last expression would be esp. appropriate here as it really means **Verrate nichts!** ('Don't divulge anything! Don't give the game away!'). Cf. **sein Gewissen einschläfern** ('to silence one's conscience') and **etwas verschweigen** ('to keep silent about something'), for which see **bergen** 4.

schwellen: 1. *Strong* forms of this verb (**schwoll, geschwollen**) are used to convey the *intrans.* sense of 'to become swollen': e.g. **Meine Backe ist** (or **Meine Füße sind**) **geschwollen**; *fig.* **Sein Herz schwoll vor Begeisterung.** Where the resultant state is added, the compd. **anschwellen** is esp. common: e.g. **Bei heftigem Regen schwillt der Bach zum reißenden Strom an—Das Geräusch schwoll allmählich zum Getöse an**; cf., as examples now regarded as incorrect, **Wenn ich die Wunder betrachte, dann schwellt** (for **schwillt**) **mir die Brust** (Gessner)—**Das Konzert schwellte volltönig an** (G. Keller). **2.** *Weak* forms are imperative when the verb is used with *factitive* force ('to cause to swell'): e.g. **Die Segel wurden vom Winde geschwellt**; fig. **Freude schwellte seine Brust—Jene stolzen Gestalten der Vergangenheit** (referring to old portraits on the wall) **schienen mit verächtlichem Lächeln um die geschwellten Lippen auf ihn zu schauen** (F. Huch: i.e. 'full *or* rounded lips', as distinct from **die geschwollenen Lippen**, 'swollen lips'). An occasional example like **Tränen schwollen ihre Augen** (Heine) should not be imitated; cf. **Ihre Augen schwollen von Tränen.**

schwerlich: see **hardly** 2.

schwindeln: 1. With the force of 'to be *or* feel giddy', this verb is now almost always used *impers.* + *dat.*: e.g. **Es schwindelt mir** (G.) or **Der Kopf schwindelt mir** ('My head reels')—**Mir schwindelt vor der grenzenlosen Stille** (Hölderlin)—**Sie wagte nicht, seinen Arm zu verlangen, obwohl ihr im plötzlichen Licht schwindelte** (A. Reiner)—**Sie küßte ihn auf den Mund; es war so unerwartet, daß ihm schwindelte** (H. Leip). The pers. use, as in **Das sterbliche Geschlecht ist zu schwach, in ungewohnter Höhe nicht zu schwindeln** (G.), is now generally avoided, as is also an accus. instead of the normal dat., as in **Mich schwindelt** (Gutzkow). With factitive force ('to cause to feel giddy') it is only used in the pres. part. in the attrib. relation: e.g. **eine schwindelnde Höhe** ('a dizzy height'); cf. **Es machte mich schwindelig** or **Ein Schwindel überkam mich** or **wandelte mich an.** **2.** In the sense of 'to swindle', **schwindeln** is only *intrans.*, the trans. being expressed by **jemanden beschwindeln** (= **jemanden um etwas betrügen**); cf. **jemandem etwas ab-** and **anschwindeln,** the former meaning 'to swindle a person out of something', the latter 'to palm something off on a person'.

schwören: 1. In early NHG this verb was sometimes used with the force of 'to curse, blaspheme (= **fluchen**), as in **Da fing ein Teil aus uns** (= **Da fingen einige von uns**) **an zu beten, das andere** (*scil.* **Teil**, i.e. 'the others') **zu schwören** (Grimmelshausen), but this use is now almost confined to the coll. combination **fluchen und schwören.** According to modern usage, **schwören** means 'to swear, take one's oath', as already in Luther's time: cf. **Da hub er an zu schwören: Ich kenne des Menschen nicht** (Matt. 26. 74—for the gen. here, see **nichts**); so one now says **Er erklärte sich bereit, einen heiligen Eid zu schwören—Willst du mir Treue schwören?—Ich will darauf** (or **auf die Bibel**) **schwören, ihn gesehen zu haben, wie er bei der Leiche stand—Er betrachtete einen Neffen als seinen geschworenen Feind** (Treitschke); cf. **die Geschworenen** ('the jury'). **2.** In spite of occasional instances of weak forms (even Sch. uses

schwörte), the historically correct *strong* forms are still firmly established. The past indic. should really be **schwur** (< MHG *swuor*), and this is still quite common, as in **Er schwur, daß er von dem Inhalt des Briefes nichts wisse** (Fr. Griese), but the form **schwor** developed in the 18th century under the influence of the part. **geschworen**, and is now in common use: cf. **Alle Bürger schworen einen Eid** (id.); in the past subj., **schwüre** is quite fixed, in order to obviate confusion with the pres. indic. and subj. **schwöre.** Both forms are also used, but with a preference for that with **o**, in the compds., esp. in **beschwören** (either 'to adjure, implore' or 'to exorcize, conjure up'): e.g. **Ich beschwur meinen Freund, er solle mir das Leben retten** (G.)—**Ich beschwor die Wache, sie sollte schweigen** (G.)—**Michael beschwor sie, nicht Unfrieden zu stiften** (Zifferer)—**Dann schlief er ein, und ein Traum beschwor ihm das Bild jener versunkenen Glanzzeit in aller Glorie zurück** (H. Hesse).

See: Distinguish between **die See** ('sea') and **der See** ('lake'), both with plur. **Seen** (disyllabic).

sehen: see **accusative and infinitive** 1, 4, and 5 (*a*); **passive voice** 3 (*a*); **look** 1. For **sehen lassen,** see **lassen** 4.

sehnen: This simple verb is now only used *reflex.* in the sense of 'to long' (for, **nach**: cf. **verlangen**): e.g. **Die Kinder sehnen sich nach den Ferien**; but two compds. are used as *trans.* verbs, viz. **ersehnen,** used esp. in the past part. ('longed-for'), as in **Der Gefangene sah seiner ersehnten Befreiung entgegen**— —and **herbeisehnen**; e.g. **Er sehnte den Augenblick herbei, wo das Gespräch ein Ende nehmen würde** (Ompteda). The infin. of the simple verb is used abs. as a verbal noun, as in **Ein unnennbares Sehnen ergriff ihn** (Tieck), but the real subst. is **die Sehnsucht** (see **Sucht** 2).

sein (verb): see **verbs (auxiliary)**; **passive voice**; **dies** 1.

seinesgleichen: see **gleich** 2.

seit: 1. This is used both as a prep. and as a conj. As a prep., it now always takes a *dat.*, a phrase like **seit des Ungewitters** (Opitz) being quite obs. But it can modify advs., so that one says not only **Ich bin erst seit gestern hier** or **Seit wann wohnen Sie hier?** but also **Ich warte schon seit morgens auf dich.** As a conj., it often takes the form **seitdem,** which can also be used, like **seither,** as an adv.: e.g. **Seit(dem) ich zuletzt hier war, hat sich alles verändert**—**Ich kam vorgestern hier an, und seitdem** ('since then') **hat es viel geregnet**; cf. 'I come to tell you things *sith then* befallen' (Shakespeare). **2.** In MHG, **seit** was *sît* or *sint,* used exactly like **seit,** but rather more common in the conj. use was *sît daz,* a combination now hardly used. Obs. now is the *causal* use of *sît* (cf. **weil** 2 (*a*)), the only survival of which is **sintemal** ('because, seeing that'), which developed out of *sint dem mâle* ('since that time') and was common in early NHG, but is now confined to poetry and archaic prose: cf. **Siehe, du wirst einen Sohn gebären . . . Da sprach Maria zu dem Engel: Wie soll das geschehen, sintemal** ('seeing') **ich von keinem Manne weiß?** (Luke 1. 31–34)—**Sintemal** (= **Da**) **uns die Adresse unsres Eidams unbekannt, soll dies Reskript ihm Kunde bringen** (Heine). For a proposition like **Vier Jahre waren vergangen, seit er nicht mehr in diese Gegend gekommen war** (Hackländer), which shows confusion between two different constructions, see **negative (pleonastic)** 2 (*b*).

seitlich: see **abseits** 3.

-sel: see **-sal** and **-selig** 2.

-selig: There are two distinct groups of words with this adj. suffix. **1.** The first group embraces those words in which the adj. **selig** is attached to nouns: e.g. **glückselig** ('blissful'), **gottselig** ('pious'), **leutselig** ('affable'), **redselig** ('talkative'). **2.** Those in the second group are the result of adding the MHG adj. ending *-ic* (> **-ig**) to nouns with the suffix *-sal* (see **-sal**), the vowel in which was then mutated to *æ* through the influence of the following *i*, so that the adj. ended in *-sælic.* Thus, **armselig** is derived from *armesal* ('poverty'), **saumselig** from *sûmesal* ('dilatoriness'), etc. In a number of such nouns the suffix *-sal* lost its vocalic force and was weakened to **-sel,** as in **Rätsel** (from *râtesal*), **Wechsel** (< *wehsal*), etc., and it may well be that the long **e** in adjs. like **mühselig** (from *müejesal*) and **trübselig** (from *trüebesal*) is historically incorrect, having crept in under the influence of the adj. **selig,** i.e. that the **e** should be short and these adjs. pronounced as dactyls (–◡◡) in the same way as **gruselig** (q.v.). To which of the two groups **feindselig** belongs seems doubtful: there is no MHG noun *vîant-* or *vîentsal* known.

September: see **Monatsnamen.**

setzen: 1. Just as **legen** is the causative of **liegen,** and **stellen** that of **stehen,** so **setzen** is the causative of **sitzen,** these last two verbs standing in the same relation to each other as do our 'set' and 'sit'; and hence **sich setzen** is 'to place oneself in a sitting position', i.e. 'to sit down' (see **put** 1 and **sitzen** 2). As explained under **accusative or dative . . .** (q.v. 1), when the simple verb **setzen** is associated with a prep. like **an, auf, in,** etc., the case after the prep. must be an *accus.*, whereas a *dat.* is really more correct when the verb is compounded with **hin-** or **nieder-**, the simple verb implying motion, the compd. rest; cf. **Setzen Sie sich hierher!** and **Setzen Sie sich hier hin!** If Tell's words **Auf dieser Bank von Stein will ich mich setzen** were not so familiar, the dat. in the prep. phrase would jar more on a sensitive ear; certainly, an examiner here would mark as wrong a proposition like **Der Apotheker ging in dem kleinen Raum hin und her, dann setzte er sich am Tischende** (A. Schaeffer: for **am Tischende hin** or **an das Tischende**). Of course, the dat. is correct in **Er setzte sich mir gegenüber. 2.** So **setzen** corresponds to our 'set' in propositions like **Man setzte ihn auf den Thron—Setze das Haus nicht in Brand** or **Flammen!—Ich werde keinen Fuß mehr in sein Haus setzen—Mehrere Liederkomponisten haben Goethes „Erlkönig" in Töne gesetzt.** But there are numerous idioms in which **setzen** has lost its orig. connexion with the idea of sitting, and here we mostly use other expressions: e.g. **Sein Betragen setzte mich in Verwunderung** ('filled me with astonishment')—**Setzen Sie** ('Put *or* Write') **Ihren Namen unter dieses Schriftstück!—Dadurch haben Sie mich in eine unangenehme Lage gesetzt** ('placed')—**Warum setzen Sie den Kerl nicht an die Luft?** (coll. 'Why don't you put *or* kick the fellow out?'); see also **außer** 3. Esp. noteworthy is the coll. impers. use in **Wenn du dich nicht benimmst, wird es Prügel setzen** (i.e. 'you'll be thrashed')—**Hat es etwas gesetzt?** ('Did you get a thrashing?' or 'Were you punished?'). For **gesetzt** used with the force of 'let us assume *or* suppose', see **accusative absolute** 2. **3.** As an *intrans.* verb, **setzen** is used with **über** + accus. (aux. **haben**) in the sense of 'to jump *or* leap over' a wall or a ditch (cf. **einen Satz tun,** 'to take a flying leap') or 'to cross' a river or lake: see **übersetzen** 1.

shoulder: German anatomists distinguish between **die Schulter,** the *upper* part of the body where the arm joins the trunk, including the top of the back, and **die Achsel,** the *lower* part: cf. **das Schulterblatt** ('shoulderblade') and **die Achselhöhle** ('armpit'). Hence one speaks esp. of **breite Schultern,** of patting a person **auf die Schulter,** of people standing **Schulter an Schulter,** etc. It is significant that the verb **achseln** ('to shoulder'), as in **Er achselte sein Bündel und machte sich auf** (Rückert), is now hardly ever used—*Duden* does not give it at all—whereas **schultern** is quite common in the *lit.* sense ('to shoulder', used fig. with objects like **Kosten, Verantwortung, Verpflichtungen,** etc., is **überne'hmen** or **auf sich nehmen**): e.g. **Die Passagiere stiegen aus, schulterten die Schneeschuhe und kletterten zum Hotel hinauf** (Kästner)—**Wir hängten den Kranz über einen Ast, den die beiden größten Mädchen schulterten** (G. Britting)—**Der Vikar wagte es nicht, den Rock auszuziehen und über den geschulterten Wanderstab zu hängen** (H. Franck). It follows that one should properly say **Ich setzte das Kind auf meine Schultern**; but an example like **Das Kind hatte auf jeder Achsel einen Vogel sitzen** (Sudermann) shows that in ordinary language the scientific distinction is not strictly observed, and indeed, in some cases either expression may be used: e.g. **Er zuckte die** (or **mit den**) **Achseln** or **Schultern** ('He shrugged his shoulders': see **zucken,** and **mit** 2); cf. **achselzuckend** ('with a shrug') and **Diesen Einfall soll mir keiner beachselzucken** (Mörike: 'Let no one shrug his shoulders at this conceit of mine'). On the whole, **Achsel** is a rather more select word, which has more or less established itself esp. in some fig. expressions: thus, **jemand über die Schulter ansehen** need not suggest more than 'to look over one's shoulder at a person', while the substitution of **Achsel** for **Schulter** here would more naturally imply 'to look down upon, *or* contemptuously at, a person'; so also one says **etwas auf die leichte Achsel** or (less commonly) **Schulter nehmen** ('to make light of something').

shy: 1. The adj. **scheu** implies a lack of boldness, a timorous nature which readily takes fright. It is particularly applicable to, and used of, animals: a high-mettled horse is **scheu**—it is apt to *shy* at what it is not familiar with (**vor dem Unbekannten scheuen**); wild creatures like deer are **menschenscheu,** owls are **lichtscheu**; cf. **Über den Schnee strich ein Wolf, scheu wie ein Gespenst** (H. Hesse). The simple word is not much used of human beings, unless the person is compared with an animal, as in **Sie ist scheu wie ein Eichhorn** (G.); but compounds like **arbeits-** and **wasserscheu** are quite common, implying that the person 'fights shy of' working or sea-bathing (**vor der Arbeit, dem Seebaden zurückscheuen**). **2.** On the other hand, **schüchtern** is more esp. used of human beings, of people who are *shy,* i.e. bashful, easily overawed: a sensitive young girl is **schüchtern** in the presence of company—**die Gesellschaft schüchtert sie ein**; when Hölderlin speaks of **der schüchterne Mond,** he is really personifying the moon, representing her as being too shy to appear from behind the clouds.

sicher: see **gewiß.**

sicherlich: see **adverbs formed from adjectives** 3.

Sicht: 1. Unlike many of its compds., most of which are in common everyday use, **Sicht** is now mainly confined to nautical and commercial lang.: e.g. **Land in Sicht!—Als wir in Sicht der Insel waren, nahm sie meinem Sohne das Steuer aus der Hand** (Ponten)—**Andern Morgens war die Küste außer Sicht—Nun war er den Frauen außer Sicht** (Frenssen)—**Wir haben eine Tratte auf lange Sicht auf Sie gezogen** ('We have drawn a bill of exchange at long date on you')—**Entnehmen Sie gefälligst auf uns durch einen Wechsel auf Sicht!** ('Please draw on us by a draft at sight!'); *fig.* **Die Italiener leben nicht auf lange Sicht, sondern für den Augenblick** (K. Edschmid: 'The Italians are not far-sighted, they live for the moment'). In ordinary lang. other expressions are much more usual: e.g. **Aus den Augen, aus dem Sinn** ('Out of sight, out of mind')—**Sie bogen um die Ecke und entschwanden unseren Blicken —In dem Gedränge verloren wir ihn aus dem Gesicht** ('In the crush we lost sight of him': see 2 (*b*)). **2.** The following neat lines bring the chief compds. together: **Wer aufwärts will, muß Einsicht haben, / Mit Umsicht brauchen seine Gaben, / Sich keiner Ansicht widersetzen, / Die Tat nach ihrer Aussicht schätzen, / Zu steter Nachsicht sich bequemen / Und täglich soviel Rücksicht nehmen, / Daß er aus Vorsicht ganz und gar / Vergißt, was seine Absicht war** (L. Fulda: 'Whoever would rise in the world must have *discernment,* must use his gifts with *discretion,* must not disagree with another's *opinion,* must estimate an action according to the *prospect* it offers, must resign himself to practise *forbearance* to others at all times, and must every day act with such *consideration* that from very *caution* he completely loses sight of his original *intention*'). (**a**) The two compds. which present some difficulty are **Ansicht** and **Aussicht.** In the rhymes just quoted both expressions are used with *fig.* force, the former in the sense of 'view, opinion', the latter in that of 'prospect, what it will lead to', but in the *lit.* sense they approach each other, differing merely in the standpoint from which a thing is regarded. While **Aussicht** (which takes a prep. phrase, not a gen.) suggests that the eye, as it were, travels *out* into the distance, **Ansicht** (which takes a gen.) indicates the aspect which the object looked at presents *to* the eye: e.g., on the one hand, **Von dieser Anhöhe aus hat man eine herrliche Aussicht auf die Stadt, in das Tal, über das Meer, nach den Bergen** (in a fig. sense always with **auf** + accus., as in **Er hat Aussicht auf baldige Beförderung,** 'He has a prospect of speedy promotion'), and on the other hand, **Hier bietet sich dem Auge eine schöne Ansicht der Stadt** ('Here a fine view *or* picture of the town presents itself to the eye'); hence always **eine Ansichtskarte,** which shows a scene viewed from a particular spot; and sim. **Die vordere Ansicht des Schlosses ist die schönste** ('The front view of the castle is the finest'). (**b**) **Gesicht** (q.v.): At one time this compd., the only *neut.* one, was commonly used with the force of the 'sense of sight', as in **Vielen Blinden schenkte er das Gesicht** (Luke 7. 21), but this use is now almost confined to a few expressions where confusion with its commonest sense of 'face' can hardly arise: e.g. **Sie hat das zweite Gesicht** ('second sight')—**Der Arme hat das Gesicht** or **das Augenlicht verloren** (= **Der Arme ist erblindet**)—**Erst als ich den schrecklichen Ort aus dem Gesicht** or **aus den Augen verlor, atmete ich wieder auf**; and esp. the phrases **zu Gesicht bekommen** ('to set eyes on') and **zu Gesicht kommen** ('to come *or* heave in sight'): cf. **Am nächsten Tage nahm er Abschied, ohne daß sie ihn noch einmal zu Gesicht bekommen hätte** (Bergengruen: cf. **ansichtig**)—**Mir ist seine Arbeit nicht zu Gesicht gekommen** (G.: 'His work has not come my way'); cf. **Gesichtskreis** ('range of vision'). Now the sense of sight is generally expressed by **der Gesichtssinn,** like **Gehör-, Geschmack(s)-, Geruchs-, Tastsinn**; cf. **Seine Sehkraft nimmt ab** ('His eyesight is failing')—**Mit der zur Hellsicht gesteigerten Sehkraft ihres Herzens erkannte sie die Eigensucht ihrer Liebe** (Bergengruen). The double compd. **Angesicht** is mainly biblical, as in **Wo soll ich hinfliehen vor deinem Angesicht?** (Ps. 139. 7); but it is still common in the phrase **von Angesicht zu Angesicht** ('face to face'), and esp. in the adv. gen. **angesichts,** used as a prep. (+*gen.*) in the sense of 'in view of': **Die Bauern flüchteten sich angesichts der drohenden Gefahr in die Stadt** (see **Tracht** 2). (**c**) The relation between **Sicht, An-** and **Aussicht** suggests that between **Blick, An-** and **Ausblick.** The fundamental sense of **Blick** is a 'look, glance': e.g. **Er warf ihr einen verliebten Blick zu**—**Ich erkannte ihn auf den ersten Blick wieder**; but it is also used like **Aussicht,** only that the 'view' is more restricted: **Von diesem Fenster hat man einen hübschen Blick auf den Garten** or **ins Gebirge. Anblick** may have verbal force, as in **Beim Anblick dieser Landschaft** (= **Als ich diese Landschaft anblickte**), **überkam mich ein Gefühl des Heimwehs**; but more commonly it expresses our 'sight, spectacle': e.g. **Ein reizender Anblick begegnete meinen Augen** ('A charming spectacle met my eyes')—**Welch ein entsetzlicher Anblick!**—cf. **Er war bestrebt, dem Blick, ja dem Anblick Schielers auszuweichen** (Bergengruen: 'He endeavoured to avoid Schieler's eye, indeed the very sight of the man'). Lastly, **Ausblick,** again more restricted than a 'prospect', and this is emphasized in **Durchblick** ('vista'): e.g. **Ich habe hier in Tübingen ein heiteres Zimmer, und zwischen der Kirche und dem akademischen Gebäude einen freundlichen, obgleich schmalen Ausblick ins Neckartal** (G.); its *fig.* force is seen in a proposition like **Der Ausblick in die Zukunft ist wenig erfreulich** ('The future *outlook* is not bright'). On the other hand, **Durchsicht** is now generally used with verbal force: **Man hat mir das Manuskript zur Durchsicht übersandt** ('They have sent me the manuscript to look through').

sichtlich: see **obvious(ly).**

siech: see **krank** 1.

sight: see **Sicht** 1, 2 (*a*), (*b*), and (*c*).

silence (verb): see **schweigen.**

single: Distinguish clearly between **einzig** and **einzeln.** Whereas **ein einziger Baum** suggests that there is one tree, and only one, **ein einzelner Baum** implies that there are a number of trees, but that the one in question stands alone, apart from the others; cf. the following pairs of examples: **Storms Gedichte sind in einem einzigen Band** ('in a single volume') **zu haben** and **Storms Werke sind in acht Bänden erschienen, die einzeln** ('separately') **käuflich sind**—**Er war unser einziger** ('only') **Gast** and **Unsere Gäste kamen einzeln** ('one by one') **an**—**Von dem, was ich sagte, verstand er nur ein einziges** ('only one') **Wort** and **Von dem, was ich sagte, verstand er nur einzelne Wörter** ('a word here and there'). Cf. also: **Du bist einzig und allein daran schuld** ('It is your blame, and yours alone')—**Dies ist einzig in seiner Art** or **einzigartig** ('unique')—**Das ist das einzig Wahre an der Geschichte** ('the only true thing in the story'); and **Die Zeugen wurden einzeln** ('individually') **verhört**—**Er prüfte die einzelnen Posten der Rechnung** ('He scrutinized each separate item in the account')—**Jeder Einzelne mußte vortreten**—**In dieser Straße ist nur ein einziges einzelnstehendes Gebäude** ('only one detached building')—**Er wurde zu zwei Tagen Einzelhaft** ('solitary confinement') **verurteilt**—**Seine Nachforschung ging ins Einzelne** or **in Einzelheiten** ('into details'). Hence, just as **ein einzelner Handschuh** is 'an odd glove', whose 'neighbour' is lost, so **ein einzelner Herr** may refer not only to a gentleman standing by himself, but also to a 'single', i.e. unmarried man; so that, in a reference to a company in which there is 'only one bachelor', it is possible, though unusual, to say **Unter den Gästen war nur ein einziger Einzelner** (for the more usual **ein einziger Unverheirateter** or **Junggeselle** or, in more archaic language, **Hagestolz**).

singular: 1. For the use of a sing. verb referring to a subj. consisting of two sing. nouns which convey a collective idea (e.g. 'life and death'), see **congruence** 1 (*c*); for a sing. verb referring to two sing. nouns connected by **(entweder) . . . oder,** see **congruence** 1 (*d*), by **weder . . . noch,** see **weder** 1. **2.** As pointed out under **congruence** 1 (*e*), **sowohl . . . als** connecting two sing. nouns standing as the subj. of a sentence properly requires the verb to be sing. The same applies to analogous expressions conveying the same idea, as in 'Charles with his brother came to see us yesterday', and in a reference to the pillars of a bridge collapsing in a flood Bürger correctly uses a sing. verb when he says **Pfeiler auf Pfeiler** (= **Ein Pfeiler nach dem anderen) zerbrach und borst.** A sing. verb would therefore be more correct in **Ein Bedienter nebst** ('along with, besides') **einem Postillion folgten mir** (G.: cf. **Nebst einem Postillion folgte mir ein Bedienter**); and sim. **Ein Harfner mit seiner Tochter gingen vor mir her** (G.)—**Der Probst mit dem Pfarrer saßen an der anderen Seite des Tisches** (Th. Mügge), where the idea that *two* people are concerned is at the back of the authors' minds. **3.** The last words just used ('the authors' minds') illustrate an English idiom which differs from that normally used in German. To express a proposition like 'They all shook their heads', a German says **Sie schüttelten alle den Kopf,** because each individual has only *one* head; and sim. **Sie standen mit offenem Munde da—Alle Anwesenden hielten die rechte Hand auf—Sie sahen mich mit blassem Gesicht an** (Frenssen)—**Wenn sie einige Bissen genommen hatten, griffen sie nach dem Bierglas** (id.)—**Die Prozession beginnt, voraus** ('at its head') **die Kardinäle im langen Gewand** (Waiblinger). *Sanders* characterizes the use of the plur. in such propositions as **„falsch“,** and it is undeniable that the distrib. sing. is more idiomatic and indeed in the very spirit of the German lang. The plur. is, in fact, a Gallicism, and to say that it is 'wrong' is to condemn the use of a foreign idiom which has gained much ground among standard German authors. Nevertheless, it would unquestionably be better German to use the sing. in the following examples: **Sie drehten die Köpfe herum** (G.)—**Alle nehmen die Hüte ab** (Sch.)—**„Sie kommen!“ flüsterten die Dirnen und drehten ihre Hälse** (usually **den Hals**) **nach dem Steige** (Storm)—**Die Kinder recken die Hälse** (Waggerl)—**Die zwei Männer sahen sich in die Gesichter** (Raabe)—**Sie standen alle mit offenen Mäulern da** (id.)—**Die Mädchen kamen mit hochroten Gesichtern vom Ballspiel hereingestürzt** (Jul. Wolff)—**Sie versteht sich darauf, den Leuten ihre Heimlichkeiten von den Gesichtern zu lesen** (Waggerl: usually **am Gesicht abzulesen**)—**Die Männer strichen sich durch die Bärte** (Blunck)—**Das Lied wird man noch singen, wenn all die jungen Leute, die heute hier tanzen, ihre silbernen Hochzeiten feiern** (Bergengruen). These examples might be multiplied almost indefinitely, so it is obviously going too far to say that all these authors are guilty of writing 'incorrect' German. All the same, students of the lang. would be well advised to use the sing. in such propositions.

sinnen: 1. Distinguish between **über etwas** (accus., less commonly dat.) **sinnen** (= **nachdenken,** 'to reflect upon something') and **auf etwas** (accus.) **sinnen** ('to meditate, plan, plot something'): cf. **Er dachte an die Säcke mit Weizen und sann über dem Preise** (usually **den Preis**), **den er zu bieten beabsichtigte** (Th. Mann)—**Er sinnt auf Flucht, auf Rache, auf mein Verderben.** Here the prep. **auf** is sometimes omitted, but this applies mainly to indef. neut. objs., as in **Was sinnst du?**—**Ich fürchte, er sinnt nichts Gutes** ('I fear he is meditating mischief')—**Sinnst du auch nichts Gefährliches?** (Sch.). **2.** With regard to the conjugation, **strong** forms (**sann, gesonnen**) are now the rule, and the past subj. is **sänne** or **sönne,** the latter being the only form given by *Sanders* (see **Ablaut** 2 (*c*)). At an earlier period *weak* forms were sometimes used, but apart from the past part. (see 3) these are now confined to southern, esp. Swiss dialects. **3.** The only weak form still in reg. use is the past part. **gesinnt,** which exists side by side with **gesonnen.** Both are used pred. with the force of 'minded, disposed' (cf. **Gesinnung,** 'disposition'), the difference being that **gesonnen** requires a following infin. with **zu,** indicating what the person is 'disposed' to do, whereas **gesinnt** is usually modified by an adj. or adv. suggesting how the person is 'minded', the two generally combining to form a compd., as in our 'noble-minded'. Thus, on the one hand, **Wie ist er gegen dich gesinnt?**—**Wir sind gleichgesinnt** ('of one mind')—**Ich bin jetzt andersgesinnt** ('of a different opinion'), and sim. **gut-, schlecht-, froh-, feindlich-, konservativ-, deutschgesinnt**; and, on the other hand,

Ich bin nicht gesonnen, in meiner Diener Schuld zu stehn (Sch.)—**Sie erklärte, sie sei nicht gesonnen, die Kinder als Verwandte anzuerkennen** (Th. Mann)—**Sie sah mich an, als fürchte sie eine Frage, die zu beantworten sie nicht gesonnen war** (Werfel)—**Der kleine Reinhold war nicht gesonnen, sich das bieten zu lassen** ('was not disposed to put up with that'): **er schrie wie ein gereizter Elefant** (O. Ernst)—**Der Lehrer war nicht gesonnen, in einen Rechtskampf einzutreten** (Zuckmayer); cf. **Serlo eröffnete ihm seine Lage: wie er nicht gesinnt** (now usually **gesonnen**) **sei, ihm nachzugeben** (G.).

sintemal: see **seit** 2.

Sitte: see **custom(ary)** 2.

sitzen: **1.** As this verb implies **rest** ('to be seated'), accompanying preps. like **an, auf, in**, etc., take a *dat.* case: hence **um den Tisch**, but **am Tisch, im Garten, über den Büchern, vor der Tür, zwischen Freunden sitzen** **2.** In southern, esp. Swiss dialects, **sitzen** is used in the sense of 'to seat oneself, sit down', in which case the *accus* is, of course, correct in such prep. phrases: e.g. **Er befahl uns, in die Wagen zu sitzen** (G.)—**Sie bat ihn, an den Ofen zu sitzen** (Federer)—**Er saß in den Wagen** (Stifter)—**Sie saßen ins grüne Gras** (Schwab). In such propositions **sich setzen** is almost invariably used in the north; but there an example like **Er hieß mich neben ihn sitzen** (G. Keller) would rather take the form **Er hieß mich neben ihm Platz nehmen**, to avoid the awkwardness of **Er hieß mich mich neben ihn setzen.** Here the second **mich** is sometimes dropped, the result being neither one thing nor another; and examples even occur in which the omission of the reflex. is quite unnecessary, as in **Dort zog sie ihn hin und hieß ihn** (insert **sich**) **neben sie setzen** (Hofmannsthal). But while **sitzen** does not ordinarily imply motion in the north, it should be noted that some of its compds. are reg. so used there: see **ab-, auf-, ein-**, and **niedersitzen.** **3.** Like other verbs suggesting a posture or attitude (**stehen, liegen**, etc.), **sitzen** takes the aux. **haben** in the north, where one says **Ich habe oft hier gesessen**—**Als ich lange allein gesessen hatte, gesellte sich ein Fremder zu mir.** It is again mainly in the south that **sein** is used in such propositions, and on the whole this should be avoided: cf. **Ich bin letzte Woche acht Stunden im Karzer gesessen** (spoken by Mörike in a story of H. Hesse's)—**O wie gern wäre er jetzt zu Hause gesessen!** (Federer: in the north, **O wie gern säße er jetzt zu Hause!**); it may have been as a result of his correspondence with Mörike that Storm sometimes used **sein**, as in **Er ist in ihrer Kammer gesessen.** **4.** As a *trans.* verb, **sitzen** is only used (**a**) with a pers. subj. in expressions like **Ich habe mich krumm und lahm gesessen** ('From sitting so long I am stiff all over') or **Ich habe mir die Beine steif gesessen** ('I have sat so long in one position that my legs are stiff')—cf. **Er streckte die steifgesessenen Beine und dehnte die Schultern** (Kolbenheyer); and (**b**) reflex., with **es** as subj., as in **Es saß sich so gemütlich in der Küche** (L. Winder: 'It was so cosy sitting in the kitchen'); otherwise, the trans. use is confined to a few compd. verbs: e.g. **Als Volontär saß er seine Pflichtstunden ab** (A. Eloesser: 'In his apprenticeship he sat through the prescribed office-hours')—**Thomas Mann folgte der Mutter nach München, nachdem er sich** (*dat.*) **das Einjährigenzeugnis ersessen hatte** (id.: '. . . after he had sat the examination and obtained the certificate exempting him from more than one year's service with the forces')—**In einem der Zimmer standen drei Stühle, die durchgesessen waren** (Fontane: '. . . the seats of which were worn through').

sitzenbleiben: see **bleiben** 2 (*b*).

slip: **1.** With the *intrans.* force of 'to lose one's footing', this verb should be rendered by **ausgleiten** (see **gleiten**), but where it means 'to glide *or* steal' (e.g. into a room, out of the house, etc.), the correct expression is **schlüpfen**: hence, on the one hand, **Sie glitt (mit dem Fuß) auf dem Eise aus**, and on the other hand, **Die Maus schlüpfte in ihr Loch**—**Das erste Küchlein** (in the north usually **Küken**) **ist eben aus dem Ei geschlüpft**—*fig.* **Er schlüpfte mir durch die Finger**; so also the common compound **entschlüpfen** + dat. ('to slip out of a person's clutches'), as in **Der Dieb wurde verhaftet, entschlüpfte aber dem Schutzmann**, or *fig.* **Verzeihen Sie, das Wort entschlüpfte** (or **entfuhr**) **mir** ('. . . slipped out'). **2.** Where 'to slip' has *trans.* force, it must be rendered in other ways: e.g. **Ich drückte ihm eine Mark in die Hand** ('I slipped a shilling into his hand')—**Da niemand öffnete, schob ich den Brief unter die Tür**

('. . . I slipped the letter under the door') —**Der Name ist mir im Augenblick entfallen** ('The name has slipped my memory for the moment').

so: 1. (**a**) The commonest uses of **so** are as an independent adv. of manner or degree, and as a modifier of adjs. and advs.: e.g. **So' war es nicht gemeint** ('It was not meant that way')—**Sie tut nur so** ('She is only pretending')—**Wie du mir, so ich dir** (prov.: 'Tit for tat')—**Es geht ihr bald so, bald so** ('She is fairly well one day, not so well the next')—**Komm so schnell wie möglich!**—**Ein so** (or **So ein**) **unartiges Kind sollte gezüchtigt werden.** (**b**) As a modifier of advs. like **bald, lange,** etc., **so** has become an unaccented prefix, the two words being written as one when the combination is used as a subord. conj. (cf. **as . . . as** 1): e.g. **Lachen Sie nur, sovie'l und sola'nge Sie mögen!** (J. Grosse: 'Laugh away, as much and as long as you like!'): see **als = 'as'** 2 (*b*) and **wie** 2 (*b*). Hence distinguish between the following pairs of examples: **Soba'ld ich ihn sah, lief ich auf ihn zu** and **Um drei Uhr? Nein, so' bald** ('as early as that') **kann ich nicht kommen**—**Sola'nge ich im Ausland war, erhielt ich keine Nachricht von zu Hause** and **Ich blieb so' lange, daß ich den Zug verpaßte**—**Soo'ft ich ihn auch besuche, er ist selten zu Hause** and **Einmal die Woche? Nein, so' oft besuche ich ihn nicht**—**Sovie'l ich weiß** ('As far as I know') **ist er gesund** and **Nein, so' viel Geld** ('as much money as that') **habe ich nicht**—**Ich gehe oft ins Theater, das heißt, sowei't es mir meine Mittel erlauben** (see **soviel**) and **Geh nur allein: so' weit** ('as far as that') **kann ich nicht gehen**; elsewhere the two words remain separate, as in **Ich hob mein Licht so ho'ch ich konnte** (Rilke). **2.** In a proposition like **Ist dein Freund treu, wird er dir beistehen,** in which both clauses have the same word-order, it is not immediately clear that the first is a *cond.*, the second a *princ.* clause ('If your friend is faithful, he will stand by you'). In such a context the princ. clause is usually introduced by **so**: e.g. **Forsche ich nach weiteren Jugendeindrücken, so gedenke ich des Tages, da ich zum erstenmal meine Eltern ins Theater begleiten durfte** (Th. Mann); cf., with a vivid indic. in the princ. clause, **Hätte sie durch Mauern sehen können, so sah sie ihn an der Gruft des Vaters knien** (C. F. Meyer). This applies particularly to contexts in which the subord. clause is a *cond.* one; but **so** is also often inserted after a *causal* or a *concess.* clause: e.g. **Da er nicht kam, so ließ ich ihn rufen** (Storm)—**Ob man gleich** (= **Obgleich man**) **über den erfochtenen Sieg das Tedeum anstimmte, so gestand doch Wallenstein selbst seine Niederlage** (Sch.). On the other hand, **so** is now rarely inserted, as it once commonly was, after *temp.* clauses (cf. **da** 1 (*b*)): one no longer says **Als ich hinausging, so wollte ich bei einem Nachbar vorsprechen** (Immermann) or **Nachdem die Prinzessin ihre Frauen hatte abtreten lassen, so begann sie folgendermaßen zu sprechen** (Platen); cf., as an unusual modern example, **Als ich ihr erzählte, daß ich in Ravenna gewesen sei, so fragte sie, ob ich im Museum den Platz gesehen hätte, wo die Andenken berühmter Männer lagen** (A. Schaeffer). The reason why this use of **so** is esp. common after cond. clauses, and really out of place after temp. ones, is evident if one realizes how this use orig. arose. In a proposition like **Ist dein Freund treu, so wird er dir beistehen,** the first clause was orig. a *question*, so that the proposition might take the form **Ist dein Freund treu? Wenn dem so ist** ('If that is so'), **wird er dir beistehen.** In such propositions **so** is often replaced by **dann,** just as we often insert 'then', and this can be explained thus: **Ist dein Freund treu? So?** ('Is that so?'). **Dann** ('In that case') **wird er dir beistehen.** For **so doch** after a neg. cond. clause, see **doch** 2 (*d*). **3.** Another common use of **so** is to introduce a *concess.* clause, and here an unaccented **auch** is generally inserted: e.g. **Sie wollte ihre eigene Herrin bleiben, so knapp es auch im Hause hergehen mochte** (R. v. Gottschall: '. . . however straitened the circumstances in the house might be') —**So stark ich auch ritt, überfiel mich doch die Nacht** (G.). Where the concess. clause stands first, as in this last example, the following princ. clause may idiomatically have *normal* word-order (see **word-order** 1 (*d*)), so that, in the example from R. v. Gottschall, the two clauses might be transposed without any other change; sim. **So wichtige Gründe der Minister auch vorbringen mochte, der König achtete nicht auf seine Worte** (Sch.)—**So unlieb es meinem Vater war, er mußte die Nacht dableiben** (Immermann). **4.** (**a**) Almost obs. now, esp. in the north, is the use of **so** to replace a *rel. pron.*, which was common in early NHG and even later, esp. in poetry: e.g. **Segnet die, so euch verfluchen** (Luke 6. 28)—**Keiner war, der Kundschaft gab, von allen, so da kamen** (Bürger)—**Röschen, so der Stolz des Dorfes war** (Hölty); in modern prose it is sometimes used in the south: cf. **Wir setzten uns zu einem fröhlichen Abendessen, welches aus den Fischen bestand, so die Vettern ausgewählt hatten** (G. Keller)—**Ich besah mir das Dutzend Bücher, so der alte Herr besaß** (id.)—**Wer selbst keine Hühneraugen hat, der ist doch häufig mit Angehörigen begabt, so welche haben** (H. Kurz: '. . . who have some'), in connexion with which see **welch (indefinite)**; in the proposition **Mit Goethe beruft sich Thomas Mann auf die Genialität der Wirklichkeit, die denen, so sehen und greifen können, alle Hände voll zu tun gibt** (A. Eloesser), the author may have wished to avoid the combination **die denen, die . . .**, but if so, he surely should have used **welche.** (**b**) Practically obs. is also the early use of **so** in the sense of 'if', as in **Das alles will ich dir geben, so** (cf. 'if *so* be that') **du niederfällst und mich anbetest** (Matth. 4. 9)—**So du kämpfest ritterlich, freut dein alter Vater sich** (Stolberg); but it is still firmly established in the expression **so Gott will** ('if it please God, God willing').

sobald: see so 1 (*b*).

sodann: see dann 1.

sofort, sogleich: see **bald**; **gleich** 2.

solange: see so 1 (*b*).

solch: 1. Whereas an indef. art. cannot precede, but can only follow **manch** (q.v. 2), it may either precede or follow **solch,** in the former case always remaining uninflected: hence, **solch ein** (or **ein solcher**) **Mann,** gen. **solch eines** (or **eines solchen**) **Mannes. 2.** Without the art., when not followed by an attrib. adj. (see 3), the gen. sing. masc. and neut. is either *strong,* as in **Wir fanden genug solches Hagels** (G.), or—but only if the noun has the strong gen. ending—*weak.* As the weak ending is fixed in **solchenfalls** ('in such a case')—cf. **allen-, jeden-, keinenfalls**—it seems strange that *Sanders* should say that the *weak* form in **Leute, die solchen Vermögens nicht bedürfen** (M. Hartmann) is **„im allgemeinen besser zu meiden"**—cf. **welch (interrog.)** 2 (*b*)—and the more so as he does not suggest the avoidance of the weak form in the case of **manch** (q.v. 3). Modern authors certainly use it quite freely, and in many contexts the weak ending undoubtedly is more euphonious: e.g. **Wie bin ich solchen Friedens seit lange nicht gewohnt** (Storm)—**Er entschied sich dahin, unbeschadet solchen Gottvertrauens, als Mensch zu handeln** (H. Franck); and the strong ending would sound very harsh in examples like **Unser Geist schweift umher nach einem Sinn solchen Geschehens** (Hofmannsthal) and **Solchen Zwanges bin ich nun entledigt** (E. Wiechert). **3.** If a strongly inflected **solch** is followed by an attrib. adj., the latter now as a rule has a *weak* ending, as after **manch** (q.v. 5): quoting **Unsere Frauen in Weimar bedürfen solcher fremder Erscheinungen** (G.), *Sanders* says explicitly that **fremder** is used **„statt fremden".** The determining factor would seem to be euphony, and it is undeniable that weak adj. endings would sound better in examples like **Der Erfolg solcher männlicher Lockungen reizte ihre Neugier** (St. Zweig) and esp. **Er war nicht gewohnt zu denken, daß ein solches schönes Fräulein nicht ihre Meinung sagen sollte** (G. Keller). So also in the nom. and accus. plur. a weak ending is to be recommended, as in **Solche alten Jungfern haben eine hohe Meinung von ihrer Familie** (Fontane) and **Man erblickt solche makellosen älteren, schon weißhaarigen Herren auf den Plakaten unserer Sektfirmen** (G. v. d. Vring). These two examples might be multiplied indefinitely; but it is only fair to say that examples like the following, although better avoided, are by no means uncommon: **Solche verliebte Leute sind mir zuwider** (Tieck)—**Solche hingeworfene Worte machen mich unglücklich** (Hauff)—**Wie oft hatte er solche junge, sichere Personen gesehen** (H. Hesse)—**Haben Sie solche unreife Ansichten, dann kann ich Ihnen nicht helfen** (Ompteda)—**Gegen solche arme Personen wird kein König ein Zorngefühl im Herzen nähren** (Bruno Frank)—**Solche nutzlose Gedanken gingen ihm durch den Kopf** (Kafka).

sollen: Like the other 'modal auxiliaries', this is one of the **past-present verbs** (q.v.), as seen from the different stem-vowels in the pres. indic. of the orig. forms of the verb: MHG *ich sal* (later *sol*), *wir suln.* **1.** Contrasted with **wollen,** which expresses the will of the subj., **sollen** always expresses the will of somebody or something else (see **müssen** 1): cf. **Ich will** and **Ich soll das Rauchen aufgeben** (the former 'I am going to', the latter 'I am to'); so also in the Commandments, **Du sollst nicht töten**, etc. (where the modern 2nd sing. form replaces MHG *du solt*)—**Sag' den Kindern, sie sollen ruhig sein!**—**Sollen wir jetzt nach Hause gehen?** ('Shall we go home now?' a seemingly innocent question, by means of which the speaker, who thinks it is time to go home, tries to communicate his will to the others); in the past subj., to suggest the duty of the subj., or to convey to a person what one regards as his duty: **Ich sollte eigentlich Briefe schreiben** ('I should really be writing letters')—**Sie sollten spazierengehen**; so also with an impers. subj., **Was soll das heißen?** ('What is the meaning of that?' lit. 'What does that want to convey?'): cf. **wonder** 1. It may also refer to future time: **Die Leute sollten sehen, daß er immer reicher wurde** (Auerbach: 'The people should see', i.e. 'He would show them that he was getting richer every day'); so also in **Ich bin selber schuld: es soll nicht wieder vorkommen** (Fontane: 'I am to blame: I'll see that it does not occur again') and in the common toast, e.g. to a bridal couple, **Hoch sollen sie leben!** ('May they have—i.e. May Providence grant them—long life and happiness!'). **2.** Esp. idiomatic is the use of **sollen** in propositions like **Er soll krank sein** ('He is said to be ill') and **Ein sonderbares Abenteuer sollte mir beschert sein** (G.: 'I was destined to have a strange adventure'). In the former example a report wants people to accept the statement as true; in the latter fate 'wills' that the author should experience something. The same idea of an outside force acting on a person is seen in everyday expressions like **Er wird wohl nicht kommen, aber es würde mich freuen, wenn er do'ch kommen sollte** ('. . . if he *should* come', i.e. if circumstances decreed that he should come) and **Das sollte unser letztes Zusammentreffen sein** ('That was destined to be our last meeting'); cf., with a pleonastic neg., **Da soll einer nicht verrückt werden!** ('That is enough to drive one mad!'). **3.** (**a**) The *infin.* form now generally replaces the past part. in a compd. tense containing a second dep. infin., as in **Sie hätte nicht allein gehen sollen** ('She ought not to have gone alone'), which is much more idiomatic than **Sie sollte nicht allein gegangen sein** (Lessing). But the part. form should be used where the dep. infin. is understood, as in **Aus der Geschichte habe ich nicht soviel behalten, als ich wohl gesollt hätte** (G.: 'I have not retained as much knowledge of history as I suppose I ought to have done'); the use of the infin. form here is now avoided, so that one no longer says **Er sagte, er habe getan, was er nicht sollen** (G., for **was er nicht gesollt**, or better **was er nicht hätte tun sollen**). (**b**) In German, a phrase containing a part., the equivalent of a rel. clause, can be used attrib. to qualify the antecedent of such a clause, as in **ein mit Talent begabter junger Mann** (= **ein junger Mann, der mit Talent begabt ist**). This idiom has a much wider application in German than in English: where we can only form compds. like 'peace-loving, disease-carrying, broken-hearted, star-spangled', etc., a German can make a much freer use of such attrib. expressions, and some authors are apt to overload their sentences with them: cf. the example from Th. Mann given under **participle (past)** 1 (*a*). This idiom is applied to the pres. part. of **sollen** with a dep. infin. in a proposition cited by *Duden*, viz. **Er machte eine höflich sein sollende Bewegung** ('He made a gesture which was meant to be a polite one'). While this is quite in the spirit of the German lang., it seems a rather clumsy way of saying **Er machte eine Bewegung, die höflich sein sollte**; and the following example seems to emphasize the clumsiness of this idiom: **Wie oft bin ich diese Treppen hinauf- und hinabgeklettert, einen, wie ich glaubte, Furore machen sollenden Leit-Artikel in der Tasche** (Raabe: 'How often have I climbed up and down these stairs with a leading article in my pocket which I believed was bound to cause a sensation'), surely an unnecessarily ponderous way of saying **einen Leitartikel in der Tasche, der, wie ich glaubte, Furore machen würde**, or better **von dem ich glaubte, daß er Furore machen würde** (see **von** 5 *ad fin.*).

some: see **deren** 1 (*b*); **einig**; **etwas**; **welch** (**indefinite**).

somebody: see **jemand**.

sondergleichen: see **-gleichen** 1.

sondern: see **aber** 1.

sonst: **1.** Qualifying a pron. or indef. expression, this word conveys the sense of our 'else', but generally precedes the word it qualifies, except in the case of an interrog. pron.: e.g. **„Haben Sie sonst etwas zu berichten?" „Nein, sonst nichts"**

('Have you anything else to report?' 'No, nothing else'). Here the reference is to something *in addition*; but sim. expressions may suggest something as an *alternative* or *substitute*, as in 'I don't want that: give me something else', and in such contexts a German prefers to use **etwas** or **nichts anderes** (see **ander** 1), although **sonst** can have the same force, as in **„Das muten Sie mir zu?" „Wem sonst?"** ('You expect *me* to do that?' 'Whom else?'). The idea of an alternative is also seen in a proposition like 'We must hurry, or (else) we shall be too late'. Here 'or (else)' really has conditional force (= otherwise, if we don't), and **sonst,** with the word-order of a question, exactly corresponds to this conditional 'or (else)': **Wir müssen uns beeilen, sonst kommen wir zu spät** (cf. **ander** 2; **fail** 1). In such contexts **sonst** is sometimes rather loosely replaced by **oder,** but this is mainly characteristic of the coll. style and better avoided in the best prose: cf. **Ich rief ihm zu, er solle zurückbleiben, oder ich würde** (= **sonst würde ich**) **nach ihm schießen** (G.); and sim. **Du sollst mir gehorchen, oder es gibt ein Unglück** (A. Wilbrandt), with which cf. **Geh, es gibt sonst Unheil!** (A. Schaeffer)—**Hör auf, oder ich laufe zu dir hinüber** (R. Herzog)—**Nimm den Zug** ('move' in a game of chess) **zurück, oder deine Königin ist verloren** (Jul. Wolff). **2.** Other meanings of **sonst** are 'at one time, formerly, at other times' and 'in other circumstances': e.g. **Hier ist alles wie sonst** ('Here everything is as it was in the old days')—**Warum ist sie wohl so verschlossen? Sie war doch sonst nicht so** ('I wonder why she is so reserved: she didn't use to be like that'). Incidentally, our 'else' was at one time used in the same way: cf. 'The crust of ice on the else rippling brook was transparent' (Dickens: **Die Eiskruste auf dem sonst rieselnden Bächlein war durchsichtig**).

sooft: see **so** 1 (*b*).

sort: for 'a sort of' see **Art.**

sound: 1. (**a**) The most comprehensive term for this noun is **Schall,** which denotes any sound that strikes the ear; hence its regular use in *physics*: **die Lehre vom Schall** ('acoustics'), **Schallwellen** ('sound waves'); cf. **Sei wie das tote Sprachrohr** ('speaking-trumpet'), **das den Schall empfängt und wiedergibt und selbst nicht höret** (Sch.). Apart from this technical use, **Schall** usually implies a *loud* sound: cf. **Welch ein Schall überbraust** ('drowns the roar of') **den Wasserfall?** (G.)—**Es erfolgte ein schallendes Gelächter** ('. . . a roar of laughter')—**Er versetzte mir eine schallende Ohrfeige** ('He gave me a resounding box on the ear'); and so, if it is used in connexion with musical instruments (see 2 (*b*) and (*c*)), it should be confined to the louder kinds (e.g. **Trompeten-, Trommel-, Zimbelschall**). (**b**) When a sound is reflected by some object which is near enough to make the original and the reflected sounds confused and practically indistinguishable (as in an empty room), the **Schall** becomes a **Hall** (cf. **In einem leeren Zimmer hallt die Stimme**); but when the object reflecting the sound is far away, so that the two sounds are distinct and separate, the **Schall** is succeeded by a **Widerhall,** i.e. an 'echo' (see **widerhallen**). **2.** More specific sounds are suggested by the following: (**a**) **Laut,** which denotes a sound produced by the voice of a *living*, not necessarily human, being (cf. 4): e.g. **Ein tierischer Laut drang an mein Ohr**—**Lautlos verließ er das Zimmer** (i.e. without *uttering* a sound: cf. 3 (*a*)); hence its use, of course, in *phonetics*: e.g. **An-, In-, Auslaut** ('initial, medial, final sound'), **Umlaut** ('vowel-mutation'), **Kehl-, Zischlaut** ('guttural, sibilant'), etc. Cf. **Lautmalerei,** the representation of a natural phenomenon by the use of appropriate sounds, as when Bürger says **Der Tauwind . . . schnob durch Welschland trüb' und feucht**). For the corresponding verb, see **lauten.** (**b**) When the vibrations of a sounding body are regular and periodic, the result is a sound that can be distinguished from others of higher or lower *pitch*. Such a sound is called a **Ton,** which is therefore regularly used in connexion with *music*: e.g. **Tonart** ('key'), **Tonleiter** ('scale'), **Grundton** ('key-note'); cf. **Tonmalerei** ('descriptive music')—**Dieses Klavier hat einen schönen Ton**; also of the intervals in a scale: **ein ganzer, halber Ton** ('a tone, semitone'). Then it is also applied to the *accent* in a spoken language, which follows the modulation of the voice: e.g. **Tonsilbe** ('accented syllable'), **tonlos** ('unaccented', as contrasted with **betont**); to warm or cold 'tones' in painting; and finally to social etiquette: **der gute** or **feine Ton** (*le bon ton*, the manners of good society), **den Ton angeben** (either lit. 'to sound the key-note', or fig. 'to set the fashion'). (**c**) But sounds do not differ only in intensity or pitch, they also differ in *quality*, as when the same note is produced by two different instruments. Viewed from this standpoint, a sound is a **Klang** (cf. **Klangfarbe,** 'timbre', with **Tonhöhe,** 'pitch'), which is more specifically used of a bright, metallic *ring*: e.g. **Glocken-, Schwerterklang,** etc.—cf. **Freunde kommen an, die das häusliche Mahl durch den Klang der Gläser beleben** (G.). The verb **klingen,** however, has come to be used in quite a general way, and has, indeed, largely displaced **tönen:** e.g. **Kennst du das alte Liedchen? es klingt so süß** (Heine)—**Dieser Name klingt komisch** ('This name has a funny sound'); see also **aushallen,** esp. 2. **3.** Passing from musical sounds to *noises*, we find, of course, a great variety of expressions, but at least two of these are commonly rendered by 'sound': (**a**) **Geräusch,** now generally used of *gentle* sounds: e.g. **Eben hörte ich ein Geräusch, als schliche jemand im Hause herum**—**Geräuschlos verließ er das Zimmer** (i.e. without *making* a sound: cf. 2 (*a*)). On the other hand, a *loud* noise is **Lärm** (from the old battlecry of the Latin nations: Ital. *all' arme*, 'to arms'—cf. **Lärm blasen, rufen, schlagen,** 'to sound, give the alarm'), which is therefore often used for 'din, uproar'. (**b**) A *rustling* sound should not be rendered by **Geräusch**; the correct expression should be **Gerausche** (from **rauschen,** 'to rustle', like **Geläute,** from **läuten,** etc.), but this form is hardly ever used, being replaced by the verbal noun **Rauschen:** e.g. **In der Ferne hörte ich das Rauschen des Meeres** ('the sound of the sea'); cf. **Die Damen, alle in Abendtoilette, kamen durch den Saal gerauscht** (suggesting the rustling sound of ladies' silk evening frocks).

soviel, soweit: see **so** 1 (*b*); for **soweit,** cf. **Es soll nicht wieder vorkommen, soweit** ('in so far as') **ich's hindern kann** (Fontane).

sowohl: The German for 'as well as' depends on the sense in which the English phrase is used. The proposition 'He speaks French as well as a Frenchman' is **Französisch spricht er so gut wie ein Franzose** (cf. **Das ist so gut wie abgemacht,** 'That is as good as settled'); but 'My parents as well as my brothers were there' is **Sowohl meine Eltern** (or **Meine Eltern sowohl**) **als** (or **wie**) **meine Brüder waren da.** If the nouns in this last example were *sing.*, the verb should strictly stand in the *sing.* also (**Sowohl mein Vater als mein Bruder war da**), but the idea of plurality is so strong that a plur. verb is quite common (see **als** = **'as'** 2, and esp. **congruence** 1 (*e*)), **as in Sowohl Effi wie die Geheimrätin waren emsig bei ihrer Handarbeit** (Fontane), where a sing. verb would obviously be impossible if 'both' were inserted (**waren beide emsig**); sim. **Line sowohl wie er haben es nicht gemerkt** (G. Engel), although this would more usually be expressed by **Weder Line noch er hat es gemerkt.** Instead of **sowohl . . . als,** one can use **wie** or **sowie** in the same sense, inserted *between* the two nouns or prons.: e.g. **Scheune wie Stall wiesen noch die althergebrachte Strohbedachung auf** (Ponten: 'Both the barn and the stable still showed the traditional thatched roof')—**Johanna sowie das Gesinde drängten an dem Burschen** ('urged the young fellow': much more usually **drangen in den Burschen**—see **drängen** 1), **das alte Spiel wieder aufzunehmen** (Spielhagen). Cf. the example from H. Ilgenstein given under **congruence** 1 (*e*), and see **samt.**

spalten: see **falten** 2.

spare: 1. (**a**) It is only in a few expressions that 'to spare' can be rendered by **sparen,** the real force of which is 'to practise economy', trans. 'to save' money: e.g. **Man muß für sein Alter sparen**—**Dadurch, daß er das Rauchen aufgegeben hat, spart er viel Geld**; but it can also be used in the sense of 'to use sparingly', as in **Wer die Rute spart, verzieht das Kind** ('Spare the rod and spoil the child'), and in that of 'to save *or* spare' expense, trouble, etc., although **scheuen** is more usual of expense, and **ersparen** in other contexts (cf. 2 (*b*)): cf. **Bei dem Neubau hat man keine Unkosten gescheut** ('No expense has been spared in the erection of the new building')—**All diese Mühe hättest du dir (er)sparen können** ('You might have saved yourself all that trouble')—**Erspare mir die Wiederholung meines Berichts!** ('Spare me the repetition of my report!')—**Hätte sie sich umgewandt, wäre ihr ein gelinder Schreck über seine Erscheinung nicht erspart geblieben** (H. Leip: '. . . she would not have been spared a slight shock at his appearance'); cf. **Theo van Gogh sparte sich** (*dat.*) **das Geld für den Lebensunterhalt**

seines Bruders ab (J. Karsten: i.e. stinted himself in order to support his brother). (**b**) An expression like 'I have no time to spare' is best rendered by the use of the adj. **übrig** or (in more formal lang.) of the verb **erübrigen**: see examples under **übrig** 1 and 2. **2.** (a) Where 'to spare' means 'not to hurt *or* damage', as in 'Woodman, spare that tree!', the reg. expression is **schonen,** implying lenient, considerate treatment: e.g. **Diese Bäume sollen geschont werden** (i.e. are to be left standing: cf. **Das Betreten dieser Schonung ist verboten,** 'No admittance to this young plantation *or* nursery of trees'); so also *fig*. **Er muß sich** (or **seine Gesundheit, Kräfte**) **schonen** ('He must spare himself, see to his health, conserve his strength')—**Schone meine Gefühle, ich müßte sonst erröten!** ('Consider my feelings and spare my blushes!'); but 'to spare a person's life' usually takes the form **jemandem das Leben schenken** or (in more choice style) **fristen.** The MHG verb *schônen* took a *gen.* obj., which is the invariable construction in the Bible: **Herr, schone deines Volks** (Joel 2. 17)—**Ich will ihrer schonen, wie ein Mann seines Sohnes schont** (Mal. 3. 17); and the gen. is found later also, but the accus. is now the rule in prose: for the gen., cf. **Hättest du doch meiner Jugend, meiner Unschuld noch vier Wochen geschont!** (G.)—**Schonen Sie meines Herzens!** (Sch.)—**Schone jetzt des Mädchens!** (Zschokke). (**b**) In the compd. **verschonen** the prefix stresses the idea of warding off harm (cf. **verhüten, verwahren,** etc.), and hence the verb is commonly used with the prep. **von**: e.g. **Von den Greueln des Krieges blieben die Schweizer verschont** ('The Swiss were spared the horrors of war')—**Der Krieg verschont niemand** ('War spares no one' *scil.* from hardship); and it is also common with **mit** in coll. expressions like **Verschone mich mit deinen gutgemeinten Ratschlägen!** (= **Erspare mir deine . . . Ratschläge!** 'Spare me your well-meant advice!')—**Er schreibt wohl von einzelnen Ungezogenheiten? Verschone mich damit!** (G.: 'I suppose he refers to individual cases of misconduct? Spare me that part of his letter!').

sparen: see **spare** 1 (*a*).

Spessart: see **Harz.**

spielen: The MHG verb *spiln* took a gen. obj.: where we now say **Ball** (or **mit dem Ball**) **spielen,** one formerly said *des balles spiln*; and so also, of playing an instrument, *der harpfen spiln* (cf. Fr. *jouer de la harpe*). The orig. construction has come down to modern times in references to playing games, as in **Greifens** (Kosegarten: 1758–1818), **Fangens** (Auerbach) and **Haschens spielen** (Spielhagen), all meaning 'to play catch-as-catch-can *or* tig' (= **Zeck**), but in such expressions the gen. **-s** ending is now usually dropped. The same applies to **Verstecken** (or, esp. in the north, **Versteck**) **spielen** ('to play hide-and-seek'); but the following examples show that the old gen. (which *Duden* represents as **„seltener"**) is by no means obs.: **Ich mußte an den Sommer denken, wo ich mit Hans Versteckens spielte** (Fontane)—**Wir haben nicht Zeit, miteinander Versteckens zu spielen** (Spielhagen)—**Die Schatten spielten Versteckens miteinander** (Immermann)—**Der Mond spielte Versteckens mit den Wolken** (Hebbel); cf., as unusual, **Wir spielen Zählens** (G.: 'We're going to play a counting game').

spotten: In ordinary lang. this verb is used intrans. with **über** + accus. ('to mock *at*'), in more elevated prose with a gen. ('to make a mock *of*'); for **Er spottete mein** (G.), one usually says **Er spottete über mich**; and sim. in **Es sind nicht alle frei, die ihrer Ketten spotten** (Lessing). But the *gen.* is quite established in propositions like **Die Überschwemmung spottet jeder Beschreibung** ('The flood defies description') or **Der Sack Kartoffeln spottete all(er) meiner Bemühungen, ihn zu heben**; and so also **Gott läßt seiner und seiner Erwählten nicht spotten** (A. Schaeffer), and in the pass., **Das heilige Wort Heimat wurde mit Verachtung genannt und des Vaterlandes wurde gespottet** (Frenssen). At one time it could be used with an accus., as in **Irret euch nicht, Gott läßt sich nicht spotten** (Gal. 6. 7), but with trans. force modern usage requires the use of **verspotten.** Rather unusual is a proposition like **Zitt're für dein Leben, weil du mich Herzog spottest** (Sch.), where **spottest** is used for **spottend** (or **spöttisch**) **nennst** ('because you mockingly call me Duke').

Sprichwort: see **Wort** 1 (*a*).

sprießen: **1.** This verb, used of plants in the sense of 'to sprout, shoot (up)', is *strong*, and occasional examples of weak forms (esp. with the prefix **auf-**) should not be imitated: cf. **Üppige Pflanzen**

sprießten auf (Scheffel: for **sprossen auf**)—**Ich hab's oft im Walde bemerkt, daß die kleinen Stämmchen, die zu gleicher Zeit aufgesprießt sind** (for **aufgesprossen sind**), **nicht einerlei Wachstum haben** (E. Wichert). **2.** On the other hand, **sprossen,** which has the same meaning, is *weak*: e.g. **Eine Lillie sproßte aus dem Boden** (G.)—**Der Baum des Lebens sproßt wieder** (Heyse); it is commonly used fig. of the first growth on a youth's face, as in **Ihm sproßte kaum der erste Flaum ums Kinn** (Sch.) and **Über des Jünglings Lippen sproßte schon der erste Flaum** (C. F. Meyer).

Sproß, Sprosse: The *strong* noun **der Sproß** (gen. **Sprosses,** plur. **Sprosse**) and the *weak* noun **der Sprosse** (gen. and plur. **Sprossen**) are really two forms of the same word, meaning 'sprout, shoot', but the weak noun is now mainly confined to the expression **Brüsseler Sprossen** (= **Rosenkohl,** 'Brussels sprouts'). On the other hand, the commonest use of the strong noun is now 'offspring, descendant', as in **Er war der letzte Sproß** (cf. our 'the last sprig') **aus diesem adligen Geschlecht.** —These should not be confused with **die Sprosse,** used of a 'rung' of a ladder (**Diese Leiter hat fünf Sprossen**), or of a 'spot *or* mark' on a person's skin, seen esp. in **Sommersprossen** ('freckles').

sprossen: see **sprießen** 2.

spuken: see **impersonal verbs** 2; **umgehen** 1.

spüren: This verb properly means 'to find *or* try to find the track (**Spur**) of' something, used specifically of a game-dog, then more generally of somebody 'searching for' a person or thing, in this sense usually intrans., **nach jemand spüren**; cf. trans. **ausspüren** ('to hunt up, track down'). A later meaning of the simple verb is 'to sense, notice, be dimly aware of', as in **Die Tür schnappte so leise ein, daß ich es kaum spürte** (G.), and esp. 'to have a vague feeling', either abs. or with accus. objs. like **Schmerz, Hunger, Lust,** etc., where **verspüren** is also used. Eventually **spüren** came to be used much like **fühlen,** the result being that the *accus. and infin.* construction, rare until comparatively recent times, is now used freely by modern authors: e.g. **Sie mußte sich abwenden, weil sie ihre Stimme zittern spürte** (St. Zweig)—**Er hatte plötzlich etwas durch seinen Körper zucken gespürt: er wußte, es war ein Vorbote des Todes** (H. E. Busse)—**Ich spürte einen Hauch der Ewigkeit durch die dämmernde Stube fluten** (H. Hesse)—**Sie hatte beide Hände auf meine Brust gelegt: ich spürte das Blut in ihren Adern pochen** (Fr. Thiess)—**Er spürte die Enttäuschung als einen brennenden Schmerz in seinem Inneren wüten** (W. Kramp). The alternative construction is a subord. clause introduced by **wie,** but the accus. and infin. is to be preferred where another **wie**-clause occurs, as in **Sie spürte Gesichter vorbeigleiten, wie** ('as') **sie vorwärts lief** (St. Zweig): cf. **Indem sie vorwärts lief, spürte sie, wie Gesichter an ihr vorbeiglitten.**

stampfen: see **mit** 2 (*b*).

Statt: 1. (a) As an independent noun, **die Statt** (really the same word as the historically incorrect **Stadt**) is now only used with a preceding gen. in a prep. phrase introduced by **an,** with the force of 'in place *or* lieu of' (whence the prep. **anstatt,** q.v.). Where the noun standing in the gen. is masc. or neut., the art. is generally omitted, as in the commonest expression of this kind, **jemand an Kindes Statt annehmen** ('to adopt a child'): cf. **Unter natürlichen Erben versteht das Gesetz Blutsverwandte oder solche, die durch Annahme an Kindes Statt zu Abkömmlingen geworden sind** (Bergengruen: 'The law takes natural heirs to mean blood relations or such as have become descendants by adoption'); and sim. **Der Burgherr sagte, er wolle ihn an Sohnes Statt annehmen** (Sch.)—**Ich bin Regent im Land an Kaisers Statt** (id.); but in the fem., **Lange wünschte die Mutter ein Mädchen im Hause, das ihr hülfe an der früh verlorenen Tochter Statt** (G.). Otherwise its use is mainly limited to a few expressions like **an Eides Statt** ('instead of an oath') or **an Zahlungs Statt** ('in lieu of payment'), the final **-s** in the latter phrase suggesting a real compd., as in **Zahlungsfrist, -mittel,** etc. Indeed, we even find occasional examples in which **Statt** and its preceding gen., although written as separate words, are treated as a loose compd., a qualifying adj. agreeing not with the gen. but with **Statt,** as in **Der Alte hatte schon alles besorgt, was nötig war, um den Enkel an eigener Kindes Statt anzunehmen** (Sudermann). Apart from its independent use, **Statt** is now only found in a few compds. like **Statthalter** ('regent, viceroy') and **Werkstatt** (see (*b*) below); cf. also **Walstatt** ('field of battle': see **Wal-**). **(b)** Much more common now is the form **Stätte,** which is really the plur. of **Statt** (MHG *stat*, plur. *stete*), but which, like **Fährte, Schläfe,** and **Trümmer** (qq.v.), has acquired an independent existence as a *sing.*, with the new plur. **Stätten.** It is now used esp. with the force of a 'fixed, abiding place', as in the biblical phrase **keine bleibende Stätte haben** (in Heb. 13. 14 the modern version has **Wir haben hie keine bleibende Stadt,** but Luther wrote **keine bleibende stat**); sim. **jemand an geweihter Stätte begraben** (cf. the more choice expression for 'to bury': **bestatten**)—**So ruhen die Liebenden nebeneinander: Friede schwebt über ihrer Stätte** (G.)—**An heil'ger Stätte ist sie** (Tell's cross-bow) **aufbewahrt** (Sch.); and so also in many common compds. like **Grab-, Ruhe-, Lager-, Wohn-, Heimstätte** ('home*stead*': cf. 'farm*stead*' and Scots '*steading*') and **Werkstätte,** for which **Werkstatt** is still used. **2.** The prefix has a somewhat different origin in the verbs **stattfinden,** less commonly **statthaben** ('to take place, be held': of meetings, etc.): see **participle** (past) 1 (*b*). Here **statt** is from MHG *state*, really a 'suitable place' or 'favourable occasion'; and the same applies to the not very common **stattgeben** (+ dat., 'to grant', esp. of requests), as in **Er schien von meiner Bitte entzückt, bedauerte aber, ihr nicht stattgeben zu können** (G. v. d. Vring: = **sie nicht gewähren zu können** or **sie abschlagen zu müssen**)—**Dieser Bitte hatte der Herzog stattgegeben** (Fr. Griese). Here belongs also **gestatten** (properly 'to give an opportunity', i.e. 'to allow'), **vonstatten gehen** (of things: 'to progress, pass off') and **zustatten kommen** ('to stand in good *stead*' or 'to come *à propos*'): e.g. **Gestatten Sie!** (a polite phrase used when one has not room to pass a person, like our 'Excuse me!')—**Die Aufführung ging glatt vonstatten** ('went without a hitch')—**Er beschloß, eine Maske aus Wachs zu machen, und es verwunderte ihn, wie leicht das Werk vonstatten ging** (P. Zifferer)—**Er sagte, die Umgestaltung des Ortes in einen Kurplatz müsse der ganzen Umgebung zustatten kommen** (id.) —**Geld habe ich im Augenblick nicht, also kommt mir deine Einladung zum Abendessen gut zustatten.**

Stätte: see **Statt** 1 (*b*).

stattfinden, -geben, -haben: see **Statt** 2; for the first and third, see also **participle** (past) 1 (*b*).

staunen: see **wonder** 4.

stecken: 1. With *trans.* force, this verb is always *weak*. It is really the factitive of the strong verb **stechen** ('to pierce, prick, sting'), so that its basic force is 'to cause to stick by piercing', as when a dressmaker sticks pins (**Stecknadeln**) in the material, or a chef fixes meat on a spit for roasting (**Fleisch an den Spieß stecken**); then, with more general application, 'to put in a secure place', so that it cannot fall, escape, etc. To the examples given under **put** 1 may be added: **Sie steckte ihre kleinen Füße in rote Pantöffelchen** (Immermann)—**Ich steckte das Geld zu mir** ('I pocketed the money, concealed it on my person')—**Wer seine Nase in die Politik steckte, den hießen wir einen Kannegießer** (Storm: 'Whoever poked his nose into *or* dabbled in politics, we dubbed an alehouse politician')—**Wollt ihr mein Haus in Brand stecken?** (Möser: 'Do you want to set my house on fire?'); so also with a pers. obj.: **jemand ins Gefängnis stecken** (coll. **jemand einstecken**) or **unter die Soldaten stecken** ('to make a soldier of a person' or 'to make some one join the forces'). **2. (a)** With *intrans.* force, it properly means 'to be sticking', as in **Der Schlüssel steckt in der Tür** or **im Schlüsselloch**—**Er hatte eine Blume im Knopfloch stecken**—**Der Wagen blieb im Schlamm stecken** (fig. **Er blieb in seiner Rede stecken,** 'He broke down in his speech'); but it is also used in a number of coll. idioms in which it often means little more than 'to be': e.g. **Er steckt bis über die Ohren in Schulden** ('He is over head and ears in debt')—**In diesem Jungen steckt etwas** ('There's something in this boy', i.e. he is clever)—**Wo hast du denn den ganzen Tag gesteckt?**—**Dahinter steckt etwas** ('There's more in this than meets the eye')—**Sie stecken unter ei'ner Decke** ('They are accomplices, have a secret understanding'). **(b)** The *strong* forms of this verb (always *intrans.*) are historically incorrect, having probably arisen through confusion with **stechen.** Of these, the pres. indic. **du stickst, er stickt,** and the past part. **gestocken** are now quite obs. (cf. Schiller's **Nun, Hauptmann, wo stickst du?** '. . . where have you been so long?'), but the past tense forms **stak,** subj. **stäke** (with *long* stem-vowels) are still in common use: e.g. **Mitten in der Brust des**

Reihers stak der Pfeil (Jul. Wolff)—**Aus dem Sumpfboden staken verkohlte Stämme** (M. Eyth: 'Charred tree-trunks stuck up out of the swamp')—**Eine Kohlenkarre stak mit den Rädern in einem Loch** (R. Herzog: 'The wheels of a coal-cart had got stuck in a hole')—**Ich stak mitten in dem Menschenknäuel und riß an meinem Koffer, der zwischen den Knien eines Herrn stak** (M. Eyth: 'I was jammed in the dense crowd and tugged at my portmanteau which had got wedged between a gentleman's knees')—**Aus der Brusttasche staken Bleistifte hervor** (H. Hauser)—**Ein Zigarrenstummel stak zwischen seinen Lippen** (Th. Mann)—**Seine Stimme klang, als stäke ein Bissen in seiner Speiseröhre** (id.: 'His voice sounded as if some food *or* a crumb had stuck in his throat'); cf. the common coll. expression **Das Kind schrie, als wenn es am Spieße stäke** ('as if it were sticking on the spit', i.e. 'at the top of its voice'). In particular, these strong past tense forms are much used in references to the human body or parts of the body (esp. hands and feet), which are clothed or encased in something: e.g. **Jetzt merkte er erschreckt, daß er noch in den Kleidern stak** (St. Zweig: i.e. that he had not undressed yet) —**Die Männer staken in ihren Abendmahlröcken** (Speckmann)—**Er stak in einer Lederkleidung, die den Hals nackt ließ** (Kafka)—**Seine Beine staken in einer engen grauen Arbeitshose** (J. Schlaf)—**Ihre Beine staken in braunen Gamaschen** (H. W. Geissler)—**Ihre nackten Füße staken in hölzernen Pantoffeln** (Bonsels) —**Von den Hüften bis zu den Füßen, die in grobem Schuhwerk staken, verriet er die ländliche Herkunft** (R. Schickele)—**Seine Finger staken in grauen Zwirnhandschuhen** (Zifferer)—**Ihr glatt frisiertes Haar stak in einem großmaschigen Netze** (Th. Mann). But, quite common as these strong past tense forms are, the historically correct *weak* forms are perhaps even more often used by modern authors, as in **Der Doktor war ein dicker Mann, der voll guter Einfälle steckte** (Immermann: '. . . who was full of bright ideas') and **Auf dem Festplatz steckten die Bäume voll bunter Lampen** (Keyserling); and esp. again in references to the human body: e.g. **Nie hatte sie Frauen gesehen, die in solchen Kleidern steckten** (H. Hauser)—**Der Erbprinz steckte in einer schwarzen Uniform** (Bruno Frank)—**Die Königin steckte in kostbaren Gewändern** (E. Wichert)—**Er trug Schaftstiefel, in denen die Hosen steckten** (A. Schaeffer)—**Seine Hände steckten in Fäustlingen** (Werfel)—**Sie hob ihm flehend die Muff** (q.v.) **entgegen, in der ihre beiden Hände steckten** (Th. Mann)—**Die Füße steckten in Goldpantoffeln** (Dauthendey), **in dicken Filzsocken** (Schreckenbach), **in blauen Gummischuhen** (E. Brüning), **in langen schwarzen Reitstiefeln** (G. Britting); cf. the example from Hofmannsthal given under **congruence** 1 (*b*).

steckenbleiben: see **bleiben** 2 (*b*).

Steg: Some confusion has arisen between the nouns **Steg, Steig(e)** and **Stieg(e)**. **1.** Apart from a number of technical uses (e.g. the 'bridge' of a violin or of spectacles, etc.), **der Steg** is for the most part confined to the meanings 'footpath' (= **schmaler Fußweg**) and 'footbridge' (= **Bretterbrücke**). The compd. **Stegreif,** formerly used of a 'stirrup' (see 2), now occurs only in the phrase **aus dem Stegreif** with a verb like **reden** or **dichten,** suggesting a speech or verses given 'impromptu'. **2. Steig** (masc.) is now only used of a narrow, generally steep 'footpath'; the idea of ascent is emphasized in **Steigbügel** ('stirrup'), **Bahnsteig** ('platform', from which you step up into a train), **Bürgersteig** ('pavement, sidewalk', to which one steps up from the street-level). **3. Steige** (fem.) is now for the most part supplanted by **Stiege** (see 4), but is still in fairly common use in the sense of either a 'step-ladder' (esp. a sloping plank with cross-pieces, as seen in building operations or in a hen-house), or a 'stile' (= **Zauntritt**). **4.** Whereas **Stieg** (masc.) is now practically limited to comp. nouns like **Auf-, Abstieg** ('ascent, descent'), **Stiege** (fem.) is used in various senses, esp. those of (**a**) a narrow, usually steep 'staircase': e.g. **Wütend sprang ich die Stiegen hinunter auf die Straße** (G.)—**Sie wurden eine Stiege hinaufgewiesen in ein Erkerstübchen** (W. Schäfer)—**Als ich den Roman zu schreiben anfing, saß ich in Rom drei Stiegen hoch** (Th. Mann); (**b**) a 'score' (= **zwanzig Stück**); (**c**) a 'shock' or 'stook' of sheaves: **eine Stiege Garben = ein Garbenhaufen** or **eine Hocke** (see **Getreide** 2).

stehen: 1. The modern forms **stehen, stand** (subj. **stände**), **gestanden** differ considerably from the standard MHG *stân, stuont* (subj. *stüende*), *gestanden* (sometimes contracted *gestân*). The infin. form *stên* occurs as an alternative of *stân*, and gradually asserted itself more and more until it became firmly established as **stehen**; and the historically incorrect past tense **stand** gradually displaced **stund,** which was the standard form in early NHG, and which was still common in the classical period, but is now obs.: cf. **Die Augen stunden ihm voll Tränen** (G.)—**Niemand verstund die Sache zu schlichten** (G.: 'No one knew how to settle the dispute'). On the other hand, the past subj. **stünde** is still fairly common in rather choice style: for examples, see **past subjunctive** 2 (*c*). **2.** Like **liegen, sitzen** and other verbs suggesting an attitude (see **liegen** 1, **sitzen** 3, and cf. **knien**), stehen is used in the north with the aux. **haben,** as in **Ich habe oft auf diesem Hügel gestanden.** In such contexts the south prefers **sein** (see 3), so naturally Goethe uses the Swiss idiom in his *Schweizerlied*: **Uf'm Bergli bin i gesässe . . . in a Garte bin i gestande** (= **Auf einem Hügel habe ich gesessen . . . in einem Garten habe ich gestanden**). To some extent the southern idiom has spread to other parts, but is not to be recommended: cf. **Am Kirchhof dort bin ich gestanden** (Lenau)—**Das Haus war damals noch dagestanden** (Storm)—**Ein dutzendmal war ich auf dem Punkte gestanden, ihn allein gehen zu lassen** (Spielhagen). **3.** The use of **stehen** implying motion (= **treten**) was established in MHG: one distinguished between *ich hân gestanden* ('I have stood') and *ich bin gestanden* ('I have stepped'), and sim. one said *in daz venster sitzen* (= **sich an das Fenster setzen**: cf. **sitzen** 2). This use of **stehen** = **treten** occurs very occasionally later, as in **Er muß vor seinen Richter stehen** (Sch.) and **Sagt, wo ich hinstehn soll!** (id.: = **Sagt, wo ich mich hinstellen soll!**), but this is now confined to some southern dialects: cf. **„Halt!" donnerte er und stand vor sie hin** (Federer). It should be noted, however, that just as some compds. of **sitzen** (q.v. 2) imply motion, so do several compds. of **stehen,** which then, of course, take the aux. **sein**: see esp. **auf-, ein-** and **entstehen,** and the double compd. **auferstehen. 4.** For **Es steht zu hoffen** or **zu befürchten,** see **infinitive** 3 (*a*).

stehenbleiben: see **bleiben** 2 (*b*); **stop (verb)** 1 (*f*).

Steig(e): see **Steg** 2 and 3.

steigen: see **climb.**

Stelle: see **place (noun)** 3.

stellen: 1. Although this verb is used in many set expressions, e.g. with objs. like **Antrag** ('to make a motion'), **Bedingung** ('to stipulate'), **Frage** ('to put a question'), **Uhr** ('to set a clock'), etc., its fundamental force is 'to place upright' (see **put** 1 and 3), and hence **sich stellen** means 'to take up a standing position': where we say 'The child was ordered to go and stand in the corner', a German says **Dem Kinde wurde befohlen, sich in die Ecke zu stellen,** the idea of 'going' being suggested by the accus. in the prep. phrase; so also fig. **Wie stellen Sie sich zu dieser Frage?** ('What is your attitude *or* standpoint towards this question?'). **2.** But **sich stellen** is also used in the sense of 'to pretend' (cf. **tun** 3), either with a pred. adj. or with an 'as if'-clause ('to do as if . . .'): e.g. **Sie stellte sich taub** (*not* **taub zu sein**: 'She pretended to be deaf *or* not to hear')—**Der Junge stellte sich** (or **tat**), **als ob er krank wäre.** In the *abs.* use, on the other hand, **sich anstellen** or **verstellen** is more usual, as in **Stelle dich doch nicht an!** ('Don't pretend!'); cf. **Der Ausdruck von unverstelltem** ('unfeigned, genuine') **Schmerz auf seinem Gesicht war schauerlich für alle Anwesenden** (Mörike). From what has been said above it follows that **sich jemandem gegenüberstellen** may have two quite different meanings: cf., on the one hand, **Ich stellte mich ihr gegenüber** ('I took up a position facing her'), and on the other hand, **Sie stellte sich, ihm gegenüber, als hoffe sie auf eine Tochter** (K. Edschmid: 'She pretended to him that she hoped her child would be a girl').

sterben: 1. This verb is now always strong and intrans., the MHG weak trans. *sterben* ('to kill') having long been obs. For the past subj. **stürbe,** see **Ablaut** 2 (*a*). **2.** Constructions: **(a)** a *cognate accus.*, as in **einen natürlichen Tod sterben** (cf. *b*), and always in **den Tod fürs Vaterland sterben**; **(b)** a *gen.*, notably in the expression **Hungers sterben** ('to die of starvation'), otherwise mainly where 'death' is qualified by an attrib. adj.: e.g. **Man sagt von der Gemse** ('chamois'), **daß sie lieber Hungers stirbt, als eine Pflanze benagt, woran sie die Berührung einer Menschenhand wittert** (Riehl)—**Er ist eines natürlichen Todes gestorben**—**Man sprach schon lange davon, daß die beiden eines unnatürlichen Todes gestorben seien** (W. v. Scholz)—**In Freytags „Ahnen" sterben**

viele eines gewaltsamen Todes (P. Lindau)—**Im Mai geschah es, daß Onkel Gotthold eines schweren Todes starb** (Th. Mann)—**Eines herrlichen, wilden Todes waren sie gestorben** (Kellermann). In view of the fact that **Hungers sterben** is quite fixed, it seems strange that Luther's **Nun muß ich Dursts sterben** (Judges 15. 18) has never become established (see *c*); (**c**) a *prep. phrase*, **an** being used of diseases (which nearly all require a def. art.), **vor** of other causes: cf., on the one hand, **Er starb an der Pest** ('of the plague'), **an der Schwindsucht** ('of consumption'), **am Schlage** ('of apoplexy'); and on the other hand, **Sie starb vor Liebe, vor Sehnsucht, vor** (sometimes **aus**) **Gram** ('of grief'), **vor Hunger und Durst, vor Langeweile** ('She was bored to death'), **vor Lachen** ('She died with laughing'); cf., as rather unusual, **Valentina von Orleans starb Kummers** (Rilke). **3.** Rather strange is the *impers. reflex.* use of the verb, as in **Es stirbt sich nicht leicht** ('To die is not an easy thing'); and sim. **So stirbt sich's schön, die Waffen in den Händen** (Sch.: 'To die sword in hand is a beautiful death')—**Hierher kommen die Leute, um zu leben, ich würde eher meinen, es stürbe sich hier** (Rilke: '. . . I should rather regard it as a place to die in'). **4.** Compds. in common use are **absterben** (esp. of plants, also of limbs which become atrophied), **aussterben** (lit. of families which become extinct; fig. of localities which are 'silent as the grave'), **ersterben** (esp. of sounds which 'die away'), and the past part **verstorben** ('deceased'). A very unusual compd., which should be avoided, is **besterben,** as used in **Die Fliegen warfen sich irgendwohin, und endlich bestarben sie das ganze Zimmer** (Rilke: '. . . and filled the room with their dead bodies').

Steuer: Distinguish between **das Steuer** ('helm, rudder'), with plur. unchanged, and **die Steuer** ('tax, impost'), with plur. **Steuern.**

stieben: This intrans. verb is chiefly used of dust, sparks, fragments, etc., in the sense of 'to fly up *or* off', then more generally 'to scatter, disperse'. *Duden* allows both strong and weak forms, but the latter seem to be rather rare: cf. **Es stiebte zwischen Regen uud Schnee** (G.: 'There came a shower, half rain, half snow'). Much more usual are still the orig. *strong* forms: e.g. **Mein Hund kam mit jähem Satz durchs offene Fenster herein, wobei viel Kies ins Zimmer stob** (Th. Mann)—**Die Funken stoben aus meiner Pfeife** (Kellermann)—**Er schüttelte sich, daß die Wassertropfen stoben** (I. Seidel); esp. with an appropriate prefix: **Vom Boden stoben unter seinen Tritten kleine Staubwolken ab** (Bergengruen). **Entsetzt waren die Kinder davongestoben** (Zifferer)—**Der Eber rannte gegen ein Häuflein Treiber an, das eiligst auseinanderstob** (E. Wichert: 'The boar charged a small group of beaters, who scattered in all directions'). Less common is its use with a sing. subj. meaning 'to rush *or* dash off', as in **Laut aufschreiend stob das Kind davon** (Hofmannsthal) and **Sogleich war der Wagen in die Nacht abgestoben** (Fr. Griese).

Stieg(e): see **Steg** 4.

Stift: Distinguish between **der Stift** ('peg' or short for **Bleistift,** 'pencil'; also 'youngster, apprentice'), with plur. **Stifte**—and **das Stift** ('foundation'; also 'asylum, home' for the poor or aged), with plur. **Stifte** or **Stifter.**

still(e): see **adverbs formed from adjectives** 1.

Stock: This *masc.* noun, with plur. **Stöcke,** has a large number of meanings, e.g. '(walking-)stick', 'stem' of a plant (also the plant itself, as in **Rosen-, Weinstock**), 'stump' of a tree, 'bee-hive' (**Bienenstock**), 'mountain-mass' (as in the Swiss mountain **Rurirotstock**; cf. **über Stock und Stein laufen,** 'to make a beeline across country'), etc. Another common meaning is a 'storey, floor' in a building, in which sense it is sometimes *neut.*; and here, when used as a measure, it remains unchanged in the plur. (see **nouns of measure** 1): e.g. **Das Gebäude hat zehn Stock—Es ist ein Haus von drei Stock**; elsewhere it is better to use the plur. of the alternative compd. **Stockwerk,** as in **Nach den Stockwerken zu urteilen** ('To judge from the number of floors'), **muß das Gebäude sehr geräumig sein.**

stop: 1. *Intransitive*: (**a**) The cessation or discontinuance of an action or state is suggested by **aufhören:** e.g. **Endlich hat der Regen** (or **hat es zu regnen**) **aufgehört**—**Höre doch endlich zu weinen auf!**—cf. the coll. expression **Da hört aber alles auf!** ('That is the absolute limit! That beats all!'). Here the discontinuance is, or is intended to be, complete, not a pause (see *b*): one does not say **Der Redner hörte einen Augenblick auf, um zu Atem zu kommen.** (**b**) On the other hand, a temporary stoppage, a break or pause is expressed by **innehalten** (q.v.) or **einhalten** (cf. *c*): e.g. **Der Redner hielt inne und fuhr dann fort—Man sah, wie die Frauen in ihrer Arbeit einhielten** (B. E. Werner)—**Er hält im Schritt inne** (Blunck: cf. 2 *b*)—**Er fing an zu laufen und hielt erst bei einem Baum ein, um sich zu verschnaufen** (Ric. Huch)—**Der Pfarrer hielt ein, um den Knecht zu segnen** (Waggerl); because of its greater resonance, the prefix **ein-** is more effective in the imperat.: **Halt ein!** (**c**) When the reference is to a train, bus, etc., coming to a standstill, the simple verb **halten** is the usual expression: e.g. **An dieser Station halten nur Personenzüge—Hält dieser Zug in Blumenberg?**—cf. **Haltestelle** (a 'halt' on the railway, a 'bus-stop'); and it may also indicate the duration of the stoppage: **Wielange hält der Zug hier?** In other contexts **anhalten** is used here, orig. a *trans.* verb (cf. 2 *b*) with its obj. understood: **Der Kutscher hielt an** really = **Der Kutscher hielt die Zügel** or **die Pferde an** ('reined in his horses'), and this led to **Der Wagen hielt an**; sim. **Ein Auto hat eben jemand überfahren, hat aber nicht angehalten** (cf. *d*)—**Er hielt** (*scil.* **den Atem**) **beim Lesen an.** Strangely enough, this verb may imply the very opposite: **Der Sturm hielt lange an** is 'The storm lasted a long time', and **anhaltendes Regenwetter** is 'prolonged rain'. (**d**) Used of vehicles, **stoppen**—the LG form of **stopfen** (see 2 *a*) and really *trans.* like **anhalten**—was orig. only used of ships (a Prussian naval regulation reads **Jedes Dampfschiff muß, wenn nötig, stoppen**), but is now popularly used of cars: one says **Er stoppte das Auto** and **Das Auto stoppte**; cf. **Alle Buchveröffentlichungen sind durch das Ministerium gestoppt** (B. E. Werner)—**Wir hatten vor einem Abgrund abgestoppt** (Kellermann). (**e**) An *abrupt* stoppage, esp. with reference to sounds, is suggested by **abbrechen**: e.g. **Mit einem vollen Akkord brach die Musik ab—In seiner Erzählung brach er plötzlich ab—Schnell brach das Mädchen in ihrem Lied ab** (Hackländer). (**f**) Much like **anhalten** is **stehenbleiben**, which means not only 'to remain standing', but also 'to come to a standstill': e.g. **Er blieb auf einmal stehen und kehrte um—Meine Uhr ist stehengeblieben: ich habe vergessen, sie aufzuziehen.** **2.** *Transitive*:—(**a**) Where the verb 'stop' has the force of 'to plug', it is rendered by **stopfen** or one of its compounds: e.g. **ein Leck stopfen** ('to stop a leak')—**Sie preßte sich gegen die Mitte der Doppeltür, als wollte sie die Fuge verstopfen** (A. Schaeffer: 'She pressed her body against the middle of the double door, as if she wished to close the gap')—cf. the coll. expression **jemandem den Mund stopfen** ('to stop a person from speaking, silence him') and **Strümpfe stopfen** ('to darn stockings'); but 'to stop' a tooth = **einen Zahn füllen** or **plombieren.** (**b**) Very frequently, 'to stop' means to prevent from proceeding or functioning, and here a number of expressions are used, according to the context: e.g. **jemand auf der Straße anhalten** ('to stop a person in the street', whereas **aufhalten** = 'to detain')—**den Schritt anhalten** or **hemmen** (of a pedestrian coming to a standstill, the former properly suggesting a sudden stoppage, the latter rather a gradual slowing down)—**jemand von einem Versuch ab-** or **zurückhalten** ('to stop a person from making an attempt')—**eine Maschine anhalten** or **abstellen** or **außer Betrieb setzen** ('to stop a machine')—**Zahlungen einstellen** ('to stop, suspend payment')—**die Arbeit einstellen** ('to stop work')—**jemandes Lohn einbehalten** ('to stop a person's wages')—**Mißbräuchen Einhalt tun** ('to stop abuses').

stopfen: see **stop** 2 (*a*).

stoppen: see **stop** 1 (*d*).

stoßen: **1.** A strange mistake which students are apt to make with this verb is to conjugate it as if it belonged to the same class as **bieten, fliegen,** etc., i.e. to say **stießen, stoß, gestoßen!** What they should impress on their minds is that it is one of the **reduplicating verbs** (q.v.), which all have the same stem-vowel in the infin. and the past part. (here **ō**) and **ie** in the *past* tense. **2.** The only other difficulty is in connexion with the aux. in a compd. tense. (**a**) Of course, when the verb has *trans.* force, the aux. is **haben**: e.g. **Die Ziege hat das Kind mit den Hörnern gestoßen—Ich habe mir den Fuß gegen einen Stein** or **den Ellbogen an der Tischkante gestoßen** (but **Ich bin mit dem Fuß** or **Ellbogen . . . gestoßen**: see *b* below)—**Du scheinst dir einen Splitter in den Finger gestoßen zu haben—Er hat**

dem Gegner den Dolch in die Brust gestoßen; and sim. with expressions like **jemand von sich stoßen** (= **fortstoßen**), **jemand zur Tür hinausstoßen**, etc. (**b**) Where the verb has *intrans.* force, there is some fluctuation. One always says **Der Jäger hat ins Horn gestoßen** (because it really means 'has blown air into the horn')—**Der Schiffer hat vom Ufer abgestoßen** ('has put off from the shore', because it implies pushing the boat off with an oar or a boathook: see **abstoßen**)—**Er hat nach mir gestoßen** ('He made a thrust *or* lunged at me': because a weapon is really understood). On the other hand, the aux. **sein** is generally used with expressions such as **auf Schwierigkeiten** or **Hindernisse stoßen** ('to come up against difficulties, obstacles') and **auf einen alten Bekannten stoßen** ('to come across *or* happen to meet an old acquaintance'); and **sein** is quite established where the verb implies a clash between opposing forces or is used with the prep. **zu** in the sense of 'to attach oneself to, unite with, join': e.g. **Das Schiff ist auf eine Klippe gestoßen—Die zwei Heere sind zusammen-** or **aufeinandergestoßen—Er hat sich aus der Gefangenschaft befreit und ist zu seinem Regiment gestoßen—Während dieses Gespräches war der Adjutant zu seinem Kommandeur gestoßen** (Binding).

strafen: Besides the ordinary sense of 'to punish', this verb formerly also had the force of 'to reprimand' (= **tadeln, verweisen**), as in **Da das seinem** (*scil.* Joseph's) **Vater gesagt ward, strafte ihn sein Vater** (Gen. 37. 10: 'his father rebuked him'). This earlier use survives only in the expression **jemanden Lügen strafen** ('to give the lie to a person', lit. 'to reprove a person for [telling] a lie'). Here the word **Lügen** is an old *gen. sing.* (in MHG, a 'lie' was *lüge* or *lügen*), and sometimes this is clearly brought out: e.g. **Ich strafe euch keiner Lüge** (Lessing)—**Ich antwortete, wenn er wieder ungerechte Worte gegen mich brauchte, so würde ich ihn der Lügen strafen** (G.); but it is much more usual to leave the old gen. unqualified, as in **Euer eigenes Herz straft euch Lügen** (Sch.)—**Ich strafe das Orakel Lügen** (Tieck); and this applies equally to an abstract obj.: e.g. **Diese Mitteilung straft seine Behauptung Lügen** ('This information belies his statement')—**Der Erfolg hat meine Erwartungen Lügen gestraft**; so also in the *pass.*, **Der Glaube an mein Glück ist in meinem Innersten stets lebendig gewesen, und ich kann sagen, daß er nicht Lügen gestraft worden ist** (Th. Mann).

Strauch: The plur. form of this masc. noun fluctuates between **Sträuche** and **Sträucher**: cf. **Sie trug das Kind zwischen jungen Blumen und Sträuchen her** (G.) and **Hier wachsen keine Bäume: an den Gebirgen flechten sich kleine Sträucher durcheinander** (G.). Nowadays the form **Sträucher** is almost established; *Duden* gives **„Sträucher (auch: Sträuche)"**. On the other hand, the neut. compd. **Gesträuch** has the plur. form **Gesträuche**, but this is naturally rather rare, as the sing. has collect. force: cf. **Die Bäume und Gesträuche hatten lange Ruten und Zweige hervorgeschossen** (Stifter).

Strauß: Distinguish between **der Strauß** ('bouquet' or 'fight, conflict'), with plur. **Sträuße**, and **der Strauß** ('ostrich'), with plur. **Strauße**: cf. **Urweisheit trieb die Strauße, ihre Eier in den heißen Sand zu scharren, wo die Sonne sie ausbrütete** (A. Döblin).

Streit: This masc. noun orig. meant 'fight' (with weapons), but in this sense it is now almost confined to poetry, as in **Die Trommel schlug zum Streite** (Uhland), its modern force being either 'quarrel, dispute' or 'contest'. The MHG plur. *strîte* was quite common, but **Streite** was rare even in early NHG: it is significant that where Luther used **Streite** in Num. 21. 14 the modern version has **Kämpfe**. According to modern prose usage, the plur. **Streite** is only used in the case of compds. suggesting 'contest', e.g. **Wett-, Wortstreit**, etc., being replaced in the sense of 'quarrels' by **Streitigkeiten**. Very common is the combination **Zank und Streit**, and these two nouns show a similarity in that the little used plur. **Zänke** is usually replaced by **Zänkereien**.

Stube: see **room** 2 and 3.

Stück: **1.** see **nouns of measure** 1 (*a*) and (*b*); **genitive of material** 1, 2 (*b*), 3 (*a*) and (*b*). **2.** In early NHG a phrase like 'about ten days' was often expressed by **ein Tag oder zehn**; cf. **Hast du ein Brot oder fünf, die gib mir in die Hand** (1 Sam. 21. 3). This is now obs., but coll. dialects have preserved an analogous idiom, the noun being given the termination **-er** or **-ner**, and the word **oder** being dropped, a possible explanation of which is that **ein Tager zehn** is a corrupt form of **ein Tag**

oder zehn; cf. **In Tagner drei bis acht bin ich zurück** (H. v. Kleist). This coll. idiom, which is, of course, not used in good prose (Erich Schmidt characterizes the example from Kleist just given as **„vulgär"**), is esp. common in the case of **Stück**: e.g. **„Deshalb hast du dich mit allen geschlagen?" „Nein, nur mit ein Stücker viere"** (Storm: 'You fought with all of them for that?' 'No, only with three or four of them')—**Es mag jetzt ein Stückener acht Wochen her sein** (G. Engel)—**Es mochte ein Stückener fünfzehn Jahre her sein, daß ich das Nest nicht gesehen hatte** (Schlaf: 'It might be some fifteen years since I last saw the hamlet').

stünde: see **past subjunctive** 2 (*c*).

stürzen: **1.** With *intrans.* force, this verb is used in two senses: cf. **Er stürzte fort** ('rushed off'), **um den Arzt zu holen** and **Der Reiter stürzte** ('fell'), **als das Pferd scheute,** implying a more violent fall than **fallen** does; it follows that a proposition like **Sie stürzte die Treppe hinunter** is ambiguous. In this last example **hinunter** might be replaced by **hinab** (not **ab**); but **abstürzen** is exceptional in that, unlike **abfallen** (q.v.), it is hardly ever used with *fig.* force, so that one can say **Der Flieger stürzte ab** ('crashed') or **Der Bergsteiger ist abgestürzt** (but only **Der Steiger ist die steile Bergwand hinabgestürzt**). **2.** As a *trans.* verb, **stürzen** is used in various specific, esp. technical, senses (**ein Feld stürzen** is 'to plough *or* break up a field'), **die Kasse stürzen** is 'to empty and count the contents of the cash-box', **Nicht stürzen!** is stamped on crates containing fragile articles, much like our 'With care: this side up!'), but otherwise mainly with fig. force, as in **jemand ins Verderben stürzen** ('to ruin a person')—**die Regierung stürzen** ('to overthrow the government'). Esp. common here is the *reflex.* **sich stürzen**, which, thus differing from the *intrans.* **stürzen,** always implies a deliberate action: hence distinguish between **Er stürzte** ('fell headlong') **in den Fluß** and **Er stürzte sich** ('plunged') **in den Fluß**; sim., without the idea of downward motion, the *reflex.* verb is used with prep. phrases like **auf den Feind** ('to hurl oneself on the enemy'), **in Vergnügungen** ('to indulge in a gay round of pleasures'), **in Schulden** ('to run headlong into debt'), **ins Elend** ('to bring misery on oneself'), **ins Unglück** (to rush into trouble').

subjunctive mood: **1.** While the indic. is the mood of reality, certainty or fact, the subj. is that of unreality, possibility or doubt. That is why the subj. is used in propositions like 'He behaves as if he were mad' (which he is not: see **als = 'as if'**) and 'Be that as it may' (it may be so or it may not: see **concessive clauses**); and that is why it is used in reported speech, because the speaker is expressing another person's ideas or thoughts without necessarily agreeing with him or believing the statement. **2.** The reported speech should properly retain the tense of the direct speech. A boy might say, **Ich will es nicht wieder tun, wenn man mich diesmal nicht schlägt,** which becomes **Der Junge sagte, er wolle es nicht wieder tun, wenn man ihn diesmal nicht schlage**; but this is by no means strictly observed, indeed, in the ordinary lang. of the north the past tense forms **wollte** and **schlüge** would almost invariably be used here, the pres. subj. being usually avoided. Where there are several subord. clauses, one not infrequently finds that some of the verbs are pres. and some past, as if the choice had been a haphazard one, or a form chosen because the author thought it sounded better in that particular context. Thus, in the following proposition there are seven subord. clauses, and three of the verbs in them are pres. and four past: **Er sann über sich selbst nach und meinte, daß er für sein Alter noch nicht gefestigt genug sei, daß ihm sichere Ansichten fehlten, daß er nicht genug Selbstzucht hätte, daß er unwissend sei, keinen rechten Glauben besäße, daß er in manchen Menschen sich täusche und nie ein guter Offizier werden könnte** (Ompteda). Here *all* the verbs might just as well have been past, and *all but one* (**fehlten**) have been pres., the important point being that a pres. subj. should be avoided—and always is in the north—if it is identical in form with the pres. indic., as **fehlen** would be. **3.** For past subj. forms like **hülfe, stürbe, bewöge, höbe, begänne** or **begönne,** etc., see **Ablaut** 2; for **stünde, bestünde,** etc., see **past subjunctive** 2 (*c*).

such: see **solch**; **like** 2 (*c*) (ii).

Suche: Apart from its use as a term of the chase, as in **Der Hund hat eine gute Suche** ('ranges well', i.e. is good at locating game), the noun **Suche** is mainly confined to a few phrases like **auf der Suche nach etwas sein** and **auf die Suche nach**

etwas gehen ('to be *or* go in quest of something'). Otherwise it is not much used: cf. **Nach mühevoller Suche** (usually **Nach mühevollem Suchen**) **gelang es mir, den Onkel auszufinden** (H. Risse)—**Glauben Sie, daß die Suche nach den gestohlenen Miniaturen aufgegeben werden muß?** (G. v. d. Vring), more naturally **daß der Versuch, den . . . Miniaturen nachzuspüren, aufgegeben werden muß?** ('that the effort to trace the stolen miniatures will have to be given up?').

Sucht: 1. This fem. noun properly means 'disease', but in this sense it is now practically confined to compds. pointing to specific diseases or pathological conditions, and hence is mainly used in the *sing.* One might still say **Es gibt verschiedene „Süchte", z. B. Bleich-** ('chlorosis, green-sickness'), **Fall-** ('epilepsy'), **Gelb-** ('jaundice'), **Mond-** ('somnambulism'), **Schwind-** ('consumption') **und Wassersucht** ('dropsy'); but otherwise the plur. is rare. According to modern usage, **Sucht** means 'mania, craze, passion' (for, **nach**): e.g. **Die jungen Leute haben heutzutage eine wahre Sucht nach Vergnügungen**—**Er leidet an einer Sucht nach Geld** (= **an Geldsucht**) or **an einer Sucht, Kunstwerke zu sammeln. 2.** There are numerous other compds. in common use, such as **Eifer-** ('jealousy' with **auf** + accus.), **Hab-** ('greed') and **Selbstsucht** ('selfishness'), all used only in the sing. Here belongs also **Sehnsucht** ('yearning after' [**nach**]), also used mainly in the sing.: *Duden* characterizes the plur. forms **Sehnsüchte** and **Sehnsuchten** as **„selten"**, but the former at least seems to be gaining some ground in modern works: cf. **Wo der Rhein Sehnsüchte weckt, da bringt die Mosel Erfüllung** (Binding)—**Die ewige Stadt war seit langem eine der größten Sehnsüchte ihres Lebens** (H. Franck)—**Er hatte nach den Wochen im Krankenhaus tagelang nichts zu essen und keine anderen Sehnsüchte als seinen Hunger** (W. Schäfer).

Süd(en), südlich: see **Nord.**

suffer: see **dulden** 1 and 2; **leiden** 2.

surprise: 1. A feeling of astonishment is suggested by **Verwunderung** (see wonder), as in **Zu meiner großen Verwunderung erhielt ich heute eine Gehaltszulage** ('To my great surprise I got a rise in my salary to-day'), and 'to surprise' a person in this sense is **jemand in Verwunderung setzen.** The verb **verwundern** is used in the pred. infin. in the expression **Das ist nicht zu verwundern** ('That is not surprising'), but esp. in the past part. to indicate a state of astonishment, as in **Ich war über sein Betragen sehr verwundert**; otherwise it is mainly used *reflex.*: **Ich habe mich über Ihren Brief etwas verwundert.** On the other hand, 'I should not be surprised if he arrived to-day' is **Es sollte mich nicht wundern** (q.v.) or **wundernehmen, wenn er heute ankäme. 2.** The verb **überraschen** properly suggests a sudden, unexpected surprise (**rasch** = 'quick'), as in **Unsere Truppen überraschten den Feind,** and **jemandem eine Überraschung bereiten** is 'to prepare a surprise for somebody'; so also **Es dauerte einige Zeit, bis ich mich von meiner Überraschung erholte** ('It was some time before I recovered from my astonishment'). But **Überraschung** has a wider application than **Verwunderung**: it may be used of something concrete, as in **Ich habe dir eine kleine Überraschung mitgebracht,** referring to a small gift, where **Verwunderung** would be quite incorrect; and the pres. part. of the verb is reg. used as an adj. or adv.: e.g. **Der Vorsitzende machte einen überraschenden Vorschlag** ('The chairman made an astonishing proposal')—**Der Versuch war überraschend erfolgreich** ('The attempt was surprisingly successful'). **3.** Analogous is the verb **ertappen,** used esp. of surprising or catching a person unawares in the act of committing a theft, telling a lie, neglecting a duty, etc.: e.g. **Der Schutzmann ertappte den Dieb auf frischer Tat** ('in the very act')—**Jetzt habe ich dich auf einer Lüge ertappt**—**Der Lehrer ertappte den Schüler dabei, von seinem Nachbar abzuschreiben** ('The teacher caught the pupil copying from the next boy').

swindle: see **schwindeln** 2.

T

t (inorganic): In many German words a *t*-sound has crept in, which has little or no historical justification, the change having, no doubt, in most cases been made for the sake of euphony. Characteristic examples are seen in nouns like **Axt** (< MHG *ackes*), **Habicht** (< *habech*: see **Käfig**), **Hüfte** (< *hüffe*, plur. of *huf*), **Mond** (< *mâne*), **Obst** (< *obez*), **Palast** (< *palas*), **Papst** (< *bâbes*); in the adj. **gewohnt** (< *gewon*: see **accustom** 1); in the pron. **jemand** (< *ieman*) and the adv. **jetzt** (< *ie-zuo, ieze*); in **anderthalb** (< *anderhalp*), **allenthalben**, **meinetwegen** (< *von mînen wegen*), **ihretwillen**, etc. (see **halb** 1 and 3 (*b*)); and esp. before **-lich**, as in **eigentlich** (< *eigenlich*), **geflissentlich** (< *gevlizzenlich*: see **befleißigen**), **öffentlich** (< *offenlich*), **ordent-**, **namentlich** (q.v.), **wesent-**, **wissent-**, **wöchentlich**, etc.

Tag: see **nouns of measure** 1 (*b*); cf. **Stück** 2. For the difference between **-tägig** and **täglich**, see **-ig**.

Tal: For the plur. of this noun, cf. **Wir sagen jetzt in der Mehrheit** (usually **Mehrzahl**) **„Täler"; ehedem sagte man unendlich wohlklingender „Tale"** (Bürger). Actually, the plur. form **Tale** is still used in poetry and choice prose: e.g. **Wenn ich hier sitze, kann ich denken: in fernen Talen leben Menschen, die meine Gedanken in sich tragen** (Auerbach)—**Von der Kuppe überschaute ich Gebirg und grüne Tale** (H. Hesse). In MHG the phrase *ze tal* was used adv. with the force of 'down', not only in *den Rîn ze tal varn* ('to sail down the Rhine'), but even in *ûf eine banc ze tal gesitzen* ('to sit down on a bench') and *den schilt ze tal setzen* ('to lay down one's shield'); as used in the last two examples, this is now quite obs., but Rhine steamers still sail **zu Tal** (= **flußabwärts**) and **zu Berg** (= **flußaufwärts**).

Tanne: see **Kiefer** 2 (*b*).

taste: **1.** The *noun* 'taste' is generally rendered by **Geschmack**, suggesting either what one perceives through one's 'sense of taste' (**Geschmacksinn**), as in **Die Suppe hat einen säuerlichen Geschmack**, or a person's artistic, aesthetic taste, and the pleasurable sensation derived from what suits his taste: e.g. **Sie zeigt wenig Geschmack, sich zu kleiden—der französische Geschmack** ('French taste, fashion')—**Dafür habe ich keinen Geschmack—Der modernen Musik kann ich wenig Geschmack abgewinnen. 2.** The *verb* 'taste' is represented by two expressions which must be carefully distinguished: **(a)** The word **schmecken** is used with either trans. or intrans. force. As an *intrans.*, it can only refer to things, meaning 'to (give off a) taste, to savour [of]' (cf. our '*smack*'), or specifically 'to taste good': thus, the first example given under 1 above could be expressed by **Die Suppe schmeckt säuerlich**; sim. **Der Kognak schmeckt, wenn ich nicht irre, nach Seife** (Kästner)—**Der Wein schmeckt nach dem Pfropfen** ('The wine is corked')—**Das schmeckt!** ('That's good!')—**Das Schwarzbrot schmeckt mir nicht** ('I don't like the taste of black bread')—**Ich setzte mich zu Tisch und ließ es mir schmecken** ('I sat down to table and enjoyed a good meal'). With *trans.* force it is only used of persons, meaning 'to perceive *or* recognize by the sense of taste': e.g. **Schmeckst du Knoblauch an der Suppe?** ('Do you taste garlic in the soup?')—**Wenn ich stark erkältet bin, kann ich nichts schmecken. (b)** The verb **kosten** (for 'to cost', see **kosten**) is only used with *trans.* force in the sense of 'to try by tasting': e.g. **Koste mal!** ('Have a taste! Try this!')—**Wenn die Köchin dies gekostet hätte, so hätte sie Zwiebel daran geschmeckt**; cf., with fig. force, **Wir haben das Glück der Zufriedenheit gekostet** ('We have tasted the joys of contentment').

tatsächlich: see **really** 1.

tatter(ed): see **rag** and **ragged**.

taugen: see **past-present verbs** 3.

tauschen: see **change** 2 (*b*).

täuschen: see **deceive**.

Tausend: see **Dutzend**.

Teil: **1.** According to *Duden*, the gender of this noun is either masc. or neut., but in practice a distinction is often made between the two genders (cf. 2). Most authors seem to distinguish between **der Teil** ('the *part*') and **das Teil** ('the *share*'): cf., on the one hand, **Der erste Teil von Goethes „Faust" erschien im Jahre 1808** (one never speaks of **das Teil eines Buches**, **Dramas**, etc.), and on the other hand, **Er wollte dem kleinen David sein Teil des**

Kuchens verleiden, damit sein eigenes größer bliebe (Waggerl). So also Luther says **Maria hat das gute Teil erwählet** (Luke 10. 42), which was no doubt in the authors' minds when they wrote **Bertha du hast das bessere Teil erwählt** (Sch.) and **Die Mutter befand sich beinahe immer auf dem Felde, während die Tochter das leichtere Teil erwählte und im Haus waltete** (G. Keller); sim. **Das schwierigste Teil der Arbeit werde ich auf mir haben** (Federer). In a phrase like 'I for my part' either gender is allowed, perhaps with a preference for the *neut.*: **Ich für mein(en) Teil bin mit dem Vorschlag einverstanden**; on the other hand, the uninflected neut. is practically fixed in **ein gut Teil**, as in **Es gehört ein gut Teil Mut** ('a good deal of courage') **dazu, so etwas zu unternehmen.** **2.** With various prefixes: (**a**) *masculine*: **Anteil** ('part, interest' or esp. 'sympathy': e.g. **An dem Unternehmen hatte ich nur geringen Anteil—August hatte Anspruch auf einen mäßigen großmütterlichen Anteil, dessen Genuß jetzt an ihn fiel** (H. Hesse)—**An Ihrem Kummer nehmen wir innigen Anteil**); **Bestandteil** ('component part, ingredient'); **Erdteil** and **Weltteil** ('part of the world'); **Nachteil** ('disadvantage, detriment': e.g. **Dieser Verlust hat mir großen Nachteil gebracht**) and its opposite **Vorteil** ('advantage, profit': e.g. **Er ist auf den eigenen Vorteil bedacht**, 'He is out for his own gain, has an eye to the main chance'); (**b**) *neuter*: **Abteil** ('compartment' in a train); **Gegenteil** ('opposite, reverse'); **Urteil** (q.v.: not really a compound of **Teil**); (**c**) *with fluctuating gender*: **Altenteil** (perhaps preferably neut.: **Das Altenteil heißt, was die Eltern, wenn sie ihr Gehöft an die Kinder abtreten, sich zu Unterhalt und Wohnung vorbehalten**, i.e. what parents reserve for their keep and lodging when they make over the farm to their children: and sim. **sich aufs Altenteil setzen**, 'to retire to the old people's quarters'); **Erbteil** ('share in an inheritance') and **Pflichtteil** ('legitimate portion', what an inheritor can legally claim), both preferably *neut.*; **Hinterteil** ('back part, hinder portion', usually *masc.*, but cf. **Manchmal tauchen die Enten plötzlich unter, Kopf und Körper verschwinden und nur das Hinterteil steht auf der Oberfläche**: E. Brüning) and sim. **Ober-, Vorder-, Unterteil.** **3.** In ordinal numerals **Teil** is *masc.*, except in the contracted form **-tel** which is always *neut.*: cf. **der vierte Teil** and **das Viertel.**

teuer: This adj. is used in both senses of 'dear': cf. **Er war mir ein teurer Freund** and **Alles ist heute sehr teuer.** A noteworthy idiom is **teuer zu stehen kommen,** used with an impers. subj. and generally with *fig.* force: e.g. **Sein Betragen wird ihm teuer zu stehen kommen** ('He will pay dearly for his behaviour')—**Warte nur, das soll dir teuer zu stehen kommen!** ('Just you wait, I'll make you pay *or* smart for that!'). Here the *dat.* of the person is fixed: in the proposition **Doktor Hoffmann besitzt eine Eigenschaft, die einen Arzt teuer zu stehen kommt: er leidet alle Leiden seiner Kranken mit** (W. Kramp), the *accus.* **einen Arzt** is presumably a misprint, unless the author had the accus. construction of **kosten** (q.v.) in mind.

than: see **als** = **'than'**; **denn** 2 (*b*).

thank(s): see **Dank** and **danken.**

that (demonstrative): see **dies** 2.

the (before a compar.): In a proposition like 'The more money he has, the more he spends', the two words 'the' were orig. the locative or instrumental case of a rel. and dem. pron. respectively (= 'By how much more his money increases, by so much more is the amount he spends'). For the German way of expressing such propositions, see **je** 3.

then: **1.** This adv. is used in a variety of ways, and to render it into German one requires almost as many different expressions. It may suggest a definite, specified time, as in 'I hope to call on you at one o'clock tomorrow: will you be at home *then*?'—see 2 (*b*); it may indicate a time subsequent to some action, as in 'I must finish this letter first; *then* I can go out with you'—see 2 (*a*); it may lose its temporal force and express a condition, as in 'We might invite him, but even *then* (= even if we did) I don't think he would come'—see 2 (*a*); it may convey an inference, as in a question like '*Then* we must give up our plan?'—see 2 (*c*); and it may have limiting or contrasting force, as in 'He hasn't studied French, but *then* he doesn't need to pass an examination in that language'—see 2 (*d*). **2.** (**a**) The word **dann** (q.v. 1) never indicates a definite point of time: it either points to a time subsequent to an action (e.g. **Erst wäge, dann wage!**—lit. 'First ponder, then venture', i.e. 'Look before you leap!'), or takes on conditional force (e.g. **Einladen könnten wir ihn schon, er käme aber auch da'nn nicht**). (**b**) Where a definite point of time is referred to, **da** is generally used if the time is recent, and **damals if** it is remote; but **zu der Zeit** (with **der** accented) may be used in either case: e.g. **Wo ich um vier Uhr war? Da war ich im Garten—Als er mich neulich aufsuchte, traf er mich nicht an: ich war zu der Zeit verreist—Der Siebenjährige Krieg brach 1756 aus: damals regierte Friedrich der Große**—cf. **Der damalige Krieg legte den Grund zu Preußens Größe.** Here belong phrases like *by then, since then, till then*: e.g. **Ich wurde ihm gestern abend vorgestellt; bis dahin** ('till then') **hatte ich ihn nie gesehen—Wir sehen uns also morgen abend im Theater: bis dahin leben Sie wohl!** ('good-bye till then!')—**Kommen Sie um 7 Uhr: bis dahin** ('by then') **bin ich mit meiner Arbeit fertig—Ich begegnete ihm letzten Sonntag, habe ihn aber seitdem** (or **seither** or **seit der Zeit**) **nicht wieder gesehen.** (**c**) To express an inference, where 'then' may be replaced by an introductory 'so' ('Then we must give up our plan?' = 'So we must give up our plan?'), the Germans use **also,** or an introductory **so** with a subsequent **denn**: e.g. **Also müssen wir** (or **Wir müssen also** or **So müssen wir denn**) **unseren Plan aufgeben?** (**d**) The combination *'but then'*, with limiting or contrasting force, is best rendered by **aber . . . ja auch**: e.g. **Französisch hat er nicht studiert, aber in dieser Sprache braucht er sich ja auch nicht prüfen zu lassen.**

these, those: see **dies** 1 and 2.

till: see **bis**; **then** 2 (*b*).

tippen: see **mit** 2 (*b*).

tired: see **müde** 1 and 2; **satt**; **verdrießen.**

Ton: see **sound** 2 (*b*).

too: Our use of 'too' as a modifier of adjs. and advs. with a following infin. clause is expressed in German by **zu** followed by an infin. with **um . . . zu**, as in **Das ist zu schön, um wahr zu sein** ('That is too good to be true') and **Dieses Gedicht ist zu lang, (um) auswendig gelernt zu werden** ('This poem is too long to be learned by heart'). To use an *act.* infin. in this last example and say **Dieses Gedicht ist zu lang, (um es) auswendig zu lernen,** although to some extent sanctioned by usage, is strictly incorrect: the infin. construction should properly be confined to propositions in which the subjs. of the two clauses are *the same*, and it is more correct, and more idiomatic, to say **Dieses Gedicht ist zu lang zum Auswendiglernen**; sim. **Das Mädchen ist noch zu jung zum Heiraten.** In any case, the use of the infin. in propositions where the subjs. are *different* should only be allowed where the first subj. is an indef. neut. expression, as in **Es ist zu früh, eine Entscheidung zu treffen** ('It is too soon to decide'). For the correct rendering of other propositions with different subjs., see **als daß** 2.—For 'too' used in the sense of 'also', see **auch.**

Tor: Distinguish between **der Tor** ('fool') with gen. and plur. **Toren,** and **das Tor** ('gate, gateway') with gen. **Tor(e)s,** plur. **Tore.**

Tracht: The nouns **Tracht** and **Betracht** have different origins, the former coming from **tragen** ('to bear', then 'to wear'), the latter from **trachten** (+**nach,** 'to make something one's aim *or* object'). **1. Tracht** is *fem.* and suggests something 'carried' or 'worn': e.g., on the one hand, **Anna trat mit ihrer Tracht Wasser in die Küche** (Hebbel), i.e. with the ordinary quantity of water carried in from the pump, two pailfuls, possibly suspended from a 'yoke' (**eine Trage**)—**eine Tracht Holz** ('a load of wood')—fig. **eine Tracht Prügel** ('a sound thrashing', as much as one can bear); and on the other hand, **die schottische Nationaltracht,** i.e. the kilt (see **clothes** 4). **2. Betracht** is *masc.*: e.g. **Lamprecht ist in gewissem Betracht** ('in a certain respect') **der Treitschke der deutschen Kulturgeschichtsschreibung geworden** (H. F. Helmolt)—**Ein Dichter ist ein . . . in jedem Betracht anrüchiger Scharlatan** (A. Eloesser). Actually, it is now rather rare in such contexts (modern usage prefers **Hinsicht**), being mainly confined to a few set prep. phrases, esp. without an art., so that the gender is left open: e.g. **Diese Frage kommt hier nicht in Betracht** ('This question is irrelevant, does not arise here')—**Man muß die jetzige internationale Lage in Betracht ziehen or nicht außer Betracht lassen** ('One must take the present international situation into consideration, must not leave it out of account'). The double compd. **Anbetracht** is now only used in the phrase **in Anbetracht** (+ *gen.*), like **angesichts** (see **Sicht** 2 *b*), in the sense of 'in view of, considering': cf. **In Anbetracht seiner Jugend** (or **In Anbetracht der Tatsache, daß er noch jung ist,**) **wollen wir ihn nicht**

bestrafen. Rather less common now, although dating from the 17th century, is the use of **in Ansehung** with the same force, as in **Ihm war, als solle er in Ansehung des gütigen Schicksals, das ihn hatte gesund bleiben lassen, die Hände falten** (H. Leip).

träge: see **idle.**

trampeln: see **mit** 2 (*b*).

Trank: see **trinken** 2 (*b*).

tränken: see **fressen** 2.

trappeln: see **mit** 2 (*b*).

trauen: 1. The simple verb **trauen** means either 'to trust' or (like **sich verlassen**) 'to rely', taking a *dat.* in the former case (cf. **impersonal verbs** 3), **auf** (+ *accus.*) in the latter: e.g. **Ihm ist nicht zu trauen** ('He is untrustworthy')—**Ich traue ihm nicht über den Weg** or **um die Ecke** ('I only trust him as far as I can see him')—**Bei dieser Nachricht traute man seinen Ohren nicht** (Moltke: 'At this news the people could not believe their ears')—coll. **Ich traue dem Frieden nicht** ('The present state of affairs fills me with misgivings'); **Wohl dem, der auf den Herrn trauet** (Ps. 34. 9), with which cf. **Herr Zebaoth, wohl dem Menschen, der sich auf dich verläßt** (Ps. 84. 13)—**Geh! Traue auf Gott!** (Sch.). **2.** (**a**) As a *trans.* verb with an accus. obj., **trauen** is only used of the person who joins a couple in marriage (see **marry** 1 *c*): hence distinguish between **Ich habe ihnen getraut** ('I trusted them') and **Ich habe sie getraut** ('I married them'). (**b**) Out of the idea implied in **trauen** + dat. (see 1) there developed the sense of 'to trust in *or* rely on one's ability' to do something, hence 'to venture', and with this force **trauen** is sometimes used with **zu**+infin., as in **Die Bauern trauten nicht zu folgen** (G.); but more in accordance with modern usage here is the *reflex.* verb, esp. the compd. **sich getrauen:** e.g. **Wußte ich ihn unter den Zuhörern, getraute ich mich nicht zu sprechen** (G.); cf., with the infin. understood, **Sie wird sich nicht ins Feld** (*scil.* **zu gehen**) **getrauen** (Heyse). Actually, the orig. construction here was **sich eines Dinges getrauen**, which is still used in elevated style, as in **Rudolf meinte, er würde sich dessen nicht getrauen** (C. F. Meyer). It is easily understandable that in the phrase **sich's getrauen** the contracted gen. **'s** came to be regarded as an *accus.*, with the inevitable result that the accus. **sich** was treated as a *dat.* (cf. **remember** 3 (*d*)), which explains examples like **Tell, wenn du dir's getrautest, uns zu helfen, so möcht' ich dich der Bande entled'gen** (Sch.)—**Ich getraue mir, den Vagabunden einzufangen** (Hebel). Both the accus. and the dat. are now officially recognized, but the dat. is imperative where the gen. **es** is replaced by a specific accus. noun or pron.: one can only say **Das getraue ich mir—Getraust du dir den Versuch, den Ertrinkenden zu retten? 3.** (**a**) The compd. **vertrauen** is a stronger form of the simple verb and has the same meanings and constructions. Noteworthy here are the verbal noun **Vertrauen** (the ordinary expression for 'trust, confidence') and the past part. **vertraut** (used as an adj. with the force of 'familiar'): e.g. **Ich habe Vertrauen zu ihm—Er hat sein Vertrauen in mich gesetzt—im Vertrauen gesagt** ('in confidence, between ourselves'); **Mit diesen Dingen bin ich nicht vertraut —Diese Gegend kommt mir vertraut vor —Sie stehen auf vertrautem Fuße** ('They are on terms of intimacy')—**Er ist ein Vertrauter des Königs** ('He is an intimate friend of the king's'). For the double compd. **anvertrauen** ('to entrust'), see **anerkennen** 1 and 2. (**b**) The compd. **zutrauen** is esp. used with a dat. of the person and an accus. of the thing in the sense of 'to think a person capable of something': e.g. **Ich traue ihm jede Bosheit zu** ('I believe him capable of any wickedness')—**So etwas hätte ich ihm nicht zugetraut—Hier ist der Freund, der die hübschen Verse gemacht hat, die ihr ihm nicht zutrauen wollt** (G.). While the verb is little used for 'to trust', the verbal noun is quite common: one says **Ich habe Zutrauen zu ihm**, but not **Ich traue ihm zu.** (**c**) For **mißtrauen**, see **miß-** 2.

traulich: see **comfortable** 2.

träumen: This verb is used either pers. or impers.: e.g. **Ich träumte** (or **Mir träumte**) **vergangene Nacht, ich wäre noch ein kleines Kind.** It is not used with the accus. and infin., but this construction seems to be the only likely explanation of its use with a following pred. adj., as in **Ich träumte mich glücklich** (with **sein** understood?); and sim. with a pred. past part. (see **accusative and participle**), as in **Er träumte sich in seine Kindheit zurückversetzt—Ich träumte dich verunglückt** ('I dreamt you had met with an accident')—**Sie träumte den Geliebten in die wilde See hinaus verschlagen** (Mörike: 'In a dream she saw her lover driven out over the storm-tossed sea'). Noteworthy is the coll. idiom sich (dat.) **etwas nicht träumen lassen** (lit. 'not to let something occur to one in a dream'): e.g. **So etwas hätte ich mir nie träumen lassen!** ('I should never have dreamt of such a thing *or* never have believed such a thing possible!'); cf. **Das wäre mir nie im Traume eingefallen** ('That would never have entered my head')—**Was? Bei diesem Wetter ausgehen? Das fällt mir nicht im Traume ein!** ('What? Go out in this weather? I wouldn't dream of it!' i.e. 'No fear!').

Trauung: see **marry** 2 (*a*).

treffen: **1.** In the sense of 'to meet', properly implying a prearranged or expected meeting (see **begegnen** 1 (*a*)), this verb is derived from its basic force of 'to hit, not to miss', either *lit.* or *fig.*: e.g. **die Scheibe treffen** (cf. **ins Schwarze treffen**, 'to score a bull's-eye', *fig.* 'to hit the mark')—**den Nagel auf den Kopf treffen** (lit. and fig.)—**jemanden mit der Faust ins Gesicht, mit dem Stock auf die Schulter treffen**; *fig.* **Der Künstler hat Sie gut getroffen** ('The artist has caught your likeness')—**Er fühlte sich von meiner Bemerkung getroffen** ('He felt that my remark was aimed at *or* was a hit at him') —**Er war wie vom Blitz getroffen** ('He was thunderstruck')—**Du hast's getroffen!** ('Right! You've hit it!'). Noteworthy expressions here are **ein Abkommen mit jemand treffen** ('to come to an arrangement *or* to terms with a person'), **Anstalten treffen** ('to make preparations'), and sim. with **Maßregeln** ('to take measures *or* steps'), **Vorkehr** or **Vorkehrungen** ('to take precautions'), **seine Wahl** ('to make one's choice'), etc. Of course, **treffen** takes the aux. **haben**; but intrans. compds. like **eintreffen** ('to arrive' q.v.) and **zusammentreffen** take **sein**: cf. **Der Fabrikant pries den Zufall, mit dem Baurat zusammengetroffen zu sein** (H. Leip). **2.** Another meaning of **treffen** is 'to happen to, befall suddenly', as in **Heute traf uns ein schwerer Schlag** ('Today we received a hard blow') and **Der Schlag hat ihn eben getroffen** ('He has just had a stroke'). It is also used in ordinary lang. in the sense of 'to come upon, find' a person doing something or engaged in some occupation, and here, on the analogy of **finden**, the *accus. and infin.* construction (q.v. 1 (*a*)) is now quite common: e.g. **Er traf den Küster, die Küsterin und die Magd um den Tisch stehen** (Immermann)—**Vor dem Tor traf er ein weinendes Frauenzimmer unter einem Weidenbaum sitzen** (G. Keller)—**Einmal traf sie Helene im Garten vor einer Blume knien** (Stehr). But the accus. and part. (q.v.), esp. a *pres.* part., so common in English ('I found him sitting at the fire'), is generally avoided: cf. **Er traf den Freund noch wach am Kamine sitzend** (Mörike)—**Als sie heimkam, traf sie ihn am Tisch stehend** (Zuckmayer); a *past* part., however, is quite common, as in propositions like **Ich traf sie schon angekleidet und im Begriff, auszugehen**: cf., as an example with both part. forms, **Er traf den Freund noch wach am Kamin sitzend** (better **sitzen**): **„Recht, daß du kommst!" sagte dieser, du triffst mich mit ernsthaften Betrachtungen über dich beschäftigt** (Mörike). **3.** The reflex. **sich treffen** is used in the sense either of 'to meet one another' (recip.) or, with an impers. subj., of 'to happen *or* chance': e.g. **Mein Freund und ich trafen uns am verabredeten Ort—Es traf sich, daß wir mit demselben Zug fuhren** ('It so happened that we travelled in the same train')—**Es trifft sich gut, daß du gekommen bist** ('It is a lucky chance that you have come').

treten: Where this verb means 'to (take a) step', implying motion in a certain direction, it requires the aux. **sein**, but it takes **haben** when used with trans. force, as in **Er hat sich** (*dat.*) **die Füße wund getreten—Ich habe mir einen Dorn in den Fuß getreten** ('I have run a thorn into my foot')—**Er hat mich getreten** (either = **Er hat mir einen Fußtritt versetzt**, 'He has kicked me', or slang 'He has dunned me for repayment of the money he lent me'). It should also properly take **haben** where it means 'to tread, set one's foot' on a thing, as in **Er hat auf eine Raupe getreten** (H. Paul) and **Neugierige mochten glauben, es hätte ein kleines Hindernis im Wege gelegen, auf das wir getreten hätten** (Rilke); but this is not insisted on, **sein** being quite common: cf. **Ich bin in eine Glasscherbe getreten** (Hebel)—**Du bist mir auf mein Kleid getreten** (Fulda). Instead of the pers. dat. in the last quotation, the accus. is sometimes used, as in **Ihr habt mich auf den Fuß getreten** (Scheffel), but the dat. is much more usual: e.g. **Er trat dem Windspiel** ('greyhound') **auf die Füße**

(Gutzkow)—**Warum hast du mir auf das Hühnerauge** ('corn') **getreten?** (Klinger); so also in fig. expressions like **Man hat mir auf den Schwanz getreten** (G.: i.e. 'I have been insulted') and **Er hat der Hydra der Revolution auf den Nacken getreten** (Gutzkow: 'He has stamped on the neck of *or* crushed the hydra of revolution').

triefen: MHG *triefen* ('to drip') was always strong, but weak forms gradually crept in, and *Duden* now gives „**troff** (**jetzt auch: triefte**), **getrieft** (**selten noch: getroffen**)". Actually, the form **getroffen** fell into almost complete disuse because of possible confusion with the past part. of **treffen**—a confusion which did not exist in MHG, the past part. of *treffen* being *troffen* (without *ge-*). But the strong past tense is still quite common, although the modern tendency is towards weak forms throughout. With regard to the construction, the verb is used both of that which drips down and of that from which a thing drips, so that one says either **Der Schweiß troff ihm von der Stirn** (R. Herzog) or **Wir troffen von Schweiß** (I. Kurz); so also, in the former sense, **Das Pflaster war naß, von den Giebeln troff es** (Th. Mann), and in the latter, **Die Gräser troffen** (Stifter: '. . . were dripping wet')—**Er sah, wie die Leute vom Regen trieften** (Storm)—**Sie kam aus dem Wasser, ihr Badeanzug triefte** (E. Brüning)—**Das Boot troff von Wasser** (Kellermann)—fig. **Er triefte heute von Lebensweisheit** (M. Eyth: 'He fairly oozed worldly wisdom today'); for the fluctuation, cf. **Ich triefte von Grauen . . . Mein Körper war in Schweiß ausgebrochen, daß ich troff** (A. Schaeffer).

trinken: 1. (a) This verb is normally used of human beings and birds, the corresponding word for beasts being **saufen** (see **fressen** 2). The following are a few of the commonest coll. idioms connected with **trinken: Ehe wir nach Hause gehen, wollen wir noch eins** (or **einen**) **trinken** or **genehmigen** ('. . . we'll have one more drink')—**Er hat einen über den Durst getrunken** ('He has had a drop too much': cf. 'He has had one over the eight')—**So, Sie haben heute Geburtstag? Da müssen wir** (**auf**) **Ihre Gesundheit trinken** ('Then we must drink your health')—**Als ich auf sein Wohl getrunken hatte, trank** (or **tat**) **er mir Bescheid** ('. . . he pledged me in return')—**Er und ich haben eben Brüderschaft getrunken** (see **du** *ad fin.*)—**Abwarten und Tee trinken!** ('Keep cool and be patient!'). (b) Distinguish between **betrinken** and **ertrinken**: the former is only used *reflex.* in the sense of 'to become intoxicated', the past part. expressing a state of inebriation, while the latter is *intrans.* (aux. **sein**), meaning 'to be drowned': e.g. **Er betrinkt sich fast jeden Abend** (or **wird fast jeden Abend betrunken**)—**Auf der Überfahrt nach Amerika fiel er vom Schiff und ertrank. 2.** (a) The most comprehensive expression denoting liquids for drinking purposes, irrespective of quality or quantity, is **Getränk,** which, although really the collect. of **Trank** (see *b* below), may be used of a single beverage, as in **ein wärmendes Getränk** (which might be a cup of hot milk or a glass of toddy); cf. **geistige Getränke** ('spirituous liquors') and **alkoholfreie Getränke** ('soft drinks'). (b) **Trank** does not point to any particular kind of drink, but has the general force of what a person drinks, as contrasted with solid food: hence the ordinary combination **Speise und Trank.** More specifically, it is used of a 'draught' or 'potion' taken or administered for a special purpose: hence compds. like **Gift-, Liebes-, Zaubertrank,** etc. (cf. *c*). (c) **Trunk** (which in independent use generally implies alcoholic liquors) is either the 'habitual addiction to strong drink' (e.g. **sich dem Trunk ergeben,** 'to take to drink') or a 'draught' in the sense of the normal quantity of a liquid, as when one asks for 'a drink of water'. It follows that **Trunk** may approach **Trank** very closely: **Schlaftrunk** views the 'sleeping-draught' from the standpoint of dose or quantity, **Schlaftrank** from that of purpose or efficaciousness. In Goethe's ballad **Der Sänger** the minstrel, after draining the goblet, says **O Trank voll süßer Labe!** (referring quite generally to the refreshing power of the wine), and continues later: **Danket Gott so warm, als ich für diesen Trunk euch danke!** (suggesting rather the quantity, 'this gobletful'); so also **Es ist der zweite Tag, daß die Gefangenen nicht Speise, nicht Trank erhalten; nicht einmal einen Trunk aus Brunnen oder Graben hat man ihnen gestattet** (Freytag).

trommeln: see **mit** 2 (*b*).

Tropf(en): With the force of a 'drop' of liquid, etc., the forms **Tropf** and **Tropfe** were used in earlier periods (Heine still uses **ein Tropfe Regenwasser**), but neither of these forms is now so used, being replaced by **Tropfen** (gen. Tropfens): a proverb says **Steter Tropfen** (or **Stetes Tröpfeln**) **höhlt den Stein** ('Constant dropping wears the stone'); the plur. has no mutation of the root-vowel: **Von dieser Arznei sind zehn Tropfen zu nehmen.** But the form **Tropf** (plur. **Tröpfe**) is still fixed in the sense of 'simpleton, oaf': Goethe speaks of **ein Tropf, ein dummer, schwerfälliger Bursche** ('a stupid clodhopper'); it is used esp. in a compassionate way: **Er ist ein armer, armseliger, elender Tropf** ('a poor, miserable wretch'), **ein gutherziger Tropf** ('a goodnatured fool'). For a similar distinction between two forms of the same word, see esp. **Lump(en).**

trotz: 1. The standard MHG form of the noun **Trotz** ('defiance') was *traz* (the modern stem-vowel **o** originated in Central Germany), which was used as an exclamation, as in Nithart's *übellîchen sprach er 'traz!'* (i.e. 'Roused to anger he said, I defy *or* challenge you!'). This is supposed to be the origin of the prep. **trotz** ('in spite of'), but another possible explanation is that it is a corruption of the phrase **zum Trotz** (as in **Er tat es mir zum Trotz,** 'He did it to spite me'). Be the origin what it may, modern usage is fixed: it is a prep. which takes either a *dat.* or a *gen.*, the latter being unhistoric, an expression like **trotz seiner schneeweißen Haare** (Raabe) having probably crept in as a result of confusion between the gen. and the dat. sing. of a *fem.* noun, as in **trotz all meiner Mühe** ('in spite of all my trouble'). The dat. is firmly established in **trotzdem** (see 2) and after **trotz** used in a sense which developed later: the idea of a challenge led to its use with the force of 'in competition with', where we commonly use 'as . . . as': e.g. **Sie schaute durch die Nelkenstöcke herein, die vor dem Fenster standen, und ihr Gesicht glühte trotz den Nelken** (G. Keller: '. . . her face vied in brightness with the carnations')—**Er malte zu seinem Vergnügen in Öl und war geschickt trotz einem Künstler** (id.: 'He painted in oils for his own amusement and was as expert as any professional artist')—**Der alte Hinrich war ein Querkopf trotz seinem Jungen** ('Storm: 'Old Henry was as stubborn as his son'—cf. **quer** 1 (*b*)). **2.** The word **trotzdem** is used either as an *adv.* ('nevertheless')—cf. **doch** (adverb) 1 (*b*)—or as a *conj.* ('notwithstanding, although'): e.g. **Ich hatte gesagt, ich würde nicht mitgehen, aber ich ging trotzdem** ('but I went notwithstanding what I had said')—**Er hat allerlei Gründe angegeben, weswegen ich nicht mitgehen sollte, aber ich ging trotzalledem** ('but I went all the same'); **Ich ging mit, trotzdem** (= **obgleich, obwohl**) **ich mich etwas unwohl fühlte,** where **daß** may be inserted after **trotzdem,** as in **Unsere Stimmung blieb gedrückt, trotzdem daß wir unter uns waren** (O. Roquette: 'We remained depressed although we were alone', i.e. although no outsiders were present).

Trübsal: see **-sal,** and cf. **-selig** 2. With regard to the gender, the neut. was formerly quite common, and Luther sometimes even used it as a masc., as in **Wir wollen euch nicht verhalten unsern Trübsal, der uns in Asia widerfahren ist** (2 Cor. 1. 8); but in the modern version the *fem.* has been substituted throughout in such propositions and has, in fact, become almost the rule in modern prose: e.g. **Wenn ich denken müßte, daß ich Euch das Herz schwer gemacht hätte mit meiner Trübsal, würde ich noch elender sein** (Heyse)—**Die kleine Seejungfer in Andersens Märchen nannte er seine Schwester in der Trübsal** (Th. Mann).

trügen: see **betrügen.**

Truhe: see **box** 4.

Trümmer: 1. MHG *drum*, later *trum*, had the force of 'bit, splinter, fag-end, stump'; cf. **von trumb zu endt** (Hans Sachs), used in the sense of 'from one *end* (of the village) to the other'. **Trum** is still a technical term in mechanics ('pulley-belt') and mining—cf. **Oft lockt den Bergmann ein betrügliches Trum** ('side-seam leading to a dead end'?) **aus der wahren Richtung** (Novalis)—and **Trumm** is used as a provincialism in the orig. sense of *trum*: e.g. **Der Vater langt mit der Gabel zuerst zu, und flink hat dann jeder sein Trumm auf dem Teller** (J. A. Lux: 'Father is the first to take his fork and dive into the pot, and in no time every one has his bit of meat on his plate')—**Zwischen den Gräsern waren alte Baumtrümme** ('tree-stumps') **verwest; einer derselben war ganz ausgehöhlt, und aus dem Trumm blühte die herrlichste Blume empor** (Immermann); so also **Er ist ein Trumm von einem Kerl** (Spindler: 'He is a big strapping fellow'); cf. 'I wish that my knife had cut nothing but worsted *thrums*' (Scott's *Fair Maid of Perth,* ch. 16) and the title of Barrie's early novel 'A Window in *Thrums*', which concealed the identity of his native Kirriemuir, once famous for weaving. **2.** Trümmer ('bits, fragments, ruins') is actually the plur. of Trumm (< MHG *trümer*), but as the sing. fell into disuse, **die Trümmer** came to be regarded as a *fem. sing.*, as in **Es lag in der Nische einer Mauertrümmer** (Stifter), which led to the new plur. form **Trümmern**, as in **Wir tragen die Trümmern hinüber** (G.). Its use as a sing. noun is now rare, and better avoided (cf. **Das alte Schloß ist jetzt eine Ruine, ein Trümmerhaufen**), and the orig. plur. form is still the more usual: e.g. **Da liegen die Trümmer** (Sch.)—**Überall, wo eins der alten Trümmer aufhörte, begann ein Bretterzaun** (Gutzkow)—**Drüben sahen sie die Trümmer der alten Burg heraufragen** (Heyse)—**Hier ist Trier, die älteste Stadt Deutschlands: drei Kulturen lagern hier übereinander, alle in Trümmer** (Binding: why not **in Trümmern**? perhaps a past part. like **verfallen** is understood—unless it is a misprint); so also one usually says **Er schlug alles in Trümmer** or **zu Trümmern.** Unusual is the unhistoric plur. form with unmutated root-vowel, as when Freytag speaks of **die Trumme gesplitterter Speere.** For other sing. words which were orig. plur. forms, see **Fährte.**

Trunk: see **trinken** 2 (*c*).

Tuch: Distinguish between the two plur. forms of this neut. noun. **Tuche** is only used of different 'kinds of cloth', as in **wollene, schwere Tuche**, etc. On the other hand, **Tücher** is used of pieces of material made into special articles, in the abs. use esp. of 'neckcloths, scarves, shawls', etc., specifically in compds. like **Bettücher** ('sheets'), **Handtücher** ('towels'), **Staubtücher** ('dusters'), **Taschen-** or **Schnupftücher** ('handkerchiefs'), **Tischtücher** ('tablecloths'), **Wischtücher** ('dishcloths'), etc.

tun: **1.** Our use of the verb 'to do' with an infin. is quite established: e.g. '*Do* you *do* much reading?' 'No, I *do* not *read* much'. In German this construction is used: (i) in propositions containing **nichts als**, as in **Er tut den ganzen Tag nichts als lesen** ('He does nothing but read all day'); and (ii) as a coll. idiom, in propositions in which, for emphasis, the infin. stands *first* in its clause: e.g. **Le'sen tut er nicht viel, er ist ja fast blind—Viel tun tut sie nicht** (Sudermann: 'She doesn't do much') —**„Er sieht gut aus." „Ja, gut aussehen tut er; gut aussehen tun die meisten hier"** (Fontane); cf. **„Er spielt gut Klavier, nicht wahr?" „Ja, das tut er."** This use—which probably developed out of an introductory question: 'Read much? No, that he doesn't'—is esp. common in northern dialects, as in **Mein Herr sagte, er könnte nicht aussprechen, wie lieb er sie haben tät** (Immermann: 'My master said he couldn't find words to say how fond he was of her'); the present author once heard a farmer's wife say in LG to a maid who had said 'Yes' on being told to do something: **„Ja, ja-seggen deihst du wol, aber dau'hen deihst du et man immer nich!"** i.e. **Ja, ja-sagen tust du wohl, aber tu'n tust du es nur immer nicht!"** ('Ay, you say Yes, only you never do it!'). **2.** In many expressions **tun** is used with objs. where we use other verbs than 'to do'. The following are a few characteristic examples: **Ich bin gekommen, um Abbitte zu tun** ('I have come to ask pardon *or* forgiveness, to apologize')—**Die Gäste taten** (or **tranken**) **ihrem Gastgeber Bescheid** ('The guests pledged their host, drank his health')—**Ich habe noch ein paar Gänge zu tun** ('I have still one or two errands to go')—**Sie tat einen Kniefall** ('She went down on her knees')—**Er tat einen Satz über den Graben** ('He took a flying leap over the ditch')—**Von der Arznei tat** (or **nahm**) **ich nur einen Schluck** 'I only took a mouthful of the medicine') —**Er tat** (or **leistete**) **einen feierlichen Schwur** ('He took a solemn oath')—**Er tat einen tiefen Zug aus der Flasche** ('He took a deep draught out of the bottle')—**Das Meer hob und senkte sich, wie wenn es regelmäßige Atemzüge täte** (A. Wilbrandt: '. . . as if it took regular breaths'). To these must be added expressions in which **tun** has the force of 'to put', used with objs. to which **legen, setzen,** and **stellen** do not apply, as explained and exemplified under **put** 2; other examples are—**Meine einzige Tochter tat ich in Pension** (G.)—**Sie riet der Mutter, ihre Töchter zu der alten Kummerfelden zu tun** (Böhlau: 'She advised the mother to send her daughters to the old dame Kummerfeld') —**Er tat es in seine linke Hosentasche** (Schmidtbonn)—**Wenn Euer Sohn einige Jahre älter ist, tun** (= **schicken**) **wir ihn nach Paris** (G. Keller). **3.** With a pred. adj., **tun** conveys the sense of 'to act *or* behave' in a certain way, as in **Er tat verdrossen wie ein eigensinniges Kind** (St.

Zweig: 'He carried on like a peevish, stubborn child'); and this may lead to **tun** having much the same force as **sich stellen**, viz. 'to pretend', with a pred. adj. or a following 'as if' clause (see **stellen** 2): e.g. **Sie tut immer so schüchtern** ('She is always pretending to be so bashful')—**Wollt Ihr noch unschuldig und verwundert tun?** (Jul. Wolff: 'Are you still going to pretend to be innocent and astonished?'—**Er tat, als hätte er mich nicht verstanden**—**Tu doch nicht so!** ('Come on, don't pretend!').

turn out: for expressions like 'to turn out to be an impostor', see **prove**.

U

übel: **1.** The opposite of **gesund** is **krank**, the opposite of **wohl** is **übel**: cf. fig., **An diesen Abenden mußte auch Tony sich wohl oder übel beteiligen** (Th. Mann: 'Tony had willy-nilly to be present on these evenings'). So **übel** does not suggest a specific disease: **Mir ward übel** = **Eine Übelkeit überkam mich** ('I felt sick, squeamish'). In fact, **übel** is chiefly used *fig.* in expressions like **Er hat einen üblen Ruf** ('a bad reputation')—**Ich befinde mich in einer üblen Lage** ('in an awkward situation, in a fix')—**Der Versuch nahm ein übles Ende** or **hatte üble Folgen** ('ended in failure, disastrously')—**Der arme Kerl ist übel dran** ('in a bad way')—**Warte nur, das wird dir übel bekommen** ('Just wait, you'll pay dearly for that')—**Er hat meine Bemerkung übelgenommen** ('He has taken offence at my remark'). So also the adj.-subst.: **Hat jemand Übles von mir geredet?** ('Has any one made disparaging remarks about me?'—cf. **afterreden**). **2.** The form **Übles** should not be confused with **Übels**, which is the gen. of the neut. subst. **Übel**, sometimes used *lit.* esp. in a proposition like **Er leidet an einem unheilbaren Übel** ('He is suffering from an incurable disease'), but again generally *fig.*: e.g., in the Lord's Prayer, **Erlöse uns von dem Übel** (Matt. 6. 13) and **Das ist ein notwendiges Übel** ('a necessary evil'). In the proposition **Seid nur nicht bang, daß ich jemand** (dat.) **Übels zufüge!** (Mörike: 'Now don't be afraid that I shall do harm to any one!') the gen. construction is probably the same as in **Aufhebens machen** (see **aufheben** 2); cf. **jemandem ein Leids antun** (see **Leid**).

über: **1.** A *dat.* is used with this prep. where the context implies (**a**) a state of rest in a position lying 'over, above' something: e.g. **Das Bild hängt über dem Sofa**—**Eine dunkle Wolke stand über der Stadt**—**Gefahr schwebt über meinem Haupte**—**Er hockt immer über seinen Büchern**—fig. **Erich sitzt über mir in der Klasse**; (**b**) a state of rest at a point lying 'across, on the other side of' (a river, street, etc.), a use mainly characteristic of the coll. lang., replaced in good prose by **jenseits** (q.v.): e.g. **Wir müssen vor Sonnenuntergang über den Grenzen sein** (Sch.)—**Es kam mir in den Sinn, daß nicht weit von hier, über der Grenze, ein paar Verwandte meiner Mutter wohnten** (Mörike)—**Drüben überm Fluß** (= **am jenseitigen Ufer**) **stand das Auto** (Binding)—**Der „Goldene Drachen" ist über der Straße** (M. Eyth); it was probably because he felt the dat. to be awkward here that Goethe wrote **Der Wirt wohnte nur über die Straße**, the idea being that you had only to go across the street to get to his house; (**c**) the temporal force of 'during' (cf. **unter**): e.g. **Über dem Auspacken verging die Zeit** (G.)—**Über dem Essen** (= **Während der Mahlzeit**) **kamen Dinge zur Sprache, die mir gleichgültig waren** (Mörike)—**Über diesem Geschäft wurde ich überrascht** (G. Keller); sim. **Über dem Lärm erwachte der Alte** (G.)—**Über der angestrengten Beschäftigung kommen die Mädchen nicht dazu, aufzusehen** (Rilke)—**Über der Krankheit des Kindes hatte ich das Ferienmachen ganz vergessen** (H. Hesse)—**Er vergaß alles über dem Anblick einer in die Straße einbiegenden Gestalt** (Binding), although in the last three examples, where the prep. has causal force, the accus. would seem more appropriate (see 2 *e*). **2.** In all other contexts **über** takes an *accus.* and this case may imply (**a**) motion towards a point lying 'above' something, or motion extending 'over' a specified surface or 'beyond' a certain limit: e.g. **Das Flugzeug stieg über**

die Wolken—Die Flut ergoß sich über das flache Land—Der Vogel flog über unseren Garten (i.e. passed over our garden; but flog eine Weile über unserem Garten herum)—Der Wind wehte über die Heide (but cf. Frenssen's Ein kalter Wind kam überm Wald her, 'A cold wind blew *from beyond* the wood'); fig. Das geht über meine Kräfte—Er ist über die Kinderjahre hinaus; (b) mental activity covering some subject: e.g. Der Redner verbreitete sich über ('enlarged on') dieses Thema—Ein neues Buch über die Romantische Schule ist erschienen—Über seinen Vorschlag habe ich ernstlich nachgedacht; unusual are examples like Über dieser (for diese) Frage disputierte ich oft mit ihm (Heine)—Er dachte an die Säcke mit Weizen und sann über dem Preise (for den Preis), den er zu bieten beabsichtigte (Th. Mann), and Beständig brütet C. F. Meyer über den Rätseln des Lebens (H. Hart); (c) excess in number, weight, time, etc.: e.g. Es waren über ('more than') zwanzig Männer in dem Zimmer—Das Paket wiegt über ein Pfund—Er wohnt schon über zwei Jahre hier (but Er wohnt schon seit über zwei Jahren hier)—Er blieb über Nacht (but usually den Tag über and die ganze Zeit über) bei mir—Wir wollen heute übers Jahr ('this day next year') wieder zusammenkommen—Ich habe es ihm einmal über das andere ('time and again') gesagt; (d) power, authority or supervision over somebody: e.g. Wir siegten über den Feind—Cäsar herrschte über die Römer—Er hat die Aufsicht über die Gefangenen übernommen; (e) cause: e.g. Über das schöne Wetter haben wir vergessen, daß wir im November leben (G.)—Ich erstaunte über diese Nachricht—Rege dich doch über so eine Kleinigkeit nicht auf! (f) in exclamations: e.g. O über die leichtsinnigen Männer! (G.: 'Oh, how credulous men are!')—Ach, über die jungen Leute heutzutage! ('Oh, young people nowadays!').

über- : **1.** Like **durch-**, **um-**, **unter-**, etc., this verbal prefix is either *sep.* (accented) or *insep.* (unaccented). It would go beyond the scope of the present volume to discuss every verb compounded with **über-**: only the commonest ones and those requiring special care are treated under their various heads. Broadly speaking, it can be said that a verb has *lit.* force when the prefix is sep., *fig.* force when it is insep. Actually, in the case of über- examples of the former are comparatively rare, the *lit.* sense of motion 'across' nearly always requiring the use of the lengthened prefixes **herüber-** or **hinüber-**: one says Er ging zur Hauptpost hinüber (not über), and a proposition like the following, in which ü'bergehen is used *fig.* although the prefix is sep., is exceptional: Ihr überrei'zter Zustand schien in Wahnsinn ü'bergehen zu wollen (E. T. A. Hoffmann: 'Her distraught condition seemed to be going to develop into insanity': see übergehen 1). **2.** The following are some typical examples of verbs implying motion which are only or generally used *fig.*, and which are not specially discussed in the present volume: Er eilte zu mir herüber, um mir die Nachricht zu überbri'ngen ('He hurried across in order to pass on the news to me'), but Sie brauchen sich nicht zu überei'len ('You don't need to be in such a hurry')—Als der Fährmann mich am anderen Ufer sah, holte er mich herüber, but Der Knabe strengte sich an, seine Mitschüler zu überho'len ('The boy strove to outstrip his classmates')—Ich nahm das Paket zur Post hinüber, but Er trug Bedenken, die Verantwortung zu überneh'men ('He hesitated to take on the responsibility') and Es hieß, daß er sich überno'mmen habe (Th. Mann: 'that he had overexerted himself')—Er schritt zu mir herüber, but Es ist verboten, die Schwelle zu überschrei'ten ('It is forbidden to cross the threshold') and Er überschri'tt die Schranken des Zeremoniells (E. T. A. Hoffmann: 'He overstepped the bounds of ceremonious etiquette')—Ich sah zum jenseitigen Ufer hinüber, but Wenn man viele schriftliche Arbeiten du'rchsehen muß, ist es leicht, Fehler zu überse'hen ('When one has a lot of written work to read through, it is easy to overlook mistakes')—Er stürzte zur Polizei hinüber, but Das Auto lief Gefahr, sich zu überstü'rzen ('The car was in danger of overturning')—Die Kirchenglocke tönte zu uns herüber, but Er hob die Stimme gellend, um den knatternden Motor zu übertö'nen (H. Leip: 'He raised his voice to a shout in order to drown the rattle of the engine')—Der Schäfer trieb seine Schafe auf die Wiese hinüber, but Sie neigt dazu, ihre Sorgen zu übertrei'ben ('She is inclined to exaggerate her troubles')—Das Mädchen warf den Ball zu ihrer Freundin hinüber, but Er scheint entschlossen, sich

mit seinen Freunden überwe'rfen zu wollen ('He seems determined to fall out with his friends')—**Die Familie zog in die angrenzende Wohnung hinüber**, but **Wir haben uns entschlossen, den Lehnstuhl neu zu überzie'hen** ('We have decided to make a new cover for the armchair') and **Die Möbel waren mit geblümtem Kattun überzo'gen** (Th. Mann).

überall: The ordinary sense of this adv. is 'everywhere', but just as **jeder** may idiomatically express 'any', so **überall** may express 'anywhere': see **jeder** 2 (*b*).

überanstrengen: The simple verb **strengen** is now obs., but **anstrengen** and **überanstrengen** are in common use. In both cases the accent falls on **an**, which is always *sep.* in **anstrengen:** e.g. **Strenge dich doch an!**—**Obwohl er sich bisher nicht sehr angestrengt hat, scheint er sich jetzt mehr anzustrengen.** In **überanstrengen**, on the other hand, *both* prefixes are far more commonly treated as *insep.*: e.g. **Du überanstrengst dich doch nicht?** (Ompteda), where no one would ever say **Du strengst dich doch nicht überan?**—**Er überanstrengte sich** (Rilke). Occasional examples of separation do occur in the infin. and past part., as in **Zum Baumeister soll man einen Mann wählen, der die Handwerker abhalten kann, sich überanzustrengen** (Frenssen) and **Ich war immer ein überangestrengter Mann** (Fulda), but modern usage very definitely favours non-separation here also: e.g. **Sie geriet in Furcht, sich zu überanstrengen** (Werfel)—**Du hast dich überanstrengt** (Blunck)—**Das Gesicht sah überanstrengt aus** (A. Zweig)—**Beim Examen hatte er sich überanstrengt** (A. Eloesser)—**Die überanstrengten Kräfte der Truppen begannen nachzulassen** (J. Thorwald)—**Das Mädchen war durch die Krankenpflege überanstrengt** (K. Edschmid)—**Er fühlte, daß sein überanstrengter Geist die Fähigkeit nicht hatte, seine Erlebnisse zu bewältigen** (W. v. Scholz).

überantworten: This verb has the trans. force of 'to hand over, deliver' (= **übergeben**), **über-** being always unaccented and *insep.*: e.g. **Es versteht sich, daß ich die Handschrift nicht dem Drucker zu übera'ntworten gedenke** (Th. Mann: 'I need not say that I do not intend to place the MS. in the hands of the printer'); it is a favourite word of Luther's, as in **Christus ward den Hohenpriestern übera'ntwortet, daß sie ihn kreuzigten**, and **Man übera'ntwortete den Verbrecher dem Gericht** is still the reg. expression for 'delivering a criminal to justice'.

überarbeiten: Used with the intrans. force of 'to work extra *or* overtime', this verb has the main stress on the prefix, which is then *sep.*: e.g. **Ich habe zwei Stunden ü'bergearbeitet**—**Ich war genötigt, diese Woche mehrere Stunden ü'berzuarbeiten.** But more common is the trans. force of 'to overwork' (a person or oneself), 'to overtax' (one's strength, nerves, etc.) or 'to revise' (a work, manuscript, etc.), and here the prefix is unaccented and *insep.*: e.g. **Er sieht übera'rbeitet aus**—**Ehe ich meine Flugschrift** ('pamphlet') **drucken lasse, wird es ratsam sein, sie nochmal gründlich zu übera'rbeiten.**

überbringen: see **über-** 2.

überdies: This adv., meaning lit. 'beyond this', is now only used in the sense of 'moreover, in addition' (= **noch dazu** or **obendrein**, q.v.), as in **Er hatte eine geschwollene Oberlippe, welche noch überdies aus ihrer Richtung gewichen war** (Sch.). An alternative form, which is confined to the south and should *not* be used, is seen in **Prinz Eugen war ein Fürstensohn und hatte über diesem eine fürstliche Seele** (Hofmannsthal).

überdrüssig: see **müde** 2.

übereilen: see **über-** 2.

übereinkommen, übereinstimmen: see agree 4 (*a*).

überessen: This verb means 'to eat too much'. **1.** The proposition 'My doctor has warned me against overeating' is **Mein Arzt hat mich davor gewarnt, mich zu übere'ssen:** in other words, when used in this sense, the verb is always *reflex.*, the prefix *insep.* and unaccented, as in **Kinder, übere'ßt euch nicht!** and in a compd. tense, **Der Arzt meinte, ich hätte mich wohl überge'ssen.** If the food of which too much has been taken is referred to, it is expressed by **an** + *dat.*: e.g. **Ich fürchte, ich habe mich an Kartoffeln überge'ssen**—**Junge, überi'ß dich nicht an Süßigkeiten!**—*fig.* **Ich kann das Predigen nicht vertragen: ich glaube, ich habe in meiner Jugend mich daran überge'ssen** (G.: '. . . I can't stand preaching, I think I had a surfeit of it in my youth'). **2.** When the prefix is *sep.* and accented, the dir. obj. of the verb is the food taken, and a dat. reflex. pron. is added, the meaning being 'to eat so much of a dish that one hates the sight of it': e.g. „Darf ich Ihnen einige Erdbeeren anbieten?" „Danke sehr ('No, thank you'), ich habe mir Erdbeeren ü'bergegessen!"—Wenn die Erdbeeren reif sind, laufe ich immer Gefahr, sie mir ü'berzuessen! 3. Strangely enough, **übertrinken** is much less common, but when used it is treated exactly like **überessen.** The following example seems significant: **An der fürstlichen Speise überi'ßt man sich, und den süßen Wein trinkt man sich** (dat.) **zuwider** (Bodenstedt: '. . . of the sweet wine one drinks so much that one loathes the taste of it': see **zuwider**).

überfahren: This verb is now little used with a *sep.* accented prefix, except in the coll. idiom **Er ist übergefahren** or more commonly **übergeschnappt** ('He has a slate loose *or* a bee in his bonnet'). 'To convey a person across' in a car, boat, etc., is now **jemand hinüberfahren** (see **her-, hin-** 3, and cf. **überfliegen, -führen,** etc.). With an *insep.* unaccented prefix, it is used in several ways: e.g. **Das kleine Schiff hat den Ozean glücklich überfahren** ('crossed')—**Der Lokomotivführer überfuhr ein Signal** ('overran a signal')—**Man kann kaum die Fassade der Kathedrale von Paris betrachten ohne Gefahr, überfahren zu werden** (Rilke: 'of being run down *or* over')—**Der Bauer überfährt den Acker mit Mist** ('is manuring his field'); impers., **Es überfuhr** (or **überlief**) **mich kalt** ('A shiver ran through me, My blood ran cold'). In „**Dummes Zeug! Wer ist denn der Mann, der solche Geschichten erzählt?" überfu'hr sie ihn mit einer Schärfe, die nicht zu überhö'ren** (q.v. 2) **war** (K. Edschmid), does it mean 'she stormed *or* raged at him'?—if so, **fuhr sie ihn . . . an** would be much more usual.

Überfall, überfallen: see **attack** 4.

überfliegen: This verb is no longer used with *sep.* prefix. To express a proposition like 'She flew (= rushed) across the street', one uses the simple verb: **Sie flog** (or **stürzte**) **über die Straße,** and where there is no prep. phrase, as in 'She saw her friend on the other side of the street and flew across', one says **Sie . . . flog hinüber** (see **her-, hin-** 3). On the other hand, **überflie'gen** (with *insep.* prefix) is a common expression and has a number of meanings: e.g. **Er war der erste, der den Atlantischen Ozean überflog** ('He was the first to fly the Atlantic')—**Der Flieger hat das Ziel überflogen** ('overshot his mark'); fig. **Er öffnete den Brief und überflog ihn** (Fontane: 'glanced through *or* ran his eye over it')—**Ein Lächeln überflog ihre marmorkalten Züge** (Häusser: 'A smile passed over her stone-cold features', they relaxed into a smile).

überführen: Much the same applies to this verb as to **überfahren** and **überfliegen** (qq.v.). One says **Der Blinde wollte die Straße überque'ren** (or **überkreu'zen**), **also führte ich ihn hinüber;** so also, in **Ein Fahrzeug lag bereit, sie nach Salerno überzuführen** (Wieland), one would now use **hinüberzuführen.** With *insep.* prefix it is used in several ways: e.g. **Der Sarg wurde feierlich zum Kirchhof überführt** ('conveyed')—**An dieser Stelle beabsichtigt man, die Autobahn über die Eisenbahn zu überführen** ('At this point the intention is to make the motor-road overpass the railway')—**Ein solcher schnell entstehender Strom überführt** ('covers') **Felder und Wiesen mit Steinen und Kies** (G.)—**Der Markt ist überführt worden** ('has been overstocked, glutted'); *fig.* **Ich habe ihn von der Notwendigkeit überführt** (= **überzeugt,** 'convinced'), **eine Entscheidung zu treffen;** with a *gen.*, **Pheidias wurde des Diebstahls überführt** ('convicted of theft') **und in das Athener Gefängnis gesteckt** (Th. Mann).

übergehen: 1. with *sep.* prefix: As in the case of other common verbs of motion (see **her-, hin-** 2 and 3; **eingehen,** etc.), so here also the simple prefix gives *fig.* force to **gehen,** the *lit.* idea of 'to go across' (e.g. to the other side of the street) properly requiring a double prefix: cf., on the one hand, **Er ging zum anderen** (or **auf das andere**) **Ufer hinüber,** and on the other hand, **Er ging zur Gegenpartei über** ('He went over to the opposition, crossed the floor of the House'). Other examples of the fig. use of this verb are: **Gehen wir zur Tagesordnung über!** ('Let us proceed to the order of the day!')—**Sie ging von dem besonderen Falle zum allgemeinen über** (Th. Mann: 'She passed from the particular to the general'; cf. **über-** 1)—**Das Geschäft ist in andere Hände übergegangen** ('The business has changed hands')—**Gelb, Grün, Rot und Violett gingen ineinander über** (H. Grimm: '. . . merged into each other')—**Beim Waschen sind die Farben ineinander übergegangen** ('The colours have run in the wash')—**Der zweite Satz des Quartetts geht in D-dur über** ('The second movement . . . goes into D major')—**Die Augen gingen ihr über** (poet., 'Her eyes filled with tears'). **2.** with *insep.* prefix: Although always trans. (aux. **haben**), this cannot be used in the *lit.* sense of 'to cross' (a threshold, frontier, etc.), which is suggested by **überschrei'ten,** but always has *fig.* force, esp. that of 'to pass over (without mention)', as in **Man einigte sich, diesen Vorfall mit Stillschweigen zu überge'hen** ('It was agreed to pass over this incident in silence') or **Bei der Beförderung war er der einzige, der überga'ngen wurde** ('His name was the only one to be omitted on the promotion list'); cf. miss 3. It is no longer used, as it once was, in the sense of 'to surpass' (**übertre'ffen**) or 'to transgress' (**übertre'ten**).

überhängen: For the mutated **a**, see **hängen. 1.** With *sep.* prefix: (**a**) *intrans.*, always with *strong* forms, 'to hang over, hang suspended, project': e.g. **Einige Felsstücke sind heruntergestürzt, andere hängen noch ü'ber** (G.)—**Der Apfelbaum im Garten nebenan stand so nahe an der Mauer, daß viele Äpfel auf unserer Seite ü'berhingen:** (**b**) *trans.*, past tense **hängte** (or **hing**) **ü'ber**, past part. **ü'bergehängt:** 'to hang (something) over (an object)': e.g. **Damit die neuen Möbel nicht schmutzig werden, haben wir Laken ü'bergehängt—Es regnet: hänge dir den Regenmantel ü'ber! 2.** With *insep.* prefix, always *trans.*: (**a**) used like **be-, verhängen** (qq.v.), 'to cover, drape', with past tense **überhä'ngte** (less commonly **überhi'ng**), past part. **überhä'ngt** (implying an action) or **überha'ngen** (implying a state or condition): e.g. **Er überhä'ngte den Altar mit Flor—Man hat den Altar mit Flor überhä'ngt—Die Rosse waren mit Waldrappen** ('saddle-cloths') **überha'ngen** (G.); (**b**) always with *strong* forms: 'to project beyond, overhang, overshadow': e.g. **Das Zelt überhi'ng die ganze Ausdehnung des Teppichs** (Chamisso: i.e. the tent more than covered the whole carpet, extended beyond it on all sides)—**Wenn wir das Zelt aufgeschlagen hätten, so hätte es die ganze Rasenfläche überha'ngen—Den Mund überhi'ng leicht ein blonder Schnurrbart** (Th. Mann); cf. **Die Felswand hing so weit ü'ber** (according to 1 *a*), **daß sie den Strand zum Teil überhi'ng** ('The cliff jutted out so far that it partially overhung the beach').

überhaupt: 1. This expression—which always has a strong accent on the *last* syllable—seems originally to have been used in connexion with the buying and selling of cattle, when a herd was sold *collectively*, irrespective of the value of particular 'heads' of cattle. It is now used to express a statement *in quite general terms, without reference to any specific case or to particular circumstances.* The following are some characteristic examples: **Nächst Hamburg war Leipzig zur bedeutendsten Handelsstadt des Deutschen Reichs, ja zu einem der wichtigsten Handelsplätze der Welt überhaupt geworden** (i.e. the *whole* world, not this or that part of it)—**Hoffentlich gibt es bald besseres Wetter, nicht nur, weil ich Ende dieser Woche in die Ferien gehe, sondern überhaupt** (i.e. not only because I want good weather for my holidays, but for the general good)—**Als er sagte, dies sei das erste Mal, daß er London besuche, glaubte ich, er meine das erste Mal in diesem Jahre, aber er sagte: nein, überhaupt** (i.e. it was his very first visit, not his first visit this year or any other year)—**„Kommt Vater bald wieder?" fragte Asmus. „Ich weiß es nicht", sagte die Mutter. „Kommt er überhaupt wieder?"** ('O. Ernst: 'Will he be coming back at all?'—as distinct from **bald** or **nach längerer Zeit**); so too, at the end of an argument, one speaker might say **Überhaupt, was nützt das viele Reden?** (i.e. Anyway, apart from this or that argument, we'll never agree, so what's the use of all this talking?). **2.** It is especially common *in negative or potentially negative propositions*: e.g. **Auf meine Frage, was für Romane er gern lese, antwortete er, Romane lese er überhaupt nicht** (i.e. he did not read *any* novels, as distinct from any special kind of novel)—**Dieser Schüler macht keine groben Fehler, ja er macht überhaupt keine** (i.e. no mistakes at all, neither bad nor slight ones)—**Er meinte, sie hätte das im Beisein ihrer Schwester vielleicht nicht sagen sollen; sie hätte es aber überhaupt nicht sagen sollen** (i.e. she should not have said it in any case, whether her sister was present or not)—**Vor Ende der Woche wird er nicht kommen, wenn er überhaupt kommt** ('if he comes at all', implying that he may *not* come, either this or any other week)—**Die Kinder des Arztes gingen nicht in unsere Schule: sie gingen überhaupt in keine Schule, denn es hieß, daß der Arzt unsere Schule, überhaupt alle Schulen für**

erbärmlich halte (Ponten). It will be observed that such negative propositions can often be rendered by 'not at all', but that is not to say that **überhaupt nicht** and **gar nicht** are exactly synonymous. In an example like **Dumm ist dieser Schüler gar nicht, er ist nur faul,** the reference is clearly to a *particular* case, to a pupil who was *by no means* stupid; **Dumm ist dieser Schüler überhaupt nicht** would imply a previous statement that the pupil had shown himself stupid in some way or other, an assertion then denied by the statement that he was not stupid *at all*, in *any* way. The same applies to 'Not at all!' as a reply to a question like 'Are you suggesting that he is stupid?' where **Überhaupt nicht!** would be quite impossible, and where even **Gar nicht!** although not incorrect, would generally be replaced by a stronger expression like **Durchaus nicht!** or **Keineswegs!** or more coll. by **Bewahre!** (for **Gott bewahre mich davor!**) or **I wo!** (for which see **wo** 1: lit. 'Heavens, whither are your thoughts tending?' i.e. 'Good gracious, how can you think of such a thing?').

überholen: see **über-** 2.

überhören: 1. This verb never has the force of English 'to overhear' what is not intended for one's ear. The correct rendering of this idea depends on whether one merely happens to hear what is said, or hears it by eaves-dropping: in the former case, **zufällig hören** is used, in the latter **belauschen** or **erlauschen,** according as the obj. is the person speaking or the words spoken, while **ablauschen** is used with a dat. of the person and an accus. of the thing (see **lauschen**): e.g. **Ich ging eben an ihnen vorbei und hörte zufällig, was er ihr zuflüsterte—Wer sollte so vermessen sein, Karlos zu belauschen, wenn er sich unbelauscht glaubt?** (Sch.)—**Da du mich belauscht hast, ist es nicht länger zu verheimlichen** (G.)—**Ich schlich näher und erlauschte ihr Geheimnis** (or **lauschte ihnen ihr Geheimnis ab**). **2.** As contrasted with our 'to overhear', **überhö'ren** (*insep.*) has two meanings, viz. either 'to hear' the lessons a pupil has learned (rather more commonly expressed by **abhören**) or 'not to hear, not to catch' what a person says (cf. **miss** 3): e.g., on the one hand, **Der Lehrer fing damit an, uns** (accus.) **die Vokabeln zu überhören:** see **accus. (double)** 1 (*c*)—**Der Lehrer hat uns** (dat.) **das Gedicht, das er uns zum Auswendiglernen aufgab, nicht abgehört;** and, on the other hand, **„Ist der Priester oben?" Sie schien die Frage überhört zu haben** (Heyse)—**Er lag im tiefen Schlaf und überhörte es auch, daß der Hund bellte** (id.)—**Seine kleinen Augen sehen alles, seine spitz nach oben zulaufenden Ohren überhören nichts** ('. . . hear everything, miss nothing').

überklettern: see **climb** 2 (*b*).

überkommen: In this verb, as in most other verbs of motion (cf. **her-, hin-** 3), **über-** is now little used as a *sep.* prefix: in the proposition **Auf dem Schiff kam ich glücklich nach Amsterdam über** (Grimmelshausen), one would now prefer **hinüber;** sim. **Komm' herüber!** (coll. **Komm' 'rüber!**)—**Es war ein so starker Verkehr auf der Straße, daß es schwer war, hinüberzukommen** ('to get across'). With **über-** *insep.*, the verb formerly could have the force of 'to overcome, gain the mastery over', as in **Ich befürchte, daß Attila uns überkommen wird** (Freytag), but this has fallen into disuse. According to modern practice, it is used in three ways: (**i**) *intrans.* (aux. **sein**), with the force of 'to come *or* be handed down': e.g. **In den Schriftwerken der Alten ist uns** (dat.) **keine genaue Kunde überko'mmen** (H. Hettner: better **überlie'fert**); (**ii**) *trans.*, with a *pers.* subj., much like **bekommen** ('to obtain'), but used esp. of things inherited or handed down: e.g. **Wenn man mit Schopenhauer meint, daß die Söhne den Charakter von dem Vater erben, so hatte Lenau die Neigung zu einem wüsten Leben schon bei der Geburt überko'mmen** (R. v. Gottschall: i.e. that the tendency to lead a dissolute life had been bequeathed to him by his father)—so also **überko'mmene Sitten** ('old customs' inherited from one's forefathers); (**iii**) With an *impers.* subj., used of feelings, etc., which 'come over' one (cf. **überfahren** and esp. **überlaufen** 2): e.g. **Ein freudiges Wohlgefühl überka'm mich** (Auerbach); here the aux. is normally **haben,** as in **Eine erste Ahnung der Vielfältigkeit des Lebens hatte ihn überko'mmen** (St. Zweig), but **sein** has crept in in modern times: cf. **Sie stand noch immer unbeweglich: sie wußte nicht, was sie überko'mmen war** (Storm)—**Er hätte noch länger gesprochen, wenn ihn nicht ein Husten überko'mmen wäre** (Gutzkow: 'if a fit of coughing had not seized him').

überlassen: see **leave (verb)** 4.

überlaufen: This verb is somewhat exceptional in that it is in common use with both sep. and insep. prefix. **1.** With **über-** *sep.* and *accented*, it is not used of a person 'running across' to the other side of a street, an idea which requires the use of **herüber-** or **hinüber-laufen** (see **her-**, **hin-** 3). Its correct uses are seen in the following examples: **Fülle den Eimer nicht zu voll, sonst läuft das Wasser über** ('Don't fill the pail too full or the water will run over'), and by metonymy, **Wenn du den Hahn nicht abdrehst, wird der Eimer überlaufen** ('If you don't turn the tap off, the pail will run over')—**Die Suppe ist übergelaufen** ('The soup has boiled over')—*fig.* **Die Galle lief mir über** ('My blood was up, I gave vent to my anger')—**Die zwei Farben sind ineinander übergelaufen** ('The two colours have run together')—**Er hat gedroht, zur Gegenpartei überzulaufen** or **überzugehen** ('He has threatened to go over to the Opposition *or* to cross the floor of the House'). **2.** With **über-** *insep.* and *unaccented*, it has several shades of meaning: e.g. **Im Sommer ist dieser Badeort überlaufen** ('In summer this watering-place is overrun')—**Ich bin in letzter Zeit von Bettlern geradezu überlaufen worden** ('I have been positively pestered with beggars of late')—**Dieses Pferd hat alle die anderen überlaufen** ('This horse has outrun *or* beaten all the others')—**Er überlief den Brief** ('He glanced through the letter': cf. **überfliegen**); with *impers.* subj., used of feelings (cf. **überfahren**): **Es überlief ihn kalt** ('A cold shudder ran through him')—**Sie warf mir einen Blick zu, der mich kalt überlief** (A. Wilbrandt: '. . . which sent cold shivers down my spine')—**Den Onkel Peter überlief eine Gänsehaut** (E. Kästner: cf. O. W. Holmes' 'A goose-flesh shiver ran over my skin').

übernehmen: see **über-** 2.

überqueren: see **quer** 1 (*a*).

überraschen, Überraschung: see **surprise** 2.

überschreiten: see **über-** 2.

übersehen: see **über-** 2.

übersetzen: **1.** With **über-** *sep.* and *accented*, this verb is used *intrans.* to suggest the idea of getting over or across some obstacle. The simple verb is used in this sense with **über** + accus. (aux. **haben**), the compd. when the obstacle has been previously referred to or is assumed: cf. **Ich setzte über den Graben** ('I jumped across the ditch') and **Ich kam an einen Graben und setzte ü'ber**; sim. **Das Pferd setzte über alle die Hürden** ('The horse cleared all the hurdles') and **Als das Pferd an die erste Hürde kam, weigerte es sich, ü'berzusetzen.** The commonest obstacle is a river or lake: e.g. **Wir zogen auf dem linken Ufer der Maas aufwärts, um an die Stelle zu gelangen, wo wir ü'bersetzen sollten. . . . Wir hatten über die Maas gesetzt** (G.). But the compd. can also be used with the *trans.* force of 'to take *or* ferry a person across', so that the first sentence in the last example might have ended with **wo man uns ü'bersetzen sollte**; sim. **„Um Gottes willen, Fährmann, Euren Kahn! . . . Setzt mich ü'ber!"** (Sch., the reference being to the Lake of Lucerne). **2.** With **über-** *insep.* and *unaccented*, it is now mainly used in one sense, like **übertra'gen**, viz. 'to translate', esp. into another language: **Überse'tzen Sie diesen Satz ins Deutsche!—Dieser Satz ist ins Französische zu überse'tzen.** At a first glance one might be inclined to think that there was a bad grammatical mistake in the proposition **Wir haben Homer vortrefflich im Deutschen übersetzt** (Börne), yet it is actually quite correct, although not very well expressed: **haben** here is not an aux., the meaning being 'We possess excellent translations of Homer in German' (**Wir haben im Deutschen vortreffliche Übersetzungen des Homer**).

übersiedeln: **1.** The prefix of this verb is *insep.* when the verb has *trans.* force, meaning either (**a**) 'to transfer to new quarters': e.g. **Es war nicht auszudenken, wie man den Kranken übersie'deln sollte** (Kafka)—cf., as contrary to accepted usage, **Dorthin hatte er alle seine Pflanzen ü'bergesiedelt** (Stifter: for **übersie'-delt**); strangely enough, the reflex. **sich übersie'deln**, as in **Ich übersie'delte mich** ('I removed') **in meine neue Wohnstätte** (id.) is rare, the intrans. being much more usual in this sense (see 2); or (**b**) 'to colonize, overspread' a country, an idea more usually expressed by **besiedeln**; cf., with *sep.* prefix, **sich irgendwo ansiedeln** ('to settle down somewhere'), as in **Sie siedelten sich bei Hall in Tirol an** (Edschmid). **2.** Where the verb has *intrans.* force ('to remove to new quarters'), there is considerable fluctuation (see **umsiedeln**). Here *Duden* gives the prefix as *sep.*, and the following examples bear this out: **Bald darauf siedelten Lenaus**

Eltern nach Csatád ü'ber (M. Koch)—**Ich verkaufe meine Güter und siedele in die Marken ü'ber** (E. Wichert)—**Er ermunterte sie, dorthin ü'berzusiedeln, wo sie Familienanhang hatte** (Ric. Huch)—**Haben Sie Lust, zu uns ü'berzusiedeln?** (Th. Mann)—**Er war in eine Privatwohnung ü'bergesiedelt** (M. Eyth)—**Der Herzog ist vor zwei Stunden nach Hoym ü'bergesiedelt** (W. v. Kügelgen)—**Ihre Mutter war vor einem Jahr zu ihr ü'bergesiedelt** (W. Kramp). But *Sprach-Brockhaus* allows both sep. and insep. forms here, and the following examples of the insep. intrans. use might be multiplied almost indefinitely, so that it seems very strange that *Duden* should not allow it: **Mein Vater übersie'delte nach Wien** (Stifter)—**Kurzum, er übersie'delte nach England** (Fontane)—**Um diese Zeit übersie'delte sie zu ihren Freunden** (Ebner-Eschenbach)—**Er nahm Hab und Gut und übersie'delte nach der Insel** (E. Brüning)—**Mörike entschloß sich, nach Lorch zu übersie'deln** (E. v. Sallwürk)—**Die Marchese erklärte, übermorgen nach Rom zu übersie'deln** (Zobeltitz)—**Sie ist mit den Kindern hierher übersie'delt** (Schnitzler)—**Als mein Bruder nach den Vereinigten Staaten übersie'delt war, erklärte er: „Wo ich bin, ist die deutsche Kultur"** (H. Mann)—**Es war der vor kurzem nach Neustadt übersie'delte Barbier** (P. Keller). For the fluctuation, cf. **An dem Tage übersie'delte Beate in das kleine Zimmer neben Frau Lotten . . . Sobald es anging, siedelte sie in das obere Stockwerk ü'ber** (Zifferer).

überspringen: see miss 3 and pass 2; cf. **Er kommt die Treppen herauf, indem er immer zwei Stufen überspri'ngt** (Th. Mann: i.e. three steps at a time).

übersteigen: see climb 2 (*b*).

überstürzen: see über- 2.

übertönen: see über- 2.

übertragen: This is not used in the lit. sense of 'to carry (something) across (a street, field, etc.), which requires **herüber-** or **hinübertragen**: e.g. **Ich saß im Auto, der Kaufmann trug das Paket zu mir herüber**—**Gestatten Sie, daß ich Ihnen das Paket hinübertrage.** The fundamental force of **übertragen** is 'to transfer, transmit', and the prefix has sometimes been treated as *sep.*, as in **Sie waren damit beschäftigt, alte Denkmäler auszumessen und in getreue Abbildungen ü'berzutragen** (F. Kugler). But this is not in accordance with modern usage, the prefix being now always *insep.*: e.g. **Das Amt des Schriftführers, das ich bisher bekleidete, hat man meinem Assistenten übertra'gen**—**Man scheint vergessen zu haben, diese Posten ins Hauptbuch zu übertra'gen** ('to transfer these entries to the ledger')—**Es ist möglich, diese Krankheit auf andere zu übertra'gen**—**Wir beabsichtigen, Ihre neue Komposition demnächst (durch den Rundfunk) zu übertra'gen** ('We propose to broadcast your new composition in the near future').

übertreiben: see über- 2.

übertrinken: see überessen 3.

überwerfen: see über- 2.

überzeugen, Überzeugung: see satisfaction (*d*).

überziehen: see über- 2.

üblich: see custom(ary) 3.

übrig: **1.** This adj. suggests what remains or is left over, often expressing 'the rest': e.g. **Wo ist das übrige Geld?** ('Where is the rest of the money?')—**So ist es in Frankreich, im übrigen Europa** ('in the rest of Europe') **ist es anders**—**Du weißt nun, was du zu tun hast, alles übrige** ('everything else') **kannst du mir überlassen**—**Ihr übrigen** ('The rest of you') **zerstreut euch im Walde** (Sch.)—**Es ist mir keine Wahl übriggeblieben** ('I have no choice left')—**Sie haben alles aufgegessen und nichts übriggelassen**; cf. **ein übriges tun** ('to do more than is needful, stretch a point') and **im übrigen** or—now more commonly—**übrigens** (= **nebenbei bemerkt**, 'by the way, incidentally'). The phrase **übrig haben** is used in two senses: (i) *lit.*, as in **Für so etwas habe ich kein Geld übrig** ('I can't afford that sort of thing') and **Haben Sie ein paar Minuten für mich übrig?** ('Can you spare me a few minutes?': see 2); (ii) *fig.*, **Du hast für ihn immer was (= etwas) übrig gehabt** (Wildenbruch: 'You have always been rather fond of *or* had a soft side for him'), esp. in a neg. proposition, as in **Für Vorträge hatte unsere Bevölkerung grundsätzlich nichts übrig** (Th. Mann: 'On principle our people had no use [*coll.* no time] for lectures')—**Ich habe für den Kerl nichts übrig** ('I can't put up with that fellow'). **2.** The verb **erübrigen** was orig. used only with the force of 'to save *or* lay by' money: e.g. **Ich habe mir soviel erübrigt, daß ich mir ein Bauerngut kaufen kann** (Auerbach)—**Er konnte seine Schulden bezahlen und noch ein Ziemliches**

erübrigen (Möser: 'He could pay his debts and still lay by a tidy sum'). Later it came to be used also like **übrig haben** in the sense of 'to spare' time: **Können Sie mir einen Augenblick erübrigen?** The simple verb **übrigen** is now to all intents and purposes obs.: in **Es übrigt noch, Euch des Klosters Bücherei zu zeigen** (Scheffel: 'It now only remains to show you the monastery's library') one would now use **Es erübrigt . . .** Quite modern is the impers. use of the reflex. **sich erübrigen** with the force of 'to be unnecessary *or* superfluous': e.g. **Daß unser Abschied kühl war, erübrigt sich wohl zu sagen** (Th. Mann: 'I suppose I need not add that our parting was not a cordial one'); and the same applies to the trans. use of **erübrigen** in the sense of 'to render unnecessary', as in **Meine Eltern hatten mir ein Vermögen hinterlassen, das sich als reichlich genug erwies, um mir den Gedanken an Erwerb zu erübrigen** (St. Zweig).

um: 1. (**a**) The prep. um requires an *accus.* case, and even where the context clearly implies *rest*, as in 'We sat round the campfire', a dat. is historically unjustifiable. So an expression like **die Welt um mir her** (Börne) is quite incorrect, and occasional examples to be found in more recent authors should certainly not be imitated: cf. **Weiße Mondschleier weben um den Bäumen** (Stehr) and **Unsere modernen Maler sollten den ewigen Schöpfungsduft malen, der um den Dingen ist** (Scheffler). Even the zeugmatic use of two preps. which take *different* cases, connected by **und** or **oder**, is hardly to be recommended, although the neatness of such phrases may perhaps excuse it: cf. a correct proposition like **Die Abbildung zeigte die Explosion einer Fabrik und bestand nur aus einem mächtigen Dampfkegel, um welchen und über welchem Mauerstücke durch die Luft sausten** (H. Hesse) with examples like **Er hörte nicht das Geschrei der Möwen, die um** (better insert **ihn**) **und über ihm flogen** (Storm) and **Der Bürgermeister kam, den durch den Sturm angerichteten Schaden in und um die Stadt** (for **in der Stadt und um dieselbe**) **zu beschauen** (Raabe); cf. mit 1. (**b**) Special care must be taken in rendering propositions like 'We strolled round the town' or 'I walked round the room and looked at the pictures'. The phrase **um die Stadt** means 'round *the outer circumference of* the town', as in **Um die Stadt erstrecken sich dichte Wälder,** so it is incorrect to say **Wir schlenderten um die Stadt** or **Ich ging um das Zimmer** (for **in der Stadt** or **im Zimmer herum**). (**c**) In the combination **um . . . willen** ('for the sake of'), **willen** is really the accus. of **der Wille,** and should be preceded by a *gen.* case, as in **um Gottes willen.** Where the gen. is a poss., as in 'for my sake, for whose sake', one now generally uses forms with an excrescent t, with **willen** as a suffix: e.g. **um meinet-, seinet-, euret-, wessent-, dessentwillen**; the true gen. forms are now only used in prose in phrases like **um meiner selbst willen** or **um unser beider willen**: cf. **Ob du ein Recht hast, mich einen Dichter zu nennen, darüber wirst du zu urteilen haben, wenn ich dir erzähle, was um deiner, nein, auch um meiner selbst willen, also: was um unser beider willen erzählt werden muß** (H. Franck). The omission of **willen** here, so that **um** seems to take a gen. case, is not to be recommended: cf. **Wie lieb' ich dich um dieser Treue gegen meinen Bruder!** (Sch.)—**Schon um** (better **wegen**) **der Wurzeln ritten wir im Schritt** (Fontane). (**d**) Of the various other meanings of **um**—e.g. 'about' (of time or numbers), 'concerning' (as in **Es handelt sich um eine Erbschaft**), 'for' (indicating the purpose in view, as in **um Verzeihung bitten** or **sich um eine Stellung bewerben**)—the most noteworthy is 'by' (indicating the measure of difference): e.g. **Er überragte alle um Haupteslänge** (Ompteda: 'by a head')—**Der Wind drehte sich um einige Striche** (Kellermann: 'The wind veered a few points')—cf. **Ich bin in meinen Studien um etwas weniges vorgerückt** (G.), where one would now rather say **um ein weniges**; here belongs the expression **um so** before a compar., for which see **als** = 'as' 4, and **um so** 2. **2.** Esp. common is the use of **um** followed by **zu** + infin. ('in order to'). This should be confined to propositions in which the subjs. of the two clauses refer to the same person or thing, as in **Er kam, um mir zu gratulieren.** Where the two subjs. refer to different persons or things, *umbe daz* was used in MHG, but this is now obs., being replaced by **damit**: hence, cf., on the one hand, **Er kam, um mir die Nachricht sofort zu überbringen,** and on the other hand, **Er kam, damit ich sofort erführe, was sich ereignet hatte**;

it is taking a liberty with the lang. to say **So öffnet sich den Freunden des Orients eine Pforte nach der anderen, um die Geheimnisse jener Urwelt kennenzulernen** (G.), where the **um**-clause should read either **damit sie die Geheimnisse . . . kennenlernen können,** or better **um ihnen die Geheimnisse . . . zu enthüllen** ('in order to disclose the secrets . . . to them').

um-: What is said under **über- 1** applies equally to the verbal prefix **um-**, and as in the case of **über-**, so here also only those verbs are discussed in detail which are used in several ways and require special care. In some cases **um-** is like **nieder-**, suggesting a *downward* motion as in **umbrechen** (q.v.) and **umfallen,** and in others it indicates *change*, as in **umsatteln, umsiedeln, umsteigen** and **umziehen** (qq.v. and cf. **Umlaut,** 'mutation' of vowels); but the commonest meaning of **um-** is *round* or *around*, as in **umarmen, umgeben, umgehen, umlaufen** and **umwandeln** (qq.v.). Taken by and large, the prefix is *sep.* when the idea it suggests is more important than that suggested by the simple verb, and *insep.* when it gives the verb fig. force or makes an intrans. verb trans.; but in many cases the prefix is either sep. or insep., as in **umgehen** and **umreißen,** and most of these are treated under their respective heads.

umändern: see **change 1** (*a*).

umarmen: This trans. verb means 'to put one's arms round, embrace', its prefix being invariably *insep.*, as in **Als sie sich trafen, uma'rmten sie sich,** and this applies equally to two other verbs used in much the same sense, viz. **umfa'ngen** and **umfa'ssen,** which latter is treated separately. The former is not so common in the lit. sense of people embracing, but is rather used with an impers. or abstract subj. which 'surrounds, envelops' a person, a subj. like atmosphere, darkness, etc.: cf. **Der müde Wanderer atmete auf, als er in den Wald trat und sich von dem Halbdunkel umfa'ngen fühlte**—(poet.) **Die Fülle des Lebens umfi'ng mich** (Hölderlin)—**War mein Herz nicht einzig da, um ihres zu umfa'ngen?** (id.).

umbrechen: With *sep.* prefix, this means 'to break down' (trans. or intrans.), as in **Der Sturm hat den Baum u'mgebrochen** and **Infolge des Sturmes ist der Baum u'mgebrochen,** or 'to break, dig, plough up', as in **Sie brachen den Acker u'm** (Immermann: which might have taken the form **Sie waren dabei, den Acker u'mzubrechen**). With *insep.* prefix, it is only used in the printing trade with the force of 'to fix the page-limits in a proof', as in **Er hatte das Morgenblatt umbro'chen** (or **Er hatte sich damit beschäftigt, das Morgenblatt zu umbre'chen,**) **und hielt noch die nassen Druckfahnen** ('galley-proofs') **in der Hand** (K. Edschmid).

umfangen: see **umarmen.**

umfassen: The prefix here is *sep.* only when the verb is used in the sense of 'to reset, alter the setting of' precious stones or a piece of jewellery, as in **Ich habe den Juwelier beauftragt, den Schmuck etwas u'mzufassen.** Otherwise the prefix is *insep.*, whether the verb has lit. or fig. force: e.g. **Sie warf sich vor ihm nieder und umfa'ßte** ('clasped') **seine Knie—Das Brautpaar hielt sich zärtlich umfa'ßt** or **uma'rmt** ('were clasped in a fond embrace')—**Der Feind hatte seine Stellung so schwach befestigt, daß unsere Truppen sie leicht umfa'ssen konnten** ('The enemy had fortified their position so badly that our forces could easily encircle it')—**Unser Briefwechsel umfa'ßte** ('embraced, covered') **einen Zeitraum von etwa anderthalb Jahren** (Bergengruen); very common is the pres. part. used adj., as in **Er ist ein Mann von umfa'ssender Bildung** ('of wide culture') and **Die jetzige Lage fordert umfa'ssende Maßnahmen** ('The present situation demands measures on a large scale').

umgeben: This is not used in the sense of 'to give *or* hand round' (e.g. copies of a document to people sitting round a table), an idea which is expressed by **heru'mgeben** or **-reichen.** The only sense in which **u'mgeben** (with *sep.* prefix) can be used is like that of **u'mhängen** (q.v.), viz. 'to put *or* hang (a covering) round' a person, 'to help (a person) on with' (a coat or cloak): e.g. **Da es regnete und ich keinen Schirm mitgebracht hatte, gab man mir einen Regenmantel um.** Otherwise the prefix is always *insep.*, the meaning of the compd. being 'to surround': e.g. **Eine hohe Mauer umgi'bt das Gefängnis** or **Das Gefängnis ist mit einer hohen Mauer umge'ben—Fichtenwälder umge'ben das Dorf—Von seinen Hofleuten umge'ben, betrat der König den Saal.**

umgehen: 1. With *sep.* prefix, this is always *intrans.*, used lit. of going a roundabout way (**einen Umweg machen**), or with an impers. subj. of going round, circulating: e.g. **Wir sind einige Meilen u'mgegangen—Übertriebene Gerüchte gingen um** (Th. Mann); here belongs its application to spirits, ghosts 'walking', often with the non-committal subj. **es**, as in **In dem alten Schloß geht es** (= **ein Gespenst**) **um** or **spukt es** ('This old castle is haunted'). With fig. force it is used in propositions like **Er geht mit Künstlern um** ('He associates with artists')—**Er geht mit dem Gedanken um, nach Amerika auszuwandern** ('He is thinking of emigrating to America'). The pres. part. **u'mgehend** is used of answers 'by return', as in **Wir bitten um eine umgehende Antwort** or **eine Antwort mit umgehender Post.** **2.** With *insep.* prefix it always has *trans.* force, either *lit.* as in **Wir haben den Marktplatz umga'ngen** ('We skirted the market-place') or *fig.* as in **Er versuchte das Gesetz zu umge'hen** ('He tried to circumvent the law') and **Auf diese Weise umge'hen wir viele Unbequemlichkeit** ('In this way we avoid much inconvenience').

umhängen: For the mutated root-vowel in pres. tense forms, see **hängen.** This compd. and esp. **überhängen** (q.v.) present even greater difficulty than **ab-, an-, aufhängen,** etc., because their prefixes may be either sep. or insep. **1.** With *sep. accented* prefix: (**a**) *intrans.*: really only used in the infin. in phrases like **Er hatte einen Mantel u'mhängen** ('He had a cloak hanging round his shoulders'); (**b**) *trans.*: past tense **hängte um** (or **hing um,** see **hängen** 2 *b*), past part. **umgehängt:** 'to hang (something) round (some object)', the latter standing in the *dat.*: e.g. **Gelingt ihm das, so mag der König ihm seinen höchsten Orden u'mhängen** (Schreckenbach)—**Er hängte** (or **hing**) **ihr die Kette um—Regine hat mir das Kettchen u'mgehängt** (Fontane)—**Käthe präsentierte sich in Rembrandthut und Staubmantel samt u'mgehängter Reisetasche** (id.); the strong past part. here is now little used in the north, cf. **Sich selbst hatte er ein Meßgewand u'mgehangen** (C. F. Meyer). **2.** With *insep. unaccented* prefix: always *trans.*, the dir. obj., as with **be-** and **verhängen,** being the thing round which some article is hung: past tense **umhä'ngte** (or **umhi'ng**), past part. **umhä'ngt** (denoting an *action*) or **umha'ngen** (denoting a *state*): e.g. **Er umhä'ngte** (or **umhi'ng**) **die Dame mit einer Kette, hat sie mit einer Kette umhä'ngt—Sie war mit einer Kette umha'ngen;** cf. fig. **Der reifende Knabe kann jenes abgelegene waldumha'ngene Tal nicht vergessen** (Carossa)—**Für ein Kind der Ebene sind sieben Ellen Höhe und sieben Ellen Tiefe eine traumumha'ngene Gebirgswelt** (O. Ernst).

umher-: If the proposition 'They strolled *round* the town' is meant to convey the idea that they strolled *about in* the town, this would be expressed by **Sie schlenderten in der Stadt herum** (or **umher**); but if 'strolling round' implies movement *round the circumference of* the town, it would be expressed by **Sie schlenderten um die Stadt herum** (*not* **umher**). In neither case would a German omit the prefix of motion: he would instinctively add it in the first sentence because of the *dat.* in the prep. phrase (see **accusative or dative . . .** 1), and in the second because the prep. **um** alone does not necessarily imply complete encirclement: of a person walking round a room to look at the pictures on the wall, one says **Er ging im Zimmer herum** (not **um das Zimmer,** nor yet **im Zimmer um**—see **umgehen**). From the two first examples given above it is clear that **herum-** has a wider application than **umher-:** either may suggest a haphazard movement, now in one direction now in another, but **umher-** cannot express a completely encircling movement, an idea which can be suggested by the use of the adv. **rings,** as in **Wir fuhren rings um die Stadt.** It follows, therefore, that **herum-** is a much commoner prefix than **umher-,** the latter being a slightly more select expression and having, as *Eberhard* says, **„eine edlere Färbung“.** The following are some characteristic examples in which **umher-** could not be substituted for **herum-:—Drake war der erste, der um die Erde herumsegelte** ('. . . the first to circumnavigate the earth')—**Als wir uns im Kreise hingesetzt hatten, reichte ich die Photographien herum—Man ließ den Hut herumgehen** ('passed the hat round'), **um Geld zu sammeln—Ein Graben zog sich um die Burg herum** ('A moat ran round the castle'); and in many cases where **umher-** might be used, **herum-** is much more usual, esp. in coll. expressions: e.g. **Gehen Sie nicht wie die Katze um den heißen Brei herum!** ('Don't beat about the bush!')—**Er versuchte, mich an der Nase herumzuführen** ('He tried to lead me by the nose')—**Ich lasse mir nicht auf der Nase herumtanzen** ('I'm not going to be made game of')—**Knaben balgen sich gern herum** ('Boys like to romp about')—**Wo hast du dich denn den ganzen Tag herumgetrieben?** ('Where have you been gadding about all day?').

umhin: Seeing that **umher** (q.v.) is such an everyday expression, it is strange that the use of **umhin** is so limited. In MHG *umbehin* suggested a detour round something to avoid contact with it (cf. the English coll. 'He manages to get round all the rules'), but the modern word is only used as a sep. prefix of the verb **können** in a *neg.* proposition with **zu** + infin., meaning 'to be unable to avoid doing something', as in **Ich konnte nicht umhin, zu lachen** ('I could not help laughing': cf. **helfen** 1 *b*): sim. **Es war hier etwas Sonderbares, das zu empfinden wohl niemand umhinkonnte** (Th. Mann: 'There was something strange here, which probably no one could help feeling *or* could fail to feel', i.e. which every one was almost bound to feel); in the past part., **Er sagte, er habe nicht umhingekonnt, die Einladung anzunehmen** ('He said he had been unable to get out of accepting the invitation').

umlauern: 1. The simple verb **lauern** (with auf+accus.) means 'to wait expectantly' (for something), esp. but not necessarily with evil intent: e.g. **Er lauerte auf die entscheidende Antwort des Prinzen** (Gutzkow)—**Der Dieb lauerte unter den Bäumen auf eine günstige Gelegenheit, einzubrechen** ('The thief lurked under the trees, waiting for a favourable opportunity to break in'); so **irgendwo heru'mlauern** (sep.) is 'to hang about somewhere'. This idea can also be expressed by the compd. **umlauern,** but only with *trans.* force, the prefix being always *insep.*: e.g. **Seine Besuche blieben aus, aber er umlau'erte öfters das Haus** (R. v. Gottschall: 'He stopped calling at the house, but frequently hung about the place'). **2.** This use of an insep. prefix to give trans. force to an intrans. verb is also seen in **umlaufen** (q.v.), **umspringen** and **umstehen** (q.v.): cf. **Er freute sich an den Hunden, die ihn umspra'ngen** (W. v. Scholz: = **die um ihn heru'msprangen**).

umlaufen: 1. With *sep.* prefix, this is used *intrans.* in the sense of 'to run *or* spin round, revolve' (as in **ein u'mlaufendes Rad**) or 'to circulate' (esp. of money, reports, etc.); used of persons, it only means 'to run *or* go a round-about way' (e.g. off a prescribed course) or simply 'to go out of one's way': e.g. **In dem Querfeldeinlauf** ('cross-country race') **lief einer der Bewerber eine Meile um—Wir wären rechtzeitig angekommen, wenn wir nicht etwas u'mgelaufen wären** ('if we had not gone a bit off our way'). With *trans.* force it means 'to run down, knock down while running', as in **Als der Dieb die Polizei hinter sich herkommen sah, stürzte er die Straße entlang und lief** (or **rannte) mehrere Leute um. 2.** With *insep.* prefix, the verb takes on trans. force, as in **Er umlie'f den ganzen Park,** but is mostly used *fig.*, as when we say 'A bench ran round the tree': e.g. **Er hatte mit eigenen Händen die Bank gezimmert, die den Stamm des Baumes umlie'f** (Bergengruen) —**In der Mitte des Hofes stand eine von einer grünen Bank umlau'fene alte Linde** (Th. Mann)—**Das Bett stand mitten im Raum und war von einer breiten schwarzen Stufe umlau'fen** (id.: 'was surrounded by a broad black step').

Umlaut: As distinct from **Ablaut** (q.v.), the word **Umlaut** is used to express the change from **a, o, u** and **au** to **ä, ö, ü** and **äu** respectively. In point of fact, there are other such 'mutations' or 'modifications', as when the noun **Erde** gives the adjs. **irden** and **irdisch,** or when the **a** in the past tense **brannte** is 'mutated' to the **e** in the infin. **brennen** (q.v.); but to discuss these changes in detail would go beyond the scope of the present volume. The cause of these vowel-changes can as a rule not be seen in modern German: in order to understand them, one requires to go back to the earlier stages of the lang. To put it broadly, what happens is that a vowel in a word 'mutates' through the influence of another vowel which occurs in a subsequent syllable: if a vowel pronounced in the front of the mouth (e.g. i) follows one pronounced in the back of the mouth (e.g. **a, o,** or **u**), it tends to shift the place of articulation of the vowels **a, o, u** more towards the front of the tongue—cf. **Ost** and **östlich, Kunst** and **künstlich.** The same applies to the mutation of **a** to **ä,** as in the plur. of **Gast** and **Lamm,** viz. **Gäste** and **Lämmer,** because there was formerly an **i** in the second syllable (OHG *gast,* plur. *gesti—lamb,* plur. *lembir*; so also **länger, längst** < OHG *lengiro, lengisto*).

umreißen: The prefix of this trans. verb is either sep. or insep. When it is *sep.*, the verb means either 'to tear *or* blow down, demolish' or 'to plough up' (land), 'turn up' (soil): cf., on the one hand, **Der Sturm hat viele Bäume or mehrere Häuser u'mgerissen**, and, on the other hand, **Im flachen Lande hält sich der Knecht, der mit Pferden pflügt, für besser als den andern, der den Acker mit Ochsen u'mreißt** (G.). With *insep.* prefix the verb has the force of 'to sketch, outline, delineate' (lit. or fig.): e.g. **Er hat die Gabe, Gestalten in Lebensgröße zu umreißen** (G.)—**Mit seinem** (*scil.* Hans Sachs') **Namen verbindet sich im Bewußtsein unseres Volkes eine klar umri'ssene Persönlichkeit** (Erich Schmidt: 'The name H. S. conjures up in our people's minds a sharply defined picture of his personality')—**Durch die Kraft, die persönliche Besonderheit der Hauptgestalten rasch zu umrei'ßen, heben Uhlands Balladen sich von der Poesie der Romantiker ab** (A. E. Schönbach: 'Uhland's ability to delineate in a few strokes the individual character of his chief figures makes his ballads stand out against the poetry of the Romantics')—**Ich werde versuchen, das Wesentliche dieser Ergebnisse zu umrei'ßen** (Th. Mann).

umsatteln: This verb, of which the prefix is always *sep.*, is used either trans. in a *lit.* sense, as in **ein Pferd u'msatteln** ('to change a horse's saddle'), or intrans. in the *fig.* sense of 'to change one's trade, switch over to another profession, curriculum', etc. The aux. here is usually **haben**, less commonly **sein**: e.g. **Sie haben geschwind umgesattelt** (G.)—**Er war einer ihrer Musikschüler gewesen, hatte aber umgesattelt und war Maler geworden** (H. Leip); **Meine Frau hat es nie verstanden, daß ich nicht umgesattelt bin** (Elfriede Brüning).

umschaffen: see **schaffen** 1 (*b*).

umschlagen (intrans.): see **change** 3.

umsetzen (reflex.): see **change** 3.

umsiedeln: This verb is used, like **u'mziehen**, in the intrans. sense of 'to remove to other quarters'. Whereas, in the alternative **übersiedeln** (q.v. 2), the prefix is either sep. or insep., that of **u'msiedeln** is invariably *sep.*: cf. **So siedelte der Greis zwei- bis dreimal um** (Rilke).

um so: 1. In this combination, when followed by **zu**+infin., **so** is an adv. of manner meaning 'thus, in that way, by doing so', being slightly accented: e.g. **Ich glaube, wir haben uns verirrt: halten wir uns also mehr nach links, um so wieder auf den rechten Weg zu kommen. 2.** Much more common is the use of **um so** (unaccented) before a compar. adj. or adv., with the same force as **desto** (cf. **erst** 2 *d*): e.g. **Wenn wir uns hier mehr nach links halten, kommen wir um so eher** (or **früher**: 'all the sooner') **zu Hause an**; sim. **„Was ich sagen wollte, ist etwas Heikles". „Das macht mich um so neugieriger"** (Fontane: 'What I was going to say is a delicate subject.' 'That makes me all the more curious')—**Je schneller wir gehen, um so schneller werden wir nach Hause kommen** (see **je** 3). For such compar. expressions followed by a causal **als**-clause, as in 'I am glad you have come, the more so as I have something to discuss with you', see **als** = **'as'** 4.

umspringen: see **umlauern** 2.

umstehen: With **um-** *sep.*, this is only used in the *pres. part.*, esp. in commercial lang., as in **Die Preise sind u'mstehend** (or **auf der u'mstehenden Seite**) **angegeben** ('The prices are quoted overleaf'); so also one can say **Die U'mstehenden rührten sich nicht** ('The bystanders stood stockstill'), but not **Viele Leute standen um** (for **herum**). With **um-** *insep.*, the verb is *trans.*, meaning 'to stand round *or* surround' something: e.g. **Nun umsta'nden sie weinend das Sterbebett des Vaters** (Th. Mann)—**Alle Familienmitglieder eilten herbei, um den Sterbenden zu umste'hen**—**Der Platz war von schützenden Steinwänden umsta'nden** (Stifter); cf. **Der Teich lag, weidenumsta'nden, nur etwa zehn Minuten Weges vom Hause entfernt** (Th. Mann: 'The pond, surrounded by willows, was only a matter of ten minutes' walk from the house').

umsteigen: see **change** 3.

umwandeln: see **change** 1 (*b*); **wandeln.**

umwechseln: see **change** 2 (*a*).

um . . . willen: see **Wille** 3; **um** 1 (*c*).

umziehen: With *sep.* prefix, this is mainly used either in the *intrans.* sense of 'to remove to other quarters', or in the *trans.* (esp. reflex.) sense of 'to re-clothe' (cf. **change** 3 *ad fin.*): e.g., on the one hand, **Die Familie beabsichtigte u'mzuziehen, ist vielleicht schon u'mgezogen**, and, on the other hand, **Da der kleine Junge ins Wasser gefallen war, zog** (or **kleidete**) **ihn die Mutter schnell um**—**Ich habe keine Zeit, mich u'mzuziehen** ('I haven't time to change'). Other occasional uses are trans. **'to pull down'**, e.g. a tree or a pole with ropes (usually **herunterziehen**) and intrans. 'to march in procession' through the town (better **in der Stadt herumziehen**). With *insep.* prefix, it is almost confined in good prose to the reflex. use in the sense of 'to become overcast', as in **Der Himmel umzo'g sich** (mit Wolken), **hat sich umzo'gen, scheint sich zu umzie'hen**; but here **sich überzie hen** is much more usual. In military lang. it is used with the force of 'to surround', e.g. a fortress with a ditch or with barbed wire: **Man hat die Festung mit einem Graben, mit Stacheldraht umzo'gen.**

unangesehen: see **ungeachtet** 2.

unbedingt: see **dingen** 2.

unbeschadet: see **ungeachtet** 2.

unbescholten: see **schelten.**

Unbill: This noun, connected with **billig** (q.v.), and meaning 'wrong, injustice, injury, hardship', as in **jemandem Unbill antun** or **zufügen** ('to do wrong *or* injury to a person'), has shown considerable fluctuation in gender, but the *fem.* is now firmly established. It is mostly used in the sing.; where a plur. is required the form **Unbilden** is used, really the plur. of another noun now little used in the sing. (< MHG *unbilde*): cf. **die Unbilden des Wetters** or **des Klimas** ('the severity of the weather *or* climate').

unerachtet: see **ungeachtet.**

ungeachtet: The way in which this expression and the alternative **unerachtet** (which latter *Duden* characterizes as **„veraltend"**) are now used is the result of a misconception. Obviously, **geachtet** and **erachtet** are past part. forms of trans. verbs, and one ought to say **Er ging, das Wetter ungeachtet, spazieren** ('Regardless of the weather, he went for a walk'), where the part. phrase is a so-called **accus. abs.** (q.v.); Luther rightly uses **dasselbe ungeachtet.** But modern usage has lost sight of the true construction here and treats these expressions either as preps. or as conjs. with the force of 'notwithstanding'. **1.** (**a**) As *preps.*, they could at one time be freely used with a preceding *dat.* (cf. **trotz**), and this case is still occasionally found, as in **Grete hatte gebeten, das Puppenspiel besuchen zu dürfen, und es war ihr, allem Abmahnen Trudes unerachtet, gestattet worden** (Fontane); but much more common is the *gen.* (the only case given by *Duden*), either preceding or following the word they govern: e.g. **Er ging ungeachtet des Regens in den Garten** (G.)—**Unerachtet alles Zorns konnten sie sich des Lachens nicht enthalten** (E. T. A. Hoffmann)—**Es stand nun fest, daß der alte Verwalter des Hauses dasselbe, seines Leugnens unerachtet, nicht allein bewohnte** (id.)—**Ungeachtet des Zeitunterschieds erkennen wir in Mörike den typischen Ausdruck moderner Kunst** (E. v. Sallwürk); cf. **Die Frau hatte für die Raritäten ihres Mannes geringe Achtung, doch gelang es, ihre Meinung von deren Wert zu verbessern; demungeachtet** ('in spite of that') **blieben sie in einer abgelegenen Kammer verwiesen** (Mörike), where **dessenungeachtet** would be more in accordance with modern usage. (**b**) As *conjs.*, although not as common as **obgleich, trotzdem,** etc., they are often used without **daß** (see **nun** 2 and **zumal**): e.g. **Sie ist gesund, unerachtet sie wie eine Kranke gepflegt wird** (E. T. A. Hoffmann)—**Wie oft hatte er sich über die kümmerliche Beleuchtung geärgert, ungeachtet die Mutter ihm immer das Lämpchen vor die Nase geschoben** (G. Keller)—**Unerachtet ich die Ersparnisse der letzten Jahre hingab, gelang es mir nicht, den Kampf mit der Armut siegreich zu beendigen** (Storm)—**Sie durchflocht ihr Haar mit Blumen, und so erschien sie selbst am Sonntag in der Kirche, ungeachtet ihr die Mutter den Putz zornig abriß** (Heyse)—**Ungeachtet er sich vorgenommen hatte, zurückhaltender gegen sie zu sein, verfiel er bald in ein seliges Schwatzen** (Ric. Huch); see also **ohnerachtet**, and cf. **ungefähr. 2.** A sim. misunderstanding has led to the use as preps. (+ *gen.*) of the expressions **unangesehen** ('regardless of') and **unbeschadet** ('without prejudice to, consistently *or* compatibly with'). These are mainly characteristic of the **Kanzleisprache**, i.e. official or legal phraseology, but they do sometimes occur in the literary lang.: e.g. **Den Einwohnern Karlsbads blieben jene Festlichkeiten verwehrt, die man zuweilen für alle Gäste unangesehen des Standes gab** (Kolbenheyer: 'The inhabitants of Karlsbad continued to be debarred from attending those festivities which were sometimes arranged for all visitors irrespective of their station in life')—**Er sagte das im Ton eines Soldaten, der zu seinen Vorgesetzten, unbeschadet des schärfsten Gehorsams, in einem vertraulichen Respektsverhältnis steht** (Werfel: 'The tone of voice in which he spoke these words was that of a soldier who is on terms of such respectful intimacy with his superior officers as are compatible with the strict carrying out of orders').

ungefähr: This word is derived from MHG *âne gevaere,* meaning lit. 'without danger' (now always **ungefährlich**) but esp. *fig.* 'without deceit, sincerely, frankly'. Until comparatively recent times it was spelled **ohngefähr** (cf. **ohnerachtet**), as in **ohngefähr soviel wie nichts** (H. v. Kleist: 'approximately nothing'), and this sense is quite in accordance with modern usage: e.g. **Das ist (so) ungefähr was er sagte** ('That is pretty much what he said')—**Es kostete ungefähr** (or **etwa**) **100 Mark** ('100 marks or so'). It is also common in the expression **von ungefähr,** as in **Es traf sich ganz von ungefähr** ('quite by chance'), and is even used as an adj.: e.g. **Man hat mir einen ungefähren Kostenanschlag geschickt** ('I have been sent a rough estimate of the cost').

ungegessen: for this, and other sim. past parts. used with act. force, see **essen** 2.

ungemein: see **gemein** 2.

ungeschoren: see **scheren.**

Unkosten: see **Kost(en)** 2.

unlängst: see **längst** *ad fin.*; **recent** 1 (*a*).

unless: This is usually expressed by a neg. cond. clause introduced by **wenn** (q.v.); for other renderings, see **denn** (adverb) 3, and cf. **except** 2 (*b*).

unpaß, unpäßlich: see **krank** 1; **adjectives (indeclinable)** 5.

unscheinbar: see **scheinbar** 1 *ad fin.*

unser: This is used in two ways. **1.** As a *pers. pron.,* it is the gen. plur. of **ich,** just as **euer** is the gen. plur. of **du.** The gen. sing. fem. and the gen. plur. of all genders of the 3rd pers. pron. (**er, sie, es**) was *ir* in MHG, and Luther still wrote **Der Herr bedarf ir** (Matt. 21. 3), but this is now obs. and is replaced by **ihrer.** After the analogy of **ihrer,** the longer forms **unserer** (cf. 2) and **eu(e)rer** crept in, and despite the grammarians' protests—both *Sanders* and *Duden* condemn them: the former says explicitly **„Erbarme dich unser (nicht: unserer)"**—they have become fairly common: e.g. **Wir sind nur unserer drei** (Jul. Wolff)—**Wir sind nur noch der Schatten unserer selbst** (Gutzkow)—**Die Zeit wäre gekommen, daß du dich unserer geschämt hättest** (Ompteda)—**Eine leise Ernüchterung bemächtigte sich unserer** (Bonsels); sim. **Die Tafel wartet Eurer, Herr König** (Wildenbruch). But on the whole it is perhaps advisable to use the historical forms **unser** and **euer.** **2.** As a *pron. adj.,* it is the poss. corresponding to **wir,** meaning 'our', being inflected like the indef. art., **mein, dein,** etc. Here it is important to note that the forms **unser** and **euer** have *no* inflexional ending, but only look as if they had; hence, in the nom. sing. masc. and neut., and the accus. sing. neut., a following attrib. adj. must be *strongly* inflected: just as one says **ein armer Mann** and **mein guter Freund,** so one can only say **unser alter** (not **alte**) **Vater** and **euer lieber Onkel.** But where these words are used as prons. ('ours, yours'), they must be inflected: **Euer verstorbener Onkel war älter als uns(e)rer,** where, however, there are the alternative forms **der uns(e)re** and **der uns(e)rige**; sim. **Unser neues Haus ist größer als eu(e)res** or **das eu(e)re** or **das eu(e)rige,** etc.

unsereiner, unsereins: see **eins** 3.

unseresgleichen: see **-gleichen** 1.

unter: Of all the preps. which can take both a dat. and an accus., this one presents least difficulty. **1.** The fundamental difference between the two cases is, of course, that the dat. indicates *rest,* the accus. *motion*: cf. **Der Hund lag unter dem Tisch,** but **legte sich unter den Tisch** (or **unter dem Tisch hin** or **nieder**: see **accusative or dative . . .** 1); so also, with the sense of 'among', **Unter all meinen Freunden ist er der beste,** but **Ich zähle ihn unter meine Freunde** ('I include him among my friends', lit. 'I put him into my circle of friends'). If the motion proceeds, not *to* a spot which lies below something, but continues *beyond* that spot, the *dat.* is used and a suitable verbal prefix added (cf. 2 (*b*)): e.g. **Ein Bach rann unter dem Zaun hindurch** (Wassermann). **2.** The *dat.* is also used idiomatically: **(a)** to suggest that two things happen at the same time: e.g. **Unter diesen Gesprächen** ('While these conversations were being carried on') **waren die Freunde eine gute Strecke weitergetrabt** (C. F. Meyer)—**Unter Tränen meiner Mutter** ('While my mother shed tears') **verabschiedete ich mich** (Kerner)—**Unter dem Schnarchen des Kaufmannes** ('Accompanied by the merchant's snores') **rollte die Postchaise das Tal abwärts** (Kolbenheyer); **(b)** to indicate the place *from below* which the motion proceeds, in which case a verbal prefix of motion is added: e.g. **Sein blondes Haar quoll unter**

der Tuchmütze hervor (Storm)—**Aus dem wettergebräunten Gesicht schauten die Augen unter buschigen Brauen hervor** (Wildenbruch). **3.** A *gen.* after **unter** is used in a few more or less set phrases in some (mainly southern) dialects, but these should not be used in good prose: e.g. **In der Wohnung war viel Besuch unter Tags** (G. Hauptmann: 'during the day')—**Er sitzt im Dunkel der Fichten; unter Tags** (= **tagsüber**) **lag er im Heidekraut** (Waggerl)—**Die Aufregung nahm einen solchen Grad an, daß kein weibliches Wesen unter Lichts das Haus zu verlassen wagte** (Stehr: presumably 'in daylight')—**Du brachtest den Hund zu mir, ohne ihm unter Weges** (for **auf den Weg**) **etwas zu fressen zu geben?** (Stifter). Actually, this last phrase **unter Weges** has become established as the adv. **unterwe'gs** ('on the way': cf. **ha'lbwegs**). The MHG for this was *under wegen*, and this was used by Luther and is retained in the modern Bible, as in **Als er unterwegen war, kam ihm der Herr entgegen** (Exod. 4. 24); and we even find another form in **Er sagte zu Herrn Julian, er solle mich mit sich nehmen, unterwegens wolle man von einigen Werken sprechen** (G.); but these have been entirely displaced in good prose by **unterwegs.** The commonest gen. form, however, is **unterdessen** ('in the meantime': see **indessen**); this is much more common than the shorter form **unterdes,** although the latter is historically more correct: the MHG was *under des* or more usually *under diu* (the instrumental case).

unterbringen: see **herunter-.**

unterdessen: see **unter** 3.

unterhalb: see **außerhalb** 2.

unterkommen: see **herunter-.**

unterlaufen: 1. As a *trans.* verb, this is sometimes used (with *insep.* prefix) in the sense of 'to trip up', but usually in that of 'to avoid (a blow) by swerving, dodging, ducking', as in **Er stieß mit dem Dolch nach mir, aber ich unterlie'f den Stoß. 2.** With *intrans.* force, it is not used of running down a hill or downstairs, an idea which requires a lengthened prefix: **Als ich sie rief, kam sie (die Treppe) heruntergelaufen—Er ließ mich oben stehen und lief den Berg hinunter.** Its chief intrans. use is in connexion with errors, inexactitudes, etc., which 'creep *or* slip in' when calculations or statements are made, accounts made up, etc. (cf. 'to make a slip'). In this sense, the prefix should really be *sep.*, as in **Einige Fehler sind auf meiner Seite mit u'ntergelaufen** (Lessing: 'Some of the mistakes that have crept in are of my doing'), and *Duden* gives only **Es sind einige Fehler u'ntergelaufen.** On the other hand, strangely enough, *Duden*'s *Stilwörterbuch* only gives examples of the *insep.* prefix here, viz. **Bei dieser Arbeit sind einige Irrtümer unterlau'fen** and **Dieses Wort ist mir unterlau'fen** (cf. 'a slip of the tongue'); and the following recent examples seem to point to the use of the *insep.* prefix as the tendency in modern times: **Ich fürchte, in dieser Rechnung ist dir ein Fehler unterlau'fen** (Bergengruen)—**Oft unterlau'fen ihm** (*scil.* E. T. A. Hoffmann) **Unwahrscheinlichkeiten** (id.: 'Improbable incidents often slip into his stories')—**An diesem Nachmittag mußte sich Herr Tonnard sagen lassen, daß ihm in seiner Ansprache ein Irrtum unterlau'fen sei** (Carl Rothe).—Its other common meaning is seen in the use of the past part. (with *insep.* prefix) in the pred. with **sein,** to indicate that a person's skin is suffused with blood under the surface: **Er bekam solche Schläge, daß sein Körper an einigen Stellen mit Blut unterlau'fen war—Ihre Augen sind mit Blut unterlau'fen** (or **sind blutunterlaufen:** 'Your eyes are bloodshot').

unterordnen: Accepted usage treats the prefix of this verb (meaning 'to subordinate') as *sep.*: e.g. **Er hielt es für eine Pflicht, den Gästen den Vortritt zu lassen, und dieser Pflicht ordnete er sein Verlangen unter** (Bergengruen)—**Sie zwang sich, jeden anderen Gedanken dieser Absicht unterzuordnen** (K. Edschmid). Apart from the common past part., as in **Dieser spielte in dem deutschen Literaturwesen eine sehr untergeordnete Rolle** (G.), its commonest use is with a reflex. pron.: e.g. **Goethe ordnete sich seinem fürstlichen Freunde unter** (W. Bode)—**Dein milder Sinn ist auf dem besten Wege, sich diesem Taugenichts unterzuordnen** (Gutzkow). Occasional, mainly southern, examples of non-separation of the prefix should not be imitated: cf. **In dem Neuen Testamente unterordnen sich sämtliche Verfasser einer Persönlichkeit** (Auerbach)—**In Rechtsfragen halte ich Euch für unbestechlich und unterordne mich Eurem Urteil** (C. F. Meyer)—**Man lebte und schaffte in Karlsbad für Menschen, die**

kamen und gingen, für Stände, denen man sich unterordnet (for untergeordnet) fühlte (Kolbenheyer).

unterrichten: see lehren 1 and 3.
untertan: see adjectives (indeclinable) 2.
unterwegs: see unter 3.
unterweisen: see lehren 3.
until: see bis; after a neg., see erst 2 (*c*).
unvergessen: see vergessen 2.
unverhohlen: see bergen 4.
unwidersprochen: see widersprechen.
unwillig, unwilling: see Wille 2; willig.
unwohl: see krank 1.
Urlaub, Ursprung: see leave (noun).
Ursache: see Grund 2.
ursprünglich: see really 2.
Urteil: see leave (noun).
utmost: see utter(ly).
utter (verb): see äußern.
utter(ly): For the various possible renderings of this expression, cf. **Wir befanden uns in vollständiger Dunkelheit** ('in utter darkness')—**Ich bin hier ganz fremd** ('I am an utter stranger here')—**Die Stadt wurde gänzlich zerstört** ('The town was utterly destroyed')—**Zu meinem größten** or **grenzenlosen Erstaunen** ('To my utter amazement') **erfuhr ich, daß er gestorben war**—**Das ist eine glatte Unmöglichkeit** or **Das ist schlechterdings** (see allerdings 2 (*b*)) **unmöglich** ('That is an utter impossibility')—**Du redest glatten** or **den reinsten Unsinn** ('You are talking utter nonsense'); cf. **Das ist von äußerster Wichtigkeit** ('That is of the utmost importance')—**Ich habe mein Möglichstes** or **Äußerstes** (or **alles Menschenmögliche**) **getan** ('I have done my utmost')—**Ich tat es mit äußerster Kraftanstrengung** ('I did it to the utmost of my power').

V

ver-: This insep. verbal prefix has developed an unusually large number of meanings, because it represents three Goth. forms, viz. *fair* (pronounced fĕr), *faur* (pronounced fŏr) and *fra*. **1.** The first of these forms has intensifying force (**vergrößern, -kürzen, -mehren, -stärken**), often suggesting 'continuation to the end', with resultant 'change of state' (**verändern, -blühen, -folgen, -heeren, -hexen, -sumpfen, -wandeln, -welken, -wüsten**). **2.** The second form implies 'cover, concealment', hence 'prevention' (**verbergen, -hehlen, -heimlichen, -hindern, -hüllen, -hüten, -meiden, -nageln, -schweigen**); see 4. **3.** The third form is the most productive. Its fundamental force is 'from, away' (**verdrängen, -kaufen, -mieten, -reisen, -scheuchen, -treiben**), hence 'astray' (**verführen, -leiten**). Out of this have come various shades of meaning, e.g. 'error, loss, deterioration' (**verlernen, sich verrechnen** or **-zählen, -salzen**), 'loss of individuality, fusion' (**verheiraten, -loben, -mählen, -mischen**), and esp. 'consumption' (**verbrauchen, -brennen, -zehren**), leading to 'spending, waste' (**vergeuden, -leben, -plaudern, -schwenden-, -tändeln**). This last idea has been extended in modern times and produced examples like **Wir verphantasierten manche Stunde** (G.)—**Die Vögel in den Bäumen verzwitscherten den Nachmittag** (Stifter)—**Er verfrühstückte das Erbe seiner Tochter** (Th. Mann)—**Den ganzen Vormittag hatten sie verdisputiert** (H. W. Geissler)—**Sie schüttelte den Kopf: „All das verstudierte Geld!"** (A. Schieber). **4.** The idea of 'cover, concealment' referred to under 2 readily suggests that of 'disappearance, invisibility', and here a grammatical point arises when the verb is combined with a prep. which may take either an accus. or a dat. In such contexts usage fluctuates between the two cases, according as the writer thinks of the object as *passing out of* sight (accus.) or projects himself forward, as it were, to the moment when the object is *already lost to* sight (dat.): for examples, see ein- 4, er- 3 (*b*), sammeln 2, and esp. **verbergen, -kriechen, -lieren, -schwinden, -sinken, -stecken, -tiefen.**

verabreden: see beanspruchen 1 (*b*); agree 4 (*b*).
verabschieden, verabscheuen: see beanspruchen 1 (*b*).
veranlagen: see beanspruchen 1 (*b*).
veranlassen: This verb (meaning 'to cause, induce, oblige') is not really the strong verb **lassen** to which **ver-** and **an-** have been prefixed, but is formed by prefixing **ver-** to the noun **Anlaß** and giving it a verbal ending. Being formed

from a noun, it is an *insep. weak* verb (see **beanspruchen** 1 and 2): hence **Er veranlaßte** (not **veranließ**) **mich, Sie aufzusuchen** ('He induced me to look you up')—**Wer hat ihn dazu veranlaßt, diesen Vorschlag zu machen?—Ich hoffe, ihn zu veranlassen, Medizin zu studieren.** It follows that the root-vowel does *not* mutate in the 2nd and 3rd sing. of the pres. indic.: cf. **Er überlegt im stillen, was ihn veranlaßt, gerade diesem Menschen Vertrauen zu schenken** (C. Bulcke), where **veranlaßt** may be the 3rd sing. of the pres. indic. but is probably the past part. with the aux. **habe** understood.

veranschlagen: This verb is treated in the same way, and for the same reason, as **veranlassen** (q.v.): formed from the noun **Anschlag** (here meaning 'calculation, estimate'), it is a *weak* verb: e.g. **Er veranschlagt** (not **veranschlägt**), **veranschlagte** (not **veranschlug**) **die Kosten auf hundert Mark** ('He estimates, estimated the cost at five pounds')—**Er hat die Kosten zu hoch veranschlagt—Die Franzosen veranschlagten den Ruhm,** *la gloire*, **sehr hoch** (Th. Mann: 'set great store by glory').

veranstalten, verausgaben: see **beanspruchen** 1 (*b*).

Verband: As one meaning of this word is a 'bandage', one would almost assume that, on the analogy of **Band** (q.v.) in the sense of 'ribbon', it was a neut. with plur. **Verbänder**, but actually it is *masc.* with plur. **Verbände**; and the same applies to its other common meaning, an 'association, corporation, union': cf. **Gewerkverbände** or **-vereine** ('trade-unions').

verbergen: For two different shades of meaning of this verb, see **bergen** 2 and 3. When its use implies, as that of **verstecken** (q.v.) does, a deliberate act of concealment, and it is accompanied by a prep. phrase indicating the hiding-place, preps. like **in, hinter,** etc., may take either an accus. or a dat., according as the idea of putting the object into the hiding-place, or of its being already concealed, is prominent in the author's mind (cf. **ver-** 2, **verkriechen, verschwinden,** etc.). Thus, **Sie verbarg sich hinter die Mädchen** (G. Keller) is much like 'She slipped behind the girls so as not to be seen', while **Wir müssen den Besen im Holze verstecken** (id.) rather suggests 'We must find a hiding-place in the wood for the broomstick'. On the whole, the dat. is probably more usual: children playing 'hide-and-seek' (see **spielen**) would say **Wo** (not so readily **Wohin**) **sollen wir uns verstecken?** and sim. **Verbirg dich hinter diesen Steinen!** (Wieland)—**Wie jammert mich ein Jüngling, der das Feuer, das ihn erwärmen sollte, in seinem Busen verbergen muß** (G.); less natural is **Sie verbarg ihre Augen ins Schnupftuch** (G.).

verbieten: 1. It is important to distinguish, both in conjugation and in sense, between **verbieten (verbot, verboten)** and **verbitten (verbat, verbeten).** They agree only in both wishing something *not* to be done, but while **verbitten** expresses a *request* (**Bitte**), **verbieten** implies an *order* (**Gebot**): cf. **Das verbat ich mir** ('I deprecated that', i.e. begged that it might not occur again) and **Das verbot er mir** ('He forbade me that'). **2. (a)** Whereas **verbitten** is used with a dir. accus. obj. and usually a reflex. dat., as in **Solche beleidigenden Bemerkungen verbitte ich mir** ('I deprecate such insulting remarks'), **verbieten** may take either an accus. obj. or a dependent clause, as in **Er verbot mir den Eintritt in sein Haus** or **Er verbot mir, sein Haus zu betreten.** As such propositions imply a negation, the dependent clause should be *pos.*, and a pleonastic neg., although fairly common at one time, and still used coll., is not to be recommended—see **negative (pleonastic)** 2 (*a*): in a proposition like **Man verbot ihnen, daß sie keine Waffen in ihren Häusern haben sollten** (Lessing), **keine** should be omitted, or **gebot (befahl)** substituted for **verbot**; but better still would be **Man verbot ihnen, Waffen in ihren Häusern zu haben. (b)** The same applies, of course, to the noun **Verbot:** cf. **Die Männer lasen ihm ein Verbot vor, bei Strafe nicht mehr das Haus zu betreten** (G. Keller), where the dependent clause would better take the form **das Haus hinfort zu betreten.** As *Sanders* suggests, the 'ten commandments', being all neg., would more correctly be called **die zehn Verbote,** not **Gebote.** For the pleonastic neg., see also **hindern, hüten** 2 and **warnen.**

verbitten: see **verbieten.**

verblichen: see **bleichen** 2.

verblühen: see **aushallen** 3.

Verbot: see **verbieten** 2 (*b*).

verbs (auxiliary): 1. The only aux. verbs (**Hilfszeitwörter**) in the narrow sense are **haben** and **sein**; in the wider sense they include **werden, lassen, helfen** and the so-called **modal auxiliary verbs** (q.v.). The broad distinction between **haben** and and **sein** is that the former is used with trans. verbs, esp. those which imply rest, and the latter with intrans. verbs, esp. those which imply change of place, state or condition. But there are numerous exceptions and fluctuations. Thus, **sein** and **bleiben**, although they imply rest, always take **sein**; many verbs have different meanings according to whether they are used with **haben** or with **sein** (e.g. **fortfahren**); many are used with **haben** in one part of the country, with **sein** in another part, esp. those suggesting a posture or attitude (**stehen, sitzen, liegen, knien, hängen**, etc.), which take **haben** in the north, **sein** esp. in the south; many implying change of place take **sein** to convey the idea of getting to some place, **haben** to indicate that the action suggested by the verb is undertaken as an exercise or sport (**reiten, schwimmen**, etc.). Such differences will be found explained under the various verbs. **2.** At one time the aux. (indic. and subj.) was almost regularly omitted in subord. clauses—cf., as an extreme example, the following proposition from Chamisso, in which the aux. is omitted at least four times: **Er erzählte mir, daß er, wie er mich nicht finden gekonnt** (*scil.* **hätte**), **nach Hause zurückgekehrt** (*scil.* **wäre**), **wo bald der Pöbel herangestürmt** (*scil.* **wäre**), **die Fenster eingeschlagen und seine Zerstörungslust gebüßt** (*scil.* **hätte**). An occasional omission of the aux. is still allowed, but is not nearly as common as it used to be, and on the whole it is advisable to insert it, except (i) in short contracted **wie**-clauses like **wie bekannt** ('as is well known'), **wie gesagt** ('as I said before'), **wie oben angeführt** ('as quoted above'), etc.; (ii) in propositions in which the same aux. form would occur twice, one immediately after the other, a good example of which is **Als er ihn vorher vorbeiwandern gesehen** (*scil.* **hatte**), **hatte er nicht gewagt, ihn anzureden** (Immermann). **3.** But there is one kind of clause in which the omission of the aux. is now definitely avoided, viz. where a subord. clause contains two infin. forms standing together, of which the second represents a past part., as in princ. clauses like **Ich hätte es nicht tun sollen—Ich habe ihn fortlaufen sehen—Man hat mich lange warten lassen**—etc. Here also the aux. was formerly often dropped: e.g. **Ich zitterte, ihn zu erblicken, der sich den Frevel erlauben dürfen** (Lessing)—**Erinnerst du dich, welche Abenteuer ich dir bestehen helfen?** (G.)—**Des Herzogs Gegenwart hätte den Eintretenden zurückgetrieben, wenn es sich noch tun lassen** (Alexis). This is not in accordance with present-day usage, which inserts the aux. before the two infin. forms, or exceptionally drops the aux. and makes the second infin. assume its real part. form: e.g. **Das ist etwas, was ich nicht hätte tun sollen** or **was ich nicht tun gesollt.** The latter alternative is not nearly so idiomatic, indeed, in some cases almost sounds wrong, as in **Ihn rührte das Schicksal des armen Vogels, welcher so schnell sein Leben lassen gemußt** (G. Keller: for **sein Leben hatte lassen müssen**); and somehow this seems particularly objectionable in a princ. clause, as in **Wie oft habe ich über diese Fragen mit meinen Freunden streiten und doch über ihren Patriotismus mich freuen gemußt** (E. M. Arndt). Incidentally, if the first infin. is understood, the second infin. takes the *part.* form and the aux. goes to the *end*: e.g. **Aus der Geschichte habe ich nicht soviel behalten, als ich wohl gesollt hätte** (G.: or **als ich wohl hätte tun sollen**).

verdanken: see **danken** 1 (*a*).

verderben: **1.** *Strong* forms of this verb (for **verdürbe**, see **past subjunctive** 2 *c* (i)) are used when it has the *intrans.* force of 'to suffer damage, be spoiled, go to ruin', or the *trans.* force of 'to spoil, damage' (see 2): e.g. (intrans.) **Priams großer Heldenstamm verdirbt** (Sch.)—**Unkraut verdirbt nicht** (proverb: cf. 'Ill weeds grow apace')—**In schlechter Gesellschaft verdirbt man**; (trans.) **Knipse doch das Licht an, sonst verdirbst du dir die Augen**—**Er hat sich den Magen verdorben** (i.e. has indigestion)—**Diese Bilder verdarben mir die Einbildungskraft** (G.)—**Du hast einen verdorbenen Geschmack**; cf. **An ihm ist ein Arzt verdorben** ('He would have made a good doctor'). **2.** *Weak* forms (esp. the past part.) are fixed when the verb means 'to spoil *morally*, demoralize, corrupt': e.g. **Sie begriff nicht, daß ihr Mann so ruhig bleiben konnte: war er denn so verderbt, war aller natürliche Sinn in ihm tot?** (Ponten)—**Er genoß jenes Gefühl der Zufriedenheit, das verderbte Menschen nach einer geglückten Missetat zu haben pflegen** (H. W. Geissler)—**Es war da eine Person mit Schleppkleid und**

„Fladuse": ein lächerliches Wort, worin das französische *flûte douce* **verderbt ist** (Th. Mann)—**Er bezeichnete sie als unerwünschte Ausländer, die verderbte Sitten mitbrächten** (Carl Rothe)—**Der Herr Professor besserte mit vielem Scharfsinn, wo der Text verderbt überliefert war** (Speckmann: '. . . where the MS. was in a corrupt state'); cf. **Ein Hagelwetter . . . beschädigte die Möbeln** (see **Möbel**) **und verderbte** (usually **verdarb**) **einige schätzbare Bücher** (G.)—**„Wasser und Wein?" fragte er mißbilligend; „damit verderbt** (for **verdirbt**) **man das Wasser"** (Wassermann).

Verdienst: Distinguish between **der Verdienst** ('earnings'), mainly used in the sing., and **das Verdienst** ('merit'), with plur. **Verdienste.**

verdingen: see **dingen** I.

verdrießen: At one time there was some fluctuation in the construction of this verb: cf., on the one hand, **Es verdrießt ihm, daß er nicht streiten soll** (Lessing) and **Ich ließ mir keine Mühe verdrießen** (id.: 'I grudged no pains'), and, on the other hand, **Es hat ihn lange nichts so verdrossen** (G.) and **Das verdrießt mich** (Sch.). In point of fact, neither of these constructions is historically correct: in MHG, 'it grieves *or* vexes me' was *es verdriuzet mich*, where *es* is a *gen.*, and **das verdrießt mich** was the result of confusion between *ez* and *es* (see **es** I). The dat. construction is quite obs., the gen. almost so, but a proposition like **Es verdrießt mich des Lebens** ('I am tired *or* sick of life': cf. **satt** and **überdrüssig**) was still in use in comparatively recent times; cf. **Er wird seines Lebens müde und verdrossen** (Luther).

vererben: see **erben.**

verfehlen: see **fail** 5; **miss** I (*a*) and (*b*).

verführen: see **verleiten.**

vergessen: 1. (a) The MHG verb *vergezzen* took a *gen.*, and this was the rule in early NHG also, as in **Sie vergaßen Gottes, ihres Heilands** (Ps. 106. 21). But the only example of this still used in ordinary lang. is **das Vergißmeinnicht**, otherwise it is confined to poetry and choice prose (cf. 2): e.g. **Der Herr hat mein noch nie vergessen; Vergiß, mein Herz, auch seiner nicht!** (in a hymn of Gellert's)—**Besonders unzufrieden zeigten sich die Barone, denen die Königin ihre Befreiung zu danken hatte und deren sie zu vergessen schien** (Platen)—**Er ließ die Kränze liegen und vergaß ihrer beinah ganz** (Fontane)—**Der Anblick machte ihn alles übrigen** (usually **alles übrige**) **vergessen** (Alverdes); cf. as a strange example of fluctuation, **Gott hatte seine Erde noch nie vergessen, er würde ihrer auch jetzt nicht vergessen** (Viebig). (**b**) In southern dialects the accus. obj. is mostly replaced by **an** + accus. (on the analogy of **denken** q.v. I (*c*)) or esp. **auf** + accus., but examples like the following are rightly condemned by *Duden* as **„nicht schriftdeutsch"**, and by *Sanders* as **„falsch und durchaus zu vermeiden": Die Angst hatte sie daran vergessen lassen** (St. Zweig)—**Er bot das Bild eines Sängers, der sich am Klavier begleitet, plötzlich aber daran vergißt und ohne Begleitung weitersingt** (Bruno Frank)—**Kindchen, auf dich hatte ich ja ganz vergessen** (G. Keller)—**Sie sollten nicht ganz auf ihn vergessen** (Rosegger)—**Er schien auf die Unterredung völlig vergessen zu haben** (Stifter)—**Morgen ist mein Geburtstag! Wenn das Kind nicht hier wäre, würde man auf so was vergessen** (P. Keller)—**Erinnere mich des öfteren an den Ernst des Lebens, sonst vergess' ich am Ende auf meinen verheirateten Zustand!** (H. W. Geissler). In spite of all these examples, the prep. construction should never be used in good prose. **2.** An isolated expression like **seines Eides vergessen** may have two meanings, according as **vergessen** is an infin. or a past part. In the former case there is no difficulty: the phrase can only mean 'to forget one's oath', where in ordinary lang. one would say **seinen Eid vergessen.** On the other hand, where **vergessen** is a past part., the idiom is a strange one in that the past part. has *act.* force, so that the phrase means 'forgetful of one's oath', much like **uneingedenk seines Eides.** The idiom can only be explained by regarding the past part. either as a mutilated pres. part., the final **-d** having been lost, or as the actual past part. with **habend** understood ('having forgotten one's oath'). In any case it is noteworthy that the *gen.* is firmly established here, which is the more surprising as it would be quite possible to use the *accus.*, in which case the phrase would be an example of the **accusative absolute** (q.v.), with the force of 'one's oath forgotten'. Actually, this idiom is not very common: it is mainly poet., as in **Seiner Menschlichkeit vergessen, Wagt er mit**

Dämonen sich zu messen (Sch.: 'Forgetting that he is a human, he dares to be a match for demons') but it also occurs in prose: e.g. **„Ihr müßt nicht alles, was er sagt, für ernst nehmen", lachte sie, ihres Kopfwehs vergessen** (Jul. Wolff); and it is esp. common in a number of compd. adjs., like **eidvergessen, pflichtvergessen** ('forgetful of one's duty'), and esp. **selbstvergessen** ('forgetting oneself, thinking of others, unselfish'). Here belongs the neg. expression **unvergessen,** which usually means 'unforgotten', but may mean 'not forgetting, mindful of'; and where this is used abs., i.e. without a gen., it may be very misleading: a good example of this is seen in the proposition **Der Hofrat verlangte, daß man die geborgten Sachen zeitig zurückgeben solle: er war in solchen Dingen unvergessen und ließ es an Erinnerungen nicht fehlen** (G.), i.e. he did not forget such things, and did not hesitate to remind the borrower to return what he had borrowed. **3.** The reflex. **sich vergessen** can, of course, be used with a pers. subj. like English 'to forget oneself', as in **Ich vergaß mich so weit, ihn zu schlagen** (or **daß ich ihn schlug**); cf., with the old gen., **Sie überließ sich einer jeden Neigung, wenn sie nur ihrer selbst vergessen konnte** (G.). But it is also idiomatically used with an impers. subj. to suggest the pass.: e.g. **Solche Beleidigungen vergessen sich nicht leicht** or **lassen sich nicht leicht vergessen** ('Such insults are not easily forgotten').

vergewissern: At first sight one might think this was a verb with two insep. prefixes, but this would obviously be incorrect, there being no verb **wissern** to which prefixes could be attached: it is formed by prefixing **ver-** to the compar. of the adj. **gewiß** and giving it a verbal termination, much in the same way as **vergewaltigen** ('to commit a criminal assault on') and **versichern** ('to assure') are formed. Its lit. meaning, therefore, is 'to make more certain, confirm', but it is mostly used with a pers. obj., esp. a reflex. pron., in the sense of 'to convince', as in **Ich mußte mich vergewissern, ob es mit der Sitzung Ernst werden würde** (M. Eyth: 'I had to convince myself *or* make sure that the proposal to hold a meeting would prove to be a serious one'). Instead of a subord. clause, as in this example, a gen. of the thing can be used, or the prep. **von** or **über** (+ accus.): e.g. **Ich habe mich dessen** (or **davon** or **darüber**) **vergewissert** ('I have made sure of that').

vergleichen: see **gleich** 5.

vergnügen: This verb is no longer used as much as it once was, modern usage generally preferring other expressions. Still in fairly common use is the reflex. **sich vergnügen** ('to amuse oneself'), as in **Er besaß ein Paar Schlittschuhe, also vergnügte er sich einige Stunden auf dem Eise** (E. Wichert), but even there one would ordinarily use **sich amüsieren.** Much less common is **jemand vergnügen** ('to amuse a person'), and in a proposition like **Eines Abends laden ihn die Bauern zum Schnaps ein: es vergnügt sie, zu sehen, wie er sich betrinkt** (E. Toller) one would rather say **es macht ihnen Vergnügen** (q.v.) or, to bring out the idea of hilarity, **es belustigt sie**; and the same applies to **Gespräch und Scherz vergnügen ihn** (Ranke). In **Sie besaß, was nur immer eine Frau vergnügen kann** (Varnhagen v. Ense) it presumably has its orig. force of 'to satisfy' (it being derived from **genug**: cf. **genügen,** 'to suffice', and **sich mit etwas begnügen,** 'to be contented with something'), but this is now almost obs.: the proposition **Er vergnügte des Jagens Begier** (Sch.: 'He gratified his craving *or* appetite for the chase') would ordinarily take the form **Er befriedigte seine Jagdlust,** and **Sie vergnügen ihre Neugier an deinem Schmerz** (Rilke) sounds distinctly archaic. The part of the verb in most frequent use is the past part. **vergnügt,** used as an attrib. or pred. adj.: e.g. **Wir waren alle sehr vergnügt** ('merry')—**Er war heute in vergnügter Laune** ('in a cheery mood') or **machte ein vergnügtes Gesicht** ('looked amused')—**Es war eine vergnügte Gesellschaft** ('a jolly party')—**Wir verbrachten einen vergnügten Abend**; cf. fig. **Wie vergnügt funkeln die Lämpchen!** (Heine: 'How cheerily the little lamps twinkle!').

Vergnügen, Vergnügung: 1. The abstr. noun **Vergnügen** expresses a pleasurable sensation or state: e.g. **Wenn er mich gebeten hätte, würde ich ihm mit Vergnügen** ('gladly, with pleasure') **geholfen haben**—**Ich wünsche Ihnen viel Vergnügen** ('I hope you will enjoy yourself *or* have a good time')—**Am Bergsteigen finde ich kein Vergnügen** ('I don't like *or* enjoy mountaineering'). Although one can speak of **ländliche Vergnügen** ('the pleasures of country life'), the plur. is actually not much used, which is natural as the word is the verbal infin. of **vergnügen** (q.v.). **2.** On the other hand, **Vergnügung** points not to a feeling or state of pleasure but to a specific cause of such feeling or state: thus, social functions, dances, visits to the theatre, etc., are **Vergnügungen,** and a person addicted to such entertainments is **vergnügungssüchtig** ('pleasure-loving'). For the difference between the two expressions cf. **In dem Volke** ('Among the common people') **ist von den Vergnügungen das Vergnügen noch nicht verbannt** (Immermann: i.e. they still enjoy their pleasures).

vergönnen: see **permit** 4.

vergraben: see **verkriechen** *ad fin.*

verhallen: see **aushallen** 1.

Verhältnis: see **relation** 3.

verhängen: 1. Like **behängen** (q.v.), **verhängen** is always trans., its dir. obj. being that which is covered, not that which is used as a covering: cf. **Ich hänge ein Tuch über den Spiegel** and **Ich verhänge den Spiegel mit einem Tuch.** It has a stronger force than **behängen,** its prefix implying more complete concealment (cf. **ver-, verbergen, verstecken**). **2.** The past tense is sometimes **verhing,** but much more commonly **verhängte,** always so when used *fig.*; the past part. **verhängt** properly implies an action, **verhangen** a state, but this distinction is not always strictly observed, as in the following examples where **verhangen** would really be more correct: **Ich richtete meinen Blick auf die verhängten Fenster** (E. T. A. Hoffmann)—**Die Kommode war mit weißen Tüchern verhängt** (H. Hauser)—**Er saß an dem weißverhängten Fensterchen** (Sudermann). The following examples observe the distinction: (i) *Weak* forms: **Handwerker hatten die Spiegel mit Flor verhängt** (Dauthendey)—**Man hatte die Fenster mit Vorhängen aus Damast verhängt** (Werfel)—**Das Fenster war zum Teil verhängt worden** (Bonsels)—**Ich verhängte dem Pferde die Zügel** ('I gave my horse his head' by letting the reins hang loose), hence **mit verhängtem** (never **verhangenem**) **Zügel reiten** ('to ride at full gallop, hell for leather': cf. **nachhängen**); so also always with *fig.* force: **Ich unterwarf mich dem Geschick, das Gott über mich verhängte** (Sch.: 'I submitted to the fate which God decreed as my lot')—**Ich nahm, was geschehen war, als verhängt (= als mein Verhängnis) an** (Chamisso: 'I accepted what had happened as my fate')—**Du tust, als verhängte ich ein abscheuliches Los über dich** (Bruno Frank: 'You act as if I were condemning you to an awful fate'); sim. **der verhängte Tag** ('the Day of Wrath', = **der Tag, den Gott über uns verhängt hat**); (ii) *Strong* forms: **Sie verhing** (usually **verhängte**) **das Fenster und entkleidete sich** (Immermann)—**Die langen Haare verhingen ihm das Gesicht** (Raabe)—**Ich ging in den Garten, den ein Nebel verhing** (Carossa); esp. in the past part.: **Der Himmel war fast zur Hälfte verhangen** (H. Hesse)—**Die Tür war mit einer Sicherheitskette verhangen** (Bruno Frank)—**Wir traten in ein grünverhangenes Stübchen** (Immermann)—**Die Welt, gestern noch grau und nebelverhangen, glitzerte in Rauhreif und Sonne** (Speckmann)—**Man sah es durch die unverhangenen Fenster** (Storm).

verhehlen: see **bergen** 4.

verheimlichen: see **bergen** 5.

verheiraten, Verheiratung: see **marry** 1 (*b*) and 2 (*d*).

verheißen: see **promise** 3.

verhindern: see **hindern.**

verhören: see **accusative (double)** 1 (*c*).

verhüten: see **hüten** 2 (*b*).

verirren: see **irre** 2 (*b*) (ii).

verklingen: see **aushallen,** esp. 2.

verköstigen: see **Kost(en)** 1.

verkriechen: This verb is only used *reflex.* with the force of 'to crawl into *or* crouch in' a corner, hiding-place, etc., preps. like **in, hinter, unter** taking either an accus., suggesting the action of crawling, or (perhaps rather more commonly) a dat., pointing to the final crouching position: e.g. **Sie verkroch sich hinter dem Altare** (Novalis)—**Er suchte sich die dunkelste Laube aus und verkroch sich in ihrem hintersten Winkel** (Sudermann)—**Der Junge verkroch sich hinter dem Rock der Mutter** (Ompteda); cf. the following two examples: **Die Schlangen hatten sich in den Binsen verkrochen** (G. Britting) and **Die Tiere hatten sich in das Gebüsch verkrochen** (Ponten). The same applies to **sich vergraben:** cf. **Ich habe mich im Heu vergraben** (Chamisso) and **Um das Feuer herum lagen die Leute auf Schütten Stroh** ('bundles of straw'), **in das sie sich vergraben hatten** (Ompteda).

verlangen: Orig. this compd. of **langen** (q.v.) was an *impers.* verb, with the force of 'to wish to reach', i.e. 'to long for' (see **sehnen, Sucht** 2, and cf. **gelüsten**): e.g.

Herr, . . . mich verlangt nach dir (Ps. 143. 8), and this impers. use is still found, sometimes with a dat. of the person, as in **Ich finde, daß du teilnahmsvoller sein könntest: wenn du wüßtest, wie mir gerade danach verlangt!** (Fontane). But **mich verlangt nach etwas** gradually lost some of its force, and in **Wie die Spangen dir gefallen werden, verlanget mich zu sehen** (Lessing) it means little more than 'I am curious'. Much more common now is the *pers.* use of the verb, suggesting an eager desire for something, as in **Der Kranke verlangt nach dem Arzt,** and this led to its commonest modern use with an accus. obj. in the sense of 'to demand'. Here it approaches **fordern,** but this suggests a stronger demand, implying that the person has a claim to what he demands: cf., on the one hand, **Der Kranke verlangt etwas Nahrung** and **Diese Arbeit verlangt viel Geduld,** and, on the other hand, **Der Offizier fordert unbedingten Gehorsam.**

verlassen: see **leave (verb)** 2.

verleiden: see **leiden** 1 (*b*).

verleihen: see **borgen** 2.

verleiten: This compd. of **leiten** (cf. **leiden** 1 (*a*)) properly means 'to mislead', implying the use of specious arguments which lead a person into doing something which he had not intended to do, or which it was not in his nature to do, while **verführen** means 'to tempt, seduce', implying the use of false representations in order to weaken a person's will-power, esp. by exciting his desires or passions. But **verleiten** need not necessarily suggest that a person deliberately sets out to mislead—an innocent remark may cause another person to act injudiciously—whereas **verführen** almost always implies a deliberate intention to lead astray: cf. on the one hand, **Er ließ sich durch das, was gesagt wurde, zu einer unvorsichtigen Bemerkung verleiten** (i.e. he was led into making a thoughtless remark), and on the other hand, **Er ließ sich durch Vorspiegelung eitler Hoffnungen verführen** (i.e. he was tempted by having vain hopes held out to him)—**Das Mädchen hat sich von dem Kerl verführen lassen.**

verleugnen: see **deny** 2 (*c*).

verlieren: The only grammatical point in connexion with this verb is when it is used *reflex.* with a prep. phrase in the sense of 'to lose one's way in *or* mix with' (a crowd), fig. 'to become lost in' (thought), and with an impers. subj. like a sound, 'to die away'. Here, as with analogous verbs compounded with **ver-** (q.v. 2), either an accus. or a dat. is used after the prep., according as the action or the resultant state is in the writer's mind: e.g. **Der Jüngling hatte sich in den Wald verloren** (Novalis)—**Er verlor sich in süßen Fantasien** (id.)—**„Guten Tag!" sagte ich ins Leere hinein** (referring to a shop in which no shopgirls were to be seen), **und noch höre ich, wie der Klang meiner Stimme sich in der Stille verlor** (Th. Mann); for the fluctuation, cf. **Man verlor sich in die alte Gewerbstadt, besonders markttages** ('on market days') **in dem Gewühl, das sich um die Kirche herum versammelte** (G.).

verloben: With an accus. and a dat., this verb means 'to betroth a person *or* promise a person's hand in marriage to somebody', as in **Sie verlobten ihre Tochter einem reichen Gutsbesitzer** ('They arranged their daughter's engagement to a rich landowner'). In the case of the more common reflex. **sich verloben** ('to get engaged'), the dat. is replaced by the prep. **mit:** e.g. **Sie hat sich mit ihrem Jugendfreund verlobt**—cf., with both act. and pass., **Du hast dich verlobt, sagst du: wem willst du das weismachen?** (see **weis-** (*a*)). **Sie hat sich verlobt, du bist bloß verlobt worden** (Fontane: 'You say you have got engaged: whom do you think you will fool with that story? It's *she* who has got engaged, *you* have just been forced into it'). The reflex. is sometimes still used with the prep. **zu** (or with **zu** + infin.) with the force of 'to bind *or* pledge oneself' to (do) something, but in this sense **sich verpflichten** is much more common.

verlohnen: see **lohnen** 1.

verlöschen: see **löschen** 2.

verlustig: see **adjectives (indeclinable)** 5; **miss** 1 (*d*).

vermachen: see **leave (verb)** 3 (*b*).

vermählen, Vermählung: see **marry** 1 (*b*) and 2 (*d*).

vermessen: The prefix of this strong verb may convey two different meanings: it may either have intensifying force (see **ver-** 1) or suggest an error (see **ver-** 3): the former is seen in the use of the verb with the force of 'to take exact measurements of' something, e.g. a room, a field, etc., while the reflex. may mean 'to make a mistake in measuring'. But the commonest use of **sich vermessen** is in the fig. sense of 'to dare', esp. 'to presume' to do something, as in **Der lose Mann vermaß sich, der Christen Gott zu lästern** (G.). The 2nd sing. of the imperat. is properly **vermiß!** but to avoid confusion with the weak verb **vermissen** (q.v.), the weak form is sometimes used, as when Faust, in a monologue, says **Vermesse dich, die Pforten aufzureißen, vor denen jeder gern vorüberschleicht!** (G.), a passage referred to in **Goethe hat den „Werther" geschrieben, der sich vermißt, „die Pforten aufzureißen, an** [*sic*] **denen jeder gern vorüberschleicht"** (F. A. Hohenstein). Common is the use of the past part. **vermessen** as an adj. ('daring, venturesome, presumptuous'): **Wer sollte so vermessen sein, den Karlos zu belauschen?** (Sch.).

vermissen: see miss 2 (*b*).

vermöge: This prep. (+ *gen.*), meaning 'by virtue *or* reason *or* the authority of, on the strength of', occurs first in the 16th century and is probably a corrupt form of the verbal subst. **Vermögen,** before which a prep. has dropped out: Luther uses **nach Vermögen des päpstlichen Briefes.** This explanation is supported by the NHG prep. **kraft** (+ *gen.*), which has much the same force and seems to have developed out of **in Kraft**: cf. **Er regiert nicht in Kraft eines verliehenen Amtes** (Fr. v. Raumer, 1781–1873) and **Er hatte sich in Kraft der Millionen, die er gewann, ein prächtiges Haus gebaut** (Wieland). Usage is now firmly established: e.g., in a well-known hymn, **Reiß mich aus den Ängsten kraft deiner Angst und Pein** (P. Gerhard); so also **kraft meines Amtes** ('by virtue of my office')—**kraft des Gesetzes—kraft meiner väterlichen Gewalt** (Heyse). While **kraft** implies the exercise of human power or authority, **vermöge** suggests an inborn or inherent natural force: **Vermöge seiner Schwere fällt ein Stein zu Boden—Vermöge seines Scharfsinns kann er die schwierigsten Rätsel lösen.**

vermögen: This verb is used in two ways. **1.** With **zu** + infin., it has the force of 'to be able *or* in a position, to have it in one's power'. Whereas the verbal noun **Vermögen** is an everyday expression, not so much in the sense of 'ability' (although **nach bestem Vermögen** is the usual way to express 'to the best of one's ability') as in that of 'fortune, wealth, means', and whereas the pres. part. **vermögend** is mostly used as an adj. meaning 'wealthy', the verb itself is comparatively little used in ordinary lang.: instead of **Ich vermag nicht ihn zu überreden,** one generally says **Ich kann ihn nicht überreden** or **Ich bin nicht imstande, ihn zu überreden.** Rather more common is its use with an indef. obj.: **Das vermag ich nicht—Ein väterlicher Rat vermag bei einer Tochter viel** (Sch.: 'A father's advice to his daughter can achieve much, do a world of good'). An important grammatical point here is that in a compd. tense the past part. can never assume the infin. form, as that of the simple verb does: cf. **Ich habe das nicht tun mögen** ('I did not like to do that') and **Ich habe das nicht zu tun vermocht. 2.** The other standard use of **vermögen** is in the sense of 'to induce' (= **bewegen,** q.v. 1 (*b*)): e.g. **Nur die Vorstellung, daß ihr Zustand bessere Kost forderte, konnte sie vermögen, etwas Wein zu genießen** (E. T. A. Hoffmann: 'Only the representation that her condition demanded a more nourishing diet could induce her to take some wine')—**Knirschend** ('Grinding his teeth': cf. **mit** 2 (*b*)) **war er gegangen, und nichts hätte ihn vermocht, die Schwelle wieder zu betreten** (Heyse)—**Er hatte einen Kameraden vermocht, bei ihm zu bleiben** (R. Herzog); so also with the *prep.* **zu** instead of the infin. with **zu,** as in **Diese Beweggründe vermochten ihn zur Einwilligung** (= **vermochten ihn, einzuwilligen** or **seine Einwilligung zu geben**: 'These arguments prevailed upon him to give his consent') —**Diese Ereignisse vermochten ihn kaum zu einem Achselzucken** (Th. Mann: 'These events hardly caused him to shrug his shoulders'); and in the comparatively rare *pass.*, **Die Königin schlug ihren Sitz im Castel Capuano auf, das zur Übergabe vermocht wurde** (Platen: 'The queen took up residence in the C.C., which was forced to capitulate').

vermuten: This is a LG word (< MLG *vormôden*) taken over into HG. Used with a reflex. pron., it has the force of 'to suppose, conjecture, suspect' (see **ahnen** 2), and the orig. **Ich hätte mich dessen nicht vermutet** gradually led to **Ich hätte mir das nicht vermutet** (see **es** 2), which is now the recognized idiom. A curious periphrastic idiom is seen in propositions like **Was gilt's, das warst du nicht vermuten?** (Lessing: 'I bet you didn't expect that?') or **Ihr Fuhrwerk wär' ich am mindesten**

vor meiner Tür vermuten gewesen (Storm: 'Your conveyance is the one I should least have expected to see at my door'): here **vermuten** has dropped a final **-d**, the idiom being **sich** (dat.) **etwas** (accus.) **vermutend sein**, an expression used chiefly in the pre-classical period, but occasionally found in modern works, where it has a distinctly archaic flavour: e.g. **Ich war mir Sie in dem Vorzimmer nicht vermutend** (Lessing)—*Bon soir, messieurs,* **gewiß sind Sie mich hier nicht vermutend** (Carossa)—**Der schlichte Mann, der alle Hände voll zu tun hatte, war sich solche Auszeichnung nicht vermutend gewesen** (Th. Mann).

verneinen: see **deny** 1.

verpassen: see **miss** 1 (*c*).

verpflichten: see **verloben** *ad fin.*

verquer: see **quer** 1 (*b*).

verrichten: see **richten** 2 (*c*).

versagen: **1.** The fundamental sense of this verb is 'to refuse, deny' (a person something), as in **jemandem den Gehorsam versagen** ('to refuse to obey some one') or **jemandem eine Bitte versagen** ('to refuse a person's request'); sim. **Der Bäcker versagte uns einiges Brot auf die Reise und verwies uns in den Gasthof** (G.: 'The baker refused to give us some bread for our journey and directed us to the inn')—**Als einziges, verzogenes** ('spoiled') **Kind reicher Eltern war er nicht gewohnt, sich etwas zu versagen** (G.: '. . . was not accustomed to deny himself anything')—**Den Engländern ist der Farbensinn versagt** (Heine: 'The English are denied, i.e. lack, colour-sense')—**Ich bedaure, mir dieses Vergnügen versagen zu müssen** ('I am sorry to have to forgo this pleasure'). **2.** As used above, **versagen** can often be replaced by **verweigern** (see **weigern** 2); but this is impossible where **versagen** is apparently used in the *intrans.* relation. In such cases, there is really an accus. obj. like **Dienst** or **Hilfe** understood ('to refuse to serve *or* help'), but, with the obj. unexpressed, the verb comes to mean 'to refuse to function' (cf. **fail** 4): e.g. **Ich drückte ab, aber das Gewehr versagte** ('I pulled the trigger, but the rifle misfired')—**Meine Stimme versagte** ('My voice broke down')—**Er war so verwirrt, daß ihm alle Worte versagten** (A. Wilbrandt)—**Meine Kräfte versagten mir** ('My strength failed me')—**Ich wußte mich kaum zu fassen, meine Knie, mein Verstand wollten mir versagen** (G.). **3.** It may seem strange at first that in certain contexts **versagen** conveys the very reverse meaning of 'to refuse', yet the association of ideas becomes clear when one considers that a girl who *gives* her hand to one of several admirers must *refuse* it to the others. So, a father who is asked for the hand of his daughter may say **Meine Tochter hat sich** (or **ihre Hand**) **schon versagt**; sim. in common expressions like **Ich kann Ihre Einladung leider nicht annehmen, ich bin für heute abend schon versagt** ('. . . I have a previous engagement for this evening')—**Ich bat sie um den nächsten Tanz, sie war aber schon versagt** ('. . . she had promised the dance to somebody else')—**Die ausgeschriebene Stelle ist bereits versagt** ('The advertised post has already been filled').—The context will generally make it clear which of the two contradictory meanings the author wishes to convey; where ambiguity may arise, as in **Sie hat sich ihm versagt**, it is advisable to use **verweigern** for 'to refuse'.

versalzen: see **falten** 3.

versammeln: see **sammeln** 2.

versäumen: see **miss** 1 (*c*); **fail** 5.

verschaffen: see **schaffen** 2 (*b*).

verschallen, verschollen: see **schallen** 2.

verschieden: see **scheiden**.

verschonen: see **spare** 2 (*b*).

verschroben: see **schrauben**.

verschweigen: see **bergen** 4; cf. **schweigen** *ad fin.*

verschwinden: When this verb is accompanied by a prep. phrase indicating the place where something disappears, an accus. is used if the idea of motion out of sight is implied, a dat. if that of being already lost to view is in the writer's mind (cf. **ver-** 2, and **versinken**): e.g. **Er verschwand in dieselbe Tür, in die vor acht Jahren Heiderieter verschwand** (Frenssen)—**Die beiden verschwanden im Walde** (id.)—**Er sah zu, wie die zwei Herren im Direktionszimmer verschwanden** (Kafka)—**Sie schaute rundherum und verschwand zwischen den Häusern** (Waggerl).

versehen: **1.** There is no fundamental difference between **versehen** and **versorgen**: both mean 'to supply, provide', the former implying that one *sees* to it that something is provided, the latter that one takes *trouble* to provide it or have it provided; either can be used with objects like **Amt** or **Posten** ('to fill a post'), **Dienst** ('to discharge a duty'), **Gottesdienst**

('to conduct a service'), **Geschäfte** ('to transact business'), etc. But **versehen** refers esp. to providing what one presumably requires *for a specific purpose*, while **versorgen** has a more general application: e.g. **Die Kinder wollen einen längeren Ausflug machen, ich habe sie mit den nötigen Nahrungsmitteln versehen—Die Haustür ist mit einer Notkette versehen—Die Römer errichteten den berühmten Pont du Gard, um die Stadt Nimes mit Wasser zu versorgen**; cf., on the one hand, **Er hat seine Tochter mit einer Eintrittskarte zur Oper versehen** and, on the other hand, **Er hat seine Tochter gut versorgt** ('He has made good provision for his daughter'). **2.** Used with a *reflex.* pron., **versehen** has several meanings, the three commonest being: (**a**) 'to provide oneself' with something (see 1); (**b**) 'to make a mistake, do something inadvertently' (see **ver-** and cf. **aus Versehen,** 'by mistake'): e.g. **Ich bitte um Entschuldigung, ich habe mich bei der Ausstellung der Rechnung versehen** ('I beg pardon, I have made a mistake in making up the account'); (**c**) 'to expect' something of *or* from a person (cf. **unversehens,** 'unawares, unexpectedly'); here the thing expected originally stood in the *gen.* case, and the reflex. pron. in the *accus.*, the person from whom the thing was expected being expressed by **zu** (now commonly **von**): e.g. **Zu einem Professor hätte ich mich dessen nicht versehen** (Lessing: 'I should not have expected that from a professor')—**Wessen soll man sich zu euch versehen?** (Sch.: 'What shall we look to you for?')—**Er sprach im Namen eines Herrn, von dem wir uns eines Besseren versehen hätten** (Fontane: '. . . from whom we should have expected something better')—**Viele Herren und Damen waren mit ihrer Dienerschaft in die Stadt gekommen, von denen sich Gastwirte und Geschäftsleute mancher Einnahmen versahen** (Bergengruen); but a phrase like **sich** (accus.) **es** (gen.) **versehen** came to be misunderstood, the orig. gen. **es** being taken to be an *accus.*, and hence the accus. **sich** to be regarded as a *dat.* (see **es** 2): e.g. **Dieses Unglück hätte ich mir nicht versehen** (Lessing). Nowadays **sich versehen** with this force is a rather choice expression; it is really only common in the phrase **ehe man sich's versieht** ('before one expects it, before you can say Jack Robinson, in less than no time'): e.g., in the first person, **Ehe ich mich's versehe** (G.) or **Ehe ich mir's versehe** (Gutzkow)—**Ehe ich mir's versah, war ich wieder eingesperrt** (Dauthendey).

versichern: 1. With the force of 'to insure' (life, property, etc.), this takes an accus. obj., as in **Ich habe mich gegen Unfall** or **mein Haus gegen Feuer versichern lassen. 2.** Used in the sense of 'to assure' a person, i.e. give him reliable information, the person stands either in the accus. or (now rather more commonly) in the dat.: e.g. **Er versicherte mir** (or **mich**), **daß er unschuldig sei—Berlin wird immer schöner: so versichern einem wenigstens alle, die nichts Besseres kennen** (Fontane). But the proposition 'He assured me of his innocence' is rendered by **Er versicherte mich** (not **mir**) **seiner Unschuld**; and so also one can say **Er hat mich dessen** ('of it') **versichert,** a more formal way of expressing **Er hat mir das versichert.** How this last construction developed is interesting. We occasionally find examples of a double accus. in such propositions, as in **Ist das die Liebe, die du mich versichert hast?** (Spielhagen) and **Das kann ich Sie versichern** (Droste-Hülshoff), but this is not to be recommended, being really the result of a misconception. In a proposition like **Er ist ein Ehrenmann, ich versichere es Sie** (W. Alexis), the old gen. **es** (q.v.) has come to be treated as an accus., and once this was accepted, it was natural that the pers. accus. should become a dat.: cf. 'I assure *you of it*' and 'I declare *it to you*'; for a similar development, see **remember** 3 (*d*) and the verbs referred to there *ad fin.*

versinken: Whereas the simple verb **sinken** requires an *accus.* in expressions like **ins Meer, auf die Knie, in einen tiefen Schlaf sinken** and **die Hände in den Schoß sinken lassen,** the compd. **versinken** more commonly takes a *dat.* in such prep. phrases, esp. (cf. **vertiefen**) where the past part. is used to suggest the state of being engulfed, submerged, lost to view (see **ver-** 2, and cf. **verkriechen**): e.g. **Deine Füße werden in dem weichen Boden versinken** (Raabe)—**Sie glaubte, ihren Sohn aus den Träumereien reißen zu müssen, in denen sie ihn versunken sah** (Novalis); and so also **in trüben Gedanken versunken** is more natural than **in düsteres Sinnen versunken** (Heyse). For the accus. here, cf. the example from Spindler given under **Gicht.**

versorgen: see **versehen** 1.
versprechen: see **promise** 1 and 2.
verständigen: see **agree** 4 (*a*).
verstecken: This verb implies a deliberate act of concealment, being a more everyday expression for **verbergen** (q.v.). As with the latter verb, preps. like **in, hinter, unter**, etc., indicating the place of concealment, may take either an accus. or a dat. In the proposition **Der Pfarrer nahm das Bild von der Wand und versteckte es in die hinterste Ecke** (Mörike), the action is regarded as not yet completed (much like our coll. 'shoved it away into the corner'); **in der hintersten Ecke** would imply a completed action, the picture being already quite concealed. The past part., used as an adj., may mean 'secluded', as in **Kein Tal war so versteckt, ich spähte es aus** (Sch.: i.e. 'I scoured every valley, no matter how secluded'); cf. fig. **eine versteckte Anspielung** ('a veiled hint'). Applied to persons, it has come to mean 'sly, underhand': e.g. **Ich bin offen und gutmütig, du bist versteckt und still** (G.).
Verstecken(s): see **spielen**; cf., as unusual, **Der Baum war hohl und bot in seinem Inneren geräumigen Platz für ein Versteckens dar** (Immermann), where it is used for **ein Versteck** ('a hiding-place').
verstehen: For the form **verstünde**, see **past subjunctive** 2 (*c*). The most important points in connexion with this verb are the various uses of **sich verstehen**, esp. with a prep. phrase: (**a**) In the abs. use, the force of the pron. may be either *recip*. (e.g. **Wir verstehen uns**, 'We understand each other') or *reflex*. (e.g. **Das versteht sich**, 'That's a matter of course'; common in commercial language: **Unsere Preise verstehen sich ohne Verpackung**, i.e. are to be understood as excluding packing); (**b**) with **auf** (+ *accus.*): 'to have a thorough knowledge of': e.g. **Er soll sich aufs Klavierspielen verstehen** ('He is said to be an expert piano-player')—**Sie versteht sich nicht aufs Kochen** ('She's no great cook'); (**c**) with **mit**: 'to be of the same opinion as', hence 'to agree, get on with': e.g. **Ich finde es schwer, mich in dieser Angelegenheit mit ihm zu verstehen** ('I find it difficult to agree with him in this matter')—**Mit solchen Menschen habe ich mich nie verstanden** ('I have never got on with such people'); (**d**) with **zu**: 'to agree to', sometimes 'to condescend to' (like **sich herablassen**): e.g. **Wir haben uns zu einer Zusammenkunft verstanden** ('. . . agreed to come together')—**Der Fürst verstand sich zu einer Unterredung mit den Aufrührern** ('. . . condescended to a conference with the rebels').
verstellen (reflex.): see **stellen** 2; cf. **pretend.**
vertauschen: see **change** 2 (*b*).
vertiefen: This verb is used with the force of 'to make deeper', as in **ein zum Bade vertiefter Raum** (G.), referring to the part of a river where the current has deepened the water and made a pool suitable for bathing. But it is mainly used *reflex*. (cf. **verkriechen**), either in the lit. sense of 'to become deeper', as in **An dieser Stelle vertieft sich der Fluß**, or esp. with the *fig*. force of 'to become absorbed, engrossed' in some occupation, the accompanying prep. **in** generally taking an *accus*. where the action of engrossing oneself is suggested, but a *dat*. where the state of being engrossed is implied, the latter esp. in the case of the past part. (cf. **versinken**): e.g. **Mutter und Sohn vertieften sich in ein leises Gespräch** (Novalis)—**Sie setzten sich in eine Ecke und vertieften sich ins Kartenspiel** (F. Kafka); so also an accus. would seem more natural in **Dann vertiefte er sich in dem dunkelsten Walde** (Sudermann), but one usually says **Er saß im Lehnstuhl, in seiner Lektüre vertieft.**
vertragen: see **agree** 2.
vertrauen: see **trauen** 3 (*a*).
vervollkommnen: This *weak* verb, meaning 'to perfect', is formed in much the same way as **bewillkommnen** (q.v.), except that the word to which **ver-** is prefixed is not a noun but an adj. (**vollkommen**). It is noteworthy that the form **vervollkommnen** is quite established: there is *no* contracted form **vervollkommen** corresponding to the alternative form **bewillkommen.**
verwahren: see **behalten** 3.
verwalten: cf. **walten** *ad fin.*
verwandeln: see **change** 1 (*b*).
Verwandtschaft: see **relation** 2.
verweben: see **weben**, and cf. **In „Tausendundeine Nacht" ist die kühnste Geistigkeit und die vollkommenste Sinnlichkeit in eins verwoben** (Hofmannsthal).
verwechseln: see **change** 2 (*a*).
verwegen, verwogen: see **wiegen** 4(*c*).
verweisen: This verb, now always *strong*, represents two quite distinct MHG verbs (one strong, the other weak), which

accounts for the fact that the modern word has two very different meanings. **1.** Its one sense (< MHG *verwîzen*, strong) is 'to rebuke, reprimand' a person for something, generally with a dat. of the person and an accus. of the thing, much less commonly an accus. of the person and a prep. phrase, probably the result of confusion with the other sense of the verb (see 2): e.g. **Ich habe ihm sein anstößiges Benehmen verwiesen** ('I have rebuked him for his offensive behaviour')—**Die Kinder mochten nicht mit dem Jungen spielen: „Er ist zu häßlich", sagten sie, der sie darob** (= **deswegen**) **verwies** (Ziferer). **2.** Its second sense (< MHG *verwîsen*, weak) was orig. 'to direct wrongly, lead astray', but now 'to direct' in a certain direction or towards some place: e.g. **Der Wirt entschuldigte sich: er müsse die Gäste in die weiter hinaufliegende Herberge verweisen** (G.)—**Der Kaiser verwies ihn auf Lebenslang ins Exil** (Wieland: see below)—**Der Leser wird auf das vorige Kapitel verwiesen** ('The reader is referred to the previous chapter')—**„Gestohlen hat er!" schrie der Fabrikant, ward aber sofort zur Ruhe verwiesen** (H. Hesse: '. . . but was promptly directed to be silent, called to order'); and so also 'to direct' away from a place, as in **Wie er mich von dem Bahnhof verweisen wollte, hielt ich ihm meinen Paß hin** (W. Schäfer), esp. 'to exile' (= **verbannen**), the place from which the person is banished standing in the *gen.*: e.g. **Ich begreife, daß Ihr ihn des Landes verweisen mußtet** (C. F. Meyer); cf. **einen Schüler (aus der Schule) verweisen** ('to expel a pupil') and **einen Studenten verweisen** ('to rusticate a student, send him down').

verwirren: The orig. strong conjugation of this verb is now only represented by the past part. **verworren,** which exists side by side with the weak form **verwirrt.** When the reference is to a person, *Sanders* rightly distinguishes between **„Jemand ist verwirrt, augenblicklich außer Fassung gebracht"** (i.e. temporarily confused, upset) and **„Jemand ist verworren, dauerndkonfus, der Klarheit und Ordnung des Denkens ermangelnd"** (i.e. constitutionally muddle-headed); cf., on the one hand, **Diese Nachricht hat mich ganz verwirrt** (not **verworren**) and, on the other hand, **Er ist ein verworrener** (not **verwirrter**) **Kopf.** The difference is well brought out in **Er hörte verworren zu . . . Diese gehässigen Reden verwirrten ihn** (St. Zweig), where the first proposition suggests inability to think clearly, the second a state of bewilderment. Actually, **verworren** is much more commonly used of things: e.g. **Aus diesem verworrenen Bericht werde ich nicht klug** ('I cannot make head or tail of this confused, rambling report')—**Die Sache wird immer verworrener** ('The case is becoming more and more complicated')—**Er redete allerlei verworrenes Zeug** ('He talked a lot of nonsense'); **cf.** the last example given under **kreuzen 2.**

verwesen: see **wesen.**

verwundern, Verwunderung: see **wonder** 2 and 3; **Wunder 1.**

verwünschen: Here the prefix **ver-** (q.v. 1) implies a change. The proper force of the verb is 'to enchant, bewitch, transform by witchcraft' (= **verzaubern**): e.g. **Zahlreich sind die Märchen, in denen es sich um die Erlösung eines Menschen handelt, der in ein Tier verwünscht ist** (P. Zaunert); sim., with an impers. obj., **Man erzählt, hier habe ein verwünschtes** ('enchanted') **Schloß gestanden** (Heine). In the former example, where the action of laying a spell is suggested, the reg. weak past part. is quite fixed; but in the latter, where the enchanted state is implied, the strong *unmutated* past part. **verwunschen** is now much more usual: e.g. **Da kamen verwunschene Prinzen und Zwerge durch die Waldesnacht gezogen** (Speckmann)—**Sage jedem ledigen Manne, auf dem Berg säße eine verwunschene Jungfrau, die auf einen Freier wartete** (Jul. Wolff)—**Der Torweg des Parks kam ihm wie verwunschen vor** (Binding)—**Es war wie in jenen Märchen, in denen ein einsamer Wanderer von Geistermusik in ein verwunschenes Haus gelockt wird** (Zuckmayer)—**Alle Straßen waren verschneit, die Dächer winterlich verwunschen** (Fr. Schnack: '. . . the roofs magically clad in their winter cloak'). A later development is the now common use of the verb with the trans. force of 'to curse' (= **verfluchen**), and in this sense the weak form is well established: e.g. **Verwünscht!** ('Confound it!')—**Diese verwünschten Steuern!** ('These accursed taxes!')—**Er dünkt sich verwünscht** (or **verteufelt**) **gescheit** ('He thinks himself deuced clever'); **cf.**, as very unusual, **„Der Tag soll verwunschen sein!" rief er** (Waggerl: 'Cursed be the day!').

verzeihen: It is strange that this compd.

is so common and has become one of the established expressions in polite conversation, seeing that the simple verb is now almost rare. Both are strong, but whereas **zeihen** (q.v., 'to accuse') takes an accus. of the person and a gen. of the thing, **verzeihen** ('to excuse, pardon') takes a dat. of the person and an accus. of the thing: cf. **Sie zeihen mich der Schreibfaulheit; ich bekenne meine Schuld und bitte Sie, mir diese Schwäche zu verzeihen**; and of course the accus. obj. may be a subord. clause, as in **Er hat mir verziehen, daß ich ihm so lange nicht geschrieben habe.** Both verbs can be used in the *pass.*, but here the accus. obj. of **zeihen** becomes a nom., while the dat. object of **verzeihen** remains a dat. (see **impersonal verbs** 3).

Verzierung: see **ornament** 3 (*b*).

viel: 1. *Uninflected*: **(a)** Like most other MHG indef. neut. expressions, *vil* was really a noun, but unlike *niht* ('nothing') which could be inflected (see **nichts**), *vil* was indeclinable. Such words normally required a partitive gen. (e.g. *hie ist vil rôter bluomen*, 'Here there is a wealth of red flowers'), and we still use this idiom when we say **viel Leute,** only that we no longer recognize **Leute** as a gen., but treat it as a nom. or accus. qualified by uninflected **viel,** and hence use a plur. verb: **Hier sind viel Leute.** But a few expressions in which **viel** precedes what is clearly a gen. sing. are still in common use: thus, rather archaic as it sounds, Luther's **viel Volks**—cf. '*Much people* of the city *was* with her': Luke 7. 12—is officially recognized, as in **Er ging in eine Seitengasse, durch die viel Volks heranströmte** (W. v. Scholz); and the same applies to **viel Leids,** as in **Es war ihm zu eng in dem Hause, wo er soviel Leids erfahren hatte** (Heyse: see **Leid**)—cf., as a more choice expression, **Ich bin meiner Weisheit überdrüssig wie die Biene, die des Honigs zuviel gesammelt hat** (Nietzsche). **(b)** Esp. common are examples of **viel** with the gen. of unmodified *verbal nouns*: e.g. **Wie heilsam ist es mir, unter einem Volke zu leben, über das soviel Redens und Schreibens ist** (G.: '. . . to live among a nation that is so much spoken and written about')—**Wir brauchen nicht viel Redens zu machen** (Heyse: 'We don't need to make a long story of it')—**Sie werden kaum von diesen Leuten gehört haben, denn viel Redens machen sie nicht von sich** (Speckmann); sim. **Er machte viel Rühmens** (q.v.) **von dem Reichtum seines Herrn** (I. Kurz: 'He boasted of his master's wealth')—**Was ist da viel Rühmens?** (Federer: 'What is there in that to brag about?')—**Da er hörte, daß ich Griechisch könnte, kramte er viel Wissens aus** (G.: '. . . he made a show of great erudition')—**Es war viel Lärmens, Springens und Jubilierens** (Immermann)—**Diese Stelle im Kant hat mir viel Kopfbrechens gemacht** (Heyse)—**Unter uns gesagt, die Harmonielehre macht mir viel Gähnens** (Th. Mann: 'Between you and me, the theory of harmony makes me yawn no end'). Here belong esp. the three verbal nouns **Aufheben, Federlesen** and **Wesen** (qq.v.). **(c)** That all feeling for the origin of such expressions has been lost is evident from the fact that some of these gen. forms can be used *without* the very word on which the gen. depends, i.e. as nouns which, while retaining the gen. ending, are used as nom. or accus. (cf. **nichts** 4): e.g. **In der Schule sammelte sich allerlei Volks an** (C. Rothe: cf. **Hand** 1 (*c*))—**Die Gräfin machte Rühmens von seiner Kunst** (C. Hauptmann: cf. **ohne** 1). So completely independent have these gen. forms become that they can even be qualified by an art. or other attributive word (see esp. **Aufheben, Federlesen, prahlen, Rat** and **Wesen,** and cf. **spielen**). **(d)** What has been said of **viel Leute** (see 1 (*a*) above) applies equally to **viel Gutes** (< MHG *vil guotes*, lit. 'much of good'), but here again **Gutes** has become a neut. adj.-subst. (cf. **nichts** 2): hence **In diesem Roman findet sich neben viel Gutem auch viel Schlechtes** (cf. 2 (*d*) below). Of course, a phrase like **viel Gutes** cannot be used as a gen., only as a nom. or accus., the only possible gen. form being **vieles Guten**; but the uninflected **viel** can stand before an attrib. adj.: **viel frisches Obst** (gen. **viel frischen Obstes**)—**viel bunte Blumen** (gen. **viel bunter Blumen**). The uninflected **viel** is now more usual in the *sing.*, esp. with monosyllabic nouns (see 2 (*a*)): e.g. **Dazu ist viel Geld nötig**—**Ich wünsche Ihnen viel Glück**—**Das Kind muß viel Milch trinken**; but always **Vielen Dank!** ('Many thanks!'). **2.** *Inflected*: **(a)** Unlike MHG *vil*, **viel** can be inflected in the ordinary way, and this is imperative when it is preceded by the def. art., a possessive or a demonstrative, and nearly always when used with subst. force in the *plur.*: e.g. **das viele Geld—sein vieles Reden** (gen. **seines vielen Redens**)—**meine vielen Bücher—diese vielen Menschen—viele meiner Freunde** or **von meinen Freunden.** Otherwise, either the inflected or, rather more coll., the uninflected form may be used attrib. before most plur. nouns: e.g. **Sie haben viel(e) Dienstboten—Er hat nicht viel(e) Freunde**; it is significant that one says **viel Zeit,** but **viele Wochen** or **Jahre.** Of course, inflexion is imperative in the gen., and also practically fixed in the dat.: e.g. **die Anwesenheit vieler Menschen—vor vielen Jahren—bei vielen Gelegenheiten.** (**b**) The normal masc. and neut. gen. sing. is **vieles** (used with *subst.* force **viel** has *no* gen.); the form **vielen** is only possible when the following noun has the strong **-(e)s** ending, and this is esp. common in the case of a verbal noun, as in **trotz vielen Sträubens.** (**c**) Where an attrib. adj. follows an inflected **viel,** there is much fluctuation: cf. **einig** 2 (*b*). In the *gen. plur.* there seems to be a preference for *weak* endings in the adj., as in **vieler vortrefflichen jungen Männer** (Sch.); but examples like **vieler anderer vornehmer Personen** (Fr. Griese) are not uncommon in modern works. On the other hand, in the *nom. and accus. plur.* there is a marked preponderance of opinion in favour of *strong* endings, indeed, *Sanders* explicitly characterizes weak endings here as **„falsch"**: e.g. **Serge ist ein Vorname, den viele russische Großfürsten führen** (Fontane), and sim. **viele intelligente katholische Priester** (Stehr), and with an adj.-subst., **Draußen vor der Kirche standen trotz der Kälte viele Neugierige** (Bergengruen). (**d**) In the case of a neut. adj.-subst. following **viel,** the usual **viel Gutes** (see 1 (*d*)) may be replaced by **vieles Gute,** so where Goethe says **Unter vielem Verhaßten ist mir das Schreiben das Verhaßteste,** it would be possible, although perhaps rather less common, to say **Unter viel Verhaßtem . . .**; cf. **Dieser Roman** (*scil.* Hauff's *Lichtenstein*) **hat große Schönheiten, es ist der Keim zu vielem Guten darin** (Schwab). In the gen. there is no choice: the only possible form is **vieles Verhaßten.**

vielerlei: see **Hand** 2 (*b*).

vier: cf. **zwei** 2 (*c*).

view: see **Sicht** 2 (*a*) and (*c*).

Volk: For propositions like **Viel Volks stand da versammelt** (Th. Mann), see **viel** 1 (*a*) and (*b*).

voll: **1.** A dependent noun which has no inflected modifier may remain uninflected after **voll** in the pred.: e.g. **Auf dem Tisch stand ein Glas voll Wein** or **eine Schüssel voll Eier,** but the dat. is sometimes used here in the plur., as in **Im Wald war ihnen alles neu und voll Wundern** (Frenssen) and **Was malt er denn? eine trübe Welt voll Gespenstern, Zauberern, Elfen und dergleichen Fratzen** (Mörike). The dat. is even used by some authors in the case of an inflected modifier: e.g. **Wir bekommen einen großen Topf voll schönem Fleisch und einen großen Becher voll reinem Wasser** (id.)—**Voll Begeisterung und einem Eifer, als gelte es, die Welt zu erobern, gingen wir an die Arbeit** (Stehr)—**Es war ein prächtiges Bauernhaus, voll Stichen, Spindeln und geschnitzten Schränken** (K. Edschmid). But the dat. is not a generally accepted construction of **voll,** and *Sanders* is not far wrong when he says **„Fehlerhaft ist die Verbindung von ‚voll' mit dem Dativ und Akkusativ".** He is certainly right so far as the accus. is concerned, and examples like the following should not be imitated: **Es ist so wenig was er besitzt, nur ein Arm voll altes Gerümpel** (Waggerl)—**Ihr hängt eure Zimmer voll echte Gobelins und verrostete Waffen** (H. Mann). In the former example a very simple change would make the proposition unobjectionable: it is quite correct to say **ein Armvoll altes Gerümpel,** just as one says **zwei Handvoll grobes Mehl,** where the construction is *appositional* (see **genitive of material** 1), as it is in **Es war ein Stück blauer Himmel zu sehen** (Britting). **2.** The standard constructions of **voll** are a *gen.* (esp. where the dependent noun has an inflected modifier) and, in the language of every day, the prep. **von.** In examples like **Er war voll Dankes für alles, was er erfahren hatte** (C. Rothe) and **Das Weib war so häßlich, daß der alte Mann voll Schreckens davonlief** (G. Keller) the uninflected forms would certainly be more usual; but **Heute will ich ein farbiges Blatt malen, wie ein Zauberspiegel, voll blühenden Lebens, voll träumenden Sehnens und lächelnden Träumens** (Raabe) and **Das ganze Haus war voll von jungen, schmucken Menschen** (Frenssen) are quite in accordance with established usage. **3.** Where we now say **Er kam gesund ans Land** ('He came safely to land') and **Ich verließ ihn gesund** ('I left him in good health'), one said in

MHG *er kam gesunder an daz lant* and *ich liez in gesunden,* because, contrary to modern usage, a pred. adj. was normally inflected at that time. Remnants of this are still probably seen in the stereotyped forms **voller** and **halber** (for the latter, see **halb** 3 (*c*)). Just as one formerly said *er was voller guotes muotes* ('He was full of good spirits'), so one can still say **Der Himmel war voller lautlos ziehender weißer Wölkchen** (Stehr), where **voller,** orig. a nom. sing. masc. agreeing with **Himmel,** is no longer recognized as such but has become a fossilized form, applicable to any gender or person; and sim. **Von der Truppe habe ich die Smeraldina gesehen, eine kleine, dicke Figur, voller Gesundheit und guten Humors** (G.)—**Wie er mit der Braut über die Kirchschwelle trat, war sein Herz voller Stolzes und Ehrgeizes** (Volkmann-Leander)—**Sie waren immer voller verwunderlicher Fragen** (Frenssen). It is noteworthy that this form, which is little used in the lang. of every day, is only used in the pred. and is always associated with the gen., never with **von.**

voll-: This verbal prefix may be either sep. or insep., the former where **voll** is really a pred. adj. and has its lit. force (in which case it should strictly be written as a separate word), the latter where it has fig. force, suggesting the idea of bringing something to completion. It is *sep.* (and therefore accented) in verbs like **vo'llgießen** or **vo'llschenken** ('to fill [a glass] full') and **vo'llstopfen** ('to stuff'): e.g. **Schenke die Gläser bis zum Rande voll!**—**Er hat sich vollgestopft** ('He has gorged himself'); so also, in a reference to the wooden horse of Troy, Schiller uses **die vollgestopften Wände.** On the other hand, the prefix is *insep.* (and unaccented) in **volle'nden, vollfü'hren** (= **au'sführen**), **vollstre'cken** and **vollzie'hen,** the last two esp. of 'executing, carrying out' orders, judgements, sentences, etc.: e.g. **Er hofft, sein Werk bald zu vollenden**—**Das ist eine vollendete Tatsache** ('an accomplished fact')—**Die Darstellung war geradezu vollendet** ('perfect')—**Haben Sie Ihren Plan vollführt?**—**Das Todesurteil ist an ihm vollstreckt worden** ('His death sentence has been carried out')—**Ich darf nicht abreisen, ohne seinen letzten Willen zu vollziehen** (Lessing)—**„Der Kaiser hat gerichtet, seinen Willen vollstrecken wir". „Den blutigen Spruch muß man nicht rasch vollziehen"** (Sch.).

voller: see **voll** 3.

von: 1. Despite the grammarians' protests, the use of **von** as a substitute for the gen. case has undoubtedly gained ground in the lang. of the common people and in familiar conversation: the man in the street almost instinctively says **Der Vater von diesem Jungen ist Arzt.** But in good prose this is only allowed in special cases: (**a**) after numerals and superlatives, to indicate a part of a whole: e.g. **einige von uns**—**drei von meinen Freunden**—**der Klügste von allen**; but to avoid a repetition of **von,** a gen. is preferable in **Ich habe es von einem meiner Freunde erfahren**; (**b**) in expressions like **der König von Preußen** or **die Königin von Schottland,** where the gen. is much less common; (**c**) above all, where a gen. would be unrecognizable as such, e.g. before indecl. words, etc.: e.g. **Wie lange dauerte die Belagerung von Paris?**—**Grün entsteht aus einer Mischung von Gelb und Blau**—**Er wird innerhalb von vier Wochen** (cf. **innerhalb dreier Wochen**) **zurückkommen.** Specially noteworthy here is the obligatory use of **von** in rendering phrases like 'the day of his father's death', *a Saxon gen. being impossible in German before a noun which is itself in the gen.* (cf. the example from Exod. 20. 17, given under **gelüsten**): hence **der Tag von seines Vaters Tod** (*not* **der Tag seines Vaters Todes**)—**Es geschah im Beisein von meines Freundes älterem Bruder.** This should be esp. noted where the Saxon gen. forms **dessen** and **deren** (q..v.) are used: the expression **dessen Gattin** ('his *or* whose wife') may be any case *except a gen.*, so it is correct to say **Er begehrte, den Burgherrn allein zu sprechen, zur großen Verwunderung von dessen Gattin** (Jul. Wolff), but really incorrect to say **Sie machte ihn eines Abends mit Hilfe der Schwester und deren Liebsten betrunken** (Frenssen: for **mit Hilfe von der Schwester und deren Liebstem**). In this connexion it is important to bear in mind that a neut. adj.-subst. (**Gutes, Schönes,** etc.) has *no gen.*, unless preceded by an inflected attrib. word: cf. **Sie hatten mancherlei Wichtiges zu besprechen** and **Es erfolgte eine Besprechung von mancherlei Wichtigem** ('There followed a discussion of various important matters'). **2.** (**a**) Quite fixed is the use of **von** in expressions corresponding to our 'her rascal of a husband', where the relationship is really appositional, the first noun having adj. force (= 'her rascally husband'): e.g. **Sie ist ein Teufel von einem Weib**; cf. **Die Kuh war nicht größer als ein Kalb, eine Zwergin von einer Kuh** (Kellermann). Here the appos. noun much more commonly drops its art. in German: e.g. **Von den Pflichten einer Hausfrau konnte so ein Kiekindiewelt von Mädchen** ('such a chit of a girl') **nicht viel wissen** (E. T. A. Hoffmann)—**Nach Jahren machte sie sich auf, sich ihren Schlingel von Schwiegersohn** ('her scoundrel of a son-in-law') **einmal anzuschauen** (Feuchtwanger)—**Du alter Schlaukopf von Vater sollst deine Freude an deinem Söhnlein haben!** (Raabe)—**Der Damm hat ein Leck bekommen, und der Racker von Fluß tut das seinige, das übrige nachstürzen zu lassen** (Wildenbruch: 'The dam has sprung a leak, and the rascally river is doing all it can to make the rest collapse')—**Im Sturm wurden die Risse in unserem Scheuerlappen von Segel breit und klaffend** (Kellermann: 'In the gale the rents in our rag of a sail gaped wider'). If the appos. noun is *weak*, or an *adj.-subst.*, it is better to insert the art.: e.g. **Satan von einem Jungen, du kneipst mir den Arm!** (Droste-Hülshoff) —**Während wir tafelten, hat sich der Hund von einem Juden erhängt** (id.); where the art. is not inserted, usage fluctuates: cf. **ein Schlingel von Lohnbedienter** (Heine) with **ein armer Teufel von Philologe** (Schücking) and **ein dummer Teufel von Deliquenten** (Droste-Hülshoff); sim. **Es war ihr gleichgültig, daß sie an den Lumpen von Neffen ihr Gut verschwendet hatte** (Werfel: 'She was unconcerned at having wasted her substance on that scamp of a nephew of hers'); in **Sie werden es dem Halunken von Ihrem Neffen verzeihen** (G. Keller) it would be more usual to say **Sie werden es Ihrem Halunken von (einem) Neffen verzeihen** (cf. **Art**). **(b)** Analogous is the fixed use of **von** without an art. in expressions indicating people's quality, rank, breeding, etc.: e.g. **Er ist ein Mann von Bildung** ('of good breeding *or* culture'), **von Ehre** ('of honour'), **von Fach** ('a professional man, specialist'); sim. **Leute von Stand** ('the quality')—**Man merkt es, daß er eigentlich kein Mann von Familie** ('of good stock') **ist und eine vornehme Erziehung nicht genossen hat** (Th. Mann). **3.** A *part. gen.* as the obj. of a verb (cf. Longfellow's 'Give me *of your bark*, o birchtree') was a very common MHG construction: e.g. *ich gap im mînes brotes* ('I gave him some of my bread'). In NHG this use, so common in French, is confined to poetry, as in **Es schenkte der Böhme des perlenden Weins** (Sch.), but **deren** (q.v. 1 ((*a*) and **ihrer** ('of them') are occasionally found in prose—see **welch (indefinite)** (*b*): e.g. **Ich entschloß mich, eine Menagerie anzulegen, und baute eine Menge Käfige: mit vielem Fleiße verfertigte ich deren** ('some') **aus Pappe und Holz** (G. Keller)—**Die Furlaner** ('men of Friuli') **sind verläßliche Dienstmänner: Sie finden ihrer am Rialto** (Hofmannsthal)—**Wölfe? Ei nun, wir haben ihrer, die sich sehen lassen können** (L. Goldammer: 'Wolves? Oh yes, we have some good specimens'). But instead of the part. gen., **von** is by no means uncommon here, although purists condemn it as a Gallicism: e.g. **Hier kommen von den redlichen Männern!** (G.)—**In der Mappe dort haben Sie ohne Zweifel von Ihren Zeichnungen: darf ich sie sehen?** (Heyse)—**Abends steckte sie sich von den weißen Maililien in ihr schwarzes Haar** (Storm)—**Wollt Ihr mir von den schönen Blumen pflücken?** (E. Wichert). **4.** Difficulty arises in forming the gen. of noble titles like **Götz von Berlichingen** (cf. **derer** 2). The word after **von** was orig. not a surname, but the name of a locality with which the person was associated (cf. 'Kitchener of Khartum'), and in such a case one should obviously say **das Leben Götzens von Berlichingen** (G.); and sim. **die Gedichte Walthers von der Vogelweide, die Dichtungen Wolframs von Eschenbach, die Werke Hoffmanns von Fallersleben, das Leben Wilhelms von Oranien,** etc. Quite different is the modern insertion of **von** before a *surname*: correct here are **die Werke Leopold von Rankes, das Zeitalter Otto von Bismarcks,** etc., and it is really incorrect to give a biography of the dramatist Kleist the title **Das Leben Heinrichs von Kleist** (O. Brahm). Actually, as the orig. idea of adding **von** and a place-name as a distinguishing mark has now lost its force, the tendency is to give the last word the **-s** ending, and this is quite fixed in the Saxon gen.: **Wolfram von Eschenbachs Dichtungen. 5.** The use of **von** is also established in connexion with verbs of knowing, believing, supposing, hoping, expecting, wishing, etc., inserted in a *rel.* clause. The proposition 'I know him to be honest' is **Ich weiß, daß er ehrlich ist**; but to express 'He is a man whom I know to be honest' (cf. **accusative and infinitive** 6), *two* subord. clauses are required in German, a rel. clause introduced by **von**, and another clause in which the rel. pron. is referred to by a *pers.* pron. or its equivalent: lit. 'He is a man of (**von**) whom I know that *he* is honest' (**Er ist ein Mann, von dem ich weiß, daß er ehrlich ist**); sim. 'Here is a present which I wish you to accept' takes the form 'Here is a present of which I wish that you will accept it' (**Hier ist ein Geschenk, von dem ich wünsche, daß du es annehmen wirst**). Where 'I hope' occurs in such a proposition, it is ordinarily rendered by the adv. **hoffentlich**, as in **Ich habe einen Vorschlag, auf den Sie hoffentlich eingehen werden** ('I have a proposal to which I hope you will agree'); but this might take the form **Ich habe einen Vorschlag, von dem ich hoffe, daß Sie darauf eingehen werden.** This construction is occasionally found in English, but whereas there it sounds ponderous (cf. Scott's 'They were aware of three horses, held by one concerning whom they could only see that he was tall, strong and accoutred in the dress of a man-at-arms'), it does not do so in German, and examples like the following are quite commonplace: **Man schwelgt im Anblick dieser Augusttage wie im Genusse einer erregenden Musik, von der man weiß, daß sie plötzlich abbrechen wird** (H. Hesse)—**Sie sahen in ihm eine Merkwürdigkeit, von der sie nicht wußten, was sie davon halten sollten** (Böhlau: 'In him they saw an eccentric whom they did not know what to make of')—**Ich landete an einer Insel, von der mir bewußt war, daß daselbst** ('on it') **die schönsten Fasanen zu haben seien** (G.)—**Hiermit erhalten Sie ein Werk, von dem ich wünsche, daß es Ihnen gefallen möchte** (G.)—**Sie hatte ein Geheimnis, von dem sie wünschte, daß ich es erriete** (Roquette)—**Sie unterhielten sich in einer asiatischen Sprache, von der sie voraussetzen konnten, daß ein Deutscher nichts davon verstand** (Alexis: 'They conversed in an Asiatic language which they could assume a German did not understand'). The same construction is possible with verbs of declaration, as in **Dies ist ein Gedicht, von dem behauptet wird, Heine habe es geschrieben,** but here the use of **sollen** (q.v. 2) is more idiomatic: **Dies ist ein Gedicht, das Heine geschrieben haben soll. 6.** With the force of 'by' in a pass. proposition, **von** points to the *agent*, **durch** to the *means*: e.g. **Maria Stuart wurde von ihren Richtern verurteilt, durch den Henker mit dem Beil hingerichtet zu werden.**

vonstatten: see Statt 2.

vor: 1. The preps. **vor** and **für,** although now clearly distinguished, must have had a common origin: the Goth. forms were *faura* and *faur* respectively, the former taking a dat., the latter an accus. The corresponding MHG forms were *vŏr* and *für*, and a definite distinction was made between *vor dem künic stân* (> **vor dem König stehen**) and *für den künic gân* (> **vor den König treten**). That some confusion resulted is not surprising: down to the classical period, and even now in dialects, **für** was sometimes used with a *dat.*, not with local force, but to express propositions like **Ich habe Furcht vor ihm** or **Das betrifft ihn vor allen anderen** ('That applies to him before, *i.e.* more than, any one else'): e.g. **Für meinem Zorn haben Sie Ruhe** (Sch.: 'You are safe from my anger')—**Schiffsleute sind ein Volk, das am Aberglauben für anderen hängt** (Herder: 'Seamen cling to superstitious beliefs more than any other class')—**Ihre Anhänglichkeit an die Religion hatte sie für allen Lustbarkeiten der Welt bewahrt** (Jung-Stilling). This use of **für** is now quite obs., but the earlier confusion survives in one or two expressions, such as **sich Schritt für** or **vor Schritt durch die Dunkelheit tasten** ('to grope one's way step by step through the darkness')—**Fürsorge** or (more commonly) **Vorsorge treffen** ('to take precautionary measures')—**mit etwas fürlieb-** or **vorliebnehmen** ('to be content *or* put up with' a thing), esp. common in coll. speech in propositions like **Kommen Sie herein! Setzen Sie sich mit uns zu Tisch und nehmen Sie mit dem fürlieb, was die Kelle gibt!** ('Come in! Join us at our meal and take potluck!'); cf. as obs. **Der Abt zog einen alten Brief herfür** (Sch.: now **hervor**). **2.** Of the many uses of the prep. **vor,** two are esp. noteworthy: **(a)** with words denoting time, to express our 'ago': e.g. **heute vor acht Tagen** ('a week ago today')—**vor ein paar Wochen** ('two or three weeks ago')—**vor kurzem** ('not long ago'); for 'no longer ago than . . .', see **erst** 2 (*c*); **(b)** with nouns or verbs of warning, protecting, guarding, etc., to express our 'against': e.g. **Vor Taschendieben wird gewarnt!** ('Beware of pickpockets!')—**Hüte dich vor den Torheiten der Liebe!** (Platen: see **Hut** and **hüten** 2)—**Alter schützt vor Torheit nicht** (prov. 'Age is not proof against folly')—**Das treue Weib muß ich vor deiner Wut beschützen** (Sch.).

vorbehalten: In this double compd. of **halten,** meaning 'to reserve' something (e.g. a right, a course of action, etc.) to oneself, the first prefix should always be treated as *sep.*: e.g. **Ich behielt mir das Recht vor, gegen ihn gerichtlich vorzugehen** ('I reserved the right to take legal proceedings against him')—**Die Schuldigen zu begnadigen, behält der Papst sich vor** (Ranke)—**Ich bestand darauf, mir die letzte Entscheidung vorzubehalten.** The same should really apply to **vorenthalten,** 'to withhold' something from a person (dat.), as in **Man enthielt den Arbeitern ihren Lohn vor** ('The workers' pay was kept back'), but here the southern use of the prefix as insep. has spread to the north, not to the same extent as with **anerkennen** (q.v.) but at least so extensively that *Duden* gives **„ich enthalte vor (auch: ich vorenthalte)"** and *Sprach-Brockhaus* **„ich vorenthalte es ihm, häufiger: ich enthalte es ihm vor"**—alternatives which, strangely enough, they do not give for **vorbehalten.** Separation of **vor-** in either case is certainly to be recommended, in spite of examples like the following: **Nicht allein die Menschen, sondern auch die Götter vorenthalten euch euer rechtmäßiges Erbteil** (G.)—**Vorenthalten Sie uns nicht länger diesen Ohrenschmaus!** (Tieck)—**Dies vorenthielt sie als Unterpfand** (G. Keller); in the infin. with **zu,** separation is firmly established, as in **Sollen wir ihn nicht bitten, uns das ganze Gedicht nicht vorzuenthalten?** (G.)—**Zu Hause verschwieg ich die neue Bekanntschaft, doch auch meinen Kameraden suchte ich sie vorzuenthalten** (Bergengruen).

vorbei, vorüber: Like **entlang** (q.v.), these words were orig. advs.: cf. **Morgen sind die Ferien vorüber** ('over, at an end'). With verbs of motion (cf. **pass** 2) they are now real sep. prefixes (probably **-gegangen** is understood in the above example), being usually combined with a prep. phrase (esp. **an**+*dat.*), less commonly now with a simple dat.: e.g. **Er schritt, ohne zu grüßen, an mir vorbei—Wir fuhren langsam am Rathaus vorüber—Die Kinder sind eben hinter** (or **hinten an**) **unserem Hause vorbeigelaufen—Lege den Schmuck an und spaziere dem** (now usually **an dem**) **Spiegelglas vorüber!** (G.); sim. **Er ging dem Hause seines Vaters und auch den übrigen vorbei** (Storm)—**Es flog ihm durch den Kopf, ob sie ihm vorbeitanzen würde** (id.)—**Kaum ein Wagen ging mir vorbei** (Wildenbruch)—**Fast mechanisch blickte sie hinauf, und ein flüchtiges Erinnern zog ihr vorüber** (Wassermann: '. . . a fleeting memory passed through her mind'). At an earlier period an *accus. of extent* was used with such verbs, but this is now avoided, certainly in the lit. sense: one no longer says **An Sonntagen schlenderte man keinen** (for **an keinem**) **Lustort vorbei, ohne einen Haufen zum Tanze versammelt zu finden** (G.) or **Der Wagen fuhr ein paar Bauernhöfe vorbei** (Schreyvogel: 1829) or **Ich möchte unsere schöne Gegend nicht an die Stadt vertauschen, wo man so viele Straßen vorbeilaufen muß, um in das freie Feld zu sehen** (Gessner). The accus. sounds less objectionable when the verb has the force of 'to pass by *or* over' without notice or mention, 'to overlook', although even then modern usage prefers to use a word like **überge'hen:** e.g. **Ha, Würger!** (Death, the 'Strangler') **du kannst nur die Glücklichen töten, die Lebenssatten gehst du vorüber** (Sch.: '. . . those tired of life you pass by')—**Der Tod ging ihn vorbei** (Mörike)—**Kleinigkeiten, die andere vorübergehen, dienen uns zu neuen Unterhaltungen** (Gellert)—**Ein richtiger Reisender soll solcherlei Seltsamkeiten** ('such quaint objects of interest': probably accus., but possibly dat.) **nicht vorbeigehen** (Storm); so also in the pass. **Das wird als bekannt vorbeigegangen** (Lessing); cf. **miss** 3.

vorbenannt: see **folgen** 3.

vorenthalten: see **vorbehalten.**

vorerwähnt: see **folgen** 3.

Vorfall, vorfallen: see **occur** 3 (*d*).

Vorgang, vorgehen: see **occur** 3 (*d*).

vorhanden: see **existence** 2; **Hand** 1.

vorher, vorhin. It is important to distinguish between these two expressions. **1.** (**a**) The sep. compd. **vorhersagen** means 'to foretell' some event, thus indicating two points of time, the first when the person says that something will take place, the second when it does take place. This idea is always implied by the use of the adv. **vorher,** both points of time lying either in the past or in the future, e.g., in the former case, **Ich habe gestern einen Brief an ihn abgeschickt, hatte ihm aber schon vorher** ('before that') **geschrieben**; in the latter case, **Ich hoffe, ihn nächste Woche zu besuchen, werde ihm aber vorher** ('before then') **meinen Besuch anmelden.** (**b**) The same idea applies to **nachher,** the antith. of **vorher:** e.g., on the one hand, **Als ich ihm letzte Woche zufällig begegnete, sagte er, er würde mich andern Tags** ('next day') **treffen, aber kurz nachher** (or **kurz darauf,** 'shortly afterwards') **wurde er von einem Auto überfa'hren**; and, on the other hand, **Ich gehe morgen abend ins Konzert, könnte dich aber nachher** ('afterwards') **irgendwo treffen.** The use of **nachher** to indicate a point of time before the present moment only seems to be contrary to the rule: when I say **Was der Arzt sagte, werde ich dir nachher erzählen,** it implies that I have something else I want to do or say first. **2.** Quite different is **vorhin,** which can never refer to future time. At an earlier period it could be used much like **vorher,** as in **Jakob . . . hieß die Stätte Beth-El, vorhin** ('before that', the English version has 'at the first') **aber hieß die Stadt Lus** (Gen. 28. 19); but this is now obs. According to modern usage it always refers to a point of time shortly before the present moment: e.g. **Ich nehme, was ich vorhin sprach, zurück** (Sch.: 'I retract what I said a little while ago'). See **recent** 2 (*b*).

vorkommen, Vorkommnis: see **occur** 1 and 3 (*g*).

vorläufig: see **erst** 1 (*b*) (i).

vorliebnehmen: see **vor** 1.

vorliegen: Whereas the simple verb **liegen** is used to express propositions like 'The valley lay spread out before us' (**Das Tal lag vor uns ausgebreitet**), the compd. **vorliegen** is used of what 'lies before' one and claims one's attention, consideration, etc.: e.g. **Das Problem, das uns vorliegt, ist schwierig** ('The problem before us is a difficult one')—**Ein Antrag liegt der Versammlung vor** ('A motion is before, *or* has been submitted to, the meeting')—**Es lag nichts Dringendes vor** ('There was no urgent business to be discussed *or* dealt with')—**Es liegt uns kein triftiger Grund vor, ihn zu verhaften** ('We have no cogent reason for arresting him'). Esp. common is the pres. part. used as an attrib. adj.: e.g. **im vorliegenden Fall** ('in the present case'); often used without an art. (cf. **folgen** 3), as in **vorliegender erste(r) Bericht** ('the first report before us') and **vorliegender erste(r) Band dieses Werkes** ('the first volume of this work now issued').

Vormund: This masc. noun (plur. **Vormunde** or **Vormünder**) and its corresponding fem. **Vormünderin** are derived from an old word *munt,* as explained under **Mund** 2. It denotes the 'guardian' of a **Mündel** ('ward') who is not yet **mündig** ('of age'), i.e. one who has not yet attained his 'majority' and so has no legal authority to act for himself. The sing. masc. form **Vormünder,** as in **Er war der Vormünder aller Waisen und Witwen** (G. Keller), is not recognized in the north.

vorrücken: see **advance** 1 and 2.

vorschreiten: see **advance** 2.

vorsprechen: This verb is used either trans. or intrans., the former in the sense of 'to say (something) to a person, for him to repeat', the latter in that of 'to look, call *or* drop in' to see a person (like **einsprechen** q.v.): e.g., on the one hand, **Der Lehrer sprach dem Schüler das kleine Gedicht vor und forderte ihn auf, es ihm nachzusprechen,** and, on the other hand, **Auf dem Heimwege habe ich bei meinem Freunde vorgesprochen—Um die beginnende Abendstunde sprach er im Hofe vor** (Frank Thiess).

vorstehend: see **folgen** 3.

Vorteil: see **Teil** 2 (*a*).

vortreten: see **advance** 4.

vorüber: see **vorbei.**

vorwärts: see **-wärts.**

vorweg: see **weg** 2.

wackeln: see **mit** 2 (*b*).

wägen: see **wiegen** 2; **Ablaut** 2 (*b*).

wahren: see **behalten** 2 (*a*).

währen: There were actually three MHG verbs *wërn*: one meant 'to grant'—another 'to protect', then also 'to prevent'—the third 'to last, endure'. In NHG the first is confined to the compd.

gewähren (e.g. **jemandem eine Bitte gewähren**); the second is seen in **sich wehren** ('to protect oneself') and **sich erwehren** (+gen., as in **Ich konnte mich des Lachens nicht erwehren**, 'I could not help laughing'); the third is now **währen.** It is strange that **währen** has become a rather select expression seeing that **während** (q.v.) and **fortwährend** ('continuous, continually') are in everyday use. In ordinary lang. it is replaced by **dauern** (q.v. 1), but one still says **Es währte nicht lange, bis . . .** ('It was not long before . . .'); cf. the prov. **Ehrlich währt am längsten** ('Honesty is the best policy, is the best in the long run').

während: 1. *Preposition*: **(a)** This pres. part. of the verb **währen** (q.v.) was orig. not a prep. at all: it is quite unknown in MHG. But it is easy to see how the prep. use arose: the phrase **während des Krieges** developed out of the adv. phrase seen in an example like **So lebten die Herren währendes Krieges** (Lessing: '. . . while the war was going on'), where the gen. phrase corresponds to the Lat. 'ablative absolute' in *bello durante* and to early modern English '*This siege during*, there were many skirmishes' (Lord Berners, 1523— in modern spelling). This earlier use of **während** is now out of fashion but examples do still occasionally occur: e.g. **Eine gemischte Empfindung ist währenden Redens** ('while I have been speaking') **in mir aufgestiegen** (Immermann)—**Ein Jahr nach dem anderen ging dahin, und in währender Zeit** ('in the passage of time') **verblühte die schöne jugendliche Frau** (Storm)—**Von Sternberg kam die Nachricht, daß der Graf den Prediger dort bei währendem Gottesdienst** ('while divine service was in progress') **angefallen habe** (Fr. Griese). **(b)** The normal construction of the prep. **während** is with the *gen.* case, but the last example quoted under **(a)** gives some indication as to how the *dat.* crept in, **bei währendem Gottesdienst** being corrupted into **während dem Gottesdienst.** The *gen.*, however, is certainly the construction which modern usage favours; but this case is not always possible, and it is questionable whether *Duden* is justified in illustrating his contention that the *gen.* is the correct case to use by the example **„während fünf Jahre (weniger gut: während fünf Jahren)"**, for despite propositions like **Sie waren während fünf Monate nicht in unserem Hause** (Frenssen), the fact remains that standard literary usage favours the *dat.* where the gen. form coincides with that of the nom. or accus.: it is, e.g., incorrect to say **Das Jahr, während welches ich in Bonn war, werde ich nie vergessen** (for **während dessen** or **welchem**—see **deren** 2 *b*); cf. **Erinnerst du dich jenes Gewitters, während welchem ich dich dort traf?** (Raabe). The same applies to propositions in which a sing. masc. or neut. noun is qualified by a 'Saxon genitive': it is, of course, correct to say **Er sagte es während meiner Anwesenheit** (where the case may be either gen. or dat.), but a standard modern author would say **Das Unglück ereignete sich während meines Freundes Aufenthalt** (not **Aufenthalts**) **in Italien**; and sim. **Er hörte von dem Tode seines Freundes während dessen Aufenthalt in Italien**—**Der Überfall fand während des Heeres Rückzug statt.** According to *Duden* the dat. is **„zulässig"** (allowed) in Austria, but authors from other parts often use it, too, and not only for the sake of euphony, as in **Während dem Laufe des siebzehnten Jahrhunderts mag die italienische Poesie sich verschlimmert haben** (G.: where **während des Laufes des siebzehnten Jahrhunderts** would sound very harsh), but also where there would be no such objection, as in **Während diesem Gespräche sah ich die übrige Gesellschaft in dem tiefsten Stillschweigen** (G.). **2.** *Conjunction*: As a subord. conj. **während** is used in two senses, having either *temporal* or *adversative* force: e.g., on the one hand, **Während** ('while') **ich in Bonn war, lebte mein Bruder in Paris**, and, on the other hand, **Ich bin zur Zeit in Bonn, während** ('whereas') **mein Bruder in Paris lebt.** With temporal force, **während daß** (like **kaum daß**—see **kaum**) was commonly used earlier in the period, as in **Während daß Gott sein erwähltes Volk durch alle Staffeln** ('stages') **einer kindischen Erziehung führte, waren die anderen Völker ihren Weg fortgegangen** (Lessing) and **Gegen Abend, während daß die Armee hereinkam, trat dieser treffliche Mann zu mir** (G.), but this is now rare, if not obs.; but **währenddessen** and **währenddem** are still sometimes so used: e.g. **Währenddem sie sprach, drohte sie mit dem Finger** (Böhlau).

wahrlich: see **adverbs formed from adjectives** 3.

wahrnehmen: Like **gewahren** (q.v.), this

verb now usually takes an *accus.* obj., both in the lit. sense of 'to perceive' and in the fig. sense of 'to take advantage of, seize' (an opportunity, etc.), the prefix **wahr-** being always *sep.* The orig. *gen.* construction is characteristic of a choice literary style: cf. **Nimm der** (in ordinary lang. **die) Stunde wahr, eh sie entschlüpft!** (Sch.). Unlike other verbs of perception, it should not be used with the accus. and infin. construction: cf., as a rare example, **Er nahm alles nach physischen Gesetzen entstehen wahr** (Kant), for **Er nahm wahr, daß alles . . . entstand.**

wahrsagen: In propositions like **Bei unserm Gott, da sagst du wahr!** (Lessing) and **Sie sagt wahr: nicht frohe Zeichen sind's** (Sch.) the verb is used with *sep.* prefix in the sense of 'to speak the truth', but in this sense it is now little used, being replaced by **die Wahrheit sprechen** or **sagen,** the latter esp. fig. in expressions such as **jemandem die Wahrheit (ins Gesicht) sagen** ('to be outspoken *or* blunt with a person'). According to present-day usage **wahrsagen** means 'to foretell, augur' (= **voraussagen**), esp. 'to tell fortunes', the prefix being now treated as *insep.*: e.g. **Grauer Tag, wahrsage mir nicht Schlimmes!** (Mörike)—**Es wurde heftig gewahrsagt** (Krieger: 'There was a lot of lively, exciting fortune-telling' at the party)—**Die Zigeunerin erbot sich, mir zu wahrsagen**; an example like **Sie wissen, den Leuten schlecht wahrzusagen** (Lessing) now sounds old-fashioned (cf. **weissagen:** see **weis-** *b*).

Wal-: There are two MHG nouns *wal*: the one (neut. or masc.) means 'slaughter', the other (fem.) 'choice'. From the former come the words **Walplatz** or **Walstatt** ('place of slaughter, battle-field') and **Walküre** ('Valkyrie', a handmaiden of Odin's sent to select heroes who have fallen in battle and convey them to **Walhalla**); cf. **der Anblick eines leichenvollen Walplatzes** (Sch.). These expressions should not be used, as they sometimes are, with the spelling **Wahlstatt,** etc.; on the other hand, of course, this spelling is correct in expressions like **Wahllokal** ('polling-station'), **Wahlbude** or **Wahlzelle** ('polling-box or -booth'), etc.

wallfahr(t)en: Although both forms of this verb are officially recognized, there seems now to be a definite preference for the longer form **wallfahrten.** In either case the verb is *weak,* the prefix *insep.*: hence, in the pres. indic., **er wallfahrtet** (less commonly **wallfahrt,** *not* **wallfährt**). Derived from MHG *walvarn* (contracted from *walle-varn*), its proper force is 'to go on a pilgrimage' (aux. **sein**), as in **Das Mädchen war mit ihrer Mutter nach Maria Einsiedel gewallfahrtet** (G.) and **Nach dem Tode der Schwester baute er ihr einen kleinen Tempel und wallfahrtete oft dahin** (Freytag); but it frequently loses its specific religious sense and comes to mean little more than **wandern** (cf. the coll. use of **pilgern** with the force of 'to trudge, hike'): e.g. **Sie wallfahrteten durch die Gemächer, schlugen Türen auf und zu** (Musäus)—**Von nah und fern wallfahrtet es jetzt in Ruperts Schloß** (A. Grün: 'From far and near people are now flocking into Rupert's castle')—**Der Schauspieler stahl sich ein geistliches Gewand und wallfahrtete** ('trekked') **als Pfarrer nach der Küste** (W. v. Scholz).

walten: This was orig. one of the *reduplicating verbs* (q.v.): the past tense of Goth. *waldan* was *wa-wald,* which became *wialt* in OHG., *wielt* in MHG. This last form was still used by Hans Sachs, but even then weak forms were in use and are now firmly established. Its basic sense is 'to rule, govern, hold sway', but it is not used in ord. lang. except in a few expressions like **jemand schalten und walten lassen** ('to let a person do as he pleases, conduct his affairs in his own way') and **Gnade walten lassen** (lit. 'to let clemency prevail', i.e. 'to be merciful'). It orig. took a *gen.*; but instead of the MHG gen. *es* in *got walde es* ('God dispose *or* arrange it, determine the course of events') one now uses the *accus.*, as in **Das walte Gott!** ('God grant it!'), and a modern example like **Die Frau waltete des Vorrechts, den ersten Gang der Mahlzeit selbst auszugeben** (C. Rothe: 'The lady of the house exercised her privilege of serving the first course of the meal herself') sounds old-fashioned. In modern prose it is used esp. intrans. in propositions such as **Ein Unstern waltete über all seinen Unternehmungen** (lit. 'An evil star dominated all his enterprises', i.e. 'Ill luck attended everything he undertook'). It is strange that the simple verb is so little used, the more so as the trans. compd. **verwalten** ('to manage, direct, have charge of') and the expression **unter obwaltenden** Umständen (see **ob-** I) are so common.

wandeln: In the proposition **Mein Gott, wie das alles gewandelt ist!** (Jul. Rodenberg), the simple verb is used in the intrans. sense of 'to change', but here one far more commonly says **Wie sich das alles verwandelt hat!** (see **change**), the compd. really implying a radical change, a transformation, so that it would be more appropriate in **Mir kommt es vor, als könne ein Augenblick den Menschen wandeln** (W. v. Scholz). Actually, **wandeln** is now a rather precious expression, not only as used above, but also when used intrans. in the lit. sense of 'to walk leisurely'—cf. **lustwandeln** (q.v.)—and with fig. force in propositions like **Über die Nebel der Schluchten wandelte das kühle Mondlicht** (H. Hesse) and **Scharf getrennt sind die Wege, die Goethe und Schiller bis dahin gewandelt waren** (J. Wychgram). It is very common in the Bible: e.g. lit. in **Stehe auf, nimm dein Bette und wandele!** (Mark 2. 9), and fig., with the aux. **haben,** to suggest a way of life, a mode of conduct (**Lebenswandel**), in **Gedenke doch, Herr, wie ich vor dir gewandelt habe in der Wahrheit** (Jes. 38. 3), a passage referred to in **Er las das 38. Kapitel des Buches Jesaja, aber schon nach einigen Sätzen unterbrach der König: „Wie kann ich sagen, daß ich vor dem Herrn gewandelt habe in der Wahrheit?"** (A. Neumann); cf. also **Jetzt wachte ich auf und glaubte, im Schlaf gewandelt zu haben** (Waiblinger), an idea usually expressed by **nachtwandeln** (with *insep.* prefix, aux. **sein** or **haben**). That the simple verb **wandeln** is now little used in ordinary prose is all the more strange as some of its compds. are quite common, not only those already mentioned, but also esp. **anwandeln** (q.v.); less common in everyday lang. are **durchwandeln** (q.v.) and **umwa'ndeln** (trans. with insep. prefix), as in **Der Chor umwa'ndelt des Theaters Rund** (Sch.: 'The chorus passes slowly round the stage')—for **u'mwandeln,** see **change** 1 (*b*).

wandern: In contrast with the rather precious **wandeln** (q.v.), this is a very common word, used not only of people travelling on foot but also of thoughts or glances straying, and somewhat humorously of articles which are relegated to the lumber-room, the rubbish-heap, etc.: e.g. **Ich bin** (see below) **den ganzen Weg hierher zu Fuß gewandert—Wäre er nicht ertappt worden, so wäre er ohne Zweifel erhobenen Hauptes seinen Pfad** (or **seines Weges**) **gewandert** (Th. Mann: 'Had he not been detected, he would no doubt have gone on his way with head erect')—**Sie ließ ihren Blick im Saale herumwandern—Die alten Stühle sind in die Rumpelkammer gewandert—Da es an Mitteln fehlte, blieb nichts anderes übrig, als einige Möbel aufs Leihhaus wandern zu lassen** ('. . . to send some of the furniture to the pawnshop'). The normal aux. is **sein,** but **haben** is often used where the idea of getting to a specific place is not implied, esp. of strolling players, wandering musicians, travelling scholars or journeymen, etc., as in **Der Geselle hatte in seinen jungen Jahren lange gewandert** (Wieland); cf. **Daher kam es, daß ihm alles Land, das er strebend und ringend durchwa'ndert war** (or **hatte**: cf. **durchwandeln**), **zum Friedhof wurde** (Stehr). Of course, **haben** is necessary where the verb is used *trans.*, as in **Ich habe mich müde** (or **mir die Füße wund**) **gewandert.**

wann: Whereas the MHG word *wan* was used in a variety of ways—e.g. with the force of **sondern, denn, weil,** and **als** ('than')—**wann** has a very limited application today: apart from its adv. use in **dann und wann** (see **dann** 1) and its very occasional use as a conj., as in **Wenn und wann** ('If and when') **du nach Berlin kommst, hoffe ich dich zu sehen,** it is the reg. expression for our *interrog.* 'when', both in dir. and indir. propositions: **„Wann fährt denn der Zug ab?" „Ich weiß nicht genau, wann er abfährt."—Ich versicherte ihr, es würde mir eine Ehre sein, jetzt und wann sie immer wolle** ('whenever she wished'), **ihr zu dienen** (St. Zweig). In the classical period, and even later, **wenn** was used in this way (see **when** 1), but this is now obs., and examples like the following should not be imitated: **„Roller ist gehangen—" „Roller? seit wenn?"** (Sch.)—**„Liebes Fräulein, wenn wollen Sie mir antworten?"** (Gellert). Even more limited is the use of **wannen,** an old-fashioned word which—like **dannen** (see **dann** 2)—is only used after **von** in the sense of **woher?** ('from where?'): e.g. **Der Wind bläset, . . . aber du weißt nicht, von wannen er kommt** (John 3. 8)—**Niemand wußte zu sagen, von wannen Benno gekommen war** (Musäus: = **woher B. stammte,** 'where B. hailed from').

warnen: The following two propositions are of special interest: **Er warnte mich,**

auf meiner Hut zu sein (Sch.)—**Doch warn' ich dich, dem Glück zu trauen** (id.). The two propositions agree in essentials: their structure is the same, and in either case the verb **warnen** has a dependent infin. clause. And yet they differ fundamentally: in the first example the infin. clause has *pos.* force ('He warned me to be on my guard'), in the second it has *neg.* force ('Nevertheless, I warn you *not* to trust in Fate'). So **warnen** differs somewhat from other verbs implying prevention, restraint, etc.: a neg. word inserted in a subord. clause depending on **hindern, sich hüten, verbieten,** etc. (qq.v.) is pleonastic, as explained under **negative (pleonastic)** 2 (*a*), these verbs in themselves implying negation ('I forbid you to do it' = 'I order you not to do it'; 'I prevented him from doing it' = 'I took steps to see that he did not do it'). The verb **warnen** really has a sim. implication ('I warned him against doing it' = 'I urged him not to do it'), but where its dependent clause is intended to have neg. force, it is advisable, in view of possible ambiguity, to make this clear by the insertion of a neg. expression—cf. **Die Sorge warnt mich, den König nicht zu betrügen** (G.)—**Von einigen war er gewarnt, daß er meinem Bruder nichts sagen sollte** (G.).

warten: The orig. meaning of this verb was 'to look out' for something, an idea still preserved in **Warte** (a 'look-out, watch-tower') and **Sternwarte** ('observatory'); but in this sense it is now obs., being usually replaced by **nach etwas ausschauen:** see **look (verb)** 1 (*a*). According to modern usage it has two meanings: **1.** Its commonest meaning is 'to wait' (cf. **harren** 1), as in **Ich werde warten, bis Sie zurückkommen** and **Warte nur, du wirst Schläge bekommen!** or **es wird Schläge setzen!** ('Just you wait, you'll get a thrashing!') That for which one waits is now expressed by **auf** + accus., as in **Er läßt immer lange auf sich warten** ('He always keeps people waiting for ages'). This construction was sometimes used in early NHG, as in **Sei stille dem Herrn und warte auf ihn** (Ps. 37. 7), but much more common here was a *gen.* case, which is still used in poetry and choice prose: e.g. **Isegrimm stand und wartete meiner** (G.)—**Sie eilte nach dem Wäldchen, wo sie den Wagen zu erblicken wähnte, der ihrer wartete** (Musäus)—**Sie wartete des günstigsten Moments** (R. Waldmüller: now usually **Sie wartete den günstigsten Moment ab**)—**Fern an der russischen Grenze wartete meiner noch immer die Heimat** (Sudermann)—**Er wartete des Erfolges seiner Fangvorrichtung** (H. Seidel). **2.** The other modern meaning is 'to attend to, look after', often still with the orig. *gen.*: e.g. **Heute warte jeder des eigenen Amtes!** (C. F. Meyer: 'Today let every man look to the duties of his office!')—**Sie wollte allein bleiben und der Lampe warten** (G.: '. . . tend the lamp')—**Da saß ein Mann und wartete der Fähre** (Sch.: i.e. the man who worked the ferry-boat, not someone waiting to be ferried across, in which case it would have been **wartete auf die Fähre**)—**Er saß vor dem Dorf und wartete der** (= **hütete die**) **Ziegen** (Mörike)—**Der Nürnberger Stadtrat meinte, er** (Hans Sachs) **solle lieber seines Amtes und Schuhmachens warten** (Erich Schmidt). But here the *accus.* is now becoming quite common, esp. where **warten** has the force of 'to tend, care for' (invalids, plants, etc.): e.g. **Er wartete den Kranken wie ein Kind** (Bruno Frank: cf. **betreuen**)—**Inmitten des Hofes stand ein Rosenstock: ein Kastellan wartete ihn** (Th. Mann).

-wärts: 1. This adv. suffix (Lat. *versus*) implies direction to-*wards*, the specific direction being suggested by what precedes the suffix: e.g. **nord-, südwärts,** etc., **vor-** and **rückwärts** (see 2), **auf-** and **abwärts,** the last two of which can be attached to nouns, as in **flußabwärts** ('downstream') and **talaufwärts** ('up the valley'); cf. **Geh du linkwärts, laß mich rechtwärts gehen** (Sch.), which last expressions are now, however, little used, being superseded by **(nach) links** and **rechts.** The forms **nord-, südwärts,** etc., can also be used as preps.: one can say **ostwärts des Rheins** (*Sanders* characterizes **nordwärts dem Rhein** as **„oberdeutsch"**, i.e. South German), although it is more usual to say **ostwärts** or **östlich vom Rhein. 2.** The form **rückwärts** has developed more than the other expressions referred to above. Its orig. sense of motion is seen in **Vorwärts mußt du, denn rückwärts kannst du nicht mehr** (Sch.), but it is also used of rest, when it has exactly the same force as **hinten** ('at the back'), as in **Rückwärts im Garten stand ein uralter Turm** (R. v. Gottschall) and **Aus dem Vorsaal lief ein Gang mitten durchs Haus nach rückwärts** (Hofmannsthal).

Moreover, it is the only one of the words referred to which has produced a common *adj*. viz., **rückwärtig,** formed on the analogy of **gegenwärtig** (see **presence** 3) and **widerwärtig** ('repugnant'): e.g. **Er trat vom Hof durch die rückwärtige Tür** (= **Hintertür**) **ins Haus** (Bergengruen)—**Sie gingen in eins der rückwärtigen Zimmer** (id.); cf. **Endlich fand er die schwarze Krawatte: er hatte sie in die rückwärtige** (usually **hintere**) **Hosentasche gesteckt** (L. Winder). In this connexion see also **auswärts.**

was (indefinite): In good prose 'something' is **etwas,** for which **was** is only used in the coll. lang.: e.g. **Weißt du was Neues?** ('Have you any news?')—**Das ist was Rechtes!** (ironical: 'That's not much to brag about!' or 'I think precious little of that!')—**Ich will dir was sagen: wir machen morgen eine Landpartie** ('I'll tell you *what*: we'll go for a picnic tomorrow'); so also after preps., as in **Sie hatte etwas vorspringende Augen** ('somewhat protruding eyes'), **die beständig nach was zu suchen schienen** (Fontane)—**Der Leipziger Sekundaner kann es noch zu was bringen** (G. Keller in a letter to Storm: '. . . may yet get on in the world, make a success of it').

was (interrogative): **1. (a)** Just as we say 'What *are* these men by profession?' so a German says **Was sind diese Männer von Beruf?** because the real subj. is **Männer,** while **was** is the pred.: **Diese Männer sind von Beruf—was?** **(b)** Like our 'what', **was** has no plur.; when a plur. is implied, **alles** is often inserted: **Was hast du in den Ferien alles gelesen?** (cf. **all** 8). **2.** The gen. of MHG *waz* was *wes*, but apart from **weshalb** and **weswegen,** the form **wes** is now confined to a few old expressions: e.g. **Wes Geistes Kind ist er?** ('What sort of a person is he?'): cf. **welch (interrogative)** 2 (*b*); so also **Wer seid Ihr? wes Namens, Standes, Wohnorts?** (H. v. Kleist)—**Ihre Mutter war einer armen Frauen Kind, Ihr wisset all', wes Landes und Glaubens** (Fontane), where **Frauen** is an old weak gen. (cf. **Erde**); sim. often with concess. force: **Hört mich an, wes Standes und Amtes ihr sein möget** (Kopisch: '. . . whatever your social standing and occupation may be')—**Wir sind angewiesen, keinen Fremden, wes Standes und Geschlechts er auch sei, zu behausen** (Lessing)—**Das versteht die Frau Rat, es einem Gast, wes Alters er auch sei** ('no matter of what age'), **in ihrem Hause wohl sein zu lassen** (F. A. Hohenstein). Elsewhere **wes** is now replaced by **wessen**: e.g. **Hier stehe ich wie ein armer Sünder, wessen angeklagt?** (R. Huch)—**Wer ihn jetzt sah, hätte ahnen können, wessen er fähig war, wenn er beleidigt war** (Polenz). The form **wessent-,** prefixed to **wegen** and **(um) . . . willen,** can only be used of *persons*, hence distinguish between **wessentwegen?** ('for whose sake?') and **weswegen?** ('for what reason?'). **3. (a)** The neut. **was** has *no dat.*, **wem** being only used of persons. This want is supplied in coll. lang. by using **was** after preps. (cf. *b* below): e.g. **An was ist er denn gestorben?** (H. Hesse) —**„Nun wird also nichts daraus?“ „Aus was denn?“** (Böhlau: 'So nothing will come of it?' 'Come of what?')—**Sie brachte uns einen Teller, ich weiß nicht, mit was allem** (G. Britting: '. . . a plate with goodness knows what on it')—**Solchen Menschen ist es gleichgültig, mit was und mit wem sie ihre Zeit verbringen** (Auerbach)—**Weißt du, nach was ich mich sehne?** (K. Sloboda)—**Von was hängen Glück und Segen ab?** (G. Keller)—**Ich habe Angst, ohne zu wissen, vor was** (F. Huch)—**Zu was ist er nütze?** (G.). **(b)** In good prose the dat. **was** is replaced by **wo(r)-** prefixed to a prep.: **Woran erkenne ich ihn?**—**Wonach sehnst du dich?** —**Wovon spracht ihr?**—**Wozu dient das?** Some of these forms, of course, also represent an accus., as in **Woran denken Sie?** and in this connexion it is noteworthy that the correct substitute for **um was** is **worum**: e.g. **Renate wußte kaum, worum es sich handelte** (Wassermann)—**Er hat mich neulich um etwas gebeten, ich entsinne mich aber nicht, worum**; cf. **Als er vernommen, warum** (incorrect for **worum**) **es sich handelte, erwiderte er . . .** (G. Keller). **4. (a)** MHG *waz* was used, like other indef. prons., with a part. gen. (see **nichts** 2), as in *waz êren* ('what [in the way] of honours') and *waz sneller degene* ('what [a lot] of brave warriors'); and in the Bible we find examples like **Was Danks habt ihr davon?** (Luke 6. 34). But this is now only used in the case of a neut. adj.-subst., where, however, the gen. is no longer regarded as such, the construction being treated as *appos.*: e.g. **Was haben Sie Interessantes erlebt?**—**Einige kamen, um zu sehen, was es Neues gebe** (G. Keller); cf. **Was hast du hier Geschäfte?**

(Storm), where **Geschäfte** is probably the old gen., and **Was Wunder, wenn er nicht kommen will?** (see **Wunder** 2). (**b**) For MHG *waz mannes ist er?* ('What sort of a man is he?') one now says **Was für ein Mann ist er?**—cf. **welch (interrogative)** 4 —where **für** is not treated as governing a case, the case of the following noun depending on whether it is a subj. or an obj.: e.g. **Was für einem Freunde bist du begegnet?—Mit was für einer Arbeit sind Sie jetzt beschäftigt?—Zu was für einem Zweck hat man dieses Loch gegraben?** Here the indef. art. follows **für** when the reference is to a single object, and where the art. represents a noun, it must have strong inflexion: **„Ich habe mir ein neues Buch gekauft." „Was für eins denn?"—„Es ist ein neuer Lehrling da." „Was ist's für einer?"** (Freytag). But when the reference is to a plur., an abstract idea, a material or a collect. sing., the art. drops out: **Was für Bücher hast du dir gekauft?—Ich gewahrte, daß ich einen kleinen Tisch umgeworfen hatte mit weiß der Himmel was für zerbrechlichen Gegenständen** (Rilke: '. . . with heaven knows what breakable objects')—**Was für Unsinn redet er da?—Was für Leder ist dies?—Was für Obst haben Sie im Garten?—Was für Vieh hat dein Onkel?** In the subst. relation here, **ein** is replaced by the strongly inflected **welch**: e.g. **„Eine Kiste Wein ist angekommen." „Was für welcher?"** ('What sort of wine?') **—Ich soll den Korb mit Obst füllen, ich weiß aber nicht, mit was für welchem— So, Sie haben neue Bücher gekauft? Was für welche denn?** In the nom. and accus., **was** and **für** are often separated in coll. speech, as in the example from Freytag given above and in **Was ist das für eine Frage?** (Lessing); but they should not be too widely separated, as is the case in **Wenn der Mann hätte voraussehen können, was aus der Erbschaft, die er den seinen hinterließ, sich für Unsegen entwickeln würde!** (Polenz: better **was für Unsegen sich aus der Erbschaft . . . entwickeln würde!**). Actually, there was orig. no close connexion between **was** and **für**, indeed, the coll. separation is strictly more correct: in **Was hast du für Bücher gekauft?** the noun was governed by **für**, the meaning being 'What have you bought in the way of books?', and it was inability to understand the idiom that led to propositions like **Mit was für Büchern hast du dich beschäftigt?** **5.** To express a question like 'What is still *to be done*?' the Germans use the *act.* infin. with **zu**, the so-called 'gerundive infinitive' (see **infinitive** 2 and 3): **Was ist noch zu erledigen?** (see below). But one must be on one's guard in rendering a proposition like 'I don't know *what to do*': it is quite incorrect to say **Ich weiß nicht, was zu tun** (for **was ich tun soll**), but in vivid lang. one can say **Ich weiß nicht, was tun —Die große Frage war: was jetzt tun?** (Ompteda)—cf. **Nach dem Essen saß er verlassen da und wußte nicht, was anfangen** (H. Hesse)—**Er wußte nicht, wohin gehen** (Hofmannsthal: 'He did not know *where to go*'). Here, however, it is easy to be misled: while it is wrong to say **Ich weiß nicht, was zu tun,** it is correct to say **Sie sagten, die Fürstin sollte entscheiden, was jetzt zu tun** (E. T. A. Hoffmann), because here the word **sei** or **wäre** is understood, the meaning being 'They said the princess should decide what *was to be done*' (not 'what to do'); cf. the example from Scheffel given under **Richtung.** On the whole, it is advisable to insert the aux. in such propositions.

was (relative): **1.** Like our 'what', **was** may represent both antecedent and rel. (= *that which*): e.g. **Endlich fand ich, was ich suchte.** But one important point here is that a German rendering of a proposition like 'At last I *came upon what* I was looking for' cannot take the form **Endlich stieß ich auf was ich suchte,** but requires the insertion of an antecedent: **Endlich stieß ich auf das, was ich suchte;** and sim. **Trifft nicht alles mit dem überein, was ich erzählt habe?** (G.: 'Does not everything agree *with what* I have told you?')—**Wie sollte die Frau nach dem fragen, was sie nicht kannte?** (G. Keller) **—Ich beruhigte mein Gewissen wegen dessen, was ich angerichtet hatte** (Speckmann). It is noteworthy that in such cases **auf das, mit dem,** etc., cannot be replaced by **darauf, damit,** etc. **2.** (a) The antecedent of **was** should *not* be a def. concrete object: it is contrary to accepted usage to say **Sie tat, als suchte sie nach dem Programm, was** (for **das** or **welches**) **sie in der Hand hielt** (C. Hauptmann); sim. **Er war erfreut, in ein Land zu kommen, was er sich wie ein irdisches Paradies gedacht hatte** (Novalis)—**Wer das Gold nicht greift, was ihm die Sterne zuwerfen, dem schleudern sie nachher Kot hin** (W. Alexis)

—**Der Garten bot das merkwürdigste Schauspiel dar, was man sehen konnte** (E. T. A. Hoffmann). Correct as antecedent is an indef. neut. pron., a neut. adj.-subst. (esp. in the superlative), or the idea contained in a whole clause: e.g. **Es gibt allerlei, was man nicht erklären kann**—**Das ist das Beste, was wir tun können**—**Mein Freund spielt Geige, was ich nicht kann**—**Er behauptet, ich sei zu nachsichtig, was auch wahr sein mag**; sim. it is correct to say **Möge dir das neue Jahr alles Gute bringen, was du dir nur wünschst!** but strictly incorrect to say **Er bewirtschaftet das Gut** ('estate'), **was** (for **das**) **der Vater hinterlassen hat** (Freytag). Where the antecedent is the idea contained in a single word, **welches** is correct—see **welch (relative)** 5—but **das**, which is still occasionally found in accordance with earlier usage, should not be used: cf. **Sie bat mich, einige Äpfel anzunehmen, das** (now **was**) **ich tat** (G.). Where the rel. pron. is governed by a prep., this is generally expressed by **wo(r)-** (q.v.): e.g. **Er sagte manches, woran ich nie gedacht hätte**—**Ich möchte allerlei tun, wozu ich nicht Zeit habe**—**Er meint, ich sei zu nachsichtig, worin er vielleicht nicht ganz unrecht hat.** On the whole, these compds. of **wo(r)-** are best used with reference to indef. or abstract antecedents; they may be used with reference to concrete objects, but *not*, as they once were, to *persons*, as in **Es waren Nachbarskinder, womit** (now **mit denen**) **ich einst gespielt hatte** (Heine) and **In der Schenke sitzen jetzt die Männer, womit ich sonst zusammenzusitzen pflegte** (Hebbel). (**b**) It is often hard, of course, to draw a line between the definite and the indefinite: what is definite to the speaker may be indefinite to the listener. Thus, in an example like **Es handelt sich um etwas Wichtiges, das Allerwichtigste, das es für mich gibt** (Kellermann), the reference is obviously to something which is very definite to the speaker, so that from *his* standpoint **das** is more correct than **was** would be; and the same applies to **Eines gab es in diesem Leben, das er ernst nahm** (Ebner-Eschenbach)—**In diesem Augenblick erschien sie ihm wie das Köstlichste, das er auf dieser Erde erringen könnte** (Binding). But even where the reference is to something definite, the speaker often prefers to make his statement more dramatic by *not* making the reference clear at the outset, and in a proposition in which the logical subj. is associated with the verb **sein** and a pred. containing a rel. clause, he can do this most effectively by placing the pred. *first* and using the *indef.* rel. pron.: e.g. **Das erste, was ich sah, als ich hinaustrat, war eine Katze**; and sim. **Das einzige, was ihm Freude macht, ist die Musik**—**Alles, was er behauptet, ist Lüge.** That the logical subj. stands last here becomes obvious when it is a plur.: **Was vom Stamme noch übrigblieb, waren nur dürre Äste** (W. Alexis)—**Was sie las, waren einfache, vertraute Dinge** (Th. Mann). (**c**) But one must guard against being misled here by clauses in which **was** *seems* to refer to a masc. or fem. noun combined with **sein.** In an example like **Reue war es nicht, was er empfand** (Polenz), **was** is correct, because the real subj. is the word **das** which is implied in **was**, and **Reue** is the pred. (= **Das, was er empfand, war nicht Reue**); sim. **Nicht die helle Jugend, sondern eine Verklärtheit war es, was den Augen diesen Ausdruck gab** (Fontane); and so also where the pred. noun stands between **es** and the rel. clause: **Es war mehr Galgenhumor als Ärger, was er empfand** (W. Schäfer)—**War es Hoffnung, was da aufstieg?** (Viebig)—**Es war nicht eben** ('exactly') **Furcht, was ihn überlief** (R. Huch)—**Das Gesicht glüht ihm, und man weiß nicht, ist es Lebenslust oder nur seine Schönheit, was ihn so glühend macht** (P. Keller)—**Es war nicht der stolze Ton, was ihn erschütterte** (J. Frey)—**Es war nicht bloß Altersschwäche, was die Alte darniederwarf** (Th. Mann); a rel. pron. agreeing in gender with the pred. noun is strictly incorrect: cf. **War es Freude, die er empfand?** (Wassermann). But **was** is *not* used when the pred. is a plur. referring to *persons*: cf., on the one hand, **Zu dem Fest lud er alles aus dem Städtchen, was nur kommen wollte** (E. T. A. Hoffmann), and, on the other hand, **Ehrliche Leute sind es nicht, die in dieser Weise handeln.** The rel. pron. **was** seems peculiarly appropriate where there are two alternative pred. nouns of different sexes or numbers: e.g. **Ein paar Sekunden lang glaubte er, daß nicht sie sondern ihr Großvater es sei, was da vor ihm kauerte** (Voigt-Diederichs). **3.** As in the case of the interrog.—see **was (interrogative)** 2—the old gen. **wes** is only used in **weshalb** and **weswegen**; elsewhere **wessen** is the recognized form as a rel. pron.: e.g. **Es handelt sich nicht um das, wessen du bedarfst, sondern um das, wessen die Kinder bedürfen** (Fontane). But where the speaker has something *definite* in mind, **dessen** is quite correct, as in **Das war das einzige, dessen er Erwähnung tat.** In practice, **wessen** is almost always used where it includes the antecedent, and **dessen** where the antecedent is expressed: cf. **Er nahm, wessen er bedurfte** and **Er nahm alles, dessen er bedurfte**; in the example from Fontane given above, **wessen** is certainly preferable, if only for reasons of euphony, the combination **das, dessen** having a distinctly unpleasant sound.

Wäsche: see **clothes** 5.

was für: see **was (interrogative)** 4 (*b*).

Wat: see **clothes** 6.

watch: For propositions like 'We watched the children playing', see **zusehen,** and cf. **look (at).**

weben: This verb was orig. *strong*, and **wōb, gewōben** (< MHG *wăp, gewĕben*) are still used, esp. in poetry and elevated prose. But *weak* forms are displacing these more and more, and are quite fixed in the intrans. **leben und weben** ('to be alive and full of energy'): cf. **Von Geistervolk lebte und webte alles** (Raabe). Weak forms are now more usual also in other contexts, with both lit. and fig. force: e.g. **Die Dämmerung webte einen dichten Flor um uns her** (Roquette)—**Ich habe die Spinnen durch Stunden beobachtet, wenn sie webten** (A. Schaeffer)—**Der Schnee sank wie ein dichtgewebter Schleier nieder** (R. Herzog)—**An einer der Wände hing ein gewebter Teppich** (W. Kramp); sim. in compds.: **Er hatte ein Kleid mit seltsamen Figuren hineingewebt** (Novalis)—**Ein Stern war in das Tischtuch eingewebt** (M. Hausmann)—**Die Bande der Familie sind mit dem inneren Dasein verwebt** (Ranke: see **verweben**); esp. in the insep. **durchwe'ben** ('to interweave'), often used fig.: e.g. **Das Grün des Gesträuchs ist mit roten Blüten durchwebt** (Waiblinger)—**Sie hielt viele mit allerlei Interjektionen durchwebte Selbstgespräche** (Raabe)—**Die Oper „Fidelio" ist mit Motiven völlig durchwebt** (K. Lamprecht).

wechseln: see **change** 2 (*a*).

wedding: see **marriage** 2.

wedeln: see **mit** 2 (*b*).

weder: 1. The pos. combination **entweder . . . oder** ('either . . . or'), when connecting *sing.* nouns, requires a *sing.* verb (see **entweder**), and the same should, of course, apply to the corresponding neg. combination **weder . . . noch** ('neither . . . nor'). But actually a plur. verb with **weder . . . noch** is surprisingly common in modern works, an author who writes **Weder er noch sein Bruder sind gekommen** no doubt having the pos. idea that 'Both brothers failed to come' at the back of his mind. The following long list of striking examples from recognized modern authors shows how wide-spread this use of a plur. verb has become: **Weder ich noch mein Mann wußten mit dem Gelde umzugehen** (Gellert)—**Ich ließ in den Büchern nachschlagen** ('I caused the books to be consulted'), **aber weder sein Name noch meiner kamen darin vor** (Grillparzer)—**An meine Reise wagten weder sie** (sing. fem.) **noch ich zu rühren** (Storm)—**Weder der Wirt noch die Mutter gingen auf den Vorschlag ein** (Auerbach)—**Macpherson ist ein verhutzeltes** ('wizened') **Männchen, auf das weder sein Clan noch Walter Scott stolz sein würden** (Fontane)—**Weder Marie noch ich dachten daran, was noch kommen sollte** (Heyse)—**Weder Himmelsblau noch Sonnenschein kamen ihrem Gesichtchen gleich** (Raabe)—**Weder Regina noch Tante Katharina waren zu sehen** (I. Seidel)—**Weder Alter noch Blindheit hatten ihm zu einer abgeklärten Betrachtung des Lebens verholfen** (Werfel)—**Weder er noch Beate hatten bisher ein Wort gesprochen** (Ziferer)—**Volksbibliothek? dachte Tonio, denn er fand, daß hier weder das Volk noch die Literatur etwas zu suchen hatten** (Th. Mann)—**Hast du daran gedacht, daß weder du noch ich eine Ahnung von Haushalten haben?** (K. Edschmid)—**Weder das Mädchen noch Victor hatten ähnliches Papier zu ihren Briefen benutzt** (A. Schaeffer)—**Weder Monika noch ihr Vater ließen jemand ins Haus** (H. E. Busse)—**Weder Vater noch Mutter hatten genaue Kunde von ihnen** (E. Wiechert)—**Ich gestehe, daß weder mein Herr noch ich erstaunt sind** (A. Neumann)—**Weder Hitler noch Goebbels wollten einsehen, daß der Krieg verlorenging** (J. Thorwald). Purists, of course, frown upon this **„falsche Konstruktion"** (*Sanders*), which is based on the sense of the context, not on strict grammar rule, but when it is so freely used by reputed authors from all parts of the German-speaking countries, it now seems unreasonable to condemn it outright. **2.** As explained under **negative (pleonastic)**, two neg. expressions now cancel each other in German: **nicht unmöglich = möglich.** To this rule there is at least one important exception, viz. that a neg. proposition like **Ich habe keine Nachricht** can be followed by **weder von ihm noch von seinem Bruder** without these two neg. ideas cancelling each other and making the proposition a pos. one. This we can render by 'I have *no* news *either* from him *or* from his brother', but this is not possible in German: **entweder . . . oder** could not be substituted for **weder . . . noch** in the example just given. Another important point here is that **weder . . . noch** must *follow* the other neg. word: otherwise the proposition can only take the form **Weder von ihm noch von seinem Bruder habe ich irgend welche** (not **keine**) **Nachricht** or **habe ich etwas** (not **nichts**) **gehört**: cf. **entweder** 2. The following are good examples of this double neg. idiom taken from modern authors: **Du sollst nicht eher dieses Kind weder sehen noch berühren, bis du sagst, wo du es gestohlen hast** (G.)—**Nichts weder in der Natur noch im Gebiete des Wissens läßt Kant gleichgültig** (W. v. Humboldt)—**Alles dies schien ihm wunderbar, da er noch nie den Wald, weder bei Tag noch bei Nacht, gesehen hatte** (G. Keller)—**Er stand in Ansehen, obwohl er nie weder ein bürgerliches Amt bekleidet noch, nach einem solchen getrachtet hatte** (Jak. Frey)—**Niemals machte weder er noch ich die leiseste Anspielung darauf** (H. Hesse)—**Goethe schätzte das alte Diktum, daß sich jeder seinen eigenen Gott macht, und daß niemand den seinigen weder nehmen kann noch soll** (W. Bode)—**Er hatte keine Freude mehr, weder an seiner Pferdezucht noch an Haus und Hof** (H. v. Kleist)—**Diese Menschen haben kein Ohr weder für Takt noch für Musik überhaupt** (Heine)—**Keiner von ihnen erwähnte weder seiner noch des anderen Krankheit** (Voss)—**Das Mädchen erinnerte in keinem Zuge weder an den Bruder noch an den Vater** (Storm)—**Für einen Mann wie Sie ist kein Mädchen weder zu gut noch zu schön** (Spielhagen); cf., with **weder** understood, **Von ihm war längere Zeit nichts zu hören noch zu sehen** (Blunck). For a pleonastic neg. inserted in propositions *implying* a negation, see **negative (pleonastic)** 2 (*a*) and (*b*).

Weg: The only interesting grammatical points in connexion with this noun are its uses in the *gen.* Apart from the common advs. **kei'neswegs** ('by no means, on no account') and **unterwe'gs** ('on the way'), there are a number of idioms in which the gen. is used, notably **seines Weges** (or **seiner Wege**) **gehen** ('to go on one's way'), **ein großes Stück** (or **eine gute Strecke**) **Weges zurücklegen** ('to cover a good bit of ground': see **genitive of material** 2 (*b*)), and the coll. expressions **Woher des Wegs?** ('Where have you come from?') and **Wohin des Wegs?** ('Whither away? Where are you bound for?'). For **gerade(n)wegs** ('in a beeline'), see **gerade** 2 (*b*); for **halben Wegs** (= **auf halbem Wege,** 'halfway'), see **halb** 2 (*b*) and **halbwegs.**

weg: **1.** This adv. is < MHG *en-wec* (orig. used of what was thrown out 'on the road') and hence means 'away', being more coll. than **fort.** Apart from its common use as a sep. prefix of verbs like **gehen, laufen, werfen,** etc., it is used as an independent adv. in a few coll. idioms, notably **frisch von der Leber weg reden** ('to speak bluntly, not to mince matters') and **von jemand** (or **etwas**) **ganz weg sein** ('to be carried away by, smitten with . . .'). **2.** It also forms a few compds., as in the following examples: **Die Preise sind du'rchweg** ('generally, altogether') **zu niedrig** (Benedix)—**Der Graf bewährte durchweg** ('throughout') **eine untadelhafte Harmlosigkeit** (Treitschke)—**Es waren durchwegs** ('without exception') **ältere Männer** (Kafka: the form with **-s** is South German, esp. Austrian); **In der Figur Napoleons sehen Tolstoi und Dostojewski schle'chtweg den Angelpunkt, um den ihr Dasein sich dreht** (Hofmannsthal: i.e. they 'see the *very* cardinal point on which their existences hinge'), where **schlechtweg = schlechthin** (q.v.) or **geradezu** (see **gerade** 2 (*b*)); **Die Prozession kommt bergauf, vorwe'g** ('in front') **die kleinsten Kinder** (G.)—**Das nahm ich ihm vorweg** ('In that I forestalled him').

wegen: **1.** This prep. normally takes a *gen.* (cf. 2), the gen. either preceding or (now usually) following the prep. It was orig. not a prep. at all: in MHG it was the dat. plur. of the noun *wec* (> **Weg**), and 'for your sake' was *von iuwer wegen.* The combination **von wegen** was in common use until recent times, and is indeed still preserved in coll. lang.: cf. **Ich habe ihm**

schon von wegen meiner Novelle geschrieben (Chamisso: 'I have already written to him in connexion with my short story')—**Ich bin von wegen der Nachfrage nach Ihrem Befinden hergekommen** (Gutzkow: 'I have come to ask how you are keeping')—esp. now in a few set expressions: **Von Amts wegen hat er sich um die Herstellung dieser Wohnungen zu kümmern** (F. A. Hohenstein: 'By reason of his official position he is obliged to make it his business to see to the erection of these dwelling-houses')—**Sie kennen das Leben sowohl als Mensch wie von Berufs wegen** (Th. Mann: i.e. 'professionally')—**Von Rechts wegen ist kein Mensch steuerfrei** (Bismarck: 'No one is by right exempt from paying taxes')—**Das hätten Sie von Rechts wegen** (much like **eigentlich**, 'by rights') **nicht tun sollen.** But **von** gradually dropped out, as in **Nicht Streitens wegen kam ich her** (Sch.) and **Er hatte nur der Form wegen gefragt** (Th. Mann: 'for form's sake'), so that **wegen** became a real prep. and assumed the normal position before the word it governed (but see 3), as in **Wegen Mangels an Geld mußte ich zu Fuß gehen** and **Er ist wegen Diebstahls angeklagt worden. 2.** Instead of the gen., a *dat.* is common in coll. speech, but in good prose style this should only be used where the gen. would not be recognizable, or where the governed word is preceded by a Saxon gen.: e.g. **Sie will mich wegen Sommerkostümen um Rat fragen** (Fulda)—**Wegen meines Freundes plötzlichem Tode mußte ich meinen Plan aufgeben**; so the dat. **Händeln** would be preferable in **Beim Regiment saß ich oft wegen Händel auf der Wacht** (Spindler), and 'because of something else' can only take the form **wegen etwas anderem. 3.** The use in good prose of **wegen** governing a *pron.*, esp. a pers. pron., is disliked in the north, where one avoids propositions like **Wegen dir lass' ich alle meine Kameraden laufen** (A. Widmann). Instead of **wegen meiner** or **mir**, one uses **meinetwegen** (q.v.); and sim. **deinet-, unsert-, ihretwegen**, etc., and with other prons., **des-, wes-, dessent-, derentwegen** (cf. deren 3).

wehklagen: The prefix of this verb, meaning 'to grieve, lament', although always accented, is *insep.*, as in **Er riß sich los und ging fort: seine Eltern wehklagten und vergossen Tränen** (Novalis); so also **Es ist kein Grund, über diese Nachricht zu wehklagen** (not **wehzuklagen**, as used by Wieland). It should not be used trans.: 'to lament a person's death' is **über jemandes Tod wehklagen** or **jemandes Tod beklagen** or **um einen Verstorbenen trauern.** This last expression may also mean 'to wear *or* be in mourning for a person': cf. **Trauer anlegen** ('to go into mourning').

Wehr: The fundamental force of this *fem.* noun is 'defence, resistance' (plur. **Wehren**), the idea of 'warding off' an attack (**einen Angriff abwehren**). This is seen esp. in the common phrase **sich zur Wehr setzen** ('to offer resistance, defend oneself'), as in **Glaubt ihr, ich werde mich zur Wehr setzen, wenn ihr mich binden wollt?** (Sch.); also in the adj. **wehrlos** ('defenceless') and compds. like **Landwehr** ('militia, territorial army'), **Wehrpflicht** ('obligation to serve in the forces' in defence of one's country) and **Wehrmacht** (the modern expression for 'all the armed forces'); cf. **in der** (usually **aus**) **Notwehr handeln** ('to act in self-defence'). A natural development was the sense of something concrete affording protection, as seen in Luther's **Ein' feste Burg ist unser Gott, ein' gute Wehr und Waffen** ('a trusty shield and weapon' in Carlyle's translation) and in **eine Brustwehr** ('a breastwork, parapet'). This then led to its specific use with the force of 'dam, weir, lock, sluice', a contrivance for keeping back the natural flow of water, in which sense the *neut.* gender (with plur. **Wehre**) is now firmly established, as in **Drüben rauscht das Wehr** (Uhland). The proposition **Über die Wehre stürzt der Wildbach** (Heyse) now at once suggests a plur., but it may be a now unusual sing., as MHG had both forms, *die wer* and *die were.*

Weib: see **Mädchen** 1 and 2.

weigern ('to refuse'): **1.** This verb was originally used with a *gen.* of the thing and a *dat.* of the person: e.g. MHG *ich mōht es* (gen.) *im geweigert hân* ('I could have refused it to him'). But the gen. here is now quite obs., being replaced by the *accus.*: e.g. **Meine erste Bitte kann er mir nicht weigern** (Sch.)—**Eurer Tapferkeit kann er den wohlverdienten Preis nicht weigern** (id.)—**Der Adel weigerte ihm die Steuern, die er ausschreiben ließ** (Fr. Griese). Even this construction, however, is somewhat limited, being confined for the most part to a few expressions like the ones just given (but see 3). **2.** Much more usual here in modern times is the compd. **verweigern,** which has a wider application: e.g. **Der Schüler wurde bestraft, weil er dem Lehrer den Gehorsam verweigert** (or **versagt**: see **versagen**) **hatte —Man kann einem großen Verbrecher eine Art Achtung nicht verweigern** (G.)—**Wie erstaunte ich, als er es verweigerte, sich ihr zu nähern** (E. T. A. Hoffmann)—**Ich verweigerte die Annahme des ungenügend frankierten Briefes** ('I refused acceptance of the insufficiently pre-paid letter'). **3.** On the other hand, the reflex. **sich weigern** (not **sich verweigern**) is always used with **zu** + *infin.*, and the last two examples given under 2 might be expressed **Wie erstaunte ich, als er sich weigerte, ihr zu nahen—Ich weigerte mich, den ungenügend frankierten Brief anzunehmen.** A remnant of earlier usage is seen in **Dem Müller war der Antrag gestellt worden, seine Mühle zu verkaufen; er hatte sich dessen geweigert** (A. Meissner), i.e. **er hatte den Antrag abgelehnt.**—It follows that **Weigerung** is now generally used with **zu** + infin., **Verweigerung** always with a gen.: cf. **Meine Weigerung, sein Anerbieten anzunehmen, verdroß ihn** and **Meine Verweigerung seines Anerbietens verdroß ihn** ('My refusal of his offer vexed him').

weigh: see **wiegen** 1 and 2.

Weih: This masc. noun is the name for the bird which we call a 'harrier', but it is commonly applied to the 'kite', which is properly **Gabelweih**: cf. '*Forktail*, of old time used in England for the Kite' (Newton, Dictionary of Birds). The form **der Weih** (strong) is the usual one in the north, but **der Weihe** (weak) is also allowed. The bird is also called **die Weihe** in the south (*Brockhaus*'s Encyclopaedia says **Die häufigste der Weihen ist die Kornweihe,** i.e. 'the hen harrier'); but the fem. is confined in the north to the sense of 'consecration, ordination', or the 'unveiling' of a monument, etc. For a 'kite' which children fly, see **Drache.**

Weihnachten: In MHG, the noun *naht* did not mutate the stem-vowel in the plur. (see **Nacht**), and **Weihnachten** is a remnant of the earlier unmutated plur. Actually, it is the *dat.* plur., the result of dropping the prep. and the art. in the phrase *zen wîhen nahten* (= **zu den heiligen Nächten,** 'in the holy nights'), the plur. being explained by the fact that the Christmas festival lasted several days (cf. 'the twelve days of Christmas'); and the same applies to the other chief church festivals, **Ostern** (Easter), **Pfingsten** (Pentecost, Whitsun) and **Fasten** (Lent: cf. Scots *Fastens-een*, Shrove Tuesday). These, then, were plur. forms; the sing. **die Weihnacht,** as in Storm's **Otto versteht so gut, Weihnacht zu feiern,** is a later development and has never approached, far less displaced, the plur. form in popular favour although it is always used in compounds: **Weihnachtsbaum, -geschenk, -mann,** etc. But in course of time the names for these festivals came to be felt as *sing.* forms, with the result that there was considerable fluctuation in gender. One would have expected that when **die Fasten** became a sing., it would automatically be *fem.*, but in point of fact the fem. is very rare: in an example like **Sie spielen hier in der Fasten geistliche Opern** (G.), the author may have had **in der Fastenzeit** in his mind. Where these festival names have no art. or other qualifying word, they are usually treated as *sing.* nouns: e.g. **Weihnachten ist nun wieder abgelaufen** (W. v. Kügelgen)—**So kam wieder Weihnachten heran** (Frenssen)—**Pfingsten war das freudvollste aller Jubelfeste, freudvoller als Weihnachten und Ostern** (Werfel)—**Ostern war vorüber** (Speckmann)—**Ostern stand vor der Tür** (Zuckmayer: 'Easter was close at hand'). Elsewhere the *plur.* forms are much more usual: e.g. **Sie war, wie vorige Weihnachten, so auch diesmal wieder verreist** (Fontane)—**Die Weihnachten dieses Jahres brachten eine Freudenbotschaft** (Sudermann)—**Um die Pfingsten begann ihr der Schlaf zu fehlen** (id.)—**Wie waren es diesmal andere Pfingsten!** (Stifter)—**Die Zeit rückte weiter, und nach den Ostern war jetzt das Pfingstfest herangekommen** (Storm)—„**Langweilige Ostern waren das bei uns**", **klagte sie** (Werfel)—**Eines Abends in den Fasten traf er einen fremden Mann bei der Krämerin** (Waggerl); for the fluctuation, cf. **Weihnachten stand vor der Tür, die ersten Weihnachten nicht zu Haus!** (Ompteda.) But the *sing.* use is by no means rare here, the noun then being either masc. or neut.: e.g. **Wenigstens sollte er bis zum nächsten Ostern warten** (Voigt-Diederichs)—**Paul schenkte ihm zu jedem Weihnachten einen neuen Kalender** (Sudermann); *masc.*, **Du siehst,**

daß ich an deinen Weihnachten gedacht habe (id.)—Ich komme diesen Weihnachten (Storm)—Ein Bilderalbum hatte ich letzten Weihnachten von ihm (Voigt-Diederichs); *neut.*, Es war ein so schönes Weihnachten! (H. W. Geissler)—Auf ein frohes Weihnachten! (Fontane)—Ein Pfingsten, wie ich's jetzt beschreiben will, trifft man wohl nirgends an (Jean Paul); cf. Fr. *à Pâques prochain* or *prochaines*.

weil: **1.** This subord. conj. now always has *causal* force (see 2). At one time it was used with *temp.* force ('while, as long as'): e.g. **Freie um die Witwe, weil sie noch trauert** (Lessing)—**Weil ich fern bin** ('During my absence'), **führe du das Regiment des Hauses!** (Sch.); sim. in the well-known lines **Freut euch des Lebens, weil noch das Lämpchen glüht!** (Usteri). In MHG this was expressed by the adv. accus. *die wîle*, sometimes by the gen. *der wîle*, like 'the while' in examples like 'Mr. Chuckster bade him go in, he would mind the chaise the while' (Dickens) and 'She knelt before him, beseeching him, the while his hand she wrung, to change his purpose' (Keats). The MHG expressions became **dieweil** (see 2) and **derweil(en)**, both common in early NHG and still in use: e.g. (adv.) **Zum Bühle da rettet euch, harret derweil!** (G.)—**Lest das Papier, derweilen will ich Umschau halten** (Raabe); (conj.) **Torheit ist in ihrem Herzen, dieweil sie leben** (Eccles. 9. 3)—**Ich erschlug den Wicht, derweil ihr schliefet** (Uhland). **2.** (**a**) It is rather strange that **weil** has become such an everyday word, as MHG *die wîle* was rare in the sense of 'because', this being then usually expressed by *sît* or *sît daz* (see **seit** 2), and it may be that **weil** developed out of **dieweil**: cf. **Dieweil er ein göttlich Leben führte, nahm ihn Gott hinweg** (Gen. 5. 24). In any case, whereas **weil** has lost its temp. force, **seit** has lost its causal force. (**b**) As **weil** now only means 'because', it closely approaches **da**; but although these two expressions are sometimes used more or less indiscriminately, they really differ: **weil** gives the *true* reason for a statement, **da** the *logical* reason from which the statement is deduced—cf. also **denn (conjunction)** 3. Thus, in the proposition **Da der Hahn kräht, ist es Morgen**, it would be quite wrong to use **weil**, because that would imply that the dawn depended on the cock-crow! So also **Da** (not **Weil**) **das Thermometer gestiegen ist, ist es wärmer geworden**, but **Weil** (not **Da**) **es wärmer ist, ist das Thermometer gestiegen**—**Da Holz auf Wasser schwimmt, ist es leichter als Wasser**, but **Weil Holz leichter ist als Wasser, schwimmt es darauf**—**Da diese Werke in keiner Bibliothek zu finden sind, sind sie vermutlich nie gedruckt worden**, but **Weil diese Werke nie gedruckt wurden, sind sie in Vergessenheit geraten.**

weis-: This verbal prefix is really the adj. **weise** ('wise'), so it is wrong to spell it as **weiß-**; cf. the adj. **naseweis**, orig. used of a game-dog with a keen scent, but now only used of a 'pert, saucy' child who gives himself grown-up airs. The prefix is now confined to two verbs: (**a**) **weismachen** ('to try to make a person believe what is untrue'); its force is not unlike the American coll. 'to put a person wise to something', so one would expect it to take an accus. of the person, but it now takes a *dat.* of the person and an *accus.* of the thing, the prefix being *sep.*: e.g. **So etwas Dummes macht mir niemand weis** ('No one is going to delude me into believing anything as silly as that')—**Er maßte sich an, mir das weiszumachen** ('He presumed to fool me with that')—**Wer hat dir das weisgemacht?** (cf. the example from Fontane under **verloben**). (**b**) **weissagen** ('to prophesy': cf. **wahrsagen**), the prefix here being *insep.* throughout: e.g. **Es hätte so kommen können, wie uns** (dat.) **der Herr weissagte** (Tieck)—**Sie haben mir einen Sohn geweissagt** (G.)—**Ich werde mich hüten zu weissagen!** ('Catch me prophesying!')—**Die Feinde rückten immer näher: vorübereilende Flüchtlinge weissagten Mord und Brand** (Spindler).

weiß: For the subst. use of this adj., see **colour**, and cf. **das Weiße im Ei** (= **das Eiweiß**, 'the white of an egg': see **gelb**).

weit, Weite: see **distance** 2.

welch (indefinite): Grammarians are apt to condemn the use in good prose of **welch** with the force of 'some, any' in references to something previously mentioned; but although it is true that this use is mainly characteristic of the coll. speech of the north (where it is, indeed, a general favourite), its sweeping condemnation is hardly supported by actual practice. **1.** It is used in the *sing.* in references to materials, etc.: e.g. **Trink ein Glas Wein: da ist welcher!** (Spielhagen: '. . . here is some!')—**Trinkst du gern Branntwein? Gibt dir die Mutter zuweilen welchen?** (Droste-Hülshoff)—

Es fehlte an Geld; um welches zu schaffen, vergriff man sich am Kapital (Th. Mann: '. . . in order to procure some they laid hands on part of the capital')—**Ich bin stark für Musik, kriege aber selten welche zu hören** (Speckmann: 'I am keen on music, but seldom get to hear any'). In the example from Th. Mann, **einiges** might conceivably be substituted for **welches**, but in the other examples any change would sound stilted. **2.** Esp. common is this use of **welch** in the *plur.*, and the following examples might be multiplied indefinitely: **Wohin sollte er gehen? Zu Bekannten, deren er welche hier hatte, traute er sich nicht** (Viebig)—**Wir besuchen jetzt weder Gesellschaften, noch geben wir selbst welche** (Th. Mann: 'We don't go to parties now, nor do we give any ourselves')—**Wie wenige vollkommene Gedichte gibt es; aber daß ihrer überhaupt welche entstehen, ist es nicht wie ein Wunder?** (Hofmannsthal)—**Gab es Worte für dieses Ereignis, so war ich zu klein, welche zu finden** (Rilke)—**„Man sollte niemals Sporen tragen", dachte er, „der König trägt nie welche"** (Bruno Franck)—**„Betrachte die Steine da: sehen sie nicht aus wie Leichensteine?" „Es sind auch welche"** (id.: = **Das sind sie auch**, 'And so they are')—**Ich hasse die Hagestolze und wundere mich nur, daß es überhaupt welche gibt** (Jul. Wolff)—**Von den Nachbarn sind welche, die schon fortgezogen sind, und welche, die hier bleiben wollen** (H. Grimm)—**Der Bauer liest keine Bücher; die Herren aus der Stadt lesen welche** (Waggerl)—**Die Erbsen haben kleine Schoten, und junge Mohrrüben hab' ich auch schon welche** (H. Krieger)—**Hier wohnten zuletzt welche aus dem Bayrischen** (Blunck: 'Among the last people who lived here there were some who hailed from Bavaria')—**Es gibt keine Handwerker im Ort; und wenn es welche gibt, kommen sie nicht** (K. Edschmid)—**In diesem Ledergurt** ('belt') **stecken die Patronen, welche mit grobem Schrot für Hasen, welche mit feinem für Rebhühner** (Speckmann).

welch (interrogative): **1.** Whether used with adj. or subst. force, in dir. or indir. questions, or in exclamations (which were orig. questions), **welch** as a rule is *strongly* inflected. The only exceptions are when it stands before **ein**, or before an attrib. adj.; in the former case it is never inflected, in the latter it may remain uninflected (the adj. then requiring strong inflexion) or be strongly inflected (the adj. then mostly having weak inflexion: cf. **manch, solch**): e.g. **Welcher Knabe** (or **Welcher von euch Knaben**) **hat das getan?**—**Ich fragte ihn, welchem Freunde** (or **welchem guten Freunde**) **er begegnet sei**—**Welch (ein) herrlicher Ausblick!** or **Welcher herrliche Ausblick!**—**Welch hübsche Blumen!** or **Welche hübschen Blumen!**—**O, welche wonnevollen Stunden habe ich hier verlebt!** (Jul. Grosse)—**Infolge welcher besonderen Umstände ist er um Urlaub eingekommen?** ('In consequence of which special circumstances has he applied for leave?'). Occasional examples of a strong adj. ending here in the nom. and accus. plur. are not to be recommended: cf. **O, welche tiefe** (for **tiefen**) **Quellen liegen verborgen!** (Auerbach) and **Himmel! welche entsetzliche Wortfügungen!** (Heine). **2.** (**a**) The gen. sing. masc. and neut. can only be used with *adj.*, not with subst. force: cf. **Welches Knaben Buch ist dies?** and **Wessen** ('Whose': not **Welches**, as that would mean 'Which') **Buch ist dies?** (**b**) Sometimes the standard gen. **welches** is replaced by the weak form **welchen** when the following noun has the strong **-s** or **-es** ending as in **Die Bestimmung lautete** ('The decision was'), **daß der Redner der geistig selbständigste Mann in der ganzen Landschaft sein sollte, einerlei welchen Standes oder Berufs** (Frenssen: '. . . no matter of what station or profession')—**Er besaß den fünften Sinn, die Qualität eines Mannes, gleichgültig welchen Berufs, zu wittern** (K. Edschmid: 'He had the fifth sense, the faculty of sizing up the character of a man, whatever his profession might be'). According to *Sanders*, this weak form should not be imitated (**verdient keine Nachahmung**); but although **wes Standes** is certainly more common—see **was (interrogative)** 2—to condemn the weak form in such phrases (cf. **solch** 2) seems rather extravagant, the more so as **welchen Standes** is much more euphonious than **welches Standes**. **3.** The invariable form **welches** is used in questions with identifying force in combination with the verb **sein**: just as one says **Dies ist eine Rose** and **Das sind Nelken**, so also one says **Welches sind deine Lieblingsblumen?** **4.** The interrog. **welch** approaches **was für**—see **was (interrogative)** 4 (*b*), and cf. **Gab es**

Worte für dieses Ereignis, so war ich zu klein, welche zu finden (Rilke)—yet they really differ, **was für** asking about a kind of thing, **welch** about a particular thing: there is an obvious difference between **Was für Bücher** ('What sort of books') **haben Sie gekauft?** and **Welche Bücher** ('Which books') **haben Sie gekauft?**

welch (relative): **1.** Orig. **welch** was not an independent rel. pron.: MHG *swelh* (< *sô+welh*) meant 'whoever, anybody who', and Luther still said **Welcher** (now **Wer**) **isset, der verachte den nicht, der da nicht isset** (Rom. 14. 3) and **Welchen** (now **Wen**) **der Herr lieb hat, den züchtiget er** (Heb. 12. 6). Gradually, however, it came to be used as a rel. pron., and as such it is now mainly characteristic of the written lang.: *Wustmann* goes so far as to say **Niemand spricht „welcher", es wird nur geschrieben,** adding in a footnote **Nur in Süddeutschland und Österreich wird „welcher" auch gesprochen, aber immer nur von Leuten, die sich „gebildet" ausdrücken möchten**; and it is true that the ordinary conversational style of the north almost demands the use of **der** as the rel. pron., **welcher** there sounding formal and almost pedantic. And even in the written lang. there are contexts where **welch** cannot be used, notably in the gen. (sing. and plur.) when the gen. precedes the noun on which it depends, as in **Wie heißt der Herr, dessen** (not **welches**) **Adresse Sie ausfindig machen möchten?** (cf. 2) or **Er schrieb Chöre, deren Texte der Bibel entnommen waren** (Th. Mann). On the other hand, **welch** is the only possible expression when the relation is an *adj.* one. But this use is almost confined to a few phrases like 'which latter', esp. prep. phrases such as 'for which reason', 'in which case', 'to which end', etc.: e.g. **Sie brachte Backwerk und Früchte, zu welchen letzteren sogar spanische Trauben gehörten** (Gutzkow: '. . . among which latter there were even grapes from Spain') —**Ich habe mir eine Erkältung zugezogen, aus welchem Grunde ich zu Hause bleiben muß; ich hoffe aber, daß ich mich bis morgen erholt haben werde, in welchem Fall ich dich, wie verabredet, treffen werde.** Elsewhere this construction is better avoided: even we say 'He asked me the time, a question which (*rather than* which question) I could not answer.' And even in the written lang. of the north **welch** is not nearly as common as **der** (but cf. 3); it is very useful, however, where two or more rel. clauses occur in the same proposition, as in **Es ist eine Reihe von Jahren her, als zu dem Regiment, welches hier in Garnison stand, ein Hauptmann versetzt wurde, der aus dem Westen Deutschlands kam** (Wildenbruch), or where the rel. **der** might at first be confused with the def. art., as in **Die Kirche, die Fichten umgeben, steht auf einer Anhöhe über dem Dorf** (W. Alexis). **2.** In independent use the masc. and neut. gen. sing. of the rel. **welch** is now avoided: one no longer says **Ich machte ein Zeichen, ungeachtet welches** ('despite which') **Werther ihn küßte** (Immermann), where modern usage demands **dessen**; cf. Spielhagen's reference to **ein Terrain, innerhalb welches keine neuen Entdeckungen gemacht werden konnten.** **3.** The only case where **welch** is probably more common than **der** is where the antecedent is **derjenige** ('he who': see **dies** 2 (*d*)). But **derjenige** is undeniably a prosaic expression, common in official documents (*Wustmann* characterizes it as **„eigens für die Papiersprache erfunden"**), and most stylists prefer **der, der . . .** to **derjenige, welcher . . .**; and there is even no stylistic objection to propositions like **Der, der der Freunde entbehrt, ist zu beklagen** or **Die, die die Schweiz besucht haben, schwärmen fast alle dafür**, which, when correctly intoned (with a slight pause after the determinative) are in the very spirit of the lang. In this connexion cf. **wer** 2 (*b*). **4.** On the other hand, the rel. **welch** is now generally avoided where the antecedent is a 1st or 2nd pers. pron.: see **der (relative)** 1, and cf. **Du Tor, welcher** (now **der**) **Du glaubst, den Narren spielen zu können!** (Raabe). **5.** Where the antecedent is not a definite concrete object, but an idea contained in a single word, **welches** is correct, as in **Er ist reich, welches ich nicht bin**; but where the antecedent is an idea contained in a whole clause, the usual expression now is **was**—see **was (relative)** 2 (*a*) —and **was** would be more in accordance with modern usage than **welches** in examples like **Ich ließ die Kardinäle aussperren, welches sie mir übelnahmen** (G.) —**Der Ring an einer Pforte lud sie ein zu klopfen, welches Felix etwas unsanft verrichtete** (G.)—**Ich sah ihn die Unterlippe zwischen die Zähne klemmen, welches er nur tut, wenn er am grimmigsten ist** (Sch.)

—**Alle waren nach der Mode des Jahres 1760 gekleidet, welches einen wunderlichen Eindruck machte** (E. T. A. Hoffmann)—**Ich stieg die Treppen hinauf, welches sehr langsam ging** (Raabe).

wenig: 1. The MHG word *wênec* was—like *etewaz, niht, vil,* etc.—an indef. neut. pron. which could take a gen. of material, as in *wênec goldes* and *wênec müeje* ('little trouble'). When a person now says **Das macht mir wenig Mühe** or **Er hat nur wenig Mittel,** he is actually using the MHG idiom (see **nichts** 2); but as neither **Mühe** nor **Mittel** can be recognized as a gen., the construction has come to be regarded as *appositional* and to be applied to nouns whose gen. would be recognizable, as in **wenig Brot** (< *wênec brôtes*). The same is true of propositions like **Er hatte nur wenig Neues zu berichten** ('He had but little that was new to report') and **Von den Menschen** (*scil.* **in Nord-Italien) wüßte ich wenig Erfreuliches zu sagen** (G.: 'As for the inhabitants, there is not much I could say in their favour'), where the adj.-substs. were orig. gen. but are now treated as accus.; and hence, in the dat., **Wir haben von wenig Neuem gesprochen.** But the historical gen. is still in use, esp. in the case of prons.: e.g. **Die Arbeiter kamen: es schienen ihm ihrer zu wenig** (G.: '. . . there seemed to him to be too few of them'). **2.** But in this last example, **wenig** might be inflected, as it is in **Ich hatte einen Widerwillen gegen feuchtkalte Hände, und bei jeder neuen Hand, die sich mir entgegenstreckte, fürchtete ich, eine dieser Art zu fassen, erwischte ihrer auch nicht wenige** (D. Speckmann: '. . . I was afraid I should grasp one of these clammy hands, and I did in fact clasp not a few of them'). In point of fact, **wenig** can in most cases be inflected or not, the one notable exception being when it is qualified by the def. art. or a poss., in which case it is always inflected: e.g. **Dies ist das wenige Geld, was ich besitze** (Raabe)—**Ich malte es mir aus mit der wenigen Phantasie, die mir gegeben** (Ompteda)—**Meine wenigen Freunde sind jetzt alle verreist.** On the other hand, one usually says **ein wenig** (like **ein bißchen** or **ein paar**), and **Er hob sich ein weniges von seinem Stuhl** (G. Britting) sounds unnatural, to say the least. But one must be on one's guard here: thus, **weniger** may be a nom. sing. masc., a gen. sing. fem. or gen. plur., or a *compar.*, so that it is better to express the proposition 'That requires little courage' by **Dazu gehört wenig Mut** (not **weniger Mut,** which would in the first instance suggest 'less courage'). So also distinguish between **Dieser Roman ist wenig** (adv.) **bekannt** ('not well-known') and **nur wenigen bekannt** ('known to only a few people'); cf. **Der Richter sprang auf und seine sonst wenig auffallenden Augenbrauen** ('his eyebrows, which ordinarily attracted little attention') **drängten sich buschig über seinen Augen** (Kafka). **3.** An attrib. adj. following an *un*inflected **wenig** must, of course, have a strong ending: one can only say **Ich habe wenig gute neue Romane gelesen.** When **wenig** is inflected, there is some fluctuation, but a following adj. far more commonly has a weak ending in all cases except the nom. and accus. plur.: e.g., on the one hand, **Das würde ich nur im Beisein weniger guten Freunde sagen**; on the other hand, **Ich habe jetzt wenige gute Freunde**—**Theodor Manns wenige literarische Beziehungen konnten nur auf Anerkennung der Leistung beruhen** (A. Eloesser); so also **wenige Deutsche,** gen. **weniger Deutschen**—**Dem Dichter** (*scil.* Fritz Reuter) **wird ein Glück zuteil, mit dem nur wenige Sterbliche begnadigt sind: er lebt auch nach dem Tode in seinem Volke fort** (Freytag). If for no other reason, it is better to use **weniger guten Freunde** meaning 'of few good friends', because **weniger gute Freunde** would at once suggest a nom. or accus. plur. with the force of '*fewer* good friends'. **4.** Adv. expressions: (**a**) The prep. phrase **mit wenigem** is used in rather choice style like **mit wenig Worten,** as in **Diese Frau verdient, daß wir ihrer mit wenigem hier gedenken** (Mörike). (**b**) The commonest expression in the north for 'at least', whether suggesting the lowest admissible amount or conveying the idea 'at any rate, at all events', is **wenigstens,** while the south rather prefers **mindestens**: e.g. **Ich habe ihn wenigstens dreimal angerufen**—**Er wird vor acht Uhr hier sein, wenigstens hat er das gesagt.** A more modern expression here is **zumindest**: e.g. **Sie war schon recht bei Jahren, Ende fünfzig zumindest:** (Th. Mann)—**Es konnte nur ein Zeichen tiefer Demütigung sein, oder es mußte zumindest so aufgefaßt werden** (Kafka). (**c**) Our 'not least' is best expressed by **nicht zum wenigsten**: e.g. **Ich war noch**

nicht gereist, so kam mir alles neu vor, und nicht zum wenigsten, wie sich die Bauart der Häuser mählich veränderte (W. Schäfer: 'not least the fact that the style of architecture gradually changed') —**Daß der Kranke wieder zu Kräften kam** ('regained his strength'), **dankte er nicht zum wenigsten der treuen Hilfe seiner beiden Kameraden** (W. Kramp). **(d)** Our 'least' used with compar. force is **am wenigsten,** as in **Bei dem Unfall wurde keiner schwer verletzt, ich am wenigsten** (or stronger **ich am allerwenigsten,** 'I least of all').

wenn: see **wann; when** 1, 2 (*c*) and 3; also **als = 'as if'** 1; **als = 'than'** 4; **except** 2 (*b*). As **wenn** may mean either 'if' or (with a pres. tense) 'when', it is not wrong to say **Wenn ich nicht zu Hause sein sollte, wenn er vorspricht, bitte ihn, mich heute abend anzurufen** ('Should I be out when he calls, ask him to ring me up tonight'). On the whole, however, it would be better here to re-word the cond. clause and say **Sollte ich nicht zu Hause sein, wenn er vorspricht, . . .**; and sim., in a proposition like 'I should be sorry if he called when I am out', it is advisable to begin with the cond. clause: **Sollte er vorsprechen, wenn ich nicht zu Hause bin, würde es mir leid tun** (better than **Es würde mir leid tun, wenn er vorsprechen sollte, wenn ich nicht zu Hause bin**).

wer: 1. (a) With gen. **wessen,** dat. **wem,** accus. **wen,** this is the standard interrog. pron. corresponding to 'who?', and is used as both masc. and fem.: e.g. **Wem** (or **Welcher**) **von den Damen gehören diese Handschuhe?**—In MHG *wes* was used both of persons and of things; now **wessen** is used of persons, **wes** of things —see **was (interrogative)** 2: e.g. **Wessen Handschuhe sind dies?** But **wessent** is prefixed to **wegen** and **willen:** cf., on the one hand, **Um wessentwillen** ('For whose sake') **quälen wir uns mit solchen Sachen?** (Fontane) and, on the other hand, **Weswegen** ('For what reason') **haben Sie den Brief nicht beantwortet?**—The form **wer** used as a dat. fem. only occurs very occasionally and should *not* be used: cf. **„Du bist so eine Art Bruder von ihr." „Von ihr? von wer?"** (A. Wilbrandt). **(b)** To convey the idea of plurality, we say 'Who *are* coming tonight?', but a German cannot say **Wer kommen heute abend?**—to make it plur., he uses the sing. verb and adds **alles,** a form which applies to *all* cases: e.g. **Wer kommt alles heute abend?—Wen sollen wir alles einladen?—Wem bist du alles unterwegs begegnet?** A plur. verb in such questions is only possible in the nom. with the verb **sein** and a following noun, as in **Wer sind diese Leute?** where **Leute** is really the grammatical subj., and **wer** the pred. introducing the proposition, just as it is in **Schauspieler sind diese Leute. 2.** The other uses of **wer** are: **(a)** with *concessive* force ('whoever'): see **immer** 3; **(b)** as a *rel.* pron. including its antecedent (= 'he who', **derjenige welcher**), as in **Wer morgen spät kommt, soll bestraft werden;** this is esp. common in prov. expressions like **Wer wagt, gewinnt** ('Never venture, never win') and **Wer anderen eine Grube gräbt, fällt selbst hinein** (cf. 'A biter is bit'); **(c)** in *coll.* lang., with the force of **jemand:** e.g. **Hat wer angerufen?** ('Has any one rung up?')—**Er sagte, er wäre wem begegnet, aber wem, weiß ich nicht** ('He said he had met somebody, but I don't know whom')—**Ich wisse doch, erzählte sie, er habe nie mit wem andern gesprochen** (St. Zweig: see **jemand** 2).

werben: see **marry** 1 (*d*); for the subj. form **würbe,** see **past subjunctive** 2 (*c*) (i).

werden: 1. This is the only verb left which can still show the most striking characteristics of several classes of MHG strong verbs, viz. different stem-vowels in the sing. and plur. of the past tense (**ich ward, wir wurden**); but even here, for the sake of greater uniformity, the sing. form **ich wurde** has come to supplant **ich ward** in ordinary lang., the latter being used only in poetry and elevated or intentionally archaic prose. For a similar vowel-change in *pres.* tenses (**ich darf, wir dürfen, etc.**), see **past-present verbs. 2.** One of the main ideas suggested by the prefix **ge-** (q.v.) is that of completeness, of the end of one action or state and the beginning of another (cf. 4), and this explains why it came to be the special characteristic of the *past part.,* which implies completion. But some verbs of themselves imply the passing into a new state, e.g. **kommen** and **werden,** and in MHG such verbs required *no* prefix *ge-*: one said *er ist ze hûse komen* ('He has come home') and *si ist kranc worden* ('She has become unwell'). **3.** Of such past part. forms without **ge-,** the only one which has survived in good prose is **worden,** the use of which, however, is strictly limited. Down to the classical period, and even later, it was often used exactly as in MHG, esp. in spoken language: e.g. **Schatzmeister bin ich worden** (Lessing)—**Wohl Euch, daß Ihr mit dem Verräter nicht näher verwandt worden** (G.)—**Bist du wahnsinnig worden?** (Sch.)—**Euer Vater ist eines schweren Verbrechens schuldig worden** (Hauff); cf., as characteristic of the lang. spoken early in the 18th century, **Es war gut Wetter worden** (Storm). But this use is now obs.: the established form of the past part. in *independent* use is **geworden,** while the form without **ge-** is used as an *aux.* verb to form the perf. tense of the **passive voice** (q.v.). Hence distinguish between **Er ist gelehrt worden** ('He has been taught') and **Er ist gelehrt geworden** ('He has become learned')—**Er ist geschickt worden** ('He has been sent') and **Er ist geschickt geworden** ('He has become skilful'); in a strictly incorrect example like **Auf der Dorfstraße war man der Fremden gewahr worden** (Zifferer), the **ge-** may have been deliberately omitted for the sake of euphony, to avoid **gewahr geworden. 4.** In standard MHG the verb *werden* was not yet used with an infin. to form the future tense: at that period future time was expressed either by a pres. tense (esp. with the prefix *ge-*) or by *suln* (> **sollen,** *shall*). But *werden* was used with a pres. part. to suggest the end of one action or state and the commencement of another: thus, *si wart weinende* meant 'She began to weep', and this idiom was frequently used by Luther, as in **Da ward das ganze Heer laufend** (Judges 7. 21) and **Moses aber ward zitternd** (Acts 7. 32). As explained under **participle (present)** 1, this use is now obs. in good prose (but see **vermuten**). It is, however, preserved in the popular lang. of the north (really LG), but the part. has lost its final **-d** and assumed the form of the infin. In this coll. idiom, used esp. in spoken narrative, **werden** + infin. at once suggests a *future* tense, but actually has *past* force: the narrator, as it were, re-lives the moment when he was just on the point of acting, which makes the narrative more vivid and alive: e.g. **Ich also nach Tannenberg gemacht, und werde gleich auf sein Zimmer gehen und ihn richtig treffen, wie er eben seinen Koffer packt: „Guten Tag!" werde ich sagen . . .** (Spielhagen: 'So I set off for T. and *went* at once to his room, and sure enough, I *came* on him just as he was packing his bag: "Good day!" I *said*'); sim., with a historic pres., **Er greift den Kleinen am Halse, und nun werden die beiden anfangen, sich mitten in der Stunde zu hauen** (Wildenbruch: 'He seized the little one by the neck, and then the two boys *started* to fight in the middle of the lesson'). **5.** In **werden** + infin. with future force, the infin. is also a corrupt form of the pres. part., **Ich werde schweigend** becoming **Ich werde schweigen.** In conditional propositions **ich werde** becomes **ich würde,** but this circumlocution should only be used in *princ.*, not subord. clauses, as students are often tempted to do when they are not sure as to the form of the past subj. of the verb: it is bad German to render 'I should be surprised if he were to do it' by **Ich würde mich wundern, wenn er es tun würde** (for **wenn er es täte**); so also **Wenn Sie es dem Richter sagen würden** (for **sagten**), **würden Sie ausgelacht** (Kafka), where the double **würden** is particularly objectionable.

werfen: see **mit** 2 (*b*); **open** 1; for the form **würfe,** see **past subjunctive** 2 (*c*) (i).

Werk: Formerly the gen. **Werks** was used as an obj. of **machen** in exactly the same way as **Aufhebens, Federlesens** and **Wesens,** as explained under **aufheben** 2. But whereas these three expressions are still in reg. use, **Werks** is peculiar to some southern dialects: cf. **Was macht man nicht für Werks!** (J. Ch. Günther [early 18th century]: 'What a fuss is being made!')—see **negative (pleonastic)** 3.

Wermut: This noun, meaning 'wormwood', is masc., but has no connexion with **Mut:** it is, in fact, not **Wer-mut,** but **Werm-ut** (it may be connected with **warm**), its termination being the same as in **Arm-ut** (see **Mut**). Our 'wormwood' is a corrupt form of Anglo-Saxon *wermod.*

wert: The orig. construction of this adj. was a *gen.*, as in **Dieser Mensch hat nichts getan, das des Todes oder der Bande wert sei** (Acts 26. 31), and this case is still quite common in good prose: e.g. **Du kannst nichts leisten, was des Antritts eines Amtes wert wäre** (Stifter)—**Es geschah nichts mehr, was des Erzählens wert wäre** (W. v. Scholz)—**Den Haufen Geld ließ er liegen und hielt Umschau, was etwa des Mitnehmens wert sein möchte** (H.

Hesse). The gen. is also common in prov. expressions such as **Eigner Herd ist Goldes wert** ('There is no place like home') and **Eine Gefälligkeit ist der anderen wert** ('One good turn deserves another'), and in compd. adjs. like **beklagenswert** ('deplorable'), **wünschenswert** ('desirable'), etc. But the *gen.* in **nichts wert** (see **nichts**) came to be treated as an *accus.*, and this was extended, first, to other indef. neut. expressions, as in **Ihr habt mich zu lieb, ich bin das nicht wert** (Mozart), and then to other common words: no one now says **Es ist nicht eines Pfennigs wert** (C. F. Meyer), just as no one would use a gen. in **Er war keinen Schuß Pulver wert** (Heyse: 'He wasn't worth powder and shot'). So also an accus. would be at least as common in ordinary lang. as the gen. in examples like **Was ich getan habe, ist keiner Rede wert** (Stifter: cf. the everyday expression **Das ist nicht die Rede wert**)—**Er hätte dieser Äußerung widersprochen, wenn er es der Mühe wert gefunden hätte, ihr zu widersprechen** (H. Hesse).

wes: see **was** (interrogative) 2; **welch** (interrogative) 2 (*b*); **wer** 1 (*a*).

Wesen: **1.** Although the verb **wesen** (q.v.) is now obs. in pres. tense forms, the infin. is in reg. use as a verbal noun, **ein lebendes Wesen** corresponding exactly to our 'a living being', and **das höchste Wesen** to 'the Supreme Being'. But its basic force is 'essence', that part of a thing which *is* (as distinct from what *seems*), and without which it would cease to be: e.g. **Wesen nennen wir das, was ist** (Schelling)—**Es gibt viele verständige Männer, welche die Fähigkeit haben, das Wesen von dem Scheine zu unterscheiden** (Ranke)—**Ihrem Wesen nach stimmen diese zwei Ansichten überein** ('These two opinions are essentially *or* fundamentally the same'). It was not till the NHG period that it came to be applied to the nature, character or personality of a human being: e.g. **Sie hat ein einnehmendes Wesen** ('an engaging personality')—**Er hat ein mürrisches Wesen** ('a surly nature, gruff manner'); so also **sein Wesen treiben** is properly 'to carry on in one's characteristic way', but esp. 'to be up to one's old tricks'. Out of this last phrase has developed the expression **Wesen machen** ('to make a fuss *or* ado'), as in **Was macht er für Wesen?** (G.) and **Sie machte kein Wesen von ihrer Schönheit** (Gutzkow); but much more common here is **Wesens machen**, used exactly like **Aufhebens** or **Federlesens machen** (see **aufheben** 2), the gen. form being dependent on an expressed or understood indef. neut. like **viel** or **wenig** (cf. **viel** 1 (*a*) and (*b*)): e.g. **Besonders macht man viel Wesens von seiner ältesten Tochter** (G.)—**Ich wunderte mich, daß sie soviel Wesens von unseren Kranken machte** (Frenssen)—**Man hat schließlich seine Nerven, wie wenig Wesens man auch daraus macht** (Spielhagen: 'After all, we are all subject to fits of nerves, no matter how little fuss we make of them')—**Kinderkrankheiten vergehen, und zwar um so schneller, je weniger Wesens man davon macht** (E. Wiechert)—**Die Großmutter hatte sich mit der Gattin Napoleons geduzt, jedoch wurde davon kein Wesens gemacht** (K. Edschmid). **2.** The verbal noun is also in common use in numerous compds.: e.g. **Anwesen** (= **Besitztum**, 'estate, property'), **Unwesen** (= **Unfug**, 'disturbance, disorderly conduct, mischief'), and esp. those with the prefixes **Armen-** ('poor relief'), **Gemein-** ('common weal'), **Kirchen-** ('church matters'), **Kriegs-** ('military affairs'), **Schul-** ('educational system'), etc.

wesen: There were two verbs meaning 'to be' in MHG, viz. *sîn* and *wesen*, but even then the latter was little used in pres. tense forms, its special function being to supply *sîn* with the past tense forms which this lacked, viz. *ich was* (> **ich war**), *wir wâren, gewesen*. The verb **wesen** is, in fact, now obs. so far as pres. tense forms are concerned, the only remnants still in reg. use being the pres. parts. **ab-** and **anwesend**, the noun **Wesen** (q.v.) and two compds. **verwesen** (both weak), the one *intrans.* meaning 'to decompose, putrefy' (really 'to cease to be'), the other *trans.* 'to manage' (esp. in **jemandes Amt verwesen**, 'to act as somebody's substitute', where **ver-** is really a corrupt form of **vor-**). But that **wesen** was still used in comparatively recent times is seen from examples like **Ottilie west** (= **ist, lebt**) **nun in Berlin** (G., in a letter to Zelter) and, in a reference to some youths who went about in a state of nature, **Man machte ihnen begreiflich, sie weseten** (= **wären, lebten**) **nicht in der uranfänglichen Natur** (G.).

weshalb: see **was** (interrogative) 2; **wer** 1 (*a*); **weswegen**.

wessen, wessent-: see **was** (**interrogative**) 2; **was** (**relative**) 3; **wer** 1 (*a*).

West(en), westlich: see **Nord.**

weswegen: see **wegen** 3; **was** (**interrogative**) 2; **wer** 1 (*a*). Besides its reg. use as an interrog., it can also be used as a *rel.*: e.g. **Ich bin diesen ganzen Sommer sehr beschäftigt gewesen, weswegen** (or **weshalb**, 'for which reason') **ich auch nicht in die Ferien habe reisen können.**

wett: This word, meaning 'equal, even', is now only used as an independent adj. in the pred. with **sein** in the sense of 'to be quits' (Scots 'to be evens'); with other verbs it has become a prefix, the commonest being **wetteifern** ('to vie, contend, compete'), **wettmachen** ('to balance, make good, compensate'), **wettlaufen** and **wettrennen** ('to race'). The only question that arises here is whether to treat the prefix as sep. or insep., and in this respect usage fluctuates to some extent. The only ones which are quite established are **wetteifern,** which is always *insep.*, and **wettmachen,** which is always *sep.*: e.g., on the one hand, **Die zwei Knaben scheinen jetzt an Fleiß miteinander zu wetteifern** (R. Herzog: The two boys now seem to vie with one another as to who will be the more diligent') and, on the other hand, **Er trug den Kopf krampfhaft nach links gedreht und schielte, wie um dieses Übel wettzumachen, mit beiden Augen stark nach rechts** (Stehr: 'He held his head twisted rigidly to the left, and as if to counteract this deformity he squinted sharply with both eyes to the right'); so also **Du hast mich nicht geliebt, ich dich auch nicht: das macht uns wett!** (Grillparzer). The two verbs **wettlaufen** and **-rennen** are represented by *Duden* as sep., but this seems more than doubtful: a proposition like **Ich lief mit ihm wett** is certainly not in accordance with established usage, and does not agree with examples like **Sie wettrannten in Eile** (Rückert) and **Wenn ich wettrennen soll, so wettrenne ich** (M. Eyth). In point of fact, these two verbs are generally avoided in those parts in which separation would take place, being replaced by **mit jemandem um** (in Austria also **in**) **die Wette laufen** (< MHG *ze wette loufen*). Incidentally, the nouns corresponding to these verbs are **der Wettlauf** and **das Wettrennen,** the latter having a wider application, e.g. to horse-racing, etc.

wetterleuchten: This artificially formed compd. verb, suggesting distant lightning with no audible thunder, is always treated as *insep.*: e.g. **Am fernen Horizonte wetterleuchtete es** (Alexis)—**In der Tiefe lag die finstere Masse eines Buchenwaldes: von dort aus wetterleuchtete es manchmal** (Storm)—**Der Mond war hinter schwarzen Wolken verschwunden, auch wetterleuchtete es in der Ferne** (W. Schäfer)—fig. **In seinem Antlitz blitzte und wetterleuchtete es wie an einem schwülen Gewitterhimmel** (Jul. Grosse); so also **Es fing zu wetterleuchten an—Es hat soeben gewetterleuchtet.** Another way to express this idea is seen in **Die Nacht war sehr schwarz, ab und zu leuchtete ein Wetter auf** (Keyserling), the noun **Wetter** sometimes having the force of '(thunder)storm' (= **Gewitter** or **Unwetter**), as in **Vorgestern hatten wir ein gewaltiges Wetter mit Donner, Blitz und Regengüssen** (G.); cf. **Donnerwetter!** as a coll. exclamation of astonishment, irritation or anger.

when: **1.** The accepted expression for 'when', used as an *interrog. adv.*, is now **wann,** whether in dir. or indir. questions: e.g. **„Wann erwarten Sie ihn?" „Ich weiß nicht, wann der Zug ankommt"—„Seit wann stehen Sie im Briefwechsel mit ihr?"—„Bis wann gedenken Sie in der Schweiz zu bleiben?"** At an earlier period **wenn** was used here (see **wann**), as in **„Liebes Fräulein, wenn wollen Sie mir antworten?"** (Gellert); but this is now only used by the uneducated or in dialects: a character in one of G. Hauptmann's plays asks **„Wenn geht der beste Zug?"** **2.** (a) Used as a *subord. conj.*, 'when' is rendered by **als** when the reference is to an actual occurrence or real state of affairs in the *past* (but see 3): e.g. **Leider war ich verreist, als er bei mir vorsprach—Als ich eben ausgegangen war, fing es zu regnen an.** A *pres.* tense after **als** is only permissible where the pres. is 'historic', which is merely a vivid way of expressing a completed action: e.g. **„Was bringt Ihr mir?" „Als ich das Vorgemach durchgehe, hör' ich** (= **durchging, hört' ich**) **von einem schrecklichen Gerüchte, das mir unglaublich deucht"** (Sch.)—**Sie eilt durch die Felder zu ihren Kindern; als sie dort angelangt ist, fragt sie nicht, was geschah** (H. Franck)—**„Also in drei Wochen", ruft er seinem Sohn nach, als der Wagen startet** (G. Bäumer)—**Er hat eines Tages, als er guter Laune ist, ein großes Grund-**

stück gekauft (C. Bulcke); cf. the stage-direction **Als die Vorhänge sich öffnen, sieht man ein prächtiges Lager** (G.), which *Sanders* represents as **„erklärbar gleichsam als** *praesens historicum*". But where the action or state is still proceeding (see (*b*)), **als** should not be used, and examples like the following should not be imitated: **Es ist spät in der Nacht, als ich dieses schreibe** (Raabe)—**Am Anfang, als seine** (an artist's) **Kunstsprache nur wenig Worte besitzt, gebraucht er keine fremden Ausdrücke** (Rilke). (**b**) Where the reference is to a still uncompleted action or state, either **da** or (rather more coll.) **wie** (q.v. 2 (*e*)) can be used: e.g. **Du kommst eben, da ich reisen muß** (G.)—**Wie ich das schreibe, erfahre ich, wie** ('how') **gut sie Bescheid wußte** (Raabe). Another alternative here is **wo** (see **da** 2 (*b*)), which, having *rel.* force, is esp. applicable in propositions like **Damals, wo wir noch jung waren, lebte man glücklicher als jetzt; heutzutage, wo alles so anders ist, ist man nicht so glücklich**; and so the example from Raabe given above at the end of (*a*) might have taken the form **In dem Augenblick, wo ich dieses schreibe, ist es spät in der Nacht.** For da used with *temp.* force, as in the example from G. above, see **als** = **'than'** 4. (**c**) Where the reference is to *fut.* time, the reg. expression is **wenn** (q.v.): e.g. **Wenn ich in Berlin ankomme, schreibe ich dir** (see 3); and sim. in the indef. sense of 'whenever', as in **Ich besuche ihn jedesmal, wenn ich nach Berlin gehe.** **3.** Special care is necessary in rendering propositions such as 'He promised to let me know *when he arrived* in Berlin' or 'I said I hoped that *when he had stayed* a month in the mountains, he would be restored to health.' Here the action is obviously *not* completed, so that **als** would be quite incorrect. In dir. speech the italicized words in these examples would be *when I arrive* (= shall have arrived) and *when you* (will) *have stayed*; and in indir. speech the same conj. must be used as in the actual spoken words: hence **Er versprach, mich wissen zu lassen, wenn er in Berlin ankäme**—**Ich sagte, ich hoffte, daß, wenn er sich einen Monat in den Bergen aufgehalten hätte, seine Gesundheit wiederhergestellt sein würde.** **4.** For normal word-order in a princ. clause following an introductory **als**-clause, see **so** 3.

wider-; **1.** A certain confusion has arisen between the prefixes **wider-** and **wieder-**, the latter of which developed out of the former. In point of fact, **wieder-** ought never to have become a verbal prefix at all, it should have remained an independent adv. of time meaning *'again'* (cf. 3); but it has come to be used as a sep. prefix when it has the force of *'back'* (**zurück**), as in words like **wie'derbekommen, -bringen, -geben, -gewinnen, -holen** (q.v.)—cf. **Ich habe das entliehene Buch endlich wie'derbekommen** ('I have at last got back the book I had lent') and **Ich habe wieder einen Schnupfen bekommen** ('I have caught a cold in the head again'). To this class belongs **wie'derkehren,** but it seems significant that, while the noun **Wiederkehr** is commonly used for **Rückkehr** or **Zurückkunft,** one does not say **Sie kehrte nach Hause wieder,** but **Sie kehrte nach Hause zurück,** a proposition in which the adv. of time is often inserted, but then *before* the prep. phrase: **Sie kehrte wieder nach Hause zurück** (like our 'She returned home *again*'); on the other hand, **wiederkehren** is generally used of things that occur over and over again, that are repeated: e.g. **Am Schluß jeder Strophe des Gedichts kehrt derselbe Vers wieder**—**Die immer wiederkehrenden Anfälle des Kranken lassen das Schlimmste befürchten** ('The recurring fits of the invalid give rise to fears for the worst'). **2.** On the other hand, **wider-** is a true *insep.* prefix (but see **widerhallen** and **widerspiegeln**) with the force of 'back' or 'against' in verbs like **widerfa'hren** (see **occur** 3 (*b*)), **-le'gen** (e.g. **Ich habe seine Behauptung widerlegt,** 'I have refuted his statement'), **-ra'ten** (e.g. **Ich habe es ihm widerraten,** 'I have dissuaded him from it'), **-ru'fen** (e.g. **Man hat den Befehl widerrufen,** 'The order has been countermanded'—**Das Gesetz ist widerrufen worden,** 'The law has been repealed'), reflex. **-se'tzen** (e.g. **Er hat sich meinem Vorschlag widersetzt,** 'He has opposed my proposal'), **-spre'chen** (q.v.), **-ste'hen** (e.g. **Ich habe der Versuchung widerstanden,** 'I have resisted the temptation'), **-stre'ben** (e.g. **Das widerstrebt mir** or **meinen Gefühlen,** 'That is repugnant to me'). **3.** Special cases in which **wieder** should not have become a prefix are doubly compounded verbs like **wiederau'frichten, -he'rstellen,** in which, however, the force of 'again' closely approaches that of 'back': in a proposition like **Das Gebäude ist wiederaufgerichtet** or **wiederhergestellt**, the fundamental idea is that of restoring the building *back* into its original completed state. But the idea of 'again' seems quite fixed in **wie'dererkennen** (**Ich habe Sie sofort wiedererkannt**, 'I recognized you at once'), in **wie'derkäuen** ('to chew the cud'), and esp. in **Auf Wie'dersehen!** ('I'll be seeing you!') and the modern **Auf Wie'derhören um 8 Uhr!** ('We shall be on the air again at 8 o'clock!').

widerhallen: This verb is exceptional in that the prefix, which is usually *insep.* (see **wider-** 2), may also be *sep.*: *Duden* gives **„wi'derhallen, wi'dergehallt; (seltener:) widerha'llen, widerha'llt"**. Usage is practically fixed in the rather rare case of the verb having *trans.* force, the prefix then being *sep.*, as in **Die Wände des öden Raumes hallten meine Schritte wider.** But much more common is the *intrans.* use of the verb, and it is here that there is considerable fluctuation. In point of fact, most authors seem to distinguish between the *sep.* use of the prefix when the subj. is the original sound or what produces it, as in 'Musical instruments resounded through the house' (**Musikinstrumente hallten im Hause wider**), and the *insep.* use when the subj. is what reflects the sound, as in 'The house resounded with musical instruments' (**Das Haus widerhallte von Musikinstrumenten**). Thus, in the former case, **Das Lied hallte im Felstal wider** (Uhland) —**Welche Klänge hallen von den Klüften wider?** (Chamisso)—**Wunderbar hallte die Flöte in den Klippen wider** (B. Kellermann)—**Die Schritte hallten an den Wänden wider** (Thoma)—**Ihre Schritte hallten im verlassenen Gang wider** (Bruno Franck) —**Die Schritte hallten hell vom Asphalt wider** (E. Brüning); and, in the latter case, **Die Höfe, die sie durchschritten, widerhallten** (Gutzkow)—**Der Palast widerhallte von seinem Rufen** (Zschokke)—**Platz und Straßen widerhallten von tobendem Geschrei und Waffengerassel** (Wassermann)—**Die Diele widerhallte von meinen Schritten** (Th. Mann)—**Das Haus widerhallte von Wehmutsliedern** (C. Hauptmann). Much less common are examples in which this distinction is not observed: cf., on the one hand, **Er zog die Glocke: der ungewohnte Klang widerhallte im ganzen Hause** (I. Frapan)—**Die verwegene Sprache, die er führte, widerhallte von jeder Wand** (Carossa); and, on the other hand, **Von diesen Tönen hallte der nächtliche Wald wider** (Bonsels)—**Der Saal hallte vom Gelächter hungriger Menschen wider** (E. Kästner)—**Das ganze Dorf hallte von Schüssen wider** (J. Thorwald).

widerlich: see **zuwider.**

widerspiegeln: This verb is exceptional in that, although it means 'to reflect', i.e. 'to throw *back*' (see **wider** 2), its prefix is now almost invariably treated as *sep.*, so that an example like **Die Poesie widerspie'gelt die Welt** (Auerbach) is rare; cf., as examples of the practically established modern usage, **Eine purpurne Lohe wälzte sich her übers Meer, der Himmel spiegelte die Feuersbrunst wi'der** (Kellermann)—**Auf ihrem Antlitz hatte sich Schrecken wi'dergespiegelt** (Gutzkow).

widersprechen: The person or thing 'contradicted' now always stands in the *dat.*: one no longer says **Das ist ein das** (now **dem**) **Evangelium widersprechender Gedanke** (Blencke) or **Ich kann dir das** (now **darin** or **in diesem Punkt**) **nicht widersprechen** (Lessing); so also in the *pass.* (see **impersonal verbs** 3): **Diesem** (not **Dieses**) **Gerücht wurde amtlich widersprochen** ('This rumour was officially contradicted'). But the pers. pass. construction is allowed, as with **folgen** and **schmeicheln** (qq.v.), in propositions like **Ich hörte mich widersprochen** ('I heard myself being contradicted'), with which cf. **Ich hörte mir widersprechen** ('I heard [somebody] contradict me'). This applies esp. to contracted clauses, as in **Von den katholischen Reichsteilen widersprochen, erhielt die Versicherung keine Gesetzeskraft** (Sch.), and is particularly common in the neg. **unwidersprochen:** e.g. **Bis hierher hatte er den Geistlichen unwidersprochen gehen lassen** (Stehr: 'So far he had let the parson talk on without contradicting him')—**Sie wollte alles über sich ergehen lassen und die Verachtung der Familie unwidersprochen hinnehmen** (H. Franck: 'She would put up with everything and suffer the family's contempt without protest').

widerstehen: 1. This *insep.* verb, which only takes a *dat.*, means either 'to oppose, resist, withstand' (not so much with an obj. like an enemy, where **Widerstand leisten** or **sich widerse'tzen** is more usual, but esp. with objs. like requests, temptations, etc.) or, with an impers. subj., 'to be distasteful *or* repugnant'

(= **zuwider sein**): e.g., on the one hand, **Ich finde es schwer, dieser Versuchung zu widerstehen,** and, on the other hand, **Solches Betragen widersteht mir**; cf. **Jede Art fratzenhafter Verzerrung war mir von jeher zuwider; was mir widersteht, davon wend' ich den Blick weg** (G.). In a compd. tense the standard aux. is **haben** (as with **stehen**); it is mainly in the south that **sein** is used. For the *passive*, see **impersonal verbs** 3. **2.** Analogous is **widerstre'ben,** also insep. and requiring a dat., used esp. of what is repugnant to a person or goes against the grain, as in **Es widerstrebt mir, Ihnen diese Mitteilung machen zu müssen** ('I am loath to have to communicate this to you'); cf. **Er ging langsam mit widerstrebendem Fuß den Pfad hinauf** (Hofmannsthal). So also the infin. used as a verbal noun: **Ich tat es mit dem größten Widerstreben** ('with the greatest reluctance').

widerstreben: see widerstehen 2.

widerwillig: see **willig.**

widrig, widrigenfalls: see **zuwider.**

wie: 1. Expressed in English by '*how*': e.g. in questions: **Wie geht es Ihnen?—Wie oft muß ich dir das sagen?—Er fragte mich, wie alt ich wäre—Ich weiß nicht, wie es kommt** ('how it is'), **aber ich werde jetzt leicht schwindlig**; in exclamations: **Ach, wie schön!—Junge, wie siehst du aus!** (i.e. 'what a sight you are!'). Here belong also propositions like 'I know how to persuade him', in connexion with which it is important to remember that **wie** *cannot* stand before an infin. with **zu** (see **wissen** 3 (*d*)): hence, either **Ich weiß, ihn zu überreden** or **Ich weiß, wie ich ihn überreden kann. 2.** Expressed in English by '*as*': **(a)** For the difference between **als** and **wie** in a proposition like 'I advise you as a friend', see **als** = **'as'** 1 (*a*). In a contracted expression like **ein Mann wie ich,** we often use 'such a man as I' or 'a man such as I', more ordinarily 'a man like me'; for such expressions, esp. when used in an oblique case (should '*to* a man like me' be **einem Manne wie ich** or **wie mir**?), see **like** 2 (*c*). Here belong sentences like 'This is a novel such as one seldom comes across', and in such contexts the noun in the princ. clause to which the **wie**-clause refers is idiomatically repeated in the latter in the form of a pers. pron., not only in the nom., as in **Die Wirklichkeit in der deutschen Literatur, wie sie sich im Roman darstellt, ist eine ganz andere als die der anderen Nationen** (Paul Fechter), but also in oblique cases: e.g. **Dies ist ein Roman, wie man ihm selten begegnet—Die „Aeolsharfe"** (Mörike's poem) **ist ein poetischer Triumph, wie ihn noch wenige errungen haben** (H. Kurz, in a letter to the poet)—**Er fing an, Dinge zu sagen, wie er sie noch niemals hatte laut werden lassen** (Th. Mann). The same applies to propositions in which a neg. **wie**-clause containing a compar. adj. or adv. is used to suggest a superl. idea: e.g. **Heute hat sie gesungen, wie ich sie nie besser habe singen hören** ('Today she sang as well as I have ever heard her sing')—**Vom Gipfel hat man eine Aussicht, wie man sie nirgends schöner haben kann** ('From the summit you get as fine a view as you will get anywhere'). **(b)** In expressions like 'He is as strong as a horse', the first 'as' is **so,** the second **wie** (cf. **als** = **'as'** 2 and 3): **Er ist so stark wie ein Pferd**; and sim. **Das ist nicht so einfach, wie es scheint—Es gibt keinen anderen Menschen, der so allein ist wie ich** (Raabe)—**Ich lief so schnell wie möglich.** When **so** modifies words like **bald, oft, lange, viel, weit,** etc., the two words are now written as one, and **wie** is commonly dropped, so that **sobald** (q.v.), **sooft,** etc., become subord. conjs.: see **so** 1 (*b*) and cf. **Sooft man das Erwachen des Frühlings auch erlebt hat, in jedem Jahre ist es ein neues Wunder** (Speckmann: see 3)—**Die jetzige Lage, soweit ich sie beurteilen kann, ist etwas heikel** ('As far as I can judge, the present situation is rather delicate'); sim. **sowohl . . . als** or **wie** (see **sowohl** and **congruence** 1 (*e*)). **(c)** It is much used in contracted, often parenthetical, phrases: e.g. **Er ist, wie gesagt** ('as I said before'), **zur Zeit verreist—Er kam, wie erwartet, spät zurück—Also abgemacht: du nimmst die Einladungen nach wie vor an** (Fontane: 'So that's settled: you will go on accepting the invitations as you have been doing'); and sim. in short complete clauses: **Der Inhalt des Berichts ist kurz, wie folgt—Ich bin, wie Sie sehen, sehr beschäftigt—Der Plan ist, wie vorauszusehen war, gescheitert. (d)** For **wie** in the sense of 'as if', see **als** = **'as if'** 1 and 3, and cf. **Sie stürzte wie besessen** ('like one possessed') **zur Tür hinaus—Mit einem Male war sie wie umgewandelt** (Fontane: 'like a different person')—**Von den Arien im „Fliegenden Holländer" war sie wie**

benommen (id.: 'as though entranced')—**Wie vom Schlage gerührt** ('As if seized with a stroke'), **schüttelte er unaufhörlich seinen Kopf hin und her** (Th. Mann). **(e)** With *temp.* force (see **when** 2): e.g. **Wie ich eben auf die Straße trat, stießen zwei Autos aufeinander.** Here, where the two actions proceed simultaneously, **wie** is strictly more correct than **als**, but in practice little or no distinction is made: **wie** is only a rather more everyday expression. Where the actions are not simultaneous, **wie** expresses a closer relation in time: cf. **Wie er das erfuhr, ging er gleich fort** and **Einige Minuten später, als er das erfahren hatte, ging er fort.** But only **als** (not **wie**) is used in contexts like **Kaum hatte er begonnen, einen Blick in die Zeitung zu tun, als an die Tür gepocht wurde** (Th. Mann: = **da wurde an die Tür gepocht**). **(f)** For a proposition like 'The place is not the same *as when* I was here last', see **als** = **'as'** 4. **3.** With *concessive* force, where an unaccented **auch** is usually added: e.g. **Wie dem auch sei** (or **Sei dem, wie ihm wolle**), **ich werde gegen den Antrag stimmen** ('Be that as it may, I shall vote against the motion')—**So dumm er auch ist, das kann er verstehen**—**Wie sich dies auch verhalten mag, gewiß ist es, daß dieser Wind bei vielen Menschen Änderungen des Gemütszustandes heraufführt** (Bergengruen: 'However that may be, the fact is that this wind effects changes in many people's mental and emotional state'). **4.** In a few cases **wie** has *rel.* force, notably after **Art** or the now very common combination **Art und Weise**: e.g. **Er nahm eine Prise, und in der Art, wie er schnupfte, lag ein unaussprechliches Behagen** (Auerbach: 'He took a pinch of snuff, and the way [in which] he sniffed it up his nostrils betokened an enjoyment beyond the power of words to express')—**Mir mißfällt die Art und Weise, wie er sich benimmt** ('I dislike the way he behaves'); see also the example from Ompteda quoted under **handhaben.** **5.** For **wie** used in the sense of 'than', see **als** = **'than'** 1, 4, and 5, and cf. **Es ist mir mehr vertraut wie meiner Mutter Wiegenlieder** (G. Hauptmann)—**Einem schöneren Jüngling wie diesem Gottfried bin ich nicht begegnet** (Suttner); cf. **apposition** 1 (*d*) and **like** 2 (*c*) (ii).

wieder: see **wider-** 1 and 3.

wiederholen: With a *sep.* prefix this verb has the force of 'to fetch *back*' (cf. **wider-** 1), an idea more commonly expressed by **zurückholen**; with the force of 'again' **wieder** should really not be a prefix but an independent adv.: cf. **Bitte hole wieder etwas Wasser vom Brunnen** ('Please go to the well again and fetch some more water'). With an *insep.* prefix it means 'to say again': e.g. **Er wiederho'lte seine Frage, hat seine Frage wiederho'lt** (but see **repeat**).

wiederkehren: see **wider-** 1.

wiegen: The three verbs **wiegen, wägen** and **wogen** show some confusion, and the confusion goes far back. In MHG the usual expression for 'to rock' (a child to sleep) was *wăgen* (weak); the form *wĭgen* was so rare that the corresponding NHG **wiegen** is probably formed from the sing. indic. of *wĕgen* (viz. *ich wĭge, er wĭget*: past tense *ich wăc, wir wâgen*: past part. *gewĕgen*), meaning either 'to weigh' or 'to move', which latter sense is seen in **bewegen** (see **move** 1, and cf. 'to wag'); the MHG strong past part. is only preserved in **verwegen** (see 4 *c*); the form **wägen** is probably the result of a mistaken idea that *wĕgen* was derived from *wâge*. Modern usage is practically fixed, viz.—**1.** **(a)** With *strong* forms, **wiegen (wōg, gewōgen)** means either 'to weigh' (something in scales) or 'to be of a certain weight': e.g. **„Hast du das Paket gewogen?"** **„Ja, es wog drei Pfund."**; **(b)** with *weak* forms, it means 'to rock, cause to swing *or* sway': e.g. **Die Mutter wiegte ihr Kind in den Armen**—**Das Korn wiegte säuselnd die Ähren** (Immermann: but cf. the first example under 3)—**Er wiegte die Arme hin und her, gleichsam um ihre Kraft zu prüfen** (id.: i.e. he swung them about)—**Er wiegte sich zögernd von einem Fuß auf den anderen** (Th. Mann)—**Sie wiegte sich in den Hüften** ('She swung her hips')—**Sie hat einen wiegenden Gang** ('a swaying gait'); cf. **Hast du die Petersilie gewiegt?** ('Have you chopped the parsley?': from an old-fashioned double-bladed chopper which was rocked to and fro). **2.** The corrupt form **wägen,** which is either *strong* **(wōg, gewōgen)** or now quite commonly *weak,* although the strong forms are really fixed in the case of **erwägen,** means 'to weigh' in one's mind: e.g. **Erst wäge, dann wage!** (lit. First weigh the pros and cons, then venture, i.e. 'Look before you leap!')—**Er wägte alles bedächtig** (G.)—**Ich erwog, was das**

Beste sei ('I debated with myself what was the best thing to do'); cf. the common phrase **alles erwogen** ('all things considered') and **etwas in Erwägung ziehen** ('to take . . . into consideration'). **3.** On the other hand, **wōgen** (*weak*) is always *intrans.* and means 'to wave, sway' (e.g. in the wind): e.g. **Das Korn wogte im Winde—Die Menschenmenge (Der Kampf) wogte hin und her—Die Straßen wogten von Menschen—Er sank nieder, seine Brust wogte** (Immermann: 'his breast heaved'); fig. **Wie soll ich es anfangen, Ihnen alles, was mir im Herzen wogt, auszusprechen ?** (id.: '. . . to express what agitates my heart'). **4.** Specially noteworthy are the adj. uses of the *past part.* forms: (**a**) **gewogen** ('well-disposed, favourably inclined'): e.g. **Ich bin dem Mädchen sehr gewogen** (G.: 'I entertain affectionate feelings towards the girl')—**Diesem jungen Maler war mein Vater besonders gewogen** (Roquette); cf. the coll. expression at parting **Bleib mir gewogen!** (lit. 'Remain kindly disposed towards me!' but usually iron. 'Clear out! I prefer your room to your company!'); (**b**) **gewiegt** ('shrewd, clever, cute'): e.g. **ein gewiegter Kaufmann** ('a shrewd businessman')—**Im Grunde ist doch der gewiegteste Maschinenbauer nur ein Lehrling dessen, der den Hammer erfand** (Waggerl)—**ein gewiegter Kunde** ('an artful dodger'); (**c**) **verwegen** or (in dialects) **verwogen** ('daring, reckless'): e.g. **ein verwegenes Unternehmen** ('a foolhardy undertaking')—**ein verwegenes Spiel treiben** ('to play a risky game')—**Ein verzweifeltes Übel will eine verwegene Arznei** (Sch.: 'A desperate evil calls for a bold remedy')—**in des Wortes verwegenster Bedeutung** (id.: 'in the most daring sense of the word')—**Der verwogene** (usually **verwegene**) **Gesell hatte mit dem Mädchen schöngetan** (Heyse: 'The impudent fellow had carried on *or* played about with the girl')—**Der Jägerhut verlieh ihm ein sehr verwogenes Aussehen** (J. Schlaf).

wieviel: This is used in everyday expressions like **Wieviel haben Sie für diese Bücher bezahlt?—Vor ein paar Jahren kosteten die Lebensmittel soundso viel; wieviel mehr heute!—Ich weiß nicht, wieviel Uhr es ist** ('I don't know what time it is'); in the plur., **Wie viele** or (now usually) **Wieviel Mitglieder wohnten der Versammlung bei?** ('How many members attended the meeting?') and esp. **Wievielmal** ('How many times') **sind Sie in Deutschland gewesen?** where **Wie viele Male** sounds rather clumsy.—To express 'What day of the month is this?' a form like that of most of the ord. nums. is used: just as one says **Heute haben wir den vierten** (*scil.* **Tag des Monats**), so also **Den wievielten haben wir heute ?** but here the alternative form **wievielsten** is also allowed: cf. **Er ist Leutnant im, ich weiß nicht wievielsten Regiment** (Ompteda: lit. 'He is a lieutenant in I don't know the how many-eth regiment', i.e. 'I don't know the number of his regiment').

wiewohl: see **obgleich** 1 and 2.

Wille: 1. The nom. form **der Willen,** which was once quite common (see **Balken**) and is still allowed in Austria, is now hardly used in the north, but the **-n** is fixed in the oblique cases: e.g. **Sei deines Willens Herr und deines Gewissens Knecht!** (Ebner-Eschenbach)—**Er bestand auf seinem Willen, hat seinen Willen durchgesetzt—Es sprach sich herum** ('The rumour went round'), **daß der Alte seinen Willen machte** (Zuckmayer: '. . . was making his will'); so also after a prep.: **Er tat es wider Willen** (or **widerwillig,** 'reluctantly')—**Sie war ihm in allem zu Willen** ('She complied with his every wish'); cf. **„Ich weiß nicht", sagte er mit Widerwillen** ('with a bad grace'), **und doch wider Willen gefesselt** ('unwillingly fascinated'), **„warum Sie es für nötig halten, mir diese Ideen vorzutragen** (Bruno Frank). **2.** (**a**) The gen. is used pred. with **sein** (esp. in a neg. proposition) and **zu** + infin. in the sense of 'to be (un)willing', being now written with a small letter: e.g. **Sie waren nicht willens, sich von einem offenbar Verrückten das Eisen durch den Leib rennen zu lassen** (id.: 'They were unwilling *or* not disposed to let themselves be stabbed by one who had obviously gone mad')—**Er war nicht in der Lage oder nicht willens, einen nahezu erwachsenen Sohn unbeschäftigt herumsitzen zu lassen** (H. Hesse). (**b**) Analogous is the expression **gewillt** (the past part. of an otherwise obs. verb **willen**), used like **willens** in the sense of 'willing, disposed, minded': e.g. **Bist du gewillt, dies Blatt zu unterschreiben ?** (Sch.)—**Der Kurfürst scheint nicht gewillt zu sein, dem Schwedenkönig zu helfen** (E. Wichert)—**Ludwig XIV. war nicht im Schwanken**

über die Gewalt, die er Europa zu geben gewillt war (Hofmannsthal); in this connexion see **adjectives (indeclinable)** 2; **willig. 3.** Here belongs also the expression **um . . . willen,** a sort of prep., which requires a *gen.* to be inserted between the two words, as in **um des Friedens willen** ('for the sake of peace'). Where the gen. is a poss. or rel. pron., **willen** is now suffixed to the gen., which takes an inorganic **t**, as in **um meinetwillen** (< **um meinen Willen** < MHG *durch mînen willen*); so also **Dies ist der Mann, um dessentwillen** (or **die Frau, um derentwillen** (**ich Sie um Unterstützung bat** (cf. **deren** 3).

willfahren: This is the NHG form of MHG *iemens willen vâren,* 'to strive to do somebody's will', hence 'to comply with a person's wishes': now esp. in a phrase like **einer Bitte** (dat.) **willfahren,** ('to grant a request' (= **eine Bitte gewähren**). Being formed from a noun, it is an *insep. weak* verb (see **beanspruchen,** 1 and cf. **ratschlagen**): e.g. **Er bat sie, in ihrem Vortrage fortzufahren, worin sie ihm sofort willfahrten** (G.)—**Er willfahrte dem Gesuche** (Heine). The infin. form **willzufahren** (Schlegel) is incorrect for **zu willfahren,** but in the past part. two forms are officially recognized, according to the accent, viz. **Der Bitte wurde willfa'hrt** or **gewi'llfahrt:** cf. **Nach vielem Einreden und Widerstreben wurde ihr willfa'hrt** (Auerbach).

willig: This adj. is used esp. in the attrib. and abs. relations: e.g. **Er tat' es mit willigem Mut—Bist du nicht willig, so brauch' ich Gewalt** (G.). It is not nearly so much used with a dependent infin. clause, as in **Ich bin willig, jede geistliche Belehrung anzunehmen** (Bergengruen), where **willens** or **gewillt** is much more usual (see **Wille** 2). The same applies to its compds: one can say **Er ist immer bereitwillig** ('willing') and **Er tat es bereitwillig** ('willingly'), but usually **Er ist immer bereit** (see **ready**) or **willens, mir zu helfen;** propositions like **Die Leute in dem Schiff schienen bereitwillig, ihn nach der verlangten Gegend zu fahren** (Novalis) and **Das Mädchen war bereitwillig, der neuen Wendung des Gesprächs zu folgen** (Spindler) are not nearly as common as they once were. So also **Ich tat es widerwillig** or **mit Widerwillen** ('reluctantly'), but 'I was reluctant to **tell it to him'** is **Es widerstrebte mir** (not **Ich war widerwillig**), **es ihm zu sagen—Ich war nicht willens** ('unwilling'), **ihm beizustehen;** what is quite wrong is to render 'I was *or* felt unwilling' by **Ich war unwillig** or **Ich empfand einen Unwillen,** as these expressions mean 'I was *or* felt indignant'; cf. **Er machte seinem Unwillen in Worten Luft** ('He gave vent to his indignation').

Winkel: see **Ecke.**

winken, wippen: see **mit** 2 (*b*).

wirklich: see **really** 1.

Wirkung: see **Grund** 2.

wish: see **wünschen; wollen** 1.

wissen: 1. This is one of the *past-present verbs* (q.v.): **ich weiß** orig. had past force. One set phrase may be a remnant of this: 'so far as I know' is **soviel ich weiß,** but the corresponding neg. uses the *past subj.*: e.g. **„Du bist ein schmucker Gesell, in den sich gewiß schon manch ein Mädchen vergafft hat, wie?" „Nicht daß ich wüßte"** (Jul. Wolff). **2.** Whereas **kennen** is 'to know *or* be familiar with' (Fr. *connaître*), **wissen** is 'to know *or* not be ignorant of' (Fr. *savoir*): cf. **Ich kenne diesen Weg** and **Ich weiß den rechten Weg;** sim. **Weißt du seine Adresse? 3.** (**a**) Apart from its use with **von** (cf. (*b*) below) or **um** to suggest 'to know *about* something', **wissen** normally requires an accus. obj., often an indef. neut.: e.g. **Wissen Sie das Neuste?** ('Have you heard the latest?')—**Man muß schon etwas wissen, um verbergen zu können, daß man nichts weiß** (Ebner-Eschenbach)—**Woher weißt du das?** ('How do you know that?'); for **wissen lassen,** see **lassen** 4. Interesting here are the idioms **sich** (dat.) **nicht Rats wissen** ('to be at a loss': see **Rat** 2) and esp. **es jemandem Dank wissen** ('to be grateful to somebody for something': cf. Fr. *je lui en sais gré*). In examples like **Er sorgte für sie, und sie wußte es ihm Dank** (Fontane) and **Wenn Ihr mir heute nachgebt, werdet Ihr es mir morgen Dank wissen** (Jul. Wolff), **es** was orig. a *gen.* (see **es** 1) but came later to be regarded as an *accus.*, which explains examples like **Wer wird ihm diese kleine Üppigkeit nicht Dank wissen?** (Lessing) and **Ich weiß dir deine Freigebigkeit großen Dank** (A. König), where, however, as a result of inability to understand the idiom, modern usage favours the use of **für,** as in **Wozu den Herren unnütze Arbeit machen? Sie würden ihm wenig Dank dafür wissen** (Sudermann). (**b**) Otherwise the obj. of **wissen** most frequently takes the form of a subord. clause introduced by **daß, ob, wie,** etc. In MHG *wizzen* could take a simple infin., as in *er wiste schaden gewinnen* ('He knew he would suffer'), where one would now say **Er wußte, daß er Schaden erleiden würde.** And even the *accus. and infin.* construction has not so far really established itself, although modern examples like the following seem to show that this construction is gaining ground: **Ich hatte eine Empfindung, daß ich ihren Blick auf mir ruhen wußte** (H. Hesse)—**Sie trat in das Rondell, wo sie den Dichter sitzen wußte** (id.)—**Ich bin daran gewöhnt** (see **accustom** 2), **daß du dir wenig daraus machst, mich irgendwo auf dich warten zu wissen** (id.)—Scholz **wußte ein unnaturalistisches Blut in sich rauschen** (H. M. Elster)—**Es fehlt mir die Befriedigung, jemanden mit teilnehmen zu wissen** (R. Herzog)—**Ich empfand Mitleid mit Anna, die ich jetzt schlafen wußte** (G. Keller)—**Ich ging in den Keller, den Kübel zu holen, den ich da stehen wußte** (G. Britting)—**Es drängt mich, ein Menschenherz aufzusuchen, das ich unfern schlagen weiß** (O. Knoop). Despite such examples, modern usage still strongly favours a subord. clause, and here special care is required where **wissen** occurs in a *rel.* clause, as in the last three examples just given. Here it is necessary to use the circumlocution with **von** (q.v. 5) explained under **glauben** 4 (*b*): to express 'He is a man whom I know to be married', a German says 'He is a man of whom I know that he is married': **Er ist ein Mann, von dem ich weiß, daß er verheiratet ist** (cf. **hoffen** and **wünschen**), unless 'I know' is inserted parenthetically: **Er ist ein Mann, der, wie ich weiß, verheiratet ist.** But the use of **von** is to be preferred, as in **Es kam ihr ein Einfall, von dem sie nicht wußte, ob sie ihn mitteilen sollte** (Zschokke)—**Ich tat etwas, von dem ich wußte, daß es die Mutter nimmer zugeben würde** (G. Keller)—**Sie sahen in ihm eine Merkwürdigkeit, von der sie nicht recht wußten, was sie davon halten sollten** (Böhlau: '. . . a queer fish they didn't quite know what to make of')—**Es klingt wie ein Duett in der Dämmerung, von dem man wünscht, daß es immer dauern möge, und von dem man doch weiß, daß es, ach, so kurz ist** (H. W. Geissler); cf. also the example from H. Hesse given under **von** 5 (*b*). **(c)** More in accordance with modern usage than the accus. and infin. here is the *accus. and past part.* (cf. **glauben** 4), probably the accus. and infin. with the infin. unexpressed: just as one can say **Ich weiß ihn glücklich** (with **sein** understood?), so also one says **Ich weiß ihn geborgen** ('I know him to be safe'); and sim. **Was für eine Erlösung, die Alte gerettet zu wissen!** (Bruno Frank: 'What a relief to know that the old lady has been saved!')—**Er sank erschöpft zusammen, wie einer, der sein Tagewerk getan weiß** (Sudermann); and here we often use 'to see' instead of 'to know': e.g. **Er wollte um alles in der Welt die Wahrheit nicht verraten wissen** (Zschokke: 'Not for anything in the world did he want to see the truth divulged')—**Der Oheim wollte jedes Talent seiner Neffen ausgebildet wissen** (W. Müller)—**Der Vater verwies uns das Lachen, denn er wollte diese Dinge mit Andacht betrachtet wissen** (Th. Mann). A *pres.* part. here, on the other hand, is little used: cf. **Er ging um das Haus herum, in dem er sie tanzend wußte** (O. Ludwig). **(d)** A phrase like **Lügen, die man Lügen zu sein weiß** (Lessing) is quite contrary to modern usage, which requires **Lügen, von denen man weiß, daß sie Lügen sind**; and so also it is incorrect to say **Ich weiß nicht, was zu sagen** (for **was ich sagen soll**): see **was (interrogative)** 5. The infin. with **zu** is correct, however, when rendering 'He knows *how* to behave', but only with the word **wie** *omitted*, as **etwas zu tun wissen** means 'to know how to do something'; so the choice is between **Er weiß sich zu betragen** and **Er weiß, wie er sich betragen muß**; and sim. **Ich weiß mich zu wehren** ('I know how to defend myself')—**Er weiß mit Tieren umzugehen** ('He knows how to handle animals'). **4.** The verbal noun **Wissen** ('knowledge, learning') is mainly used in a few set expressions: e.g. **meines Wissens** ('so far as I know')—**ohne mein Wissen** ('unknown to me')—**wider mein besseres Wissen** ('against my better judgement')—**nach bestem Wissen (und Gewissen) urteilen** ('to judge to the best of one's knowledge'). For the expression **viel Wissens**, see **viel** 1 (*b*). At one time **Wissenschaft** was used in the sense of 'knowledge', as in **Ihr hattet Wissenschaft von allem** (Sch.: 'You knew all about it'), and this sometimes occurs in more recent times, as in **Woher kam ihr die**

Wissenschaft, daß seine Seele der Rettung bedürftig sei? (Fontane); but it is now for the most part avoided in this general sense, and confined to the more specific one of 'science': cf. **Wissenschaft und Kunst** ('science and art'), **Handels-, Kriegs-, Natur-, Rechts-, Religionswissenschaft**, etc.

Wissen, Wissenschaft: see **wissen** 4.

without: see **ohne**; for 'to be, do without', see **miss** 2 *(a)* and *(c)*.

wo: 1. The orig. force of **wo** (< MHG *wâ*), and still its commonest meaning, is 'where' (interrog. or rel.), corresponding to **wohin** ('whither') and **woher** ('whence'): e.g. **„Wo ist das Buch?" „Ich habe es da hingetan, wo niemand es finden wird."** Here presumably belongs the coll. exclamation **I wo!** ('No fear! Catch me!'), as in **„Du gehst doch mit?" „I wo!"** where **I** is the LG form of **Ei** (< Lat. *eia*) and **wo** an elliptical interrog. proposition like **Wo denkst du hin?** (lit. 'Whither are your thoughts going?' i.e. 'How can you think that?'). For **wo** prefixed to preps., see **wo(r)-. 2.** In NHG **wo** often has the temp. force of 'when', but only in a *rel.* clause (see **da** 2 *(b)*): e.g. **Das geschah zu der Zeit, wo ich noch auf der Schule war —Von dem Augenblick an, wo der Schutzmann erschien, hörte die Schlägerei auf— Eine Zeit wird kommen, wo** ('when') **man nicht mehr richten wird hinter düstern Mauern, wo** ('where') **niemand zugegen ist als der Richter selbst** (A. Meissner). **3.** At one time **wo** was also used with cond. force (= **wenn**), as in **Wo** ('If') **du den Gottlosen warnest und er sich nicht bekehret . . ., wird er um seiner Sünde willen sterben** (Ezek. 3. 19) and **Es stand ihr fest, daß die beiden verunglückt seien, wo sie nicht gar Hand an sich selbst gelegt hätten** (Heyse: '. . . if they had not actually taken their lives'); but this is now for the most part confined to the neg. 'if not' in propositions like **Ich kann, wo nicht fließend Deutsch sprechen, doch wenigstens mich verständlich machen** ('I am able, if not to speak German fluently, at least to make myself understood')—**Was die Alten darüber gesagt, hatte ich, wo nicht studiert, doch sprungweise gelesen** (G.)—**Ich hielt ihn für einen aufdringlichen Schwätzer, wo nicht gar für einen Schelm** (Mörike). Here belongs the adv. **womöglich,** which has developed out of **wo möglich** ('if possible', now usually **wenn möglich**) and taken on the modern sense of 'possibly' (= **möglicherweise**) or 'perhaps' (**vielleicht**): e.g. **Bei diesem Nebelwetter wird der Zug womöglich Verspätung haben. 4.** In the coll. lang. **wo,** often prefixed with **irgend-,** is used in the sense of 'somewhere': e.g. **Ich glaubte, das Buch läge irgendwo im Studierzimmer, aber es muß wo anders** ('somewhere else') **liegen.** Definitely not to be imitated is the use in dialects of **wo** as a rel. pron. (= **der, welcher**): e.g. **Der Meister nimmt das schlechteste Messer, wo** (for **das** or **welches**) **er hat** (Hebel)—**Wenn ich zur Messe geh', sehn mich allerlei Männer an, auch solche, wo** (for **die**) **eine Frau zu Hause haben** (H. Leip: spoken by a Bavarian peasant girl); cf. **was (relative)** 2 *(a)*.

wöchentlich: for the difference between this and **-wöchig,** see **-ig.**

wogen: see **wiegen** 3.

wohl: 1. This adv. corresponds to the adj. **gut,** as our 'well' does to 'good', but like 'well' it has come to be used as a pred. adj. in references to bodily or mental health, as in **Ich bin** (or **befinde mich**) **wo'hl,** and in this sense it has the reg. degrees of comparison: **Ich fühle mich heute etwas wo'hler** (or **besser**)—**In lustiger Gesellschaft fühlt er sich am wo'hlsten. 2.** As an *accented* adv., it has several shades of meaning, but it is *not* used as an introductory exclamation as in our 'Well, how are you?' or 'Well, I never!' (for which see **nun** 3). Instead of **Seid Ihr wohl?** one can say **Ist Euch** (dat.) **auch wo'hl, Vater? Ihr seht so blaß** (Sch.: now **Ihr seht so blaß aus**), where **auch** (q.v. 3) has explanatory force, the question being prompted by the father's pale face; so also **Mir ist wo'hl zumute** ('I'm in good humour'). Other common expressions belonging here are: **Leb' wo'hl!** ('Farewell!')—**Wo'hl bekomm's!** (lit. 'May it agree with you!' esp. 'Here's your good health!')—**Schlafen Sie wo'hl!—Ich wünsche Ihnen, wo'hl geruht zu haben!** ('I hope you have had a good night's rest!'), where **Ihnen** is often, but really ungrammatically, omitted; cf. **Morgen muß ich, wo'hl oder ü'bel, nach Berlin** ('Whatever happens, Whether it suits me or not, I have got to go to Berlin tomorrow'). It is also effectively used before **aber** to introduce and stress a pos. clause which contrasts with a previous neg. one: e.g. **Heute hörte er kein Nachtigallenlied, wo'hl aber** ('what he did hear was') **das Heulen des Windes,**

das Rollen des Donners (Hackländer)—**Daß ich lebe, ist nicht notwendig, wo'hl aber daß ich tätig bin** (Friedrich der Große). **3.** *Unaccented*: (**a**) It frequently has *concessive* force, thus approaching **zwar** (q.v. 1) but expressing a rather less decided opinion than that word: e.g. **Da's mag wohl sei'n** or **Da's ist wohl mö'glich** ('That may be so, I admit')—**Da der Bildschnitzer keinen Geschäftssinn hatte, gab er seine Schnitzwerke fort, wohl nicht umso'nst** ('not for nothing certainly'), **aber für einen so kleinen Preis, daß er aus seiner Armut nicht herauskam** (Stehr); sim. with other adv. particles: **Er ist wohl a'rm, aber so' arm ist er doch ni'cht?** ('He is no doubt poor, but surely he is not as poor as all that?'), while **do'ch nicht** here would suggest '. . . but he is not as poor as that, whatever you may say to the contrary'. This concessive force leads to its use to express a *conjecture*, with a tacit admission that the statement may possibly not be in accordance with the facts: e.g. **Er wird wohl mo'rgen zurückkommen** ('I fancy he'll be back tomorrow')—**Es ist wohl zu spä't, noch auszugehen?** ('I suppose it's too late to go out now, isn't it?') (**b**) Its other idiomatic use is in a real or a rhetorical question, where we use 'I wonder' or 'I ask myself': e.g. **Waru'm er wohl nicht geko'mmen ist? Ob er wohl kra'nk ist?** (see **wonder** 1). **4.** It was a natural development that **wo'hl** in the sense of 'well' became a prefix to certain nouns, esp. verbal nouns, and to a number of adjs.: e.g. **Wohlbefinden** ('good health'), **Wohlfahrt** ('welfare'), **Wohlwollen** ('good will'), **Wohlsein** (esp. in **Auf Ihr Wohlsein!** 'Here's to you!'); **wohlfeil** ('cheap'), **wohlhabend** ('well off'), **wohltätig** ('beneficent, charitable'), etc.; and so also prefixed to many parts., esp. past parts., although not to the same extent as in English, where 'well-' is used in a number of expressions which a German would render with **gut** as an adv.: e.g. **Sie ist immer gut gekleidet** ('well-dressed', not **wohlgekleidet**)—**Sie wären gut beraten** ('well-advised'), **das Anerbieten abzuschlagen**—**Das Geld ist gut angewandt** ('well-spent'). But in many cases **wohl-** is quite common, esp. in **wohlbekannt** ('well-known'), **wohlerzogen** ('well-bred'), **wohlgesinnt** or **gut gesinnt** ('well-disposed'), **wohlverdient** ('well-earned'), **wohlüberlegt** ('well-considered'), **wohlgemeint** or **gut gemeint** ('well-meant'). Such adjs. have normal degrees of comparison: e.g. **Dieser Händler verkauft wohlfeiler als alle anderen** ('charges less than all the others')—**Er ist der wohlhabendste Mann in der Stadt.** But in some cases the compar. and superl. are not formed in the reg. way, esp., of course, but not exclusively, where **gut** is used in the pos. degree: e.g. **Sie ist besser gekleidet** (not **wohlgekleideter**) **als die anderen Damen**; but one also says **Obwohl er erst vor kurzem hierher übergesiedelt ist, ist er schon besser bekannt als mancher Einheimische—Er ist einer der bestbekannten Schriftsteller**; and sim. with **wohlgemeint, wohlgesinnt**, etc.

wollen: 1. This 'modal auxiliary' differs from the other **past-present verbs** (q.v.) in that, while **ich mag, kann**, etc., were orig. past indics., **ich will** was a past *subj.*, which explains the modern idiom **Ich wollte, ich wäre zu Hause!** (cf. **wünschen** 2 (*c*)). But although we now always say 'I *wish* I were at home!', a poet prefers to say '*Would* I were in Grantchester!', where the 1st pers. pron. is understood: cf. '*I would* thou wert cold or hot (Rev. 3. 15). **2.** The following are the chief uses of **wollen**: (**a**) Contrasted with **sollen** (q.v.), it expresses the *will* of the *subj.*, taking an accus. obj. (generally an indef. neut.), a simple infin., or (if the subjs. of the two clauses differ) a subord. **daß**-clause: e.g. **Ich will Arzt werden—Das wolle Gott verhüten!** ('May God be pleased to avert that!' i.e. 'God forbid!')—**Er will, daß ich spreche** ('He wants me to speak'), *not* **Er will mich sprechen**, which means 'He wants to see me' on business. Occasional examples of the infin. with **zu** are to be condemned: cf. **Er gab vor, müde zu sein und nach Hause zu gehen zu wollen** (Spielhagen). In ordinary lang. the dep. infin. is often left unexpressed: e.g. **Willst du Geld?—Wo wollen Sie denn hin?** ('Where are you bound for?')—**Sie wollte mit der Sprache nicht heraus** (G.: 'She was reluctant to speak')—**Der harmloseste Mensch hätte gemerkt, worauf ihre Andeutungen hinauswollten** (J. Schlaf: 'The most innocent person would have seen what she was driving at')—**Sie will mir nicht aus dem Sinn** ('I cannot get her out of my mind'). Here belongs the idiomatic use of **wollen** with the infin. **sein** to express the **pass. voice** (q.v. 2 (*b*) (iii)), often with an impers. subj., the inanimate object being, as it were, endowed with human will-power: e.g. **Ihr Vorschlag will besprochen sein** ('Your proposal calls for discussion')—**Das will ernst genommen sein** ('That demands serious consideration')—**Das Stück will geübt sein** (Sch.: 'The play needs to be rehearsed')—**Das Geld wollte binnen 24 Stunden bezahlt sein** (Sudermann: 'The money was required to be paid within 24 hours')—**Mit einer nagenden Angst auf der Seele mutig zu lächeln, will gelernt sein** (M. Eyth: 'To show a brave smile when fear is gnawing at your heart needs to be learned'). (**b**) Out of the *will* to do something came the *intention* to do it, as in **Ich wollte ihn heute aufsuchen, kam aber nicht dazu** ('I meant to look him up today, but didn't manage to'), and this led to the idea of something being *about to happen*: e.g. **Ich wollte eben ausgehen, als ein Gewitter aufzog** ('I was on the point of going out when a thunderstorm came up')—**Die Uhr schrillte, wenn sie schlagen wollte** (Gutzkow: 'The clock made a high grating sound just before striking')—**Der Krieg schien sich auf deutschem Boden spielen** (usually **abspielen**) **zu wollen** (Sch.: The war, it seemed, was going to be fought out on German soil'); sim. in *neg.* propositions, as in **Man wartete auf den Haarkünstler, der nicht kommen wollte** (Kolbenheyer: here not 'who wouldn't come', but 'who seemed never to be coming')—**Der Wald wollte kein Ende nehmen** (Baumbach: 'The forest seemed never to come to an end')—**Von dem Arzt wollten keine Nachrichten kommen** (G.: 'Would word from the doctor never come?')—**Mörikes Erwartungen, daß bald eine zweite Auflage seiner Gedichte nötig sein werde, wollten sich nicht erfüllen** (E. v. Sallwürk). (**c**) It often expresses a *claim* made by the subj.: e.g. **Er will es nicht getan haben** ('He maintains that he did not do it'), not to be confused with **Er wird es nicht getan haben** ('He won't have done it') or **Er hat es nicht tun wollen** (see 3)—**Man wollte wissen** ('It was maintained'), **daß er nachts auf dem Zimmer des Grafen gewesen** (E. T. A. Hoffmann)—**Sie wollte wissen, ihr Bruder habe früher viel gesungen** (H. Hesse)—**Er beschrieb den Weg, den er genommen haben wollte** (Sudermann: '. . . the road he claimed to have taken')—**Er erzählte von der Zeit, in der er Rittmeister in der preußischen Garde gewesen sein wollte** (M. Eyth)—**Er wollte das Opernwerk wiedergehört haben, hatte es möglicherweise wirklich wiedergehört** (Th. Mann); and here the verb often assumes *pretending* force: e.g. **Diese Bemerkung will ich überhört haben** ('I'll carry on as if I hadn't heard that remark') —**Er sitzt und sitzt an seinem Pult . . . großer Gott, vielleicht ist es wirklich nötig: ich will nichts gesagt haben** (Th. Mann: '. . . disregard what I have just said, I take it back'). (**d**) Some care is necessary in connexion with **etwas . . . haben wollen** with a past part. inserted before **haben**, as such propositions can have quite different meanings. Thus, **Er will die Rechnung beglichen haben** may mean either 'He claims to have settled the account' or 'He wants to have the account settled'. The context will generally make the meaning clear: **Die Kinder umdrängten mich und wollten Geschichten erzählt haben** (Th. Mann) can hardly convey any other sense than 'The children crowded round me and wanted to have stories told them'. **3.** In a compd. tense the past part. **gewollt** is used when the verb has independent force, or when the aux. or the dependent infin. is unexpressed, as in **Du mußt vollführen, was du gewollt** (Auerbach)—**Das Bett oben hatte sich als zu klein erwiesen, also legte man ihn auf den Teppich, denn hinunter hatte er nicht gewollt** (Rilke: '. . . as he refused to be taken downstairs')—**Wenn er gewollt hätte, hätte er es tun können** ('He could have done it if he had liked')—**Wenn ich in diesem Zimmer** ('Goethe's Room' in the Ilmenau inn) **nicht übernachten gewollt, so sah ich nunmehr, daß es sich gar wohl darin frühstücken lasse** (Jul. Rodenberg). But when the dependent infin. is expressed, the past part. assumes the infin. form **wollen** (see **accusative and infinitive** 4), and in this case, in a clause introduced by a subord. conj., the aux. *precedes* both infin. forms as well as any modifiers of the first infin.: e.g. **Ich habe ihn eingeladen, aber er hat nicht kommen wollen—Ich habe ihn öfters sagen hören, daß er schon seit Jahren habe nach Amerika fahren wollen.** **4.** The pres. part. is only used in the compds. **wohl-** and **übelwollend** (cf. **Wille** 2, and **willig**) and in **nicht enden wollend** used attrib.: cf. the example from M. Eyth given under **participle (present)** 1.

womöglich: see **wo** 3.

wonder: 1. The verb **wundern** always has *trans.* force, meaning 'to astonish, excite surprise in' a person. A proposition like 'I wonder that he has not come yet' expresses *surprise*, and this is suggested in German by the impers. or reflex. use of **wundern**: one says **Es wundert mich** (or **Ich wundere mich**), **daß er noch nicht gekommen ist** (see also **Wunder** 1). On the other hand 'I wonder whether he will come' implies *curiosity*, and such a proposition presents some difficulty in German. The most idiomatic rendering is obtained by the impers. use of the modal aux. **sollen**, but it is important to note that this is only possible in a *pres.* tense (which may be a past tense in indir. speech): **Es soll mich wundern, ob er kommen wird**—**Sie sagte, es solle** (or **sollte**) **sie wundern, ob er kommen werde** (or **würde**). The corresponding *past* tense of **sollen**, on the other hand, conveys a different sense: **Es sollte mich wundern, wenn er käme** means 'I should be surprised if he came'. In a past tense in a narrative or in dir. speech, the idea of curiosity is expressed by **sich wundern**: e.g. **Ich wunderte mich, warum ich nicht schon an der vorletzten Station ausgestiegen war** (W. Schäfer)—**Seit wann regt sich denn Fritz über die kirchliche Lage auf, wunderte sich seine Schwester** (G. Bäumer), where the last clause might take the form **fragte sich seine Schwester verwundert** (see 2). An alternative *coll.* way of rendering propositions like 'I wonder what time it is' or 'I wonder whether it is going to rain' is to omit 'I wonder' and use a question introducing an unaccented **wohl**: e.g. **Wieviel U'hr mag es wohl sein?**—**Ob es wohl re'gnen wird?** and sim. **Welch ein liebenswürdiges Mädchen! ob sie wohl Vermö'gen hat?** (H. Grimm). Then there is another difficulty in connexion with this idea of curiosity. In rendering a proposition like 'He looked at the passers-by and wondered about them', one cannot use **Er . . . wunderte sich über sie**, because this would mean 'He . . was surprised at them' (see 2), and in such cases one must have recourse to a paraphrase. A man who set off at dawn with a friend says **Ich möchte wissen, wieviel Leute jetzt schon unterwegs sind** (Fr. Schnack): this exactly expresses 'I wonder how many people are abroad at this early hour', and sim. 'He wondered about them' might be rendered by **Er hätte gern etwas von ihnen wissen mögen**; cf., as a possible alternative rendering, **Er war neugierig auf sie** ('curious about them'). **2.** The compd. **verwundern** is a stronger form of the simple verb (see surprise): e.g. **Sein Betragen verwundert mich**—**Wenn der Geizige auf einmal freigebig wird, so verwundert man sich, aber bewundern** ('admire') **kann man ihn nicht** (Lessing); and its past part. is always used to express a state of astonishment: **Ich war verwundert** (not **gewundert**). To express 'to be astonished *at*' something, one now uses **sich (ver)wundern über** + *accus.*, the old gen. being obs. in prose: cf. **Alle, die ihm zuhöreten, verwunderten sich seines Verstandes und seiner Antworten** (Luke 2. 47)—**Wir konnten uns nicht genug des Anblicks verwundern** (Tieck). But very common is the expression **Es ist (nicht) zu verwundern** ('It is [not] to be wondered at'): e.g. **Da sie nicht nur schön, sondern auch gut von Herzen war, ist es nicht zu verwundern, daß der Jüngling sich in sie verliebte** (G. Keller)—**War es zu verwundern, daß es mir zumute war, als ob ich noch immer träumte?** (M. Eyth). **3.** Rather less strong than **verwundern** is **befremden** ('to fill with a mild surprise'), used of what strikes one as strange (**fremd**). The gradation is well brought out in **Er sah die Mienen des Fürsten aus Befremdung in Verwunderung, aus Verwunderung in Bestürzung ü'bergehen** (Spielhagen: 'He saw the prince's expression pass from surprise to astonishment, from astonishment to consternation'). **4.** Stronger than any of the verbs referred to above is **staunen**, which implies a *state of amazement*, while the compd. **erstaunen** suggests *passing into* such a state (but see below). The simple verb is always *intrans.*, as in **Ich staunte über sein Betragen**; on the other hand, **bestaunen** and (more commonly) **anstaunen** are always *trans.* ('to stare in amazement at') as in **Die Kinder bestaunten den Mann** (C. F. Meyer) and **Sie hält sich viel zu vornehm, um sich anstaunen zu lassen** (Heyse). Orig. **erstaunen** was only used *intrans.*, and this is really still the rule, the corresponding trans. being **in Erstaunen setzen** (incidentally, the verbal subst. **Erstaunen** has practically displaced **Erstaunung**): cf. **Ich erstaunte über das, was er sagte** and **Was er sagte, setzte mich in Erstaunen**—**Hatten ihn die Kinder in**

Verwunderung gesetzt, so erfüllte ihn das, was ihm jetzt zu Augen kam, mit Erstaunen (G.). The use of **erstaunen** as a *trans.* verb had occurred only sporadically until recent times, as in **Diese Übereinstimmung muß einen jeden erstaunen** (G.), and although many standard modern authors use it freely, the fact remains that it is not yet generally accepted, so that **Das setzte mich in großes Erstaunen** is still the best rendering of 'That astounded me'. But the following examples give some indication of the extent to which the trans. use has spread in recent times: **Ich bin mir nicht ganz klar darüber, was mich bewegt, zu Ihnen zu kommen: es erstaunt mich selbst** (Wassermann)—**Daß er so ungeniert seine Meinung herausplauderte, erstaunte mich** (H. Hesse)—**Mich erstaunten die Menschenmassen vor den Schaufenstern** (Dauthendey)—**Sie sagte es mit einer Leidenschaftlichkeit, die ihn erstaunte** (F. Huch)—**Später ereignete sich etwas Außerordentliches, das Anna im höchsten Grade erstaunte** (Th. Mann)—**Da sah er ein Schauspiel, das ihn erstaunte** (Bruno Frank)—**Daß eine lange Kette herunterhing, sah ich, ohne daß es mich erstaunt hätte** (A. Schaeffer)—**Der Fremde sagte ihm nichts Neues, was ihn erstaunt hätte** (W. v. Scholz)—**Es hätte sie nicht erstaunt, wenn er über den Zaun gesprungen wäre** (K. Edschmid). It seems significant that the reflex. use (as in Fr. *s'étonner*) is very rare —cf. **Es blieb mir keine Zeit, mich groß zu erstaunen** (P. Keller)—and that the pres. part. is generally avoided in the attrib. adj. relation: instead of **ein erstaunendes Gedächtnis** (Sch.) one now prefers to use **ein erstaunliches Gedächtnis.**

wo(r)-: Just as **da(r)-** (q.v.), when prefixed to a prep., properly represents a *pers.* pron., so **wo(r)-** represents an *interrog.* or *rel.* pron., the antecedent in the latter case being preferably indef. or abstract: e.g. **Womit bist du beschäftigt?—Wozu brauchst du soviel Geld?—Das ist das einzige, worauf ich mich freue—Es ist etwas Wichtiges, worum es sich handelt —Das sind Sachen, worein ich mich niemals mische** (see **darein** 1 (*b*) and 2); cf., as incorrect, **Sooft sie sich zu dem Paketchen beugte, worein** (for **worin** or **in dem**) **das Kind zappelte, wurde sie stiller** (Federer). It is esp. noteworthy that such expressions should not be used in references to persons—see **was** (relative) 2 (*a*), and cf. **was** (interrogative) 3 (*b*)—and that the rel. clause must be a finite one when **wo(r)-** is expressed: e.g. **Er gab mir etwas, womit man Ungeziefer umbringen kann** ('with which to destroy vermin': not **womit Ungeziefer umzubringen**)—**Ich habe nichts, worüber ich mich beklagen kann** ('nothing to complain of': not **worüber mich zu beklagen**).

word-order: As the most important point in connexion with the order of words in a German sentence is the position of the *verb*, the present article will regard the question from that angle and consider in detail the four distinct word-orders, generally referred to as 'normal', 'inverted', 'question' (a misleading term) and 'transposed'. **1. Normal order: (a)** Here the subj. with its modifiers stands in the first place, and the verb (in a compd. tense the pers., i.e. finite, part or the aux.) in the second place, followed by the modifiers of the verb: e.g. **Die überall in der Welt gefeierte Liedersängerin, die wir lange nicht haben singen hören** (subj. with modifiers) **wird** (pers. part of the compd. verb) **nächste Woche, wie uns berichtet wird, hier bei uns auftreten** (modifiers of the verb); so also in questions introduced by the interrog. word or phrase, as in **Wer hat das behauptet?** and **Wessen deutsche Bücher sind dies?** It is important here that the verb must follow the subj. and its modifiers *immediately*; in English, an adv. may separate the subj. from the verb in a declaratory statement, as in 'I sometimes go for a walk in the evening' or 'He readily agreed to my proposal', but this is impossible in German: **Ich gehe manchmal abends spazieren—Er stimmte meinem Vorschlag bereitwillig zu.** It is, therefore, quite irregular to say **Der Knecht nach langem Suchen findet endlich seinen Herrn** (Heine); but it is quite correct to say **Ich wenigstens bin anderer Meinung** or **Ich blieb sitzen, er jedoch verließ das Zimmer,** because the advs. here only modify the subjs., not the whole sentence (cf. 2 (*a*)); and this is extended to expressions like 'I said' or 'he replied' in reporting spoken words, as in **„Du", sagte er, „bist der letzte, der so etwas vorschlagen sollte"** (cf. 2 (*b*)). **(b)** It is quite contrary to accepted usage to start a sentence with an adv. expression or a subord. clause and follow it up with normal order: an example like **Im Garten die Nachtigallen riefen ängstlich** (Heyse) is unorthodox, to say the least, and an examiner would certainly not pass it. It is true that this use—or rather misuse—seems to be gaining ground, but it is anything but recognized, far less established, so that it is definitely inadvisable to imitate it: cf., as further examples, **In der Mitte der Kern der Finsternis lag still** (Hofmannsthal)—**An der Türe der Pförtner klapperte mit seinen Schlüsseln** (Bruno Frank)—**Im Park die Terriers und Collies tummelten sich auf den Wiesen** (id.)—**An einem Fenster die Gardinen teilten sich** (E. Toller)—**Über ihnen der Himmel war blaugefleckt** (Britting)—**Wie sie schritten, das Glas der Fensterscheiben strahlte von hundert Sonnenstrahlen** (H. Kesten). (c) But there are cases where normal order is legitimately used to replace other word-orders. Thus, while it is taking an inexcusable liberty with the spirit of the German prose language to use normal order in a subord. **daß**-clause in which **daß** is expressed (see 2 (*a*) and 4), as in **Es ist schwer zu denken, daß fremde Leute wohnen in dem alten Herrenhaus** (Rilke), which again no examiner would pass, normal order is imperative here when **daß** is omitted, as in **Er sagte, er käme erst morgen an**, and in the second of two such co-ord. clauses where **daß** is expressed in the first, a connecting **und** being dropped: e.g. **Er sagte, daß er uns erst morgen besuchen würde, er könne heute nicht abkommen.** And so it is possible to have a princ. and two dependent subord. clauses, *all* with normal order, as in **Ich habe viel über die Todesfurcht nachgedacht: ich glaube, ich kann sagen, ich habe sie gefühlt** (Rilke). Normal order after an introductory *conditional* clause is permissible, though rather choice, as in **Wenn ich in dieser Stunde stürbe, sie würde nicht betrübt sein!** (H. Hesse), with a slight pause between the two clauses, suggesting the likely explanation of this deviation from the rule, namely, that another clause is really understood there: cf. **Wenn ich in dieser Stunde stürbe,** [**ist eins gewiß** ('one thing is certain'):] **sie würde nicht betrübt sein!** But normal order is common in the second of two *conditional* clauses connected by **und**, with **wenn** introducing the first but dropped in the second: e.g. **Mir will es das Herz abdrücken, wenn ich meinem Bruder und seinen Kindern begegne und darf nicht mit ihnen reden** (Auerbach)—**Was sollen die Leute später sagen, wenn man den Krieg mitgemacht hat und hat nicht einmal das Eiserne Kreuz bekommen?** (W. v. Scholz); and even with different subjs. in the two clauses, as in **Wenn sie auf der Terrasse säße und ich käme aus dem Garten, würde sie mich spöttisch ansehen** (Hofmannsthal) and **Man muß an die Eltern zurückdenken, die man kränken mußte, wenn sie einem eine Freude brachten und man begriff sie nicht** (Rilke); at one time this was also possible after other subord. conjs., but this is now avoided: cf. **Er gab ihnen Macht über die unsaubern Geister, daß sie die austrieben und heilten allerlei Krankheit** (Matt. 10. 1), and as a modern example, which should not be imitated, **Mir kommt vor, daß alle beschäftigt sind und nicht achtgeben, als ob eine Sternschnuppe fiele und es sieht sie keiner** (Rilke), for **und keiner sie sähe.** (d) Idiomatic is the use of normal order after a *concessive* clause, esp. common when the latter is introduced by **so** (q.v. 3): e.g. **Sooft sie auch aufschaute** ('However often she looked up'), **die bekannte Gestalt ließ sich nicht blicken** (E. Wichert)—**„Herr Schmitz, ich habe Ihnen etwas zu offenbaren!" So verdrießlich er war, diese Anrede machte ihn aufmerksam** (Immermann)—**So merklich auch die Jahre ihre Spuren auf sein Gesicht schrieben, er blieb jung im Herzen** (H. W. Geissler)—**So wunderlich es scheinen mag, der Mensch des Mittelalters war in gewissem Sinne freier als der moderne** (A. E. Schönbach); so also after other kinds of concess. clauses, as in **Sie mochte vorschlagen, was sie wollte** ('No matter what she proposed'), **man war immer dabei, ihre Ideen durchzuführen** (Böhlau)—**Man lege die Sache aus, wie man will, ich halte es nicht für meine Aufgabe, darüber nachzudenken** (Th. Mann: 'Put whatever construction you like on the matter, I do not regard it as my business to worry about it')—**Wenn sie auch mehrmals versuchte, sich auf die Fußspitzen zu stellen** ('However often she tried to stand on tip-toe'), **sie konnte nichts sehen** (Werfel)—**Was Bergengruen auch immer sagt, sei es im kleinen Gedicht, sei es in hymnischer Form, es ist bedeutend und machtvoll** (W. Grenzmann). Here again there is a short pause suggesting a clause that is understood: the first of these examples just given, with such a clause inserted, might read **Sooft sie auch aufschaute,** [**war sie jedesmal enttäuscht:**] **die bekannte Gestalt ließ sich nicht blicken**; and sim. **Wenn sie auch mehrmals versuchte, sich auf die Fußspitzen zu stellen,** [**hatte es keinen Zweck:**] **sie konnte nichts sehen.** The same applies to a proposition like **Was mich betrifft, ich muß zugeben, daß ich den Versuchungen in gewisser Beziehung erlegen bin** (Rilke: 'As for myself, I must admit that I have yielded to these temptations in some respects'), where there is a sim. pause: cf. **Was mich betrifft,** [**will ich eins nicht verschweigen:**] **ich muß zugeben, daß ich den Versuchungen . . . erlegen bin.** (**e**) In a declaratory statement a sep. prefix, or a word which has become one, normally goes to the end, as in **Er machte die Tür auf** or **Das Kind stand mitten auf der Straße still.** Orig. this was not necessary, as when Luther says **Er hebt auf den Dürftigen** (1 Sam. 2. 8); but **Er machte auf die Tür** as a rendering of 'He opened the door' would now be considered wrong. In other contexts a certain freedom is allowed: **Er blickte zurück, das Haus hob sich nicht ab von der dunklen Fläche** (Viebig) is quite common, esp. in a longer sentence like **Wir gingen ab von dem Weg, der uns, wie man behauptete, schneller an unser Ziel bringen würde.** Some expressionists even want prefixes never to be separated: cf. **Daran vorüber knarrte die brüchige Treppe, aufging oben das kleine Zimmer** (H. Mann)—**In der Ferne aufleuchtete die Gralsburg von** *Sacré Cœur* (Werfel)—**Heiliges Morgenland! Wer dich anschaut, dem stillsteht das Herz** (A. Schaeffer); but this is now only allowed in the case of a few verbs like **anerkennen, obliegen,** etc. (qq.v.). **2. Inverted order:** (**a**) As in normal order, so here also the pers. part of the verb (or the aux.) stands in the *second* place but is *followed* by the subj., the proposition being introduced, often for emphasis, by some other word or phrase, such as an obj., a pred. adj., an adv. expression, an infin. or part. forming a link with what has preceded: e.g. **Mich hat er nicht eingeladen—Freunde hat er so gut wie keine** (Fr. Huch)—**So leicht ist diese Aufgabe nicht—Abends gehe ich selten aus—Ihre Heiterkeit konnte sich in mancher Weise äußern, aber lange sich verbergen konnte sie nicht** (H. Hesse)—**„Tut sie viel?" „Nein, viel tun tut sie nicht"** (Sudermann)—**„Hat er dich besucht?" „Besucht hat er mich nicht, aber er hat mich zu morgen eingeladen**; and so also in *questions* which begin with the obj., as in **Was hat er dir gesagt?** If the subj. is a pers. pron., it should follow the verb immediately, but not necessarily otherwise: cf. **Heute bekam ich zu meinem Entsetzen eine Todesanzeige** and **Heute lief zu meinem Entsetzen eine Todesanzeige ein.** These last two examples illustrate another important point in connexion with inverted order, namely, that *one* introductory idea is sufficient to fix the position of the verb. It is quite correct to say **Heute früh, so um 7 Uhr, als ich eben aufgestanden war, sah ich, wie zwei Autos draußen zusammenstießen** or **Auf dem Weg zur Stadt, ein paar Kilometer von hier, an einer scharfen Krümmung, ereignete sich ein schlimmer Unfall,** because in either case there is a close connexion between the three adv. expressions with which the propositions begin; on the other hand, where there is no such connexion the verb should stand immediately after the *first* expression, and that is why one does not say **Heute zu meinem Entsetzen bekam ich eine Todesanzeige,** unless commas are inserted before and after the prep. phrase, in which case this phrase is a sort of parenthetical addition. But one must not be misled by an introductory adv. which modifies only one word or phrase in the statement, and not the statement itself: cf. the inverted order in **Anfangs sind Schüler oft fleißig, werden aber später faul** with the normal order in **Anfangs fleißige Schüler** ('Pupils who are diligent at first') **werden später oft faul,** and the inverted order (because the obj. stands first) in **Anfangs willfährige Hausgehilfinnen hatte sie schon mehr als einmal gehabt** (L. Winder: 'Family helps who were willing at first she had already had more than once'); so also after an introductory subord. clause or its equivalent (but see 1 (*c*)): e.g. **Ein regelmäßiger Teilnehmer an unseren Abendgesellschaften** (really a contracted causal clause), **genoß er große Achtung bei allen unseren Gästen** (Th. Mann). Here belong certain advs., notably **auch, schon, vielleicht,** and **wenigstens,** which can take either inverted or normal order according as they modify the whole statement or only one word in it, as in the following pairs of examples: **Ich hatte keine Lust, auszugehen, auch fühlte ich mich etwas unwohl** and **Die meisten Leute stimmten gegen den Antrag, und auch ich war dagegen**—**Schon war mir der Gedanke gekommen, ehe mein Freund ihn aussprach** and **Schon der Gedanke erschreckt mich** ('The very idea frightens me')—**Vielleicht gibt es kein zuverlässiges Mittel gegen Seekrankheit** and **Vielleicht das zuverlässigste Mittel gegen Seekrankheit ist diese**—**Ich glaube es, wenigstens** ('at all events') **haben zwei von meinen Freunden es behauptet** and **Wenigstens zwei** ('At least two') **von meinen Freunden haben das behauptet.** (**b**) Inverted order is reg. used in circumlocutions beginning with **es,** as in **Es ist jemand draußen** or **Es war einmal ein König**; sometimes in exclamatory statements like **Wie herrlich leuchtet mir die Natur!** (G.), where other word-orders are more usual in ordinary lang., as in **Welch ein herrlicher Blick bietet sich dem Auge hier!** (normal) and **Junge, wie groß du geworden bist!** (transposed: see 4 (*d*)); and in parenthetical expressions like 'he said' or 'I think' inserted in spoken words, as in **„Nein", sagte er, „abends gehe ich selten aus"** and **„Er ist, glaube ich, augenblicklich verreist",** so that it is taking an unwarrantable liberty to say **Es war nichts in dem Raum zu finden als eine alte Büste, die, ich glaube, den Admiral Juel darstellte** (Rilke). (**c**) Where there are two or more co-ord. clauses, the first of which is introduced by an adv. expression, etc., inversion is usually confined to the first, but is used in the others also if the adv. expression is intended to apply to all, or for reasons of emphasis: e.g., on the one hand, **Im gestrigen Konzert trug die Sängerin Brahms-Lieder mit großem Ausdruck vor, und der Klavierspieler begleitete sie mit Gefühl**—**Eines Abends klopfte es an meiner Tür und ich erschrak ein wenig** (H. Hesse); and, on the other hand, **Schön war die Stadt niemals, ist sie auch nicht geworden und wird sie nie werden** (Jensen)—**Auf Nebentischen standen Blechbüchsen voll feiner Biskuits, waren glänzende Honigkuchen übereinandergeschichtet, erhoben sich Glasschalen mit überzuckerten Früchten** (Th. Mann)—**Bei seiner Rückkehr aus Amerika hat er fast alle Freunde besucht, mich aber hat er nicht aufgesucht.** (**d**) The only introductory expressions which do *not* cause inversion are short exclamations and certain advs., really weak exclamations, which are followed by a short pause indicated by a comma: e.g. **O weh! ich habe einen Tintenklecks gemacht!**—**„Gehst du mit ins Konzert?" „Bewahre! ich werde mich hüten!"** (see **behalten**)—**Ach, das waren herrliche Tage!**—**„Hat er das wirklich gesagt?" „Gewiß** (or **Freilich**), **ich habe es deutlich gehört"**—**„Sagte er, er würde kommen?" „Allerdings, ich verlasse mich auch darauf"**—**Wie ich mein Leben in Südamerika entwickelte, soll hier unbetrachtet bleiben: genug** ('suffice it to say'), **ich bin mit den Jahren zu Reichtum gekommen** (Bergengruen). **3. Question order:** Here the finite part of the verb stands in the first place, the subj. generally (necessarily if it is a pers. pron.) in the second place. The term 'question order' is rather unfortunate, as it might mislead one into assuming that it applied to *all* questions, and *only* to questions, which is very far from being the case (cf. 1 (*a*) and 2 (*a*)). Question order is used: (**a**) in *interrog.* propositions other than those referred to in 1 (*a*) and 2 (*a*): e.g. **„Ist er verlobt?" „Weswegen wollen Sie das wissen?"**; (**b**) in *conditional* clauses not introduced by **wenn**: e.g. **Hätte ich das gewußt, (so) wäre ich zu Hause geblieben**; this was presumably first used in a pres. tense and was orig. a question: cf. **Hast du deine Schularbeiten gemacht[?], dann darfst du spielen**; (**c**) in clauses introduced by **als** = **'as if'** (q.v. 1); (**d**) in *concessive* clauses not introduced by a conj.: e.g. **Sei dem, wie ihm wolle, mich geht die Sache nicht an** ('Be that as it may, the matter does not concern me')—**Mochte er sich auch noch soviel Mühe geben, der Versuch gelang ihm nicht** ('However much trouble he took, he failed in the attempt'): for the normal order in the second clauses, see 1 (*d*); (**e**) in *imperative* propositions: e.g. **Laß mich allein!**—**Seien Sie so gut und helfen Sie mir über die Straße!**—**Glauben Sie mir, mit nüchternem Magen** ('on an empty stomach') **trifft man immer falsche Entschlüsse!** (B. E. Werner); (**f**) in *optative* propositions: e.g. **Möge es Ihnen gut gehen!**—**Leben Sie wohl!** (**g**) in narrative style, to state something in a lively way in order to excite interest, nearly always with **da** inserted immediately after the introductory verb: e.g. **Wird da eines Tages Wieland zu der Aufführung eines Dramas „Eurydice"**

eingeladen (F. A. Hohenstein)—**Kommt da vorigen Herbst der Landrat auf einen Hof gefahren und wünscht den Bauern zu sprechen** (Speckmann)—**Bei der nächsten Pfadkrümmung scheute das Pferd vor einem menschlichen Körper: lag da in der Sonne der Beppo und schlief seinen Rausch aus** (Zifferer); (**h**) in the second of two statements with the adv. **doch** inserted, explaining the reason for the first statement: e.g. **Auf den dunklen Gassen war groß Gewimmel, war doch am Nachmittage der neue Galgen aufgerichtet worden** (Storm)—**Endlich kam der Tag, wo er seine Freiheit forderte, konnte er doch darauf verweisen, daß er die gestellten Bedingungen erfüllt hatte** (Wassermann)—**Ihre Worte hatten ihn erschüttert, war er doch so lange der Zeuge ihrer stummen Leiden gewesen, und kannte er doch deren geheimen Grund** (E. Wichert)—**Diese Jahre entbehrten nicht der äußeren und inneren Stürme, mußte er** (*scil.* Storm) **doch jahrelang das Brot der Fremde essen** (A. Biese). **4. Transposed order:** (**a**) Here the pers., i.e. the finite, part of the verb (or the aux.) stands at the *end*, the proposition being generally introduced by a subord. conj. or a rel. or interrog. word. When a subord. conj. introduces the clause, it must be followed immediately by the subj. if this is a pers. pron., not necessarily otherwise. An introductory rel. or interrog. need not be the subj., so that the clause *may* begin with a prep. The following examples illustrate these points: **Er schrieb, daß er mich bald kennenzulernen hoffe**—**Es wurde mir mitgeteilt, daß infolge der Erkrankung des Dirigenten das Konzert verschoben werden müsse**—**Er wußte nicht, wessen er sich versehen sollte** ('He did not know what to expect')—**Ich bin noch unsicher, mit welchem Zuge ich fahren werde**—**Ich erteilte ihm die gewünschte Auskunft, worauf er sich höflich grüßend verabschiedete** (not **worauf höflich grüßend er sich verabschiedete**). Through the omission of **daß**, certain advs. have come to be used also as conjs. in which case the verb must necessarily go to the end: see esp. **kaum** 1, **nun** 2, **ungeachet** and **zumal.** For normal order in the second of two co-ord. **daß**-clauses, see 1 (*c*). (**b**) A very important point arises where one dependent clause is inserted in another, and here learners often go wrong. The proposition 'If it rains, we ought to stay at home' is **Wenn es regnet, sollten wir zu Hause bleiben,** whereas 'He said that we should stay at home' is **Er sagte, daß wir zu Hause bleiben sollten** (cf. 1 (*c*)). When the two are combined to form the proposition 'He said that if it rained we ought to stay at home', the important thing in the German word-order is that, with **daß** *inserted*, the verbs in *both* dependent clauses must go to the *end*: it is quite wrong to say, as learners are so apt to do, **Er sagte, daß, wenn es regnete, sollten wir zu Hause bleiben.** In practice, where the subj. of the **daß**-clause is a pers. pron., this pron. is almost necessarily brought forward and placed *before* the inserted clause: **Er sagte, daß wir, wenn es regnete, zu Hause bleiben sollten**; and sim., with an infin. clause inserted, **Er war der Ansicht, daß, wir, anstatt auszugehen, zu Hause musizieren sollten.** (**c**) There is one important exception to the rule that in a dependent clause the finite verb must stand at the end, namely, where the clause is a compd. one with two infin. forms, of which the second replaces a past part. This occurs with the 'modal auxiliaries' and with **brauchen, heißen, hören, lassen,** etc. (qq.v.). When a proposition like **Er hat es tun müssen** becomes a subord. **daß**-clause, the aux. *precedes* not only the two infin. forms but also any modifiers of the first infin.: e.g. **Er sagte, daß er es habe tun müssen**—**Der Zeuge sagte aus, daß er den Angeklagten etwas habe zu sich stecken sehen** ('The witness stated in evidence that he had seen the accused conceal something on his person')—**Der Bauer bestand darauf, daß er den Arzt habe unverzüglich kommen lassen** ('The farmer insisted that he had sent word to the doctor to come without delay'; with **unverzüglich** *preceding* **habe,** the meaning would be 'The farmer insisted that he had immediately sent for the doctor'). In this connexion it should be noted that if the past part. is used instead of the second infin., the aux. must stand in its normal place at the *end*: cf. the last four examples given under **accusative and infinitive** 5 (*a*). (**d**) Transposed order is used coll. in lively *questions* (often with **nur** inserted, implying surprise and eagerness to know the facts) and *exclamations*: e.g. **Wo er nur so lange bleibt?** ('Where on earth can he be all this time?')—**Wie er nur so etwas tun konnte?** ('How could he possibly do such a thing?')—

Ach, wie krank der Herr aussieht! Here, as in the case of normal order after a concess. or cond. clause (see 1 (*c*)), there is really an introductory clause understood: cf. **[Wenn ich nur wüßte,] wo er so lange bleibt!**—**[Sieh nur,] wie krank er aussieht!** **(e)** In a complex sentence, with one or two subord. clauses inserted in another one, the strict observance of the rule that the verbs should go to the end would result in a bewildering accumulation of verbs at the end of the sentence. This is now avoided, as it tends to make the sense obscure: cf. as a striking example, **Der Knabe gefiel mir und ich behielt ihn bei mir, als der Vater, nachdem seine Ränke, die mich in einen meine Ehre vernichtenden Kriminalprozeß verwickeln sollten, entdeckt worden, fliehen mußte** (E. T. A. Hoffmann), better **. . . ich behielt ihn bei mir, als der Vater fliehen mußte, nachdem seine Ränke . . . entdeckt worden waren.**

worein, worin: see **wo(r)-**; **da(r)-** 2; **darein** 2.

Wort: 1. (a) In the plur. of this noun, distinguish between **Wörter,** single disconnected words, and **Worte,** words connected in the spoken or written lang.: e.g., on the one hand, **In diesem Kapitel kommen zwei Wörter vor, die nicht im Wörterbuch** ('dictionary') **stehen**—**Dieser Dichter prägt gern neue Wörter** ('likes to coin new words'); and, on the other hand, **Ich traue seinen Worten nicht**—**Mendelssohns Lieder ohne Worte** (i.e. without an accompanying text)—**mit** ('in') **anderen Worten.** The only exception here is **Sprichwort** ('proverb'), the plur. of which is not **Sprichworte,** but **Sprichwörter,** while the Proverbs in the Bible are **die Sprüche Salomos. (b)** In the proposition **Ich war erschöpfter, als ich es wahr haben wollte** (Roquette), the expression **es wahr haben wollen** is used with the same force as **zugestehen** (cf. **confess** 2): 'I was more exhausted than I would admit'. More in accordance with modern usage here is the substitution of the noun **Wort** for the adj. **wahr,** the accepted idiom being **es** or **etwas nicht Wort haben wollen,** as in **Der Großherzog wollte seine Großmut nicht Wort haben** (Mörike: 'The Grand Duke would not admit that he had been generous') and **Sie wollte** (with or without **es**) **nicht Wort haben, daß sie ihn nicht bemerkt hätte** (G.: 'She denied that she had not noticed him'). **2.** Whereas **Wort** is *neut.*, its comp. **Antwort** is now always *fem.* Actually, this has a historical basis: in MHG there were two forms, viz. *die antwurt* and *daz antwürte,* and Luther used both genders. That the neut. persisted through later periods is evident from Lessing's **Antworts genug.**

worum: see **was** (interrogative) 3 (*b*).

Wunder: 1. The fundamental force of this noun, viz. '(a feeling of) astonishment', is now almost confined to one verb, being otherwise expressed by **Verwunderung** (see **surprise** and cf. **wonder** 2 and 3). The verb in question is **wundernehmen,** which has developed out of the expression **Es nimmt mich Wunder,** where **Es** (q.v. 1) was orig. a dependent *gen.*, the lit. meaning being 'Astonishment because of it takes possession of me'; but through misunderstanding, **Es** came to be regarded as a nom., and **Wunder** to be written with a small letter and treated as a real sep. prefix: hence, **Das nimmt mich wunder** ('That surprises me')—**Sein Betragen scheint dich wunderzunehmen** ('His behaviour seems to astonish you')—**Bei der Wohnung angelangt, fand er die Haustüre nur angelehnt, was ihn sehr wundernahm** (Mörike). **2. Wunder** then came to be used of what *causes* a feeling of astonishment, esp. of what is or seems marvellous, like the miracles wrought by Our Lord: e.g. **Du bist der Gott, der Wunder tut** (Ps. 77. 14)—**Wisse, Königin, daß dir zum Troste Gott ein Wunder verrichten kann** (Sch.)—**Die Bildsäule Jupiters von Phidias galt als eins der sieben Wunder der Welt**; cf. the coll. expression **Du wirst dein blaues Wunder erleben** ('You'll have the surprise of your life'), which *Sanders* thinks may have originated from seeing the wonders of the deep. Here belong also a number of coll. expressions, in some of which the noun is now written with a small letter: e.g. **Es ist kein Wunder** (or simply **Kein Wunder,** like our 'No wonder'), **daß er sich erkältet hat**—**Es wäre ein Wunder, wenn er sich nicht erkältet hätte**—**Was Wunder, daß** (or **wenn**) **heutzutage soviel Leute arm sind?** ('Is it to be wondered at that so many people are poor nowadays?')—**Sie glaubt wunder wie anziehend sie ist** ('She thinks herself mighty fascinating')—**Du bildest dir wunder was ein!** ('You think no small beer of yourself!')—**Als ob ich wunder was verrichtet hätte** ('As though

I had done something wonderful'), **zog ich hochvergnügt dem Dorfe zu** (G. Keller); and even with a *gen.* ending, probably depending on **was** understood, as in **Du stellst dir wunders vor, was ein König von Preußen ist** (Bruno Frank: 'You think a king of Prussia is a prodigy').

wundern: see **surprise** 1; **wonder** 1.

wundernehmen: see **surprise** 1; **Wunder** 1.

wünschen: 1. The noun **Wunsch** has lost some of its orig. force. In MHG, *wunsch* implied the highest, most perfect thing one could desire: thus, the stock phrase *ze wunsche wol getân* was used esp. of a lovely woman, with perfect features and figure, and *ze wunsche wol gekleidet* meant 'most beautifully dressed'. The noun could also suggest the ability to perform something extraordinary or miraculous, a sense still seen in **Wünschelrute** ('magic wand', esp. 'divining-rod'). **2.** Constructions of **wünschen**:—(**a**) The desired obj. orig. stood in the gen. case (now obs.), a pers. accus. being only used of 'wishing a person to some place', as we say 'I wished him miles away *or* to the devil'. The NHG verb takes an accus. of the thing and a dat. of the person, as in **jemandem Glück wünschen** (cf. **jemanden beglückwünschen,** 'to wish a person good luck' or 'to congratulate a person'). (**b**) We can say 'I wish to go' and 'I wish you to go'; in the former case, where the two verbs refer to the same person, a German uses the infin. with **zu,** in the latter he can only use a subord. clause introduced by **daß** (cf. the example from Roquette given under **von** 5). It follows that the proposition **Er wünscht dich zu sprechen** does *not* mean 'He wishes you to speak', but 'He wishes to speak to *or* see you (on business)'. The polite expression **Ich wünsche wohl geruht zu haben** ('I hope you have slept well') should really be **Ich wünsche or hoffe, daß Sie wohl geruht haben,** but though strictly incorrect it is sanctioned by usage. (**c**) The accus. and infin. (without **zu**) is never used, but the accus. and *past part.* (with **zu sein** understood) is in regular use, and a good example of this is **Das Haus ist alt: ich tue vielleicht Unrecht, wenn ich es erhalten wünsche** (R. Waldmüller: not '. . . in wishing to preserve it', which would require **zu erhalten,** but '. . . in wishing it to be preserved'); and sim. **Den Dichter hoffte sie besonders zu verbinden** ('to oblige'), **weil sie einige Lieder von ihm an sie gerichtet wünschte** (G.: '. . . . because she wished some of his poems to be addressed to her')—**Er machte mich aufmerksam auf das, was er besonders hervorgehoben wünschte** (G. Keller: 'He drew my attention to what he wished to be specially emphasized'). (**d**) Noteworthy is the use of the **past subjunctive** (q.v. 3) in expressions like **Ich wünschte** (more ordinarily **wollte**: see **wollen** 1), **ich wäre zu Hause** ('I *wish* I were at home'); sim. **Ich wünschte, du ständest neben mir und hieltest meine Hand** (K. Edschmid).

Wurm: The plur. of this noun was orig. **Würme** (< OHG *wurmi*), and this form occurs occasionally even in modern times, as in a reference to **ein Bücherhauf, den Würme nagen** (G.); but this is now almost obs., the recognized form being **Würmer**—cf. **jemandem die Würmer aus der Nase ziehen** ('to *worm* a secret out of a person', from Fr. *tirer les vers du nez à quelqu'un*). Incidentally, the phrase **es wurmt mich** ('it vexes *or* annoys me') is presumably derived from the feeling of discomfort occasioned by the presence of tape-worms (**Bandwürmer**) in the intestine.—With regard to the gender, **Wurm** is properly *masc.*, and so also in **Bücher-, Glüh-, Lindwurm** ('winged dragon'), etc.; but when used coll. of a little child (cf. **Ding**), it is now perhaps more commonly *neut.*: in the north one usually says **Ach, das arme kleine Wurm!** and where the neut. **Kind** has just been referred to, the masc. sounds rather strange, as in **Als ich das Kind zur Taufe hielt, ließ ich den armen Wurm auf den Taufstein fallen** (Hebbel) and **„Sie werfen eben ein neugeborenes Kind in den Fluß". „Gehen wir hinunter: vielleicht ist der arme Wurm noch zu retten!"** (Fr. v. Bülow.)

Z

Zahl: This noun properly denotes an arithmetical 'number, cipher' (see **figure** 2, and cf. **gerade** 1), but it is often used loosely of a 'number' of people, etc., where strictly **Anzahl** would be more correct: cf. **Mehrzahl** ('majority') and

Unzahl ('countless number'). For a plur. verb in propositions like **Es waren eine große Anzahl Leute anwesend,** see congruence 1 (*a*) and (*b*), and cf., on the one hand, **Eine Unzahl Kaiser fanden sich nicht entehrt, auf Kupferpfennigen zu erscheinen** (G.: 'A countless number of emperors did not feel dishonoured by having their likenesses represented on copper pennies'), and, on the other hand, with **Anzahl** followed by a recognizable *gen.*, **Seinen Fahnen folgte eine große Anzahl Freiwilliger** (Sch.: which might have been . . . **folgten eine große Anzahl Freiwillige**); and sim. **Eine Anzahl zerstreuter Blätter lag unter den Händen der Schlafenden** (Mörike).

Zeh(e): The MHG expression for 'toe' was *diu zêhe*, and **die Zehe** is still the recognized form, as in **Mich schauerte es vom Wirbel bis zur Zehe** (G. Keller: 'I shuddered from head to foot, from top to toe'). The form **der Zeh** (weak or more usually strong) was at one time not uncommon and is still used in some parts, but this should, on the whole, be avoided: cf. **Mose nahm seines Blutes** (i.e. some of the ram's blood) **und tat' s Aaron auf . . . den großen Zehen** (sing.; Lev. 8. 23)—**Er fragte ängstlich, ob Ihr versehrt** ('wounded') **wäret: ich sagte, „Er ist ganz** ('unhurt'), **von der äußersten Haarspitze bis zum Nagel des kleinen Zehs** (G.). The plur. **die Zehen** is practically fixed: one says **Um besser zu sehen, stellte ich mich auf die Zehen** ('I stood up on tiptoe') and, of course, **Der Räuber schlich auf den Zehen ins Haus.**

Zeichen: for the expression **seines Zeichens** ('by trade *or* profession'), see **genitive** (adverbial) 3 (*b*) *ad fin.*

zeigen: The usual constructions after this verb can be seen from the following examples: **Sie zeigte mir ihre Geburtstagsgeschenke**—**Man zeigte ihm die kalte Schulter** ('He was cold-shouldered')—**Die Uhr zeigt auf drei** ('points to three')—**Der Wegweiser zeigt nach Süden**—**Er hat sich immer freundlich gegen mich gezeigt**—**Es zeigte sich** ('Events showed'), **daß ich mich getäuscht hatte.** It is important to note that a finite subord. clause is necessary in rendering a proposition like 'Show me what to do!' the infin. construction being impossible in German: **Zeige mir, was ich machen muß!** and sim. **Er zeigte mir, wie ich es machen mußte** or **wie es zu machen war** ('He showed me how to do it'). Quite foreign to present-day usage, certainly in the north, is the *accus. and infin.* construction, as in **Man zeigte uns das Schloß Chanvan blinken** (G.), where one would now use the rel. clause **das herüberblinkte**; even in the south a proposition like **Das Jahrhundert zeigt ihn im Pilgerkleid von Kirche zu Kirche ziehen** (Rilke) is very rare and not to be recommended.

zeihen: 1. This strong verb, meaning 'to accuse' somebody (*accus.*) of something (*gen.*), is from the same root as **zeigen** (cf. **jemand als Dieb anzeigen,** 'to denounce someone as a thief'). It was a favourite word of Luther's, and later of Schiller's, but it is now confined to poetry and choice prose, in which respect, as well as in construction, it stands in marked contrast with the common compd. **verzeihen** (q.v.): e.g. **Welcher unter euch kann mich einer Sünde zeihen?** (John 8. 46)—**Er zieh sich der Eitelkeit** (Gutzkow). Occasional examples of a weak past tense are not recognized: cf. **Das Verbrechen, dessen ich Sie zeihte, ich beging es selbst** (Sch.)—**Wer zeihte ihn der Mutlosigkeit?** (Alexis). In ordinary prose one now uses **jemand eines Diebstahls beschuldigen, eines Mordes anklagen** (see **accuse**). **2.** Almost as choice as **zeihen** is **bezichtigen,** which has the same meaning and construction: **Wer bezichtigt ihn des Verbrechens?**—**Er ist eines Attentats bezichtigt worden** ('He has been charged with an attempt on somebody's life'); at an earlier period the form **bezüchten** was used, as in **Will solcher Taten mich jemand bezüchten, tu' er's mit redlichen Zeugen** (G.), but this is now quite obs.

zerfetzt, zerlumpt: see **ragged** 2.

Zeug: The ordinary meaning of this noun is 'material, cloth', as in **Ich habe mir Zeug zu einem neuen Anzug gekauft**; but MHG *ziuc* had several other meanings, e.g. 'instrument' (> **Werkzeug**), 'weapon, armour' (> **Zeughaus,** 'arsenal, armoury'), 'witness' (> **Zeuge**), etc. The idea of material or stuff is seen in fig. expressions like **Er hat das Zeug dazu, ein Kunstwerk zu schaffen** (G. Keller: 'He has the makings of *or* is cut out for a great artist')—**Der Kaiser will mir am Zeuge (et)was flicken** (Bürger: '. . . wants to pick holes in my coat, to find fault with me')—**Er strengte sich an, was das Zeug halten wollte** ('He strove with might and main, strained every nerve')—**Jetzt werden die Weiber auf uns**

schimpfen, was nur das Zeug halten will (Auerbach: 'Now our wives will be tearing us to pieces *or* running us down for all they're worth'); on the other hand, the early sense of 'armour' is probably seen in **sich für jemand ins Zeug legen** ('to take up the cudgels for a person'). But in modern times **Zeug** has come to be used more and more disparagingly, just as our 'stuff' has: e.g. **Ach, dummes Zeug!** ('Oh, stuff and nonsense!')—**Sie redet immer dummes Zeug** ('She's always talking nonsense': cf. our slang 'rot')—**Wider Willen schluckte ich das Zeug** ('Reluctantly I swallowed the horrid stuff'); and so also contemptuously even of people: **Die jungen Mädchen lustwandelten im Freien, aber es war meist halbwüchsiges Zeug, das er keines Blickes würdigte** (Speckmann: 'The girls were taking the air, but they were mostly half-baked young things that he didn't deign to glance at'). In this disparaging sense the form **Zeugs** is now very common in familiar lang., being applied, like **Dings** (see **Ding** 1), to worthless, trumpery things: e.g. **Sie warfen das Zeugs weg** (Stifter: 'They flung the rubbish away')—**„Klatschrosen! Was das Zeugs dies Jahr gedeiht!"** (Böhlau: 'Poppies! How that stuff is thriving this year!')—**Meinen Sie denn, ich wollte mir den Kopf mit dem Zeugs vollpfropfen?** (Klinger: 'Do you imagine I wanted to cram my head with that useless lumber?')—**Sie taten viel verrücktes Zeugs** (Stifter: 'They did all sorts of mad things'); and even **Ich bin nie in New York gewesen, ich weiß nicht mal genau, wo das Zeugs liegt** (Tieck: '. . . I don't even know exactly where the wretched hole is').

Zier(de), Zierat, zieren: see **ornament** 3.

Ziffer: see **figure** 2.

-zig: 1. This corresponds to our '-ty', being suffixed to the cardinal numerals from 2 to 9 to express multiples of ten, additional numbers under ten being prefixed, as in 'two-and-twenty': cf. **dreiundneunzig** with **hundertunddrei.** Irreg. in form are **zwanzig** (instead of **zweizig**: (< MHG *zweinzec*), **dreißig** (not **dreizig**) and **sechzig** (not **sechszig**), while **siebenzig** is now almost always contracted to **siebzig.** Incidentally, although the vowel in **vier** is long (close), that in **vierzig** (as in **vierzehn** and **Viertel**) is short (open). The corresponding ord. nums. end in **-zigst** (adj., inflected in the normal way) and **-zigstel** (noun, neut. but masc. in Switzerland): e.g. **Der neunundzwanzigste Februar kommt nur in Schaltjahren vor—Ich habe nur ein Zwanzigstel des Geldes erhalten. 2.** The suffix **-ziger** expresses the decades of time or of human life. **(a)** Used as an *adj.*, it remains uninflected: e.g. **Seit den vierziger Jahren bin ich nicht in Deutschland gewesen—Mein Sohn steht in den zwanziger Jahren.** **(b)** Used as a *noun*, it is inflected when it refers to a man in his twenties, thirties, etc., the corresponding fem. taking the additional ending **-in:** e.g. **Er ist ein Fünfundsechziger** ('a man of sixty-five')—**Ich habe eben die Lebensgeschichte eines Neunzigers** (or **zweier Neunzigerinnen**) **gelesen**; cf. **Mütterchen bringt uns ein Gläschen Dreiundachtziger her** (G.: i.e. wine of the '83 vintage). As a noun expressing the decades of a person's age, it remains uninflected in the *gen.* and *accus.*: e.g. **Sein Vater hat die Sechzig nicht erreicht** (Frenssen)—**Er war älter als Stoltenkamp, Mitte der Fünfzig** (R. Herzog); less commonly **Sie stand am Ende der Dreißiger** (Th. Mann). In the *dat.* it may also remain uninflected, but here the form with **-zigen** is quite common: e.g. **Der Direktor näherte sich den Vierzig** (id.)—**Er war den Fünfzig nahe** (Bruno Frank)—**Er mochte stark in den Vierzigen sein** (G.)—**Er war ein Fünfziger, das heißt hoch in den Fünfzigen** (Immermann)—**Er näherte sich den Achtzigen** (G. Keller)—**Sie war so in den Vierzigen** (Droste-Hülshoff: 'She was somewhere about in her forties'). *Sanders* condemns the dat. form with **-zigern** in the sense of decades (he says expressly **„jemand ist in den Zwanzig oder Zwanzigen, nicht Zwanzigern"**), but *Duden* allows it, and modern authors use it quite freely: e.g. **Er war tief in den Fünfzigern** (Heine)—**Der in den Vierzigern stehende Herr sah kaum wie ein Dreißiger aus** (W. v. Scholz)—**Er war ein überaus gepflegter Mann in den Dreißigern** (Bruno Frank)—**Sie alle hatten die Vierzig überschritten, während die Hausherrin ziemlich weit über die Sechzig hinaus war und die Konsulin sich schon in den Siebzigern befand** (Th. Mann).

Zimmer: see **room** 3.

Zoll: When this noun has the force of 'toll, duty', its plur. is **Zölle,** but as a measure in the sense of 'inch', it has the plur. **Zolle** when used distrib., **Zoll** when used collect. after nums. (see **nouns of measure**

1 (*a*)): e.g. **Meine Abgaben und Zölle habe ich bezahlt** (G.)—**Das Brett ist drei Fuß** (q.v.) **zwei Zoll lang—Ich habe die Bretter nach Zollen gemessen** (cf. **Pfund**).

zu: 1. For the main uses of the *prep.* **zu,** see **nach** 2 and 3. In the construction commonly referred to as the 'infin. with zu', the infin. is really a gerundive, the equivalent of a verbal subst.: in the proposition **Dieser Junge ist immer zu lügen bereit** ('This boy is always ready to tell a lie'), the pred. might be **zum Lügen bereit** (Lat. *ad mentiendum paratus*). For a detailed explanation of this, see **infinitive,** under which head (3 (*b*)) the *attrib.* use of **zu** + infin., as in **Hier ist das auswendig zu lernende Gedicht** ('Here is the poem that has to be learned by heart') is also explained. **2.** For the *adv.* use of **zu** before adjs. and advs., as in **Der Weg ist zu lang** and **Sie besuchen uns zu selten,** see **too** and **als daß** 2.

zucken, zücken: These verbs both suggest a quick, convulsive movement, a jerk or twitch. Although there was formerly some fluctuation between the two forms, modern usage is practically fixed, **zucken** being used with *intrans.*, **zücken** with *trans.* force. Thus, on the one hand, **Es zuckt mir in allen Gliedern —Dem Vater zuckte der Mund** (Freytag) **—Seine Augen zuckten** (Gutzkow)—cf. **Blitze zuckten durch die Nacht** and (trans.) **Mein Herz durchzu'ckte ein Blitz bei ihrem ersten Anblick** (Heine); and, on the other hand, **Er zückte den Dolch** ('He whipped out his dagger')—**Der Jüngling rannte durch die lange Reihe der Zimmer, der Soldat mit gezücktem** ('drawn') **Degen hinter ihm her** (Wassermann); cf. **Du weißt noch, wie du jenem Reiter den Kopf spaltetest, da er eben den Säbel über mich zuckte** (Sch., for the modern **zückte**). The only exception here is the phrase **die Achseln zucken** (not **zücken,** 'to shrug one's shoulders'), where the alternative **mit den Achseln zucken** would be more in accordance with established present-day usage (see **mit** 2 (*b*)); cf. **An der Tür zuckte er, als hätte er etwas vergessen, mit dem Kopf herum** (St. Zweig: i.e. he sharply turned his head).

zuerkennen: see **anerkennen** 2 (*a*).

zuerst: see **erst** 2 (*e*).

zufällig: see **happen.**

zufrieden: This adj., which does not occur before about 1700, has developed out of the adv. phrase **zu Frieden,** an idea which is still seen in **Laß mich zufrieden!** ('Leave me in peace!'), which in MHG would have taken the form *lâ mich mit vride!* Gradually it became a real adj., used both attrib. and pred.: **Er ist ein zufriedener** ('contented') **Mensch—Er hat seine Gläubiger zufriedengestellt** ('He has satisfied his creditors')—**Gib dich damit zufrieden!** ('Rest content with that!')—**Ich bin mit meinem Los zufrieden** ('I am contented with my lot'). At one time a *gen.* was commonly used instead of the prep. **mit,** as in **Ich bin des Dienstes zufrieden, den sie mir geleistet** (G.), but this is now confined to indef. neut. expressions, as in **Ich bin dessen zufrieden;** and so also **Sie waren es zufrieden** (Alverdes) and **Er war alles zufrieden** (R. Herzog), where, however, the old gens. **es** and **alles** have come to be treated as *accus.*, so that one ordinarily says **Ich bin das zufrieden.** But even so, the prep. **mit** is preferable in good prose: cf. **Wir sind die** (better **mit der**) **Probe zufrieden** (Rückert). The prep. **von** here is now obs.: one no longer says **Er war zufrieden von seiner Reise** (G.).

Zufriedenheit: see **satisfaction** (*b*) and (*e*).

Zufriedenstellung: see **satisfaction** (*c*).

zugeben, zugestehen: see **confess** 2.

zugleich: see **gleich** 5.

zuhanden: see **Hand** 1.

Zuhause: see **Heim** 2 (*a*).

zulassen: see **permit** 3.

zumal: This word and its compd. **allzumal** (a favourite expression of Luther's) are no longer used in good prose, as they once were, with the force of 'together', as in **Sie sind allzumal Sünder** (Rom. 3. 23) **—Wie singen die Vöglein allzumal!** (G.); cf. **Sie steckten die Stadt an dreiunddreißig Ecken zumal** (now **zugleich,** 'simultaneously') **in Brand** (Sch.). The only sense in which **zumal** is now used is 'especially': e.g. **In diesem Jahr ist das Obst gut gediehen, zumal die Pflaumen—Ich gehe gern spazieren, zumal wenn die Sonne scheint.** In such propositions **zumal** may be replaced by other expressions, e.g. **besonders** and **namentlich** (q.v. 2 (*b*)); but there is one good use of **zumal** which does not apply to these other expressions, viz. its use as a *causal conj.* Thus, one can only say **Aus mehreren Gründen kann ich Sie heute nicht treffen, besonders weil ich für diesen Tag schon versagt bin** ('. . . especially because I have a previous engagement for today'), where **weil** could not be omitted; but **zumal** does not require the addition of a word like **weil** or **da**, being used independently with causal force, as the following examples show: **Sie bog in die steile Straße zur Rechten ein; viele gingen ihr nach, zumal die Straße ungewöhnlich belebt war** (Heyse)—**Als er heiratete, meinte man, er werde nun für ein besseres Logis sorgen, zumal es ihm an Mitteln nicht fehlen konnte** (E. Wichert)—**Er ging, zumal seine Frau sich oft schwach fühlte, allein spazieren** (W. v. Scholz)—**Die Kinder kamen nicht oft mit ihrer Mutter in Berührung, zumal sie nicht an der elterlichen Tafel teilnahmen** (Th. Mann)—**Er wußte nicht recht, was er antworten sollte, zumal er annahm, daß der Meister eine Schmeichelei verlangte** (A. Neumann). In this connexion see **nun** 2 and **ungeachtet**, which are commonly used as independent conjs. with the force of 'now that' and 'although' resp., and cf. **except** 2 (*b*) and **kaum** 1.

zumindest: see **wenig** 4 (*b*).

zumute: see **anmuten** 2.

zunächst: This word is used either as a prep. or as an adv. **1.** As a prep., meaning 'nearest *or* next', it could once take a *gen.*: e.g. **In einem Gasthof zunächst des Meeres verzehrten wir ein frugales Mahl** (G.)—**So wurde denn auf dem Rasen unter den blühenden Bäumen zunächst des Hauses getanzt** (G. Keller); but this is now almost obs. The recognized construction is now the *dat.*, and **zunächst** may either precede or follow a noun but always follows a pron.: e.g. **Er beugte sich über den Herrn, der ihm zunächst** (not **zunächst ihm**) **saß** (Bruno Frank)—**Dem Eingang zunächst stand eine Gruppe kleinerer Leute** (Th. Mann)—**Unser Weg führte uns durch die zunächst der Bühne gelegene Loge des Theaterdirektors** (id.); and even where it seems to assume adv. force, it is really a prep.: cf. **Das Mädchen bemühte sich, von dem Baume herunterzukommen: sie streckte den einen Fuß nach dem zunächst tieferen Zweige aus** (Jul. Wolff: '. . . she stretched her one foot down towards the branch nearest to the one on which she was standing'). **2.** As an adv., it has temporal force, meaning not 'next' (q.v.) but 'in the *first* instance, first and foremost' (cf. **erst** 2 (*e*)): e.g. **Als ich in Berlin ankam, sah ich mich zunächst nach einem Gasthof um** ('. . . the first thing I did was to look for a hotel')—**Zunächst müssen wir entscheiden, ob der Versuch überhaupt gemacht werden soll** ('To begin with we must decide whether the attempt is to be made at all')—**Herr Marini war zunächst** ('in the first place') **Dirigent des Gesangvereins; alsdann** ('then also') **brachte er den Töchtern der Stadt die Kunst des Klavierspiels bei** (R. Herzog).

zunichte: see **nichts** 1.

zurück: see **wider-** 1 and 3.

zurückerinnern: see **remember** 3 (*d*).

zurückhalten: see **stop** 2 (*b*).

zurücklassen: see **leave (verb)** 3 (*a*).

zurückschrecken: see **schrecken** 1 and 2.

zusammenhängen: In ordinary lang. *pres.* tense forms now always have **ä** (see **hängen** 2 (*a*)): **1.** *trans.*, with *weak* forms (in the past tense also **hing**: see **hängen** 2 (*b*)): occasionally 'to hang (things) together, beside each other' (e.g. **Sie hat die Kleider zusammengehängt**, i.e. **nebeneinander aufgehängt**), but usually 'to connect, join together': e.g. **Durch Brücken sind die Türme zusammengehängt** (G.)—fig. **Der Pfarrer hat Gelegenheit, die Sünden seiner Gemeine mit Naturbegebenheiten zusammenzuhängen** (id.). **2.** *intrans.*, always *strong*: 'to be connected': e.g. **Mein historisches Wissen hing nicht zusammen** (G.), i.e. 'was disconnected, showed gaps'—**Unsere Absicht ist, zu untersuchen, wie so seltsam Widersprechendes zusammengehangen hat** (id.); cf. **Die Naturforscher sagen, an dieser Stelle habe einst Irland mit Schottland zusammengehängt** (Rodenberg), according to modern usage **zusammengehangen** (implying a *state*).

zusammenschrecken: see **schrecken** 1 and 2.

zuschauen: see **zusehen.**

zusehen: **1.** As stated under **look (verb)** 1 (*a*), **schauen** is mainly characteristic of the south, **sehen** of the north. The same applies to the compds., and it is strange that, although **zuschauen** is comparatively little used in the ordinary lang. of the north, the established expression for a 'spectator' is **Zuschauer.** On the other hand, the adv. for 'visibly' is always **zusehends,** used esp. in propositions like **Seine Kräfte nehmen zusehends ab** (i.e. one can almost see him getting weaker, his strength is rapidly failing). **2.** The verb **zusehen** means 'to look on, be a spectator, watch', and is used either abs. or with a *dat.* obj.: e.g. **Ich habe (dem Spiel) nur zugesehen, nicht mitgespielt;**

cf. **Die anderen bekamen Geschenke, ich hatte das Zusehen** (i.e. I got nothing). It is often followed by a subord. clause introduced by **daß** or **wie,** less commonly **ob**: e.g. **Seht zu** (much like **Seht euch vor), daß ihr euch nicht überschla'gt!** ('See *or* Take care you don't fall head over heels!') —**Sieh zu** (more commonly **nach), ob der Vater noch nicht kommt!** ('Go and see whether your father isn't coming yet!'). A **wie**-clause is esp. common where we use a pres. part., as in 'We watched the men working': one says **Wir sahen den Männern bei der Arbeit zu** or **Wir sahen zu, wie die Männer arbeiteten.** As an obj. of this verb always stands in the dat., the accus. and infin. construction is obviously inapplicable, but a dat. and infin. in such cases has no historical foundation whatever, and it is taking a very dubious liberty with the lang. to say **Ich beobachte, wie der alte Mann dem Vieh trinken zusieht** (Hofmannsthal), for **dem Vieh beim Trinken zusieht** or **zusieht, wie das Vieh trinkt.**

zusprechen: This has various shades of meaning, the commonest being: (**a**) with a *dat.* of the person and an *accus.* of the thing, esp. a word like **Mut** or **Trost**: e.g. **Er sprach mir Mut zu** ('He tried to cheer me up, spoke encouragingly to me')—**Alle haben mir Trost zugesprochen** ('Everybody has spoken words of comfort to me'); the accus. is often implied: **Er sprach mir freundlich zu**; (**b**) with a *dat.* of the thing, 'to apply oneself to' (esp. food and drink): e.g. **Wir sprachen dem Wein fleißig zu** ('We did not spare the wine')—**Diesem Gericht spreche ich immer zu** ('I always have a liberal helping of this dish'); (**c**) with a prep. phrase, like the more usual **ein-** or **vorsprechen** (qq.v.), 'to drop in' on a person: e.g. **Ein Reisender bot einen hohen Preis für das Bild: er wollte bei der Rückkehr in vier Wochen wieder zusprechen** (Tieck).

zustatten: see **Statt** 2.

zustimmen: see **agree** 1 (*a*).

zustoßen: see **occur** 3 (*e*).

zutragen (reflex.): see **occur** 3 (*e*).

zuträglich: see **agree** 5.

zutrauen: see **trauen** 3 (*b*).

zutreten: see **advance** 3.

zuwider: This word is properly a prep., meaning 'contrary to, not in accordance with', and always *follows* a dependent *dat.* With one or two verbs it has become a sep. prefix, as in **Er hat dem Gesetz zuwidergehandelt** ('He has contravened the law') and **Die jetzige auswärtige Politik droht dem Nationalgefühl zuwiderzulaufen** ('The present foreign policy threatens to run counter to national feeling'). But it is esp. common with the verb **sein,** as in **Wir haben eine Schlacht verloren: das Glück war uns zuwider** (Sch.: 'fortune was against us'), and this applies esp. to its later fig. meaning, **viz.** 'distasteful, unpalatable, repellent, repulsive': e.g. **Knoblauch ist meinem Geschmack zuwider** ('I don't like the taste of garlic')—**Mir ist kein Geschöpf so zuwider als eine Spinne** (Sch.)—**Wie vertraut und fremd zugleich waren mir diese alten Kupferstiche Dürers, wie zuwider und wie lieb zugleich!** (Hofmannsthal); cf. **überessen** 3 *ad fin.* Here it has practically become a pred. adj., and, indeed, in southern dialects, esp. in Bavaria, it is even used as an attrib. adj., as in **ein zuwideres Weib** (Spindler), but this is definitely contrary to modern literary usage—in other words, it is **der heutigen gebildeten Schriftsprache zuwider!** In the attrib. relation one now uses **widrig** (lit. or fig.) or **widerlich** (fig.), as in phrases like **ein widriger Wind** ('a contrary wind') and **ein widriger** or **widerlicher Kunde** ('a loathsome specimen'); cf. **Solches Betragen widert mich an** ('That sort of behaviour disgusts me') and **Wir ersuchen Sie, unsere Rechnung binnen drei Tagen zu begleichen, widrigenfalls** ('failing which') **wir Sie verklagen werden**; cf. the example from R. Huch given under **infinitive** 3 (*a*) *ad fin.*, and **fail** 1.

zwanzig: see **-ig.**; **-zig.**

zwar: This adv. has developed out of MHG *ze wâre* ('in truth') but is no longer used merely to emphasize the truth of a statement. It is not used, as it often is by learners, in rendering propositions like 'a *really* kind lady' (**eine wirklich liebenswürdige Dame**): see **really** 1. Nowadays it is used in two ways: **1.** Like **allerdings, freilich** (qq.v.), it can have *concessive* force, being followed by a limiting 'but'-clause (cf. also **wohl** 3 (*a*)): e.g. **Dieser Roman ist zwar gut geschrieben, zieht sich aber zu sehr in die Länge** ('This novel is no doubt well written, but too long drawn out'); in such propositions **zwar** is sometimes omitted, but it is more idiomatic to insert it, and it is reg. inserted when the clause is a contracted one used attrib.: **Unser Patient wird morgen**

ausgehen dürfen, als ein zwar blasser, aber doch geheilter Mann (Immermann)—**Vor ihr stand ein junger, zwar sauber, aber einfach gekleideter Mann** (Jak. Frey). **2.** After **und** or **so,** it has *particularizing* force, adding some specific details to a previous vague or indefinite statement: e.g. **Mein Freund wohnt in der Hochstraße, und zwar** ('to be exact') **Nummer 25, drei Treppen hoch—Ja, er spricht Deutsch, und zwar sehr gut** ('and very well too')—**Es ist unumgänglich notwendig, zu handeln, und zwar unverzüglich** ('It is absolutely necessary to act, and that promptly')—**Sie trugen silberne Halsketten, deren Glieder abwechselnd die Gestalt von Falken und von Reihern hatten: so zwar, daß die Falken auf die Reiher zu stoßen schienen** (Bergengruen), i.e. the chain-links represented hawks and herons, and were arranged alternately in such a way that the hawks seemed to be pouncing on the herons; so also with a neg.: **Sie sang uns einige Lieder von Schumann vor, und zwar gar nicht schlecht** ('and not badly either').

zwei: 1. In MHG this cardinal num. had different forms for the three genders, viz. masc. *zwêne*, fem. *zwô*, neut. *zwei*, and these were the reg. forms in use down to the 18th century: e.g. **Man entzog ihm zween Tage das Brot** (Gellert: 1746)—**Es ist unmöglich, daß zwo grade Zahlen miteinander verbunden eine ungrade Zahl ausmachen** (Breitinger: 1740). The fem. **zwo** is still used in giving telephone numbers, etc., to obviate possible confusion between **zwei** and **drei**, and the three forms are still in use in southern spoken dialects: a little boy from the Saar, on being shown two apples, two forks, and two knives, and asked to name them, is reported to have said unhesitatingly **Zween Ebbel, zwo Gawweln, zwei Messere.** Gradually, however, the instinctive feeling for the three forms was lost, so that incorrect forms were often used: in Storm's *Aquis submersus*, the scene of which is laid in Holstein in the latter half of the 17th century, we find **zwo** (for **zween**) **Köter** and **zwo** (for **zwei**) **Bilder**, these incorrect forms being no doubt used deliberately in accordance with the confusion then prevailing. **2.** (**a**) The nums. **zwei** and **drei** must be strongly inflected in the *gen.*, when no other word clearly marks the case: e.g. **Durch zweier Zeugen Mund wird allerwegs die Wahrheit kund** (G.)—**Goethe erzählte mir von dem Besuch zweier Russen** (Eckermann)—**„Liederbuch dreier Freunde"** (the early poems of Storm and the brothers Mommsen). Followed by an attrib. adj. with a strong ending, the num. may remain uninflected, but actually a gen. phrase like **zwei junger Mädchen** is rather unusual, inflexion of the num. being much more common, and here the inflexion of the adj. fluctuates. On the whole, there is perhaps a slight preference for a *weak* ending, but usage is by no means fixed: cf., on the one hand, **Ich spreche von dem Einklang zweier gleichgestimmten Seelen** (Heine)—**Was gehen uns die letzten Stunden zweier armen gerichteten Sünder an?** (Böhlau)—**„Iphigenie" ist das Ergebnis einer Verschmelzung zweier scheinbar weitgetrennten Kunstwelten** (G. Witkowski)—**Die Rede zweier Vorübereilenden schreckte sie auf** (Hebbel); and, on the other hand, **Sein Untergesicht lag im Schatten zweier vorspringender Backenknochen** (Fontane)—**Er vernahm das Lachen zweier junger Stimmen** (Storm)—**Er hatte seine Freude an der Neigung zweier unschuldiger Menschenkinder** (C.F.Meyer)—**Im Jahre 1840 wurde Fontane Mitglied zweier literarischer Vereine** (R. Pechel)—**Tony hatte ihren Platz inmitten zweier anderer Pensionärinnen erhalten** (Th. Mann)—**Sie sah seine Gestalt vom Licht zweier großer altertümlicher Laternen umflossen** (Binding). This point does not arise, of course, where a strongly inflected word precedes the num., in which case usage is quite fixed: **Ich erwarte den Besuch meiner zwei ältesten Freunde—Der Preis dieser drei deutschen Bücher beträgt 30 Mark.** (**b**) In the *dat.*, **zwei** and **drei** should be inflected when used subst.: e.g. **Laß eine Chaise zu dreien anspannen!** (G.: 'Have a chaise and three harnessed!')—**Zu zweien und dreien** ('In twos and threes': cf. (*c*)) **kamen die Leute vom Dorf** (Frenssen)—**Der Erzbischof sah den dreien nach** (Ric. Huch)—**Uns dreien war nicht wohl zumute** (H. Hoffmann)—**Der verdammte Bursch schneidet schon die Cour, und gleich dreien auf einmal** (Ebner-Eschenbach: 'The confounded young fellow is courting already, and no fewer than three girls at the same time'); so also **Er hatte mit zweien seiner Leute dort übernachtet** (A. Neumann), although the num. before a gen. or **von** is often left uninflected (**mit zwei von meinen Freunden**). On the other hand, non-inflexion of the num. is now the rule when it qualifies a noun or is qualified by a word indicating the case (but cf. 3), and examples like the following should not be imitated: **Die Hängelampen leuchteten nur zweien Gästen** (Mörike)—**Die Frau wurde mit dreien Kindern vom Lande erwartet** (id.)—**Das Haus gehörte zweien Brüdern** (Hofmannsthal)—**Wenn zweien Gatten die Trennungsstunde schlägt, gibt's keinen dritten auf der Welt** (Sudermann)—**Nicht ein Tropfen Blutes ist diesen zweien gemeinsam** (C. F. Meyer). (**c**) An alternative expression for **zu zweien** (**dreien**) is **zu zweit** (**dritt**), and this applies also to the other nums.: e.g. **Zu fünft verließen wir das Haus** (Schickele)—**Zu viert stehen die Hofleute auf den Tennen und dreschen** (Waggerl); cf. **Man saß zu elfen** (or **elft**) **an der Tafel** (Mörike). **3.** Apart from the cases given above, inflexion of the num. is now avoided in good prose but common in coll. speech, esp. in some set phrases (but see **-zig**): e.g. **Er hat alle neune geworfen** (in skittles)—**Er stand an der Kegelbahn und sah den Wechselschicksalen der neune zu** (H. Kurz)—**Die Kinder krochen auf allen vieren**—**Das Tier streckte die viere** (usually **alle viere**) **von sich** (Sudermann: 'stretched itself full length')—**Es waren unser dreie** or **drei von uns** ('There were three of us')—**Es schlägt eben zwölfe** (G.). For **alles dreies**, see **drei**.

zweierlei: see **Hand** 3.

zweifelsohne: see **ohne** 1.

zwinkern: see **mit** 2 (*b*).

zwischen: The only contexts in which an *accus.* is used with this prep. are those which express or imply motion up to, but not beyond, a point situated between two objects, as in **Goethe setzte sich zwischen die beiden Schwestern** (Böhlau); it is incorrect to say **Ich setzte mich zwischen meinen beiden Meistern, dem Maurer- und Zimmermeister** (Storm, in a letter to G. Keller), which would be correct if the prefix **hin-** or **nieder-** were added (see **accusative or dative . . .** 2 (*a*)). In all other contexts **zwischen** requires a *dat.* case, including those which imply motion through between two objects to a point beyond these, where, however, a prefix of motion is almost always used: e.g. **Er saß zwischen den zwei Schwestern**—**Das kann man zwischen den Zeilen lesen** ('That can be read between the lines')—**Ich erbot mich, zwischen den zwei Parteien zu vermitteln** ('I offered to mediate between the two parties')—**Er ritt zwischen den zwei Menschenreihen entlang**—**„Erlauben Sie", sagte er und ging eilig zwischen den Wächtern durch in sein Zimmer** (Kafka)—**Seine Nase sprang scharf zwischen den eingefallenen Wangen hervor** (Th. Mann)—**Heinrich blickte zwischen ihr und dem Herzog hindurch auf das helle Fenster** (id.); cf. **Sie wandelte zwischen den Gräbern** (Heer), where one would ordinarily add **herum**.

Zwischenraum: see **distance** 6.

APPENDIX

A list of the chief authors from whose works the examples have been taken

Alexis (Willibald) = Wilhelm Häring: 1798–1871.
Allmers (Hermann): 1821–1902.
Alverdes (Paul): 1897–
Arens (Hanns): 1902–
Arnim (Achim v.): 1781–1831.
Auerbach (Berthold): 1812–82.
Bauer (Josef Martin): 1901–
Bäumer (Gertrud): 1873–1954.
Beethoven (Ludwig van): 1770–1827.
Bergengruen (Werner): 1892–
Binding (Rudolf G.): 1867–1938.
Blunck (Hans Friedrich): 1888–
Bode (Wilhelm v.): 1845–1929.
Böhlau (Helene): 1859–1940.
Böll (Heinrich): 1917–
Bonsels (Waldemar): 1881–1952.
Borchert (Wolfgang): 1921–47.
Börne (Ludwig) = Löb Baruch: 1786–1837.
Brahm (Otto): 1856–1912.
Braun (Otto): 1897–1918.
Brentano (Clemens): 1778–1842.
Breuer (Robert): 1909–
Britting (Georg): 1891–
Brüning (Heinrich): 1885–
Bulcke (Carl): 1875–1936.
Bülow (Margarete v.): 1860–84.
Bürger (Gottfried August): 1747–94.
Carossa (Hans): 1878–1956.
Chamisso (Adalbert v.): 1781–1838.
Dahn (Felix): 1834–1912.
Dauthendey (Max): 1867–1918.
Döblin (Alfred): 1878–1957.
Droste-Hülshoff (Annette v.): 1797–1848.
Duden (Konrad): 1829–1911.
Ebner-Eschenbach (Marie v.): 1830–1916.
Eckermann (Johann Peter): 1792–1854.
Edschmid (Kasimir) = Eduard Schmidt: 1890–
Eloesser (Arthur): 1870–1938.
Engel (Eduard): 1851–1938.
Engel (Georg): 1866–1937.
Ernst (Paul): 1866–1937.
Eyth (Max): 1836–1906.
Fallada (Hans) = Rudolf Dietzen: 1893–1947.
Federer (Heinrich): 1866–1928.
Fichte (Johann Gottlieb): 1762–1814.
Flake (Otto): 1880–
Fontane (Theodor): 1819–98.
Forster (Georg): 1754–94.
Franck (Hans): 1879–
Frank (Bruno): 1887–1945.
Frank (Leonhard): 1882–
Frapan [-Akunian] (Ilse): 1852–1908.
Freiligrath (Ferdinand): 1810–76.
Frenssen (Gustav): 1863–1945.
Frey (Jakob): 1824–75.
Freytag (Gustav): 1816–95.
Geibel (Emanuel): 1815–84.
Geissler (Horst Wolfram): 1893–
Gellert (Christian Fürchtegott): 1715–69.
Gerstäcker (Friedrich): 1816–72.
Gessner (Salomon): 1730–88.
Goethe (Johann Wolfgang v.): 1749–1832.
Goldammer (Leo?): ?
Gotthelf (Jeremias) = Albert Bitzius: 1797–1854.
Gottschall (Rudolph v.): 1823–1909.
Greif (Martin) = Friedrich H. Frey: 1839–1911.
Griese (Friedrich A. H.): 1890–
Grillparzer (Franz): 1791–1872.
Grimm (Hermann): 1828–1901.
Grimmelshausen (Hans J. C. v.): 1625(?)–76.
Grosse (Julius): 1828–1902.
Gutzkow (Karl): 1811–78.
Hackländer (Friedrich Wilhelm): 1816–77.
Halbe (Max): 1865–1944.
Hahn (Friedrich) = E. Freiherr v. Münch-Bellinghausen: 1806–71.
Hansjakob (Heinrich): 1837–1916.
Harnack (Otto): 1857–1914.
Hartmann v. Aue: 1160 (?)–1210 (?).
Hauff (Wilhelm): 1802–27.
Hauptmann (Carl): 1858–1921.
Hauptmann (Gerhart): 1862–1946.
Hauser (Heinrich): 1901–55.
Hausmann (Manfred G. A.): 1898–
Hebbel (Friedrich): 1813–63.
Hebel (Johann Peter): 1760–1826.
Heine (Heinrich): 1797–1856.
Heinse (J. J. Wilhelm): 1746–1803.
Herder (Johann Gottfried): 1744–1803.
Herzog (Rudolf): 1869–1943.
Hesse (Hermann): 1877–
Heygrodt (Robert Heinz): 1893–1928.
Heyne (Moritz): 1837–1906.
Heyse (Paul): 1830–1914.

HOFFMANN (E. T. Amadeus): 1776–1822.
HOFFMANN (Hans): 1848–1909.
HOFMANNSTHAL (Hugo v.): 1874–1929.
HOHENSTEIN (Friedrich August): 1875–
HÖLDERLIN (Friedrich): 1770–1843.
HOPFEN (Hans): 1835–1904.
HUCH (Friedrich): 1873–1913.
HUCH (Ricarda): 1864–1947.
HUMBOLDT (Wilhelm v.): 1767–1835.
ILGENSTEIN (Heinrich): 1875–1935 (?).
IMMERMANN (Karl Lebrecht): 1796–1840.
JUNG-STILLING = Johann H. Jung: 1740–1817.
KAFKA (Franz): 1883–1924.
KÄSTNER (Erich): 1899–
KAUFMANN (Maré): 1897–
KELLER (Gottfried): 1819–90.
KELLER (Paul): 1873–1932.
KELLERMANN (Bernhard): 1879–1951.
KERNER (Justinus): 1786–1862.
KEYSERLING (Eduard Graf v.): 1855–1918.
KINKEL (Gottfried): 1815–82.
KLABUND = Alfred Henschke: 1891–1928.
KLEIST (Heinrich v.): 1777–1811.
KLOPSTOCK (Friedrich Gottlieb): 1724–1803.
KOLBENHEYER (Erwin Guido): 1878–1958 (?).
KOPISCH (August): 1799–1853.
KRAMP (Willy E.): 1909–
KRIEGER (H.): ?
KÜGELGEN (Wilhelm v.): 1802–67.
KUGLER (Franz): 1808–58.
KÜRNBERGER (Ferdinand): 1823–79.
KURZ (Isolde): 1853–1944.
LAMPRECHT (Karl): 1856–1915.
LEIP (Hans K. H. G.): 1893–
LENAU (Nikolaus) = N. Niembsch v. Strehlenau: 1802–50.
LESSING (Gotthold Ephraim): 1729–81.
LEWALD (Fanny): 1811–89.
LEYEN (Friedrich v. d.): 1873–
LILIENCRON (Detlev v.): 1844–1909.
LÖNS (Hermann): 1866–1914.
LUDWIG (Otto): 1813–65.
LUTHER (Martin): 1483–1546.
MANN (Heinrich): 1871–1950.
MANN (Thomas): 1875–1955.
MAYNC (Harry): 1874–1947.
MEYER (Conrad Ferdinand): 1825–98.
MEYER (Julius): 1876 (?)–
MÖRIKE (Eduard): 1804–75.
MÖSER (Justus): 1720–94.
MÜGGE (Theodor): 1806–61.
MÜLLER (Johann v.): 1875–1944.
MUSÄUS (Johann Karl): 1735–87.
NECKER (Moritz): ?
NEUMANN (Alfred): 1895–
NIETZSCHE (Friedrich Wilhelm): 1844–1900.
NORDAU (Max) = Max Südfeld: 1849–1923.
NOVALIS = Friedrich v. Hardenberg: 1772–1801.
OKEN (Lorenz): 1779–1851.
OMPTEDA (Georg Freiherr v.): 1863–1937.
PERKONIG (Joseph Friedrich): 1890–
PLATEN (August) = Graf Hallermünde: 1796–1835.
POLENZ (Wilhelm v.): 1861–1903.
PONTEN (Josef): 1883–1940.
PRUTZ (Robert): 1816–72.
RAABE (Wilhelm): 1831–1910.
RANKE (Friedrich): 1882–
RATZEL (F.): 1844–1904.
REINER (Anna): ?
RIEHL (Wilhelm Heinrich): 1823–97.
RILKE (Reiner Maria): 1875–1926.
RODENBERG (Julius): 1831–1914.
ROQUETTE (Otto): 1824–96.
ROTH (Joseph): 1894–1939.
ROTHE (Carl): 1900–
SACHS (Hans): 1494–1576.
SALLWÜRK (Ernst v.): 1839–1926.
SALTEN (Felix): 1869–1945.
SANDERS (Daniel): 1819–97.
SCHAEFFER (Albrecht): 1885–1950.
SCHÄFER (Wilhelm): 1868–1952.
SCHAFFNER (Jakob): 1875–1944.
SCHAIDENREISSER (Simon): ? (early 16th cent.).
SCHEFFEL (Joseph Viktor v.): 1826–86.
SCHELLING (Friedrich Wilhelm v.): 1775–1854.
SCHIEBER (Anna): 1867–1945.
SCHILLER (Friedrich v.): 1759–1805.
SCHLAF (Johannes): 1862–1941.
SCHLEGEL (August Wilhelm): 1767–1845.
SCHLEGEL (Friedrich): 1772–1829.
SCHLIPPENBACH (A. Graf v.): 1859– ?
SCHMIDT (Erich): 1853–1913.
SCHMIDT (Julian): 1818–86.
SCHNACK (Friedrich): 1888–
SCHNEIDER (Manfred): 1884–1935.
SCHOLZ (Wilhelm F. J. v.): 1874–
SCHRECKENBACH (Paul): 1866–1923.
SCHÜCKING (Levin): 1814–83.
SCHWAB (Gustav): 1792–1850.
SEUME (Johann Gottfried): 1763–1810.
SPECKMANN (Diedrich): 1872–1938.
SPIELHAGEN (Friedrich): 1829–1911.
SPINDLER (Karl): 1796–1855.
STAHR (Adolf): 1805–76.
STEHR (Hermann): 1864–1940.

STIFTER (Adalbert): 1805–68.
STORM (Theodor): 1817–88.
STROBL (Karl Hans): 1877–1946.
SUDERMANN (Hermann): 1857–1928.
SÜTTERLIN (Ludwig): 1863–1917.
SYBEL (Heinrich v.): 1817–1895.
TAMSEN (M.): ?
THIESS (Frank): 1890–
THORWALD (Jürgen): 1916–
TIECK (Ludwig): 1773–1853.
TOLLER (Ernst): 1893–1939.
TREITSCHKE (Heinrich v.): 1834–96.
UHLAND (Ludwig): 1787–1862.
VARNHAGEN V. ENSE (Karl August): 1785–1858.
VIEBIG (Clara): 1860–1952.
VILLINGER (Hermine): 1849–1917.
VOIGT-DIEDERICHS (H.) = Helene Diederichs, née Voigt: 1875–
VOLKMANN-LEANDER (Richard): 1830–89.
VOSS (Johann Heinrich): 1751–1826.
VRING (Georg v. d.): 1889–
WAGGERL (Karl Heinrich): 1897–
WAGNER (Richard): 1813–83.
WAIBLINGER (Wilhelm): 1804–30.
WALDAU (Gustav): 1871–1958.
WALDMÜLLER (Ferdinand): 1793–1865.
WALTHER v. d. VOGELWEIDE: 1170 (?)–1230 (?).
WALZEL (Oskar): 1864–1957 (?).
WASSERMANN (Jakob): 1873–1934.
WEIGAND (Wilhelm): 1862–1949.
WEISS (Ernst): 1884–
WERFEL (Franz): 1890–1945.
WERNER (Bruno E.): 1896–
WICHERT (Ernst): 1831–1902.
WIECHERT (Ernst Emil): 1887–1950.
WIELAND (Christoph Martin): 1733–1813.
WILBRANDT (Adolf): 1837–1911.
WILDENBRUCH (Ernst v.): 1845–1909.
WILDERMUTH (Ottilie): 1817–77.
WINDER (Ludwig): 1889–1946.
WOLFF (Julius): 1834–1910.
ZAHN (Ernst): 1867–1952.
ZIFFERER (Paul): 1879–1929.
ZOBELTITZ (Fedor v.): 1857–1934.
ZSCHOKKE (Heinrich): 1771–1848.
ZUCKMAYER (Carl): 1896–
ZWEIG (Arnold): 1887–
ZWEIG (Stefan): 1881–1942.